Corporate Finance and Governance

Corporate Finance and Governance

Cases, Materials, and Problems for an Advanced Course in Corporations

THIRD EDITION

Lawrence E. Mitchell
JOHN THEODORE FEY RESEARCH PROFESSOR OF LAW
GEORGE WASHINGTON UNIVERSITY

Lawrence A. Cunningham
PROFESSOR OF LAW AND BUSINESS
LIBBY SCHOLAR AND ACADEMIC DEAN
BOSTON COLLEGE LAW SCHOOL

Jeffrey J. Haas
PROFESSOR OF LAW
NEW YORK LAW SCHOOL

CAROLINA ACADEMIC PRESS
Durham, North Carolina

Paperback 978-1-5310-2168-9
LL 978-1-5310-2096-5
ISBN 1-59460-162-3
LCCN 2005937597

CAROLINA ACADEMIC PRESS
700 Kent St.
Durham, NC 27701
Telephone (919) 489-7486
Fax (919) 493-5668
www.cap-press.com

Printed in the United States of America
2020 Reprint

For Alex
L.E.M.

To the memory of my father
L.A.C.

For Peter (happy 3rd birthday!)
J.J.H.

Contents

Contents

Table of Cases

Preface to the Third Edition

The study of corporate finance by lawyers has exploded. At one time the subject was limited principally to an examination of the legal capital rules in a segment of the basic course on corporations. Today, a separate course in corporate finance is part of the business curriculum at most law schools, and the study ranges from the lawyer's traditional world of legal capital to market-based methods of valuation once reserved to the business school curriculum.

There are a number of reasons for this development. One is the increasing complexity and sophistication of the American and world financial markets, with the proliferation of new financial instruments having uncertain legal characteristics. Another is the humble rise of securitization as a means of financing beginning in the 1970s and its evolution into a more than $6 trillion industry. Yet another is the effect of the takeover boom of the 1980s, not only on the development of financing techniques such as original issue junk bonds but on the rights of security holders in target corporations and the legal understanding of the nature of the corporate form. Of further importance has been the influence of law and economics, first on academic lawyers and, increasingly, on judges and legislators. The result of these factors has been a radical rethinking of the nature of the corporate form, basic principles of corporate governance, the rights of security holders and, correspondingly, the duties of corporate management.

There are a number of reasons for corporate lawyers to study corporate finance. The first, and most practical, is that finance is the essence of any corporate law practice. Private placements, public offerings, debt issuances, securitizations, stock issuances, leveraged transactions, mergers, recapitalizations and the like are all important financing techniques, and the lawyer who lacks at least a rudimentary understanding of the basic business principles involved will be inadequately prepared to draft contracts and financial instruments, let alone counsel her client. The legal consequences of these financing techniques are themselves a part of the cost/benefit analysis that goes into the decision to undertake them, so the lawyer, to have meaningful input into the decisionmaking process, must be equipped to assist in this evaluation. Finally, on a broader professional level, the theory and practice of corporate finance has significant societal consequences, both internal and external to the corporation, and an understanding and appreciation of these consequences is the responsibility of every business lawyer.

This book is centered around two organizing themes. The first is that none of the difficult questions of corporate law (including the scope of corporate law itself) can be resolved without an underlying theory of the corporation. We suspect that judges mostly assume a theory of the corporation in resolving disputes which rarely is explicit in the opinion (or even consciously acknowledged by the judge). The same is often true of corporate scholars, and appears particularly true of legislators. Finance theory also is influenced by, or influences, the theory of the corporate form. We thus begin by presenting a variety of theories of the corporation, both of ancient (in terms of corporate law) and recent vintage, to serve as an organizing theme for the materials that follow.

The second organizing theme of this book is that most difficult corporate law questions revolve around the tension created between principles of fiduciary duty and contract upon which corporate law is based, and that judicial decisionmaking reveals a constant readjustment of these principles within the context of corporate law. The extent to which one predominates in a given case is often a reflection of the judge's theory of the corporation, but again it rarely is acknowledged. A self-conscious analysis of this issue ought to bring greater understanding to corporate law problems and result in more coherent resolutions of those problems.

What has changed in the Third Edition?

In addition to updating the materials presented in the *Second Edition*, we have streamlined and reorganized those materials in order to make learning easier. In particular:

- **chapter 1** (The Corporate Form: Theories and Consequences) and **chapter 2** (Limited Liability—A Central Problem in Corporate Finance) have been reduced in length without, in our view, any meaningful reduction in the substance they convey.

- **chapter 3** (Valuation) has been reorganized and enhanced in recognition of the central role that valuation plays in corporate finance. We also added a section on behavioral finance and its impact on investor behavior.

- **chapter 4** (Managing Risk (Hedging) with Derivatives) is a new chapter that includes the derivative materials formerly found in chapter 3. In addition to reorganizing the materials, we provide enhanced coverage of the four building blocks of derivatives—options, forwards, futures and swaps. We also discuss derivatives as tools for both risk reduction and speculation. We finish by examining how the courts are adjudicating disputes involving derivatives.

- **chapter 5** (The Rights of Contract Claimants—Part 1: Holders of Debt Securities) has been completely reorganized. We lead with materials on the use of leverage and the characteristics of debt securities generally that had previously appeared in chapter 7. We then discuss the valuation of debt securities before launching into an extended section addressing the legal treatment of debt securities. We then added a section addressing other participants in debt offerings, to wit, underwriters, indenture trustees and rating agencies. We then provide materials on the bankruptcy rights of debtholders. We finish by focusing on advanced debt topics, including a new subsection on asset-backed securitization.

- **chapter 6** (The Rights of Contract Claimants—Part 2: Preferred Stock) has been significantly reorganized and expanded. Included at the chapter's end is an excerpt from Larry Mitchell's seminal article on preferred stock: "The Puzzling Paradox of Preferred Stock (And Why We Should Care About It)," 51 Bus. Law. 443 (1996). This excerpt thoughtfully ties together all of the themes presented earlier in this chapter.

- **chapter 7** (The Rights of Contract Claimants—Part 2: Convertible Securities) is a new chapter that brings all the materials on convertible securities together in one place. The chapter begins with an explanation of the economics of, and justifications for, convertible securities (both convertible debt and convertible preferred stock). It then provides and extended discussion of, and substantial materials covering, the obligation of an issuer to protect the conversion rights of its convertible securityholders.

- **chapter 8** (The Rights of Ownership Claimants—Part 1: General Concepts) begins with a discussion of the nature of fiduciary duty generally. It then provides extensive coverage of a variety of substantive topics: dividend policy and the legal rules affecting dividends; redemptions and repurchases of common stock; preemptive rights and dilution; and recapitalizations and restructurings. It finishes with materials addressing the intersection between fiduciary duty and corporate democracy.

- **chapter 9** (The Rights of Ownership Claimants—Part 2: Mergers and Acquisitions) is essentially a new chapter dedicated to legal issues arising in mergers and acquisitions. In this context, the duty of care and the business judgment rule are first explored. A board's duty of loyalty is then examined in light of its decision to sell the company, adopt defensive strategies, and enter into transactions with controlling stockholders. The chapter finishes with a discussion of antitakeover legislation and the *de facto* merger doctrine.

Leading the charge on the *Third Edition* is our new co-author, Jeffrey J. Haas. Jeff brings a wealth of both real world and scholarly insights to the book. In addition to updating and reorganizing all of the materials, he was responsible for enhancing the chapters and materials on valuation, derivative instruments, asset-backed securitization, convertible securities and mergers and acquisitions.

At the same time, we wish to thank our former co-author, Lewis D. Solomon, who worked on the first two editions of this book. We wish Lew well with the exciting new projects he is pursuing.

L.E.M.
L.A.C.
J.J.H.
January 1, 2006

Acknowledgments

Each of the people and organizations listed below has helped to make this project a reality, and each of them is a part of this book.

Third Edition (2006)

The lion's share of the work on the *Third Edition* took place during the Summer of 2005. It could not have happened without the Herculean efforts of the following New York Law School student research assistants: Matthew Rench ('06), Antar P. Jones ('06), Lucia Freda ('07) and Patricia E. Cleary ('06). In addition, sincere thanks go out to the New York Law School library staff, particularly Grace E. Lee. The financial support of New York Law School, and the personal support and encouragement of Dean Richard A. Matasar and Associate Dean Stephen J. Ellmann, are also gratefully acknowledged.

Second Edition (1996)

Special thanks are due to Pat Ryan, whose insightful comments and feedback based on his usage of the prior edition were very helpful to us in improving the book. Additional thanks are due in the second edition to Geoffrey Barrow whose research help was very valuable, and Ross Issacs whose formatting of the manuscript saved us weeks of work. Thanks are also due to Andrew Buck, who proofread parts of the manuscript, to students at the Benjamin N. Cardozo School of Law who helped test portions of the manuscript in class, and to former Cardozo Dean Frank J. Macchiarola, who also provided generous financial support. The financial support of Cardozo's Samuel and Ronnie Heyman Center on Corporate Governance is also gratefully acknowledged.

First Edition (1992)

A number of people helped make this project a reality and are due our sincerest thanks. Alex Seita, of the Albany Law School faculty, was patient in helping us with aspects of bankruptcy law. Bob Tymann sat through the first course in which the materials were taught, and offered helpful insights on the teachability of the book. On the research assistant front (all of whom are or were students at Albany Law School during the progress of this book) Arete Kontogiannis and Laurie Marsh helped get the book started. Mike Williams and Matt Walko did the lion's share of work as consummate professionals and without either of them this project would have suffered, both professionally and in terms of enjoyment. Mike is equally responsible with us for the development and preparation of chapter 3 and it is fair to say that without his dedication and insight it would have been substantially harder to complete this book. Jim Barriere was helpful in putting together much of chapter 6 and in keeping us abreast of current developments in corporate theory. Russ Siddiqui kept us up to the minute on business developments and provided creative insight into much of the takeover materials. Renee Doyle provided important information on a variety of topics and was of tremendous help in producing the manuscript. Finally, Abbie Baynes, a student at the National Law Center of George Washington University, contributed her efforts to section 1 of chapter 7.

The staff of the Schaffer Law Library at Albany Law School was very patient, and particular thanks are due Mary Wood, who promptly filled all our inter-library loan requests, and Bob Emery, who seems to know everything! Dean Martin H. Belsky of Albany Law School provided generous financial support.

Michelle Sasso continued to prove her infallibility in typing the manuscript and Theresa Colbert (who typed part of the manuscript) was helpful in her secretarial assistance and ability to keep us organized. Dave Foss contributed his efforts in pulling together the final product.

I resist any thing better than my own diversity....

Walt Whitman
Song of Myself

Corporate Finance and Governance

Introduction and Problem—
The Enormous Room

If you become a corporate lawyer, at some point in your career you will attend a special kind of meeting in an enormous room somewhere on the upper floor of a large building in a large American city. The room will be full of people. They will not be smiling. You have been working very hard prior to this meeting. If your client is the corporation that is the subject of the meeting, you and its officers will be especially tense. In fact, if you close your eyes and let your imagination wander, you may picture yourself and your client's officers in the middle of the desert, tired, hot and thirsty, with hundreds of vultures sitting on the cliffs above you. The vultures will each have a face and it will be the face of somebody else in the room. This is a meeting with your client's creditors. Your client is going down the tubes.

The creditors' meeting illustrates in fairly bold relief what this book is all about. Sitting at the meeting will be representatives of senior secured debtholders, senior unsecured debtholders, subordinated debtholders, convertible debtholders, general trade creditors, preferred stockholders, equipment lessors, employees' unions, and, foremost in your mind as counsel to the corporation, common stockholders. Why common stockholders are foremost in your mind is a major subject of this book. Of course there will also be lawyers for each of these participants, as well as accountants and investment bankers. Their duties also will be explored in this book.

There are interesting ethical and legal issues that are posed by meetings of this type. If you represent the corporation, what is your obligation as counsel to that corporation with respect to each of those various classes? And, of course, what is the obligation of your client and its management? In any event, whether you are there to liquidate the corporation or reorganize it, each of these interests is going to be fighting for as much of the corporate pie as it can get.

Nobody comes to the table unarmed. This isn't a free-for-all. Each representative of each of the various interests will carry with him or her a contract, negotiated in more optimistic times, which defines the rights and the covenants designed to protect the value of those interests in the corporation. And these contracts form the basis of each party's negotiating position.

You might well ask: why doesn't each of these parties simply demand that the corporation fulfill the terms of the contract? If it fails to do so, surely the contracts provide remedies enforceable in court. The simple answer is, it can't. Your client is a limited liability corporation with insufficient assets to fulfill its obligations. Even if it is able to fulfill the terms of one contract, it is unlikely to be able to satisfy all of them. And although bodies of law such as the bankruptcy code are designed to help resolve

3

the conflict created by limited liability (and limited resources) in this setting, the practical reality of the situation is that at least some of the parties are likely to want to bargain to keep the corporation able to satisfy its obligations.

Other forms of conflict arise among classes of corporate claimants during the life of the corporation. Dividends paid to stockholders diminish the wealth available to other claimants. Risky projects undertaken to maximize stockholder profit may upset the expectations of creditors by decreasing the value of their investments. Corporate restructurings to avoid hostile takeovers may require plant closing that result in massive layoffs. And stockholder wealth maximization through control transactions might harm a variety of corporate claimants.

In each of these contexts, and others that your will encounter in this book, the traditional principles of stockholder primacy and limited liability produce conflicts among the corporation, its stockholders, and its other financial claimants. Central to resolving these conflicts is an understanding of the role of corporate management. Thus the pervasive question that forms the doctrinal basis for this book is: what are the rights and obligations of each of these actors to one another in an organization with limited financial resources?

On one level that's what this book is all about. We start off mentioning the corporation's demise because it is at that point that the financial structure of the corporation is all in place. The construction of this financial structure does not occur at once, but in stages over the life of the corporation. Only at death does this structure become static. And, as you'll see, not even then.

In determining how these competing interests coexist, we'll also concern ourselves with how they get to be interests in the first place. How do you create them? What are the normal characteristics of these instruments and how do they vary? What are the concerns of the people who own them? In order to introduce you to the types of problems you'll be addressing, we ask you to think about the following:

Problem

You are the consultant to the government of Bondolia, a former communist country that has decided to move to a market-based free enterprise system of finance and government. Based on your knowledge of, and experience with, American public corporations, you have been asked to draft a memorandum describing the types of issues that arise in creating a financial and governance structure for corporations in that type of society. In preparing your memorandum, please be sure to identify the concerns of each of the following corporate actors, and discuss how they might be addressed:

    (1) common stockholders;
    (2) debtholders, including holders of debt that is
        (a) secured;
        (b) unsecured;
        (c) senior;
        (d) subordinated;
        (e) convertible;
        (f) non-convertible;
    (3) preferred stockholders;
    (4) directors;

(5) officers;
(6) current employees;
(7) retirees;
(8) customers and suppliers; and
(9) local communities in which the corporation will operate.

Chapter 1

The Corporate Form:
Theories and Consequences

Use of the corporate form as a method of conducting business[1] in America did not become common until well into the nineteenth century,[2] although its historical origins date back to medieval English ecclesiastical and municipal corporations, and even to Roman times.[3] By the early Twentieth Century, the corporation had become well established as a vehicle for raising capital and conducting business.

The legal rules and principles by which this form was to be organized and its activities regulated developed with the increasing use of the form. However, the largely pragmatic legal consensus on the rules of the game, designed to accommodate industrial growth in the new era, were predicated on a centuries-old reification of the corporate form developed in the context of municipal and ecclesiastical corporations. The notion of the corporation as a "person" or an "entity" formed the fundamental, if largely unspoken, assumption on which modern corporation law is based.

This fundamental assumption has been challenged significantly at two points during the Twentieth Century. In the early part of that century, realist philosophers and the new legal realists challenged the personification of the corporation in an outpouring of literature on the subject,[4] while Berle and Means[5] provided the evidence of the increasing isolation of management as the center of the corporate form. The focus of corporate jurisprudence from their time to ours largely has been the mooring of the management entity to its stockholder roots.

The second "great awakening" has its roots in the early 1960s and has mushroomed over the 1980s. This time the spur was law and economics scholarship (led by modern financial

---

1. Douglas and Shanks, Insulation from Liability Through Subsidiary Corporations, 39 Yale L.J. 193, 194 (1929) ("Little will be gained by seeking to ascertain what a corporation is. It is not a thing. It is a method.").

2. Mitchell, Close Corporations Reconsidered, 63 Tulane L. Rev. 1301 (1989); E. Dodd, American Business Corporations Until 1860 (1954).

3. For those with an antiquarian bent, the development of the corporate form is nicely traced in S. Kyd, A Treatise on the Law of Corporations (1793 and Photo Reprint 1988). *See also* A. Berle, Studies in the Law of Corporation Finance (1928); Williston, History of the Law of Business Corporations Before 1800—Parts 1 & 2, 2 Harv. L. Rev. 105 (Part 1), 149 (Part 2) (1888). *See also* Dodd, *supra* note 2.

4. *See generally* Mark, The Personification of the Business Corporation in American Law, 54 U. Chi. L. Rev. 1441 (1987); Horwitz, Santa Clara Revisited: The Development of Corporate Theory, 88 W. Va. L. Rev. 173 (1985); J. Hurst, The Legitimacy of the Business Corporation in the Law of the United States 1780–1970 (1970).

5. Berle and Means, The Modern Corporation and Private Property (rev. ed. 1967).

economists) whose theoretical focus was the deconstruction of the corporation into a nexus-of-contracts.[6] That is to say, the nature of the form was that there was no form! The implications of this in terms of corporate ownership, managerial duties, governmental regulation, and social responsibility are striking, and has led those who disagree with this approach to attempt to justify more traditional or newer theories of the corporation.

For the most part, judicial opinions and legislation do not identify the theory of the corporation upon which they are based. Often a single judge will rely upon conflicting theories in a single opinion. This leads to inconsistent policies and unclear precedent.

Consequently, one premise upon which this book is based is that corporate law questions cannot be resolved satisfactorily without some theory of the nature of the corporation[7] as a key starting point. This is especially important in the field of corporate finance, which largely revolves around issues of who's "in" and who's "out" (and what's "in" and "out") of the corporate framework. As you will see, this basic issue even is manifest in various financial theories of valuation which play a significant role in corporate law. Thus (and without further ado), this chapter will present some theories of the purpose and nature of the corporation to serve as a matrix for your analysis and discussion throughout the rest of the book.

Section 1
The Ownership Model

Trustees of Dartmouth College v. Woodward
17 U.S. (Wheat.) 518, 627, 636–39, 668–69, 671–72 (1819)

[During the reign of George III, a corporate charter was granted to 12 persons denominated "The Trustees of Dartmouth College," incorporating them for the purpose of founding and operating Dartmouth College. Forty-seven years later, in 1816, the New Hampshire legislature passed a bill amending the charter, in effect making Dartmouth College a state institution, for the purpose of expanding the college into a university. The Trustees of Dartmouth College sued, in effect to invalidate the bill as violating the clause in the United States Constitution prohibiting states from passing any laws "impairing the obligation of contracts." Chief Justice Marshall began his opinion for the Court by stating: "It can require no argument to prove, that the circumstances of this case constitute a contract." After briefly examining the meaning of the contract clause, he identified the real issue as being whether the business conducted by the corporation was public or private, concluding that it was the latter. He then turned to the question of whether the act of incorporation itself altered the character of the institution.]

.... A corporation is an artificial being, invisible, intangible, and existing only in contemplation of law. Being the mere creature of law, it possesses only those properties which the charter of its creation confers upon it, either expressly, or as incidental to its very existence. These are such as are supposed best calculated to effect the object for which it was created. Among the most important are immortality, and, if the expression may be allowed, individuality; properties, by which a perpetual succession of

---

6. Butler & Ribstein, Opting Out of Fiduciary Duties: A Response to the Anti-Contractarians, 65 Wash. L. Rev. 1 (1990) (explaining this theory).

7. Throughout this book the phrase "nature of the corporation" is used as a shorthand for issues of form, purpose, ownership, governance, regulation, and social responsibility.

many persons are considered as the same, and may act as single individual. They enable a corporation to manage its own affairs, and to hold property, without the perplexing intricacies, the hazardous and endless necessity, of perpetual conveyances for the purpose of transmitting it from hand to hand. It is chiefly for the purpose of clothing bodies of men, in succession, with these qualities and capacities, that corporations were invented, and are in use. By these means, a perpetual succession of individuals are capable of acting for the promotion of the particular object, like one immortal being. But this being does not share in the civil government of the country, unless that be the purpose for which it was created. Its immortality no more confers on it political power, or a political character, than immortality would confer such power or character on a natural person. It is no more a state instrument, than a natural person exercising the same powers would be. If, then, a natural person, employed by individuals in the education of youth, or for the government of a seminary in which youth is educated, would not become a public officer, or be considered as a member of the civil government, how is it, that this artificial being, created by law, for the purpose of being employed by the same individuals, for the same purposes, should become a part of the civil government of the country? Is it because its existence, its capacities, its powers, are given by law? Because the government has given it the power to take and to hold property, in a particular form, and for particular purposes, has the government a consequent right substantially to change that form, or to vary the purposes to which the property is to be applied? This principle has never been asserted or recognized, and is supported by no authority. Can it derive aid from reason?

The objects for which a corporation is created are universally such as the government wishes to promote. They are deemed beneficial to the country; and this benefit constitutes the consideration, and in most cases, the sole consideration of the grant. In most eleemosynary institutions, the object would be difficult, perhaps unattainable, without the aid of a charter of incorporation.... The benefit to the public is considered as an ample compensation for the faculty it confers, and the corporation is created. If the advantages to the public constitute a full compensation for the faculty it gives, there can be no reason for exacting a further compensation, by claiming a right to exercise over this artificial being, a power which changes its nature, and touches the fund, for the security and application of which it was created. There can be no reason for implying in a charter, given for a valuable consideration, a power which is not only not expressed, but is in direct contradiction to its express stipulations.

From the fact, then, that a charter of incorporation has been granted, nothing can be inferred, which changes the character of the institution, or transfers to the government any new power over it. The character of civil institutions does not grow out of their incorporation, but out of the manner in which they are formed, and the objects for which they are created. The right to change them is not founded on their being incorporated, but on their being the instruments of government, created for its purposes. The same institutions, created for the same objects, though not incorporated, would be public institutions, and, of course, be controllable by the legislature. The incorporating act neither gives nor prevents this control. Neither, in reason, can the incorporating act change the character of a private eleemosynary institution.

* * *

[Justice STORY concurred:]

.... Another division of corporations is into public and private. Public corporations are generally esteemed such as exist for public political purposes only, such as towns, cities, parishes and counties; and in many respects, they are so, although they involve some private interests; but strictly speaking, public corporations are such only as are founded by the government, for public purposes, where the whole interests belong also to the government. If, therefore, the foundation be private, though under the charter of the government, the corporation is private, however extensive the uses may be to which it is devoted, either by the bounty of the founder, or the nature and objects of the institution. For instance, a bank created by the government for its own uses, whose stock is exclusively owned by the government, is, in the strictest sense, a public corporation. So, an hospital created and endowed by the government for general charity. But a bank, whose stock is owned by private persons, is a private corporation, although it is erected by the government, and its objects and operations partake of a public nature. The same doctrine may be affirmed of insurance, canal, bridge and turnpike companies. In all these cases, the uses may, in a certain sense, be called public, but the corporations are private; as much so, indeed, as if the franchises were vested in a single person.

This reasoning applied in its full force to eleemosynary corporations.

When, then, the argument assumes, that because the charity is public, the corporation is public, it manifestly confounds the popular, with the strictly legal, sense of the terms. And if it stopped here, it would not be very material to correct the error. But it is on this foundation, that a super-structure is erected, which is to compel a surrender of the cause. When the corporation is said, at the bar, to be public, it is not merely meant, that the whole community may be the proper objects of the bounty, but that the government have the sole right, as trustees of the public interests, to regulate, control and direct the corporation, and its funds and its franchises, at its own good will and pleasure. Now, such an authority does not exist in the government, except where the corporation, is in the strictest sense, public; that is, where its whole interests and franchises are the exclusive property and domain of the government itself....

Questions

1. Do Marshall and Story seem to share the same theory of the corporation? If not, what are the differences?

2. Why does the state create corporations? What are the corporate attributes essential to achieving these purposes? What problems are raised by these purposes or attributes, and how would you resolve them?

3. What are the implications of Marshall's and Story's views for the rights and obligations of management, shareholders, and creditors? For the corporation's role in society?

4. The *Dartmouth College* case arose out of a highly charged local political dispute (with significant national overtones.) *See* Stites, Private Interest and Public Gain: The Dartmouth College Case, 1819 (1972), for an excellent recounting of the factual setting. To what extent did the political context inform the opinions? If you were a Justice of the Supreme Court in 1819, faced with attempted legislative revision of the charter of a business corporation, would you have written the same opinions as Marshall or Story? How would you differ? *See generally* Friendly, The Dartmouth College Case and the Public/Private Penumbra (1969).

5. As discussed by Professor O'Melinn:

The celebrated *Dartmouth College* decision of 1819 announced a sea change in corporate theory and law that was already well under way. Relying on familiar principles of American political and constitutional theory, the case declared that the corporation was an immortal being with a soul—a group of trustees endowed with the power to govern the corporation. As Chief Justice Marshall wrote, the *primary purpose* of incorporation was to create an immortal being with the capacity to pursue great ends:

> "It is chiefly for the purpose of clothing bodies of men, in succession, with these qualities and capacities, that corporations were invented, and are in use. *By these means, a perpetual succession of individuals are capable of acting for the promotion of the particular object, like one immortal being.*"[22]

His pronouncement stood at odds with the theory of the corporation that had dominated the law for at least 400 years—the concession theory. This view had been espoused most famously by the English jurist Sir Edward Coke, who maintained that corporations "cannot commit treason, nor be outlawed, nor excommunicated, for they have no souls."[23] The difference between the two could hardly be greater—Coke's insistence that the corporation was soulless contrasts sharply with Marshall's vision of corporate immortality, and the contrast marks a true revolution in American corporate law.

O'Melinn, Neither Contract Nor Concession: The Public Personality of the Corporation, forthcoming 74 G.W. L. Rev. __ (2006).

Dodd, For Whom Are Corporate Managers Trustees?
45 Harv. L. Rev. 1145, 1046–48, 1052–53, 1156–57, 1159–60, 1161–63 (1932)

[I]t is undoubtedly the traditional view that a corporation is an association of stockholders formed for their private gain and to be managed by its board of directors solely with that end in view. Directors and managers of modern large corporations are granted all sorts of novel powers by present-day corporation statutes and charters, and are free from any substantial supervision by stockholders by reason of the difficulty which the modern stockholder has in discovering what is going on and taking effective measures even if he has discovered it. The fact that managers so empowered not infrequently act as though maximum stockholder profit was not the sole object of managerial activities has led some students of corporate problems, particularly Mr. A. A. Berle, to advocate an increased emphasis on the doctrine that managerial powers are held in trust for stockholders as sole beneficiaries of the corporate enterprise.[a]

The present writer is thoroughly in sympathy with Mr. Berle's[b] efforts to establish a legal control which will more effectually prevent corporate managers from diverting

---

22. [*Dartmouth Coll.*, 17 U.S. (4 Wheat.) at 636] (emphasis added).
23. Case of Sutton's Hospital, (1612) 77 Eng. Rep. 960, 973 (K. B.).
a. *See* Berle, Corporate Powers as Powers in Trust, 44 Harv. L. Rev. 1049 (1931).
b. *See id.* at 1074, in which Mr. Berle argues:
   In this concept, corporation law becomes in substance a branch of the law of trusts. The rules of application are less rigorous, since the business situation demands greater flexibility than the trust situation. Probably the requirements as to motive and clean-mindedness on the part of the persons exercising the powers are substantially similar. The requirements of exactitude in apportioning or assessing ratable differences must yield to the necessary approximations which business entails. But the fundamental requirements follow similar lines.

profit into their own pockets from those of stockholders, and agrees with many of the specific rules which the latter deduces from his trusteeship principle.[6] He nevertheless believes that it is undesirable, even with the laudable purpose of giving stockholders much-needed protection against self-seeking managers, to give increased emphasis at the present time to the view that business corporations exist for the sole purpose of making profits for their stockholders. He believes that public opinion, which ultimately makes law, has made and is today making substantial strides in the direction of a view of the business corporation as an economic institution which has a social service as well as a profit-making function, that this view has already had some effect upon legal theory, and that it is likely to have a greatly increased effect upon the latter in the near future.

* * *

If, however, as much recent writing suggests, we are undergoing a substantial change in our public opinion with regard to the obligations of business to the community, it is natural to expect that this change of opinion will have some effect upon the attitude of those who manage business. If, therefore, the managers of modern businesses were also its owners, the development of a public opinion to the effect that business has responsibilities to its employees and its customers would, quite apart from any legal compulsion, tend to affect the conduct of the better type of business man. The principal object of legal compulsion might then be to keep those who failed to catch the new spirit up to the standards which their more enlightened competitors would desire to adopt voluntarily. Business might then become a profession of public service, not primarily because the law had made it such but because a public opinion shared in by business men themselves had brought about a professional attitude.

Our present economic system, under which our more important business enterprises are owned by investors who take no part in carrying them on—absentee owners who in many cases have not even seen the property from which they derive their profits—alters the situation materially. That stockholders who have no contact with business other than to derive dividends from it should become imbued with a professional spirit of public service is hardly thinkable. If incorporate business is to become professionalized, it is to the managers, not to the owners, that we must look for the accomplishment of this result.

* * *

The view that those who manage our business corporations should concern themselves with the interests of employees, consumers, and the general public, as well as of the stockholders, is thus advanced today by persons whose position in the business world is such as to give them great power of influencing both business opinion and public opinion generally. Little or no attempt seems to have been made, however, to consider how far such an attitude on the part of corporate managers is compatible with the legal duties which they owe the stockholder-owners as the elected representatives of the latter.

---

6. That directors are fiduciaries for their corporations is indisputable....
It may be questioned, however, whether some of the problems which Mr. Berle treats as fiduciary problems—e.g., that relating to dividends on non-cumulative preferred stock—are not questions of contract rather than of fiduciary law. Cf. Wabash Ry. v. Barclay, 280 U.S. 197 (1930)....

No doubt it is to a large extent true that an attempt by business managers to take into consideration the welfare of employees and consumers (and under modern industrial conditions the two classes are largely the same) will in the long run increase the profits of stockholders.... If the social responsibility of business means merely a more enlightened view as to the ultimate advantage of the stockholder-owners, then obviously corporate managers may accept such social responsibility without any departure from the traditional view that their function is to seek to obtain the maximum amount of profits for their stockholders.

And yet one need not be unduly credulous to feel that there is more to this talk of social responsibility on the part of corporation managers than merely a more intelligent appreciation of what tends to the ultimate benefit of their stockholders. Modern large-scale industry has given to the managers of our principal corporations enormous power over the welfare of wage earners and consumers, particularly the former. Power over the lives of others tends to create on the part of those most worthy to exercise it a sense of responsibility. The managers, who along with the subordinate employees are part of the group which is contributing to the success of the enterprise by day-to-day efforts, may easily come to feel as strong a community of interest with their fellow workers as with a group of investors whose only connection with the enterprise is that they or their predecessors in title invested money in it, perhaps in the remote past.[30] Moreover, the concept that the managers are merely ... "attorneys for the investors" leads to the conclusion that if other classes who are affected by the corporation's activities need protection, that protection must be entrusted to other hands than those of the managers. Desire to retain their present powers accordingly encourages the latter to adopt and disseminate the view that they are guardians of all the interests which the corporation affects and not merely servants of its absentee owners.

Any clash between this point of view and the orthodox theory that the mangers are elected by stockholder-owners to serve their interests exclusively has thus far been chiefly potential rather than actual. Judicial willingness—which has increased of late—to allow corporate directors a wide range of discretion as to what policies will best promote the interests of the stockholders, together with managerial disinclination to indulge a sense of social responsibility to a point where it is likely to injure the stockholders, has thus far prevented the issue from being frequently raised in clear-cut fashion in litigation.[31]

* * *

---

30. Some of our most successful industrial corporations have for years obtained all the additional capital which they needed out of surplus profits without any further issue of securities. See, e.g., The General Electric Co., Moody's Manual of Investments, Industrial Securities (1931) 971, indicating that the only outstanding bonds of that corporation were issued in 1902 and that no stock has been issued since 1920 except as a stock dividend or split-up.

31. It was raised in the case of Dodge v. Ford Motor Co., [204 Mich. 459, 170 N.W. 668 (1919)], in which Mr. Ford's expressions of an intention to share profits with the public through a reduction in prices were relied upon as justifying a decree compelling the declaration of a dividend out of the large surplus of the company. Neither the language of the opinion nor the relief granted necessarily involves an unqualified acceptance of the maximum-profit-for-stockholders formula. The opinion states that "a business corporation is organized and carried on primarily for the profit of the stockholders" and that directors cannot lawfully "conduct the affairs of a corporation for the merely incidental benefit of shareholders and for the primary purpose of benefiting others." 204 Mich. at 507, 170 N.W. at 684. Despite testimony of Mr. Ford that he planned to expand the enterprise in the interest of consumers rather than of stockholders, the court was careful so to limit its decree as not to interfere seriously with the expansion program. Its avowed reason for so doing was that expansion might be made profitable despite Mr. Ford's expressed indifference to profit. One may suspect that it was also motivated, consciously or unconsciously, by a reluctance to prevent the growth of a socially important enterprise.

Such a view is difficult to justify if we insist on thinking of the business corporation as merely an aggregate of stockholders with directors and officers chosen by them as their trustees or agents. It is not for a trustee to be public-spirited with his beneficiary's property. But we are not bound to treat the corporation as a mere aggregate of stockholders. The traditional view of our law is that a corporation is a distinct legal entity. Unfortunately, its entity character has been thought of as something conferred upon it by the state which, by a mysterious rite called incorporation, magically produced "*e pluribus unum*." The present vogue of legal realism breeds dissatisfaction with such legal mysteries and leads to insistence on viewing the corporation as it really is. So viewing it we may, as many do, insist that it is a mere aggregate of stockholders; but there is another way of regarding it which has distinguished adherents. According to this concept any organized group, particularly if its organization is of a permanent character, is a factual unit, "a body which from no fiction of law but from the very nature of things differs from the individuals of whom it is constituted."

If the unity of the corporate body is real, then there is reality and not simply legal fiction in the proposition that the managers of the unit are fiduciaries for it and not merely for its individual members, that they are … trustees for an institution rather than attorneys for the stockholders. As previously stated, this entity approach will not substantially affect our results if we insist that the sole function for the entity is to seek maximum stockholder profit. But need we so assume?

* * *

…. If we think of it as an institution which differs in the nature of things from the individuals who compose it, we may then readily conceive of it as a person, which, like other persons engaged in business, is affected not only by the laws which regulate business but by the attitude of public and business opinion as to the social obligations of business. If business is tending to become a profession, then a corporate person engaged in business is a professional even though its stockholders, who take no active part in the conduct of the business, may not be. Those through whom it acts may therefore employ its funds in a manner appropriate to a person practicing a profession and imbued with a sense of social responsibility without thereby being guilty of a breach of trust.…

The legal recognition that there are other interests than those of the stockholders to be protected does not, as we have seen, necessarily give corporate managers the right to consider those interests, as it is possible to regard the managers as representatives of the stockholding interest only. Such a view means in practice that there are no human beings who are in a position where they can lawfully accept for incorporated business those social responsibilities which public opinion is coming to expect, and that these responsibilities must be imposed on corporations by legal compulsion. This makes the situation of incorporated business so anomalous that we are justified in demanding clear proof that it is a correct statement of the legal situation.

Clear proof is not forthcoming. Despite many attempts to dissolve the corporation into an aggregate of stockholders, our legal tradition is rather in favor of treating it as an institution directed by persons who are primarily fiduciaries for the institution rather than for its members. That lawyers have commonly assumed that the managers must conduct the institution with single-minded devotion to stockholder profit is true; but the assumption is based upon a particular view of the nature of the institution which we call a business corporation, which concept is in turn based upon a particular view of the nature of business as a purely private enterprise. If we recognize that the attitude of law and public opinion toward business is changing, we may then properly modify our ideas as to the nature of such a business institution as the corporation and hence as to the considerations which may properly influence the conduct of those who direct its activities.

Questions

1. What is the debate between Berle and Dodd? What are the implications of each theory for the rights and duties among directors, shareholders, and creditors? Which view do you think leads to better social policy?

2. Is any particular theory of the corporation important to Dodd's argument?

3. For more of the Berle-Dodd debate, see Berle, For Whom Corporate Managers Are Trustees: A Note, 45 Harv. L. Rev. 1365 (1932); Dodd, Is Effective Enforcement of the Fiduciary Duties of Corporate Managers Practicable?, 2 U. Chi. L. Rev. 194 (1935); Dodd, Book Review, 9 U. Chi. L. Rev. 538 (1942); Berle, The 20th Century Capitalist Revolution 169 (1954). For a study of the Berle-Dodd debate, see Weiner, The Berle-Dodd Dialogues on the Concept of the Corporation, 64 Colum. L. Rev. 1458 (1964). For a powerful statement by business leaders largely accepting Dodd's approach, see The Business Roundtable, Statement on Corporate Responsibility (1981).

4. Should the purpose of the corporation be shareholder primacy? Consider the view of Professor O'Melinn:

> .... Shareholder primacy has thus frequently been advanced as the desideratum of corporate law. If the business corporation is required to acknowledge the work that other institutions have done for it, it becomes obvious that shareholder primacy has little currency as a foundational norm. Many advances in corporate law were achieved on behalf of corporations without any shareholders, such as colleges and churches. These organizations quite clearly attained corporate privileges on account of the important public services that they performed. Further, shareholder primacy is closely associated with individualistic notions of property ownership that are incompatible with both the law and the facts of corporate life. American law has recognized the importance of property primarily because it expresses the moral personality of the corporation, and not because of each individual corporator's entitlement to her property.

O'Melinn, Neither Contract Nor Concession: The Public Personality of the Corporation, forthcoming 74 G.W. L. Rev. __ (2006).

———

Note on Unocal Corp. v. Mesa Petroleum Co., Revlon, Inc. v. MacAndrews & Forbes Holdings, Inc. and Paramount Communications, Inc. v. Time Incorporated

In Unocal Corp. v. Mesa Petroleum Co., 493 A.2d 946 (Del. 1985),[1] Mesa, owner of 13 percent of Unocal's stock, made a two-tier front loaded cash tender offer for approximately 37 percent of Unocal's outstanding stock. The back end of the merger was to be paid in junk bonds.[2] As part of its defensive effort to keep control of the corporation,

———

1. The *Unocal* opinion is set forth *infra* at chapter 9, section 2b(i).
2. Junk bonds are treated *infra* at chapter 5, section 2b(ii).

the Unocal board of directors authorized an exchange offer to be made to all of Unocal's shareholders except Mesa, in which the corporation exchanged its own debt for 49 percent of the outstanding stock.

The Delaware Supreme Court upheld this selective self-tender against Mesa's challenge that excluding it from the self tender was a breach of the directors' fiduciary duty to it. In so doing, the court suggested that among the factors the board could consider in implementing a defensive measure was "the impact [of the tender offer] on 'constituencies' other than shareholders (i.e., creditors, customers, employees, and perhaps even the community generally)...." *Id.* at 955.

Notwithstanding this suggested broadening of the scope of management's responsibilities, the tenacity of the traditional view was demonstrated the next year in Revlon, Inc. v. MacAndrews & Forbes Holdings, Inc., 506 A.2d 173 (Del. 1986). Among the criticisms levied by the court at Revlon's directors for wrongfully deploying their defensive arsenal was that they had considered the interests of a class of noteholders rather than those of the shareholders exclusively. The notes in question were issued as part of a defensive exchange offer, in which Revlon traded the notes for outstanding stock. Thus, stockholders of Revlon acquired the notes in exchange for their stock in a transaction designed to keep Revlon independent. Not only did the court disregard the identity (at least in theory)[3] of the noteholders in describing the board's proper focus as the interests of the stockholders, but it further ignored the fact that, under the proration rules of the Williams Act,[4] the noteholders probably continued to hold Revlon stock as well. Was the court correct in disregarding these facts?

In Paramount Communications, Inc. v. Time Incorporated, 571 A.2d 1140 (Del. 1990), the Delaware Supreme Court affirmed the Chancellor's[5] denial of plaintiff's request to enjoin defendant Time's tender offer for 51% of Warner Communication, Inc. Time had been negotiating a business combination with Warner since 1987, following four years during which its executive board explored a variety of expansion possibilities (including consideration of a merger with plaintiff, which was not pursued). In any event, Time and Warner negotiated a merger, which was interrupted by plaintiff's hostile tender offer commenced on June 7, 1989. Time resisted, and recast its transaction with Warner as a tender offer by Time, at least in part to deprive Time shareholders of the right to vote on the deal.[6] Prior to Paramount's tender offer, Time's board had also adopted several defensive measures to ward off unwanted bidders.

The Court held that, under *Revlon,* the Time board had not put the company "up for sale" by engaging in the Warner deal. Rather, it rejected the Paramount bid in a manner consistent with its long-term strategic business plan, the key to which was the Warner transaction. In fact, the court applied the business judgment rule to Time's defensive measures, noting that its insistence on the Warner deal (or none at all) as consistent with its corporate "culture" (designed to preserve Time magazine's journalistic integrity) and long-term strategic objectives was proper under Delaware law regardless of the stockholders' desires.

---

3. As a practical matter, most of the notes and Revlon stock probably were in the hands of arbitrageurs.

4. Securities Exchange Act of 1934, §14d(6); 17 C.F.R. §240.14d-8.

5. The Chancellor's opinion is set forth *infra* at chapter 9, section 2b(i).

6. Voting was not required under Delaware law but was required by the New York Stock Exchange Rules to which Time was subject. 571 A.2d at 1146.

Question

Whose interests are served by the preservation of a corporation's "culture"? What are the broader implications of *Time*? *See infra* chapter 5, section 7, for a discussion of constituency statutes.

* * *

American Law Institute, Principles of Corporate Governance: Analysis and Recommendations
(1994)[a]

Section 2.01 The Objective and Conduct of the Corporation

(a) Subject to the provisions of Subsection (b) ... [a] corporation ... should have as its objective the conduct of business activities with a view to enhancing corporate profit and shareholder gain.

(b) Even if corporate profit and shareholder gain are not thereby enhanced, the corporation, in the conduct of its business:

(1) Is obliged, to the same extent as a natural person, to act within the boundaries set by law;

(2) May take into account ethical considerations that are reasonably regarded as appropriate to the responsible conduct of business; and

(3) May devote a reasonable amount of resources to public welfare, humanitarian, educational, and philanthropic purposes.

Question

What is the ALI's position in the debate?

See Schwartz, Defining the Corporate Objective: Section 2.01 of the ALI's Principles, 52 Geo. Wash. L. Rev. 511 (1984); White, How Should We Talk About Corporations? The Languages of Economics and of Citizenship, 94 Yale L.J. 1416 (1985); Solomon & Collins, Humanistic Economics: A New Model for the Corporate Social Responsibility Debate, 12 J. Corp. L. 331 (1987).

Section 2
Economic Theories:
The Agency/Contract Model

The central corporate law problem throughout most of the twentieth century has been to ensure that corporate management conducts the business and affairs of the corporation

---

in the interests of its owners.[1] The fact that stockholders in the modern public corporation tend to be widely dispersed and own relatively small proportions of the corporation's stock[2] suggests that they are unlikely to have an incentive to supervise management. And the relatively greater security of other financial claimants of the corporation suggests that their monitoring incentives may be even weaker. So the problem of ensuring managerial fealty to the corporation exists.

You are familiar from your previous study of corporations with the basic principles and doctrines that corporate law has developed to deal with this problem based on the traditional entity theory of the corporation. Recently economists, and lawyers influenced by them, have begun to look at this problem in the context of a different understanding of the corporation. The common theory underlying these approaches treats the corporation as a web, or "nexus," of contracts, in which "the corporation" is nothing more than a state-sanctioned device for coordinating the contractually supplied inputs it requires to conduct its business, with management as one of these inputs whose task is to contract for, coordinate, and monitor the supply of the other inputs.[3] Although this nexus-of-contracts theory does not appear to be an indispensable foundation for all of the economic theories of internal corporate behavior, it is upon the basis of this model that these theories are best explained.

Although the economic literature is too vast and diverse to summarize, it is fair to say that the central problem these theories attempt to resolve is restraining managerial self-dealing (including in that term nonfeasance) at the lowest possible cost.[4] Thus the excerpt of Professor Fama's article attempts to deal with this problem in the context of a market-based economic model centered principally on the market for managerial services. Professors Easterbrook and Fischel discuss this approach in the language of corporate law. Professor Williamson, on the other hand, addresses the problem in the context of minimizing the transaction costs of corporate governance. As you consider these views and the others presented in this section, measure them against the traditional model of the corporation and the means of managerial restraint with which you are familiar.

---

1. The traditional approach has been to treat the stockholders as the owners. We, however, use the term "owners" in lieu of stockholders because the question of who owns the corporation has become a matter of serious debate in corporate law. See, e.g., Baird & Jackson, Corporate Reorganization and the Treatment of Diverse Ownership Interests: A Comment on Adequate Protection of Secured Creditors in Bankruptcy, 51 U. Chi. L. Rev. 97 (1984) (including within the concept of owners all those with rights to a portion of the corporation's wealth). Professor Fama, whose seminal article is excerpted infra, argues that ownership is itself an irrelevant concept.

2. This may well be changing with the rise of the institutional investor. See Black, Shareholder Passivity Reexamined, 89 Mich. L. Rev. 520 (1990); Brancato, The Pivotal Role of Institutional Investors in Capital Markets: A Summary of Economic Research at the Columbia Institutional Investor Project (1990); Conard, Beyond Managerialism: Investor Capitalism?, 22 U. Mich. J.L. Ref. 117, 132–34 (1988); Eisenberg, The Structure of the Corporation: A Legal Analysis §§5.3–5.6 (1976), for studies of the increased concentration in institutional stockholding. The role of institutional investors in corporate governance is a subject of continuing debate.

3. See generally Butler, The Contractual Theory of the Corporation, 11 Geo. Mason L. Rev. 99 (1989) (describing the contractual theory of the corporation).

4. The term "agency costs" is used to define the costs arising from the separation of functions within the corporation, including the cost incurred by stockholders in monitoring management, the cost of devices employed by management to guarantee its loyalty ("bonding costs"), and the cost of self-dealing that is simply too expensive to prevent. See Klein & Coffee, Business Organization and Finance 176-83 (9th ed. 2004); Fama & Jensen, Agency Problems and Residual Claims, 26 J. Law & Econ. 327 (1983).

Fama, Agency Problems and the Theory of the Firm
88 J. Pol. Econ. 288 (1980)[a]

Economists have long been concerned with the incentive problems that arise when decision making in a firm is the province of managers who are not the firm's security holders. One outcome has been the development of "behavioral" and "managerial" theories of the firm which reject the classical model of an entrepreneur, or owner-manager, who single-mindedly operates the firm to maximize profits, in favor of theories that focus more on the motivations of a manager who controls but does not own and who has little resemblance to the classical "economic man." ...

More recently the literature has moved toward theories that reject the classical model of the firm but assume classical forms of economic behavior on the part of agents within the firm. The firm is viewed as a set of contracts among factors of production, with each factor motivated by its self-interest. Because of its emphasis on the importance of rights in the organization established by contracts, this literature is characterized under the rubric "property rights." ...

The striking insight ... is in viewing the firm as a set of contracts among factors of production. In effect, the firm is viewed as a team whose members act from self-interest but realize that their destinies depend to some extent on the survival of the team in its competition with other teams. This insight, however, is not carried far enough. In the classical theory, the agent who personifies the firm is the entrepreneur who is taken to be both manager and residual risk bearer. Although his title sometimes changes—for example, Alchian and Demsetz call him "the employer"—the entrepreneur continues to play a central role in the firm of the property-rights literature. As a consequence, this literature fails to explain the large modern corporation in which control of the firm is in the hands of managers who are more or less separate from the firm's security holders.

The main thesis of this paper is that separation of security ownership and control can be explained as an efficient form of economic organization within the "set of contracts" perspective. We first set aside the typical presumption that a corporation has owners in any meaningful sense. The attractive concept of the entrepreneur is also laid to rest, at least for the purposes of the large modern corporation. Instead, the two functions usually attributed to the entrepreneur, management and risk bearing, are treated as naturally separate factors within the set of contracts called a firm. The firm is disciplined by competition from other firms, which forces the evolution of devices for efficiently monitoring the performance of the entire team and of its individual members. In addition, individual participants in the firm, and in particular its managers, face both the discipline and opportunities provided by the markets for their services, both within and outside of the firm.

The Irrelevance of the Concept of Ownership of the Firm

To set a framework for the analysis, let us first describe roles for management and risk bearing in the set of contracts called a firm. Management is a type of labor but with a special role—coordinating the activities of inputs and carrying out the contracts agreed among inputs, all of which can be characterized as "decision making." To explain the role of the risk bearers, assume for the moment that the firm rents all other factors of production and that rental contracts are negotiated at the beginning of each production

---

period with payoffs at the end of the period. The risk bearers then contract to accept the uncertain and possibly negative difference between total revenues and costs at the end of each production period.

When other factors of production are paid at the end of each period, it is not necessary for the risk bearers to invest anything in the firm at the beginning of the period. Most commonly, however, the risk bearers guarantee performance of their contracts by putting up wealth ex ante, with this front money used to purchase capital and perhaps also the technology that the firm uses in its production activities. In this way the risk bearing function is combined with ownership of capital and technology....

However, ownership of capital should not be confused with ownership of the firm. Each factor in a firm is owned by somebody. The firm is just the set of contracts covering the way inputs are joined to create outputs and the way receipts from outputs are shared among inputs. In this "nexus of contracts" perspective, ownership of the firm is an irrelevant concept. Dispelling the tenacious notion that a firm is owned by its security holders is important because it is a first step toward understanding that control over a firm's decisions is not necessarily the province of security holders. The second step is setting aside the equally tenacious role in the firm usually attributed to the entrepreneur.

Management and Risk Bearing: A Closer Look

... [A]ny given set of contracts, a particular firm, is in competition with other firms, which are likewise teams of cooperating factors of production. If there is a part of the team that has a special interest in its viability, it is not obviously the risk bearers.... The risk bearers, as residual claimants, also seem to suffer the most direct consequences from the failings of the team. However, the risk bearers in the modern corporation also have markets for their services—capital markets—which allow them to shift among teams with relatively low transaction costs and to hedge against the failings of any given team by diversifying their holdings across teams.

Indeed, portfolio theory tells us that the optimal portfolio for any investor is likely to be diversified across the securities of many firms. Since he holds the securities of many firms precisely to avoid having his wealth depend too much on any one firm, an individual security holder generally has no special interest in personally overseeing the detailed activities of any firm. In short, efficient allocation of risk bearing seems to imply a large degree of separation of security ownership from control of a firm.

On the other hand, the managers of a firm rent a substantial lump of wealth—their human capital—to the firm, and the rental rates for their human capital signaled by the managerial labor market are likely to depend on the success or failure of the firm. The function of management is to oversee the contracts among factors and to ensure the viability of the firm. For the purposes of the managerial labor market, the previous associations of a manager with success and failure are information about his talents. The manager of a firm, like the coach of any team, may not suffer any immediate gain or loss in current wages from the current performance of his team, but the success or failure of the team impacts his future wages, and this gives the manager a stake in the success of the team.

The firm's security holders provide important but indirect assistance to the managerial labor market in its task of valuing the firm's management. A security holder wants to purchase securities with confidence that the prices paid reflect the risks he is taking and that the securities will be priced in the future to allow him to reap the rewards (or punishments) of his risk bearing. Thus, although an individual security holder may not have a strong interest in directly overseeing the management of a particular firm, he has a strong interest in the existence of a capital market which efficiently prices the firm's securities. The signals provided by an efficient capital market about the values of a firm's securities are likely to be important for the managerial labor market's revaluations of the firm's management.

We come now to the central question. To what extent can the signals provided by the managerial labor market and the capital market, perhaps along with other market-induced mechanisms, discipline managers? ...

The Viability of Separation of Security Ownership and Control of the Firm: General Comments

The outside managerial labor market exerts many direct pressures on the firm to sort and compensate managers according to performance. One form of pressure comes from the fact that an ongoing firm is always in the market for new managers. Potential new managers are concerned with the mechanics by which their performance will be judged, and they seek information about the responsiveness of the system in rewarding performance. Moreover, given a competitive managerial labor market, when the firm's reward system is not responsive to performance the firm loses managers, and the best are the first to leave.

* * *

Each manager has a stake in the performance of the managers above and below him and, as a consequence, undertakes some amount of monitoring in both directions.

All managers below the very top level have an interest in seeing that the top managers choose policies for the firm which provide the most positive signals to the managerial labor market. But by what mechanism can top management be disciplined? Since the body designated for this function is the board of directors, we can ask how it might be constructed to do its job. A board dominated by security holders does not seem optimal or endowed with good survival properties. Diffuse ownership of securities is beneficial in terms of an optimal allocation of risk bearing, but its consequence is that the firm's security holders are generally too diversified across the securities of many firms to take much direct interest in a particular firm.

If there is competition among the top managers themselves (all want to be the boss of bosses), then perhaps they are the best ones to control the board of directors. They are most directly in the line of fire from lower managers when the markets for securities and managerial labor give poor signals about the performance of the firm. Because of their power over the firm's decisions, their market-determined opportunity wages are also likely to be most affected by market signals about the performance of the firm. If they are also in competition for the top places in the firm, they may be the most informed and responsive critics of the firm's performance.

Having gained control of the board, top management may decide that collusion and expropriation of security holder wealth are better than competition among themselves. The probability of such collusive arrangements might be lowered, and the viability of the board as a market-induced mechanism for low-cost internal transfer of control might be enhanced, by the inclusion of outside directors. The latter might best be regarded as professional referees whose task is to stimulate and oversee the competition among the firm's top managers. In a state of advanced evolution of the external markets that buttress the corporate firm, the outside directors are in their turn disciplined by the market for their services which prices them according to their performance as referees. ...

This analysis does not imply that boards of directors are likely to be composed entirely of managers and outside directors. The board is viewed as a market-induced institution, the ultimate internal monitor of the set of contracts called a firm, whose most important role is to scrutinize the highest decision makers within the firm. In the team or nexus of contracts view of the firm, one cannot rule out the evolution of boards of directors that contain many different factors of production (or their hired representatives), whose common trait is that their marginal products are affected by those of the top decision makers. On the other hand, one also cannot conclude that all such factors will naturally show up on boards since there may be other market-induced institutions, for example, unions, that more efficiently monitor managers on behalf of specific factors. All one can say is that in a competitive environment lower-cost sets of monitoring mechanisms are likely to survive. The role of the board in this framework is to provide a relatively low-cost mechanism for replacing or reordering top managers; lower cost, for example, than the mechanism provided by an outside takeover, although, of course, the existence of an outside market for control is another force which helps to sensitize the internal managerial labor market.

* * *

.... The viability of the large corporation with diffuse security ownership is better explained in terms of a model where the primary disciplining of managers comes through managerial labor markets, both within and outside of the firm, with assistance from the panoply of internal and external monitoring devices that evolve to stimulate the ongoing efficiency of the corporate form, and with the market for outside takeovers providing discipline of last resort.

The Viability of Separation of Security Ownership and Control: Details

.... We now examine somewhat more specifically conditions under which the discipline imposed by managerial labor markets can resolve potential incentive problems associated with the separation of security ownership and control of the firm.

To focus on the problem we are trying to solve, let us first examine the situation where the manager is also the firm's sole security holder so that there is clearly no incentive problem.... The manager ... pays directly for consumption on the job; that is, as manager he cannot avoid a full ex post settling up with himself as security holder.

In contrast, when the manager is no longer sole security holder, and in the absence of some form of full ex post settling up for deviations from contract, a manager has an incentive to consume more on the job than is agreed in his contract. The manager perceives that, on ex post basis, he can beat the game by shirking or consuming more perquisites than previously agreed. This does not necessarily mean that the manager profits at the expense of other factors. Rational managerial labor markets understand any shortcomings of available mechanisms for enforcing ex post settling up. Assessments of ex post deviations from contract will be incorporated into contracts on an ex ante basis; for example, through an adjustment of the manager's wage.

Nevertheless, a game which is fair on an ex ante basis does not induce the same behavior as a game in which there is also ex post settling up. Herein lie the potential losses from separation of security ownership and control of a firm. There are situations where, with less than complete ex post settling up, the manager is induced to consume more on the job than he would like, given that on average he pays for his consumption ex ante.

Three general conditions suffice to make the wage revaluation imposed by the managerial labor market a form of full ex post settling up which resolves the managerial incentive problem described above. The first condition is that a manager's talents and his tastes for consumption on the job are not known with certainty, are likely to change through time, and must be imputed by managerial labor markets at least in part from information about the manager's current and past performance. Since it seems to capture the essence of the task of managerial labor markets in a world of uncertainty, this assumption is no real restriction.

The second assumption is that managerial labor markets appropriately use current and past information to revise future wages and understand any enforcement power inherent in the wage revision process. In short, contrary to much of the literature on separation of security ownership and control, we impute efficiency or rationality in information processing to managerial labor markets. In defense of this assumption, we note that the problem faced by managerial labor markets in revaluing the managers of a firm is much entwined with the problem faced by the capital market in revaluing the firm itself. Although we do not understand all the details of the process, available empirical evidence ... suggests that the capital market generally makes rational assessments of the value of the firm in the face of imprecise and uncertain information. This does not necessarily mean that information processing in managerial labor markets is equally efficient or rational, but it is a warning against strong presumptions to the contrary.

The final and key condition for full control of managerial behavior through wage changes is that the weight of the wage revision process is sufficient to resolve any potential problems with managerial incentives. In this general form, the condition amounts to assuming the desired result....

* * *

Conclusions

... The important general point is that in any scenario where the weight of the wage revision process is at least equivalent to full ex post settling up, managerial incentive problems—the problem usually attributed to the separation of security ownership and control of the firm—are resolved.

No claim is made that the wage revision process always results in a full ex post settling up on the part of the manager. There are certainly situations where the weight of anticipated future wage changes is insufficient to counterbalance the gains to be had from ex post shirking, or perhaps outright theft, in excess of what was agreed ex ante in a manager's contract. On the other hand, precise full ex post settling up is not an upper bound on the force of the wage revision process. There are certainly situations where, as a consequence of anticipated future wage changes, a manager perceives that the value of his human capital changes by more than the wealth changes imposed on other factors, and especially the firm's security holders, by his current deviations from the terms of his contract.

The extent to which the wage revision process imposes ex post settling up in any particular situation is, of course, an empirical issue. But it is probably safe to say that the general phenomenon is at least one of the ingredients in the survival of the modern large corporation, characterized by diffuse security ownership and the separation of security ownership and control, as a viable form of economic organization.

Questions

1. Does Fama have a theory of the corporation? What is the theory upon which the excerpt is based?

2. What are the problems Fama is trying to confront? Are they the same problems addressed by corporate law? How, if at all, does corporate law deal with these problems? How does Fama propose to deal with them?

3. What are the normative considerations underlying Fama's theory? What are his underlying assumptions?

4. What are the implications of this theory for the duties of management to shareholders and creditors? What do you think Fama would view as the goal of corporate law? The appropriate governance structure of corporations?

Easterbrook & Fischel, The Corporate Contract
89 Colum. L. Rev. 1416, 1419–22 (1989)[a]

The corporation and its securities are products to as great an extent as the sewing machines or other things the firm makes. Just as the founders of a firm have incentives to make the kinds of sewing machines people want to buy, they have incentives to create the kind of firm, governance structure, and securities people value. The founders of the firm will find it profitable to establish the governance structure that is most beneficial to investors, net of the costs of maintaining the structure. People who seek resources to control will have to deliver more returns to investors. Those who promise the highest returns—and make the promises binding, hence believable—will obtain the largest investments.

The first question facing entrepreneurs is what promises to make, and the second is how to induce investors to believe the promises. Empty promises are worthless promises. Answering the first question depends on finding ways to reduce the effects of divergent interests; answering the second depends on finding legal and automatic enforcement devices. The more automatic the enforcement, the more investors will believe the promises.

What promises will the entrepreneurs make in order to induce investors to hand over more money? No set of promises is right for all firms at all times. No one thinks that the governance structure used for a small business will work well for Exxon or Hydro Quebec. The best structure cannot be derived from theory; it must be developed by experience. We should be skeptical of claims that any one structure—or even a class of structures—is best. But we can see the sorts of promises that are likely to emerge in the competition for investments.

Some promises entail submitting to scrutiny in advance of action. Outside directors watch inside ones; inside directors watch other managers; the managers hire detectives to watch the employees. At other times, though, prior monitoring may be too costly in relation to its benefits, and the most desirable methods of control will rest on deterrence, on letting people act as they wish but penalizing certain conduct. Fiduciary obligations and litigation are forms of subsequent settling-up included among these kinds of devices. Still other methods operate automatically. Managers enjoy hefty salaries and perquisites of office; the threat of losing these induces managers to act in investors' interest.

Managers in the United States must select the place of incorporation. The fifty states offer different menus of devices (from voting by shareholders to fiduciary rules to deriv-

---

ative litigation) for the protection of investors. The managers who pick the state of incorporation that is most desirable from the perspective of investors will attract the most money. The states that select the best combination of rules will attract the most corporate investment (and therefore increase their tax collections). So states compete to offer—and managers to use—beneficial sets of legal rules. These include not only rules about governance structures but also fiduciary rules and prohibitions of fraud.

Managers select when to go public. Less experienced entrepreneurs start with venture capital, which comes with extensive strings. The venture capitalists control the operation of the firm with some care. Only after the managerial team and structure have matured will the firm issue public securities.

Entrepreneurs make promises in the articles of incorporation and the securities they issue when they go public. The debt investors receive exceptionally detailed promises in indentures. These promises concern the riskiness of the firm's operations, the extent to which earnings may be paid out, and the domain of managerial discretion. These promises benefit equity investors as well as debt investors. The equity investors usually receive votes rather than explicit promises. Votes make it possible for the investors to replace the managers. (Those who believe that managers have unchecked control should ask themselves why the organizers of a firm issue equity claims that enable the investors to replace the managers.) The managers also promise, explicitly or otherwise, to abide by the standards of "fair dealing" embedded in the fiduciary rules of corporate law. Sometimes they make additional promises as well.

To sum up: self-interested entrepreneurs and managers, just like other investors, are driven to find the devices most likely to maximize net profits. If they do not, they pay in lower prices for corporate paper. Any one firm may deviate from the optimal measures. Over tens of years and thousands of firms, though, tendencies emerge. The firms and managers that make the choices investors prefer will prosper relative to others. Because the choices do not generally impose costs on strangers to the contracts, what is optimal for the firms and investors is optimal for society. We can learn a great deal just by observing which devices are widely used and which are not.

It is important to distinguish between isolated transactions and governance structures. There are high costs of operating capital and managerial markets, just as there are high costs of other methods of dealing with the divergence of interests. It is inevitable that a substantial amount of undesirable slack or self-dealing will occur. The question is whether these costs can be cut by mechanisms that are not themselves more costly. We accept some costly conduct because the costs of the remedy are even greater. We also use deterrence (say, the threat of punishment for fraud) rather than other forms of legal control when deterrence is the least-cost method of handling a problem. Deterrence is a particularly inexpensive method. The expensive legal system is not cranked up unless there is evidence of wrongdoing; if the anticipated penalty (the sanction multiplied by the probability of its application) is selected well, there will not be much wrongdoing, and the costs of the system are correspondingly small. A regulatory system (one entailing scrutiny and approval in advance in each case) ensures that the costs of control will be high; they will be incurred even if the risk is small.

Markets that let particular episodes of wrongdoing slide by, or legal systems that use deterrence rather than structural change to handle the costs of management, are likely very effective in making judgments about optimal governance structures. Governance structures are open and notorious, unlike the conduct they seek to control. Costs of information in knowing about a firm's governance are low. Firms and teams of managers can compete with each other over time to design governance structures and to build in penalties for malfeasance. There is no substantial impediment to the operation of the competitive process at the level of structure. The pressures that operate in the long run are exactly the forces that shape structure. Contractual promises and fiduciary rules arise as a result of these considerations.

... Today's task is to step back and ask whether corporation-as-contract is a satisfying way of looking at things even in theory. No one portrays the relation between trustee and beneficiary as one of arm's-length contracting, and legal rules impose many restrictions that the trustee cannot avoid. Why think about corporations differently?

Question

What do Easterbrook and Fischel think are the legal implications of Fama's theory?

O'Melinn, Neither Contract Nor Concession: The Public Personality of the Corporation
forthcoming 74 G.W. L. Rev. __ (2006)

.... [A]lthough courts are required at least to pay lip service to Justice Marshall's literal contractual language [in *Dartmouth College*[a]], they are loath to adhere to it. The corporate charter *is* a contract as a matter of constitutional law, and courts have continued to say so, albeit often with obvious regret.[210] Nonetheless, they have also been happy to uphold alterations and have repeatedly issued decisions that would clearly contravene corporate contractual rights if such rights existed.

More importantly, their skepticism accorded with the shift from special incorporation to general incorporation, which brought about a change in the fundamental theory under which incorporation was granted. To depart from special incorporation was also to move away from the theory of contract. Under acts of special incorporation there was some reason to consider the corporation as a contract between the corpora-

a. Trustees of Dartmouth College v. Woodward, 17 U.S. (Wheat.) 518 (1819).
210. As Justice Brown put it in 1896, the *Dartmouth College* proposition has "become firmly established as a canon of American jurisprudence." Pearsall v. Great N. Ry. Co., 161 U.S. 646, 660 (1896). That does not mean, however, that courts have been happy to be bound by *Dartmouth College*. In *Stone v. Mississippi*, the Court voiced very clear resignation on the binding force of *Dartmouth College*:
   "It is now too late to contend that any contract which a State actually enters into when granting a charter to a private corporation is not within the protection of the clause in the Constitution of the United States that prohibits States from passing laws impairing the obligation of contracts. The doctrines of *Trustees of Dartmouth College v. Woodward*, announced by this court more than sixty years ago, have become so imbedded in the jurisprudence of the United States as to make them to all intents and purposes a part of the Constitution itself."
Stone v. Mississippi, 101 U.S. 814, 816 (1879). Explicit attempts to repudiate *Dartmouth College* have by and large failed. Chief Justice Dow of the New Hampshire Supreme Court, for example, took an antagonistic stance. *See* Dow v. N. R.R., 67 N.H. 1, 36 Atl. 510 (1887) .... So did Justice Grice of the Georgia Supreme Court. *See* Barnett v. D. O. Martin Co., 11 S.E.2d 210, 213 (Ga. 1940)....

tors and the state, for the state typically extracted a *quid pro quo* in the form of some public benefit — such as bridge-building — from corporators in exchange for privileges not available to noncorporators. There was thus consideration. Under general incorporation, the situation changed drastically, for the corporators incurred no obligation sufficient to furnish consideration, and any *de facto* privilege they received was available to all comers.[213]

Over time, this theoretical shift manifested itself in the transfer of sovereignty from the government to the corporation, and general incorporation made it inevitable that the "corporate contract" would be violated on a regular basis. Recognition of the moral personality of the corporation called for acknowledgment of corporate capacity as well, which included the management of corporate affairs. The demands of corporate life and public policy were incompatible with the contractual theory, which reserved to each contractor enormous powers to obstruct change, so the law gave corporate management and majorities the power to rule over the objections of dissenters. However legitimate the dissenters' grievances might be if measured in terms of contractual expectation, it was just as true in business as in religion that they were not allowed to stand in the way of the increasingly powerful personality of the corporation.

Williamson, Corporate Governance
93 Yale L.J. 1197, 1200–1205 (1984)[a]

The microanalytic approach within which I propose to examine the issue of corporate governance is that of "transaction cost economics." I have set out the attributes of this approach elsewhere.[14] In essence, the approach regards the transaction as the basic unit of analysis and contends that a leading but widely neglected purpose of economic organization is to economize on the costs of transacting over time. Applications include intermediate product market organization, labor market organization, and regulation.

Neoclassical economics, which regards the firm as a production function, holds that nonstandard forms of organization have monopoly purpose and effect. Transaction cost economics, which regards firms, markets, and hybrid "mixed modes" as alternative governance structures, maintains instead that the institutions of contract ought mainly to be regarded in economizing terms. Assigning transactions to governance structures in such a way as to accomplish an economizing result is what transaction cost economics is all about. Since any issue that can be posed as a contracting problem is usefully addressed in transaction cost economizing terms, and since corporate governance falls within this description, the subject of corporate governance becomes grist for the transaction cost economics mill.

The study of corporate contracting is complicated by interdependencies within and between contracts; changes in one set of terms commonly require realignments in others....

---

213. Dodd makes a similar argument.... [*See* Dodd, Dissenting Stockholders and Amendments to Corporate Charters, 75 U. Pa. L. Rev. 585, 594-95 (1927).] ...

a. Reprinted by permission of The Yale Law Journal Company and Fred B. Rothman & Company from Yale Law Journal, Vol. 93, pp. 1197–1230.

14. Williamson, *Credible Commitments: Using Hostages to Support Exchange*, 73 Am. Econ. Rev. 519 (1983) ...; Williamson, *Transaction Cost Economics: The Governance of Contractual Relations*, 22 J.L. & Econ. 233 (1979)....

A. *A Contractual Schema*

The most important attribute for assessing whether a transaction requires a special governance structure is the degree to which the parties must invest in transaction-specific assets to facilitate the proposed exchange of goods or services. Transaction-specific assets are ones whose value is much greater in the given transaction than in their next-best use or by their next-best user. Failure to distinguish among transactions with respect to asset specificity has been responsible for much confusion and error in public policy.

Economists of all persuasions recognize that the terms of an initial bargain depend on whether qualified suppliers will submit noncollusive bids. If there is only a single highly qualified supplier, then the terms of the contract will be monopolistic; if there are many such suppliers, then the terms will be competitive. Transaction cost economics fully accepts this description of pre-contract bidding competition, but also insists that the study of contracting be extended to include post-contract features. Thus, initial bidding merely sets the contracting process in motion. A full assessment requires scrutiny of both contract execution and competition at the contract renewal interval.

In contrast to earlier theories, transaction cost economics suggests that a large number of bidders at the outset does not necessarily imply that there will be a large number thereafter. The efficacy of competition after the initial period depends on whether the good or service in question requires durable investments in transaction-specific assets, either human or physical. An initial winning bidder who makes no specialized investments realizes no advantage over rivals. Although it may continue to supply for a long period of time, this is only because, in effect, it is continuously meeting competitive bids from qualified rivals.

There is no longer parity with rivals, however, once the initial supplier undertakes substantial investments in durable transaction-specific assets. In such cases, both buyers and suppliers have a strong interest in preserving the continuity of the exchange, since economic values would be sacrificed if the ongoing supply relation were to be terminated. Rivals who lose the bid are unavoidably at a disadvantage if it is important to preserve the particular buyer/seller relation once the original contract has been awarded. Accordingly, what was a competitive market with a large number of bidders at the outset is effectively transformed into one of bilateral monopoly thereafter.

The convenient fiction of faceless contracting is thereby upset. Adapting to changing circumstances in bilateral trading poses a serious dilemma in contracting. Joined as they are in a condition of bilateral monopoly, both buyer and seller can bargain over the disposition of any incremental gain whenever a proposal to alter the contract is made by the other party. Although buyer and seller have a long-term interest in effecting adaptations that make both parties better off, each party also has an interest in appropriating as much of the gain as he can from each adaptation. Efficient adaptations may thus be made only with costly haggling or may even go unmentioned because one party fears that the other's opportunism will dissipate the gains. The parties therefore have an incentive to develop governance structures that help prevent opportunism and infuse confidence.

* * *

The safeguards to which I refer normally take one or more of three forms. The first is the realignment of incentives, commonly through some type of penalty for premature termination. The second is the creation of a specialized governance structure to resolve disputes. "Private ordering," rather than litigation in the courts, is thus characteristic of ... [this type of] governance. The third is the introduction of trading regularities that support and signal intentions of continuity.

Question

How does Williamson's approach differ from Fama's? How do the implications of each approach differ (if at all) for corporate law?

Section 3
The Neo-Traditional Response

Clark, Agency Costs versus Fiduciary Duties
(1985)[a]

A closer focus on actual rather than presumed legal doctrines and concepts might do much to refine our current theory of the firm. This paper begins by exploring some problems with economists' customary presentation of agency costs theory, and then examines the law's concept of the fiduciary duty of loyalty as an attempted solution to the so-called problem of agency costs.

Pitfalls of the Agency Costs Approach

Lawyers and economists often study the same phenomena but approach them in different ways. In some contexts their awareness of these differences can be mutually enlightening. The received agency costs literature describes managers as "agents" of stockholders and the corporation as a "center of contracts." But the important relationships and real problems that engage the "agency costs" commentators are conceived by legal authorities in a subtly different way, because the legal system has evolved its own unique strategy for dealing with them. The precise characteristics of the legal strategy, I believe, are often unknown or misunderstood, and could usefully be subjected to a close economic analysis.

Much of the economic literature talks about "firms" rather than "corporations," and does not distinguish sharply between closely held business organizations (whatever their legal form) and publicly held corporations. For a number of reasons, failure to make this distinction clearly can be a source of almost fatal confusion. Throughout this paper, I will be referring only to publicly held (or "public") business corporations, which of course account for the great bulk of business revenues of the United States. Some apparently different approaches by legal commentators to the theory of business organizations, such as William Klein's emphasis on bargaining under constraints, may be compatible with mine, once this restriction is appreciated.[3]

---

a. From John W. Pratt and Richard J. Zeckhauser, eds., Principals and Agents: The Structure of Business. Boston: Harvard Business School Press, 1985. Reprinted by permission.
3. See William A. Klein, "The Modern Business Organization: Bargaining Under Constraints," Yale Law Journal 91 (1982); 1521.

Managers Are Not Agents of Stockholders

To an experienced corporate lawyer who has studied primary legal materials, the assertion that corporate managers are agents of investors, whether debt holders or stockholders, will seem odd or loose. The lawyer would make the following points: (1) corporate officers like the president and treasurer are agents of the corporation itself; (2) the board of directors is the ultimate decision making body of the corporation (and in a sense is the group most appropriately identified with "the corporation"); (3) directors are not agents of the corporation but are sui generis; (4) neither officers nor directors are agents of the stockholders; but (5) both officers and directors are "fiduciaries" with respect to the corporation and its stockholders.

These legal characterizations are not just semantic differences from the usual terminology of the agency costs literature. To see the distinction, let us first contrast the legal conception of the agent with that of the corporate director and then examine the more general legal concept of the fiduciary.

Though lawyers use the concept of agency in a variety of senses, the core legal concept implies a relationship in which the principal retains the power to control and direct the activities of the agent. Typically, the principal sets the ultimate objective and general strategy for the agent to pursue, occasionally specifies details of the agent's behavior, and stands ready to countermand specific acts of the agent.

A review of elementary corporate law shows that this power of the principal to direct the activities of the agent does not apply to the stockholders as against the directors or officers of their corporation. By statute in every state, the board of directors of a corporation has the power and duty to manage or supervise its business. The stockholders do not. To appreciate the point fully, consider the following activities: setting the ultimate goal of the corporation—for example, whether its legal purpose will be to maximize profits; choosing the corporation's lines of business—for example, whether it will engage in retailing general merchandise or refining oil; hiring and firing the full-time executives who will actually run the company; and exercising supervisory power with respect to the day-to-day operations of the business. Stockholders of a large publicly held corporation *do not* do these things; as a matter of efficient operation of a large firm with numerous residual claimants they *should not* do them; and under the typical corporate statute and case law they *cannot* do them....

Thus, the legal relationship between the stockholder and the manager is very different from the legal relationship between the ordinary principal and agent. So what? the reader might ask. Do these differences have any bearing on the kinds of problems that have been at the heart of the agency costs literature? To some degree, yes. Ignoring the legal restrictions on stockholders' decision making power makes it easier to talk as if stockholders and managers "bargain" over and "contract" about the terms of their relationship, or "implicitly" or "virtually" do so—and this is the next, more serious pitfall of the agency costs literature....

My basic proposition is that an important but neglected job for agency costs theories is to try to understand, in economic terms, the main features of the actual legal relationship between stockholders and managers. They should theorize about the conditions under which such features are likely to come about, test their theories against empirical data, and assess whether these features are likely to be efficient or not. A modest stab at this problem is made later in this paper. Everyone will agree that there is still an ample virgin territory to be explored.

A Corporation Is Not a Nexus of Actual Contracts

While Coase saw the essence of the firm in coordination of activities by "fiat" rather than in "market" transactions, subsequent writers in the same general tradition have often gone out of their way to disagree. Alchian and Demsetz insisted that the firm "has no power of fiat, no authority, no disciplinary action any different in the slightest degree from ordinary market contracting between any two people." They went on to say that the distinctive feature of the employer-employee relationship, as contrasted with that between a sole proprietor and his customer, lies "in a *team* use of inputs and a centralized position of some party in the contractual arrangements of *all* other inputs. It [the firm] is the *centralized contractual agent in a team productive process*—not some superior authoritarian directive or disciplinary power...."

These remarks might be interpreted simply as an exaggerated way of pointing out that employees of modern firms are not slaves: They have the legal option of refusing to get into or stay in a relationship with someone who might give them orders (a boss). But the more important point seems to be a much broader one—that all relationships that make up a firm are "contractual." In their influential and often illuminating article on the theory of the firm, Jensen and Meckling drive home this point and are worth quoting at length:

> The private corporation or firm is simply one form of *legal fiction which serves as a nexus for contracting relationships and which is also characterized by the existence of divisible residual claims on the assets and cash flows of the organization which can generally be sold without permission of the other contracting individuals*. While this definition of the firm has little substantive content, emphasizing the essential contractual nature of firms and other organizations focuses attention on a crucial set of questions.... Viewed this way, it makes little or no sense to try to distinguish those things that are "inside" the firm from those things that are "outside" of it. There is in a very real sense only a multitude of complex relationships (i.e., contracts) between the legal fiction (the firm) and the owners of ... inputs and the consumers of output.

Jensen and Meckling's view that the corporation is "only" a multitude of contracts becomes important to them when they attempt to establish certain conclusions. It helps them argue that the "original owner-manager" of a firm that later goes public bears all of the agency costs thereby generated, and that agency costs are at an optimal or efficient level. Both of these propositions, and others that they assert in their article, may have important consequences for policy making.

But is it realistic or useful to view the modern public corporation as consisting only, or even principally, of a set of contracts? I think not. This extreme contractualist viewpoint is almost perverse. It is likely to blind us to most of the features of the modern public corporation that are distinctive, puzzling, and worth exploring. To see this, we must first consider the notion of contract, and then note the extent to which the corporation, considered as a multitude of legal relationships, consists of noncontractual legal relationships.

The term *contract* is more frequently used, even by lawyers, in varying senses than is the term *agency*, so it would be neither right nor prudent for me to claim that one particular specification of the term is the definitive legal notion of contract. For example, lawyers and judges often talk of contractual terms that are "implied" by law or custom, and courts often declare and enforce rights and duties between contracting parties that relate to matters neither party actually contemplated or bargained about. It is easy to speak of such rights and duties as being "part" of the parties' "contract." Nevertheless, the core notion of contract, and the most relevant for theorizing about the optimality of commercial relationships, is that the rights and duties between the two parties are specified and fixed by their own voluntary and actual agreement. Let me refer to a set of legal relationships determined solely in this way as constituting an "actual contract."

Most of the particular rules that make up the legal relationships among corporate officers, directors, and stockholders—that is, the relationships that constitute corporate law and give operational meaning to the legal concept of the corporation—are not the product of actual contracts made by the persons subject to them. Furthermore, they are often not the product of "implicit" contracts between these people, if by that term we mean that the individuals actually understood the governing rules but simply did not advert to them when entering their roles as officers, directors, or stockholders.

But some will insist that contracts may be implicit in a more remote but meaningful sense: Such as a contract exists if the parties, assuming they are rational and reasonable, would have agreed to the rules in question, if they had thought and bargained about them beforehand. Moreover, the whole set of legal relationships that make up corporate law may well be seen as a large-scale "standardized contract" or "form contract"—a miniature version of the libertarian philosophers' social contract—to which various people "consent" when they voluntarily step into the standardized roles of the officer, director, or stockholder. But I would insist that the use of the term contract in connection with "implicit contracts" and "standardized contracts" is metaphorical, and (as I will argue below) that the metaphor is seriously misleading.

Most corporate case law deals with alleged breaches of fiduciary duties by managers, though a given opinion might focus as readily on a question of procedure or process as on a question of definition or application of the duty. Fiduciary duties are sometimes waivable by stockholders and sometimes not waivable. But in either event the duties are highly unlikely to have been the result of any actual compact or understanding between manager and investor.

Since actual voluntary consent to the governing rules of a relationship is the essence of my notion of actual contracts, let me restate my view in terms of three grades of consent that might be given to corporate law by participants in the modern public corporation. The first level is consent to the *role* of officer, director, or stockholder. Many millions of people in the United States have voluntarily entered these roles, often with some vague awareness of, and lack of objection to, the fact that they thereby become subject to an unspecified, large, and perhaps arcane assortment of legal rights and duties. This acceptance of the legal rules, however, does not explain their origins. Most of these millions of people play no direct part in articulating, justifying, criticizing, changing, getting established as law, or enforcing the myriad particular rules that govern and define the roles they play.

The second level is consent to particular deviations from the otherwise governing rules in particular situations. Sometimes, for example, an officer will want to buy a "corporate opportunity" for himself—that is, to exploit for himself an opportunity that he would normally be expected to recommend to the corporation. In an earlier era, around 1900, directors who wished to engage in dealings with their corporations might have to, and often would, seek the explicit approval of the "disinterested" directors. But while such things do happen with some frequency, they do not explain the creation of the ground rules to which they are exceptions. Moreover, lawyers, courts, and commentators often argue over the extent to which such expressions of consent are informed, uncoerced, and untainted by conflicts of interest, and thus whether they should be declared legally valid.

The third level of consent is bargaining about and creation of the particular terms of a particular relationship among participants in a public corporation. A chief executive officer, for example, may bargain with a board of directors about compensation and terms of employment. Other important examples are hard to come by.

With these qualifications and understandings, I suggest again that the legal relationships among participants in the modern public corporation are not primarily the product of actual contracts.

Questions

1. What are the theories of the corporation upon which Clark's excerpt is based?

2. What are the normative considerations underlying his theory?

3. What are the implications of these theories for the duties of management to shareholders and creditors?

Problems

1. In your capacity as consultant to Bondolia, the former communist country described in the Introductory Problem to this book, you have been asked to assist in preparing a summary of the various theories of the American corporation. Prepare an outline of the various theories, considering the implications of each with respect to the duties of management to stockholders and creditors.

2. Review the Introductory Problem preceding this chapter. Which theories of the corporation are most attractive to which types of claimant, and why?

Section 4
Corporate Form and Corporate Governance:
The Current Debate

Bebchuk, The Debate on Contractual Freedom
in Corporate Law
89 Colum. L. Rev. 1395, 1395–98 (1989)[a]

I. The Freedom-To-Opt-Out Challenge To Corporate Law Theory

Corporate law has always included a substantial body of mandatory rules. To be sure, as state corporate law has increasingly taken an "enabling" approach, the set of issues with respect to which opting out is possible has expanded. Both state and federal corporate law, however, still include many significant mandatory rules; indeed, such rules govern most of the important corporate arrangements.

While it has long been taken for granted that corporate law has a substantial mandatory core, this feature of corporate law has in the last decade come under heavy theoretical

---

attack. A significant camp in corporate law scholarship has put forward the proposition that corporations should largely be free to opt out of corporate law rules.[7] The freedom-to-opt-out advocates start from the premise that a corporation should be viewed as essentially a contractual creature, a "nexus of contracts."[8] They argue—and we will see that this argument is disputable—that the contractual view of the corporation implies that the parties involved should be totally free to shape their contractual arrangements. The primary function of corporate law, they suggest, should be to facilitate the private contracting process by providing a set of nonmandatory "standard-form" provisions, with private parties free to adopt charter provisions that opt out of any of these standard arrangements.

Because many important corporate rules are mandatory, the freedom-to-opt-out view has considerable practical implications. For example, the freedom-to-opt-out advocates have proposed allowing companies to opt out of all doctrines concerning managerial fiduciary duties and out of all insider trading rules. If such unconstrained freedom to opt out were granted, it presumably would bring significant change to corporate life.[11]

The freedom-to-opt-out advocates have already had much influence. On the practical side, they have had an impact on the direction of law reform and law change. The American Law Institute Reporters, for example, recently proposed permitting opting out with respect to some significant issues.[12] The SEC recently requested comments on a proposal to provide companies with substantial freedom to opt out of federal takeover rules.[13] And the state of Delaware recently permitted corporations to adopt charter provisions that eliminate or restrict director liability for breach of their duty of care.[14]

---

7. See, e.g., R. Posner, Economic Analysis of Law 372 (3d ed. 1986); Carlton & Fischel, The Regulations of Insider Trading, 35 Stan. L. Rev. 857 (1983); Easterbrook & Fischel, Voting in Corporate Law, 26 J.L. & Econ. 395 (1983); Easterbrook & Fischel, Corporate Control Transactions, 91 Yale L.J. 698 (1982); Fischel, The Corporate Governance Movement, 35 Vand. L. Rev. 1259 (1982); Macey, From Fairness to Contract: The New Direction of the Rules Against Insider Trading, 13 Hofstra L. Rev. 9 (1984); Winter, State Law, Shareholder Protection, and the Theory of the Corporation, 6 J. Legal Stud. 251 (1977).

8. On this view, the contractual entity is nothing more than a metaphor for a conglomeration of voluntary agreements among the various participants in the enterprise. On the contractual view of the corporation, see Alchian & Demsetz, Production, Information, Costs, and Economic Organization, 62 Am. Econ. Rev. 777 (1972); Fama & Jensen, Separation of Ownership and Control, 26 J.L. & Econ. 301 (1983); Jensen & Meckling, Theory of the Firm: Managerial Behavior, Agency Costs and Ownership Structure, 3 J. Fin. Econ. 305 (1976); Klein, The Modern Business Organization: Bargaining Under Constraints, 91 Yale L.J. 1521 (1982); Williamson, Corporate Governance, 93 Yale L.J. 1197 (1984). The contractual approach goes back to Coase, The Nature of the Firm, 4 Economica (n.s.) 386 (1937). . . . .

11. While most people would accept without question the importance of the issue under consideration, Bernard Black disputes this importance in an interesting and provocative article. See Black, Is Corporate Law Trivial?: A Political and Economic Analysis[, 84 Nw. U. L. Rev. 542 (1990)]. Black's view stems from his more general position, which he develops in this article, that corporate law is on the whole not that important. While I disagree with Black's general position, I wish here only to point out that even he would presumably agree with the view ... that the question of contractual freedom is one of the most important questions in corporate law (whatever the importance of this area of the law may be).

12. See, e.g., Principles of Corporate Governance: Analysis and Recommendations §5.09 (Tent. Draft No. 7, 1987) (effect of officer's reliance on a standard of the corporation); id. §7.17 (limitation on damages for certain violations of duty of care).

13. See Concept Release on Takeovers and Contests for Corporate Control, Exchange Act Release No. 230,486 [1986–1987 Transfer Binder] Fed. Sec. L. Rep. (CCH) ¶84,018 (July 31, 1986).

14. See Del. Code Ann. tit. 8, §102(b)(7) (Supp. 1988).

On the intellectual side, the freedom-to-opt-out advocates have had a substantial impact on corporate law scholarship and its agenda. The longstanding mandatory nature of American corporate law—and, to the best of my knowledge, the corporate law of all the other major market economies as well—can no longer be accepted without question and reflection. Corporate law scholars have had to wrestle with the freedom-to-opt-out view, and have been faced with the need to either accept it or give reasons for rejecting it. The articulation of the freedom-to-opt-out position has challenged scholars who support mandatory rules to put forward a systematic theory that provides a rationale for mandatory rules, as well as criteria for deciding which rules should be mandatory. Several articles working toward this goal have already been published,[15] and several others appear in this issue.

Note

The literature discussing the corporation as contract is large and continues to grow. Some of the contributions include: Rosenberg, Making Sense of Good Faith in Delaware Corporate Fiduciary Law: A Contractarian Approach, 29 Del. J. Corp. L. 491 (2004); Joo, Corporations Theory and Corporate Governance Law: Contract, Property, and the Role of Metaphor in Corporations Law, 35 U.C. Davis L. Rev. 779 (2002); Brudney, Contract and Fiduciary Duty in Corporate Law, 38 B.C. L. Rev. 595 (1997); Butler and Ribstein, Opting Out of Fiduciary Duties: A Response to the Anti-Contractarians, 65 Wash. L. Rev. 1 (1990); Butler, The Contractual Theory of the Corporation, 11 Geo. Mason L. Rev. 99 (1989); Butler & Ribstein, The Contract Clause and the Corporation, 55 Brooklyn L. Rev. 767 (1989); Symposium: The Corporation as Contract, 89 Colum. L. Rev. 1395–1774 (1989).

Consider the implications of the power model developed in the next excerpt on the theory of the corporation, and the implications of this theory for the duties of management to shareholders and creditors.

Dallas, Two Models of Corporate Governance:
Beyond Berle and Means
22 U. Mich. J. L. Ref. 1, 30–31 (1988)

The power model depicts the firm as an institution with its own internal structure that seeks to decrease its uncertainty by increasing its own autonomy and discretion over its environment. Unlike a wheat market, it utilizes various strategies to decrease its dependence on its environment, thus muting the effects of market constraints. According to the power model, not "only are organizations [perceived as] constrained by the political, legal, and economic environment, but, in fact, law, legitimacy, political outcomes, and economic climate [are understood to] reflect, in part, actions taken by organizations to modify these environmental components for their interests of survival and growth." Thus, the firm is not merely reactive with respect to its environment, but proactive.

---

15. See Bebchuk, [Limiting Contractual Freedom in Corporate Law: The Desirable Constraints on Charter Amendments, 102 Harv. L. Rev. 1820 (1989)]; Brudney, Corporate Governance, Agency Costs, and the Rhetoric of Contract, 85 Colum. L. Rev. 1403 (1985); Clark, Agency Costs Versus Fiduciary Duties, In Principals and Agents: The Structure of Business (J. Pratt & R. Zeckhauser eds. 1985); Coffee, No Exit?: Opting Out, The Contractual Theory of the Corporation, and the Special Case of Remedies, 53 Brooklyn L. Rev. 919 (1988).

Firm behavior results from a contest for control among power coalitions comprised of groups of individuals in specific relationships to the firm and with each other. Power derives from numerous sources.... The important bargaining takes place in the context of political and social relationships among groups rather than through individual or atomistic exchanges. The objective is to become part of the dominant coalition, which generally consists of management and some other groups, depending on the decision involved and the power of various groups. "Internal" coalitions consist of top management and employees of various divisions and departments. "External" coalitions include shareholders, customers, and suppliers.

Under the power model, the dominant coalition emerges as "the firm," thus the corporation does not disappear as an actor. The most important question becomes not "what is the objective of the firm?" but "who is in the dominant coalition?"

The corporate scandals of 2002, beginning with the collapse of Enron, did more than simply help crash the stock market bubble of the late 1990s, result in the passage of the Sarbanes-Oxley Act of 2002, and lead to widespread distrust of corporate America, from the CEOs of *Fortune* 500 companies to securities analysts on Wall Street. What implications do these scandals have for Fama's belief in the efficacy of "managerial labor markets"? And for the desirability of fully embracing the "opt out" model discussed by Bebchuk?

Not unexpectedly, the scandals gave rise to public debate, not only in the major media but in law schools, business schools, think tanks, and public policy groups, of the appropriate nature and role of the corporation in the twenty-first century. In particular, the 1990s (and, to a lesser extent, the 1980s), saw the rise of a short-term culture in investing and managing catalyzed by a number of different developments.

The dominance of institutional investors, once thought by legal scholars to solve the problems of the separation of ownership and control, turned out instead to result in extraordinary pressure on corporate managers to keep stock prices rising (largely through ever-increasing earnings per share), a result we believe largely caused by the way in which institutional money managers are compensated. In addition, the tax code change of 1993, which prohibited corporate tax deductions of executive cash salaries in excess of $1 million, led (as it was intended to do) to the proliferation of executive stock options as the principle form of executive compensation.

At the height of the 1990s stock market bubble, the average *Fortune* 1000 CEO earned substantially more each year in stock than in cash. Again, this was initially heralded by the corporate community as aligning managerial with stockholder interests. Instead, the consequence was to focus executives on increasing stock prices, especially since many of their options could be exercised within the relatively short-term, allowing executives (perhaps most famously Enron's Kenneth Lay) to develop annual programs of exercising options and selling stock. Finance came to dominate business management, as corporate executives found ways to manipulate both their businesses and financial statements (often legally) to make earnings appear better than they really were, or at least to sacrifice long-term business health (like, for example, investment in workers and research and development) for short-term gain.

On top of this, the mania of high-tech stocks, especially those of unproven Internet start-ups, resulted in initial public offerings in which stock prices shot through the roof within the first days of issuance, and price-earnings multiples reached levels never before seen. This brought into the market new and inexperienced investors, who expected ever increasing earnings and stock prices and who deserted stocks in droves at the first sign of lower than expected earnings—another incentive for managers to keep stock prices up. Finally there was unprecedented noise trading[1] from day traders, who traded solely on price movements and whose investment strategy was purely speculative and short-term, comprising at the height of the bubble fully 15% of the public market. The destabilizing effect caused by these traders again led managers to worry about stock price in the short term.

It is extraordinarily difficult for any business to beat its earnings estimates quarter after quarter. As a consequence, many corporations turned to financial manipulations to maintain the appearance of increasing earnings. While many of these were within the bounds of GAAP and SEC rules, others clearly were not. But the damage was not simply in the loss of trust engendered in the investment community when these manipulations were uncovered. The real damage has not yet been assessed, for it lies in cost-cutting measures like massive layoffs at all levels of worker, demoralizing and destabilizing the work force and long-held expectations about the employment bargain, underinvestment in research and development, and a variety of other business practices that threaten the long-run health of American business.

While the Sarbanes-Oxley Act aimed at some of the abuses by demanding greater disclosure, changing accounting practices, and instituting some corporate governance reforms, it failed to address the incentives that led to these problems in the first place. With the American economy in a shambles and the stock market flailing back and forth around significantly lower indices, the future is unclear. What is clear is that the responsibility of American corporations not only to their stockholders but to their workers, the environment, their creditors and preferred stockholders, and the American public, is on the table for debate in a way that it hasn't been since the Crash of 1929. These basic issues are important for you to keep in mind as you study the materials in this course, for they present them at each point in the book.

For a deeper discussion of these issues see Mitchell, Corporate Irresponsibility: America's Newest Export (2001).

O'Melinn, Neither Contract Nor Concession: The Public Personality of the Corporation

forthcoming 74 G.W. L. Rev. __ (2006)

I. Contract, Concession, and the Inadequacy of Corporate Theory

.... This article challenges the two preeminent theories of the corporation—contract and concession—by arguing that the corporation is a special kind of moral personality for which the law has made extensive accommodation. It makes three points of fundamental importance: First, although many of the most important developments in corporate law have resulted from the efforts of the nonprofit institution, the business corporation has undeservedly received the exclusive attention of corporate law theorists. Corporate law is the result of a common course of development shared by profit and nonprofit organizations, but the business corporation, by achieving pride of place as *the* corporation, has become divorced from its heritage and has been allowed to masquerade

---

1. For a discussion of noise theory and trading, see *infra* chapter 3, section 5c(iv).

as a purely private institution. Second, given the important role that the nonprofit institution has played in the growth of corporate law, it is clear that shareholder primacy cannot be the ultimate goal of corporate law. Third, the public character of the corporation justifies greater regulation of corporate activity in the public interest.

The inability of legal theory to account for the character of the corporation is a long-standing problem. In their seminal work, *The Modern Corporation and Private Property*, Adolf Berle and Gardiner Means began the modern debate on corporate governance with a call to recognize the public nature of the modern corporation. In the many years that have passed, hardly a step has been taken in that direction.... Theorists continue to hold that the corporation is the product either of a concession or a contract.[3] According to the view that a corporation has its legal origin in a concession by the state, the corporation is a creature of the government and is thus properly subject to regulation.[4] According to the contractual theory, the corporation represents an agreement, or series of agreements, among private parties. The duty of the corporation is to satisfy the expectations of these individual contractors, and the corporation should thus not be regulated extensively by the state.

In recent years the contractual view has become increasingly dominant .... As Michael DeBow and Dwight Lee put it, the debate over the nature of the corporation pits those who know what a corporation is—the contracts theorists—against those who do not—the concession theorists: "For years now, debates over the proper scope of and content of corporate behavior and corporate law have exhibited much regularity: they almost always involve a clash between those who treat corporations as contractually-based, profit-maximizing entities, *and those who wish corporations could be made to be something else.*"[8]

This article argues that the corporation *is* something else. Neither contract nor concession can explain the place that the corporation holds in American law, and neither view accounts for the extraordinary development of the corporation in America .... With the active help of the law, the corporation sought to overcome the defects of contract and individualism and to replace them with an *institution* with corporate capacities and endowed with powers of sovereignty. The effort succeeded beyond all imagination. Not only did corporate management attain a power of government over its own membership, it has also begun to acquire a power of sovereignty over the public—and this too in the name of contract.

.... The corporation has truly become a new kind of juristic person defying the traditional categories of law and occupying a privileged place akin to that of an aristocracy.[9] Once the corporation attained this status, the next question to be addressed by corporate theory should have been obvious: by what law should this new juristic person be governed?

---

3. Not all theorists use the language of contract and concession, with several preferring "property" and "entity," but the contract and property theories are roughly the same, as are the concession and entity theories. The contractual or property-based view sees the corporation as the product of private enterprise and believes that corporate law should ensure that the fruits of that enterprise inure to the benefit of the individual investor. . . . The concession or entity-based view maintains that the corporation has a more public dimension that justifies regulation in the public interest....

4. [Michael E. DeBow & Dwight R. Lee, Shareholders, Nonshareholders and Corporate Law: Communitarianism and Resource Allocation, 18 Del. J. Corp. L. 393, 397 (1993)] . . . .

8. DeBow & Lee, supra note [4], at 393 (emphasis added).

9. Just as Berle and Means noted the failure of traditional theory to keep pace with the claims of the corporation, so Frederic Maitland once called for an investigation of the corporation as an en-

That question has never been squarely answered. Instead, the corporation has been allowed to masquerade as a purely private enterprise dedicated only to the economic welfare of the individual "contractors" who compose it. This masquerade, although based on an almost purely fictional account of the development of corporate law, has been surprisingly successful.

. . . . Berle and Means demanded the recognition of a new relationship between the corporation and the greater society, a recognition far afield from the shareholder primacy ideal. The real question of corporate governance, in their view, was not a question directed primarily either to directors or to shareholders, but to the public at large. The replacement of shareholder ascendancy with managerial ascendancy pointed in the direction of the ascendancy of the *public* over the corporation: "The control groups have ... placed *the community in a position to demand that the modern corporation serve not alone the owners or the control but all society.*"[12]

"Community." The word that makes corporate law scholars shudder. Accompanied by the word "society," it was bound to call for a narrowing construction of the Berle and Mean's position and for a return to more familiar and comfortable terms of debate....

This article charts the course of this revolution by beginning with Chief Justice Marshall's decision in *Trustees of Dartmouth College v. Woodward*[16].... The decision heralded a recognition of the force of the moral personality of the corporate entity, as a consequence of which the corporation went from being the humble servant of the state to being its virtual master. This change was incompatible with either a true contractual theory or a concession theory.

.... One of the few decisions involving nonprofit organizations to be included in the canon of business corporation decisions, [*Dartmouth College*] actually shows that the concerns of business were largely irrelevant to many of the most important developments in corporate law. *Dartmouth College* thus points to the greatest deficiency in corporate law scholarship: the tendency to focus on the business corporation as *the* corporation, with an almost inevitable tendency to see corporate law only as a device for

---

tity that challenged the traditional categories of the law. . . . A legal historian and active participant in the debate over corporate personality, Maitland pointedly noted that the modern corporation was making the conventional legal categories of status and contract irrelevant, and that the corporation was furnishing a new kind of person who received exceptional treatment from the law:

> You know that classical distribution of Private Law under three grand rubrics—Persons, Things, Actions. Half a century ago the first of these three titles seemed to be almost vanishing from civilised jurisprudence. No longer was there much, if anything, to be said of exceptional classes, of nobles, clerics, monks, serfs, slaves, excommunicates or outlaws. Children there might always be, and lunatics; but women had been freed from tutelage. The march of the progressive associates was from status to contract. And now? And now that forlorn old title [i.e., the law of persons] is wont to introduce us to ever new species and new genera of persons, to vivacious controversy, to teeming life; and there are many to tell us that the line of advance is no longer from status to contract, but through contract to something that contract cannot explain, and for which our best, if an inadequate, name is the personality of the organised group.

[Frederic W. Maitland, Moral Personality and Legal Personality, in 3 Collected Papers of Frederic William Maitland 304, 315 (H.A.L. Fisher ed., 1981)].

12. [Adolf A. Berle & Gardiner C. Means, The Modern Corporation and Private Property 312 (rev. ed. 1967)] (emphasis added).

16. Trs. of Dartmouth Coll. v. Woodward, 17 U.S. (Wheat.) 518 (1819).

satisfying the needs of the businessman and to miss the true significance of the institutional rights that were actually vindicated.

* * *

This article concludes by assessing the public character of the corporation in two ways. First, the corporation has literally become an outlaw, exempt from the operation of some parts of the law and imbued with a power to impose law on its members. Not only has the corporation acquired a power of sovereignty over its membership through a steady delegation of sovereign power from the state; it has also managed to attain real powers of government over the broader public. Now a broad range of people who are not parties to the "corporate contract," including consumers and employees, are subject to the corporation's sovereignty through the enforcement of restrictive provisions in standard form contracts, notably in clickwrap and shrinkwrap end-user "agreements."

The corporation escaped the bounds of the conventional categories of concession and contract, becoming an extraordinary kind of person with legal privileges to rival those of the state. These privileges, seen most powerfully in the exercise of corporate sovereignty over noncontractors, illustrate just how shallow the language of the corporate contract is and how tenuous is the route toward shareholder primacy. The corporation's supposed mission to cater only to its shareholders' economic interests is the result of a misconception of its character. The business corporation gained its ascendancy under the law because of the public interest—as a consequence of its affinity with the college and the church—but by virtue of the contractual theory's triumph over its weak and un-American rival, the concession theory, it has been allowed to pose as a purely private actor.

Section 5
Close Corporations: A Different Result?

Donahue v. Rodd Electrotype Co. of New England
328 N.E.2d 505 (Mass. 1975)

[Euphemia Donahue, minority shareholder in the corporation, sued to invalidate the corporation's repurchase of its former president's stock. The remainder of the stock was held by members of the president's family, some of whom were directors and officers. In analyzing Mrs. Donahue's claimed right to an equal opportunity to sell her shares to the corporation, the court had this to say about the corporate form and its consequences:]

TAURO, Chief Justice,

* * *

A. Close Corporations. In previous opinions, we have alluded to the distinctive nature of the close corporation ... but have never defined precisely what is meant by a close corporation. There is no single, generally accepted definition. Some commentators emphasize an "integration of ownership and management." ... Others focus on the number of stockholders and the nature of the market for the stock. In this view, close corporations have few stockholders; there is little market for corporate stock. The Supreme Court of Illinois adopted this latter view in Galler v. Galler, 32 Ill. 2d 16, 203 N.E.2d 577 (1965): "For our purposes, a close corporation is one in which the stock is held in a few hands, or in a few families, and wherein it is not at all, or only rarely, dealt in by buying or selling." Id. at 27, 203 N.E.2d at 583.... We accept aspects of both definitions. We deem a close corporation to be typified by: (1) a small number of stockholders; (2) no ready market for the corporate stock; and (3) substantial majority stockholder participation in the management, direction and operations of the corporation.

As thus defined, the close corporation bears striking resemblance to a partnership. Commentators and courts have noted that the close corporation is often little more than an "incorporated" or "chartered" partnership.... The stockholders "clothe" their partnership "with the benefits peculiar to a corporation, limited liability, perpetuity and the like." ... In essence, though, the enterprise remains one in which ownership is limited to the original parties or transferees of their stock to whom the other stockholder have agreed,[13] in which ownership and management are in the same hands, and in which the owners are quite dependent on one another for the success of the enterprise. Many close corporations are "really partnerships, between two or three people who contribute their capital, skills, experience and labor." ... Just as in a partnership, the relationship among the stockholders must be one of trust, confidence and absolute loyalty if the enterprise is to succeed. Close corporations with substantial assets and with more numerous stockholders are no different from smaller close corporations in this regard. All participants rely on the fidelity and abilities of those stockholders who hold office. Disloyalty and self-seeking conduct on the part of any stockholder will engender bickering, corporate stalemates, and, perhaps, efforts to achieve dissolution....

Although the corporate form provides the above-mentioned advantages for the stockholders (limited liability, perpetuity, and so forth), it also supplies an opportunity for the majority stockholders to oppress or disadvantage minority stockholders. The minority is vulnerable to a variety of oppressive devices, termed "freeze-outs," which the majority may employ.... An authoritative study of such "freeze-outs" enumerates some of the possibilities: "The squeezers [those who employ the freeze-out techniques] may refuse to declare dividends; they may drain off the corporation's earnings in the form of exorbitant salaries and bonuses to the majority shareholder-officers and perhaps to their relatives, or in the form of high rent by the corporation for property leased from majority shareholders ...; they may deprive minority shareholders of corporate offices and of employment by the company; they may cause the corporation to sell its assets at an inadequate price to the majority shareholders...." F. H. O'Neal and J. Derwin, Expulsion or Oppression of Business Associates, 42 (1961). In particular, the power of the board of directors, controlled by the majority, to declare or withhold dividends and to deny the minority employment is easily converted to a device to disadvantage minority stockholders....

The minority can, of course, initiate suit against the majority and their directors. Self-serving conduct by directors is proscribed by the director's fiduciary obligation to the corporation.... However, in practice, the plaintiff will find difficulty in challenging dividend or employment policies. Such policies are considered to be within the judgment of the directors. This court has said: "The courts prefer not to interfere ... with the sound financial management of the corporation by its directors, but declare as a general rule that the declaration of dividends rests within the sound discretion of the directors, refusing to interfere with their determination unless a plain abuse of discretion is made to appear." ...

---

13. The original owners commonly impose restrictions on transfers of stock designed to prevent outsiders who are unacceptable to the other stockholders from acquiring an interest in the close corporation. These restrictions often take the form of agreements among the stockholders and the corporation or by-laws which give the corporation or the other stockholders a right of "first refusal" when any stockholder desires to sell his shares.... In a partnership, of course, a partner cannot transfer his interest in the partnership so as to give his assignee a right to participate in the management or business affairs of the continuing partnership without the agreement of the other partners....

Judicial reluctance to interfere combines with the difficulty of proof when the standard is "plain abuse of discretion" or bad faith ... to limit the possibilities for relief. Although contractual provisions in an "agreement of association and articles of organization" ... or in by-laws ... have justified decrees in this jurisdiction ordering dividend declarations, generally, plaintiffs who seek judicial assistance against corporate dividend or employment policies do not prevail. ...

Thus, when these types of "freeze-outs" are attempted by the majority stockholders, the minority stockholders, cut off from all corporation-related revenues, must either suffer their losses or seek a buyer for their shares. Many minority stockholders will be unwilling or unable to wait for an alteration in majority policy. Typically, the minority stockholder in a close corporation has a substantial percentage of his personal assets invested in the corporation. ... The stockholder may have anticipated that his salary from his position with the corporation would be his livelihood. Thus, he cannot afford to wait passively. He must liquidate his investment in the close corporation in order to reinvest the funds in income-producing enterprises.

.... [T]he the minority stockholder in a close corporation becomes manifest. He cannot easily reclaim his capital. In a large public corporation, the oppressed or dissident minority stockholder could sell his stock in order to extricate some of his invested capital. By definition, this market is not available for shares in the close corporation. In a partnership, a partner who feels abused by his fellow partners may cause dissolution by his "express will ... at any time" ... and recover his share of partnership assets and accumulated profits. ... If dissolution results in a breach of the partnership articles, the culpable partner will be liable in damages. ... By contrast, the stockholder in the close corporation or "incorporated partnership" may achieve dissolution and recovery of his share of the enterprise assets only by compliance with the rigorous terms of the applicable chapter of the General Laws. ... "The dissolution of a corporation which is a creature of the Legislature is primarily a legislative function, and the only authority courts have to deal with this subject is the power conferred upon them by the Legislature." ... To secure dissolution of the ordinary close corporation subject to G. L. c. 156B, the stockholder, in the absence of corporate deadlock, must own at least fifty per cent of the shares ... or have the advantage of a favorable provision in the articles of organization. ... The minority stockholder, by definition lacking fifty per cent of the corporate shares, can never "authorize" the corporation to file a petition for dissolution under G. L. c. 156B, §99(a), by his own vote. He will seldom have at his disposal the requisite favorable provision in the articles of organization.

Thus, in a close corporation, the minority stockholders may be trapped in a disadvantageous situation. No outsider would knowingly assume the position of the disadvantaged minority. The outsider would have the same difficulties. To cut losses, the minority stockholder may be compelled to deal with the majority. This is the capstone of the majority plan. Majority "freeze-out" schemes which withhold dividends are designed to compel the minority to relinquish stock at inadequate prices. ... When the minority stockholder agrees to sell out at less than fair value, the majority has won.

See also Galler v. Galler, 32 Ill. 2d 16, 203 N.E.2d 577 (1964) (permitting parties to contract to some extent around corporation statute to permit greater flexibility in close corporation governance). But see Boss v. Boss, 98 R.I. 146, 200 A.2d 231 (1964) (rejecting imposition of fiduciary duty on majority stockholders of close corporation as inconsistent with structure of corporate governance).

Mitchell, Close Corporations Reconsidered
63 Tulane L. Rev. 1143, 1144–48 (1989)

Close corporation law has reached maturity. Although it lacks the venerable and ancient common law history of such seemingly timeless bodies of law as property and crimes, close corporation law has developed in the twentieth century to the point where it has engendered a voluminous body of case law and literature.

Review of close corporation materials reveals an overwhelming focus on one central question: How can we adapt formalistic general incorporation statutes to fulfill the needs of this hybrid form of business organization? In particular, how can we adapt a form that separates ownership and control (and is premised on that separation) to an organization in which that separation is typically minimal, if not absent? The judicial and legislative responses to the needs of close corporation shareholders, although somewhat varied, essentially address the problems of close corporations within the traditional corporate framework.

Past attempts to develop a law of close corporations have been misdirected. Legislation, case law, and commentary have focused on the problems of minority shareholders and the adaptation of the corporate structure to a less formal relationship. Legislators, judges, and commentators have devoted little attention to the theoretical and societal problems of close corporations, and how those problems affect the treatment of close corporations within the traditional corporate context.

* * *

The time has come to reassess the law of close corporations and to resolve some underlying questions—questions rarely asked and even more rarely answered: *Should* the law accommodate the desires of close corporation shareholders for freedom to alter the corporate form? Is the close corporation truly a "corporation" in the economic and behavioral sense in which our society has come to conceptualize that term? Do close corporations serve the same efficiency and social functions as more widely held corporations? Are the characteristics of corporations, reflected in general incorporation statutes, mere technical formalities, or do those characteristics serve some other functions? And is it appropriate to dispense with these characteristics in close corporations?

The answers to these questions depend upon a theoretical understanding of close corporations. In attempting to reach such an understanding, I propose a restructuring of business organization law. Instead of working to modify the corporate structure, we should abandon the attempt to develop a separate body of corporate law governing close corporations and should encourage business persons to select only those forms of business organization that balance their needs with society's legitimate concerns. The underlying theoretical perspective of my proposal is the unity of ownership and control in close corporations. This perspective is applied particularly to the policy of limited liability. On examination, the only way the close corporation fulfills the modern notion of the corporate form is through its possession of a certificate of incorporation. This analysis reveals that close corporations should not exist as corporations at all.

.... The logical determinant of the proper form of organization of a business is whether ownership and control are separated—that is, the presence of passive investment. Passive investment marks the distinction between close and public corporations and ultimately justifies the distinctive characteristics of corporations. Thus, shareholders should only be permitted to acquire the traditional corporate characteristics of limited liability, centralized management, free transferability of shares, and perpetual succession when ownership and control are separated significantly.

Questions

1. In what sense is a close corporation a "corporation"? How does it fit within the theories you have examined in the rest of this chapter?

2. Are the relationships among directors, officers, and shareholders in close corporations similar to those in publicly held corporations?

3. Is use of the corporate form for closely held businesses efficient? Are the laws governing the rights of shareholders and creditors, and the obligations of management, appropriate to close corporations? Consider this question again as you study the consequences of limited liability in chapter 2 and the problems raised in chapters 5, 6 and 8.

4. For statutory responses to the issues facing close corporations, consider: Del. Gen. Corp. Law §§ 341-56; N.Y. Bus. Corp. Law § 620; and Cal. Gen. Corp. Law §§ 158 & 418.

5. Other analyses of the close corporation form include Siegel, Fiduciary Duty in Close Corporate Law, 29 Del. J. Corp. L. 377 (2004); Crago, Fiduciary Duties and Reasonable Expectations: Cash-Out Mergers in Close Corporations, 49 Okla. L. Rev. 1 (1996); Chittur, Resolving Close Corporation Conflicts: A Fresh Approach, 10 Harv. J.L. & Pub. Pol'y 129 (1987); Easterbrook & Fischel, Close Corporations and Agency Costs, 38 Stan. L. Rev. 271 (1986).

6. As identified in *Donahue*, one of the main problems with the close corporation form is shareholder oppression: the ability of the majority shareholder to "freeze-out" the minority. Due to the nature of the close corporation form, the minority shareholder is placed in a difficult position. There is no ready market for a minority interest in a closely held corporation. Furthermore, a stockholder in a close corporation may only achieve dissolution and recovery of his or her investment through rigid compliance with the applicable statutory law. *See, e.g.,* Del. Gen. Corp. Law § 301.

By contrast, most of the original limited liability company ("LLC") statutes provided a solution to this dilemma. By statute, members of an LLC were given the right to withdraw from the LLC and receive the fair market value of their interest, absent an agreement to the contrary. A growing number of the newer LLC statutes, however, have eliminated members' right to withdraw prior to dissolution and winding up or have otherwise eliminated the members' right to be paid the fair market value of their interest. *See* Miller, What Buy-Out Rights, Fiduciary Duties, and Dissolution Remedies Should Apply in the Case of the Minority Owner of a Limited Liability Company, 38 Harv. J. on Legis. 413 (2001).

Chapter 2

Limited Liability — A Central Problem in Corporate Finance

Section 1
The Basic Conflict between Creditors and Stockholders

Perhaps the most cogent explanation of the basic conflict between creditors and shareholders created by limited liability is Manning's and Hanks' analysis in the following excerpt.

Manning and Hanks, A Concise Textbook on Legal Capital
(3d ed. 1990), 5-7, 10-16, 17-18

The interests of creditors of a corporation and the interests of shareholders of a corporation are adverse whenever assets of shareholders are to be committed to the corporation's treasury and whenever assets are to be distributed to shareholders from the corporate treasury....

A. THE CREDITOR'S PERSPECTIVE

1. Creditors — General

The legal term "creditor" expresses a single basic proposition. A creditor has, subject to the special terms of the credit, a higher and prior claim to the assets of his debtor than the debtor has himself (leaving aside extraordinary circumstances as when, for example, a debtor has received a bankruptcy discharge or holds a homestead exemption). When a loan or other class of creditor's claim has become due and payable, the creditor may, in normal course, enlist the engines of the law to compel his debtor to pay the debt, regardless of the consequent diminution of the assets that "belong" to the debtor.

Though the term "priority" is usually reserved in the law to describe relationships among claimants other than the debtor, in a basic sense it may be said that the creditor's claim against the assets of his debtor is "prior" to the debtor's own claim to "his" assets. "Prior" in this sense has no relationship to the concept of time; it relates to hierarchy of claim. If the debtor has just enough assets to pay the creditor's claim, the creditor gets them all, *i.e.*, his claim is "prior," and the debtor gets nothing.

General creditors are those creditors who are not secured creditors. A *secured* creditor is a creditor who, in addition to his creditor's claim, has "collateral"—a mortgage or other security interest in particular assets of the debtor. Since all claims of all creditors to the assets of the debtor have priority over the debtor's claim, the secured creditor does not by force of his security interest in particular assets of the debtor gain in priority vis-à-vis his *debtor*. The purpose and effect of the collateral obtained by the secured creditor is to achieve a preferred position as against, not the debtor, but other creditors. If, at the critical time for payment, the debtor has enough assets to pay all creditors, the secured creditor's security is irrelevant since he will be paid in any case. But if the debtor's assets are not sufficient to pay all the creditors' claims outstanding against him, some creditors will come out short. The creditor who has in some manner obtained a lien on particular assets of the debtor has the opportunity to claim those assets for the full payment of the debt owing to him, even if they are the only assets around so that the application of the collateral to his debt means that other creditors will receive nothing at all. Until paid, the secured creditor is "prior" to general creditors to the extent of the value of the assets that are subject to the secured creditor's lien. The general creditors have no claim against the assets under the secured creditor's lien except to the extent that the value of the assets exceeds the secured creditor's claim.

Creditors compete among themselves not only for an interest in specific assets of the debtor but also, to the extent they are unable to achieve a fully-secured position, for priority among themselves in right of payment. The creditor, or class of creditors may, of course, be negotiated into agreeing (in advance or later) that its claim against the debtor's assets will rank below that of some or all other creditors or classes of creditors— though always, of course, ahead of the debtor's claim to the assets. Such a creditor is said to have "subordinated" his claim, he is referred to as a "subordinated creditor" and his claim is "subordinated debt." Reflecting this relative priority of claims, creditors are often referred to as "senior" or "junior."

Thus, from the perspective of any single *general* creditor:

- he is more likely to be paid and is thus better off the more assets the debtor has on the payment date;
- he is adversely affected by an increase in the aggregate of outstanding claims of general creditors against the debtor since, in any ultimate showdown, all the general creditors will share equally in the finite assets of the debtor; and
- he is more adversely affected still by the creation or existence of secured creditors, for in the showdown, the secured creditors will, to the extent of their security, be able to assert a claim prior to all general creditors.

* * *

3. The Creditor of the Corporation

Much is usually made of the proposition that the hallmark of the corporate form of business enterprise is "limited liability." The statement is not untrue, but it deserves somewhat closer attention than is usually given to it.

As a matter of history, it is at least worth noting that the feature of limited liability, so much emphasized today, played little or no part in the development of modern corporation law....

History aside, the key point is not that the shareholder has been granted some special thing called limited liability. The real point is that in the case of creditor claims against an enterprise in corporate form, *the corporation is the debtor*, not those who hold claim to the proprietorship capital in the enterprise. Once that conceptual step is taken, the creditor law of the corporation exactly parallels the law of individual indebtedness and of creditors of individuals. The corporation has no limited liability at all. As in the case of any debtor, the creditors of the corporation have a claim to the assets of the corporation that is prior to the corporation's own claim as "owner." The creditors' claim to the corporate assets is thus automatically prior to the claim of the proprietorship investors—the shareholders. And the creditors' claim extends to *all* the assets of the debtor corporation. If necessary, the entire assets of the corporation must be devoted to payment of creditors of the corporation, even though nothing is left for the corporation or, *a fortiori*, its proprietorship owners. Furthermore, as in the case of almost all debtors, the creditors of the corporation must, in usual course, find their payment from the pool of assets that belong to the debtor corporation. If the assets of the corporation are insufficient to pay the claims, then, in the absence of some special guaranty, a creditor can no more expect to pursue assets beyond the debtor corporation's assets than a creditor of an individual can expect that payment of a debt owed by that individual can be extracted from some other individual.

Thus, the creditor of a corporation has the same kind of economic interest as the creditor of a human being and is subject to the same kinds of risks as the creditor of the individual. Similarly, the corporate creditor tries to resort to many of the same devices to enhance the likelihood that his corporate debtor will have sufficient funds in hand to pay off the debt when maturity comes.... In the usual case ... it will be a matter of major concern to the creditor of the corporation to seek four objectives—precisely as in the case of the lender to an individual debtor.

(1) The creditor will be happier if his corporate debtor has substantial assets in the corporate till at the time he extends credit and thereafter;

(2) The creditor will want to restrict the corporation from incurring debts to other general creditors with whom he might have to share the corporation's limited assets;

(3) The creditor will want the corporate assets to be free and unencumbered of any lien interests of a prior (secured) creditor; and

(4) The creditor will want to preserve a cushion of protective assets, and will want to see to it that no claimants who rank junior to him (usually shareholders, but sometimes subordinated debt holders) make off with assets of the corporation while the creditor's claim is still outstanding and unpaid.

Note again that even if the creditor should happen to be so fortunate as to achieve all four of these protections—which he will seldom be able to exact in full measure—still he has, by making the loan, put his funds at risk of the basic *commercial* vicissitudes of the debtor enterprise. If the market for the enterprise's product disappears, or the market value of the assets it holds drops through the floor, the creditor is apt to be left to whistle for his claim.... In the long pull, there is no security for enterprise creditors (or any other investors) other than the initial capital unspent and profitability of the enterprise. This uncontrollable, inherent commercial risk of the enterprise stands in marked contrast to the creditor's other risks—the risk that the corporate debtor might incur additional debt, or might distribute assets to the junior proprietorship investors, the shareholders. Those managers who control the business affairs of the corporate enterprise cannot determine what will happen to the general market, but they can determine whether indebtedness or distributions occur. Since the occurrence or non-occurrence of these events *are* amenable to managerial decision, they can be proscribed or limited by contract or by general law. And they often are.

* * *

B. THE SHAREHOLDER'S PERSPECTIVE
1. Payouts to Shareholders

The ideal world as conceived by the creditor of the corporation is a world that is normally wholly unacceptable to the shareholder. The investor who buys shares of stock in the incorporated enterprise and the investor who lends money to the incorporated enterprise, are, as a matter of economics, engaged in the same kind of activity and are motivated by the same basic objectives. They are both making a capital investment; they both expect or hope to get their investment back in the long run, either by liquidating pay-out or by sale of the security; and they both expect and hope to receive income from their investment in the interim before their capital is returned to them in full.

In the stereotypic model transaction, the investor who chose to take a shareholder's position rather than a creditor's position in a particular transaction simply made a calculated economic judgment that was different from the creditor's. The shareholder estimated that he could make more money by relinquishing to creditor investors a "prior" claim for interest and a fixed principal payment on maturity, and, by opting for uncertain "dividends" and the residual claim to the assets of the enterprise that would remain after all creditors, with their fixed claims, had been paid off.

The shareholder is willing to admit the "priority" of the creditor's interest claim and claim for principal payment on maturity. That does *not* imply, however, that the shareholder is willing to stand by chronologically until such time as the creditors have been paid in full. The shareholder will usually insist, that if, as he hopes, the enterprise makes money (and perhaps even if it does not), the shareholders will receive some return on (or of) their investment from time to time, regardless of the fact that there are creditor claims outstanding. Such periodic payments to shareholders are characterized as "dividends"; and, in the usual and normal case of the healthy incorporated enterprise, it is assumed that some assets will be regularly distributed out from the corporate treasury to the shareholder investors in dividend form.

Simple as this observation may be, its implications are far-reaching. If it were the case that all creditors had to be paid off before *any* payment could be made to shareholder investors, and if shareholders received nothing until ultimate liquidation of the enterprise when they would divide the residuum left after payment of all creditors—if, in other words, the terms "prior" and "before" were chronological as well as hierarchical—the creditor would not have to worry about assets being drained away into the hands of junior claimants and he would sleep better at night. But that arrangement would be wholly unacceptable to shareholders. Shareholders insist—and ultimately must concede—that, *during the life* of the creditor's claim, assets may be passed out to an investing group that hierarchically ranks below the creditors. The question becomes unavoidable: How much of the assets in the treasury of the incorporated enterprise may be distributed to shareholders, when, and under what circumstances?

While "dividends" are the most common form in which distributions are made to shareholders out of corporate assets, the distributive process is potentially Protean. If it is decided that an incorporated enterprise should be broken up, or that some of its assets or separable operations should be sold for cash, extraordinary cash distributions may be made to shareholders; these will be referred to as liquidating distributions, or distributions in partial liquidation. Similarly, the decision-makers in a going economic enterprise may conclude that the company has more cash or other liquid assets on hand than it needs, that no interesting investment opportunities are visible, and that the best thing to do is to distribute the excess assets to the shareholders; such a transaction may be referred to as a partial return of capital. Substantially the same transaction may occur where, for one reason or another, it seems desirable to those who are making the decisions to transfer a major nonliquid asset (such as a parcel of land or a separable business operation) to the shareholders, either by transferring to each shareholder a proportionate undivided interest in the asset, or by putting the asset into a subsidiary and distributing the subsidiary's shares to the parent's share-holders. Or those in control of an incorporated enterprise may decide to "buy in" or "repurchase" some of the outstanding stock of the corporation—a transaction that pays assets out of the corporate treasury to shareholders but brings in to the corporation nothing but pieces of paper in the hands of the corporation....

These instances do not exhaust the numbers of ways in which assets can be transferred by corporate managers out of a corporate till into the hands of shareholders.... In all these instances, and others, the problem of the creditor of the corporation is the same. Assets have left the corporate pot, have gone beyond his reach, and, worst of all, have been paid out to that group of investors whose claim to the assets of the corporation is junior to his.

Finally, it must be observed, there are two other factors that contribute to the creditor's unease. It is not just that there are many ways by which corporate assets *can* be channeled out of the corporate pot and into the shareholders' pockets. More worrisome is the shareholders' keen desire and incentive to do just that. The shareholder knows that so long as his money is at stake in the enterprise he will be the last one paid—or will not be paid at all—if the weather gets stormy. His instinct is to limit that risk by arranging for some kind of payout of at least his initial investment as soon as possible.

A closely related consideration is the dynamic known as "leverage." The creditor wants a thick equity cushion under him; the equity investors tend to prefer a thick debt slice in the company's capitalization, up to the capacity of the enterprise to meet the carrying charges of the debt. The shareholder sees an obvious advantage in a funding plan under which he puts in $1 and the lender puts in $2, the lender agreeing to a fixed return of 5¢ for each dollar loaned; if the enterprise earns 10¢ on each of the three dollars invested, the end result is that the creditor's $2 investment yields him 10¢ while the shareholder's $1 investment yields him 20¢. Shareholders greatly relish such leveraged arrangements under which the entrepreneurial harvest, if any, will come to them while the risk of capital loss is largely that of lenders.

The second thought that disturbs the sweet slumber of the creditor is the knowledge that virtually all responsibility and power for the conduct of the enterprise is in the hands of the members of the board of directors, who are elected by and mainly interested in the shareholders, and of corporate officers selected by the board. As the creditor sees it, hungry goats have been set to watch the cabbages.

* * *

C. THE CREDITOR'S AND SHAREHOLDER'S PERSPECTIVES COMBINED

It will now be seen that a corporate financial "model" has begun to appear.... It is well to pause here, however, to emphasize ... that the analytic corporate financial model discussed here is just that. The model does not purport to be fully descriptive of reality—of the actual way in which corporate creditors and shareholders go about their business of making investment decisions and protecting their positions. Reality is much more complex, often involving special factors that are determinative in the particular situation.

Moreover—and this point deserves special underscoring—the whole model we are using here presents a fundamentally skewed picture because of its emphasis upon the creditor's concern about the *ultimate* payment of his claim out of his debtor's assets in liquidation or bankruptcy. Creditors *are* concerned about that of course. And debtors *do* sometimes wind up in liquidation proceedings that set all the claimants against one another in a Donnybrook over who gets what from the insufficient carcass. But such events are not normalcy in the conduct of business. They bear the same relationship to daily business as a train wreck bears to a train trip. It *could* happen; one may do well to carry some travel insurance against it, perhaps even sit in the middle of the car; but if one knows, or seriously suspects, that a train may wreck, he does not usually take extra protective precautions—he stays off the train.

In the usual case, creditors expect to be paid, and are actually paid, on an ongoing basis out of the cashflow of the enterprise. The depression of the 1930s and the repeated wipe-out of gold-plated "fully secured" bond issues of blue chip railroads drove the point home at last; enterprise debt is not ultimately paid out of balance sheet assets but rather out of cash, which usually means operating profits. Security interests, mortgages, liquidation preferences and the like, are disaster remedies—like emergency exits. When an enterprise asks to borrow money, the prospective lender's primary interest will be in the economic prospects of the enterprise—the *dynamics* of the enterprise—the estimated cash flow, the chances of profitability, quality of management, markets for the product, competition, assembly of production components, labor relations, adequacy of financing, technological leads—to name but some. The model outlined here is distorted, for analytic purposes, in its pervasive implication that balance sheet assets are foremost in the creditor's mind, and in the essentially static character of the model.

Note

Halpern, Trebilcock and Turnbull have summarized Posner's view on how lenders factor limited liability into their lending practices:

> Posner ... contend[s][a] that in general lenders are fully compensated by the higher interest rates that the corporation must pay by virtue of enjoying limited liability. At the time the contract is made, the required or expected rate of return will compensate the lender for the anticipated risk. In order to determine the required or expected rate of return, the lender must form an accurate assessment of the risk, which will necessitate collecting information about the existing and expected assets and liabilities of the borrowing corporation, in so far as these assets and liabilities affect the lender's ability to obtain repayment. After the signing of the contract between the lender and the borrowing corporation, actions by the corporation might increase the risk of default to the creditor. To the extent that such actions were unanticipated, the corporation will have been able to borrow funds at a rate which does not fully compensate the creditor for the risk. In an attempt to minimize this type of risk various forms of constraints can be stipulated in the creditor's contract with the corporation restricting the actions of the corporation. The difficulty of specifying such constraints in sufficient detail to provide protection against all the possible means by which the corporation could increase the risk to creditors limits the usefulness of such a strategy. However, Posner argues that monitoring costs would be much greater in the case of unlimited liability. Here the information costs entailed in creditors mon-

---

a. The Rights of Creditors of Affiliated Corporations, 43 U. Chi. L. Rev. 499 (1967); and Posner, Economic Analysis of Law (2d ed. 1977), at chpt. 14.

itoring the wealth of a constantly changing body of shareholders (at least in large corporations) are likely to be substantial. Landers' proposals, if implemented, would entail similar costs, as creditors of one corporation would often be compelled to monitor the activities of several corporations.

Halpern, Trebilcock & Turnbull, An Economic Analysis of Limited Liability in Corporate Law, 30 U. Toronto L.J. 117, 124-25 (1980).

Problem — The Term Sheet

Oilcan Corporation ("Oilcan"), an integrated oil company, needs money to expand its refining capacity. Specifically, it needs $100,000,000 to buy land for, and build, a new refinery and storage facility. Oilcan has two other refineries in the continental United States, as well as pipeline, exploration leases, and a number of producing oil wells. Oilcan's common stock is listed on the New York Stock Exchange, and Oilcan has 3,000,000 shares of common stock outstanding, most of which is dispersed widely throughout the public. However, members of the Hatfield family of Possum Hollow, the founders and original owners of the corporation, own a total of 10 percent of this stock, subject to a shareholders' agreement covering voting and transfer.

The company has $100,000,000 in publicly held long-term subordinated debt, and another $50,000,000 of privately held debt secured by a mortgage on one of the refineries. Oilcan pays 6 percent a year in dividends on its common stock, and never has missed an interest payment on any of its debt. Oilcan's current net book value is $500,000,000.

Oilcan has asked The Possum Hollow National Bank and Trust Company either to lend it the full $100,000,000 or, as is more likely, syndicate the loan among a number of banks. McCoy, the lending officer, is new to commercial banking and has called you as counsel to draft a term sheet.

1. What are the basic protections that you will recommend? In coming up with a list, distinguish between those you believe are essential and those of lesser importance.

2. After completing this task, put yourself in the role of Oilcan's general counsel. After reviewing the term sheet prepared by the bank, draft a brief memorandum explaining to Oilcan's CFO the position you think Oilcan should take with respect to each of the proposed terms.

Please be sure to save your work. It will provide an interesting comparison with what you come up with after studying chapter 5 on corporate debt.

Section 2
The Origins and Purposes of Limited Liability

Mitchell, Close Corporations Reconsidered
63 Tulane L. Rev. 1143, 1155-68 (1989)

III. THE SIGNIFICANCE OF LIMITED LIABILITY
A. A Brief Inquiry into the Origins of Limited Liability

Modern courts and commentators often speak of limited liability as having developed as an incentive to industrial growth. Without limited liability, they say, investors would be unwilling to risk their personal wealth in an uncertain business venture. This conclusion seems intuitively correct to the modern lawyer and businessperson. Yet, although this rationale appears historically as one justification for limited liability, little evidence supports the view that it caused the adoption of that policy. At best, the rationale is only one of many reasons why limited liability became an accepted principle of corporate law. At worst, it is a rationalization of that principle.

Neither Coke, Blackstone, nor Kyd, the best known of the early commentators, specifically identified limited liability as a characteristic of corporateness. Kyd actually demonstrated that none of the characteristics commonly identified with corporations was unique to corporations—what was unique was the peculiar combination of characteristics. Thus, he identified the "essence" of all corporations as follows:

> 1. To have perpetual succession under a *special* denomination and under an *artificial* form. 2. To take and grant property, to contract obligations, and to sue and be sued by its corporate name, in the same manner as an individual. 3. To receive grants of privileges and immunities, and to enjoy them in *common*. These alone are sufficient to the *essence* of corporation....

The common thread underlying these characteristics is the unity and independent identity of the corporate form, a unity and identity that Kyd later emphasized: "The capacity of a corporation, and of the members of which it is composed, as individuals, is totally distinct...."

This unity and identity was not sacrosanct. Indeed, the law would sometimes look solely to the corporation's members for recompense, primarily when the corporation acted in a manner beyond its legally constituted capacities. Thus, wrote Kyd, a corporation could not commit a crime, not because of "the quaint observations frequent in the old books" that a corporation has no soul, but rather because it is beyond the corporation's capacity to do so. However, the crime did not go unpunished. Instead, the corporation's members could themselves be punished. Kyd stated that the same principle applied to other corporate incapacities.

Thus, the corporation's hallmark was its independence from its members, although that independence was limited to those cases in which the corporation legally could act. This independence was significant to the development of limited liability. Although the early commentators did not specifically identify limited liability as a corporate characteristic or privilege, some form of that principle did exist. Blackstone and Kyd concurred in the following statement:

> The debts of a corporation, either to or from it, are totally extinguished by it's [sic] dissolution; so that the members thereof cannot recover, or be charged with them, in their natural capacities: agreeable to that maxim of civil law, "*si quid universitati debetur, singulis non debetur; nec, quod debet universitas, singuli debent*" [If anything is owed to an entire body, it is not owed to the individual members, nor do the individual members owe what is owed by the entire body].

Neither commentator gave the reason for this rule, but two sources of it appear. The first source was a case cited by both Blackstone and Kyd, *Edmunds v. Brown & Tillard*, a paragraph-long opinion in which, without citing authority, the court dismissed a suit by a creditor of a dissolved corporation against its members to recover a debt. The second source was the Roman civil law from which the maxim Blackstone quoted was taken. The reason for the rule, implicit in the language of the maxim, appears to lie in the model of the corporation as a separate entity. This entity theory of the corporation formed the basis for judicial adoption of the modern principle of limited liability.

In addition to this early form of limited liability, the seventeenth-century case of *Salmon v. The Hamborough Company*[61] suggests a broader version of that principle. In that case, individual members of a trading corporation were served to answer for the corporation's unpaid debts. Kyd stated that, in demurring, these individuals pleaded that they were not liable for the corporation's debts in their individual capacities, suggesting the modern notion of limited liability. The defendants ultimately were held to answer for these debts, but the judgment was based on grounds other than their own direct liability. Thus, the case suggests that a broader principle of limited liability was known at an early stage of corporate law development. Whether the principle actually existed as law is unclear.

But if a broad form of limited liability was a corporate characteristic in Restoration England, the question remains: Why? Surely the reason could not have been to encourage industrial growth, because industrial growth does not appear to have been a predominant concern of that era. Nor would industrial growth have been of contemporary concern, because the essential impetus for such growth—the development of factories—was lacking. Where did the members of the Hamborough Company get their defense? The best answer appears to have been the unity and identity of which Kyd spoke: the concept of the corporate entity.

The concept of the corporate entity has a long tradition in common-law jurisprudence and has served as a fertile ground for philosophical debate. Yet the concept's roots do not appear to be in the common law at all, but rather in civil law and, in particular, the law governing ecclesiastical corporations. Although conceptually distinct from the theory that a corporation exists only by virtue of governmental concession, the concept of corporate entity, through the course of its history, became closely identified with this concession theory. The entity concept was, in that interdependent form, embraced by the courts of the new United States. Thus conceptualized, the corporation was a person, separate from its members, with separate existence, behavior, and identity. The characteristics the corporation possessed were those, and only those, enumerated in its charter granted by the state.

The entity theory clearly predated modern limited liability, and the concession theory also was of early vintage. Taken alone, the former theory suggests that, at least in fulfilling its corporate purpose, the corporation incurred liabilities for which it alone was responsible. Combined with the concession theory, this conclusion becomes less certain. For although the corporation was indeed conceived as separate from its members, the characteristics attributed to a particular corporation could not be discerned absent an examination of the legislation constituting it an entity and defining that corporation's relationship to its members and the state. If that legislation were silent, what of limited liability?

American courts began to answer this question in the late eighteenth century similarly to the English courts that had dealt with it. By the second decade of the nineteenth century, at least in the manufacturing states, courts generally held that silence in a corporate charter implied the existence of limited liability. The basis for these holdings is unclear; the sparse reasoning that exists is quite varied. What is clear, however, is that the American policy of limited liability initially was, like its English

61. 1 Ch. Cas. 204 (1691).

progenitor, a distinctly judicial development. As indicated earlier, a logical extension of the entity theory suggests that the shareholders of a corporation could not be held liable for the corporation's debts, but Professor Dodd wrote that this conclusion was not a necessary one. In any event, the courts of those states in which industrialization was nascent followed this approach.

The legislative response to the judicial presumption of limited liability is revealing. Rather than adopt this presumption as a term in corporate charters or permit it to exist unimpeded, state legislatures at first did just the opposite. Although the shareholders of public corporations[82] generally were granted limited liability, legislators usually denied that privilege to the shareholders of manufacturing corporations organized in the early nineteenth century. The conditions imposed on all corporations of that era were stringent. Professor Berle attributes this severity to the legislators' general fear of corporations stemming from their governmental sanction and utility as a center of power. Thus, requirements of minimum capital and limitations on maximum capital, limited duration, and carefully circumscribed corporate purposes were imposed as conditions to the grant of incorporation. All these limitations were geared originally toward checking the power that the corporation could amass.

The critical question, however, is how the imposition of unlimited liability served the goal of checking corporate power. One possibility is that it did so by creating disincentives for growth through debt financing for, by evading maximum capital requirements through the liberal use of leverage, shareholders exposed themselves to significant personal liability. Another explanation might be that the imposition of unlimited liability was not directed to these limited ends at all, but was instead an early means of protecting creditors. However, a coherent and reasoned policy dealing with shareholders' liability had not yet developed.

Dodd traces the development of limited liability in the industrializing states. He demonstrates that it was not until the 1840s that legislatures consistently recognized and applied limited liability as a principle of corporate law. His evidence and analysis provide the most detailed and comprehensive treatment available of this piece of legal history. Dodd's evidence and analysis do not support, by his own admission, the thesis that limited liability was an essential, or even important, motivator of early industrial growth, nor that it was necessarily designed to be such. In fact, his recounting of the debates in the Massachusetts legislature over the issue of limited liability sounds a wryly familiar note. It seems that New Hampshire provided for limited liability to shareholders of manufacturing corporations at an earlier stage than did Massachusetts. Coincidentally, or perhaps because of this, New Hampshire corporations began attracting significant amounts of capital from Massachusetts investors. In a foreshadowing of the "race to the bottom" of corporate law that Delaware led in the twentieth century, Massachusetts legislators insisted upon the necessity of limited liability as a means of retaining Massachusetts capital in that state. Dodd minimizes the legitimacy of this argument and points to other reasons for the attractiveness of New Hampshire industry. He cites Rhode Island as an example of a state that succeeded in developing substantial industry, despite the rather late guaranty of limited liability, to suggest that limited liability was not an important factor in early industrial growth. However, Dodd does not reach any

---

82. The phrase "public corporation" had, in the early nineteenth century, a very different meaning than the contemporary one. Historically, secular corporations were defined according to their purpose, with public corporations defined as those undertaking a governmental or quasi-governmental function and private corporations existing solely for private gain....

firm conclusions or definitively state the reasons for the acceptance of the principle of limited liability.

Dodd and other historians and commentators are quite clear that limited liability had very little effect on the predominant corporate type of that era and of ours: the small, closely held corporation. They identify other corporate characteristics, especially perpetual succession, as serving a far more important function for the small businessperson. Professor Hurst suggests another important reason for the desire to incorporate: the availability (with the advent of general incorporation laws) of a standard contract setting forth the relationships among corporate constituents....

The history of the development of limited liability, while inconclusive, has significant implications for the law of close corporations. Most significant is that the policy did not arise out of a concern for industrial growth or as a result of any carefully considered policy judgment by a legislative body. As a legislative matter, the development of limited liability clearly was a reaction to, and gradual acceptance of, the common-law principle. And as a common-law principle, the justification for its application to close corporations is weak. The notable failure of the early cases to discuss the reasons underlying limited liability suggests that the policy may have been taken for granted. The evidence indicates that the entity theory was the basis for this acceptance. Thus, it is reasonably clear that limited liability grew out of a reification of the corporate form that is inappropriate today with respect to the public corporation and even more inappropriate to the close corporation.

For additional historical analyses of the origins of limited liability, *see* Blumberg, Limited Liability and Corporate Groups, 11 J. Corp. Law 573, 577-81, 585-87 (1986); Dodd, American Business Corporations Until 1860, 364-437 (1954); Handlin & Handlin, Origins of the American Business Corporation, 5 J. Econ. Hist. 1 (1945); Jenkins, Skinning the Pantomime Horse: Two Early Cases on Limited Liability, 34 Cambridge L.J. 308 (1975); Presser, Thwarting the Killing of the Corporation: Limited Liability, Democracy, and Economics, 87 Nw. L. Rev. 148 (1992).

In the following excerpt, the authors undertake their own analysis of limited liability and posit their own conclusions:

Halpern, Trebilcock & Turnbull, An Economic Analysis of Limited Liability in Corporate Law
30 U. Toronto L.J. 117, 147-50 (1980)

* * *

.... We now attempt to derive some implications ... for the form of an efficient liability regime for corporations.

First, in the case of large, widely held companies, a limited liability regime, as a general rule, is the most efficient regime. By skewing the distribution of business risks amongst different shareholders, an unlimited liability regime would create a significant measure of uncertainty in the valuation of securities and threaten the existence of organized securities markets, thus inducing costly attempts by creditors and owners to transact around the regime. The case for a limited liability regime for this class of company is very compelling. The attenuated nature of the moral hazard factor[a] in widely held companies does not create a strong countervailing consideration.

Second, in the case of small, tightly held companies, a limited liability regime will, in many cases, create incentives for owners to exploit a moral hazard and transfer uncompensated business risks to creditors, thus inducing costly attempts by creditors to reduce these risks. An unlimited liability regime[51] for this class of enterprise (perhaps the 'private company,' recognized by many corporation statutes with respect to financial disclosure and securities regulation exemptions, having fewer than, say, fifty shareholders, restrictions on share transfers, and no right to make public offerings)[52] would seem to be the most efficient regime. The availability of an organized securities market is not, of course, a major countervailing factor with this class of company.

A major effect of adopting an unlimited liability regime in this context would be to shift to the corporation and its owners the onus of proposing contractual arrangements to creditors which limit the liability of the owners (where these are desired). Requiring explicit negotiation of such arrangements is likely to improve information flows to creditors about allocation of risks and sharpen the focus of creditors' incentives to monitor a corporation's activities. We acknowledge that the case for an unlimited liability regime for this class of company is not as compelling as the case for limited liability for large, widely held companies, given that in the former case, with fewer parties involved, most creditors and owners can contract around either regime at low cost, thus making the choice of liability regime relatively inconsequential. We also recognize that difficulties may be associated with attempting to distinguish by law small from large corporations for the purpose of applying different liability regimes, and that the distinction may induce some perverse and wasteful incentive effects as firms seek to manipulate internal structures to ensure compliance with the requirements of the preferred regime. However, our empirical intuition remains that, on balance, an unlimited liability regime is the most efficient regime for small, closely held companies.

Third, in cases where, as a general rule, a limited liability regime is the most efficient regime (large, widely held corporations, in our analysis), there is a case for a limited number of exceptions to the regime where some form of unlimited liability seems desirable. These exceptions might embrace the following classes of case:

A. MISREPRESENTATION

An exception is called for in the case of misrepresentation to creditors as to the legal status of a firm or its financial affairs.... Here the party responsible for the misrepresentation should be personally liable for corporate debts induced by the misrepresentation,

---

a. "Moral hazard" is a term that is used by economists to refer "to risk-sharing under conditions in which individuals can take private actions that affect the probability of the distribution of the outcome." Etzioni, The Moral Dimension: Toward a New Economics 239, 240 (1988). Examples include the increased carelessness of persons who take out insurance policies in performing the activities they have insured, such as driving. *Id.*

51. We contemplate an unlimited liability regime where creditors must first sue the company and, in the event of non-payment, petition the company, into bankruptcy, following which the trustee in bankruptcy can enforce unmet creditors' claims against shareholders on a joint and several basis. Contracting out would be permitted.... *See* Palmers Company Law, [(22nd ed. 1976)], at 32, 33.

52. This type of enterprise will, like a partnership, typically entail active owner involvement in management activities (hence the moral hazard problem) while involving a small and relatively stable number of owners, thus minimizing monitoring and enforcement costs for owners and creditors under an unlimited liability regime....

but, in addition, as we elaborate below, the directors of the corporation might be made personally liable (subject to offsetting insurance or compensation arrangements) to strengthen management incentives to have this form of behaviour monitored by corporate officers and employees.

B. THE INVOLUNTARY CREDITOR

In cases such as *Walkovsky v. Carlton*,[55] transaction costs are such that a firm can transfer uncompensated business risks to this class of creditor. *Rockwell Developments Ltd. v. Newtonbrook Plaza Ltd.*,[56] where a firm unilaterally imposed costs on another party through unmeritorious legal proceedings, involved similar considerations. Again, it can be argued that the directors of the company should be personally liable to this class of creditor. In the large, widely held corporation where this exception would apply, such a rule would minimize the information costs that owners would face in monitoring each other's wealth, would reduce creditors' transaction costs in enforcing claims, and would focus incentives to adopt cost-justified avoidance precautions on that body of persons (the directors) in such a class of corporation best able to respond to those incentives.

C. THE EMPLOYEE

Amongst corporate creditors, employees, as a class, probably face the most severe informational disabilities, have the least ability to diversify risk of business failure, and may have the strongest equity argument (in terms of relative capacity to absorb losses). This proposition is not universally true, as some employees will possess both superior information on corporate finances and high job mobility (e.g., corporate executives and professional employees), while some trade creditors may be afflicted with similar disabilities to those of the less informed, less mobile corporate employees. However, fashioning a rule that clearly differentiates these situations is likely to be difficult, and present rules governing the liability of directors for limited amounts of unpaid wages of 'employees' in the Canada Business Corporation Act may represent defensible approximations of optimal rules.[59]

The net effect of these proposals would seem to be to obviate the need for the elaborate veil-piercing, subrogation, and consolidation rules in corporate bankruptcies advocated by Landers. In the case of small, tightly held corporations, the unlimited liability regime which we have proposed would seem responsive to many of the parent-subsidiary and affiliated company problems with which he is concerned. In the case of large, widely held companies, involuntary creditors and employees, under our proposals, receive special protection. Other creditors, prejudiced by intra-group transactions induced by moral hazard considerations, would have to rely on the misrepresentation exception. This exception is necessarily a much more limited response to creditor problems than the unlimited liability regime proposed for small, closely held corporations because any substantial move in the direction of unlimited liability in the case of large, widely held companies will engender the kind of costs that have led us generally to reject such a regime in this case.

---

55. Supra note 8 [223 N.E.2d 6 (1966); noted 76 *Yale L. J.* 1190 (1967)].
56. Supra note 14 [30 O.R. (2nd) 199 (Ont. C.A. 1972)].
59. For reasons noted above, we would again focus the liability rule on directors, rather than owners-at-large....

Easterbrook & Fischel, Limited Liability and the Corporation
52 U. Chi. L. Rev. 89, 93-97 (1985)

People can conduct economic activity in many forms.... Limited liability for equity investors has long been explained as a benefit bestowed on investors by the state. It is much more accurately analyzed as a logical consequence of the differences among the forms for conducting economic activity.

Publicly held corporations typically dominate other organizational forms when the technology of production requires firms to combine both the specialized skills of multiple agents and large amounts of capital. The publicly held corporation facilitates the division of labor. The distinct functions of managerial skills and the provision of capital (and the bearing of risk) may be separated and assigned to different people—workers who lack capital, and owners of funds who lack specialized production skills. Those who invest capital can bear additional risk, because each investor is free to participate in many ventures. The holder of a diversified portfolio of investments is more willing to bear the risk that a small fraction of his investments will not pan out.

Of course this separation of functions is not costless. The separation of investment and management requires firms to create devices by which these participants monitor each other and guarantee their own performance.... The costs of the separation of investment and management (agency costs) may be substantial. Nonetheless, we know from the survival of large corporations that the costs generated by agency relations are outweighed by the gains from separation and specialization of function. Limited liability reduces the costs of this separation and specialization.

First, limited liability decreases the need to monitor. All investors risk losing wealth because of the actions of agents. They could monitor these agents more closely. The more risk they bear, the more they will monitor. But beyond a point more monitoring is not worth the cost. Moreover, specialized risk bearing implies that many investors will have diversified holdings. Only a small portion of their wealth will be invested in any one firm. These diversified investors have neither the expertise nor the incentive to monitor the actions of specialized agents. Limited liability makes diversification and passivity a more rational strategy and so potentially reduces the cost of operating the corporation....

Second, limited liability reduces the costs of monitoring other shareholders. Under a rule exposing equity investors to additional liability, the greater the wealth of other shareholders, the lower the probability that any one shareholder's assets will be needed to pay a judgment. Thus existing shareholders would have incentives to engage in costly monitoring of other shareholders to ensure that they do not transfer assets to others or sell to others with less wealth. Limited liability makes the identity of other shareholders irrelevant and thus avoids these costs.

Third, by promoting free transfer of shares, limited liability gives managers incentives to act efficiently.... So long as shares are tied to votes, poorly run firms will attract new investors who can assemble large blocs at a discount and install new managerial teams. This potential for displacement gives existing managers incentives to operate efficiently in order to keep share prices high.

Although this effect of the takeover mechanism is well known, the relation between takeovers and limited liability is not. Limited liability reduces the costs of purchasing shares. Under a rule of limited liability, the value of shares is determined by the present value of the income stream generated by a firm's assets. The identity and wealth of other investors is irrelevant. Shares are fungible; they trade at one price in liquid markets. Under a rule of unlimited liability, as Halpern, Trebilcock, and Turnbull emphasized, shares would not be fungible. Their value would be a function of the present value of future cash flows *and* of the wealth of shareholders. The lack of fungibility would impede their acquisition....

Fourth, limited liability makes it possible for market prices to impound additional information about the value of firms. With unlimited liability, shares would not be homogeneous commodities, so they would no longer have one market price. Investors would therefore be required to expend greater resources analyzing the prospects of the firm in order to know whether "the price is right." When all can trade on the same terms, though, investors trade until the price of shares reflects the available information about a firm's prospects. Most investors need not expend resources on search; they can accept the market price as given and purchase at a "fair" price.

Fifth, as Henry Manne emphasized, limited liability allows more efficient diversification. Investors can minimize risk by owning a diversified portfolio of assets. Firms can raise capital at lower costs because investors need not bear the special risk associated with nondiversified holdings. This is true, though, only under a rule of limited liability or some good substitute. Diversification would increase rather than reduce risk under a rule of unlimited liability. If any one firm went bankrupt, an investor could lose his entire wealth. The rational strategy under unlimited liability, therefore, would be to minimize the number of securities held. As a result, investors would be forced to bear risk that could have been avoided by diversification, and the cost to firms of raising capital would rise.

Sixth, limited liability facilitates optimal investment decisions. When investors hold diversified portfolios, managers maximize investors' welfare by investing in any project with a positive net present value. They can accept high-variance ventures (such as the development of new products) without exposing the investors to ruin. Each investor can hedge against the failure of one project by holding stock in other firms. In a world of unlimited liability, though, managers would behave differently. They would reject as "too risky" some projects with positive net present values. Investors would want them to do this because it would be the best way to reduce risks.[12] By definition this would be a social loss, because projects with a positive net present value are beneficial uses of capital.

Both those who want to raise capital for entrepreneurial ventures, and society as a whole, receive benefits from limited liability. The equity investors will do about as well under one rule of liability as another. Every investor must choose between riskless T-bills and riskier investments. The more risk comes with an equity investment, the less the investor will pay. Investors bid down the price of equity until, at the margin, the risk-adjusted returns of stock and T-bills are the same. So long as the rule of liability is known, investors will price shares accordingly.[13] The choice of an inefficient rule, however, will shrink the pool of funds available for investment in projects that would subject investors to risk. The increased availability of funds for projects with positive net values is the real benefit of limited liability....

---

12. In the jargon of portfolio theory, when investors are or can be diversified, managers should consider only systematic risk in making decisions. When investors cannot diversify their holdings, managers should consider both systematic and unsystematic risk. The consideration of unsystematic risk may lead them to forgo profitable investments. [These issues are discussed *infra* at chapter 3, section 5a.—Eds.]

13. This is an implication of the Coase Theorem. Coase, *The Problem of Social Cost*, 3 J.L. & Econ. 1 (1960).

Professor Stephen Presser argues that, while Easterbrook and Fischel's six factors (and underlying economic efficiency considerations) were important in the evolution of the doctrine of limited liability, they do not provide a full explanation. Presser, Thwarting the Killing of the Corporation: Limited Liability, Democracy, and Economics, 87 Nw. U. L. Rev. 148, 155-163 (1992). Presser attacks Easterbrook and Fischel's theory on three grounds.

First, Presser disagrees with their claim that unlimited liability produces high monitoring costs that discourage investment. He contends that even in an unlimited liability regime, shareholders would still invest if the return on their investment were high enough; they would simply base their investment on the corporation's proven business strategies or the self-monitoring abilities of management.

Presser's second objection arises from Easterbrook and Fischel's contention that unlimited liability would lead to increased costs arising from the need to monitor other investors. He notes that monitoring would be required only where unlimited liability was joint and several. He believes that it is likely, however, that an unlimited liability regime would involve pro rata liability for shareholders so that any individual shareholder would be liable only in the proportion that her investment bore to the total investment in the firm. Under such a system, the need for monitoring other shareholders disappears because the wealth of other shareholders is irrelevant. The only important criterion is investment in the firm.

Third, Presser notes that the benefits of diversified investments, such as the increased incentives for managers to invest in risky projects and a concomitant decrease in investment costs, could be obtained in other ways apart from limited liability. For example, diversification could be achieved at the firm level, if firms had sufficient capital to invest in a wide range of opportunities.

Presser looks to the historical justification for limiting liability and concludes that "the imposition of limited liability was perceived as a means of encouraging the small-scale entrepreneur, and of keeping entry into business markets competitive and democratic." Coupled with economic efficiency, Presser concludes that business democracy explains the continuing appeal of limited liability.

In chapter 3, section 5a, we will take up the issue of investment diversification versus concentration that implicitly divides some of the foregoing theories about limited liability.

Stone, The Place of Enterprise Liability in the Control of Corporate Conduct
90 Yale L.J. 1, 70-74 (1980)[a]

.... [W]e should not underestimate the continuing potential of limited liability to work social mischief. The problems extend far beyond the financially unaccountable taxicab companies that supply the paradigm case for the law schools; I have in mind, even more troublesomely, the firms that produce and handle such products as toxic chemicals. As long as limited liability is available as a protection, it is precisely in such areas of substantial third-party risk that we can expect to find a disproportionate population of small, financially unaccountable companies. Major firms will incline to externalize the risks of their more jeopardous undertakings by establishing subsidiaries; by leaving the "dirty business" to small, specialized outfits that are themselves questionably

---

a. Reprinted by permission of The Yale Law Journal Company and Fred B. Rothman & Company from *The Yale Law Journal*, Vol. 90, pp. 1-77.

capitalized; or by creating "independent suppliers" whose umbilical cord to the firm is a loan and output contract, rather than stock, so that the major company that in reality stands behind the operation may be able to avoid some of the entanglements of being a technical stockholder-parent.

To deal with some of the situations where limited liability most strongly conflicts with fundamental law-enforcement goals, prosecutors and plaintiffs can, with varying degrees of satisfaction, circumvent the doctrine. In close corporation contexts, for example, where the firm's investors are often also its managers, there is the possibility of holding the key individuals directly accountable, both in crime and in tort, on the basis of their personal participation. Particularly where a subsidiary is involved, plaintiffs can allege a joint tort, a conspiracy between the two entities, or aiding and abetting. There are, moreover, special legislative possibilities that would deal with some of these problems on an area-by-area basis: mandatory insurance, for example, or, where licensing is required, a condition that companies engaged in high-risk ventures demonstrate financial capability adequate to meet the expected liability claims.

Whatever the merits of these various options, none of them can be regarded as the functional equivalent of piercing the corporate veil. It is one thing to hold investors secondarily liable for judgments secured against the corporation for the corporation's wrongs, and quite another and more difficult task, especially where criminal-law burdens of proof are concerned, to establish their independent culpability by showing a conspiracy or aiding and abetting. Moreover, while mandatory insurance for companies engaged in high-risk activities may be appropriate to advance compensation goals, it would not be well suited for specific deterrence, since the consequences of intentional wrongdoing are generally uninsurable.

* * *

The better approach would be to reverse the present presumption that limited liability is the norm, at least when applied to certain corporate delicts....

Even if increased investor liability could improve deterrence, its potential is restricted by ... efficiency and morality constraints.... Particularly as share ownership diversifies, with all the problems of high monitoring costs for large numbers of investors, each with a relatively small stake, the level of monitoring we can realistically expect from the investors declines. In all likelihood, the added legal risk to investors would increase the cost of equity capital without significant reduction in unwanted behavior (other than through some unlamentable decrease in investment available for jeopardous activities). And from a moral perspective, there are the same reservations about imposing vicarious punitive liabilities on superior agents—in this case, the investors. Indeed, one wonders whether the imposition of a "penalty" on the numerous, faceless shareholders of a defunct corporation would advance any of the real moral goals of the law.

But if these are, as I assume, the considerations that form the true basis for the present presumption in favor of limited liability, they constitute not so much warrants for protecting shareholders from liability absolutely, as for protecting them from the peculiarly onerous character of the joint and several liability that would prevail in the absence of limited liability. That is, if the limited liability rules are withdrawn, the only option that exists in present law may be to treat the investors, *inter se*, as partners, in which case each shareholder of a corporation like the Penn Central would have to stand behind every delict judgment in its indivisible entirety. This would surely be unacceptable. But our choice need not be restricted to limited liability or ordinary partner's liability as the only alternatives. As a compromise, we could provide that when an insolvent corporation has unpaid debts arising from a criminal fine or punitive damage award, or perhaps even civil liabilities arising under federal statutes whose policies do not appear fully discharged by compensation, shareholders would be held liable on the debt as guarantors but not as partners: each would be liable only in proportion to his or her equity interest.

Problem — The Policy of Limited Liability[a]

The government of Bondolia has been so pleased with your work thus far that it has requested that you prepare a corporations code to be presented to the new legislature. The finance minister of Bondolia, who studied law and business in the United States, suggests that you treat close corporations separately, and gives you a draft of the following statute:

(a) A close corporation is a corporation with voting stock of all classes held of record by no more than thirty persons.

(b) Each stockholder of a close corporation who is an officer, director, or holder of issued and outstanding stock of such corporation possessing 10 percent or more of the voting power of all classes of stock outstanding shall be deemed a "managing stockholder." Each other stockholder of a close corporation shall be deemed a "passive stockholder."

(c) Each managing stockholder of a close corporation has the liabilities of a partner in a general partnership with respect to third parties.

(d) A passive stockholder is not liable for the obligations of a close corporation unless, in addition to the exercise of his (or her) rights and powers as a passive stockholder, he (or she) participates in the control of the business. However, if the passive stockholder participates in the control of the business, he (or she) is liable only to persons who transact business with the close corporation reasonably believing, based upon the passive stockholder's conduct, that the passive stockholder is a managing stockholder.

Prepare a memorandum evaluating the desirability of adopting this statute as part of the Bondolia Corporations Code. In particular, address:

(i) the desirability of limiting the liability of stockholders in close corporations;

(ii) whether tort and contract liability should be treated similarly;

(iii) whether voting power or managing control are effective criteria for imposing general liability;

(iv) whether compulsory insurance should be required as a substitute for limited liability, and whether self-insurance is acceptable;

(v) whether limited liability should be statutorily abrogated with respect to specific problems it causes, or whether exceptions to the principle should be judicially developed;

(vi) whether relevant and substantive differences exist between close corporations and partnerships that justify different liability regimes; and

(vii) whether relevant differences exist between close and public corporations that justify a difference in liability regime.

------

a. Adapted from Note, Should Shareholders Be Personally Liable for the Torts of their Corporations?, 76 Yale L.J. 1190, 1205 (1967).

Section 3
Legal Limitations — Limited Liability and Corporate Structure

The preceding section set out some of the developmental background and policy considerations underlying limited liability. This section deals with limitations the law has placed on that principle. Since you undoubtedly already have been exposed to some of this material, we have attempted to provide an overview of the issues most relevant to questions of corporate financial structure, and some of the more unusual doctrinal permutations.

The legal tests involved in establishing limits to the principle of limited liability, commonly known as "piercing the corporate veil," are amorphous, difficult to apply and certainly not predictive. In fact, it is not always clear that courts actually are applying the tests they are articulating in determining that limited liability does or does not survive in a particular case. Nevertheless, the cases are at least significantly policy-driven, as should be illustrated by those presented in this chapter. In addition, the cases will discuss the different tests purportedly used in veil piercing cases.

The traditional situation in which the veil is pierced in some form is when a creditor of the corporation attempts to hold its shareholders personally liable for obligations of the corporation. Not surprisingly, the almost exclusive context of this approach is in close corporations[1] (including parent-subsidiary relationships). Favour Mind Ltd. v. Pacific Shores, Inc., a more modern analog to the oft-assigned Walkovszky v. Carlton, provides a thorough discussion of the law in this area.

Veil piercing, however, is occasionally applied in other factual contexts. For example, the concept of *reverse piercing the veil*, which is discussed in section 3a(ii) below, occasionally has been accepted, where the shareholders of a close corporation have argued that their individual identification with the corporation leads to the conclusion that some right of the corporation is in reality their personal right. Also, some cases present the situation in which a creditor of the corporation or an insider of the corporation attempts to hold somebody outside the corporation liable for the corporation's debts on the theory that that person has exercised dominion or control over the corporation. One type of case—involving the so-called doctrine of "lender liability"—occurs when third parties attempt to hold creditors of the corporation liable for the corporation's debts.

Thus, this section provides an overview of the tests used in veil piercing and the variety of situations in which it is applied. As you read the materials that follow, consider whether the policy considerations underlying veil piercing in the traditional cases equally underlie veil piercing in other contexts in which it has applied. Certainly, as a theoretical matter, one thing should be apparent: the tenacity of the entity theory of the corporation. Consider as you study these materials whether the analysis would change if the nexus of contracts theory of the corporation were more generally accepted in the case law.

Would a contractual approach to limited liability help resolve some of the policy concerns raised in the preceding section? Why would shareholders ever be willing to contract around limited liability and, if they did so, what types of concerns would they need to address?

---

1. Thompson, Piercing the Corporate Veil: An Empirical Study, 76 Cornell L.Rev. 1036, 1039 (1991) (" … piercing occurs only in close corporations or within corporate groups; it does not occur in public corporations.")

a. Veil Piercing under Corporate Law

(i) Traditional Veil Piercing

Problem—Structuring the Corporation[a]

Frank and Stanford were classmates in architecture school. Frank now has an active architecture practice. Stanford has a small contracting business specializing in the renovation of urban residential real estate. They have decided to go into business together. To begin, they intend to purchase and renovate six contiguous townhouses on the edge of a run-down neighborhood in Usonia. The houses currently are empty shells, all of which are owned by O. M. Pie. Frank and Stanford believe that they can purchase the shells for an average cost of $25,000 each. They estimate that renovation will cost between $50,000 and $80,000 for each house, assuming no structural defects. Their capital contribution will consist of $5,000 each per house (the difference between what a bank will lend for construction and the anticipated cost of purchase and renovation) for a total capital contribution of $30,000 each. Frank and Stanford will be the only officers and directors.

Stanford presently has the assets of his contracting business, having a net worth of about $20,000, in a corporation, Stanford Builder's, Inc., of which he is the sole shareholder, officer, and director. Although he is working on three other jobs, he plans to devote full time to the project with Frank when he's finished. If their first project is successful, they expect to undertake similar projects on a full-time basis.

Frank and Stanford have come to you for advice on structuring their undertaking. They have discussed the following alternatives:

(i) Creating a single new corporation in which they will invest equal amounts (for equal shares) that will purchase and renovate all six houses;

(ii) Setting up six separate corporations, in which they will each invest $5,000 for equal shares. Each corporation will purchase and renovate one house; and

(iii) Having the stock of the six corporations discussed in (ii) above owned by a single holding company, the stock of which will be owned equally by Frank and Stanford.

They would like your advice on the corporate structure. They want to minimize the risks for the overall business, and protect their own investment (and personal wealth) to the extent possible (and therefore, of course, a partnership is out of the question). Which of these alternatives do you recommend, and why?

Favour Mind Ltd. v. Pacific Shores, Inc.

2004 U.S. Dist. LEXIS 637 (S.D.N.Y. 2004)

GEORGE B. DANIELS, District Judge:

This is an action by Plaintiff, Favour Mind Limited ("FML"), a Hong Kong corporation which manufactures, exports, and distributes garments, against Pacific Shores, Inc. ("Pacific Shores"), Alpine Apparel Group d/b/a Cameron Roberts, Ltd. ("Alpine Ap-

---

a. Adapted from Solomon, Schwartz, Bauman, and Weiss, Corporations: Law and Policy, Materials and Problems, 337-38 (3d Ed. 1994).

parel"), and Defendant Robert Czwartacky ("Czwartacky"). Plaintiff seeks $216,408.06 in unpaid invoices for garments that it manufactured, asserting breach of contract, fraud, and unjust enrichment. Plaintiff also seeks a declaratory judgment allowing it to pierce the corporate veil of Pacific Shores and Alpine Apparel to hold Defendant Czwartacky personally liable for the outstanding debt. On May 7, 1999 Plaintiff was granted default judgments against Pacific Shores and Alpine Apparel with respect to the breach of contract claim for $216,408.06, on the basis that neither answered Plaintiff's complaint.

.... Presently before this Court is Defendant Czwartacky's Rule 56 motion for summary judgment of Plaintiff's remaining cause of action seeking a declaratory judgment allowing Plaintiff to pierce the corporate veil to hold Defendant Czwartacky liable for the debts of Pacific Shores and Alpine Apparel. Fed R. Civ. P. 56. For the following reasons, Defendant Czwartacky's motion for summary judgment is hereby GRANTED.

BACKGROUND

Pacific Shores was incorporated in New York in May 1988. The company consisted of Defendant Czwartacky, the President, and Steve Kent ("Kent"), the Vice-President and Secretary.... Defendant Czwartacky and Kent were the company's sole directors and 50% shareholders.... Defendant Czwartacky managed Pacific Shores' day-to-day operations.... Defendant Czwartacky invested $50,000 to start up Pacific Shores and Kent invested $100,000. Both later invested $15,000 and Defendant Czwartacky subsequently invested $5,000 or $10,000 on several occasions.

In or about mid-1991, Pacific Shores ordered sample garments from Plaintiff. The samples were billed to Pacific Shores on open credit terms. After Pacific Shores approved the sample order, it ordered production goods. Plaintiff required Pacific Shores to obtain a letter of credit to pay for the production goods, or else wire transfer funds before shipment. The production goods were paid for by letters of credit issued by Pacific Shores' factor, Finova Capital Corporation ("Finova"). Plaintiff subsequently invoiced and expected payment from Pacific Shores. As Plaintiff became Pacific Shores' sole overseas supplier, Pacific Shores gradually became slow in paying for samples. In December 1993, Pacific Shores asked Plaintiff to allow it to pay two-thirds of the invoices of production goods by letter of credit and one-third by wire transfers some time after shipment. Plaintiff agreed to this request to help Pacific Shores expand its business and enable it to pay the outstanding sample charges faster, so that Plaintiff might receive more business from Pacific Shores.

* * *

Throughout 1994, Plaintiff continued to sell goods to Pacific Shores, while constantly pursuing Pacific Shores for payment. By December 6, 1994, Plaintiff threatened to cut off Pacific Shores' credit because of slow payment. By April 1995, due to Pacific Shores' slow payments, Plaintiff rescinded its agreement to allow Pacific Shores to wire transfer one-third of the invoiced value after shipment. It instead reverted to the original requirement that Pacific Shores provide a letter of credit for the full amount of the invoice before shipment. Plaintiff also insisted upon payment of the past due amount before it would ship any further goods.... Plaintiff continued to ship samples to Pacific Shores on credit to help keep it in business.

By April 25, 1995, Pacific Shores had become Plaintiff's largest account debtor, owing Plaintiff over $200,000.... On June 1, 1995 Defendant Czwartacky wrote to Plaintiff that "I [have] become cash poor." ...

In May 1995, Defendant Czwartacky incorporated Cameron & Roberts under New York law. He was the President, sole shareholder, and managing director. There is no evidence that Defendant invested any money other than the payment of the incorporation fee. Cameron & Roberts licensed its name to Alpine Apparel, an unrelated New York corporation of which Defendant Czwartacky was never a shareholder, officer, or employee. Under the terms of the License Agreement, Alpine Apparel would pay a 6% royalty to Cameron & Roberts.

On September 5, 1995 Pacific Shores advised Plaintiff that Finova would no longer amend its letter of credit for payments to Plaintiff. As Pacific Shores would therefore be unable to purchase goods, it advised Plaintiff the next day that it was going out of business. On September 25, Pacific Shores informed Plaintiff that it lost $6,118 over the eight-month period ending August 31, 1995.

Pacific Shores advised Plaintiff that Alpine Apparel would open a letter of credit for the purchase of additional goods. In fact, Defendant Czwartacky named Cameron & Roberts as the corporation that would assume Pacific Shores' debt to Plaintiff.... On January 25, 1996, Alpine Apparel opened a letter of credit to Plaintiff. Plaintiff thereafter made two shipments of goods to Alpine Apparel amounting to $122,261.25, which were paid for by letter of credit....

In March 1996, Pacific Shores and Cameron & Roberts went out of business, though Pacific Shores was never formally dissolved. At that time, Alpine Apparel owed Plaintiff $3,486.50 for samples and Pacific Shores owed Plaintiff $100,000 to $200,000, all or most of which were for samples. Defendant Czwartacky took $700 from Cameron & Roberts' bank account because "it was my money that I put in there in the first place." ... Defendant also withdrew $200 to $300 from Pacific Shores' bank account.

Defendant Czwartacky has not produced any stock certificates, record books, minutes of shareholders, officers, and/or directors meetings, or financial records except tax returns for Pacific Shores and Cameron & Roberts. He claims that minutes of Pacific Shores' directors meetings were not kept after the initial meetings. He also explains that Pacific Shores' final tax return for 1996 showed its address as his own home address in South Carolina because, by the time of filing taxes, Pacific Shores was out of business and had no offices.

DISCUSSION

* * *

Defendant Czwartacky argues that he is entitled to summary judgment dismissing Plaintiff's cause of action seeking a declaratory judgment piercing the corporate veil to hold him liable for the debts of Pacific Shores and Alpine Apparel. Defendant Czwartacky argues that Plaintiff cannot show that he committed a fraud or wrong against Plaintiff, this being a required showing in order to pierce the corporate veil.

New York courts disregard the corporate form where it is necessary to do so in order "to prevent fraud or to achieve equity." Walkovsky v. Carlton, 18 N.Y.2d 414, 223 N.E.2d 6, 276 N.Y.S.2d 585, 587 (1966) (quoting International Aircraft Trading Co. v. Manufacturers Trust Co., 297 N.Y. 285, 292, 79 N.E.2d 249, 252 (1948)). Under New York law, a company's corporate form may be disregarded and the corporate veil may be pierced where the party seeking to do so makes a two-part showing: "(i) that the owner exercised complete domination over the corporation with respect to the transaction at issue; and (ii) that such domination was used to commit a fraud or wrong that injured the party seeking to pierce the veil." American Fuel Corporation v. Utah Energy Development Company, Inc., 122 F.3d 130, 134 (2d Cir. 1997) (citing Morris v. New York

State Dep't of Taxation & Fin., 82 N.Y.2d 135, 623 N.E.2d 1157, 1160-61, 603 N.Y.S.2d 807 (1993))…. An employee/shareholder who uses his control of the corporation to further his own personal business rather than that of the corporation may be held liable for the corporation's acts. Id. For example, an employee may be deemed liable where he exercises complete domination and control over the corporation. Austin Powder Co. v. McCullough, 216 A.D.2d 825, 826, 628 N.Y.S.2d 855 (1995).

While control or complete domination of the corporation is an essential factor in determining whether to pierce the corporate veil, it is not enough to only show such domination, standing alone-there must also be "some showing of a wrongful or unjust act toward [the party seeking piercing]." Id., (citing Morris, at 1161). Further, the test for piercing the corporate veil is not disjunctive in that piercing the corporate veil does not depend upon a showing of either domination or a fraud or wrong. Id. The test is instead conjunctive-in order to pierce the corporate veil, a showing of both domination and fraud or wrong is required. Id., (citing Morris, at 1160-61).

1. Control/Domination

In determining corporate domination, a court may consider several factors, including:

> (1) whether corporate formalities are observed, (2) whether the capitalization is adequate, (3) whether funds are put in and taken out of the corporation for personal rather than corporate purposes, (4) whether there is overlap in ownership, officers, directors, and personnel, (5) whether the corporate entities share common office space, address and telephone numbers, (6) the amount of business discretion displayed by the allegedly dominated corporation, (7) whether the alleged dominator deals with the dominated corporation at arms length, (8) whether the corporation is treated as an independent profit center, (9) whether others pay or guarantee debts of the dominated corporation, and (10) whether the corporation in question had property that was used by the alleged dominator as if it were the dominator's own.

William Passalaqua Builders, et al. v. Resnick Developers South, Inc., et al., 933 F.2d 131, 139 (2d Cir. 1990)….

Plaintiff contends that Defendant Czwartacky is personally liable for Pacific Shores' and Alpine Apparel's corporate debt because Defendant Czwartacky as shareholder used the corporation for his own personal business and exercised complete domination. A defendant may be held liable only where he has used the corporation "to perpetrate a fraud or has so dominated and disregarded [the corporation's] corporate form that [the corporation] primarily transacted [his] personal business rather than its own corporate business." Kirno Hill Corp. v. Holt, 618 F.2d 982, 985 (2nd Cir. 1980). However, the Second Circuit has denied personal liability for the shareholder even where the corporation is thinly capitalized, kept no separate books or files, and had no offices distinct from the shareholder's other corporations. Garter v. Snyder, 607 F.2d 582 (2nd Cir. 1979). The Garter court also refused to render dispositive the fact that the corporation paid some of the shareholder's personal expenses, noting that the payment was petty. Id. at 587. More was needed to evince control. The corporate form could be disregarded only where a corporation's "separate identity [is] so disregarded, that it primarily transacted the dominator's business rather than its own and can be called the other's alter ego." Id. at 586.

With respect to Pacific Shores, there is no evidence that corporate formalities were generally observed as no meetings or records have been produced. Pacific Shores did not appear to display much business discretion independent of Defendant Czwartacky's will. With regard to the exchange of personal and corporate funds, although Plaintiff's employee concluded that Pacific Shores' payments came from Defendant Czwartacky personally, this employee's testimony does not evince an appreciation of the difference between Defendant Czwartacky's payments in his personal capacity and those that he made as "the boss" of Pacific Shores. Also, as in Garter, supra, the $200 to $300 that Defendant used for personal or showroom expenses was petty. Though Pacific Shores' initial capital investment was only $10,000, at least $170,000 was additionally invested. Also, Pacific Shores existed as a profit center independent of Defendant Czwartacky, and Finova issued Pacific Shores' letters of credit. There is no evidence that Defendant Czwartacky used Pacific Shores' property as his own personal property.

The Second Circuit in American Fuel Corporation, supra, found that the defendant shareholder did not dominate the subject corporation because he was only a 50% owner, the other shareholder was active in the business, and the defendant had not taken corporate funds for his own use. It did so despite the fact that the corporation had no contracts, no employees, no independent office space, it used the defendant shareholder's home address on the corporation letterhead, it had no separate bank account, capital, or assets at the time of trial, and the shareholder had personally paid corporate expenses and kept no records of the expenditures.

* * *

2. Fraud/Wrong

The second part of the piercing inquiry concerns whether domination was used to commit a wrongful, fraudulent, or unjust act towards the Plaintiff. In the present case, it cannot be shown that Defendant Czwartacky committed any such fraud or wrong against Plaintiff. Therefore, Plaintiff has not satisfied the required showing in order to pierce the corporate veil.

Since early in Plaintiff's relationship with Pacific Shores. Plaintiff perceived signs of and was informed of the credit risks that Pacific Shores posed. As early as the start of the parties' relationship, Plaintiff was significantly aware of the corporate structure and financial condition of the entity with which it sought to do business. The Dun & Bradstreet's March 6, 1991 credit report on Pacific Shores [which Plaintiff saw] showed that Pacific Shores had three employees, that it lost $30,365 in 1989 on gross sales of $866,294, that it lost $31,325 in retained earnings, that its initial capital investment was $10,000, and that it carried a Financial Appraisal Ranking of "3." Plaintiff knew of these risks. Nonetheless, just two-and-a-half years into Plaintiff's relationship with Pacific Shores, even after Pacific Shores was slow in making payments to Plaintiff, Plaintiff agreed to accept only one-third of Pacific Shores' production goods payment via wire transfer and two-thirds by letter of credit.

Further, throughout 1994, Plaintiff continued to sell goods to Pacific Shores even though Plaintiff had to "chase" after Pacific Shores for payment of these goods and at times, was worried about being paid.... By April 25, 1995, Pacific Shores had become Plaintiff's largest account debtor, owing Plaintiff in excess of $200,000. Plaintiff continued to sell to Pacific Shores on open credit terms.... On September 5, 1995 Pacific Shores advised Plaintiff that Finova would no longer amend its letter of credit for payments to Plaintiff.... As Pacific Shores would therefore be unable to purchase goods, it advised Plaintiff the next day that it was going out of business.... On September 25, 1995, this time enclosing a copy of Pacific Shores' Profit and Loss Statement for the eight month period ending on August 31, 1995, showing a loss of $6,118, Pacific Shores again apprised Plaintiff of its financial situation....

Pacific Shores then advised Plaintiff that Alpine Apparel would open a letter of credit for the purchase of additional goods.... Alpine Apparel was a company that had licensed the name of Cameron & Roberts, Ltd, which Defendant Czwartacky had incorporated in May 1995 and of which he was the President and sole shareholder. Despite previous warning signs, Plaintiff thereafter agreed to do business with Alpine Apparel.... On January 25, 1996, Alpine Apparel opened a letter of credit to Plaintiff.... Plaintiff thereafter made two shipments of goods to Alpine Apparel amounting to $122,261.25, which were paid for by letter of credit.

Where a party is aware of the risks of dealing with a corporation, that party has assumed the risk of such dealings.

* * *

In the present case, Plaintiff knew of Pacific Shores' poor 1991 Dun & Bradstreet ranking, its losses, and its $10,000 initial capital investment. Plaintiff's decision to do business with Pacific Shores in light of this knowledge indicates an informed decision. After Plaintiff was alerted to signs that Pacific Shores needed help in paying its bills, Plaintiff's unabated business with Pacific Shores indicates a ratification of its previous decision and evinces a deeper appreciation of the risks involved. Plaintiff's decision to accept one-third of the payment for production goods after shipment most notably evidences Plaintiff's assumed responsibility.

There is no evidence that Plaintiff ever had any reasonable expectation that Defendant Czwartacky would be personally liable for payment. Nor did he conceal the nature of his personal relationship and involvement with either Pacific Shores or Alpine Apparel. Plaintiff's employee indicated Plaintiff's assumption of the risk when it indicated that it made no sense to inquire of Defendant Czwartacky as to whether he had any money.... This employee concluded that "we make a wrong decision, we have to bear the result." ... In light of this knowledge of risk and assumption of responsibility, it cannot be said that Defendant Czwartacky committed a fraud or wrong against Plaintiff. Therefore, though Plaintiff ultimately did lose $216,408.06, this loss cannot be attributed to a fraud or wrong that Defendant Czwartacky visited upon Plaintiff.

CONCLUSION

Pacific Shores and Alpine Apparel have been held liable for their debts to Plaintiff. Defendant Czwartacky's involvement in Pacific Shores does not rise to the level of domination used to inflict a fraud or wrong upon Plaintiff. Defendant Czwartacky's summary judgment motion to dismiss Plaintiff's claim for declaratory judgment piercing the corporate veil with respect to Pacific Shores is therefore GRANTED. Defendant's summary judgment motion to dismiss Plaintiff's claim for declaratory judgment piercing the corporate veil with respect to Alpine Apparel is also GRANTED.

Notes and Questions

1. Minton v. Cavaney, 56 Cal. 2d 576, 15 Cal. Rptr. 641, 364 P.2d 473 (Cal. 1961), is the seminal case in which undercapitalization appears to have been the real determinant in a finding of liability.[1] Does the "contract" among the state, the corporation and its

---

1. It should be obvious that in all of the veil piercing cases the corporation has insufficient capital to pay the claims of plaintiffs. This, of course, is not the equivalent of undercapitalization.

shareholders require the corporation or the shareholders to maintain adequate capital in exchange for the privilege of limited liability?

Courts using undercapitalization as a test for veil piercing focus on the initial relationship between the corporation's assets and the risks associated with its business activities. The undercapitalization doctrine requires that a corporation begin its activities with sufficient financial resources so that it can satisfy any losses likely to be generated by its ventures. See Radaszewski v. Telecom Corp, 981 F.2d 305, 309 (8th Cir. 1992) ("The whole purpose of asking whether a subsidiary is 'properly capitalized,' is properly to determine its 'financial responsibility.'"). Typically, capital consists of the shareholders' equity. In a tort context, capital also may include insurance coverage. See id. (in discussing the policy of preventing a parent corporation from using an undercapitalized subsidiary to commit fraud, the court stated "Insurance [coverage obtained by the subsidiary] meets this policy just as well, perhaps even better, than a healthy balance sheet."). Moreover, it is not uncommon for one or more of the principal shareholders to lend the corporation substantial amounts of money; whether such loans will be considered capital depends on the totality of the circumstances, including the risks of the new venture and the proportion that the loans bear to the other capital of the corporation. See Arnold v. Phillips, 117 F.2d 497 (5th Cir. 1941), cert. denied, 313 U.S. 583 (1941).

The question of undercapitalization involves the adequacy of the capital when the corporation is formed. Courts have concentrated generally on initial capitalization, although they may consider a corporation undercapitalized if it grows substantially without enjoying a corresponding increase in its capital. However, a corporation is not required to increase its capital base simply because it loses money. See Truckweld Equip. Co. v. Olson, 618 P.2d 1017, 1022 (Wash. Ct. App. 1980) ("We know of no rule of law requiring a corporate stockholder to commit additional private funds to an already faltering corporation."). See generally Hackney & Benson, Shareholder Liability for Inadequate Capital, 43 U. Pitt. L. Rev. 837, 898-99 (1982).

Professor Thompson argues that undercapitalization is not a significant factor in veil piercing cases. He finds that undercapitalization was present in only 19% of the contract cases and 13% of the tort cases in which the corporate veil was pierced. This data suggests that when considering undercapitalization, context does not matter greatly. Nevertheless, undercapitalization may affect the outcome when it is present; in the cases in which undercapitalization was found, the corporate veil was pierced almost three-quarters of the time. Thompson, Piercing the Corporate Veil: An Empirical Study, 76 Cornell L. Rev. 1036, 1066 (1991). The Ninth Circuit, interpreting California law, has stated that "undercapitalization alone will justify piercing the corporate veil." Nilsson, Robbins v. Louisiana Hydrolec, 854 F.2d 1538, 1544 (9th Cir. 1988). See also Slottow v. Fidelity Federal Bank, 10 F.3d 1355 (9th Cir. 1993) (holding same in the context of a parent-subsidiary arrangement). This statement is dubious, given the California Court of Appeals' statement that "Evidence of inadequate capitalization is, at best, merely a factor to be considered by the trial court in deciding whether or not to pierce the corporate veil…." Arnold v. Browne, 103 Cal. Rptr. 775, 783 (Cal. Ct. App. 1972).

2. What is the relationship of limited liability to corporate structure and other corporate rules? Is non-compliance with some or all of these inconsistent with the idea of limited liability? For an affirmative answer to this question, see Mitchell, Close Corporations Reconsidered, 63 Tulane L. Rev. 1143 (1989). For an argument that both close corporation constituents and society in general expect less of close corporations in terms

of public responsibility, *see* Soderquist, Reconciling Shareholders' Rights and Corporate Responsibility: Close and Small Public Corporations, 33 Vand. L. Rev. 1387 (1980).

Easterbrook and Fischel argue that the economic efficiency rationales for limited liability begin to break down when applied to close corporations. Because these are companies owned by a small number of investors who often are also managers, there is much less separation of management and risk bearing than there is in public corporations. Limited liability becomes unnecessary to reduce monitoring costs because the managers who would need to be monitored are also those who supply the capital. Moreover, the lack of liquidity in a close corporation makes irrelevant the need for limited liability to create an efficient market for the corporation's stock. There is also no threat of new investors replacing the existing management in close corporations because the management and risk-bearing functions are united. Finally, limited liability is more likely to encourage risk taking by close corporations because the decisionmakers in a close corporation have more to gain personally by shifting losses to creditors than do managers of a public company. Thus, limiting shareholders' liability for close corporations is likely to generate external costs. Easterbrook and Fischel conclude that a court can reduce the extent to which third parties bear these costs by disregarding limited liability in close corporations when there has been an abuse of the privilege. Easterbrook and Fischel, The Economic Structure of Corporate Law 55-56 (1991).

Professor Presser does not agree that the argument for piercing the corporate veil is stronger for close corporations than publicly held corporations. He contends that Easterbrook and Fischel ignore the principal historical justification for limited liability— promoting individual investment in smaller firms. Thus, it is precisely in the context of such firms that limited liability should be most protected. Presser, Thwarting the Killing of the Corporation: Limited Liability, Democracy, and Economics, 87 Nw. U. L. Rev. 148, 163-65 (1992).

Professor Thompson concludes that there is a relationship between the number of shareholders and the courts' willingness to pierce the corporate veil. He finds that in almost 50% of the cases in which there was only one shareholder, the court pierced the veil, but that this percentage decreased to about 35% where the corporation had more than three shareholders. Thompson, Piercing the Corporate Veil: An Empirical Study, 76 Cornell L. Rev. 1036, 1054-55 (1991).

3. In *Favour Mind*, there clearly were written contracts between the plaintiff and defendant corporations that allowed the plaintiff to sue for breach of contract upon the defendants' payment default. After receiving default judgments against the two corporations (which, of course, they could not pay), plaintiff then went after the personal assets of the individual defendant under a traditional veil piercing theory. But what about the involuntary creditors of the world, such as pedestrians who "slip-and-fall" on the snowy sidewalk outside the front door of an incorporated store? Unlike the plaintiff in *Favour Mind*, they clearly did not "assume the risk" of the store's financial woes. Are involuntary creditors more likely to successfully invoke veil piercing than voluntary creditors? Should they be? The Tenth Circuit, applying Utah law, addressed this issue head-on in Cascade Energy and Metals Corp. v. Banks, 896 F.2d 1557, 1577-78 (10th Cir. 1990):

> [T]he analysis of corporate veil issues is different in a consensual transaction, such as a breach of contract case, than in a nonconsensual transaction, such as many tort cases:
>
>> The issues of public policy raised by tort claims bear little relationship to the issues raised by a contract claim. It is astonishing to find that this fundamental

> distinction is only dimly perceived by many courts, which indiscriminately cite
> and purport to apply tort precedents in contract cases and vice versa.

Hamilton, The Corporate Entity, 49 Tex. L. Rev. 979, 984-85 (1971). The obvious difference between consensual and nonconsensual transactions is that the claimants in consensual transactions generally have chosen the parties with whom they have dealt and have some ability, through personal guarantees, security agreements, or similar mechanisms, to protect themselves from loss.... But in nonconsensual cases, there is "no element of voluntary dealing, and the question is whether it is reasonable for businessmen to transfer a risk of loss or injury to members of the general public through the device of conducting business in the name of a corporation that may be marginally financed." Id.

.... The upshot is that Utah courts, like courts generally, appear less likely to pierce a corporate veil when a consensual, contract-like transaction is involved than when a nonconsensual, tort-like transaction is involved. See, e.g., Centurian Corp. v. Fiberchem, Inc., 562 P.2d 1252, 1253 (Utah 1977) (piercing not allowed in sales contract dispute); Dockstader v. Walker, 510 P.2d 526, 528 (Utah 1973) (piercing not allowed in employment contract dispute).

See also U.S. Fire Ins. v. Peerless Ins. Co., 18 Mass. L. Rep. 64 (Mass. Super. Ct. 2004); Ziegler v. Del. County Daily Times, 128 F. Supp.2d 790 (E.D. Pa. 2001); Torco Oil Co. v. Innovative Thermal Corp., 763 F. Supp. 1445 (N.D. Ill. 1991); Wheeling-Pittsburgh Steel Corp. v. Intersteel, Inc., 758 F. Supp. 1054 (W.D. Pa. 1990).

In a contractual arrangement, a creditor can adjust his return so as to account for the perceived risks of lending to the corporation. This means of self-protection is not available to the tort claimant who is an involuntary creditor of the corporation. Thus it might be expected that courts would protect tort victims more than contract creditors when considering whether to disregard limited liability.

A comprehensive study casts considerable doubt on that expectation. Professor Thompson analyzed 1600 cases through 1985 and, counterintuitively, found that courts pierced the corporate veil more often in contract cases (about 42% of the cases) than in a tort actions (about 31% of the cases). Professor Thompson concluded that his results depart from traditional expectations primarily because many contract cases involve alleged misrepresentations that would effectively obviate the basis for the parties' contract. However, even without the misrepresentation cases, Thompson found that courts pierce in 34% of the nonmisrepresentation contract cases and only 27% of the nonmisrepresentation tort cases. Thompson, Piercing the Corporate Veil: An Empirical Study, 76 Cornell L. Rev. 1036, 1058, 1069 (1991).

Thompson's findings may provide support for Professors Hansmann and Kraakman who strongly advocate disregarding limited liability in cases involving involuntary tort creditors. Hansmann and Kraakman, Toward Unlimited Shareholder Liability for Corporate Torts, 100 Yale L.J. 1879 (1991). Hansmann and Kraakman favor eliminating limited liability in tort cases because limited liability gives the managers of a corporation incentives to incur too much risk, knowing that some of the costs of the corporation's activities will be externalized. With limited liability, the corporation can disregard the expected tort costs of a project and thus will invest in projects whose total social costs exceed total social benefits.

Hansmann and Kraakman would replace limited liability with a rule that subjects shareholders to a pro-rata liability for tort damages in excess of the firm's resources. A pro-rata rule overcomes the major objections to unlimited liability in the tort context, to wit, joint and several liability. If shareholders, on a pro-rata basis, faced full liability for such damages, share prices would decline to reflect the potential additional personal liability. Managers would then have a greater incentive to consider the full expected social costs of the firm's torts and adjust the company's behavior accordingly.

4. Should it make a difference if a creditor seeks to pierce the veil of a subsidiary corporation, thus exposing the assets of its parent corporation, as opposed to seeking to pierce the veil of a stand-alone corporation, thus exposing the assets of individual shareholders? Is it legally (and morally) easier to "raid" the parent corporation's treasury as opposed to seizing assets (monies in a retirement account, a car, etc.) of a natural person? On the issue of piercing a subsidiary corporation's veil, see Yoder v. Honeywell Inc., 104 F.3d 1215 (10th Cir. 1997), and Fletcher v. Atex, Inc., 68 F.3d 1451 (2d Cir. 1995). For an argument that all the assets of a conglomerate should be available to satisfy creditor claims of any insolvent subsidiary of that conglomerate, see Berle, The Theory of Enterprise Entity, 47 Colum. L. Rev. 343 (1947).

What if the creditor is the U.S. government seeking to recoup costs incurred to remediate a toxic waste site putatively owned and operated by the subsidiary of a parent corporation? In U.S. v. Bestfoods, 524 U.S. 51 (1998), the Supreme Court addressed whether a parent corporation that actively participated in, and exercised control over, the operations of a subsidiary may, without more, be held liable as an "operator" of a polluting facility owned or operated by the subsidiary under the Comprehensive Environmental Response, Compensation, and Liability Act of 1980 (CERCLA), 42 U.S.C. §9601 *et seq.* This case, which includes the Supreme Court's analysis of veil piercing, is presented in section 4a below.

5. Sandy and Ken are siblings. Sandy owns 51 percent of each of four corporations; Ken owns the remaining 49 percent. Both are directors (and are the only directors) of each corporation. Sandy is the president of each corporation, and is in complete control of its affairs. Ken is secretary of each corporation, but has an independent career as a proctologist. If a court agrees, at the instance of a creditor of one of the four corporations, that the veil of the corporation in question should be pierced, must it hold Sandy solely liable for the corporation's debts or can it hold Ken jointly (and/or severally) liable? *Cf.* Stacey-Rand, Inc. v. J. J. Holman, Inc., 527 N.E.2d 726 (Ct. App. Ind. 1988).

(ii) Reverse Veil Piercing

Reverse veil piercing involves an attempt by the shareholders of a close corporation to argue that their individual identification with the corporation leads to the conclusion that some right of the corporation is in reality their *personal right*. Instead of the typical situation whereby a creditor of the corporation seeks to disregard corporate existence to get at the personal assets of shareholders, reverse veil piercing generally involves an attempt by a shareholder to disregard corporate existence in order to get at the assets of a third party with unpaid obligations owed to the corporation.

In Crum v. Krol, 425 N.E.2d 1081, 1088-89 (Ill. App. Ct. 1981), the court defended its decision to reverse pierce the corporate veil to permit plaintiff sole shareholder to recover funds owed by defendant to the corporation:

 .... Disregarding the corporate entity is an equitable remedy generally imposed to rectify an abuse of corporate privilege. (See Wikelund Wholesale Co. v. Tile World Factory Tile Warehouse, (1978), 57 Ill. App. 3d 269, 14 Ill. Dec. 743, 372 N.E.2d 1022.) Thus in the usual situation, the doctrine is invoked by a creditor of the corporation to reach an individual who has used the corporation as an instrument to defraud creditors.... The pending case, however, requires a different application of the theory, which may be characterized as a "reverse pierce." In *Roepke*,[a] the Minnesota Supreme Court recognized the fairness of allowing an "insider" to pierce the corporate veil from within the corporation under appropriate circumstances.

We believe that the circumstances of the present case justify treating Crum and his corporation as a single entity with respect to the damages claim against defendant. While we realize that the concept of a "reverse pierce" has not been at issue in the overwhelming number of the corporate veil cases, we believe the same equitable considerations of preventing injustice should apply when it is a third party, rather than a shareholder or officer, who attempts to use the corporate entity as a shield....

We agree with the rationale of *Earp* and with dicta from a more recent case which notes that the doctrine of corporate separation "is a legal theory for the convenience of the business world [and] cannot be extended to a point beyond its reason and policy * * *." (*Wikelund* 57 Ill. App. 3d at 272-73, 14 Ill. Dec. at 745, 272 [sic] N.E.2d at 1024.) To refuse to pierce the corporate veil in this case would be to permit Krol's escape from liability, an unjust result. We conclude, therefore, that the trial court did not abuse its discretion in allowing Crum and Thomas Crum & Associates to be treated as a single entity.

In refusing to reverse pierce the corporate veil in Cascade Energy and Metals Corp. v. Banks, 896 F.2d 1557, 1577 (10th Cir. 1990), the court wrote:

The reverse-pierce theory presents many problems. It bypasses normal judgment-collection procedures, whereby judgment creditors attach the judgment debtor's shares in the corporation and not the corporation's assets. Moreover, to the extent that the corporation has other nonculpable shareholders, they obviously will be prejudiced if the corporation's assets can be attached directly. In contrast, in ordinary piercing cases, only the assets of the particular shareholder who is determined to be the corporation's alter ego are subject to attachment. *See* 1 Fletcher Cyc. Corp. §41.20 at 413 (1988 Supp.) ("[A] necessary element of the [alter ego] theory is that the fraud or inequity sought to be eliminated must be that of the party against whom the doctrine is invoked, and such party must have been an actor in the course of conduct constituting the abuse of corporate privilege—the doctrine cannot be applied to prejudice the rights of an innocent third party."). Absent a clear statement by the Supreme Court of Utah that it has adopted the variant reverse piercing theory urged upon us here, we are inclined to conclude that more traditional theories of conversion, fraudulent conveyance of assets, respondeat superior and agency law are adequate to deal with situations where one seeks to recover from a corporation for the wrongful conduct committed by a controlling stockholder without the necessity to invent a new theory of liability.

Who is right? Do the same practical, theoretical, economic, and policy considerations apply in reverse piercing cases as in cases of forward piercing? What about the contexts in which each is likely to arise? Are the differences enough to warrant different treatment? Or are the problems truly symmetrical? Once a court has decided to disregard the entity concept under some circumstances, how strong is the argument that the

---

a. Roepke v. Western Nat'l Mutual Ins. Co., 302 N.W.2d 350 (Minn. 1981).

entity ought to be respected for other purposes? *See* Norman v. Murray First Thrift & Loan Co., 596 P.2d 1028, 1032 (Utah 1979), quoting Cooperman v. California Unemployment Ins. Appeals Bd., 122 Cal. Rptr. 127, 132 (Cal. Ct. App. 1975): "The fact that a corporate entity has been disregarded for some purposes in an action does not mean that it will be disregarded for all purposes." *See also* United States v. Goldberg, 206 F. Supp. 394 (E.D. Pa. 1962).

Notes and Questions

1. The doctrine of reverse piercing is rarely used, and the jurisdictions which have considered the issue are about evenly split as to its wisdom. *Compare* Cascade Energy and Metals Corp. v. Banks, 896 F.2d 1557, 1576 (10th Cir. 1990) (holding that "it is far from clear that Utah has adopted the doctrine of 'reverse' piercing ..."); In re Wilson, 90 B.R. 208, 212-13 (Bankr. E.D. Va. 1988) (noting that the Fourth Circuit at least implicitly has rejected the concept of reverse piercing);[1] Hogan v. Mayor & Alderman of Savannah, 171 Ga. App. 671, 320 S.E.2d 555, 557-58 (Ga. App. 1984) (rejecting the concept of reverse piercing under Georgia law); Kiehl v. Action Mfg. Co., 535 A.2d 571 (Pa. 1987) (refusing to reverse pierce veil to permit parent corporation to claim that it and its subsidiary were a single employer under Workmen's Compensation Act), *with* State Bank v. Euerle Farms, Inc., 441 N.W.2d 121 (Minn. Ct. App. 1989); Crum v. Krol, 425 N.E.2d 1081 (Ill. App. Ct. 1981).

2. In Wodogaza v. H & R Terminals, Inc., 411 N.W.2d 848 (Mich. Ct. App. 1987), plaintiffs appealed from the trial court's grant of defendants' request for summary judgment. Stephen Wodogaza was injured while operating a forklift during the course of his employment with Preston Trucking Company, Inc. The tractor was owned by one subsidiary of Preston, and the premises on which the accident occurred were owned by another. After receiving workers' compensation benefits from Preston, Wodogaza sued the subsidiaries on theories of negligence and statutory violation. Defendants successfully argued in the trial court that Michigan's Workers' Disability Compensation Act, which provided an exclusive remedy against a plaintiff's employer, provided Wodogaza's exclusive remedy, because Preston and its subsidiaries were one entity and were therefore collectively Wodogaza's employer.

The appeals court reversed, and in so doing refused to reverse pierce the subsidiaries' veils to treat them as one with the present employer. The court applied an economic reality test to determine whether the subsidiaries were Wodogaza's employer, examining the following factors: "'control of a workers' duties; (2) payment of wages; (3) the right to hire, fire, and discipline; and (4) the performance of the duties as an integral part of the employer's business toward the accomplishment of a common goal.'"

The court also rejected defendants' argument on the equities, principally on the ground that no injustice would result from respecting the separate corporate entities of the parent and subsidiaries.

---

1. The *Wilson* court cites Terry v. Yancey, 344 F.2d 787, 790 (4th Cir. 1965), and Picture Lake Campground Inc. v. Holiday Inns, Inc., 497 F. Supp. 858, 863 (E.D. Va. 1980) as authority for an implicit rejection of reverse piercing. As a matter of internal corporate law, the entire question of piercing ordinarily would be a matter of state concern, and one would expect that federal courts would thus apply the law of the state of incorporation. See the discussion of this issue in Cascade Energy and Metals Corp. v. Banks, 896 F.2d at 1575 n.18.

Wodogaza stands in contrast with Woodson v. Rowland, 373 S.E.2d 674 (N.C. Ct. App. 1988), a wrongful death action in which plaintiff not only sued decedent's corporate employer but its sole shareholder as well. In holding that the sole shareholder, who "made all of the decisions concerning the corporation including which jobs to bid, who to hire, and salaries ..." was the "corporate alter ego," and was therefore protected by the exclusivity provision of the Workers' Compensation Act, the court reasoned that "[t]o do otherwise would effectively negate the exclusivity provision of the [North Carolina Workers' Compensation] Act as to small businesses." *Id.* at 677-78. Given the typical judicial reluctance to pierce the corporate veil, this court's decision, predicated on one sentence of factual analysis, is striking, and clearly illustrates the importance of policy and equitable considerations in veil piercing cases.

3. Nunn v. Chem. Waste Mgmt., Inc., 856 F.2d 1464 (10th Cir. 1988), illustrates the relationship between the concept of reverse piercing and the question of whether a plaintiff shareholder's claim is derivative in nature or direct. After affirming the district court's holding that the former shareholders of National Industrial Environmental Services, Inc. ("NIES") had breached their warranties made in selling the stock of NIES to Chemical Waste, the court, *id.* at 1470, wrote:

> We cannot affirm, however, that portion of the damage award which was intended to compensate the defendants for their lost profits. The contractual warranties contained in the acquisition agreement were made by the former owners to Chemical Waste. Therefore, Chemical Waste was directly injured by the breach of those warranties. The lost profit injury, on the other hand, was not suffered by Chemical Waste. Rather, the profits were lost by a separate corporate entity, the subsidiary corporation NIES. As a matter of law, it was erroneous for the trial court to disregard the separate entity status of the defendant corporations and the injured corporation.... Accordingly, we reverse the award of damages insofar as that award reflects profits lost by NIES, a corporate entity which was not made a party to this lawsuit.

b. Lender's Liability for Corporate Debts

Problem—Lender's Liability for Corporate Debts

1. Sherman, Grant, and McClellan, respectively the president, vice president, and controlling stockholder of Manassas Corporation (all of whom are directors), took Manassas private in a leveraged buy-out (the "LBO") five years ago.[1] Following the LBO, Grant, Sherman, and McClellan were the company's only three stockholders, officers, and directors. Although much of the debt financing was provided through a public issue of unsecured subordinated debt, almost a third of the financing was done in the form of secured debt privately issued by the corporation to a consortium of banks led by the Shiloh National Bank and Trust Company. Assume you were counsel to the bank at the time of the LBO. What kinds of protections would you have required? Review your response to Problem—The Term Sheet, *supra* at section 1.

---

1. A leveraged buy-out is the acquisition of all of the stock of a corporation, either by a management or outside group, financed largely by debt which is assumed by the acquired corporation and secured by its assets.

2. Ultimately, Shiloh negotiated a very strong series of restrictive covenants, detailing Manassas' continuing financial requirements in terms of net worth, working capital, financial ratios, and the like. The loan agreement prohibited Manassas from raising capital, selling assets, or restructuring in any way without Shiloh's consent, as agent for the lending banks, and precluded any change in business without Shiloh's consent. Four years ago, after Manassas experienced particularly severe losses and defaulted on some financial covenants, Shiloh demanded that the three stockholders place their stock in a voting trust with Shiloh as trustee. The stockholders complied, to avoid having Shiloh accelerate the debt. As voting trustee, Shiloh elected Sherman, Grant, and McClellan as directors, but increased the size of the board to four and added a Shiloh senior vice president as a director. Thereafter, all Manassas corporate decisions effectively were subject to Shiloh's veto.

Two years ago, Manassas, unable to pay its debts, decided to liquidate in bankruptcy. After paying the claims of senior creditors (including those of the Shiloh group), there were sufficient funds to pay other creditors only ten cents on the dollar. Grant, Sherman, and McClellan lost all of their personal wealth as a result of the bankruptcy. The trustee in bankruptcy is considering a suit against the Shiloh syndicate in an attempt to hold it liable for the balance of Manassas' debts. Will the trustee succeed? Should she? *See* In re W. T. Grant Co., 699 F.2d 599 (2d Cir.), *cert. denied*, 464 U.S. 822 (1983) and the following case. What additional information should the trustee consider?

Krivo Indus. Supply Co. v. Nat'l Distillers & Chem. Corp.
483 F.2d 1098 (5th Cir. 1973), *modified and petition for reh'g denied*, 490 F.2d 916 (5th Cir. 1974)[a]

RONEY, Circuit Judge:

Plaintiffs, ten creditors of [Brad's Machine Products, Inc.,] a now [insolvent] corporation, individually sued National Distillers and Chemical Corp., the major creditor of that corporation, on their debts.... The alleged liability of National Distillers was predicated upon the rule that, when one corporation controls and dominates another corporation to the extent that the second corporation becomes the "mere instrumentality" of the first, the dominant corporation becomes liable for those debts of the subservient corporation attributable to an abuse of that control. After hearing plaintiffs' evidence, the District Court granted a directed verdict in favor of National Distillers. We affirm....

I. The Law

* * *

The "Instrumentality" Doctrine

We note at the outset that the case before us involves only the question of National Distillers' liability under the "instrumentality" theory....

* * *

.... A corporation may become liable for the debts of another corporation in two ways. First, expressly or impliedly, it may assume responsibility for those debts by

---

a. The original 5th Circuit opinion, as modified by the 5th Circuit's subsequent opinion, is presented herein.

indicating to the creditors of the other corporation that it stands behind those debts as a guarantor. In this situation, one separate and distinct corporation becomes responsible for the debts of another separate and distinct corporate entity. The corporate form of each remains intact and liability is not predicated upon disregarding the corporate form of the debtor. Second, a corporation may be held liable for the debts of another corporation when it misuses that corporation by treating it, and by using it, as a mere business conduit for the purposes of the dominant corporation.... The rationale for holding the dominant corporation liable for the subservient corporation's debts is that, since the dominant corporation has misused the subservient corporation's corporate form by using it for the dominant corporation's own purposes, the debts of the subservient corporation are in reality the obligations of the dominant corporation.... Plaintiffs' claim in this case is based on this second theory of liability.

In formulating a basis for predicating liability of a dominant corporation for the acts or omissions of another corporation, courts have developed various legal theories and descriptive terms to explain and to describe the relationship between a dominant and a subservient corporation. For example, under the "identity" theory the separate corporate identities are disregarded and both corporations are treated as one corporation.... Alternatively, a subservient corporation may be labeled the instrument, agent, adjunct, branch, dummy, department, or tool of the dominant corporation.... "Instrumentality" is perhaps the term most frequently employed to describe the relationship between a dominant corporation and its subservient corporation....

Nevertheless, the mere incantation of the term "instrumentality" will not substitute for rigorous, tough-minded analysis....

* * *

.... Although the Alabama courts have yet to delineate a more precise test, the parties in the case at bar agree, and we agree, that two elements are essential for liability under the "instrumentality" doctrine. First, the dominant corporation must have controlled the subservient corporation, and second, the dominant corporation must have proximately caused plaintiff harm through misuse of this control....

In considering the first element, that of control, the courts have struggled to delineate the kind of control necessary to establish liability under the "instrumentality" rule. Two problem areas have persistently troubled the process of ascertaining the extent of control. First, to what extent is stock ownership critical, and second, how much weight should be given to the existence of a creditor-debtor relationship in those cases where the debtor corporation is alleged to be the "instrumentality" of its creditor?

As to the effect of stock ownership, an examination of the case law in this area indicates that the fact that the allegedly dominant corporation held an ownership interest in another, allegedly subservient, corporation does not, *per se*, resolve the question of control. For example, in *Owl Fumigating Corp. v. California Cyanide Co.*, 24 F.2d 718 (D. Del. 1928), aff'd, 30 F.2d 812 (3d Cir. 1929), the allegedly dominant corporation owned all of the stock of another corporation. The District Court, in rejecting attempt to establish liability on the part of the defendant by disregarding the corporate form of the allegedly subservient corporation, found that defendant had done nothing beyond the authority legally vested in it as a creditor and a stockholder.

On the other hand, the fact that the allegedly dominant corporation held *no* stock ownership interest in the allegedly subservient corporation has not precluded application of the "instrumentality" rule where actual and total control has been otherwise established.

* * *

As with stock ownership, a creditor-debtor relationship also does not *per se* constitute control under the "instrumentality" theory. The general rule is that the mere loan of money by one corporation to another does not automatically make the lender liable for the acts and omissions of the borrower.... The logic of this rule is apparent, for otherwise no lender would be willing to extend credit. The risks and liabilities would simply be too great. Nevertheless, lenders are not automatically exempt from liability under the "instrumentality" rule. If a lender becomes so involved with its debtor that it is in fact actively managing the debtor's affairs, then the quantum of control necessary to support liability under the "Instrumentality" theory may be achieved.

An examination of "instrumentality" cases involving creditor-debtor relationships demonstrates that courts require a strong showing that the creditor assumed actual, participatory, total control of the debtor. Merely taking an active part in the management of the debtor corporation does not automatically constitute control, as used in the "instrumentality" doctrine, by the creditor corporation.

* * *

Not all "instrumentality" cases that involve creditor-debtor pressures result in findings of no liability. But in the cases resulting in "instrumentality" liability for the creditor, the facts have unmistakably shown that the subservient corporation was being used to further the purposes of the dominant corporation and that the subservient corporation in reality had no separate, independent existence of its own.

* * *

In summary, then the control required for liability under the "instrumentality" rule amounts to total domination of the subservient corporation, to the extent that the subservient corporation manifests no separate corporate interests of its own and functions solely to achieve the purposes of the dominant corporation.... No lesser standard is applied in "instrumentality" cases involving a creditor-debtor relationship. As the Court said in *In re Kentucky Wagon Mfg. Co., 3 F. Supp. 958, 963 (W.D. Ky. 1932)*, aff'd, *71 F.2d 802 (6th Cir.)*, cert. denied, *Laurent v. Stites, 293 U.S. 612, 55 S. Ct. 142, 79 L. Ed. 701 (1934)*, "it is to be noted that it is not 'controlling influence' that is essential. It is actual control of the action of the subordinate corporation."

In addition to actual and total control of the subservient corporation, the "instrumentality" rule also requires that fraud or injustice proximately result from a misuse of this control by the dominant corporation.... Alabama emphatically rejects actual fraud as a necessary predicate for disregarding the corporate form.... [See] *Forest Hill Corp. v. Latter & Blum, Inc.,[249 Ala. 23, 29 So.2d 289, 302 (Ala. 1947)]*.

This is the better rule, for the theory of liability under the "instrumentality" doctrine does not rest upon intent to defraud. It is an equitable doctrine that places the burden of the loss upon the party who should be responsible. The basic theory of the "instrumentality" doctrine is that the debts of the subservient corporation are in reality the obligations of the dominant corporation.

II. The Factual Background

Because the facts are critical in cases under the "instrumentality" rule, we detail the events and transactions tending to illuminate the relationship between the defendant National Distillers and Brad's Machine Products, Inc., for whose debts the plaintiff creditors seek to hold National Distillers responsible.

Brad's Machine Products, Inc., was a California corporation that began its existence as a machine shop in Stanton, California. Employing approximately 25 persons, Brad's was owned by John C. Bradford and his wife Nola. In addition to the machine business, Bradford's investments included a championship quarter horse, racing boats, airplanes, an Arizona bar, an Alabama motel, Florida orange groves, and oil wells. In addition, Bradford, a country and western singer, formed a motion picture company, Brad's Productions, Inc., through which he produced a film that featured him as a singer. All of these investment activities were funded by his income from the machine shop.

.... In 1966, Bradford saw potential profit in the munitions industry, so he employed Arnold Seitman to guide his entry into the Government contracting system. Seitman ... soon obtained for Brad's a 2.7 million dollar contract for the production of M-125 fuses, the principal component of which was brass.

* * *

For a brief time, Brad's appeared to prosper. Bradford's wide-ranging investments, however, soon became a severe financial drain on the Brad's operation.... By the end of 1968, Brad's was headed for financial distress.

The M-125 booster fuse assembly was the major product manufactured by Brad's, accounted for ninety percent of its gross sales, and required substantial quantities of brass rods. In the beginning Brad's had purchased its brass requirements from three sources: Revere Brass Company, Mueller Brass Company, and Bridgeport Brass Company. Brad's principal source of supply was Bridgeport, and Brad's was one of Bridgeport's larger customers. Bridgeport is a division of the defendant, National Distillers and Chemical Corporation.

In early 1969, Bridgeport was shipping approximately $400,000-$500,000 worth of brass rod to Brad's every month. In March, 1969, Brad's owed Bridgeport approximately $1,000,000 and Bridgeport, at the request of Brad's, agreed to convert this arrearage to a promissory note. On March 28, 1969, Bridgeport accepted Brad's note, secured by (1) the personal guaranties of John C. Bradford, Chairman of the Board and sole stockholder of Brad's, and his wife and (2) a mortgage on real property owned by J-N Industries, Inc., a subsidiary of Brad's located in Tucson, Arizona....

* * *

On August 1, 1969, Bradford, Brad's President E. J. Huntsman, and Brad's Comptroller Roy Compton, went to New York to confer with representatives of National Distillers, including Assistant General Counsel and Secretary John F. Salisbury. The representatives of Brad's stated that its current financial situation precluded continued operation unless it received additional assistance, including working capital. They blamed the unsuccessful attempts to diversify Brad's as the reason for the company's financial straits. Moreover, they needed immediate assistance because the Government had threatened to cancel the current fuse contract if the financial condition of Brad's continued to worsen. Bradford offered to put up all the assets he and the company had in exchange for the additional funds and for National Distillers' intervention with the Government on behalf of Brad's.

At the close of the August 1, 1969, meeting, National Distillers and Brad's reached an oral agreement in line with Bradford's requests. . . .

Salisbury immediately telephoned a Government official in Birmingham, Alabama, whose job included monitoring for the Defense Contract Administration Service the financial ability of Brad's to perform its Government contracts, and assured him of National Distillers' intent to aid Brad's. On August 4, 1969, Brad's executed notes for the $600,000 in cash and for the $630,000 in unpaid accounts receivable, with National Distillers taking a real estate mortgage on the Gadsden plant and premises and a security agreement covering the plant's furniture and fixtures. Brad's and Bradford also assigned to National Distillers certain shares of capital stock of other corporations, several oil and gas leases, and all of the capital stock of Brad's Productions, Inc. These assets were to be sold and the proceeds were to be returned to the operating capital of Brad's. To help the financial management at Brad's, Leon Rudd, one of National Distillers' "Internal Auditors" was sent to Gadsden to oversee its finances and to establish control procedures for managing cash and investments. Finally, Salisbury assigned one of his assistants to help him and Brad's dispose of the assets assigned to National Distillers and other assets not so assigned. Under the terms of several agreements, both formal and informal, National Distillers agreed that any income or proceeds from these unassigned assets would be used for certain designated purposes in aid of Brad's other creditors and then either would revert to Brad's or to Bradford or would belong to National Distillers outright.

Rudd remained with Brad's for fifteen months, during which National Distillers loaned Brad's an additional $169,000 in cash and deferred another $667,131.28 in accounts payable by Brad's to Bridgeport. Despite these transfusions, Brad's ceased its operations in December, 1970. These suits resulted from debts left unpaid by Brad's.

III. The Decision

[W]e conclude that the evidence was not "of such quality and weight that reasonable and fair-minded men in the exercise of impartial judgment might reach different conclusions," Boeing v. Shipman, [411 F.2d 365, 374 (5th Cir. 1969)], on the issue of control. Keeping in mind that the kind of control prerequisite to liability under the "instrumentality" rule is actual, operative, total control of the subservient corporation, the evidence here was wholly insufficient to support a jury decision that Brad's had "no separate mind, will or existence of its own and [was] but a business conduit" for National Distillers. . . . Hence, the motion for a directed verdict in favor of defendants was properly granted.

In cases involving the "instrumentality" rule, we must take a broad approach to the question of control, examining all of the plaintiffs' evidence to ascertain if the allegedly subservient corporation in fact had no separate corporate purposes or existence. In the case before us, plaintiffs presented evidence of (1) National Distillers' ownership of majority control of Brad's, (2) National Distillers' view of its relationship to Brad's, (3) the scope of National Distillers' control over Brad's. . . .

1. Although stock ownership is not *per se* determinative of the issue of control, . . . it is a factor to be considered in assessing the relationship between two companies sought to be linked under the "instrumentality" rule.

Plaintiffs attempted to prove that the stock ownership of Brad's had been transferred from John C. Bradford to National Distillers. Plaintiffs introduced (1) letters indicating that National Distillers intended to enter into an agreement with Bradford to assign the stock to National Distillers, (2) a memorandum dated August 13, 1969, and written by

National Distillers' credit manager, Zimmerman, indicating that the stock transfer was "in process," and (3) a guaranty executed by National Distillers promising to repay a loan made to Brad's, that referred to National Distillers as "a mortgage holder" of the Brad's stock. Significantly, no one testified that the Brad's stock was ever actually assigned. On the other hand, National Distillers' Salisbury testified that, despite his earlier intent to take the stock, the transfer was never consummated because he feared endangering National Distillers' mortgage interest.... Hence, plaintiffs failed to create an issue of fact on this point.

2. According to plaintiffs, the evidence shows that National Distillers believed that it had the power to control Bradford and his corporation and acted accordingly. A careful examination of this evidence, however, makes clear that National Distillers considered control of Brad's to be, at most, only partly shared between National Distillers and Brad's.

First, a letter from National Distillers' Salisbury to the general manager of the movie company, Brad's Productions, Inc., stated: "As I am sure you are aware, National Distillers and Chemical Corporation has taken an active role in the management and control of Brad's Machine Products, Inc., and various other undertakings of John C. Bradford." This letter, however, is not inconsistent with National Distillers' argument, which we conclude is correct, that the evidence shows that Brad's voluntarily *shared* control with National Distillers. The letter does not say that National Distillers had taken control of Brad's....

Second, according to Compton's testimony, National Distillers' credit manager, Zimmerman, told him that National Distillers "had the power, authority to fire Bradford and run him off." But the evidential importance of this statement is clarified by Compton's preceding testimony: "he (Zimmerman) said that Mr. Bradford should be fired and control taken away from him, and the plant be run properly." This language indicates that, although an employee of National Distillers may have felt that they should have taken control of Brad's away from John Bradford, they had not done so....

Third, plaintiffs quote Seitman's testimony that states that Salisbury at one time threatened to "fire" both Seitman and Bradford and run the Brad's operation itself. A complete reading of Seitman's testimony indicates that he believed that National Distillers' so-called power or authority to "fire" lay in its "control of the purse strings." Seitman testified that National Distillers could not "have told Brad's who its officers were to be," and he then stated that he understood Salisbury to mean that National Distillers would cease extending credit to Brad's if certain contracts were not fulfilled. Thus, it is plain that National Distillers could have "fired" Brad's personnel only by cutting off credit or loans, thereby putting Brad's out of business....

3. As to the scope of National Distillers' alleged control, the evidence shows only that National Distillers' activities were narrowly restricted to safeguarding its interests as a major creditor of Brad's, that National Distillers participated in the corporate decision-making at Brad's only to a limited degree, and that at no time did National Distillers assume actual, participatory, total control of Brad's.

The thrust of plaintiffs' contention here is that Leon Rudd, who was sent to the Gadsden plant by National Distillers in August, 1969, and who remained until late November, 1970, actively dominated the Brad's decision-making apparatus during his stay.

A reading of the testimony, especially that of the Brad's comptroller Compton, compels a conclusion that Rudd's activities were much more circumscribed than appellants argue. Rudd, an internal auditor employed by National Distillers, was transferred to Brad's in response to John Bradford's request for assistance in establishing a system of internal controls. Rudd was not thrust upon Brad's unwanted or unneeded.

.... According to Compton's testimony, Rudd suggested, and they all "readily agreed," that no purchase orders be sent out without his prior approval. Also, Rudd's signature was made mandatory on all checks from the Brad's accounts. From these "controls," plaintiffs would extrapolate the theory that National Distillers, through Rudd, was in charge of Brad's. Such a conclusion is untenable.

First, the evidence showed that, in fact, Rudd's prior approval of purchase requisitions was not always necessary for purchases....

Second, assuming that Rudd in fact enjoyed such an all-powerful veto over purchases, this power was never exercised where Brad's proper business purposes were involved. Rather, Rudd voiced his displeasure only when expenditures were contemplated that were unrelated to the Brad's machine shop operation.

Third, Rudd's powers were essentially negative in character. The testimony showed that his function was to monitor the finances and to help Compton fend off aggressive, unhappy creditors. Although plaintiffs contend that Rudd "participated in the management" of Brad's, the evidence shows that he did so only in a limited sense. Only those decisions having an immediate effect on Brad's financial position were subject to Rudd's primary attention. He attended management meetings solely in that capacity. The record contains no evidence that he was ever substantially involved in personnel or production decisions. Rudd left the delicate task of renegotiating Government contracts to Compton....

Fourth, Rudd's position as a required signatory on all checks drawn against the Brad's general account provides little support for plaintiffs' theory. Besides Rudd's signature, the checks also required one other signer from Brad's. Hence, Rudd again had but a veto power.

* * *

Rudd's activities while at Brad's simply do not amount to active domination of the corporation.... Although he kept a fairly tight rein on disbursements, the evidence shows that his role was that of providing a centralized control over purchases and disbursements. His job was two-fold: (1) to eliminate costly duplication, e.g., multiple orders of the same supply, and (2) to eliminate all disbursements not directly and immediately related to the machine shop business. These controls were strong, and Rudd was not afraid to exercise his power, but we cannot conclude from the evidence before us that his activities could justify a jury verdict that found control....

* * *

After considering the plaintiffs' evidence in the most favorable light, it is plain that Brad's never became an "instrumentality" of National Distillers. Although National Distillers' position as a major creditor undoubtedly vested it with the capacity to exert great pressure and influence, we agree with the District Court that such a power is inherent in any creditor-debtor relationship and that the existence and exercise of that power, alone, does not constitute control for the purposes of the "instrumentality" rule.... Plaintiffs had to show the exercise of that control in the actual operation of the debtor corporation. Accordingly, because plaintiffs failed to produce substantial evidence of such actual operative control, we affirm the directed verdict granted by the District Court.

* * *

AFFIRMED.

Notes and Questions

1. When a business debtor begins to encounter financial difficulty, its dominant creditor often will attempt to secure its investment by requiring the business to submit to creditor control over its operations or its management. However, despite the initial attractiveness of this technique, the lender should be cautious because this new relationship may change a formerly arm's length transaction into one where the creditor has incurred fiduciary obligations—both as to the debtor and to third party creditors. If the debtor files in bankruptcy, the bankruptcy trustee and other creditors may ask the court to subordinate the controlling creditor's claims to theirs in order to avoid unfairness in distributing the assets of the debtor. See 11 U.S.C. § 510 (2000).

Ordinarily a creditor owes no fiduciary obligation to his debtor or his fellow creditors. Knapp v. Amer. Gen. Fin., Inc., 111 F. Supp.2d 758 (S.D. W. Va. 2000); Overseas Private Inv. Corp. v. Industria de Pesco, 920 F. Supp. 207 (D.D.C. 1996). However, if a lender's actual control reaches a pervasiveness such that the lender was "in substance the owner" of the bankrupt, then a fiduciary duty will be imposed and any unfair or inequitable conduct on the lender's part will cause its claims to be equitably subordinated. In re Process-Manz Press Inc., 236 F. Supp. 333 (N.D. Ill. 1964), rev'd on jurisdictional grounds, 369 F.2d 513 (7th Cir. 1966). See Taylor v. Standard Gas & Electric Co., 306 U.S. 307 (1939); In re KDI Holdings, Inc., 277 Bankr. 493 (Bankr. S.D.N.Y. 1999); In re Beverages Int'l, Ltd., 50 Bankr. 273 (Bankr. D. Mass. 1985).

The basic test for equitable subordination was set forth in In re Mobile Steel Co., 563 F.2d 692, 700 (5th Cir. 1977):

(i) The claimant must have engaged in some type of inequitable conduct.

(ii) The misconduct must have resulted in injury to the creditors of the bankrupt or conferred an unfair advantage on the claimant.

(iii) Equitable subordination of the claim must not be inconsistent with the provisions of the Bankruptcy Act.

(citations omitted). See also In re Osborne, 42 Bankr. 988 (Bankr. W.D. Wis. 1984). Recently some courts have abandoned the misconduct standard. See Burden v. U.S., 917 F.2d 115 (3d Cir. 1990); Virtual Network Services Corp. v. U.S., 902 F.2d 1246 (7th Cir. 1990).

2. Professor Lawrence argues that the specter of lender control liability has been exaggerated by commentators and misapplied by courts because of a failure to appreciate the purposes for which control liability is imposed. Lawrence, Lender Control Liability: An Analytical Model Illustrated with Applications to the Relational Theory of Secured Financing, 62 S. Cal. L. Rev. 1387 (1989). As he points out: "The most grievous, fundamental error has been to treat control as a generic concept." Id. at 1388. Rather, control in a particular circumstance is a function of the legal theory of liability to which it is relevant, and the elements of control possessed or exercised by a lender should lead to liability only when related to the theory under which liability is sought to be imposed. Applying this insight to the relational theory of secured financing,[1] he discusses the types of control possessed by a secured relational lender and those types of control (and

_____

1. This theory posits the inability of detailed contracts to specify and prohibit opportunistic behavior over the life of a long-term contract, and suggests that a lender's floating security interest in the debtor's assets combined with an exclusive financing arrangement commits the debtor to pursue the lender's interests.

abuses thereof) giving rise to liability under the Bankruptcy Code for voidable preferences, agency theory, equitable subordination, federal securities laws, the Internal Revenue Code, and tort law.

Does Lawrence's approach help to explain the outcome in the CERCLA cases discussed in section 4 below?

3. For general discussions on equitable subordination and the problems of creditor control, see Triantas and Daniels, The Role of Debt in Interactive Corporate Governance, 83 Cal. L. Rev. 1073 (1995); Hynes, Lender Liability: The Dilemma of the Controlling Creditor, 58 Tenn. L. Rev. 635 (1991); Lawrence, Lender Control Liability: An Analytical Model Illustrated with Applications to the Relational Theory of Secured Financing, 62 S. Cal. L. Rev. 1385 (1989); Haas, Insights into Lender Liability: An Argument for Treating Controlling Creditors as Controlling Shareholders, 135 U. Pa. L. Rev. 1321 (1987).

As Professor Lawrence's article suggests, the question of lender liability for corporate debts often is a question that goes beyond the boundaries of internal corporate law.

4. One issue that has become increasingly important (and controversial) is lender's liability for the cleanup of a debtor's toxic waste under the Comprehensive Environmental Response, Compensation, and Liability Act (CERCLA). CERCLA liability is explored in more detail in section 4 below.

Section 4
Limited Liability and Environmental Claims

Depending on the circumstances, the limited liability provided by the corporate form may not protect shareholders from liabilities relating to the cleanup of environmental waste and contamination imposed by Federal and state governments. On the Federal level, shareholders, including parent corporations, must be cognizant of the Comprehensive Environmental Response, Compensation, and Liability Act, 42 U.S.C. §9601 et. seq. ("CERCLA"). CERCLA places financial responsibility for cleaning up hazardous waste sites on, among others, any person who owned or operated such a site at the time it was contaminated. Thus, not only are shareholders potentially at risk, but so too are creditors who exercise too much control over their debtors. In this section, we explore the liability of an "owner" and "operator" of a contaminated site, a "successor" to a company that operated such a site, and a creditor of a debtor that operated such a site.

a. "Owner" and "Operator" under CERCLA

U.S. v. Bestfoods
524 U.S. 51 (1998)

Justice SOUTER delivered the opinion of the Court.

The United States brought this action for the costs of cleaning up industrial waste generated by a chemical plant. The issue before us, under the Comprehensive Environmental

Response, Compensation, and Liability Act of 1980 (CERCLA), 94 Stat. 2767, as amended, 42 U.S.C. §9601 *et seq.*, is whether a parent corporation that actively participated in, and exercised control over, the operations of a subsidiary may, without more, be held liable as an operator of a polluting facility owned or operated by the subsidiary. We answer no, unless the corporate veil may be pierced. But a corporate parent that actively participated in, and exercised control over, the operations of the facility itself may be held directly liable in its own right as an operator of the facility.

* * *

In 1957, Ott Chemical Co. (Ott I) began manufacturing chemicals at a plant near Muskegon, Michigan, and its intentional and unintentional dumping of hazardous substances significantly polluted the soil and ground water at the site. In 1965, respondent CPC International Inc. incorporated a wholly owned subsidiary to buy Ott I's assets in exchange for CPC stock. The new company, also dubbed Ott Chemical Co. (Ott II), continued chemical manufacturing at the site, and continued to pollute its surroundings. CPC kept the managers of Ott I, including its founder, president, and principal shareholder, Arnold Ott, on board as officers of Ott II. Arnold Ott and several other Ott II officers and directors were also given positions at CPC, and they performed duties for both corporations.

In 1972, CPC sold Ott II to Story Chemical Company, which operated the Muskegon plant until its bankruptcy in 1977. Shortly thereafter, when respondent Michigan Department of Natural Resources (MDNR) examined the site for environmental damage, it found the land littered with thousands of leaking and even exploding drums of waste, and the soil and water saturated with noxious chemicals. MDNR sought a buyer for the property who would be willing to contribute toward its cleanup, and after extensive negotiations, respondent Aerojet-General Corp. arranged for transfer of the site from the Story bankruptcy trustee in 1977. Aerojet created a wholly owned California subsidiary, Cordova Chemical Company (Cordova/California), to purchase the property, and Cordova/California in turn created a wholly owned Michigan subsidiary, Cordova Chemical Company of Michigan (Cordova/Michigan), which manufactured chemicals at the site until 1986.

By 1981, the federal Environmental Protection Agency had undertaken to see the site cleaned up, and its long-term remedial plan called for expenditures well into the tens of millions of dollars. To recover some of that money, the United States filed this action under §107 in 1989, naming five defendants as responsible parties: CPC, Aerojet, Cordova/California, Cordova/Michigan, and Arnold Ott. (By that time, Ott I and Ott II were defunct.)....

* * *

It is a general principle of corporate law deeply "ingrained in our economic and legal systems" that a parent corporation (so-called because of control through ownership of another corporation's stock) is not liable for the acts of its subsidiaries.... Thus it is hornbook law that "the exercise of the 'control' which stock ownership gives to the stockholders ... will not create liability beyond the assets of the subsidiary. That 'control' includes the election of directors, the making of by-laws ... and the doing of all other acts incident to the legal status of stockholders. Nor will a duplication of some or all of the directors or executive officers be fatal." [*Id.* at 196.] [N]othing in CERCLA purports to reject this bedrock principle, and against this venerable common-law backdrop, the congressional silence is audible....

* * *

But there is an equally fundamental principle of corporate law, applicable to the parent-subsidiary relationship as well as generally, that the corporate veil may be pierced and the shareholder held liable for the corporation's conduct when, *inter alia,* the corporate form would otherwise be misused to accomplish certain wrongful purposes, most notably fraud, on the shareholder's behalf.... Nothing in CERCLA purports to rewrite this well-settled rule, either. CERCLA is thus like many another congressional enactment in giving no indication "that the entire corpus of state corporation law is to be replaced simply because a plaintiff's cause of action is based upon a federal statute," [*Burks v. Lasker,* 441 U.S. 471, 478 ... (1979)], and the failure of the statute to speak to a matter as fundamental as the liability implications of corporate ownership demands application of the rule that "in order to abrogate a common-law principle, the statute must speak directly to the question addressed by the common law." [*United States v. Texas,* 507 U.S. 529 ... (1993)].... The Court of Appeals was accordingly correct in holding that when (but only when) the corporate veil may be pierced, may a parent corporation be charged with derivative CERCLA liability for its subsidiary's actions.

* * *

If the act rested liability entirely on ownership of a polluting facility, this opinion might end here; but CERCLA liability may turn on operation as well as ownership....

* * *

Under the plain language of the statute, any person who operates a polluting facility is directly liable for the costs of cleaning up the pollution. *See* 42 U.S.C. §9607 (a)(2). This is so regardless of whether that person is the facility's owner, the owner's parent corporation or business partner, or even a saboteur who sneaks into the facility at night to discharge its poisons out of malice. If any such act of operating a corporate subsidiary's facility is done on behalf of a parent corporation, the existence of the parent-subsidiary relationship under state corporate law is simply irrelevant to the issue of direct liability....

* * *

This much is easy to say; the difficulty comes in defining actions sufficient to constitute direct parental "operation." ... To sharpen the definition for purposes of CERCLA's concern with environmental contamination, an operator must manage, direct, or conduct operations specifically related to pollution, that is, operations having to do with the leakage or disposal of hazardous waste, or decisions about compliance with environmental regulations.

* * *

The well-taken objection to the actual control test, however, is its fusion of direct and indirect liability; the test is administered by asking a question about the relationship between the two corporations (an issue going to indirect liability) instead of a question about the parent's interaction with the subsidiary's facility (the source of any direct liability). If, however, direct liability for the parent's operation of the facility is to be kept distinct from derivative liability for the subsidiary's own operation, the focus of the enquiry must necessarily be different under the two tests. "The question is not whether the parent operates the subsidiary, but rather whether it operates the facility, and that operation is evidenced by participation in the activities of the facility, not the subsidiary. Control of the subsidiary, if extensive enough, gives rise to indirect liability under piercing doctrine, not direct liability under the statutory language." [Oswald, Bifurcation of the Owner and Operator Analysis under CERCLA, 72 Wash. U. L.Q., 223, 269 (1994)]....

In addition to (and perhaps as a reflection of) the erroneous focus on the relationship between CPC and Ott II, even those findings of the District Court that might be taken to speak to the extent of CPC's activity at the facility itself are flawed, for the District Court wrongly assumed that the actions of the joint officers and directors are necessarily attributable to CPC....

* * *

.... The Government would have to show that, despite the general presumption to the contrary, the officers and directors were acting in their capacities as CPC officers and directors, and not as Ott II officers and directors, when they committed those acts. The District Court made no such enquiry here, however, disregarding entirely this time-honored common law rule.

* * *

In our enquiry into the meaning Congress presumably had in mind when it used the verb "to operate," we recognized that the statute obviously meant something more than mere mechanical activation of pumps and valves, and must be read to contemplate "operation" as including the exercise of direction over the facility's activities....

* * *

Identifying such an occurrence calls for line drawing yet again, since the acts of direct operation that give rise to parental liability must necessarily be distinguished from the interference that stems from the normal relationship between parent and subsidiary. Again norms of corporate behavior (undisturbed by any CERCLA provision) are crucial reference points. Just as we may look to such norms in identifying the limits of the presumption that a dual officeholder acts in his ostensible capacity, so here we may refer to them in distinguishing a parental officer's oversight of a subsidiary from such an officer's control over the operation of the subsidiary's facility. "Activities that involve the facility but which are consistent with the parent's investor status, such as monitoring of the subsidiary's performance, supervision of the subsidiary's finance and capital budget decisions, and articulation of general policies and procedures, should not give rise to direct liability." Oswald 282. The critical question is whether, in degree and detail, actions directed to the facility by an agent of the parent alone are eccentric under accepted norms of parental oversight of a subsidiary's facility.

* * *

Notes and Questions

1. Parent control of a polluting subsidiary is insufficient to produce CERCLA liability on the parent. Nor is it enough that employees shared by parent and subsidiary controlled the subsidiary's polluting facility. Necessary for parental CERCLA liability as an operator of a subsidiary's polluting facility is that parent's own personnel controlled the facility or participated in its operations. How does one determine the capacity in which dual employees are acting for the parent or the subsidiary? Consider this footnote omitted from the report of the Court's opinion excerpted above:

We do not attempt to recite the ways in which the Government could show that dual officers or directors were in fact acting on behalf of the parent. Here, it is prudent to say only that the presumption that an act is taken on behalf of the corporation for whom the officer claims to act is strongest when the act is perfectly consistent with the norms of corporate behavior, but wanes as the distance from those accepted norms approaches the point of action by a dual officer plainly contrary to the interests of the subsidiary yet nonetheless advantageous to the parent.

Bestfoods, supra, n. 13.

2. *Bestfoods* leads Federal courts applying CERCLA into state corporate law principles. Consider this summary from *Browning-Ferris Indus. v. Ter Maat,* 195 F.3d 953, 959-961 (7th Cir. 1999) (Posner, C.J.):

The general rule ... is that a shareholder qua shareholder, and a parent, subsidiary, or other affiliate, qua affiliate, is not liable for a corporation's debts. That is the principle of limited liability and it serves the important social purpose of encouraging investment by individuals who are risk averse and therefore will not invest (or will insist on a much higher return) in an enterprise if by doing so they expose their entire wealth to the hazards of litigation. But in some circumstances the corporate veil is pierced and the corporation's debtor allowed to collect his debt from the shareholder or affiliate.

In the case of a voluntary creditor, for example someone who had lent money to the corporation, the strongest case for piercing the veil is presented when the corporation had led potential creditors to believe that it was more solvent than it really was.... [I]t is hard to see how a voluntary creditor can complain if he knows that his debtor lacks sufficient assets to be certain to be able to pay the debt when it comes due.

Analysis is more difficult in the case of an involuntary creditor.... In such a case there is no issue of protecting reliance induced by misrepresentations by the debtor.... In these circumstances we can think of only two arguments for piercing the corporate veil. The first is that the owners may have so far neglected the legal requirements (requirements not intended solely for the protection of creditors) for operating in the corporate form that they should be taken to have forfeited its protections.... [I]f the formalities have been flouted, it becomes hard to see how the investors could reasonably have relied on the protections of limited liability; they would have known they were skating on thin ice....

Second, it could be argued that enterprises engaged in potentially hazardous activities should be prevented from externalizing the costs of those activities, by being required to maintain or at least endeavor to maintain a sufficient capital cushion to be answerable in a tort suit should its activities cause harm for which liability would attach, on pain of its shareholders' and affiliates' losing their limited liability should the corporation fail to do this. This argument has not carried the day in any jurisdiction that we are aware of, presumably because of the risks that it would impose on shareholders and because the potential victims of the corporation's hazardous activities can be protected without making inroads into limited liability by requiring enterprises engaged in such activities to post a bond large enough to assure that any judgment against the corporation will be collectible. Courts do, it is true, frequently mention "undercapitalization" as a separate ground from neglect of corporate formalities for piercing the corporate veil. They do not do so on the basis of unusual risks to potential tort victims or other involuntary creditors, however, though conceivably such concerns are in the background of their thinking.

The clearest case—here merging, though, with neglect of corporate formalities—for forfeiture of limited liability on this ground is where the corporation has failed to maintain the minimum capitalization required by law.... The cases in which undercapitalization has figured in the decision to pierce the corporate veil are ones in which the corporation had so little money that it could not and did not actually operate its nominal business on its own.... Even there the court did not pierce the veil on the basis of undercapitalization alone, but cited also a persistent neglect of corporate formalities. Undercapitalization is rarely if ever the sole factor in a decision to pierce the corporate veil, ... and we think is best regarded simply as a factor helpful in identifying a corporation as a pure shell....

3. In U.S. v. Kayser-Roth Corp., Inc., 910 F.2d 24 (1st Cir. 1990), Kayser-Roth appealed from a district court decision holding it liable for the costs incurred by the United States Environmental Protection Agency in cleaning up a spill of trichlorethylene occurring at a textile plant owned by Kayser-Roth's wholly-owned subsidiary, Stamina Mills, Inc. Stamina Mills had been dissolved after the spill occurred but before it was discovered. The district court imposed liability on the grounds that Kayser-Roth was both an "owner" (direct liability) and an "operator" (indirect liability) of the plant within the meaning of CERCLA. The appellate court rejected Kayser-Roth's argument that, as a matter of law, the parent of a dissolved subsidiary cannot be held liable for the latter's obligations on either ground, holding that Kayser-Roth was an "operator" of the facility and therefore liable. After concluding that "a fair reading of CERCLA" permitted a court to find such liability, the court went on to examine whether the district court was correct in concluding that Kayser-Roth was an "operator":

.... Without deciding the exact standard necessary for a parent to be an operator, we note that it is obviously not the usual case that the parent of a wholly owned subsidiary is an operator of the subsidiary. To be an operator requires more than merely complete ownership and the concomitant general authority or ability to control that comes with ownership. At a minimum it requires active involvement in the activities of the subsidiary.

The district court's excellent opinion found that "Kayser-Roth ... exerted practical total influence and control over Stamina Mills' operations." *United States v. Kayser-Roth Corp.*, 724 F. Supp. 15, 18 (D.R.I. 1989). The court summarized the evidence as follows:

Kayser-Roth exercised pervasive control over Stamina Mills through, among other things: 1) its total monetary control including collection of accounts payable; 2) its restriction on Stamina Mills' financial budget; 3) its directive that subsidiary—governmental contact, including environmental matters, be funneled directly through Kayser-Roth; 4) its requirement that Stamina Mills' leasing, buying or selling of real estate first be approved by Kayser-Roth; 5) its policy that Kayser-Roth approve any capital transfer or expenditures greater than $5000; and finally, its placement of Kayser-Roth personnel in almost all Stamina Mills' director and officer positions, as a means of totally ensuring that Kayser-Roth corporate policy was exactly implemented and precisely carried out.

Id. at 22. Kayser's control included environmental matters including the approval of the installation of the cleaning system that used the TCE.[8] The district court found

> Kayser had the power to control the release or threat of release of TCE, had the power to direct the mechanisms causing the release, and had the ultimate ability to prevent and abate damage. Kayser-Roth knew that Stamina Mills employed a scouring system that used TCE; indeed [it] approved the installation of that system ... [and] was able to direct Stamina Mills on how the TCE should have been handled.

Id. Such control is more than sufficient to be liable as an operator under CERCLA.

How does the 1st Circuit's analysis measure up against the standards contained in *Bestfoods*? Would it withstand appellate scrutiny today?

In Joslyn Mfg. Co. v. T. L. James & Co., 893 F.2d 80 (5th Cir. 1990), a case relied upon unsuccessfully by defendant in *Kayser-Roth*, the court refused to interpret CERCLA as directly imposing the liabilities of wholly owned subsidiaries on parent corporations as "owners." Furthermore, the court declined to pierce the subsidiary's corporate veil, holding that it "faithfully adhered to basic corporate formalities by keeping its own books and records and holding frequent shareholder and directors meetings." Indeed, the operations of the two companies were kept separate, the officers were separate, and the corporations owned and used their own property, filed separate tax returns, paid their own bills, and provided their own employee benefits.

How would the 5th Circuit's analysis hold up against the standards contained in *Bestfoods*, particularly its point on veil piercing?

b. Successor Liability under CERCLA

North Shore Gas Co. v. Salomon, Inc.
152 F.3d 642 (7th Cir. 1998)

CUDAHY, Circuit Judge. Who should assume responsibility for the cost of an environmental cleanup is the first messy question in what is generally a messy business....

* * *

Beginning in the early part of this century, the S.W. Shattuck Chemical Company (Old Shattuck) operated a mineral ore processing plant in Denver, Colorado (the Denver Site). In 1969, Salomon[, Inc.'s] predecessor-in-interest purchased Old Shattuck and renamed it the S.W. Shattuck Chemical Company, Inc. (New Shattuck). From 1969 to 1984, New Shattuck operated the Denver Site as a mineral processing facility. Unfortunately, the activities at the Denver Site were not without environmental costs. In 1983, the Environmental Protection Agency (EPA) placed the Site on its national priorities list. In 1992, the EPA ordered New Shattuck, the current owner of the Site, to remove certain hazardous substances.... At the time of this appeal, remediation costs had exceeded $20 million.

---

8. Although indicia of ability to control decisions about hazardous waste are indicative of the type of control necessary to hold a parent corporation liable as an operator, we do not think the presence of such indicia is essential, assuming there are other indicia of the pervasive control necessary to prove operator status.

After the EPA charged New Shattuck with liability, the company embarked on a search for entities that might contribute to response costs. It discovered that from 1934 to 1942, North Shore Coke & Chemical Company (the Coke Company) owned 60% of Old Shattuck. In the mid-1930s, the Coke Company had formed North Continent Mines, which mined mineral ores containing vanadium and uranium. North Continent Mines regularly transported radium slimes—a waste product as hazardous as its name suggests—to the Denver Site for processing and disposal.

The Coke Company was incorporated in 1927 by William Baehr, the then-manager (and later president) of the North Shore Gas Company (the Gas Company), which supplied gas to communities around Waukegan, Illinois. In 1928, the Coke Company built a coke oven plant in Waukegan. The Coke Company sold all of the gas generated at the Waukegan plant to the Gas Company, furnishing more than 80% of the Gas Company's total supply. The Coke Company was also a source of coke for the Gas Company, as well as for other purchasers. The ore processed by Old Shattuck and North Continent Mines was not used to manufacture gas or coke.

From 1927 to 1942, the Coke Company and the Gas Company were closely related entities. Virtually all of the Coke Company's stock was owned by North Continent Utilities Corporation, a holding company that Baehr formed in 1922; North Continent Utilities also owned 100% of the Gas Company's common stock and 2.28% of its preferred stock. The financial reports of North Continent Utilities listed the Coke Company and the Gas Company as consolidated subsidiaries. And the Coke and Gas Companies had virtually identical officers and directors. The companies even issued joint bonds, which were secured by a lien on the assets of both companies. In 1940, a consultant deftly summarized the companies' connection:

> The actual operations of the properties are interdependent. One is dependent on the other as a source of supply. One company is dependent on the other as a market for one of its primary products....

* * *

.... The Coke and Gas Companies thus shared far more than the typical arms-length relationship of most purchasers and suppliers.

This happy union began to unravel in 1940. The companies were facing financial difficulties, since they anticipated that they would be unable to redeem the joint bonds that were due to mature in 1942. In addition, the dividend requirements of the Gas Company's preferred stock were exceeding the company's earning ability. And a committee representing the preferred stockholders of the Gas Company had asserted various mismanagement claims against the Coke Company, North Continent Utilities and Baehr. The Coke Company had also run afoul of the Public Utility Holding Company Act of 1935, 15 U.S.C. §79 (k), which sought to eliminate nonutility investments from the utility system. In an effort to address these difficulties, the Coke and Gas Companies submitted a "Plan of Reorganization" to the Securities and Exchange Commission in 1941 (the 1941 Plan). Under the Plan, the Coke Company sold all of its assets to the Gas Company—except the stock in North Continent Mines and Old Shattuck, certain debt owed to the Coke Company and $45,000 in cash—in exchange for shares of the Gas Company. The Coke Company transferred its interest in Old Shattuck and North Continent Mines to North Continent Utilities. The Plan also settled all mismanagement claims by the preferred shareholders, refunded the bonds issued by the Gas and Coke Companies, and recapitalized the Gas Company so that it had only a single class of stock (common).

When New Shattuck went looking for parties to contribute to CERCLA costs, it discovered that the Coke Company was liquidated in 1942, pursuant to the 1941 Plan. North Continent Utilities dissolved in 1954. So New Shattuck seized on North Shore Gas—the only company remaining from the once formidable triumvirate—and demanded that it help pay for the cost of cleaning up the Denver Site. Eventually North Shore Gas filed an action against Salomon in an Illinois federal district court, seeking a declaration that it was not liable for remediation costs associated with the Site....

* * *

... [W]e are assuming *arguendo*, as did the district court, that the Coke Company incurred CERCLA liability as an operator of Old Shattuck and North Continent Mines.... Given CERCLA's prohibition on transferring liability (in the absence of an in-demnification agreement or similar arrangement), the Coke Company would be unable to divest itself of this direct liability by conveying the "dirty" businesses to North Continent Utilities.... The Coke Company's liability, however, is by no means a foregone conclusion. *See United States v. Bestfoods*, [524 U.S. 51] ... (1998) (explaining that a parent corporation incurs direct liability only if it manages, directs or conducts the operations of the subsidiary's facility that are specifically related to pollution). On remand, the district court will have to determine whether the Coke Company was in fact an "operator"—or in other words, whether there were any CERCLA liabilities to which North Shore Gas could succeed....

Whether a successor corporation may be liable for the cost of a CERCLA cleanup is a question of first impression in this circuit. The issue is not resolved by the plain language of CERCLA, which imposes liability on "covered persons." 42 U.S.C. §9607(a).... As the Third Circuit has noted, it is unsurprising that "as a hastily conceived and briefly debated piece of legislation," CERCLA fails to expressly address corporate successor liability. *Smith Land & Improvement Corp. v. Celotex Corp.*, 851 F.2d 86, 91 (3d Cir. 1988). However, every circuit confronted with the question has determined that Congress intended successor liability to apply in the context of CERCLA....

When Congress enacted CERCLA, it enabled the federal government to provide an efficacious response to environmental hazards and to assign the cost of that response to the parties who created or maintained the hazards. Accordingly, Congress was unlikely to leave a loophole that would enable corporations to die "paper deaths, only to rise phoenix-like from the ashes, transformed, but free of their former liabilities." *Mexico Feed*, 980 F.2d at 487. Moreover, there is no concern—at least theoretically—about punishing the successor for the acts (or omissions) of the predecessor; CERCLA is a remedial measure which is aimed only at correcting environmentally dangerous conditions.... The reasoning of our fellow circuits is persuasive.

* * *

.... [H]olding the successor corporation liable for the cost of cleanup is not necessarily unfair, since the successor and its shareholders likely will have derived some benefit from the predecessor's use of the pollutant and the savings that resulted from the hazardous disposal methods. We therefore reach the same result as the other circuits that have considered this issue—that Congress intended the equitable doctrine of successor liability to apply under CERCLA....

Most circuits which have construed CERCLA to incorporate successor liability have concluded that the parameters of the doctrine should be fashioned by federal common law ... because of the need for national uniformity with respect to CERCLA, and the possibility that parties would frustrate the aims of CERCLA by choosing to merge or consolidate under the laws of states "which unduly restrict successor liability." *Smith Land*, 851 F.2d at 91.

Until recently, only the Sixth Circuit had concluded that state law provided the rule of decision for successor liability under CERCLA.... The Ninth Circuit, however, recently overruled one of its prior decisions and held that it would look to the law of the relevant state to decide issues of successor liability. *See [Atchison, Topeka & Santa Fe Ry. Co. v. Brown & Bryant*, 132 F.3d 1295, 1301-02 (9th Cir. 1997) (noting that state law is largely uniform and that there is no reason to think a state will change its law to become a haven for liable companies).] ...

.... [W]e think it prudent to reserve the choice-of-law question until we are confronted with a case in which the parties have argued the issue....

* * *

The intuitive response to the question of North Shore Gas' liability might be that as a result of the 1941 Plan, North Continent Utilities—not North Shore Gas—received Old Shattuck and North Continent Mines, and that therefore any liability should succeed to North Continent Utilities. But remember that we are assuming that the Coke Company incurred direct CERCLA liability as a result of its activities with respect to Old Shattuck and North Continent Mines. Thus the question that we address in the following discussion is *not* whether North Shore Gas incurred responsibility for the liabilities of Old Shattuck and North Continent Mines, but instead whether North Shore Gas succeeded to the *direct* liabilities of the Coke Company....

The general rule is that an asset purchaser such as the Gas Company does not acquire the liabilities of the seller. There are, however, four exceptions to this general rule: (1) the purchaser expressly or impliedly agrees to assume the liabilities; (2) the transaction is a de facto merger or consolidation; (3) the purchaser is a "mere continuation" of the seller; or (4) the transaction is an effort to fraudulently escape liability.... Salomon argues that North Shore Gas is liable under the first, second and third exceptions. The district court, however, decided that none of these exceptions applied and granted summary judgment to North Shore Gas. We review this decision de novo....

* * *

Turning to the exceptions themselves, we agree with the district court that the Gas Company did not agree to assume the Coke Company's direct CERCLA liabilities....

.... The 1941 Plan provided that the Gas Company "shall take said business, properties and contract and other rights subject to all liens, claims, and charges thereon, and *shall assume liabilities and obligations of every kind and character (other than the Debentures and interest thereon, hereinafter mentioned) of the [Coke] Company accrued to or existing on the date of transfer."* ... The use of the word "existing" "fairly obviously forecloses the possibility that [the purchaser] agreed to assume any contingent liabilities, much less the environmental liabilities at issue here." ... As for the use of "accrued to," *Black's Law Dictionary* states that it means "due and payable; vested." Black's Law Dictionary 20 (6th ed. 1990)....

.... As the district court recognized, two of the requirements for a de facto merger are that "there is a continuation of the enterprise of the seller in terms of ... management, personnel, physical location, assets and operations" and that "the purchasing corporation assumes the obligations of the seller necessary for uninterrupted continuation of business operations." ... The Holding Company Act—one of the primary reasons the companies entered into the Plan—sought to "limit the operations of holding companies ... to a single integrated public-utility system, and to such other businesses as are reasonably incidental, or economically necessary or appropriate to the operations of such integrated public-utility system." *15 U.S.C. §79k(b)(1).* The Gas Company therefore did not assume (and could not assume) the Coke Company's nonutility assets—Old Shattuck and North Continent Mines. Thus, taking a narrow view, the de facto merger exception might not be available because a federal statute, the Holding Company Act, required divestment of the mining businesses. Or, put slightly differently, compliance with the Holding Company Act might effectively defeat CERCLA liability, since the Holding Company Act requires the divestment that may make the de facto merger exception inapplicable. This result would be unsatisfactory for two reasons.

The first relates to what actually happened as a result of the 1941 Plan. If we abandon a "slavish adherence to multi-factor tests" ... the transaction between the Coke and Gas Companies strongly resembles a de facto merger. Before the 1941 Plan, the Coke and Gas Companies were in effect two divisions of the same utility business.... After the Plan, the Coke and Gas Companies became a vertically integrated public utility system in form as well as in fact, with the Gas Company continuing all of the Coke Company's utility-related operations. In literal terms, this means that what was formerly the Coke Company continued to manufacture gas and coke for the Gas Company, and that the Gas Company continued to distribute gas in the Waukegan area. And this continuation of the status quo is unsurprising, since the 1941 Plan was widely viewed as a merger of the Gas and Coke Companies.... Of course, in light of the Holding Company Act, the SEC would not have approved the merger if the Coke Company had continued to hold its non-utility assets. Given the necessity of compliance with the Act, it may be reasonable to view the transfer of Old Shattuck and North Continent Mines to North Continent Utilities as merely the preliminary step in the de facto merger between the Coke and Gas Companies.

CERCLA itself is the second reason why a straightforward de facto merger analysis is unsatisfactory. North Shore Gas asserts that a "de facto merger between [the Gas Company's] and [the Coke Company's] *utility* operations would not render North Shore Gas liable for liabilities relating to the ... *non-utility* operations [of the 'dirty' businesses]." ... But this contention runs contrary to CERCLA, which generally prohibits a party from transferring away its direct liabilities.... If we were to conclude that there were no de facto merger solely because the Coke Company transferred Old Shattuck and North Continent Mines to North Continent Utilities—and that hence the Gas Company could not succeed to the Coke Company's direct liabilities—we would essentially allow the Coke Company to circumvent CERCLA's prohibition on the transfer of direct liability.

Because we are also able to find the Gas Company responsible for the Coke Company's CERCLA liabilities under the mere continuation exception, we will not pursue at further length the complexities surrounding the de facto merger issue ... If the case for de facto merger were not so strong, our approach to the mere continuation exception might be different. In a sense, then, our analysis is a hybrid, in which we rely on both the rationale for the de facto merger exception and on the underlying basis of the mere continuation exception as well.

.... The mere continuation exception allows recovery when the purchasing corporation is substantially the same as the selling corporation.... Courts have identified a number of factors that suggest that the seller's corporate entity has continued on after the sale of assets. These factors include "an identity of officers, directors, and stock between the selling and purchasing corporations," ... as well as a continuity of ownership and control.... Courts also consider whether only one corporation exists after the transfer of assets, ... and whether the purchaser paid adequate consideration for the assets....

In this case, continuity of ownership and control is the linchpin of our conclusion that the Coke Company merely continued on in the Gas Company after implementation of the 1941 Plan.... Prior to the Plan, North Continent Utilities owned more than 99% of the Coke Company's common stock and 91.47% of its preferred stock; it also controlled 100% of the Gas Company's common stock and 2.28% of its preferred stock. Because North Continent Utilities (a Baehr family vehicle) owned the vast majority of stock, it called the shots with respect to the activities of the Gas and Coke Companies. After the 1941 Plan—which reduced claims on the Gas Company's earnings by eliminating preferred stock from the Gas Company's capital structure and substituting common stock for the non-Baehr interest—North Continent Utilities owned slightly more than 35% of the Gas Company's common stock. The former owners of the Gas Company's preferred stock (the public) owned the remaining 65%. A crude assessment of the numbers might suggest to the financially untutored that North Continent Utilities suffered a precipitous loss of control over both the Gas Company and the assets that formerly belonged to the Coke Company. But the decline in the percentage of common stock owned by North Continent Utilities is, of course, deceptive. No other single entity or individual owned a percentage of the Gas Company's common stock that came close to rivaling that of North Continent Utilities. Thus, as the Securities and Exchange Commission noted after reviewing the effects of the 1941 Plan, the 35% share was "for all practical purposes ... sufficient to insure control of the Gas Company ... by North Continent and Baehr." ...

.... And although the preferred shareholders had various mismanagement claims against Baehr, there is no indication that they sought to wrest control away from him....

Because North Continent and Baehr remained in control after the 1941 Plan, the next factor that the case law identifies as important—an identity of officers and directors between the selling and purchasing corporations—declines in significance. In evaluating this factor, courts traditionally look to the number of officers and directors from the selling corporation who serve on the board of the purchasing corporation after the sale of assets.... Here, for example, the 1941 Plan provided that the Gas Company's preferred shareholders would elect five individuals to serve on the post-1941 board of directors, and that North Continent Utilities would elect four. This board would be in place only until early 1943, however, at which time North Continent Utilities (with 35% of the Gas Company's stock) would be "insured control" of the board because shareholders had the right to cumulate their votes in elections for directors.... We can assume, of course, that North Continent would, or could if circumstances demanded, install a majority of directors that were attentive to its interests. Whether these were the same directors that had served at the board of the Coke Company seems less probative of corporate identity—the important point is that both the old directors of the Coke Company and the new directors of the Gas Company were subject to the marching orders of North Continent Utilities and Baehr.

But even if the post-Plan Gas Company were not controlled by North Continent Utilities and Baehr and we looked to its officers and directors as personalities in their own right, we could find an identity between the post-1941 Gas Company and the Coke Company. North Shore Gas emphasizes that before the 1941 Plan, five of the Coke Company's nine officers and directors were on the board of the Gas Company; while after the Plan, only two of the Coke Company's officers and directors assumed roles on the nine-member board of the Gas Company.... Prior to its sale of assets, the Coke Company had nine officers and directors. After implementation of the 1941 Plan, two of these individuals served on the board of the post-1941 Gas Company. And six of the officers and directors of the Coke Company became or continued on as officers and directors of North Continent Utilities.... Because North Continent Utilities controlled the post-1941 Gas Company, the practical and immediate effect of the 1941 Plan was that seven of the nine directors of the defunct Coke Company became influential in the affairs of the rejuvenated Gas Company (one via the board of the Gas Company, five via the board of North Continent Utilities and one via the boards of the Gas Company and North Continent Utilities)....

The other factors emphasized by the case law warrant less discussion. Although neither party argues the point, there was identity of stock after the sale of the assets because holders of the Coke Company's preferred stock received common shares (the sole surviving class of equity securities) of the post-Plan Gas Company. There was also only one corporation after the purchase of assets; as we have already stated, the 1941 Plan specified that the Coke Company was to be liquidated "as soon as may be conveniently done." ...

We note, as North Shore Gas argues, that there is no evidence that the Gas Company paid inadequate consideration for the Coke Company's assets. But given the circumstances of this particular case, the amount of consideration is not strongly probative of whether the Coke Company's corporate entity continued on after the sale of assets. Presumably courts look to consideration to help determine whether a sale of assets was a genuine transaction between the purchasing and selling corporations, and not a mere change of garb. Here, the negotiations were between a committee representing the preferred shareholders in the Gas Company, North Continent Utilities (the owner of the Coke Company as well as the Gas Company's common stock) and the bondholders.... It was these interests that determined how many shares of the Gas Company the Coke Company would receive in exchange for its assets. But regardless of the legitimacy of these negotiations, the bulk of the evidence suggests that the 1941 Plan only served to update the wardrobe of the Gas and Coke Companies. Prior to the Plan, the companies had virtually identical boards of directors and both were controlled by North Continent and Baehr; after the Plan, North Continent and Baehr maintained control. And throughout it all, the Gas Company and the assets that constituted the Coke Company continued to supply gas to the Waukegan area. In the face of these corporate realities, adequacy of consideration should not be determinative.

Finally, because successor liability is an equitable doctrine ... we say a word or two about the equities of this case (which we regard as the crucial and decisive element of our analysis). North Shore Gas argues vigorously that before and after the 1941 Plan, it neither contributed to nor profited from the contamination at the Denver Site. But this argument ignores the close relationship between the Gas and Coke Companies and several facts about their shared history. This is not a case in which we are holding an arms-length purchaser responsible for the environmental sins of its supplier.... Given this serendipity, it seems that to the extent that the Coke Company benefitted [sic] from involvement in the mining industry, the Gas Company benefitted [sic] as well.

* * *

To conclude, we note that one of North Shore Gas' main defenses throughout is that, since the mining businesses were severed from the utility operations pursuant to the Holding Company Act, environmental liability should attach to North Continent

Utilities instead of North Shore Gas. But, as we have tried to emphasize, the shedding of direct environmental liability is not a matter entirely within the control of the party seeking to hand off (or avoid) liability. And to allow direct liability to be conveyed away under the circumstances of this case would violate CERCLA's clear policy that once direct liability attaches, it cannot be cast off through the mere transfer of property.

In any event, we leave to the district court the task of determining whether the Coke Company incurred direct CERCLA liability from its activities relating to Old Shattuck and North Continent Mines.

* * *

Notes and Questions

1. Who pays? Is that fair? Efficient?

2. Do you see any doctrinal defect in the court's conclusion that a *de facto* merger occurred? The Gas Company did not buy the mining assets. Is that possible in a merger? Does the "mere continuation" inquiry seal the crack? Or are there defects in that analysis too? Is there such a thing as a "corporate sibling liability" doctrine? Is equity the answer?

3. The court assumes that the Coke Company is liable as a parent of the mining companies for purposes of its analysis. Whether it is will depend on analyzing factors examined in U.S. v. Bestfoods, 524 U.S. 51 (1998), *supra* at section 4a.

c. Lender Liability for Environmental Claims

One issue that has become increasingly important (and controversial) is lender's liability for the cleanup of a debtor's toxic waste under the Comprehensive Environmental Response, Compensation, and Liability Act (CERCLA). Consider the following case and the notes and questions that follow.

Monarch Title, Inc. v. City of Florence
212 F.3d 1219 (11th Cir. 2000)

HALL, Senior Circuit Judge:

The instant case requires us to determine whether a governmental body that acquires indicia of ownership in a property for the purpose of fostering private economic development thereon, but which retains those indicia for the purpose of securing repayment of the development bonds that financed the property's acquisition, can qualify for the Comprehensive Environmental Response, Compensation, and Liability Act's ("CERCLA's") "secured creditor" liability exception, 42 U.S.C. § 9601 (20)(A). Because we hold that such a governmental body can qualify for the secured creditor exception, we affirm the judgment of the district court.

I.

Appellee, the City of Florence, is a municipal corporation organized under the laws of Alabama. In 1952, Appellee purchased a parcel of land and leased it to Stylon, a corporation wishing to construct and operate a ceramic tile manufacturing factory on said parcel. Appellee acquired the property for the purpose of encouraging industrial development within the county. By purchasing the property and leasing it to a factory operator, that factory operator would benefit from certain tax savings that could be passed along through Appellee. Appellee issued bonds to finance the purchase of the parcel and mortgaged the parcel to First National Bank of Florence ("Trustee"), pledging that Stylon's rent payments from the property would be used to secure the repayment of principal and interest on the bonds held by Trustee. Three years later, Appellee entered into a similar arrangement with respect to an adjoining property. Stylon operated a tile manufacturing facility at the property until its bankruptcy in 1973. From 1973 to 1988 Appellant, Monarch Tile, Inc., leased the property in question from Appellee, with Appellee retaining title. In 1988 Appellant purchased the two parcels from Appellee and a related municipal body for approximately $60,000.

From 1953 to 1973 Stylon discharged substances that are hazardous within the meaning of § 101(14) of CERCLA, 42 U.S.C. § 9601(14). The discharge of these substances left the property and the neighboring watershed significantly contaminated. Appellant's activities further contaminated the property, although Appellant apparently was not responsible for most of the pollution. Appellant first discovered some levels of contamination on the property in 1987, but apparently did not come to realize the full scope of the problem until several years later. Upon learning of the contamination, Appellant notified the Environmental Protection Agency, and was directed to clean up the facility under CERCLA. Appellant brought suit against Appellee, alleging that Appellee owes Appellant contribution under CERCLA, 42 U.S.C. § 9613(f), which provides that prior owners can be financially responsible to subsequent owners who must bear the costs of cleaning up contaminated facilities.

The district court granted summary judgment in Appellee's favor, holding that Appellee was exempted from liability under 42 U.S.C. § 9601(20)(A), which exempts from CERCLA liability any person who, without participating in the management of the facility, holds indicia of ownership primarily to protect security interests in the vessel or facility. Appellant filed a timely appeal. We ... review the grant of summary judgment de novo....

II.

CERCLA is a broad, remedial statute animated by a sweeping purpose to ensure that those responsible for contaminating American soil shoulder the costs of undoing that environmental damage.... "An essential purpose of CERCLA is to place the ultimate responsibility for the clean-up of hazardous waste on those responsible for problems caused by the disposal of chemical poison." *Florida Power & Light Co. v. Allis Chalmers Corp.*, 893 F.2d 1313, 1317 (11th Cir.1990) (internal quotations omitted). "CERCLA holds the owner or operator of a facility containing hazardous waste strictly liable to the United States for expenses incurred in responding to the environmental and health hazards posed by the waste in that facility." *United States v. Fleet Factors Corp.*, 901 F.2d 1550, 1554 (11th Cir.1990).[2] The terms "owner" and "operator" do not have any special meaning under

---

2. While much of *Fleet Factors'* reasoning and holding remain intact, Congress has abrogated the part of *Fleet Factors'* holding that deals with the liability of lenders who participate in the management of properties operated by polluting firms. *Fleet Factors* held that lenders and other parties who participated "in the financial management of a facility to a degree indicating a capacity to influence the corporation's treatment of hazardous wastes" could be liable for cleaning up pollution created by an operator's activities. Largely in response to the perceived overbreadth of the *Fleet Factors* rule, Congress amended CERCLA in 1996, narrowing somewhat the sweep of lender liability under CERCLA. *See, e.g.,* 42 U.S.C. § 9601(F)(i)(II) (noting that the term "participate in management" does not include "merely having the capacity to influence ... facility operations.")....

CERCLA, but are to be given their "ordinary meanings." *Redwing Carriers, Inc. v. Saraland Apartments,* 94 F.3d 1489, 1498 (11th Cir. 1996).

CERCLA contains a smattering of exceptions to this broad liability for owners, one of which is the "secured creditor" exception carved out in 42 U.S.C. § 9601(20)(A). The last sentence of that subsection states that the term "owner or operator" does not "include a person, who, without participating in the management of a vessel or facility, holds indicia of ownership primarily to protect his security interest in the vessel or facility." That clause is very much at issue in this case. Appellant argues that the district court erroneously held that Appellee could qualify for this exception. Appellee, not surprisingly, sees it the other way. In the instant case, Appellee had the burden of establishing its entitlement to that exemption. *See Fleet Factors,* 901 F.2d at 1555. And it is undisputed that Appellee did not participate in the management of the facility. Therefore, in order to prevail on its appeal, Appellant must show that Appellee failed to prove that Appellee held indicia of ownership primarily to protect its security interest.

In determining whether Appellee met its burden of proving that it qualifies for the exception, the district court relied heavily on the Ninth Circuit's opinion in *In re Bergsoe Metal Corp.,* 910 F.2d 668 (9th Cir.1990). The *Bergsoe* court confronted facts virtually identical to those before us today. The Port of St. Helens, a municipal corporation in Oregon, issued bonds for the economic development of the St. Helens area. The Port sold 50 acres of land to Bergsoe, upon which Bergsoe operated a lead recycling plant. Bergsoe gave the Port a promissory note and a mortgage on the property.... Like the present transactions, the Bergsoe transactions involved a commercial bank as an intermediary. The bank purchased the Port's revenue bonds and, in exchange, the Port assigned to the bank "all its rights under, and revenues to be generated from, the leases." *Id.* at 670. Although the Port all the while retained title to the property, the Court found the Port not liable under CERCLA because it held indicia of ownership primarily to protect a security interest. The Court emphasized that "the leases give to Bergsoe all other traditional indicia of ownership, such as responsibility for the payment of taxes and for the purchase of insurance," as well as "the risk of loss from destruction or damage to the property," and that Bergsoe's rent "was equal to the principal and interest due under the bonds." *Id.* at 671....

Appellant's effort to distinguish *Bergsoe* is unconvincing. Appellant correctly points out that the 1996 amendments to CERCLA introduced a new definition of the term "security interest." The new definition is as follows:

> The term "security interest" includes a right under a mortgage, deed of trust, assignment, judgment lien, pledge, security agreement, factoring agreement, or lease and any other right accruing to a person to secure the repayment of money, the performance of a duty, or any other obligation by a nonaffiliated person.

42 U.S.C. § 9601(20)(G)(vi). Appellant argues that Appellee did not "hold" a security interest, but rather "gave" a security interest to Trustee. The *Bergsoe* court adequately dealt with this objection. It held that where a party held bare title, and devoted the lease revenues to pay off the development bonds that had financed the property's acquisition, the party held a "security interest" within the meaning of § 9601(20)(A). There is nothing in the 1996 amendments suggesting that Congress sought to constrain the definition of a "security interest" so as to preclude the type of security interest identified in *Bergsoe*. To the contrary, it appears that the amendment's broad language "any other right accruing to a person to secure the repayment of money ... or any other obligation" encompasses the

activity occurring here. We therefore view the type of "security interest" identified in *Bergsoe* as having survived the enactment of 42 U.S.C. §9601(G)(vi).

* * *

Appellant ... argues that the fact that Alabama law limited Appellee to purchasing the property in question for a public purpose (the development of industry within the county) precludes Appellee from arguing that it held title to the property primarily to protect a security interest. The district court rejected this contention by noting that Appellee indeed acquired the property to spur industrial development, but subsequently held title to ensure that Appellee's bonds, held by Trustee, were backed by adequate security.... Plainly, governments will never acquire property for the purpose of protecting a security interest in that same property. Governments acquire property to further some public purpose, be it economic development, environmental protection, or flood control. Once those public purposes are met, however, as it was in this case when a tile manufacturing factory began operating on the property, the government often holds title or other indicia of ownership during the duration of a long-term lease so that it can ensure that its investment is repaid. The district court, recognizing this dynamic, drew a distinction between Appellee's motivations for *obtaining* and *retaining* the property. The district court's bifurcation was quite elegant in its simplicity, and we endorse it wholeheartedly. The fact that a government's initial motivation for purchasing land was to further economic development will not preclude it from qualifying for the secured creditor exception as long as it "holds indicia of ownership primarily to protect" its security interest in the property during the period when the pollution occurs.

III.

For the foregoing reasons, the judgment of the district court is
AFFIRMED.

Notes and Questions

1. What is the wisdom of imposing liability on a secured creditor which has some financial managerial involvement in the business of its debtor?

2. In U.S. v. Fleet Factors, 901 F.2d 1550 (11th Cir. 1990), which is discussed in footnote 2 of *Monarch Title*, the government had urged the court to adopt a narrow and strictly literal interpretation of the secured creditor exemption to CERCLA liability that would exclude from its protection any secured creditor that participates in any manner in the management of a facility. Fleet Factors, in turn, urged an adoption of a standard that would permit certain permissible participation in the day-to-day or operational management of a facility without fear of losing the exemption. The 11th Circuit, however, chose an intermediate standard:

> [A] secured creditor may incur ... liability, without being an operator, by participating in the financial management of a facility to a degree indicating a capacity to influence the corporation's treatment of hazardous wastes. It is not necessary for the secured creditor to actually involve itself in the day-to-day operations of the facility in order to be held liable.... Nor is it necessary for the secured creditor to participate in management decisions relating to hazardous waste. Rather, a secured creditor will be liable if its involvement with the management of the facility is sufficiently broad to support the inference that it could affect hazardous waste disposal decisions if it so chose.

Id. at 1557-58. Not surprisingly, *Fleet Factors* was not greeted warmly by the American banking community. *See* Statement of the American Bankers Association on the Lender Liability Act of 1990, before the Senate Committee on Banking, Housing, and Urban Affairs (July 19, 1990); Statement of the New York State Bankers Association on S. 2827, The Lender Liability Act of 1990, before the Senate Committee on Banking, Housing, and Urban Affairs (July 19, 1990).

In 1992, the EPA issued long-awaited rules on lender liability that attempted to clarify the scope of the "security interest" exemption. (57 Fed. Reg. 18, 382 (Apr. 29, 1992)). However, they were struck down in Kelley v. EPA, 15 F.3d 1100 (D.C. Cir. 1994), on the ground that it was the role of the courts and not the EPA to determine the scope of CERCLA liability. Congress responded in 1996 by amending Section 9601 to include the following:

(F) Participation in management. For purposes of subparagraph (E) —

    (i) the term "participate in management" —

        (I) means actually participating in the management or operational affairs of a vessel or facility; and

        (II) does not include merely having the capacity to influence, or the unexercised right to control, vessel or facility operations;

    (ii) a person that is a lender and that holds indicia of ownership primarily to protect a security interest in a vessel or facility shall be considered to participate in management only if, while the borrower is still inpossession of the vessel or facility encumbered by the security interest, the person —

        (I) exercises decisionmaking control over the environmental compliance related to the vessel or facility, such that the person has undertaken responsibility for the hazardous substance handling or disposal practices related to the vessel or facility; or

        (II) exercises control at a level comparable to that of a manager of the vessel or facility, such that the person has assumed or manifested responsibility —

        (aa) for the overall management of the vessel or facility encompassing day-to-day decisionmaking with respect to environmental compliance; or

        (bb) over all or substantially all of the operational functions (as distinguished from financial or administrative functions) of the vessel or facility other than the function of environmental compliance;

    (iii) the term "participate in management" does not include performing an act or failing to act prior to the time at which a security interest is created in a vessel or facility; and

    (iv) the term "participate in management" does not include —

        (I) holding a security interest or abandoning or releasing a security interest;

        (II) including in the terms of an extension of credit, or in a contract or security agreement relating to the extension, a covenant, warranty, or other term or condition that relates to environmental compliance;

        (III) monitoring or enforcing the terms and conditions of the extension of credit or security interest;

        (IV) monitoring or undertaking 1 or more inspections of the vessel or facility;

        (V) requiring a response action or other lawful means of addressing the release or threatened release of a hazardous substance in connection with the vessel or facility prior to, during, or on the expiration of the term of the extension of credit;

(VI) providing financial or other advice or counseling in an effort to mitigate, prevent, or cure default or diminution in the value of the vessel or facility;

(VII) restructuring, renegotiating, or otherwise agreeing to alter the terms and conditions of the extension of credit or security interest, exercising forbearance;

(VIII) exercising other remedies that may be available under applicable law for the breach of a term or condition of the extension of credit or security agreement; or

(IX) conducting a response action under section 107(d) [42U.S.C. §9607(d)] or under the direction of an on-scene coordinator appointed under the National Contingency Plan, if the actions do not rise to the level of participating in management (within the meaning of clauses (i) and (ii)).

3. Assume you represent a commercial lender. What precautions would you advise your client to take to avoid incurring CERCLA liability? For a prescriptive argument favoring self-regulation through coordination and collaboration among participants in business ventures that pose environmental risks, see Thomas, The Green Nexus: Financiers and Sustainable Development, Geo. Int'l Envtl. L. Rev. 899 (2001); Bregman & Jacobson, Environmental Performance Review: Self-Regulation in Environmental Law, 16 Cardozo L. Rev. 465 (1994).

Chapter 3

Valuation

The importance to a lawyer of understanding valuation principles is not necessarily obvious. From a business perspective, valuation lies at the heart of corporate finance. Without an appreciation of an asset's worth (including the worth of the capital asset we call the corporation), the corporate manager would be unable to make investment decisions or financing decisions.[1]

To the lawyer as well, valuation principles have great significance. On the most fundamental level, the lawyer who helps to plan and implement corporate investment and financial policy must thoroughly understand the interests of her client in order to effectively structure a transaction and negotiate and draft the necessary papers. An appreciation of the client's evaluative processes is helpful to this. In order to draft a buy/sell agreement among close corporation shareholders, or an earn-out clause in a corporate acquisition agreement, it is important to be familiar with the principles of valuation. Furthermore, valuation lies at the heart of a number of legal proceedings as diverse as appraisals, corporate dissolutions, liquidations and reorganizations, distributional disputes among stockholders, estate and gift tax matters, and even divorce proceedings. Ultimately valuation principles help to tell us whether, on the prevailing view of corporate governance, corporate directors are fulfilling their responsibilities by maximizing value. Consequently, the lawyer must understand not only valuation principles and legal principles, but also how the two interact.

On a more conceptual level, familiarity with these valuation matters reveals the ephemeral nature of the concept of value. The apparent numerical precision of the end-product of valuations masks the significant subjectivity of the conclusion. A large variety of factors influence the determination of value, not the least of which is the method used to make the determination. In a sense, valuation decisions potentially are the financial economist's equivalent of "the chancellor's foot."

Not only are valuation determinations inherently imprecise, but the various methodologies are predicated on their own normative concepts. For example, the market-based approaches presented in section 5 of this chapter both derive from and are predicated upon the idea that informed participants in a well-developed market determine value through their trading activities. The difference between market-based and fundamental approaches to valuation underlying the various theories lead to differing notions about the theory of the corporation, the proper role of law in regulating corporate financial matters, and the nature and role of the corporation in modern society. Ultimately the theoretical perspective from which a decision-maker operates significantly influences her views of the appropriate structure of corporate governance. So, as you study the

---

1. It should here be noted that generally it is considered best to keep investment decisions separate from financing decisions because the criteria governing the prudence of these two kinds of decisions are different.

materials that follow, please keep in mind these issues as well as the technical and doctrinal matters that will become a part of your daily practice.

Section 1
Introduction to Valuation

a. The Idea of Capital

Perhaps you have a vague idea of what the term capital means from your corporations course. You may even have noticed that its meaning depends on the purpose for which it is being defined or from whose perspective one is defining it. For example, capital has a precise legal meaning to a lawyer applying a state corporate statute to determine whether a corporate client can declare and pay a dividend. Capital also has a precise but different meaning for the accountant concerned with calculating the shareholders' equity accounts. Economists use the term capital in yet another sense and businesspersons may understand the concept in a sense different from all these groups. Since the concept of capital is at the heart of many valuation problems in corporate law, consider the following summary of these different conceptions, modeled on 1 Dewing, The Financial Policy of Corporations 45-52 (5th ed. 1953).

Classical economics defined capital as that part of material wealth that has been accumulated by the skill of labor and that is dedicated to the production of increases in material wealth. In a general sense, this is the same conception of capital many people use in thinking about corporations. Corporations employ material wealth in their enterprises with the view toward increasing that wealth. As Professor Dewing puts it, "capital is the economic substance of a corporation." And Adam Smith recognized, at the heart of his economic theory, that all such wealth was traceable back to the input of labor, regardless of whether the capital originated from the sale of stock or was borrowed from lenders. This general perspective also implies that the fundamental idea of corporate capital is wealth. We need to be more specific, however, about the variety of ways in which the concept of capital has been used.

Accountants assume that economic values correspond to money values. This assumption is a functional necessity in order to meet the accountant's task of presenting an infinitely complex variety of financial transactions in a useable form comparable to the forms used by a wide variety of business enterprises. One consequence of this assumption is that accountants recognize only those transactions that can be stated fairly and accurately based on some objective exchange in monetary terms. So while accountants record and report in financial statements items of value such as property, plant and equipment, they do so only on the basis of what it cost in some exchange (unless prevailing market values are lower) and they do not record the value of such "assets" as employee or customer relations.

Accountants also assume an identity between a corporation's total value in terms of money, on the one hand, and its total obligations in terms of money, on the other. This assumption implies that accountants are not especially concerned with who contributed the value or to whom the corporation may owe a claim with respect to that value. As a result, the accountant's conception of capital is a statement of the net money value of the corporation's property without regard to who contributed it or how it was obtained.

The accountant's conception of capital is also not concerned with whether or to what extent property is in fact capable of being used to generate more wealth. For example, the accountant's conception of capital would include the money value of environmentally contaminated wasteland and would exclude the appreciated value of real estate and other fixed assets.

Law is of course ultimately concerned precisely with the rights and duties of individuals and other juridical entities. Corporate law seeks to define the rights and duties of those who own the corporation's property, those who deploy it and others who may claim some entitlement to it. Perhaps the oldest mechanism through which corporate law has sought such definition is the concept of legal capital. The principle of limited liability, reviewed in chapter 2, holds that the owners of stock in a corporation are not generally liable for the corporation's debts. To operationalize this hoary principle required defining the portion of the corporation's property available to satisfy its debt obligations. This was called capital.

The concept of legal capital has become anachronistic for many reasons (see chapter 8, section 2a), including that the business world's conception of capital is far more expansive. It is also more expansive than the idea of capital used by accountants. It more nearly resembles the idea of capital held by the classical economists. But because businesspeople use the term in a wide variety of ways, it remains important to evaluate the concept as it is used in particular contexts.

In its broadest sense, capital to the businessperson means all the productive resources available for deployment in profit-making enterprises, from whatever source. Unlike the lawyer's concern with tracing precisely who has a claim to capital, the businessperson is more interested in its availability (although we shall see that from a financial planning perspective, determining the mix of owned and borrowed capital can have significant consequences). Unlike the accountant's concern with valuing resources in money terms, capital to the businessperson may include all sorts of items having intangible value. Among these are employee and customer relations, as well as trademarks, patent rights and other intellectual property that are not generally the concern of the accountant's conception of capital. In addition, businesspersons would also include in capital the market value of assets that exceed their historical cost.

Many resources that accrue to a corporation other than through market exchanges may also be viewed by businesspersons as capital. Consider the recently-graduated computer whiz kid who moves to Silicon Valley and starts a small software business with her summer savings. After years of experimenting with hyper-high-density computer software, she designs a bionic package that overwhelms the industry. Her only cost in producing the package was her time and labor but this nonmaterial wealth has generated more wealth. And so it may be considered as capital because it contributes to the earnings potential of the enterprise.

b. The Idea of Valuation

Now that you know what capital is (do you?), you will want to consider how to go about placing a value on it. However, you will first need to know exactly what sort of capital we are going to go about valuing. We start in this essay with common stock. We present two theories of valuing common stock that tend to dominate thinking on the subject: the firm foundation theory and the castles in the air theory, both of which are also summarized in Malkiel, A Random Walk Down Wall Street (8th ed. 2003), at 28-32, on which this essay is based.

The firm foundation theory starts with the proposition that all investments, including common stock, have an "intrinsic value." The idea is that by carefully studying the present conditions relevant to some investment and then carefully thinking about how the future might affect that investment, you can come up with the "right" value of the investment. In the case of common stock, hundreds of thousands of people watch stock markets every day. If enough of them are careful enough and pay close enough attention, maybe something like an intrinsic value for common stock could be found.

But what, exactly, are these people supposed to be studying so carefully? One important benefit of owning common stock is that from time to time the directors of the corporation will declare dividends on it. The payment of dividends is a kind of value. So one might try to forecast the probable future dividend payment stream and come up with some plausible value for the common stock that creates the right to that stream. In doing so, however, one must of course keep in mind that the payments are going to be made in the future and not today. To take account of that, one applies to that probable future stream of payments a simple process called *discounting*.

Discounting starts from the idea that money in hand today is worth more than the same amount of money to be paid at any future time. Assume you deposit $1,000 in your savings account today, leave it on deposit for one year, and the bank is paying interest on savings accounts of 5% per year. As of the end of the year, your $1,000 balance will have grown to $1,050. Another way of looking at things is to ask how much your balance of $1,050 as of the end of the year is worth today. The answer, $1,000, is given by our starting point. You can ask the same question about what some amount paid at the end of two years is worth today and at the end of three years and four years and so on. In this process you are calculating the present value of some future payment or series of payments. So once you have forecast a dividend payment stream on a share of common stock, you can calculate its present value by discounting it.

Financial economists and investment managers use this technique to calculate the intrinsic value of common stock. It is the cornerstone of what Malkiel identifies as the "firm foundation theory" of valuing common stock. The basic assumption, of course, is that the value of a share of common stock should be based on the future stream of income that it is expected to generate through the payment of dividends. The chief difficulty resides in forecasting the future. The past dividend history of a share of common stock is a good place to start. But care must be taken to consider whether any extraordinary circumstances affected the payment of dividends in the past and consideration given to the probability of those or other extraordinary circumstances repeating in the future.

The firm foundation theory gives the appearance of a certain objectivity, and may even resemble a science. The "scientific" emphasis may be seen to ignore the subjective dimension of investing, or the part that more nearly resembles art. The "castles-in-the-air theory" focuses on this side of the story.[2] It was coined by John Maynard Keynes in the period after the Great Depression and the stock market crash of 1929. Keynes, General Theory of Employment, Interest and Money (1936). Keynes was skeptical of the

---

2. Although as you will see in section 5, modern finance theory attempts to quantify this subjective element in "scientific" terms. When you study that material, consider whether that attempt succeeds.

degree to which market traders relied on examining the intrinsic values of common stocks. He thought it equally likely that they were interested in figuring out what other people thought about the value of a share of common stock rather than what its so-called intrinsic value was.

Keynes's idea goes back to a famous book by Charles MacKay called Memoirs of Extraordinary Popular Delusions and the Madness of Crowds (1841). People were seen to act impulsively, sometimes overly optimistically and sometimes overly pessimistically. The great investor, according to Keynes, would watch for the building up of crowd sentiment and, when excessive optimism characterized the crowd, the market would build "castles in the air." Malkiel reports that Keynes practiced what he preached:

> While London's financial men toiled many weary hours in crowded offices, he played the market from his bed for half an hour each morning. This leisurely method of investing earned him several million pounds for his account and a tenfold increase in the market value of the endowment of his college, King's College, Cambridge.

Malkiel, at 31. Keynes was particularly concerned about the uncertainty under the firm foundation theory of using dividend payment histories to forecast future payment streams. This way of calculating intrinsic value was wrought with intrinsic infirmities! Instead of wasting time and energy in such a pseudo-science, Keynes thought it better and more likely that investors would gauge general investor sentiment and make investment decisions based on principles of mass psychology rather than on principles of the dismal science of economics.

Keynes revealed the intuitive appeal of his theory in terms of a popular game played by his English contemporaries. Newspapers of the period held beauty contests featuring scores of contestants. Readers were to select the six most beautiful contestants. The winning readers were those whose selections were closest to the overall selections made by all participating readers. The optimal strategy for the reader, therefore, was to evaluate the contestants based on prevailing sentiments about beauty, rather than about one's own sense of fundamental beauty.

With respect to common stock, the castles-in-the-air theory rests on the belief that investors are willing to pay a given price because they expect that someone else at some other time will be willing to pay a higher price. In this story of value, the search for intrinsic value is a diversion because, to paraphrase Samuel Butler, "The value of a thing is exactly what it will bring."

Notes and Questions

1. Under what circumstances would the "value" of a share of common stock determined under the firm foundation theory be equal to the "value" of the same share of common stock determined under the castles-in-the-air theory? How often would you expect those circumstances to obtain in actual public capital market trading?

2. As you study the succeeding materials in this chapter, keep these two perspectives on valuation in mind and consider how those materials are informed by one theory or the other and the implications of each theory for law and public policy. In particular, consider what each of these theories of valuation suggest with respect to the goals of corporate law.

3. See Manning, Reflections and Practical Tips on Life in the Boardroom After Van Gorkom, 41 Bus. Law. 1 (1985), where, in discussing the decision of the Delaware

Supreme Court in Smith v. Van Gorkom, 488 A.2d 858 (Del. 1985), in which the court held Trans Union's directors liable for breach of the duty of care for accepting a cash-out merger offer at less than the stock's "intrinsic value" he states:

> Something must be said about the court's talk about the "intrinsic value" of the Trans Union stock. It is disappointing to see a modern court, especially a commercially oriented Delaware court, lapse into anachronistic language of "true value," as though we have learned nothing from 150 years of market economy analytics. And one wonders just how the lower court on remand will go about determining the "intrinsic value" of the Trans Union stock to set the benchmark for the directors' liability.

Id. at 4.

Section 2
Risk and Return

Much of the focus of valuation in corporate law is on determining the value of an individual share of stock. The need to do this arises in a variety of legal contexts. One of the most important legal implications of the ability to determine value, whether of a share of stock or of the corporation as a whole, is to determine whether the corporation's directors are fulfilling their various duties explored throughout the rest of this book. Much of the balance of this chapter is devoted to exploring the methods employed by financial analysts in making this determination. Your task is to evaluate how well these methods work.

Before doing so, however, we wish to note several important points. First, although the following methods are described in the context of stock valuation, some are equally useful in valuing other productive assets. In particular, the present value and risk concepts are used by businesspersons in making internal investment decisions for the corporation. In this respect, traditional valuation principles treat corporate securities much as they do other types of assets.

One area in which this proposition is debatable is in the development of the capital asset pricing model and its supporting theories, particularly the efficient capital market hypothesis, which are discussed in section 5. These are valuation models developed expressly in the context of functioning markets. The depth and efficiency of markets for different types of assets may differ, thus limiting the theories' utility.

This brings us to our second, and more important, introductory point. The valuation method you select is based upon, and has implications for, a distinct set of normative principles. For example, the traditional valuation methods usually applied in the cases and which are the subject of this section are based upon a traditional notion of the corporation as a unique, independent entity. By contrast, the market-based methods of analysis discussed in section 5 largely sever the security from its specific corporate mooring and try to locate its value in a functioning, efficient marketplace where its worth is expressed in much more relative terms. Each of these approaches has significant implications for the structure of corporate governance, and the rights and duties of directors, stockholders, officers, and other corporate constituents. Try not to lose sight of this insight as you study these materials (and we will periodically remind you of its importance).

a. Introduction to Risk and Return

The fundamental components of financial analysis are the related concepts of risk and return. Return on an investment is a function of two basic components: (i) the time value of money, or the return available from a risk-free investment, and (ii) risk, or the possibility that the expected return will not materialize. The following materials are included to introduce you to the basic concepts.

Discounting, discussed further in section 2b(ii) below, is a fundamental concept in finance. Underlying that process is the idea of the time value of money—that any amount of money in hand today is worth more than the same amount to be paid at any future time. Suppose your professor were to offer you $1,000 in exchange for reading this book (setting aside the legal problem of past consideration) and gave you the choice of being paid immediately upon completing the task or being paid one year later.[1] Which would you choose? We guess you, like most people, would choose immediate payment. But what if the offer were for either $1,000 paid upon completion ... or $1,100 one year later? Or $1,500 one year later?

Two questions arise. First, why should people generally prefer earlier payment of money to deferred payment of money? Second, in terms of our example, at what amount of money to be paid in the future would you, or most people, opt for the future sum instead of the present sum? With respect to why people should generally prefer earlier payment of money to deferred payment of money, there are four sorts of reasons: inflation, utility, risk and opportunity cost.

Inflation is an increase in the general level of prices of goods and services over time. Inflation, therefore, causes the erosion of the dollar's purchasing power. Inflation is caused by too many dollars chasing too few goods and services. This occurs during periods of economic expansion when the economy is flush with cash and consumer spending is in full swing. In order to balance the supply and demand for goods and services, merchants and service providers raise their prices until demand levels off to match supply. Accordingly, in choosing between your professor's offer to pay $1,000 upon completing reading or a greater sum one year later, you must take into consideration the anticipated rate of inflation over the ensuing year. Indeed, at a minimum any future sum you could receive should at least have the same purchasing power as the sum you could receive today.

Utility is the notion that things of value satisfy desire and immediate possession of the thing can satisfy immediate desire. With the payment of $1,000 upon reading this book, you could throw a party for your classmates or take a trip to Italy. If this satisfies your desires more than getting even a larger sum when you are about to graduate from law school, then you may opt for earlier payment rather than later payment. But your friends may have a different set of preferences, or different utility, for entertainment and gratification now as opposed to deferring entertainment and gratification until a year on. Despite these different preferences, however, in order to be indifferent about payment now and payment in the future, most people would insist on a greater amount in the future.

Risk. In choosing between your professor's offer to pay $1,000 upon completing reading this book (say this semester) and to pay $1,100 one year later, you will be

---

1. We draw this example and discussion from Stevenson and Jennings, Fundamentals of Investments 111-113 (3d ed. 1988).

concerned about the possibility of breach. That is, in thinking about opting for the future payment, you will be concerned about the possibility of not getting it. Perhaps you will have graduated from law school and are so busy doing deals and making money that you forget all about it. Or perhaps your professor will be running the law school's Moscow program next year and forget all about it. Or (heaven forfend) your professor may declare personal bankruptcy during the course of the year and simply not have the $1,100 to pay you then. All these hypotheticals pose the problem of *risk*—the risk of nonpayment of the future sum, for whatever reason. What emerges is the hackneyed adage that a bird in hand is worth two in the bush. But, as with utility, there will be some amount of additional money to be paid in the future that will induce you to accept the risk of nonpayment.

Opportunity cost is a fundamental concept in economic theory. It recognizes that people have all sorts of opportunities available to them but that some of these are mutually exclusive. In choosing one opportunity, other opportunities are foreclosed. In the context of the time value of money, the idea is that you may have available to you the opportunity to invest the $1,000 paid this semester and earn interest on that amount. Recall from the previous discussion of discounting that you could deposit the $1,000 in your savings account and earn $50 during the year it is on deposit (assuming an interest rate of 5%). If that is right, then you would be indifferent between receiving $1,000 upon completing reading and receiving $1,050 one year hence, subject of course to the question of risk. But if your savings account is insured by the federal government so that your investment and the earnings thereon are in effect riskless, you would remain indifferent. In any event, if you considered the risk of losing the $1,000 investment in your insured savings account to be equivalent to the risk of your professor not paying you the $1,050 in one year's time, then you would again be indifferent as between these opportunities. In this example, the opportunity cost of foregoing the payment now is $50 and you would insist on being paid in the future that additional amount in order to be indifferent between these choices.

Our second question—what amount of money to be paid in the future would lead you, or most people, to opt for the future sum instead of the present sum—can be answered directly in terms of the time value of money.

b. Return as a Function of Present Value

The time value of money generally is expressed in terms of the concept of *present value*. Present value tells us what the right to receive a certain sum at some point in the future is worth to us today. Similarly, present value allows us to determine the rate of return we will receive on our investment if we anticipate receiving a particular sum of money in the future. By determining the present value of an investment, we can thus compare it not only with the right to receive a sum of money today, but with the present value of other investments that are available to us. To understand present value, it is first useful to understand the related concept of *future value*.

(i) Future Value

Annual Compounding. Assume you have $100 that you decide to deposit in a savings account that is paying 8% interest annually. What will your account balance be at the end of the year (assuming no deposits or withdrawals)? It will be $108. You may have been able to calculate that result in your head. How did you do it? Probably by multiplying $100 by .08 to determine the interest and then adding that to the $100 balance with which you started. How would you respond if we asked what your balance would be at the end of two years? You would repeat the foregoing calculation and then in addition add to your new balance of $108 an amount equal to 108 times .08 to reflect the interest to be earned during the second year. That would be 108 + (108 × .08) and would equal $116.64. If we asked, what about for three years, four years, five years and so on, you would probably just keep doing the series of calculations. That is fine, but there is an easier and less time-consuming way. You could use a single formula:

$$FV_n = x(1+k)^n$$

This formula says that your balance (which we have abbreviated FV, standing for the phrase "future value") at the end of some future year (denoted by n) is equal to the amount you started with (which we have called x) times a function of the interest rate (which we have called k) and the number of years in the future we are considering. That is, the term $(1 + k)^n$ (which is called the *future value factor*) is a way of avoiding the problem of repeating a series of calculations by instead just doing one calculation.

Let's try this for the two examples we just did. Your account balance at the end of one year would be:

$$FV_1 = x(1+k)^1$$
$$= \$108$$

Your account balance at the end of two years would be:

$$FV_2 = x(1+k)^2$$
$$= \$116.64$$

Continuing, your account balance at the end of three years would be:

$$FV_3 = x(1+k)^3$$
$$= \$125.97$$

Using this formula makes things clearer and also makes the calculation simpler because it can be done very easily using a basic calculator. Things are even simpler than that, you may be happy to know. Look at Table 1. It shows the results of using the future value formula for $1 for various years at various interest rates. No more need for a calculator—just use the table. For the future value of $100 at an interest rate of 8% at the end of 3 years, use Table 1 as follows: go down the year row to 3, go across the percentage column to 8% and you are given the future value of $1. It is equal to $1.2597. Multiply that by the $100 you are interested in and you get the same result we just got in our calculation: $125.97.

Compounding and Future Values. Notice that the key operation in the foregoing calculations turns on the future value factor. In particular, what is crucial in the formula is that we are adding to your account balance interest earned at the end of each year and then using that new balance (which includes the previously earned interest) to calculate the interest to which you are entitled in the next year and so on. This process is called *compounding*. It means that you in effect earn interest on interest over time. We have assumed that you are getting the interest payments added to your balance at the end of each year and not more frequently. This is called *compounding annually*.

Some bank accounts and other investments make the interest calculations and payments more often than each year, however. For example, your bank may make the calculation and

Table 1 Future Value of $1 at the End of n Periods

	4%	5%	6%	7%	8%	9%	10%	11%	12%	13%	14%	16%	17%	18%	19%	20%
1	1.0400	1.0500	1.0600	1.0700	1.0800	1.0900	1.1000	1.1100	1.1200	1.1300	1.1400	1.1600	1.1700	1.1800	1.1900	1.2000
2	1.0816	1.1025	1.1236	1.1449	1.1664	1.1881	1.2100	1.2321	1.2544	1.2769	1.2996	1.3456	1.3689	1.3924	1.4161	1.4400
3	1.1249	1.1576	1.1910	1.2250	1.2597	1.2950	1.3310	1.3676	1.4049	1.4429	1.4815	1.5609	1.6016	1.6430	1.6852	1.7280
4	1.1699	1.2155	1.2625	1.3108	1.3605	1.4116	1.4641	1.5181	1.5735	1.6305	1.6890	1.8106	1.8739	1.9388	2.0053	2.0736
5	1.2167	1.2763	1.3382	1.4026	1.4693	1.5386	1.6105	1.6851	1.7623	1.8424	1.9254	2.1003	2.1924	2.2878	2.3864	2.4883
6	1.2653	1.3401	1.4185	1.5007	1.5869	1.6771	1.7716	1.8704	1.9738	2.0820	2.1950	2.4364	2.5652	2.6996	2.8398	2.9860
7	1.3159	1.4071	1.5036	1.6058	1.7138	1.8280	1.9487	2.0762	2.2107	2.3526	2.5023	2.8262	3.0012	3.1855	3.3793	3.5832
8	1.3686	1.4775	1.5938	1.7182	1.8509	1.9926	2.1436	2.3045	2.4760	2.6584	2.8526	3.2784	3.5115	3.7589	4.0214	4.2998
9	1.4233	1.5513	1.6895	1.8385	1.9990	2.1719	2.3579	2.5580	2.7731	3.0040	3.2519	3.8030	4.1084	4.4355	4.7854	5.1598
10	1.4802	1.6289	1.7908	1.9672	2.1589	2.3674	2.5937	2.8394	3.1058	3.3946	3.7072	4.4114	4.8068	5.2338	5.6947	6.1917
11	1.5395	1.7103	1.8983	2.1049	2.3316	2.5804	2.8531	3.1518	3.4785	3.8359	4.2262	5.1173	5.6240	6.1759	6.7767	7.4301
12	1.6010	1.7959	2.0122	2.2522	2.5182	2.8127	3.1384	3.4985	3.8960	4.3345	4.8179	5.9360	6.5801	7.2876	8.0642	8.9161
13	1.6651	1.8856	2.1329	2.4098	2.7196	3.0658	3.4523	3.8833	4.3635	4.8980	5.4924	6.8858	7.6987	8.5994	9.5964	10.699
14	1.7317	1.9799	2.2609	2.5785	2.9372	3.3417	3.7975	4.3104	4.8871	5.5348	6.2613	7.9875	9.0075	10.147	11.420	12.839
15	1.8009	2.0789	2.3966	2.7590	3.1722	3.6425	4.1772	4.7846	5.4736	6.2543	7.1379	9.2655	10.539	11.974	13.590	15.407
16	1.8730	2.1829	2.5404	2.9522	3.4259	3.9703	4.5950	5.3109	6.1304	7.0673	8.1372	10.748	12.330	14.129	16.172	18.488
17	1.9479	2.2920	2.6928	3.1588	3.7000	4.3276	5.0545	5.8951	6.8660	7.9861	9.2765	12.468	14.426	16.672	19.244	22.186
18	2.0258	2.4066	2.8543	3.3799	3.9960	4.7171	5.5599	6.5436	7.6900	9.0243	10.575	14.463	16.879	19.673	22.901	26.623
19	2.1068	2.5270	3.0256	3.6165	4.3157	5.1417	6.1159	7.2633	8.6128	10.197	12.056	16.777	19.748	23.214	27.252	31.948
20	2.1911	2.6533	3.2071	3.8697	4.6610	5.6044	6.7275	8.0623	9.6463	11.523	13.743	19.461	23.106	27.393	32.429	38.338
21	2.2788	2.7860	3.3996	4.1406	5.0338	6.1088	7.4002	8.9492	10.804	13.021	15.668	22.574	27.034	32.324	38.591	46.005
22	2.3699	2.9253	3.6035	4.4304	5.4365	6.6586	8.1403	9.9336	12.100	14.714	17.861	26.186	31.629	38.142	45.923	55.206
23	2.4647	3.0715	3.8197	4.7405	5.8715	7.2579	8.9543	11.026	13.552	16.627	20.362	30.376	37.006	45.008	54.649	66.247
24	2.5633	3.2251	4.0489	5.0724	6.3412	7.9111	9.8497	12.239	15.179	18.788	23.212	35.236	43.297	53.109	65.032	79.497
25	2.6658	3.3864	4.2919	5.4274	6.8485	8.6231	10.835	13.585	17.000	21.231	26.462	40.874	50.658	62.669	77.388	95.396
26	2.7725	3.5557	4.5494	5.8074	7.3964	9.3992	11.918	15.080	19.040	23.991	30.167	47.414	59.270	73.949	92.092	114.48
27	2.8834	3.7335	4.8223	6.2139	7.9881	10.245	13.110	16.739	21.325	27.109	34.390	55.000	69.345	87.260	109.59	137.37
28	2.9987	3.9201	5.1117	6.6488	8.6271	11.167	14.421	18.580	23.884	30.633	39.204	63.800	81.134	102.97	130.41	164.84
29	3.1187	4.1161	5.4184	7.1143	9.3173	12.172	15.863	20.624	26.750	34.616	44.693	74.009	94.927	121.50	155.19	197.81
30	3.2434	4.3219	5.7435	7.6123	10.063	13.268	17.449	22.892	29.960	39.116	50.950	85.850	111.06	143.37	184.68	237.38

add it to your account balance every six months rather than every year. When they do that, it is called *compounding semi-annually* (every six months). It has the effect of letting you earn interest on your interest more frequently. Hence the future value of your initial deposit under semi-annual compounding will be greater than under annual compounding. To calculate by how much, we can work with the same formula we just used with one refinement.

If you are getting 8% compounded semi-annually, that means that at the end of every six months your balance will be paid interest for that six months equal to 4% and then that additional interest amount will be added to your balance. To reflect this idea in our formula, we just indicate the frequency of compounding in the $(1 + k)^n$ term by dividing the k term by the number of times per year that interest will be paid and keeping track of the frequency for the number of periods by modifying *n*, the exponent. So the formula becomes the following:

$$FV_n = x(1+k/m)^{mn}$$

This modification to the formula means that the interest you are paid (k) will be calculated and added to your balance m times per year. So if your bank is giving you semi-annual compounding, then m in the formula will be equal to 2. (Note that if your bank were giving you annual compounding, then m = 1 and has no effect on the result of the computation—we would be back to the basic formula for annual compounding.) Let's see how this works for the examples we just did. Your account balance at the end of the first 1/2 year would be:

$$FV_{1/2} = 100(1+.08/2)^1$$
$$= \$104$$

Your account balance at the end of one year would be:

$$FV_1 = 100(1+.08/2)^2$$
$$= \$108.16$$

Notice the consequence on the future value of your $100 of semi-annual compounding as compared to annual compounding. At the end of one year with semi-annual compounding your $100 balance is now $108.16 whereas with annual compounding it was only $108. *Thus, more frequent compounding results in higher future values.*

What would be the future value at the end of one year of your $100 deposit if your bank were to pay 8% interest compounded quarterly (every three months)? (Solve this problem on your own before consulting the following solution.) Your account balance at the end of one year would be:

$$FV_1 = 100(1+.08/4)^4$$
$$= \$108.24$$

Repeat this problem for a future value of your $100 at the end of three years.[2]

(ii)   Present Value

Now that you understand how to calculate future values, we can perform the opposite procedure to work from future values to present values. Here we ask not how much will our money today grow to in the future (what is its future value) but rather how much is some amount to be paid in the future worth today (what is its present value). This question can be asked of both some lump sum amount that you expect to receive in the future and also of some lump sum amount that you will be obligated to pay in the future. Of the first sort of questions you may ask what some investment with a fixed payment such as a bond is worth today; of the second sort of questions you may ask how much money you need to set aside today in order to pay for college for your three-year-old son.

You may have an intuitive sense that determining present values is the opposite of determining future values. To confirm that intuition, ask yourself this question: If you need to make a payment of $116.64 exactly two years from today, how much would you have to deposit in your savings account (bearing interest of 8% compounded annually) to have that amount at that time? Answer: $100. This relationship between future values and present values is the whole idea of the time value of money.

(A) Present Value of a Lump Sum

Annual Compounding. The formula for determining the present value (PV) of a lump sum (which we call x) to be paid at the end of some future year (which we again call n) is:

$$PV = x_n/(1+k)^n$$

---

2. A fascinating mathematical implication arises in the context of compounding at more and more frequent intervals. It is that as m, the frequency of compounding, approaches infinity, the term $(1 + k/m)^{mn}$ approaches e^{kn} where e is a universal constant equal to approximately 2.71828. The discovery of the universal constant e has been traced to the seventeenth century work of Mark Napier, who invented logarithms to simplify many mathematical operations. The intellectual history and practical application of e in finance and other fields is lucidly discussed in Major, e The Story of a Number (1994).

Notice that this is a mathematical confirmation of your intuition about the relationship between future values and present values. That is, in the future value formula we *multiplied* x by the $(1 + k)^n$ term and here in the present value formula we *divide* x by the $(1 + k)^n$ term. And now that term is called the *present value factor*. The result is that future values are reciprocals of present values.

A notable semantic difference between the future value and the present value formula is how we characterize k. In the future value formula and related discussion we called k the interest rate. It was the amount of interest your bank was going to pay you. In the case of present values, we call k the *discount rate* rather than the interest rate. Despite the different labels, they are both taking account of the four factors discussed in the previous essay concerning why people prefer earlier payment of a sum of money to later payment of the same sum: inflation, utility, opportunity cost and risk. More particularly, each incorporates two discrete factors. The first is the pure time value of money. It is the idea that if you had the money today you could invest it profitably in a federally-insured savings account or other risk-free instrument. The second, which we will discuss in more detail in the next essay, is the risk that you will fail to receive all or a portion of the money you expect to receive at the end of the period. The discount or interest rates are intended to compensate for each of these elements: the risk-free time value of money and the additional risk of the particular investment being considered.

Take an example of how the present value formula works. What is the present value of $100 to be received at the end of year two, assuming a discount rate of 8% compounded annually?

$$PV = 100/ (1 + .08)^2$$
$$= \$85.73$$

As with the future value calculations, there are tables that show the present value of lump sums to be paid in the future under various discount rates. Look at Table 2. All you need to do is select a discount rate and the number of years in the future until payment, and *multiply*[3] this rate by the amount of money to be received. (As with the future value table, the present value table gives the present value of $1.00 for each discount rate and time period.) For example, the present value of $100 to be received in five years discounted by 8% is: $100 × .6806 (the discount rate for $1 discounted at 8% for five years), or $68.10 (rounded up).

Compounding and Present Values. Recall that the future value of a lump sum today will be greater if compounding occurs more frequently than annually. Similarly, but with opposite effect, the present value of a lump sum to be paid in the future (or of an annuity to be paid over future time) will be lower if compounding occurs more frequently than annually. To calculate by how much, we can modify the present value formula (in an analogous way to the way we modified the future value formula). In particular, we modify the $(1 + k)^n$ term by adding a term, m, to the formula to denote the number of times per year interest is compounded, as follows:

$$PV = \frac{x_n}{(1 + k/m)^{mn}}$$

---

3. As a technical matter, you are required to multiply rather than divide because the figures set forth in Table 2 are the reciprocals of the present value factors. For example, 0.8573 (the number listed under the 8% column for 2 periods of time) represents 1 *divided by* $(1 + .08)^2$.

Table 2 Present Value of $1 due at the End of n Periods

	4%	5%	6%	7%	8%	9%	10%	11%	12%	13%	14%	16%	17%	18%	19%	20%
1	0.9615	0.9524	0.9434	0.9346	0.9259	0.9174	0.9091	0.9009	0.8929	0.8850	0.8772	0.8621	0.8547	0.8475	0.8403	0.8333
2	0.9246	0.9070	0.8900	0.8734	0.8573	0.8417	0.8264	0.8116	0.7972	0.7831	0.7695	0.7432	0.7305	0.7182	0.7062	0.6944
3	0.8890	0.8638	0.8396	0.8163	0.7938	0.7722	0.7513	0.7312	0.7118	0.6931	0.6750	0.6407	0.6244	0.6086	0.5934	0.5787
4	0.8548	0.8227	0.7921	0.7629	0.7350	0.7084	0.6830	0.6587	0.6355	0.6133	0.5921	0.5523	0.5337	0.5158	0.4987	0.4823
5	0.8219	0.7835	0.7473	0.7130	0.6806	0.6499	0.6209	0.5935	0.5674	0.5428	0.5194	0.4761	0.4561	0.4371	0.4190	0.4019
6	0.7903	0.7462	0.7050	0.6663	0.6302	0.5963	0.5645	0.5346	0.5066	0.4803	0.4556	0.4104	0.3898	0.3704	0.3521	0.3349
7	0.7599	0.7107	0.6651	0.6227	0.5835	0.5470	0.5132	0.4817	0.4523	0.4251	0.3996	0.3538	0.3332	0.3139	0.2959	0.2791
8	0.7307	0.6768	0.6274	0.5820	0.5403	0.5019	0.4665	0.4339	0.4039	0.3762	0.3506	0.3050	0.2848	0.2660	0.2487	0.2326
9	0.7026	0.6446	0.5919	0.5439	0.5002	0.4604	0.4241	0.3909	0.3606	0.3329	0.3075	0.2630	0.2434	0.2255	0.2090	0.1938
10	0.6756	0.6139	0.5584	0.5083	0.4632	0.4224	0.3855	0.3522	0.3220	0.2946	0.2697	0.2267	0.2080	0.1911	0.1756	0.1615
11	0.6496	0.5847	0.5268	0.4751	0.4289	0.3875	0.3505	0.3173	0.2875	0.2607	0.2366	0.1954	0.1778	0.1619	0.1476	0.1346
12	0.6246	0.5568	0.4970	0.4440	0.3971	0.3555	0.3186	0.2858	0.2567	0.2307	0.2076	0.1685	0.1520	0.1372	0.1240	0.1122
13	0.6006	0.5303	0.4688	0.4150	0.3677	0.3262	0.2897	0.2575	0.2292	0.2042	0.1821	0.1452	0.1299	0.1163	0.1042	0.0935
14	0.5775	0.5051	0.4423	0.3878	0.3405	0.2992	0.2633	0.2320	0.2046	0.1807	0.1597	0.1252	0.1110	0.0985	0.0876	0.0779
15	0.5553	0.4810	0.4173	0.3624	0.3152	0.2745	0.2394	0.2090	0.1827	0.1599	0.1401	0.1079	0.0949	0.0835	0.0736	0.0649
16	0.5339	0.4581	0.3936	0.3387	0.2919	0.2519	0.2176	0.1883	0.1631	0.1415	0.1229	0.0930	0.0811	0.0708	0.0618	0.0541
17	0.5134	0.4363	0.3714	0.3166	0.2703	0.2311	0.1978	0.1696	0.1456	0.1252	0.1078	0.0802	0.0693	0.0600	0.0520	0.0451
18	0.4936	0.4155	0.3503	0.2959	0.2502	0.2120	0.1799	0.1528	0.1300	0.1108	0.0946	0.0691	0.0592	0.0508	0.0437	0.0376
19	0.4746	0.3957	0.3305	0.2765	0.2317	0.1945	0.1635	0.1377	0.1161	0.0981	0.0829	0.0596	0.0506	0.0431	0.0367	0.0313
20	0.4564	0.3769	0.3118	0.2584	0.2145	0.1784	0.1486	0.1240	0.1037	0.0868	0.0728	0.0514	0.0433	0.0365	0.0308	0.0261
21	0.4388	0.3589	0.2942	0.2415	0.1987	0.1637	0.1351	0.1117	0.0926	0.0768	0.0638	0.0443	0.0370	0.0309	0.0259	0.0217
22	0.4220	0.3418	0.2775	0.2257	0.1839	0.1502	0.1228	0.1007	0.0826	0.0680	0.0560	0.0382	0.0316	0.0262	0.0218	0.0181
23	0.4057	0.3256	0.2618	0.2109	0.1703	0.1378	0.1117	0.0907	0.0738	0.0601	0.0491	0.0329	0.0270	0.0222	0.0183	0.0151
24	0.3901	0.3101	0.2470	0.1971	0.1577	0.1264	0.1015	0.0817	0.0659	0.0532	0.0431	0.0284	0.0231	0.0188	0.0154	0.0126
25	0.3751	0.2953	0.2330	0.1842	0.1460	0.1160	0.0923	0.0736	0.0588	0.0471	0.0378	0.0245	0.0197	0.0160	0.0129	0.0105
26	0.3607	0.2812	0.2198	0.1722	0.1352	0.1064	0.0839	0.0663	0.0525	0.0417	0.0331	0.0211	0.0169	0.0135	0.0109	0.0087
27	0.3468	0.2678	0.2074	0.1609	0.1252	0.0976	0.0763	0.0597	0.0469	0.0369	0.0291	0.0182	0.0144	0.0115	0.0091	0.0073
28	0.3335	0.2551	0.1956	0.1504	0.1159	0.0895	0.0693	0.0538	0.0419	0.0326	0.0255	0.0157	0.0123	0.0097	0.0077	0.0061
29	0.3207	0.2429	0.1846	0.1406	0.1073	0.0822	0.0630	0.0485	0.0374	0.0289	0.0224	0.0135	0.0105	0.0082	0.0064	0.0051
30	0.3083	0.2314	0.1741	0.1314	0.0994	0.0754	0.0573	0.0437	0.0334	0.0256	0.0196	0.0116	0.0090	0.0070	0.0054	0.0042

Let's try another example. What is the present value of a lump sum of $100 to be received at the end of year two, assuming a discount rate of 8% compounded semi-annually?

$$PV = \frac{100}{(1 + .08/2)^{2 \times 2}}$$
$$= \$85.48$$

Notice the consequence for present values of semi-annual compounding as compared to annual compounding. The present value of a lump sum payment of $100 at the end of two years was $85.73 under annual compounding (discussed above) but with semi-annual compounding it declines to $85.48. As we would expect, this is the opposite of what happens when future values are compounded more often than annually.

(B) Present Value of an Annuity

Now that you have mastered the basic concept of present value with respect to a lump sum to be paid in the future, consider the slightly more complicated problem of determining the present value of a *stream of payments* over time. For example, what is the present value of the right to receive $10 at the *end* of each of the next five years?

The payment of a constant sum at fixed intervals over a period of years is called an *annuity*. The cash flows in an *ordinary annuity* occur at the *end* of each period (in "arrears"). Thus, an ordinary annuity is also called a "deferred" annuity. The cash flows of an *annuity due*, by contrast, occur at the *beginning* of each period.

(1) Ordinary Annuity

Annual Compounding. It should be evident that determining the present value of an annuity requires calculating the present values of each payment. You could therefore determine the present value of an annuity by applying the basic present value formula as follows:

$$PV = \frac{x_1}{(1 + k)^1} + \frac{x_2}{(1 + k)^2} + \frac{x_3}{(1 + k)^3} + \cdots + \frac{x_n}{(1 + k)^n}$$

thus determining the present value for each individual payment and adding them together. We could then express the formula more simply, using the summation (capital Sigma) symbol:

$$PV_a = \sum \frac{x_n}{(1 + k)^n}$$

Alternatively, you could determine the present value of each payment using Table 2 and add them together. Once again, lucky us, tables have been developed to give us the present value factor to apply to annuity payments. As a result, the easiest way to calculate the present value of an annuity is to use Table 3. It sets forth the present value of annuity payments in much the same way that Table 2 sets forth the present value of lump sum payments.

To use Table 3, all you need to do is select a discount rate and the number of years over which the future payments are to be made, and *multiply* this rate by the amount of money to be received. For example, the present value of $10 to be received at the end of each of the next five years discounted by 8% is: $10 × 3.9927 (the present value factor for $1 to be paid at the end of the next five years, discounted at 8%), or $39.93.

Many investments contain both the promise of a lump sum payment and the promise of an annuity. To calculate the present value of such instruments, one values the lump sum component using the present value Table 2 as described above and then separately values the annuity component using the present value Table 3 as described above. Then, the two present values are added together. For example, a $100 bond with a maturity date of five years that pays interest of $10 per year at the end of each of the next five years has a present value equal to the sum of $68.06 (the present value of the lump sum component) plus $39.93 (the present value of the annuity component) or a total of $108.00.

Compounding and the Ordinary Annuity. What if an annuity calculation assumed more frequent compounding than annual? Suppose interest was compounded semi-annually? How would this affect the calculation? Based on what we know about discounting, more frequent compounding would result in a lower present value than that calculated using less frequent compounding.

Let's assume that an ordinary annuity pays $150,000 per year during a ten-year period, and that the interest rate is 8% compounded semi-annually. Calculating the PV of an ordinary annuity based on compounding more frequent than annual is a two-step process. First, you must determine what the effective annual interest rate (EAIR) is, because a portion of the annual interest is being compounded. EAIR is calculated as follows:

$$EAIR = (1 + k/m)^m - 1$$

where: k is the annual interest rate
            m is the number of compounding periods per year

Table 3   Present Value of an Annuity of $1 per Period for n Periods

	4%	5%	6%	7%	8%	9%	10%	11%	12%	13%	14%	16%	17%	18%	19%	20%
1	0.9615	0.9524	0.9434	0.9346	0.9259	0.9174	0.9091	0.9009	0.8929	0.8850	0.8772	0.8621	0.8547	0.8475	0.8403	0.8333
2	1.8861	1.8594	1.8334	1.8080	1.7833	1.7591	1.7355	1.7125	1.6901	1.6681	1.6467	1.6052	1.5852	1.5656	1.5465	1.5278
3	2.7751	2.7232	2.6730	2.6243	2.5771	2.5313	2.4869	2.4437	2.4018	2.3612	2.3216	2.2459	2.2096	2.1743	2.1399	2.1065
4	3.6299	3.5460	3.4651	3.3872	3.3121	3.2397	3.1699	3.1024	3.0373	2.9745	2.9137	2.7982	2.7432	2.6901	2.6386	2.5887
5	4.4518	4.3295	4.2124	4.1002	3.9927	3.8897	3.7908	3.6959	3.6048	3.5172	3.4331	3.2743	3.1993	3.1272	3.0576	2.9906
6	5.2421	5.0757	4.9173	4.7665	4.6229	4.4859	4.3553	4.2305	4.1114	3.9975	3.8887	3.6847	3.5892	3.4976	3.4098	3.3255
7	6.0021	5.7864	5.5824	5.3893	5.2064	5.0330	4.8684	4.7122	4.5638	4.4226	4.2883	4.0386	3.9224	3.8115	3.7057	3.6046
8	6.7327	6.4632	6.2098	5.9713	5.7466	5.5348	5.3349	5.1461	4.9676	4.7988	4.6389	4.3436	4.2072	4.0776	3.9544	3.8372
9	7.4353	7.1078	6.8017	6.5152	6.2469	5.9952	5.7590	5.5370	5.3282	5.1317	4.9464	4.6065	4.4506	4.3030	4.1633	4.0310
10	8.1109	7.7217	7.3601	7.0236	6.7101	6.4177	6.1446	5.8892	5.6502	5.4262	5.2161	4.8332	4.6586	4.4941	4.3389	4.1925
11	8.7605	8.3064	7.8869	7.4987	7.1390	6.8052	6.4951	6.2065	5.9377	5.6869	5.4527	5.0286	4.8364	4.6560	4.4865	4.3271
12	9.3851	8.8633	8.3838	7.9427	7.5361	7.1607	6.8137	6.4924	6.1944	5.9176	5.6603	5.1971	4.9884	4.7932	4.6105	4.4392
13	9.9856	9.3936	8.8527	8.3577	7.9038	7.4869	7.1034	6.7499	6.4235	6.1218	5.8424	5.3423	5.1183	4.9095	4.7147	4.5327
14	10.5631	9.8986	9.2950	8.7455	8.2442	7.7862	7.3667	6.9819	6.6282	6.3025	6.0021	5.4675	5.2293	5.0081	4.8023	4.6106
15	11.1184	10.3797	9.7122	9.1079	8.5595	8.0607	7.6061	7.1909	6.8109	6.4624	6.1422	5.5755	5.3242	5.0916	4.8759	4.6755
16	11.6523	10.8378	10.1059	9.4466	8.8514	8.3126	7.8237	7.3792	6.9740	6.6039	6.2651	5.6685	5.4053	5.1624	4.9377	4.7296
17	12.1657	11.2741	10.4773	9.7632	9.1216	8.5436	8.0216	7.5488	7.1196	6.7291	6.3729	5.7487	5.4746	5.2223	4.9897	4.7746
18	12.6593	11.6896	10.8276	10.0591	9.3719	8.7556	8.2014	7.7016	7.2497	6.8399	6.4674	5.8178	5.5339	5.2732	5.0333	4.8122
19	13.1339	12.0853	11.1581	10.3356	9.6036	8.9501	8.3649	7.8393	7.3658	6.9380	6.5504	5.8775	5.5845	5.3162	5.0700	4.8435
20	13.5903	12.4622	11.4699	10.5940	9.8181	9.1285	8.5136	7.9633	7.4694	7.0248	6.6231	5.9288	5.6278	5.3527	5.1009	4.8696
21	14.0292	12.8212	11.7641	10.8355	10.0168	9.2922	8.6487	8.0751	7.5620	7.1016	6.6870	5.9731	5.6648	5.3837	5.1268	4.8913
22	14.4511	13.1630	12.0416	11.0612	10.2007	9.4424	8.7715	8.1757	7.6446	7.1695	6.7429	6.0113	5.6964	5.4099	5.1486	4.9094
23	14.8568	13.4886	12.3034	11.2722	10.3711	9.5802	8.8832	8.2664	7.7184	7.2297	6.7921	6.0442	5.7234	5.4321	5.1668	4.9245
24	15.2470	13.7986	12.5504	11.4693	10.5288	9.7066	8.9847	8.3481	7.7843	7.2829	6.8351	6.0726	5.7465	5.4509	5.1822	4.9371
25	15.6221	14.0939	12.7834	11.6536	10.6748	9.8226	9.0770	8.4217	7.8431	7.3300	6.8729	6.0971	5.7662	5.4669	5.1951	4.9476
26	15.9828	14.3752	13.0032	11.8258	10.8100	9.9290	9.1609	8.4881	7.8957	7.3717	6.9061	6.1182	5.7831	5.4804	5.2060	4.9563
27	16.3296	14.6430	13.2105	11.9867	10.9352	10.0266	9.2372	8.5478	7.9426	7.4086	6.9352	6.1364	5.7975	5.4919	5.2151	4.9636
28	16.6631	14.8981	13.4062	12.1371	11.0511	10.1161	9.3066	8.6016	7.9844	7.4412	6.9607	6.1520	5.8099	5.5016	5.2228	4.9697
29	16.9837	15.1411	13.5907	12.2777	11.1584	10.1983	9.3696	8.6501	8.0218	7.4701	6.9830	6.1656	5.8204	5.5098	5.2292	4.9747
30	17.2920	15.3725	13.7648	12.4090	11.2578	10.2737	9.4269	8.6938	8.0552	7.4957	7.0027	6.1772	5.8294	5.5168	5.2347	4.9789

Thus, when the annual interest rate is 8% and compounding is semi-annual, EAIR is calculated as follows:

$$EAIR = (1 + .08/2)^2 - 1$$
$$= .0816$$

The second step of the calculation is to perform the regular calculation for an ordinary annuity, except you now replace "k" with "EAIR." However, because EAIR is unlikely to be a whole number, you must use a *financial calculator* rather than the table to perform the calculation:

$$PV_a = \sum \frac{\$150,000}{(1 + .0816)^{10}}$$
$$= \$150,000 \times 6.6619$$
$$= \$999,285$$

How does this result compare to the same calculation done based on *annual* compounding? Upon doing the math, you would see that the calculation done based on annual compounding is $7,230 more than if interest was compounded semi-annually. Because more frequent compounding yields lower present values, this result is not surprising.

(2) Annuity Due

The cash flows in an ordinary annuity occur at the end of each period (in "*arrears*"). Annuities where the cash flows occur at the *beginning* of each period are called *annuities due.* Thus, while the same number of payments are received in an ordinary annuity and an annuity due, the first payment in the annuity due is received *one time period earlier.* Because of this, the present value of the cash flow of an annuity due is exactly one interest payment *greater* than the present value of an ordinary annuity. Therefore, an annuity due is more valuable to the holder than an ordinary annuity.

In an annuity due, each payment is discounted for one less period. Thus, to calculate the present value of an annuity due, simply multiply the present value of an *ordinary* annuity by 1 plus the interest rate:

$$PV_{ad} = \sum \frac{x_n}{(1 + k)^n} \cdot (1 + k)$$

Notice the difference in present values below when the facts of the previous example involving $150,000 annual payments are applied to a series of cash flows that occur at the beginning of the period rather than at the end:

Period	Cash Flow	Rate	Factor Ordinary Annuity	Factor Annuity Due	Amount* Ordinary Annuity	Amount* Annuity Due
1	$150,000	8%	0.92593	1.00000	$ 138,890	$ 150,000
2	$150,000	8%	0.85734	0.92593	128,601	138,890
3	$150,000	8%	0.79383	0.85734	119,075	128,601
4	$150,000	8%	0.73503	0.79383	110,255	119,075
5	$150,000	8%	0.68058	0.73503	102,088	110,255
6	$150,000	8%	0.63017	0.68058	94,525	102,088
7	$150,000	8%	0.58349	0.63017	87,525	94,525
8	$150,000	8%	0.54027	0.58349	81,040	87,525
9	$150,000	8%	0.50025	0.54027	75,037	81,040
10	$150,000	8%	0.46319	0.50025	69,479	75,037
					$1,006,515	$1,087,036

* Amounts may be off by $1 due to rounding errors

Study the Tables. It will repay studying the accompanying Tables to get a feel for the relationship between future values and changes in interest rates, the relationship between present values and changes in discount rates and the relationship between present values and future values. For example, notice that the future values given in Table 1 are the *reciprocals* of the present values given in Table 2. For another example, notice that the higher the discount rate, the lower the present value; and the higher the interest rate, the greater the future value. Select any "Year" line on the present value table and look across at the present value of $1 at different discount rates. The higher the discount rate, the lower the present value. The reason, again, is that discount rates reflect the opportunity cost of capital. The higher the rate of return available to you today, the more value you have sacrificed in waiting to receive your payment.

Note on Inflation and Taxes. The foregoing discussion of the future value formula, the present value formula and the related Tables has addressed the effects of inflation by factoring the anticipated rate of inflation into the interest rate or discount rate. We have not, however, factored in taxes. This is deliberate. To be more accurate, we would need to consider whether differential tax treatments affect the results. This complex subject is beyond the scope of our present discussion.

Problems

Most of the following problems can be answered by direct reference to the various Tables discussed above and accompanying this essay, although a couple require additional calculations using the formulas discussed above. In each case, make your calculations without regard to any potential effect of inflation or taxes.

1. Rachel is a thirty-five-year-old lawyer who has just been informed by her precocious 8-year-old son Josh that he wishes to attend Yale when he graduates from high school ten years from now. Assume Rachel now has $10,000 in a savings account, paying 10% interest compounded annually. What will her balance be when Josh graduates, assuming no deposits or withdrawals? What would her balance be if interest were compounded semi-annually instead of annually?

2. X Corp. has obtained a twenty-five year mortgage on land that it just acquired. The mortgage terms call for a balloon payment of $125,000 due at the end of the twenty-fifth year. How much money does X Corp. have to deposit in a savings account today to have enough on deposit to make the balloon payment, assuming it expects to receive 8%, compounded annually, on its savings?

3. Joe owns a retail store and has $25,000 of accounts receivable, due in one year. However, Joe needs cash now, so he contacts Harry who is seeking to invest some cash. Harry agrees to buy Joe's receivables. They agree that the receivables will be discounted at 12% (which incorporates the rate Harry could get at a bank plus a risk premium to compensate Harry in case some of Joe's customers are deadbeats). What price will Harry pay for the receivables?

4. Y Corp. is starting a retirement fund for its employees. It estimates that total annual disbursements to retired employees to be paid out of the fund will be $32,000 for each of the next ten years. If the retirement fund will earn 9% compounded annually and the payments will be made at the end of each year, how much will Y Corp. have to contribute to the fund now to make the estimated payments over the next ten years?

5(a). Lucky Laura received a letter from Fred McCann notifying her that she has just won third prize in a major sweepstakes. Fred gives Laura a choice of two prizes: $15,000 in cash awarded immediately or $1,800 in cash paid at the end of each year for the next ten years. Assume that Lucky Laura would deposit the $1,800 annual payments in a bank account earning 12% compounded annually. Which prize should Laura choose?

5(b). What would your answer be if the interest on Lucky Laura's savings account were compounded semi-annually instead of annually?

c. Risk as a Function of Probability

Economists and others are fond of saying that "there is no such thing as a free lunch." The fact that differences exist among rates of return on various investments leads one to suspect that there must be a reason. And there is a reason: risk. One of the things one sacrifices in foregoing a payment today in favor of a payment in the future is the security of having the money in hand. Certain investments, called *risk-free investments*, provide the functional equivalent, by providing security that the expected return will materialize as the actual return.[1] The greater the risk that some or all of the expected return will not be paid, the higher the return an investor will demand for making the investment. The size of this increase in return over the risk-free rate, called the *risk premium*, obviously will vary depending upon the riskiness of the particular investment. It is thus important to factor risk into our calculations of value.[2]

Risk is defined in *The American Heritage Dictionary* as "the possibility of suffering harm or loss." It is the chance that something bad will happen and is a fact of life in a friction-filled world. You take chances throughout your life and virtually every day: when you tried out for the varsity team in high school, when you applied to law school, when you go waterskiing, when you go mountain climbing, when you bet money on the Super Bowl or the World Series, and indeed, when you invest money, whether in education, real estate or public capital markets. When you buy a share of common stock, you take a risk of losing all or part of your investment. You take the risk of suffering harm or loss in exchange for the possibility of enjoying some benefit or gain.[3]

Different kinds of investments pose different degrees of risk. Consider an investment of $20,000 used to buy short-term government bonds having a yield to maturity of 10%. Government bonds are considered to be risk-free investments because the chance of default is virtually zero—even in times of Federal budget deadlocks. As a result, the 10% yield to maturity on the bonds is a very good estimate of its expected rate of return.

In contrast, consider an investment of $20,000 in a new corporation one of your law school friends has formed to buy and operate a restaurant and nightclub near the law school campus. The return on this investment is harder to estimate. Your friend may tell you that, as a statistical matter based on comparable start-up businesses, the *expected* rate of return on your investment is 20%. But, your friend's statistical acumen and entrepreneurial skills notwithstanding, who knows whether the joint will boom or

---

1. Risk-free investments are traditionally understood as either obligations of the United States federal government or private obligations guaranteed by the United States federal government (such as federally insured savings accounts up to $100,000). As the savings and loan debacle of the late 1980s suggests, these obligations are not entirely risk *free* (*see* The Junkification of American T-bonds, Economist, May 27, 1989, at 77), but the risk of loss is considered to be so low that no risk premium (defined in the following essay) need be paid to induce people to make such investments. Consequently, the return on such an investment is said to reflect the pure time value of money.

2. There are many different types of risk that can affect the expected return on a security, but they can be classified into two categories. The first category involves risk not specific to the particular corporation, such as market risk, which is associated with fluctuations in the market as a whole. These fluctuations can be caused by a bad economic forecast, political turmoil or general pessimism as to the expected performance of the market. Other types of risks in this category are: interest-rate risk, which is caused by changes in the interest rates paid on government securities, and purchasing-power risk or the uncertainty of the value of money based on the inflation rate.

The second category is risk which is particular to a corporation or a specific industry. Such risk consists of business risk and financial risk. Business risk can be subdivided into external and internal business risk. External business risk is risk that is caused by outside influences such as government regulations on a specific industry. Internal business risk is that associated with the operating efficiency of a corporation. Financial risk involves the strategy used by a corporation to finance its business. *See generally* Fischer & Jordan, Security Analysis and Portfolio Management 70-76 (6th ed. 1995). We will examine the consequences of distinguishing these types of risk in section 5a.

3. A distinction can be drawn between the *risk* that is involved with investing and the *uncertainty* of investing. "'Risk' is ... used to refer to variation depending purely on chance ... or, more broadly, to measurements as to which there is a large body of data or experience so that the probable outcomes can be estimated in a purely mechanical way. 'Uncertainty,' by contrast, refers to estimates made in situations where there is so little experience that the process of estimation is highly intuitive." Klein and Coffee, Business Organization and Finance 241 (9th ed. 2004).

bust? In other words, there is some chance that the venture will be splashingly success-ful but there is also some chance that it will never get off the ground. So your *actual* re-turn on the investment could range from losing your $20,000 investment entirely (a 100% loss) to quadrupling it (a 400% gain) or even better. It is this chance that your *ac-tual* return could be substantially below the *expected* return that makes this investment *relatively risky* or *speculative*.

As a matter of intuition, therefore, gauging the relative risk of this and other invest-ments depends on the probability of earning a rate of return lower than the expected re-turn. The more probable it is that your actual return will be lower than the expected re-turn, the more risky the investment is said to be. This intuition can be formalized in more precise terms to express a measurement of the relative risk of an investment in terms of probabilities.

Probability is simply a way to measure the chance that something will occur or not occur. Weather forecasters make probabilistic statements all the time. For example, they might say: "There is a 40% chance that it will rain tomorrow, a 35% chance that it will snow tomorrow and a 25% chance that it will be dry (no precipitation) tomorrow." The universe of possible future events can then be arrayed for analysis along what is called a *probability distribution*. A simple probability distribution of the foregoing weather fore-cast about precipitation would be as follows:

Event	Probability
Rain	.40
Snow	.35
Dry	.25
	1.00

This simple example lists under the event column all possible states of the world (rain, snow or dry) and the probability of each state occurring (.40, .35 and .25, the decimal equivalents of the percentage chance of each event occurring). The probabilities of each state of the world sum to 1, since all possible states of the world are being forecasted (we are ignoring for the moment gradations of precipitation such as sleet and hail).

We can adapt this very simple example to the context of investments in common stock. Let us compare two alternative investments, one in the common stock of The Bionic Computer Company ("Bionic") and one in the common stock of Burgers Are Us, Inc. ("Burgers"). Bionic designs, manufactures and distributes high-tech computer software for the high-end of the telecommunications industry. That is a growth industry whose de-mand for Bionic's products fluctuates as the business cycle ebbs and flows. As a result, Bionic's sales are also cyclical, its profits fluctuate with the business cycle and dividend payments are sporadic. Bionic's market is extremely competitive and a new entrant into the market with superior software products could send Bionic into a business tailspin.

Burgers owns and operates a chain of fast-food stores with thousands of outlets throughout North America. In several regions, it is the dominant seller of burgers and faces virtually no serious competition in those regions and only limited competition in its other regions. Burgers is also virtually immune from the business cycle (its fare is whole-some and inexpensive) and so its sales, profits and dividend payments are stable over time.

We can compose probability distributions for the rates of return for Bionic and Burgers. We can stipulate that the events that bear on the rates of return are states of the economy over the next year (the analogue to states of the weather tomorrow). We can draw on eco-nomic forecasts that are publicly available and determine, let us assume, that there is a

Table 4   Probability Distributions for Bionic and Burgers

		Rates of Return Given Event	
Event	Probability (P_i)	Bionic (k_i)	Burgers (k_i)
Boom	.40	100%	30%
Normal	.25	15	15
Bust	.35	−70	10
	1.00		

40% chance that the economy will boom this upcoming year, a 35% chance that it will bust and a 25% that it will be normal (neither boom nor bust).

In a boom economy, Bionic and Burgers will both have higher earnings and pay higher dividends compared to a normal economy. In a bust economy, both will have lower earnings and pay lower dividends compared to a normal economy. But given the nature of the businesses in which these two companies operate, Bionic will do smashingly well in a boom economy compared to a normal economy but also face grave difficulties in a bust economy. In contrast, Burgers will do only somewhat better in a boom economy than it would in a normal economy and only slightly worse in a bust economy than in a normal economy. As a result, Bionic's rate of return can vary far more widely than Burgers's rate of return. Let's say that it can range from 100% in a boom economy to 270% in a bust economy, whereas Burgers's rate of return can range from 30% in a boom economy to 10% in a bust economy. Table 4 depicts this information in a probability distribution.

All we have done so far is shown how actual rates of return could vary on each of these investments depending on probabilities of future states of the economy. What we really want to know, however, is the expected rates of return on each of these investments. Calculating expected rates of return requires two steps. First, multiply each possible outcome (that is, the rates of return given each event as shown in the right-hand column of Table 4 for each of Bionic and Burgers separately) by the probability of the occurrence of each event (i.e., of a boom, normal or bust economy). Second, add together the results.

These two steps can be expressed by the following formula, where k is the expected rate of return, P_i is the probability of each event (each event being called the $_i$th event) and k_i is the rate of return given each separate event:

$$k = \sum_{i=1}^{n} P_i k_i$$

This formula is therefore a calculation of the weighted average of the probabilities, which is the *expected rate of return*, given by k. Using this formula for Bionic works as follows:

$$k = (P_1)(k_1) + (P_2)(k_2) + (P_3)(k_3)$$
$$= (.40)(100) + (.25)(15) + (.35)(-70)$$
$$= 40 + 3.75 + (-24.50)$$
$$= 19.25\%$$

For Burgers, it works this way:

$$k = (P_1)(k_1) + (P_2)(k_2) + (P_3)(k_3)$$
$$= (.40)(30) + (.25)(15) + (.35)(10)$$
$$= 12 + 3.75 + (3.50)$$
$$= 19.25\%$$

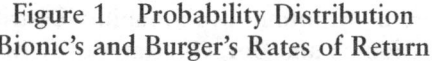

Figure 1   Probability Distribution
Bionic's and Burger's Rates of Return

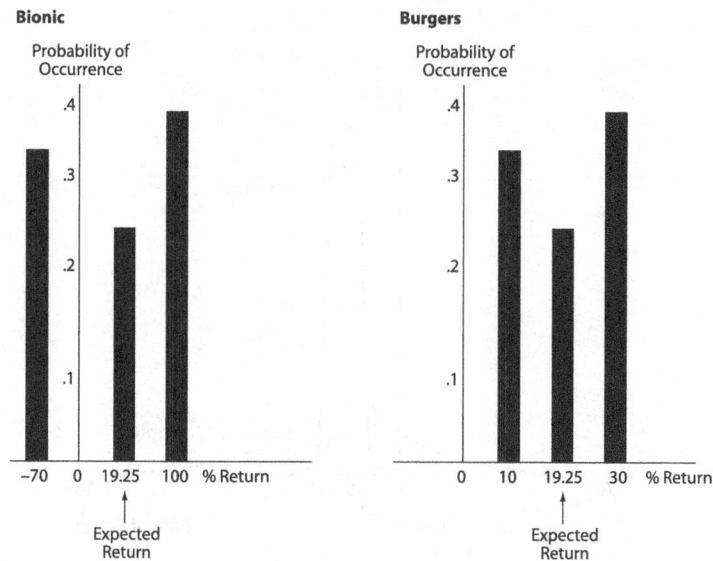

Notice that the expected rates of return on the common stock of Bionic and Burgers are the same, even though as the probability distribution table (Table 4) shows, the variation in the possible returns differs significantly. A comparison of the expected rates of return and this variation in range can be depicted graphically in images using bar charts, as shown in Figure 1. The height of each bar depicts the probability of the occurrence of each outcome given each event. The expected return for each of Bionic and Burgers is 19.25%, but the range of probable returns for Bionic is from 100% to -70%, whereas the range for Burgers is far narrower (from 10% to 30%).

We noted above that these probability distributions could be created when all states of the world (in terms of our events) were defined. In our weather example, we assumed that the universe of meteorological states of the world was exhausted by the set rain, snow or dry and noted that we were in effect ignoring sleet, hail and other grades of precipitation. Similarly, in our Bionic and Burgers example we have assumed that the universe of economic states of the world was exhausted by the set boom, bust or normal. In fact, however, in each of these contexts the gradations can be much more refined. We could assign separate probabilities to a whole series of possible weather patterns, from blizzard, to thunderstorm, to hail storm, to drizzle, to overcast, to bright and sunny and we could do the same for a whole range of economic conditions from economic bubbles, to robust growth, to modest growth, to weak growth, to recession or to depression.

When we do this fine tuning, we can create what are called *continuous probability distributions*. To do this, we assign a probability to every possible state of the economy in a series of fine gradations ranging from hyperboom to hyperbust, with the sum of all probabilities still being equal to 1.0. We also define a rate of return on each stock for each state of the economy. Then we can use the formula we used in the three-states-of-the-world

Figure 2   Continuous Probability Distribution
Bionic's and Burgers' Rates of Return

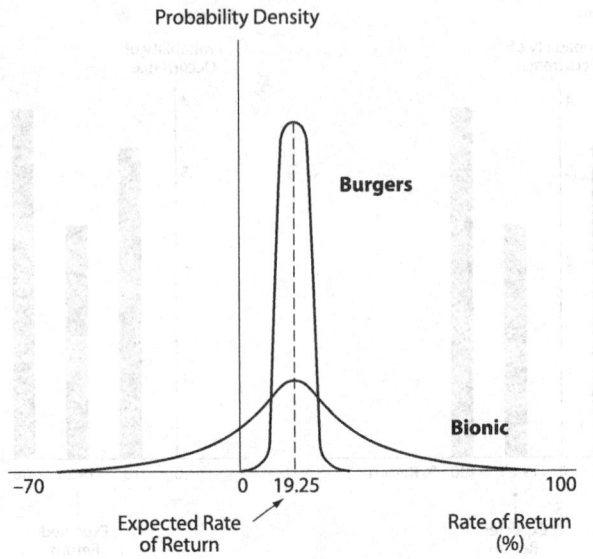

model but now will be calculating many more equations. The results when depicted graphically will appear as a continuous curve rather than the bar charts that reflected just three equations. Figure 2 shows what we mean.

Continuous probability distribution curves having a tighter, or more peaked, band are those in which the probability of the actual return being close to the expected return is relatively high. A broader or more flattened band indicates a lower probability that the actual return will be close to the expected return. In other words, the tighter and more peaked a probability distribution, the less risk exists in the investment depicted and the broader and more flattened a probability distribution, the greater risk exists in the investment depicted. In our example, Burgers's probability distribution curve shows that Burgers's common stock is a less risky investment than Bionic's common stock.

While the graphical depictions of the range of possible rates of return on Bionic and Burgers common stock give us a good sense of the related risk, it would be more helpful if we could quantify that risk in a simple numerical form that could be used to compare risks across a range of investments. What we are looking for is a way to measure the graphical notion that tighter probability distributions of expected returns imply smaller total risks of an investment than broader ones, and vice versa. A simple way to do this is to use what statisticians call the *standard deviation*.

The standard deviation is calculated by the following steps. First, the expected return is calculated as described above (in the case of Burgers and Bionics in the three-states-of-the-world model, 19.25%). Second, the expected rate of return is subtracted from each possible outcome, both those above and below the expected rate of return (also as done above for Burgers and Bionics). Third, in order that all these results can be summed together, each result is squared (with the result that negative numbers will become positive so that the results can be summed). Fourth, each such "deviation" is multiplied by the probability of its occurrence. Fifth, add up those results. At this point, we have what statisticians call the *variance*. The final step is to take the square root of the variance, and this result is the standard deviation.

The standard deviation, usually denoted by σ (lower case sigma), thus provides a uniform benchmark with which to compare the risk of different investments. Technically, it is a probability-weighted average deviation from the expected return. More intuitively, it gives a measure of the dispersion of the actual returns around the expected return—in short, it is a measure of risk that can be usefully compared across investments. Since tighter and more peaked probability distributions exhibit less dispersion of actual returns around the expected return, they will have smaller standard deviations. Conversely, broader and more flattened probability distributions will have larger standard deviations. In our example, the standard deviation of Bionics is about 65% and the standard deviaton of Burgers is about 4%. As such, Bionics stock would be said to be more risky and more volatile and Burgers stock would be said to be less risky and less volatile.[4]

For purposes of an intuitive sense of the relationship between standard deviation and various investments about which you may have some familiarity, consider the following data. From January 1999 through December 2003, the standard deviations of the common stock of ExxonMobil and Heinz were about 18% and 24%, respectively; Ford and Microsoft were about 44% and 48%, respectively; and Dell and Amazon.com were about 53% and 73%, respectively. *See* Brealey, Myers & Allen, Principles of Corporate Finance 160, Table 7.3 (8th ed. 2006).

Section 3
Valuation Methods:
Putting Risk and Return to Work

Now that you understand the basic elements of valuation—risk and return—we can turn to the actual process of valuing a share of common stock using these tools. Several different valuation models are used by analysts, investors and judges and lawyers. Among these are (1) balance sheet based methods such as book value, adjusted book value and net asset value, (2) income statement based methods such as the capitalization of earnings and (3) cash flow based methods such as the dividend discount model (DDM) and discounted cash flow (DCF) analysis. Each of these methods seeks to determine the "intrinsic" value of the stock, referred to in section 1b. We will elaborate on each of these methods after providing a short overview of accounting concepts and presenting a problem which will be used to operationalize and critique these valuation methods.

---

4. You may be wondering whether this concept of standard deviation is really a precise measure of risk at least as risk is being defined in terms of the chance that an actual return turns out to be less than the expected return. After all, standard deviation measures dispersion of returns in both directions—that is both actual returns below expected returns and actual returns greater than expected returns. There are two answers to your wonder. First, there are more refined ways of calculating only the chances of actual returns being less than expected returns (they are called semivariance measures) but they are a lot harder to work with than standard deviations. Second, if the probability distribution is fairly symmetric (as our examples of Bionic and Burgers are and as are most investment alternatives), then standard deviation remains a pretty good measure (and is exactly as good as any semivariance measure).

a. A Brief Introduction to Basic Accounting Principles

Throughout this book, we encounter various accounting terms and financial statements. A few introductory words concerning these terms and statements are in order.

Accountants have devised three basic forms to present financial information: the balance sheet, the income statement, and the statement of cash flows. These documents report the financial and other information necessary for shareholders, creditors, and anyone else who deals with the business to evaluate the entity's financial condition and performance.

The financial statements are prepared from the internal day-to-day records of the entity by the employees and managers of the entity. The day-to-day records are maintained by recording the financial transactions in which the entity engages each day. Those daily transactions are periodically summarized, usually at the end of each month, then quarterly, and then cumulatively at the end of each year. The annual financial statements in turn usually form a part of an annual report that also includes a narrative commentary on the financial condition and performance of the entity for the year and summary reports of other statistical data.

The balance sheet is like a snapshot of an entity at a specific date. It is intended to reflect the *financial condition* of that entity *as of that specific date*. It lists the entity's assets as of a specified date and the entity's liabilities as of that date and then shows the difference between these totals. *Assets* are probable future economic benefits obtained or controlled by an entity resulting from past transactions or events. *Liabilities* are probable future sacrifices of economic benefits arising from present obligations to transfer assets or render services in the future. *Equity* is the difference between assets and liabilities (and is sometimes also called *book value* or *net worth*). It represents the ownership claims on the firm.

As a matter of convention, the assets are listed on the balance sheet in the order of their *liquidity*, beginning with cash (the very definition of liquid), and going through to such relatively illiquid assets as real property, and other things not expected to be converted into cash for a significant period of time. Similarly, the liabilities are listed on the balance sheet beginning with obligations having the shortest due date (such as accounts payable, usually due in 30 days) through those with the longest due date (such as long-term bonds, often not due for 10 or more years). The owners' equity is listed next and it will always equal the total assets minus the total liabilities.

The income statement is like a motion picture of the enterprise over a defined period of time, such as one year, and is intended to reflect the *financial performance* of the entity *during that period of time*. It lists the total revenues generated by the entity during the period; the total expenses incurred by the entity during that period; and the difference between these totals. *Revenues* are increases in equity resulting from asset increases and/or liability decreases from delivering goods or services or other activities that constitute the entity's ongoing major or central operations. They include sales of merchandise, fees for services, commission received on transactions and so on. *Expenses* are decreases in equity from asset decreases or liability increases from delivering goods or services, or carrying out any activities which constitute the entity's ongoing major or central operations. They include the costs of goods made or bought for sale, and costs associated with marketing and selling and administrative affairs.

The difference between revenue and expense during each reporting period is called the entity's *net income* for the period (or, when expenses exceed revenues, the *net loss*).

It measures the financial performance of the entity during the period. The net income is also referred to as *earnings* and can be broken down according to the portion allocable to each ownership interest in the entity, a breakdown called *earnings per share*. Items included in net income are sometimes displayed in various classifications, including income from continuing operations, income from discontinued operations, extraordinary items, or income due to the cumulative effect of changes in accounting principles. Income (or loss) ultimately leads to changes in owners' equity.

The cash flow statement is also like a motion picture of the entity over the same period covered by the income statement, only the lens of the camera is more focused. It lists the total cash that flowed into the entity during the period and the total cash that flowed out of the entity during the period. These cash amounts may be different from the revenue and expense amounts listed on the income statement because not all items of revenue or expense are paid for in cash (for example, some customers may buy goods from the entity on credit). The difference between cash inflows and cash outflows gives a measure of an entity's ability to pay its debts as they come due.

Supplementing these basic financial statements are footnote disclosures intended to explain some of the accounting principles used or to furnish other information useful to a reader of the financial statements.

Generally accepted accounting principles (GAAP) is a mix of principles and rules. Dozens of organizations contribute to their promulgation, led by the national standard setter called the Financial Accounting Standards Board (FASB) and strongly influenced by the Securities and Exchange Commission (SEC) in its oversight role. FASB has articulated a series of broad principles constituting its spirit and bedrock (issuing 7 "Statements of Financial Accounting Concepts"—SFACs—since 1973) against which more detailed rules are gauged (through mid-2005 FASB issued 154 "Statements of Financial Accounting Standards"—SFASs—and thousands of other detailed "Interpretations" and "Technical Bulletins", which are not technically part of GAAP though they inform it). Evolving practice and professional judgments constitute an important part of GAAP as well.

At the most general level, GAAP seeks to report business conditions and results according to a "fair presentation" (or "fairly presents"). The term is not defined by GAAP or law in the US, reflecting a common law sensibility in leaving to professional judgment the ultimate application of general rules to specific situations. The operational function of the standard entails that compliance with applicable accounting principles will presumptively but not invariably meet the standard. Achieving the view means tracking revenues and expenses using the accrual system (matching items of revenue with the expenses incurred to generate them) and historical cost accounting conventions (listing acquired assets at cost rather than at any higher market value). These methods should result in reports mirroring external business activity—lumpy or smooth. The standard may then call for adjustments when applying those conventions to particular events fogs the mirror.

Accountants sometimes distinguish between financial accounting and managerial accounting. Financial accounting concerns the content of GAAP and its application to produce financial statements intended for external users of financial information, including stockholders and creditors. Managerial accounting refers to more informal principles applied to assist internal managers with making capital allocation and other internal financing and business decisions. Compliance with GAAP can entail significant costs and as a result many small or closely-held businesses will not adhere to it but instead follow a set of managerial accounting principles for both internal use and summary financial reporting. Indeed, the only source of law in the US that requires applying GAAP to prepare financial statements are those rules applicable to SEC registrants (public companies). Even there, moreover, GAAP itself is not the sole talisman of financial reporting.

SEC regulations require that "the overall financial disclosure fairly presents, in all material respects, the company's financial condition, results of operations and cash flows." The SEC clarifies that the certification is not limited to an attestation that the financial statements accord with GAAP, emphasizing instead the broader requirement of "overall material accuracy and completeness." In other words, "presenting financial information in conformity with generally accepted accounting principles may not necessarily satisfy obligations under the antifraud provisions of the federal securities laws." A "fair presentation" is not about results alone but also about:

> the selection of appropriate accounting policies, proper application of appropriate accounting policies, disclosure of financial information that is informative and reasonably reflects the underlying transactions and events and the inclusion of any additional disclosure necessary to provide investors with a materially accurate and complete picture of an issuer's financial condition, results of operations and cash flows.

For SEC registrants and private companies, corporate managers bear the responsibility for preparing financial statements. This entails maintaining a system of internal reporting, internal controls, systems for measuring economic activity, aggregating the data, and reporting it. To generate assurance that these systems are effective, all companies invariably, and SEC registrants must, obtain an independent audit of their financial reports, including an independent test of the internal control systems used to collect data and prepare the reports. Audits are thus a central feature of financial reporting, constituting a hinge on which capital is allocated and attracted using securities markets as the vehicle. Outside auditors examine internal controls and financial statements, applying a variety of tests and conducting selected reviews of management personnel, processes, and systems. They then deliver an opinion as to whether the reports comply with GAAP, exhibit a true and fair view, and otherwise meet requisite standards.

Audits are not foolproof and they cannot constitute guarantees of the accuracy of the reported data. Managers are given substantial discretion in choosing applicable accounting principles and deciding a variety of issues of timing, measurement, and classification that can fall within a range of legitimacy and also extend beyond it. An old joke is that a business manager asks his accounting manager how much is two plus two. The accounting manager wryly replies, "How much do you want it to be?" The joke reflects more than inevitable reality that accounting involves judgment: that inevitable quality also creates the possibility of accounting alchemy. Using any set of financial data thus requires awareness of both its potential power and its potential for obfuscation.

The 1990s saw the dominance of finance over business management for the purpose of raising stock prices. One way corporate managers presented earnings that appeared better than economic reality was to issue quarterly earnings statements in the form of "EBITDA"—earnings before interest, taxes, depreciation, and amortization. Some of these, like interest and taxes, obviously were cash expenses the company would have to pay. Depreciation and amortization, by contrast, are non-cash charges to earnings. All of these are deducted under GAAP to produce the final number that represents earnings per share. By eliminating these deductions to earnings, managers thus presented earnings as higher than they really were (and to some extent cash flow higher than it really was). These statements were permissible if accompanied by appropriate (perfunctory) warnings. Moreover, any investor or analyst with a modicum of financial sophistication should have understood that these earnings did not represent the corporation's actual economic performance. Nonetheless, EBITDA earnings reports became widely-accepted as the standard by which a company's stock rose or fell on Wall Street. Following the corporate scandals of 2002, the Sarbanes-Oxley Act restricted the utility of these non-GAAP financial reports, requiring managers to explain precisely why they were issuing them and the extent to which they believed these statements actually reflected company finances. As a result, the utility of these statements as a means of hiding lackluster earnings should diminish.

Many of the cases in the ensuing materials draw on accounting data. Debates arise as to which data are most relevant to an analysis. The foregoing insights will be useful in navigating this terrain. For most lawyers, however, a full-fledged introductory accounting course is recommended to develop a full appreciation for the nature, limits, and uses of accounting data. *See generally* Cunningham, Sharing Accounting's Burden: Business Lawyers in Enron's Dark Shadows, 57 Bus. Law. 1421 (2002).

Problem — Smith Drugstores, Part I

Thirty-four years ago, after working as a pharmacist for a number of years in Phil's Pharmacy, Jerome Smith bought his own drugstore. Over the next five years, Jerome bought four other drugstores in neighboring communities. Jerome was helped in this early expansion of his business by his son Harry and one of his first employees, Mike, who had also been instrumental in starting the business. Twenty-nine years ago, Jerome decided to incorporate his business in the State of Delaware under the name Smith Drugstores Inc. ("the Company"), and to reward Harry and Mike for their hard work. One million shares of common stock were issued, with Jerome owning 60%, Harry owning 20%, Mike owning 10%, and ten of their friends and employees owning the remaining 10%. As a result of a number of stock splits, the number of shares increased to 50,000,000 as of nine years ago and has since then remained at that level. The ownership percentages have remained the same throughout. During this same period, the board of directors has consisted of Jerome, Harry, and Mike, with Jerome serving as chairman and chief executive officer, Mike as president, and Harry as executive vice president and secretary.

As you can see from the financial statements appearing in the next few pages, the business was enormously successful. As of 14 years ago, Smith Drugstores Inc. had stores in over 1,000 locations throughout the South and Midwest. As of seven years ago, that number had expanded to 1,400 with operations on the West Coast. As of this year, the Company had 1,750 drugstores (including a number of new locations in New England), and had also developed a significant business packaging and marketing its own line of over-the-counter pharmaceutical products.[1] Jerome, who was in charge of site acquisitions for drugstores, had shrewdly acquired property near developing residential areas in each city in which the Company did business. Consequently, when real estate prices spiraled throughout much of the country in the past decade, the Company's land holdings became very valuable indeed.

---

1. The products are made by commercial drug manufacturers licensed by Smith Drugstores Inc., and packaged under the "Smith" label.

This past year, Mike wanted to withdraw his wealth from the Company and retire. There had been an informal arrangement among the shareholders that if someone wished to sell his or her shares, the Company or the other shareholders would have the option to purchase those shares at fair value. The other shareholders have agreed that the Company will buy Mike's shares and now need to determine the value of these shares. The Company has hired you. In preparation for a meeting with the Company and its financial advisors and Mike, his counsel and his financial advisors, you need to have in mind an appropriate value for these shares, as well as some understanding of how Mike's financial advisors might choose to value them and how the Company's financial advisors might choose to value them.

1. Value Mike's shares in the Company using: (a) book value, adjusted book value and net asset value; (b) the capitalized earnings approach; and (c) the dividend discount model.

2. In studying and using the accompanying financial data for Smith Drugstores Inc., and comparable information for other drugstore chains, consider whether all of the corporations should be used in your analysis or only some of them and consider what factors you should use in selecting comparable companies.

3. As and after you have made your calculations, consider: (a) which of the valuation methods you believe produces the most accurate results and why; (b) whether all or any of these approaches adequately reflect the "true value" of Mike's stock; and (c) which approaches will be emphasized or deemphasized by Mike on the one hand and the Company on the other.

---

b. Valuation Methods

(i) Balance Sheet Based Valuation

Balance sheet based valuation methods utilize the numbers contained in a company's balance sheet to determine a company's value. Because virtually all businesses, including small businesses, create a balance sheet at least once a year, balance sheet based valuation methods are popular valuation methods. For example, it is usual to see a balance sheet based valuation method appear within a "shareholders' agreement" or "buy-sell agreement" entered into by the stockholders of a small, privately-held company. Such an agreement often requires a stockholder to sell her shares back to the company upon the occurrence of certain events; therefore, having a pricing formula or method specified in the agreement is imperative.

(A) Book Value

Book value is simply the excess of the total assets of a company as set forth on the balance sheet over the total liabilities of a company, also as set forth on the balance sheet. Thus:

$$\text{Book Value (BV)} = \text{Total Assets (TA)} - \text{Total Liabilities (TL)}$$

To determine book value on a per share basis, simply take a company's book value on a given date and divide it by the number of outstanding shares of common stock on that date:

$$\text{BV per share} = \frac{\text{BV}}{\text{\# of o/s shares}}$$

Smith Drugstores Inc.

Balance Sheet as at December 31, Year 10
(Dollars in thousands)

Assets

Current Assets

Cash & Equivalents		20,000
Pharmacy & Other Receivables[1]		75,000
Inventories		250,000
Other Current Assets		55,000
Total Current Assets		400,000

Fixed & Other Assets

Total Property, at Cost[2]	150,000	
Less Accumulated Depreciation	55,000	
Property, Net		95,000
Trademark		5,000
Total Assets		500,000

Liabilities

Current Liabilities

Accounts Payable	50,000
Short-Term Debt	100,000
Accrued Salaries, Wages and Other	25,000
Total Current Liabilities	175,000
Long-Term Debt	25,000
Total Liabilities	200,000

Stockholders' Equity

Common Stock (Par Value $1)	
(50,000,000 shares outstanding)	50,000
Retained Earnings	130,000
Paid-in Capital	120,000
Total Stockholders' Equity	300,000
Total Liabilities & Stockholders' Equity	500,000

---

1. For the last ten years, on average 5 percent of the Company's receivables have been deemed uncollectible. The amount listed on the balance sheet for Pharmacy and Other Receivables is net of an allowance for doubtful accounts equal to the historical average.

2. As part of a study conducted by the Company in Year 10 to evaluate the advantages of selling some of its real estate and leasing it back, an extensive valuation was performed to establish the fair market value of real property owned by the Company. The study, which was concluded on September 1, Year 10, estimated the fair market value of the property to be $700,000,000.

Smith Drugstores Inc.

Income Statement Three Years Ended Dec. 31, Years 10, 9, 8
(Dollars in thousands, except per share amounts)

	Year 10	Year 9	Year 8
Gross Revenue	2,500,000	2,100,000	2,000,000
Costs & Expenses[3]	2,225,000	1,875,000	1,850,000
Operating Income	275,000	225,000	150,000
Interest Expense	100,000	60,000	20,000
Net Income before Taxes	175,000	165,000	130,000
Income Tax[4]	40,000	37,000	30,000
Net Income after Taxes	135,000	128,000	100,000
Earnings Per Share (50,000,000 outstanding)	2.70	2.56	2.00

Historical Income Statement Data (Seven Previous Years)
(Dollars in thousands, except per share amounts)

Year	Gross Revenue	Net Income after Taxes	Earnings Per Share
7	1,910,000	95,000	1.90
6	1,750,000	73,000	1.46
5	1,575,000	84,000	1.68
4	1,225,000	72,000	1.44
3	1,100,000	60,000	1.20
2	985,000	50,000	1.00
1	900,000	40,000	.80

Historical Dividend Information

Year	Dividends Per Share	Payout Ratio (%)	Growth Rate (%)
10	.40	15	14
9	.35	14	25
8	.28	14	12
7	.25	13	25
6	.20	14	11
5	.18	11	20
4	.15	10	50
3	.10	8	25
2	.08	8	60
1	.05	6	—

3. Depreciation expense has been recorded on a straight line basis over time and has equalled $5,000,000 in each of Years 10, 9, 8 and 7 and had equalled $4,000,000 in each prior year reported.

4. Of the total income tax reported, a portion is deferred, equal to $3,000,000 in each of Years 10, 9, 8, and 7 and equal to $1,000,000 in each prior year reported.

Other Drugstore Chains

Selected Financial Data (Year 10, Except Forecasts)
(Dollars in millions, except per share amounts)

Financial Data and Market Ratios

Firm	Gross Revenue	Net Income	EPS[1]	P/E Ratio[2]	M/B Ratio[3]	ROE[4]
A	5,380.1	154.2	2.50	16.1	3.01	18.7
B	574.1	10.4	.68	17.7	2.71	15.3
C	3,172.8	81.9	1.97	17.9	2.08	11.6
D	2,110.6	61.3	3.01	13.8	2.53	18.3
E	669.6	7.1	.70	14.5	2.05	14.1
Average			1.77	16.0	2.48	15.6

Dividend Data / Forecasted Earnings Data

Firm	Div./Share[5]	Payout Ratio (%)[6]	Div. Yield Year 10[7]	Div. Yield Year 11[8]	EPS Year 11[9]	EPS Year 12[10]	EPS Trend[11]
A	.71	28	1.8	1.83	2.83	3.25	3.14
B	.19	28	1.6	2.62	.82	.96	1.35
C	.82	42	2.3	2.54	2.65	3.03	2.70
D	.92	31	2.2	2.91	3.10	3.37	3.79
E	0	0	0	0.00	.40	.80	.42
Average	.53	25.80	1.58	1.98	1.96	2.28	2.28

1. "EPS" is earnings per share determined by dividing Year 10 net income by the number of common shares outstanding at the end of Year 10.

2. "P/E Ratio" is equal to the closing price per share of common stock on the last trading day of Year 10 divided by EPS.

3. "M/B Ratio" is equal to the closing price per share of common stock on the last trading day of Year 10 divided by the book value of the company per share as of that date.

4. "ROE" is return on equity, determined by dividing EPS by book value of the company per share as of the end of Year 10.

5. "Div./Share" is equal to the sum of the annual cash dividends paid per share of common stock during Year 10 based on the weighted average number of shares of common stock outstanding during that year.

6. "Payout Ratio (%)" equals the percentage equivalent of Div./Share divided by EPS for Year 10.

7. "Div. Yield Year 10" equals the Div./Share divided by the closing price per share of the common stock on the last trading day of Year 10.

8. "Div. Yield Year 11" is the indicated annual dividend for Year 11, obtained by dividing Div./Share by the closing price of the common stock on November 30, Year 11.

9. "EPS Year 11" is the forecast of earnings per share for Year 11 reported by financial analysts following the stock.

10. "EPS Year 12" is the forecast of earnings per share for Year 12 reported by financial analysts following the stock.

11. "EPS Trend" is an estimate of earnings per share based on reported earnings for the prior 5 years.

But accounting conventions require that assets be reported on the balance sheet at their historical cost (or lower current market value if value has been permanently impaired). To the extent that some asset has increased in value under current market conditions, it will not be properly valued using the book value measure. This may result from inflation in the market prices of assets over time, for example, which accounting book value does not reflect.

(B) Adjusted Book Value

The adjusted book value approach attempts to keep the simplicity of the book value method while eliminating that method's emphasis on conservative asset valuation. For example, the line items on the balance sheet for such assets as property, plant and equipment could be increased to reflect current market values. Under the adjusted book value approach, asset values listed on the balance sheet are restated to reflect their current market value. Once this is done, the adjusted asset values are plugged into the basic book value formula.

However, the adjusted book value approach still fails to give an accurate measure of a company's value, because it fails to value the company as a going-concern. Indeed, as one court noted, a company's total assets are usually "worth more than the sum of their parts, because they include qualities useful in the context of a particular business that they would lose if put to different uses."[1]

(C) Net Asset Value

The net asset value method seeks to improve upon the book value and adjusted book value methods by valuing the business as a going concern. It does so by determining what it would cost to *replicate* the company in question. Thus, it considers more than simply what it would cost to purchase the same group of assets. It also considers the costs associated with establishing name recognition, training the company's employees, developing its products, creating brand awareness, and attracting and retaining its customer base, among other things. All of these reflect the "going concern" concept.

Another way to consider "going concern" value is to consider the accounting concept of *goodwill*. Goodwill reflects the value of a business as a going concern, and it typically arises in the context of a corporate acquisition. Whenever an acquiror pays more to purchase a target company than the target company's book value, the *overage* is called goodwill.[2]

Goodwill thus represents the "going concern" value of the target company, because presumably an acquiror would only pay book value or adjusted book value for a target company that had no future as a viable, earnings-generating enterprise. Once the acquisition is completed, accounting rules require the acquiror to reflect the amount of overage on its balance sheet as an intangible asset called "goodwill."

Precisely how one conducts the hypothetical replication of the company being valued will vary from company to company, but exercising substantial amounts of judgment will be unavoidable. Perhaps the easiest way to determine the net asset value of a

---

1. In re Spang Industries, Inc., 535 A.2d 86, 89 (Super. Ct. Pa. 1987).
2. For a detailed discussion of the measurement of goodwill in the context of a closely held company, see Donahue v. Draper, 491 N.E.2d 260 (Mass. App. 1986), *infra* at section 4c.

company is to use a *benchmark*. One useful benchmark is the *market to book ratio* (the *M/B Ratio*). The M/B Ratio is calculated in two steps. First, the book value per share of the company is calculated by dividing its book value by the number of common shares outstanding. Second, the market price per share of the company is divided by the book value per share of the company:

$$M/B \text{ Ratio} = \text{Market price per share/Book value per share}$$

The M/B Ratio for any particular company can be used in two ways. First, it may be compared with that of other publicly traded companies in the same industry to give a measure of how investors regard the subject company compared with other companies or the industry average. Higher M/B Ratios mean that investors regard the stock more favorably.

Second, the industry average can be used to give a possible measure to be used in valuing a company whose stock is not publicly traded. For example, the market price per share of a comparable publicly traded company (or the industry average) could be plugged into the M/B Ratio formula together with the book value per share of the privately held company to determine the privately held company's M/B Ratio. In other words, deliberately mix apples and oranges to determine a more accurate value for the privately held company.

Two empirical facts are worth noting about M/B Ratios. First, most M/B Ratios exceed 1. This should not surprise you given the foregoing discussion of the limitations on using book value as a measure of a company's actual value. Second, the average M/B Ratio for publicly traded companies has recently been in the range of 2-2.5, with older, industrial companies (such as steel companies) sometimes trading at M/B Ratios near or below 1 and newer, technology oriented companies (such as computer software manufacturers) sometimes trading at M/B Ratios as high as 10 or more.

Limitations on Balance Sheet Based Valuation. Subject to the possible use of the M/B Ratio as described above, even if one could overcome the limitations that accounting conventions impose on book value, give some measure to a company's internal synergies through adjusted book value, or divine some reasonably objective measure of net asset value, a final problem would remain. This is that, unless we are valuing a company for purposes of liquidating it, what we want to know is not what its assets cost or what they could attract if sold but rather what those assets, and the enterprise taken as a whole, can do for us. That is, we are interested in knowing what it can generate in terms of returns over time. Rather than sticking with the balance sheet, therefore, we should consider looking at the income statement.

(ii)   Income Statement Based Valuation

The primary income statement based valuation method is capitalization of earnings. Capitalizing earnings requires two primary steps. The first is to come up with a representative annual earnings figure. The second is choosing a capitalization rate which somehow reflects the stability and predictability of the company's earnings. We consider each of these problems in turn, and address the related concept of price-earnings ratios.

The Earnings Estimate. The capitalization of earnings method of valuation first requires making an estimate of earnings. Several issues arise. First, what does "earnings" mean? Earnings are defined by accountants in a variety of ways and are a function of a variety of accounting conventions. The purest sense of accounting earnings is the actual "bottom line" earnings reported on the income statement. Such accounting earnings are the result of subtracting from gross revenue all expenses, both cash expenses and all non-cash expenses such as depreciation and deferred taxes.

However, just as assets reported on a balance sheet based on accounting conventions do not reflect our interest in value, earnings reported on an income statement are also a product of those same accounting conventions. Earnings over time can be adjusted by altering accounting conventions that a company employs from time to time. For example, changes in the method of accounting for inventory, in the method of accruing tax liabilities and the method of depreciating fixed assets all impact accounting earnings. Moreover, these and many other accounting conventions are not concerned with tracking precisely the "value" of the assets being addressed. For example, the accounting convention of depreciation seeks to allocate the cost of a fixed asset over its assumed useful life. But there is no necessary relationship between the annual depreciation expense and a firm's reinvestment in the assets being depreciated.

To use accounting earnings as a basis for the valuation exercise would therefore give an inaccurate picture. But in the same way that the basic infirmities of the balance sheet based techniques of valuation can be improved somewhat, so too can the income statement based approach. The objective would be to reverse engineer the income statement report of accounting earnings in order to ascertain their actual economic significance. In particular, we could seek to restate the earnings figure as defined by accounting conventions in terms of actual cash inflows and cash outflows. The technique is to add back to accounting earnings all non-cash expenses reported during a particular period, such as depreciation and deferred taxes.

After so modifying accounting earnings one still must consider what earnings should be used—past earnings, present earnings or future earnings? Past earnings may enable us to tell what the corporation was worth in the past. But should we not be interested in what the corporation will do for us in the future? If so, then should we not want to consider future earnings? Probably, but how can we forecast what these will be other than with reference to the past? And how can we be sure that past earnings will be a guide to the future? What if extraordinary events have occurred in the past that are unlikely to be repeated in the future? One way to attempt to minimize these difficulties is to compute what are called normalized earnings. *Normalized earnings*, often used for companies whose earnings are cyclical in nature, are an average of earnings over the past five years or so that can be used to forecast future earnings.

The Capitalization Rate. Once a representative earnings figure is selected, a suitable capitalization rate (referred to as the *cap rate*) must be chosen based upon the risks involved in the company and its industry. The question an investor faces is what amount of money is she willing to pay for a specified return. Assume a stock having expected earnings per share (in the sense described above) of $1 per year for every year in the future. The price we are willing to pay will be a function of the rate of return on which we will insist in light of the risk that the $1 per year will not materialize. The higher the risk, the greater the rate of return we will insist upon and the lower the risk the lower the rate of return we will insist upon. If the risk justified a 10% rate of return, then the per share value of earnings would be $10 ($1/.10 = $10). But if the risk justified a 5% rate of return, then the per share value of earnings would be $20 ($1/.05). Accordingly, the value of the share of stock would range between $10 and $20 depending upon the risk involved.

A number of rules of thumb have been developed for setting cap rates given various levels of risk. In general, the lower the risks involved in a particular type of business, the lower the cap rate. For example, if there is a high degree of certainty that the company will continue to perform as it has in the past, then a cap rate in the range of up to around 12.5% would be appropriate. For companies that present moderate degrees of risk, a cap rate in the range of 15-25% would be more appropriate. And for particularly risky companies, those where uncertainty about sustained success is great, an appropriate cap rate could range from 30 or 40% up to 100%. *See generally* Amling, Investments, An Introduction to Analysis and Management, 525-26 (6th ed. 1993); 1 Dewing, The Financial Policy of Corporations 390-91 (5th ed. 1953).

For any given company, these rules of thumb should be tailored to address the particular risks it faces. Indeed, the cap rate would have to be adjusted depending on how future risks the company faces, or is likely to face, differ from historical risks. If future risks are greater, then the cap rate would have to be increased and vice versa.

Application. Once we have an earnings estimate and a cap rate, we simply divide the earnings by the cap rate to get an estimate of value, using the following formula:

$$V_e = E \, / \, R$$

where: V_e is the valuation based on earnings
          E is the earnings figure
          R is the cap rate

Given the difficulties in selecting both a representative earnings figure and the cap rate, we would want to make such a calculation using a range of earnings figures and perhaps even cap rates. That is, we could develop a probability distribution table under which we stipulate to a cap rate and then calculate a range of values based on a range of earnings figures, such as low, high and average (or normalized).

The Price-Earnings Ratio. Beyond the rules of thumb referred to above for choosing an appropriate cap rate, another risk measurement can be drawn from the way public markets price common stocks for companies with various earnings. This measure reflects risk by comparing the price of a share of common stock with the earnings per share of that common stock. This device, which is widely used by investors and analysts, is called the price-earnings ratio (the "P/E ratio"). Like the M/B Ratio, the P/E ratio is not itself a measure of the intrinsic value of the common stock but, rather, is a method of assessing risk based upon the relationship between a stock's market price and its earnings. Also as with the M/B Ratio, for close corporations there is no P/E ratio (and even for thinly traded stocks any P/E ratio that exists is not particularly meaningful). However, the P/E ratios of publicly-traded companies that are otherwise comparable to the subject company could still be used as a benchmark of the market's collective appraisal of the risks associated with a particular kind of business.

The P/E ratio is computed by dividing the current price of a share of common stock by the company's earnings per share. A stock trading at $40 per share for a company with earnings equal to $2 per share has a P/E ratio of 20. Stock prices fluctuate in part as expectations about the future change, including expectations about future earnings. Therefore, stock prices may be expected to some degree to reflect current expectations about future earnings as much as or more than past earnings histories. Accordingly, the price earnings ratio should also be calculated based on current expectations of future earnings. If analysts believe that the earnings per share of the company in the foregoing example will rise to $2.50 per share in the upcoming year, then its price earnings ratio given those expectations would not be 20 but instead would be 16. In effect, the market is saying that it believes that this company's earnings potential is strong, that uncertainty surrounding its prospects is relatively lower than in previous periods.

The reason that various levels of the P/E ratio tell us something about how the market is appraising risk is that the P/E ratio is mathematically the reciprocal of the cap rate. That is, in the foregoing example of a company with a stock price of $40 and earnings per share of $2, we have a P/E ratio of 20. The reciprocal of 20 is 1/20, which is the fraction equivalent of 5%. Thus the P/E ratio of 20 is the equivalent of a cap rate of 5%. So you can translate all P/E ratios into cap rates, as follows:

P/E Ratio	Cap Rate (%)
100	1
50	2
25	4
20	5
12.5	8
10	10
5	20
4	25
2	50

Because the cap rate is the reciprocal of the P/E ratio, the P/E ratio enables us to go out into the market and determine what the market collectively has judged is the cap rate for various companies under consideration. From that measure, we could then come up with appropriate cap rates for other companies that we deem in some sense comparable to a company in which we are especially interested. For comparative purposes, we would want to consider companies in the same industry, of approximately the same size, of similar maturity and having similar growth histories and so on.

More generally, once the P/E ratio for a corporation is calculated, it can be compared to either the P/E ratio of a market index (such as the Dow Jones Industrial Average), a similar company in the same industry, or the past P/E ratio of the company in question. This comparison will show the relationship of the stock's risk to the risk of securities with which it is being compared. Some securities analysts consider a high P/E ratio to be favorable because the market price of the stock reflects a belief by investors that the company has good earnings potential. Consequently, two corporations with the same earnings may have widely divergent values.

Just as "earnings" for purposes of the basic calculation may be distorted, so too may the resulting price-earnings ratio one uses to gauge the related risk in choosing a cap rate. The problem here is exacerbated for several reasons. Since P/E ratios are used as a comparison tool, the analyst must be consistent in the earnings figure used for different corporations. If different methods are employed to calculate earnings — both in terms of the way accounting earnings are calculated or adjusted and in the period over which the earnings figure is calculated — any comparisons made are useless. For example, The Wall Street Journal publishes the P/E ratios for all stocks listed on the major exchanges. These P/E ratios are determined based upon the *current reported earnings* of the corporation. Consequently, any analysis performed using the P/E ratios given in The Wall Street Journal would have to be done using the current earnings-per-share figure, as reported in the company's financial statements. Otherwise, the figures will be noncomparable.

The Earnings Estimate Revisited. As you recall, the purest sense of accounting earnings is the actual "bottom line" earnings reported on the income statement. Such accounting earnings are the result of subtracting from gross revenue all expenses, both cash expenses and all non-cash expenses such as depreciation and deferred taxes. One expense, often a large expense for closely held corporations, is executive compensation. Those in control of the closely held corporation often work for the corporation, and hence are in charge of setting their own salaries. How should a shareholder of a closely held corporation take this into consideration when valuing her shares utilizing an income statement based valuation method? Consider the following problem.

Problem — Smith Drugstores, Part II

In the course of negotiating over the value of Mike's shares, it was pointed out that the three senior executives of the company, Jerome, Harry and Mike, were all well paid and had all enjoyed numerous "perqs" in connection with their positions. With respect to cash salaries in the most recent year, Jerome was paid $780,000; Harry was paid $520,000; and Mike was paid $390,000 (and had worked only ten months of the year). For comparative purposes, the following compensation information for the most recent year was provided with respect to the three highest paid executives of the drugstore chains referred to in conjunction with Smith's financial statements. Amounts include total cash compensation and any performance bonuses or benefits compensation.

OTHER DRUGSTORE CHAINS
Comparative Executive Compensation Data
(three highest paid executives)

A	960,833	816,304	556,053
B	458,174	261,346	223,789
C	980,000	542,692	397,923
D	536,092	410,326	321,816
E	425,300	361,000	348,600

In addition to the salaries paid to Jerome, Harry and Mike, each of them was also provided with (i) a Company car at a cost that has never exceeded $32,500 per year; (ii) membership in one country club and one luncheon club, at an aggregate cost which has not exceeded $26,000 per year; (iii) unlimited use of a company-owned jet; (iv) use of company-owned apartments in each major city in which the Company has done business (Miami, Dallas, New Orleans, Chicago, Atlanta, Los Angeles, Phoenix, San Francisco, Las Vegas, among others); and (v) an expense account which has never exceeded $260,000 per year.

You have now been asked to evaluate the extent to which this information bears on the question of the valuation of Mike's shares. How does this information affect an earnings based valuation of his shares? If you represented Mike, what arguments would you formulate to advance his demand for a greater per share valuation? How would you counter these arguments if you represented the Company? Compare your analysis to that of the expert in Donahue v. Draper, 491 N.E.2d 260 (Mass. App. 1986), *infra* at section 4c.

Limitations of Income Statement Based Valuation. In the same way that balance sheet based methods of valuation fail to give effect to the earnings potential and are therefore regarded as inferior methods of valuation, the income statement based method of capitalizing earnings (and its utilization of P/E Ratios) also has significant limitations. In addition to the issues raised by the preceding problem, the calculation is constrained by potentially artificial accounting conventions. Moreover, it fails to recognize whether earnings will be paid out to shareholders in the form of dividends or will be retained in the corporation for internal purposes that are not of immediate benefit to shareholders. As a result of these limitations, yet another alternative to valuation looks beyond both the balance sheet and the income statement and toward cash flows.

(iii) Cash Flow Based Valuation

(A) Dividend Discount Model

The limits of the income statement based valuation methods point directly to valuation based on determining the present value of the expected stream of future dividends that will be paid to stockholders in cash. The cash-dividend based approach to valuation was championed by John Burr Williams, who argued as follows in his The Theory of Investment Value, 57-58 (1938):

> Earnings are only a means to an end, and the means should not be mistaken for the end. Therefore we must say that a stock derives its value from its dividends, not its earnings. In short, a stock is worth only *what you can get out of it.*
>
> * * *
>
> In saying that dividends, not earnings, determine value, we seem to be reversing the usual rule that is drilled into every beginner's head when he starts to trade in the market; namely, that earnings, not dividends, make prices. The apparent contradiction is easily explained, however, for we are discussing permanent investment, not speculative trading, and dividends for years to come, not income for the moment only. Thus, DDM assumes you're not going to sell. Of course it is true that low earnings together with a high dividend for the time being should be looked at askance, but likewise it is true that these low earnings mean low dividends *in the long run.* On analysis, therefore, it will be seen that no contradiction really exists between our formula using dividends and the common precept regarding earnings.

The conventional cash flow based method of valuation is called the dividend discount model (DDM). It involves little more than a particularized application of the present value concept we have already explained. Predicated on the notion that the value of a share of common stock is equal to the expected flow of the dividends it produces, the model seeks to discount to present value that anticipated flow. Several steps are required, each of which requires careful consideration.

Forecasting Expected Dividends. The first step in using the DDM is to forecast expected dividends to be received in the future. The annuity model we developed earlier assumed a steady stream of defined payments at definite intervals. Not so with dividends. As you will recall from your corporations or business associations course, and as we explore in detail in chapter 8, dividends are payable almost solely in the discretion of the corporation's board of directors, are subject to the arcane set of rules governing legal capital, and depend sensitively upon the corporation's financial position, growth plans, and future prospects. Thus, although past dividends may serve as some guide, future dividends are mere predictions. Therefore, it should be no surprise to realize that different analysts may reach different conclusions regarding a stock's value based upon their evaluation of the corporation's dividend prospects.

Choosing The Discount Rate. The second step is choosing a discount rate. This raises a factor which reemerges from our discussion of the present value concept: risk. The discount rate used in the DDM must incorporate both the time value of money, as well as the measurement of risk, which now assumes great importance. In choosing a discount rate for use in the DDM, the analyst must attempt to evaluate quantitatively the likelihood that the actual returns in the form of dividends will differ from the expected returns. We will present a method for doing so below.

Alternative Dividend Growth Rates. The third step requires taking account of whether it is expected that dividends will be the same amount in future years, will grow at a constant rate in future years or will grow at a nonconstant rate over time. After presenting the generalized DDM, we will refine it to account for growth rates of various kinds.

Terminal Values. For how many years into the future must we discount to present value the expected stream of cash dividends? Does the valuation differ if we expect to hold the stock for a definite period of years (say 3) as compared to holding it forever (in our lifetime and through our heirs)? The answer, perhaps surprising at first, is: no, it does not matter. This is because for any investor the value of the stock consists in the stream of payments she expects to receive plus any gain on reselling it. But the only reason there will be any gain on reselling it is because some other investor notices that there will be a stream of payments to him after he buys it and so on. As a result, the value of a share of common stock under the DDM resides solely in its expected stream of cash dividends.

Nevertheless, we could also cut off our time period as at the end of any given future year. But if we did, the valuation result would be the same. The only difference would be that some portion of the total value would consist in the present value of the stream of expected payments and the rest would consist in the present value of the expected (higher) prevailing price (which, in turn, would of course be based on then-prevailing expected returns). Accordingly, we will proceed to present the formula based on the assumption of an indefinite stream of payments over time, with two caveats: first, we will also show a more intuitive way of dealing with the conceptual proposition of an infinite payment stream and later we will return to the question by presenting two methods of valuation using terminal values to cut off the payment stream short of infinity.

The DDM Formula. The DDM formula is this:

$$V = \frac{D_1}{(1+k)^1} + \frac{D_2}{(1+k)^2} + \cdots + \frac{D_{25}}{(1+k)^{25}} + \cdots + \frac{D_\infty}{(1+k)^\infty}$$

where: D_n is the expected cash dividends in a given year
     k is the discount rate
     ∞ is infinity

You will note that this is a particularized application of the present value formula for an *annuity* discussed above in section 3b(ii)(B). The difference is that this formulation extends out to infinity rather than for a definite period of years. It is a *perpetuity* rather than an annuity. In the same way we generalized the present value formula for an annuity, we can generalize the DDM formula as follows:

$$V = \sum_{t=1}^{\infty} \frac{D_t}{(1+k)^t}$$

Application to Zero Growth Stock. Let us now apply the DDM formula by considering a common stock on which dividends are expected to remain constant in the future. Assume

an expected dividend stream of $1.00 per year and a discount rate of 10%. The value of
the stock using the DDM is as follows:

$$V = \frac{\$1.00}{(1.10)^1} + \frac{\$1.00}{(1.10)^2} + \cdots + \frac{\$1.00}{(1.10)^{25}} + \cdots + \frac{\$1.00}{(1.10)^{50}}$$

$$V = .91 + .83 + \cdots + .09 + \cdots + .01 \cdots$$

One then extends the sum out through infinity, adds up the results and gets a
value for the stock. You may not be surprised (but will be relieved) to know that
there is a formula for doing this. As noted, it is the formula for calculating the present value of a perpetuity and just involves a minor variation on the formula we discussed above for determining the present value of an annuity. The formula for determining the present value of a perpetuity is the annual payment amount divided by
the discount rate. In the context of a zero growth stock, that formula is specified as
follows:

$$V = \frac{D}{k}$$

In the foregoing example, the value of our share of stock is therefore equal to

$$\frac{\$1.00}{0.10} = \$10$$

As promised, for those of you who are having difficulty accepting the conceptual
proposition of a stock with a dividend payment stream extending out to infinity, consider the following. Assume you will hold the stock for 50 years only, instead of forever (through your heirs). Using the present value table for annuities (see Table 3 in
section 2b(ii)(B)(1)), what is the value of our stock? Going down the year row to 50
and across the discount rate column to 10%, you are given an answer of $9.9148. This
is very close to our answer of $10. Why is it both so close yet so far away? It is because
the portion of the present value of our stock attributable to dividends being paid beyond year 50 is very slight indeed.

The Discount Rate Revisited. Before proceeding to modify the DDM for the case of
growth stocks, let us take a minute to observe a way in which the DDM can be used to
help derive an appropriate discount rate. It is by adapting the foregoing perpetuity formula. That formula was $V = D / k$. We can transpose that formula to give $k = D / V$.
What does this mean? This means that the discount rate that the market is implicitly
using for the stock (k) is equal to the dividends being paid (D) divided by the stock
price (V). So, if the stock in our previous example were publicly traded, we could look
up in a newspaper its prevailing price and latest dividend to give us the expected return
on the stock. In other words, if we bought the stock for $10 and expected dividends at a
constant future rate of $1 per year, we would be getting an expected rate of return of
10%. For close corporations or thinly-traded corporations, these computations can be
used as comparative tools in the same way the M/B Ratio and the P/E Ratio can be used
as comparative tools.

Application to Constant Growth Stock. Let us now apply the DDM formula to a
common stock on which dividends are expected to grow at a constant rate over time.
It is customary to expect that the constant rate of growth for growth stocks is equal to
the percentage increase in some measure of gross product (either gross domestic

product or gross national product) plus an amount equal to the percentage rate of inflation. Let us assume that this amounts to 8%. The formula for incorporating the constant growth rate is a simple adaptation of the formula for future values discussed above in section 2b(i):

$$D_n = D_0(1 + g)^n$$

where D_n is the future dividend amount in year n, D_0 is the dividend in the prior year and g is the growth rate. Therefore, if a stock paid a $1 dividend last year, then its expected dividends in future years are as follows:

Year	Expected Dividend		
1	$1.00 (1 + .08)	=	$1.08
2	$1.00 (1 + .08)^2	=	$1.17
3	$1.00 (1 + .08)^3	=	$1.26
4	$1.00 (1 + .08)^4	=	$1.36

You can see this by referring to the table for calculating future values (see Table 1 in section 2b(i)).

To determine the value of a share of common stock expected to pay future dividends according to this growth rate, we adapt the basic DDM formula set forth above for constant growth rates. We do this by reflecting our more precise definition of D_n, which is now equal to $D_0 (1 + g)^n$. The formula becomes:

$$V = \frac{D_0(1 + g)^1}{(1 + k)^1} + \frac{D_0(1 + g)^2}{(1 + k)^2} + \cdots + \frac{D_0(1 + g)^3}{(1 + k)^3} + \cdots + \frac{D_0(1 + g)^\infty}{(1 + k)^\infty}$$

Just as we restated the DDM formula for the zero growth stock as $V = D / k$, we can restate the formula for the constant growth stock. It is $V = D_1 / k - g$. The new term, g, simply gives effect to the fact of expected growth. To see this, notice that in the case of no growth, the term g in this latter formula would be zero, and that is the same thing as using the no growth formula.

Now we can finish our example of valuing the constant growth stock, having a latest dividend of $1, a discount rate of 10% and a growth rate of 8%:

$$V = \frac{D_1}{k - g}$$

$$V = \frac{\$1.08}{.10 - .08}$$

$$= \frac{\$1.08}{.02}$$

$$= \$54$$

The Discount Rate Revisited (Again). In the same way that we paused to consider a way to determine the implied discount rate used in the market in the case of the no growth stock, we also pause to consider the implied discount rate used in the market for the constant growth stock. The idea is conceptually the same, except we must account for the expected growth rate, g. Now the formula is:

$$k = \frac{D_1}{V} + g$$

Using this formula for the preceding example, we have:

$$k = \frac{\$1.08}{\$54} + 8\%$$

$$= 2\% + 8\%$$

$$= 10\%$$

Growth: Payout Versus Plowback. You may be wondering why the dividends on some stocks are not expected to grow and the dividends on other stocks are expected to grow. The answer depends primarily on the manner in which a company chooses to allocate its earnings available for distribution to shareholders between *payout* (in dividends) and *plowback* (retained earnings used for reinvestment). A firm that allocates its entire earnings to payout will be expected to experience no growth in either earnings or dividends over time whereas a firm that allocates some portion of its earnings to plowback will be expected to experience growth in both dividends and earnings.

For a firm that makes some allocation to plowback, then, we can use the foregoing formula to be more precise about the expected return on a constant growth stock. A portion of the value consists of payout, which is called the *dividend yield*, and is given by D/V; and a portion of the value consists of plowback, which gives a measure of the growth rate and is captured by g. In the foregoing example, the dividend yield is 2% and the growth rate is 8%.

Estimating g is the tricky part of the project. A conventional way of doing so involves the following steps. First, calculate the *payout ratio*, which is the ratio of dividends per share to earnings per share. Assume a company that has historically had a payout ratio of about 30%. Each year the company pays out about 30% of its earnings in dividends and plows back about 70% of its earnings in reinvestment. Second, calculate the *return on equity (ROE)*, which is the earnings per share divided by the book value per share. Assume that our company's ROE has historically been around 11%. Third, if we assume that our company is relatively stable and mature and that its payout ratio and ROE will continue as historically, then we are assuming that the company will earn 11% of its book value per share (its ROE) and reinvest 70% of that. As a result, we would expect its book value per share to increase by $.70 \times .11 = .077$ or about 8% (rounding up).

Dividends Versus Earnings. This perspective furnishes an alternative intuitive understanding for why earnings as such are excluded from the DDM. Since it is believed that future dividends reflect the consequences of the retention and reinvestment of earnings, then one cannot include them as part of the DDM model or else one would be double-dipping—counting the reinvested earnings twice! In other words, it is *incorrect* to say that the value of a share of stock is equal to the present value of the earnings per share. Rather, it is correct to say that the value of a share of stock is equal to the present value of the expected cash dividends per share. These two amounts will only be the same for a no growth stock, where all earnings are paid out and none are plowed back. For companies that both payout and plowback, if you claimed to have valued the share based on its earnings per share, you have claimed the rewards of investment in the form of increased earnings without having acknowledged the burdens of investment in the form of plowback.

Nonconstant Growth Stocks. We have left out what you may be thinking is probably the most realistic kind of stock, that of a company expected to experience increasing growth in the next few years and then level off thereafter. Its dividends are expected to grow at an increasing rate for some years (supernormal growth) in the future and then settle into a period of constant growth. The growth rate during the supernormal growth period could, of course, vary from year to year. Moreover, several different supernormal growth periods could occur (*e.g.*, 25% for 3 years, then 15% for three years, and then a constant 7%).

Many examples of companies that experienced supernormal growth come easily to mind. Steel companies experienced this growth at the turn of the nineteenth century, automobile manufacturers in the early twentieth century, and high technology companies at the turn of the twentieth century. What do you think the growth stock of the 2040s will be?

There are three steps in the valuation process for nonconstant growth stocks, all of which are applications of what we have presented above. First, calculate the present value of the expected dividends during the period of nonconstant growth. Second, calculate the expected price at the end of the nonconstant growth period based on the expected dividends from that point forward. Third, add the results together. For an example, see Brigham, Fundamentals of Financial Management 323-25 (8th ed. 1998).

Terminal Values (Revisited). We noted in the beginning of our discussion of the DDM that it does not matter for purposes of valuing a share of common stock whether an investor intends to hold it indefinitely or only for a limited period of time. We said this because the value of a share of common stock under the DDM is a function solely of its expected cash flows and that as a result it does not matter for valuation purposes that an investor plans to hold the stock for a definite period of years and then sell it. We promised to return to this question by presenting two methods for cutting the expected payment stream short and adding to its value the terminal value as of that time. This may be useful as a practical matter for two reasons. First, the reliability of any forecast of dividend flows necessarily diminishes as they become more remote. Second, in determining the value of a business enterprise as a whole, rather than an individual share of common stock, it is conventional to bifurcate the components of valuation in this manner and examine separately the expected payment stream over a definite period and the terminal value at the end of that period, which is called the *horizon*. The formula for this two-part valuation is as follows:

$$V = \sum_{t=1}^{n} \frac{D_t}{(1 + k)^t} + \frac{V_n}{(1 + k)^n}$$

This formula says that the present value of an asset (such as a share of common stock or an entire business) that is to be held for n years equals the discounted sum of all cash flows thereon expected during that period *plus* the present value of what it could be sold for at the end of year n—that is, its terminal value at the horizon. We have called this V_n in the formula. The present value of the terminal value is called the *horizon value*. The first half of this formula is simply an application of the discounting method we have been pursuing. The second half is new. It requires an estimate of the terminal value, which can be estimated in a number of ways, of which we will present two.

The first way of estimating terminal value is to compare the P/E ratios of comparable businesses that have reached the stage of maturity that the business in which we are interested will reach at the horizon. Assume for example that we are examining what has been a growth company and want to define its horizon as the time it reaches maturity. We would look to the current P/E ratios of companies who have now reached that stage to derive both a basis for calculating the expected price for our stock at the horizon and an appropriate discount rate to calculate the horizon value. For example, assume a business maturation point will occur in year four, that earnings in year four are projected to be $2.00 per share, and that the industry average P/E ratio for mature companies is 10. Terminal value would therefore equal $2.00 × 10 or $20. The horizon value would therefore be as follows:

$$\frac{V_n}{(1 + k)^n}$$

$$= \frac{\$20}{(1.10)^3}$$

$$= \frac{\$20}{1.33}$$

$$= \$15.03$$

This horizon value would then be added to the discounted value of the dividends expected in years one through three to give a total value for the asset. Notice that this method of calculating horizon value requires a projection of earnings for the terminal year, which creates the difficulties noted above. While it is true that making earnings estimates will usually form a part of the valuation exercise anyway, drawing on the income statement based method of valuation does fly in the face of the theoretical justification for using expected cash flow rather than earnings in the dividend discount model.

The second way of estimating terminal value is to use the constant growth variation of the DDM and a dividend projection for the terminal year. We would forecast the dividend to be paid in the terminal year, which in this example is year four, and then select a long-term growth rate, g, in the manner discussed above. For example, assume an expected year four dividend of $.66, a growth rate of 5%, and a discount rate of 10%. The formula for determining horizon value in this approach is:

$$\frac{1}{(1 + k)^n} \times \frac{D_{n+1}}{k - g}$$

where n = the last year for which dividends have been discounted. Incorporating our numbers, we get

$$= \frac{1}{(1.10)^3} \times \frac{\$.66}{.10 - .05}$$

$$= \frac{1}{1.33} \times \$13.20$$

$$= \frac{\$13.20}{1.33}$$

$$= \$9.92$$

Again one would add to this the discounted value of expected dividends up through the year preceding the terminal year to give a total value. In some instances these two approaches to estimating terminal value and calculating horizon value will give different results (as seen above). When this happens, the results could be averaged arithmetically or on a weighted basis if it is believed that one or the other method is more reliable.

(B) Discounted Cash Flow Method

The dividend discount model is a specialized application of more general methods called discounted cash flow (DCF) analysis. The basic technique can be adapted to apply to any future stream of cash flows, including the cash flows of a business, as we suggested in the foregoing discussion of horizon value. This more direct method of valuation for a business is particularly useful for companies that are not projecting the payment of any dividends and indeed for companies that are not expected to generate earnings, either in an accounting sense or an adjusted sense.

Calculating a company's value based on DCF involves four steps:

- *First*, forecast the company's annual net cash flows for the time period you expect to own shares of its common stock.
- *Second*, estimate a terminal or residual value of the company at the end of your holding period.
- *Third*, discount at an appropriate discount rate the present value of each of (a) the projected net cash flows determined in step one and (b) the terminal value determined in step two.
- *Fourth*, add the discounted net cash flows to the discounted terminal value to arrive at the present value of the company.

For example, suppose that you acquired all the outstanding shares of PNH Corp. on December 31, 2006. You plan to hold your shares for five years and then sell them all. You project that PNH will provide $100 million in cash flow during 2007, and that PNH's cash flow will increase at an annual rate of 10% over the next five years. PNH's projected terminal value on December 31, 2011 is expected to be $1.61 billion based on a cash flow multiple of 10 in its fifth year of the forecast. Assume further that the rate of return for companies with a risk profile similar to PNH's is 5%. What is the value of PNH today applying DCF?

First, calculate the present value of the projected cash flows discounted at the discount rate for companies with a similar risk profile as PNH's (dollar amounts are in millions):

$$PV_{cash\ flow} = \frac{\$100}{1.05} + \frac{\$110}{1.05^2} + \frac{\$121}{1.05^3} + \frac{\$133}{1.05^4} + \frac{\$161}{1.05^5}$$

$$= \$95.24 + \$99.77 + \$104.52 + \$109.42 + \$126.15$$

$$= \$535.10$$

Next, calculate the present value of the terminal value discounted at the discount rate for companies with a similar risk profile as PNH's (dollar amounts are in millions):

$$PV_5 = \frac{\$1,610}{1.05^5}$$

$$= \$1,261.47$$

Finally, add the two present values together:

$$\$535.10 + \$1,261.47 = \$1,796.57 \ (or\ \$1,796,570,000)$$

Like DDM, DCF suffers from several flaws. First, you must forecast future cash flows, a process that is inherently subjective and rarely accurate. Second, you must subjectively choose an appropriate discount rate. Once again, you can use a discount rate that reflects a rate of return for a company with a comparable level of risk as the company you are valuing. If the company is privately held, you can use the cap rate of a comparable, *publicly traded* company. This is simply the reciprocal of that public company's P/E Ratio. Lastly, estimating a terminal value for a company in the future is very difficult because of the myriad of uncertainties in the business, financial and economic environment.

For cases discussing the application of DCF and its limitations, see Le Beau v. M.G. Bancorporation, Inc., 1998 WL 44993 (Del. Ch. 1998), *aff'd in part & remanded in part*, 737 A.2d 513 (Del. 1999); In re Zenith Electronics Corp., 241 B.R. 92 (D. Del. Bankr. 1999); Cede & Co. v. Technicolor, Inc., C.A. No. 7129, slip op., 1990 WL 161084 (Del. Ch. 1990).

c. Capital Budgeting

Up until this point we have explained only how an investor or analyst values the common stock of a company and the role that present value formulae play in that valuation. However, these same present value concepts are used by corporate officers in making internal investment decisions for the corporation. Capital budgeting is the process of valuing projects and investment opportunities available to the corporation. The projects that are selected are those that add value to the firm based on the capital budgeting analysis. Two of the most popular capital budgeting methods are the net present value method (NPV) and the internal rate of return method (IRR), both of which utilize present value concepts.

The NPV method is similar to the dividend discount model used in valuing common stock. It is used to determine the present value of all future cash flows (both negative and positive) that are expected to be generated from the project. The discount rate used in the determination is based on the company's opportunity cost of capital, which is the expected rate of return that can be obtained by investing instead in financial securities with equivalent risk to the project. If the NPV is positive, the project will add value to the company and should be selected. Conversely, if the NPV is negative, the project should be rejected because it will decrease, rather than add to, the corporation's wealth.

The IRR method is used to calculate the discount rate required to equate the present value of expected cash inflows generated by the project with the present value of its cash outflows. In other words, the IRR is that discount rate that makes net present value equal to 0. The internal rate of return is then compared to the opportunity cost of capital. If the internal rate of return exceeds the opportunity cost, the project should be selected.[1]

---

1. The IRR method expressed as a formula is as follows:

$$C_0 = \sum_{t=1}^{n} \frac{C_t}{(1 + k)^t}$$

where: C_o is the inital cash outlay
C_t is the net cash flow at time t
k is the internal rate of return
n is the last period in which cash flow is expected

A corporation can usually use either method in its capital budgeting analysis and achieve the same results. However, under certain circumstances, the results can be different. Discrepancies most often occur when only one of the projects under consideration may be selected. The NPV method properly ranks projects when exclusivity is a factor, whereas the IRR method often does not. One of the reasons for the difference is that each method uses a different reinvestment rate. The NPV method assumes that the cash inflows are reinvested at the opportunity cost of capital. The IRR method, however, assumes that such inflows are reinvested at the internal rate of return, which is not always a true reflection of the rate at which funds can be reinvested.

A second disadvantage of the IRR method is that it does not take into account the size of the initial cash outlay, and therefore does not measure the size of the return to be expected from the project. The IRR method only calculates the expected rate of return of a project. In contrast, the NPV method does reflect, in absolute terms, the amount by which a given project will increase (or decrease) net present value. Although one project may have a higher rate of return than another, it may not add as much value to the corporation as the other which has a lower rate of return but a significantly higher initial cash outlay, and consequently a larger cash return. For more on capital budgeting using the NPV and IRR methods, *see* Brealey, Myers & Allen, Principles of Corporate Finance, 20-25 (8th ed. 2006); Van Horne, Financial Management and Policy, 141-46 (12th ed. 2001).

Questions

As you know, under the business judgment rule courts give boards of directors wide discretion in their management of the corporation. Should the law require some correlation between an average measure of volatility of a corporation's stock over some defined period of time and the riskiness of projects approved by the board in assessing whether the directors have discharged their duty of care? Or, put another way, should a prudent board of directors seek to pursue only those projects whose riskiness somehow correlates with the riskiness of the company's stock measured by the standard deviation?

For example, in the essay above concerning probability distributions and standard deviations using Bionics and Burgers, we said that Burgers's standard deviation was approximately 4%. Should a Burgers's stockholder have an action for breach of duty of care if Burgers's board of directors vote to undertake a substantial project with a standard deviation of 70%, the project fails and causes Burgers significant losses? What are the advantages and disadvantages of such an approach? Does your answer depend upon whether you are dealing with a close corporation or a widely held public corporation? Reconsider this question after studying section 5: Does the efficient capital market hypothesis provide an answer?

Section 4
Fundamental Valuation in Legal Context

Valuation principles are central to resolving a variety of legal problems. Judges are called upon to determine the value of shares in the hands of a given stockholder in three main situations. First, a judge must value shares in an appraisal proceeding commenced by a stockholder who dissents to a merger involving her company. Second, a judge must interpret a valuation formula set forth in a shareholders' agreement when a stockholder challenges it. Finally, a judge must value shares in other legal contexts, such as in liquidation, divorce, or tax proceedings.

a. Valuation in Appraisal Proceedings

Sometimes referred to as *dissenter's rights* or *buy-out rights*, *appraisal rights* entitle stockholders who disfavor certain mergers to seek a judicial determination of the fair value of their shares. Once that determination is made, the surviving entity must then pay that amount to these stockholders in cash.

The origin of the appraisal remedy is tied to a shift in stockholder voting rights. Historically, corporate law required unanimous stockholder approval of all fundamental corporate transactions. Over time, the law moved away from unanimity to mere majority approval. The law embraced appraisal rights as a quid pro quo for taking away a stockholder's veto power over such transactions. Any stockholder who did not want to go along with the transaction could cash out for fair value and move on.

(i) Valuation Methodology

(A) Historical Context

Prior to the seminal case of Weinberger v. UOP, Inc., 457 A.2d 701 (Del. 1983), the Delaware courts, as well as other state courts, used the *Delaware block method* of valuation as the exclusive method to determine fair value in an appraisal proceeding. For example, Piemonte v. New Boston Garden Corporation, 387 N.E.2d 1145 (Mass. 1979), provided an elaborate explanation of the Delaware block method and its application.

Piemonte involved an appeal from an appraisal proceeding following the merger of Boston Garden Arena Corporation (Garden Arena) on July 19, 1973, into New Boston Garden Corp. Among Garden Arena's assets were the stock of two corporations (one of which held a National Hockey League while the other held an American Hockey League franchise), the Boston Garden Sports Arena and the stock of a corporation that operated the Garden's food and beverage concessions. Both sides appealed from the trial judge's determination that the fair value of a share of Garden Arena stock as of the date preceding the merger was $75.27.

In making his determination, the trial judge applied the "Delaware block method" of valuation which requires that the court determine value by taking a weighted average of the market value, earnings value and net asset value of the stock. The court's calculation was as follows:

	Value ($)	Weight (%)	Result ($)
Market Value:	26.50	10	2.65
Earnings Value:	52.60	40	21.04
Net Asset Value:	103.16	50	51.58
	Total Value Per Share:		75.27

Id. at 1148 n.3.

In challenging these conclusions, plaintiffs argued that the judge should have disregarded market value because trading in the stock was so limited as to make it undeterminable. Defendants, on the other hand, argued that he should have reconstructed market value based on comparable companies. The court had this to say:

> Market value may be a significant factor, even the dominant factor, in determining the "fair value" of shares of a particular corporation under G.L. c. 156B, §92. Shares regularly traded on a recognized stock exchange are particularly susceptible to valuation on the basis of their market price, although even in such cases the market value may well not be conclusive.... On the other hand, where there is no established market for a particular stock, actual market value cannot be used. In such cases, a judge might undertake to "reconstruct" market value, but he is not obliged to do so.[7] Indeed, the process of the reconstruction of market value may actually be no more than a variation on the valuation of corporate assets and corporate earnings.

In this case, Garden Arena stock was traded on the Boston Stock Exchange, but rarely. Approximately ninety per cent of the company's stock was held by the controlling interests and not traded. Between January 1, 1968, and December 4, 1972, 16,741 shares were traded. During this period, an annual average of approximately 1.5% of the outstanding stock changed hands. In 1972, 4,372 shares were traded at prices ranging from $20.50 a share to $29 a share. The public announcement of the proposed merger was made on December 7, 1972. The last prior sale of 200 shares on December 4, 1972, was made at $26.50 a share. The judge accepted that sale price as the market price to be used in his determination of value.

The judge concluded that the volume of trading was sufficient to permit a determination of market value and expressed a preference for the actual sale price over any reconstruction of a market value, which he concluded would place "undue reliance on corporations, factors, and circumstances not applicable to Garden Arena stock." The decision to consider market value and the market value selected were within the judge's discretion.

Id. at 1149.

Next, both parties objected to the judge's determination of earnings value, which he determined by averaging Garden Arena's earnings per share for the five fiscal years ending before the merger date and applying a multiplier of 10. The court described the process of earnings valuation as follows:

> Delaware case law, which, as we have said, we regard as instructive but not binding, has established a method of computing value based on corporate earnings. The appraiser generally starts by computing the average earnings of

---

7. The Delaware cases require the reconstruction of market value only when the actual market value cannot be determined and a hypothetical market value can be reconstructed. Compare *Application of Del. Racing Ass'n*, 213 A.2d 203, 211-212 (Del. 1965), with *Universal City Studios, Inc. v. Francis I. duPont & Co.*, 334 A.2d 216, 222 (Del. 1975).

the corporation for the past five years.[8] ... Extraordinary gains and losses are excluded from the average earnings calculation.... The appraiser then selects a multiplier (to be applied to the average earnings) which reflects the prospective financial condition of the corporation and the risk factor inherent in the corporation and the industry.... In selecting a multiplier, the appraiser generally looks to other comparable corporations. *Universal City Studios, Inc. v. Francis I. duPont & Co., supra* at 219 [334 A.2d 216, 219-21 (Del. 1875)] (averaging price-earnings ratios of nine other motion picture companies as of date of merger).... The appraiser's choice of a multiplier is largely discretionary and will be upheld if it is "within the range of reason." *Universal City Studios, Inc. v. Francis I. duPont & Co., supra* at 219 (approving a multiplier of 16.1).... [9]

Id. at 1150.

The court deferred to the trial judge's choice of a multiplier based upon his evaluation of "'the specific situation and prospects of the Garden Arena,'" rather than providing greater emphasis on comparable corporations. The court also deferred to the trial judge's exclusion of Garden Arena's dividend record from consideration, noting that dividend policy was implicitly included in consideration of market value, and that separate consideration of dividends was unnecessary since the latter "tend to reflect the same factors as earnings." The court also held that the trial judge had not abused his discretion in including expansion income rather than excluding it as extraordinary, based upon the historical role of expansion income in Garden Arena's business.

Finally, the court evaluated the parties' objections to the trial judge's determination of net asset value as follows:

> The judge determined total net asset value by first valuing the net assets of Garden Arena apart from the Bruins franchise and the concession operations at Boston Garden. He selected $9,400,000 (the June 30, 1973, book value of Garden Arena), as representing that net asset value. Then, he added his valuations of the Bruins franchise ($9,600,000) and the concession operation ($4,200,000) to arrive at a total asset value of $23,200,000, or $103.16 a share.[10]

* * *

> The defendant objects to the judge's refusal to deduct $1,116,000 from the $9,400,000, that represented the net asset value of Garden Arena (exclusive of the net asset value of the Bruins franchise and the concession operation). The defendant's expert testified that the $9,400,000 figure included $1,116,000 attributable to the goodwill of the Bruins, net player investment, and the value of

---

8. A 1976 amendment to the Delaware statute requires the court to appraise the stock rather than appoint an appraiser. 60 Del. Laws, c. 371, Del. Code tit. 8, §262(f).

9. Although Delaware courts have relied on, and continue to rely on, Professor Dewing's capitalization chart (see 1 A.S. Dewing, The Financial Policy of Corporations 390-391 [5th ed. 1953]), they have recognized that it is somewhat outdated and no longer the "be-all and end-all" on the subject of earnings value. See *Universal City Studios, Inc. v. Francis I. duPont & Co., supra* at 219; *Swanton* v. *State Guar. Corp.*, 42 Del. Ch. 477, 483-484, 215 A.2d 242 (1965). [The capitalization chart referred to by the court consisted of Professor Dewing's suggested capitalization rates for various types of businesses, which is set forth in Note 3 at the end of this subsection.—Eds.]

10. $23,200,000 / 224,892 (the number of outstanding shares).

the AHL franchise. The judge recognized that the items included in the $1,116,000 should not be valued twice and seemingly agreed that they would be more appropriately included in the value of the Bruins franchise than in the $9,400,000. He was not plainly wrong, however, in declining to deduct them from the $9,400,000, because, as is fully warranted from the testimony of the defendant's expert, the judge concluded that the defendant's expert did not include these items in his determination of the value of the Bruins franchise. The defendant's expert, whose determination the judge accepted, arrived at his value of the Bruins franchise by adding certain items to the cost of a new NHL franchise, but none of those items included goodwill, net player investment, or the value of an AHL franchise. Acceptance of the defendant's argument would have resulted in these items' being entirely omitted from the net asset valuation of Garden Arena.[12]

The plaintiffs object that the judge did not explicitly determine the value of the Boston Garden and implicitly undervalued it. Garden Arena had purchased the Boston Garden on May 25, 1973, for $4,000,000, and accounted for it on the June 30, 1973, balance sheet as a $4,000,000 asset with a corresponding mortgage liability of $3,437,065. Prior to the purchase, Garden Arena had held a long-term lease which was unfavorable to the owner of the Boston Garden.[13] The existence of the lease would tend to depress the purchase price.

The judge stated that the $9,400,000 book value "*includes* a reasonable value for Boston Garden" (emphasis supplied). He did not indicate whether, if he had meant to value the Boston Garden at its purchase price (with an adjustment for the mortgage liabilities), he had considered the effect the lease would have had on that price. While we recognize that the fact-finding role of the judge permits him to reject the opinions of the various experts,[14] we conclude, in the absence of an explanation of his reasons, that it is possible that the judge did not give adequate consideration to the value of the Garden property. The judge should consider this subject further on remand.

A major area of dispute was the value of the Bruins franchise. The judge rejected the value advanced by the plaintiffs' expert ($18,000,000), stating that "[a]lthough the defendant's figure of [$9,600,000] seems somewhat low in comparison with the cost of expansion team franchises, *the Court is constrained* to accept defendant's value as it is the more creditable and legally appropriate expert opinion in the record" (emphasis supplied). Although the choice of the word "constrained" may have been inadvertent, it connotes a sense of obligation. As the trier of fact, the judge was not bound to accept the valuation of either one expert or the other. He was entitled to reach his own conclusion as to value....

---

12. One of the points on which we will remand this case is the valuation of the Bruins franchise. Since, as discussed below, the judge need not have felt constrained to accept the defendant's expert's opinion on this issue, on remand he will be free to determine the value of the franchise based on such evidence as he chooses to accept. Assignment of a different value to the franchise may require an adjustment in the net asset value of Garden Arena if the franchise value determined by the judge includes some or all of the items supposedly included in the $1,116,000.

13. The lease, which ran until June 1, 1986, contained a fixed maximum rent and an obligation on the lessee to pay only two-thirds of any increase in local real estate taxes. In a period of inflation and rising local real estate taxes, the value of the lease to the lessor was decreasing annually.

14. The lowest value expressed by any expert for the plaintiffs was $8,250,000 (exclusive of mortgage liabilities), based on depreciated reproduction cost. The defendant offered no testimony concerning the value of the property on July 18, 1973.

Because the judge may have felt bound to accept the value placed on the Bruins franchise by the defendant's expert, we shall remand this case for him to arrive at his own determination of the value of the Bruins franchise. He would be warranted in arriving at the same valuation as that advanced on behalf of the defendant, but he is not obliged to do so.

The defendant argues that, in arriving at the value of the assets of Garden Arena, the judge improperly placed a separate value on the right to operate concessions at the Boston Garden. We agree with the judge. The fact that earnings from concessions were included in the computation of earnings value, one component in the formula, does not mean that the value of the concessions should have been excluded from the computation of net asset value, another such component.

The value of the concession operation was not reflected in the value of the real estate. Real estate may be valued on the basis of rental income, but it is not valued on the basis of the profitability of business operations within the premises.... Moreover, it is manifest that the value of the concession operation was not included in the value placed on the Boston Garden. The record indicates that Garden Arena already owned the concession rights when it purchased the Boston Garden. The conclusion that the value of the concession operation was not reflected in the value of the Boston Garden is particularly warranted because the determined value of the right to operate the concessions ($4,200,000) was higher than the May 25, 1973, purchase price ($4,000,000) of the Boston Garden.

We do conclude, however, that the judge may have felt unnecessarily bound to accept the plaintiffs' evidence of the value of the concession operation. He stated that "since the defendant did not submit evidence on this issue, the Court will accept plaintiffs' expert appraisal of the value of the concession operation." Although the judge did not express the view that he was "constrained" to accept the plaintiffs' valuation, as he did concerning the defendant's valuation of the Bruins franchise, he may have misconstrued his authority on this issue. The judge was not obliged to accept the plaintiffs' evidence at face value merely because no other evidence was offered....

On remand, the judge should reconsider his determination of the value of the concession operation and exercise his own judgment concerning the bases for the conclusion arrived at by the plaintiffs' expert. However, the evidence did warrant the value selected by the judge, and no reduction in that value is required on this record.

Id. at 1151-53.

The court then determined that the weights assigned by the trial judge to each value determined were "reasonable and within the range of the judge's discretion," remanding the case for clarification and further consideration in accordance with its opinion.

———————

The Delaware Supreme Court abandoned the Delaware block method in *Weinberger v. UOP, Inc.,* 457 A.2d 701 (Del. 1983). Although not an appraisal proceeding, *Weinberger* dealt with the fiduciary duty of a parent corporation to the minority shareholders of its subsidiary in a parent-subsidiary merger. In announcing its new valuation approach, during its analysis of the fair price component of the entire fairness test, the court indicated that this approach would apply to appraisal proceedings:

Turning to the matter of price, plaintiff also challenges its fairness. His evidence was that on the date the merger was approved the stock was worth at least $26 per share. In support, he offered the testimony of a chartered investment analyst who used two basic approaches to valuation: a comparative analysis of the premium paid over market in ten other tender offer-merger combinations, and a discounted cash flow analysis.

In this breach of fiduciary duty case, the Chancellor perceived that the approach to valuation was the same as that in an appraisal proceeding. Consistent with precedent, he rejected plaintiff's method of proof and accepted defendants' evidence of value as being in accord with practice under prior case law. This means that the so-called "Delaware block" or weighted average method was employed wherein the elements of value, i.e., assets, market price, earnings, etc., were assigned a particular weight and the resulting amounts added to determine the value per share. This procedure has been in use for decades. *See In re General Realty & Utilities Corp.*, Del. Ch., 52 A.2d 6, 14-15 (1947). However, to the extent it excludes other generally accepted techniques used in the financial community and the courts, it is now clearly outmoded. It is time we recognize this in appraisal and other stock valuation proceedings and bring our law current on the subject.

While the Chancellor rejected plaintiff's discounted cash flow method of valuing UOP's stock, as not corresponding with "either logic or the existing law" (426 A.2d at 1360), it is significant that this was essentially the focus, i.e., earnings potential of UOP, of Mssrs. Arledge and Chitiea in their evaluation of the merger. Accordingly, the standard "Delaware block" or weighted average method of valuation, formerly employed in appraisal and other stock valuation cases, shall no longer exclusively control such proceedings. We believe that a more liberal approach must include proof of value by any techniques or methods which are generally considered acceptable in the financial community and otherwise admissible in court, subject only to our interpretation of 8 Del. C. §262(h), *infra. See also* [Delaware Rules of Evidence] 702-05. This will obviate the very structured and mechanistic procedure that has heretofore governed such matters....

Fair price obviously requires consideration of all relevant factors involving the value of a company. This has long been the law of Delaware as stated in *Tri-Continental Corp.*, 74 A.2d [71, 72 (Del. 1950)]

> The basic concept of value under the appraisal statute is that the stockholder is entitled to be paid for that which has been taken from him, viz., his proportionate interest in a going concern. By value of the stockholder's proportionate interest in the corporate enterprise is meant the true or intrinsic value of his stock which has been taken by the merger. In determining what figure represents this true or intrinsic value, the appraiser and the courts must take into consideration all factors and elements which reasonably might enter into the fixing of value. Thus, market value, asset value, dividends, earning prospects, the nature of the enterprise and any other facts which were known or which could be ascertained as of the date of merger and which throw any light on *future prospects* of the merged corporation are not only pertinent to an inquiry as to the value of the dissenting stockholders' interest, but *must be considered* by the agency fixing the value. (Emphasis added.)

This is not only in accord with the realities of present day affairs, but it is thoroughly consonant with the purpose and intent of our statutory law. Under 8 Del. C. §262(h), the Court of Chancery:

> shall appraise the shares, determining their *fair* value exclusive of any element of value arising from the accomplishment or expectation of the merger, together with a fair rate of interest, if any, to be paid upon the amount determined to be the *fair* value. In determining such *fair* value, the Court shall take into account *all relevant factors....* (Emphasis added.)

See also Bell v. Kirby Lumber Corp., Del. Supr., 413 A.2d 137, 150-51 (1980) (Quillen, J., concurring).

It is significant that section 262 now mandates the determination of "fair" value based upon "all relevant factors." Only the speculative elements of value that may arise from the "accomplishment or expectation" of the merger are excluded. We take this to be a very narrow exception to the appraisal process, designed to eliminate use of *pro forma* data and projections of a speculative variety relating to the completion of a merger. But elements of future value, including the nature of the enterprise, which are known or susceptible of proof as of the date of the merger and not the product of speculation, may be considered. When the trial court deems it appropriate, fair value also includes any damages, resulting from the taking, which the stockholders sustain as a class. If that was not the case, then the obligation to consider "all relevant factors" in the valuation process would be eroded. We are supported in this view not only by *Tri-Continental Corp.*, 74 A.2d at 72, but also by the evolutionary amendments to section 262.

* * *

Although the Chancellor received the plaintiff's evidence, his opinion indicates that the use of it was precluded because of past Delaware practice. While we do not suggest a monetary result one way or the other, we do think the plaintiff's evidence should be part of the factual mix and weighed as such. Until the $21 price is measured on remand by the valuation standards mandated by Delaware law, there can be no finding at the present stage of these proceedings that the price is fair. Given the lack of any candid disclosure of the material facts surrounding establishment of the $21 price, the majority of the minority vote, approving the merger, is meaningless.

In Leader v. Hycor, 395 Mass. 215, 479 N.E.2d 173 (1985), the Massachusetts Supreme Judicial Court affirmed the propriety (but not exclusivity) of the Delaware block method of valuation as set out in its opinion in *Piemonte* and notwithstanding its rejection by the Delaware court in *Weinberger*. After remanding the issue of fair price to the trial judge for an explanation of his reasoning, the court stated:

> Because the issue of the continuing validity of the "Delaware block method" of stock valuation is likely to arise on remand, we express our opinion on this matter. We do not agree that the "Delaware block method" for valuing closely held stock ... is outmoded. Citing *Weinberger v. UOP, Inc.*, 457 A.2d 701 (Del. 1983), the plaintiffs contend that the Delaware Supreme Court has rejected this valuation method. The *Weinberger* court stated that this method is outmoded "to the extent it excludes other generally accepted tech-

niques used in the financial community and the courts" and that it would no longer "*exclusively* control such proceedings" (emphasis added). *Weinberger, supra* at 712-713. We need not accept judicial interpretations of Delaware law made subsequent to our Legislature's adoption of c. 156B. *Id.* at 723. In any event, we have never held that the Delaware block method is the only approach that a judge may employ in valuing stock. In *Piemonte*, we stated that a judge "might appropriately follow" this general approach. *Id.* at 723-724.

Id. at 224, 479 N.E.2d 173, 178-79 (1985).

Notes and Questions

1. What virtue does the Massachusetts court apparently see in the Delaware block method? Would corporate management prefer the *Weinberger* approach or the Delaware block method? Why? What about shareholders and their lawyers?

2. For examples of courts continuing to apply the Delaware block method, see Genesco v. Scolaro, 871 S.W.2d 487 (Tenn. Ct. App. 1993); Sarrouf v. New England Patriots Football Club, 492 N.E.2d 1122 (Sup. Jud. Ct. Mass. 1986); Beerly v. Dep't of Treasury, 768 F.2d 942 (7th Cir. 1985).

3. The capitalization chart referred to in footnote 9 of the *Piemonte* opinion is as follows:

> Summary Statement of Capitalization of Earnings.... [I]t is possible to throw industrial businesses into diverse categories in accordance with which we can form some estimate of the value of a business by capitalizing its earnings. These categories could be described in the following manner:
>
> 1. Old established businesses, with large capital assets and excellent goodwill— 10%, a value ten times the net earnings. Very few industrial enterprises would come within this category.
>
> 2. Businesses, well established, but requiring considerable managerial care. To this category would belong the great number of old, successful industrial businesses—large and small—12½%, a value eight times the net earnings.
>
> 3. Businesses, well established, but involving possible loss in consequence of shifts of general economic conditions. They are strong, well established businesses, but they produce a type of commodity which makes them vulnerable to depressions. They require considerable managerial ability, but little special knowledge on the part of the executives—15%, a value approximately seven times the net earnings.
>
> 4. Businesses requiring average executive ability—and at the same time comparatively small capital investment. These businesses are highly competitive, but established goodwill is of distinct importance. This class include the rank and file of medium-sized, highly competitive industrial enterprises—20%, a value approximately five times the net earnings.
>
> 5. Small industrial businesses, highly competitive, and requiring a relatively small capital outlay. They are businesses which anyone, even with little capital, may enter—25%, a value approximately four times the net earnings.
>
> 6. Industrial businesses, large and small, which depend on the special, often unusual skill of one, or of a small group of managers. They involve only a

small amount of capital; they are highly competitive and the mortality is high among those who enter the competitive struggle—50%, a value approximately twice the net earnings.

7. Personal service businesses. They require no capital, or at the most a desk, some envelopes and a few sheets of paper. The manager must have a special skill coupled with an intensive and thorough knowledge of his subjects. The earnings of the enterprise are the objective reflection of his skill; and he is not likely to be able to create "an organization" which can successfully "carry on" after he is gone. He can sell the business, including the reputation and the "plan of business," but he cannot sell himself, the only truly valuable part of the enterprise—100%, a value equal, approximately, to the earnings of a single year.

This summary of categories is not a classification in the sense of clearly defined and marked classes. There are innumerable intermediate stages. These seven categories are of the nature of nodal points in the organization of industry, according to the relation of earnings and value. There may be businesses so highly stabilized, so immune to the shocks of industrial depression and incompetent management, that they are worth more than ten times their annual earnings; there may be businesses so peculiar and individual that they are, in the hands of another, not worth even the earnings of a single year.

1 Dewing, The Financial Policy of Corporations 390-91 (5th ed. 1953).

4. On what theory of the corporation is the appraisal remedy based? How does the traditional limitation of appraisal rights to certain forms of merger, sales of all or substantially all the assets, and material charter amendments reflect upon this? *Consider* Manning, The Shareholder's Appraisal Remedy: An Essay for Frank Coker, 72 Yale L.J. 223, 244-48 (1962):[a]

> There is nothing economically baneful about a merger; it may, frequently will, greatly benefit the shareholder. Of course economic loss *can* follow from the merger, but in this respect the merger is not distinguishable from any other transaction [of a variety enumerated by Dean Manning as to which appraisal rights are not given.] ... So why the merger?

> The answer must be sought not in economics but in ideology....

> * * *

> .... Monuments often outlive the philosophies they were built to glorify. The pyramids are one example. The appraisal statutes are another. To the nineteenth century mind contemplating such matters, a corporate merger was a major and significant event. In the first place it involved a species of corporate assassination. A "corporation" died. A three-dimensional thing, created by the sovereign legislature, had passed away. These things were not matters to be taken casually. But something else happened, too. The shareholders of corporation A somehow became shareholders of corporation B and no longer shareholders of corporation A. The mere statement of such a preposterous proposition did violence to fundamental principles. How *could* a man who owned a horse suddenly find that he owned a cow? Furthermore—or perhaps this is but another statement of the same point—even if this transmutation could somehow be brought off,

---

a. Reprinted by permission of The Yale Law Journal Company and Fred B. Rothman & Company from The Yale Law Journal, Vol. 72, pp. 223-65.

surely it could not constitutionally be done without the owner's consent. You might try to persuade him to sell his horse or to exchange it for a cow, but surely you could not whisk it away from him. Freedom of contract, rights of property, Constitution, law, and morals would forbid it, even if the *leger domain* for the conversion had been mastered. Given a nineteenth century view of freedom of contract this line of reasoning required only one premise: a "corporation" is just like a horse. The law of the last century had no doubt that it was.

Nebulous suspicions about big economic combinations helped to reinforce this jaundiced view of the merger. Mack the Knife says somewhere in the Three Penny Opera: "I rob banks. Is it worse to rob a bank than merge a bank?" Whether Brecht was just flaying capitalists, slyly supporting Stalin's role in the Georgian banking operations, or merely writing a sharp line for audience response, is hard to say. But it is certain that the public, even the most educated public, has had no success at all in distinguishing the corporate form from the underlying economic event. Orators have always inveighed against "corporations" when they meant large enterprises; and the people have suspected "mergers" and passed laws against "trusts" when they had in mind business combines. Public education on these matters has not been accelerated by the fact that much of the time the bar, the legislatures, and the courts have had them all mixed up too.

In any case, to the nineteenth century mind, mergers were deeply suspect. When commercial pressures forced the enactment of the general merger statutes, the function of the appraisal statutes was clear. They met a conceptual and ideological problem — how to preserve the constitutionality of the merger statutes. The appraisal provisions were calculated to solve a purely conceptual need — to provide something for the shareholder who was about to undergo a *legal* trauma — a trauma deemed compensable regardless of its economic consequences upon him. By ideological assumption, no one but a shareholder could suffer this trauma; only other shareholders could inflict it; and damages were irrelevant. It never occurred to anyone to ask about the effect of the combination of enterprises on various economic groups; the problem at hand was the effect of the combination of the "corporations" upon the only group that had a stake in the "corporations" — the shareholders....

There would never have been appraisal statutes of the kind we now have if the courts had not balked at the constitutionality of the statutory merger. Under modern views of a business enterprise no court would conceivably hold a statutory merger unconstitutional because not accompanied by an appraisal opportunity. And no economic argument exists for singling out ... the particular formal device of merger for such special treatment. The appraisal remedy as applied to mergers is a pure anachronism — a residual adaptation to an extinct theological problem.

Professor Eisenberg responds to Dean Manning, Eisenberg, The Legal Roles of Shareholders and Management in Modern Corporate Decisionmaking, 57 Calif. L. Rev. 1, 77-79 (1969),[b] in part as follows:

[Manning's] thesis is open to question on at least three grounds:

(1) It has already been seen that the changes which require shareholder approval under the traditional statutes are not coextensive with the changes we

b. © 1969 by California Law Review, Inc. Reprinted from California Law Review Vol. 57 No. 1, (January 1969), pp. 77-79, by permission.

have labeled structural in the normative model. Nevertheless, when the normative model is laid alongside the traditional statutes, a strong structural motif becomes visible. It is true that at first glance this structural motif appears to relate, as Manning argues, to changes in the legal structure of the corporation (that is, changes in the corporate entity), rather than changes in the economic structure of the corporation (that is, changes in the corporate enterprise). Viewing the traditional fundamental changes in this light, it could indeed be concluded that the traditional statutes require shareholder approval for mergers and certificate amendments only because they involve rearrangement of the legal structure and for the sale of substantially all assets because it involves a de facto amendment of the certificate. So viewed, the corporate statutes would indeed seem based on economically irrelevant criteria.

But the statutes can also be viewed in another light. It is possible that the purpose of the statutes was to govern structural changes in the enterprise, and that they dealt in terms with changes in the legal structure only because such changes provided a convenient and readily identifiable handle for latching on to changes in the enterprise. Thus the statutes may have required shareholder approval for mergers, as a way of governing the restructuring of the enterprise through a combination; for certificate amendment, as a way of governing changes in the relative rights of shareholders and in the purpose of the enterprise; for dissolution, as a way of governing termination of the structure of the enterprise; and for sale of substantially all assets, as a way of governing certain transformations in the nature of the enterprise's assets....

(2) Manning's argument that appraisal rights have a constitutional genesis is at best a minority view. Most commentators hold the opinion that the legislatures conferred appraisal rights on dissenting shareholders as a matter of fairness, not as a matter of constitutional compulsion. Ballantine seems to have gone about as far as one may fairly go on the basis of existing evidence when he said that "It is not easy to ascertain whether this remedy ... is intended for the benefit and protection of the minority or for the benefit of the majority to remove any doubt about the constitutionality of fundamental changes without unanimous consent."

(3) Finally, and most important, if we look at the statutes as a whole, rather than looking only at the merger provisions, Manning's thesis — that the appraisal right is based on ideological and constitutional principles, not on economics — turns out to be wholly inconsistent with the statutes it purports to explain. If Manning's thesis is correct, it should follow that: (1) A merger would not trigger appraisal rights for the survivor's shareholders, since the entity of the survivor need not be affected by a merger, and the only necessary effect of a merger on such shareholders is an economic one; (2) An amendment of the certificate of incorporation should normally trigger appraisal rights, since it involves a change in the entity; (3) Dissolution should trigger appraisal rights for the same reason; (4) A sale of all assets should not trigger appraisal rights, since it does not affect the entity, and its only effect on the survivor's shareholders is an economic one.

The hard facts, however, are that in each case just the contrary is true: (1) A merger normally triggers appraisal rights for the survivor's shareholders; (2) Amendment of the certificate usually does not trigger appraisal rights; (3) Dissolution never triggers appraisal rights; (4) A sale of substantially all assets usually does trigger appraisal rights.

But assuming that Manning's specific criticisms are not wellfounded [sic], we are still left with the larger question he raises: Is the appraisal right desirable? Does it have any real utility? Again, it is necessary to separate out privately and publicly held corporations.

5. On appraisal rights generally, see Hossfeld, Short-Form Mergers After Glassman v. Unocal Exploration Corp.: Time to Reform Appraisal, 53 Duke L.J. 1337 (2004); Carney & Heimendinger, Doctrines and Markets: Appraising the Nonexistent: The Delaware Courts' Struggle with Control Premiums, 68 S. Cal. L. Rev. 719 (2003); Letsou, The Role of Appraisal in Corporate Law, 39 B.C. L. Rev. 1121 (1998).

(B) Modern Application

Scores of Delaware appraisal proceedings have involved application of the *Weinberger* approach. The cases reveal an explosion of valuation methodologies involving an astonishing array of variations on those set forth in Section 3. However, as seen in *Le Beau* below, litigants have increasingly argued the discounted cash flow method, or a variant thereon, in Delaware courts.

Students understandably are curious as to the exact methodology employed to value a company during an appraisal proceeding. *Le Beau* provides a vivid discussion of the "battle of the experts" that occurs in such a proceeding, as the court looks in detail at the merits and demerits of the various valuation methods that the parties' experts utilized. After reading the case, perhaps you'll agree that valuation, like the making of sausage, is better left to the imagination!

Le Beau v. M.G. Bancorporation, Inc.
1998 WL 44993 (Del. Ch. 1998),
aff'd in part & remanded in part, 737 A.2d 513 (Del. 1999)

JACOBS, Vice Chancellor:

[A group of shareholders of MGB, a Delaware-chartered bank holding company headquartered in Illinois, petitioned the court to value their shares of common stock that were eliminated in a merger of MGB with and into Southwest Bancorp, Inc. Before the merger, MGB also owned equity interests in two operating bank subsidiaries, Mount Greenwood Bank (of which it owned 100%) and Worth Bancorp, Inc. ("WBC") (of which it owned 75.5%).]

Before the Merger, Southwest owned 91.68% of MGB's common shares. On November 17, 1993, MGB was merged into Southwest in a "short form merger" under 8 Del. C. §253. Because the Merger was accomplished unilaterally, neither MGB's board of directors nor its minority shareholders were legally required to, or did, vote on the transaction. MGB's minority shareholders were offered $41 in cash per share in the Merger. The Petitioners rejected that offer, electing instead to pursue their statutory appraisal rights.

To assist it in setting the Merger price, Southwest engaged Alex Sheshunoff & Co. Investment Bankers ("Sheshunoff") to determine the "fair market value" of MGB's minority shares. In a report submitted to Southwest on or about October 28, 1993, Sheshunoff determined that the fair market value of MGB's minority shares was $41 per share as of June 30, 1993.

The Petitioners commenced this appraisal proceeding on March 15, 1994.... At trial the Petitioners' expert witness, David Clarke ("Clarke"), testified that as of the Merger date the fair value of MGB common stock was at least $85 per share. In arriving at that conclusion, Clarke used three distinct methodologies to value MGB's two operating bank subsidiaries: (i) the comparative publicly-traded company approach, (ii) the discounted cash flow ("DCF") method, and (iii) the comparative acquisition technique. Clarke then added a control premium to the values of the two subsidiaries to reflect the value of the holding company's (MGB's) controlling interest in those subsidiaries. Lastly, Clarke then added the value of MGB's remaining assets to the sum of his valuations of the two subsidiaries, to arrive at an overall fair value of $85 per share for MGB.

Clarke's comparative publicly-traded company approach involved five steps: (1) identifying an appropriate set of comparable companies, (2) identifying the multiples of earnings and book value at which the comparable companies traded, (3) comparing certain of MGB's financial fundamentals (e.g., return on assets and return on equity) to those of the comparable companies, (4) making certain adjustments to those financial fundamentals, and (5) adding an appropriate control premium. After completing the first four steps, Clarke arrived at a value for WBC of $33.059 million ($48.02 per share), and for Greenwood of $20.952 million ($30.44 per share). Clarke next determined that during the period January 1989 to June 1993, acquirors of controlling interests in publicly-traded companies had paid an average premium of at least 35%. On that basis, Clarke concluded that a 35% premium was appropriate, and applied that premium to the values he had determined for Greenwood and WBC, to arrive at fair values of $43.3 million ($62.90 per share) for WBC and $27.1 million ($39.37 per share) for Greenwood, respectively. Clarke then valued MGB's 75.5% controlling interest in WBC at $32.691 million ($47.49 per share), and MGB's 100% interest in Greenwood at $27.1 million ($39.37 per share), under his comparative company approach.

Clarke's DCF valuation analysis involved four steps: (1) projecting the future net cash flows available to MGB's shareholders for ten years after the Merger date, (2) discounting those future cash flows to present value as of the Merger date by using a discount rate based on the weighted average cost of capital ("WACC"), (3) adding a terminal value that represented the present value of all future cash flows generated after the ten year projection period, and (4) applying a control premium to the sum of (2) and (3).

Clarke did not create his own cash flow projections. He used the projections made by Sheshunoff at the time of the Merger, because Southwest's own management had accepted those projections when they fixed the Merger price. Clarke also accepted Sheshunoff's ten year projection period, because he independently had concluded that it would require ten years for MGB's cash flows to stabilize. Based on a 1996 Ibbotson Associates ("Ibbotson") study of the banking industry, Clarke concluded that the appropriate "small stock" premium to be used to determine MGB's discount rate (WACC), was 1%, and that the appropriate discount rate (WACC) for MGB was 12%. Applying that 12% discount rate, Clarke calculated the present value of WBC's future cash flows to be $17.251 million, and WBC's terminal value to be $14.824 million. Applying that same 12% discount rate, Clarke arrived at a present value of $10.937 million, and a terminal value of $9.138 million, for Greenwood.

Applying the same 35% control premium to those values of the two subsidiaries, Clarke calculated MGB's 75.5% interest in WBC at $33.824 million or $49.14 per share; and MGB's 100% interest in Greenwood at $28.3 million, or $41.11 per share.

Clarke's third valuation approach, the comparative acquisition method, focused upon multiples of MGB's last twelve months earnings and its tangible book value. Those multiples were determined by reference to the prices at which the stock of comparable companies had been sold in transactions involving the sale of control. Unlike the comparative company and DCF valuation approaches, this method did not require adding a control premium to the values of the subsidiaries because under that methodology, the parent holding company's controlling interest in the subsidiaries was already accounted for.

In valuing MGB under his third approach, Clarke identified three transactions involving community banks in the relevant geographic area that occurred within one year of the Merger. He also considered data published by The Chicago Corporation in its September 1993 issue of Midwest Bank & Thrift Survey. From these sources, Clarke determined that (i) control of WBC could be sold for a price between a multiple of 14 times WBC's last twelve months' earnings and 200% of WBC's tangible book value, and that (ii) control of Greenwood could be sold for a price between a multiple of 12 times Greenwood's last twelve months' earnings and 175% of its tangible book value. Giving equal weight to these two sets of values, Clarke valued MGB's 75.5% interest in WBC at $28.8 million (75.5% x $38.1 million) or $41.84 per share, and MGB's 100% interest in Greenwood, at $22.9 million, or $33.27 per share.

Having valued MGB's two subsidiaries, Clarke then determined the fair value of MGB's remaining net assets, which included (i) a $6.83 million note payable by Southwest, (ii) certain intangibles that Clarke did not include in his valuation, (iii) $78,000 in cash, and (iv) other assets worth $2000. These assets totaled $6.91 million, from which Clarke subtracted liabilities of $96,000 to arrive at a net asset value of $6.814 million ($9.90 per share) for MGB's remaining assets.

Clarke then added the values he had determined under each of his valuation methodologies, for (i) MGB's 75.5% interest in WBC, (ii) MGB's 100% interest in Greenwood, and (iii) MGB's 100% interest in its remaining assets. Under his comparative publicly-traded method, Clarke concluded that MGB's value was $76.59 per share with no control premium, and $96.76 per share with a control premium. Under his DCF approach, Clarke determined that MGB's value was $74.75 per share with no control premium, and $100.15 per share with a control premium. And under his comparative acquisitions method, Clarke concluded that MGB's minimum fair value was $85 per share, which represented the median of the values described above.

Respondents relied upon the testimony of Mr. Robert Reilly ("Reilly"), who opined that as of the Merger date, the fair value of MGB common stock was $41.90 per share— only 90 cents per share more than Sheshunoff's $41 valuation. Reilly arrived at that result by performing two separate valuations: a DCF analysis and a "capital market" analysis. Reilly did not include any control premium, having determined that a control premium was inappropriate in valuing a holding company such as MGB.

Reilly's DCF analysis consisted of: (1) projecting MGB's future net cash flows available to shareholders for a period of five years after the Merger date, (2) determining an appropriate discount rate and discounting those future cash flows back to the Merger date, and (3) adding a terminal value that represented the present value of all future cash flows beyond the five year projection period. Reilly used a five year period, because in his opinion any longer interval would be too speculative. Relying on a 1992 Ibbotson study that was not specific to the banking industry, he also concluded that 5.2% was the appropriate small stock size premium to use for purposes of determining the WACC for MGB.

In determining an appropriate discount rate, Reilly concluded that MGB was subject to certain company-specific risks, namely, litigation involving its data processor (BYSIS) and MGB's dependence upon a single key supplier. Reilly quantified those risks at four percentage points, and on that basis concluded that the appropriate discount rate for MGB was 18%. Applying that 18% discount rate to MGB's future cash flows, Reilly valued MGB at $29.220 million, or $42.45 per share, on the basis of his DCF approach.

Reilly's second method for valuing MGB was the "capital market" method, which involved: (1) identifying a portfolio of guideline publicly-traded companies, (2) identifying appropriate pricing multiples for those companies, (3) using the multiples for the guideline companies to calculate the appropriate pricing multiples for MGB[6] and (4) applying the multiples to the corresponding financial indicators for MGB. By this method, Reilly concluded that MGB was worth $28.4 million, or $41.26 per share, at the time of the Merger.

Reilly then averaged his DCF and capital market valuations, to arrive at an ultimate fair value for MGB of $41.90 per share.

The first [issue] is whether Reilly's "capital market" valuation approach is legally permissible in this case. The specific question is whether that valuation method is generally accepted or recognized in the financial community for purposes of valuing a bank or bank holding company.

Neither side contests the validity per se of either the comparative publicly-traded company or the DCF valuation approaches. Both sides claim that the other improperly applied those methodologies to MGB. That frames the second set of issues regarding Clarke's publicly-traded company analysis, which are: (i) did Clarke use the proper financial indicators, (ii) did Clarke erroneously rely upon stock price quotes for the six weeks preceding the Merger, and (iii) was five years an appropriate historical period to compare the financial indicators and to make future growth projections? Respecting each side's DCF analysis, the issues concern (i) the appropriate discount rate and (ii) the appropriate projection period.

It is a well-established principle of Delaware law that the objective of a section 262 appraisal is "to value the corporation itself, as distinguished from a fraction of its shares as they may exist in the hands of a particular shareholder." Based on that principle, this Court determined in its earlier Opinion that Sheshunoff's $41 valuation was impermissible under 8 Del. C. §262, because it was an appraisal not of the entire corporation as a going concern but only of a minority block of its shares. Presumably that is why the Respondents chose not to rely upon the Sheshunoff valuation or to call Sheshunoff personnel as trial witnesses. Instead, Respondents elected to rely solely upon Reilly's valuation, which resulted in the same $41 per share value that Sheshunoff had arrived at by a valuation approach found to be improper.

The fact that Reilly's per share fair value determination serendipitously turned out to be only 90 cents per share more than Sheshunoff's legally flawed $41 valuation, cannot help but render Respondent's valuation position highly suspect and meriting the most careful judicial scrutiny. As a matter of plain common sense, it would appear evident that a proper fair value determination based upon a going concern valuation of the en-

---

6. Reilly's pricing multiples were all related to the market value of invested capital ("MVIC"). Reilly computed the ratios of MVIC to: (1) earnings before interest and taxes ("EBIT"); (2) earnings before interest, depreciation and taxes ("EBIDT"); (3) debt free net income ("DFNI"); (4) debt free cash flow ("DFCF"); (5) interest income; and (6) total book value of invested capital ("TBVIC").

tire company, would significantly exceed a $41 per share fair market valuation of only a minority block of its shares. If Respondents choose to contend otherwise, it is their burden to persuade the Court that $41.90 per share represents MGB's fair value. The Court concludes that the Respondents have fallen far short of carrying their burden, and independently determines that the fair value of MGB at the time of the Merger was $85 per share.

The Court first addresses whether Reilly's capital market approach is legally permissible. That valuation approach (to repeat) involved deriving various pricing multiples from selected publicly-traded companies, and then applying those multiples to MGB, resulting in a valuation of $41.26 per share.

The Petitioners argue that Reilly's capital market valuation method is impermissible because it includes a built-in minority discount. The valuation literature, including a treatise co-authored by Reilly himself, supports that position, and Respondents have introduced no evidence to the contrary. Nor did the Respondents establish that Reilly's capital market method is generally accepted by the financial community for purposes of valuing bank holding companies, as distinguished from other types of enterprises. Reilly determined the ratio of MVIC to other financial measures such as EBIT, EBIDT, DFNI, DFCF, Interest Income, and TBVIC—ratios that the record indicates are not used to value banks.

Because Reilly's capital market method results in a minority valuation, and the Respondents have failed to establish that that approach is generally accepted in the financial community to value banks or bank holding companies, the Court must conclude that in this specific case Reilly's capital market approach is improper, and must be rejected.[18]

The Court next considers (i) whether Clarke properly applied his comparative company analysis to MGB, and (ii) whether both sides' experts properly applied their respective DCF analyses to MGB. The validity per se of these two valuation methodologies is not in dispute.

A primary issue dividing the parties concerns the companies chosen as "comparable" to the corporation being appraised. A determination of that kind is necessarily fact intensive.

In performing his comparative company analysis, Clarke selected as comparables, banks having financial ratios, geographic locations, and demographic factors similar to those of MGB's two bank subsidiaries. Reilly, on the other hand, included companies that operated outside MGB's geographic location, in different economic environments, and in different lines of business. Where the valuation exercise rests upon data derived from companies comparable to the company being valued, it stands to reason that the more "comparable" the company, the more reliable will be the resulting valuation information. The Court concludes that in this case it was sounder practice to use as comparables suburban banks located in the same geographic area (as Clarke did), rather than banks located outside of WBC's and Greenwood's immediate areas (as Reilly did). Accordingly, I find Clarke's comparable companies to be superior to Reilly's.

Another key difference between the parties' comparative publicly-traded company approaches is that Clarke used the price-to-earnings and price-to-book value financial

---

18. This conclusion should not be read as a categorical, matter-of-law determination that Reilly's capital market approach is an inappropriate method to value banks. The opposite may be true, but in this specific case the Respondents failed to discharge their burden of proof on that issue.

multiples, whereas Reilly used multiples based upon the market value of invested capital ("MVIC"). Relying upon various valuation authorities and publications, the Petitioners argue that where the enterprise being valued is a bank, the relevant ratios are price-to-earnings and price-to-book value. Reilly disagreed. He opined that it is more appropriate to compare the different financial measures as a fraction of MVIC, because that approach eliminates the distortions inherent in Clarke's financial ratios. Reilly did not elaborate on what those distortions were, however, nor did he point to specific cases where MVIC was considered an appropriate financial measure of a bank or bank holding company. Given this record, the Respondents have not persuaded the Court that MVIC is widely accepted in the financial community as a measure of the value of a bank or bank holding company.[21] Clarke's financial measures are generally accepted in the financial community for valuing banks, and the Court accepts them.

A third major difference between the parties' comparative company approaches is that Clarke used historical financial data going back five years before the Merger, whereas Reilly used historical financial data going back 2.75 years. In performing bank valuations, five year historical information is typically used. Reilly's position was that the banking industry had changed dramatically during the five years before the Merger, such that it was not appropriate to rely upon financial data going back that far.

At the heart of this dispute are the experts' differing assumptions about MGB's future growth prospects. The Respondents paint a bleak picture of MGB's future prospects for increasing its revenues; the Petitioners argue that MGB's future prospects were far brighter. Petitioners agree that a company's more recent historical economic averages are a good indicator of its future growth rate, but emphasize that a firm's financial trends are often more reliably evidenced by its performance over the past five years. I concur. Petitioners have demonstrated that MGB's historical performance, whether over the past five years, three years, or twelve months before the Merger, indicated significant future growth. Although MGB's subsidiary banks did face certain difficulties (specifically, a limited marketplace without high-potential for growth or expansion and a primarily blue-collar residential population), the Respondents have not persuaded me that this difficulty would likely prevent MGB's bank subsidiaries from maintaining their historical rates of growth.

A fourth major difference between the parties' comparative company analyses is that Reilly relied upon comparable company stock prices on the day before the Merger, whereas Clarke used price quotations six weeks before the Merger. Because the merger date (more specifically, the date before the public announcement of a merger) is normally the time that is relevant, and because the Petitioners made no effort to justify Clarke's use of stock prices going back six weeks before the Merger, the Court cannot accept Clarke's comparative company valuation, despite the validity of the technique itself. Clarke's use of six week old pre-merger stock prices represents a departure from the norm without demonstrated justification.

To summarize, Reilly's capital market approach must be rejected because it was not shown to be generally accepted in the financial community for bank valuation purposes. Clarke's comparative company valuation must be rejected because it was improperly applied in this specific case. Accordingly, the only valuation methodologies remain-

---

21. The use of MVIC as a tool to value other kinds of enterprises is, of course, widely accepted. See Rapid-American Corp. v. Harris, 603 A.2d 796 (1992). Again, the Court's conclusion that MVIC has not been shown to be an appropriate measure of a bank's value is fact-specific to this case, and by virtue of the Respondent's failure of proof.

ing to be considered are (i) Reilly's and Clarke's DCF valuations and (ii) Clarke's comparative acquisition analysis.

The parties' competing DCF analyses raise three questions. First, were the so-called "key supplier dependence" and "litigation risks" a proper basis for determining Reilly's 18% discount factor, or were those risks contrived solely for litigation purposes? Second, was it appropriate for Clarke to determine a 1% small stock size premium based on the 1996 Ibbotson study that was specific to the banking industry? Third, what cash flow projection period (five or ten years), and what growth rate after the fifth year, are appropriate assumptions for a DCF valuation of MGB?

Specifically, the parties' DCF valuations differ with respect to: (i) how many years into the future cash flows should be projected (ten years versus five years), (ii) what growth rate assumption after the fifth projection year is appropriate for MGB, (iii) should the Court credit the assumptions Sheshunoff made in valuing MGB in 1993, and (iv) what discount rate is appropriate for MGB. As more fully elaborated below, the Court finds it appropriate (a) to project future cash flows for a period of ten years into the future at a constant 4% growth rate, (b) to assign a high degree of reliability to Sheshunoff's remaining DCF assumptions (except for its minority discount), and (c) to accept neither Clarke's 12% discount rate nor Reilly's 18% discount rate.

The difference between Clarke's 12% discount rate and Reilly's 18% discount rate is attributable primarily to their different estimates of MGB's cost of equity capital, and their different assessments of the company specific risks confronting MGB at the time of the Merger. Reilly selected an equity risk premium based upon a 1992 Ibbotson study indicating that an appropriate small stock premium factor was 5.2%. Clarke relied on a 1996 Ibbotson study indicating that a premium of 1% was appropriate. The problem with the 1992 Ibbotson study was that it is not specific to the banking industry. The problem with the 1996 Ibbotson study is that although it was specific to the banking industry, the Petitioners have not shown that the data contained in that study (and relied upon by Clarke) was in existence as of the Merger date. The Court, therefore, is unable to accept the 1996 Ibbotson study, and the 12% discount rate derived therefrom.

Reilly's 18% discount rate is also flawed, however, because it rests on the unsupported assumption that at the time of the Merger, MGB was subject to certain material risks that required a steep discount of MGB's projected future cash flow. Reilly placed great emphasis upon MGB's dependence upon one key supplier and upon the pending litigation involving BYSIS, MGB's data process server as a basis to conclude that MGB involved abnormal business risk to a potential acquiror. The underlying evidence that these "risks" were material is unpersuasive. No document contemporaneous with the Merger shows that Southwest's or MGB's management or boards viewed these developments as material risks. Importantly, nowhere in its valuation report did Sheshunoff allude to those risks.... Of considerable importance also is that Sheshunoff concluded that a 10% discount factor (2% lower than Clarke's) was appropriate, and management accepted that discount assumption. Accordingly, the Court concludes that Reilly's 18% discount rate is inappropriately high and not supported by the record.

The final major difference between the parties' DCF analyses is that Clarke projected ten years of future cash flows at a constant growth rate of 4% using many of Sheshunoff's projections; whereas Reilly projected future cash flows for only five years, at a growth rate that decreased after the fifth year, using his (Reilly's) own projections. Sheshunoff used a ten year projection period for future cash flows, and assumed a constant rate of growth. Because Sheshunoff performed its valuation at the time of the

Merger, without the benefit of hindsight and when no litigation was pending, and management accepted its assumptions, the Court accepts Sheshunoff's DCF assumptions (except for its minority discount) as more appropriate than Reilly's litigation-driven (and extremely conservative) assumptions.

Because neither side has supported certain key DCF valuation assumptions by a preponderance of persuasive evidence, the Court is unable to accept either Clarke's or Reilly's discounted cash flow valuations. That leaves Clarke's comparative acquisition approach....

Having rejected Clarke's DCF and comparative company valuations, both of which involved directly adding a control premium to the values of MGB's two subsidiaries, the Court need not decide whether the direct addition of a premium is or is not mandated by *Rapid-American*. Nonetheless, the Court must address the control premium issue, but in a different context. That is, the Court must decide whether Clarke's comparative acquisition valuation, in which a control premium is implicit, is proscribed by §262. I conclude that it is not.

In *Rapid-American Corp. v. Harris*, the Delaware Supreme Court held that in valuing a holding company for §262 appraisal purposes, it was appropriate to include a control premium as an element of the fair value of the majority-owned subsidiaries. The Court said:

> Rapid was a parent company with a 100% ownership interest in three valuable subsidiaries. The trial court's decision to exclude the control premium at the corporate level practically discounted Rapid's entire inherent value. The exclusion of a "control premium" artificially and unrealistically treated Rapid as a minority shareholder. Contrary to Rapid's arguments, Delaware law compels the inclusion of a control premium under the unique facts of this case. Rapid's 100% ownership interest in its subsidiaries was clearly a "relevant" valuation factor and the trial court's rejection of the "control premium" implicitly placed a disproportionate emphasis on pure market value.

The Respondents argue that *Rapid-American* turned on the "unique fact" that its subsidiaries were involved in three different industries. I do not read *Rapid-American* to hold that that "unique" fact was in any way critical to the result. The Respondents' construction of that case is too narrow. What the Supreme Court ruled is that a holding company's ownership of a controlling interest in its subsidiaries is an independent element of value that must be taken into account in determining a fair value for the parent company. Thus, the rationale of *Rapid-American* applies to MGB, and the Respondents have not shown otherwise.

The Respondents also challenge Clarke's comparative acquisition approach on a different basis. Pointing to the command in 8 Del. C. §262(h) that fair value must be determined "exclusive of post-merger events or other possible business combinations," the Respondents urge that any valuation method that includes a control premium as an element of "fair value" necessarily represents post-merger synergies proscribed by §262(h). I cannot agree. The (implicit) control premium at issue here is not the product of post-merger synergies. Rather, that control premium reflects an independent element of value existing at the time of the merger, flowing from the fact that the parent company owned a controlling interest in its subsidiaries at that point in time. Therefore, Clarke's comparative acquisition valuation cannot be invalidated on that basis either.

Because the Respondents have not challenged Clarke's comparative acquisition approach on any valid ground, and because the Court has rejected the parties' valuations based on their other methodologies, by process of elimination the only evidence of MGB's fair value is the $85 per share Clarke arrived at by the comparative acquisition method. Having no other adjudicated basis to value MGB, the Court would be justified in accepting $85 per share as the fair value of MGB, and does so but not by default or uncritically.

The Court is mindful that $85 per share is more than double the Merger price. The Court is also aware of its role under §262, which is to determine fair value independently. In discharging that institutional function as an independent appraiser, the Court should, where possible, test the soundness of its valuation conclusion against whatever reliable corroborative evidence the record contains. On that score the record falls far short of perfection. Limited corroborative evidence is available, however, in the form of Sheshunoff's 1993 fair market valuation, (i) adjusted by Clarke to exclude Sheshunoff's minority discount and (ii) updated by Clarke to reflect value data as of November 17, 1993, the date of the Merger. When Sheshunoff's 1993 valuation is adjusted in that manner, the resulting value of MGB is $48,504,664 or $70.46 per share with no control premium. If (for purposes of illustration) a 20% control premium were added, the resulting value would be $56,842,796.80 or $82.57 per share; and if the premium were 35%, the resulting value would be $63,096,394.40, or $91.66 per share. The $85 per share fair value based upon Clarke's comparative acquisition approach fits comfortably within that (hypothetical) range of values.

.... Under §262(h), this Court is empowered to award interest in an appraisal action at whatever rate (and compounding interval, where relevant) the Court deems equitable. Because MGB's cost of debt capital at that time was 8%, the Court finds that to be the appropriate interest rate. Because the legal rate of interest had risen to 10% as of the date of the trial, the Petitioners urge the Court to award them interest at that rate. The Court declines to do so. A 10% interest rate might arguably be appropriate had the Court found undue delay on the Respondents' part, but there has been no undue delay here.

Whether or not to award simple or compound interest is a matter within the Court's discretion. While it may be true, as the Respondents point out, that "an award of compound post-judgment interest is the exception rather than the rule," in today's financial markets a prudent investor expects to receive a compound rate of interest on his investment. Therefore, it is equitable and realistic for the Court to award compound interest in this case.

Turning to the compounding interval, the Petitioners argue that it should be monthly. The Respondents do not address the issue. Having been furnished no reason to do otherwise, the Court concludes that a monthly compounding interval is appropriate.

Notes and Questions

1. Judicial appraisal cases regularly define the fair value of a share of stock based on a valuation of the business as a going concern and then divide that value by the number of shares outstanding. This is not necessarily how public capital markets determine price. A share of stock trading in a public capital market trades on the basis of a single share rather than on the basis of the business as a whole. Hence, *a single share price has, in effect, a built-in minority discount.* To that extent, it is widely recognized in takeover contests and appraisal proceedings that a premium to market price is called for, whether the share itself is traded and thus has a price or whether comparable prices are drawn on.

The situation is extended in cases, such as *Le Beau*, where a holding company controls subsidiaries and the value of that control must be added to the intrinsic value of the subsidiaries themselves. As for the experts in that case, Clarke's comparative companies and comparative acquisition valuation methods recognized such a premium whereas neither of Reilly's did. For more on minority discounts, see *infra* section 4a(ii).

2. What weight should the court give to the merger price when determining fair value in an appraisal proceeding? In M.P.M. Enterprises, Inc. v. Gilbert, 731 A.2d 790 (Del. 1999), the Delaware Supreme Court affirmed the lower court's appraisal of petitioner stockholder's shares following the merger of MPM into another company. Pointing to Del. Gen. Corp. Law § 262's language requiring the lower court to "take into account all relevant factors" when determining the fair value of petitioner's shares, MGM had argued that the lower court impermissibly ignored its proffer of "real world" valuation evidence derived from the merger itself and from prior offers for MGM. The Delaware Supreme Court disagreed:

> A merger price resulting from arms-length negotiations where there are no claims of collusion is a very strong indication of fair value. But in an appraisal action, that merger price must be accompanied by evidence tending to show that it represents the going concern value of the company rather than just the value of the company to one specific buyer. In this case, MPM failed to present this additional evidence with respect to the merger or the prior offers.[47] This led the Court of Chancery to decide that these values were of only marginal relevance, if any. In our view, this determination was not an abuse of discretion.

Id. at 797.

3. Section 262 of the Delaware General Corporation Law prescribes awarding "a fair rate of interest, if any" on damages in appraisal proceedings and the Supreme Court of Delaware interprets this to permit the Court of Chancery to award compound interest or "simple interest." Simple interest is as simple as it sounds. It means multiplying the base amount by the product of the number of years and the interest rate—no benefit of compounding arises. In *Le Beau*, the Chancery Court awarded compound interest on the grounds that "in today's financial marketplace a prudent investor expects to receive a compound rate of interest" (which, of course, is accurate).

The company objected on the grounds that no "exceptional circumstances" supported the award of compound rather than simple interest. The Delaware Supreme Court acknowledged that the Chancery Court's stance was consistent with "a developing trend toward the routine awarding of compound interest," but also emphasized that the Delaware statute (section 262) precludes a "routine application" of any standard. Instead, the Chancery Court must choose and explain its choice given the record evidence and merits of the proceeding. The Supreme Court therefore remanded the interest award portion of the case for further consideration.

If the trend seems to be toward compound interest—at least in appropriate cases—another question on the horizon will be the frequency of compounding, which could be daily, monthly, quarterly, semi-annually or annually and the court's choice can have significant financial consequences. In *Le Beau*, for example, the Supreme Court affirmed

---

47. The prior offers suffered from flaws that made them marginally useful in an appraisal under section 262, under the best of circumstances. Both were remote in time from the date of the merger and neither was actually consummated.

the Chancery Court's valuation of $85 per share nearly 7 years after the cash-out merger. The Court of Chancery awarded interest at 8% compounded *monthly* (and the Supreme Court said nothing about whether monthly was an appropriate frequency). We can do some quick math to determine what $85 per share over 7 years is, using different interest rate and compounding assumptions:

simple interest	$132.60
compounded interest	
annual	$145.68
semi-annual	$147.19
quarterly	$147.98
monthly	$148.53
daily	$148.79

The quick math is as follows. For simple interest, $85 + (.08 x $85 x 7). For compound interest, $85 $(1 + .08/m)^{m7}$ where m is the frequency of compounding per year (1 for annual; 2 for semi-annual; 4 for quarterly; 12 for monthly; and 365 for daily).

4. How effective is the use of expert witnesses, paid for by the litigants, in the valuation process? In Kahn v. U.S. Sugar Corp., 1985 WL 4449, 11 Del. J. Corp. L. 908 (Del. Ch. 1985), plaintiffs challenged the fairness of a self-tender offer at $68 per share instigated by controlling stockholders. Upon determining that the defendant directors had breached their fiduciary duties to minority shareholders, Vice Chancellor Hartnett turned to the determination of the fair value of plaintiffs' shares. In doing so, he expressed his extreme frustration with expert testimony on the issue of valuation:

> Most of the testimony adduced at trial relating to value was produced by experts retained by the litigants who expressed their opinion of the fair and intrinsic value of U. S. Sugar's stock at the time of the tender offer....

> A review of this testimony clearly shows the reason that testimony as to value by experts is of such limited use to a trier of fact.

> It has been succinctly stated:

>> "In common law countries we have the contentious, or adversary, system of trial, where the opposing parties, and not the judge as in other systems, have the responsibility and initiative in finding and presenting proof. Advantageous as this system is in many respects, its present application in the procurement and presentation of expert testimony is widely considered a sore spot in judicial administration. There are two chief points of weakness in the use of experts. The first is the choice of experts by the party, who will naturally be interested in finding, not the best scientist, but the 'best witness.' As an English judge has said:

>>> '... the mode in which expert evidence is obtained is such as not to give the fair result of scientific opinion to the Court. A man may go, and does sometimes, to half-a-dozen experts ... He takes their honest opinions, he finds three in his favor and three against him, he says to the three in his favor, 'will you be kind enough to give evidence?' and he pays the three against him their fees and leaves them alone; the other side does the same ... I am sorry to say the result is that the Court does not get that assistance from the experts which, if they were unbiased and fairly chosen, it would have a right to expect.'

>> The second weakness is that the adversary method of eliciting scientific testimony, by direct and cross-examination in open court, frequently

upon hypothetical questions based on a partisan choice of data, is ill-suited to the dispassionate presentation of technical data, and results too often in over-emphasizing conflicts in scientific opinions which a jury is incapable of resolving."

McCormick on Evidence (3rd ed.) § 17 (1984).

The valuations expressed by the several expert witnesses were all based on numerous value judgments. While the assumptions had a basis, almost every figure used, whether a base figure or a multiplier, could have just as well been a different figure and the selection of the figure to be used necessarily involved a choice or guess by the witness, who in turn was being handsomely paid by one side or the other. The range between the two sides as to the value of the shares at the time of the tender offer was from a high (expressed by one of the experts called by the plaintiffs) of $121.92 per share and the low (expressed by one of defendants' experts) of $51.82 per share. Supposedly all of the experts were evaluating the same corporation!

* * *

The ... testimony of the expert witnesses ... is in hopeless disagreement. Each expert presented impressive credentials. Each expressed an opinion as to value based on dozens of value judgment assumptions. While each assumption was based on some data, almost all of the assumptions were fairly debatable and reasonable men using the same data could conclude that a different percentage multiple, or per acreage figure, etc., should be used.

Quite frankly, there is no rational way that I as the trier of fact could conclude that one expression of value was best. All had flaws, all were based on personal assumptions and opinions and all were expressed by obviously knowledgeable and experienced experts who were retained by one side or the other.

In only one respect did the two sides come close to each other. Professor Walter, who was called by the plaintiffs, relied heavily on land appraisals prepared for defendants. Based on this information he opined that the going concern value of U.S. Sugar was $79.14 per share. Although he also opined that the liquidation value was $104 to $122 per share, the assumptions which he used to arrive at the going concern value were more persuasive than the basis he used for his liquidation value. His $79.14 per share going concern value, while also obviously based on some invalid data and questionable assumptions, was not entirely unreasonable.

* * *

Notwithstanding that none of the opinions of value expressed by the experts are conclusive or even persuasive, I must establish from the trial record the value of the stock of U.S. Sugar at the time of the tender offer.

The primary assets of U.S. Sugar are its large holdings of the unique muckland which is used primarily for the growing of sugar cane and its capital assets used in the growing, harvesting and processing of the sugar cane. I find that the expressions of value based on estimates of the value of the muckland and its improvements were the most persuasive and accurate, although certain errors of fact were pointed out by cross-examination and the values expressed represented a certain amount of puffing or discounting depending on whether the witness was retained by the plaintiffs or defendants.

After considering and weighing all the conflicting testimony, the many value judgments and assumptions (some of which were invalid), and the credentials and demeanor of the witnesses, I conclude that the fair value of the assets of U. S. Sugar at the time of the tender offer was $72 per share. The damages, therefore, are equal to $4 per share ($72 less the $68 tender offer price).

* * *

(ii) Minority and Marketability Discounts

Problem — Smith Drugstores, Part III

Recall the facts of Smith Drugstores, Part I, *supra* at section 3a. Assume that during the negotiations between Mike and the other shareholders the parties employed different valuation techniques that resulted in a wide range of possible values for Mike's shares. The meeting turned rancorous and was adjourned. During the adjournment, the shareholders asked you if there is any reason to believe that the value of Mike's shares should be discounted, either because they represent a minority position or because of a lack of marketability in the shares. But what is a "minority discount" and how does it differ from a "marketability discount"? The shareholders want first some help in explaining the finance issues raised by these questions to the other shareholders and then they want a legal analysis of the issues. There is to be a conference call on the subject and you must prepare for the call. Before doing so, review the following cases.

Cavalier Oil Corp. v. Harnett
564 A.2d 1137 (Del. 1989)

WALSH, Justice.

[Harnett, a minority shareholder in a closely held corporation, brought an appraisal proceeding pursuant to Del. Gen. Corp. Law § 262 seeking a determination of the fair value of his shares of EPIC Mortgage Servicing, Inc. ("EMSI"), after its merger into Cavalier Oil Corporation. Both parties appealed from the vice chancellor's determination of fair value. Among Cavalier's complaints was the vice chancellor's inclusion of the dissenting minority shareholder's corporate opportunity claim in appraising the fair value of the shares and the vice chancellor's "refusal to apply a minority discount in valuing Harnett's EMSI stock." The Delaware Supreme Court affirmed the vice chancellor's opinion in its entirety.

Harnett had previously filed a separate action, Harnett v. Billman, C.A. No. 83-1029-A (E.D. Va., Oct. 13, 1983), to recover damages with respect to his minority interest in a related company. That action contained numerous counts, including allegations of common law fraud, state and federal securities fraud, RICO violations and a shareholder derivative claim. That action was ultimately settled and the action dismissed under a settlement agreement expressly reserving Harnett's right to assert facts underlying the shareholder derivative claim. The facts underlying that claim as they related to Harnett's corporate opportunity claim in the present appraisal proceeding were unknown to Harnett as of the time he filed his previous action and therefore the facts were not alleged in that action and no claim was based on them. As a result, the Delaware Supreme Court rejected Cavalier's claim in the appraisal proceeding that Harnett's assertion of the corporate opportunity claim was barred by *res judicata*.]

III

Having concluded that Harnett's corporate opportunity claim was not subject to the bar of *res judicata*, we next consider the related question of whether such a claim may be asserted by a shareholder incident to a section 262 appraisal proceeding. We agree with the Court of Chancery that, under the circumstances in which such a claim evolved here and in light of the consent of the parties to accord recognition to derivative-like claims for future valuation purposes, the claim was cognizable in an appraisal action.

A shareholder who dissents from a cash-out merger is nonetheless entitled to receive the fair or intrinsic value of his shares. Under Delaware law the sole remedy available to minority shareholders in a cash-out merger, absent a challenge to the merger itself, is an appraisal under 8 *Del. C.* §262. *Weinberger v. UOP, Inc.,* Del. Supr. 457 A.2d 701, 703 (1983). An action seeking appraisal is intended to provide shareholders who dissent from a merger, on the basis of the inadequacy of the offering price, with a judicial determination of the fair value of their shares....

The standard for determining the "fair value" of the company's outstanding shares was liberalized in *Weinberger*, which broadened the process from the exclusive use of the "Delaware Block" method to include all generally accepted techniques of valuation used in the financial community.... The scope of the appraisal action is limited, with the only litigable issue being the determination of the value of petitioner's shares on the date of the merger. *Cede and Co. v. Technicolor, Inc.,* 542 A.2d [1182, 1187 (Del. 1988)]. Although the justiciable issue in an appraisal action is a limited one, as this Court held in *Weinberger* "all relevant factors" are to be considered in determining fair value of shares subject to appraisal.... In the present case, the Vice Chancellor concluded that he had authority to determine the corporate opportunity claim because it related to the value of Harnett's EMSI stock....

Cavalier argues that the Court of Chancery's decision to extend the scope of valuation to embrace Harnett's corporate opportunity claim impermissibly expands the appraisal remedy to include questions of breaches of fiduciary duty, contrary to this Court's holding in *Rabkin. See Rabkin v. Philip A. Hunt Chemical Corp.,* 498 A.2d [1099, 1106 (Del. 1985)]. Fiduciary duty/common law fraud claims have been disallowed in appraisal actions under both *Rabkin v. Philip A. Hunt Chemical Corp., id.* (unfair dealing claims, based on breaches of the duties of loyalty and care, raise "issues which an appraisal cannot address") and *Weinberger v. UOP, Inc.,* 457 A.2d at 714 (the appraisal remedy may not be adequate in cases involving fraud, misrepresentation, self-dealing, waste of corporate assets, or gross and palpable overreaching). We believe, however, that our previous rulings do not control this case.

[T]he unusual facts of this case, particularly the consent of the parties as reflected in the ... settlement order [of the previous action] providing that the derivative-like claims are viable for appraisal purposes, require that Harnett's corporate opportunity claim be considered in valuing his shares.

Nor is our decision, upholding the viability of a fraud-based claim on the present facts on the appraisal action, to be viewed as undercutting the holding in *Cede*, that derivative claims are lost in subsequent appraisal proceedings because the derivative plaintiff loses his standing to assert these claims on behalf of the corporation. It is true that this Court in *Cede* held that where allegations of fraud and breaches of fiduciary duty exist in connection with a merger, an action separate and distinct from an appraisal proceeding may and indeed must be maintained. *Cede and Co. v. Technicolor Inc.,* 542

A.2d at 1189. *See also Kramer v. Western Pacific Industries, Inc.*, Del. Supr., 546 A.2d 348, 354 (1988). In *Cede* this Court permitted a separate action for fraud in the merger itself because "... an appraisal action may not provide a complete remedy for unfair dealing or fraud ..." in the merger. *Cede and Co. v. Technicolor, Inc.*, 542 A.2d at 1187. The Court in *Cede* also noted that "[a] determination of fair value does not involve an inquiry into claims of wrongdoing in the merger." *Id.* at 1189. Further, this Court held in *Kramer* that "... direct attacks against a given corporate transaction (attacks involving fair dealing or fair price) give complaining shareholders standing to pursue individual actions even after they are cashed out through the effectuation of a merger." *Kramer v. Western Pacific Industries, Inc.*, 546 A.2d at 354.

The wrongdoing alleged by Harnett relates directly to the fair value of his stock, not the validity of the merger itself. Harnett does not dispute that there was a legitimate business purpose to be served by the merger. His claim relates strictly to the value of his shares, and is the one issue that all of the parties had agreed to preserve. His claim is thus viewed as more personal than derivative and appropriately so, in view of his status as the sole minority shareholder whose claims of fraud are directed against the two controlling shareholders. The EMSI corporate opportunity claim, if considered on its derivative merits, would inure almost entirely to the benefit of the alleged wrongdoers, an inequitable result at variance with the fair value quest of the appraisal proceeding.[a] In the present case a fair value determination in an appraisal action will satisfactorily redress the claimed wrongdoing. Additionally, the Vice Chancellor found that Harnett did not have knowledge of the basis for the corporate opportunity claim prior to the institution of the appraisal proceeding and that, as a matter of credibility, those claims were based on misrepresentations by the principal shareholders. We conclude that, under the unusual configuration of facts present here, the corporate opportunity claim was assertable in the section 262 proceeding....

IV

Cavalier contends that Harnett's "de minimus" (1.5%) interest in EMSI is one of the "relevant factors" which must be considered under *Weinberger's* expanded valuation standard. In rejecting a minority or marketability discount, the Vice Chancellor concluded that the objective of a section 262 appraisal is "to value the *corporation* itself, as distinguished from a specific fraction of its *shares* as they may exist in the hands of a particular shareholder" [emphasis in original]. We believe this to be a valid distinction.

A proceeding under Delaware's appraisal statute, 8 Del. C. §262, requires that the Court of Chancery determine the "fair value" of the dissenting stockholders' shares. The fairness concept has been said to implicate two considerations: fair dealing and fair price. *Weinberger v. UOP, Inc.*, 457 A.2d at 711. Since the fairness of the merger process is not in dispute, the Court of Chancery's task here was to value what has been taken from the shareholder: "viz. his proportionate interest in a going concern." *Tri-Continental Corp. v. Battye*, Del. Supr., 74 A.2d 71, 72 (1950). To this end the company must be first valued as an operating entity by application of traditional value factors, weighted as required, but

---

a. For the difference between derivative claims and personal claims, *see, e.g.*, Robinette v. Merrill Lynch, Pierce, Fenner & Smith, Inc., 2004 U.S. Dist. LEXIS 24537 (D. Tex. 2004); Danielewicz v. Arnold, 769 A.2d 274 (Md. Ct. App. 2001); Eisenberg v. Flying Tiger Line, Inc., 451 F.2d 267 (2d Cir. 1971); Principles of Corporate Governance §7.01 (Amer. Law Inst. 1994 & Supp. 2005); 12B Fletcher et al., Fletcher Cyclopedia of the Law of Private Corporations §§5907—5912 (perm. ed., rev. vol. 2000 & Supp. 2004).

without regard to post-merger events or other possible business combinations.... The dissenting shareholder's proportionate interest is determined only after the company as an entity has been valued. In that determination the Court of Chancery is not required to apply further weighting factors at the shareholder level, such as discounts to minority shares for asserted lack of marketability.

* * *

The application of a discount to a minority shareholder is contrary to the requirement that the company be viewed as a "going concern." Cavalier's argument, that the only way Harnett would have received value for his 1.5% stock interest was to sell his stock, subject to market treatment of its minority status, misperceives the nature of the appraisal remedy. Where there is no objective market data available, the appraisal process is not intended to reconstruct a *pro forma* sale but to assume that the shareholder was willing to maintain his investment position, however slight, had the merger not occurred. Discounting individual share holdings injects into the appraisal process speculation on the various factors which may dictate the marketability of minority shareholdings. More important, to fail to accord to a minority shareholder the full proportionate value of his shares imposes a penalty for lack of control, and unfairly enriches the majority shareholders who may reap a windfall from the appraisal process by cashing out a dissenting shareholder, a clearly undesirable result....

[Affirmed.]

Question

Minority Discount Versus Marketability Discount. Does the court in *Cavalier* properly explain the difference between a minority discount and a marketability discount? What exactly is the distinction? Will a minority position always have limited marketability? Can a majority position ever have limited marketability? Do the answers to the questions depend on whether the company is publicly traded or, like EMSI, closely held? Consider the following case and the notes and questions that follow.

Pueblo Bancorporation v. Lindoe, Inc.

63 P.3d 353 (Colo. 2003) (en banc)

JUSTICE RICE delivered the Opinion of the Court.

* * *

Petitioner, Pueblo Bancorporation ("Holding Company"), a Colorado corporation, is a bank holding company whose principal asset is The Pueblo Bank and Trust, a commercial bank with several branches throughout southeastern Colorado. In November of 1997, Holding Company had 114,217 outstanding shares, owned by thirty-eight shareholders— including twenty-nine individuals, two corporations, and seven retirement trusts.

One of Holding Company's corporate shareholders was Respondent, Lindoe, Inc. Lindoe, which is also a bank holding company, first purchased shares in 1988 and has since acquired additional shares as they became available. By November of 1997, Lindoe owned 6,525 (5.71%) of Holding Company's outstanding shares and was its sixth-largest shareholder.

[Holding Company arranged to merge with a wholly-owned subsidiary. The purpose of the merger was to enable Holding Company to elect to become an S Corporation rather than a C Corporation for Federal income tax purposes. This enabled it to be taxed as partnerships are taxed (at the owner level only) instead of as a traditional corporation is taxed (at the entity level and again at the owner level). To qualify as an S Corporation, all shareholders must agree and shareholders must possess certain characteristics not all Holding Company shareholders possessed. In the merger, qualifying shareholders were offered stock in the surviving corporation and others were paid cash and sent on their way.]

* * *

After an appraisal of the value of its shares, Holding Company offered $341 per share to the cashed out shareholders. Several shareholders accepted the amount and tendered their stock. Lindoe, however, chose to dissent and seek a higher amount. Pursuant to the procedure set out in Colorado's dissenters' rights statute, Lindoe sent a notice to Holding Company rejecting Holding Company's fair value determination and providing its own estimate of fair value: $775 per share.... Disputing Lindoe's estimate, Holding Company initiated this action in order to obtain the court's determination of the fair value of Lindoe's shares....

The trial to determine fair value was a classic battle of experts. Holding Company's expert concluded that Holding Company, as an entity, was worth $72.9 million, or $638 per share. Lindoe provided two valuation experts whose estimates regarding the value of Holding Company ranged from $82.8 million to $88.5 million, a per share value of $725 to $775. The primary source of disagreement throughout the proceeding was whether the court should apply a minority or marketability discount to determine the fair value of Lindoe's shares. Holding Company's expert, arguing that the court must apply both a minority and marketability discount in order to accurately reflect the value of Lindoe's shares, applied both discounts to arrive at his final opinion that the shares had a fair value of $344 per share. Lindoe's experts argued that application of discounts was inappropriate; the fair value of the shares in their opinion was between $725 and $775 per share.

The trial court first determined the value of Holding Company as an entity by combining the opinions of two of the experts. It concluded that the enterprise value of Holding Company was $76,087,723, or $666.16 per share. On the issue of discounts, the court was persuaded by Holding Company and applied both a minority discount and a marketability discount to arrive at its fair value determination of $362.03. Because Lindoe had already received $341 for its shares, the court entered judgment in favor of Lindoe in the amount of $137,220.75 ($21.03 times 6,525, the number of shares held by Lindoe).... [The court of appeals reversed the trial court concerning the minority discount, saying it should not be applied, but upheld application of the marketability discount, the subject of this opinion by the Colorado Supreme Court.]

* * *

[T]he statutory standard of value to which a dissenting shareholder is entitled is "fair value":

> "Fair Value", with respect to a dissenter's shares, means the value of the shares immediately before the effective date of the corporate action to which the dissenter objects, excluding any appreciation or depreciation in anticipation of the corporate action except to the extent that exclusion would be inequitable.

§7-113-101(4), 2 C.R.S. (2002).

This case requires us to determine what the General Assembly meant by "fair value." ...

* * *

In our view, the term "fair value" could reasonably be subject to one of three interpretations. One possible interpretation, urged by Lindoe, is that fair value requires the court to value the dissenting shares by looking at what they represent: the ownership of a certain percentage of the corporation. In this case, the trial court found that Holding Company, as an entity, was worth $76.1 million. Lindoe owned 5.71 percent of Holding Company and therefore, under this view, Lindoe is entitled to 5.71 percent of Holding Company's value, or just over $4.3 million. Because the proper measure of value is the shareholder's proportionate interest in the value of the entity, discounts at the shareholder level are inapplicable.

Another interpretation of fair value is to value the dissenters' specific allotment of shares, just as one would value the ownership of a commodity. Under this view, although Lindoe's shares represent ownership of 5.71 percent of Holding Company, the "fair value" of its ownership interest is only the amount a willing buyer would pay to acquire the shares. In effect, this interpretation reads fair value as synonymous with fair market value. An investor who wants to buy a minority allotment of shares in a closely-held corporation would discount the price he was otherwise willing to pay for the shares because the shares are a minority interest in the company and are a relatively illiquid investment. Likewise, under this interpretation, the trial court should usually apply minority and marketability discounts.

The third possible interpretation of fair value is a case-by-case approach which allows the trial court to adapt the meaning of fair value to the specific facts of the case. In some circumstances, fair value of a dissenter's shares will mean his proportionate interest in the corporation; in other cases it will mean the fair market value of specific shares valued as a commodity.

* * *

.... A case-by-case interpretation of "fair value" results in a definition that is too imprecise to be useful to the business community. Under a case-by-case approach, the parties proceed to trial without knowing what interest the trial court is valuing.... [T]he court's choice of which interpretation to adopt is largely determined by whichever expert the court finds more persuasive.

.... A case-by-case interpretation encourages unnecessary litigation; it is a costly and inefficient means to settle disputes between a corporation and a dissenting shareholder. A definition of "fair value" that varies from one courtroom to another is no definition at all; this could not be the scheme the legislature intended.

We conclude that a case-by-case approach to the definition of "fair value" is untenable. "Fair value" must have a definitive meaning; either it is the value of the shareholder's proportionate interest in the value of the corporation as an entity, or it is the value of the specific shares in the hands of that particular shareholder....

The interpretation of "fair value" advocated by Holding Company reads the term as synonymous with "fair market value." Under a fair market value standard a marketability discount should be applied because the court is, by definition, determining the price at which a specific allotment of shares would change hands between a willing buyer and a willing seller. However, in a dissenters' rights action, the dissenting shareholder is not in the same position as a willing seller on the open market—he is an unwilling seller with little or no bargaining power.... We are convinced that "fair value" does not mean "fair market value."

* * *

Fair market value is typically defined as the price at which property would change hands between a willing buyer and a willing seller when neither party is under an obligation to act.... If the General Assembly intended to create a fair market value measure for the price of a dissenter's shares, it knew how to provide it; the phrase has been used many times in a wide variety of other statutes....

Although the plain language of the statute is ambiguous, we conclude that "fair value" is not synonymous with "fair market value." To determine the precise meaning of the term, we next consider the purpose of the statute and the interpretation of "fair value" provided by courts and commentators around the country....

* * *

In recent years, the purpose of modern dissenters' rights statutes has been vigorously debated by commentators. The consensus that has developed among courts and commentators is that the modern dissenters' rights statute exists to protect minority shareholders from oppressive conduct by the majority....

The necessity of a dissenters' rights statute for protection of minority shareholders is illustrated by examining the situations in which the remedy is typically used today. The original concern of the appraisal remedy was for shareholders who were trapped in a post-merger investment that did not resemble their original investment. Today, financial practice and legal environments have changed such that mergers are often used solely to cash-out minority shareholders....

In a typical cash-out merger, a corporation creates a shell company which is owned by the corporation's majority shareholders. The original corporation and the shell company merge and only the majority shareholders continue as shareholders of the surviving company; the minority shareholders are involuntarily cashed out of their investment.

The dissenters' rights statute serves as the primary assurance that minority shareholders will be properly compensated for the involuntary loss of their investment....

In this case, the sole purpose of the merger between Holding Company and Merger Corp. was to cash out minority shareholders, such as Lindoe, who did not qualify to hold stock in an S corporation. The time and price at which Lindoe was cashed out was determined entirely by Holding Company.

The purpose of the dissenters' rights statute would best be fulfilled through an interpretation of "fair value" which ensures minority shareholders are compensated for what they have lost, that is, their proportionate ownership interest in a going concern. A marketability discount is inconsistent with this interpretation; it injects unnecessary speculation into the appraisal process and substantially increases the possibility that a dissenting shareholder will be under-compensated for his ownership interest....

The interpretation of fair value which we adopt today is the clear majority view. It has been adopted by most courts that have considered the issue, the authors of the Model Business Corporation Act, and the American Law Institute.

Our interpretation of "fair value" is consistent with the interpretation adopted by most courts that have considered the issue. The interpretation of other states is especially persuasive for two reasons. First, the language of the Colorado statute, because it was based on the Model Act, is nearly identical to the language of dissenters' rights statutes around the country....

Second, we believe that one of the purposes of the MBCA was to facilitate a degree of national uniformity among state corporate law. Because the General Assembly enacted Colorado's corporate code based largely on the Model Act, we presume that it intended, to some degree, to place Colorado's corporate law in step with the law of other states....

In the leading case regarding discounts, *Cavalier Oil Corp. v. Harnett*, 564 A.2d 1137 (Del. 1989), the Delaware Supreme Court held that discounts should not be used in determining the "fair value" of a dissenters' shares....

Since *Cavalier*, courts across the country have considered the issue of marketability discounts and have generally followed Delaware's lead. Of the jurisdictions with "fair value" statutes, courts in fifteen states have held that a marketability discount should not be applied in determining fair value....

In addition, five state legislatures have already adopted the 1999 amendments to the MBCA's fair value definition which explicitly prohibit minority and marketability discounts....

Finally, several other states, while not specifically addressing the issue of marketability discounts, have expressed the view that the proper interpretation of "fair value" is the shareholder's proportionate interest of the corporation as a going concern, not the specific stock valued as a commodity....

In contrast, only six states with "fair value" statutes have clearly concluded that fair value may include marketability discounts....

The clear majority trend is to interpret fair value as the shareholder's proportionate ownership of a going concern and not to apply discounts at the shareholder level....

We also find the recent amendments to the Model Business Corporation Act to be persuasive. In 1999, the MBCA amended its definition of fair value to reflect the national trend against discounts in fair value appraisals. "Fair value," according to the amended definition:

> means the value of the corporation's shares determined...(iii) without discounting for lack of marketability or minority status except, if appropriate, for amendments to the articles pursuant to section 13.02(a)(5).

Model Bus. Corp. Act 3d §13.01(4)(iii) (1984) (amended 1999). The commentary to the 1999 amendments makes clear that the change was an adoption of the "more modern view that appraisal should generally award a shareholder his or her proportional interest in the corporation after valuing the corporation as a whole, rather than the value of the shareholder's shares when valued alone." MBCA §13.01 official cmt. 2.

.... Because the legislature has consistently relied on the MBCA when fashioning the corporate laws of this state we find the views of the MBCA on this issue to be persuasive.

* * *

Finally, we are persuaded by the recommendations of the American Law Institute regarding the interpretation of "fair value." The ALI has endorsed the national trend of interpreting fair value as the proportionate share of a going concern "without any discount for minority status or, absent extraordinary circumstances, lack of marketability." A.L.I., Principles of Corporate Governance: Analysis and Recommendations §7.22(a) (1994). To determine fair value, the trial court must determine the aggregate value for the firm as an entity, and then simply allocate that value pro rata in accordance with the shareholders' percentage ownership. A.L.I. §7.22 cmt. d.

The court of appeals explicitly adopted the ALI's definition of "fair value," including the exception for "extraordinary circumstances." The extraordinary circumstances exception is "very limited" and is intended to apply only when the trial court "finds that the dissenting shareholder has held out in order to exploit the transaction giving rise to appraisal so as to divert value to itself that could not be made available proportionately to other shareholders." A.L.I. §7.22 cmt. e. In effect, the exception is intended to leave room for trial courts to exercise their equitable powers in certain extraordinary circumstances to ensure that a fair and just result is reached. The court of appeals concluded, as a matter of law, that the facts of this case did not constitute an extraordinary circumstance.

.... We hold that "fair value," for the purpose of the dissenters' rights statute, means the shareholder's proportionate ownership interest in the value of the corporation and therefore, it is inappropriate to apply a marketability discount at the shareholder level. Because the issue is not squarely before us, we do not decide the question of whether there may be an equitable exception to this rule, such as the ALI "extraordinary circumstance" exception, which would allow a trial court to apply a marketability discount under certain circumstances.

* * *

JUSTICE KOURLIS dissenting (joined by JUSTICE MARTINEZ and JUSTICE COATS):

In my view, defining "fair value" so to extinguish the possibility of marketability discounts in dissenters' rights actions represents a policy decision that the General Assembly must make. Our statute is, as the majority notes, ambiguous. Colorado courts, with the exception of the court of appeals' decision in this case, have never interpreted the language of the statute as precluding trial courts from considering a marketability discount in valuing dissenters' shares. We must presume that the General Assembly is aware of those cases.

Despite the national trend to eliminate the marketability discount and the 1999 amendments to the Model Business Corporations Act ("MBCA"), also eliminating marketability discounts, the Colorado General Assembly has made no movement to change the Colorado statute. In my view, we cannot infer from any legislative history surrounding the dissenters' rights statute that the General Assembly has or would mandatorily [sic] exclude the use of marketability discounts in arriving at valuation.

Hence, absent a clear legislative declaration, an interpretation of the term "fair value" that essentially gives a shareholder more money for its shares because of a merger than the shareholder would have received immediately prior to the corporate action does not, in my view, comport with the language of the statute or with this state's prior case law.

* * *

There can be no question that, up until the court of appeals' decision in this case, no Colorado court had interpreted the existing statute as precluding application of a marketability discount.

* * *

Our statute currently provides that the shares are valued "immediately before the effective date of the corporate action to which the dissenter objects, excluding any appreciation or depreciation in anticipation of the corporate action except to the extent that exclusion would be inequitable." §7-113-101(4), 2 C.R.S. (2002).

Without imposition of a marketability discount, the amount the dissenting share-holder will receive for his shares will exceed that which he would have received had he sold his stock for some unrelated reason prior to the corporate action. An investor seek-ing a minority interest in a closely held corporation typically discounts the amount he is willing to pay, because the minority shares represent a relatively illiquid investment. An investor would not buy minority shares in a close corporation without accounting for the relative illiquidity of the stock. So, in any arms-length transaction that might pre-cede corporate change triggering dissenters' rights, the shareholder receives only that amount that an investor is willing to pay—taking into account the illiquidity of the asset. Consequently, in a situation where that same shareholder is exercising dissenters' rights, he will collect a windfall.

Immediately before the corporate change here, if Lindoe had tried to sell its shares, the buyer would most certainly have negotiated a discount in price to account for the illiquidity of the shares. Lindoe, as a minority shareholder, had to expect the value of shares would reflect the lack of a market for them.

The majority opines that windfall is acceptable since the dissenting shareholder in a corporate action is not a "willing" seller. The underlying policy question is whether the General Assembly intends to penalize corporations for undertaking corporate change with less than unanimous shareholder approval by rewarding dissenting shareholders with a windfall. Although that would be a legitimate policy choice, I do not see the General Assembly as having made it.

Leaving marketability in the determination seems most fair to both parties—as the shareholder gets what he expected out of his investment and the corporation is not un-necessarily penalized for corporate change....

The notion that clarity and predictability are well served by narrowing the number of factors a trial court must consider has obvious merit. I would only add that the real struggle is in arriving at value for the closely-held entity in the first place. The elimina-tion of discounts from the formulation is certainly a move toward greater predictability, but does not change the fact that value is almost always disputed, with both parties' ex-perts relying on a myriad of other considerations and calculations. In sum, under the language of the present statute, it is my view that a marketability discount can be applied by the trial court if that would contribute to ascertainment of a "fair value" assessment.

* * *

Notes and Questions

1. *Minority Discount.* Consider Walter S. Cheeseman Realty Co. v. Moore, 770 P.2d 1308 (Colo. App. 1988), in which Moore, the owner of a minority block of non-voting common stock in a close corporation appealed from a judgment of valuation in an appraisal proceeding brought in connection with the corporation's dissolution. The corporation's only assets were "its substantial real estate holdings ... and some securi-ties." Moore objected, among other things, to the trial court's application of a dis-count to his shares "for lack of control and marketability." The *Cheeseman* court agreed:

> Among the jurisdictions that have considered the question, there is a diver-sity of opinion on whether and when a minority discount is appropriate. *Com-pare Brown v. Allied Corrugated Box Co.*, 91 Cal. App. 3d 477, 154 Cal. Rptr. 170 (1979) *and Woodward v. Quigley*, 257 Iowa 1077, 133 N.W.2d 38 (1965)

with *Perlman v. Permonite Manufacturing Co.*, 568 F. Supp. 222 (N.D. Ind. 1983), *aff'd*, 734 F.2d 1283 (7th Cir. 1984) and *Moore v. New Ammest, Inc.*, 6 Kan. App. 2d 461, 630 P.2d 167 (1981). Typically, the reason stated for imposing the minority discount is that a minority block of shares does not possess the "control element of value" and is, therefore, less valuable and less attractive to potential buyers. *See Perlman v. Permonite Manufacturing Co.*, *supra*; *Moore v. New Ammest, Inc.*, *supra*. However, even these cases suggest that a minority discount would not be appropriate if liquidation or sale of the company as a whole is imminent. *See Perlman v. Permonite Manufacturing Co.*, *supra*; *Moore v. New Ammest, Inc.*, *supra*.

Here, the corporate action to which Moore objects is the dissolution of the corporation and the liquidation of all corporate assets. Under these circumstances, lack of control and marketability of minority shares are not relevant factors to be considered because the corporation will not continue in existence. Just as a minority share would be no less valuable than any other share if, for example, the corporation as a whole were sold to a single buyer, so too, once the corporation decides to dissolve, any control element of value in the majority block of shares is lost. Thus, the trial court erred in applying a 35% minority discount to the value of Moore's shares.

Id. at 1312-13.

2. *Marketability Discount.* Should a court apply a discount for lack of *marketability* when a corporation buys out a minority shareholder who has filed for judicial dissolution? A New York court affirmed the application of a marketability discount in such a proceeding in Blake v. Blake Agency, Inc., 107 A.D.2d 139, 486 N.Y.S.2d 341 (2d Dep't. 1985). In *Blake*, the minority shareholder, Lawrence Blake, brought an action for judicial dissolution under N.Y. Bus. Corp. Law §1104-a claiming that he had been "frozen out" of corporate affairs, "as evidenced by the fact that he was never consulted before corporate decisions were made and the fact that he was never paid any dividends." *Id.* at 142. Blake Agency, Inc., in order to avoid dissolution, opted to purchase Lawrence's shares as was its right under N.Y. Bus. Corp. Law §1118. When the parties could not agree on a price for the minority block of shares, it was left to the court to determine the shares' "fair value."

The *Blake* court, in affirming the use of a marketability discount, but not a minority discount, to arrive at a fair price wrote:

[A] discount recognizing the lack of marketability of the shares of Blake Agency, Inc. is appropriate.... A discount for lack of marketability is properly factored into the equation because the shares of a closely held corporation cannot be readily sold on the market. Such a discount bears no relation to the fact that the petitioner's shares in the corporation represent a minority interest....

Id. at 149.

The purpose of New York's judicial dissolution statute, BCL §1104-a, is "to afford a minority shareholder the right to bring a proceeding to dissolve the corporation and to distribute its assets among the shareholders" when directors, officers, or control persons have been guilty of illegal, fraudulent, oppressive, or wasteful acts. *Id.* at 144. However, because of the severity of dissolution, the New York statute, §1118, permits the corporation or any of its shareholders to avoid this remedy by purchasing the shares of a complaining shareholder at a fair price.

How can you reconcile *Blake* and *Cheeseman*? Are they consistent with *Cavalier*?

3. *Effect of Dissolution Versus Continuation.* Does it make sense to let the application of a minority discount or a marketability discount hinge on whether the corporation is being dissolved or continuing as a going concern? For example, how would a minority discount or marketability discount impact the value of Mike's shares in Smith Drugstores, Part II, *supra* at section 3b(ii)? *See* Taines v. Gene Barry One Hour Photo Process, 123 Misc. 2d 529, 534-35, 474 N.Y.S.2d 362, 366 (Sup. Ct. 1983) (justifying applying a marketability discount by saying that "[s]ince the corporation has opted by its election to continue as a going business, the valuation should be the value of the business as a continuing entity rather than its value in liquidation").

How does choosing to apply or refusing to apply any discount based on whether the corporation is to be dissolved or continued affect the exercise of control by controlling stockholders? Consider Brown v. Allied Corrugated Box Co., 91 Cal. App. 3d 477, 486-87, 154 Cal. Rptr. 170, 176 (1979), where the court refused to apply a *minority* discount in an involuntary dissolution case:

> Under the valuation approach adopted by the majority commissioners and confirmed by the trial court ... a controlling shareholder, especially an unscrupulous one, could avoid the proportionate distribution which would follow from an involuntary dissolution simply by invoking the buy-out provisions [of the statute]. According to that approach, the minority shares would then have to be valued in relation to what they would bring in the open market, with an appropriate reduction for the fact that they do not give their purchaser control of the corporation. Further, if, as was apparently the case here, the controlling shareholder has been using his position to insure that no benefits, such as dividends or employment, ever accrue to the owners of the minority shares, then an argument could be made that the value of the minority shares should be reduced even further, perhaps to zero. Thus, the very misconduct and unfairness which provoked the minority shareholders to seek involuntary dissolution could, in this manner, be used to further oppress them. This, the statutory scheme before us cannot be read as condoning. Rather, the statutes suggest that a minority shareholder who brings an action for the involuntary dissolution of a corporation should not, by virtue of the controlling shareholder's invocation of the buy-out remedy, receive less than he would have received had the dissolution been allowed to proceed. The majority commissioners' decision here to devalue the plaintiffs' shares for their lack of control was in direct conflict with this principle.

Is the reasoning in *Brown* consistent with the court's reasoning in *Cavalier* relating to the minority shareholder's corporate opportunity claim? Could that branch of *Cavalier* be adapted to meet the concerns expressed by the *Brown* court?

Should the reasoning in *Brown* extend to deny a *marketability* discount? *See* Charland v. Country View Golf Club, Inc., 588 A. 2d 609 (R.I. 1991) (following New York and California approaches as to minority discounts but refusing to apply marketability discount, distinguishing New York approach on the basis of statutory language). *See also* King v. F.T.J., Inc., 765 S.W.2d 301 (Mo. App. 1988) (holding that the applicability of both marketability discounts and minority discounts in valuing close corporation shares rested in the discretion of the trial court).

4. *Control Premium.* Is it proper to apply a premium to reflect the value of control? *See* Comment, Valuing Closely Held Stock: Control Premiums and Minority Discounts,

31 Emory L.J. 139 (1982) (suggesting that, in general, neither control premiums nor minority discounts ought to be applied in valuations of close corporation stock).

How should a court determine market value when, prior to the merger at issue, the merged corporation was the subject of a control contest that at least temporarily drove up the market price of the corporation's shares? Can the court consider the higher market value, or must it go back to a time before the control contest commenced? *Compare* Gibbons v. Schenley Industries, Inc., 339 A.2d 460 (Del. Ch. 1975) (considering higher market value) *with* California Corporations Code §1300(a) (dissenting shareholders may require corporation to purchase for cash their shares at "fair market value," which shall be "determined *as of the day before the first announcement* of the terms of the proposed reorganization...." (emphasis added)).

5. As *Pueblo* suggests, there continues to be substantial disagreement among courts and commentators concerning the applicability of minority and marketability discounts.

Scholarly commentary includes: Moll, Shareholder Oppression and "Fair Value": Of Discounts, Dates, and Dastardly Deeds in the Close Corporation, 54 Duke L.J. 293 (2004); Carney & Heimendinger, Appraising the Nonexistent: The Delaware Courts' Struggle With Control Premiums, 152 U. Pa. L. Rev. 845 (2003); Booth, Minority Discounts and Control Premiums in Appraisal Proceedings, 57 Bus. Law. 127 (2001).

Cases include: Sieg Co. v. Kelly, 568 N.W. 2d. 794 (Iowa 1997) (holding that a minority discount should never be applied, but a marketability discount applied at the corporate level is acceptable); Lawson Mardon Wheaton Inc. v. Smith, 160 N.J. 383 (N.J. 1999) (finding that a minority discount should never be applied and a marketability discount is inappropriate in the instant case.); Balsamides v. Protameen Chem., Inc., 150 N.J. 352 (N.J. 1999) (finding that a marketability discount at the corporate level is appropriate in the instant case.); Borruso v. Communications Telesystems Intl., 752 A.2d 451 (Del. Ch. 1999) (holding that a marketability discount at the corporate level is not permissible).

(iii) Synergies and Other Benefits of the Merger
Cede & Co. v. Technicolor, Inc.
684 A.2d 289 (Del. 1996)

HOLLAND, Justice:

* * *

Technicolor engaged in a number of distinct businesses through separate operating units. Technicolor's Professional Services Group was its main source of revenue and profit. The Videocassette Duplicating Division operated one of the largest duplicating facilities in the world. The Consumer Services Group operated film processing laboratories ("Consumer Photo Processing Division" or "CPPD"), which provided film processing services to other photofinishers. CPPD also operated Standard Manufacturing Company ("Standard"), which manufactured film splicers and associated equipment. The Government Services Group ("Government Services") provided photographic and non-photographic support and management services under contract to governmental agencies. Technicolor's Gold Key Entertainment Division ("Gold Key"), licensed motion pictures and other programs for television exhibition. The Audio Visual Division ("Audio Visual") distributed film and video equipment.

Morton Kamerman ("Kamerman"), Technicolor's Chief Executive Officer and Board Chairman, concluded that Technicolor's principal business, theatrical film processing, did not offer sufficient long-term growth for Technicolor. Kamerman proposed that Technicolor enter the field of rapid processing of consumer film by establishing a network of stores across the country offering one-hour development of film. The business, named One Hour Photo ("OHP"), would require Technicolor to open approximately 1,000 stores over five years and to invest about $ 150 million. [Technicolor's board ultimately approved Kamerman's OHP proposal.]

* * *

In the months that followed [implementation], Technicolor fell behind on its schedule for OHP store openings. The few stores that did open reported operating losses. At the same time, Technicolor's other major divisions were experiencing mixed, if not disappointing, results.

[Thereafter, Ronald O. Perelman ("Perelman"), MacAndrews & Forbes Group Incorporated's (MAF's) controlling stockholder, expressed interest in acquiring Technicolor. After lengthy negotiations, Technicolor's board agreed to a two-step acquisition of Technicolor by MAF: a first-step tender offer by MAF at $23 per share for all the outstanding shares of Technicolor common stock; and a second-step merger with any remaining outstanding Technicolor shares converted into $23 per share. Following the merger, Technicolor would be a wholly-owned subsidiary of MAF.]

* * *

The merger was accomplished on January 24, 1983. [Cinerama, a beneficial owner of Technicolor common stock, sued for a judicial appraisal of its shares. Unhappy with the Court of Chancery's valuation, it appealed.] The parties agree that the appraised value of Technicolor must be fixed as of [the date of the merger]. *See Alabama By-Products Corp. v. Neal, Del. Supr.*, 588 A.2d 255, 256-57 (1991). There is a fundamental disagreement between the litigants, however, concerning the nature of the enterprise to be appraised.

Cinerama argues that the Court of Chancery should have valued Technicolor as it existed on the date of the merger and, in particular, with due regard for the strategies that had been conceived and implemented following the merger agreement by ... Perelman ("Perelman Plan"). Technicolor argues that the Court of Chancery properly considered Technicolor without regard to the Perelman Plan and only as it existed on or before October 29, 1982, with the then extant strategies that had been conceived and implemented by Technicolor's Chairman, Morton Kamerman ("Kamerman Plan"). According to Cinerama:

> Reduced to its simplest form, the dispute was whether the trial court should value Perelman's Technicolor - a company whose business plans and strategies focused on the processing and duplication of film and videotape and the provision of services to the United States Government and which planned and expected to generate $50 million in cash during 1983 from the sale of unwanted and/or unsuccessful businesses, namely, OHP, CPPD, Gold Key and Audio Visual; or Kamerman's Technicolor - a company whose business plans and strategies assumed diversification away from a concentration on film processing and videotape duplication for the professional market toward consumer oriented businesses, especially OHP.

The economic experts for both parties used a form of discounted cash flow methodology to value Technicolor.... The fundamental nature of the disagreement between the parties about the Perelman Plan and the Kamerman Plan, however, resulted in different factual assumptions by their respective experts.

The Court of Chancery recognized that the parties' disagreement about valuing Technicolor based upon either the Perelman Plan or the Kamerman Plan presented a question of law with regard to the proper interpretation of the appraisal statute. *See 8 Del. C. §262(h)*. According to the Court of Chancery, that legal

> issue is whether in valuing Technicolor as of January 24, 1983, the court should assume the business plan for Technicolor that MAF is said by [Cinerama] to have had in place at that time [Perelman Plan], or whether a proper valuation is premised upon ignoring such changes as Mr. Perelman had in mind because to the extent they create value they are "elements of value arising from the accomplishment or expectation of the merger. *8 Del. C. §262(h)*.

The Court of Chancery also recognized that legal issue was "particularly pertinent when considering One Hour Photo, Standard Manufacturing and [the Consumer Photo Processing Division]." [Cinerama's expert] assumed each of those businesses would be sold by [MAF]. [Technicolor's expert] assumed that, but for the MAF acquisition, those businesses would have continued operating. Therefore, [the valuation by Technicolor's expert] included those businesses as going concerns. Predictably, the different assumptions factored into each expert's discounted cash flow model yielded disparate valuation results.[3]

In the Court of Chancery, Cinerama argued that the Perelman Plan ... was governing the operation of Technicolor on January 24, 1983. Consequently, Cinerama argued Perelman's Plan had to govern any expert's projection of net cash flow. For example, according to Cinerama, Technicolor's previous projections of negative cash flow from OHP's operation would be irrelevant in the appraisal valuation. In support of its position, Cinerama presented evidence that, prior to the merger date, Perelman had not only formulated, but had also implemented, a plan for how OHP and certain other Technicolor assets would be sold.

Technicolor argued to the Court of Chancery that the Perelman Plan, which it admitted called for the liquidation of OHP and a number of its other businesses, was not sufficiently defined on the date of the merger to form the factual premise for the Cinerama expert's cash flow projections from asset sales. The Court of Chancery unequivocally rejected that assertion by Technicolor. The Court of Chancery made a specific factual finding that "the record supports the conclusion that MAF intended from the outset to realize by one technique or another the capital value of One Hour Photo and to terminate that division's drain on the company's cash flow. Insofar as sale of that enterprise is involved, the 'Perelman Plan' was fixed by the merger date."

In view of that adverse factual determination, Technicolor's alternative contention was a legal argument. According to Technicolor, any value attributable to the Perelman Plan as of the merger date had to be excluded as arising from the expectation of the merger. *See 8 Del. C. §262(h)*. Thus, Technicolor argued that the net cash flows which followed from the Perelman Plan should be excluded from the statutory appraisal valuation, as a matter of law.

---

3. Cinerama's expert opined that the statutory appraisal fair value of Technicolor on a per share basis as of January 24, 1983 was $62.75. Technicolor's expert opined that the statutory appraisal fair value of Technicolor at the time of the merger was $13.14 per share.

In response, Cinerama argued to the Court of Chancery that this Court had construed the statutory phrase "exclusive of any element of value arising from the accomplishment or expectation of the merger" to exclude "only the speculative elements of value that may arise from the 'accomplishment or expectation' of the merger.... But elements of future value ... which are known or susceptible of proof as of the date of the merger and not the product of speculation, may be considered." *Weinberger v. UOP, Inc., Del. Supr., 457 A.2d 701, 713 (1983).* Thus, Cinerama argued any nonspeculative element of future value that could be proven may be considered in a statutory appraisal proceeding, even if it is an "element of value arising from the accomplishment or expectation of the merger." *See 8 Del. C. § 262(h).*

The Court of Chancery acknowledged that, based upon the quoted language from *Weinberger,* Cinerama's legal argument appeared to be persuasive. The Court of Chancery concluded, however, "that reading [of *Weinberger*] is too difficult to square with the plain words of the statute to permit the conclusion that that is what was intended." The Court of Chancery then stated "in order to understand the quoted passage [from *Weinberger*] when read together with the statutory language, I assume an unexpressed phrase to the effect 'unless, but for the merger, such elements of future value would not exist." According to the Court of Chancery, the language in *Weinberger* would read: "But elements of future value, including the nature of the enterprise, which are known or susceptible of proof as of the date of the merger and not the product of speculation, may be considered [unless, but for the merger, such elements of future value would not exist]." *Weinberger v. UOP, Inc., Del. Supr., 457 A.2d 701, 713 (1983).*

In explaining the "but for" caveat that it had superimposed upon this Court's holding in *Weinberger,* the Court of Chancery reasoned that, as a matter of policy, the valuation process in a statutory appraisal proceeding should be the same irrespective of whether a merger is accomplished in one or two steps:

> .... When value is created by substituting new management or by redeploying assets "in connection with the accomplishment or expectation" of a merger, that value is not, in my opinion, a part of the "going concern" in which a dissenting shareholder has a legal (or equitable) right to participate.

> If one accepts this principle, the question arises how it is to be applied in a two-step arms'-length acquisition transaction. In such a transaction there will be a period following close [to] the first-step tender offer in which the [majority] acquirer may, as a practical matter, be in a position to influence or change the nature of the corporate business, or to freeze controversial programs until they are reviewed following the second-step merger.

Accordingly, the Court of Chancery concluded that "future value that would not exist *but for* the merger ... even if it is capable of being proven on the date of the merger," is irrelevant in a Delaware statutory appraisal proceeding....

* * *

The Delaware appraisal statute provides that the Court of Chancery:

> shall appraise the shares, determining their fair value exclusive of any element of value arising from the accomplishment or expectation of the merger or consolidation, together with a fair rate of interest, if any, to be paid upon the amount determined to be the fair value. In determining such fair value, the Court shall take into account all relevant factors.

8 Del. C. § 262(h). In *Weinberger,* this Court construed the appraisal statute. That construction required this Court to reconcile the dual mandates of Section 262(h) which direct the Court of Chancery to: determine "fair" value based upon "all relevant factors;" but, to exclude "any element of value arising from the accomplishment or expectation of the merger." In making that reconciliation, the *ratio decidendi* of this Court was, as follows:

> Only the speculative elements of value that may arise from the "accomplishment or expectation" of the merger are excluded. We take this to be a very narrow exception to the appraisal process, designed to eliminate use of *pro forma* data and projections of a speculative variety relating to the completion of a merger. But elements of future value, including the *nature of the enterprise,* which are known or susceptible of proof as of the date of the merger and not the product of speculation, may be considered....

Weinberger v. UOP, Inc., 457 A.2d at 713 (emphasis added).

After examining the evolution of the statutory text in Section 262(h), this Court concluded "there is a legislative intent to fully compensate shareholders for whatever their loss may be, *subject only to the narrow limitation that one can not take speculative effects of the merger into account." Id. at 714* (emphasis added). Therefore, in *Weinberger,* this Court held that the more liberal methodology we had just authorized in appraisal and other stock valuation cases *"must* include proof of value by any techniques or methods which are generally considered acceptable in the financial community and otherwise admissible in court, *subject only to our [narrow] interpretation of [the exclusionary language in] 8 Del. C. § 262(h),"* i.e., requiring that only speculative elements of value, which may arise from the accomplishment or expectation of the merger, be disregarded. *Weinberger v. UOP, Inc., 457 A.2d at 713* (emphasis added); *see also Kahn v. Household Acquisition Corp., Del. Supr., 591 A.2d 166, 174 (1991); Rosenblatt v. Getty Oil Co., Del. Supr., 493 A.2d 929, 940 (1985).*

* * *

.... [T]his Court has held that the corporation must be valued as an operating entity. [*Cavelier Oil Corp. v. Harnett,* 564 A.2d 1137, 1144 (Del. 1989).] We conclude that the Court of Chancery did not adhere to this principle.

The Court of Chancery determined that Perelman "had a fixed view of how [Technicolor's] assets would be sold before the merger and had begun to implement it" prior to January 24, 1983.

Consequently, the Court of Chancery found that the Perelman Plan for Technicolor was the operative reality on the date of the merger. Nevertheless, the Court of Chancery held that Cinerama was not entitled to an appraisal of Technicolor as it was actually functioning on the date of the merger pursuant to the Perelman Plan.

The Court of Chancery reached that holding by applying its majority acquiror principle and correlative proximate cause exception. The Court of Chancery excluded any value that was admittedly part of Technicolor as a going concern on the date of the merger, if that value was created by substituting new management or redeploying assets during the transient period between the first and second steps of this two-step merger, i.e., Perelman's Plan. The Court of Chancery reasoned that valuing Technicolor as a going concern, under the Perelman Plan, on the date of the merger, would be tantamount to awarding Cinerama a proportionate share of a control premium....

* * *

In a two-step merger, to the extent that value has been added following a change in majority control before cash-out, it is still value attributable to the going concern, *i.e.*, the extant "nature of the enterprise," on the date of the merger.... The dissenting shareholder's proportionate interest is determined only after the company has been valued as an operating entity on the date of the merger.... Consequently, value added to the going concern by the "majority acquiror," during the transient period of a two-step merger, accrues to the benefit of all shareholders and must be included in the appraisal process on the date of the merger....

In this case, the question in the appraisal action was the fair value of Technicolor stock on the date of the merger, January 24, 1983, as Technicolor was operating pursuant to the Perelman Plan....

The "accomplishment or expectation" of the merger exception in Section 262 is very narrow, "designed to eliminate use of pro forma data and projections of a speculative variety relating to the completion of a merger." ... That narrow exclusion does not encompass known elements of value, including those which exist on the date of the merger because of a majority acquiror's interim action in a two-step cash-out transaction....

The Court of Chancery's determination not to value Technicolor as a going concern on the date of the merger under the Perelman Plan ... permitted MAF to "reap a windfall from the appraisal process by cashing out a dissenting shareholder [Cinerama]," for less than the fair value of its interest in Technicolor as a going concern on the date of the merger....

* * *

The judgment of the Court of Chancery in the appraisal action is reversed. This matter is remanded for further proceedings in accordance with this opinion.

Notes and Questions

1. In M.G. Bancorporation, Inc. v. Le Beau, 737 A.2d 513 (Del. 1999), the Delaware Supreme Court further embraced the notion of "operative reality" as discussed in *Cede*. The court stated that "the corporation must be valued as a going concern based upon the 'operative reality' of the company as of the time of the merger." *Id*. at 525. How does one discern what a company's "operative reality" is? Does this concept clarify or further cloud the valuation exercise?

2. How should an appraising court react to subsequent events which demonstrate that its valuation may have been wrong? In Metlyn Realty Corp. v. Esmark, Inc., 763 F.2d 826 (7th Cir. 1985), plaintiffs brought an action seeking to have the district judge reopen his approval of a settlement regarding Esmark's 1974 tender offer for TransOcean Oil, Inc., and the subsequent merger of TransOcean into Esmark. The settlement, following litigation over the merger price, was based on Esmark's withholding of valuation information in its tender offer circular, and was approved by the district court in August 1979, after which TransOcean was merged into Esmark. In August 1980, Esmark sold TransOcean to Mobil Corp. for more than twice what it paid TransOcean's shareholders in the merger under the approved settlement. In addition to challenging the credibility of the testimony of Levy, a key expert witness in the district court proceeding (which challenge was rejected by the court), plaintiffs further alleged that, at the time of the settlement, Esmark's management thought the

stock was worth more than Levy had testified. About this, Judge Easterbrook said the following:

> The second prong—that Esmark had a different assessment of TransOcean's worth—goes to the evaluation of the facts rather than the information on which that evaluation was based. We certainly would be surprised if, in 1979, Esmark's managers did *not* think the stock worth more than Levy testified. Why else would they have gone ahead with the merger? It is *always* the case that an acquiring firm thinks the stock or other assets to be acquired worth more than the current price (which here exceeded Levy's estimate). The question is not whether the acquiring firm thinks the stock worth more, but whether the acquiring firm has withheld *facts* that would establish the value of the stock or assets in the absence of the acquisition. The district court found that Esmark withheld no facts.

Finally, plaintiffs argued that Esmark's higher valuation of the stock was based, at least in part, on its plan to sell TransOcean. Judge Easterbrook answered this contention as follows:

> If any beliefs of Esmark's managers stemmed from plans to change TransOcean's operations or management, or to engage in other transactions with the assets, this too would be excluded from the process of computing value. *Weinberger* held that "elements of future value" are part of the entitlement of the old investors when "known or susceptible of proof *as of the date of the merger*" (*ibid.*; emphasis added). Corporate law, like the law of property and contract, allows acquirors to keep increments of value they produce in a firm, as well as those that later arise by luck, in order to give the acquirors incentives to find and improve undervalued or poorly employed properties. Here the subsequent events—including any changes Esmark may have made in TransOcean's management or operations, and its ability to set off a bidding contest for the assets—were no more than speculation as of the time of the merger. Esmark was not required to disclose its subjective wishes and beliefs. These might have been pertinent in 1974, when investors had to decide whether to tender. In 1979, though, there was no investment decision, no prediction, to make. Only the objective value of TransOcean mattered.
>
> We, like the district court, therefore exclude from consideration the fact that Mobil paid in 1980 more than twice the value implied by the merger in 1979. Only facts known in 1979 count. After the decision developments in Iran influenced the world's markets in oil and gas. Mobil's higher bid may have been based on increases in the price of oil and gas (Levy had assumed they would increase only at the rate of inflation). The bid also may have been based on plans to change TransOcean's managers or operation. Or perhaps it showed that Mobil would accept a lower rate of return on investment, which implied a higher cash price (Mobil's internal computations may have used a rate as low as 4% rather than Levy's 8%). None of this matters. Any increment of value attributable to changes after August 1979 in the market for oil and gas, or to Mobil's willingness to make changes or bear special risks, belongs to Mobil's and Esmark's shareholders rather than TransOcean's. The investors in a firm are entitled only to what it is worth as it exists, not as it could become in other hands.

The objectors' final argument is that the district court's finding that Esmark did not have a plan in August 1979 to sell TransOcean is clearly erroneous. The objectors say that Esmark had a cash flow problem, and that the sale of TransOcean was a logical way to handle the problem; Esmark concedes that it had such a problem. The objectors point out that Esmark had some dealings in

November 1979 with a German bank concerning possible dispositions of assets; they say these dealings support an inference that Esmark planned all along to sell TransOcean. We agree with the objectors that the district court was required to consider the sale to Mobil for a very limited purpose—not because the value of TransOcean rose quickly, but because Esmark had represented in 1979 that it did not plan to sell, and this may have misled the court. But this is the end of the agreement.

The district court considered very carefully whether Esmark had planned in 1979 to sell TransOcean. It was troubled by this possibility, because it believed that an impending sale would have made the valuation exercise in which it engaged unnecessary. (We need not decide whether, in light of *Weinberger*, this is an accurate understanding.) The court reviewed the evidence with painstaking care. It was aware that the business situation "suggests a climate in which the sale of TransOcean was a logical solution. The defendants cannot dispute this business truism." Yet it also concluded that the record shows only that Esmark pondered many ways of raising cash and did not contemplate until April 1980 a substantial probability of selling TransOcean. It would extend an already tiresome opinion to rehearse the support for this conclusion. We are satisfied, though, that it is not clearly erroneous.

AFFIRMED.

(iv) Exclusivity of Appraisal Rights

Are appraisal rights an exclusive remedy? It seems clear that a dissenting stockholder, whose complaint is with the magnitude of the merger consideration she is to receive, should be limited to the appraisal remedy. However, should that same stockholder be precluded from bringing another cause of action against her corporation and its board of directors if one exists? For example, should the availability of appraisal rights cut off a stockholder's ability to claim that directors of her company approved a merger in violation of their fiduciary duties?

Cede and Co. v. Technicolor, Inc.[a]
542 A.2d 1182 (Del. 1988)

Before HORSEY, MOORE and HOLLAND, JJ.

HORSEY, Justice:

We accepted this interlocutory appeal from the Court of Chancery to address a question of first impression in this Court: the standing and right of a minority shareholder who has dissented from a cash-out merger and commenced an appraisal proceeding under 8 Del. C. §262 to assert and pursue a later-discovered individual claim of fraud in the merger through an action for rescissory damages against the participants for breach of fiduciary duty to the shareholder. This issue arises from a cash-out merger of the minority shareholders of Technicolor Incorporated ("Technicolor"), a Delaware corporation, accomplished by MacAndrews & Forbes Group Incorporated ("MAF") through the merger of its wholly-owned subsidiary, Macanfor Corporation ("Macanfor"), into Technicolor, following approval by a majority of Technicolor's shareholders.

---

a. Commonly referred to as *"Cede I."*

The appeal encompasses two suits, a first-filed statutory appraisal proceeding (the "appraisal action") and a later-filed shareholders' individual suit for damages for alleged fraud, conspiracy, self-dealing and waste of corporate assets (the "fraud action"). The plaintiffs are Cinerama, Incorporated, a beneficial owner of 201,200 shares of Technicolor common stock, approximately 4.5% of the total issued and outstanding common stock, and Cede & Company, the record owner of the shares of Technicolor owned beneficially by Cinerama.[1] Cinerama seeks to proceed to trial on both its appraisal remedy and its equitable claim against the several defendants, individual and corporate, for breach of fiduciary duty occurring in the merger.

The sole defendant in the appraisal action is Technicolor, the surviving corporation of the merger. The several individual and corporate defendants in the fraud action include Technicolor, all but two of the members of Technicolor's Board of Directors at the time of the merger,[2] and the chief architects of the merger, MAF, Macanfor, and Ronald O. Perelman, controlling shareholder and Chairman of MAF.[3]

Cinerama instituted its appraisal action pursuant to 8 *Del. C.* §262 after voting against the merger. Approximately two years later, in the course of appraisal discovery, Cinerama came upon evidence of wrongdoing by Technicolor management associated with the merger. Cinerama then filed in the Court of Chancery its fraud action, charging the above-described defendants with conspiracy, fraud, breach of fiduciary duty, and other wrongdoing in the merger.

Defendants moved to dismiss the fraud action, asserting that Cinerama lacked standing to institute a fraud action after electing appraisal relief under section 262. Cinerama countered by moving the Court for alternative relief: (1) to amend its appraisal complaint to include its fraud and unfair dealing claims asserted in its fraud action; or (2) to consolidate for discovery and trial its appraisal and its fraud actions. Technicolor opposed both motions, and all defendants moved to dismiss Cinerama's fraud action on the grounds previously stated.

By opinion and interlocutory order dated January 13, 1987, the Court of Chancery, in an unreported decision, denied all three motions. While the effect of its rulings was to permit Cinerama to pursue independently both its appraisal and its fraud actions, the Court then ruled that Cinerama, after completing discovery, would be required to elect which of its two suits to bring to trial and which suit to abandon.

Both parties appeal the Court's several rulings. Cinerama appeals: (1) the Court's denial of its motion to amend its appraisal action; (2) the Court's ruling requiring Cinerama to make a binding election before trial between its appraisal remedy and its rescissory claim for damages; and (3) the Court's denial of Cinerama's motion to consolidate its appraisal and fraud suits. The defendants cross-appeal from the Court's denial of their motion to dismiss Cinerama's fraud action as barred by loss of standing through election of its appraisal remedy. Defendants also cross-appeal from the Court's

---

1. Hereinafter, Cinerama, Incorporated and Cede & Company shall be collectively referred to as "Cinerama."

2. The only Technicolor directors not joined were Charles S. Simone, who allegedly opposed the merger, and William R. Frye, by then deceased.

3. Perelman was Chairman of the Board and Chief Executive Officer of MAF. In addition to his position in MAF, he personally owned 38.4% of the common stock of MAF and, together with the other officers and directors of MAF, collectively owned more than 50% of the common stock of MAF.

election of remedy ruling, contending that Cinerama's election should be required to be made immediately and not deferred until Cinerama announces itself ready for trial.

We affirm the Chancellor's ruling declining to dismiss Cinerama's fraud action, but we reverse the Court's ruling declining to consolidate Cinerama's appraisal and fraud actions, requiring Cinerama to make a binding election of remedies before trial. Under the facts as alleged, Cinerama should not be put to an election of such disparate remedies; rather, the actions should be consolidated for trial. If Cinerama prevails, the Court will determine the appropriate remedies warranted by its findings.

* * *

II.

For the first time, this Court addresses the standing and right of a shareholder dissenting from a cash-out merger to pursue under Delaware law both an appraisal remedy under 8 *Del. C.* §262 and a subsequent individual action for rescissory damages based on a later-discovered claim of fraud in the merger. The disparate nature of the two causes of action has been previously addressed by this Court in *Weinberger v. UOP, Inc.*, Del. Supr., 457 A.2d 701 (1983), and in *Rabkin v. Philip A. Hunt Chem. Corp.*, Del. Supr., 498 A.2d 1099 (1985). In each case, we stated that a statutory appraisal proceeding under section 262 and a rescissory suit for fraud, misrepresentation, self-dealing and other actionable wrongs violative of "entire fairness"[6] to minority shareholders serve different purposes and are designed to provide different, and not interchangeable, remedies.

An appraisal proceeding is a limited legislative remedy intended to provide shareholders dissenting from a merger on grounds of inadequacy of the offering price with a judicial determination of the intrinsic worth (fair value) of their shareholdings. *Weinberger*, 457 A.2d at 714; *Kaye v. Pantone Inc.*, Del. Ch., 395 A.2d 369, 374-75 (1978) (describing an appraisal remedy as "entirely a creature of statute"; "the sole issue raised by an action seeking an appraisal should be the value of the dissenting stockholder's stock"). Value was traditionally arrived at by determining "the true or intrinsic value" of the shareholders' proportionate interest in the company, valued on a going-concern rather than a liquidated basis. *See Universal City Studios, Inc. v. Francis I. duPont & Co.*, Del. Supr., 334 A.2d 216 (1975); *Tri-Continental Corp. v. Battye*, Del. Supr., 74 A.2d 71, 72 (1950).

Weinberger broadens or liberalizes the process for determining the "fair value" of the company's outstanding shares by including all generally accepted techniques of valuation used in the financial community, thereby supplementing the previously employed rigid or stylized approach to valuation. *See* 457 A.2d at 712-13. *Weinberger* directs that this "liberalized approach" to appraisal shall be used to determine the value of a cashed-out minority's share interest on the day of the merger, reflecting all relevant information regarding the company and its shares. *Id.* at 713. This includes information concerning future events not arising solely "from the accomplishment or expectation of the merger," 8 *Del. C.* §262(h), which, if made public, can affect the current value of the shares and "which are known or susceptible of proof as of the date of the merger...." 457 A.2d at 713; 8 *Del. C.* §262(h).[8]

---

6. In *Weinberger* we recognized that "[t]he concept of fairness has two basic aspects: fair dealing and fair price." 457 A.2d at 711.

8. Information and insight not communicated to the market may not be reflected in stock prices; thus, minority shareholders being cashed out may be deprived of part of the true investment value of their shares. *See generally* R. Clark, *Corporate Law* 507 (1986).... The issue we are addressing is not the manipulation of the transaction, *see Rabkin*, 498 A.2d at 1104-05, nor the suppression or misstatement of *material* information by insiders defrauding the market, *see Basic Inc. v. Levinson*, [485 U.S. 224 (1988), reprinted *infra* at section 5c(i). Instead, we recognize that the majority may have in-

In contrast to appraisal, entire fairness—fair price and fair dealing—is the focal point against which the merger transaction and consideration arrived at can be measured. *See Rabkin*, 498 A.2d at 1106 (unfair dealing claims, based on breaches of the duties of loyalty and care, raise "issues which an appraisal cannot address"); *Weinberger*, 457 A.2d at 714 ("[t]he appraisal remedy ... may not be adequate in certain cases, particularly where fraud, misrepresentation, self-dealing, deliberate waste of corporate assets, or gross and palpable overreaching are involved"). It is important to emphasize that "the test for fairness is not a bifurcated one as between fair dealing and price. *All aspects of the issue must be examined as a whole* since the question is one of fairness." *Id.* at 711 (emphasis added).

To summarize, in a section 262 appraisal action the only litigable issue is the determination of the value of the appraisal petitioners' shares on the date of the merger, the only party defendant is the surviving corporation and the only relief available is a judgment against the surviving corporation for the fair value of the dissenters' shares. In contrast, a fraud action asserting fair dealing and fair price claims affords an expansive remedy and is brought against the alleged wrongdoers to provide whatever relief the facts of a particular case may require. In evaluating claims involving violations of entire fairness, the trial court may include in its relief any damages sustained by the shareholders. *See Rabkin*, 498 A.2d at 1107; *Weinberger*, 457 A.2d at 713. In a fraud claim, the approach to determining relief *may* be the same as that employed in determining fair value under 8 *Del. C.* §262.[9] However, an appraisal action may not provide a complete remedy for unfair dealing or fraud because a damage award in a fraud action may include "rescissory damages if the [trier of fact] considers them susceptible of proof and a remedy appropriate to all issues of fairness before him." *Weinberger*, 457 A.2d at 714. *Weinberger* and *Rabkin* make this clear distinction in terms of the relief available in a section 262 action as opposed to a fraud in the merger suit.

III.

A.

Whether Cinerama's Subsequent Fraud Action Is Foreclosed by Its Original Election of an Appraisal Remedy

Applying these principles to the record before us, we find the Chancellor was clearly correct in refusing to dismiss Cinerama's fraud action. Given the distinctive nature of the remedies available to a cashed-out shareholder, the Chancellor properly declined to find Cinerama to lack standing to pursue its fraud claim....

---

sight into their company's future based primarily on bits and pieces of *nonmaterial* information that have value as a totality. *See* Clark, *supra* at 508. It is this information that, if available in a statutory appraisal proceeding, the Court of Chancery must evaluate to determine if future earnings will affect the fair value of shares on the day of the merger. *See* 8 *Del. C.* §262(h). To obtain this information the appraisal petitioner must be permitted to conduct a "detailed investigation into the facts that is warranted by the acute conflict of interest and the potential for investor harm that is inherent in freeze-out transactions." Clark, *supra* at 508.

9. This Court in *Weinberger* recognized that "[i]n this breach of fiduciary duty case, the Chancellor perceived that the approach to valuation was the same as that in an appraisal proceeding." 457 A.2d at 712. Although this Court overruled the exclusivity of the method used by the Chancellor, we did not reverse the Chancellor's decision to use the appraisal valuation approach for cases involving breaches of fiduciary duties.

Defendants' reliance upon *Dofflemyer v. W. F. Hall Printing Co.*, D. Del., 558 F. Supp. 372 (1983), and *Braasch v. Goldschmidt*, Del. Ch. 199 A.2d 760 (1964), is misplaced. *Dofflemyer* and *Braasch* are decisions that were based on the doctrine that, by demanding appraisal, a former shareholder elects "to withdraw from the corporate enterprise and take the value of his stock," and, as a result, is divested of the rights appertaining to his shares. *Southern Production Co. v. Sabath*, Del. Supr., 87 A.2d 128, 134 (1952). *Dofflemyer*, *Braasch*, and *Southern* derive from *Taormina v. Taormina Corp.*, Del. Ch. 78 A.2d 473 (1951), a shareholder derivative suit representing application of Court of Chancery Rule 23.1. As the Trial Court recognized, procedural requirements of standing developed to control derivative actions have no relevance to individual shareholder suits claiming a private wrong.[10] Standing to pursue a derivative claim for injury to the corporate entity should not be confused with the right of a former shareholder claimant to assert a timely filed private cause of action premised upon a claim of unfair dealing, illegality, or fraud. No one would assert that a former owner suing for loss of property through deception or fraud has lost standing to right the wrong that arguably caused the owner to relinquish ownership or possession of the property.

The Chancellor correctly equated the right of a shareholder who loses share membership through misrepresentation, conspiracy, fraud, or breach of fiduciary duty to seek redress with the right of a shareholder who dissents from a merger and seeks appraisal of his shares to seek redress after discovery of allegedly wrongful conduct. Fairness and consistency require equal recourse for a former shareholder who accepts a cash-out offer in ignorance of a later-discovered claim against management for breach of fiduciary duty and a shareholder who discovers such a claim after electing appraisal rights.

Moreover, policy considerations militate against foreclosing a shareholder electing appraisal rights from later bringing a fraud action based on after-discovered wrongdoing in the merger. Experience has shown that the great majority of minority shareholders in a freeze-out merger accept the cash-out consideration, notwithstanding the possible existence of a claim of unfair dealing, due to the risks of litigation. *See Joseph v. Shell Oil Co.*, Del. Ch., 498 A.2d 1117, 1122 (1985). With the majority of the minority shareholders tendering their shares, only shareholders pursuing discovery during an appraisal proceeding are likely to acquire the relevant information needed to pursue a fraud action if such information exists. Such shareholders, however, would not have any financial incentive to communicate their discovered claim of wrongdoing in the merger to the shareholders who tendered their shares for the consideration offered by the majority and, by tendering, have standing to file suit. Thus, to bar those seeking appraisal from asserting a later-discovered fraud claim may effectively immunize a controlling shareholder from answering to a fraud claim.

---

10. The fundamental distinction between derivative and individual claims is well established: Generally speaking, a wrong to the incorporated group as a whole that depletes or destroys corporate assets and reduces the value of the corporation's stock gives rise to a derivative action; a breach of an individual shareholder's 'membership' contract or some other interference with the rights that are traditionally viewed as incident to the individual's ownership of stock gives rise to a non-derivative, or direct, action by the injured shareholder or shareholders.

D. Block, N. Barton & S. Radin, *The Business Judgment Rule: Fiduciary Duties of Corporate Directors and Officers* at 216 (1987) (citing W. Cary & M. Eisenberg, *Cases and Materials on Corporations* 897 (5th ed. 1980); H. Henn & J. Alexander, *Laws of Corporations and Other Business & Enterprises* §360, at 1048 (3d ed. 1983)).

Defendants assert that it is inconsistent (or unfair) to permit both the fraud action and the appraisal action to proceed simultaneously. This argument is misguided. Cinerama is not seeking (nor would our courts permit) inconsistent remedial relief, but rather is simply pleading alternative causes of action. In the instant case, the merger occurred. If the merger was properly consummated, then 8 *Del. C.* §262 affords Cinerama a claim for the fair value of its Technicolor shares.... If the merger was not lawfully effected, Cinerama should be entitled to recover rescissory damages, rendering the appraisal action moot.

* * *

B.

Whether Cinerama May Assert in Its Appraisal Proceeding Its Claim of Fraud in the Merger

The Court of Chancery correctly denied Cinerama's motion to amend and enlarge its appraisal action to include its claim for rescissory relief for conspiracy, illegality, fraud, and breach of fiduciary duty.... [I]n a fraud action seeking monetary relief for unfair dealing, the focus of the suit is whether wrongdoing can be established, *see Weinberger*, 457 A.2d at 714. Hence, the necessary party defendants in a "fraud in the merger" action are the alleged wrongdoers because it is they who arguably caused the injury and should pay any damage award. To permit Cinerama to amend its statutory appraisal action to include its fraud claims would impermissibly broaden the legislative remedy. It would also fail to bring before the Court the necessary parties for the fashioning of any appropriate relief for a fraud.

Finally, to judicially expand an appraisal proceeding to include unfair dealing claims would likely create unforeseeable administrative and procedural problems for litigants and the courts....

On the several grounds stated, we conclude that the Court of Chancery did not abuse its discretion in denying Cinerama's motion to amend its appraisal action....

C.

Whether Cinerama Should Be Put to an Election of Remedies before Trial or Both Claims Should Be Consolidated for Trial

On this issue we find the Court of Chancery to have erred. Cinerama's motion to consolidate, for purposes of trial as well as discovery, its fraud and appraisal actions should have been granted....

We know of no general substantive or procedural law that should require Cinerama to be put to a binding election before trial between its statutory right to receive fair value for its shares and an opportunity to litigate its fair dealing claims....

Cinerama, therefore, is entitled to proceed simultaneously with its statutory and equitable claims for relief. What Cinerama may not do, however, is recover duplicative judgments or obtain double recovery....

Consolidation of the actions is also necessary to put Cinerama in a position equivalent to the position it would arguably be in had defendants exercised "complete candor" in disclosing all material information associated with the merger to the minority shareholders. Had Cinerama known at the time of the merger what it arguably learned through discovery, it is reasonable to assume that Cinerama would have first brought suit to enjoin the merger,[13] and if unsuccessful, Cinerama could still have perfected its appraisal rights.

To require Cinerama to make a binding election of remedies no later than the time that it announced itself to be ready for trial would deprive Cinerama of a cause of action it would have possessed had management made a full disclosure of all material information prior to the merger, as mandated by *Weinberger*. *See* 457 A.2d at 710. Assuming the defendants failed to exercise "complete candor" with the minority shareholders, the minority should not be placed in a worse position than if management had acted with "complete candor." *See Bershad v. Curtiss-Wright Corp.*, Del. Supr., 535 A.2d 840 (1987). Thus, we hold that Cinerama should be permitted to exercise its appraisal rights while seeking rescissory damages in a consolidated action, subject to the limitation of a single recovery judgment.

Accordingly, the judgment of the Court of Chancery denying defendants' motion to dismiss Cinerama's fraud action is AFFIRMED and defendant's cross-appeal (asserting Cinerama's loss of standing) fails. The judgment denying Cinerama's motion to amend its appraisal action is AFFIRMED. The judgment requiring Cinerama to make an election of remedies (implicitly denying Cinerama's motion to consolidate its appraisal and fraud actions) is REVERSED, and defendants' cross-appeal (requiring an earlier election by Cinerama) necessarily fails. The causes are REMANDED, with directions that Cinerama be permitted to consolidate its two pending actions for further discovery and trial.

Affirmed in part; Reversed in part; and Remanded.

Notes and Questions

1. Is the compensation awarded in mergers in which directors are held to have breached their fiduciary duties the same as in an appraisal proceeding? The *Weinberger* court said yes, but did the *Cede I* court agree?

In another disagreement between Delaware and Massachusetts courts, the court in Coggins v. New England Patriots Football Club, Inc., 397 Mass. 525, 492 N.E.2d 1112, 1119-20 (1986), expressed a different view and elaborated on what "rescissory damages" entail:

> *Remedy.* The plaintiffs are entitled to relief. They argue that the appropriate relief is rescission of the merger and restoration of the parties to their positions of 1976. We agree that the normally appropriate remedy for an impermissible freeze-out merger is rescission. Because Massachusetts statutes do not bar a cash freeze-out, however, numerous third parties relied in good faith on the outcome of the merger. The trial judge concluded that the expectations of those parties should not be upset, and so chose to award damages rather than rescission.
>
> We recognize that, because rescission is an equitable remedy, the circumstances of a particular case may not favor its employment. The goals of a remedy instituted after a finding that a merger did not serve the corporate purpose should include furthering the interests of the corporation. Ordinarily, we would remand with instructions for the trial judge to determine whether rescission would be in the corporation's best interests, but such a

_____

13. At this late date, there is a strong reluctance to "unwind" a merger. *See, e.g., Weinberger*, 457 A.2d at 714....

remedy does not appear to be equitable at this time. This litigation has gone on for many years. There is yet at least another related case pending (in the Federal District Court). Furthermore, other factors weight against rescission. The passage of time has made the 1976 position of the parties difficult, if not impossible, to restore. A substantial number of former stockholder have chosen other courses and should not be forced back into the Patriots corporation. In these circumstances the interests of the corporation and of the plaintiffs will be furthered best by limiting the plaintiffs' remedy to an assessment of damages.

We do not think it appropriate, however, to award damages based on a 1976 appraisal value. To do so would make this suit a nullity, leaving the plaintiffs with no effective remedy except appraisal, a position we have already rejected. Rescissory damages must be determined based on the present value of the Patriots, that is, what the stockholders would have if the merger were rescinded.... On remand, the judge is to take further evidence on the present value of the Old Patriots on the theory that the merger had not taken place. Each share of the Coggins class is to receive, as rescissory damages, its aliquot share of the present assets.

The trial judge dismissed the plaintiffs' claims against the individual defendants based on waste of corporate assets. The remedy we order is intended to give the plaintiffs what they would have if the merger were undone and the corporation were put back together again. The trial judge's finding that the sole purpose of the merger was the personal financial benefit of William H. Sullivan, Jr., and the use of corporate assets to accomplish this impermissible purpose, leads inescapably to the conclusion that part of what the plaintiffs otherwise would have benefitted by, was removed from the corporation by the individual defendants. We reverse the dismissal of the claim for waste of corporate assets and remand this question to the trial court. The present value of the Patriots, as determined on remand, should include the amount wrongfully removed or diverted from the corporate coffers by the individual defendants.

Do you agree with the Delaware approach or the Massachusetts approach? Why?

2. A majority of jurisdictions expressly provide for appraisal rights as the exclusive remedy, at least in some situations. *E.g.*, Cal. Corp. Code §1312; Conn. Gen. Stat. §33-856; Yanow v. Teal Indus., 422 A.2d 311 (Conn. 1979). Of these, a majority make an exception where fraud and/or illegality is alleged. *See* Model Bus. Corp. Act Ann. §13.02, Statutory Comparison (3rd ed. 1984 & Supp. 2000/01/02); Maine Bus. Corp. Act 13-C M.R.S. §1302; South Carolina Corps., Partnerships and Assocs., S.C. Code Ann. §33-13-102. However, in some jurisdictions, even where the appraisal remedy is made exclusive by statute, courts have denied its exclusivity. *E.g.*, *Coggins, supra*; In re Jones & Loughlin Steel Corp., 412 A.2d 1099 (Pa. 1980) (construing Pa. Bus. Corp. L. §1515(K)); *see generally* 15 Fletcher et al., Fletcher Cyclopedia of the Law of Private Corporations §7165.1 (perm. ed., rev. vol. 1997 & Supp. 2004). For cases holding the appraisal remedy to be non-exclusive where there are allegations of fraud or unfair dealing, *see* Mullen v. Academy Life Ins. Co., 705 F.2d 971 (8th Cir. 1983) (construing New Jersey law), *cert. denied*, 464 U.S. 827 (1983); Dowling v. Narragansett Capital Corp., 735 F. Supp. 1105 (D.R.I. 1990)(construing Rhode Island law); Yeager v. Paul Semonion Co., 691 S.W.2d 227 (Ky. Ct. App. 1985); Alpert v. 28 Williams St. Corp., 473 N.E.2d 19 (N.Y. 1984); Stepak v. Schey, 553 N.E.2d 1072 (Ohio 1990); Pritchard v. Mead, 455 N.W.2d 263 (Wisc. 1990).

Problem — Providing Appraisal Rights

The Bondolian legislature has decided to include in its new corporations code provisions permitting a variety of fundamental corporate changes including mergers, consolidations, sales of all or substantially all assets, dissolutions, and charter amendments for the purpose of recapitalization. In light of that nation's new-found love for private property, however, the legislature has expressed concern that such transactions be accomplished in the manner least harmful to the rights of minority stockholders. You have told them about the concept of appraisal rights, and they have asked you to draft a statute providing for such rights, defining them, delineating their scope, and providing enforcement mechanisms. Do so, and write a memo explaining your statute and the choices you have made. In drafting your statute, consider (i) when appraisal rights should be available (including transactions or events in addition to those enumerated if you believe it to be appropriate); (ii) what those rights should consist of (including valuation methods, to the extent you think they should be specified); and (iii) how those rights should be enforced (paying particular attention to the possibility that undue complexity may effectively destroy those rights). Also consider whether the statute should distinguish between close and public corporations in any of these respects (including whether appraisal rights should be available at all in each case). Finally, consider whether the availability of appraisal rights should be limited to stockholders.

After you have completed your statute, compare it with the following: §262 of the Delaware General Corporation Law; §§13.01-13.30 of the Revised Model Business Corporation Act; §§1300 and 1312 of the California Corporations Code; and §§623 and 910 of the New York Business Corporation Law. How does your statute compare with these? Which do you prefer? Why?

---

b. Valuation by Agreement

The partnership-like character of close corporations emphasizes the importance of personal relationships among close corporation participants. Consequently, one of the typically important goals of stockholders in close corporations is to control who may become stockholders of the corporation by restricting the transferability of shares of the corporation's stock. Such restrictions, particularly when coupled with the well-known lack of marketability of close corporation stock, virtually eliminates any liquidity for stockholders. One device that has been developed both to insure that stock ownership remains among the group and to provide liquidity for those stockholders who choose to withdraw is the buy-sell agreement. Such an agreement is referred to as a shareholders' agreement when it also covers other issues, such as those relating to corporate governance.

The buy-sell agreement, while it may take a variety of forms (such as a provision set forth in a company's bylaws or a broader shareholders' agreement), focuses close corporation planners on the problems of valuation, with a twist. That twist is that the time at which the stock will have to be valued is in the future. Thus planners are not only faced with the ordinary problem of selecting a valuation method (or combination of methods) that best determines present value, but also the problem of deciding whether that method (or methods) will continue to be appropriate in the future. The individual motivations of the parties will also be a factor with which planners have to contend. For example, a controlling stockholder who does not anticipate leaving the corporation may want to ensure that those who do are paid a relatively low value for their stock, while the other parties to the agreement obviously will feel differently. Even when the parties agree on valuation language, courts are required to settle disputes relating to its interpretation and overall fairness given events occurring after its adoption. Before we turn to a judicial review of valuation language, consider the following problem.

Problem — Smith Drugstores, Part IV

Forget about all the troubles that the team from Smith Drugstores has given you over the last few weeks and assume instead that you are retained by Jerome Smith, Harry Smith, and Mike Wilson to incorporate Smith Drugstores Inc. (Although the company was incorporated twenty-nine years ago, assume that the law and the state of financial theory are as they exist today.) During the course of your initial consultation, they explain their desire to restrict stock ownership to their small group (including their employees who will own 10% of the total outstanding stock), and their further intent to limit stock ownership only to those persons who are employed by the corporation.

1. You agree to draft a buy-sell provision that meets your clients' needs and to send it to them together with a memorandum explaining the choices you have made and the alternatives you have foregone. Do so, focusing on: (i) the method of valuation, and (ii) the contexts in which the agreed-upon valuation method (or the value itself) is relevant.

2. To what extent should a court respect the agreed-upon valuation method (or the value itself) in a particular context? Consider the excerpt from In the Matter of Pace Photographers, Ltd., which is set forth in Note 1 at the end of this subsection. What is the planning significance of the *Pace* case?

3. Do you have any ethical problem representing the stockholders as they have requested? Would it make a difference if you were retained by the company, which will be a party to the agreement? *See* Model Rules of Prof'l R. 1.13 & 1.7 (2004).

Allen v. Biltmore Tissue Corp.
2 N.Y.2d 534 (NY 1957)

Fuld, Chief Judge:

The by-laws of defendant corporation give it an option to purchase, in case of the death of a stockholder, his shares of the corporate stock. The enforceability [sic] of this option is one of the questions for decision.

Biltmore Tissue Corporation was organized under the Stock Corporation Law in 1932, with an authorized capitalization of 1,000 shares without par value, to manufacture and deal in paper and paper products. The by-laws, adopted by the incorporators-directors, contain provisions limiting the number of shares (originally 5, later 20) available to each stockholder (§28) and restricting stock transfers both during the life of the stockholder and in case of his death (§§29, 30). Whenever a stockholder desires to sell or transfer his shares, he must, according to one by-law (§29), give the corporation or other stockholders "an opportunity to repurchase the stock at the price that was paid for the same to the Corporation at the time the Corporation issued the stock"; if, however, the option is not exercised, "then, after the lapse of sixty days, the stock may be sold by the holder to such person and under such circumstances as he sees fit." The by-law, dealing with the transfer of stock upon the death of a stockholder (§30) — the provision with which we are here concerned — is almost identical. It recites that the corporation is to have the right to purchase its late stockholder's shares for the price it originally received for them [or,] the corporation does not, or cannot, purchase such stock, the Board of Directors shall have the right to empower such of its existing stockholders as it sees fit to make such purchase at the same price. Should the option not be exercised, then, after the lapse of ninety days, the late shareholder's legal representative may dispose of said stock as he sees fit.

Harry Kaplan ... purchased 5 shares of stock from the corporation at $5 a share. In 1936, Kaplan received a stock dividend of 5 more shares, and two years later purchased an additional 10 shares for $100. On the face of each of the three certificates, running vertically along the left-hand margin, appeared the legend,

"Issued subject to restrictions in sections 28, 29, and 30 of the By-laws."

On October 20, 1953, Kaplan wrote to the corporation stating that he was "interested in selling" his 20 shares of stock and requesting that he be given the "price" which the board of directors "will consider, so that I may come to a decision." He died five days later. Some months thereafter, in February, 1954, his son, who was also one of his executors, addressed a letter to Biltmore, inquiring whether it was "still interested in acquiring shares and at what price." ... [O]n March 4, 1954, Biltmore's board of directors voted to exercise its option to purchase the stock, pursuant to section 30 of the by-laws, and about three weeks later the executors' attorney was advised of the corporation's action. He was also informed that, although the by-law provision permitted purchase at "the same price that the company received therefor from the stockholder originally," the corporation had, nevertheless, decided to pay $20 a share, "considerably more than the original purchase price", based on the prices at which it had acquired shares from other stockholders.

Kaplan's executors declined to sell to the corporation, insisting that the stock which had been in the decedent's name be transferred to them. When their demand was refused, they brought this action to compel Biltmore to accept surrender of the decedent's stock certificate and to issue a new certificate for 20 shares to them. They contended ... the by-law is void as an unreasonable restraint. The corporation interposed a counterclaim for specific performance.... The court at Special Term granted judgment to the corporation on its counterclaim and dismissed the complaint. The Appellate Division reversed, rendered judgment directing the transfer of the stock to the plaintiffs and dismissed the defendant's counterclaim upon the ground that the by-law in question is void.

Section 176 of the Personal Property Law, which is identical with section 15 of the Uniform Stock Transfer Act, provides that "there shall be no restriction upon the transfer of shares" represented by a stock certificate "by virtue of any by-law of such corporation, or otherwise, unless the ... restriction is *stated* upon the certificate." (Emphasis supplied.) In order to comply with this statutory mandate, the corporation printed the words, "Issued subject to restrictions in sections 28, 29, and 30 of the By-laws," on the side of the certificate....

Since ... the legend on the certificate meets the statute's requirements, we turn to the validity of the by-law restriction.

The validity of qualifications on the ownership of corporate shares through restrictions on the right to transfer has long been a source of confusion in the law. The difficulties arise primarily from the clash between the concept of the shares as "creatures of the company's constitution and therefore … essentially contractual choses in action" (Gower, Some Contrasts between British and American Corporation Law, *69 Harv. L. Rev. 1369, 1377*) and the concept of the shares as personal property represented so far as possible by the certificate itself and, therefore, subject to the time-honored rule that there be no unreasonable restraint upon alienation. While the courts of this state and of many other jurisdictions … have favored the "property" concept … the tendency is, as section 176 of the Personal Property Law implies, to sustain a restriction imposed on the transfer of stock if "reasonable" and if the stockholder acquired such stock with requisite notice of the restriction.

The question posed, therefore, is whether the provision, according the corporation a right or first option to purchase the stock at the price which it originally received for it, amounts to an unreasonable restraint. In our judgment, it does not.

The courts have almost uniformly held valid and enforceable the first option provision, in charter or by-law, whereby a shareholder desirous of selling his stock is required to afford the corporation, his fellow stockholders or both an opportunity to buy it before he is free to offer it to outsiders.… The courts have often said that this first option provision is "in the nature of a contract" between the corporation and its stockholders and, as such, binding upon them. Hassel v. Pohle, … 214 App. Div. 654, 658; see, also 8 Fletcher, … § 4194, p. 736. In Doss v. Yingling … 95 Ind. App. 494, a leading case on the subject and one frequently cited throughout the country, a by-law provision against transfer by any stockholder—there were three—of any shares until they had first been offered for sale to other stockholders at *book value*, was sustained as reasonable and valid (p. 500): "The weight of authority is to the effect that a corporate by-law which requires the owner of the stock to give the other stockholders of the corporation … *an option to purchase the same at an agreed price or the then-existing book value before offering the stock for sale to an outsider, is a valid and reasonable restriction* and binding upon the stockholders." (Emphasis supplied.)

[W]hat the law condemns is, not a *restriction* on transfer, a provision merely postponing sale during the option period, but an effective *prohibition* against transferability itself. Accordingly, if the by-law under consideration were to be construed as rendering the sale of the stock impossible to anyone except to the corporation at whatever price it wished to pay, we would, of course, strike it down as illegal. But that is not the meaning of the provision before us. The corporation had its option only for a 90-day period. If it did not exercise its privilege within that time, the deceased stockholder's legal representative was at liberty to "dispose of said stock as he [saw] fit" (§ 30), and, once so disposed of, it would thereafter be free of the restriction. In a very real sense, therefore, the primary purpose of the by-laws was to enable a particular party, the corporation, to buy the shares, not to prevent the other party, the stockholder, from selling them.…

The Appellate Division, however, was impressed with what it deemed the "unreasonableness," that is, "unfairness," of the price specified in the by-law, namely, a price at which the shares had originally been purchased from the corporation. Carried to its logical conclusion, such a rationale would permit, indeed, would encourage, expensive litigation in every case where the price specified in the restriction, or the formula for fixing the price, was other than a recognized and easily ascertainable fair market value. This would destroy part of the social utility of the first option type of restriction which, when imposed, is intended to operate *in futuro* and must, therefore, include some formula for future determination of the option price.

Generally speaking, these restrictions are employed by the so-called "close corporation" as part of the attempt to equate the corporate structure to a partnership by giving the original stockholders a sort of pre-emptive right through which they may, if they choose, veto the admission of a new participant.... Obviously, the case where there is an easily ascertainable market value for the shares of a closely held corporate enterprise is the exception, not the rule, and, consequently, various methods or formulae for fixing the option price are employed in practice—e.g., book or appraisal value, often exclusive of good will ... or a fixed price ... or the par value of the stock....

In sum, then, the validity of the restriction on transfer does not rest on any abstract notion of intrinsic fairness of price. To be invalid, more than mere disparity between option price and current value of the stock must be shown.... Since the parties have in effect agreed on a price formula which suited them, and provision is made freeing the stock for outside sale should the corporation not make, or provide for, the purchase, the restriction is reasonable and valid....

The judgment of the Appellate Division dismissing the defendant's counterclaim and sustaining the plaintiff's complaint should be reversed, and that of Special Term reinstated, with costs in this court and in the Appellate Division.

Note

In Evangelista v. Holland, 537 N.E.2d 589 (Mass. App. Ct. 1989), a shareholders' agreement provided that the corporation could buy out the stock held by the estate of any deceased shareholder. The corporation brought suit against the estate of a deceased shareholder to enforce the agreement, but the executors of the estate refused to comply with the agreement. Evidence suggested that the decedant's stock was worth at least $191,000. In holding for the corporation, the court stated:

> The executors suggest that to require them to part with their interest in the business for so much less than the [value of the stock] violates the duty of good faith and loyalty owed one another by stockholders in a closely held corporation.... Questions of good faith and loyalty do not arise when all the stockholders in advance enter into an agreement for the purchase of stock of a withdrawing or deceased stockholder.... That the price established by a stockholders' agreement may be less than the appraised or market value is unremarkable. Such agreements may have as their purpose: the payment of a price for a decedent's stock which will benefit the corporation or surviving stockholders by not unduly burdening them; the payment of a price tied to life insurance; or fixing a price which assures the beneficiaries of the deceased stockholder of a predetermined price for stock which might have little market value.... When the agreement was entered into in 1984, the order and time of death of stockholders was an unknown. There was a "mutuality of risk."

Contrast the resolute judicial enforcement of the valuation provisions in *Allen* and *Evangelista* with the judicial analyses in the following two cases. What factual differences exist between *Allen*, on the one hand, and the two cases that follow, on the other? Additionally, with respect to just the following two cases, what factual differences exist between them that lead to different judicial outcomes?

Helms v. Duckworth
249 F.2d 482 (D.C. Cir. 1957)

BURGER, Circuit Judge.

Appellant, administratrix of the estate of Charles W. Easterday, sued for cancellation of a stock purchase agreement between Easterday and appellee Duckworth, by which the survivor would acquire the decedent's stock in a "two man" corporation. Both parties moved for summary judgment. The District Court granted summary judgment in favor of appellee.

The record discloses that in 1948 Easterday, then age 70, was engaged in business as a roofing and sheet metal contractor, an activity he had pursued for 45 years. Duckworth, then age 37, was employed by a roofing contractor. After negotiations the two men executed a contract in April 1948, calling for the formation of a new corporation with 1500 shares of $10 par value stock to be issued at that time, Easterday receiving 51% and Duckworth 49%. Duckworth was to pay for his shares in cash and Easterday was to pay for his by transfer of business assets. Notes were to be given by the new corporation to Easterday for transfer of other business assets having a value in excess of the cost of his shares. The new corporation was to carry on the business established by Easterday.

The contract also provided for the execution of a trust agreement by which each stockholder would place his stock in trust and agree that on his death (or sooner by mutual consent) his stock would be sold to the survivor or continuing member, "the purchase price of the stock [to the other] ... [being] the par value of $10 per share unless modified by the parties by subsequent agreement."

Shortly thereafter a formal survivor purchase agreement was executed with appellee Hamilton National Bank as trustee. This agreement spelled out the mechanics of purchasing and pricing the stock in these terms:

"Article II

"Upon the death, prior to the termination of this agreement, of whichever of the parties of the first or second parts is the first to die, the surviving party shall purchase the stock in the aforesaid corporation owned by the deceased stockholder at the time of his death and deposited hereunder, and the Trustee shall sell, transfer and deliver such stock to the surviving stockholder at the price and upon the terms and conditions hereinafter set forth.

"Article III

"The price which the surviving stockholder shall pay for the stock of the deceased stockholder shall be at the rate of $10.00 per share; provided, however, that such sale and purchase price may, from time to time, be re-determined and changed in the following manner:

"During the month of January in any year while this agreement remains in force, the parties of the first and second part shall have the right to increase or decrease the sale and purchase price by an instrument in writing signed by the parties of the first and second parts and filed with the trustee, the last paper writing so filed with the Trustee prior to the death of either of said parties to be final and conclusive in establishing such value and shall effectively fix the price at which the surviving stockholder shall purchase and the Trustee shall sell the stock of the decedent in said corporation."

It is undisputed that in 1948 when the enterprise began the $10 per share figure reflected the real net worth of the company and that as of December 31, 1955, the value of the stock was about $80 per share. There is, however, no evidence that either party ever proposed a change in price in accordance with the trust (survivor-purchase) agreement. Upon the death of Easterday in September 1956, Duckworth tendered to the trustee his check for Easterday's stock priced at $10 per share. Appellant then instituted this suit contending that unless Duckworth agreed to pay the true value of the stock as of decedent's death, i.e., approximately $80 per share, the survivor-purchase agreement should be cancelled.

In support of this contention appellant urges that Duckworth fraudulently induced Easterday to execute the trust agreement by misrepresenting that he (Duckworth) would consent to a periodic redetermination of the stock purchase price; that this misrepresentation violated the confidential relationship existing between the parties, and, in any case, the consideration was so grossly inadequate as to warrant rescission of the agreement.

Appellee Duckworth stands on the letter of his contracts, arguing that there having been no mutually agreed change in the purchase price, the trustee is obligated to transfer decedent's shares at the stipulated contract price of $10 per share.

The basic contract between Easterday and Duckworth and the formal trust agreement implementing it are in general terms typical of agreements made between partners of small businesses or stockholders of closely held corporations where the major stockholders are also the managers of the enterprise. In this case, however, three provisions are of special significance: Articles II and III of the trust agreement, quoted above, and a clause in the basic contract of April 1948, which provides:

"It is hereby understood and agreed that the majority stockholders will not vote, or cause to be voted, a dissolution of the corporation or a complete disposition of the assets of the corporation without the consent of the minority stockholders."

These three provisions in combination had several significant effects:

(a) they prohibited Easterday as the majority stockholder from dissolving the corporation without consent of Duckworth;

(b) they prohibited Easterday as the majority stockholder from voting a complete disposition of the assets without Duckworth's consent; and

(c) they required a deceased member's estate to sell and the surviving member to buy the stock pursuant to the survivor-purchase agreement.

It is equally clear that the agreement contemplated, upon the initiative of either party, a yearly adjustment of the stock price to conform with the realities of a rising or declining net worth of the corporation. The corporate books were kept on a calendar year basis and the trust agreement provided "[d]uring the month of January ... the parties ... shall have the right to increase or decrease the sale and purchase price by an instrument in writing...." Plainly this implied a periodic bargaining or negotiating process in which each party must participate in good faith.... Any other interpretation would render the procedure for adjusting the stock purchase price superfluous since parties to a contract can, at any time, mutually agree to renegotiate and modify specific terms or execute a new contract. Furthermore, absent a bona fide promise or intent to bargain in good faith, either party could at will frustrate the agreement since it provided no alternative method of adjusting the valuation if the parties did not agree on an adjusted price. The absence of a good faith intent to bargain would work especially to the disadvantage of the elderly Easterday, since, having surrendered his normal voting position as majority stockholder, including the power to sell or liquidate the corporation, he could only effect a change in the stipulated price by persuading Duckworth in negotiations. This surrender of these normal and usual powers of a majority stockholder becomes especially significant in the relations between the parties. In operation it altered Easterday's position drastically and placed him dependent entirely upon Duckworth's good faith in negotiating any change in the stock price to reflect fairly the true value.

The very heart and core, then, of this agreement was the assumed willingness of each party to bargain and negotiate in good faith whenever called upon to revise the price of the stock. Not unlike the duty to bargain in good faith imposed by statute upon employers and unions, good faith in this context "means more than merely going through the motions of negotiating; *it is inconsistent with a predetermined resolve not to budge from an initial position.*"[4] (Emphasis added.) An even higher obligation to bargain sincerely arises under a contract which is not made at arms length, but between parties bearing a relationship of trust and confidence toward each other. Cf. Restatement, Contracts, §§497, 498 (1932). While both parties are free to argue and even disagree, each must argue sincerely and in good faith, disclosing all relevant facts, with the hope of reaching a fair agreement and not with a secret intent of preventing agreement. Thus any secret intent on the part of either party to refuse to negotiate fairly and in good faith becomes of vital importance.

We have no way to discern Easterday's intent, if any, as the record is silent. The intentions of Duckworth are not left to speculation or conjecture on this record; they are manifested plainly in his own affidavit, wherein he states:

"Further, he states that provisions of article III of the trust agreement of May 20, 1948 and provisions of a fourth paragraph on page 2 of the contract of April 15, 1948, both require his consent to any change in the price at which the stock could be purchased from the bank as trustee in the event of the death of either party.

"No change was ever made in this price, that he is advised and believes no change could be made without his consent, *that it was never his intention at any time to consent to any change in this provision,* nor was any request or suggestion ever made to him by the late Charles W. Easterday that any change be made." (Emphasis added.)

It is unnecessary for this court to determine whether Duckworth fraudulently induced Easterday to execute the survivorship agreement by means of a misrepresentation or otherwise.[5] In an intimate business venture such as this, stockholders of a close corporation occupy a position similar to that of joint adventurers and partners.... We believe that the holders of closely held stock in a corporation such as shown here bear a fiduciary duty to deal fairly, honestly, and openly with their fellow stockholders and to make disclosure of all essential information.

This rule "is based upon the proposition that, under all the circumstances of the case, it was the duty of the party who obtained the consent, acting in good faith, to have disclosed the facts which he concealed." Strong v. Repide, 1909, 213 U.S. 419, 430, 29 S. Ct. 521, 525, 53 L. Ed. 853. Certainly there must be a duty to disclose information which if known to the other party might lead him either to withdraw or to insist upon some self-executing provisions for stock pricing not capable of being frustrated by the bad faith of either party. But the very nature of Duckworth's secret intent was such that

---

4. N.L.R.B. v. Truitt Manufacturing Co., 1956, 351 U.S. 149, 154, 76 S. Ct. 753, 757, 100 L. Ed. 1027, Frankfurter, J., dissenting on other grounds.

5. It is clear that a promise made with the undisclosed intention not to perform it constitutes fraud and renders the agreement voidable. Restatement, Contracts, §§473, 476 (1932). It might fairly be inferred that no rational man in Easterday's position would enter a contract with these provisions unless he relied on the agreement as an implied promise to bargain in good faith.

it had to be kept secret and undisclosed or it would fail of its purpose. Having secured Easterday's agreement not to sell his stock nor to vote his stock for the dissolution or disposition of assets and having executed a survivorship agreement with Easterday whereby the stock purchase price was subject to periodic modification, appellee's failure to disclose to his corporate business "partner" his fixed intent never to alter the original price constitutes a flagrant breach of a fiduciary duty. Standing alone this warrants cancellation of the agreement by a court of equity.

There is another basis for demanding from appellee the highest degree of good faith in this case and imposing upon him the concomitant duty of full disclosure. Duckworth was trained in both business administration and the law while the record shows nothing to indicate Easterday had any training or experience in drafting contracts. The basic contract incorporates practically verbatim a "preliminary agreement" prepared personally by appellee. The "preliminary agreement," like the subsequently executed contract, provided for adjustments in the price of the stock. The record shows Easterday had no independent legal advice or help and that no independent legal counsel acted for both parties in drafting the trust agreement which set forth the procedure for modifying the purchase price....

It is apparent on this record that Easterday relied on appellee to formulate the technical terms of their agreement. Appellee, as one trained in the law and in the formalized processes of the business world, and who undertook to draft the procedure for purchasing the decedent's stock is subject to a special duty to his associate to act in the utmost good faith and reveal any possible conflicts of their respective interests.

Since our holding rests on the breach of a fiduciary relationship it is not necessary for the appellant to excuse or justify Easterday's failure to have sought a revision of the sale price of the stock. Moreover, it is plain that any request by Easterday in this regard would have been futile. Not only the circumstances but the express and calculated utterances of appellee, made in his affidavit at a time when he could have remained silent as to his intent, make it crystal clear that any effort by Easterday to negotiate a change in the price would have been frustrated. The failure of Easterday to request an adjustment of the purchase price is therefore immaterial in the light of Duckworth's secret intent to frustrate the spirit and letter and indeed one of the basic objectives of the agreement.

* * *

The order of the District Court is reversed and the case remanded for further proceedings not inconsistent herewith.

Reversed and remanded.

Notes

1. In the Matter of Pace Photographers, Ltd., 525 N.E.2d 713 (N.Y. 1988), involved a petitioner stockholder of a close corporation who was a party to an agreement with the other stockholders. The agreement provided that during its first five years a stockholder could sell his stock only to the remaining stockholders at a price determined by a formula set forth in the agreement. The formula was designed to ensure that any such sales would be at a "deep discount." Within three years after the agreement was signed, petitioner had a falling-out with the other stockholders and brought an action for dissolution under N.Y. Bus. Corp. Law §1104-a. Shortly thereafter, the corporation elected to repurchase petitioner's shares pursuant to §1118 at the price provided in the shareholders' agreement.

Petitioner appealed the trial court's determination that the appropriate repurchase price under §1118 was that set forth in the shareholders' agreement, and the Court of Appeals reversed. The court wrote:

In purporting to fix the fair value of petitioner's shares in accordance with Business Corporation Law §1118, both the Supreme Court and the Appellate Division viewed the 1104-a petition as petitioner's voluntary offer to sell his stock, and therefore simply applied the agreed terms for a voluntary sale. Supreme Court declared that "the fair value of the stock of the petitioner is that agreed to in Section 12(d) of the shareholders' agreement." The Appellate Division, in affirming, concluded that a petitioner claiming unfairness in an agreed price must show more than a disparity between that price and current value (citing *Allen* v. *Biltmore Tissue Corp.*, 2 N.Y.2d 534, 161 N.Y.S.2d 418, 141 N.E.2d 812), and that this agreement was both voluntary and unambiguous as to terms for a buyout. Finally, the court noted that, a "'review of the record reveals that the petitioner may obtain a fair return on his investment pursuant to the buy-out provisions of the shareholder's agreement' (*Matter of Harris [Daniels Agency]*, 118 A.D.2d 646, 647, 500 N.Y.S.2d 5)." (133 A.D.2d at 830, 520 N.Y.S.2d 202.) Significantly, no evidence was taken on valuation.

As an abstract matter, it may well be that shareholders can agree in advance that an 1104-a dissolution proceeding will be deemed a voluntary offer to sell, or fix "fair value" in the event of judicial dissolution, and that their agreement would be enforced.... Participants in business ventures are free to express their understandings in written agreements, and such consensual arrangements are generally favored and upheld by the courts....

But in the absence of explicit agreement a shareholders' agreement fixing the terms of a sale voluntarily sought and desired by a shareholder does not equally control when the sale is the result of claimed majority oppression or other wrongdoing—in effect, a forced buyout (*Matter of Kemp & Beatley [Gardstein]*, 64 N.Y.2d 63, 75, 484 N.Y.S.2d 799, 473 N.E.2d 1173, *supra*....) Here, the shareholders' agreement neither provided that an 1104-a dissolution proceeding would be deemed a voluntary offer to sell, nor fixed fair value in the event of an 1118 election. The buy-out provisions were explicitly limited to the desire of any party to "sell, hypothecate, transfer, encumber or otherwise dispose of" his shares. The only event otherwise deemed a voluntary sale was the death of a stockholder. The provisions of the shareholders' agreement regarding buyout within the first five years, at a 50% discount, were expressly limited to the situation where "a stockholder desires to sell his shares of the stock to the other stockholders" (para 12[e]), contemplating a voluntary sale at the convenience of and for the benefit of the selling shareholder, without regard to the inconvenience or detriment inflicted on the corporation or other shareholders. Similarly, paragraph 14 and schedule A by their terms dealt with the value of shares for shareholders "retiring or withdrawing from the business." It is plain from these cited provisions that a sale occasioned by an 1104-a petition premised on abuse by the majority does not fall within the contemplation of this shareholders' agreement regarding a sale of stock by a shareholder to the corporation.

We therefore conclude that the stipulated price of "one-half of the formula as set forth in paragraph 15" does not in and of itself dictate the "fair value" of petitioner's shares under section 1118, and that it was error to impose those terms without further inquiry regarding valuation.

Section 1118(b) directs that, when petitioner and the corporation cannot agree upon fair value, the court upon application of either party shall stay the 1104-a proceedings and determine fair value as of the day prior to the date on which the petition was filed. While respondent's election and application stayed the 1104-a proceeding, and petitioner consented to the buyout (133 A.D.2d 829, 830, 520 N.Y.S.2d 202, *supra*), no steps were taken to fix fair value. Value "should be determined on the basis of what a willing purchaser, in an arm's length transaction, would offer for the corporation as an operating business, rather than as a business in the process of liquidation." ... In reaching such a determination, the court obviously may take into account the shareholders' agreement provisions regarding value..., petitioner's own offer to buy, the corporation's alleged efforts to sell the business earlier, and any other pertinent evidence.... In this forced sale, the court's objective will be to fix the value of the business as a going concern as of the day prior to the filing of the petition, which may be very different from the objective of a shareholders' agreement fixing value for a voluntary sale.

2. Section 2703 of the Internal Revenue Code requires that valuations provided in buy-sell agreements which are at less than fair market value, or are set forth in an agreement which otherwise restricts the right to sell stock, be disregarded for estate and gift tax purposes. The section provides exceptions for bona fide agreements which are not designed to make intra-family transfers for less than adequate consideration with terms that are comparable to those contained in arm's length transactions. *See* Solomon & Saret, New Estate Freeze Rules for Strategies Tax Planning, Tax Notes, 871, 876-77 (February 25, 1991).

c. Valuation in Other Legal Contexts

Courts are called upon to value companies in several other contexts besides those presented above. These include, among others, liquidation, oppression, divorce, tax, and probate proceedings. With this in mind, consider the following two cases.

Donahue v. Draper
491 N.E.2d 260 (Mass. App. 1986)

KAPLAN, Justice.

Douglas A. Donahue, an equal owner with Thomas F. Draper of Donahue-Draper Corporation (DDC), a "close" corporation, sued Draper and others for damages for the commission of sundry breaches of fiduciary duties and breaches of contract associated with or consequent upon his being "frozen out" of the corporation.... The jury, responding to special interrogatories, returned answers prevailingly favorable to Donahue. Thereafter the trial judge made supplemental findings, and on June 28, 1983, an amended judgment entered, conforming to the answers and findings. The defendants appeal from parts of the judgment: Draper now accepts that some of his actions were in breach of his duties toward Donahue, but he resists that conclusion as to other conduct.

In outline, the course of events, as the jury could have found it, was as follows. Until some time in 1967, Donahue through a sole proprietorship, Douglas A. Donahue Company (DAD), did business as a broker and dealer in scoured wools and noils;[5] Draper,

_____

5. Noils are a kind of waste, short fibers combed from long fibers.

through his wholly-owned corporation, Thomas F. Draper Co., Inc. (TFD), was engaged in the branch of the wool trade called top-making.[6] In 1967, the two discontinued their own enterprises and founded DDC, to be engaged chiefly in top-making. They contributed equal capital to the company, received equivalent amounts of its stock, and had an understanding between them of equal efforts, rights, and benefits. Draper became the operational, Donahue the financial partner, although there was some crossing over of functions.

By 1978, DDC had very greatly prospered. At that time, Draper was serving as president of DDC, and Donahue as treasurer, and the directors were Draper, Donahue, and Draper's wife Ethel.[7] There was a falling out between the partners in April, 1978. Being able to count on Mrs. Draper's vote, Draper had at the time a practical control of DDC. Draper caused Donahue to be dismissed as treasurer of DDC; thereafter he removed Donahue as a trustee of the DDC pension trust, and as a director and officer of W. A. McNeill & Co., Inc. (McNeill Co.), a close corporation two-thirds owned by DDC. Draper cut Donahue's DDC annual salary (as an employee) to $25,000 while taking a salary of $65,000 for himself, and he took to himself other unequal emoluments. He proceeded toward the liquidation of DDC which was formally voted at a meeting of the directors and shareholders on September 20, 1979, with Donahue joining in the vote. During a preceding period, and thereafter during actual liquidation (completed in September, 1980), Draper so acted as to further his purpose of facilitating a transition or transfer of the top-making business from DDC to TFD. The latter company, reactivated on October 1, 1979, within a short time was dealing with former customers of DDC, occupying the old premises, using similar staff and the same telephone number, and so forth.[8]

To revert to the meeting of September 20, 1979, Donahue then stated that he was not agreeable to a distribution in kind of the stock of McNeill Co. held by DDC; he wanted cash. Thereafter Draper voted the DDC-owned shares of McNeill Co. (Wesley A. McNeill, the one-third owner of the company, joining) to replace Donahue by Ethel Draper as a director of McNeill Co. The directors acted to remove Donahue as an officer and, on behalf of McNeill Co., to waive any first refusal right in respect to the DDC-owned shares. Draper then caused those shares to be distributed to Donahue and himself in equal parts as a feature of the liquidation of DDC. From October, 1979, onward, Draper by agreement with Wesley McNeill received certain benefits from McNeill Co. in alleged breach of his duty toward Donahue, now a minority shareholder of that company.

* * *

In consequence of the liquidation of DDC, Donahue received some $321,000, evidently as his share of the avails of the net tangible assets. In the present lawsuit, Donahue sought damages for—

* * *

Goodwill. The jury found a corporate goodwill of $536,750 wrongfully appropriated by Draper (answers to interrogatory 4 on "Goodwill") of which Donahue would be entitled to one-half. This is on appeal.

---

6. Top-making consists essentially of combining various types of raw ('grease') wool and having them processed into a finished quality ('top') wool which is then spun into yarn....

7. At an earlier date the third director had been a relative of Donahue's. The change to Ethel Draper was a gesture of equalization, made quite casually.

8. Donahue resumed business through DAD in the purchase and sale of scoured wools and noils and did not engage in any top-making.

1. *Goodwill.* The jury found that DDC had goodwill of the value mentioned as of a date just before April 12, 1978, the date of the quarrel (agreed by the parties to be the proper time for valuation); that Draper took this goodwill for his own use; and that TFD benefited from Draper's misappropriation. Draper argues on the present appeal that there was less or no goodwill to be taken.

(a) Harold Petersen testified as an expert on Donahue's behalf and used a conventional method (and two alternatives) for ascertaining the existence of basic goodwill as well as its amount. We may take it that goodwill is, fundamentally, the value of an enterprise over and above the value of its net tangible assets, ... a value that may derive from the allegiance of customers, prolonged favorable relations with a source of financing, and the like.[11] In the case of an ordinary "public" corporation, one could (as of a relevant date) take the net earnings as they appeared, apply to this figure an appropriate multiple, and from the product subtract the value of the net tangible assets; any positive result would be an indication of the fact, and an idea of the extent, of the company's goodwill. In the case of a "close" corporation, earnings are typically withdrawn by the partners in the form of company-paid premiums for insurance on their lives, enhanced salaries, contributions to pensions, and perhaps various fringe benefits. Thus comes about a need for adjusting or "normalizing" earnings—ascertaining the "true" earnings—in working a formula for determining basic goodwill.... Petersen projected normalized net earnings for a year of $397,462; applied a multiplier of 6.4, which he believed appropriate for the kind of business; thus reached a product of $2,543,757; from which he subtracted net tangibles at the time of $968,608, yielding a basic goodwill of about $1,574,000. In the normalization process, Petersen allowed $70,800 for the combined annual salaries of the partners as a business expense of the company; the excess paid to the partners in the form of salary he considered as part of the company earnings. (The $70,800 amount, in particular, Draper criticized, as we note below.)

As to the alternative methods, Petersen offered one that dealt expressly with inflation, and another that projected earning power ahead for ten years. These estimates converged on the $1,574,000 for basic goodwill.[12] In the end, the jury allowed a goodwill of around one-third of that figure. On the basis of all that was put before them, the jury might have considered (with respect to Petersen's first method) that it would cost something more than $70,800 per year to acquire substitutes for Donahue and Draper; that the suggested multiplier was somewhat too high, etc.

(b) Draper contends that Petersen's testimony should have been struck or in any event that it was so weak as to infect the jury's findings of goodwill.

There is no doubt that Petersen was properly held qualified to serve as an expert witness—a matter as to which the judge anyway had wide discretion....

---

11. Petersen spoke of "customer loyalty, ... loyalty of employees, ... association with suppliers, ... association with a banker or financial institution, anything that tends to lead to continued patronage or continued availability of credit...."

12. First: Take the normalized earning power of $397,462; adjust for inflation by deducting $79,366 (based on an inflation rate of 7%), yielding a remainder of $318,096; apply a multiple appropriate to this base, namely, 8.0, for a total of $2,544,768; deduct $968,608 of net tangible assets. Goodwill is $1,576,160.

Second: Earnings for ten years increasing at a 7% inflation rate amount to $4,739,166 (these are the earnings that could be withdrawn by the partners without impairing capital needed to continue to generate earnings). Discounted to the present at 16%, this comes to $2,111,712. Add $432,369, being the value of the net tangible assets as they would appear after ten years ($1,907,366), discounted to the present. The total is $2,544,081. Subtract $968,608 for the present value of the net tangible assets. Goodwill is $1,574,473....

Draper attacked Petersen's analysis of basic goodwill at the point of his adjustment of partners' salaries, arguing that Petersen had no personal knowledge of the top-making business and had used surveys and other materials about executives' salaries and perquisites that did not include data gathered from this specific industry. The use, however, of data claimed to be "comparable"—such was Petersen's claim—was quite unobjectionable; for example, it is an everyday practice of experts testifying to the value of real estate....

(c) Draper contends that the judge committed errors which unfairly or improperly blunted his efforts to bring in factors that might discredit or diminish Petersen's estimate of basic goodwill. Draper says that the judge mistakenly refused to instruct the jury to "consider" his personal skills, abilities, and attributes, and that, had the judge so instructed, the jury might have found that "no goodwill or only a nominal amount" could be ascribed to DDC. The judge declined to adopt the instructions requested by Draper ...., whose effect would have been more radical—to require the jury to find there was no DDC goodwill if the company's success was mainly dependent on this skill factor. That would not conform to the law. The existence and value of a goodwill upon one or another kind of dissolution of a partnership enterprise is a question of fact.... As appears from *Stefanski v. Gonnella*, 15 Mass. App. Ct. 500, 501-503, 446 N.E.2d 734 (1983), reviewing the decisional history, goodwill has been found in professional partnerships (accountants, architects, dentists, etc.) where individual skill may be highly important, and when found, the goodwill is "an asset of the firm, and a partner appropriating it to his own use must account for its value." *Id.* at 502, 446 N.E.2d 734, quoting from *Whitman v. Jones*, 322 Mass. 340, 343, 77 N.E.2d 315 (1948). In the present case—an alleged calculated freezeout—the judge charged, without objection: "If you find that [DDC] had a goodwill value, I instruct you that such value belonged to the corporation, and not to the stockholders individually, and in the absence of an agreement to the contrary, the goodwill of the partnership is an asset of the firm, and a partner appropriating it to its [sic: "his"] own use must account for its value. This is true whether or not the goodwill is partly derived from experience and contacts which one partner had prior to forming a joint enterprise. In such a case he is deemed to have distributed [sic: "contributed"] the goodwill to the joint enterprise and may not reappropriate it for his own use without paying for its value." ...

(d) The judge properly instructed the jury that upon "termination" of DDC, each partner would have a right to enter a new business, or reestablish an old one, or solicit the former customers of DDC; the exercise of this right would not have encompassed a "takeover" of the company's goodwill. This instruction was a virtual paraphrase of an instruction requested by Draper.... It offered the picture of a company peacefully dissolved without agreement as to goodwill, where each partner might later carry on lawfully without restraint. It was left to the jury ... to find whether the picture was different here, whether Draper had "take[n] the goodwill of [DDC] for his own benefit," i.e., unlawfully appropriated it; and the jury answered, "Yes." The jury were helped toward a rational finding by considering, according to the instruction, the line between the permissible and impermissible.

Draper appears to be arguing that the judge should have instructed the jury to put a value on Draper's right to do business, in case of some innocuous dissolution, and deduct it from the value of the goodwill improperly taken by Draper (should the jury find that he misappropriated). It is unnecessary to go further than to say that Draper did not offer an instruction on that line.... In a larger sense, we are unable to see the logic of Draper's proposition. When one partner wrongfully takes to himself the good-will of the enterprise, the other is entitled to his share of its value, and any values hypothesized as to events which did not occur can have little bearing.[15]

(e) Other matters. (i) Donahue, Draper, and DDC were parties to a stock redemption agreement by which (omitting details) in case of the death of a partner, DDC would purchase the partner's shares at a fixed value (using the proceeds of insurance carried on the partner's life), and, in case a partner proposed to transfer his shares to an outsider, would accord DDC a right of first refusal at the lower of the fixed value or the amount offered by the outsider. The value was to be fixed by agreement from time to time. [The value fixed by agreement yielded a goodwill figure of $437,049.]

* * *

Draper seems to contend that the judge should have charged that $437,049 was the ceiling on what the jury could find as goodwill. Draper did not request this instruction, which anyway would be wrong for the reason — among others — that an agreed value for the particular redemption purpose may be the product of motives and considerations that are irrelevant to fixing value for our present purpose.[a]

(ii) The judge charged, without objection, that in considering the question of goodwill the jury should disregard the fact that DDC went into liquidation. The jury found (answer to interrogatory 7) that "the breach of the working relationship between the partners" was by "mutual agreement." Liquidation became inevitable and Donahue's vote followed as a matter of course. Formal liquidation, however, does not insulate a partner from liability for the consequences of a wrongful plan to take and appropriate the goodwill of the company to his own use. The agreed date for determining goodwill was indeed just prior to April 12, 1978, well before the liquidation vote. The judge did not charge, as Draper requested, that "[g]oodwill relates to a business as a going concern and is not involved in a business in liquidation." This would have been misleading. The cases that speak of goodwill as related to a going concern can mean merely that in measuring goodwill one may project the earning power of a company as if it were to continue as a going entity.

* * *

As to goodwill, the judgment is affirmed....

So ordered.

Questions

1. What is the issue of goodwill doing in a liquidation proceeding?

2. How does the court measure goodwill? Do you agree with its methods?

3. Do you agree with Draper's argument that any goodwill was attributable to his skills and not to the business itself?

4. How does Draper's argument relate to the exercise of comparing a company's executive compensation and benefits packages with those of other companies?

---

15. As well might the jury be asked to speculate on the values involved in other events contrary to fact, e.g. a sale of the whole business to a third party where, to make the sale go, the partners might have to agree to covenants not to compete for some period of time, for which, however, they might exact a price.

a. *Cf.* In the Matter of Pace Photographers, Ltd., which is discussed in Note 1 at the end of section 4b.

Nardini v. Nardini
414 N.W.2d 184 (Minn. 1987)

COYNE, Justice.

Marguerite Nardini has obtained further review of a decision of the court of appeals affirming the trial court's valuation of a business owned by the parties to this marital dissolution proceeding [and] its characterization of one-half the value as nonmarital property belonging to Ralph Nardini.... We affirm in part, reverse in part, and remand for further proceedings in conformity with this opinion.

[Ralph claims he bought a one-half interest in the sole proprietorship Chemical Sales & Service ("Chemical") prior to his marriage to Marguerite, while Marguerite contends he bought an interest only in that part of Chemical which was engaged in servicing fire extinguishers. Later, as a married couple, the Nardini's purchased the remaining interest in Chemical and incorporated the business and changed its name to Nardini Fire Equipment Company of Minnesota ("Nardini of Minnesota"). Ralph managed the business and called on customers for over 30 years, while Marguerite contributed to the business through periodic employment and voluntary activities. At the time of dissolution of the marriage, Ralph held 60% of the shares and Marguerite held 40%.]

* * *

To determine the value of Nardini of Minnesota, Marguerite's expert, Steven Thorp, employed a comparison analysis, examining specific characteristics and financial information of similar companies. In comparing the Nardini business to publicly-traded companies and taking into account factors unique to the Nardini operation, he valued Nardini of Minnesota at $725,213.

John Hawthorne, Ralph's expert witness, estimated value by both a comparison analysis and an examination of similarly structured small fire equipment dealers operating in the metropolitan area. He, too, noted and factored the unique Nardini characteristics, but he estimated the total value of Nardini of Minnesota at $350,000. He then assumed that one-half the value was excepted nonmarital property and reduced the remaining one-half value to reflect a lack of operational control in a one-half interest. He ultimately opined that a one-half interest had a value of $135,135. Separately, Hawthorne estimated liquidation value of the corporation at $391,456. While he acknowledged that this valuation exceeded the sale valuation, he reasoned that the risks and expenses attendant on liquidation must be considered in estimating the market value of the company as a going business.

The record clearly demonstrates Ralph's contributions to the growth of the business. Working within the company since 1949 and functioning as its president and salesperson, Ralph has developed the business contacts and personally claims responsibility for 50% to 60% of the sales based upon his personal relationships with customers and his hard work. Marguerite's contributions were less tangible, taking the form of sporadic bookkeeping services and substantial community involvement.... Moreover, as indicated, she provided a stable home and family life which permitted Ralph to devote his efforts to business achievements.

The trial court found that Ralph owned a one-half interest in the common stock of Nardini of Minnesota as nonmarital property and assigned a market value of $135,135 to that one-half interest. The trial court found that the other one-half interest in the common stock of Nardini of Minnesota was marital property, which the court also valued at $135,135....

* * *

On appeal the court of appeals affirmed [the trial court's findings with respect to Nardini of Minnesota].

I.

A. *Valuation of the Family Business.*

Minn. Stat. §518.58 (1986) provides that when a marriage is dissolved, "the court shall make a just and equitable division of the marital property of the parties."... [T]he statutory mandate requir[es] the courts to consider all relevant factors in making the division:

> The court shall base its findings on all relevant factors including the length of
> the marriage, any prior marriage of a party, the age, health, station, occupa-
> tion, amount and sources of income, vocational skills, employability, estate, li-
> abilities, needs, opportunity for future acquisition of capital assets, and in-
> come of each party. The court shall also consider the contribution of each in
> the acquisition, preservation, depreciation or appreciation in the amount or
> value of the marital property, as well as the contribution of a spouse as a
> homemaker. It shall be conclusively presumed that each spouse made a sub-
> stantial contribution to the acquisition of income and property while they were
> living together as husband and wife.

Minn. Stat. §518.58 (1986)....

When the parties cannot agree on a division of the marital property, just and equitable division of an asset included in the marital property of the parties can be accomplished in one of three ways: (1) If the asset is readily divisible, the court can divide the asset and order just and equitable distribution in kind; (2) the court can order the sale or liquidation of the asset and make a just and equitable division of the proceeds of sale or liquidation; or (3) the court can determine the value of the asset, order distribution of the entire asset to one of the parties, and order the recipient to pay to the other spouse a just and equitable share of the value of the asset. Whatever the method, the goal is to place *both* parties in the optimum position. The choice of methods usually depends on the type of asset to be divided. While the first method may be an eminently suitable way to divide the shares of a publicly owned corporation, it is an unlikely choice if the corporation is closely held. The second method has the advantage of certainty and may be necessary for equitable division when an indivisible asset constitutes the bulk of the marital property. Sale or liquidation of a family-owned business may be appropriate if, for example, the parties are at or near retirement age or the dissolution of the marriage may adversely affect the business. The third method, which is in essence a forced sale by one spouse to the other in which the court sets the selling price and the terms of payment, has the greatest potential for error and unfairness, particularly where the asset is the major marital asset. It is the third method of division which gives rise to this appeal.

The principal bone of contention here, as well as in the earlier stages of these proceedings, is the value and disposition of the parties' principal asset: the family business. The book value of Nardini of Minnesota at December 31, 1984 was $565,598. The corporation held cash and cash equivalents totalling more than $100,000 and its net accounts receivable exceeded $300,000. Absent an unnoted change in accounting methods, inventory was carried at the lower of cost (first in-first out method) or market. Current liabilities, including current installments of long term debt, were less than $80,000. The consultants' estimates of the market value of Nardini of Minnesota varied from $725,000 to $350,000. The one consultant also testified that the value of a one-half interest in the common stock of the corporation must be reduced from $175,000 to $135,135 to reflect a lack of control. While we are cognizant of the difficulty and the imprecision of valuing a closely held corporation, nevertheless it is apparent that a valuation which assumes that either Marguerite or Ralph would be willing participants in a sale of Nardini of Minnesota to a third party for a price of $270,270—a sum no greater than the corporation's cash and cash equivalent, Ralph's annual salary and benefits and one year's net corporate income—is unrealistic.

First, for purposes of valuing marital property, there is no justification for discounting an undivided interest in a corporation all of whose shares are owned by one or both spouses. Although shares may be transferred from one spouse to the other, whenever the court is called on to value a business, neither any corporate asset nor any fraction of the shares of the corporation will actually be sold to an outsider. Generally, as occurred here, the corporate shares are awarded to the spouse more actively engaged in the business of the corporation, and the management and operation of the business continue essentially unchanged. In this context the establishment of a fair market value contemplates nothing more than the assignment of a fair and reasonable value to the family business as a whole to allow equitable apportionment of the marital property.

Second, Ralph's appraiser testified that the amount which could be realized by liquidating the corporation significantly exceeded its market value as a going business. Nevertheless, the trial court adopted the lesser value, which it further discounted for lack of control. The value of a family business as marital property cannot be less than a sum equal to the net proceeds which could be realized from the forced sale of the tangible assets of the business and the collection or assignment of intangibles such as accounts receivable, and after payment of all liabilities. If the corporation is to continue in operation under the management of one of the owner-spouses even though the liquidation value of the business is greater than its value as a going business, assigning the corporation the lesser value as a going business patently disadvantages the spouse who must relinquish his or her interest in the corporation and unfairly benefits the spouse to whom the marital interest in the corporation is awarded. Moreover, inasmuch as Nardini of Minnesota is a thriving and vital corporation with cash and cash assets in excess of liabilities, the worst-case scenario suggested by "down and dirty" liquidation is not a suitable measure of market value.[2] While the relinquishment of his or her interest in the family business is in effect a forced sale, the court must determine the value of the business as if the transaction were a sale of the entire business by a willing seller to a willing buyer.

There is, of course, no universal formula for determining the value of a closely held business. No matter how experienced and objective the appraiser, the valuation of a business is an art, influenced by various subtle and subjective factors. While book value may be an appropriate starting point in valuing a business such as Nardini of Minnesota, with its high liquidity and modest investment in machinery and equipment, whatever the starting point, other factors, such as the following, must be taken into consideration before a reasonable valuation can be made:

---

2. Ralph's appraiser considered $407,859 a "realistic" liquidated value for Nardini of Minnesota. His "down and dirty" liquidation figure was $391,456.

1.	The nature of the business and the history of the enterprise from its inception.

2.	The economic outlook in general and the condition and outlook of the specific industry in particular.

3.	The book value of the stock and the financial condition of the business.

4.	The earning capacity of the company.

5.	The dividend-paying capacity.

6.	Whether or not the enterprise has goodwill or other intangible value.

7.	Sales of the stock and the size of the block of the stock to be valued.

8.	The market price of stocks of corporations engaged in the same or a similar line of business having their stocks traded in a free and open market.[3]

In any case a sound valuation requires not only the consideration of all relevant facts but also the application of common sense, sound and informed judgment, and reasonableness to the process of "weighing those facts and determining their aggregate significance."[4]

Viewed in the light of the foregoing principles, it is apparent that by failing to take into consideration the relevant facts and the fundamental factors appropriate for use and analysis in the value of a closely held corporation, the trial court abused its discretion. We remand for determination of the fair and reasonable value of Nardini of Minnesota in accordance with the principles enunciated in this opinion.

* * *

Notes and Questions

1. How does the context of the valuation affect the manner in which the court makes its determination? Outside of the divorce context, what other circumstances might alter the way in which a court evaluates a corporation's worth?

2. In *Nardini*, the court states that "the value of the family business ... cannot be less than a sum equal to the net assets which could be realized from the forced sale of the tangible assets of the business and the collection or assignment of intangibles such as accounts receivable, and after payment of all liabilities." Is this true? Takeover artists in the 1980s often employed a "bust up" strategy. This would entail the acquisition of a public company (often by means of a leveraged buyout) whose share price was trading below its book value per share. Once the company was acquired, the acquiror would "bust it up" by liquidating assets and thus pocketing the difference between the price it paid for the company and the net proceeds from the asset sales. Indeed, sometimes the sum of the parts is worth more than the whole.

3. Revenue Ruling 59-60, 1959-1 C.B. 237, cited and described in the *Nardini* case, provides a procedure for determining the fair market value of stock in close corpora-

_____

3. [Internal Revenue Service] Revenue Ruling 59-60, 1959-1 C.B. 237.
4. *Id.* at 238. Although Revenue Ruling 59-60 sets out the procedure used by the Internal Revenue Service for estate and gift tax valuation, we regard the eight fundamental factors therein identified as equally appropriate for use and analysis in determining the value of a closely held corporation as marital property for purposes of equitable distribution. *E.g., Nehorayoff v. Nehorayoff,* 108 Misc. 2d 311, 437 N.Y.S.2d 584 (1981).

tions[1] for estate and gift tax purposes, where the relevant regulations define fair market value "as the price at which the property would change hands between a willing buyer and a willing seller when the former is not under any compulsion to buy and the latter is not under any compulsion to sell, both parties having reasonable knowledge of relevant facts."

For a thorough application of Rev. Rul. 59-60, see Okerlund v. U.S., 365 F.3d 1044 (D.C. Cir. 2004). *See also* Estate of Newcomer v. United States, 447 F. Supp. 1368 (W.D. Pa. 1978) (applying the guidelines set forth in Rev. Rul. 59-60 to value shares in a close corporation); Foltz v. U.S. News & World Report, Inc., 865 F.2d 364 (D.C. Cir. 1989) (affirming district court's conclusion that Rev. Rul. 59-60 did not require valuation at a control premium[2] where general purpose of Plan under which valuation occurred was to effect employee-ownership, a purpose "diametrically opposed to that of the estate tax").

4. Estate of Newhouse v. Commissioner, 94 T.C. 193 (1990), involved a proceeding brought by the executors of decedent's estate to challenge an assessment of deficiency by the Internal Revenue Service. The Newhouse enterprises were owned and operated by several closely held corporations. The most controversy in this proceeding revolved around the value of decedent's interest in Advance Publications, Inc., the largest of the Newhouse publications, which had a complex capital structure, further complicated by the fact that it was a close corporation in which individual expectations might well have influenced the rights of different classes of stock. In any event, several of the nation's most noted corporate lawyers and scholars testified on behalf of each side, with the result that the court concluded that, for valuation purposes, any potential purchaser of Advance would significantly discount the price it was willing to pay to account for the virtual certainty of lengthy and uncertain litigation over the rights of the various classes of securities.

Estate of Newhouse, which space limitations have kept us from including here, is well worth reading as a fascinating case study in valuation generally.

Section 5
Market-Based Valuation

Although it is almost impossible to study fundamental valuation without at least some market concepts creeping in (for example, P/E ratios), most of the principles of fundamental analysis you have just learned focus on the specific corporation which is (or the securities of which are) to be valued. Much of modern financial theory, in contrast,

---

1. The ruling defines "close corporation" as follows:
   .03 Closely held corporations are those corporations the shares of which are owned by a relatively limited number of stockholders. Often the entire stock issue is held by one family. The result of this situation is that little, if any, trading in the shares takes place. There is, therefore, no established market for the stock and such sales as occur at irregular intervals seldom reflect all of the elements of a representative transaction as defined by the term "fair market value."
2. Rev. Rul. 59-60 states that the "control of a corporation, either actual or in effect, representing as it does an added element of value, may justify a higher value for a specific block of stock." Revenue Ruling 59-60, 1959-1 C.B. at 242.

looks away from the particular corporation to the broader capital markets. In this context, the corporate security is itself seen as the central asset, to be traded for cash or other securities or combined with other securities as part of a larger investment strategy. The values assigned by the market, therefore, assume greater significance than the fundamental components of value looked to by traditional theory.

a. Portfolio Theory

The centerpiece of the market-based approach is portfolio theory, sometimes called modern portfolio theory, and abbreviated MPT. It is an idea with significant implications for the structure of corporate governance and the duties of corporate managers. This subsection will turn to MPT after summarizing the role of risk in stock investment decisions. And it is the *stock investment* decision which is the crucial focus now. Fundamental valuation, you will recall, largely relies on principles which are as applicable to the corporation's own investment decisions as they are to securities analysis. In contrast, modern capital asset pricing theory assumes the focus of the securities investor, although it has implications for corporate decision-making as well.

Problem — Portfolio Theory and Corporate Governance

You are an associate in a major law firm in a major city. The firm's managing partner has been asked to serve on a bar association panel devoted to the relationship between portfolio theory and corporate governance. The partner has done a lot of corporate work over the years but has not kept up with the latest thinking in finance, including portfolio theory. On the panel with your partner will be Judge Winter, who has not only extensive experience with corporate law but is also well versed in finance theory. The partner has asked you to brief him on the relationship of portfolio theory to corporate governance and has called to your attention the following discussion by Judge Winter explaining the nature of directorial liability and the underlying basis for the business judgment rule in Joy v. North, 692 F.2d 880, 885 (2d. Cir. 1982), *cert. denied*, 460 U.S. 1051 (1983):

First, shareholders to a very real degree voluntarily undertake the risk of bad business judgment. Investors need not buy stock, for investment markets offer an array of opportunities less vulnerable to mistakes in judgment by corporate officers. Nor need investors buy stock in particular corporations. In the exercise of what is genuinely a free choice, the quality of a firm's management is often decisive and information is available from professional advisors. Since shareholders can and do select among investments partly on the basis of management, the business judgment rule merely recognizes a certain voluntariness in undertaking the risk of bad business decisions.

Second, courts recognize that after-the-fact litigation is a most imperfect device to evaluate corporate business decisions. The circumstances surrounding a corporate decision are not easily reconstructed in a courtroom years later, since business imperatives often call for quick decisions, inevitably based on less than perfect information. The entrepreneur's function is to encounter risks and to confront uncertainty, and a reasoned decision at the time made may seem a wild hunch viewed years later against a background of perfect knowledge.

Third, because potential profit often corresponds to the potential risk, it is very much in the interest of shareholders that the law not create incentives for overly cautious corporate decisions. Some opportunities offer great profits at the risk of very substantial losses, while the alternatives offer less risk of loss but also less potential profit. Shareholders can reduce the volatility of risk by diversifying their holdings. In the case of the diversified shareholder, the seemingly more risky alternatives may well be the best choice since great losses in some stocks will over time be offset by even greater gains in others. Given mutual funds and similar forms of diversified investment, courts need not bend over backwards to give special protection to shareholders who refuse to reduce the volatility of risk by not diversifying. A rule which penalizes the choice of seemingly riskier alternatives thus may not be in the interest of shareholders generally.

The partner wants your views on the following issues, which he must come to grips with for purposes of debate with Judge Winter on the panel:

1. What are the theoretical bases upon which Judge Winter has grounded these reasons? How do they accord or conflict with the traditional legal model of the corporation?

2. What are the implications of this jurisprudential approach for a legal evaluation of the duties of corporate officers and directors? For the role of law in corporate governance?

3. What are some of the "opportunities less vulnerable to mistakes in judgment by corporate officers" offered by the investment markets to which Judge Winter refers in the first paragraph? Are they in fact less vulnerable to such mistakes? What are the disadvantages of such investments? Are they satisfactory alternatives to common stock (i) from an individual's perspective? (ii) from a societal perspective?

4. Is the goal of investment diversification (discussed in the ensuing essays) achieved by an individual investor purchasing and holding shares in a single mutual fund? Or must an investor diversify her mutual funds into a portfolio of funds to achieve that goal?

(i) Appetites for Risk

As discussed in section 2, the riskier a security is, the higher the return that an investor will expect to receive from owning that security. This characterizes how most investors react to risk. If two investments are expected to result in the same return, the investor will choose the one with less risk. This investor is said to be risk-averse and will not accept an increase in risk without a corresponding increase in the expected return. To a risk-averse investor, as a security becomes riskier, the expected return rises at an increasing rate. This is illustrated in Figure 3.

The curves in Figure 3 are known as *indifference curves* because the investor has no preference as to where an investment lies on the curve, since he will receive the necessary increase in return as the risk becomes greater. However, the investor will prefer an investment lying on curve 1 as opposed to curve 2 because the return is greater for less risk.

Some investors could be characterized either as risk-neutral or risk-seekers. An investor who is risk-neutral does not make investment decisions based on the risk associated with those stocks. This person's investment decision will be based solely on the expected return of each investment. A risk-neutral investor's indifference curves are shown in Figure 4. This investor would prefer a stock on line 1 rather than line 2 because it has a higher expected return, but the investor is indifferent to where the stock falls on line 1.

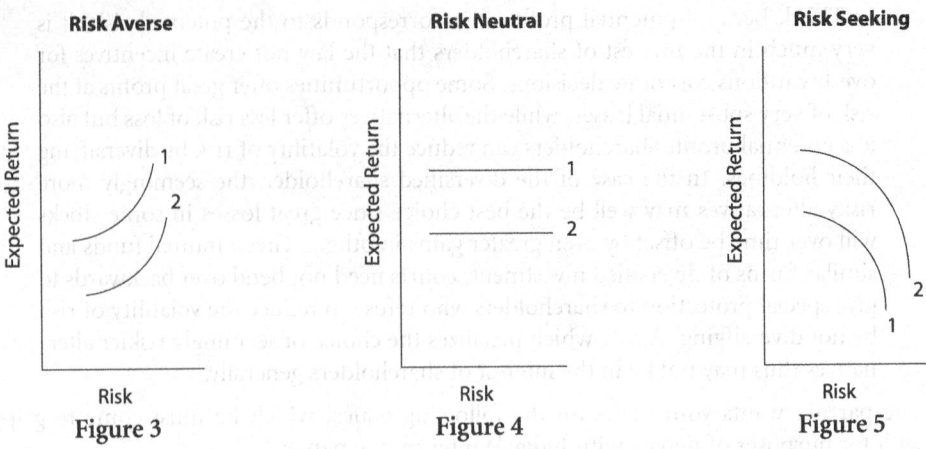

On the other hand, a risk-seeker is an investor who will actually accept a lower expected return for increased risk. Her indifference curves are shown in Figure 5. She is willing to take the small chance that the actual return will be greater than the expected return.

(ii) Risk Reduction by Diversification

Since most investors are risk-averse, they will seek ways to reduce risk and still receive a high return. In 1952, Harry Markowitz published an article, Portfolio Selection,[1] in which he developed the concept of portfolio theory and provided the risk averse investor with a "how-to" manual in investing. The theory follows from the old common-sense caution against putting all your eggs in one basket.[2] It goes further, however, recognizing that different baskets are exposed to and respond to different hazards. Recall the concepts developed in our discussion in section 2c of probability distributions and the example of Burgers and Bionics. The expected return on each stock was the same, but we said that they posed different risks because they respond differently to various states of the economy. If one were to hold only Bionics stock, one is exposed to a large risk because depending on how the economy performs, the actual return could range from 100% to -70%. But what if the same person were also to hold Burgers stock as well? Then the risk associated with holding only Bionics stock is substantially reduced because, although in a bust economy the investor stands to lose 70% on Bionics, that loss will be at least somewhat offset by the 10% gain in Burgers.

This idea of combining a number of investments into a portfolio of investments is therefore a way to reduce the risks associated with holding only a single security. Moreover, one could in fact eliminate the peculiar risks associated with any given security if it were possible to identify and buy another security that reacts in exactly the opposite manner to various future conditions. For example, suppose the only significant event

---

1. Markowitz, Portfolio Selection, Journal of Finance, vol. 7, no. 1 (March 1952), pp. 77-91. Markowitz won a Nobel Prize in Economics in 1990.

2. Of course, Mark Twain advocated a more controversial approach: "Behold the fool saith, 'Put not all thine eggs in the one basket'—which is but a manner of saying, 'Scatter your money and your attention;' but the wise man saith, 'Put all your eggs in the one basket and—WATCH THAT BASKET.'" Mark Twain, Pudd'nHead Wilson (1894) (Bantam Classics; Reissue edition February 1, 1984).

affecting the performance of Burgers stock over time is prevailing attitudes toward health. When the country is in a devil-may-care mood, people love to eat red meat, and Burgers stock flies; when anxiety about cholesterol sets in, the stock falters. The stock of Lettuce-Is-Us, a health food chain, behaves in exactly the opposite manner: flies during health crazes, falters when beef is the rage. If you assume again that the expected return on each of these stocks is the same, but now assume that they respond in exactly opposite ways to external stimuli, then buying and holding both stocks means that you have eliminated the peculiar risks associated with holding either of them alone!

These central insights of MPT can be stated more formally. First, MPT recognizes the two basic ideas we developed in section 2: the expected return on an investment is the probability-weighted average of all possible returns on it and the risk of an investment is the dispersion of possible returns on that investment around the expected return.[3] Second, MPT also recognizes that the expected return on a *portfolio of investments* is simply the weighted sum of the expected returns on the individual investments. Third—and this is the key to portfolio theory—the risk of a *portfolio of investments* is not necessarily the weighted sum of the risks (or dispersion in the returns) of the individual investments. Unless the portfolio consists entirely of investments that are expected to behave in exactly the same way in response to various external stimuli, then the risk on the portfolio will be less than the weighted sum of the risk of the individual investments.

But notice that we have been talking about eliminating risk associated with the individual investment: we said that the "peculiar" risks of each individual investment can be canceled out. Does that mean that no risks remain? Can it be possible to eliminate risks? No. All stocks in our example—Bionic, Burgers and Lettuce-Is-Us—as well as all combinations of stocks that you can assemble, are subject to certain common risks. Markets as a whole can swing very widely based on information or even speculation that has nothing to do with a particular stock. For example, the entire market was shaken when President Reagan was shot in 1981, when Pope John Paul II was shot that same year and when other calamitous world events occurred. No matter how broadly you diversify, you will always be subject to these risks. So we end up with two categories of risk: those associated with a particular stock and those associated with the market as a whole.[4]

The peculiar risks associated with individual stocks go by various names in portfolio theory, including unique risk, specific risk, diversifiable risk or unsystematic risk. The basic idea, as implied by this cluster of names, is that this is risk that an investor can do something to control! All other kinds of risk go by the names undiversifiable or systematic risk. These are risks that no investor can control in setting up his investment portfolio.

The consequence of the distinction between systematic and unsystematic risk is this: by assembling a portfolio of certain stocks—that is, by diversifying—an investor can reduce the unsystematic risk associated with each of those individual stocks and therefore only systematic risk then need factor into the decision. However, the goal of portfolio theory is not to assemble the portfolio with the lowest possible risk (which would

---

3. Recall from section 2 that risk is the "variance" of possible returns around the expected return, expressed in terms of standard deviations.
4. We alluded to these two categories of risk in our discussion in section 2c, footnote 2.

Figure 6   The Efficient Frontier

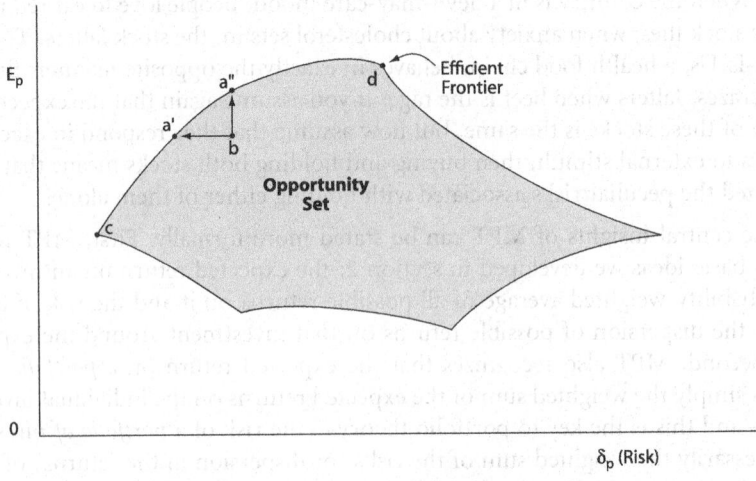

obviously provide the investor with a low average return). It is rather to assemble the portfolio with the best combination of risk and return, given both the opportunities available and the investor's appetite for risk. Let us see how this is done.

(iii) The Efficient Frontier

The concepts of expected return and risk can be expressed formally and employed to choose between alternative portfolios of investments. Let E_p denote the expected return on a portfolio and let d_p denote the risk of a portfolio. A potentially infinite number of portfolios combining various levels of E_p and d_p can be depicted on a graph such as Figure 6. Of those, an investor can envision a set of opportunities available to him under current investment alternatives, labelled on the graph as the "opportunity set." We have also depicted five possible portfolios from among that opportunity set to illustrate how to choose the most efficient ones—those that yield the greatest expected return for any given level of risk.

The thick arc we have drawn at the top of the opportunity set depicts the efficient combinations, and is called the efficient frontier. The arc extends from Point c to Point d. Point c is the terminal point at one end because it represents the portfolio having the least risk for a minimum desired expected return. Point d is the terminal point at the other end because it represents the portfolio having the greatest expected return and also very high risk. Colloquially, c is the portfolio for the chicken and d is the portfolio for the daredevil. Moreover, c is a well-diversified portfolio; d is not (and may even represent the risk-return profile for a single investment).

All points in between c and d on the arc give the optimum mix of expected return for any given level of risk. To see this, compare a portfolio offering the combined expected return and risk indicated by portfolio b. b is inferior to a' because, although both offer the same expected return, b poses greater risk. Similarly, b is inferior to a" because, although both pose the same amount of risk, a" offers greater expected return. The result is that the portfolios having the combination of expected return and risk lying on the arc are superior to all others inside the curve (and no others are available outside the curve).

Figure 7   The Efficient Frontier with Differential Lending and Borrowing Rates

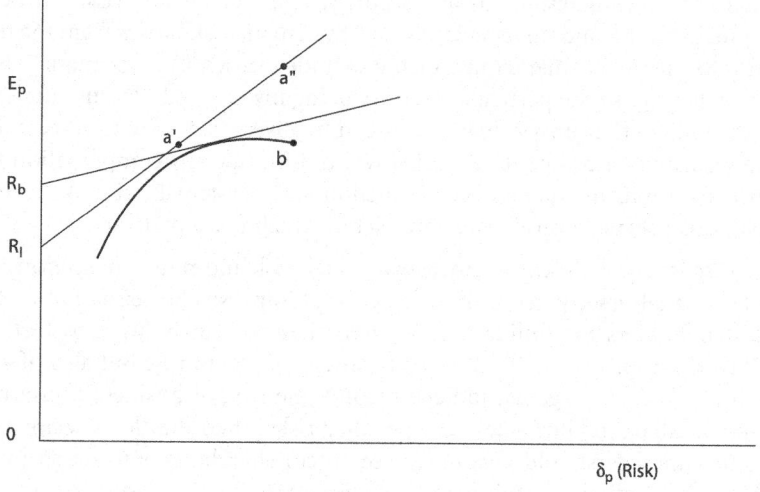

Which portfolio on the curve is suitable for a particular investor depends on their appetite for risk—whether they are more nearly a chicken or a daredevil, for example.

(iv) Lending and Borrowing

So far we have assumed that an investor plotting the efficient frontier has some capital to invest and is assembling a portfolio of investments that pose some risk. We now want to change both assumptions and consider how the efficient frontier would be affected by the availability of risk-free investments and the possibility that the investor could borrow funds to invest.[5] We make the realistic assumption that an investor cannot borrow at the risk-free rate and therefore that the borrowing rate is higher than the lending rate. We can now modify the efficient frontier by letting R_b denote the borrowing rate and letting R_l denote the lending rate.

Consider Figure 7. The two additional lines added to this figure denote, respectively, the investor's borrowing rate R_b and lending rate R_l. Adding the possibility of borrowing creates a new efficient frontier. To see this, compare point b in Figure 7 (which is on the efficient frontier without borrowing) with point a'. Point a' is superior to point b because the investor can achieve the same expected return but with less risk. Similarly, point a" is superior to point b because the investor can achieve a greater expected return but for the same risk. In each case, the investor can achieve a superior position by borrowing at his lending rate and investing in the portfolio. Put another way, if borrowing were prohibited, the investor would be stuck in a less efficient portfolio.

---

5. Recall our references throughout section 2 to the idea of risk-free investments, such as U.S. treasury securities that are held to maturity, and the precise meaning of the concept, especially our discussion in section 2c, footnote 1.

(v) Practical Consequences

As noted above, with respect to any security, two elements of risk can be distinguished: systematic risk and unsystematic risk. "Systematic risk" arises from the tendency of a security to vary as the market in which it is traded varies. "Unsystematic" risk arises from the peculiarities of the particular security being investigated. Because under MPT's diversification injunction unsystematic risks can be diversified away to zero, market returns on a security in a competitive market will not include any compensation for such risk. Thus market returns will be solely a function of the systematic risk, or the extent to which a particular security varies as the market of which it is a part varies.

We will discuss mechanisms for measuring such risk and return in section 5b when we consider capital asset pricing models. Before doing so, however, notice that the ability of shareholders to eliminate nonsystematic risks can be used to fortify arguments in favor not only of the traditional business judgment rule but also of a further strengthening of the rule against judicial second-guessing of business decisions. After all, if a shareholder can eliminate these peculiar risks, then it at least seems plausible to believe that the law should encourage (or force) shareholders to do so by further weakening judicial oversight of directorial decisions. Numerous issues arise.

Accepting this proposition requires a high degree of confidence in several elements of MPT. Chief among these is the proposition that the risk identified by modern portfolio theory as nonsystematic is capable of reasonably accurate measurement. This is not an insignificant issue and indeed we devote the next section to the subject, as noted. Even if such a measurement can be made, however, conducting the sorts of calculations required by MPT to assure that an investor is positioned on her efficient frontier is complicated. The associated risks can change daily and an investor would have to be prepared to reexamine and readjust her portfolio on a daily basis in order to exploit the benefits of diversification as fully as would be necessary to defend strengthening the business judgment rule.

Apart from these operational difficulties, the further question is whether as a matter of corporate law, a shareholder's action or inaction in diversifying her portfolio should be the basis for defining the standard of directorial obligation. Historically, shareholder action has not been used this way and the norms reflected by that history would have to be confronted by any apologist who seeks an emboldened business judgment rule on the strength of MPT.

Among critics of any effort to strengthen the business judgment rule is Professor Gevurtz, who has not only attacked the business judgment rule but has also advocated its abolition. Gevurtz, The Business Judgment Rule: Meaningless Verbiage or Misguided Notion?, 67 S. Cal. L. Rev. 287 (1994). Professor Gevurtz analyzed and rejected a series of arguments that have been advanced in defense of the business judgment rule, including that "according to currently popular financial theory, shareholders should protect themselves against the risks of mismanagement in any one company by holding a diversified portfolio of stock." Id. at 314. Professor Gevurtz responds to this argument as follows:

> To begin with, owning a portfolio of stocks only dilutes, but does not eliminate, the effects of mismanagement on the individual shareholder.[134] In

---

134. Diversification can only provide full protection against bad results from a director decision that had a net positive expected return (in other words, a decision that should not be considered negligent, ...). In that case, the positive actual returns from those decisions that pan out should eventually more than offset the losses from those that, because of bad luck, fail.... On the other

addition, the ability to protect oneself from director negligence by diversification is not entirely unique. Individuals dealing with doctors or other professionals can, and often do, get a second opinion on various judgment calls. More broadly, medical and disability insurance cushion the financial risk from personal injury much as diversification cushions the loss from bad investments. Admittedly, there are practical limits on the ability to always get a second opinion whenever dealing with a professional or to fully insure against injury. Similarly, not every investor can or will hold an efficiently diversified portfolio of stocks. This is particularly the case when dealing with closely held corporations, where it is quite common for shareholders to tie up a substantial percentage of their wealth in the stock of one company. Moreover, whatever one thinks of the acumen of the numerous investors who do not diversify, it seems questionable whether courts should gear rules of law to demand that individuals follow a particular investment strategy.

Most fundamentally, however, the diversification argument proves too much. Holding diversified portfolios also dilutes the individual stockholder's risk from any given company becoming the victim of breaches of contract by those the company does business with, of illegal trade practices by the firm's competitors, of tortious activities by those outside the firm, or of other conduct which might harm and create a cause of action in favor of a corporation. Does anyone suggest the law abolish the ability of corporations to bring lawsuits, since their stockholders could always diversify to minimize such risks? The diversification argument ... ignores the fact that one of the original purposes for creating the legal fiction of corporate entities was to allow an entity to have rights and assert causes of action independent of its owners.

Id. at 314-317.

b. Capital Asset Pricing Model

Not surprisingly, the implications of portfolio theory for the problem of valuation are significant. If the only risk for which issuing corporations sensibly will compensate investors is systematic risk (or, more accurately, the sensitivity of its stock to systematic risk), then the correct value of a share of stock must be a function of that sensitivity. This insight led to the development by Lintner and Sharpe of the capital asset pricing model (CAPM).[1] Since the early 1970s, CAPM has become one of the most popular methods utilized by financial analysts to determine the risks of investing in common stock. In this section we show how the CAPM is derived, what it means, how it is applied and then consider the assumptions on which it is based. After that, we consider what all this leads to as a matter of finance and law. To explore some of the practical consequences of the CAPM, we start by revisiting Smith Drugstores.

---

hand, if directors negligently make decisions with a net negative expected return, diversification can at best dilute the losses.

1. Sharpe, Capital Asset Prices: A Theory of Market Equilibrium Under Conditions of Risk, Journal of Finance, vol. 19, no. 3 (September 1964), pp. 425-42; Lintner, Security Prices, Risk, and Maximal Gains from Diversification, Journal of Finance, vol. 20, no. 4 (December 1965), pp. 587-616. Sharpe won a Nobel Prize in Economics in 1990.

Problem — Smith Drugstores, Part V

Reconsider the facts with respect to Smith Drugstores, Part I, *supra* at section 3a. Assume that after extensive negotiations, the company repurchased Mike's shares and that thereafter Jerome and his son Harry both retired. Also assume that the financial statements of Smith Drugstores set forth in section 3a were unaffected by these events.[2] After these events, the shareholders voted to take the corporation public by making an underwritten public offering of 50,000,000 shares of newly authorized common stock, which were issued and sold for a price equal to $18 per share.

The stock was well received in the offering and has traded actively in the past eight months on the New York Stock Exchange. A few market analysts have been following the stock regularly in part because of the appeal of the Smith brand-name, in part because of the company's stable cash flows and in part because it is seen as a promising "small-capitalization stock."[3] In the months following the initial public offering, the stock traded at around $26 per share. A few months ago a large diversified retail company made a merger proposal to the company's board of directors. The proposal, which the board unanimously and promptly approved after brief discussion, called for the company's shareholders to receive cash and stock worth $32 for each share of the company's stock. The company's stockholders approved the merger at a meeting duly called for the purpose.

Renee, a minority shareholder, believed that the merger consideration accepted by the board of directors was grossly inadequate. She brought and won an action for breach of fiduciary duty, and the court must now assess damages under the post-*Weinberger* quasi-appraisal remedy.[4] Her trial counsel has consulted you in connection with the damages branch of the case and has asked you to consider the following issues.

1. With respect to the initial public offering of the stock, what valuation techniques could be used to justify the $18 per share price? Would you have priced the offering differently? Why?

2. With respect to the fair value of the stock as of the time of the merger to which Renee has objected, what is the expected rate of return for the stock using the CAPM? Renee's counsel has informed you that the parties have stipulated that the risk-free rate of return is 7% and that the average rate of return on the market as a whole is 10%. Her counsel has also informed you that Smith Drugstores common stock had a beta (defined in the ensuing essay) of 1.10 with respect to the first six months that it traded on the New York Stock Exchange but that its beta is more like 1.35 if the entire period of its listing is included.

3. How does using CAPM to calculate the expected rate of return for Smith Drugstores common stock differ from the methods employed to determine the discount rate and capitalization rate used in the fundamental approaches to valuation, *supra* section 3b? How would using that rate of return have affected your calculations of the value of Mike's common stock using those methods?

4. Does using CAPM result in a more accurate measure of the fair value of the stock? Why? What disadvantages are posed by using CAPM? What weight is the court in the

---

2. We know this is unrealistic but it saves us from writing and you from getting acquainted with a whole new set of financials.

3. A small capitalization stock is one whose total market capitalization (current market price times shares outstanding) is significantly smaller than the market average.

4. *See supra* section 4a.

appraisal proceeding likely to give to this approach? If the court does adopt this approach in any part, what factors will influence it in settling on an appropriate beta?

(i) Derivation and Meaning of CAPM

Recall from our discussion of portfolio theory that the total risk of an investment security can be divided into two parts, systematic risk and nonsystematic risk. Recall also that portfolio theory proposes that since nonsystematic risk can be diversified away to zero, the risk for which an investor will be compensated with respect to any investment security is the systematic risk of that security. In particular, securities with greater systematic risk should be expected to offer higher expected returns. CAPM attempts to operationalize this idea by postulating that assets with the same risk should offer the same expected return. As a corollary, therefore, the price of investment securities should be expected to adjust until securities posing equivalent risks also offer identical expected returns. This will occur, it is believed, as a result of the activities of professional market participants, such as arbitragers, who constantly monitor the market in search of opportunities to exploit these deviations.

Beta. Modigliani and Pogue have illustrated the implications of this postulate in developing a way to measure the systematic risk of an investment security, designated by the Greek letter b (beta). Modigliani and Pogue, An Introduction to Risk and Return: Concepts and Evidence, 30 Fin. Anal. J. 68 (March/April 1974) and 30 Fin. Anal. J. 69 (May/June 1974). Beta is a measure of the relationship of the risk of an individual security to the risk of the market as a whole. Therefore, an investment security that poses risk equivalent to the market risk is said to have a beta equal to 1. An investment security that is deemed to pose no risk, such as a U.S. treasury security, is said to have a beta equal to 0. Accordingly, an investor who holds a risky portfolio with a beta equal to 1 should expect a return on that portfolio equal to the market return and an investor who holds a riskless portfolio (with a beta equal to 0) should expect a return equal to the risk-free rate of return.

For an investor who holds a mixed portfolio, determining the risk of that portfolio is done by calculating the beta for each individual security and weighting each according to its proportion in the portfolio as a whole. An investor who has invested in a proportional mix of risk-free assets and risky assets will therefore have a portfolio with beta equal to between 0 and 1. An investor who has borrowed at the risk-free rate and invested the proceeds in the risky portfolio will have a portfolio with beta greater than 1. (Recall the discussion in sections 5a(iii) & (iv) of the efficient frontier under differential borrowing and lending rates.)

Alpha. A way in which to assess the accuracy of a given stock's beta is through the measurement known as "alpha." Alpha measures the difference between a stock's actual return and its expected performance, given its level of risk (as measured by its beta). A positive alpha figure indicates that a stock has performed better than its beta would predict. Alternatively, a negative alpha figure indicates that a stock has under-performed, given the expectations established by the stock's beta. In other words, alpha measures the predictive accuracy of a given stock's beta.

Formal Mathematics. Beta can be expressed formally in mathematical terms. Let X equal the proportion of funds invested in the risky portfolio and (1 - X) equal the remaining proportion invested in risk-free investments. Since the beta of the risk-free assets equals 0 and the beta of the market portfolio equals 1, then the beta of such a mixed portfolio (denoted by $ß_p$) is calculated as follows (the symbol '·' in the following equations means multiplied by):

$$ß_p = [(1 - X) \cdot 0] + [X \cdot 1]$$
$$= X$$

Similarly, determining the expected return on such a mixed portfolio is done by calculating the expected return for each individual security and weighting each according to its proportion in the portfolio as a whole. This idea can also be expressed mathematically. Let $ß_p$ denote the expected return on the portfolio, let E_f denote the risk-free rate of return and let $ß_m$ denote the expected return on the market portfolio. Then:

$$E_p = [(1 - X) \cdot E_f] + [X \cdot E_m]$$

Since we know from the previous equation we used to calculate the risk of a portfolio that X is equal to $ß_p$, we can substitute $ß_p$ for X in the foregoing equation to give the following:

$$E_p = [(1 - ß_p) \cdot E_f] + [ß_p \cdot E_m]$$

Rearranging terms, this equation can be stated as follows:

$$E_p = [E_f] + [ß_p \cdot (E_m - E_f)]$$

This equation is the capital asset pricing model.

Meaning of CAPM Equation. In this form, Modigliani and Pogue explain, the CAPM formula says that "the expected return on a portfolio should exceed the riskless rate of return by an amount which is proportional to beta."

Any expected return in excess of the risk-free return is called the *expected risk premium*. There can be an expected risk premium with respect to any asset or portfolio of assets that one could assemble, including of the market as a whole. And each of those premia can also be stated mathematically. For example, the expected *market* risk premium can be stated as $P_m = E_m - E_f$ and the expected *portfolio* risk premium can be stated as $P_p = E_p - E_f$. From these two ideas the CAPM can be restated in terms of expected premium. This is done by substituting these two equations into the CAPM equation, to give the following:

$$P_p = ß_p \cdot P_m$$

This formulation says that the expected portfolio risk premium is also proportional to the beta of that portfolio.

Illustration. To illustrate these ideas and mathematical expressions, consider the following simple example offered by Modigliani and Pogue, *supra.* Assume the risk-free interest rate is equal to 6% and that the expected return on the market is 10%. The expected risk premium for the market portfolio is therefore 4% (the expected market return less the risk-free rate of return). In terms of CAPM, the beta of a portfolio of risk-free assets is by definition equal to 0 and therefore the expected return on such a portfolio under these assumptions is 6%. Similarly, the beta of the market portfolio is by definition equal to 1 and therefore the expected return of such a portfolio under these assumptions is 10%. For portfolios having betas other than 0 and 1, the expected return would be proportional to beta. Thus, for example, a portfolio with a beta of .5 would have an expected return of 8% [6% + (.5 · 4%)] and a portfolio with a beta of 1.5 would have an expected return of 12% [6% + (1.5 · 4%)]. Try a few examples for yourself.

Beta is a Measure of Risk. More concretely yet, under CAPM, securities with higher bs are more risky than securities with lower bs because they tend to swing more widely than the market—their returns exhibit greater dispersion versus market returns. They are said to be more market sensitive. Securities that are highly-sensitive to market swings will have higher betas, pose greater risks and offer a greater premium above the market return. Securities that are weakly-sensitive to market swings will have lower betas, pose less risk and offer a lower premium above the market.

Indeed, securities that are very insensitive to market swings will have betas less than 1 (i.e., less than the market), pose slight risks and therefore offer a return less than the market return.

Relation to Standard Deviation Measure of Risk. In thinking about and applying beta, it is useful to consider its relationship to standard deviation. In our discussion of fundamental approaches to valuation we noted that we sought to implement the proposition that an investor will insist on a greater return in order to assume a greater risk. This remains the working hypothesis. What changes is how risk is measured. In the standard deviation formula, the risk being captured was the total risk of the investment. In the CAPM beta formulation, the total risk is divided between systematic risk and unsystematic risk. Beta measures sensitivity to systematic risk and is intended merely to formalize the insight of portfolio theory that investors can eliminate nonsystematic risk and so can expect no returns in respect of it.

(ii) Applications

We have so far not said anything about how to calculate beta for an individual common stock. This is partly because the calculation of betas involves statistical techniques whose complexities put them beyond the scope of this book.[5] It is also partly because despite that complexity, the technical application is straightforward and essentially noncontroversial. On the other hand, what can be controversial, and what requires the exercise of sound judgment, is defining the time period over which to take the measurement. That is, beta expresses sensitivity of a common stock to market volatility and that sensitivity can be measured by applying standard statistical tools. But any such measure will have meaning only insofar as the time period used is meaningful. For example, a beta will be skewed if part of the measuring period included times when a stock price fluctuated wildly in response to extraordinary events related to it, such as the announcement of a merger or of a major technological breakthrough.

Many financial service corporations periodically calculate and publish the betas assigned to the common stocks of various corporations. The publications are called beta books and usually report betas measured over the preceding calendar year. Two of the more popular publications are produced by Merrill Lynch and Value Line and can be useful for many applications, so long as one takes care to note any extraordinary events affecting an individual stock over the measuring period. One can use these books to

---

5. For the statistically curious, the method is straight regression analysis, using least squares regression of an individual stock's return compared to the overall market return.

obtain a beta for a stock to be valued and, after doing so, all that is then required is to plug the beta figure into the CAPM. The following examples illustrate the simplicity of this process. We start by stating the CAPM formula for a particular security:

$$E_i = [E_f] + [\beta_i \cdot (E_m - E_f)]$$

where: E_i is the expected return on the security (i)
   E_f is the expected return on a riskless security
   β_i is the beta of the security (i) and
   E_m is the expected return on the market portfolio.

Assume for purposes of the following examples that the expected return on a riskless security is 7% (assume this is the current yield on U.S. Treasury securities) and that the expected return on the market portfolio is 10% (assume this has been the average return on common stocks over recent years).

Example One. Assume that the beta of Apple Computers common stock is 1.25. We now have everything we need to calculate its expected return.

$$E_i = [E_f] + [\beta_i \cdot (E_m - E_f)]$$
$$E_i = .07 + 1.25 \,(.10 - .07)$$
$$= .07 + 1.25 \,(.03)$$
$$= .07 + .0375$$
$$= 1.075$$

The expected return on Apple Computers common stock is therefore 10.75%.

Example Two. Assume that the beta of IBM common stock is .90. Again, we now have everything we need to calculate its expected return.

$$E_i = [E_f] + [\beta_i \cdot (E_m - E_f)]$$
$$E_i = .07 + .90 \,(.10 - .07)$$
$$= .07 + .09 \,(.03)$$
$$= .07 + .027$$
$$= .097$$

The expected return on IBM common stock is therefore 9.7%. Which stock is more risky, Apple Computers or IBM?

———————————

If a stock or portfolio has a beta greater than 1, then the expected return should be greater than the average return expected from the market. A security with a beta greater than 1 is riskier than the average risk for the market and therefore should have a higher expected return to compensate the investor for bearing the increased risk. Conversely, if a stock or portfolio has a beta less than 1, it has a lower expected return than the market, because it is less risky than the market as a whole and investors need less compensation to bear this level of risk.

Although in its pure form CAPM serves as a measure of relative risk, it is also useful in the valuation of a specific corporation. Recall the difficulty you had deciding upon a discount rate or capitalization rate when valuing Smith Drugstores in Part I of the problem. Your problems are solved! Once you have derived the expected return of a security using CAPM, you can use that expected return as your discount rate or capitalization rate.

For example, assume that Apple Computers common stock is expected to pay a constant dividend of $1.00 per share for the indefinite future. The value of a share of Apple

Computers stock can be determined using the DDM set forth in section 3b(iii)(A) using a discount rate of .1075—the expected return on Apple Computers stock derived from its beta. Similarly, assume Apple's average earnings over the last five years was $2.65 per share and this is expected to continue. The value of a share of Apple Computers stock can be detemined using a capitalization rate of .1075 (giving a value equal to $2.65 / .1075). Indeed, the beta-derived expected return can be used to solve all sorts of other problems, such as calculating a company's cost of capital in making capital budgeting decisions, as discussed in section 3c.

Can life really be this simple? It is doubtful. First, one still must have calculated beta. As noted above, although one can usually look this up in a beta book, one must be cautious in considering the time period over which the beta book has made its measurements. Second, what one sacrifices in relying on beta is one's own judgment about risk and replaces it with the collective risk assessment being implicitly made by the market as a whole. This is not an insignificant sacrifice, for at least two reasons: a number of assumptions underlie CAPM and its concept of beta which may bear on its integrity, and empirical tests of the validity of CAPM and beta have not always proved out. We take up each of these troubles in order.

(iii) Assumptions Underlying CAPM

CAPM, like nearly all economic models that try to capture complex reality in mathematical and theoretical terms, rests on a number of important assumptions that may or may not obtain in the real world. The integrity of CAPM has been debated in terms of the validity of these assumptions and relaxations of the assumptions have produced modifications in the model. Consider the following assumptions on which CAPM rests, as reported by Modigliani and Pogue, *supra:*

(a) The market is composed of risk-averse investors who measure risk in terms of standard deviation of portfolio return. This assumption provides a basis for the use of beta-type risk measures.

(b) All investors have a common time horizon for investment decision-making (*e.g.,* one month, one year, etc.). This assumption allows us to measure investor expectations over some common interval, thus making comparisons meaningful.

(c) All investors are assumed to have the same expectations about future security returns and risks. Without this assumption, the analysis would become much more complicated.

(d) Capital markets are perfect, in the sense that all assets are completely divisible, there are no transactions costs or differential taxes, and borrowing and lending rates are equal to each other and the same for all investors. Without these conditions, frictional barriers would exist to the equilibrium conditions on which the model is based.

As reported, these assumptions may seem innocuous enough. Let us unpack them and take a closer look.

1. *Risk Aversion.* The assumption that investors are risk averse as a general matter is the most plausible of the assumptions underlying CAPM. Investors exhibit this risk aversion in tending to follow the sage advice of not putting all of their eggs in one basket. The dramatic rise in the number and size of mutual funds and other financial intermediaries that specialize in diversifying investment positions may be seen as a striking example of the impulse to minimize risk. A separate question, of course, is whether

investors all measure risk in the same manner or in the manner suggested by beta. Whether investors did so before CAPM emerged as a popular device in financial and investing circles is an open question. It is clear, however, that many investors have employed the model and beta since it became fashionable in the mid-1970s.

2. *Risk-Free Rate of Return.* An assumption unstated by Modigliani and Pogue but which is implicit in the idea of risk is the availability of a risk-free rate of return. We have previously suggested that such a rate does not exist. Even investments widely deemed to be risk-free, such as U.S. Treasury securities, pose risks. These include risks of inflation, of adverse changes in currency exchange rates and timing problems with respect to reinvestment. As a practical matter, there is no such thing as a risk-free security.

3. *Identical Time Horizons and Expectations: Rationality.* The assumptions that investors have identical time horizons and expectations can be restated in terms of a standard assumption in financial economics known as the rational expectations assumption. It is the idea that human beings act with perfect knowledge and in a way that maximizes their own best interests. The rational expectations assumption and its subsidiary premise of identical time horizons and expectations are particularly troubling for CAPM. Indeed, a substantial volume of arbitrage activity in public capital markets goes forward on precisely the opposite assumptions. The consequence of recognizing this reality and relaxing these assumptions is that the tradeoff between expected return and risk for various combinations of risk-free investments and risky investments will vary from person to person, depending on their time horizons and expectations.

4. *Complete Divisibility of Assets.* Modigliani and Pogue noted that complete divisibility of assets is one among several assumptions necessary to postulate what economists call a perfect market. The complete divisibility of assets means that an asset can be divided into small parts and sold separately. Shares of common stock represent such divisibility of the firm as an asset. This assumption is of course crucial to both CAPM and portfolio theory, since without completely divisible assets in public capital markets portfolio diversification would be prohibitive. This assumption seems nearly as plausible for public capital markets as the risk aversion assumption.

5. *No Transactions Costs.* The assumption of no transaction costs is of course far from realistic because buying and selling securities does cost money. The cost may be relatively low, however, for large institutions and even for smaller investors the transactions costs necessary to purchase a diversified portfolio are not substantial. This is because it is commonly believed that the risk-reducing benefits of diversification can be achieved by holding as few as 15 or so different investments. Nevertheless, the consequence of recognizing the existence of transactions costs is that securities prices will not be aligned with the risk-return profile predicted by CAPM. *See* Booth, Richard A., The Efficient Market, Portfolio Theory, And The Downward Sloping Demand Hypothesis 68 N.Y.U.L. Rev. 1187 (1993) (discussing the debate as to how diverse a portfolio should be to mitigate firm-specific risk).

6. *No Differential Taxes.* Like the no transactions costs assumption, most people are well aware that taxes of various kinds and amounts are imposed on many investment transactions. The effects vary from investor to investor, thus not only affecting asset prices directly, but also affecting each investor's expectations. For example, individual investors are subject to tax at different rates than corporate investors and certain kinds of institutions are exempt from taxes altogether. Also, if some sorts of assets are taxed at

higher rates than other sorts of assets, investors may be expected to reallocate their portfolio away from the higher taxed assets and toward lower taxed assets. This also creates risk-return relationships that CAPM would not predict.

7. *No Differential Borrowing and Lending Rates.* If a risk-free security exists (see assumption 2 above), it is plausible to assume that an investor can lend (i.e., invest) at that rate. Most investors, however, cannot also borrow at that rate. (Some institutional investors with AAA credit ratings might be able to.) As we saw in section 5a(iii) when we introduced this differential, the efficient frontier changes. Accordingly, if investors face different borrowing rates, then investors will have different efficient frontiers, even if they share the same appetite for risk.

8. *Market Impact.* There is one additional assumption necessary to define a perfect market not explicitly stated by Modigliani and Pogue but with great significance for corporate law and finance. This is the assumption that no investor acting alone can have a material impact on the overall market. This assumption is true in most cases. When a client instructs a broker to trade 100 shares of IBM, the trade taken alone will have no impact on the price at which IBM trades. The assumption is not always true, however. Large block trades (such as when Fidelity's Magellan Fund decides to unload $350 million worth of IBM common stock) may have market effects and this echoes the recurring question in valuation concerning the appropriateness of recognizing minority discounts and control premiums, as we saw in section 4a(ii).

A number of other assumptions underlie CAPM, but the foregoing are regarded as the most significant. Of the foregoing assumptions, note that the last five are required by Modigliani and Pogue's broader assumption that "capital markets are perfect." Those of you have studied economics will recognize that this is a potentially heroic assumption to make about any market. In the economics of public capital markets, however, perhaps no idea has held greater sway over discussions of corporate law and policy than this: the efficient capital market hypothesis. We turn to that subject in section 5c.

Public capital markets may or may not have the characteristics assumed by the perfect market model or by CAPM. But the cardinal rule of economic forecasting holds that a model's predictive power is the only relevant test of its validity, not the assumptions underlying it. *See* Friedman, The Methodology of Positive Economics, in Essays in Positive Economics 3, 23 (1953); Blaug, The Methodology of Economics: Or How Economists Explain 104 (1980). Thus the fact that investors do not hold identical or rational expectations, for example, is not material, so long as these realities do not interfere with the predictive power of CAPM (or other capital market theories, such as portfolio theory and the efficient capital market hypothesis). With respect to the integrity of their assumptions, therefore, beta and CAPM may deserve respect, but only if those assumptions do not impair their predictive accuracy as an empirical matter. That is another question.

(iv) Empirical Testing of CAPM

Theories are wonderful things, of course, but putting theories to the test of empirical reality is the ultimate barometer of their practical usefulness. CAPM has been the subject of extensive and repeated empirical testing for the past couple of decades. Results of the early tests led to great optimism that financial economists had substantially solved the riddle of risk in public capital market trading. Over time, other tests have dampened that enthusiasm and, in many quarters, have led to downright pessimism. We start with a summary of the results of the early tests, as reported by Modigliani and Pogue, *supra*:

1. The evidence shows a significant positive relationship between realized returns and systematic risk. However, the ... relationship is usually less than predicted by the CAPM.

2. The relationship between risk and return appears to be linear. The studies give no evidence of significant curvature in the risk-return relationship.

3. Tests that attempt to discriminate between the effects of systematic and unsystematic risk do not yield definitive results. Both kinds of risks appear to be positively related to security returns. However, there is substantial support for the proposition that the relationship between return and unsystematic risk is at least partly spurious—that is, it partly reflects statistical problems rather than the true nature of capital markets.

Obviously, we cannot claim that the CAPM is absolutely right. On the other hand, the empirical tests do support the view that beta is a useful risk measure and that high beta stocks tend to be priced so as to yield correspondingly high rates of return.

One reason Modigliani and Pogue note that it is obvious that they cannot claim CAPM is absolutely right is that there are inherent practical limitations on the ability to conduct empirical testing of the model. First, all testing of a particular stock is necessarily done by comparing it to some basket or portfolio of other assets—such as all those traded on the New York Stock Exchange—whereas CAPM is expressed as a comparison against the universe of assets as a whole (including stocks, bonds, real estate and so on). This is not a crucial infirmity but it is a limitation. Second, the model hinges on some sense of investor expectations, as you no doubt have noticed throughout our discussion in the use of the phrase expected return. But how can one determine empirically what expectations are? The shortcut here is to assume that investors' expectations are rational in an economic sense—investors are fully informed about risks and returns and gauge their behavior to maximize their wealth. This limitation too is not devastating, although it does raise questions that we will consider in the next section's discussion of the efficient capital market hypothesis.

Apart from the inherent difficulties of conducting empirical tests of CAPM, the results of the tests that have been done have led in recent years to a crisis for its supporters, and the pronouncement of its death by its detractors. Among the observed results are that the following kinds of stocks all have higher returns than CAPM would predict: (1) small capitalization stocks; (2) high dividend yield stocks; (3) low P/E Ratio stocks; (4) stocks trading at below 2/3 of their net asset value; and (5) stocks regularly followed by a fewer number of market analysts rather than a larger number of market analysts. For a more complete list, *see* Lindgren, Telling Fortunes: Challenging the Efficient Markets Hypothesis by Prediction, 1 S. Cal. Interdisc. L.J. 7 (1992).

Since none of these results can be explained by CAPM, its devotees call them "anomalies." And although the anomalies are numerous and justify some skepticism in the validity of the model, the model retains substantial purchase in the financial community. This is in part because of the inherent difficulty of coming to grips with the idea of risk and the not insignificant improvements the model offers in our sense that we can understand public capital markets in some intelligent way. Perhaps it is for these sorts of reasons as well that CAPM has also been influential in court.

(v) CAPM in Court

Cede & Co. v. Technicolor, Inc.
1990 WL 161084 (Del. Ch. 1990)

ALLEN, Chancellor.

[In this appraisal proceeding following a cash-out merger of Technicolor, Inc., Chancellor Allen evaluated the probity of expert testimony concerning appropriate methodology for estimating the fair value of the common stock of Technicolor. The following is Chancellor Allen's discussion of expert testimony using the CAPM and beta as a baseline for estimating Technicolor's cost of capital, which in turn would be used as a basis for valuing the shares of stock.]

[W]hile I believe it is incumbent upon the court to examine the experts [sic] methods, where as here those methods each present a reasonable approach recognized in the world of financial analysis, other factors, such as the projection of future cash flows, the cost of capital and sources of corroboration are necessary in order to make the overall assessment concerning which opinion is more likely to estimate fair value as defined in Section 262....

The cost of capital supplies the discount rate to reduce projected future cash flows to present value. The cost of capital is a free-standing, interchangeable component of a DCF model. It also allows room for judicial judgment to a greater extent than the record in this case permits in other areas of the DCF models. Professor Rappaport used two cost of capital rates. For most of the cash flows (notably film processing and videocassette) he used a weighted cost of capital of 20.4%; for One Hour Photo and two small related businesses he used 17.3%.

Professor Rappaport used the Capital Asset Pricing Model (CAPM) to estimate Technicolor's costs of capital as of January 24, 1983. That model estimates the cost of company debt (on an after tax basis for a company expected to be able to utilize the tax deductibility of interest payments) by estimating the expected future cost of borrowing; it estimates the future cost of equity through a multi-factor equation and then proportionately weighs and combines the cost of equity and the cost of debt to determine a cost of capital.

The CAPM is used widely (and by all experts in this case) to estimate a firm's cost of equity capital. It does this by attempting to identify a risk-free rate for money and to identify a risk premium that would be demanded for investment in the particular enterprise in issue. In the CAPM model the riskless rate is typically derived from government treasury obligations. For a traded security the market risk premium is derived in two steps. First a market risk premium is calculated. It is the excess of the expected rate of return for a representative stock index (such as the Standard & Poor 500 or all NYSE companies) over the riskless rate. Next the individual company's "systematic risk" — that is the nondiversified risk associated with the economy as a whole as it affects this firm — is estimated.

This second element of the risk premium is, in the CAPM, represented by a coefficient (beta) that measures the relative volatility of the subject firm's stock price relative to the movement of the market generally. The higher that coefficient (i.e., the higher the beta) the more volatile or risky the stock of the subject company is said to be. Of course, the riskier the investment the higher its costs of capital will be.

The CAPM is widely used in the field of financial analysis as an acceptable technique for estimating the implicit cost of capital of a firm whose securities are regularly traded. It is used in portfolio theory and in capital asset budgeting decisions.... It cannot, of course, determine a uniquely correct cost of equity. Many judgments go into it. The beta coefficient can be measured in a variety of ways; the index rate of return can be determined pursuant to differing definitions, and adjustments can be made, such as the small capitalization premium, discussed below. But the CAPM methodology is certainly one of the principle "techniques or methods ... generally considered acceptable [for estimating the cost of equity capital component of a discounted cash flow modeling] in the financial community ..." *Weinberger v. UOP*, Inc. at 713. *See, e.g., Northern Trust Co. v. C.I.R.*, 87 T.C. 349, 368 (1986).

In accepting Professor Rappaport's method for estimating Technicolor's costs of capital, I do so mindful of the extent to which it reflects judgments. That the results of the CAPM are in all instances contestable does not mean that as a technique for estimation it is unreliable. It simply means that it may not fairly be regarded as having claims to validity independent of the judgments made in applying it.

With respect to the cost of capital aspect of the discounted cash flow methodology (in distinction to the projection of net cash flows and, in most respects, the terminal value) the record does permit the court to evaluate some of the variables, used in that model chosen as the most reasonable of the two (i.e., Professor Rappaport's) and to adjust the cost of capital accordingly. I do so with respect to two elements of Professor Rappaport's determination of costs of equity for the various Technicolor divisions. These businesses were all (excepting One Hour Photo, Consumer Photo Processing and Standard Manufacturing) assigned a cost of equity of 22.7% and a weighted average cost of capital of 20.4%. The remaining businesses were assigned a cost of equity of 20.4% and a weighted average cost of capital of 17.3%.

In fixing the 22.7% cost of equity for film processing and other businesses Professor Rappaport employed a 1.7 beta which was an estimate published by Merrill Lynch, a reputable source for December 1982. That figure seems intuitively high for a company with relatively stable cash flows. Intuition aside, however, it plainly was affected to some extent by the striking volatility in Technicolor's stock during the period surrounding the announcement of [the] proposal to acquire Technicolor for $23 per share. Technicolor stock rapidly shot up to the $23 level from a range of $9 to $12 in which it traded for all of September and the first week of October. Technicolor stock was thus a great deal more volatile than the market during this period. Applying the same measure of risk—the Merrill Lynch published beta—for September yields a significantly different beta measurement: 1.27. Looking at other evidence with respect to Technicolor betas I conclude that 1.27 is a more reasonable estimate of Technicolor's stock beta for purposes of calculating its cost of capital on January 24, 1983, than 1.7, even though that latter figure represents a December 1982 estimation.[52]

The second particular in which the record permits and my judgment with respect to weight of evidence requires a modification of Mr. Rappaport's cost of capital calculation relates to the so-called small capitalization effect or premium. This refers to an unexplained inability of the capital asset pricing model to replicate with complete accuracy the historic returns of stocks with the same historic betas. The empirical data show that there is a recurring premium paid by small capitalization companies. This phenomena

---

52. I have no similar reservation with respect to the 1.19 beta used for One Hour Photo, Consumer Photo Processing and Standard Manufacturing. That beta was determined by [reference to the betas of comparable companies] and was not affected by Technicolor's stock rise in the fall of 1982.

was first noted in 1981 and has been confirmed. The greatest part of the additional return for small cap companies appears to occur in January stock prices. No theory satisfactorily explaining the phenomena has been generally accepted.

Professor Rappaport classifies Technicolor as a small capitalization company and expressed the view that its cost of equity would include a 4% premium over that generated by the CAPM. The question whether the premium can be justified in this instance is difficult because of the inability of academic financial economists to generate an accepted theory of the phenomena. While Technicolor may qualify as a small cap company, the particulars of its situation are different from many small cap companies. It was an old, not a new company. It existed in a relatively stable industry—motion picture film processing. That industry was an oligopoly and Technicolor was a leader. It had "brand name" identification. Do these distinctive characteristics that Technicolor had in common with many giant capitalization companies, matter at all in terms of the "small cap" anomaly? One cannot say. Yet the impact of a 4% increase in the cost of equity (yielding a 3.44% increase in the cost of capital of the Film Processing & Videocassette divisions) would be material to the value of the company and the appraisal value of a share. In these circumstances, I cannot conclude that it has been persuasively shown that the statutory fair value of Technicolor stock would more likely result from the inclusion of a small capitalization premium than from its exclusion. In this circumstance, I conclude it should not be considered.

Thus, in summary, I find Professor Rappaport's calculation of a cost of capital follows an accepted technique for evaluating the cost of capital; it employs that technique in a reasonable way and, except for the two particulars noted above, in a way that is deserving of adoption by the court. Applying these adjustments they lead to a cost capital of 15.28% for the main part of Technicolor's cash flow and 14.13% for the One Hour Photo related cash flows.

Mr. Torkelsen suggests a range of discount rates from 9.96% (weighted average cost of capital of [the acquiring company in the merger]) to 15% (the average cost of capital for all manufacturing companies). He uses a 12.50% rate (an average of these two) to generate the $62.75 figure which he presents as his best estimation of value. This technique of estimating a discount rate is decidedly less reliable than Professor Rappaport's technique. It is not an acceptable professional technique for estimating Technicolor's cost of capital to look to the cost of capital (CAPM derived) of the acquiring company. Mr. Torkelsen's alternative of the average of all industrial concerns is far too gross a number to use except where no finer determination is feasible, which is not the case here.

Notes and Questions

1. What do you suppose is the intuition behind Chancellor Allen's statement that a beta of 1.7 for Technicolor common stock "seems intuitively high for a company with relatively stable cash flows"? To what extent did he rely on that judicial hunch to endorse the beta of 1.27? Was the inclination toward the 1.27 defensible on grounds more firm than intuition? Is it enough to cite market volatility following announcement of the merger? If intuition is playing a significant role, of what value is all the mathematical and theoretical work that goes into calculating betas in the first place?

2. Chancellor Allen referred to the small capitalization anomaly which we noted earlier along with several other anomalies. These anomalies, as we have said, led to a crisis in beta. That crisis, in turn, has led to refinements of the model, including the development of arbitrage pricing theory ("APT"). APT was developed chiefly by Stephen Ross and Richard Roll and represents CAPM's intellectual and theoretical competitor. *See*

Ross, Westerfield and Jaffe, Corporate Finance 283-85 (7th ed. 2005); Van Horne, Financial Management and Policy 93-94 (12th ed. 2001); Roll, A Critique of the Asset Pricing Theory's Tests, 4 J. Fin. Econ. 129 (1977); Ross, The Arbitrage Theory of Capital Asset Pricing, 13 J. Econ. Theory 341 (1976); Roll and Ross, An Empirical Investigation of the Arbitrage Pricing Theory, 35 J. Fin. 1073 (1980).

APT seeks to answer the question revealed by the empirical studies undermining CAPM: what factors other than risk defined in terms of beta affect returns in a way that can be measured? It does this by unpacking beta's category of systematic risks and defining the category into a whole series of sub-risks. These could include such risks as changes in the rate of inflation or changes in the rate of industrial production, and perhaps other risks such as trading by investors who do not conform to the rational expectations assumption implicit in tests of the CAPM. Under APT, each of these sub-risks gets its own beta. The APT formula becomes an extended form of the CAPM that attempts a more realistic and more precise way of measuring risk. APT is still being developed and worked out in financial theory and much work remains to be done in operationalizing it for practice. See Huang, Securities Price Risks and Financial Derivative Markets, 21 Nw. J. Int'l L. & Bus. 589 (2001); Adams & Runkle, Solving A Profound Flaw In Fraud-On-The-Market Theory: Utilizing A Derivative Of Arbitrage Pricing Theory To Measure Rule 10b-5 Damages, 145 U. Pa. L. Rev. 1097 (1997).

APT does hold out promise, however, and may indeed be the wave of the future in corporate finance. For now, we do not think it is worthwhile to pursue the mathematical complexities of this alternative approach to asset pricing and we hope that you are relieved and not disappointed. For the disappointed, we can suggest consulting the articles referenced above. After doing so, you may join the ranks of the relieved.

c. Efficient Capital Market Hypothesis

As should be obvious by this point, the market-based valuation theories built on the foundation of portfolio theory require even a deeper footing—well-functioning capital markets. The bedrock in which all these theories are anchored is the efficient capital market hypothesis (ECMH). The ECMH posits that the price of a share of stock in the market accurately reflects some level of information about that stock. As a corollary, the stock is "correctly" priced by the efficient market. The ECMH is the aspect of modern financial theory that has had the greatest impact on both legal theory and doctrinal development. Unsurprisingly, this development has not occurred without debate. Before examining the theory and debate in detail, it will be instructive to examine the highest legal level of that debate.

(i) "Fraud-on-the-Market" Theory

Basic, Inc. v. Levinson
485 U.S. 224 (1988)

Justice BLACKMUN delivered the opinion of the Court.

This case requires us to apply the materiality requirement of §10(b) of the Securities Exchange Act of 1934.... (1934 Act), and the Securities and Exchange Commission's Rule 10b-5, promulgated thereunder ... in the context of preliminary corporate merger discussions. We must also determine whether a person who traded a corporation's shares on a securities exchange after the issuance of a materially misleading statement by the corporation may invoke a rebuttable presumption that, in trading, he relied on the integrity of the price set by the market.

I

Prior to December 20, 1978, Basic Incorporated was a publicly traded company primarily engaged in the business of manufacturing chemical refractories for the steel industry. As early as 1965 or 1966, Combustion Engineering, Inc., a company producing mostly alumina-based refractories, expressed some interest in acquiring Basic, but was deterred from pursuing this inclination seriously because of antitrust concerns it then entertained.... In 1976, however, regulatory action opened the way to a renewal of Combustion's interest. The "Strategic Plan," dated October 25, 1976, for Combustion's Industrial Products Group included the objective: "Acquire Basic Inc. $30 million." ...

Beginning in September 1976, Combustion representatives had meetings and telephone conversations with Basic officers and directors, including petitioners here, concerning the possibility of a merger. During 1977 and 1978, Basic made three public statements denying that it was engaged in merger negotiations. On December 18, 1978, Basic asked the New York Stock Exchange to suspend trading in its shares and issued a release stating that it had been "approached" by another company concerning a merger.... On December 19, Basic's board endorsed Combustion's offer of $46 per share for its common stock, ... and on the following day publicly announced its approval of Combustion's tender offer for all outstanding shares.

Respondents are former Basic shareholders who sold their stock after Basic's first public statement of October 21, 1977, and before the suspension of trading in December 1978. Respondents brought a class action against Basic and its directors, asserting that the defendants issued three false or misleading public statements and thereby were in violation of §10(b) of the 1934 Act and of Rule 10b-5. Respondents alleged that they were injured by selling Basic shares at artificially depressed prices in a market affected by petitioners' misleading statements and in reliance thereon.

The District Court adopted a presumption of reliance by members of the plaintiff class upon petitioners' public statements that enabled the court to conclude that common questions of fact or law predominated over particular questions pertaining to individual plaintiffs. See Fed. Rule Civ. Proc. 23(b)(3). The District Court therefore certified respondents' class....

The Court of Appeals [for the Sixth Circuit] joined a number of other Circuits in accepting the "fraud-on-the-market theory" to create a rebuttable presumption that respondents relied on petitioners' material misrepresentations, noting that without the presumption it would be impractical to certify a class under Federal Rule of Civil Procedure 23(b)(3). See 786 F.2d, at 750-751.

We granted certiorari, 479 U.S. 1083 (1987), to resolve the split ... among the Courts of Appeals as to the standard of materiality applicable to preliminary merger discussions, and to determine whether the courts below properly applied a presumption of reliance in certifying the class, rather than requiring each class member to show direct reliance on Basic's statements.

* * *

IV

A

We turn to the question of reliance and the fraud-on-the-market theory. Succinctly put:

> "The fraud on the market theory is based on the hypothesis that, in an open and developed securities market, the price of a company's stock is determined by the available material information regarding the company and its business.... Misleading statements will therefore defraud purchasers of stock even if the purchasers do not directly rely on the misstatements.... The causal connection between the defendants' fraud and the plaintiffs' purchase of stock in such a case is no less significant than in a case of direct reliance on misrepresentations." *Peil v. Speiser*, 806 F.2d 1154, 1160-1161 (CA3 1986).

Our task, of course, is not to assess the general validity of the theory, but to consider whether it was proper for the courts below to apply a rebuttable presumption of reliance, supported in part by the fraud-on-the-market theory....

This case required resolution of several common questions of law and fact concerning the falsity or misleading nature of the three public statements made by Basic, the presence or absence of scienter, and the materiality of the misrepresentations, if any. In their amended complaint, the named plaintiffs alleged that in reliance on Basic's statements they sold their shares of Basic stock in the depressed market created by petitioners.... Requiring proof of individualized reliance from each member of the proposed plaintiff class effectively would have prevented respondents from proceeding with a class action, since individual issues then would have overwhelmed the common ones. The District Court found that the presumption of reliance created by the fraud-on-the-market theory provided "a practical resolution to the problem of balancing the substantive requirement of proof of reliance in securities cases against the procedural requisites of [Federal Rule Civil Procedure] 23." The District Court thus concluded that with reference to each public statement and its impact upon the open market for Basic shares, common questions predominated over individual questions, as required by [Federal Rule Civil Procedure] 23(a)(2) and (b)(3).

Petitioners and their *amici* complain that the fraud-on-the-market theory effectively eliminates the requirement that a plaintiff asserting a claim under Rule 10b-5 prove reliance. They note that reliance is and long has been an element of common-law fraud, see *e.g.*, Restatement (Second) of Torts §525 (1977) ... W. Keeton, D. Dobbs, R. Keeton, and D. Owen, Prosser and Keeton on The Law of Torts §108 (5th ed. 1984), and argue that because the analogous express right of action includes a reliance requirement, see, *e.g.*, §18(a) of the 1934 Act, as amended, 15 U.S.C. §78r(a), so too must an action implied under §10(b).

We agree that reliance is an element of a Rule 10b-5 cause of action.... Reliance provides the requisite causal connection between a defendant's misrepresentation and a plaintiff's injury.... There is, however, more than one way to demonstrate the causal connection. Indeed, we previously have dispensed with a requirement of positive proof of reliance, where a duty to disclose material information had been breached, concluding that the necessary nexus between the plaintiffs' injury and the defendant's wrongful conduct had been established. *See Affiliated Ute Citizens v. United States*, 406 U.S. [128 at, 153-154 (1972)]. Similarly, we did not require proof that material omissions or misstatements in a proxy statement decisively affected voting, because the proxy solicitation itself, rather than the defect in the solicitation materials, served as an essential link in the transaction. *See Mills v. Electric Auto-Lite Co.*, 396 U.S. 375, 384-385 (1970).

The modern securities markets, literally involving millions of shares changing hands daily, differ from the face-to-face transactions contemplated by early fraud cases, and our understanding of Rule 10b-5's reliance requirement must encompass these differences.

"In face-to-face transactions, the inquiry into an investor's reliance upon information is into the subjective pricing of that information by that investor. With the presence of a market, the market is interposed between seller and buyer and, ideally, transmits information to the investor in the processed form of a market price. Thus the market is performing a substantial part of the valuation process performed by the investor in a face-to-face transaction. The market is acting as the unpaid agent of the investor, informing him that given all the information available to it, the value of the stock is worth the market price." *In re LTV Securities Litigation*, 88 F.R.D. 134, 143 (ND Tex. 1980).

Accord, e.g., *Piel v. Speiser*, 806 F.2d, at 1161 ("In an open and developed market, the dissemination of material misrepresentations or withholding of material information typically affects the price of the stock, and purchasers generally rely on the price of the stock as a reflection of its value")....

B

Presumptions typically serve to assist courts in managing circumstances in which direct proof, for one reason or another, is rendered difficult.... The courts below accepted a presumption, created by the fraud-on-the-market theory and subject to rebuttal by petitioners, that persons who had traded Basic shares had done so in reliance on the integrity of the price set by the market, but because of petitioners' material misrepresentations that price had been fraudulently depressed. Requiring a plaintiff to show a speculative state of facts, *i.e.*, how he would have acted if omitted material information had been disclosed, *see Affiliated Ute Citizens v. United States*, 406 U.S., at 153-154, or if the misrepresentation had not been made, *see Sharp v. Coopers & Lybrand*, 649 F.2d 175, 188 (CA3 1981), *cert. denied*, 455 U.S. 938, (1982), would place an unnecessarily unrealistic evidentiary burden on the Rule 10b-5 plaintiff who has traded on an impersonal market....

Arising out of considerations of fairness, public policy, and probability, as well as judicial economy, presumptions are also useful devices for allocating the burdens of proof between parties.... The presumption of reliance employed in this case is consistent with, and, by facilitating Rule 10b-5 litigation, supports, the congressional policy embodied in the 1934 Act. In drafting that Act, Congress expressly relied on the premise that securities markets are affected by information, and enacted legislation to facilitate an investor's reliance on the integrity of those markets....

* * *

The presumption is also supported by common sense and probability. Recent empirical studies have tended to confirm Congress' premise that the market price of shares traded on well-developed markets reflects all publicly available information, and, hence, any material misrepresentations.[24] It has been noted that "it is hard to imagine that there ever is a buyer or seller who does not rely on market integrity. Who would knowingly roll the dice in a crooked crap game?" *Schlanger v. Four-Phase Systems Inc.*, 555 F. Supp. 535, 538 (SDNY 1982).[a] Indeed, nearly every court that has considered the proposition has concluded that where materially misleading statements have been disseminated into an impersonal, well-developed market for securities, the reliance of individual plaintiffs on the integrity of the market price may be presumed. Commentators generally have applauded the adoption of one variation or another of the fraud-on-the-market theory.[26] An investor who buys or sells stock at the price set by the market does so in reliance on the integrity of that price. Because most publicly available information is reflected in market price, an investor's reliance on any public material misrepresentations, therefore, may be presumed for purposes of a Rule 10b-5 action.

C

The Court of Appeals found that petitioners "made public, material misrepresentations and [respondents] sold Basic stock in an impersonal, efficient market. Thus the class, as defined by the district court, has established the threshold facts for proving their loss." 786 F.2d, at 751.[27] The court acknowledged that petitioners may rebut proof of the elements giving rise to the presumption, or show that the misrepresentation in fact did not lead to a distortion of price or that an individual plaintiff traded or would have traded despite his knowing the statement was false. *Id.*, at 750, n.6.

Any showing that severs the link between the alleged misrepresentation and either the price received (or paid) by the plaintiff, or his decision to trade at a fair market price, will

---

24. *See In re LTV Securities Litigation*, 88 F.R.D. 134, 144 (ND Tex. 1980) (citing studies); Fischel, Use of Modern Finance Theory in Securities Fraud Cases Involving Actively Traded Securities, 38 Bus. Law. 1, 4, n.9 (1982) (citing literature on efficient-capital-market theory); Dennis, Materiality and the Efficient Capital Market Model: A Recipe for the Total Mix, 25 Wm. & Mary L. Rev. 373, 374-381, and n.1 (1984). We need not determine by adjudication what economists and social scientists have debated through the use of sophisticated statistical analysis and the application of economic theory. For purposes of accepting the presumption of reliance in this case, we need only believe that market professionals generally consider most publicly announced material statements about companies, thereby affecting stock market prices.

a. On this point, Lynn Stout has argued:
The problem with this view is that in an inefficient trading market the odds of selling at an incorrectly low price are no greater than the chance of a windfall by selling at an incorrectly high price. Inefficient stock markets (like efficient ones) may well be a crap game, but not necessarily a crooked one. If inefficiency is as likely to lead to overvaluation as undervaluation, inefficient pricing will not affect investors' *average* returns. Consequently, inefficiency should not erode investor confidence in the market's expected returns.
Stout, The Unimportance of Being Efficient: An Economic Analysis of Stock Market Pricing and Securities Regulation, 87 Mich. L. Rev. 613, 672 (1988).

26. *See, e.g.*, Black, Fraud on the Market: A Criticism of Dispensing with Reliance Requirements in Certain Open Market Transactions, 62 N.C.L. Rev. 435 (1984); Note, The Fraud-on-the-Market Theory, 95 Harv. L. Rev. 1143 (1982); Note, Fraud on the Market: An Emerging Theory of Recovery Under SEC Rule 10b-5, 50 Geo. Wash. L. Rev. 627 (1982).

27. The Court of Appeals held that in order to invoke the presumption, a plaintiff must allege and prove: (1) that the defendant made public misrepresentations; (2) that the misrepresentations were material; (3) that the shares were traded on an efficient market; (4) that the misrepresentations would induce a reasonable, relying investor to misjudge the value of the shares; and (5) that the plaintiff traded the shares between the time the misrepresentations were made and the time the truth was revealed. *See* 786 F.2d, at 750.
Given today's decision regarding the definition of materiality as to preliminary merger discussions, elements (2) and (4) may collapse into one.

be sufficient to rebut the presumption of reliance. For example, if petitioners could show that the "market makers" were privy to the truth about the merger discussions here with Combustion, and thus that the market price would not have been affected by their misrepresentations, the causal connection could be broken: the basis for finding that the fraud had been transmitted through market price would be gone.[28] Similarly, if, despite petitioners' allegedly fraudulent attempt to manipulate market price, news of the merger discussions credibly entered the market and dissipated the effects of the misstatements, those who traded Basic shares after the corrective statements would have no direct or indirect connection with the fraud.[29] Petitioners also could rebut the presumption of reliance as to plaintiffs who would have divested themselves of their Basic shares without relying on the integrity of the market. For example, a plaintiff who believed that Basic's statements were false and that Basic was indeed engaged in merger discussions, and who consequently believed that Basic stock was artificially underpriced, but sold his shares nevertheless because of other unrelated concerns, e.g., potential antitrust problems, or political pressures to divest from shares of certain businesses, could not be said to have relied on the integrity of a price he knew had been manipulated.

V

In summary:

* * *

5. It is not inappropriate to apply a presumption of reliance supported by the fraud-on-the-market theory.

6. That presumption, however, is rebuttable.

7. The District Court's certification of the class here was appropriate when made but is subject on remand to such adjustment, if any, as developing circumstances demand.

The judgment of the Court of Appeals is vacated and the case is remanded to that court for further proceedings consistent with this opinion.

It is so ordered.

The Chief Justice, Justice SCALIA, and Justice KENNEDY took no part in the consideration or decision of this case.

Justice WHITE, with whom Justice O'CONNOR joins, concurring in part and dissenting in part.

I join Parts I-III of the Court's opinion .... But I dissent from the remainder of the Court's holding because I do not agree that the "fraud-on-the-market" theory should be applied in this case.

---

28. By accepting this rebuttable presumption, we do not intend conclusively to adopt any particular theory of how quickly and completely publicly available information is reflected in market price. Furthermore, our decision today is not to be interpreted as addressing the proper measure of damages in litigation of this kind.

29. We note there may be a certain incongruity between the assumption that Basic shares are traded on a well-developed, efficient, and information-hungry market, and the allegation that such a market could remain misinformed, and its valuation of Basic shares depressed, for 14 months, on the basis of the three public statements. Proof of that sort is a matter for trial, throughout which the District Court retains the authority to amend the certification order as may be appropriate. See Fed. Rules Civ. Proc. 23(c)(1) and (c)(4).... Thus, we see no need to engage in the kind of factual analysis the dissent suggests that manifests the "oddities" of applying a rebuttable presumption of reliance in this case....

I

Even when compared to the relatively youthful private cause-of-action under §10(b), ... the fraud-on-the-market theory is a mere babe. Yet today, the Court embraces this theory with the sweeping confidence usually reserved for more mature legal doctrines. In so doing, I fear that the Court's decision may have many adverse, unintended effects as it is applied and interpreted in the years to come.

A

At the outset, I note that there are portions of the Court's fraud-on-the-market holding with which I am in agreement. Most importantly, the Court rejects the version of that theory, heretofore adopted by some courts, which equates "causation" with "reliance," and permits recovery by a plaintiff who claims merely to have been *harmed* by a material misrepresentation which altered a market price, notwithstanding proof that the plaintiff did not in any way *rely* on that price.... I agree with the Court that if Rule 10b-5's reliance requirement is to be left with any content at all, the fraud-on-the-market presumption must be capable of being rebutted by a showing that a plaintiff did not "rely" on the market price. For example, a plaintiff who decides, months in advance of an alleged misrepresentation, to purchase a stock; one who buys or sells a stock for reasons unrelated to its price; one who actually sells a stock "short" days before the misrepresentation is made—surely none of these people can state a valid claim under Rule 10b-5. Yet, some federal courts have allowed such claims to stand under one variety or another of the fraud-on-the-market theory.

Happily, the majority puts to rest the prospect of recovery under such circumstances....

B

But even as the Court attempts to limit the fraud-on-the-market theory it endorses today, the pitfalls in its approach are revealed by previous uses by the lower courts of the broader versions of the theory. Confusion and contradiction in court rulings are inevitable when traditional legal analysis is replaced with economic theorization by the federal courts.

In general, the case law developed in this Court with respect to §10(b) and Rule 10b-5 has been based on doctrines with which we, as judges, are familiar: common-law doctrines of fraud and deceit.... Even when we have extended civil liability under Rule 10b-5 to a broader reach than the common law had previously permitted, ... we have retained familiar legal principles as our guideposts.... The federal courts have proved adept at developing an evolving jurisprudence of Rule 10b-5 in such a manner. But with no staff economists, no experts schooled in the "efficient-capital-market hypothesis," no ability to test the validity of empirical market studies, we are not well equipped to embrace novel constructions of a statute based on contemporary microeconomic theory.

The "wrong turns" in those Court of Appeals and District Court fraud-on-the-market decisions which the Court implicitly rejects as going too far should be ample illustration of the dangers when economic theories replace legal rules as the basis for recovery. Yet the Court today ventures into this area beyond its expertise, beyond—by its own admission—the confines of our previous fraud cases.... Even if I agreed with the Court that "modern securities markets ... involving millions of shares changing hands daily" require that the "understanding of Rule 10b-5's reliance requirement" be changed, *ibid.*, I prefer that such changes come from Congress in amending §10(b). The Congress, with its superior resources and expertise, is far better equipped than the federal courts for the task of determining how modern economic theory and global financial markets require that established legal notions of fraud be modified. In choosing to make these decisions itself, the Court, I fear, embarks on a course that it does not genuinely understand, giving rise to consequences it cannot foresee.

For while the economists' theories which underpin the fraud-on-the-market presumption may have the appeal of mathematical exactitude and scientific certainty, they are—in the end—nothing more than theories which may or may not prove accurate upon further consideration. Even the most earnest advocates of economic analysis of the law recognize this. *See, e.g.,* Easterbrook, Afterword: Knowledge and Answers, 85 Colum. L. Rev. 1117, 1118 (1985). Thus, while the majority states that, for purposes of reaching its result it need only make modest assumptions about the way in which "market professionals generally" do their jobs, and how the conduct of market professionals affects stock prices, ... I doubt that we are in much of a position to assess which theories aptly describe the functioning of the securities industry.

Consequently, I cannot join the Court in its effort to reconfigure the securities laws, based on recent economic theories, to better fit what it perceives to be the new realities of financial markets. I would leave this task to others more equipped for the job than we.

C

At the bottom of the Court's conclusion that the fraud-on-the-market theory sustains a presumption of reliance is the assumption that individuals rely "on the integrity of the market price" when buying or selling stock in "impersonal, well-developed market[s] for securities." ... Even if I was prepared to accept (as a matter of common sense or general understanding) the assumption that most persons buying or selling stock do so in response to the market price, the fraud-on-the-market theory goes further. For in adopting a "presumption of reliance," the Court *also* assumes that buyers and sellers rely—not just on the market price—but on the "*integrity*" of that price. It is this aspect of the fraud-on-the-market hypothesis which most mystifies me.

To define the term "integrity of the market price," the majority quotes approvingly from cases which suggest that investors are entitled to "'rely on the price of a stock as a reflection of its value'" ... (quoting *Peil v. Speiser,* 806 F.2d 1154, 1161 (CA3 1986)). But the meaning of this phrase eludes me, for it implicitly suggests that stocks have some "true value" that is measurable by a standard other than their market price. While the Scholastics of Medieval times professed a means to make such a valuation of a commodity's "worth," I doubt that the federal courts of our day are similarly equipped.

Even if securities had some "value"—knowable and distinct from the market price of a stock—investors do not always share the Court's presumption that a stock's price is a "reflection of [this] value." Indeed, "many investors purchase or sell stock because they believe the price *inaccurately* reflects the corporation's worth." *See* Black, Fraud on the Market: A Criticism of Dispensing with Reliance Requirements in Certain Open Market Transactions, 62 N.C.L. Rev. 435, 455 (1984) (emphasis added). If investors really believed that stock prices reflected a stock's "value," many sellers would never sell, and many buyers never buy (given the time and cost associated with executing a stock transaction). As we recognized just a few years ago: "[I]nvestors act on inevitably incomplete or inaccurate information, [consequently] there are always winners and losers; but those who have 'lost' have not necessarily been defrauded." *Dirks v. SEC,* 463

U.S. 646, 667, n.27 (1983). Yet today, the Court allows investors to recover who can show little more than that they sold stock at a lower price than what might have been.[7]

I do not propose that the law retreat from the many protections that §10(b) and Rule 10b-5, as interpreted in our prior cases, provide to investors. But any extension of these laws, to approach something closer to an investor insurance scheme, should come from Congress, and not from the courts.

II

* * *

Congress has not passed on the fraud-on-the-market theory the Court embraces today. That is reason enough for us to abstain from doing so. But it is even more troubling that, to the extent that any view of Congress on this question can be inferred indirectly, it is contrary to the result the majority reaches.

III

Finally, the particular facts of this case make it an exceedingly poor candidate for the Court's fraud-on-the-market theory, and illustrate the illogic achieved by that theory's application in many cases.

Respondents here are a class of sellers who sold Basic stock between October, 1977 and December 1978, a fourteen-month period. At the time the class period began, Basic's stock was trading at $20 a share (at the time, an all-time high); the last members of the class to sell their Basic stock got a price of just over $30 a share.... It is indisputable that virtually every member of the class made money from his or her sale of Basic stock.

The oddities of applying the fraud-on-the-market theory in this case are manifest. First, there are the facts that the plaintiffs are sellers and the class period is so lengthy — both are virtually without precedent in prior fraud-on-the-market cases.[9] For reasons I discuss in the margin, I think these two facts render this case less apt to application of the fraud-on-the-market hypothesis.

* * *

---

7. This is what the Court's rule boils down to in practical terms. For while, in theory, the Court allows for rebuttal of its "presumption of reliance" — a proviso with which I agree, ... *in practice* the Court must realize, as other courts applying the fraud-on-the-market theory have, that such rebuttal is virtually impossible in all but the most extraordinary case. See *Blackie v. Barrack*, 524 F.2d, at 906-907, n.22; *In re LTV Securities Litigation*, 88 F.R.D. 134, 143, n.4 (ND Tex. 1980).

Consequently, while the Court considers it significant that the fraud-on-the-market presumption it endorses is a rebuttable one, ... the majority's implicit rejection of the "pure causation" fraud-on-the-market theory rings hollow. In most cases, the Court's theory will operate just as the causation theory would, creating a non-rebuttable presumption of "reliance" in future 10b-5 actions.

9. None of the Court of Appeals cases the Court cites as endorsing the fraud-on-the-market theory ... involved seller-plaintiffs. Rather, all of these cases were brought by purchasers who bought securities in a short period following some material misstatement (or similar act) by an issuer, which was alleged to have falsely inflated a stock's price.

Even if the fraud-on-the-market theory provides a permissible link between such a misstatement and a decision to purchase a security shortly thereafter, surely that link is far more attenuated between misstatements made in October 1977, and a decision to sell a stock the following September, 11 months later. The fact that the plaintiff-class is one of sellers, and that the class period so long, distinguish this case from *any* other cited in the Court's opinion, and make it an even poorer candidate for the fraud-on-the-market presumption. *Cf., e.g., Schlanger v. Four-Phase Systems Inc.*, 555 F. Supp. 535 (SDNY 1982) (permitting class of sellers to use fraud-on-the-market theory where the class period was eight days long).

IV

In sum, I think the Court's embracement of the fraud-on-the-market theory represents a departure in securities law that we are ill-suited to commence—and even less equipped to control as it proceeds. As a result, I must respectfully dissent.

Questions

1. What do you think of the Supreme Court's use of the fraud-on-the-market theory? Which form of the efficient capital market hypothesis does it appear to accept? (The forms of the ECMH are discussed in the ensuing essays.)

2. How is a plaintiff to establish that the stock at issue was traded on an efficient market? Consider footnote 27 of the Court's opinion.

3. In footnote 24 Justice Blackmun writes:

> We need not determine by adjudication what economists and social scientists have debated through the use of sophisticated statistical analysis and the application of economic theory. For purposes of accepting the presumption of reliance in this case, we need only believe that market professionals generally consider most publicly announced material statements about companies, thereby affecting stock market prices.

What do you think of this statement? Is this an adequate basis on which to accept the fraud-on-the-market theory? Does Justice White adequately respond to the majority?

4. Did Basic's directors breach their fiduciary duty to its stockholders by their misleading disclosures? Would stockholders' wealth have been increased or diminished by accurate and early disclosure? Are other values served by the holding in *Basic*?

5. For a critical evaluation of the *Basic* opinion, *see* Marber, Griffin & Lev, The Fraud-On-The-Market Theory And The Indicators Of Common Stocks' Efficiency, 19 J. Corp. L. 285 (1994); *see also*, Macey and Miller, Good Finance, Bad Economics: An Analysis of the Fraud-on-the-Market Theory, 42 Stan. L. Rev. 1059 (1990).

6. In connection with congressional review of securities fraud litigation in the mid-1990s, various proposals for reform included legislation that would overrule the holding in *Basic* with respect to eliminating the reliance requirement in such litigation for stocks that trade in efficient markets.

For a rejection of *Basic* and the fraud-on-the-market theory as a matter of common law fraud in a securities context, see Mirkin v. Wasserman, 858 P.2d 568 (Cal. 1993), and the following case.

Kaufman v. i-Stat Corp.
754 A.2d 1188 (N.J. 2000)

The opinion of the Court was delivered by LaVECCHIA, J.

This appeal presents the question whether a class of plaintiffs in a common-law action for fraud can prove the element of reliance through the presumption of a fraud on the market. The theory of fraud on the market, as described by the United States Supreme Court in *Basic Inc. v. Levinson*, 485 U.S. 224 (1988), allows plaintiffs to bring class actions under federal securities-fraud law by excusing those plaintiffs from the burden of proving individual reliance. Instead, plaintiffs may establish the reliance element of their claims by showing that they purchased securities in the secondary markets at attractive prices that had been artificially affected by an issuer's misrepresentations and omissions.

Plaintiff Susan Kaufman held shares of defendant i-Stat Corporation ("i-Stat") over a period during which i-Stat allegedly misrepresented certain financial matters and the misrepresentations were discovered and publicized. The misrepresentations were never made to Kaufman by i-Stat or any intermediary. Kaufman relied on the price of the stock in her decisions, and now contends that, because i-Stat's misrepresentations were reflected in the share price, she can make out claims for common-law fraud and negligent misrepresentation on the basis of the share price alone.

Even though the theory of fraud on the market has a place in the securities law of this nation, it is a stranger to New Jersey's securities laws. It is also not consistent with the current requirements for a common-law action for fraud in New Jersey. Use of the fraud-on-the-market theory is not the equivalent of proof of indirect reliance that is required minimally in a common-law fraud action. Because we discern no compelling reason to deviate from our current standard of proof for the reliance element in a common-law fraud action, and because we, like many commentators, cast a jaundiced eye on the worth of the fraud-on-the-market theory, we decline to expand our common law to permit its use. Accordingly, we reverse the judgment of the Appellate Division and reinstate the trial court's dismissal of plaintiff's fraud claim....

This matter comes before the Court as a result of the Law Division's grant of summary judgment for the defendants. Accordingly, we give the plaintiff the benefit of every positive inference to be drawn from the facts as she has pled them....

i-Stat is a public New Jersey corporation ... [that] makes a hand-held blood analyzer and cartridges to test individual patients. The corporation's stock is traded on the NASDAQ National Market System. On October 31, 1995, during the events at issue in this action, i-Stat had 11,083,421 shares of common stock issued and outstanding.

On May 9, 1995, i-Stat announced its financial results for the first fiscal quarter of 1995, ending March 31. The company reported net sales of $3,359,000, as compared to reported net sales of $1,651,000 for the same period in the previous year. The company reported a net loss of $6,531,000 ($0.59 per share) for the first quarter as compared with a net loss of $6,056,000 ($0.55 per share) for the same period in the prior year. Kaufman alleges that, to produce the improved sales figures, i-Stat misrepresented acceptance of the company's products to the public by "reporting sales that were not, in fact, true sales, but were, instead, loans on a trial basis." For example, i-Stat allegedly reported "sales" to certain hospitals without disclosing that the "sales" were induced by "charitable donations" from interested third parties to the purchasing hospitals. These sales practices resulted in an exaggerated representation of the company's sales and degree of market acceptance of its products.

On May 22, 1995, Susan Kaufman purchased one hundred shares of i-Stat common stock at 21 3/4, a total investment of $2175. Meanwhile, on that date, *Forbes* magazine reported that a medical investment newsletter believed i-Stat was experiencing difficulties and that its products were not economical. On June 21, 1995, an article in *The Financial Post*, a Canadian financial publication, reported "the expected profitability and growth of the Company," citing an interview with defendant Imants Lauks. On September 21, 1995, i-Stat reached its all-time high, trading at 43 3/4.

The bubble began to burst on January 28, 1996. On that date, *The New York Times* reported that Daniel R. Frank, manager of the Fidelity Advisor Strategic Opportunities

Fund, whose successor is still the largest institutional holder of i-Stat, had made chari-table contributions to hospitals to enable them to obtain i-Stat's diagnostic equipment.

Then, on March 19, 1996, *The Wall Street Journal* reported that the Securities and Exchange Commission ("SEC") was investigating i-Stat's business. The article revealed that some of i-Stat's "sales" had been loans of the products to hospitals on a trial basis rather than actual sales. i-Stat responded with a press release confirming the SEC's in-vestigation and inquiry into its sales procedures. On that same day, i-Stat's shares, which had been declining, tumbled 2 1/2 to 28 3/4. Two million shares of i-Stat, nearly one sixth of the shares outstanding on that date, traded on March 19.

On May 20, 1996, Kaufman sold 50 shares at 20 1/4. On June 19, she filed suit as putative class representative on behalf of all purchasers of i-Stat common stock be-tween May 9, 1995, and March 19, 1996, excluding the officers and directors of the company. Kaufman alleged common-law fraud and negligent misrepresentation, con-tending that i-Stat's deliberately false and misleading statements regarding its financial status and deceptive sales practices inflated the stock price during the class period....

i-Stat filed an answer alleging various affirmative defenses. Both parties stipulated to the following: (1) Kaufman did not "actually or directly receive or rely on any commu-nication containing any misrepresentation ... nor ... actually receive or rely on any communication which omitted material facts[;]" (2) Kaufman purchased her stock through a brokerage firm and did not directly receive or rely on any communication from the brokerage firm concerning the i-Stat purchase; and (3) Kaufman "relied exclu-sively on the integrity of the market price of i-Stat stock at the time of her purchase." Therefore, Kaufman's satisfaction of the reliance element of the common-law fraud and negligent misrepresentation claims depends entirely on the fraud-on-the-market theory.

The misdeeds that plaintiff alleges i-Stat to have committed, if proven, clearly fall within the ambit of [Rule 10b-5 promulgated under the Securities Exchange Act of 1934]. Many actions based on similar claims, some using the fraud-on-the-market the-ory, have been brought before the federal courts over the last sixty years. But since 1995, plaintiffs in these actions have increasingly turned to state courts.

The change has come about neither because state courts have greater expertise in these matters nor because they are more convenient. The impetus for these state court filings was provided by Congress' passage of the Private Securities Litigation Reform Act of 1995, 109 Stat. 737 ("PSLRA"). Congress enacted the PSLRA to reduce or eliminate class-action strike suits filed by investors when the price of a stock declined. PSLRA's provisions have made litigating such cases much more difficult for plaintiffs.[a]

* * *

These changes have led plaintiffs to attempt to [bring cases in state court]. Most of those cases newly brought in state court have been, as this one is, substitutes for Rule 10b-5 actions. To maintain those actions' viability, the plaintiffs bringing them have sought to have the courts hearing them incorporate the doctrine of fraud on the mar-ket into the common law of their respective states. Plaintiff, however, has cited no case in which a state court ruling on its common law has accepted the invitation. Defen-dants, by contrast, have found several cases declining to allow the fraud-on-the-market

---

a. In addition to the difficulties plaintiffs face as a result of PSLRA, the Supreme Court, begin-ning in 1975, has steadily eroded investor protections and plaintiffs' access to the courts to redress securities law violations. Mitchell, No Business Like No Business, in Herman Schwartz, ed., The Rhenquist Court: Judicial Activism on the Right, 227 (2002). [Eds.]

theory to establish reliance at common law. The federal courts with jurisdiction in New Jersey have rejected the idea that fraud on the market can create a common-law action for fraud.

The many state-law class actions for securities fraud triggered further federal reform legislation, the Securities Litigation Uniform Standards Act of 1998.... Now, SLUSA provides that any securities action brought on behalf of a class of more than fifty individual investors, whether arising under federal, common, or blue-sky law, must be brought in federal court. Since the common law of fraud covers areas other than securities, then, the plaintiffs in this case are asking this Court to expand the common law, potentially beyond the arena of securities, in an action of a sort that Congress substantially has barred our courts from hearing in the future.

* * *

Plaintiff characterizes the fraud-on-the-market theory as no more than a reasonable application of indirect reliance principles. Indirect reliance allows a plaintiff to prove a fraud action when he or she heard a statement not from the party that defrauded him or her but from that party's agent or from someone to whom the party communicated the false statement with the intention that the victim hear it, rely on it, and act to his or her detriment....

Defendants ... argue that this Court's standard for reliance, even indirect reliance, requires that the plaintiff have actually relied on the misstatement, i.e., that the plaintiff actually received and considered the misstatement or omission, however indirectly uttered, before he or she completed the transaction....

We agree with defendants. The actual receipt and consideration of any misstatement remains central to the case of any plaintiff seeking to prove that he or she was deceived by the misstatement or omission. The element of reliance is the same for fraud and negligent misrepresentation....

Because negligent misrepresentation does not require scienter as an element, it is easier to prove than fraud. [B]ecause the Rule 10b-5 action requires a plaintiff to prove scienter, expanding fraud on the market to cover a tort without scienter would be inconsistent with the theory of recovery. Nevertheless, our law of indirect reliance, even though most recently clarified in negligent-misrepresentation cases, is the same in fraud cases, the element of reliance being the same in both....

If a party to a transaction makes a false statement to another party, intending or knowing that the other party in the transaction will hear it and rely on it, and the second party to the transaction actually hears the substance of the misrepresentation, by means however attenuated, and considers the actual content of that misrepresentation when making the decision to complete the transaction, then that person has established indirect reliance to support a fraud claim.

In this case, plaintiff has explicitly stated that she did not consider i-Stat's financial statements, either by herself or in consultation with an investment professional, but acted only on the market price. By that statement she denies that she ever considered i-Stat's sales volume in her buying decision. Thus, she has failed to establish that she relied, however indirectly, on the misstatements of i-Stat and its management. Therefore, under our traditional standard for proof of reliance, even indirect reliance, plaintiff fails to show reliance and, therefore, fails to make out a claim for fraud.

Since the Supreme Court accepted fraud on the market in *Basic, supra,* twelve years ago, no state court with the authority to consider whether *Basic* is persuasive has chosen to apply it to claims arising under its own state's laws. In considering whether to accept the theory, then, the persuasiveness of its intellectual underpinning, the Efficient Capital Markets Hypothesis, or ECMH, requires close examination. The ECMH proposes that the price of a stock reflects information known about a corporation whose securities trade publicly. The extent to which the price reflects that information is expressed by the three different forms of market efficiency—strong, semi-strong, and weak. In a strong-form efficient market, all information that exists about a company and would be of interest to a purchaser of the company's securities is reflected, nearly instantaneously, in the price of the stock, such that no individual can expect to gain a greater return from that security than from any other security, and no individual can hope to perform better than any other individual over the long term. The weak form of the ECMH, by contrast, proposes that the price of the stock eventually reflects publicly available information. There is widespread agreement among economists and investment professionals that the national stock markets of the United States display weak-form efficiency. *See* Barbara Black, Fraud on the Market: A Criticism of Dispensing with Reliance Requirements in Certain Open Market Transactions, 62 N.C. L. Rev. 435, 438, n.8 (1984).

Semi-strong efficiency, which is somewhere between the other two forms in holding that most information about a company is reflected in its price fairly quickly, appears to be the form assumed to exist by the United States Supreme Court in *Basic....*

The ECMH, perhaps because it posits that no investor can consistently outperform the market regardless of the amount of research or work undertaken beforehand, is a favorite subject for academics but is often discounted by investment professionals. For example, Warren Buffett, the well-known, successful investor, contends that proper study of a company's financial condition reveals its value far better than does the market price of its shares. Roger Lowenstein, Buffett: The Making of an American Capitalist 307-22 (1995).

The ECMH has suffered at the hands of academic writers as well:

> We think that the legal rush to embrace and apply the efficient market hypothesis has been overly precipitous and occasionally unwise.... More recent economic research and controversy about the hypothesis casts doubt on ECMH's empirical claims and theoretical underpinnings. Whether markets are efficient in the sense claimed by the initial tests is now highly suspect.... Virtually none of this doubt, however, has been reflected in the debates about the implications of the efficient market hypothesis for legal decision-making.

Jeffrey N. Gordon & Lewis A. Kornhauser, Efficient Markets, Costly Information, and Securities Research, 60 N.Y.U. L. Rev. 761, 764 (1985).

As more time has passed, and there has been greater opportunity to examine and test market efficiency, the hypothesis has shown greater weakness.

> The debate over the ECMH is fundamental because [it] is a major premise for a substantial body of corporate and securities law and scholarship [and] the United States Supreme Court has recognized the ECMH as a basis for satisfying the reliance requirement in certain securities-fraud cases. Moreover, since the late 1970s, a great deal of corporate and securities law scholarship has extolled the virtues of the ECMH and urged it as a basis to advocate many major policy prescriptions. Indeed, before the public capital market crash of October 1987,

   only a few sobering pieces stood to remind the legal community that the ECMH
   is only a hypothesis, and a dubious one at that.

Lawrence A. Cunningham, From Random Walks to Chaotic Crashes: The Linear Genealogy of the Efficient Capital Market Hypothesis, 62 Geo. Wash. L. Rev. 546, 548-49 (1994).

   Because the ECMH fails to adjust for the noise and chaos inevitable in any system created by the acts of so many participants, one observer has gone so far as to contend that
"obsolescence renders the ECMH false in all its forms." Cunningham, 62 Geo. Wash. L
Rev. at 548. Other writers have commented on causation uncertainty in understanding
market reactions, noting, among other things: how inefficiently prices reflect earnings;
how other publicly available financial information is underreflected; how other information, such as historical underperformance, affects price; and how the activities of under-
rational "noise traders" and those otherwise affected by investor sentiment distort the picture. See Victor L. Bernard, et al., Challenges to the Efficient Market Hypothesis: Limits to
the Applicability of Fraud-on-the-Market Theory, 73 Neb. L. Rev. 781, 786-92 (1994).

   Plaintiff argues that the academic debate goes to whether particular securities trade
in efficient markets and that academics and courts remain confident that the markets
are efficient. Defendants acknowledge that uncertainty whether the markets are efficient
may not be reason enough to reject fraud on the market where it has already been accepted, but argues that a theory, whose validity at best remains in question, provides
poor support for an expansion of the common law.

   Our own Chancery Division has noted the uncertainty regarding the validity of the
EMCH.... [See] Johnson v. Johnson, 515 A.2d 255 (1986).

   Other courts have also expressed misgivings about the ECMH.... Even at the time of
the Basic decision, skeptical voices were heard. Dissenting from the majority opinion,
Justice White wrote that "with no staff economists, no experts schooled in the 'efficient-
capital-market hypothesis,' no ability to test the validity of empirical market studies, we
are not well equipped to embrace novel constructions of a statute based on contemporary microeconomic theory." 485 U.S. at 253. There is no greater proof now than there
was then that the theoretical foundation for the fraud-on-the-market theory is as strong
as its proponents maintain.

   Yet now, despite there being no basis for increased acceptance of the idea of fraud on
efficient markets, plaintiff asks us to expand its use beyond the carefully balanced world
of the federal securities laws to the vastly more diverse universe of common-law fraud
claims....

                                    * * *

   Indirect reliance occurs when a single communication, an inducement to engage in
a fraudulent transaction, is clearly communicated to the defrauded party. The price of
a publicly traded stock, however, synthesizes a great variety of information and conveys
as much of that information as possible. But the information is jumbled. No one piece
of information survives clearly enough that the share price can be said to have passed it
on clearly. Until study or experience can prove that an impersonal mechanism can
communicate a single idea clearly, indirect reliance should not be expanded to include
this theoretical model of market performance and excuse this plaintiff from her obligation to show individual reliance on the alleged misrepresentation.

   Accepting fraud on the market as proof of reliance in a New Jersey common-law
fraud action would undercut the public interest in preventing forum-shopping,
weaken our law of indirect reliance, and run contrary to the policy direction of the

Legislature and Congress. We decline to expand our law regarding satisfaction of the reliance element of a fraud action on the basis of a complex economic theory that has not been satisfactorily proven. In so holding, we note that plaintiff had available to her an adequate federal remedy perfectly suited to her complaint. She chose not to pursue it.

STEIN, J., dissenting (joined by JUSTICES O'HERN and LONG):

... i-Stat issued materially misleading public statements about its financial condition and prospects, subsequent to which the price of its stock rose.... Under the principle of indirect reliance applied by this Court ... and consistent with the Restatement (Second) of Torts' position, i-Stat's intentional misrepresentation may be actionable as a common law fraud even though the authors of the false information did not communicate directly to plaintiff.

The question thus is whether the principle of indirect reliance applies in the context of purchasers of publicly traded securities where the fraud was perpetrated generally on the public with the intention that all purchasers of the securities would be defrauded. The answer to that question is found in the United States Supreme Court's analysis of the fraud-of-the-market theory in Section 10b-5 cases ...

Prior to the United States Supreme Court's 1988 *Basic* decision, to satisfy the reliance element of a fraud claim brought under Rule 10b-5 victims of fraudulent misrepresentations were required to show that they actually relied on the misrepresentations made by defendants....

In *Basic, supra*, the Supreme Court first concluded that the reliance element in a claim based on fraudulent misrepresentations under Rule 10b-5 may be satisfied by proof that the plaintiff relied on the integrity of the market price....

The fraud-on-the-market theory of reliance is but a rebuttable presumption of reliance....

Defendants may "rebut proof of the elements giving rise to the presumption, or show that the misrepresentation in fact did not lead to a distortion of price or that an individual plaintiff traded or would have traded despite his knowing the statement was false." [*Basic*, 485 U.S.] at 248. Similarly, the presumption may be rebutted by "any showing that severs the link between the alleged misrepresentation and either the price received (or paid) by the plaintiff, or his decision to trade at a fair market price" or if credible information "entered the market and dissipated the effects of the misstatements." *Id.* at 249.

.... Because most publicly available information is reflected in market price, an investor's reliance on any public material misrepresentations, therefore, may be presumed for purposes of a Rule 10b-5 action." *Id.* at 247. Thus, the fraud-on-the-market theory of reliance is sufficient to satisfy the reliance element of a Rule 10b-5 claim.

The *Basic* Court's holding that the use of the fraud-on-the-market theory may satisfy the reliance element of a Rule 10b-5 claim is not based on the specific language of the [Securities Exchange] Act. Instead, the holding relies on the fact that the reliance elements of securities law claims and common law fraud actions are virtually identical. *Basic*, at 243....

The majority refers to limitations on the fraud-on-the-market theory of reliance and notes that commentators and investors may disagree about whether the market price of a security fully reflects the present value of a company. However, adoption of the fraud-on-the-market principle does not require us to "adopt any particular theory of how quickly and completely publicly available information is reflected in market price." *Basic*, at 248, n.28. It requires merely that we accept that "the idea of a free and open public market is built upon the theory that competing judgments of buyers and sellers as to the fair price of a security brings [sic] about a situation where the market price reflects as nearly as possible a just price." *Id.* at 246. The significance of the fraud-on-the-market principle derives not from the infallibility of the market price of securities but rather from the theory's implicit acknowledgment that the investing public is entitled to assume that SEC-mandated disclosures have been made and that fraudulent misrepresentations have not unlawfully affected the market price.

The majority asserts that to accept the fraud-on-the-market theory of reliance as proof of reliance in a common law fraud suit would "undercut the public interest in preventing forum-shopping, weaken our law of indirect reliance, and run contrary to the policy direction of the Legislature and Congress." Those arguments are unpersuasive.

[C]lass action lawsuits for securities fraud are so few in number that the adoption of the fraud-on-the-market theory as a rebuttable presumption of reliance will have little or no impact on the operation of state courts.... Moreover, the enactment by Congress of legislation restricting the fora in which victims of securities fraud may sue limits further those plaintiffs who are permitted to maintain a securities fraud cause of action in state courts. Initially, in 1995 Congress passed the Private Securities Litigation Reform Act (PSLRA). PSLRA imposed many procedural restrictions on federal class-action plaintiffs. In 1998 Congress enacted the Securities Litigation Uniform Standards Act (SLUSA), which sharply limits the number of securities fraud class action suits that may be brought in state courts. SLUSA, by its terms, preempts all but a limited group of future class action common law fraud claims that would otherwise be filed in state court and requires that they be filed in federal court. SLUSA provides that the vast majority of class actions, including suits such as the one at bar, that are based on a state's statutory or common law alleging "a misrepresentation or omission of a material fact in connection with the purchase or sale of a covered security" or "any manipulative or deceptive device or contrivance in connection with the purchase or sale of a covered security" may not be brought in a state court. SLUSA prevents all but state or municipal entities, state pension funds, or classes comprised of less than fifty plaintiffs from filing suit in a state court. The majority's conclusion that "the excepted plaintiffs remaining under SLUSA, ... could still bring a significant amount of litigation" is overstated.

Nevertheless, the PSLRA and SLUSA permit specific but restricted classes of plaintiffs to maintain their causes of action in state court. In the absence of congressional intent to the contrary, those plaintiffs should be permitted to have the benefit of the fraud-on-the-market theory of reliance under our common law fraud doctrine.

(ii) The Roots and Meaning of the ECMH

Theories about public capital market behavior continue to evolve and continue to generate lively debate. While it is generally accepted that public capital markets are efficient in some sense, there is disagreement as to what it means to say that a market is efficient, and whether or why efficiency matters. Indeed, Warren Buffett anecdotally has proclaimed: "I'd be a bum in the street with a tin cup if the markets were efficient."[1]

---

1. Fortune, Apr. 3, 1995, at 68.

The following essays are intended to give you some perspective on the debate. They are adapted from Cunningham, From Random Walks to Chaotic Crashes: The Linear Genealogy of the Efficient Capital Market Hypothesis, 62 Geo. Wash. L. Rev. 546 (1994).

Economists developed the efficient capital market hypothesis in the mid-1960s as a way to explain several empirical studies that some economists thought proved successive changes in security prices are random. Based on those studies, many economists thought that there is no pattern to the price history of a security and therefore there can be no accurate prediction of future changes in security prices based on prior prices. This lack of pattern was the basis of the "random walk model" of security price behavior. The ECMH "explains" that model by hypothesizing that price changes occur as the result of changes in information concerning the security in question.

The Random Walk Model. In 1900 Louis Bachelier, a French mathematician, discovered that prices of securities traded on the French Bourse exhibited the property of a "random walk" process. In rough terms, a "random walk" process is one in which successive steps in the process are independent of prior steps in the process. The prosaic image of a drunk wandering across a football field gives you the idea of a random walk. *See* Malkiel, A Random Walk Down Wall Street (8th ed. 2003).

A more precise image is of the televised lottery drawings in which winning lottery numbers are determined by selecting numbered balls from a bin containing numerous balls with different numbers painted on them. The auditor retrieves a ball, records its number, and replaces the ball. The auditor does this a few more times, each time retrieving, recording and replacing. This process has the property of statistical independence because the numbers recorded after any retrieval indicate nothing about the numbers to be recorded subsequently. The resulting series of numbers are random and a listing of them is said to exhibit a random walk.

In the context of public capital markets, the fact that IBM common stock rises by $1 on Monday is said to tell you nothing about how its price will perform on Tuesday. This simple idea has proven enormously influential, and also controversial. Studies seeking to confirm or deny its truth have been conducted repeatedly over the decades since Bachelier's study. In an odd twist of intellectual history, however, Bachelier's work was virtually unnoticed by economists through the first half of the twentieth century. Maurice Kendall is sometimes credited with bringing the random walk model to the attention of economists in the early 1950s. But Bachelier's own work was not "discovered" by economists until the mid-1950s when Paul Samuelson and his colleagues at MIT stumbled on it in the course of doing other research.

Early Testing. The principal tests used to evaluate the truth or falsity of the random walk model of security price behavior were autocorrelation tests. These tests, which are also sometimes called serial correlation analysis, investigate whether specified data sequences move together to any degree. In the case of security prices, for example, price changes of a given security are recorded over a specified time period (say 1, 5 or more days) and a subsequent time period of the same length. These sequences, called time series data, are then compared with one another and examined to determine whether they move together to any degree (whether there is any "serial correlation"). The comparisons take the form of a mathematical calculation called correlation coefficients, which measure the degree to which the data are linearly related.

In effect, the time series of data is tested for correlation by fitting a straight line to the data and then calculating the correlation coefficient. A correlation coefficient equal to zero would constitute evidence that the data in the series had the property of "statistical independence" and correlation coefficients that are close to zero (but not equal to zero) indicate that the data are "uncorrelated." A time series of data is "random" if it is either independent or uncorrelated.

The autocorrelation analyses of the 1960s all resulted in correlation coefficients that did not differ significantly from zero. This meant that various series of actual securities market data were indistinguishable from various series of numbers generated by a random-number table, roulette wheel or other device of chance—such as lottery drawings. These findings had an important practical implication: traders cannot systematically make gains from speculative trading because, under these statistical properties, the best estimate of the future price of a security is its present price. In other words, if price changes follow the random walk model, the price change from Monday to Tuesday will not affect the probability that a particular price change will occur on Wednesday. Thus past price changes cannot be of help in predicting future price changes.

One long-known weakness of the statistical technique of autocorrelation is that the results can be skewed by a small number of extraordinary data in the time series. An alternative test that avoids this weakness is an analysis of "runs" in the data—an investigation of whether there is any persistence to the direction of successive changes.[11] Thus, instead of testing the correlation of numerical changes in the data in the series, the relationship of the direction of those changes is investigated. If price changes follow the random walk model, the number of sequences and reversals in time series data of security prices over time would be roughly equal. If the same direction persisted for a significant period, then the random walk model would be contradicted.

Professor Fama, one of the chief architects of the ECMH, found that in fact price changes tended to persist but nevertheless concluded that no trading rule or strategy could be derived with which to outperform the market consistently. Fama, The Behavior of Stock Market Prices, 38 J. Bus. 34 (1965). Accordingly, most everyone involved in the debate in the late 1960s agreed that the observed departures from randomness were negligible and believed that this constituted strong support for the random walk model.

Skeptics remained, however, and sought to disprove these results by designing trading strategies that would outperform the market. These trading strategies were the forerunner of the "chartist" or "technical" approach to security analysis and trading still prevalent today. These techniques study past prices (or other data) and seek to use it as a basis for predicting future prices. Chartists note that stock prices over time undulate between high points and low points, which they refer to as *resistance points*. Whenever a given stock's price trends downward towards the lower resistance point, technical analysts predict an upturn. Whenever the price approaches the higher resistance point, they predict a downturn. Not until a given stock's price has "broken through a resistance point" do they predict a new trading range with new resistance points.

Even though chartist trading strategies are commonly used by traders and recommended by investment advisors and brokers, many students of the random walk model and the ECMH think they are nonsense (and even refer to chartists as "witchdoctors"). They prefer a "fundamental" approach to security analysis and trading in which study is made of a company's business and financial position and prospects in search of information that will clarify the "intrinsic" value of the company's stock.

---

11. A "run" is a statistical term used in time series analysis and is defined by an absence of directional change in a statistic in the time series. Thus a new run begins any time the direction changes (*i.e.*, from negative to positive, positive to negative or unchanged to either negative or positive).

Nevertheless, it is important to recognize that a meaningful segment of investors adhere to what the chartists say. Therefore, when the price of a given stock trends downward towards its lower resistance point, many of these investors begin purchasing the stock thus creating upward pressure on its price. When the price of that stock trends upward towards its higher resistance point, many of these investors begin selling the stock thus creating downward pressure on its price. In other words, at times there are enough "believers" to make a chartist-predicted upturn or downturn in a given stock's price a self-fulfilling prophecy.

Development of the ECMH. Many have suggested that the ECMH developed in a peculiar manner uncommon in scientific development: the "proof" of the hypothesis came first, beginning with Bachelier in 1900 and proceeding through the wealth of studies reporting randomness in the early 1960s. Only then was a theory proposed to explain the randomness, beginning with the first explication of the ECMH (by Paul Samuelson in 1965).[12] Economists welcomed this "proof": the conditions necessary to produce it seemed tantalizingly near to those necessary to sustain a perfect market which, you will recall, is an important assumption underlying the CAPM.

For economists seeking empirical support concerning market conditions approximating the theoretical perfect market, the proof supporting the random walk model was very rich indeed. The perfect market is a heuristic invented by stipulating the numerous assumptions concerning a market referred to in our discussion of CAPM in section 5b(iii). These include complete divisibility of assets, the absence of transaction costs and differential tax rates, uniform borrowing and lending rates, as well as a large number of participants such that the actions of any individual participant cannot materially affect the market, participants are fully informed, have equal access to the market and act rationally. Under these assumptions, the perfect market model would predict precisely what the random walk model was implying: that prices of securities in the public capital markets should adjust instantaneously and accurately to new information concerning them.

That prediction was embodied in the ECMH as first propounded. In its broadest terms, the ECMH holds that the price of securities traded in public capital markets fully reflect all information concerning those securities. Under this broad statement, the ECMH explains more than the random walk model required: the random walk model holds simply that successive price changes are independent or uncorrelated while the ECMH explains that holding by saying that public security prices fully reflect all information—not just price histories—about a security. As a result, virtually since the emergence of the ECMH as an explanation of the random walk model, the ECMH has been divided into three forms.

Three Forms of the ECMH. The three forms of the ECMH are strong, semi-strong and weak. They were first proposed to classify empirical tests of price behavior given specified kinds of information.[13] The weak form tested the random walk model itself, using autocorrelation tests and run analysis to investigate whether past prices indicate anything about future prices. Semi-strong form testing investigated whether publicly

---

12. Samuelson, Proof That Properly Anticipated Prices Fluctuate Randomly, 6 Indus. Mgmt. Rev. 41 (1965). Samuelson won a Nobel prize in economics in 1970, the first American to be so honored.

13. Although Samuelson introduced the ECMH in 1965, the three forms of the ECMH were not introduced until 1970, when Eugene Fama published his classic work surveying efficient market scholarship. Fama, Efficient Capital Markets: A Review of Theory and Empirical Work, 25 J. Fin. 383 (1970) (crediting Harry Roberts with the idea for the three forms).

available information in addition to prices was reflected in prevailing prices. Strong form testing investigated whether private information was reflected in prevailing prices.

As the wealth of tests and discussion proceeded in the 1970s, the three forms of the ECMH came to be used to refer to the conclusions those tests suggested. The forms of the ECMH came to be specified as follows: the weak form holds that current security prices fully reflect all information consisting of past security prices; the semi-strong form holds that current security prices fully reflect all information that is currently publicly available; and the strong form holds that current security prices fully reflect all currently existing information (whether publicly available or not).[14]

The Efficiency Paradox. The basic proposition of the ECMH is therefore that information, defined in three categories, is swiftly digested and incorporated into prices. If true, however, then why would anyone spend the resources necessary to discover information? And if no one is willing to spend resources to discover information, then how will it come to be reflected in market prices? This conundrum is known as the efficiency paradox. (Is this what the *Basic* court was referring to in footnote 29 of its opinion?) Devotees of the ECMH sought to solve it by relaxing some of the bolder claims the ECMH makes. In particular, rather than claim that all information is instantaneously impounded into stock prices, efficiency should be seen as a relative matter. Markets are more efficient when more informed traders participate in information discovery and less efficient when fewer informed traders participate. Pure efficiency reigns only when all traders are fully-informed. *See* Grossman and Stiglitz, On the Impossibility of Informationally Efficient Markets, 70 Am. Econ. Rev. 393 (1980).

(iii) Empirical State of Play

The Joint Hypothesis Problem. Solving the efficiency paradox by recharacterizing efficiency in relative terms is consistent with categorizing the ECMH into three forms. Each of these forms has been tested separately, with varying results. One reason for the varying results may be inherent limitations on the ability to test the ECMH empirically. Every test of the ECMH or any of its forms must ask whether it is possible to use a specified information set to systematically achieve above-normal returns in trading. But this means we must have some basis for saying what normal returns in trading would be. We of course have such a basis: CAPM tells us what expected (meaning normal) returns are. Yet we have seen that empirical tests of CAPM have been inconclusive. Moreover, tests of CAPM make the assumption (or series of assumptions) that the market being investigated is a perfect (meaning efficient) market. The result is called the *joint hypothesis problem*: tests of the ECMH are conditional on the validity of CAPM and tests of CAPM are conditional on the validity of the ECMH!

Strong and Weak Form Testing. The joint hypothesis problem notwithstanding, tests of the ECMH have gone forward. Numerous studies have shown that corporate insiders and market specialists and others with private information can make superior returns

---

14. Professor Fama has proposed to modify this three-part categorization slightly: instead of "semi-strong form" tests he would use the term "event studies" to evaluate the adjustment of prices to public announcements; instead of "strong form" tests he would use the term "tests for private information"; and instead of "weak-form" tests, this category would be renamed and broadened to include all tests for "return predictability" (thus including in addition to tests based on past returns, tests based on other variables such as dividends and interest rates). Fama, Efficient Capital Markets II, 46 J. Fin. 1575, 1576-77 (1991).

by trading on that information.[15] The insider trading scandals of the 1980s offer proof positive that the strong form of the ECMH is false, and hardly anyone believes it, including plenty of foolish people who continue to trade in violation of laws prohibiting insider trading. On the other hand, plenty of studies tend to show that it is not possible to use price histories in any systematic way to make superior returns. This makes the weak form highly plausible, although a number of studies also show that certain kinds of historical price-related data can be used to make systematically superior gains. And empirical testing of the weak form continues with great vigor. *See* Fama, Efficient Capital Markets II, 46 J. Fin. 1575, 1609 (1991).

Semi-Strong Form Testing. The real action and controversy has centered on debate over the semi-strong form. Empirical tests investigate whether above-normal returns can be achieved using specified information sets that are publicly available. Many of these studies tend to support the ECMH by showing, for example, that new information is quickly reflected in prices so that it is not possible for most investors to use it systematically to generate above-normal returns. Also, many such studies show that the market is not fooled by changes in reported earnings based on changes in accounting conventions. Nevertheless, many studies have revealed numerous phenomena in public capital market trading that cannot be explained in terms of the ECMH. Many of these phenomena are the same sorts of things that, as we noted earlier, contradict CAPM and that CAPM cannot explain either. They are also called anomalies.

A relatively complete list of the anomalies is set forth in Lindgren, Telling Fortunes: Challenging the Efficient Markets Hypothesis by Prediction, 1 S. Cal. Interdisc. L.J. 7 (1992). Among these, in addition to those set forth in section 5b(iv) with respect to CAPM, are (1) the Value Line Investment Survey stock selections produce above-average returns; (2) above-normal returns on small capitalization stocks tend to occur in early January (this is known as the "January effect"); and (3) below-normal returns tend to occur on Monday (this is known as the "weekend effect"). There is yet other, quite surprising, evidence that factors such as hemlines and sporting news can be used successfully in forecasting market behavior! For example, if the winner of the Super Bowl was a team from the old National Football League, then the market rises during the year; otherwise, it falls! *See* Krueger and Kennedy, An Examination of the Super Bowl Stock Market Predictor, 45 J. Fin. 691 (1990). Relationships of this sort may of course be spurious, yet they do exist.

Beyond these and other anomalies, many recent studies have also demonstrated that there is simply too much trading activity in public capital markets to be attributable to information changes alone and therefore that something else is going on in markets for which the ECMH has no explanation. *E.g.,* Schiller, Market Volatility (1989). Moreover, dramatic drops in public capital markets—such as the October 1987 market crash and the October 1989 market break—cannot be explained in terms of the ECMH either. That is, the huge falls in overall market prices at such times cannot be explained in terms of new information that would justify the repricing witnessed on those days. As a result of these otherwise inexplicable phenomena, alternative explanations to the ECMH have emerged. They revive a debate to which you were introduced in section 1b: the firm foundation theory versus the castles-in-the-air-theory.

---

15. For a list, see Cunningham, From Random Walks to Chaotic Crashes: The Linear Genealogy of the Efficient Capital Market Hypothesis, 62 Geo. Wash. L. Rev. 546, 562 (1994). *See generally,* Macey, Efficient Capital Markets, Corporate Disclosure, And Enron, 89 Cornell L. Rev. 394 (2004); Ferrillo, Dunbar & Tabak, The "Less Than" Efficient Capital Markets Hypothesis: Requiring More Proof From Plaintiffs In Fraud-On-The-Market Cases, 78 St. John's L. Rev. 81 (2004).

In the contemporary formulation of this debate, the firm foundation theory is the conceptual ancestor of the ECMH. The castles-in-the-air-theory has been redefined by drawing a distinction between fundamental efficiency of the firm foundation variety on the one hand, and informational efficiency on the other. This distinction is embodied in a framework of public capital markets that goes by the name of noise theory.

(iv) Noise Theory

James Tobin explained that even if a public capital market is efficient in the sense of swiftly incorporating public information into security prices (i.e., the semi-strong form of the ECMH), that does not necessarily mean security prices in that market reflect fundamental values (i.e., the present value of expected future flows to securityholders). James Tobin, On the Efficiency of the Financial System, 153 Lloyds Bank Rev. 1 (1984).[16] The conceptual distinction Tobin makes between informational and fundamental efficiency dates to Keynes' beauty contest metaphor, discussed in section 1b. Recall that the best strategy for readers to adopt was to pick the contestants they thought others would pick (a "non-fundamental" method) rather than the contestant they thought should win on the merits (a "fundamental" method). John Maynard Keynes, The General Theory of Employment, Interest and Money 153-57 (1936). If Tobin is right, then the semi-strong form of the ECMH would itself have to be sub-divided and evaluated separately with respect to strict informational efficiency and a more refined notion of fundamental efficiency.

In this context, informational efficiency describes a market in which all public information about a security is reflected in the price of that security, without regard to the quality of that information. Thus, information that concerns the fundamental value of a security is reflected but so is information wholly unrelated to that fundamental value. This category could include all sorts of essentially extraneous data, but which has sometimes influenced trader actions, such as who won the Super Bowl and how hemline fashions are changing. Fundamental or allocative efficiency is then the more narrow proposition that security prices are accurate indicators of "intrinsic value" because what they reflect is strictly information concerning fundamental asset values.

The technical issue becomes whether the information-processing function of public capital markets is capable of distinguishing among kinds of information such that only information about fundamental value is impounded and reflected in stock prices. In human terms, the issue becomes the pervasive question whether human beings behave rationally.[17] The possibility that human beings behave irrationally has been resisted by economists for centuries, and is assumed out of modern financial theories, including portfolio theory, CAPM and the ECMH. However, the informational/fundamental distinction is so potent (both empirically and intuitively) that it had to be confronted. The result was the face-saving shelter of euphemism—Fischer Black, borrowing a term from the statistics literature, renamed irrational behavior "noise", thus enabling self-respecting economists to discuss the issue and try to model it. Black, Noise, 41 J. Fin. 529 (1986).

Noise theory models hold that the public capital markets are infected by substantial trading based on information unrelated to fundamental asset values ("noise trad-

---

16. Tobin won a Nobel Prize in Economics in 1981.
17. In the context of the ECMH, rational human behavior need not be strictly true at the individual level provided it is true in the aggregate—provided the result of the process is as if individuals had behaved rationally.

ing"). These models attempt both to explain why noise trading occurs and why its effects persist. The commonest noise theory model holds, for example, that noise trading is conducted by ill-informed investors and persists in keeping prices away from fundamental values because even sophisticated arbitragers will not fully arbitrage its influence away because (1) they are risk averse and (2) they cannot be sure that the misperceptions of the noise traders will not change adversely at any time. *See* De Long, et al., Noise Trader Risk in Financial Markets, 98 J. Pol. Econ. 703 (1990).

For other work on noise theory, see Cespa & Giovanni, A Comparison Of Stock Market Mechanisms, Rand J. Ec. 4803 (2004); Shleifer and Summers, The Noise Trader Approach to Finance, J. Econ. Persp., Spring 1990, at 19; Stiglitz, Symposium on Bubbles, J. Econ. Persp., Spring 1990, at 13; Tversky and Kahneman, Rational Choice and the Framing of Decisions, in Decision Making: Descriptive, Normative, and Prescriptive Interactions (David E. Bell et al. eds. 1988). For discussion of some of the implications of noise theory for securities regulation, see Langevoort, Theories, Assumptions, and Securities Regulation: Market Efficiency Revisited, 140 U. Pa. L. Rev. 851 (1992).

Questions

In what ways are the tensions between the ECMH and noise theory the same as or different from the tensions between the firm foundation theory and the castles-in-the-air-theory? Is noise theory simply an auxiliary model that, by explaining certain deviant phenomena, supplements but does not supplant the ECMH? Do you see a relationship between arbitrage pricing theory (discussed in Note 2 at the end of section 5b(v)) and noise theory? Does any such relationship parallel the relationship between CAPM and the ECMH?

d. Behavioral Finance

The development of noise theory has coalesced with a broader intellectual movement called behavioral finance. It blends realistic accounts of market action with insights from psychology. The following introduces the subject.

Cunningham, Behavioral Finance and Investor Governance
59 Wash. & Lee L. Rev. 767, 829-833 (2002)

Behavioral economics is emerging as an important new disciplinary adjunct to legal analysis. Encompassing a wide range of fields[,] ... behavioral economics shakes up thought and reorients scholarship laden by its progenitor, law and economics. Behavioral economics revises the received wisdom that assumed the bounded but substantial rationality of human actors and prescribed legal rules and social norms according to sterile abstractions that bore little resemblance to actual human beings, but which could be modeled in elegant and simple ways. As a result, the encrusted models have been injected with more realistic accounts of complex human behavior originally mapped in the field of cognitive psychology, subsequently adapted by economists, and lately imported by legal scholars.

One corner of this behavioral orientation ... examines the pricing of stocks in public capital markets. The knowledge being generated from this investigation has significant implications for the field of corporate governance. Corporate law and economics assume that prices of publicly traded stocks constitute the best estimate of the value of the ownership interest in the businesses they represent....

A set of cultural beliefs accompany the view that stock markets are efficient in terms of accurately pricing business value. Chief among these is the belief that the stock market itself operates as a disciplining device on corporate managers. The theory is that a company's stock price is an accurate and transparent report card on its performance: a manager who performs poorly will see his company's stock price fall and be held accountable.

* * *

[A] subdiscipline of behavioral economics has blossomed, enervating the thirty-year-old tenets of the efficient market story. Called behavioral finance, this discipline rests on two foundations. The first holds that a substantial amount of stock pricing is performed by investors who do not accurately perceive underlying business values and hence produce prices that do not reflect those values. Investor sentiment, rather than rational economic calculation, contributes significantly to price formation. The second holds that even those investors who do accurately perceive underlying business values will not always step in to offset the sentiments of those who do not because they face risks too great for such an undertaking. This limited arbitrage, when coupled with investor sentiment, yields pricing that does not equate to value, and the managerial report card seen in prices turns out often to be inaccurate, even if it remains translucent.

In the world of behavioral finance, no longer can the social or legal culture be content to rely upon market mechanisms to do the work of managerial discipline. Neither the market for corporate control nor that for managerial labor is as potent in the behavioral finance story as it was in the world where efficient stock markets ruled. Fiduciary duties, disclosure, and accounting play an important role in holding managerial feet to the fire. Capital structure and allocation decisions are far more flexible and unrestrained; dividend policy, the debt/equity mix, and stock repurchases all matter as substantive decisions and manifestations of managerial probity and intelligence. As under the efficient market theory, investors may justly rely upon market prices in allocating their investment capital. That reliance, however, remains functionally irrelevant to legal questions concerning whether a management that misleads investors should be found liable even to investors who do not directly rely on misleading information.

Commentators have predicted the death of the efficient market idea for a number of years, but the idea has held onto breath even as research steadily reveals its fatal infirmities....

Theoretical challenges to the EMH question the assumed rationality of investors. Drawing on the pioneering work of cognitive psychologists Amos Tversky and Daniel Kahneman in during the 1970s, by the mid-1980s economists speculated that many traders act, not on information, but on hunch, and that the market absorbs rationality of calculation no more than it does mere noise. More recent theorizing on investor behavior has considered the nature of investor attitudes towards risk and explanations of investors' preference for attention and memory over probabilistic analysis; further, researchers have considered how the influences of autonomous brain activity can produce judgments outside of a person's awareness.

In terms of assessing risk, investors tend not to look at levels of final wealth attainable but at gains or losses relative to a reference point. The path can be more important than the end. When considering the assumption of risk, people display loss aversion, a tendency to place an asymmetrically greater weight on losses than on gains. Investors epitomize this aversion in their reluctance to sell stocks that have suffered substantial losses and in the puzzlingly high premium returns attributable to investments in equity compared to fixed-income securities.

Related to the way reference points are created is how they influence solutions. People make different decisions depending on the framing of the problem. This frame dependence manifests itself in the observed tendency of experimental subjects to allocate more to stocks when they are shown long-term histories of high returns than when they are shown short-term histories of substantial price volatility.

Attention and memory capabilities are often incorrect, but people rely on them to such a degree as to suggest that they believe these capabilities are infallible. Thus, people constantly violate probability theory, including basic principles of Bayesian logic and statistics. One tendency is to predict by projecting a long future pattern based on a short recent history rather than to realize that the short recent history could be due to chance rather than to any emerging pattern. A good example is the late 1990s tendency to interpret several years, or even quarters, of earnings growth as portending high rates of earnings growth for years to come.

These tendencies and numerous related biases may exist across all groups of investors, from do-it-yourself individuals to sophisticated hedge fund managers. If so, these tendencies would undercut claims that nonrational investors are canceled out by rational investors. On the contrary, it is possible that these nonrational tendencies are imitated by other investors and the biases instantiated. This is especially possible when investors act as agent rather than principal and therefore worry more about the measure of their performance against their institutional peers. This promotes distortion rather than enabling investors to offset the noise. Nor can arbitrageurs be counted on. Effective arbitrage requires close substitutes for the good being arbitraged, and there are not always close (and hardly ever perfect) substitutes for securities.

The empirical challenges to the EMH were pioneered as early as 1981 by Robert Shiller, who showed that there is too much price volatility for the EMH to hold true. The studies continued, challenging the EMH at its every level....

Further, anomalies galore infect the EMH's claim about public information (called semi-strong form efficiency)....

Concerning the more general EMH claim that there should be no reactions to noninformation, it is common to note that the stock market crash of 1987 continues to have no identifiable justifying cause, nor do virtually any other major market moves of dramatic proportions....

* * *

.... The cautionary bell sounded against the EMH has been rung before, and many investors appear to be listening. Yet the attraction of the EMH's simplicity and elegance remains, not only among scholars, but also among courts and regulators. One reason for the time lag between the output of economic scholarship and its absorption by lawyers may be the current lack of a coherent model of market behavior that accounts for and incorporates criticisms of the EMH. Much of the economics literature critiquing the EMH demonstrated weaknesses or anomalies in the model rather than developing an integrated alternative view. Researchers have started to fill that void, however, and the next subpart demonstrates a version of the model that will be useful to corporate and securities law scholars as well as policymakers in evaluating a range of rules and the assumptions on which they are grounded.

These theoretical and empirical challenges to the EMH have been combined and deepened in the broader context of well-known behavioral phenomena. These traits can be seen in action in market behavior that we observe. When synthesized, they offer an attractive and general account of a range of typical market activities that the EMH struggles to explain.

The late Fischer Black ... developed a theory in the mid-1980s based on the idea that ill-informed traders (called "noise" traders) populated the market. This was a major intellectual challenge, given the dominance of efficiency theory at the time. In the noise-trader model, ill-informed traders cause mispricing of stocks and a risk for arbitrageurs that leaves mispricing in place. The trouble with Black's model was that it reached too far, providing an explanation for any kind of trading imaginable, whether or not it occurred. A better model would explain only those things that are actually observed.

Researchers building on Black's insights developed a more refined model called the "positive feedback model." Markets experience momentum, the researchers found, when new purchases are made based on recent purchases and new sales are made based on recent sales. Price changes in one direction bring pressure in that direction. This model captures the psychological phenomenon of "extrapolating trends," the notion of assuming that trends that have progressed a certain way for a period will keep going that way a while longer.

Although useful to describe extraordinary market phenomena such as bubbles and breaks, the noise-trader and positive feedback models do not address the more routine shifts between the continuation (and chasing) of trends and the correction. Refinements would also need to explain short-term continuations met by ultimate reversals.

More dynamic accounts attempt to explain both the extraordinary bubble-break phenomena and the quotidian cycles. These models are built on the premise that investors hold mistaken beliefs and make bad judgments—the behavioral finance story. Dynamic market accounts explain shifts between investor underreaction and overreaction. The main model begins by viewing investors as sharing mistaken beliefs and bad judgment. The dominant psychological forces at play are the status quo bias and the pattern-seeking bias, along with a hefty dose of overconfidence. Investors learn about their performance and what they are capable of doing in biased, self-promoting ways.

When they digest information to form a judgment, investors are not entirely sure of the precision of their analysis, but consider it reliable enough to be a basis for action. Subsequent news either confirms or refutes their judgment. Investors pat themselves on the back too much and kick themselves too little. News that confirms the judgment is seen as so powerful that investors become more confident in their ability than is justified. When news refutes the judgment, confidence wavers, but less than warranted. So bad news breeds conservatism, and good news breeds pattern seeking.

There are two versions of the "shared mistaken beliefs" model. In one, individuals digest company news as favorable, buy its stock, and see the price rise. As new information arrives that seems to confirm the accuracy of the judgment, the price rises further. Many participants do the same thing, pushing price ahead of the increase that the news justified. Investors begin to see that. A return to a more reasonable self-perception ensues, and the price settles back to a level more in line with the news. There is smoothness to the process of this hump-shaped price evolution, yielding short-term positive price trends met by long-term reversals.

* * *

The propensity of people to overlook basic lessons from statistics supports this model. When two variables are imperfectly related, extreme values on one tend to be matched by less extreme values on the other. As examples, tall parents on average have tall children but not as tall as they are; straight A high school students tend to do well in college but not quite as well as they did in high school (on average); and a company's low profit years tend to be followed by better ones and vice versa. In investing, people often get this last example backwards. Instead they believe they see trends stretching into future quarters after witnessing steady profit increases in each of the prior three quarters.

In the second version of the shared mistaken beliefs model, underreaction and over-reaction are explained by a more involved story. This story supposes earnings of a particular company (or all companies) to be random. Earnings could be up one quarter, or down, just as the flipping of a coin could be heads or tails. But investors don't fully understand probability theory and tend to substitute rules of thumb. If investors view the world this way, then it would be no surprise for them to believe (wrongly) that an earnings-trend reverse—say a series of ten-cent increases followed by a five-cent decline—signal a normal reality check (reversion to the mean). They thus underreact to the news, exhibiting status quo bias (conservatism).

The result is underreaction during short horizons and overreaction longer term. As with the hump-shaped picture in the first version of this model, the process can be quite smooth. It is also the case that the same misperceptions that drive momentum in one direction drive the longer-term reversal. That means stocks with the largest pricing momentum should get the largest pricing reversal and that stocks of businesses facing greater uncertainty should register more mispricing.

Other cognitive biases supplement this model of investor behavior. First, people who have chosen a voluntary course of action tend to resist evidence that it was ill-chosen. This commitment bias entails an unconscious shift in attitudes and beliefs to preserve consistency with the original decision. It reinforces the conservatism, or status quo bias, of individual investors who have purchased a particular stock. It also helps to explain why people cling to stocks whose fundamentals have obviously deteriorated.

Second, people tend to develop self-serving beliefs, making inferences from new data that enable them to see what they want to see. This bias reinforces both the underreaction to news associated with conservatism and the overreaction to cumulated recurring news associated with representativeness. In each case, the bias causes investors to see small changes as of low relevance and a series of them as having great relevance.

Third, overconfidence bias pertains to the pervasive tendency of people to think that they know more than they do and otherwise to overrate their own abilities. Common examples are that eighty percent of drivers think they are better than average drivers, and despite a divorce rate of fifty percent newly married couples invariably believe that they will beat the odds. For investors, overconfidence bias manifests itself in the tendency to construe investing success as confirmation of their own abilities even when the results are not due to any particular research, insight, or skill. This bias includes a tendency to underestimate the role that chance or luck played in the process and is often coupled with the commitment and self-serving beliefs biases just noted.

Reinforcing these biases and their effects is the availability bias. This describes the tendency of people to overweight events or circumstances that are at one's fingertips, as it were, be they recent, or well-publicized, or traumatic, or vivid. The risk of unprovoked shark attacks on humans, for example, remains far lower than commonly thought or than portrayed in the news media. Likewise, the risk of homicidal death is far lower than death from diabetes or stomach cancer, yet surveys routinely show that people believe the opposite. This impressionistic behavior helps explain the appeal of sector funds and other capital allocation decisions that appear upon rational reflection to make little sense. Recall the late 1990s, when the Internet was the fetish of conversation and investors flocked to tech companies in droves.

The interplay of various cognitive biases shows familiar patterns of price formation. One commonly observed phenomenon in market pricing histories is the occurrence of short-term trends followed by longer run trend reversals. The short-term trends are a product of underreaction to individual bits of information not seen as significant and are explained by the conservatism bias (the slow updating of beliefs in the face of new information). The longer term reversals of those trends are a product of overreaction to cumulated bits of information perceived as manifesting conspicuous patterns and are explained by the representative heuristic.

These trends and reversals pose undesirable price-value deviations that, although not cataclysmic, distort the capital allocation process. Other combinations of these biases can have devastating effects. Overconfidence plus representativeness, for example, can lead to feedback loop bubbles in prices. Feedback loops describe a category of observed investment phenomena including instances of price momentum, in which prices continue moving persistently in the same direction despite either no or opposite changes in fundamentals.

As prices drive upward, investors who recently bought those stocks see their judgment as being vindicated, forming beliefs about their expertise. As the prices move yet higher, investors detect a pattern of price increases. Overconfidence confirms the trend: more buying ensues and other biases—commitment and self-serving beliefs—reinforce each other in an upward spiral, or bubble.

There are, of course, separate and external causes to the spirals caused by overconfidence and representativeness. These include investors chasing trends or chasing each other. These loops can be fed by rumor, widespread publicity attendant to new technologies, or other social forces that trigger the availability bias. They produce cascading chain reactions that reinforce each successive link. These reactions often lure substantial numbers of new investors to the market, increase the dollar amount of new and borrowed funds invested, and force up trading volume and price volatility.

Technical trading strategies adopted by some investors often exacerbate feedback loops. These strategies include stop-loss orders that automatically trigger selling on price declines and margin calls that result in the involuntary liquidation of all or part of a leveraged portfolio in a declining market. A conspicuous example of a feedback-loop aggravator was the so-called portfolio insurance popular among institutional investors in the 1980s before the crash of 1987. A portfolio insurance program known as a "programmed trading directive" (much like a stop-loss order but on a vaster scale) commanded the selling of stocks as their prices fell. Cascades resulted; as the falling prices triggered the "insurance" sale, prices fell further in a downward spiral.

More generally, an entire class of investment phenomena rooted in the cognitive biases just discussed and called extrapolative expectations can set in when price declines (or rises) lead to expectations of further price declines (or rises). The expectations then become self-fulfilling prophecies. Narrative histories of price bubbles throughout financial history show this pattern repeatedly.

For several reasons, sophisticated traders cannot eliminate the price-value discrepancies this behavior creates. First, all investors, even sophisticated traders, suffer from these biases to some degree. Second, even rational traders cannot escape the wrath of the biased errors. Third, securities lack good substitutes that enable the kind of risk arbitrage that perfectly—or even substantially—efficient markets require. Fourth, in these patterns it becomes a rational choice for arbitrageurs and other "smart money" to join the crowd rather than to try to beat it. Far from stepping in to correct the mistakes of the noise trader, arbitrageurs in the ballooning of such bubbles can make more money by participating in the rise by buying on the way up and attempting to sell before the fall down. Accordingly, not only does investor sentiment drive the final nail into the EMH's coffin, this "limited arbitrage" offers the eulogy.

All these phenomena also point to a more general attribute of investors in public capital markets: they operate in these cognitive biases differently. Some display one bias more than another. Others can more easily recognize themselves as about to commit one and avoid it. When people operate under the conservatism or representativeness heuristic, their methods differ. In short, people exhibit different preferences for the same thing, an observation in tension with the usual story of the EMH and the general story of rational choice theory.

The net results of these behavioral phenomena in financial economic thought are theoretical, empirical, and psychological accounts showing that stock prices systematically deviate from values. The story of the EMH turns out to be like a fairy tale in the sense that it would be wonderful if it were true. It would be wonderful because the equation of price and value promotes optimal asset allocation, thus deploying the capital market resources of society in their most effective capacities.

Desirable policies tend to align the reality with the ideal. Recognizing justifiable skepticism that the ideal will ever be realized, behavioral finance implies a two-part program: one part that promotes the aspirational tale and another that addresses the distance that remains between the reality and that goal.

Notes and Questions

1. How should corporate law respond to theories of capital market behavior? What implications do alternative theories hold for how corporate law defines directorial fiduciary duties? If the ECMH were an accurate account of stock market behavior, would that be a basis to define those duties as requiring the maximization of stock price? If noise theory were an accurate account of stock market behavior, would that be a basis to define those duties as requiring the maximization of the firm according to fundamental valuation techniques? If we cannot be sure whether either is an accurate account, what standard of obligation should be chosen?

2. How helpful is it to define the efficiency of stock markets in relative terms? *See* Gilson and Kraakman, The Mechanisms of Market Efficiency, 70 Va. L. Rev. 549 (1984). In terms of the three forms of the ECMH, markets can be efficient with respect to certain information (such as stock price histories) and inefficient with respect to

other kinds of information (such as private information). Professors Gilson and Kraakman developed a typology of information sets on which different kinds of investors trade that they believe corresponds to the three forms. Universally informed trading is based on widely disseminated information such as current events and past stock prices and corresponds to the semi-strong form. Professionally informed trading is based on quasi-public information, most accessible to market professionals but not necessarily the general public and corresponds to the weak form. Derivatively informed trading is based on private information, such as that known only to corporate insiders, and corresponds to the strong form. Uninformed trading is based on hunches and intuition related to forecasts and predictions. Gilson and Kraakman also link this to the strong form.

Together these categories of information, trading and investors constitute the mechanisms of market efficiency, according to Gilson and Kraakman. What turns out to be important for the relative efficiency of the market, in addition to the initial distribution of information, is how and by whom new information is retrieved and digested. This in turn hinges on the cost of discovering information. Is this way of understanding the mechanisms of market efficiency helpful? How could it be used as a practical matter?

3. How important is efficiency? Should improving the efficiency of stock markets be an objective of legal policymaking? Many believe that it should and debate legal rules governing such things as insider trading, corporate disclosure, and tender offers, in terms of whether they promote or impair stock market efficiency. See Stout, The Unimportance of Being Efficient: An Economic Analysis of Stock Market Pricing and Securities Regulation, 87 Mich. L. Rev. 613 (1988). Professor Stout argues that debating corporate and securities law policy in terms of stock market efficiency is misguided because insufficient evidence supports the claim that stock markets are important in determining how capital is allocated. Do you agree that the stock market plays an unimportant role in allocating capital? Should you distinguish between the market for new securities issues from secondary market trading and from the issuance of securities by more seasoned companies? Does that distinction make a difference for purposes of the capital allocation function? If bond markets are less efficient than stock markets, should you distinguish between debt and equity? Does that distinction make a difference? See generally Stout, supra. Cf. Kahan, Securities Laws and the Social Costs of "Inaccurate" Stock Prices, 41 Duke L.J. 977 (1992).

4. In re Glosser Bros., Inc., 555 A.2d 129 (Pa. Super. 1989), was a cross appeal from a judicial determination of the fair value of appellee's stock in Glosser Bros., Inc. (the "Company"), following a management buyout of the Company.

Before the buyout, 50-60% of the Company's stock was closely held by management and the Glosser family, and the balance was listed on the American Stock Exchange. In determining the value of the stock, the trial judge assigned 65% weight to the Company's asset value and 35% weight to its investment value.

The Company objected to, among other things, the trial court's refusal to give any weight to the stock's market value based on its trading price on the American Stock Exchange. The appellate court agreed with the Company. After describing the general process of valuation (and approving the Weinberger approach discussed supra section 4a(i) for use in Pennsylvania valuation proceedings), the court wrote:

> Thus, market value is relevant to a determination of the true intrinsic value of stock on a going concern basis whenever it is reliable, i.e. whenever it represents the amount that a willing buyer is willing to pay for the stock and the amount for which a willing seller is willing to sell the stock in an open and free

market. Market value becomes less relevant as its reliability decreases and may in fact properly be deemed irrelevant where it provides no reliable information as to the true value of the stock.

* * *

[M]arket value is to be totally disregarded in determining fair value only in a limited number of situations. That is, market value is to be entirely disregarded where there is competent and substantial evidence to support the conclusion that the value at which the stock is trading is not at all reliable in gauging the stock's intrinsic going concern value.

Applying this standard to the case *sub judice,* we find that the trial court erred in concluding that market value should be totally disregarded. We arrive at this conclusion despite our cognizance of the fact that the record reveals that the market value of the Company's stock is of limited importance in assessing the stock's fair value.

The trial court justified its refusal to consider market value on the following grounds:

> ... to consider the market value approach as a valid valuation method would be improper because the corporation ... was closely held and it was not traded on the open market as a result of national research being done on the history of the Company, and as such, did not and could not reflect its true value. Nearly half of the outstanding shares were held by relatives of the Glosser family or management personnel.

* * *

We concur in the conclusion that the fact that a high percentage of the outstanding shares of a corporation are closely held by one entity or group can indicate that the market value of the remaining shares is an unreliable guide to true value.... We also agree that thin trading in the remaining shares decreases the reliability of market value.... However, under the precise facts of this case, it is unwarranted to conclude that *no* weight is to be accorded market value.

Here, only 50-60% of the stock was closely held, as compared to the 80-100% levels of control that existed in those cases where market value has been disregarded. Although trading in the remaining Company stock was admittedly thin, the stock was listed on a national exchange and was steadily traded. Moreover, ... this is not a case where there was any evidence of manipulation of the market or the exercise of control of the market by the family and management group. Finally, we do not see the relevance of the lack of "national research" having been done on the Company's stock. It would unquestionnably [sic] open a Pandora's box were we to require the trial court in every appraisal matter to investigate how much independently generated investment information was available concerning a listed stock before it was traded in order to determine how accurately the market was reflecting the stock's value....

Based on your understanding of the ECMH, is the court correct? Is its reasoning sound? Reconsider footnote 27 of the Court's opinion in *Basic, supra.*

5. CAPM and the ECMH have been increasingly used to evaluate the merits of securities fraud claims. The technique is an *event study,* used to assess whether some allegedly fraudulent disclosure or nondisclosure had a cognizable impact on the price at which a

security traded. The methodology, in brief, is as follows. First, identify the allegedly fraudulent statement or omission (called an "event"); second, define the time period over which that statement was made or the omission occurred (an "event window"); and third, compare the actual price change in that period with the price change that would have been predicted by CAPM in the absence of the event. On the technique generally and its application, see Mitchell and Netter, The Role of Financial Economics in Securities Fraud Cases: Applications at the Securities and Exchange Commission, 49 Bus. Law. 545 (1994). For criticism, see Cunningham, Capital Market Theory, Mandatory Disclosure and Price Discovery, 51 Wash. & Lee L. Rev. 843 (1994); Fisch, Picking a Winner (Review of The Genius of American Corporate Law, by Roberta Romano), 20 J. Corp. L. 451 (1995).

Note: Post-Modern Finance Theory

Does it seem difficult for you to believe that an objective observer of prevailing theoretical debates about public capital market behavior could be satisfied? Has the state of debate ultimately advanced significantly beyond the old debate between the firm foundation theorists and the castles-in-the-air theorists? It does seem that the developments over the past few decades in portfolio theory, CAPM and ECMH have been important in many respects, even if shortcomings remain. These theories have been collectively referred to as modern finance theory. As theories of capital market behavior continue to evolve, perhaps we should begin to call them post-modern finance theory. As far as we know, we are the first to make this suggestion, but it has a certain appeal. We would include in post-modern finance theory the arbitrage pricing theory—at least in some forms—and noise theory because each seeks to break out of the rational expectations paradigm and associated limitations to which CAPM and the ECMH are subject.

We would also include in this category an entirely new theory of public capital market behavior, called chaos theory. This theory has yet to be widely incorporated into mainstream finance textbooks but we and others believe that it offers the potential to improve understanding of public capital market behavior. Chaos theory comes from a branch of modern physics holding that there is pattern to the seeming randomness of physical events occurring in the universe, such as weather systems. It is therefore a misleading name: it does not mean disorder or confusion but rather the appearance of disorder masking great stability and order.

In the context of public capital markets, chaos theory accepts the basic point of the ECMH that firm-oriented information is absorbed and used by market participants in a way that affects stock prices. It also accepts the basic point of noise theory that other kinds of information are also incorporated into prices by uninformed market participants and other noise traders. Chaos theory adds to these propositions one further point, built on the distinction drawn in noise theory between these two kinds of information. It is the suggestion that capital markets are *feedback systems* in which this wide variety of information is digested and the results of that process create more information, and that gets digested, and so on. The result of such a feedback system is that the process is nonlinear, rather than linear as CAPM and the ECMH necessarily assume. And it is this insistence on linearity that contributes to the difficulties inherent in CAPM and the ECMH.

By *linear*, chaos theory means proportionality in the sense that a change in one variable causes a proportionate change in another variable. This is the point of CAPM's assertion that the expected risk premium varies in direct proportion to beta and the ECMH's assertion that information changes result in swift and unbiased price changes.

In contrast, a *nonlinear* function is one in which the relationship between variables is not necessarily proportional but is usually exponential. And we observe those sorts of relationships in many of the anomalies for which neither CAPM nor the ECMH can account and in the kinds of excessive trading activity that noise theory seeks to explain.

From the proposition that public capital markets are nonlinear systems, the relationship of price changes over time can be reexamined. Except rather than investigate for linear dependence in price changes over time—as did all the early tests of the ECMH in the 1960s and 1970s—the tests seek to determine whether there is nonlinear dependence in price changes over time. A number of studies have shown that there is nonlinear dependence in price changes over time. *See* E. Peters, Chaos and Order in the Capital Markets (1992). This is inconsistent with the ECMH and can also not be explained by noise theory. It is also inconsistent with CAPM and therefore calls for new ways of seeking to measure risk. A branch of nonlinear mathematics called fractal theory has been employed to seek such alternative measures of risk. *See* E. Peters, Fractal Market Analysis (1994).

The consequences of this way of investigating and understanding public capital market behavior are still being pursued and much work remains to be done. But, given the difficulties in testing and proving CAPM and the ECMH, the work may prove worthwhile. For more elaborate discussions of chaos theory in capital markets and its perceived implications for various corporate and securities law issues, *see* Stout, Corporate Finance: How Efficient Markets Undervalue Stocks: CAPM And ECMH Under Conditions Of Uncertainty And Disagreement, 19 Cardozo L. Rev. 475 (1997); Roe, Chaos And Evolution In Law And Economics, 109 Harv. L. Rev. 641 (1996); Cunningham, From Random Walks to Chaotic Crashes: The Linear Genealogy of the Efficient Capital Market Hypothesis, 62 Geo. Wash. L. Rev. 546 (1994); Crowell & Peters, Chaos Theory Weakens Efficient Market Idea, Pensions & Investments, June 10, 1991, at 14; Lehmann, Fads, Martingales and Market Efficiency, 105 Q. J. Econ. 1, 25 (1990).

Chapter 4

Managing Risk (Hedging) with Derivatives

The lesson of portfolio theory from the preceding chapter is that nonsystematic risks on investment securities can be eliminated by diversifying a portfolio of investments. That lesson is instructive for the perspective of the investor as a participant from outside the firm. In this chapter we turn inward to the firm to consider the variety of business and financial risks that corporate managers face as a constant part of operating the corporation and techniques for managing those risks. Those risks include changes in a firm's raw materials and product markets, interest rate changes in its lending and borrowing markets, default risk of those to whom it extends credit, and foreign exchange changes in its currency markets.

Corporate managers and their financial advisors have always had available a number of instruments to reduce those risks (i.e., "hedge," as in "hedging your bets"). For example, an airline could limit the risk of jet fuel increases by entering into a long-term supply contract that limits price escalations. Or a real estate developer could limit the risk of interest rate increases by borrowing at fixed rates.

These instruments — referred to as "derivatives" — and variations on them have proliferated in recent decades and have become standard tools for hedging, or minimizing, these risks. They are not, however, new. Indeed, Thirteenth Century shipping merchants in Venice during the time of Marco Polo are reputed to have bought and sold option contracts to protect the value of cargoes enroute by ship to and from Asia.[1]

Derivative instruments are "derivative" in nature because their value at any point in time is *derived from the value of some other asset*, the potential fluctuation in which creates the risk to be hedged. The aspiration in using these devices is to perfectly match the downside potential of one's position (rising fuel prices or interest rates, for example) with the upside potential of one's position (such as falling fuel prices or interest rates).

Investors, however, use derivative instruments for speculative purposes in addition to risk reduction. That is, investors may use derivatives to place bets on, among other things, the future direction of a given stock's price, or the movement of a particular financial variable, such as an interest rate or a currency exchange rate. During the early-1990s, betting through the use of derivatives financially impaired, or brought on the complete demise, of many otherwise viable companies, and even resulted in the bankruptcy of the famed "O.C." — Orange County, California. This led to a period of "derivaphobia," as public outcry led government regulators to seek to reign in the use of derivatives for speculative purposes.[2]

---

1. *See* Braddock, Derivatives Demystified, at v (1997).
2. *See id.* at vi-viii.

We consider here the four building blocks of derivative instruments: options, forwards, futures and swaps. Although some of these—such as futures contracts and swap contracts—may be new to you, the basic concepts underlying most of them will be familiar to you from your contracts course. In this discussion we build on those basics and explore ways in which these devices operate in corporate practice, how they may be used to hedge risks and how they are priced in the market. Thereafter, we look at some of the hazards such devices pose for the incautious or imprudent and what can be done about that.

Section 1
Types of Derivative Instruments

a. Options

(i) Overview

An option contract gives its holder the right (but not the obligation) to buy from or sell to the option writer (also known as the "counterparty") a specified asset, on or before a specified expiration or maturity date, for a specified price. The main emphasis is on the "right," not the "obligation." An option holder can choose to exercise the option or not. However, this right is not free. The option holder must pay a price—the *option premium*—for the option to the option writer.

Options are ubiquitous and are the most commonly used derivative instrument. For example, stock options are a common form of executive compensation (though these options are not publicly traded). Warrants are quasi-equity instruments that companies issue that give their holders the right to buy common stock in those companies (company-issued call options in the hands of investors). As we will see in chapter 7, convertible bonds carry a right to interest and principal repayment, but also give the holder an option to buy common stock from the company (preferred stock can likewise be made convertible for common). Bonds can be made puttable, meaning the holder has the option of requiring the issuer to buy them back. Callable bonds carry a right in the issuer to do so. And even common stock in a company with outstanding debt can be conceptualized as an option: the common (acting through the corporation's board) has the option to buy the debt (pay it off) or default! (Default effectively allows the stockholders to put the company to the debtholders.)

Investors seeking to acquire options can do so either in the private or public markets. The private market (referred to as the "over-the-counter" or "OTC" market) for options consists of individuals acquiring custom-tailored options that meet their particular needs, most typically risk reduction. The option holder's counterparty is normally a brokerage house or investment bank.

The public market for options, by contrast, consists of individuals and institutions seeking to hedge positions or engage in speculation. Instead of the options being custom-tailored, they are written by investors in accordance with guidelines established by the Chicago Board Options Exchange (CBOE (often pronounced "C-BO")). Uniformity is required because these options are listed for trading purposes. They can be bought or sold prior to their maturity based on the investment appetites of those who engage in options trading. For purposes of nomenclature, a publicly traded call option written on shares of IBM common stock with a strike price of $45 and a maturity date in January would be called the "IBM 45 January calls."

Options are comprised of the following five key variables or terms:

(1) The underlying asset upon which the option is written;

(2) Whether the option is a "put" or "call";

(3) The "strike" or "exercise" price of the option;

(4) The expiration or maturity date of the option; and

(5) The manner in which the option can be exercised.

Underlying Assets. Almost any asset can serve as the underlying asset of an option. This includes goods, real estate, intellectual property, securities and contractual rights. Most typical in the financial arena are options written on common stocks. Many other financial instruments, however, can support options, such as bonds and stock indices (e.g., the S&P 500).

Calls and Puts. Options are either "call" options or "put options."

A *call* option gives its holder the right to *buy* (or "call away," hence the term "call") the underlying asset on which that option is written from the counterparty at a specified price, called the *strike* or *exercise price*, on or before a specified date, called the *expiration* or *maturity date*. If the current market price or *spot price* of the underlying asset rises above the strike price during the term of the option, the call option becomes intrinsically valuable. The reason for this is simple. Having the right to buy a particular asset at a price below the current market price is valuable. You can exercise the option at the lower strike price and then resell the asset at the higher current market price and pocket the difference. In speculative terms, a call option is a bet that the spot price of the underlying asset will rise above the strike price of the option during the option's term.

When the spot price of the asset underlying a call option rises above the option's strike price, the option is referred to as "*in-the-money*" (i.e., it is intrinsically valuable). When that spot price exactly equals the call option's strike price, the option is "*at-the-money*." Finally, when that spot price is below the call option's strike price, the option is "*out-of-the-money*."

For illustrative purposes, suppose a hedge fund manager buys a call option on a 20-year T-Bond bearing an 8% coupon at $76 through Sept. 19 paying $1.50. The following table shows the payoff matrix for this call option.

Call Option Payoff

T-bond Price on Sept. 19	Gross Payoff on Option	Net Payoff on Option
60	0.0	-1.5
70	0.0	-1.5
75	0.0	-1.5
76	**0.0**	**-1.5**
77	1.0	-0.5
78	2.0	0.5
79	3.0	1.5
80	4.0	2.5
90	14.0	12.5
100	24.0	22.5

A *put* option gives its holder the right to *sell* (or "put to," hence the term "put") the underlying asset on which that option is written to the counterparty at the strike price on or before the expiration date. If the spot price of the underlying asset falls below the strike price during the term of the option, the put option becomes intrinsically valuable. The reason for this is simple. Having the right to sell a particular asset at a price above the current market price is valuable for obvious reasons. In speculative terms, a put option is a bet that the spot price of the underlying asset will drop below the strike price of the option during the option's term.

When the spot price of the asset underlying a put option falls below the option's strike price, the option is referred to as "*in-the-money.*" When that spot price exactly equals the put option's strike price, the option is "*at-the-money.*" Finally, when that spot price is above the put option's strike price, the option is "*out-of-the-money.*"

Consider the buyer of a put option on the same Treasury bond described above. The exercise price is $76. It can be exercised from now until Sept. 19. Assume the put costs $2.00. As the following table shows, sellers of put or call options face the exact opposite payoffs of buyers of put or call options.

Put Option Payoff

T-bond Price on Sept. 19	Gross Payoff on Option	Net Payoff on Option
60	16.0	14.0
70	6.0	4.0
75	1.0	-1.0
76	**0.0**	**-2.0**
77	0.0	-2.0
78	0.0	-2.0
79	0.0	-2.0
80	0.0	-2.0
90	0.0	-2.0
100	0.0	-2.0

Option Writers. Sellers of options are referred to as *option writers.* Their positions are said to be "written calls" or "written puts," as the case may be. For sellers of puts and calls, the upside is limited to the option's premium. For sellers of call options, the downside is unlimited (the higher the spot price of the underlying asset, the more you lose and the price has no cap). For sellers of put options, the downside is limited to the exercise price (the lower the spot price of the underlying asset, the more you lose, but the spot price can't go below zero).

Expiration or Maturity Date. In the private or "OTC" options market, the parties will negotiate over the duration or term of the particular option. Options typically run for a period of less than one year. All other things being equal, the longer the option period, the higher the option premium because of the greater likelihood that the spot price will rise above (in the case of a call) or fall below (in the case of a put) the option's strike price.

In the public options market, options are written to last for set periods of time, such as one month or three months. It is possible, however, to purchase longer term options referred to as "LEAPs" (Long-term Equity AnticiPation Securities) in the public market.

Manner of Exercise. Options can be written with one of three types of exercise: American Style, European Style or Asian Style. All publicly traded options have an *American Style* of exercise. An American Style option can be exercised by its holder at any time on or before its maturity date. Thus, if a call option is in-the-money half way through its term (because the spot price of the underlying asset has risen above the call option's strike price), its holder could exercise the option and make the spread between the spot and strike prices (i.e., the option's intrinsic value). However, rarely does this occur because by doing so the holder would be wasting the option's other element of value: its *time value*. Time value refers to the chance that the spot price could move even further into-the-money during the remaining term of the option. Because the market values both the intrinsic and time values of an option, the holder should sell the option rather than exercise it in order to reap both elements of value.

In the private options market, options can have an American, European or Asian Style of exercise. A *European Style* option can only be exercised on its maturity date. An *Asian Style* option, by contrast, can be exercised only on specified dates negotiated by the parties at the time the option is written.

All other things being equal, the price of an American Style option—its option premium—is higher than that of a European or Asian Style option. This is due to the tremendous flexibility that an American Style option provides its holder with respect to exercise. The premium associated with a European Style option is typically the lowest, because exercise is only allowed at maturity. The premium associated with an Asian Style option will vary depending on the number of exercise dates associated with it.

Physical Settlement and Cash Settlement. Exchange traded options, other than those written on stock indices, are normally settled physically. This means that the actual asset underlying the option must be physically bought or sold if the option is in-the-money when exercised. By contrast, private options are almost always settled in cash. If a private option is exercised when it is in-the-money, the counterparty must pay the intrinsic value of the option to the holder in cash. Underlying assets are not physically transferred.

(ii) Options Used for Hedging: An Example

Assume you purchased 100,000 shares of unregistered Microsoft common stock in a private placement nine months ago at $27 per share. Because these shares were not registered with the SEC, Rule 144 under the Securities Act of 1933 requires that you hold them a minimum of one year. Satisfying this holding period demonstrates that you acquired the shares for "investment purposes only" and not with a "view to distribution" (i.e., to the public). The current market price for publicly traded shares of Microsoft is now $45. Assume you believe $45 per share is about as high as Microsoft is likely to climb between now and the time your holding period expires. Therefore, you are not overly concerned about capturing continued price appreciation of Microsoft during this time; your concern, instead, is with a decline in price. How can options help you hedge or reduce your risk of a price decline?

An easy solution would be for you to purchase put options on 100,000 shares of Microsoft common stock. Assume that each put option has a strike price of $40 and a maturity date three months from now. Between now and three months from now, you will still bear the risk of the price of Microsoft falling from $45 per share to $40 per share. However, if Microsoft drops below $40 per share, your put options will have moved into-the-money. Excluding the option premium you paid, the rise in the value of your put options will directly offset the decline in the value of Microsoft stock you own below $40 per share. In the meantime, you enjoy 100% of any price appreciation in Microsoft between now and three months from now. In that event, your only out-of-pocket cost is the option premium you paid for the put options.

(iii) Options Used for Speculation: An Example

Assume you believe in your heart of hearts that Google common stock is ready for a serious run up in price over the next six months, and you'd like to tag along for the ride. One strategy would be for you to go out and purchase actual shares of Google (a so-called "long position") and hold onto them as the price (hopefully) increases over time. However, doing so ties up a lot of cash, and you are limited by your cash resources and margin requirements (assuming you want to borrow some of the money) as to how many shares you can purchase. Instead of buying actual Google shares, another strategy is for you to purchase call options on Google shares. The premium you pay for the call options covering a specified number of shares, while not chicken feed, is substantially less of a cash outlay than the one required to make an outright purchase of the same number of shares.

Suppose the current market price for Google is $300 per share. To employ an options strategy, you could purchase call options with a strike price of $320 and a maturity date six months from now. If, during the six month duration of the options, Google's price rises above $320 per share, you'll be entitled to the intrinsic value of your options less the option premium you paid for them. If, however, Google's price does not exceed $320 per share, then your options will expire out-of-the-money and thus be worthless. Plus, you'll be out the option premium you paid for the option.

(iv) Option Pricing Theory

What drives the pricing of options both in the OTC and public markets? Why would you pay a higher premium to purchase one option on IBM common stock as opposed to another? The answer is simple and intuitive: the more likely it is for a given option to move into-the-money during its term, the more you will have to pay for it.

Specifically, many variables influence the pricing of options. The principal factors are captured in a standard option pricing model influenced by the assumptions underlying modern finance theory. It is called the Black-Scholes Option Pricing Model, after the two economists who developed it. Fisher Black & Myron Scholes, The Pricing of Options and Corporate Liabilities, 81 J. Pol. Econ. 637 (1973). The model stipulates that option values are a function of the following factors:

- Change in value of optioned asset;
- Strike price;
- Optioned asset volatility;
- Interest rates and other macroeconomic variables;
- For options on common stocks, cash dividends; and
- Time to expiration (duration).

Each of these factors has a discrete effect on the value of calls, on the one hand, and puts, on the other. Changes in the value of the optioned asset define the "derivative" character of options. For stock options, as a stock price rises, the value of a call option rises. There is a greater likelihood that the option will be in-the-money. Contrariwise, as a stock price rises, the value of a put option falls. There is a lesser likelihood that the option will be in-the-money.

With to the option's strike price, the closer that price is set to the market price of the underlying asset when the option is written, the more expensive the option will be. This is because there is a greater probability that the option will move into-the-money during its term.

In terms of the volatility of the underlying asset, the more volatile that asset's price movement, the more expensive an option on that asset will be. Once again, this is because there is a greater probability that the option will move into-the-money during its term. Thus, in order to reduce the option premium payable with respect to an option being written on a volatile asset, the strike price should be set further away from the market price.

Interest rates affect option values due to the time value of money. The strike price of a call option is paid in the future upon exercise and the consideration due on a put option is received in the future. Thus the higher the relevant discount rate, the lower the present value of the exercise price of a call option (what you have to pay to exercise it) and hence the higher the call option's value. The opposite is true for put options: the higher the relevant discount rate, the lower the present value of what you receive on exercising it, and hence the lower the put option's value.

For common stocks, option values are affected by the frequency and amount of cash dividends paid on the common stock. Options that partake of a cash dividend increase in value and those that do not decrease in value. The key issue is the so-called "ex-dividend date." This refers to the date on or after which the buyer of an equity security does not acquire the right to receive a recently declared dividend. As of the ex-dividend date for common stock, the value of the stock should decline by an amount approximately equal to the amount of the cash dividend. Thus, the higher the dividends, the lower the value of a call relative to the stock and the higher the value of a put relative to the stock.

The time to expiration exposes an option's value to numerous forces. In general, however, the value of puts and call options both benefit from longer maturity periods. It is akin to the effect of volatility. Both give the holder more time to benefit from variability in the exercise price-option value relationship. On the other hand, longer expiration periods reduce the present value of the future exchange, thus increasing the value of a call and decreasing the value of a put. Likewise, longer expiration periods create a greater chance for a cash-dividend effect, reducing the call value but increasing the put value.

Summary of Option Pricing Model Valuation Factors

Variable	Change	Call Option Value	Put Option Value
Optioned Asset Price	Rising	Increases	Decreases
	Falling	Decreases	Increases
Strike Price	Higher	Decreases	Increases
	Lower	Increases	Decreases
Optioned Asset Volatility	Greater	Increases	Increases
	Lesser	Decreases	Decreases
Interest Rates	Rising	Increases	Decreases
	Falling	Decreases	Increases
Dividends	Higher	Decreases	Increases
	Lower	Increases	Decreases
Time to Expiration	Longer	Increases	Increases
	Shorter	Decreases	Decreases

Notes and Questions

1. For the "everything you wanted to know about options but were afraid to ask" book, hunt down a copy of McMillan, Options as a Strategic Investment (4th ed. 2001), which is published by the New York Institute of Finance.

2. Stock-based compensation plans are often used to compensate managers. Under the plans, stock options (all of which are call options) are granted annually to key managers and directors with strike or exercise prices equal to the market price on the date of grant or in some cases at a higher price. Grants are typically fully exercisable after three years (a so-called "vesting period") and have a fifteen-year life. Stock option compensation is said to provide additional incentives for the recipient to manage the entity well— if he or she does, the stock price should rise, generating profits for the recipient when exercising the option. (We again refer you to the discussion in chapter 1, section 4, arguing that these options can create perverse incentives for managers to run the company for the sake of the short-term stock price.)

A debate has raged over the last several years as to whether employee stock options should be expensed against earnings by the companies granting them. This would entail estimating compensation cost for the stock option plans based on the fair value of the options at the grant date and reporting on a *pro forma* basis the effect of that cost on a company's net earnings and earnings per share. A leading proponent of expensing is famed investor Warren Buffett, who argues: "When a company gives something of value to its employees in return for their services, it is clearly a compensation expense. And if expenses don't belong in the earnings statement, where in the world do they belong?"[3] Opponents, particularly technology companies whose employees often receive a large portion of their compensation in the form of stock options, countered that the expensing of stock options would unfairly penalize them as compared to non-technology companies. Still other companies were perplexed by the calculation of the expenses themselves, assuming that expensing was deemed necessary.

For now, the proponents of expensing have carried the day. In December 2004, FASB issued revised SFAS No. 123, Accounting for Stock Based Compensation, which, among other things, requires most publicly traded companies to expense employee stock options effective June 15, 2005.[4] Specifically, the Statement requires a public entity to measure the cost of employee services received in exchange for an award of equity instruments based on the grant-date fair value of the award (with limited exceptions). That cost will be recognized over the period during which an employee is required to provide service in exchange for the award—the requisite service period (usually the vesting period). No compensation cost is recognized for equity instruments for which employees do not render the requisite service.

Nevertheless, opponents of expensing continue to battle on and may yet win the war. They continue to point to the disproportionate impact expensing has on technology

---

3. Warren E. Buffett, Who Really Cooks the Books?, N.Y. Times, July 24, 2002, at A19.

4. Revised SFAS No. 123 superceded APB Opinion No. 25, Accounting for Stock Issued to Employees, which only encouraged but did not mandate the expensing of employee stock options by publicly traded companies.

companies as well as the overall difficulty of assigning requisite cost. *See* Nocera, Starting Off By Doing Right On Options, N.Y. Times, June 11, 2005, at C1.

b. Forwards

(i) Overview

A forward contract is a unique investment tool primarily designed to decrease the contracting parties' exposure to price fluctuations of the asset (typically a commodity, such as grain) covered by the contract. A forward contract imposes the obligation (not merely the right) to buy from or sell to another party (the "counterparty") a specified asset, on a specified date, for a specified price. The *buyer* of a forward contract is obligated to buy the specified asset and the *seller* of a forward contract is obligated to sell the specified asset.

As with an option, the specified asset can be almost anything. However, this is about the only feature forwards and options have in common. In particular, no premium or other money is paid by either party upon execution of a forward contract. Moreover, both parties are obligated to perform a forward, while only the option writer is obligated to perform on an option.

Forward contracts are derivative instruments because their value is derived from changes in the spot price of the underlying asset over time. As the spot price of the asset rises, new forward contracts are issued at higher forward prices than those specified in previously issued forward contracts. The value of an older forward contract in the hands of a buyer, therefore, rises as the spot price rises because it entitles (indeed, obligates) the buyer to buy the asset at the older, lower price. On the other hand, the value of an older forward contract in the hands of a seller falls as the spot price rises because it obligates the seller to sell the asset at the older, lower price. As the spot price of the forward asset falls, the converse is true with respect to buyers and sellers.

A forward contract normally requires physical delivery of the underlying asset, but it need not. Instead, the parties may simply settle their contract in cash with reference to the market price of the asset on the contract's maturity date.

As a result of the link between the value of a forward contract and changes in the spot price of the underlying asset, forwards can be used to hedge against the risk of changes in the spot price. For example, if you are worried about the risk of a fall in the spot price of some asset you sell in your business, you can hedge the risk by selling a forward contract that locks in today's spot price. If spot prices fall as you feared, you have the right to sell the asset at your contract forward price rather than at the prevailing spot price. If instead spot prices rise, it is true that you will be obligated to sell the asset at a price less than the prevailing market price, but presumably you were satisfied with the forward price when you entered into the contract.

(ii) Forward Price

Prospective parties to a forward contract negotiate over the underlying asset, the forward price and the settlement date. The forward price is typically based on three variables: (1) the spot price of the underlying asset on the date on which the parties enter into the contract; (2) the cost, if any, to carry the underlying asset; and (3) distributions (such as dividends or interest), if any, to be paid on the underlying asset. The formula for determining the forward price is thus:

$$FP = SP + CC - D$$

where: FP = forward price
         SP = spot price of the underlying asset
         CC = cost to carry the underlying asset
         D   = distributions, if any, to be received on the underlying asset

The cost to carry the underlying asset until the settlement date is determined by adding two variables: (1) the seller's opportunity cost; and (2) the seller's cost of storage. In a forward contract, the parties enter into the contract today, yet make payment and delivery at a future date. This delay imposes an opportunity cost on the seller. Theoretically, the seller could sell the underlying asset today and then reinvest the proceeds until the settlement date of the forward contract. The seller would earn interest on the proceeds during this time. The forward price, therefore, will reflect the seller's opportunity cost of waiting until the settlement date to be paid.

The cost to store the underlying asset until settlement is also a part of the seller's cost to carry. The seller of the underlying asset may incur transaction costs to hold the asset until the forward contract expires. The storage cost is typically a cost incorporated into the forward price for commodities such as wheat, oil and gold. However, in certain forward contracts, the storage cost is zero. A forward contract for financial assets, such as foreign exchange, is a prime example.

In a forward contract, the buyer receives delayed delivery of the underlying asset. Accordingly, the seller rather than the buyer will receive any distribution on that asset made during the term of the forward contract. These distributions typically consist of dividends or interest, and thus are only applicable when the underlying asset is a financial instrument rather than a commodity. Anticipated distributions are deducted when calculating the forward price the buyer must pay the seller, because the seller is entitled to receive those distributions.

(iii) Counterparty Credit Risk

Each party to a forward contract is exposed to counterparty credit or default risk. This is the risk that the other party to the contract will not be able to perform its contractual duties on the settlement date. The failure to perform may arise from internal factors, such as financial difficulty, or external factors, such as a natural disaster that affects a crop harvest. Counterparty credit risk remains a significant concern to both parties because forwards are private contracts. Accordingly, each party must assess the risk of conducting business with the other party prior to entering into a forward contract.

c. Futures

Futures contracts are essentially publicly traded forward contracts. Indeed, similar to forward contracts, futures also obligate the buyer to buy and the seller to sell a specified asset on a specified date for a specified price (here called the *futures price*). Nevertheless, the following five primary operational differences exist between forward and futures contracts that arise from the manner in which the contracts are treated in the markets:

(1) Cash Settlement;

(2) Standardized Contracts;

(3) Daily Settlement;

(4) Margin Requirements; and

(5) Elimination of Counterparty Credit Risk.

Unlike a forward contract, where physical delivery is the norm, physical delivery of the underlying asset associated with a futures contract occurs less than two percent of the time. Instead, cash settlement is the norm, as this is necessary to help establish a cash-based trading market in futures. Additionally, unlike a forward contract, the terms of which are privately negotiated, most of the terms of a futures contract are standardized by the various futures exchanges and are nonnegotiable. Thus, provisions including quantity, expiration date and underlying asset are fixed terms within the contract. This is also necessary to create an organized trading market for futures. If the standardized contracts offered by the futures exchanges do not meet the parties' needs, then a forward contract becomes necessary.

The price of a futures contract (the *futures price*) is established by traders on the floor of a commodity exchange, such as the Chicago Board of Trade (CBOT), the Chicago Mercantile Exchange (CME) or the New York Mercantile Exchange (NYMEX). Traders use the *open outcry* system. The term refers to the shouting exchanged between traders seeking to sell or buy at a particular price. Trading of a particular contract takes place in specified locations on the trading floor referred to as *pits*. When two traders connect on price, they have made a contract that will be recorded. (Think of Dan Aykroyd and Eddie Murphy first selling and then buying frozen concentrated orange juice (FJOC) futures in the trading pit in the hit movie *Trading Places*.)

Perhaps the main difference between forwards and futures lies in the terms of settlement between the parties. As noted above, forward contracts are settled only at the maturity date and before that time their value fluctuates as the spot price of the underlying asset fluctuates. In contrast, futures contracts are settled daily based on each day's changes in the spot price of the underlying asset. This process of daily settlement is called *marking-to-market*.[5] The relative profit or loss positions of the buyer and seller are calculated and recognized at the end of each day (and note that their relative positions are identical to the relative position of buyers and sellers under forward contracts). Following each day's settlement, the futures price is reset so as to equal the closing spot price of the asset. The consequence is that whereas the forward contract is initially set so that its market value is zero and thereafter its market value fluctuates, the daily settlement of futures contracts means that at the end of each day the market value of a futures contract is restored to zero. Like a forward contract, however, the only net exchange of cash would

---

5. Marking-to-market is a process undertaken by many firms in many contexts, not only in futures markets, but also in stock, bond and various asset markets, as well as derivatives markets. It may take the form of actual settlement with a counterparty, as in the futures contract situation, or of "booking" gains or losses in accounting records and presenting them in financial statements before the gain or loss is actually realized.

be the difference between the spot price of the underlying asset at the time the original contract was struck and the spot price of that asset on the contract's maturity date.

This marking-to-market feature of futures contracts is facilitated by various organized exchanges on which futures contracts are listed. Each futures contract trader is required to maintain an account, called a *margin account*, in respect of her futures contracts position.[6] The account balance is adjusted at the end of each trading day according to that day's settlement of each buyer's and seller's profit and loss positions. The exchanges require a minimum balance to be maintained in these accounts (*maintenance margin*) under their capital adequacy rules.

Futures markets essentially eliminate counterparty credit risk. Rules relating to marking-to-market and margin accounts substantially reduce that risk. These rules help ensure that traders will have adequate capital to cover positions they have taken in futures contracts as spot prices fluctuate over time. Additionally, futures transactions, while executed on the floor of a given exchange, are settled through a separate entity from the exchange called a clearinghouse. A given clearinghouse is the "financial sponsor" of all the participants who conduct daily trading on an exchange floor. The clearinghouse *guarantees* obligations of the parties to a futures contract.

The Commodity Futures Trading Commission (CFTC) enforces the laws and makes the regulations that govern futures markets in the United States. Each individual exchange must gain permission from the CFTC to list and trade futures contracts on its trading floor. The rules and regulations that the CFTC promulgates are extremely detailed and specific, and thus the U.S. futures markets are highly-regulated.

d. Swaps

Swap contracts require the parties to make a series of payments to one another over time defined with reference to some specified criteria, such as publicly available interest rate or currency exchange rate data. The parties involved in a swap sign a contract specifying each party's obligations to the other just as in a forward contract. Moreover, the contract yields the same advantages as a forward (*e.g.*, customization, privacy, etc.), as well as its disadvantages (*e.g.*, counterparty credit risk, lack of liquidity, etc.).

Swaps are most commonly used to hedge risks of fluctuations in currency rates and interest rates. More exotic swaps, however, are also possible. These include commodity swaps,[7] forward start swaps,[8] diversification swaps,[9] swaptions,[10] and credit-

---

6. Margin accounts are also required of certain participants in other capital markets, such as the stock market.

7. These swaps involve an exchange of cash flows linked to a specific commodity price or index of prices.

8. These swaps have start dates and subsequent exchanges of interest payments that are deferred to some time in the future.

9. These swaps allow an investor with unsaleable stock to enter into an equity swap with a counterparty whereby the counterparty pays the investor the total return on a specified market index and the investor pays the counterparty the total return on the unsaleable stock.

10. These are essentially option contracts on interest rate swaps with the swaps having some future commencement date.

default risk swaps.[11] For an excellent discussion of a credit-default risk swap, see Eternity Global Master Fund Ltd. v. Morgan Guaranty Trust Co., 375 F.3d 168 (2d Cir. 2004), *infra* at section 3a.

Unlike futures and certain options, swaps are private contracts that do not yet trade in any organized secondary market. These private contracts, however, can be standardized or customized. Standardized forms have been prepared by the International Swap and Derivatives Association (ISDA).

Leaving aside the exotics, the most common form of swap is the interest rate swap. An interest rate swap calls for one party to pay a fixed rate of interest to its counterparty and for the counterparty to pay a floating rate of interest in return. For example, suppose a company is seeking to raise capital through the issuance of debt securities. It finds that it can get the most attractive terms by issuing fixed rate bonds but also believes that interest rates are heading downward. To hedge against the risk of falling interest rates, it could issue the fixed rate bonds and simultaneously enter into an interest rate swap agreement with another party. Under the swap, the company would agree to pay a floating interest rate to the counterparty in exchange for the counterparty's promise to make fixed rate payments to the company. The amount of any payment would be calculated with reference to the principal amount of the issued bonds, and that amount is called the "notional amount" or "notional value" of the swap. It has no other purpose except as the multiplicand of the applicable interest rate.

Customized interest rate swaps may also contain an explicit leverage function that makes them especially sensitive to adverse changes in interest rates. A leveraged interest rate swap is one in which the payment streams to be paid based on floating interest rates vary at a greater multiple when rates go in one direction and at a lesser multiple when rates move in the opposite direction. For example, for a party paying the floating rate, base rate increases could be multiplied by say 1.5 whereas base rate decreases could be multiplied by 1.25. In such a case, if the base rate rises by 1, the payor's payment rate would increase by 1.5, whereas if the base rate falls by 1, the payor's payment rate would decrease by 1.25. In this example, the leverage ratio would therefore be 6:5 (1.5/1.25).

Currency swaps are also common. For example, many British companies desire to raise funds in non-pound currencies (especially dollars) to finance operations abroad but can get better terms if they borrowed at home in pounds. These companies simply borrow in pounds in England and then enter into a currency swap under which they agree to pay their swap counterparty in pounds in exchange for the counterparty's payment in dollars.

While no organized exchange or secondary market yet exists for swaps, they can be marked-to-market with computer models and can be unwound or terminated simply by executing a contract having mirror image terms that in effect cancels out the original payment terms. Of course, the unwinding or termination may not be costless, for a party seeking to get out of an unfavorable position may have to compensate the counterparty for giving up the offsetting favorable position.

Swaps typically provide for early termination in the event of certain adverse financial conditions afflicting one of the parties (such as bankruptcy, insolvency or payment default). Moreover, most of the credit risk in the swap market is borne by financial intermediaries who act as middlemen between corporate clients.

---

11. These swaps allow investors to hedge against the risk that the corporate issuers of the debt they purchase may default on that debt.

Section 2
The Spectrum from Hedging to Speculation

The usual objective in designing and using derivative instruments is to hedge exposure to risks. Of course, not all risks can be eliminated but many can be hedged. Trouble arises, however, when one is tempted to use derivatives not for the purpose of hedging risks but for the purpose of eliminating them. In other words, if one begins to believe that it is possible to eliminate risks, one will begin to overemphasize the upside potential of some exchange and underemphasize the downside. When this happens, a device useful for hedging becomes nothing more than a speculative gamble. Corporate managers must therefore take great care in evaluating the manner in which they deploy these hedging devices. Lawyers would also do well to pay attention, whether in advising on a bond offering that includes an interest rate swap, or acquiring a company that has engaged in significant derivatives transactions or in similar contexts.

Failure to do so has led to some great financial debacles. Among the most striking is the Singapore trader who began hedging on swings in different stock markets and ended up buying a huge amount of futures on one market without selling enough offsetting futures on another market. This led to the collapse of Barings Bank, one of the oldest and most conservative European banks, a bank that had financed the Louisiana Purchase and the Napoleonic Wars. On February 26, 1995, Barings went bankrupt as a result of a series of derivative trades made by Nick Leeson, a 28-year-old trader in the British bank's Singapore office. Leeson, whom the British Treasury Secretary Kenneth Clarke would later call a "rogue trader," was sought out for a week by police in Singapore, Malaysia and Thailand. He finally turned up in Frankfurt, Germany, only to face extradition charges by Singapore authorities.

Leeson ostensibly was doing arbitrage trading. That is, he was to notice price differentials on identical securities or baskets of securities traded on different exchanges. Leeson focused on differences in prices of Nikkei-225 futures contracts listed on the Osaka Securities Exchange (OSE) in Japan and the Singapore Monetary Exchange (SIMEX).[1] The strategy is to buy futures contracts on one market and simultaneously sell them on another. This is a low-risk strategy, because a long position in one market is offset by a short position in the other.

Leeson apparently did more than this, however. In addition to buying $7 billion in unhedged stock-index futures, he is also said to have entered into a "straddle" arrangement by simultaneously selling put options and call options on Nikkei-225 futures. Such straddles are profitable to the seller but only if the market is relatively stable. The Japanese stock markets were shaken by the Kobe earthquake in early January 1995 and later in the month plunged. Throughout the period, however, Leeson went on a spree of buying more Nikkei futures in the vain hope of propping up the Nikkei.

The market did not recover, however, and Barings's exposure on the futures contracts was estimated at a staggering $1 billion, far in excess of Barings's total capital. Many regarded it as extraordinary that a single trader could do such tremendous damage. Recall that exchanges that list futures contracts require traders to maintain

---

1. The Nikkei-225 is a market index of 225 stocks, similar in import to the Dow Jones Industrial Average and other market barometers.

margin accounts to limit default risk. How could Barings's open position on these futures contracts have been so large if its margin account was properly funded? Somehow Barings's daily margin obligations — which were then 6% of its open position — had not depleted its minimum capital requirements until after the damage was done and Leeson had fled to Germany. After the fallout, representatives of the Singapore financial community and exchange representatives took care to emphasize that the margin was adequate to cover the Bank's open positions. Singapore's finance minister later announced the need for tighter operating controls. *See* Asiaweek, Mar. 10, 1995.

But what about oversight within Barings? Or from its independent auditors? Here we see fraud. Apparently, Leeson told them the plausible story that he was hedging his long futures positions with private (over-the-counter) contracts and was also making hedged trades on behalf of a client of the bank. In fact, however, the client did not exist but was rather a completely fictitious name given to an account that Leeson had earlier invented for his own use. Leeson allegedly funded that account with proceeds from other trades and used those funds to maintain the margin account balance. He apparently also used that fictitious client account to convince Barings in London that they could provide Leeson with additional firm capital which Lesson in turn used to shore up the margin account.

Notes and Questions

1. Do you see how Leeson's actions and the Barings's bankruptcy bear on your current study of derivatives? Is this simply a case of one man's fraud in concealing financial transactions that could easily have been implemented by a variety of other devices (such as insider trading, money laundering or a whole host of other so-called "white collar crimes")? Was the trouble caused by Leeson the trader or the products he traded? *See* Braddock, Derivatives Demystified, at vi-vii (1997).

In the aftermath of the Barings Bank debacle, debates raged concerning such questions. Defenders of derivatives noted that Leeson was engaged in fraud and covering up trades and that this could be done with or without derivatives. The contrary debaters, noting the complexities of the instruments, emphasized that complexity breeds opportunity.

2. The Barings Bank debacle is recounted with characteristic cool in "The Collapse of Barings," The Economist, Mar. 4, 1995, and with less dispassion in "Going for Broke," Time, Mar. 13, 1995.

3. It is well worth noting that famed investor Warren Buffett had this to say about derivatives: "[D]erivatives are financial weapons of mass destruction, carrying dangers that, while now latent, are potentially lethal." Berkshire Hathaway Inc., 2002 Annual Report, at 15. From what you know, do you agree?

Long Term Capital Management
Cunningham, Outsmarting the Smart Money
(© McGraw-Hill 2002)

Overconfidence plagues even the brightest and clearest thinking [arbitrageurs or "arbs"] in whom efficiency theory places its confidence to keep markets efficient. Take the case of Long Term Capital Management, the fancy hedge fund run by finance's brightest and best which ran into havoc in the embroiled markets of the late 1990s.

The enigmatic John Meriwether, a veteran of the once-venerable trading powerhouse Salomon Brothers, founded Long Term in 1994. He made Salomon's arbitrage practice famous by staffing it with geniuses. He tried to do the same at Long Term. It would become famous for other reasons.

Long Term's top arbs were luminaries from academia. They included Robert C. Merton and Myron S. Scholes, two fathers of the efficient market story who won the 1997 Nobel Prize in economics for their work developing a new way to value financial hedging instruments known as derivatives.

These Nobelists along with David W. Mullins Jr., former Harvard University economics professor and retired vice chairman of the Federal Reserve Board, joined Meriwether and a dozen other impeccably credentialed arbs. Launched with $1 billion in equity, the group borrowed more than $100 billion from the world's most sophisticated commercial and investment banks.

Their plan was to discover temporary pricing differences between equivalent securities. To illustrate the plan's simplicity, imagine that a corporation issues two separate series of bonds that are identical in all respects except they were issued in different seasons of the year, say Spring and Fall, and are owned by different sorts of investors, say individuals and institutions. Each bond promises to pay $1 in present value three years from now.

Due to sentiment about Spring and Fall or to the biases of individuals versus institutions, however, the Fall bonds are trading at $0.95 and the Spring bonds at $1.05. The arbitrage play on these identical but mis-priced bonds is to buy Fall bonds and sell Spring bonds short (borrow the $1.05 bonds promising to repay with bonds bought later, for $1.00). The arb pockets a nickel on each position when eventually the prices converge to $1.

In the words of Myron Scholes, the strategy at Long Term was this simple—they were "vacuuming up nickels others couldn't see." This is precisely the arbitrage activity that efficiency fans applaud—picking up cash from the market floor to drive away inefficient pricing.

Long Term vacuumed up lots of nickels in its first few years. One dollar invested in Long Term at its 1994 founding grew to $4 by early 1998. Apparently this success went to the trader's heads. Brimming with bravado, the firm neglected to take precautions that it must have felt only less successful competitors needed to take.

The firm conducted no independent risk assessment and failed to establish any internal control. All 16 of the principals did whatever trading they chose, without oversight. Most companies require two supervisors to sign off on matters as simple as issuing a check for more than $5,000. But the ethos at Long Term saw no need to micro-manage its luminaries.

The firm borrowed an enormous amount of money to boost returns on the bets it made. After all, it is hard to make a lot of money vacuuming up nickels one at a time, but picking them up 20 at a time turns them into dollars. The firm's leverage ratio (borrowed funds listed on its balance sheet compared to funds of its principals that were at risk) was huge, regularly around 33 to 1. So for every $100 of borrowed money, the firm's owners had about $3 at stake. With lenders being paid first in the event of insolvency, this meant that if the fund's value fell $3 the owners were wiped out, a margin for error only the highly confident can bear.

The firm carried an additional layer of debt not listed on its balance sheet. It engaged in numerous "derivative" transactions, the hedging instruments at the center of the Nobel Prize awarded to Merton and Scholes. They are side-bets not reported on Long Term's financial statements. Instead of buying a bond outright, for example, the arrangement is that one party agrees to pay another a certain amount if the bond's market price rises, and the other party agrees to pay a proportional amount if the bond's price falls.

When Long Term's derivative positions are counted as part of its borrowing, its leverage ratio rose to as much as 60 to 1. Operating with this much leverage meant that if the value of the fund fell by $1.66, the firm would own nothing, lenders taking all. That basically meant the firm was operating with no margin for error and stupendous self-confidence—the slightest bump in the road would bring disaster. To put that in perspective, industrial corporations simply cannot operate with that amount of debt, and are considered too aggressive when leverage is greater than 7 to 1.

Efficiency devotees, including those at Long Term, would not recognize a leverage ratio as measuring risk. For them, risk is about price volatility. In the case of a hedge fund, risk is measured by how much net assets rise and fall. A leverage ratio of 5 could be highly risky if invested in erratically-priced securities while one of 100 could be conservative if invested in securities with narrow price fluctuations. For that matter, many Wall Street investment banks operate with leverage ratios well above the levels typical of industrial corporations, sometimes as much as 25.

Common sense suggests this approach to measuring risk overlooks significant exposure to losses. The common sense definition of investment risk is the possibility of loss. When the capital structure of an investment fund is so laden with debt that tiny vacillations in portfolio value can wipe the entire equity out of the firm, risk is high, even if invested in the most price insensitive securities.

In Long Term's case, the risk from this common sense view is even greater, for the sums involved were staggering. About $100 billion was borrowed and a mere $3 to 4 billion invested as equity. At times the firm also held positions in derivatives that exposed it to bets as high as $1 trillion. This sounds like wildly irrational behavior from members of the school of American finance so keen on rationality.

The firm committed the fundamental error of pattern seeking. Bets were made as if the experience of the recent past guaranteed a similar environment a few years later. The computer models Long Term created to help detect price discrepancies were all predicated on the direction of past price movements of securities. But past patterns are not reliable guides given the randomness of the future.

In early 1998, Long Term viewed U.S. Treasury bonds as overpriced and a host of others—junk bonds, European government bonds, and mortgage-backed securities—as underpriced. So the firm sold short the U.S. Treasuries and loaded up on mortgage backs, Euros, and junk.

Past patterns were disrupted in mid-1998. A financial crisis broke out in Asia. Stock markets fell worldwide. The Russian government defaulted on its debt and devalued its currency. Sellers flooded the market for the defaulted Russian debt. Buyers were scarce.

In a global "flight to quality," investors dumped the junk and Euro bonds Long Term held, buying U.S. Treasuries. This led the price of Treasuries to rise and their yield, which moves in the opposite direction, to fall. The decline in yields, in turn, led to a decline in the interest rate on mortgages, depressing the value of the mortgage-backed securities Long Term owned.

To recall the Spring-Fall bond example, in this berserk market it was as if the Spring bonds suddenly traded at $3.00 and the Fall bonds suddenly traded at $0.25. Long Term's nickel-sucking vacuum cleaner now worked as a pump. It lost nickels as fellow investors sold junk bonds and European issues; more as the price of U.S. Treasuries it was compelled to buy rose; and yet more as the value of its mortgage-backed securities fell.

Long Term could have absorbed much of this nickel regurgitation if it was not so leveraged. But the downside to leverage is proportional to its upside. As these nickels disappeared with the asset value, lenders started to make margin calls, demanding more nickels than Long Term had. The debacle wiped it out.

Genius and money, buoyed by past successes, led to a stupefying hubris. Long Term's strategists saw patterns that did not exist. By the fall of 1998, panic and fear set in. The geniuses sought to be rescued. The Federal Reserve brokered a bailout by 15 large financial institutions, mostly former lenders to the firm. At that time, for every dollar invested in Long Term in 1994, an investor had about five nickels left.

How could such geniuses and finance masters have been so irrational? Maybe they weren't. Maybe everyone else in the market was acting irrationally while they were acting hyperrationally. The odds of the pricing going the way it did—Spring bonds up to $3.00 and Fall bonds down to $0.25 were around 1 in 50 million. The likes of experienced men of affairs such as Alan Greenspan and then-Treasury Secretary Robert E. Rubin admitted they have never seen such a financial crisis.

In this view, Long Term's positions were not the product of overconfidence, pattern seeking, or other cognitive bias. The real irrationality in this story is the failure by other professional money managers to exploit the arbitrage opportunities. They should not have allowed the price gaps to widen so much in the first place. They certainly should not have allowed them to persist.

Whichever view you take—Long Term strategists as super star paragons of rationality or as overconfident pattern blinded human beings—the moral of Long Term's saga is the same. Arbs are not immune from cognitive bias and arbitrage is a risky business. The nickels and dollars sitting in the market are not always seen and are never free.

Section 3
Judicial Analysis of Derivatives

a. Contractual Interpretation

At their most basic, derivatives are simply contracts between two counterparties—highly complex contracts for sure—but contracts nonetheless. When counterparties have a dispute over specific contractual language, courts are required to step in and solve the dispute. But are they up for the challenge given the complexity of derivatives?

Eternity Global Master Fund Ltd. v. Morgan Guaranty Trust Co.
375 F.3d 168 (2d Cir. 2004)

DENNIS JACOBS, Circuit Judge:

Plaintiff-Appellant Eternity Global Master Fund Limited ("Eternity" or "the Fund") purchased credit default swaps ("CDSs" or "the CDS contracts") from Defendants-Appellees Morgan Guaranty Trust Company of New York and JPMorgan Chase Bank (collectively, "Morgan") in October 2001. Eternity appeals from a final judgment entered in the United States District Court for the Southern District of New York (McKenna, J.), dismissing with prejudice its complaint alleging breach of contract, fraud, and negligent misrepresentation by Morgan in connection with the CDSs. The CDS contracts were written on the sovereign bonds of Argentina and would be "triggered" upon the occurrence of a "credit event," such that if Argentina restructured or defaulted on that debt, Eternity would have the right to put to Morgan a stipulated amount of the bonds for purchase at par value.

In late November 2001, the government of the Republic of Argentina, in the grip of economic crisis, initiated a "voluntary debt exchange" in which bondholders had the option of turning in their bonds for secured loans on terms less favorable except that the loans were secured by certain Argentine federal tax revenues. Eternity informed Morgan that the voluntary debt exchange was a credit event that triggered Morgan's obligations under the CDS contracts. Morgan disagreed.

* * *

On appeal, Eternity challenges the dismissal of its claims. For the reasons set forth below, we affirm the dismissal of the fraudulent and negligent misrepresentation claims but reverse the dismissal of the contract claim and remand for further proceedings.

* * *

On behalf of its investors, Eternity trades in global bonds, equities and currencies, including emerging-market debt. During the relevant period, Eternity's investment portfolio included short-term Argentine sovereign and corporate bonds. In emerging markets such as Argentina, a significant credit risk is "country risk," i.e., "the risk that economic, social, and political conditions and events in a foreign country will adversely affect an institution's financial interests," including "the possibility of nationalization or expropriation of assets, government repudiation of external indebtedness, ... and currency depreciation or devaluation."[1] Credit risk can be managed, however. Banks, investment funds and other institutions increasingly use financial contracts known as "credit derivatives" to mitigate credit risk. In October 2001, in light of Argentina's rapidly deteriorating political and economic prospects, Eternity purchased CDSs to hedge the credit risk on its in-country investments.

* * *

A credit default swap is the most common form of credit derivative, i.e., "[a] contract which transfers credit risk from a protection buyer to a credit protection seller."[4] Protection buyers (here, Eternity) can use credit derivatives to manage particular market exposures and return-on-investment; and protection sellers (here, Morgan) generally use credit derivatives to earn income and diversify their own investment portfolios. Simply put, a credit default swap is a bilateral financial contract in which "[a] protection buyer makes[] periodic payments to ... the protection seller, in return for a contingent

---

1. Office of the Comptroller of the Currency et. al., Interagency Statement: Country Risk 1 (2002), available at http://www.occ.treas.gov/ftp/bulletin/2002-10a.pdf (Feb 22, 2002); see also Joyce A. Frost, Credit Risk Management from a Corporate Perspective, in Handbook of Credit Derivatives 89-96 (Jack Clark Francis et. al. eds., 1999) ("Frost").

4. Office of the Comptroller of the Currency & Administrator of National Banks, OCC Bank Derivatives Report Fourth Quarter 2003 5 (2004), available at http://www.occ.treas.gov/ftp/deriv/dq403.pdf (last visited June 21, 2004)....

payment if a predefined credit event occurs in the reference credit," i.e., the obligation on which the contract is written.[7]

Often, the reference asset that the protection buyer delivers to the protection seller following a credit event is the instrument that is being hedged. But in emerging markets, an investor may calculate that a particular credit risk "is reasonably correlated with the performance of [the sovereign] itself,"[9] so that (as here) the investor may seek to isolate and hedge country risk with credit default swaps written on some portion of the sovereign's outstanding debt.

In many contexts a "default" is a simple failure to pay; in a credit default swap, it references a stipulated bundle of "credit events" (such as bankruptcy, debt moratoria,[11] and debt restructurings) that will trigger the protection seller's obligation to "settle" the contract via the swap mechanism agreed to between the parties. The entire bundle is typically made subject to a materiality threshold. The occurrence of a credit event triggers the "swap," i.e., the protection seller's obligation to pay on the contract according to the settlement mechanism. "The contingent payment can be based on cash settlement … or physical delivery of the reference asset, in exchange for a cash payment equal to the initial notional [i.e., face] amount [of the CDS contract]."[14] A CDS buyer holding a sufficient amount of the reference credit can simply tender it to the CDS seller for payment; but ownership of the reference credit prior to default is unnecessary. If a credit event occurs with respect to the obligation(s) named in a CDS, and notice thereof has been given (and the CDS buyer has otherwise performed), the CDS seller must settle. Liquidity in a secondary market increases the usefulness of a CDS as a hedging tool, though the limited depth of that market "can make it difficult to offset … positions prior to contract maturity."[16]

* * *

The principal issue dividing the parties is whether the CDS contracts at issue are ambiguous in any material respect. "An ambiguity exists where the terms of a contract could suggest 'more than one meaning when viewed objectively by a reasonably intelligent person who has examined the context of the entire integrated agreement and who is cognizant of the customs, practices, usages and terminology as generally understood in the particular trade or business.'" *Alexander & Alexander Servs., Inc. v. These Certain Underwriters at Lloyd's, London, 136 F.3d 82, 86 (2d Cir. 1998)* (quoting *Lightfoot v. Union Carbide Corp., 110 F.3d 898, 906 (2d Cir. 1997)).*

In this case, we assess ambiguity in the disputed CDS contracts by looking to (i) the terms of the three credit default swaps; (ii) the terms of the International Swaps and Derivatives Association's ("ISDA" or "the Association") "Master Swap Agreement," on which those swaps are predicated, (iii) ISDA's 1999 Credit Derivatives Definitions— which are incorporated into the disputed contracts; and (iv) the background "customs,

---

7. Frost, supra, at 90 (footnote omitted).

9. Satyajit Das, Credit Derivatives—Applications, in Credit Derivatives: Trading & Management of Credit & Default Risk 125, 163 (Satyajit Das ed., 1998) ("Das").

11. Generally speaking, a debt moratorium is "an order by a government making it lawful to defer payment of all or certain kinds of debts for a certain period of time beyond the original maturity, issued in order to prevent general bankruptcy or a collapse of credit by legally protecting debtors against their creditors in times of public danger." Charles J. Woelfel, Encyclopedia of Banking & Finance 759 (10th ed. 1994).

14. Frost, supra, at 90.

16. OCC Bulletin, supra; see also [Robert S. Neal & Douglas S. Rolph, An Introduction to Credit Derivatives, in Handbook of Credit Derivatives (1999)], at 17.

practices, [and] usages" of the credit derivatives trade, id. Because customs and usages matter, and because documentation promulgated by the ISDA was used by the parties to this dispute, we briefly review some relevant background.

The term "derivatives" references "a vast array of privately negotiated over-the counter ... and exchange traded transactions," including interest-rate swaps, currency swaps, commodity price swaps and credit derivatives—which include credit default swaps. A derivative is a bilateral contract that is typically negotiated by phone and followed by an exchange of confirmatory faxes that constitute the contract but do not specify such terms as events of default, representations and warranties, covenants, liquidated damages, and choice of law. These (and other) terms are typically found in a "Master Swap Agreement," which, prior to standardization efforts that began in the mid-1980s, "took the form of separate 15-to 25-page agreements for each transaction."[19]

Documentation of derivatives transactions has become streamlined, chiefly through industry adherence to "Master Agreements" promulgated by the ISDA. In 1999, Eternity and Morgan entered the ISDA Multicurrency-Cross Border Master Agreement, which governs, inter alia, the CDS transactions disputed on appeal. Each disputed CDS also incorporates the 1999 ISDA Credit Derivatives Definitions, the Association's first attempt at a comprehensive lexicon governing credit derivatives transactions. Last year, due to the rapid evolution of "ISDA documentation for credit default swaps," the Association began market implementation of the 2003 Credit Derivatives Definitions, which evidently constitutes a work in progress....

* * *

Eternity's Global Master Fund is managed by HFW Capital, L.P., including its Chief Investment Officer, Alberto Franco. In 2001, Franco engaged Morgan to facilitate Eternity's participation in the Argentine corporate debt market. Fearing that a government debt crisis would impair the value of Eternity's Argentine investments, Franco sought to hedge using credit default swaps written on Argentine sovereign bonds. In October 2001, the Fund entered into three such contracts. Each CDS incorporated (i) the ISDA Master Swap Agreement, and (ii) the 1999 ISDA Definitions. The total value of the contracts was $ 14 million.... Except as to value and duration, the terms were virtually identical, as follows:

(i) Eternity would pay Morgan a fixed periodic fee tied to the notional value of each respective credit default swap.

(ii) The swaps would be triggered upon occurrence of any one of four credit events—as defined by the 1999 ISDA Credit Derivative Definitions—with respect to the Argentine sovereign bonds: Failure to pay, Obligation Acceleration, Repudiation/Moratorium, and Restructuring.

(iii) Each CDS called for physical settlement following a credit event, specifically:

(a) Upon notification (by either party to the other) of a credit event, and confirmation via two publicly available sources of information (e.g., the Wall Street Journal), and

(b) delivery to Morgan of the requisite amount of Argentine sovereign bonds,

---

19. Allen & Overy, An Introduction to the Documentation of OTC Derivatives 1, 2-3 (2002), available at http://www.isda.org /educat/pdf/documentation_of_derivatives.pdf (last visited June 21, 2004) ("Allen & Overy").

(c) Morgan would pay Eternity par value for the obligations tendered.

It is alleged (and we therefore assume) that Eternity entered the swaps in reliance on Morgan's representations that it would provide access to a liquid secondary market that would enable the Fund to divest the contracts prior to termination.

The parties dispute whether any of certain actions taken by Argentina with respect to its debt obligations in November and December 2001 constituted a credit event. The district court thought not, and dismissed Eternity's contract claim at the pleading stage. *Eternity II, 2003 U.S. Dist. LEXIS 12351, 2003 WL 21305355, at *4-6.* With the background and structure of the disputed CDS contracts in mind, we turn to Eternity's principal allegations.

* * *

The contracts at issue were signed in October 2001. By then, international financial markets had been speculating for months that Argentina might default on its $ 132 billion in government and other public debt. At an August 2001 meeting of bondholders in New York, Morgan acknowledged the possibility of a sovereign-debt default and advised that it was working with the Argentine government on restructuring scenarios. On October 31, 2001—after the effective date of the swap contracts at issue on this appeal—Morgan sent Eternity a research report noting that there was a "high implied probability of [a] restructuring" in which bondholders would likely receive replacement securities with a less-favorable rate of return. One day later, Argentine President Fernando de la Rua asked sovereign-bond holders to accept lower interest rates and longer maturities on approximately $ 95 billion of government debt. On November 19, 2001, the Argentine government announced that a "voluntary debt exchange" would be offered to sovereign-bond holders. According to various public decrees, willing bondholders could exchange their obligations for secured loans that would pay a lower rate of return over a longer term, but that would be secured by certain federal tax revenues. So long as the government made timely payments on the loans, the original obligations would be held in trust for the benefit of Argentina ; if the government defaulted, however, bondholders would have recourse to the original obligations, which were to "remain effective" for the duration of their life-in-trust. From late November through early December 2001, billions of dollars in sovereign bonds were exchanged for the lower-interest loans.

The complaint alleges that the debt exchange amounted to a default because local creditors had no choice but to participate, and that the financial press adopted that characterization. On November 8, 2001 Eternity served the first of three notices on Morgan asserting that the planned debt exchange was a restructuring credit event as to all three CDS contracts; but Morgan demurred.

On December 24, newly-installed interim President Adolfo Rodriguez Saa—appointed by the Argentine Congress on December 23 to replace President de la Rua—announced a public–debt moratorium. On December 27, Morgan notified Eternity that the moratorium constituted a credit event and subsequently settled the outstanding $ 2 million and $ 9 million credit default swaps (otherwise set to terminate on October 22, 2006 and March 31, 2002, respectively). According to Morgan, the third swap (valued at $ 3 million) had expired without being triggered, on December 17, 2001.

It is undisputed that the December 24 public-debt moratorium was a trigger of Eternity's outstanding swaps; in Eternity's view, however, the voluntary debt exchange had triggered Morgan's settlement obligations as early as November 8, 2001, as the Fund had been insisting throughout November and December of that year. In that same period, Eternity asked Morgan to liquidate the swaps on a secondary market. Notwithstanding Morgan's representations in February 2001 regarding the existence of a secondary market for the CDSs, it refused to quote Eternity any secondary-market pricing, though it did offer to "unwind" the contracts by returning the premiums Eternity had paid from October through November 2001.

* * *

The question is whether at this stage it can be decided as a matter of law that the voluntary debt exchange was not a "restructuring credit event" covered by the Fund's CDS contracts with Morgan.... [The court concludes that it could not be decided as a matter of law.] ...

* * *

The district court ruled, and we agree, that Morgan's representations as to (i) Eternity's ability to liquidate the credit default swaps at some future time, and (ii) Morgan's ability to assist Eternity in such a liquidation, cannot support a claim for negligent misrepresentation because they are promissory representations about future events....

* * *

For the foregoing reasons, we affirm the judgment insofar as it dismissed Eternity's claims premised on fraud and negligent misrepresentation. We reverse the judgment insofar as it dismissed Eternity's claim for breach of contract, and remand for further proceedings consistent with this opinion, on the ground that certain material terms of the contracts cannot be found unambiguous on the basis of the pleadings alone.

Note

A robust literature addresses legal issues concerning derivatives. *See, e.g.,* Partnoy, The Shifting Contours of Global Derivatives Regulation, 12 U. Pa. J. Int'l Econ. 421 (2001); Finnerty & Brown, An Overview of Derivatives Litigation, 7 Fordham J. Corp. & Fin. L. 131 (2001); Huang, Securities Price Risks and Financial Derivative Markets, 21 NW. J. Int'l L. & Bus. 589 (2001); Stout, Why the Law Hates Speculators: Regulation and Private Ordering in the Market for OTC Derivatives, 48 Duke L. J. 701 (1999).

b. Derivatives and Fiduciary Duties

Brane v. Roth
590 N.E.2d 587 (Ct. App. Ind. 1992)

This case involves a shareholders' action against the directors of a rural grain elevator cooperative for losses [LaFontaine Grain Co-op ("Co-op")] suffered in 1980 due to the directors' failure to protect its position by adequately hedging in the grain market.... Approximately ninety percent of Co-op's business was buying and selling grain....

The records show that Co-op's gross profit had fallen continually from 1977. After a substantial loss in 1979, Co-op's CPA, Michael Matchette, recommended that the directors hedge Co-op's grain position to protect itself from future losses. The directors authorized [Co-op's] manager to hedge for Co-op. Only a minimal amount was hedged, specifically $20,050 in hedging contracts were made, whereas Co-op had $7,300,000 in grain sales.

On February 3, 1981, Matchette presented the 1980 financial statement to the directors, indicating a net profit of only $68,684. In 1982, Matchette informed the directors of errors in his 1980 financial statement and that Co-op had actually experienced a gross loss of $227,329.... The directors consulted another accounting firm to review the financial condition of Co-op. Coulter found additional errors in Matchette's 1980 financial statement, which increased the gross loss to $424,038.... Coulter opined that the primary cause of the gross loss was the failure to hedge.

The court entered specific findings and conclusions determining that the directors breached their duties by retaining a manager inexperienced in hedging; failing to maintain reasonable supervision over him; and failing to attain knowledge of the basic fundamentals of hedging to be able to direct the hedging activities and supervise the manager properly; and that their gross inattention and failure to protect the grain profits caused the resultant loss of $424,038.89....

The trial court [correctly applied] the standard of care set forth in [Indiana's state statute, which] provided that a director shall perform his duties in good faith in the best interest of the corporation and with such care as an ordinarily prudent person in a like position would use in similar circumstances. The statute allows the director to rely upon information, reports, and opinions of the corporation's officers and employees which he reasonably believes to be reliable and competent, and public accountants on matters which he reasonably believes to be within such person's professional competence....

Under [the clearly erroneous] standard of review, we find that there was probative evidence that Co-op's losses were due to a failure to hedge. Coulter testified that grain elevators should engage in hedging to protect the co-op from losses from price swings. One expert in the grain elevator business and hedging testified that co-ops should not speculate and that Co-op's losses stemmed from the failure to hedge.

Further evidence in the record supports the court's findings and its conclusions that the directors breached their duty by their failure to supervise the manager and become aware of the essentials of hedging to be able to monitor the business which was a proximate cause of Co-op's losses. Although the directors argue that they relied upon their manager and should be insulated from liability, the business judgment rule protects directors from liability only if their decisions were informed ones.

[We have] stated that "a director cannot blindly take action and later avoid the consequences by saying he was not aware of the effect of the action he took. A director has some duty to become informed about the actions he is about to undertake." Here, the evidence shows that the directors made no meaningful attempts to be informed of the hedging activities and their effects upon Co-op's financial position. Their failure to provide adequate supervision of the manager's actions was a breach of their duty of care to protect Co-op's interests in a reasonable manner. The business judgment rule does not shield the directors from liability.

* * *

[D]irectors are not liable for mere errors of judgment, but ... they are liable for losses occurring through their gross inattention to the business or their willful violation of their duties.... [Duties include]: knowing the company's general financial condition, knowing its solvency position, checking or preventing improvident or dishonest conduct of managers, examining corporate records and knowing the manner in which business is conducted, and supervising managers....

The directors argue that this [duty] requires "gross negligence" before liability is exacted. We disagree with the directors' interpretation and also note that ... the proper

standard of care is that set forth in [the Indiana state statute], which is not a gross negligence standard. The trial court [found] particular breaches of duties here and [does
not imply that] gross negligence by Co-op's directors was necessary.... [T]he trial court
required more than errors in judgment before finding the directors were negligent. It
was necessary that the trial court here decide whether the directors acted as ordinarily
prudent persons in like positions in similar circumstances would have acted. The trial
court applied that standard correctly.

Notes and Questions

1. Cases holding directors liable for breach of the duty of care are about as rare as
hen's teeth. Prominent examples are Francis v. United Jersey Bank, 432 A.2d 814 (N.J.
1981) and Smith v. Van Gorkom, 488 A.2d 858 (Del. 1985), neither of which involve
derivatives. As with *Brane*, however, both concern directorial failure to become adequately informed. Should *Brane* be generalized? Should it be limited to the small universe of membership cooperatives? Should it be limited to close corporations? Should it
extend to public corporations? Consult Krawiec, Derivatives, Corporate Hedging, and
Shareholder Wealth: Modigliani-Miller Forty Years Later, 1998 U. Ill. L. Rev. 1039;
Roberta A. Romano, A Thumbnail Sketch of Derivative Securities and Their Regulation, 55 Md. L. Rev. 1 (1996); Henry T. C. Hu, Hedging Expectations: "Derivative Reality" and the Law and Finance of the Corporate Objective, 73 Tex. L. Rev. 985 (1995).

2. If it is possible for companies to hedge risks through derivatives, should the failure
to do so constitute a breach of the duty of care? Should it depend on whether the risks
to be hedged constitute unsystematic risks? If one accepts the proposition under modern portfolio theory that shareholders can themselves diversify unsystematic risks to
zero, would a firm be wasting resources by hedging such risks? Does the appropriate
hedging policy for any firm depend on how one understand's the purpose of the corporation and the precise standard of obligation owed by directors and to whom? *See* Hu,
Hedging Expectations: "Derivative Reality" and the Law and Finance of the Corporate
Objective, 73 Texas L. Rev. 985 (1995); Crawford, A Fiduciary Duty to Use Derivatives?,
1 Stan. J. L., Bus. & Fin. 307 (1995).

Should any duty to use derivatives extend to investment managers? Consider the following case:

> In *Levy v. Bessemer Trust Co.*, No. 97 Civ. 1785 (JFK), 1997 WL 431079, at *1
> (S.D.N.Y. July 30, 1997), a client of a financial management and investment ad-
> visory service sued the firm for negligence, gross negligence, negligent misrep-
> resentation, breach of fiduciary duty, breach of the duty to supervise, and fraud.
> Levy, the client, held most of his portfolio in one company's stock with restric-
> tions on his ability to sell. He repeatedly asked Bessemer Trust Company (BTC),
> his brokerage firm, to protect his investment from downward movement in the
> stock price. BTC replied that due to the restrictions on his ownership, there was
> no "immediate protection from downward price movement." A broker at an-
> other firm informed Levy some six months after hiring BTC, that indeed there
> was protection from downward price movement. The competing dealer recom-
> mended a "European options collar", a combination put and call option. If BTC
> had entered into this type of transaction for Levy six months earlier, his stock
> price would have a floor of $33.33 per share and a ceiling of $44 per share. By
> the time Levy had fired BTC and hired another broker to enter the transaction,
> however, his price floor was $24.75 per share and capped at $31.90 per share.

The district court denied the defendant's motion to dismiss, allowing the claims to go forward as sufficient to state a cause of action. Levy alleged inter alia that BTC failed to know and advise him of the availability of downside price protection; was unaware of an investment protective strategy available and did not find out about such a strategy despite his repeated inquiries; made misrepresentations about its expertise in asset management and investment advise; breached its fiduciary duty as investment advisor by giving erroneous information and thereby induced him to maintain his account with BTC and forego other advice; and that BTC knowingly made false statements about its services and expertise in order to induce Levy to retain its services.

Adams & Runkle, The Easy Case for Derivatives Use: Advocating a Corporate Fiduciary Duty to Use Derivatives, 41 Wm. & Mary L. Rev. 595, 644-45 (2000).

c. Derivatives as "Securities"

Financial fiascos occurred in the interest rate derivatives market during 1994. Among the victims were Orange County, California, a once financially venerable county driven into bankruptcy, as well as corporate giants Proctor & Gamble and Gibson Greetings. These and other firms had entered into highly leveraged interest rate swaps under which they would benefit significantly from stable or declining interest rates but would incur substantial loses if interest rates rose. In general, the gains would increase linearly if interest rates fell, but losses would increase exponentially if rates rose. During 1994, rates rose, as the Federal Reserve repeatedly raised its discount rate. Among other casualties of this volatility was Bankers Trust Co., the financial adviser to firms like Gibson Greetings. Some of Bankers Trust's activities are the subject of the following order in an enforcement action brought by the Securities and Exchange Commission. The SEC's jurisdiction, however, only covers "securities," as defined in the various Federal securities laws. But are derivatives "securities"?

In the Matter of BT Securities Corporation
58 S.E.C. Docket 1145
1994 SEC LEXIS 4041 (Dec. 22, 1994)

[The Securities and Exchange Commission ("Commission") instituted administrative proceedings pursuant to its statutory authority to determine whether BT Securities Corporation ("BT Securities") violated various provisions of the Securities Act of 1933 (the "Securities Act") and the Securities Exchange Act of 1934 (the "Exchange Act") in connection with the sale of certain derivative instruments to Gibson Greetings, Inc. ("Gibson"). In connection with the proceeding, BT Securities submitted an Offer of Settlement, which the Commission accepted. The Commission made the following findings, to which BT Securities consented but solely for the purpose of these or other proceedings involving the Commission and without admitting or denying the findings.

BT Securities, a Delaware corporation, is registered with the Commission as a broker-dealer pursuant to Section 15(b) of the Exchange Act. Bankers Trust Company ("Bankers Trust"), a New York banking corporation, was the counterparty to each derivative that BT Securities sold to Gibson and maintained on its books certain information relating to derivatives transactions with Gibson. All the outstanding stock of

Bankers Trust and BT Securities is owned by Bankers Trust New York Corporation ("BTNY"), a publicly traded New York bank holding company. For some purposes, the results of operation of Bankers Trust, BT Securities and other companies are reported on a consolidated basis by BTNY. At year-end 1993, BT Securities accounted for 28% of the consolidated assets of BTNY. Gibson, a Delaware corporation, manufactures and sells greeting cards and gift wrap in the United States and abroad. Its common stock is registered pursuant to Section 12(g) of the Exchange Act and quoted on the Nasdaq stock market.]

III.

* * *

C. FACTS

This matter involves violations of the reporting and antifraud provisions of the federal securities laws in connection with transactions in derivatives sold by BT Securities to Gibson.[2]

1. Background

In May 1991, Gibson issued and privately placed $50 million of senior notes with an interest rate of 9.33% and annual serial maturities from 1995 through 2001 ("the notes"). After the issuance of these notes, interest rates declined. Because the notes could not be prepaid for a number of years, Gibson began to explore the possibility of engaging in interest rate swaps to effectively reduce the interest rate paid on the notes. In connection with those efforts, Gibson sought proposals from a number of entities, and eventually decided to purchase derivatives from BT Securities.

From November 1991 to March 1994, representatives of BT Securities[3] proposed, and Gibson entered into, approximately 29 derivatives transactions, including amendments to existing derivatives, and terminations of derivatives or portions thereof. Over time, the derivatives sold to Gibson by BT Securities became increasingly complex, risky and intertwined. Many had leverage factors which caused Gibson's losses to increase dramatically with relatively small changes in interest rates.

The derivatives that BT Securities sold to Gibson were customized and did not trade in any market. As a result, Bankers Trust used sophisticated computer models to establish values for those derivatives. Such values, as adjusted, were reflected in the financial statements that BTNY, the parent of BT Securities, filed with the Commission.[4] Gibson, however, did not have the expertise or computer models needed to value the derivatives it purchased from BT Securities. Instead, as BT Securities knew, Gibson used the information provided by BT Securities about the value of its derivatives positions to evaluate

---

2. This matter does not involve any finding or conclusion relating to the suitability of the derivative products described herein for Gibson.

3. The BT Securities' representatives referred to in this Order were primarily the persons responsible for handling the Gibson account.

4. The value of Bankers Trust's derivatives portfolio, as reflected on BTNY's 1992 financial statements, was adjusted by general reserves intended to reflect market risk, model risk, operations cost, as well as other valuation considerations, and general credit reserves. These reserves did not reflect any differential between values quoted to Gibson and the computer model value of Gibson's positions.

particular transactions and to prepare its financial statements, which would be included in periodic reports filed with the Commission.[5]

On BTNY's 1993 financial statements, the value of Bankers Trust's derivatives portfolio was adjusted by general reserves and by specific reserves intended to reflect the differential between the "quoted values" of positions and the computer model values. With respect to Gibson, the specific reserve reflected 25% of the differential between the computer model value and the "quoted value" of Gibson's position at the end of November 1993.

BT Securities has stated that it also quoted prices at which derivatives transactions could be terminated or "torn up." These prices might vary from the computer model values to reflect, among other factors, market conditions, hedging costs, credit concerns, or discounts offered to customers for competitive reasons. Bankers Trust has stated that its policy was that it was willing to execute on the basis of a quoted termination or "tear-up" price. However, in 1993, Bankers Trust tore up only two transactions at prices below the computer model value, and none of the transactions with Gibson, except for the final restructuring transaction in March 1994, were executed at less than computer model values.

2. Provision of Inaccurate Valuations to Gibson

During the period from October 1992 to March 1994, BT Securities' representatives misled Gibson about the value of the company's derivatives positions by providing Gibson with values that significantly understated the magnitude of Gibson's losses. As a result, Gibson remained unaware of the actual extent of its losses from derivatives transactions and continued to purchase derivatives from BT Securities. In addition, the valuations provided by BT Securities' representatives caused Gibson to make material understatements of the company's unrealized losses from derivatives transactions in its 1992 and 1993 notes to financial statements filed with the Commission.

* * *

On two occasions when Gibson sought valuations for the specific purpose of preparing its financial statements, representatives of BT Securities provided Gibson with valuations that differed by more than 50% from the value generated by the computer model and recorded on Bankers Trust's books. In early February 1993, Gibson asked representatives of BT Securities for the value of its derivatives as of December 31, 1992 and stated that the information would be used in preparing Gibson's 1992 year-end financial statements. As of December 31, 1992, Bankers Trust's books reflected a negative value of $2,129,209 for Gibson's derivatives positions. BT Securities, however, provided Gibson with a "mark-to-market" value for the derivatives positions of a negative $1,025,000, a difference of $1,104,209, or 52%.

The next fiscal year, in a letter dated December 31, 1993, Gibson asked representatives of BT Securities to provide Gibson with the value of Gibson's derivatives as of that date to use in preparing Gibson's 1993 year-end financial statements. As of December 31, 1993, Bankers Trust's books reflected a negative value of $7,470,886 for Gibson's derivatives positions. Representatives of BT Securities, however, provided Gibson with a

---

5. As a public company whose securities are registered with the Commission, Gibson was required, by rules promulgated under Section 13(a) of the Exchange Act, to file with the Commission annual and periodic reports that included accurate annual and quarterly financial statements.

"mark-to-market" value for the derivatives positions of a negative $2,900,000, a difference of $4,570,886, or 61%.

3. Offer and Sale of Securities to Gibson

Certain of the derivatives that BT Securities sold to Gibson were securities within the meaning of the federal securities laws. BT Securities' representatives made material misrepresentations and omissions in the offer and sale of these securities.

a. Treasury-Linked Swap

On February 19, 1993, BT Securities sold Gibson a derivative transaction sometimes referred to as the "Treasury-Linked Swap."[6] The Treasury-Linked Swap was within the class of options that are securities, within the meaning of the federal securities laws. During late January and early February 1993, immediately before selling the Treasury-Linked Swap to Gibson, BT Securities provided Gibson with four different proposals for restructuring a derivative position held by the company known as the Ratio Swap. In connection with one of those proposals, they represented to Gibson that the Ratio Swap had a negative value to Gibson of $1,000,000.

By mid-February 1993, according to Bankers Trust's own books, the value of the Ratio Swap had improved to a negative value of $138,000 to Gibson. However, BT Securities' representatives failed to inform Gibson of this improvement in the value of the Ratio Swap. Unaware of this information, Gibson entered into the Treasury-Linked Swap on February 19, 1993 as a means of reducing the risk on the Ratio Swap.

The Treasury-Linked Swap had a term of eight months. Under the terms of the transaction, Gibson was required to pay the London Interbank Offered Rate ("LIBOR") and would receive LIBOR, plus 200 basis points, on a $30 million notional amount (the amount used to determine the periodic payments between the counterparties). At maturity, Gibson was required to pay Bankers Trust $30 million, and Bankers Trust would pay the lesser of $30.6 million or an amount determined by the following formula:

$$\$30,000,000 \times 1 - \frac{\frac{103 - 2 \text{ yr. Treas. yield}}{4.88\%} - 30 \text{ yr Treas. price}}{100}$$

In return for entering into the Treasury-Linked Swap, the maturity of the Ratio Swap was shortened from five years to four years. On February 19, 1993, the day Gibson entered into the Treasury-Linked Swap, Bankers Trust's own books and computer models indicated that the fifth year of the Ratio Swap had a negative value to Gibson of $851,700. At the time, BT Securities' representatives knew that Gibson would incur a loss of $2.1 million, composed of an unrealized loss and transactional charges, built into the structure of the Treasury-Linked Swap.

BT Securities proposed, and Gibson entered into, five amendments to the Treasury-Linked Swap. Each of the amendments was a security within the meaning of the federal securities laws. Each amendment was proposed by BT Securities as a way to improve

---

6. While called a swap, the Treasury-Linked Swap was in actuality a cash-settled put option that was written by Gibson and based initially on the "spread" between the price of the 7.625% 30-year U.S. Treasury security maturing on November 15, 2022 and the arithmetic average of the bid and offered yields of the most recently auctioned obligation of a two-year Treasury note. The option was based on a notional amount of $30 million....

Gibson's derivatives positions. In connection with entering into the amendments, representatives of BT Securities misled Gibson and, accordingly, Gibson sustained unrealized losses of approximately $2 million.

b. Knock-Out Call Option

On June 10, 1993, BT Securities sold Gibson another derivative transaction sometimes referred to as the "Knock-Out Call Option."[7] The Knock-Out Call Option was an option on a security and, thus, was a security within the meaning of the federal securities laws.

BT Securities' representatives marketed the Knock-Out Call Option to Gibson as part of a strategy to reduce Gibson's exposure on the Treasury-Linked Swap, described above, by reducing its notional amount. The transaction required Bankers Trust to pay Gibson on settlement date an amount calculated as follows: (6.876% − Yield at Maturity of 30-year Treasury security) × 12.5 × $25,000,000. If at any time during the life of the Knock-Out Call Option, the yield on the 30-year U.S. Treasury security dropped below 6.48%, the option expired, or was "knocked-out," and became worthless. The option was not exercisable until maturity.

During the summer of 1993, the yield on the 30-year U.S. Treasury security began to decline, increasing the Knock-Out Call Option's potential payout but also increasing the likelihood that the option would expire worthless. BT Securities thereafter proposed, and Gibson entered into, a number of amendments to the Knock-Out Call Option. Each of the amendments to the Knock-Out Call Option was a security within the meaning of the federal securities laws.

On August 4, 1993, Gibson agreed to enter into an interest rate swap known as the Time Swap. As part of the transaction, Gibson agreed to terminate another interest rate swap, and BT Securities agreed to lower the knock-out barrier on the Knock-Out Call Option. BT Securities' representatives had proposed that Gibson enter into the transactions to preserve an opportunity for "substantial" gain. BT Securities' representatives knew that, as a result of amending the Knock-Out Call Option in this fashion, Gibson would sustain approximately $1.4 million in unrealized losses built into the structure of the Time Swap, but failed to disclose that information to Gibson. The cost of entering into the Time Swap was almost equal to Gibson's maximum possible profit on the Knock-Out Call Option.

Approximately one week later, as the yield on the 30-year U.S. Treasury security continued to decline, BT Securities' representatives proposed that Gibson again lower the knock-out barrier of the Knock-Out Call Option, this time in exchange for adjusting the leverage factor in the Time Swap. On August 12, 1993, Gibson accepted the proposal and entered into an amendment of the Knock-Out Call Option and increased the leverage factor in the Time Swap. By entering into this amendment, Gibson unknowingly sustained unrealized losses of approximately $89,000, which were built into the structure of the amendment at the time it was entered into.

Several weeks later, BT Securities' representatives proposed that Gibson enter into yet another amendment to the Knock-Out Call Option, in exchange for restructuring the Time Swap. A BT Securities' representative told Gibson that the Time Swap "continues

---

7. The Knock-Out Call Option was a European-style, cash-settled call option that was written by BT Securities and had a return based on the yield of the 7.125% 30-year U.S. Treasury security maturing February 15, 2023. The option was based on a notional amount of $25 million....

to look pretty good." In fact, at that time, the Time Swap held a substantial negative value to Gibson.

Gibson agreed to purchase the amendment to the Knock-Out Call Option's barrier on August 26, 1993 by entering into another amendment to the Time Swap. By entering into this amendment, Gibson unknowingly incurred a loss of approximately $578,000, composed of an unrealized loss and transactional charges, built into the structure of the amendment at the time it was entered into. The next day Gibson agreed to terminate the Knock-Out Call Option and was paid $475,000 by Bankers Trust. In the three amendments to the Knock-Out Call Option, Gibson unknowingly incurred unrealized losses of $3 million built into the structure of the Time Swap. In comparison, the maximum possible payout of the Knock-Out Call Option never exceeded $2.3 million.

4. Failure to Supervise

The combination of Gibson's frequent trades on terms favorable to Bankers Trust made Gibson a particularly lucrative customer for BT Securities. During 1993 alone, the BT Securities managing director dealing with Gibson generated approximately $8 million in derivatives revenues from Gibson, out of a total of approximately $20 million from all of his derivatives customers that year. And BT Securities generated overall revenues of approximately $13 million from these transactions with Gibson.

BT Securities' managing director for the Gibson account told his supervisor in February 1994 that "from the very beginning, [Gibson] just, you know, really put themselves in our hands like 96% ... And we have known that from day one." The managing director also told the Bankers Trust relationship officer responsible for the Gibson account that "these guys [Gibson] have done some pretty wild stuff. And you know, they probably do not understand it quite as well as they should. I think that they have a pretty good understanding of it, but not perfect. And that's like perfect for us."

Despite the volume of BT Securities' transactions with Gibson and their profitability, BT Securities did not take steps to determine whether it was providing Gibson with information that accurately reflected the value of its positions. In fact, for more than one year, BT Securities' representatives provided Gibson with valuations substantially more favorable to Gibson than the values contained on Bankers Trust books and generated by its computer models. Although these valuations were not provided to Gibson, they were incorporated in the filings made with the Commission by BTNY, the parent of BT Securities.

D. LEGAL DISCUSSION
1. Causing Misstatements by Gibson in Financial Statements

As set forth above, representatives of BT Securities provided Gibson with valuations which materially understated Gibson's losses from derivatives transactions. On two occasions, Gibson asked representatives of BT Securities to provide such valuations to assist it in preparing year-end financial statements. On both occasions, BT Securities provided Gibson with valuations which were over 50% below the value of those positions reflected on Bankers Trust's books. BT Securities' representatives knew that the numbers they were giving Gibson understated Gibson's unrealized losses and would be used to prepare financial statements that would be filed with the Commission. However, those representatives never informed Gibson that the numbers they had provided did not accurately reflect the value of Gibson's positions. As a result, Gibson used the values in its financial statements, and those statements materially understated the company's losses from derivatives activities. Accordingly, BT Securities caused violations of Section 13(a) of the Exchange Act and Rules 13a-1 and 12b-20 thereunder.

2. Offer and Sale of Securities

As discussed above, the Treasury-Linked Swap, the Knock-Out Call Option, and the amendments to these derivatives, were securities under the federal securities laws. BT Securities engaged in material misrepresentations and omissions in its offer and sale of these derivative securities to Gibson. In offering and selling these securities, as set forth above, BT Securities violated Section 17(a) of the Securities Act, Section 10(b) of the Exchange Act and Rule 10b-5. As a result, Gibson engaged in a series of derivatives transactions to BT Securities' financial advantage.

3. Failure to Supervise

Section 15(b)(4)(E) of the Exchange Act authorizes the Commission to impose sanctions against a broker-dealer if the firm has "failed reasonably to supervise, with a view to preventing violations of federal securities laws, another person who commits such a violation, if such other person is subject to his supervision."

BT Securities failed to take reasonable steps to supervise its representatives. BT Securities had no procedure that could reasonably be expected to prevent or detect the violative conduct described herein. BT Securities' procedures allowed its representatives to engage in a practice of providing Gibson with values that materially understated Gibson's unrealized losses. The valuations were provided to a public company, Gibson, with knowledge that they would materially affect its financial statements filed with the Commission and relied on by the investing public. The valuations were created by and provided to Gibson by BT Securities' marketers who had an interest in having Gibson engage in derivatives transactions. In such circumstances, BT Securities failed reasonably to supervise with a view to preventing violations of the federal securities laws....

Notes and Questions

1. *Gibson's Situation.* Gibson was already locked into paying fixed rate notes that could not be prepaid under their terms for a number of years. In seeking to reduce its interest expense on those notes, was there a simpler way than that proposed under the Treasury-Linked Swap? Was that device designed to reduce Gibson's interest rate expense in respect of the pre-existing notes? Did it work?

2. *Terms of the Gibson Instruments.* Consider the last paragraph of part III.C.1 of the order, beginning with "BT Securities has stated that it also quoted prices at which derivatives transactions could be terminated or 'torn up.'" The paragraph is trying to report that BT in effect tracked two separate prices for the products, its tear up price and its computer model price, and that these two prices can vary for the reasons stated in the paragraph. The order reports that BT stated that it was willing to terminate the swaps at the tear up price. The SEC's claims of fraud rested on the discrepancy between the computer model prices and the prices BT had given to Gibson. But what if the prices given to Gibson had been the tear up prices? Then the claim of fraud depends on a conclusion that the price that mattered was the computer model price and not the tear up price. If there is no reason to believe that one or the other of these prices is the correct one, would the claim of fraud against BT have stood? Assuming that the computer model price could be calculated by any firm that engages routinely

in writing and marketing derivatives, should Gibson have contacted one of those firms and asked for its determination of the price? If it had done so, and learned of the discrepancy, how would this have affected the relationship between BT and Gibson and the resulting fallout?

3. *Gibson's Legal Exposure.* Consider the BT Securities' representative statement that Gibson's managers "have done some pretty wild stuff [that] they probably do not understand … as well as they should." If found to be true in another proceeding, would this be a basis for stockholders of Gibson to establish a breach of the duty of care on the part of Gibson's board of directors? *Cf.* Brane v. Roth, 590 N.E.2d. 587 (Ct. App. Ind. 1992), *supra*, and Graham v. Allis-Chalmers Mfg., 188 A.2d 125 (Del. 1963). How would the argument that BT Securities had breached a duty to clarify Gibson's understanding of the derivatives affect such a claim?

4. *Suitability Issues.* Footnote 2 of the SEC's findings and order announces that the SEC is taking no position on the suitability for Gibson of the instruments BT Securities sold to it. What does this mean? There are a number of so-called suitability rules applicable to transactions in securities, historically limited to individual (retail) investors. These require brokers to know their customer's needs and to avoid recommending instruments that are somehow inappropriate for that client. In the aftermath of the derivatives market shake up, Gibson, Proctor & Gamble, other large corporations and Orange County reportedly claimed that their investment brokers had violated these rules. Orange County's trustee in bankruptcy sued the County's investment banker, Merrill Lynch, claiming that its losses of more than $2 billion arose from entering into a series of "highly leveraged" instruments that were illegal for it to enter into under California law applicable to municipalities. *See* Orange County Chapter 9 Bankruptcy, (Case No. SA 94-22272-JR) (Bankr. C.D. Cal. 1995), N.Y.L.J., Mar. 16, 1995. (The lawsuit was later dismissed.) Should brokers owe to corporate clients the same know-the-customer duty owed to individual (retail) clients? Should it matter how large the corporation is? Should they have the same duty to institutional clients, such as insurance companies? What about municipalities? Should it matter whether the municipality is large or small? See Goldman, Crafting A Suitability Requirement for the Sale of Over-the-Counter Derivatives: Should Regulators "Punish the Wall Street Hounds of Greed"?, 95 Colum. L. Rev. 1112 (1995).

Jurisdictional Turf Wars

The SEC asserted jurisdiction over the BT-Gibson matter after it determined that the derivatives in question were "securities" as defined in Section 3(a)(10) of the Exchange Act. Thus, the Federal securities laws applied. The Commodities Futures Trading Commission (CFTC), however, disagreed with the SEC's determination. It conducted its own investigation into the BT-Gibson matter and commenced its own action against BT entitled In the Matter of BT Securities Corporation,1994 WL 711224 (CFTC).

The CFTC's complaint was filed pursuant to Sections 6(c) and (d) of the Commodity Exchange Act (CEA). The CFTC found that BT entered into a commodity trading advisory relationship with Gibson and made fraudulent misrepresentations and omissions in connection with derivatives. BT submitted an offer of settlement that was subsequently accepted by the CFTC. BT was ordered to cease violating the CEA and pay a $10 million civil penalty.

This was not the first jurisdictional struggle over derivative transactions between the SEC and the CFTC. Historically, the SEC and the CFTC have been at odds about how to classify certain derivative transactions, especially privately-negotiated ("over-the-counter") derivatives ("OTC derivatives"). OTC derivative transactions like those engaged in by Gibson posed a unique problem because they were not traded on any exchange. Because of this, they were exempt from SEC and CEA regulation except for antifraud and antimanipulation provisions. As of 1994, neither the SEC nor the CFTC was willing to assert jurisdiction beyond this scope. Even when enforcing antifraud and antimanipulation provisions, these agencies found it difficult to classify these complex transactions. For example, some of the underlying assets in an OTC derivative may be deemed a "security," while other underlying assets may be deemed "commodities" or may resemble a "future." These hybrid instruments, therefore, have created legal uncertainty as to whether the CFTC or the SEC may assert jurisdiction over these transactions and, if so, to what extent. The Gibson proceedings illustrated that difficulty. These agencies were not alone in their confusion, as courts also grappled with the same question as seen in Procter & Gamble Co. v. Bankers Trust Co., 925 F. Supp. 1270 (S.D. Ohio 1996), *infra*.

In response to market developments and the high profile losses surrounding OTC derivative transactions, the SEC and the CFTC embarked on separate regulatory initiatives. The SEC adopted new rules governing the disclosure of derivatives on January 28, 1997. The expanded disclosure rules were set up to keep investors informed about the risks public companies were taking through derivatives and what losses they could incur if interest rates, foreign currency exchange rates, or commodity prices fluctuated. This was the first time the SEC required reporting companies to quantify risks associated with derivative transactions.

The CFTC followed suit by issuing a concept release on May 12, 1998. In this concept release, the CFTC outlined possible reforms to the exemption policies concerning swap transactions and hybrid instruments. In particular, the CFTC sought to impose narrowly-defined exemptive conditions based on market developments. In doing so, OTC derivative transactions would have to comply with the new conditions or be subject to CFTC regulation. The sought after changes would impose a regulatory scheme on hybrid and swap transactions as a condition for exempting such products from CEA regulation. Many market leaders considered this proposal a Catch-22, as OTC derivative transactions would have to comply with some form of CFTC regulation in any event.

The SEC later released a written statement regarding the regulation of OTC derivatives, largely in response to the CFTC's concept release. In this statement, the SEC challenged any assertion of jurisdiction by the CFTC over the OTC derivatives market. It also resisted the CFTC's proposal to change the scope of the exemption provided for hybrid instruments through its exemptive authority. The SEC raised serious doubts as to whether the CFTC had the authority to regulate OTC markets since Congress had yet to articulate an intent for the CFTC to regulate off-exchange markets.

Congress attempted to resolve this turf war and the many problems surrounding OTC derivative transactions by passing the Commodity Futures Modernization Act of 2000 (CFMA), the year 2000 amendments to the CEA. The purpose of the CFMA was to eliminate the legal uncertainty surrounding derivative transactions by clarifying jurisdictional lines and statutory definitions of market instruments. The CFMA also sought to stimulate innovation and promote market efficiency for the U.S. derivatives market.

Among other things, the CFMA provided: (1) that OTC derivative transactions between "eligible contract participants" may not be voided as illegal off-exchange contracts;

(2) that a transaction that is based on prices, yields or volatilities of securities that (a) is not an option or forward on a security or (b) a swap between eligible participants will not be classified as a "security" under Federal securities laws; however, basic antifraud, antimanipulation and insider trading prohibitions will still apply; and (3) for the creation of a three-tiered regulatory structure for CFTC oversight of the derivatives market.

Despite the CFMA, some courts continue to grapple with the definition of "security" for purposes of the Federal securities laws in the context of derivatives. *See* Caiola v. Citibank, N.A., 295 F.3d 312 (2d Cir. 2002), *infra*.

Besides the SEC and CFTC, other U.S. and foreign governmental and other regulatory agencies investigated the use of derivatives during the 1990s. These included the Federal Reserve Board, the Financial Accounting Standards Board, the New York Stock Exchange, the London Stock Exchange, and The Bank of England. In addition, a number of private organizations have also emerged to develop protocols for the derivatives industry. These include the Derivatives Products Group (DPG), an organization comprised of a number of the leading firms that design derivative products and market them; the End Users of Derivatives Association (EUDA, pronounced uta), a group of industrial corporations and other entities that participate in the deriviatives markets, usually as customers of those firms; and the Global Derivatives Study Group of the Group of Thirty, an industry research and policy formulation organization. These groups have sought to develop protocols to address the numerous issues posed by the widespread use of deriviatives, including some of the issues discussed below.

Procter & Gamble Co. v. Bankers Trust Co.
925 F. Supp. 1270 (S.D. Oh. 1996)

.... This case involves two interest rate swap agreements. A swap is an agreement between two parties ("counterparties") to exchange cash flows over a period of time. Generally, the purpose of an interest rate swap is to protect a party from interest rate fluctuations. The simplest form of swap, a "plain vanilla" interest-rate swap, involves one counterparty paying a fixed rate of interest, while the other counterparty assumes a floating interest rate based on the amount of the principal of the underlying debt. This is called the "notional" amount of the swap, and this amount does not change hands; only the interest payments are exchanged.

In more complex interest rate swaps, such as those involved in this case, the floating rate may derive its value from any number of different securities, rates or indexes. In each instance, however, the counterparty with the floating rate obligation enters into a transaction whose precise value is unknown and is based upon activities in the market over which the counterparty has no control. How the swap plays out depends on how market factors change....

In the face of relentless competition and capital market disintermediation, banks in search of profits have hired financial scientists to develop new financial products. Often operating in an international wholesale market open only to major corporate and sovereign entities—a loosely regulated paradise hidden from public view—these scientists push the frontier, relying on powerful computers and an array of esoteric models laden with incomprehensible Greek letters. But danger lurks. As financial creatures are invented, introduced, and then evolve and mutate, exotic risks and uncertainties arise. In its most fevered imagining, not only do the trillions of mutant creatures destroy their creators in the wholesale market, but they escape and wreak havoc in the retail market and in economies worldwide....

[The] swaps transactions are governed by written documents executed by BT and P&G. BT and P&G entered into an Interest Rate and Currency Exchange Agreement on January 20, 1993. This standardized form, drafted by the International Swap Dealers Association, Inc. ("ISDA"), together with a customized Schedule and written Confirmations for each swap, create the rights and duties of parties to derivative transactions. By their terms, the ISDA Master Agreement, the Schedule, and all Confirmations form a single agreement between the parties.

During the fall of 1993, the parties began discussing the terms of an interest rate swap which was to be customized for P&G. After negotiations, the parties agreed to a swap transaction on November 2, 1993, which is referred to as the 5s/30s swap; the written Confirmation is dated November 4, 1993.

In the 5s/30s swap transaction, BT agreed to pay P&G a fixed rate of interest of 5.30% for five years on a notional amount of $ 200 million. P&G agreed to pay BT a floating interest rate. For the first six months, that floating rate was the prevailing commercial paper ("CP") interest rate minus 75 basis points (0.75%). For the remaining four-and-a-half years, P&G was to make floating interest rate payments of CP minus 75 basis points plus a spread. The spread was to be calculated at the end of the first six months (on May 4, 1994).... The leverage factor in this formula meant that even a small movement up or down in prevailing interest rates results in an incrementally larger change in P&G's position in the swap.

The parties amended this swap transaction in January 1994; they postponed the date the spread was to be set to May 19, 1994, and P&G was to receive CP minus 88 basis points, rather than 75 basis points, up to the spread date.

In late January 1994, P&G and BT negotiated a second swap, known as the "DM swap", based on the value of the German Deutschemark. The Confirmation for this swap is dated February 14, 1994. For the first year, BT was to pay P&G a floating interest rate plus 233 basis points. P&G was to pay the same floating rate plus 133 basis points; P&G thus received a 1% premium for the first year, the effective dates being January 16, 1994 through January 16, 1995. On January 16, 1995, P&G was to add a spread to its payments to BT if the four-year DM swap rate ever traded below 4.05% or above 6.01% at any time between January 16, 1994, and January 16, 1995. If the DM swap rate stayed within that band of interest rates, the spread was zero. If the DM swap rate broke that band, the spread would be set on January 16, 1995.... The leverage factor in this swap was shown in the formula as ten.

P&G unwound both of these swaps before their spread set dates, as interest rates in both the United States and Germany took a significant turn upward, thus putting P&G in a negative position vis-a-vis its counterparty BT. BT now claims that it is owed over $200 million on the two swaps, while P&G claims the swaps were fraudulently induced and fraudulently executed, and seeks a declaratory verdict that it owes nothing.

In the 1933 Securities Act, Congress defined the term "security" as:

     any note, stock, treasury stock, bond, debenture, evidence of indebtedness, certificate of interest or participation in any profit-sharing agreement, collateral-trust certificate, preorganization certificate or subscription, transferrable share, investment contract, voting-trust certificate, certificate of deposit for a security, fractional undivided interest in oil, gas, or other mineral rights, any put, call, straddle, option, or privilege on any security, certificate of deposit, or group or index of securities (including any interest therein or based on the value thereof), or any put, call, straddle, option, or privilege entered into on a national securities exchange relating to foreign currency, or, in general, any interest or instrument commonly known as a "security", or a certificate of interest or participation in, temporary or interim certificate for, receipt for, guarantee of, or warrant or right to subscribe to or purchase, any of the foregoing.

15 U.S.C. §77b(1). The definition section of the 1934 Act, 15 U.S.C. §78c(a)(10), is virtually identical and encompasses the same instruments as the 1933 Act. *Reves v. Ernst & Young*, 494 U.S. 56, 61 n.1, 108 L. Ed. 2d 47, 110 S. Ct. 945 (1989).

P&G asserts that the 5s/30s and DM swaps fall within any of the following portions of that definition: 1) investment contracts; 2) notes; 3) evidence of indebtedness; 4) options on securities; and 5) instruments commonly known as securities.

Congress intended a broad interpretation of the securities laws and flexibility to effectuate their remedial purpose of avoiding fraud. *SEC v. Howey*, 328 U.S. 293, 90 L. Ed. 1244, 66 S. Ct. 1100 (1946). The United States Supreme Court has held, however, that Congress did not "intend" the Securities Acts "to provide a broad federal remedy for all fraud." *Marine Bank v. Weaver*, 455 U.S. 551, 556, 71 L. Ed. 2d 409, 102 S. Ct. 1220 (1982). The threshold issue presented by P&G's securities fraud claims is whether a security exists, i.e., whether or not these swaps are among "the myriad financial transactions in our society that come within the coverage of these statutes." [*United Housing Federation, Inc. v. Forman*, 421 U.S. 835, 849 (1975)].

Economic reality is the guide for determining whether these swaps transactions that do not squarely fit within the statutory definition are, nevertheless, securities. [*Reves v. Ernst & Young*, 494 U.S. 56, 62 (1990)]. In order to determine if these swaps are securities, commodities, or neither), I must examine each aspect of these transactions and subject them to the guidelines set forth in Supreme Court cases.

For purposes of the federal securities laws, an "investment contract" is defined as "a contract, transaction or scheme whereby a person invests his money in a common enterprise." *Howey*, 328 U.S. at 298-99. Stated differently, the test whether an instrument is an investment contract is whether it entails "an investment in a common venture premised on a reasonable expectation of profits to be derived from the entrepreneurial or managerial efforts of others." *Forman*, 421 U.S. at 852. The U.S. Court of Appeals for the Sixth Circuit has interpreted the *Howey* test as a "flexible one 'capable of adaptation or meeting the countless and variable schemes devised by those who seek the use of the money of others on the promise of profits.'" *Stone v. Kirk*, 8 F.3d 1079, 1085 (6th Cir. 1993), quoting *Howey*, 328 U.S. at 299.

BT argues that the swaps are not investment contracts because 1) neither P&G nor BT invested any money; rather, they agreed to exchange cash payments at future dates; 2) the swaps did not involve an investment in a "common enterprise," which involves the pooling of funds in a single business venture; and 3) any gains to be derived from the swaps were not "profits," which are defined as "capital appreciation" or "participation in earnings" of a business venture. BT contends that cash payments to be made arise not from the efforts of others, but from changes in U.S. and German interest rates.

P&G counters that the swaps are investments of money because an investment exists where an investor has committed its assets in such a way that it is subject to a financial loss and that the commitment to make future payments is sufficient to constitute an investment; further, that the swaps meet the "common enterprise" tests because its swaps, when combined with those of other parties, became part of the capital used to support BT's derivatives business. Specifically, P&G argues, BT combines its sales in one hedge book to offset all of its customers' transactions, and unwind prices reflect BT's overall portfolio risk. P&G further contends that its profit motive was its desire to reduce its overall interest costs and that it expected to derive profits from the efforts of BT in structuring and monitoring the swaps.

While the swaps may meet certain elements of the *Howey* test whether an instrument is an investment contract, what is missing is the element of a "common enterprise." P&G did not pool its money with that of any other company or person in a single business venture. How BT hedged its swaps is not what is at issue—the issue is whether a number of investors joined together in a common venture. Certainly, any counterparties with whom BT contracted cannot be lumped together as a "common enterprise." Furthermore, BT was not managing P&G's money; BT was a counterparty to the swaps, and the value of the swaps depended on market forces, not BT's entrepreneurial efforts. The swaps are not investment contracts.

BT asserts that the swaps are not notes because they did not involve the payment or repayment of principal. P&G responds that the counterparties incurred payment obligations that were bilateral notes or the functional equivalent of notes.

As with the test whether an instrument is an investment contract, these swap agreements bear some, but not all, of the earmarks of notes. At the outset, and perhaps most basic, the payments required in the swap agreements did not involve the payment or repayment of principal.

In *Reves*, 494 U.S. at 64-67, the Supreme Court set out a four-part "family resemblance" test for identifying notes that should be deemed securities. Those factors are: 1) the motivations of the buyer and seller in entering into the transaction (investment for profit or to raise capital versus commercial); 2) a sufficiently broad plan of distribution of the instrument (common trading for speculation or investment); 3) the reasonable expectations of the investing public; and 4) whether some factor, such as the existence of another regulatory scheme, significantly reduces the risk of the instrument, thereby rendering application of the securities laws unnecessary....

There is no "neat and tidy" way to apply [the first] prong of the test, in part because P&G and BT were counterparties, not the typical buyer and seller of an instrument. BT's motive was to generate a fee and commission, while P&G's expressed motive was, in substantial part, to reduce its funding costs. These motives are tipped more toward a commercial than investment purpose. As to P&G, there was also an element of speculation driving its willingness to enter a transaction that was based on its expectations regarding the path that interest rates would take. Thus, this prong of the *Reves* test, standing alone, is not a sufficient guide to enable one to make the determination whether the 5s/30s and DM swaps were notes within the meaning of the Securities Acts.

The second prong of the *Reves* test examines the plan of distribution of the instrument "to determine whether it is an instrument in which there is 'common trading for speculation or investment.'" *Id.* While derivatives transactions in general are an important part of BT's business, and BT advertises its expertise in putting together a variety of derivatives packages, the test is whether the 5s/30s and DM swaps in particular were widely distributed. These swaps are analogous to the notes that were held not to be securities on the basis that the plan of distribution was [limited]. The 5s/30s and DM swaps were customized for Procter & Gamble; they could not be sold or traded to another counterparty without the agreement of BT. They were not part of any kind of general offering. Thus, I conclude that the 5s/30s and DM swaps were not widely distributed and do not meet the second prong of the *Reves* test.

Application of the third *Reves* factor—the public's reasonable perceptions—does not support a finding that these swap agreements are securities. They were not traded on a national exchange, "the paradigm of a security." *Reves*, 494 U.S. at 69.... [W]hat is relevant is the perception of those few who enter into swap agreements, not the public in general. P&G knew full well that its over-the-counter swap agreements with BT were not registered with any regulatory agency. P&G's "perception" that these swap agreements were securities did not surface until after it had filed its original Complaint in this case. Thus, I conclude that the 5s/30s and DM swaps do not meet the third prong of the *Reves* test.

The fourth *Reves* factor is whether another regulatory scheme exists that would control and thus reduce the risk of the instrument, making application of the securities laws unnecessary. At about the time these swaps were entered into, the guidelines of the Office of the Comptroller of Currency ("OCC") and the Federal Reserve Board went into effect.... While these guidelines are useful in regulating the banking industry, their focus is the protection of banks and their shareholders from default or other credit risks. They do not provide any direct protection to counterparties with whom banks enter into derivatives transactions. While the 5s/30s and DM swaps may meet this prong of the *Reves* "family resemblance" test, this is not enough to bring these transactions within the statutory definition of a "note" for purposes of the securities laws. Balancing all the *Reves* factors, I conclude that the 5s/30s and DM swaps are not notes for purposes of the Securities Acts.

P&G argues that if the swaps are not notes, they are evidence of indebtedness because they contain bilateral promises to pay money and they evidence debts between the parties. It argues that the counterparties promised to pay a debt, which consists of future obligations to pay interest on the notional amounts. Indeed, BT now claims that it is owed millions of dollars on the swaps. P&G points out that the phrase "evidence of indebtedness" in the statute must have a meaning other than that given to a "note" so that the words "evidence of indebtedness" are not redundant. Thus, it argues, without citation to authority, that if the swaps are not notes, then they should be construed as an evidence of indebtedness "either because they may contain terms and conditions well beyond the typical terms of a note and beyond an ordinary investor's ability to understand, or because the debt obligation simply does not possess the physical characteristics of a note."

I do not accept P&G's definition of "evidence of indebtedness" in large part because that definition omits an essential element of debt instruments—the payment or repayment of principal. Swap agreements do not involve the payment of principal; the notional amount never changes hands.

An option is the right to buy or sell, for a limited time, a particular good at a specified price. Five-year notes and thirty-year Treasury bonds are securities; therefore, P&G contends that the 5s/30s swap is an option on securities. It argues that because the 5s/30s swap spread was based on the value of these securities, it falls within the statutory definition: "any put, call, straddle, option or privilege on any security, group or index of securities (including any interest therein or based on the value thereof)." It describes the 5s/30s swap as "a single security which can be decomposed into a plain vanilla swap with an embedded put option. The option is a put on the 30-year bond price with an uncertain strike price that depends on the level of the 5-year yield at the end of six months."

BT contends that the 5s/30s swap is not an option because no one had the right to take possession of the underlying securities. BT argues that although both swaps contained terms that functioned as options, they were not options because they did not give either party the right to sell or buy anything. According to BT, the only "option-like" feature was the spread calculation that each swap contained; that any resemblance the spread calculations had to options on securities does not extend to the underlying swaps themselves, which had no option-like characteristics. I agree that the 5s/30s swap was not an option on a security; there was no right to take possession of any security.ᵃ

The definition of a "security" in the 1933 and 1934 Acts includes the parenthetical phrase "(including any interest therein or based on the value thereof)," which could lead to a reading of the statute to mean that an option based on the value of a security is a security. Legislative history, however, makes it clear that that reading was not intended.... Even though ... the P&G 5s/30s swap derived their values from securities (Treasury notes), they were not options. While these swaps included option-like features, there is a missing essential element of an option. These swaps were exchanges of interest payments; they did not give either counterparty the right to exercise an option or to take possession of any security. Neither party could choose whether or not to exercise an option; the stream of interest payments under the swap was mandatory. Consequently, I conclude that the 5s/30s swap is not an option on a security or an option based on the value of a security.

Finally, P&G contends that both the 5s/30s and the DM swaps are securities simply because that is how these instruments were offered and how they have become known through a course of dealing.... In determining whether the 5s/30s and DM swaps are instruments commonly known as securities, P&G's own pleadings are telling in defining how P&G viewed these transactions. In recent motions, P&G asserts that it knew of the alleged fraud in the 5s/30s swap in mid-April 1994. Yet, P&G did not bring securities claims when it filed its original Complaint in October 1994. P&G did not assert a claim for securities violations until January 1995.... If P&G itself had really thought it was dealing with securities, it is fair to assume that P&G would have included securities counts in its original Complaint. In any event, the contracts between P&G and BT do not meet the *Howey* criteria, particularly because there is no way that they can be construed to be a pooling of funds in a common enterprise. These swap's [sic] do not qualify as securities....

[The court also held that the swaps are not within the definition of a "security" in Ohio "blue sky" laws regulating securities in that state.]

The Commodity Exchange Act ("CEA") includes in its definition of a commodity "all services, rights, and interests in which contracts for future delivery are presently or in the future dealt in." 7 U.S.C. §1a(3). BT asserts that the swaps are not futures contracts; P&G claims that they are.

Under the CEA, The Commodity Futures Trading Commission has exclusive jurisdiction over "accounts, agreements ... and transactions involving contracts of sale of a commodity for future delivery traded or executed on a contract market ... or any other board of trade, exchange, or market, and transactions [in standardized contracts for

---

a. The court apparently wasn't briefed on cash-settled options, which do not involve the physical delivery of the underlying asset. *See* Caiola v. Citibank, N.A., 295 F.3d 312 (2d Cir. 2002), *infra*, for the Second Circuit's analysis of whether cash-settled options are "securities." [Eds.]

certain commodities]." As of January 19, 1996, the CFTC had "not taken a position on whether swap agreements are futures contracts." Letter from Mary L. Schapiro, Chair of U.S. Commodity Futures Trading Commission to Congressmen Roberts and Bliley, p.4 (Jan. 19, 1996). This opinion does not decide that issue because the 5s/30s and DM swaps are within the Swaps Exemption to the CEA and because P&G has not stated a claim under §4b, §4o, or 17 C.F.R. §32.9....

Even if the 5s/30s and DM swaps are defined as commodities, swap agreements are exempt from all but the antifraud provisions of the CEA under the CFTC Swap Exemption. Title V of the Futures Trading Practices Act of 1992 granted the CFTC the authority to exempt certain swaps transactions from CEA coverage. 7 U.S.C. §6(c)(5)....

To qualify for exemption, a transaction must fit within the CFTC's definition and meet four criteria. The CFTC defines a "swap agreement" as

(i) An agreement (including terms and conditions incorporated by reference therein) which is a rate swap agreement, basis swap, forward rate agreement, commodity swap, interest rate option, forward foreign exchange agreement, rate cap agreement, rate floor agreement, rate collar agreement, currency swap agreement, cross-currency rate swap agreement, currency option, any other similar agreement (including any option to enter into any of the foregoing);

(ii) Any combination of the foregoing; or

(iii) A master agreement for any of the foregoing together with all supplements thereto.

17 C.F.R. §35.1(b) (1993). The 5s/30s and DM swaps fit within this definition [and] meet these criteria. First, the definition of "eligible swap participants" in 17 C.F.R. §35.1(b)(2) includes a "bank or trust company (acting on its own behalf or on behalf of another eligible swap participant)" and corporations with total assets exceeding $10,000,000. BT and P&G are within this definition. Second, these swaps are customized and not fungible as they could not be sold to another counterparty without permission. Third, creditworthiness is a consideration of the parties. Fourth, the swaps are private agreements not traded on any exchange.

While exempting qualified swap agreements from CEA requirements such as trading only on an exchange, the CFTC specifically reserved the antifraud provisions in Sections 4b and 4o of the Act and Commission Rules 32.9, 17 C.F.R. §32.9 (1992)....

Thus, even if the 5s/30s and DM swaps are exempt from other provisions of the CEA, they may be subject to the antifraud provisions (§4b and §4o).

P&G contends that BT's advertisements and representations are promises that BT would use its experience, sophistication and expertise on behalf of its clients to advise them in the complex financial area of leveraged derivatives.... BT was not acting for or on behalf of P&G as that relationship is generally construed in the customer-broker context. As counterparties, P&G and BT were principals in a bilateral contractual arrangement. This is not to say that BT had no duties to P&G ... [but that] P&G has no private right of action under §4b.

Section 4o, 7 U.S.C. §6o, provides:

(1) It shall be unlawful for a commodity trading advisor ... by use of the mails or any means or instrumentality of interstate commerce, directly or indirectly ...

(A) to employ any device, scheme or artifice to defraud any client or participant or prospective client or participant; or

(B) to engage in any transaction, practice, or course of business which operates as a fraud or deceit upon any client or participant or prospective client or
participant.

... [T]he CEA defines "commodity trading advisor" as: any person who

(i) for compensation or profit, engages in the business of advising others, either directly or through publications, writing, or electronic media, as to the
value of or the advisability of trading in ...

(I) any contract of sale of a commodity for future delivery made or to be made
on or subject to the rules of a contract market;

(II) any commodity option authorized under section 6c of this title; or

(III) any leverage transaction authorized under section 23 of this title; or

(ii) for compensation or profit, and as part of a regular business, issues or promulgates analyses or reports concerning any of the activities referred to in clause (i).

Section (I) of the definition does not apply because the 5s/30s swaps were not traded
on any contract market and are not subject to the rules of any contract market under
the Swaps Exemption. Section (II) refers to commodity options authorized under section 6c. This provision prohibits all option trading in commodities unless authorized by
CFTC rules. 7 U.S.C. §6c. Because of the Swaps Exemption, swaps are specifically exempt from CFTC rules. Thus, Section (II) may not be applicable. Section (III) does not
apply, because the 5s/30s and DM swaps do not fit within the CFTC's regulations for
leverage contracts referred to in 7 U.S.C. §23(a).

A commodity trading advisor is one who is "in the business of advising others on the
value or advisability of trading in the purchase or sale of futures contracts or options" or
as an "investment adviser." *F.D.I.C. v. Hildenbrand*, 892 F. Supp. 1317, 1324–35 (D. Colo.
1995). I recognize that representatives from BT Securities had conversations with P&G
regarding market conditions, past performance of Treasury notes and bonds, prognosti-
cations for the future, and the like. There is also evidence that these representatives gave
P&G a sales pitch regarding the potential benefits of their product. These representatives
also discussed P&G's view of interest rates. Thus, while BT Securities representatives
came close to giving advice, P&G representatives used their own independent knowledge
of market conditions in forming their own expectation as to what the market would do
in the 5s/30s and DM swaps. That expectation (central to the two swaps) was not based
on commodity trading advice. That expectation was clearly P&G's sole decision....

Section 32.9 of the CFTC Rules, 17 C.F.R. §32.9, provides:

It shall be unlawful for any person directly or indirectly:

(a) To cheat or defraud or attempt to cheat or defraud any other person;

(b) To make or cause to be made to any other person a false report or statement thereof ...;

(c) To deceive or attempt to deceive any other person by any means whatsoever, in or in connection with an offer to enter into, the entry into, or the confirmation or the execution of, any commodity option transaction.

BT argues that there is no private right of action under the CFTC Rules. Courts are
divided on this question .... The better reasoned rule of law is that §32.9 is applicable
only to CFTC enforcement actions and does not give rise to a private cause of action for
violation of that Regulation....

* * *

P&G contends that a fiduciary relationship existed between it and BT. It argues that it agreed to the swap transactions because of a long relationship it had with BT and the trust that it had in BT, plus the assurance that BT would take on the responsibility of monitoring the transactions and that BT would look out for its interests.

P&G points to its trust in BT in that it divulged confidential corporate information to BT. By entering into complex swaps transactions with BT, which represented itself as experts in such transactions, P&G relied on that expertise and BT statements that it would tailor the swaps to fit P&G's needs. Even accepting these contentions as true, these contentions fail. New York case law is clear [that no fiduciary relationship exists where parties are contracting at arm's length, as here].

This does not mean, however, that there are no duties and obligations in their swaps transactions. Plaintiff alleges that in the negotiation of the two swaps and in their execution, defendants failed to disclose vital information and made material misrepresentations to it....

Since plaintiff's Amended Complaint is based on allegations of defendants' fraud and material misrepresentations, I must determine what the duties and obligations of the parties are to each other.

This requires 1) an analysis of the written contracts between the parties, *i.e.*, the International Swap Dealers Association ("ISDA") Agreement of January 20, 1993, the Schedule and Definitions appended to it, and the detailed Confirmations as to each swap; 2) the statutes and case law of New York (the parties in the ISDA Agreement and Part 4 of the Schedule, having contracted that "this Agreement will be governed by, and construed and enforced in accordance with, the laws of the State of New York without reference to choice of law doctrine"); and 3) the Uniform Commercial Code as well as the Restatement (Second) Contracts, the Code having been made a part of New York statutory law and the principles of the Restatement having been accepted by New York courts.

.... The sections in the ISDA Agreement that appear to be relevant to these swap transactions are as follows:

In Section 3.(a)(v), this appears: "Obligations Binding. Its obligations under this Agreement ... to which it is a party constitute its legal, valid and binding obligations, enforceable in accordance with their respective terms...."

Section 4., which reads: "Each party agrees with the other that so long as it has or may have any obligation under this Agreement ... to which it is a party: (a) It will deliver to the other party: (ii) any other documents specified in Part 3 of the Schedule or any Confirmation."

Section 9.(d), which reads: "Except as provided in this Agreement, the rights, powers, remedies, and privileges provided in this Agreement are cumulative and not exclusive of any rights, powers, remedies, and privileges provided by law." ...

Under Section 4., each party must furnish specified information and that information must also relate to any documents specified in any Confirmation. Documents that are referred to in the Confirmation (here I allude specifically to the documents that will enable a party to determine the correlation between the price and yields of the five-year Treasury notes and thirty-year Treasury bonds, the sensitivity tables, the spreadsheets regarding volatility, and documents relating to the yield curve) should be provided.

.... The Uniform Commercial Code, as part of New York statute law, particularly Section 1-203, states: "Every contract or duty written in this Act imposes an obligation of good faith in its performance or enforcement." New York has also adopted the principles in the Restatement (Second) Contracts, §205, that every contract imposes upon each party a duty of good faith and fair dealing in its performance and enforcement. *Id.*

New York case law establishes an implied contractual duty to disclose in business negotiations. Such a duty may arise where 1) a party has superior knowledge of certain information; 2) that information is not readily available to the other party; and 3) the first party knows that the second party is acting on the basis of mistaken knowledge. [D]efendants had a duty to disclose material information to plaintiff both before the parties entered into the swap transactions and in their performance, and also a duty to deal fairly and in good faith during the performance of the swap transactions....

New York case law demonstrates that [P&G's claims of negligent misrepresentation and negligence] are not available to P&G.... BT and P&G are sophisticated corporations whose dealings were on a business level. Theirs was not a "special relationship" that would support a claim of negligent misrepresentation under New York law. [The court also declines to find malpractice under Restatement (Second) Torts, §299A and related case law.]

Caiola v. Citibank, N.A.
295 F.3d 312 (2d Cir. 2002)

PARKER, J:

... Louis S. Caiola brought federal securities fraud and state law claims against defendant-appellee Citibank, N.A., New York arising from extensive physical and synthetic investments. The District Court ... granted Citibank's motion to dismiss the Complaint ..., finding that Caiola lacked standing under Rule 10b-5 to allege a violation of section 10(b) of the Securities Exchange Act of 1934 (the "1934 Act") because he was not a purchaser or seller of securities, his synthetic transactions were not "securities" as defined by the 1934 Act, and he failed to plead material misrepresentations.... [We reverse and remand.]

... Caiola, an entrepreneur and sophisticated investor, was a major client of Citibank Private Bank, a division of Citibank, from the mid-1980s to September 1999.... Beginning in the mid-1980s, Caiola undertook high volume equity trading, entrusting funds to Citibank who in turn engaged various outside brokerage firms. Caiola specialized in the stock of Philip Morris Companies, Inc. ("Philip Morris") and regularly traded hundreds of thousands of shares valued at many millions of dollars. To hedge the risks associated with these trades, Caiola established option positions corresponding to his stock positions.

As Caiola's trades increased in size, he and Citibank grew increasingly concerned about the efficacy of his trading and hedging strategies. Caiola's positions required margin postings of tens of millions of dollars and were sufficiently large that the risks to him were unacceptable unless hedged. But the volume of options necessary to hedge effectively could impact prices and disclose his positions—effects known as "footprints" on the market. In early 1994, Citibank proposed synthetic trading. A synthetic transaction is typically a contractual agreement between two counterparties, usually an investor and a bank, that seeks to economically replicate the ownership and physical trading of shares and options. The counterparties establish synthetic positions in shares or options, the values of which are pegged to the market prices of the related physical shares or options. The aggregate market values of the shares or options that underlie the synthetic trades are referred to as "notional" values and are treated as interest-bearing loans to the investor. As Citibank explained to Caiola, synthetic trading offers significant advantages to investors who heavily concentrate on large positions of a single stock by reducing the risks associated with large-volume trading. Synthetic trading alleviates the necessity of posting large amounts of margin capital and ensures that positions can be established and unwound quickly. Synthetic trading also offers a solution to the "footprint" problem by permitting the purchase of large volumes of options in stocks without affecting their price.

Taking Citibank's advice, Caiola began to engage in two types of synthetic transactions focusing on Philip Morris stock and options: equity swaps and cash-settled over-the-counter options. In a typical equity swap, one party (Caiola) makes periodic interest payments on the notional value of a stock position and also payments equal to any decrease in value of the shares upon which the notional value is based. The other party (Citibank) pays any increase in the value of the shares and any dividends, also based on the same notional value.

For example, if Caiola synthetically purchased 1000 shares of Philip Morris at $50 per share, the notional value of that transaction would be $50,000. Because this notional value would resemble a loan from Citibank, Caiola would pay interest at a predetermined rate on the $50,000. If Philip Morris's stock price fell $10, Caiola would pay Citibank $10,000. If the stock price rose $10, Citibank would pay Caiola $10,000. Citibank also would pay Caiola the value of any dividends that Caiola would have received had he actually owned 1000 physical shares.

Caiola also acquired synthetic options, which were cash-settled over-the-counter options. Because these options were not listed and traded on physical exchanges, their existence and size did not impact market prices. Caiola and Citibank agreed to terms regarding the various attributes of the option in a particular transaction (such as the strike price, expiration date, option type, and premium). They agreed to settle these option transactions in cash when the option was exercised or expired, based on the then-current market price of the underlying security.

Caiola and Citibank documented their equity swaps and synthetic options through an International Swap Dealers Association Master Agreement ("ISDA Agreement") dated March 25, 1994. The ISDA Agreement established specific terms for the synthetic trading. After entering into the ISDA Agreement, Caiola, on Citibank's advice, began to enter into "coupled" synthetic transactions with Citibank. Specifically, Caiola's over-the-counter option positions were established in connection with a paired equity swap, ensuring that his synthetic options would always hedge his equity swaps. This strategy limited the amount he could lose and ensured that his risks would be both controllable and quantifiable.

Citibank promised Caiola that as his counterparty it would control its own risks through a strategy known as "delta hedging." Delta hedging makes a derivative position, such as an option position, immune to small changes in the price of an underlying asset, such as a stock, over a short period of time.... The "delta" measures the sensitivity of the price of the derivative to the change in the price of the underlying asset. Specifically, "delta" is the ratio of the change in the price of the derivative to that of the underlying asset.... Thus, if an option has a delta of .5, a $1 change in the stock price would result in a $.50 change in the option price. Caiola's synthetic positions contained a number of components, such as a stock position plus one or more option positions. For each of these coupled or integrated transactions a "net delta" was calculated which helped Citibank determine the amount of securities necessary to establish its "delta core" position. By maintaining a "delta core" position in the physical market, Citibank could achieve "delta neutrality," a hedge position that would offset Citibank's obligations to Caiola.

Effective delta hedging is a sophisticated trading activity that involves the continuous realignment of the hedge's portfolio. Because the delta changes with movements in the price of the underlying asset, the size of the delta core position also constantly changes. Although a certain delta core position might sufficiently hedge Citibank's obligations at one point, a different delta core position may become necessary a short time later. Thus, as markets fluctuate, the net delta must be readjusted continuously to ensure an optimal exposure to risk.[a] Citibank told Caiola that as his counterparty it would continuously adjust its delta core positions to maintain delta neutrality. Also, Caiola routinely altered his transactions to account for their effect on Citibank's delta core positions. This arrangement was satisfactory so long as Citibank adhered to its delta hedging strategy, which involved comparably small purchases in the physical market. However, if Citibank fully replicated Caiola's stock and option positions in the physical market instead of delta hedging, the benefits of synthetic trading would disappear and he would be exposed to risks that this strategy was designed to avoid.

Each synthetic transaction was governed by an individualized confirmation containing a number of disclaimers. A confirmation for Caiola's purchase of 360,000 cash-settled over-the-counter options dated December 9, 1998 ("Confirmation"), for instance, provides that each party represents to the other that "it is not relying on any advice, statements or recommendations (whether written or oral) of the other party," that each is entering the transaction "as principal and not as an agent for [the] other party," and that "[Caiola] acknowledges and agrees that [Citibank] is not acting as a fiduciary or advisor to [him] in connection with this Transaction." Further, [in addition to a "merger" or "integration" clause,] the ISDA Agreement and accompanying Schedule, which governed the overall synthetic relationship, provides:

* * *

> [Caiola] has such knowledge and experience in financial, business and tax matters that render him capable of evaluating the merits and risks of this Agreement and the Transactions contemplated hereunder; [Caiola] is able to bear the economic risks of this Agreement and the Transaction contemplated hereunder; and, after appropriate independent investigations, [Caiola] has determined that this Agreement and the Transactions contemplated hereunder are suitable for him....

In October 1998, Citicorp, Citibank's parent company, merged with Travelers Group, Inc. ("Travelers"). Caiola feared that Salomon Smith Barney ("SSB"), a Travelers affiliate, might become involved in his account. At a November 18, 1998 meeting, Citibank informed Caiola that SSB would become involved in Caiola's synthetic equities trading. At this meeting, Caiola stated that he did not wish to become a client of SSB and that, unless his relationship with Citibank were to continue as it had previously existed, he would terminate it. Citibank assured Caiola then and subsequently that their relation-

---

a. A concept referred to as "dynamic hedging." [Eds.]

ship would continue unchanged and, specifically, that his synthetic trading relationship with Citibank would remain unaltered by SSB's involvement.

Relying on these assurances, Caiola maintained his account at Citibank and continued to establish sizeable positions with the understanding that they would be managed synthetically, with Citibank continuing to serve as the delta hedging counterparty....

However, after November 1998, and contrary to its representations and unknown to Caiola, Citibank had secretly stopped delta hedging and transformed Caiola's synthetic portfolio into a physical one by executing massive trades in the physical markets that mirrored Caiola's synthetic transactions. In other words, when Caiola sought to open an integrated synthetic position in shares of synthetic stock and synthetic options, Citibank, instead of delta hedging, simply executed physical trades on stock and options.[2] These transactions, Caiola alleges, exposed him to the risks—"footprints" and a lack of liquidity—that synthetic trading was intended to avoid.

On March 12, 1999, Citibank told Caiola that it intended to early exercise certain options in his portfolio for physical settlement, a demand inconsistent with a synthetic relationship. One week later Citibank for the first time refused to establish a synthetic option position Caiola requested. Growing concerned, on March 26, 1999, Caiola inquired and was told that SSB was unwilling to assume the risks associated with synthetic trading. During this time period, although Caiola had taken a large position in Philip Morris stock that was declining in value, he wrote options expecting to recoup his losses and to profit from an anticipated rise in the value of the shares. The strategy, Caiola claims, failed because Citibank had secretly and unilaterally terminated synthetic trading. This termination cost Caiola tens of millions of dollars because the price of Philip Morris rebounded as he had expected.

At this point, Caiola investigated and discovered that Citibank had ceased treating his investments synthetically as early as November 1998. Two Citibank officers informed Caiola that "many" of his trades had been executed on the physical market, although they had been submitted and accepted by Citibank as synthetic transactions.

Caiola unearthed additional evidence that Citibank had transformed his portfolio when he attempted to unwind his account in September 1999. When Caiola placed unwind transactions, Citibank refused to execute the trades without a commission—a further indication to Caiola that what he thought were synthetic positions were being handled by Citibank as physical transactions. In addition, as Citibank executed certain option transactions during this unwind period, Citibank sent Caiola confirmations reflecting that the transactions were for physical, instead of cash, settlement. Caiola also was told by a Citibank official that it was holding hundreds of thousands of physical shares of Philip Morris stock in his account and that Citibank had executed certain unwind transactions by going to the physical market to sell millions of options and shares. Finally, when Citibank failed to completely unwind a certain swap position, it told

---

2. Caiola offers the following illustration:

> For example, on March 9, 1998 [sic], Mr. Caiola submitted an order to establish a synthetic position consisting of (i) a long position in 2 million notional shares of Philip Morris stock; (ii) a long position in 2 million synthetic Philip Morris put options, and (iii) a short position in 2 million synthetic Philip Morris call options. Had Citibank still been delta hedging, it would only have needed to purchase approximately 100,000 shares of Philip Morris stock to adjust its delta core position as a result of this transaction. But, as publicly available trading records reveal, Citibank actually bought huge quantities of real physical options on the American Option Exchange in order to open this position.

Caiola that hundreds of thousands of physical shares—for which he had no hedge protection and was financially responsible—were being sold on his behalf.

In July 2000, Caiola sued Citibank alleging violations of section 10(b) and Rule 10b-5. He also asserted state law claims for fraud, breach of fiduciary duty, and breach of contract. Generally, the Complaint alleged that Citibank violated section 10(b) and Rule 10b-5 when it misrepresented that it would continue its pre-existing synthetic trading relationship but secretly abandoned its role as delta hedging counterparty and, instead, bought and sold exchange-traded stock and options on Caiola's behalf. Caiola further claims that Citibank's misrepresentations were material, he relied on them, and, as a result, he experienced massive losses.

Citibank moved to dismiss under Rule 12(b)(6) on the grounds that Caiola was neither a purchaser nor a seller of securities, that the synthetic transactions were not "securities," and that the confirmations established that neither party was entitled to rely on the representations of the other. [The discussion below is confined to the question of whether the synthetic transactions are "securities" within the meaning of section 10(b) and Rule 10b-5. The court addresses separately the two types of instruments used: cash-settled over-the-counter options and equity swaps, after first reviewing the federal law concerning the interpretation of the word "security."]

The anti-fraud provisions of the federal securities laws cover options on securities. Section 3(a)(10) of the 1934 Act defines "security" to include "any put, call, straddle, option, or privilege on any security, certificate of deposit, or group or index of securities (including any interest therein or based on the value thereof)...." 15 U.S.C. §78c(a)(10) (2000).... Options have been covered under section 10(b) since the 1934 Act was amended in 1982.... The Supreme Court has cautioned that "in searching for the meaning and scope of the word 'security'... the emphasis should be on economic reality." *United Hous. Found. v. Forman*, 421 U.S. 837, 848, 44 L. Ed. 2d 621, 95 S. Ct. 2051 (1975) (quoting *Tcherepnin v. Knight*, 389 U.S. 332, 336, 19 L. Ed. 2d 564, 88 S. Ct. 548 (1967)). The definition of security is construed in a "flexible" manner, so as to "meet the countless and variable schemes devised by those who seek the use of the money of others on the promise of profits." *SEC v. W.J. Howey Co.*, 328 U.S. 293, 299, 90 L. Ed. 1244, 66 S. Ct. 1100 (1946).

Under section 3(a)(10) "security" includes (i) an option on any "security," (ii) an option on any "certificate of deposit," and (iii) an option on any "group or index of securities." Therefore, "option" under section 3(a)(10) is not limited to "conventional" exchange-traded options. It applies to both exchange-traded as well as over-the-counter options and does not distinguish between physically-settled and cash-settled options. Nor does the definition distinguish between options documented as swaps as opposed to options documented in some other fashion.

We find further support for our conclusion in section 3(a)(10)'s definition of "security" to include an option on any "group or index of securities." An option on a security can be physically settled by delivery of physical stock. An index of securities, however, is simply a benchmark against which financial performance is measured. An option on an index of securities is settled by cash since physical delivery is not possible. *See* 5 Louis Loss & Joel Seligman, Securities Regulation 2650 (3d ed. 1999). Consequently, the right to take possession does not define an "option" under section 3(a)(10), which covers options that can be physically delivered as well as those that cannot.

Both the District Court and Citibank rely heavily on [*Procter & Gamble Co. v. Bankers Trust Co.*, 925 F. Supp. 1270 (S.D. Oh. 1996)] for their conclusion that cash-settled over-the-counter options are not securities. *Procter & Gamble*, however, held that a very different type of transaction—swaps linked to the price of Treasury notes—were not securities. The plaintiff in *Procter & Gamble* argued that even though the instrument in question was technically an interest rate swap—it had option-like features and thus could be characterized as an "option on a security" under section 3(a)(10). The court, however, rejected this argument because the swap "did not give either counterparty the right to exercise an option or to take possession of any security." *Id.* at 1822. The District Court imported this language from *Procter & Gamble*, finding it dispositive. Unlike the plaintiff's argument in *Procter & Gamble* that an interest rate swap with option-like features could be characterized as an option on a security, Caiola's transactions involve the much more straightforward question of whether a cash-settled over-the-counter option on Philip Morris stock—similar to options commonly traded on the market—is an option on a security. *Procter & Gamble* does not address this issue.

Further, *Procter & Gamble* concluded that a critical feature of an option was the right to exercise and to take possession of the security because the parenthetical "based on the value thereof" in section 3(a)(10) applied only to the immediately preceding phrase, "group or index of securities" and not to "any security." *Procter & Gamble*, 925 F. Supp. at 1281-82. We believe this conclusion is incorrect, and we decline to follow its lead. We hold that the parenthetical applies to "any security." The text of the statute itself includes cash-settled options by defining "option" to include an option on a "group or index of securities." This provision is sufficiently clear that a resort to legislative history is not necessary.[7] ...

In December 2000, Congress enacted the [Commodity Futures Modernization Act ("CFMA")] to, among other things, clarify the status of swap agreements under the securities laws. CFMA §2, 114 Stat. at 2763A-366. Sections 302 and 303 of the CMFA define "swap agreements" and then expressly exclude them from the definition of "securities," but amend section 10(b) [of the 1934 Act] to reach swap agreements. *Id.* §§302, 303, 114 Stat. at 2763A-452. Had Caiola entered into his synthetic stock transactions after the enactment of the CFMA, they clearly would now be covered under Rule 10b-5. To prevail on a retroactivity argument, Caiola faces a substantial burden.... We find it unnecessary to resolve whether Caiola has overcome this hurdle because he failed to raise the issue properly in the District Court and we generally do not consider arguments not raised below....

Caiola's Complaint, we conclude, easily satisfies [the federal securities law element of] materiality. Caiola alleges that Citibank falsely told him that their trading relationship would not change subsequent to the Travelers merger, and that had he known that the relationship would change, he would have closed his account. Indeed, Caiola alleges that Citibank knew this information was material, since a Citibank representative informed him "that he understood that Citibank's conduct was totally inconsistent with Mr. Caiola's hedging investment strategy and that he understood that if Mr. Caiola had known the truth he would have ... 'run like a rabbit' from Citibank." ...

---

7. The District Court examined the CFMA and its legislative history for insight into the status of Caiola's transactions, which were entered into prior to the enactment of the CFMA. Because section 3(a)(10) is clear, that inquiry was unnecessary. In any event, we disagree with the District Court's conclusion that Caiola's options were "security based swap agreements" exempted from the CFMA's definition of security. The CFMA provides that a "swap agreement" is not a security under section 3(a)(10) of the 1934 Act. CFMA §303, 114 Stat. at 2763A-452-57. However, section 301 of the CFMA excludes from the definition of "swap agreement" "any ... option ... on any security ... or group or index of securities, including any interest therein and based on the value thereof." *Id.* §301, 114 Stat. at 2763A-450. Thus, options based on the value of a security are not "swap agreements;" they are securities. The District Court's analysis failed to account for this exclusion.

Caiola alleges that Citibank continued to mislead him as it abandoned delta hedging and bought and sold exchange-traded stock and options on his behalf without disclosing these activities to him. These misrepresentations are clearly sufficient under Rule 10b-5 because they are the sort that "a reasonable person would consider [] important in deciding whether to buy or sell shares." *Azrielli v. Cohen Law Offices*, 21 F.3d 512, 518 (2d Cir. 1994).

Relying on various provisions of the ISDA Agreement and the Confirmation, Citibank argues that a reasonable investor of Caiola's sophistication would not have relied upon Citibank's oral misrepresentations in light of the disclaimers. In particular, the Confirmation specifically provided that Caiola would not be relying on Citibank's advice or recommendations, that he would make his own investment decisions, and that Citibank would not be his fiduciary or advisor.

We are not persuaded that these disclaimers barred Caiola from relying on Citibank's oral statements. A disclaimer is generally enforceable only if it "tracks the substance of the alleged misrepresentation...." *Grumman Allied Indus., Inc. v. Rohr Indus., Inc.*, 748 F.2d 729, 735 (2d Cir. 1984). The disclaimer provisions contained in the Confirmation fall well short of tracking the particular misrepresentations alleged by Caiola. Caiola specifically alleges that Citibank offered false assurances that after the Travelers merger the parties' existing trading relationship would not change and that Citibank would continue to act as a delta hedging counterparty. The disclaimer in the Confirmation states only in general terms that neither party relies "on any advice, statements or recommendation (whether written or oral) of the other party." This disclaimer is general, not specific, and says nothing about Citibank's commitment to delta hedging.

Finally, we deem irrelevant Citibank's contention that the disclaimers meant that it owed Caiola no duty to disclose its hedging strategy. Whether Citibank had such a duty in the first instance is irrelevant because Caiola alleges that Citibank chose to disclose its hedging strategy. Caiola alleges that Citibank affirmatively spoke and, in doing so, made material misrepresentations concerning this strategy ...

Assuming Caiola can prove these allegations, the lack of an independent duty is not, under such circumstances, a defense to Rule 10b-5 liability because upon choosing to speak, one must speak truthfully about material issues. Once Citibank chose to discuss its hedging strategy, it had a duty to be both accurate and complete.

d. Accounting for Derivatives

Under GAAP, entities must recognize all derivatives as either assets or liabilities on the balance sheet and measure them at fair value. Yet the fair value of such a financial instrument can change over time with market conditions, alternately representing an asset of the entity (when the value is positive to it) or a liability to it (when the value is negative to it). These changes in value of the instrument have the effect of generating gains or losses. The changing market value therefore needs to be reflected by recording gains or losses on the investment in the income statement in accordance with GAAP's "matching principle" (which generally requires that items of revenue be allocated to the same periods as the items of expenses incurred to generate them). To do so, GAAP distinguishes between types of derivatives.

Fair value hedges address exposure to changes in asset or liability values (such as an interest rate swap intended to hedge the risk that rising interest rates will decrease the fair value of a debt investment), and gains or losses on such contracts are recognized as part of net income when they occur. In contrast are *cash flow hedges*, which address exposure to variable cash flows of a forecasted transaction (such as a currency swap calling for one party to pay in US dollars and its counterparty to pay in Euros). Gains or losses on these are recorded as a part of "other comprehensive income" when they occur and are later reclassified into net income when the related (hedged) transaction affects earnings. (Other comprehensive income is a specialized category of income reported separately from income generated by an entity's main business activity.)

Apart from the direct inclusion of fair values of derivatives on the balance sheet and associated recognition of gains and losses on both the derivative and the hedged asset or liability on the income statement, GAAP calls for certain footnote disclosure. Entities must disclose their objectives in holding or issuing derivative instruments, the context needed to understand those objectives, and their strategies for achieving the objectives. This disclosure must distinguish between fair value hedges, cash flow hedges, as well as various types of analogous foreign currency hedges. This disclosure must also describe the entity's risk management policy for each type of hedge, including a description of the types of transactions that are hedged.

Enron, Derivatives and Accounting

Cunningham, The Sarbanes-Oxley Yawn: Heavy Rhetoric, Light Reform
(And It Might Just Work)
35 Conn. L. Rev. 915 (2003)

Enron Corp. became a notorious household word in the early 2000s as a series of accounting and other deceptions emerged that plunged the large company into bankruptcy. During the economic boom years of the late 1990s, Enron engaged in thousands of transactions designed to house volatile trading activity in separate entities to insulate the company's earnings and hence stock price from the short-term gyrations of its trading activities. Using special purpose entities [SPEs] is perfectly legitimate and lawful as matters of accounting and commercial and securities laws, so long as rules are observed.

To obtain off-balance treatment, the special purpose entities must satisfy general well-known rules of consolidation accounting and particular arcane rules applied to these entities. The general rule provides that to avoid full consolidation of an entity, a third-party must control a majority of that entity's equity; the arcane rule says that at least 3% of the total capital of the special purpose entity must be equity (capping the debt:equity ratio at 33:1).

In early transactions, Enron followed both rules, capitalizing SPEs with a debt:equity ratio no greater than 33:1 and placing a majority of the equity with a third party. In subsequent deals, however, one or both requirements went unmet, and in most of these either Enron, an affiliate or an Enron executive held the equity. This meant that all the deals constituted related party transactions and all should have been consolidated on Enron's books. None were. The amount of debt housed in these controlled entities ran to billions of dollars, the security was often Enron's own stock, and when business conditions turned adverse, its stock price weakened, the debts came home to roost in cascades leading to bankruptcy.

Much of the trading activity to be housed in the SPEs and much of Enron's direct activity centered on the risk management business pursued through the development and trading of derivative securities. In this area, accounting rules calling for real-time valuation of these instruments (called mark-to-market rules) required Enron to assign values to these instruments. The tendency was for Enron to use excessively rosy assumptions and aggressive allocation judgments. Managers assigned high asset values on exchanges and listed those amounts on the balance sheet and correspondingly high and theoretical profits in the income statement. In other cases managers treated borrowed funds not as loans but as sale-and-purchase transactions—a modern version of a classic trick from the accounting fraud cookbook.

These were characterized as synthetic transactions that exploit forms to portray balance sheet deals (such as loans) as income statement deals (as sales). A standard commercial loan is recorded on the borrower's books as an increase in cash (a debit in bookkeeping parlance) and an increase in debt (a credit). Recasting the deal, a con artist treats the fund infusion as the sale of some financial asset (called anything you want, but usually using the word derivative) and the purchase of that same asset with slightly modified terms such as a 10% mark-up to be paid a year later. The con-man records the infusion as a debit to cash and a credit to revenue.

For the standard case, the balance sheet absorbs debt on origination, and is adjusted as payments are made. For the con-man case, the income statement sports revenue on origination, and no debt appears. A double comparative benefit magically sprouts: no debt and a revenue boost. This is a "revenue-ization" of cash. The Ponzi characteristic of the charade is the lender/buyer thinks it is in on a big thing, assured of its 10% (or better) return, with no risks. But the risks are real, because the company behind the con man isn't.

Chapter 5

The Rights of Contract Claimants — Part 1: Holders of Debt Securities

The legal treatment of common stockholders is familiar to every student of corporate law and fundamentally is based on fiduciary principles. Although the phrase "fiduciary duty" embraces a rich variety of conceptual variations, it rests upon a firm foundation requiring that corporate officers, directors and controlling stockholders act in the best interests of their corporation and, in some circumstances, the stockholders themselves. Ultimately, and regardless of phraseology, the law has come largely to equate the best interests of the corporation with the best interests of its stockholders.[1] The essential theoretical underpinning for this doctrine is, of course, the received understanding that stockholders are the corporation's owners and, therefore, the rightful focus of management's concern.

The transformation from the formulation that accords primacy to the *corporation's* interests, predicated on the traditional entity model of the corporation, to that which centers on the *shareholders'* interests, which largely deconstructs that model, was not inevitable. People other than shareholders have significant interests in the corporation's welfare. Although the investments of debtholders and preferred stockholders are, unlike the residual character of common stock investments, less risky due to their inherent character, both of these groups of corporate investors depend upon the careful and loyal management of the corporation to ensure the security of their returns.

The law has not traditionally recognized this interest, at least in the case of debtholders. Debtholders, and to a lesser extent preferred stockholders, are dependent upon the terms of their investment contract as the source of their protection.[2] This approach, based historically on the non-equity character of the former type of investment and the contractually defined nature of the latter, has been rigorous and well settled.

The student approaching this lengthy chapter is well justified in asking, why the extended treatment?

---

1. *See, e.g.,* Principles of Corp. Gov. § 2.01 (Amer. L. Inst. 1994). *But see* Schwartz, Defining the Corporate Objective: Section 2.01 of the ALI's Principles, 52 Geo. Wash. L. Rev. 511, 512 (1984) (noting confusion engendered by § 2.01's reference both to *corporate* profit and *shareholder* gain).

2. Common stockholders also can be seen to have an investment contract, with fiduciary duty as an implied term. Easterbrook & Fischel, Corporate Control Transactions, 91 Yale L.J. 1 (1982). Courts have been far more reluctant to imply fiduciary terms into the contracts of debtholders and preferred stockholders.

Several factors have led us to lavish a large amount of attention on the rights of contract claimants.[3] First, debt securities and preferred stock are important techniques of corporate finance, with widely varying characteristics, and nowhere else in the corporate law curriculum (except perhaps in a course in corporate reorganization) are they typically studied. Second, we believe that this material offers students an opportunity to reexamine the theoretical underpinnings, and thus legitimacy, of a settled body of law, particularly in light of the new theoretical and analytical tools presented earlier in this book. Finally, although the basic law of contract claimants has been settled for well over a century, recent legal and business developments have stimulated courts and scholars to question the assumptions upon which the traditional doctrines are based. In particular, the wave of leveraged acquisitions that swept over corporate America during the 1980s revealed the vulnerable nature of contract investments to stockholder interests through the expropriation of wealth.

Before we begin our journey, a note on organization is in order. We have purposely chosen to provide a full discussion of convertible securities, including the economics underlying them, in a separate chapter. Therefore, to learn about convertible securities, including convertible debt securities, see *infra* chapter 7.

Section 1
The Concept and Consequences of Leverage

An important financial question, and one which has been the subject of considerable debate, is whether there is a correct or optimal capital structure for a corporation. If there is, then adopting such a structure should enhance stockholder welfare, and may create new dimensions of directors' duties. The following materials examine some of the competing positions in this debate.

Graham, Dodd & Cottle, Security Analysis (4th ed. 1962)
539-43

In our discussion of key ratios in [financial] statement analysis, ... we commented briefly on the significance of the "common-stock ratio," which shows the ratio of common-stock equity to total capital funds. We indicated that—other things being equal—the higher this ratio, the better the credit standing of the company; the higher in turn the "quality" of the stocks issue [sic]; and the higher—other things being equal—the multiplier to be applied to earnings per share. At the same time we commented that this did not necessarily mean that an all-common-stock capital structure was the most advantageous one for the owners of the business. We return to this subject now, as part of our discussion of factors governing the multiplier of per-share earnings and dividends.

---

3. The term "contract claimants" is a bit of a misnomer, since preferred stockholders do possess equity interests and fiduciary rights. We feel justified in treating them as such, however, because, with respect to the *preferred* characteristics of their investment, they are treated much the way debtholders are. *See* Jedwab v. MGM Grand Hotels, Inc., *infra* at chapter 6, section 4. We have conceded their differences by putting preferred stockholders' rights in a separate chapter.

Table 40-1

Capital Structure	Company A	Company B	Company S
Bonds:			
5 percent		$3,500,000	
6 percent			$10,000,000
Book value of common	$10,000,000	6,500,000	0
Total capital fund	$10,000,000	$10,000,000	$10,000,000
Net before taxes and interest	1,500,000	1,500,000	1,500,000
Interest		175,000	600,000
Balance	$ 1,500,000	$1,325,000	$ 900,000
Income tax (52 percent)	780,000	689,000	468,000
Balance for common	$ 720,000	$ 636,000	$ 432,000
Value of common at 13.9 times earnings	10,000,000	8,840,000	6,000,000
Value of bonds at par		3,500,000	10,000,000
Total value of enterprise	$10,000,000	$12,340,000	$16,000,000
Times interest earned before taxes		8.5 ×	2.5 ×

The subject divides itself into two questions, viz: (1) What should be, in theory, the effect of variations in capital structure on the multipliers for earnings and dividends? (2) What relationship actually exists in the markets between one factor and the other? ...

Possible Results from Variations in Capital Structure. Let us begin by assuming three similarly situated industrial companies, A, B, and S—each of which has $10 million of capital funds and earns $1.5 million before income taxes. Company A's only securities are 100,000 shares of common stock, without par value. Company B has the same stock issue, plus $3.5 million of 5 percent bonds. Company S has the same common stock, plus $10 million of 6 percent bonds. For our first approach let us assume that regardless of capital structure the market is willing to pay 13.9 times earnings for each common stock, and that the bonds would be worth par. The figures would work out as shown in Table 40-1.

These results, if actually realized in the market, would be extraordinary. Company A would sell for the amount invested, Company B, for 23.4 percent more, and Company S, for 60 percent more. These wide differences in the enterprise value would be due solely to variations in the capital structure, including the differing tax burdens flowing therefrom. If our postulates as to price relationships were valid it would be obvious that stockholders would gain most by issuing the largest possible amount of bonds, and that the much-praised "clean" capital structure would be a costly mistake.

Of course, our assumptions are not correct. The common stocks of all three companies would *not* sell at the same multiplier of earnings, nor would both the bond issues necessarily be quoted at par.

Let us now make an alternative assumption. This is that since all the companies are in exactly the same position as to capital invested, earnings before taxes, and prospects, they should all sell at the same aggregate or enterprise valuation, except to the extent that interest charges reduce the tax burden. In other words, we assume in these examples that they would all sell in the aggregate at the same 13.9 multiplier of earnings on capital after income tax. For simplicity, we assume further that the bond issues would sell at par. The resultant enterprise valuations and common-stock valuations are shown

Table 40-2   Effect of Differences of Capital Structure, Assuming a Constant Multiplier of Total Earnings after Tax and Par Value of Bonds

Capital Structure	Company A	Company B	Company S
Earnings after taxes	$ 720,000	$ 636,000	$ 432,000
Interest		175,000	600,000
Earnings after taxes before interest	$ 720,000	$ 811,000	$ 1,032,000
Assumed multiplier	13.9 ×	13.9 ×	13.9 ×
Value of enterprise	$10,000,000	$11,270,000	$14,340,000
Less par value of bonds		3,500,000	10,000,000
Resultant value of common	$10,000,000	$ 7,770,000	$ 4,340,000
Resultant multiplier of common earnings	13.9 ×	12.2 ×	10.0 ×

in Table 40-2. In accordance with our assumptions, the enterprise value increases as the bond component rises, by reason of the tax saving. But the multiplier of the common stock declines, as required to offset the "leverage" advantage from the use of bonded debt.

Two Schools of Thought. The foregoing hypothetical illustrations somewhat roughly depict the two broad theoretical points of view which presently exist. In essence, one group (represented—and also exaggerated—by Table 40-1) holds that capital structure can affect the aggregate market valuation of a firm's securities, even apart from the tax impact, whereas the other group (represented by Table 40-2) considers that—except for the tax factor—capital structure has *no* effect on the aggregate market valuation of a company's securities. The fundamental differences between these two schools of thought have been aptly set forth by David Durand. He treats them in reverse order of that employed above. Durand points out that the proponents of the second, or "entity," approach, "argue that the totality of risk incurred by all security holders of a given company cannot be altered by merely changing the capitalization proportions. Such a change could only alter the proportion of the total risk borne by each class of security holder." In regard to the first, or "optimal," approach he states, "Those who adhere strictly to this method contend: first, that *conservative* increases in bonded debt do not increase the risk borne by the common stockholders; second, that a package of securities containing a conservative proportion of bonds will justifiably command a higher market price than a package of common stock alone." (Certainly, insofar as Companies A and B are concerned, Table 40-1 is representative of this point of view.)

We do not propose here to enter into the details of the controversy, with its elaborate mathematical calculations; we seek rather to point up some of the practical implications of the question.

Our Own View. Let us call attention first to a significant fact which appears to have been given too little consideration in the theoretical discussions. This is that a good part of *any* suggested gain in enterprise value through creating or increasing the debt component will be accounted for (under existing legislation) by the factor of tax savings—a benefit apparently conceded by those who deny the other claimed benefits. Thus we find that having the bond issue raises the total value of Company B 23.4 percent over that of Company A in our Table 40-1—which illustrates the "optimal" theory—but it also raises the value by 11.3 percent under our Table 40-2—which presents the "entity"

Table 40-3 Effect of Differences of Capital Structure, Assuming Probable Market Prices for the Bonds and Stock Issues

	Company A	Company B	Company S
Assumed price of bonds		100	70
Resultant value of bond issue		$3,500,000	$7,000,000
Assumed multiplier of earnings of common stock	12.5 ×	12.0 ×	6.0 ×
Resultant value of stock issue	$9,000,000	7,630,000	2,590,000
Resultant enterprise value	$9,000,000	$11,130,000	$9,590,000

theory. In other words, the tax saving *alone* resulting from the use of debt was sufficient to increase the value of Company B by about as much as could be expected from the leverage factor. Since the tax saving is not in dispute, the great controversy—from a practical standpoint—seems to reduce to a calculation of the amount by which a given *acceptable* bond component will raise the total value.

In our opinion the advantages to stockholders from the *appropriate* proportion of corporate debt will go beyond the indubitable tax saving and will fall close to those shown in Table 40-1. The appropriate amount of debt is that which the company can safely borrow, which in turn is no more and very little less than investors may safely lend to it.... For such a company the market's multiplier of its share earnings should be only slightly, if any, less than that of a similar company without bonds (Company A).

In Table 40-3 we seek to present the valuation picture more realistically, in terms of the market's probable reaction to the corporate structures of Company A and Company B (together with a *possible* valuation of Company S). The previous assumptions accepted a valuation of Company A equal to the book value of the common stock. We now suggest that, since the concern earned only 7.2 percent thereon after taxes—a subnormal rate—the market might well apply a multiplier as low as 12½, thus producing a value less than book value for the enterprise. Company B, on the other hand, will show earnings of about 10 percent on its common-stock component. Thus a multiplier of 12 for these earnings might be a reasonable expectation. (In fact, it might well be somewhat higher.) The two multipliers of 12½ and 12, respectively, produce total values of $9,000,000 for Company A and $11,130,000 for Company B—an advantage of over 23 percent in favor of the one with a moderate debt proportion. To this final figure the tax saving and the "leverage" factor contribute about equally.

If these conclusions are correct, two important consequences ensue. The first is that where debt (and/or preferred stock) is conservative, the security analyst need not adjust his earnings and dividend multiplier downward for the debt factor. Thus he can virtually disregard the senior securities in selecting the capitalization rate. The second consequence relates to corporate financial policy. It suggests that frequently the stockholders will be better off if the company has a moderate amount of debt than if it has none.

In Cottle, Murray & Block, Graham & Dodd's Security Analysis, 592 (5th ed. 1988), the authors reaffirm their conclusion in the preceding excerpt that a moderate debt level for creditworthy corporations enhances the value of the enterprise. They describe their "Principle of the Optimal Capital Structure" as being that most corporations should borrow approximately that amount of debt that "careful financial institutions would be ready to lend, at the going rate for sound risks...."

Klein & Coffee, Business Organization and Finance
(9th ed. 2004), 338-41, 346-47

A. INTRODUCTION

Thus far we have assumed, at least implicitly, that the total market value of a firm's securities is equal to the value of the firm determined independently of its capital structure—independently, that is, of the relative amounts of common stock (equity), bonds (debt), and other securities. In other words, it has been assumed that the total value of all securities is the same regardless of the proportions of each. We now turn to an examination of the validity of that assumption. From a managerial perspective..., the issue can be framed in terms of whether the cost of capital is affected by the firm's capital structure. From an investor perspective the same issue would more likely be framed in terms of whether the value of the equity interest can be increased by a judicious use of debt. Regardless how the issue is framed, the possibility that capital structure does affect the total market value of securities has a number of obviously important ramifications. To emphasize that observation, consider one of the more dramatic of these ramifications. Suppose that a corporation is financed entirely with common stock, consisting of 1,000,000 shares with a market price of $100 per share, or a total market value of $100,000,000. Now suppose that the corporation could sell $60,000,000 worth of bonds and use this money to redeem half of its common stock (500,000 shares) at $120 per share, on the assumption that it would wind up with 500,000 shares of common stock worth $60,000,000 and debt worth $60,000,000 (with no other change in the nature of the corporation or its investments or prospects). In other words, suppose that by a readjustment of the capital structure alone, the total value of the securities of the corporation could be increased by 20 percent. This corporation, among other possibilities, would be a prime candidate for a take-over by speculators. A speculator could buy enough common stock to gain control of the corporation; cause the corporation to change its capital structure in the manner suggested; and then sell the common stock for a fast 20 percent profit.

B. PURE LEVERAGE EFFECT

Suppose that you know of two (moderately) risky investment opportunities with identical characteristics. The cost of each is $100,000 and the expected annual return (net) on each is $12,000 (including expected annual appreciation, if any). You have just inherited $100,000 and have no other assets and no debts. You can borrow $50,000 (with recourse) to finance the purchase of either investment, at an interest rate of 8 percent. Disregard taxes and transaction costs.

One possibility is that you simply use your $100,000 to acquire one of the risky investments. Your expected return is $12,000 or 12 percent.

A second possibility is to borrow $50,000 on each of two investments, using your own $100,000 to pay for the remaining $50,000 cost of each. Your expected net return from the two investments is now $24,000 before the payment of interest. The interest obligation is $8,000 per year (8 percent on the total borrowings of $100,000). Your expected net return after the interest payment is $16,000 ($24,000 less $8,000) or 16 percent. You have increased your expected rate of return by 4 percent. You have borrowed money at 8 percent to finance an investment that is expected to yield 12 percent—which seems to be an easy road to riches.

To take the illustration one step further, suppose that you could borrow $75,000 on each $100,000 investment and that four investment opportunities were available. You might buy all four, using, for the purchase of each one, $25,000 of your own money and $75,000 of borrowed funds. Your expected return would be $48,000 before interest; the interest payment would be $24,000 (8 percent of $300,000); and the net expected return after interest would be $24,000. The expected rate of return on your $100,000 equity would now be 24 percent.

Obviously this kind of progression cannot continue indefinitely—for example, to a point where you could borrow $95,000 at 8 percent on each of 100 investments and have an expected return of 88 percent. One reason why this possibility seems too good to be true should be easy to see—no one would lend you money at 8 percent with only a 5 percent equity cushion, unless the investment were virtually free of risk. If such a risk-free investment were available, the lender would invest in it directly; the lender could earn the 12 percent itself and would not be willing to lend to you at 8 percent no matter how much equity you put up. In other words, an 8 percent borrowing rate is inconsistent with the availability of risk-free investments yielding 12 percent. All of which suggests that, up to now, the discussion has avoided a crucial element—risk.

C. LEVERAGE AND RISK

We will now take all the hypothetical facts used in the immediately preceding discussion and add the critical omitted element—namely, the variance of the expected return.... Suppose that the expected return of $12,000 is the product of the following set of outcomes and probabilities:

Probability	Amount	Value
$\frac{1}{3}$	$ 3,000	$ 1,000
$\frac{1}{3}$	12,000	4,000
$\frac{1}{3}$	21,000	7,000
1.0		$12,000

Consider the possible outcomes with various investment strategies. If you simply acquire one investment, with no debt (no leverage), the range of possible outcomes is, of course, $3,000 to $21,000 (by hypothesis) and the expected return is $12,000.

Now suppose that you borrow $100,000 and acquire two investments (each with the expected return and variance set forth above). Assume further that each of the investments is identically affected by all risk factors, so that the outcome will always be the same for each; if one earns $3,000, the other earns $3,000; if one earns $12,000, the other earns $12,000; and so on. The expected return before interest charges is now simply doubled, as is the return for each possible outcome. The effects, after taking account of interest (at 8 percent on the $100,000 debt), are:

Probability	Total Return	Interest	Net	Value
$\frac{1}{3}$	$6,000	$8,000	($ 2,000)	($667)
$\frac{1}{3}$	24,000	8,000	16,000	5,333
$\frac{1}{3}$	42,000	8,000	34,000	11,333
1.0				16,000

The expected return has now increased from $12,000 (12 percent) to $16,000 (16 percent), but only at the price of an increase in the range of possible outcomes (that is, at the price of an increase in volatility risk or variance) from $3,000-$21,000 to ($2,000)-$34,000.

If the total investment were increased to $400,000, with $300,000 debt (75 percent) and $100,000 equity (25 percent), then, assuming no increase in the interest rate, the effect would be as follows:

Probability	Total Return	Interest	Net	Value
⅓	$12,000	$24,000	($12,000)	($ 4,000)
⅓	48,000	24,000	24,000	8,000
⅓	84,000	24,000	60,000	20,000
1.0				$24,000

The expected return is now $24,000 (24 percent on equity), but the range of possible outcomes has increased to ($12,000)-60,000. That should show how, with leverage, people can get very rich, or very poor.

The principles should be clear. Assuming an expected return higher than the interest rate, the use of debt (leverage) to increase the total investment will increase the expected return. But since there will be variance in the expected return, leverage will increase risk; it will magnify the variance. At the same time that it increases the expected return, leverage magnifies the range of possible outcomes (that is, it magnifies the risk or variance). Another way to describe leverage is to note that debt is a fixed obligation; equity has the residual claim after the fixed obligation is met. The greater the relative amount of the fixed obligation, the greater will be the changes in the return on (and value of) the residual associated with any change in the total return on (and value of) the investment.

* * *

F. LEVERAGE AND WEALTH

Again, assume that you have just inherited $100,000, which sum has just been deposited in your checking account. The $100,000 is your total wealth, or net worth. Your expected return, for the moment, is zero. Next, you use the $100,000 to buy a U.S. Treasury obligation with a yield of 8 percent; that 8 percent is now your expected return. Your wealth is still $100,000. The ratio of your wealth, which might also be referred to as the price of your asset, to your expected return, which might be called your earnings on that asset, is 12.5 to 1. That is, the wealth/return or price/earnings ratio is 12.5 to 1.

Next, you sell the Treasury obligation for $100,000 and buy the risky investment with its expected return of $12,000 or 12 percent. The ratio of price to earnings is now 8.33 to 1. Your wealth is still $100,000. You may feel that you are better off now than you were when you held the Treasury obligation; your personal assessment may be that, for you, the risky investment is more valuable than the Treasury obligation. But that does not affect your wealth (as measured by the price at which you could sell).

Finally, you acquire two risky $100,000 investments, borrowing $50,000 at 8 percent against the security of each. Your net expected return is now $16,000 ($24,000 expected return less the interest of $8,000) or 16 percent. Your net worth is still $100,000. The ratio of wealth to expected return (or, if you will, of the price of your equity to your expected earnings) is now 6.25 to 1. Again, you may be happier with the expected return of $16,000 than with the expected return of $12,000, despite the greater risk. But the market value of your wealth remains constant.

The moral of this little story is that the introduction of leverage does not increase the market value of your wealth. Why not? Suppose that you are convinced that the increase in risk resulting from the leveraging does not justify an increase in required rate of return to 16 percent; that instead an increase to 14 percent is sufficient compensation for the risk. You go to a stranger and convince her of this fact. Then you offer to sell her your equity position in the two risky investments for $114,286, which you have arrived at by capitalizing the $16,000 expected return at the 14 percent rate that you both agree is the proper rate to use. The stranger should turn you down cold. In fact, she should refuse to pay you more than $100,000, not because she challenges your private assessment of value, but rather for the simple reason that by hypothesis she can acquire the same leveraged investment herself for $100,000. Assuming that there is nothing unique about your risky investment and that, consequently, she can buy the same kind of investment for $100,000, and assuming that she can create her own leverage on the same terms that were available to you, she would be foolish to pay more than $100,000 for the investment that you offer her. In other words, there is no reason why she should pay you a profit of $14,286 for creating leverage when she can easily create her own leverage.

Notes and Questions

1. The assertion that leverage does not increase stockholders' wealth was first theoretically developed by Franco Modigliani and Merton Miller in The Cost of Capital, Corporation Finance and the Theory of Investment, 48 Am. Econ. Rev. 261 (1958). The theory has been studied extensively and has been the subject of some controversy. *See, e.g.,* Modigliani, MM—Past, Present, Future, 2 J. Econ. Persp. 149 (1988); Miller, The Modigliani-Miller Propositions After Thirty Years, 2 J. Econ. Persp. 99 (1988); Ross, Comment on the Modigliani-Miller Propositions, 2 J. Econ. Persp. 127 (1988); Bhattacharya, Corporate Finance and the Legacy of Miller and Modigliani, 2 J. Econ. Persp. 135 (1988). *See generally* Brealey, Myers, & Allen, Principles of Corporate Finance 446-51 (8th ed. 2006).

MM hypothesize that the value of the firm is independent of its capital structure. The theory is that, all other characteristics of two corporations being exactly the same, different capital structures cannot result in different firm values, because investors will arbitrage their investments, incurring their own debt and investing in an unleveraged firm that requires a lower capital investment for the same return (or, as Klein & Coffee put it in the preceding excerpt, no one will pay you for leverage they can create themselves).

The following example should illustrate this theory: Assume Firm A has no debt and $66,667 in equity (on which there is an expected return of 15 percent), while Firm B has $30,000 of 12 percent bonds outstanding and $40,000 in equity (on which there is an expected return of 16 percent). If an investor in Firm B owns 1 percent of its stock, worth $400, she should sell her stock in Firm B, borrow $300 at a 12 percent rate of interest (which replicates her 1 percent interest in the debt issued by Firm B), and buy 1 percent of the stock of Firm A for $666.67. The expected return on Firm A stock is 15 percent, or $100 which, after the $36 interest payable on the $300 debt, gives the investor a net return of $64, the same return as that on her original investment in Firm B. However, she has had to invest only $366.67 of her own money to obtain this return from Firm A ($336.67 + $300 (borrowed) = $667.67), whereas the same return cost her $400 out-of-pocket in Firm B. (This example of the arbitrage effect is developed in Van Horne, Financial Management and Policy 258-60 (12th ed. 2002)). As investors recognize this opportunity, selling stock in Firm B and buying stock in Firm A, the values of the two firms will be driven to equilibrium.

2. Of particular importance in evaluating Modigliani and Miller's theory is understanding the assumptions on which it is based. One important assumption is that of perfectly efficient capital markets lacking transaction costs and populated by rational investors. Modigliani & Miller, 48 Am. Econ. Rev. at 266-67. (Another is the absence of taxes, an assumption they later relax.) Is this a valid assumption in the real world? Even if not, is there still power to the Modigliani and Miller theory?

3. Copeland, Koller & Murrin, Valuation 93-94 (1990), report that leverage-increasing transactions had a positive impact on stock prices, regardless of their effect on the corporation's earnings per share and, conversely, leverage-decreasing transactions had a negative impact on stock prices. They cite this evidence as support for their theory that the market values cash flow, not earnings-per-share, and further suggest that leverage-increasing transactions provide a signal to the market that management expects the corporation's cash flow to remain strong.

4. If Modigliani and Miller are correct, what are the implications of their theory, if any, for the rights of senior security holders, both relative to management and to common stockholders? Put another way, what does it suggest about the nature of the corporation and its various financial constituents?

5. If Modigliani and Miller are wrong, and if the sole goal of the corporation is corporate/stockholder wealth maximization, should the failure of a corporation's management to carry a reasonable amount of debt be a breach of the duty of care? With what remedy?

Section 2
The Characteristics of Debt

a. Types and General Attributes

Klein and Coffee, Business Organization and Finance
(9th ed. 2004), 248-51

.... Bonds and debentures are manifestations of commitments of funds to a firm for a relatively long period of time (generally, five years or more). Shorter-term obligations are usually referred to as notes. The commitment reflected in the bonds and debentures is, however, of limited duration: there is a fixed date, called the maturity date, at which the firm must pay the principal sum. This will seldom be more than 30 or 40 years in the future and generally will be sooner.

A long-term obligation secured by a mortgage on some property of the issuer is generally referred to as a *bond,* while a long-term unsecured obligation is generally referred to as a *debenture.* In the financial literature and in this book, the distinction is sometimes ignored, or rejected, and the term "bond" often used to refer to both types of obligation. When we speak of a corporation selling or issuing bonds to the public, what we mean is that the corporation is borrowing money from people and that those people may receive a fancy certificate as tangible evidence of the corporation's obligation to pay interest, to repay principal, and to abide by certain terms and conditions that are spelled out in part on the certificate and more fully elsewhere. Ordinarily a person who owns a bond (that is, a creditor with a set of rights normally associated with bonds) can sell the bond to any other person for any price they agree upon. Corporate bonds and debentures are usually issued in *denominations* of $1,000, though, as we have seen, they will not necessarily be sold at that price.... The denomination, *face value*, or *par value*, of a bond may be thought of, then, simply as the amount that must be paid on maturity (that is, at the end of the term of the loan). Regardless of the face value or denomination of the bond, the price quoted in the financial pages will be the price per $100 face value. Thus, if one reads that the price of a bond is 98½, one would normally assume that the bond is in the denomination of $1,000 and that consequently the price is $985.

A bond will manifest the borrower's obligation to pay a *fixed* amount of *interest* at regular intervals (commonly every six months) as well as to pay the face amount at maturity. The total annual interest payment, when expressed as a percentage of the face amount or denomination, is the nominal interest rate (as distinguished from the true interest rate or yield, which will be different if the bond is not bought and sold at par). This nominal interest rate is sometimes called the *coupon rate*. Thus, if a bond obligates a company to pay $85 per year and $1,000 at maturity, the coupon rate would be 8.5 percent; the original sale price and the current market price do not affect the coupon rate. The term coupon rate is a relic of an era when a purchaser of a bond usually received a large, sturdy piece of paper, part of which was divided into small segments called coupons, each of which reflected the obligation of the borrowing company to pay a fixed amount of money (the interest payment) on a particular date, with one coupon for each interest payment date. The owner of the bond collected interest by cashing in the appropriate coupon, usually at a bank. These days, most bonds are registered; the owner's name is registered with the debtor company and the interest payment goes in the mail by check to the registered owner. The term coupon rate is still widely used, however, and reveals the annual dollar amount that the borrower is required to pay. With that information, the current price of the bond, and the length of time to maturity, one can calculate yield.

The *duration* of a bond is a more complex concept than one might imagine. Suppose there are two $1,000 bonds, each with a maturity date ten years hence. Bond A pays interest of $100 per year while Bond B pays interest of $200 per year. Suppose that because Bond B has a much higher risk of default than Bond A, the two bonds sell for the same price. At a naive level it may be thought that the two bonds have the same duration, since they are both scheduled for redemption at the end of ten years. A more sophisticated, and more accurate, measure of duration takes account of the difference in promised cash payments. Bond B's cash payments are weighted more heavily toward the early years than Bond A's, and for purposes of comparison of the two bonds, this difference must be taken into account. In sophisticated market analysis of debt obligations, the concept of duration that is used is a weighted average of the time to each cash payment, so Bond B's duration is shorter than Bond A's. This approach is part of a broader perspective on analysis of debt, a perspective in which each payment—each interest payment and the principal payment at maturity—is seen as a separate obligation.

.... Debt may be issued to, and held by, a large number of people or institutions—that is, it may be "publicly issued" and held. The issuance of debt to the "public"[4] will require, among other things, the filing of a registration statement

---

4. The term "public" in the context does not imply individuals. The fact is that most publicly issued corporate bonds (especially high-yield, or "junk," bonds) are held by institutions such as mutual funds, pension funds, savings and loan institutions, and insurance companies....

with the SEC and the use of investment bankers and brokers to sell the securities (or, if you will, to find the lenders). The holders of the debt generally will not know each other or communicate effectively among themselves. The basic terms of the debt, such as duration, interest rate, and the call feature ... generally will be worked out by the issuer and the investment banker. Other terms, such as the duties of the indenture trustee..., the manner in which the call feature is exercised, and the manner of calculating any limitation on the payment of dividends, will tend to follow standardized forms. Innovations as to details, though perhaps important to particular borrowers (issuers), and potentially acceptable to the well-informed public investors, will be costly to adopt.

Where special circumstances call for the negotiation of non-standardized terms, the borrower may find it advantageous to use a private placement — that is, to borrow from a single lender or a small number of lenders. The lender may be a wealthy individual or a partnership of wealthy individuals, a mutual fund, an insurance company, or a savings and loan institution. Private placements, which are widely used, not only avoid some of the costs of registration with the SEC, and certain administrative costs, but also allow the issuer and the lender to bargain in ways that benefit both. For example, an issuer seeking a loan that will have a high risk of default may be willing to agree to maintain a certain ratio of assets to liabilities.[5] In return for that agreement, the lender may be willing to accept a lower rate of interest than would otherwise be required. Both the borrower and the lender may consider themselves better off with the combination of the financial-ratio obligation and the lower interest rate than without it. In a public placement it might be impossible to convey to the potential buyers of the debt an adequate understanding of the nature or the importance of the issuer's obligation. Thus, the issuer's willingness to accept a financial-ratio burden might not be met by a sufficient willingness on the part of the buyers to accept a lower interest rate. Moreover, the borrower might be reluctant to agree to a tough obligation without some realistic prospect of negotiation with the lender of some relief (that is, some alternative to default) in the event the obligation is not met, and such negotiation may not be feasible (and possibly not legally permissible) when the debt is publicly held. This observation suggests another general advantage to private placements: the greater ability to negotiate changes in the obligation when circumstances change.

As one might expect, the public-versus-private dichotomy, like most dichotomies, can be misleading: problems of coordination among holders increase gradually as the number of holders increases. Moreover, in many cases, where debt is initially issued to a small number of holders, those holders may contemplate selling some or all of the obligations to larger numbers of investors in the near or distant future. Where that is so, the initial holders, though small in number, may bargain for terms that will be suitable for public offerings.

---

5. Failure to maintain the ratio would be an act of default, which ordinarily would make the debt due and payable. A borrower that has failed (or is about to fail) to maintain the ratio, might, in order to avoid the consequences of the failure, be forced to raise new equity capital or to grant some new concession to the lender.

Questions

Why do corporations issue debt? What are the advantages and disadvantages of debt as compared with common stock?

b. The Changing Nature of Corporate Debt

(i) Generally

Klein and Coffee, Business Organization and Finance
(9th ed. 2004), 281-82

.... In recent years, there has been considerable innovation in various terms of debt instruments. A few of the more popular innovations are described below, but the degree of creativity is remarkable.

a. *Rates.* The traditional fixed interest rate has been varied in a number of ways. The most widely used variation is the floating-rate note, in which the interest rate is periodically adjusted to reflect changes in some well-established market interest-rate index such as LIBOR (London InterBank Offered Rate). Interest payments (and other payments as well) may also be linked to a particular stock, a set of stocks, a stock index, or a commodity such as gold or oil. The effect is to shift the risk of change in the market rate of interest (or some other economic indicator) from the lender to the borrower. Another innovation is a rate that changes to reflect changes in the risk of default, as measured, for example, by some accounting ratio. This type of provision shifts the risk of a decline in creditworthiness to the borrower and thereby not only protects the lender but also provides an appropriate incentive to the borrower. Still another innovation is to determine the interest payment in a foreign currency.

Another innovation is the increasing rate note. For example, a note might provide for a basic interest rate plus a rate increase of half a percent each quarter for the first year and a quarter of a percent per quarter thereafter. The basic rate might be tied to a market index. Such notes are generally callable at par within six months of issuance. They are used for short-term financing, but the borrower has the option to extend them by, in effect, paying a penalty.

b. *Duration.* A debt obligation may be made "puttable" or "extendible" by the holder. For example, a debenture with a six year maturity can be made puttable by the holder at the end of three years, which means simply that at the end of three years the holder may demand repayment, but is not required to do so. Alternatively, essentially the same result can be achieved by issuing a three-year debenture that is extendible by the holder for an additional three years.

c. *Combinations.* The innovations as to rate and duration can, of course, be combined. Consider, for example, the "extendible reset" obligation. The initial duration is relatively short, but the issuer has the option to extend the due date, at periodic intervals, subject to a limit. If the issuer extends, the holder must be allowed to demand redemption unless the interest rate is reset. The reset rate may be either (i) a new rate based on changes in a market index or (ii) a new rate set (by an investment banker) to cause the obligation to trade at a specified price (usually 101 or 102). Under the latter formula the reset rate will vary with changes in default risk as well as market rate and the similarity to short-term debt is strong.

(ii) The Rise (and Fall?) of High-Yield Debt Securities

Pitt and Groskaufmanis, A Tale of Two Instruments: Insider Trading in Non-Equity Securities
784 PLI/Corp 347 (Aug. 17-18 1992)

* * *

Corporate debt, unlike equity, is issued with some qualitative assessment of the issuer's viability. When corporate debt is issued, rating services have made an assessment of the issuer's creditworthiness. A secondary market for such bonds exists either via trading on the New York Stock Exchange ("NYSE") or through dealers in the over-the-counter ("OTC") market. The NYSE accounts for only one half of one percent of the OTC market volume; most institutional investors find it easier to place large orders in the OTC market.

Traditionally, corporate bonds were viewed as instruments sufficiently secure for widows and orphans.... In this market, there was less of a pressing need to maintain the close watch on an issuer which is required when holding a company's stock. The market for suitably-rated corporate debt became a familiar haven for institutional investors.

3. "Equity in Drag": The Evolution of the Junk Bond Market

The traditional notions of corporate debt were dashed by the evolution of a burgeoning market in so-called junk bonds. The evolution, sparked by a perceptive financial insight, produced a debt instrument which carried many attributes of equity. This market and its primary proponent became emeshed in the most extensive white collar prosecution in American history. The legacy of the junk bond saga—replete with meteoric ascents and tragic falls—is an enduring market.

Junk bonds are high yielding bonds rated below investment grade. Such bonds are rated either BB+ or less by Standard and Poors or Baa or below by Moody's. Before 1977, this market consisted entirely of "fallen angels"—the bonds of companies that once earned investment grade ratings but had fallen on harder times. In 1977, the market was transformed by new issues of corporate debt with subinvestment grade ratings. In an effort to entice investors to these "junk" offerings, issuers offered a premium over investment grade bonds. In the 1980s, this $9-billion market grew to $200-billion, spurred by $145-billion in offerings initially rated below investment grade. The distribution of junk debt at the end of 1988 mirrored the distribution of investment grade securities. About 30 percent was held by insurance companies and mutual funds, pension funds—15 percent; foreign investors—9 percent; thrift institutions—7 percent; individuals—5 percent. By the end of the decade, the junk market accounted for one fifth of publicly-held corporate debt.

The growth of this market was fueled by Drexel, Burnham, Lambert's Michael Milken. He observed that investment in the corporate debt markets often reflected a herd instinct; investors stuck solely to investment grade securities. Milken believed that the herd instinct was flawed in several important ways. As a process, it was based largely on a company's historical performance. A Congressional report noted that "[t]he rating agencies have always emphasized size, historical record, industry position and ratio analysis. However, qualitative considerations such as management's ability, its vision of the future and its attitude towards public security holders may be more important." Junk bonds required an investor to look at the company to determine whether this upstart or this fallen angel had the means to endure and meet the payments. Milken also tapped demand for debt financing in the vast majority of public companies which had no access to the traditional long-term debt market. Drexel provided the means for this market to function by issuing the lion's share of these bonds and nurturing a secondary market to ensure their ongoing liquidity.

One result was a security which in many ways resembled common stock. One Congressional witness characterized the bonds as "equity in drag."[168] While a triple A rating in itself would sell an investment grade issue, a C rating required an extensive pitch about the issuer. Like equity securities, junk bonds were valued with an eye on the company's fundamentals, as much as prevailing interest rates. Drexel observed that "[t]he values of all high-grade or government bonds in a portfolio will decline when interest rates rise. The values of high-yield bonds, on the other hand, are somewhat less sensitive to changes in the interest rate because they respond to changes in the financial outlooks of the individual underlying companies." These securities also traded like equities—both in volume and volatility. Moreover, trading patterns in junk bonds reflected the economic cycle in a manner comparable to stocks. These similarities prompted some commentators to question whether the interest paid on junk bonds should be eligible for deductibility in a manner comparable to more traditional forms of corporate debt. "In short, junk bonds behave much more like equity, or shares, than old-fashioned corporate bonds."[175]

It was symbolic that purveyors of these bonds could never shake the "junk" moniker. In a rare interview, Milken acknowledged that junk bonds were viewed dimly by the public. Although the "junk" terminology had been used since the 1970s, its lingering use in the 1980s mirrored two factors—the transformation by junk bonds of the market for corporate control and the government's most sweeping investigation ever of securities fraud. These two factors fundamentally altered the nature of the market for junk bonds.

Junk bonds played a vital role in the corporate takeover battles of the 1980s. This new pool of financing allowed individual investors to make credible takeover bids for significant corporations, bids that only a few years earlier, would have been laughable.... Pantry Pride's acquisition of Revlon in 1985 marked a significant turning point. After that, corporate managements often responded with leveraged buyouts which used junk bonds as an integral part of their financing. These transactions drew a storm of criticism. Supporters contended that this market discipline revived dormant management which up until was immune from any accountability. Critics responded that paper charades crippled companies with no productive result.

Concurrently, Drexel and Milken were targets in the most extensive government enforcement action in the history of securities regulation. The financial scandals of the

---

168. The term surfaced in the testimony of Professor Laurence H. Summers:

[W]hen corporations borrow at rates 10 or more percent above the safe rate of return, when they offer a risk premium greater than common stocks, make no commitment to pay cash for 5 to 10 years, and issue 90 percent of their balance sheet in the form of debt securities, the are, in the words that investment bankers frequently use, "offering equity in drag."

"Leveraged Buyouts and Corporate Debt: Hearing Before the Committee on Finance," U.S. Senate, 100th Cong., 1st Sess. 28 (Jan. 25, 1989) (statement of Laurence H. Summers, Nathaniel Ropes Professor of Political Economy, Harvard University).

175. M. Lewis, [Liar's Poker 217 (1989)].

1980s set off a series of dominos that ended with Milken and his employer. In testimony before Congress, SEC Chairman Richard Breeden characterized the case against Drexel as a "felony insider trading case." The Commission's 174-page complaint alleged four separate instances of insider trading activity, and a panoply of other securities law offenses. It was likely the specter of vast forfeiture available to the government under the Racketeer Influenced Corrupt Organizations Act ("RICO") prompted Drexel to settle with the government in late 1988. The cost was steep: a $650-million settlement and a vast restructuring of Drexel's operations.

RICO's potent force became prominent in the March 1990 indictment of Milken, his brother Lowell and Bruce Newberg. Paralleling the Commission's complaint, the criminal case added the demand for a RICO forfeiture of $1.8-billion. About one year later, Milken entered a guilty plea to counts that did not involve insider trading allegations and agreed to pay a $600-million fine. A downturn in business and the shriveling of its capital sources caused Drexel to seek bankruptcy protection on February 13, 1990. Federal Judge Kimba Wood provided the tale with its surprising epitaph—a ten year jail sentence for Milken.

These developments undermined severely the market for junk bonds. With Drexel's demise, a primary market-maker became unavailable for thousands of junk bond issues. Regulatory distaste for junk bonds drove out other market participants. The Financial Institution Reform Recovery Enforcement Act ("FIRREA"), introduced in 1989, required savings institutions to divest themselves of their junk bond holdings by 1994. The collapse of Executive Life stiffened the resolve of state insurance regulators to limit investment by such institutions in high yield securities. An economic recession, moreover, boosted default rates in 1990 to a record high 8.5 percent....

Note

The following statement from a CRS Report for Congress: Winch, Innovative High Yield Securities (Cong. Res. Service May 19, 1989), illustrates the growth of junk bond financing through the 1980s.

> In the late 1970s most junk bonds were "fallen angels," that is, bonds which had once been issued as investment grade securities but had subsequently been downgraded to speculative rating. At present, the main source of junk bonds are new issues, that is bonds which are unrated or rated below investment grade when they are publicly offered. They first passed the 5 percent level of all outstanding corporate bonds in 1980, when these newly issued junk bonds were at the start of their rapid growth phase.
>
> The rising and waning significance of high yield bonds is evident when comparing the aggregate par value of all (nonconvertible) public corporate debt, to that of junk bonds (see Table 1). The relative shift in importance of junk bonds from 1979 to 1989, shifting from 4 percent to over 20 percent, and their decrease to 12.8% in 1993, is evident in Table 1, based on data prepared by the investment banking firm Morgan Stanley. This tally of junk bonds includes all issues with a straight coupon, i.e., all non-convertible bonds, including floating rates issues and other variations. Morgan Stanley does not include preferred stock, exchange offers, secondary offerings, tax-exempts, convertibles, government agencies, mortgage- or asset-backed issues, or debt of non-domestic issuers in its high yield bond totals.

Table 1 Public Straight Debt Outstanding 1970-1993 $ Million

Year	Corporate Debt Estimate of Par Value Outstanding[1]	High Yield Debt Estimate of Par Value Outstanding[2]	Percentage of Total Debt
1993	1,560,769	199,190	12.8
1992	1,254,093	179,216	14.3
1991	1,033,350	158,448	15.3
1990	901,559	168,207	18.7
1989	843,172	170,200	20.2
1988	730,242	143,141	19.6
1987	606,256	112,986	18.6
1986	500,840	82,946	16.6
1985	358,181	49,915	13.9
1984	350,771	34,371	9.8
1983	310,515	19,338	6.2
1982	285,600	18,536	6.5
1981	255,300	17,362	6.8
1980	265,100	15,125	5.7
1979	269,900	10,675	4.0
1978	252,200	9,401	3.7
1977	237,800	8,479	3.6
1976	219,200	8,015	3.7
1975	200,600	7,720	3.8
1974[3]	167,000	8,401	5.0
1973[4]	154,800	8,082[4]	5.2
1972	145,700	7,106	4.9
1971	132,500	6,643	5.0
1970	116,200	6,996	6.0

Source: Morgan Stanley, IDD Information Systems, Standard & Poor's *Bond Guide* and Moody's *Bond Record*, July issues of each year. Defaulted railroads excluded. High yield futures also include non-rated debt of equivalent status to rated debt of speculative grade companies.

Notes: 1. Investment grade debt amounts adjusted to exclude maturities.

2. Amount outstanding is adjusted to exclude maturities, repurchases and exchanges.

3. Excludes $2.7 billion in Consolidated Edison debt.

4. Estimates for 1973 and earlier based on linear regression of this column versus the Federal Reserve's Corporate Bonds Outstanding figures (Federal Reserve Bulletin).

Comment, Junk Bonds: Do They Have a Value?
35 Emory L.J. 921, 922-25, 927-32, 942 (1986)

I. WHAT ARE JUNK BONDS?

A. *Types of Junk Bonds*

Junk bonds are high yield, high risk bonds which can be classified into two major categories. The first category is that of bonds which were investment-grade when originally issued, but which have subsequently been downgraded. The second category is that of bonds originally issued as low-grade bonds. This second category can be further subdivided into two sub-categories—bonds issued by low-rated companies simply as a means of financing ordinary operations, and junk bonds issued in connection with more extraordinary corporate takeover transactions. As discussed more fully below, much of the concern about junk bonds as investment vehicles relates to the possibility of investors failing to make a distinction between the two major categories, and thereby failing to evaluate accurately the risk connected with the securities they are purchasing.

Originally, the term "junk bond" was applied to bonds rated as investment grade[10] when first issued, but the rating of which subsequently fell due to a decline in the issuer's creditworthiness. As it became apparent that these securities still yielded acceptable returns, investors became accustomed to buying low-rated or non-rated bonds. Consequently, the demand for such securities increased, and today companies issue large volumes of bonds rated below investment grade at the time of issuance.

B. *Historical Rates of Return on Junk Bonds*

Junk bonds appeal to a certain segment of the investment community because they have historically provided higher returns than less risky alternatives. Yields on junk bonds have historically averaged 3 to 5 percentage points above higher quality instruments. These higher yields are due to the greater risk that the issuer will default on the payment of either interest or principal. A higher risk of default means a lower expected return to the purchaser of the bond, all other factors being held equal. Investors will only accept a greater risk if compensated by a higher expected return; therefore, if a bond is to remain equally attractive to investors as its risk of default increases, it must offer a higher return to an investor contemplating the purchase of the bond.

C. *How Junk Bonds Are Used in Corporate Takeovers*

A corporation seeking to acquire another corporation must make a number of choices.... Early in the analysis process, the Bidder must decide whether to approach the Target Company on a friendly or hostile (unfriendly) basis....

The Bidder must also choose the structure of the offer for the Target Company's shares. A tender offer is often the most advantageous method for the Bidder to obtain the stock of the Target. Since an element of surprise is generally necessary, or at least helpful, for the success of a tender offer, the possibly greater flexibility available in issuing junk bonds may be advantageous in a hostile tender offer situation....

---

10. Investment grade securities are generally defined as those having ratings above BB (Standard and Poor's) or Ba (Moody's). *Junk Bonds Aren't Just for Highrollers*, Bus. Wk., May 6, 1985, at 141.

Tender offers involving junk bonds typically proceed in several steps. First, the Bidder establishes an asset-free subsidiary corporation (a "shell corporation"), which will ultimately own the Target Company if the acquisition of Target Company shares is completed. Next, the Bidder, in consultation with its investment banker, creates a junk bond package, which the shell corporation will market in order to obtain the funds necessary to finance the acquisition. The investment banker obtains advance commitments from investors to purchase the bonds. These investors are typically third party investors (i.e., investors not otherwise connected with either the Bidder or the Target Company), and the cash acquired in exchange for the bonds is then used to purchase the shares of the Target Company. Such an offering would, in most instances, be considered a public offering under the Securities Act of 1933, so that the filing of a registration statement would be required. A frequently-used alternative is to issue the bonds in some form of "private placement," an offering which avoids the registration requirement. This approach is the most advantageous, if it is available to the Bidder, since it avoids both the expense and the delay associated with the registration of a public offering. Buyers of the privately placed bonds may get a covenant from the issuer guaranteeing a later registration of the bonds for resale. After the Bidder has completed the initial arrangements for the financing, or possibly even before the financing is completed, the Bidder commences a tender offer for the shares of the Target Company. After the tender offer is complete, the Bidder often sells parts of the Target, to raise cash in order to pay down [some of] the junk bond debt.

Several variations on this basic theme are possible in individual transactions, and either the source of the financing or the structure of the bid may distinguish one transaction from another. On the financing side, junk bonds may be issued directly to shareholders of the Target Company in exchange for their shares of the Target. Alternatively, the Bidder may issue junk bonds in exchange for cash, in order to raise a "war chest" in advance of a planned tender offer. The tender offer may be funded entirely by junk bonds, or the Bidder may combine partial junk bond financing with a bank loan. On the structure side, the tender offer may be presented as a bid of 100% of the Target's shares....

Another arrangement is the "leveraged buy-out" (LBO)[a], in which the Bidder purchases the shares of the other shareholders, securing the acquisition debt with the assets of the Target. The only significant difference between junk bonds and LBOs is the fact that LBO financing does not involve the issue of marketable securities in small denominations, and the buyers of the notes are traditional institutional lenders, such as banks, insurance companies, and commercial finance companies. Leveraged buyouts have traditionally been friendly transactions, because it is usually important to keep existing management in place to increase the company's chances of success after the buyout. Management groups have often been the Bidders in these transactions....

Booth, Junk Bonds, the Relevance of Dividends and the Limits of Managerial Discretion
Colum. Bus. L. Rev. 553, 554-57 (1987)

[I]t may be that investors find junk bonds attractive primarily because the issuer-bidder promises more generous cash distributions than the target's current management has

---

a. Leveraged buy-outs are analyzed *infra* at section 8a.

seen fit to pay. That is, it may be that the higher return paid on a junk bond is not so much a reflection of increased risk as it is of the fact that the same segment of returns that previously were claimed by shareholders are now being promised to a new class of junior bondholders. In short, the crucial word is not "junk" but rather "bonds." Junk bonds are not really riskier bonds, but rather are stock which includes a promise to pay.

In the end, the only difference between a bond and a share of stock is that the bond-holder gets paid first and is assured of a regular, agreed return. Thus the only reason one would invest in stock is the prospect of being paid more. However, there is a risk that the company may not make enough money to pay more, or that the management may choose not to pay dividends and may indeed use the money to invest in new business that the shareholder may not regard as sufficiently profitable.

Junk bonds offer a compromise that amounts to a hybrid investment. With a junk bond the investor gets higher returns than on other debt instruments together with the corporation's promise to declare "dividends." The popularity of junk bonds strongly suggests that investors find this deal quite attractive.

Experience supports this hypothesis. For example, the attempted takeover of Gulf Oil by Mesa Petroleum, which was financed largely with junk bonds, was prompted by the perception that Gulf was using available cash to explore for additional oil at a time when the market simply did not justify further drilling. The use of junk bonds to finance the offer was thus perfectly consistent with the motivation for the tender offer. What Mesa offered was a firm policy of cash distributions.

The thesis of this Article, then, is that junk bonds have become an important takeover tool because investors view them as a means of assuring themselves that the target company will pay dividends. In other words, the use of junk bonds is simply an expression of the bidder's belief (together with that of the investors who back up the bidder) that the target company should be paying dividends rather than retaining its cash and pursuing a growth strategy.

Notes and Questions

1. What are the advantages and disadvantages of junk bond financing both within and outside of the corporate takeover context? Are junk bonds really different in nature than traditional corporate bonds? Even if they are, do the differences justify different legal treatment?

2. The large interest payments that resulted from junk bond financing overburdened some corporations in the late 1980s and early 1990s. During the 1980s the percentage of total capital represented by debt of non-financial corporations increased from 34 percent to 49 percent, and interest coverage went from 4.6 to 3.3[1] Several large corporations acquired through LBO deals have ended up in bankruptcy court after defaulting on payments due on high interest junk bonds and other debt. The largest such failure occurred in January 1990 when Campeau Corporation filed for bankruptcy after failing to service the debt that it incurred after acquiring Allied Stores following a bidding war with R. H. Macy & Co.[2] According to one commentator,

---

1. Curran, Hard Lessons from the Debt Decade, Fortune, June 18, 1990, at 76.
2. Financial Adviser Says Bankruptcy Laws Fail to Protect LBO-Related Bondholders, BNA, Inc., Sec. Reg. & L. Rep., Feb. 2, 1990, Vol. 22, No. 5 at 166.

Critics of the debt-heavy deals are now having a field day, saying Campeau's difficulty in making interest payments on its 7.2 billion dollar debt symbolizes all that was wrong with high leverage for Wall Street and the U.S. economy....

"Campeau was symptomatic of the foolishness of the junk bond market during the 1980s, which drove the deals," said Lewis Lowenstein, a professor at Columbia University Law School. "No rational person would have bought these bonds."[3]

3. With failures of large LBO deals in the early 1990s, many critics restated their criticisms of LBOs and the large amount of debt incurred by American corporations during the 1980s. In January and February 1989, the Senate Committee on Finance and the House Committee on Ways and Means held hearings on the issue of leveraged buy-outs. In testimony before the Senate Committee, then Treasury Secretary Nicholas Brady, countering a proposal to limit tax deductions for interest on debt, suggested instead eliminating double taxation of corporate income in order to equalize somewhat the tax treatment of debt and equity. Addressing the issue of corporate recapitalizations as well as LBOs, he identified the appropriate focus of inquiry as whether LBOs improve the competitive position of American business. Brady noted the efficiency gains of LBOs (including tax benefits, the provision of mechanisms to distribute excess cash, and the ability to discipline management with large debt burdens) but further noted that these explanations could not fully account for the dramatic increase in LBO activity because the efficiency considerations had existed long before the rise in LBOs. He thus identified several factors he believed to have contributed to the LBO boom, including (i) the creation of a junk bond market, (ii) an increase in arbitrage activity, (iii) the increased perception that the stock of many corporations is undervalued by the market, (iv) the success of some early LBOs, and (v) the substantial fees available to banks, underwriters, and LBO fund managers from LBOs. Recognizing the advantages of corporate management freed from the pressures of capital markets, he nevertheless suggested that privatization through LBOs would not achieve this goal because pressure on management to service heavy debt would continue to result in a short-term focus. Ultimately he called for further study of the LBO phenomenon, and the exploration of a variety of regulatory solutions.

SEC Chairman David Ruder also testified, focusing principally on the disclosure aspects of LBOs, and particularly on disclosure of financing risks. Suggesting that SEC rulemaking authority was sufficient to address issues of concern, he concentrated on the problem of fairness opinions, a concern also voiced by Secretary Brady, who criticized the practice of linking fairness opinion fees to the successful completion of a transaction.

In February 1990, legislation was introduced in the Senate "to limit takeovers and leveraged buyouts." Sens. Sanford, Sasser Introduce Bill to Limit Takeover, Leveraged Buyouts, 5 BNA Corp. Counsel Weekly 3 (Feb. 28, 1990). The focus of this proposal was on the disclosure aspects of takeovers, and included disclosures of financing arrangements, application of the short-swing trading provisions to bidders owning 5 percent of a target (in contrast to the current statutory requirement of 10 percent) and requiring independent appraisals of "going-private" transactions.[4]

---

3. Fromartz, Wall Street Craze for Company Buyouts Fades, Reuters, Jan. 28, 1990.
4. Leveraged Buyouts and Corporate Debt, Sen. Hearing 101-54, Pt. 1, Hearing Before the Committee on Finance, United States Senate (January 24, 1989).

As the use of junk bonds declined during the early 1990s, critical attention paid to them waned. Thus, most of the legislative proposals were moved to the back burner and ultimately dropped.

4. The correlation presented in chapter 3, section 2, between risk and return should suggest to you the reason that junk bonds provide relatively high rates of interest: their risk of default also is relatively high.

Moody's Investors Service, Inc.[1] has compiled and presented empirical data on the default rates of corporate bonds during the period 1970-1989. Some of the information contained in this report is examined below, with the emphasis placed on the default rates of speculative-grade ("junk") bond issuers.

The economic expansion of the 1980s, fueled in part by junk bonds, resulted in many companies assuming more debt in proportion to total capital than they had previously.

For nonfinancial corporations, net interest expense as a percentage of earnings before interest and taxes (EBIT) rose from 18.2% in 1979 to 42.9% by year-end 1989. Similarly, net cash flow fell from 25.5% of total debt in 1979 to 17.4% in fourth-quarter 1989. Finally, total debt soared from 53.6% of net worth at year-end 1979 to 90.5% by year-end 1989. On average, leverage has increased and the protection of interest and principal has declined.[2]

This lessened protection manifested itself in higher overall default rates for all issuers of corporate debt, realizing a twenty-year high in 1989 with fifty-two rated corporate issuers defaulting on long-term debt obligations. This figure is in contrast to the previous high of thirty-three defaults set in 1986.[3] Much of this increase in the default rates of issuers of corporate bonds is attributable to the increased use of junk bonds as a major financing tool.

5. No matter what issues junk bonds raise apart from their use in takeovers, they seem to be at least similar in kind (if not degree) to the issues raised generally with respect to the legal treatment of debt. Although their use may be somewhat specialized, their principal function is, like ordinary debt, to serve as a method of corporate finance. The same takeover phenomenon that gave rise to the popularity of junk bonds has, however, also given rise to the use of corporate debt for non-financial purposes, that is, as a means of defending against hostile takeovers.

Clemons, Poison Debt: The New Takeover Defense, 42 Bus. Law. 747-53 (1987), describes a number of ways in which debt has been used to prevent or defeat unwanted takeovers. He notes that poison debt is particularly useful when the hostile bidder is financing the attempted acquisition with significant amounts of high interest debt (i.e., junk bonds) that require for repayment significant cash flow from the target. Some of the ways in which a target can disrupt such a takeover include: (i) issuing note purchase rights to stockholders permitting them to exchange stock for debt if a bidder acquires a threshold percentage of the target's stock (typically 20 or 30%), thus significantly increasing the target's debt burden; (ii) providing debt issued in connection with such a rights plan with a short maturity, requiring prompt repayment, or a longer term together with burdensome restrictive covenants; (iii) providing such debt with floating interest rates that increase with the target's leverage; (iv)

---

1. Moody's Special Report, Corporate Bond Defaults and Default Rates, 1970-1989, (April 1990).

2. Id. at 6.

3. Id. at 1.

providing such debt with covenants restricting the sale of the target's assets, its ability to incur new debt, and/or similar limitations that would make it difficult for a bidder to finance the acquisition; and (v) limiting the redeemability of debt to prevent a bidder from redeeming the debt to eliminate restrictive covenants, or provide for mandatory redemption upon changes in control to impose a financial burden on the bidder.

Does issuing debt for the purpose of preventing control transactions raise issues of bondholders' rights that differ from those arising in connection with the traditional use of debt for financing? If so, what are these issues, and how should they be resolved?

6. In his book Junk Bonds: How High Yield Securities Restructured Corporate America (1991), economist Glenn Yago makes the case in favor of junk bonds: "Far from undermining our economy, junk bonds promoted the economic objectives Americans value: efficiency, productivity, profit, and growth. The most degrading or destructive aspect of junk bonds has been the language used to describe them." Among other benefits provided by junk bonds, Yago sees them as democratizing the capital markets by providing access to capital for the large majority of American corporations whose debt is not investment grade, and assisting corporations in providing equity ownership for management and employees. He argues that the junk bond market "eliminated many of the advantages of corporate size," thus dispersing corporate power among a wide variety of participants. Furthermore, by encouraging managers to eliminate unprofitable investments and "deconglomerate," junk bonds permitted decentralization of management at the operating level while at the same time permitting substantial employee equity ownership, thus "reintegrat[ing] ownership and control in corporations." Finally, junk bonds gave access to capital to higher risk technologically and scientifically oriented corporations whose access to debt was limited by the conservative lending practices of commercial banks, and permitted the managers of low-growth corporations to restructure.

Looking back with historical hindsight, do you agree with Yago's assessment of the utility of junk bonds? Or is he wearing rose-colored glasses?

Section 3
Valuation of Debt Securities

If the original purchaser of a debt security, such as a bond, holds that debt security until its maturity, she will receive the full face value of the debt security (typically $1,000) plus, of course, interest along the way. However, that purchaser need not hold on to the debt security until its maturity. Instead, she can resell it to another investor either over an exchange (if the debt security has been registered and is listed for trading purposes) or privately (over-the-counter). The important question is: "at what price?"

Although the corporate issuer is obligated to pay interest at the debt security's coupon rate to any subsequent purchaser of the debt security, investors seeking to buy debt securities in the secondary market demand an interest rate (a *yield to maturity* or *YTM*) competitive with the current market rate on similar, newly-issued debt securities. That rate, however, may be higher or lower than the existing bond's coupon rate. Because the existing debt security's coupon rate generally is fixed, the only way to raise or lower its YTM in response to current market conditions is for the debt security to sell above (*i.e.*, at a *premium*) or below (*i.e.*, at a *discount*) its $1,000 face value.

Valuing debt securities involves the use of present value concepts discussed in chapter 3, section 2b(ii). To determine the value of a debt security requires computing the present value of both the interest flow and the repayment of principal upon maturity. In other words, we must compute the present value of an annuity (*i.e.*, the interest stream) and add to that the present value of a lump sum (*i.e.*, the principal component).

To give an example, let's take a 30-year bond with a face value of $1,000, a 9% annual coupon (thus paying $90 interest per year) and five years remaining until maturity. Suppose that today, due to evolving credit conditions for the bond issuer and the general market, the appropriate discount rate applied to this issuer is 11%. What is the value of the bond in the secondary market?

To determine the present value of the principal, use Table 2, found in chapter 3, section2b(ii)(A) (or the related formula). In Table 2's cell for the present value of $1 at the end of 5 years using a discount rate of 11%, the Table indicates a present value factor of .5935. Applied to the $1,000 face value of this bond gives us $593.50. To determine the present value of the interest stream use Table 3, found in chapter 3, section 2b(ii)(B)(1) (or the related formula). The 5-year/11% cell in Table 3 for a $1 annuity shows a present value factor of 3.696, indicating a value for the interest stream of $332.64 (that is, 3.696 x $90). The value of the bond is the sum of these two pieces ($593.50 + $332.64), giving a total of $926.14.

Thus, this bond should sell at a discount to its face value in the secondary market. *The reason for this is that bond values in the secondary market fluctuate inversely with changes in interest rates.* When interest rates increase beyond the coupon rate of an existing bond ("Bond A"), Bond A's value in the secondary market declines. Those selling Bond A at that time must do so at a discount to its face value, as in the previous example. This occurs because investors will discount Bond A's value at the current (and higher) coupon rate of a similar, newly-issued bond, thus leading to a market value for Bond A below its face value. When considered with Bond A's below-market coupon rate, the discounted price an investor pays will cause Bond A's YTM to match the higher coupon rate of a similar, newly-issued bond.

When interest rates decrease below the coupon rate of Bond A, Bond A's value increases in the secondary market. Those selling Bond A at that time charge a price greater than Bond A's face value, because investors will pay a premium for a bond with an above-market coupon rate. When considered with Bond A's above-market coupon rate, the premium price an investor pays will cause Bond A's YTM to match the lower coupon rate of a similar, newly-issued bond.

For an explanation of how to calculate yield to maturity, see Van Horne, Financial Management and Policy 24-25 (12th ed. 2002). For an additional bond valuation illustration, see Klein & Coffee, Business Organization and Finance 321 (9th ed. 2004).

Section 4
The Legal Treatment of Debtholders

Common stock is an instrument which, once identified as such, has a limited and clearly defined set of characteristics.* Not so with corporate debt. Unlike common

---

* *See* Landreth Timber Co. v. Landreth, 471 U.S. 681 (1985), for a discussion of the characteristics of "stock" under the Securities Act of 1933.

stock, which is the beneficiary of extensive statutory and common law refinement, corporate debt is very much a creature of the contract defining it. Partly as a consequence of this, as well as of other considerations to which you will be introduced, courts have tended to treat the rights of debtholders as limited to those set forth in the specific contract at issue. This section is designed to give you a flavor of the manner in which courts approach the rights of debtholders.

a. Debtholders as Contract Claimants

Simons v. Cogan
549 A.2d 300 (Del. 1988)

WALSH, Justice:

This is an appeal from a decision of the Court of Chancery, 542 A.2d 785, granting a motion to dismiss a class action brought by Louise Simons ("Simons"), a holder of convertible subordinated debentures,[a] against the issuing corporation, Knoll International, Inc. ("Knoll"), its controlling shareholder, Marshall S. Cogan ("Cogan"), and other related corporate constituents. Simons' complaint asserted claims based on violations of fiduciary duty, breach of indenture and common law fraud. In granting the motion to dismiss, the Court of Chancery determined that the issuing corporation and its directors do not owe a fiduciary duty to the debenture holders. In addition, the court ruled that the restrictive provisions of the indenture agreement precluded a claim for breach of indenture.... We agree with the reasoning and holding of the Court of Chancery and accordingly affirm the judgment in all respects.

I

* * *

The transaction challenged in this case involves the merger of two related corporations, Hansac, Inc. ("Hansac") and Knoll.[1] The merger which was completed on January 22, 1987, left Knoll, the surviving corporation, as the wholly owned subsidiary of Knoll Holdings. The merger caused the minority shareholders of Knoll to be eliminated through a $12 cash tender offer.

Significantly, the merger also resulted in the execution of a supplemental indenture which eliminated the right of Knoll's convertible debenture holders to convert their debentures into shares of its common stock. The supplemental indenture, which was executed by Knoll and the indenture trustee, provided that in lieu of the right to convert into the common stock of Knoll, the debentures would be convertible into $12.00 cash for each $19.20 principal amount of debenture. An additional supplemental indenture

---

a. For a full discussion of convertible securities, including the economics underlying them, see *infra* chapter 7.

1. Hansac is a wholly owned subsidiary of GFI Nevada, Inc. ("GFI Nevada"). GFI Nevada is wholly owned by General Felt Industries, Inc. which is in turn wholly owned by Knoll International Holding, Inc. ("Knoll Holding"). Knoll Holding through its subsidiary GFI Nevada controls approximately 90.5 percent of the voting stock of Knoll. Marshall S. Cogan, an individual defendant, controls 51.5 percent of the voting interests of Knoll Holding giving him effective control of both Hansac and Knoll.

was also executed increasing the interest rate on the debentures from 8½ percent to 9⅛ percent per annum.[b]

Simons filed a class action on behalf of the holders of Knoll's convertible debentures asserting as a primary cause of action that the defendants, in terminating the right to convert the debentures into the common stock of Knoll, breached a fiduciary duty to the debenture holders. In support of this claim the complaint essentially alleges: (1) Cogan, as the controlling shareholder of both Knoll and Hansac, unilaterally set the $12 conversion price without negotiating with a representative of the debenture holders; (2) there were conflicts of interest among Knoll's directors and no special committee of independent directors was formed to evaluate the transaction; (3) Knoll's directors did not seek other offers to acquire Knoll; and (4) the transaction was timed to take advantage of the 1986 low point in the trading price of Knoll's shares and debentures. Moreover, it is claimed that the $12 conversion price was unfair and inadequate.

The complaint also contains claims sounding in breach of contract. It is alleged that Knoll breached the terms of the indenture by changing the conversion feature without the approval of all debenture holders as required by section 15.02 of the indenture. Further, the complaint premises a breach of contract claim on the allegation that Knoll also violated section 15.02 by entering into a supplemental indenture without obtaining the required consent of the holders of not less than a majority of the aggregate principal amount of debentures outstanding.

* * *

Defendants filed a motion to dismiss the complaint on the grounds that it failed to state a valid cause of action. In granting the motion the Chancellor ruled that Simons, as a debenture holder, did not share in a fiduciary relationship with the issuing corporation or its directors.... He also held that the "no recourse" provision of the indenture barred an action based on breach of indenture against all defendants except the issuing corporation and the terms of the indenture barred Simons from bringing suit on the indenture without initially making a demand on the indenture trustee on behalf of 35 percent of the outstanding debentures.[c]

II

The first issue presented in this appeal, whether the directors of the issuing corporation owe a fiduciary duty to the holders of convertible debentures, requires that we revisit a question addressed indirectly in an earlier opinion of this Court, *Harff* v. *Kerkorian*, Del. Supr., 347 A.2d 133 (1975).[d]

This Court's holding in *Harff* is best understood in the context of the Court of Chancery decision which it reviewed. In *Harff*, the plaintiffs had sought relief in the

_____

b. The Chancery Court opinion gave the trading history of the common stock and debentures as follows: "Knoll's Class A common was trading at 9¼ on the day before announcement of the $12 cashout transaction; the 8¼%[sic] debentures were trading at 86 at that time.... The debentures, however, allegedly declined in value upon announcement of the supplemental indenture, trading at 73¼ immediately thereafter...." 542 A.2d at 787-88, n.3.

c. The court's discussion of the demand provision is set forth *infra* at section 4d(ii).

d. The *Harff* case is reproduced *infra* at section 4d(i).

Court of Chancery, both derivatively and on behalf of a class. *Harff v. Kerkorian*, Del. Ch. 324 A.2d 215 (1974). Regarding plaintiff's first claim, the Chancellor held that convertible debenture holders did not have standing as "stockholders" for purposes of maintaining a derivative action. *Id.* at 219. The court reasoned that, until the conversion feature is exercised, the debenture holders stand as creditors of the corporation with their rights determined by the indenture contract. The plaintiff in *Harff* also sought to assert class action rights, independent of the indenture, based on an alleged fiduciary duty owed by the director defendants to the debenture holders. In rejecting that assertion, the Chancellor concluded that such independent claims must be based on "special circumstances":

> It is apparent that unless there are special circumstances which affect the rights of the debenture holders as creditors of the corporation, e.g., fraud, insolvency, or a violation of a statute, the rights of the debenture holders are confined to the terms of the Indenture Agreement pursuant to which the debentures were issued.

324 A.2d at 222 (citations omitted).

On appeal, this Court, in a *per curiam* opinion, did not directly consider the broad question of whether a fiduciary obligation extends to debenture holders. Instead this Court reversed on the narrow ground that the Court of Chancery improperly granted summary judgment against the plaintiffs on their fraud claim....

Our decision in *Harff*, if read against the enlarged holding of the Court of Chancery, does not support the inference that, under Delaware law, a fiduciary duty is owed to debenture holders. In dismissing the class claim, the Chancellor found no fiduciary relationships but noted that the class, as creditors of the corporation and apart from the debenture provisions, could seek recovery for "fraud, insolvency or a violation of a statute." Since the plaintiffs in *Harff* conceded the absence of insolvency or statutory violation, the sole focus of the Chancellor was upon the claim of fraud. He concluded that fraud was not alleged in the complaint. On appeal, this Court reached a contrary conclusion as to the fraud allegation and remanded for a factual determination. We did not differ, however, with the Chancellor's substantive analysis. In effect, this Court permitted the class action in *Harff* to proceed because plaintiffs had brought themselves within the fraud exception, not because the complaint stated a cause of action for breach of fiduciary duty.

Notwithstanding the clear inference of our holding in *Harff*, we deemed it advisable to address directly the fiduciary claim asserted by Simons here and in the Court of Chancery. In order to determine whether a holder of a convertible debenture is owed a fiduciary duty by the issuing corporation and its directors we must begin our analysis with an examination of the nature of the interest or entitlement underlying a convertible debenture. A debenture represents a long term unsecured debt of the issuing corporation convertible into stock under certain specified conditions.... A debenture is a credit instrument which does not devolve upon its holder an equity interest in the issuing corporation.... Similarly, the convertibility feature of the debenture does not impart an equity element until conversion occurs. This distinction was noted by the Chancellor in *Harff*:

> "That a bond is convertible at the sole option of its holder into stock should no more affect its essential quality of being a bond than should the fact that cash is convertible into stock affect the nature of cash. Any bond, or any property, for that matter, is convertible into stock through the intermediate step of converting

it to cash.... [C]ase law indicates that a convertible debenture is a bond and not an equity security until conversion occurs."

Harff v. *Kerkorian*, 324 A.2d at 220 (quoting *In re Will of Migel*, Sup. Ct., 71 Misc. 2d 640, 336 N.Y.S.2d 376, 379 (1972)) (citations omitted). In sum, a convertible debenture represents a contractual entitlement to the repayment of a debt and does not represent an equitable interest in the issuing corporation necessary for the imposition of a trust relationship with concomitant fiduciary duties....

Simons argues that this traditional analysis has been softened by cases which have held that convertible debenture holders possess an interest in the underlying corporation sufficient to warrant the imposition of fiduciary duties. Typical of this expansive theory is *Green* v. *Hamilton Int'l Corp.*, S.D.N.Y., 76 Civ. 5433 (July 13, 1981).

Interpreting the significance of the opinion in *Harff*, the court in *Green* reasoned:

> [*Harff*] supports two propositions relevant to the matter before this Court. First, under Delaware law, convertible debenture holders do not possess all the rights of shareholders with respect to actions taken by corporate directors or majority shareholders. Second, in certain circumstances, a holder of a convertible debenture is entitled to different treatment from a mere creditor of a corporation, and a cause of action for breach of fiduciary duty may lie under Delaware law apart from the express terms of an Indenture Agreement.
>
> * * *
>
> As holders of convertible debentures, plaintiffs were part of the entire community of interests in the corporation—creditors as well as stockholders to whom the fiduciary duties of directors and controlling shareholders run.

Id. (citations omitted).

As previously indicated, we do not believe that our holding in *Harff* supports an inference that a fiduciary duty is owed to holders of convertible debentures. Nor are we persuaded by the reasoning in *Green*. In relying on an expectancy interest created by the conversion feature of the debenture, the *Green* court misperceives the type of interest required for the imposition of fiduciary duties under Delaware law. As this Court recently noted in *Anadarko Petroleum Corp.* v. *Panhandle Eastern Corp.*, Del. Supr., 545 A.2d 1171 (1988)[e] a mere expectancy interest does not create a fiduciary relationship. Before a fiduciary duty arises, an existing property right or equitable interest supporting such a duty must exist. The obvious example is stock ownership. Until the debenture is converted into stock the convertible debenture holder acquires no equitable interest, and remains a creditor of the corporation whose interests are protected by the contractual terms of the indenture.

* * *

III

We next consider whether the "no recourse" provision of the indenture operates to insulate all defendants except the issuing corporation from liability for breach of the indenture.[2] As the Chancellor correctly noted, the "no recourse" provision found in Arti-

---

e. The *Anadarko* case is reproduced *infra* at chapter 8, section 3c.

2. The "no recourse" provision, found in article 13 of the indenture, provides in part:

No recourse shall be had for the payment of the principal of, premium, if any, or the interest on any Debentures, or any part thereof, or for any claim based thereon or otherwise in respect thereof, or of the indebtedness represented thereby, or upon any obligation, covenant or agreement of this Indenture, against any incorporator, or against any

cle 13 of the indenture is a standard provision that enjoys general acceptance. *See Continental Illinois National Bank*, slip op. at 13-14 (discussing the recognition and parameters of a "no recourse" provision). *Cf. Harff* v. *Kerkorian*, Del. Ch., 324 A.2d at 217 ("no recourse" provision as an absolute defense to actions by debenture holders against directors). *See also* 3A H. Schlagman, *Fletcher Cyclopedia of the Law of Private Corporations* §1241.1 (perm. ed. 1986). The meaning of the "no recourse" provision is clear — it extends broad immunity to stockholders, directors and officers of the issuing corporation. Accordingly, we agree with the Court of Chancery that since the "no recourse" provision of the indenture limits liability for breach of contract to Knoll, the issuing corporation, the motion to dismiss the contractual claim against the individual defendants must be granted.

IV

[The court's discussion of Section 8.08 of the indenture barring the debentureholders from bringing suit against the corporation other than through the trustee (except under limited circumstances) is set out in full *infra* at section 4d(ii).]

* * *

The decision of the Court of Chancery dismissing Simons' complaint is AFFIRMED.

Questions

1. The supplemental indenture executed in connection with the Knoll/Hansac merger made each $19.20 principal amount of debenture convertible into $12.00 cash. On the face of it, isn't this a grossly unfair price? Does the increase in interest rate from 8½ percent to 9⅞ percent eliminate all unfairness?

2. Upon what theory of the corporation does the court base its opinion? Would different theories of the corporation suggest different results?

3. What is a fiduciary relationship? Why does the existence of such a relationship lead to the imposition of special duties on the fiduciary? Why does it require "an existing property right or equitable interest"? Does such a requirement necessarily lead to the conclusion that bondholders are not in a fiduciary relationship with corporate management?

4. The court writes that "a mere expectancy interest does not create a fiduciary relationship." What is the "expectancy interest" to which the court refers? Do you agree with this statement?

5. Does modern financial theory suggest an alternative means of bondholder protection? If so, is it satisfactory?

---

stockholder, officer or director, as such, [sic] past, present or future, of the Company, or of any predecessor or successor corporation, either directly or through the Company or any such predecessor or successor corporation, whether by virtue of any constitution, statute or rule of law, or by the enforcement of any assessment or penalty or otherwise; it being expressly agreed and understood that this Indenture and all the Debentures are solely corporate obligations, and that no personal liability whatsoever shall attach to, or be incurred by, any such incorporator, stockholder, officer or director, past, present or future of the Company....

Pitt and Groskaufmanis, A Tale of Two Instruments:
Insider Trading in Non-Equity Securities
784 PLI/Corp 347 (Aug. 17-18, 1992)

* * *

C. Classic Bond Doctrine: Attack on Another Citadel?
1. The Citadel: The "Bond Doctrine"

.... Under the prevailing view, debtholders are limited to those rights they have secured by contract. More importantly, the traditional view expressly rejects the notion of any fiduciary link between issuers and bondholders.

The classic view treats the rights of debtholders as starkly distinct from those of equity investors. Morey McDaniel outlines the "tidy concepts" that extend from this compartmentalization. The stockholders are the corporation's owners; the debtholders are its creditors. Corporate law is for stockholders; contract law is for the debtholders. Corporate directors are charged with protecting stockholder interests; the indenture represents the debtholders' protection.[215] The Delaware courts, the chief arbiters of American corporate law, have held that "in the absence of fraud, insolvency or a statutory violation, a debenture holder's rights are defined by the terms of the indenture."[216]

An important corollary to the traditional view holds that issuers owe no fiduciary duty to debtholders. Chancellor Allen's articulation of this viewpoint in Simons v. Cogan starts with the observation that "among the duties owed by directors of a Delaware corporation to holders of that corporation's debt instruments, there is no duty of the broad and exacting nature characterized as a fiduciary duty."[217] Chancellor Allen warned that introducing this "powerful abstraction" to carefully negotiated and copiously documented commercial relationships would "risk greater insecurity and uncertainty than could be justified by the occasional increment in fairness that might be hoped for."[218] Courts adopting this position reason that "bondholders make a 'knowledgeable gamble' from an equal bargaining position and bear only the risks they pay to bear."[219] This position concludes that it is far more efficient to enforce complex arrangements made in advance than to impose "deadweight losses" on participants who must litigate "an inherently and endlessly ambiguous concept" after the fact.[220]

The absence of a fiduciary link mandates that protections bondholders fail to negotiate remain unavailable to them. The disparity in the standing of debt and equity holders became apparent in the litigated takeover cases of the 1980s. The Delaware Supreme Court determined that "obtaining the highest price for the benefit of the

---

215. *See* McDaniel, "Bondholders and Corporate Governance," 41 Bus. Law. 413, 413 (1986).

216. *Simons* v. *Cogan*, 542 A.2d 785, 788 (Del. Ch. 1987), aff'd, 549 A.2d 300 (Del. 1988)....

217. *Simons*, 542 A.2d at 786....

218. *Simons*, 542 A.2d at 791.

219. Bratton, *The Economics and Jurisprudence of Convertible Bonds*, 1984 Wisc. L. Rev. 667, 697 (1984).

220. Scott, "The Law & Economics of Event Risk, John M. Olin Program in Law & Economics," Working Paper No. 62, June 1990, at 25.

stockholders should [be] the central theme guiding director action."[221] At the same time, Delaware courts recognized that some restructurings that maximize shareholder value "may in some instances have the effect of requiring bondholders to bear greater risk of loss and thus in effect transfer economic value from the bondholders to stockholders." The fact that this maximization came "'at the expense' of others * * * does not for that reason constitute a breach of duty."[222] "Courts traditionally have directed bondholders to protect themselves against … self-interested issuer action with explicit contractual provisions."[223]

Metropolitan Life Insurance Co. v. RJR Nabisco, Inc.[224] represented the triumph of the classic doctrine in a new milieu. The case centered on Kohlberg Kravis Roberts & Co.'s record $24-billion leveraged buyout of RJR Nabisco, Inc. The tremendous debt inevitable in such a transaction caused RJR Nabisco's existing bonds to plummet in value. Metropolitan Life Insurance Company filed suit against the company alleging a series of amorphous tort violations. Judge Walker identified the "heart" of these claims as an alleged breach of an implied covenant of good faith and fair dealing.[227] Included among the other counts alleging fraud, tortious interference with contract or property and fraudulent conveyance was a claim "in equity" which the court equated to a claim for a breach of fiduciary duty. The plaintiffs asserted that RJR Nabisco fostered "investment grade" ratings for its debt, emphasized its solid capital structure and made representations about future creditworthiness which were not reflected in the indentures.

The court's rejection of this claim was implicit in its opening observation that the corporate parties to this litigation "are among the country's most sophisticated financial institutions."[230] Metropolitan Life, Judge Walker noted, had itself invested in LBOs as early as 1980 and had extensive memoranda in its files about the risks posed by such transactions to debtholders.[231] Finding Simons "persuasive," the court agreed that RJR Nabisco owed no fiduciary duty to these investors. In fact of all the parties to whom such a "special and rare" duty could be owed—including trade creditors and employees—"these informed plaintiffs least require a Court's equitable protection; not only are they willing participants in a largely impersonal market, but they also possess the financial sophistication and size to secure their own protection."[232]

Metropolitan Life's claims were dismissed.

2. The Assault on the Bond Doctrine Citadel

By exposing the harsh operation of the traditional bond doctrine, Metropolitan Life (and other instances involving comparable fact patterns) have prompted a scholarly reassessment of the traditional bond doctrine. Some commentators assert that heavily leveraged transactions amount to an outright expropriation from bondholders to the

---

221. *Revelon, Inc.* v. *MacAndrews & Forbes Holdings, Inc.* 506 A.2d 173, 182 (Del. 1986). (The court noted that a board could guard the interests of its other "constituencies," including bondholders, "provided there are rationally related benefits accruing to the stockholders.").

222. *Katz v. Oak Industries, Inc.,* 508 A.2d 873, 879 (Del. Ch. 1986).

223. *Simons,* 542 A.2d at 789 (quoting Bratton, The Economics and Jurisprudence of Convertible Bonds, 1984 Wisc. L. Rev. 667, 668 (1984)), aff'd, 549 A.2d 300 (Del. 1988).

224. *See* 716 F. Supp. 1504 (S.D.N.Y. 1989).

227. *Metropolitan Life Insurance,* 716 F. Supp. at 1507.

230. *Id.* at 1505.

231. *Id.* at 1511.

232. *Id.* at 1524-25.

benefit of shareholders.[233] By the mid-1980s, a Barron's editorial noted that "bondholders, after years of suffering in sullen silence, are showing signs of growing mutinous."[234] Both institutional investors and some academics have championed a wholesale reassessment of the antiquated principles. At the core of this argument is the contention that the traditional concept does not comport with the realities of the current marketplace. While these arguments have not gained widespread judicial approval, they provide a broader conceptual framework for the narrow exceptions crafted by some courts when an issuer is insolvent or has issued convertible securities.

Proponents of fiduciary rights for debtholders maintain that such rights are needed because the core precept of the bond doctrine—that debtholders contract to protect themselves—is grounded in a fiction. [D]ebtholders do not participate in the crafting of indentures because they do not yet exist; the rights of the investors are delineated by underwriters and indenture trustees who owe their position to the issuer. The Metropolitan Life court recognized this fact.[238] In this context fraught with potential conflicts of interest, ... fiduciary obligations are particularly apt. The increased activity in the secondary market adds to the number of investors with no means to develop contractual protections.

Proponents of fiduciary rights for bondholders note further that the same pragmatic review of bondholder covenants reveals the sparse protection offered by such provisions. The bond indenture enjoys a dubious notoriety in the legal lexicon for its length and complexity; the indenture is criticized "for its ridiculous proportions and its extravagantly complicated phraseology exemplifying the worst obscurantism of the law."[241] In reality, McDaniel observes, "[c]ovenants are in decline, presumably because they proved too costly in lost opportunities."[242] McDaniel surveyed the bond contracts of Fortune 100 companies and found that not one had a restriction on the disposition of assets.[243] Even with the country's largest industrial corporations, "indenture restrictions on unsecured debt and dividends are the exception, not the rule."[244]

Given this reality, the proponents conclude, the lot of bondholders (not entirely unlike that of shareholders) is uniquely suited to the protections afforded by a fiduciary standard. The issuer's management exercises "control, discretion, expertise; on the bondholder side, there is reliance."[245] Offering such protection would not be completely without precedent. State corporate statutes have been amended to afford directors latitude in considering various constituencies besides shareholders in reaching decisions. The law of trusts provides just one example in which a fiduciary serves more than one master. Finally, fiduciary obligations are permeating multiple relationships which were once governed by black letter principles. Indeed, proponents note that early corporate commentators found strange the absence of such an obligation.[249] The modern corporate bondholder, these commentators conclude, represents one context in which such a

---

233. *See, e.g.* McDaniel, "Bondholders and Stockholders, 13 J. Corp. L. 205, 205 (1988) ("We also are witnessing a massive transfer of wealth from bondholders to stockholders, possibly the largest expropriation of investors in American business history.")....

234. Bondholders, Unite!, Barrons, Nov. 24, 1986, at 9....

238. *See Metropolitan Life Ins. Co.* v. *RJR Nabisco, Inc.,* 716 F. Supp. 1504, 1509 (S.D.N.Y. 1989).... *Cf. Katz* v. *Oak Indus., Inc.,* 508 A.2d 873, 879 (Del. Ch. 1986)....

241. McDaniel, *supra* note 215, at 423....

242. McDaniel, *supra* note 233, at 236.

243. McDaniel, *supra* note 215, at 425-26.

244. *Id.* at 426....

245. McDaniel, *supra* note 233, at 273....

249. *See, e.g.,* McDaniel, *supra* note 233, at 220....

transition is necessary because the common law standard offers inadequate remedies in the modern markets.[250]

* * *

Questions

1. Why do bond indentures offer diminished protection to bondholders? Does it matter? Might there be reasons for this diminished contractual protection that suggest this fact is not a cause for alarm? Do the facts that bond trading has increased and that bond ownership increasingly is by institutional investors suggest an answer? Is it a good answer as a policy matter?

2. Assuming that we can identify some level of protection for corporate bondholders that is "adequate," can such protection be structured within the current legal framework, that is to say, can the bond contract provide adequate protection for bondholders?

3. Even if the traditional treatment of bondholders was appropriate as a policy matter through the first half of this century, the 1980s saw an extraordinary proliferation of corporate debt, largely in the form of junk bonds issued in connection with corporate acquisitions. Does the modern bond environment call for different treatment of bondholders, or does the traditional view still make sense?

4. For an excellent discussion on the bond doctrine/fiduciary duty debate, see Schwarcz, Rethinking a Corporation's Obligations to Creditors, 17 Cardozo L. Rev. 647 (1996).

b. Interpreting the Debt Contract

It should be obvious by now that the principal, if not exclusive, source of bondholders' rights is the bond contract. Of course contracts are made up of words and, as Theodore Dreiser wrote: "... words are but the vague shadows of the volumes we mean."[1] But what are the words in the first place? And how are those words interpreted? We begin with the first question and then turn to the second.

(i) Key Contractual Terms and Protective Provisions

A. The Promise to Pay and Provisions Designed to Support It

Every debt indenture sets forth the issuer's promise to repay debtholders the borrowed funds along with interest. This promise is fully enforceable in contract by those debtholders, as it was given by the issuer in a bargained for exchange in return for the loaned funds.

Besides relying on the issuer's naked promise to repay its debt, many investors insist on additional indenture provisions designed to reduce the risk or impact of a payment default. One way to reduce this risk is to *collateralize* the debt securities.

---

250. *See* McDaniel, *supra* note 233, at 315....
1. Dreiser, Sister Carrie 6 (Piger, ed. 1970).

Whether debt is collateralized is the subject of negotiations between the issuer and prospective debtholders (or their agent). If the issuer defaults, and that default is not cured in a timely fashion, debtholders through the indenture trustee can seize the collateral supporting the issuer's payment obligation, sell it, and pay themselves back with the proceeds.

Almost any of an issuer's assets can secure its debt securities. Examples include land, accounts receivable, inventory and equipment. An exception would include assets that require governmental approval to own, such as a casino gaming license. In order to ensure the ability to seize collateral, debtholders through the trustee must "perfect" a security interest in that collateral in accordance with Article 9 of the UCC.

A second way investors can protect themselves against non-payment is by demanding a *guarantee* from a third party. Guarantees take many forms. Most typical is a payment guarantee, whereby the guarantor must pay if the issuer does not. More unusual guarantees include an equity infusion guarantee, whereby a third party commits to infusing equity capital into the issuer in the event the issuer's debt-to-equity ratio becomes dangerously unbalanced.

Parties closely affiliated with the issuer typically provide guarantees. They do so because of the indirect benefits they receive when the issuer gains access to the loaned funds. Most typical is a guarantee from a controlling stockholder, whether an individual or a parent company. However, when the issuer is a holding company, debtholders demand guarantees from the holding company's operating subsidiaries. Because the holding company is almost entirely dependent on those subsidiaries up-streaming cash to pay off the holding company's debt, it makes sense to obtain the guarantees from them.

A third way investors can protect themselves is through the creation of a *sinking fund*. A sinking fund indenture provision requires the issuer to periodically deposit a percentage of its cash flow into a custodial account (the "sinking fund") typically maintained by the indenture trustee. The goal of this provision is to assure investors that the issuer will have the funds necessary to repay the principal on the debt securities when those securities mature.

Sinking funds, however, are often a mixed blessing. On the one hand, debt securities supported by a sinking fund are less risky than those without. On the other hand, an issuer that is required to make sinking fund payments cannot use those funds to grow its business. This works to the detriment not only of stockholders but debtholders as well.

B. Ranking

When an issuer has multiple classes of debt securities outstanding (*e.g.*, bonds and debentures), the priority in which debtholders of different classes are repaid is crucial. Ranking among classes is particularly important when the issuer declares bankruptcy or seeks to liquidate.

The concept of *subordination* refers to one debtholder class standing behind another in order of payment. A given issuer, for example, may have senior debt securities, senior subordinated debt securities, and subordinated debt securities outstanding at any given time. Holders of the senior debt securities rank ahead of the holders of the other two classes of debt securities. Holders of the senior subordinated debt securities rank ahead of the holders of the subordinated debt securities. Thus, in terms of the repayment "food chain," holders of subordinated debt securities are at the bottom when it comes to debt securityholders.

Where a given issue of debt securities ranks vis-á-vis another issue is purely a matter of contract law.[1] For a given issue to be subordinated, its indenture must so provide. Thus, subordination is a topic of negotiation. In return for accepting the additional risk relating to subordination, investors in subordinated debt demand a higher rate of interest. In fact, subordinated debt securities are referred to as both *high-yield* debt securities and *junk* bonds. These bonds are considered high in yield because they yield about three hundred to five hundred basis points more than regular investment grade bonds.

C. Covenants

A debt indenture typically contains two types of covenants: affirmative and negative. Covenants are designed to ensure that the issuer operates in a way most conducive to fulfilling its promise to repay the debtholders.

Affirmative covenants are promises that an issuer makes to perform specified, affirmative acts. For example, an issuer may promise to: (1) maintain its properties and corporate existence; (2) pay its taxes; (3) deliver its financial information to the indenture trustee; (4) obtain and maintain insurance on its properties; (5) deliver a compliance certificate to the trustee annually stating that the issuer is in compliance with all indenture covenants and conditions; and (6) give prompt notice to the trustee of the occurrence of certain specified events, such as a default.[2] Most indentures contain standard affirmative covenants regardless of the type of debt securities being issued or the credit quality of the issuer.

Negative covenants, by contrast, are issuer promises not to engage in specified acts. They often are referred to as "thou shalt nots." Negative covenants include:

Limitation on the Incurrence of Indebtedness. This covenant prevents the issuer from increasing its debt load unless it is generating enough cash flow to easily satisfy its principal and interest payments on the debt securities in question. "Indebtedness" as used in this covenant is broadly defined.[3] The definition brings within it both conventional and unorthodox leverage. Conventional leverage covers, among other things, new debt securities or bank loans. Unorthodox leverage, by contrast, would include an issuance of stock (often referred to as *disqualified stock*) that is redeemable by the issuer prior to the maturity of the debt securities in question. Redeemable preferred stock is a prime example. This covenant, however, typically allows the issuer to incur additional indebtedness if certain financial ratios are met.

Restricted Payments. The purpose of this covenant is to keep money within the issuer for use in servicing the debt securities in question. The covenant typically prohibits the issuer from (a) distributing its cash to its equity holders either through the payment of dividends or through repurchases of stock or (b) purchasing or redeeming any indebtedness of the issuer subordinated to the debt securities in question. The covenant, however, typically allows the issuer to make some restricted payments if the issuer is in good financial health and the payment in question is reasonable in amount.

---

1. *See* Ad Hoc Committee for the Revision of the 1983 Model Simplified Indenture, Revised Model Simplified Indenture, 55 Bus. Law. 1115, 1125 (2000) (definition of "Senior Debt") [hereinafter "Revised Model Simplified Indenture"].

2. *See id.* at 1133-34 (Article 4).

3. *Id.* at 1124-25 (definition of "Debt").

Asset Sales. This covenant prohibits an issuer from selling substantial assets unless (a) no default or event of default exists, (b) the issuer receives consideration for the assets at least equal to the fair market value (as determined in good faith by the issuer's board) of the assets sold, and (c) a high percentage (typically 90%) of the consideration received is cash or cash equivalents. To the extent the asset purchaser assumes liabilities of the issuer as part of the transaction, the amount of assumed liabilities is typically deemed to be "cash" for purposes of clause (c) above. Sales of assets less than a specified deminimus amount ($500,000 is typical) are usually carved-out from the covenant altogether. Any asset sale that constitutes a sale of "all or substantially all" of the issuer's assets, however, is covered by the "Merger, Consolidation or Sale of Assets" covenant described below.

When an asset sale is permitted under this covenant, it often further requires the issuer to reinvest the proceeds from that sale in its core operations within a specified period of time (usually 180 days after receipt). If the issuer fails to do so and unreinvested proceeds from all asset sales exceed a specified amount, the issuer often is required to offer to buy back a portion of the debt securities in question at a small premium with the excess proceeds.

Merger, Consolidation or Sale of Assets. This covenant prevents the issuer from consolidating, merging or selling all or substantially all of its assets to any other person unless certain conditions are met. These conditions may include: (1) the issuer must be the surviving entity or, if not, the surviving entity must be a company existing under the laws of the United States or any of its states; (2) the surviving entity (if not the issuer) must assume all of the issuer's obligations under the indenture pursuant to a supplemental indenture or otherwise; (3) the valuation of the issuer or, if the issuer is not the surviving entity, the surviving entity after the transaction must not be less than the issuer's valuation prior to the transaction; (4) immediately after the transaction no default or event of default must exist; and (5) the issuer or, if the issuer is not the surviving entity, the surviving entity must at the time of the transaction and after giving pro forma effect thereto be permitted to incur at least $1.00 of additional indebtedness under the "Limitation on the Incurrence of Indebtedness" covenant.[4]

The main purpose of this covenant is to restrict the issuer from engaging in a reorganization in which either the issuer does not survive or the surviving entity is financially weaker than the issuer. Additionally, this covenant prevents the surviving entity from purchasing the issuer's assets without also assuming the indebtedness related to the debt securities in question. Because of this covenant, the debt securities must follow the assets that produce the revenue needed to service them.

Dividend and Other Payment Restrictions on Subsidiaries. This covenant typically appears when a holding company is the issuer of debt securities. In this event, the holding company is dependent on its subsidiaries up-streaming the monies necessary for it to service those securities. Thus, this covenant prohibits the issuer (holding company) and its subsidiaries from entering into any contract or arrangement that could impede the subsidiaries from up-streaming cash to the holding company.

Transactions with Affiliates. This covenant ensures that any issuer-affiliate transaction is done on an arms'-length basis, thus preventing "sweetheart deals" that siphon off issuer funds.

Restrictions on Liens. This covenant, often referred to as a "negative pledge clause," typically appears when the issuer has issued secured (collateralized) debt securities. The

---

4. *Id.* at 1134-35 (Sections 5.01 and 5.02).

covenant prohibits the issuer from permitting liens on its assets unless certain conditions are met. It protects the holders of the secured debt securities by minimizing the likelihood that other creditors will have liens on the same assets as those holders. Certain exceptions to this covenant are typically negotiated (so-called *permitted liens*), such as one allowing pledges or deposits under worker's compensation laws. For an example, see the second part of Problem—Balancing the Rights of Debtholders and Stockholders in the Bond Indenture, which follows subsection E below.

Line of Business. An indenture may include a covenant that prohibits the issuer from engaging in any business activity other than those specified in the indenture.

With respect to bond indenture covenants, compare the Table of Contents of the American Bar Foundation's Model Debenture Indenture (1971) with that of the Revised Model Simplified Indenture, 55 Bus. Law. 1115 (2000). For a further discussion of covenants, see Klein & Coffee, Business Organization and Finance 252-256 (9th ed. 2004).

D. Redemption

The indenture relating to a particular issuance of debt securities may provide for optional and/or mandatory redemption of those securities by the issuer prior to their maturity date. Once an issuer fixes a date for redemption, debt securities no longer earn interest beyond that date. Thereafter, debtholders are only entitled to receive the redemption price from the issuer. Debtholders, therefore, have an incentive to turn in their debt securities on or before the redemption date.

Optional Redemption. The ability to pay off debt securities prior to their maturity is something most issuers seek, and against which most investors fight. When interest rates fall, an issuer may seek to refinance existing debt with lower interest rate debt. Doing so, however, prevents existing debtholders from continuing to receive their now above-market return. Indeed, if existing debtholders are paid off early, any newly-issued debt securities they purchase with the proceeds will be lower yielding than their previous investment.

Indentures ordinarily contain a compromise. The issuer receives the ability to redeem its debt securities early, but only after a period of years transpires during which redemption is prohibited. This period of years is referred to as the debtholders' *call protection*, because the issuer is prohibited from "calling away" the debt securities from the debtholders during this period. Thereafter, the issuer has the option of redeeming some or all of the securities at a premium that declines to zero over subsequent years, plus accrued and unpaid interest (if any) to the date of redemption.

For example, the indenture for 20-year debentures might provide the issuer with the ability to redeem those debentures in accordance with the following schedule:

Years 1-3	Call Protection (no redemption allowed)
Years 4-7	103% of principal (3% premium)
Years 8-11	102% of principal (2% premium)
Years 12-14	101% of principal (1% premium)
Years 15-20	100% of principal (no premium)

Mandatory Redemption. Many indentures require an issuer to offer to redeem some or all of the debt securities prior to their maturity upon the incurrence of certain events. For example, an indenture may require the issuer to offer to repurchase debt securities if the issuer's cash flow from operations is greater than a predetermined benchmark. The "Assets Sales" covenant discussed above may also give rise to a mandatory offer of redemption. If the issuer has not redeployed excess proceeds from asset sales within a specified period of time, then it must offer to buy back debt securities with those excess proceeds.

Another mandatory redemption trigger is a *change in control*. If a change in control (as defined) occurs, the issuer has to offer to purchase all the outstanding debt securities at a purchase price usually equal to 101% of their aggregate principal amount, plus accrued and unpaid interest (if any) to the date of purchase. This change in control "put," as it is sometimes referred to, effectively forces a potential acquiror to either negotiate with the debtholders over how the debt securities will be treated in the overall transaction or face having to buy back all those securities at a small premium after acquiring control of the issuer.

"Change in control" is a carefully defined term. Ordinarily, several events qualify, including:

(a) The sale of all or substantially all of the assets of the issuer;

(b) Any person becomes the beneficial owner of a specified percentage (typically 25% to 35%) of the issuer's voting stock through a tender offer made to the issuer's public stockholders; or

(c) Any time that a majority of the issuer's board of directors is not comprised of *continuing directors*. Continuing directors are members of the board on the issuance date of the debt securities and any subsequent members of the board nominated by those members or any such subsequent members.

In situations where a controlling stockholder exists on the issuance date of the debt securities, the "change in control" definition often includes the consummation of any transaction the result of which any person or group holds more of the issuer's voting stock than is owned by the controlling stockholder.

E. Events of Default

All debt indentures define *event of default* and specify the consequences of the occurrence of such an event.[5] The following events typically fall within that definition:

Default in the Payment of Interest or Principal. The failure of an issuer to make a scheduled interest or principal payment (referred to as a *payment default*) is the most fundamental event of default. A grace period may attach to a default on an interest payment (typically 30 days), but not on a principal payment. If the issuer misses a principal payment, or fails to make an interest payment following the expiration of the grace period, the indenture trustee may declare the full principal amount of the debt securities, plus any accrued and unpaid interest, immediately due and payable. This is known as *acceleration* of the debt.

Breach of a Covenant, Warranty or Representation. An issuer's breach of any of its covenants, warranties or representations qualifies as an event of default. The issuer is usually given a grace period (typically 30 days) to state in writing that it will cure the breach. If the issuer shows no inclination to cure, does not cure, or refuses to engage in any dialogue with the indenture trustee within the grace period, the indenture trustee may accelerate the debt.

---

5. Revised Model Simplified Indenture, *supra* note 1, at 1135-36 (Section 6.01).

Bankruptcy/Insolvency. An involuntary order or decree resulting in an issuer's bankruptcy or insolvency or a voluntary filing of a bankruptcy petition by the issuer constitutes an event of default. When the issuer is involved in an involuntary insolvency (*i.e.,* one commenced by the issuer's creditors), the issuer typically has a grace period (typically 60 consecutive days[6] before this event becomes an event of default. This gives the issuer time to dismiss the proceedings and prevent the acceleration of the debt. If the issuer voluntarily engages in insolvency proceedings, however, it is immediately in default under the terms of the indenture.[7]

Cross-Default. An indenture may contain a cross-default provision if the issuer has other significant debt besides the debt securities in question. This provision provides that any default by the issuer under any other agreement evidencing indebtedness generally constitutes an event of default under the indenture for the debt securities in question. If an issuer triggers the cross-default provision under one agreement, the indenture trustee can take action even if those debt securities in question are not yet in default.

Problem — Balancing the Rights of Debtholders and Stockholders in the Bond Indenture

Jock, Inc. ("Jock"), is a diversified manufacturer and distributor of sporting goods and clothing and children's toys. It also owns a majority interest in Golf Resorts, Inc., a publicly held corporation that owns a chain of golf resorts in the southeastern United States. Jock itself is publicly owned, with 50,000,000 common shares and 1,000,000 shares of 7 percent Series A Preferred Stock (with a liquidation preference of $10 per share) traded on the New York Stock Exchange. As at December 31, 2006, Jock had a net worth of $500,000,000. Dividends over the past five years have been steady at $0.80 per share annually. The only debt Jock has outstanding is a $15,000,000 unsecured working capital loan with the Resolution Bank & Trust Company.

Jock is the defendant in an action pending in federal court by a competitor for trademark infringement which is currently in discovery proceedings. Jock's litigation counsel has opined that Jock has about a 50 percent chance of winning, and that if Jock loses, the likely financial consequence will be a loss of approximately $15,000,000. Plaintiff has also requested a preliminary injunction preventing Jock from disposing of any assets relating to the litigation pending the outcome of the case, and litigation counsel has opined that plaintiff's motion is likely to succeed.

Despite its excellent financial health (including a good cash flow), Jock's assets are fairly illiquid. Jock's board of directors would like to borrow money in the public debt market to enable it to expand its operations, through a combination of developing new product lines and, possibly, acquiring corporations in related businesses. The amount of money the board thinks Jock will need is $150,000,000, and it would like to keep the debt outstanding for fifteen years with the option to redeem all or part of the issue at any time after five years. In addition, Jock is in the process of negotiating

---

6. The drafters of the Revised Model Simplified Indenture advocate shortening the 60 day period to 15 or at most 30 days. They argue: "Such a lengthy period [60 days] is inconsistent with the exigencies of the modern world. A 'pre-packaged' bankruptcy case can be taken from filing to confirmation of a plan in less than 60 days." *Id.* at 1192.

7. *Id.* at 1187-88.

for the acquisition of Sweat, Inc. ("Sweat"), a small chain of sporting goods stores in the Midwest, for $50,000,000, and the sellers have agreed (tentatively) to take $30,000,000 of the purchase price in debt secured by Sweat's assets. Jock's board does not expect to complete this deal for nine months, by which time they hope to have issued the new debt.

1. You represent Junque Bustup & Co., the lead underwriter for the debt issue. Draft a term sheet for the proposed offering, describing the types of covenants you would like included in the indenture. Then give your term sheet to a classmate, who represents Jock. After your classmate has had an opportunity to review your proposal, the two of you should discuss the terms for the purpose of reaching a mutually satisfactory deal. Then redraft the term sheet, reflecting your agreement.

2. You now represent Jock, Inc. Assume that one term on which you and the underwriters agree is that the indenture will include a negative pledge clause. Counsel for Junque Bustup has included the following as part of the indenture:

Limitation on Liens.[*]

The Company will not, and will not permit any Subsidiary to,

A. create, assume or incur or suffer to be created, assumed or incurred or to exist any mortgage, lien, charge or encumbrance of any kind upon, or pledge of, any of the property of any character of the Company or any Subsidiary, whether owned at the date hereof or hereafter acquired; or

B. acquire or agree to acquire any property of any character under any conditional sale agreement or other title retention agreement (including any lease in the nature of a title retention agreement); or

C. by transfer to any Subsidiary, subject to the prior payment of any Debt other than that represented by the Debentures, any property of any character of the Company or any Subsidiary; or

D. give its consent to the subordination of any right or claim of the Company or any Subsidiary to any right or claim of any other person; or

E. sign or file a financing statement under the Uniform Commercial Code which names the Company or any Subsidiary as debtor or sign any security agreement authorizing any secured party thereunder to file such financing statement; or

F. suffer to exist any Debt of the Company or of any Subsidiary or any claims or demands against the Company or any Subsidiary, which, if unpaid, might (in the hands of the holder or anyone who shall have guaranteed the same or who has any right or obligation to purchase the same) by law or upon bankruptcy or insolvency or otherwise, be given any priority whatsoever over its general creditors; excluding, however, from the operation of the foregoing:

(1) mortgages, liens, charges, pledges or other security interests or encumbrances created by any Subsidiary as security for Debt owing to the Company;

(2) (a) pledges or deposits to secure obligations under workmen's compensation laws or similar legislation, including liens of judgments thereunder which are not currently dischargeable;

---

[*] Adapted from American Bar Foundation, Commentaries on Indentures §10-10 (1971).

(b) deposits to secure public or statutory obligations of the Company or any Subsidiary;

(c) materialmen's, mechanics', carriers', workmen's, repairmen's, or other like liens arising in the ordinary course of business, or deposits to obtain the release of such liens; and

(d) leases made, or existing on property acquired, in the ordinary course of business.

After reviewing this language, meet with your classmate representing Junque Bustup to negotiate and reach a mutually acceptable provision. You should come to this meeting with proposed language revising or amending the provision as drafted.

(ii) Judicial Interpretation of the Debt Contract

A contract can, of course, be more or less elastic depending upon the manner in which it is interpreted. Moreover, it is impossible to contract for every contingency that may arise in a long-term relationship, so contractual gaps are certain to exist. Consequently, the manner in which a court approaches the task of contract interpretation will have a significant impact on debtholders' rights. The following materials are designed to give you some insight into the interpretive process.

Sharon Steel Corp. v. Chase Manhattan Bank, N.A.
691 F.2d 1039 (2d Cir. 1982), *cert. denied*,
460 U.S. 1012 (1983)

WINTER, Circuit Judge:

This is an appeal by Sharon Steel Corp. ("Sharon") and UV Industries, Inc. ("UV"), trustees of the UV Liquidating Trust (collectively the "UV Defendants") from grants of a directed verdict and summary judgment by the United States District Court for the Southern District of New York (Henry F. Werker, Judge) in favor of the Trustees of certain UV indentures ("Indenture Trustees") and intervening holders of debentures issued pursuant to certain of those indentures ("Debentureholders").... Judge Werker held that UV's liquidation and unsuccessful attempt to assign its public debt to Sharon rendered UV liable for the principal and accrued interest on the debentures. The Indenture Trustees and Debentureholders cross-appeal from other parts of the judgment.

We affirm in part and reverse in part.

BACKGROUND
1. The Indentures

Between 1965 and 1977, UV issued debt instruments pursuant to five separate indentures, the salient terms of which we briefly summarize. In 1965, UV issued approximately $23 million of 5⅜% subordinated debentures due in 1995, under an indenture naming The Chase Manhattan Bank, N.A. ("Chase") as the trustee ("First Chase Indenture"). The current principal amount of the debentures outstanding under that indenture is approximately $14 million.

[The court's description of the other four debt issues has been omitted. The trustees in addition to Chase were Union Planters National Bank of Memphis, Manufacturers Hanover Trust Company, and United States Trust Company of New York.]

The debentures, notes and guaranties are general obligations of UV. Each instrument contains clauses permitting redemption by UV prior to the maturity date, in exchange for payment of a fixed redemption price (which includes principal, accrued interest and a redemption premium) and clauses allowing acceleration as a non-exclusive remedy in case of a default. The First Chase Indenture,[4] the Port Huron Lease Guaranty, the Union Planters Lease Guaranty, the Manufacturers Indenture and the U.S. Trust Indenture each contains a "successor obligor" provision allowing UV to assign its debt to a corporate successor which purchases "all or substantially all" of UV's assets. If the debt is not assigned to such a purchaser, UV must pay off the debt. While the successor obligor clauses vary in language, the parties agree that the differences are not relevant to the outcome of this case.[a]

2. The Liquidation of UV

During 1977 and 1978, UV operated three separate lines of business. One line, electrical equipment and components, was carried on by Federal Pacific Electric Company ("Federal"). In 1978, Federal generated 60% of UV's operating revenue and 81% of its operating profits. It constituted 44% of the book value of UV's assets and 53% of operating assets. UV also owned and operated oil and gas properties, producing 2% of its operating revenue and 6% of operating profits. These were 5% of book value assets and 6% of operating assets. UV also was involved in copper and brass fabrication, through Mueller Brass, and metals mining, which together produced 13% of profits, 38% of revenue and constituted 34% of book value assets and 41% of operating assets. In addition to these operating assets, UV had cash or other liquid assets amounting to 17% of book value assets.

On December 19, 1978, UV's Board of Directors announced a plan to sell Federal. On January 19, 1979, the UV Board announced its intention to liquidate UV, subject to

---

4. Section 13.01 of the First Chase Indenture reads as follows:
  Nothing in this Indenture or any of the Debentures contained shall prevent any merger or consolidation of any other corporation or corporations into or with the Company, or any merger or consolidation of the Company (either singly or with one or more corporations), into or with any other corporation, or any sale, lease, transfer or other disposition of all or substantially all of its property to any corporation lawfully entitled to acquire the same or prevent successive similar consolidations, mergers, sales, leases, transfers or other dispositions to which the Company or its successors or assigns or any subsequent successors or assigns shall be a party; provided, however, and the Company covenants and agrees, that any such consolidation or merger of the Company or any such sale, lease, transfer or other disposition of all or substantially all of its property, shall be upon the condition that the due and punctual payment of the principal of, interest and premium, if any, on, all of the Debentures, according to their tenor, and the due and punctual performance and observance of all the terms, covenants and conditions of this Indenture to be kept or performed by the Company shall, by an indenture supplemental hereto, executed and delivered to the Trustee, be assumed by any corporation formed by or resulting from any such consolidation or merger, or to which all or substantially all of the property of the Company shall have been sold, leased, transferred or otherwise disposed of (such corporation being herein called the "successor corporation"), just as fully and effectively as if the successor corporation had been the original party of the first part hereto, and such supplemental indenture shall be construed as and shall constitute a novation thereby releasing the Company (unless its identity be merged into or consolidated with that of the successor corporation) from all liability upon, under or with respect to any of the covenants or agreements of this Indenture but not, however, from its liability upon the Debentures....
  a. Consequently, we have omitted footnotes setting forth the language of all of these provisions except footnote four which sets forth the language of Section 13.01 of the First Chase Indenture.

shareholder approval. On February 20, 1979, UV distributed proxy materials, recommending approval of (i) the sale of Federal for $345,000,000 to a subsidiary of Reliance Electric Company and (ii) a Plan of Liquidation and Dissolution to sell the remaining assets of UV over a 12-month period.[9] The proceeds of these sales and the liquid assets were to be distributed to shareholders. The liquidation plan required "that at all times there be retained an amount of cash and other assets which the [UV Board of Directors] deems necessary to pay, or provide for the payment of, all of the liabilities, claims and other obligations ..." of UV. The proxy statement also provided that, if the sale of Federal and the liquidation plan were approved, UV would effect an initial liquidating distribution of $18 per share to its common stockholders.

On March 26, 1979, UV's shareholders approved the sale of Federal and the liquidation plan. The following day, UV filed its Statement of Intent to Dissolve with the Secretary of State of Maine, its state of incorporation. On March 29, the sale of Federal to the Reliance Electric subsidiary for $345 million in cash was consummated. On April 9, UV announced an $18 per share initial liquidating distribution to take place on Monday, April 30.

The Indenture Trustees were aware that UV contemplated making an $18 per share liquidating distribution since at least February 20, 1979 (the date the proxy materials were distributed).[10] On April 26, representatives of Chase, Manufacturers and U.S. Trust met with UV officers and directors and collectively demanded that UV pay off all the debentures within 30 days or, alternatively, that UV establish a trust fund of $180 million to secure the debt. There was testimony that at least one of the Indenture Trustees threatened to sue to enjoin UV from paying the $18 liquidating distribution on the grounds that a liquidating distribution prior to payment of UV's debts would violate Maine law,[11] which provides, as to a liquidating corporation, that:

> *After* paying or adequately providing for the payment of all its obligations, the corporation shall distribute the remainder of its assets ... among its shareholders....

Me. Rev. Stat. Ann. Tit. 13-A, §1106(4) (1971) (emphasis added).

The outcome of this meeting was an "Agreement for Treatment of Certain Obligations of UV Industries, Inc.," dated April 27, 1979, between UV and the Indenture Trustees ("April Document"). Under the April Document, UV agreed, *inter alia*, to set aside a cash fund of $155 million to secure its public debt and to present a proposal for the satisfaction and discharge of that debt to the Indenture Trustees within 90 days. The

---

9. Completion of the Liquidation Plan within 12 months was necessary for tax reasons. If so completed, UV would avoid recognition of any taxable gain on the sale of Federal and its other assets and UV shareholders could treat liquidation distributions as capital gains rather than ordinary income.

10. During this period, Chase, Union Planters and U.S. Trust each wrote to UV concerning its plans with respect to its long-term debt. In response to a letter from a Chase officer dated March 26, UV replied on April 9 that the debentures "will be provided for in the liquidation according to the respective Indentures and the covenants therein." Immediately following UV's announcement on April 9 that the $18 distribution would be made on April 30, U.S. Trust and Union Planters each wrote to ask UV about the payment of the debt instruments. By letter of April 20, UV replied to Union Planters stating simply that "UV will contact the trustees at a future time, when it is prepared to advise the trustees as to the mechanics of honoring its commitments." An identical letter was sent to Chase; U.S. Trust never received a reply to its inquiry.

11. The Indenture Trustees apparently concede that as of the April 26 meeting none of the Indentures was in default and the forthcoming $18 distribution would not be a default under any of the indentures....

Indenture Trustees agreed not to seek an injunction against the payment of the $18 per share liquidating distribution. The April Document provided that all obligations thereunder would terminate upon the payment of UV's public debt or upon UV's abandonment of the plan of liquidation.

On July 23, 1979, UV announced that it had entered into an agreement for the sale of most of its oil and gas properties to Tenneco Oil Company for $135 million cash. The deal was consummated as of October 2, 1979 and resulted in a net gain of $105 million to UV.

3. The Sale to Sharon Steel

In November, 1979, Sharon proposed to buy UV's remaining assets. Another company, Reliance Group (unrelated to Reliance Electric), had made a similar offer. After a brief bidding contest, UV and Sharon entered into an "Agreement for Purchase of Assets" and an "Instrument of Assumption of Liabilities" on November 26, 1979. Under the purchase agreement, Sharon purchased all of the assets owned by UV on November 26 (i.e., Mueller Brass, UV's mining properties and $322 million in cash or the equivalent) for $518 million ($411 million of Sharon subordinated debentures due in 2000—then valued at 86% or $353,460,000—plus $107 million in cash). Under the assumption agreement, Sharon assumed all of UV's liabilities, including the public debt issued under the indentures. UV thereupon announced that it had no further obligations under the indentures or lease guaranties, based upon the successor obligor clauses.

On December 6, 1979, in an attempt to formalize its position as successor obligor, Sharon delivered to the Indenture Trustees supplemental indentures executed by UV and Sharon. The Indenture Trustees refused to sign. Similarly, Sharon delivered an assumption of the lease guaranties to both Chase and Union Planters but those Indenture Trustees also refused to sign.

4. The Proceedings in the District Court

By letters dated December 24, 1979, Chase, U.S. Trust and Manufacturers issued virtually identical notices of default as a result of UV's purported assignment of its obligations to Sharon. Each demanded that the default be cured within 90 days or that the debentures be redeemed. Chase and U.S. Trust brought separate actions in New York County Supreme Court against UV and Sharon for redemption of the debentures; Manufacturers subsequently initiated a similar lawsuit. On December 26, 1979, Sharon initiated this action against Chase, U.S. Trust and Manufacturers. The state court actions have been stayed pending disposition of this case.

The amended complaint, in effect, raises five claims: (i) the April Document is of no force because it was procured by coercion and lacks consideration; (ii) the April Document expired upon Sharon's purchase of all UV's assets and assumption of UV's liabilities since it does not apply to a successor corporation; (iii) Manufacturers and Chase conspired to force UV and Sharon to redeem the debentures in violation of Section 1 of the Sherman Act; (iv) Manufacturers, Chase and U.S. Trust improperly refused to execute supplemental indentures, issued default notices and demanded immediate redemption of the debentures; and (v) Chase and Union Planters improperly refused to execute supplemental lease guaranties and demanded repayment of the debt. Chase, U.S. Trust and Manufacturers sought specific performance of the redemption provisions by counterclaim.

* * *

.... [T]he Debentureholders sought leave to intervene to assert claims against UV and Sharon. The Court granted intervention and subsequently certified them as the representatives of all holders of such debentures pursuant to Fed. R. Civ. P. 23 (b)(2).

During February and March, 1980, the Indenture Trustees and the Debentureholders moved for dismissal of Sharon's amended complaint and for summary judgment. In an opinion dated September 3, 1980, reported at 88 F.R.D. 38 (S.D.N.Y. 1980), the District Court denied these motions.

A jury trial was held during April and early May, 1981, at which Sharon submitted voluminous testimony and other evidence. The Indenture Trustees and Debentureholders moved for a directed verdict, and on May 11, 1981, the District Court granted the motion and dismissed Sharon's claims. The Indenture Trustees and Debentureholders subsequently moved for summary judgment on their claims and counterclaims, which was granted on June 2, 1981. A judgment encapsulating these determinations was filed on August 18, 1981.

The judgment orders: (i) dismissal with prejudice of Sharon's amended complaint; (ii) judgment in favor of the Indenture Trustees and Debentureholders on their claim that the debentures were due and payable; (iii) payment to the Debentureholders of an allocable share of the interest earned on the $155 million fund created pursuant to the April Document; (iv) an award of costs and expenses to the Indenture Trustees (including attorney's fees); (v) an award of attorneys' fees and expenses to the Debentureholders to be paid out of the recovery; (vi) dismissal of the claims of the Indenture Trustees and the Debentureholders for a redemption premium; and (vii) impression of a constructive trust for the Debentureholders on the $155 million fund sufficient to satisfy the debt (plus $2 million as an estimate of costs) and remission of funds in excess of that amount to Sharon.

Sharon and the UV Defendants appeal various portions of judgment. The Indenture Trustees and Debentureholders cross-appeal from the denial of the redemption premium. The Debentureholders cross-appeal from the denial of legal fees and expenses to be paid by UV and Sharon, rather than from the class recovery.

DISCUSSION
1. The Successor Obligor Clauses

Sharon Steel argues that Judge Werker erred in not submitting to the jury issues going to the meaning of the successor obligor clauses. We disagree.

Successor obligor clauses are "boilerplate" or contractual provisions which are standard in a certain genre of contracts. Successor obligor clauses are thus found in virtually all indentures. Such boilerplate must be distinguished from contractual provisions which are peculiar to a particular indenture and must be given a consistent, uniform interpretation....

Boilerplate provisions are ... not the consequence of the relationship of particular borrowers and lenders and do not depend upon particularized intentions of the parties to an indenture. There are no adjudicative facts relating to the parties to the litigation for a jury to find and the meaning of boilerplate provisions is, therefore, a matter of law rather than fact.

Moreover, uniformity in interpretation is important to the efficiency of capital markets. As the Fifth Circuit has stated:

> [U]niformity of the indentures that govern competing debenture issues is what makes it possible meaningfully to compare one debenture issue with another,

focusing only on the business provisions of the issue (such as the interest rate, the maturity date, the redemption and sinking fund provisions in the conversion rate) and the economic conditions of the issuer, without being misled by peculiarities in the underlying instruments.

Broad v. Rockwell International Corp., 642 F.2d 929, 943 (5th Cir.), *cert. denied*, 454 U.S. 965, 102 S. Ct. 506, 70 L. Ed. 2d 380 (1981). Whereas participants in the capital market can adjust their affairs according to a uniform interpretation, whether it be correct or not as an initial proposition, the creation of enduring uncertainties as to the meaning of boilerplate provisions would decrease the value of all debenture issues and greatly impair the efficient working of capital markets. Such uncertainties would vastly increase the risks and, therefore, the costs of borrowing with no offsetting benefits either in the capital market or in the administration of justice. Just such uncertainties would be created if interpretation of boilerplate provisions were submitted to juries sitting in every judicial district in the nation.

Sharon also argues that Judge Werker erred in rejecting evidence of custom and usage and practical construction as to the meaning of the successor obligor clauses. While custom or usage might in some circumstances create a fact question as to the interpretation of boilerplate provisions, the evidence actually offered by Sharon simply did not tend to prove a relevant custom or usage. Sharon's experts both conceded that so far as the meaning of successor obligor clauses and the language "all or substantially all" are concerned, the UV/Sharon transaction was unique. Their testimony was thus limited to use of such clauses and such language in very different contexts. Because context is of obvious and critical importance to the use of particular language, the testimony offered did not tend to prove or disprove a material fact.

Sharon's proffer of evidence as to practical construction also fails. At best, it amounted to a few statements over a two-week period by Indenture Trustees or Debentureholders implying that a purchaser such as Sharon might become a successor obligor. Sharon's offer of proof falls woefully short of the kind of mutual understanding over a period of time which is necessary for practical construction to become relevant to interpretation.... Particularly where boilerplate is concerned, a more deliberate and enduring course of conduct is necessary to utilize practical construction.

We turn now to the meaning of the successor obligor clauses. Interpretation of indenture provisions is a matter of basic contract law.... Contract language is thus the starting point in the search for meaning and Sharon argues strenuously that the language of the successor obligor clauses clearly permits its assumption of UV's public debt. Sharon's argument is a masterpiece of simplicity: on November 26, 1979, it bought everything UV owned; therefore, the transaction was a "sale" of "all" UV's "assets." In Sharon's view, the contention of the Indenture Trustees and Debentureholders that proceeds from earlier sales in a predetermined plan of piecemeal liquidation may not be counted in determining whether a later sale involves "all assets" must be rejected because it imports a meaning not evident in the language.

Sharon's literalist approach simply proves too much. If proceeds from earlier piecemeal sales are "assets," then UV continued to own "all" its "assets" even after the Sharon transaction since the proceeds of that transaction, including the $107 million cash for cash "sale," went into the UV treasury. If the language is to be given the "literal" meaning attributed to it by Sharon, therefore, UV's "assets" were not "sold" on November 26 and the ensuing liquidation requires the redemption of the debentures by UV. Sharon's literal approach is thus self-defeating.

The words "all or substantially all" are used in a variety of statutory and contractual provisions relating to transfers of assets and have been given meaning in light of the particular context and evident purpose. *See Campbell v. Vose*, 515 F.2d 256 (10th Cir. 1975) (transfer of sole operating asset held to be a sale of all or substantially all of the corporation's assets even though two-thirds of asset book value in the form of bank balances, promissory notes and an investment portfolio was retained); *Atlas Tool Company v. Commissioner*, 614 F.2d 860 at 865-66 (3rd Cir. 1980). ("Substantially all" requirement is chiefly determined by the transfer of operating assets). Sharon argues that such decisions are distinguishable because they serve the purpose of either shareholder protection or enforcement of the substance of the Internal Revenue Code.[b] Even if such distinctions are valid, these cases nevertheless demonstrate that a literal reading of the words "all or substantially all" is not helpful apart from reference to the underlying purpose to be served. We turn, therefore, to that purpose.

Sharon argues that the sole purpose of successor obligor clauses is to leave the borrower free to merge, liquidate or to sell its assets in order to enter a wholly new business free of public debt and that they are not intended to offer any protection to lenders. On their face, however, they seem designed to protect lenders as well by assuring a degree of continuity of assets. Thus, a borrower which sells all its assets does not have an option to continue holding the debt. It must either assign the debt or pay it off.... The single reported decision construing a successor obligor clause, *B.S.F. Company v. Philadelphia National Bank*, 42 Del. Ch. 106, 204 A.2d 746 (1964), clearly held that one purpose of the clause was to insure that the principal operating assets of a borrower are available for satisfaction of the debt.

Sharon seeks to rebut such inferences by arguing that a number of transactions which seriously dilute the assets of a company are perfectly permissible under such clauses. For example, UV might merge with, or sell its assets to, a company which has a minuscule equity base and is debt heavy. They argue from these examples that the successor obligor clause was not intended to protect borrowers from the kind of transaction in which UV and Sharon engaged.

We disagree. In fact, a substantial degree of protection against diluting transactions exists for the lender. Lenders can rely, for example, on the self-interest of equityholders for protection against mergers which result in a firm with a substantially greater danger of insolvency. So far as the sale of assets to such a firm is concerned, that can occur but substantial protection exists even there since the more debt heavy the purchaser, the less likely it is that the seller's equityholders would accept anything but cash for the assets. A sale to a truly crippled firm is thus unlikely given the self-interest of the equityholders. After a sale, moreover, the lenders would continue to have the protection of the original assets. In both mergers and sales, complete protection against an increase in the borrower's risk is not available in the absence of more specific restrictions, but the self-interest of equityholders imposes a real and substantial limit to that increase in risk. The failure of successor obligor clauses to provide even more protection hardly permits an inference that they are designed solely for the benefit of borrowers.

---

b. The Delaware Chancery Court, in interpreting the "all or substantially all" language of §271 of the Delaware General Corporation Law (providing for stockholder voting in the case of a sale of all or substantially all of the assets"), did not distinguish between the stock situation and bond indentures. In fact, in *Katz v. Bregman*, 431 A.2d 1274 (Del. Ch. 1981), *appeal ref'd sub. nom. Plant Indus., Inc. v. Katz*, 435 A.2d 1044 (Del. 1981), the court relied in part upon the interpretation of similar language in a bond indenture. *See Philadelphia National Bank v. B.S.F. Co.*, 199 A.2d 557 (1969), *rev'd on other grounds*, 204 A.2d 746 (1964). *See also* 2 Ward, Welch & Turezyn, Folk on the Delaware General Corporation Law §271 (4th ed. 1998 & Supp. 2005-1). [Eds.]

Sharon poses hypotheticals closer to home in the hope of demonstrating that successor obligor clauses protect only borrowers: *e.g.*, a transaction involving a sale of Federal and the oil and gas properties in the regular course of UV's business followed by an $18 per share distribution to shareholders after which the assets are sold to Sharon and Sharon assumes the indenture obligations. To the extent that a decision to sell off some properties is not part of an overall scheme to liquidate and is made in the regular course of business it is considerably different from a plan of piecemeal liquidation, whether or not followed by independent and subsequent decisions to sell off the rest. A sale in the absence of a plan to liquidate is undertaken because the directors expect the sale to strengthen the corporation as a going concern. A plan of liquidation, however, may be undertaken solely because of the financial needs and opportunities or the tax status of the major shareholders. In the latter case, relatively quick sales may be at low prices or may break up profitable asset combinations, thus drastically increasing the lender's risks if the last sale assigns the public debt. In this case, for example, tax considerations compelled completion of the liquidation within 12 months. The fact that piecemeal sales in the regular course of business are permitted thus does not demonstrate that successor obligor clauses apply to piecemeal liquidations, allowing the buyer last in time to assume the entire public debt.

We hold, therefore, that protection for borrowers as well as for lenders may be fairly inferred from the nature of successor obligor clauses. The former are enabled to sell entire businesses and liquidate, to consolidate or merge with another corporation, or to liquidate their operating assets and enter a new field free of the public debt. Lenders, on the other hand, are assured a degree of continuity of assets.

Where contractual language seems designed to protect the interests of both parties and where conflicting interpretations are argued, the contract should be construed to sacrifice the principal interests of each party as little as possible. An interpretation which sacrifices a major interest of one of the parties while furthering only a marginal interest of the other should be rejected in favor of an interpretation which sacrifices marginal interests of both parties in order to protect their major concerns.

Of the contending positions, we believe that of the Indenture Trustees and Debentureholders best accommodates the principal interests of corporate borrowers and their lenders.... We hold, therefore, that boilerplate successor obligor clauses do not permit assignment of the public debt to another party in the course of a liquidation unless "all or substantially all" of the assets of the company at the time the plan of liquidation is determined upon are transferred to a single purchaser.

The application of this rule to the present case is not difficult. The plan of liquidation was approved by UV's shareholders on March 26, 1978.... The question then is whether "all or substantially all" of the assets held by UV on that date were transferred to Sharon. That is easily answered. The assets owned by UV on March 26 and later transferred to Sharon were Mueller Brass, certain metals mining property, and substantial amounts of cash and other liquid assets. UV's Form 10-K and Sharon's Form S-7 state that Mueller Brass and the metals mining properties were responsible for only 38% of UV's 1978 operating revenues and 13% of its operating profits. They constitute 41% of the book value of UV's operating properties. When the cash and other liquid assets are added, the transaction still involved only 51% of the book value of UV's total assets.

Since we do not regard the question in this case as even close, we need not determine how the substantiality of corporate assets is to be measured, what percentage meets the "all or substantially all" test or what role a jury might play in determining those issues.

Even when the liquid assets (other than proceeds from the sale of Federal and the oil and gas properties) are aggregated with the operating properties, the transfer to Sharon accounted for only 51% of the total book value of UV's assets. In no sense, therefore, are they "all or substantially all" of those assets. The successor obligor clauses are, therefore, not applicable. UV is thus in default on the indentures and the debentures are due and payable. For that reason, we need not reach the question whether the April Document was breached by UV.

* * *

3. The Redemption Premium

Judge Werker held that the redemption premium under the indentures need not be paid by UV. His reasoning was essentially that UV defaulted under the indenture agreement and that the default provisions provide for acceleration rather than a redemption premium. We do not agree. The acceleration provisions of the indentures are explicitly permissive and not exclusive of other remedies. We see no bar, therefore, to the Indenture Trustees seeking specific performance of the redemption provisions where the debtor causes the debentures to become due and payable by its voluntary actions.

This is not a case in which a debtor finds itself unable to make required payments. The default here stemmed from the plan of voluntary liquidation approved on March 26, 1979, followed by the unsuccessful attempt to invoke the successor obligor clauses. The purpose of a redemption premium is to put a price upon the voluntary satisfaction of a debt before the date of maturity. While such premiums may seem largely irrelevant for commercial purposes in times of high interest rates, they nevertheless are part of the contract and would apply in a voluntary liquidation which included plans for payment and satisfaction of the public debt. We believe it undermines the plain purpose of the redemption provisions to allow a liquidating debtor to avoid their terms simply by failing to take the steps necessary to redeem the debentures, thereby creating a default. We hold, therefore, that the redemption premium must be paid.

CONCLUSION

We affirm Judge Werker's dismissal of Sharon's amended complaint and award of judgment to the Indenture Trustees and Debentureholders on their claim that the debentures are due and payable. We reverse his dismissal of the claim for payment of the redemption premium.... We affirm his granting of attorney's fees and expenses to the Debentureholders out of the judgment recovered. The Indenture Trustees shall be awarded their full costs. The Debentureholders shall be awarded one-half their costs.

Note and Questions

1. Why do the trustees object to permitting Sharon to assume the debt?

2. How does Judge Winter's approach to interpreting the bond contract differ from that applied in other cases?

3. The *Sharon Steel* case required the court to interpret the phrase "all or substantially all" of the corporation's assets. As our "note b" in the case indicates, this language is also used in corporation statutes. For example, §271(a) of the Delaware General Corporation Law permits the board of directors to sell "all or substantially all" of the corporation's assets "when and as authorized by a resolution adopted by a majority of the outstanding stock of the corporation entitled to vote thereon...." *Cf.* New York Business

Corporation Law §909(a) (establishing similar requirements for a sale of "all or substantially all the assets of a corporation, if not made in the usual or regular course of the business actually conducted by such corporation ..."); Rev. Model Bus. Corp. Act §12.02 (requiring shareholder approval if the sale of assets "would leave the corporation without a significant continuing business activity"); *but see* Rev. Model Bus. Corp. Act §12.01 (permitting board to authorize sale of "all, or substantially all" of the corporation's assets if "in the usual and regular course of business"). Not only is it important to determine whether a sale of assets constitutes "all or substantially all" of those assets for purposes of stockholder voting, but whether appraisal rights (which are dealt with in more detail *supra* at chapter 3, section 4a) are available may also depend on this determination. *See, e.g.,* Rev. Model Bus. Corp. Act §13.02(a)(3) (providing for dissenter's rights where sale of "all, or substantially all" of assets if stockholder permitted to vote); N.Y. Bus. Corp. Law §910 (same); *but see* Del. Gen. Corp. Law §262 (not providing appraisal rights for this type of transaction).

As the *Sharon Steel* case illustrates, such language in the bond indenture may govern mandatory redemptions. Yet, despite the obvious importance of this language, its meaning remains unclear. 6A Fletcher et al., Fletcher Cyclopedia of the Law of Private Corporations §2949.4 (perm. ed., rev. vol. 1997 & Supp. 2004). In Katz v. Bregman, 431 A.2d 1274 (Del. Ch. 1981), *appeal ref'd sub. nom. Plant Indus., Inc. v. Katz,* 435 A.2d 1044 (Del. 1981), the court interpreted the language in Del. Gen. Corp. Law §271 as including a sale of a majority of the corporation's assets constituting its historical principal business when the corporation intended to alter that line of business following the sale. *See also* Philadelphia National Bank v. B.S.F. Company, 199 A.2d 557 (Del. Ch. 1964), *rev'd,* B.S.F. Company v. Philadelphia National Bank, 204 A.2d 746 (1964) (applying Pennsylvania Law) (chancery court and supreme court agreeing that sale of 75 percent of the corporation's assets constituting its principal business was a sale of substantially all of the assets within the meaning of the indenture. In reaching this conclusion the court looked for interpretive guidance to the Pennsylvania Business Corporation Law's sale of assets provision.). In Dukas v. Davis Aircraft Products Co., 131 A.D.2d 720, 576 N.Y.S.2d 781 (App. Div. 1987), the court identified the purpose of Section 909(a) of the New York Business Corporation Law as being "to prevent a corporation from disposing of a major portion of its property without obtaining prior approval of its shareholders...." *Id.* at 782. Consequently, the court dismissed the complaint against defendant corporation in an action to set aside a conveyance of defendant's property where it had exchanged one manufacturing building for another without changing the nature of its business.

Rudbart v. North Jersey District Water Supply Commission
605 A.2d 681 (N.J. 1992)

PER CURIAM.

We granted certification, 122 N.J. 137, 584 A.2d 210 (1990), primarily to consider the contention of First Fidelity Bank, N.A., New Jersey (Fidelity) that "in a published decision without precedent in the United States the Appellate Division had ruled that every investment security, whether a stock, bond, note or in some other form, is a contract of adhesion subjecting every term of the agreement to post hoc review for fairness." The Bank's petition for certification recited that "[n]ot only does this decision threaten to wreak havoc with the federally-regulated national securities market, but it would lead to the courts of this state being inundated with a group of law suits—securities litigation—that is among the most complex known to the bar."

* * *

The decision has the potential of opening to scrutiny by the courts the terms and conditions of notes and securities that have been sold to the public by governmental agencies throughout the State. The transfer of securities in the primary and secondary market hinges upon the certainty of the terms of such securities, and the assurance that those terms cannot be overridden by judicial fiat. The broad implications of the decision by the Appellate Division could adversely affect on the sale of securities in this State.

.... We agree that the doctrine of adhesion contracts should not be extended to regulated securities transactions. We now reverse the judgment of the Appellate Division, which was based on that court's holding that the subject securities constituted a contract of adhesion, but remand the matter to the Law Division for resolution of the remaining claims asserted by the plaintiffs.

I

These consolidated class actions were brought on behalf of holders of notes issued by defendant North Jersey District Water Supply Commission (Commission) to recover damages arising from an early redemption of the notes effected by newspaper notice. Plaintiffs' central claim was that notice by publication, although specifically provided for in the notes, was inadequate and unconscionable.

A.

The Commission, a public corporation, operates and maintains a public water system serving northern New Jersey.... By resolutions adopted April 25 and May 23, 1984, the Commission authorized the issuance of $75,000,000 in new project notes to provide interim financing for a portion of the cost of constructing a new water-supply facility and to pay certain outstanding obligations.... The Commission and its underwriters, one of which was defendant Fidelity, negotiated the terms of the notes; Fidelity also was designated as the indenture trustee ... and as registrar/paying agent for the notes. The underwriters agreed to purchase the notes at the discounted price of $73,800,000, intending to sell them on the secondary market at face value. The project notes were issued on June 15, 1984. Issued in registered form, without coupons, in denominations of $5,000 or multiples thereof, the notes bore tax-free interest at the rate of 7% per annum payable on June 15th and December 15th. The notes fixed a June 15, 1987, maturity date, but, as set forth in both the Commission's authorizing resolutions and the Official Statement offering the issue to the public, were subject to earlier optional redemption:

> The Notes are subject to redemption prior to maturity as a whole at the option of the Commission on 30 days published notice in a newspaper or newspapers of general circulation in the City of Newark, New Jersey and in the City of New York, New York on the dates and at the prices below:

Redemption Period (both dates inclusive)	Redemption Price (percent of par value)
June 15, 1986 to December 14, 1986	101%
December 15, 1986 and thereafter	100½%

If on the date fixed for redemption sufficient monies are available to the Trustee to pay the redemption price plus interest accrued to the date of redemption, the Notes shall cease to bear interest and shall not be deemed to be outstanding from such date. The back of each of the issued notes bore similar language.

In the summer of 1985, the Commission decided to redeem the notes prior to maturity. In keeping with the procedures established in its 1984 resolutions, the Commission entered into an escrow deposit agreement with Fidelity, effective September 26, 1985, for the redemption of the notes on June 23, 1986. Among its other terms, the agreement provided for the Commission to deposit with Fidelity an escrow sum sufficient to pay the redemption price and interest until the redemption date, and for Fidelity to publish a notice of redemption in accordance with the note terms.

Although regular interest payments were mailed to registered noteholders on December 15, 1985, and June 15, 1986, neither those nor any other mailings informed the noteholders of the forthcoming early redemption. Fidelity did, however, provide the required notice by publication in The Star-Ledger, The New York Times, and The Wall Street Journal on May 23 and again on June 9, 1986. The June 3, 1986, issue of Moody's Municipal & Government Manual also contained the call notice.

As of December 15, 1986, the holders of approximately $10,000,000 of the notes still had not redeemed. A number of noteholders apparently made inquiries and complaints when they failed to receive their anticipated December 15, 1986, interest payments. Fidelity, at the Commission's request, mailed notice in early 1987 to those holders who had not yet redeemed, but declined the Commission's request to put the unredeemed funds in an interest-bearing account. The late-redeeming noteholders received the redemption price (101% of face value) and interest from June 15 to June 23, 1986, the date of redemption. Plaintiffs filed separate actions in February and April 1987 on behalf of noteholders who allegedly had not learned of the redemption until after December 15, 1986. On various theories of negligence, conversion, breach of trust, constructive trust, and reformation, plaintiffs demanded that they be paid interest at the 7⅞% rate from June 23, 1986, until the dates that they submitted their notes for redemption or other appropriate relief. The two actions were consolidated for trial.

* * *

The parties in the present actions then cross-moved for summary judgment on liability, based on a filed stipulation of facts. In a letter opinion, the Law Division held that "the notice provision clearly indicates that the newspaper publication method outlined would be the only type of notice given to the bond [sic] holders," and that "the failure to mail a notice to the plaintiffs when they could have, at the time they sent out interest checks," did not give rise to a cause of action. The Law Division granted summary judgment for defendants, finding that "the agreed upon notice by publication is binding on the plaintiffs and * * * such a method is not deficient as a matter of law." ...

Before the Appellate Division, plaintiffs urged that the early-redemption notice by publication "was insufficient as a matter of law" and that the Commission and Fidelity had "converted [plaintiffs'] monies." They argued that the noteholders "had no power to negotiate with either the Commission or First Fidelity regarding the terms of the notes or the redemption provisions thereof," and that "[t]his is a classic example of a contract of adhesion." That was plaintiffs' first and entire reference to that theory of liability.

The Appellate Division adopted that theory. It reversed, holding that "a note or other security sold to the general investing public pursuant to standard form contractual provisions is a contract of adhesion"; that "[c]onsequently, if the security contains an unfair provision or the issuer fails to deal fairly with the investors, the issuer and its agents may be liable for any resulting damages"; and that "the failure * * * to give mail notice of the early redemption of the project notes was unfair." Rudbart v. North Jersey Dist. Water Supply Comm'n, 238 N.J. Super. 41, 47, 568 A.2d 1213 (1990). The court reasoned that investment securities are generally "drafted by the issuer and presented to the purchaser on a take it or leave it basis," that the offering statements are "lengthy and difficult to understand," and that "members of the general investing public cannot reasonably be expected to understand the entire offering statement before deciding whether to purchase a particular security." Id. at 49, 568 A.2d 1213. Accordingly, courts should intervene "to afford protection to purchasers of securities from unconscionable contractual terms and other forms of overreaching by the issuers and their agents." Ibid. The Appellate Division went on to hold that "the notice by publication provided by defendants did not constitute fair notice of the early redemption," id. at 51, 568 A.2d 1213, and that "defendants did not show any legitimate business reason for failing to give notice by mail." Id. at 56, 568 A.2d 1213. The court thus reversed and remanded for the determinations of damages and their allocation as between the Commission and Fidelity. Id. at 57, 568 A.2d 1213....

II

Plaintiffs do not contend that the project notes are ambiguous, nor do they claim that the Commission or Fidelity committed fraud or violated federal or state securities laws. Ordinarily, then, contract law would make the terms of the notes fully binding on plaintiffs. That law, based on principles of freedom of contract, was well stated in Fivey v. Pennsylvania Railroad, 67 N.J.L. 627, 52 A. 472 (E. & A. 1902), in which the court enforced a release incorporated in a standard-form contract:

> A party who enters into a contract in writing, without any fraud or imposition being practiced upon him, is conclusively presumed to understand and assent to its terms and legal effect....

If an agreement is characterized as a "contract of adhesion" however, nonenforcement of its terms may be justified on other than such traditional grounds as fraud, duress, mistake, or illegality.... Although the term "has acquired many significations," ... the essential nature of a contract of adhesion is that it is presented on a take-it-or-leave-it basis, commonly in a standardized printed form, without opportunity for the "adhering" party to negotiate except perhaps on a few particulars.... We have previously defined "contract of adhesion" in just those terms: "[a] contract where one party * * * must accept or reject the contract * * *." Vasquez v. Glassboro Serv. Ass'n, 83 N.J. 86, 104, 415 A.2d 1156 (1980). Such a contract "does not result from the consent of that party." Ibid.... The distinct body of law surrounding contracts of adhesion represents the legal system's effort to determine whether and to what extent such nonconsensual terms will be enforced....

The project notes involved here unquestionably fit our definition of contracts of adhesion. That is, they were presented to the public on standardized printed forms, on a take-it-or-leave-it basis without opportunity for purchasers to negotiate any of the terms.[1] But the observation that the notes fit the definition of contracts of adhesion is

---

1. The Commission and the underwriters negotiated the terms of the notes. However, although the underwriters presumably sought to enhance the attractiveness of the offer to prospective purchasers, the record does not indicate whether the negotiation addressed the interests of individual

the beginning, not the end, of the inquiry: we must now determine as a matter of policy whether to enforce the unilaterally-fixed terms of the notes.

We have discussed those considerations in a number of earlier cases. The seminal case is [Henningsen v. Bloomfield Motors, Inc., 32 N.J. 358, 161 A.2d 69 (1960)], in which we invalidated an automobile manufacturer's standard-form disclaimer of its implied warranty of merchantability. In justifying that deviation from ordinary contract-law principles, we noted that a car is "a common and necessary adjunct of daily life," id. at 387, 161 A.2d 69, that the disclaimer form was used by the manufacturers of virtually all American passenger cars, id. at 390, 161 A.2d 69, that the "gross inequality of bargaining position * * * is thus apparent," id. at 391, 161 A.2d 69, and that the disclaimer represented "a studied effort to frustrate" the legislative grant of implied-warranty protection. Id. at 404, 161 A.2d 69.

In Ellsworth Dobbs, Inc. v. Johnson, 50 N.J. 528, 236 A.2d 843 (1967), we similarly invalidated a provision of a standardized real-estate-brokerage contract that obligated the seller to pay a commission even if the buyer was financially unable or unwilling to complete the transaction. Relying on the "undue advantage" that arose from "monopolistic or practical control in the business transaction involved," id. at 553, 236 A.2d 843, we held that the offending contractual term would "thwart" the judicially-declared public policy of the State. Id. at 552, 555, 236 A.2d 843. Such a contractual provision accordingly is unenforceable "[w]henever there is substantial inequality of bargaining power, position or advantage between the broker and the other party involved." Id. at 555, 236 A.2d 843.

We applied similar principles in Shell Oil Co. v. Marinello, 63 N.J. 402, 307 A.2d 598 (1973), cert. denied, 415 U.S. 920, 94 S.Ct. 1421, 39 L.Ed.2d 475 (1974), to invalidate the termination provision of an oil company's lease and dealer agreement. We described the oil company as "the dominant party," and found that its relationship with its dealer "lacks equality in the respective bargaining positions"; moreover, a dealer who has operated the station for a period of years "cannot afford to risk confrontation with the oil company." Id. 408, 307 A.2d 598. Because the parties' "grossly disproportionate bargaining power" had produced a "grossly unfair" term that contravened "the extant public policy of this State," we did not enforce that term. Id. at 408-09, 307 A.2d 598.

We again explored contracts of adhesion in Vasquez, supra, 83 N.J. 86, 415 A.2d 1156, in which we denied enforcement of a provision in a migrant worker's contract permitting eviction of a worker immediately on termination of his employment. We noted that contracts should be enforced where "the parties are in positions of relative equality and * * * their consent is freely given." Id. at 101, 415 A.2d 1156. However, we found that the migrant farmworker was in a position "analogous to that of a consumer who must accept a standardized form contract to purchase needed goods and services." Id. at 103, 415 A.2d 1156. We also found that the eviction terms of the standard-form contract conflicted with the demonstrated policy of the New Jersey courts and Legislature "in providing legal protection for migrant farmworkers." Id. at 99, 415 A.2d 1156. Because the contract "[did] not result from the [worker's] consent," we invalidated its "unconscionable" eviction provision. Id. at 104, 415 A.2d 1156; see also Kuzmiak v. Brookchester, Inc., 33 N.J. Super. 575, 111 A.2d 425 (App.Div.1955) (lease provision exculpating residential landlord from liability held contrary to public policy).

---

noteholders with respect to the form of early redemption notice or otherwise. See Lawrence E. Mitchell, The Fairness Rights of Corporate Bondholders, 65 N.Y.U. L. Rev. 1165, 1183 (1990). We thus reject defendants' suggestion that the noteholders had in fact negotiated the notice provision through the underwriters.

Thus, in determining whether to enforce the terms of a contract of adhesion, courts have looked not only to the take-it-or-leave-it nature or the standardized form of the document but also to the subject matter of the contract, the parties' relative bargaining positions, the degree of economic compulsion motivating the "adhering" party, and the public interests affected by the contract. Applying those criteria to the project notes, we find insufficient reason to invalidate the notice-by-publication term.

III

The three considerations that lead us to that conclusion derive primarily from the fact that the project notes were publicly-traded securities. First, no investor was under any economic pressure to buy the notes. The notes were not consumer necessities. Prospective investors could choose from a vast selection of alternative equity and debt investments, including bonds and notes with various call and notice provisions. They were not driven to accept the Commission's notes because of a monopolistic market or any other economic constraint. Accordingly, the Commission did not enjoy a superior bargaining position permitting it to dictate its own terms. In short, the principal justifications for invalidating terms of a contract of adhesion are simply not present in a fully open and competitive securities market....

* * *

Second, although securities are offered to the public on a take-it-or-leave-it basis, enforcement of their terms advances rather than contravenes well-established and important public policies. Securities are governed by Article 8 of the Uniform Commercial Code, N.J.S.A. 12A:8-101 to -408. See N.J.S.A. 12A:8-102; N.J.S.A. 12A:8-105(1). The Legislature has mandated that terms incorporated in such instruments shall be effective "[e]ven against a purchaser for value and without notice." N.J.S.A. 12A:8-202(1). That provision, unique to investment securities and unlike the general Uniform Commercial Code principle that "[a] person 'knows' or has 'knowledge' of a fact when he has actual knowledge of it," N.J.S.A. 12A:1-201(25), is designed to provide certainty and stability in the marketing of securities. Its purpose is explained in the Official Comment:

> A purchaser must have some method of learning the terms of the security he is purchasing. The printing on the certificate or on the initial transaction statement ("ITS") is designed to notify the purchaser of those terms. If he purchases without examining the certificate or ITS, he does so at his peril, since he is charged with notice of terms stated thereon. [U.C.C. § 8-202 cmt. 1 (1977).]

We have recently observed that "the U.C.C. represents a comprehensive statutory scheme that satisfies the needs of the world of commerce, and courts should pause before extending judicial doctrines that might dislocate the legislative structure." Spring Motors Distribs., Inc. v. Ford Motor Co., 98 N.J. 555, 577, 489 A.2d 660 (1985). The aim of Article 8 is to confer negotiability on securities; the statutory provisions should be implemented to ensure "'the freedom of transferability which is essential to the negotiability of investment securities.'" 8 Anderson, Uniform Commercial Code § 8-105:3, :4 (3d ed. 1985) (quoting E.H. Hinds, Inc. v. Coolidge Bank & Trust Co., 6 Mass.App. 5, 372 N.E.2d 259, 263 (Mass.App.Ct.1978)). Subjecting the terms of Article 8 securities to continual judicial determinations of fairness would seriously impair the reliability and transferability of such instruments.[2]

---

2. Subjecting Commission notes to a judicial-fairness review could also undermine the statutory assurance that "[all] * * * provisions" of such obligations are "valid and legally binding contracts * * * enforceable by any * * * holder or holders." N.J.S.A. 58:5-48.

Third, judicial review of the fairness of negotiable securities would be inconsistent with federal and state securities laws. Central to those statutes is the requirement of full disclosure of all material facts and the prohibition of fraudulent conduct in connection with the purchase or sale of securities. See 15 U.S.C.A. § 78j(b); N.J.S.A. 49:3-52(a) and (b). Both Congress and our Legislature have chosen to protect investors by assuring that they be given all materials necessary to make an informed decision; accordingly, the federal and state legislative schemes do not provide for governmental review—judicial or otherwise—of the risk, fairness, good sense, or other substantive qualities of the offered security. Introducing a judicial-fairness review would effectively reject those legislative judgments in favor of a view that full disclosure does not provide adequate protection to an investor.[3] Similarly inappropriate is the Appellate Division's suggestion that terms of securities should be subject to a judicial-fairness review because the documents "are lengthy and difficult to understand." 238 N.J. Super. at 49, 568 A.2d 1213. The forms of documents are dictated by, and their sufficiency is reviewable under, the securities laws.

We are satisfied that in light of the considerations we have stated, the asserted unfairness of the notice provision is not sufficient to justify judicial intrusion. Notice by publication does not contravene or frustrate any legislative policy. Moreover, although such notice may be constitutionally insufficient in certain settings, see, e.g., Mullane v. Central Hanover Bank & Trust Co., 339 U.S. 306, 70 S.Ct. 652, 94 L.Ed. 865 (1950), plaintiffs have not demonstrated any established judicial policy against contractual provisions for notice by publication. We recognize that the Securities and Exchange Commission's recent guidelines for bond redemptions, SEC Exchange Act Release No. 23, 856 (Dec. 3, 1986), encourage notice by mail and that the Model Debenture Indenture Provisions of the American Bar Foundation, American Bar Foundation Corporate Debt Financing Project, Model Debenture Provisions—All Registered Issues §1105 at 68 (1967), also suggest that notice of early redemption should be given to registered holders by mail. Moreover, we have no doubt that notice by mail here would have been preferable. But those considerations are not of sufficient weight to overcome the policy considerations that properly restrain judicial oversight of the terms of publicly-held securities.[4]

We do not read Van Gemert v. Boeing Co., 520 F.2d 1373 (2d Cir.), cert. denied, 423 U.S. 947, 96 S.Ct. 364, 46 L.Ed.2d 282 (1975), relied on by plaintiffs, as holding that a court may properly invalidate a notice-by-publication term of a security. In Van Gemert, holders of Boeing's convertible debentures challenged as unreasonable the published notice given by Boeing of redemption of the debentures. Although the plaintiffs argued that the indenture agreement was "in the nature of a contract of adhesion" and thus any "unconscionable features * * * are unenforceable as a matter of policy," id. at 1380, that court did not agree. Rather, it found that the newspaper notice was inadequate because the investors had not been adequately informed "by the prospectus or by the debentures" of the notice to be given. Id. at 1383. The court clas-

---

3. The ability of the courts to conduct such evaluations of securities is, at the very least, questionable. Some state securities laws do provide for a fairness review, commonly performed by a specially-constituted executive commission prior to the issuance of a security. That procedure not only provides some degree of expertise and consistency but also assures that an investor can still rely on the express terms of the security once issued....

4. We also note that in the special circumstances of this case, invalidation of the "notice" provision might have a peculiarly unfortunate effect: the Commission, a public agency, and hence its ratepayers, might be required to pay interest on an escrow fund that was not under its control and that may have generated no income for the Commission.

sified the limited scope of that holding in its later opinion after remand. See 553 F.2d 812 (1977). There the court stated that it had found "significant * * * the fact that the debentures did not explicitly set forth the type of notice [that the debenture holders] could expect" in the event of an early redemption, and accordingly had "held as a matter of law" what notice the debenture holders "were entitled to expect." Id. at 815....

As we have already noted, plaintiffs here do not dispute that the notes and the Official Statement fully disclosed that notice of redemption would be given by publication. If anything, Van Gemert suggests that such a fully disclosed term should be enforced.

We therefore conclude that although the project notes fit our literal definition of contracts of adhesion, plaintiffs are bound by the provision for notice by publication because of the unique policy considerations attendant on securities offerings.

* * *

The judgment of the Appellate Division is reversed. The matter is remanded to the Law Division for further proceedings in accordance with this opinion.

The Chief Justice, Justices Handler and O'Hern, and Judges Gaulkin and Keefe join in Parts I, II, and III of the opinion....

Judge Petrella dissents from Parts I, II, and III of the opinion and files a separate opinion.

* * *

PETRELLA, P.J.A.D. (temporarily assigned), concurring in part and dissenting in part.

Because I am unable to agree fully with the Court's conclusions ... I dissent from parts I through III. In my view, the "contract" under which the registered bearer notes were purchased by individuals or institutions is one of adhesion. That the notice provisions of the contract are not necessarily "unconscionable" does not resolve the issue of whether those provisions, if patently unfair to registered note holders under the circumstances, warrant judicial intervention.

* * *

I disagree with the majority's notion that it is significant that investors were not under any economic pressure to buy the project notes. Contrary to the majority opinion's view, the fact that consumer necessities are not involved should not be determinative of the issue. Contracts of adhesion are not limited to contracts for necessities or policies of insurance unless the Legislature, or perhaps a court, so declares based on stated policy reasons. In my view, there is neither viable reason nor necessity to exclude securities from contract scrutiny. Hence, applying definitional terms, investment securities of the type involved in this case are contracts of adhesion and should be treated as such unless specifically provided otherwise by statute.

.... The issue is the fairness or reasonableness of notice to a registered note holder solely by publication....

It is unnecessary to conclude that the notice by publication provision, despite any inherent unfairness or unreasonableness, is unconscionable. The organic law of this State and its statutes and case law apply, including the provisions of Article 1 of the UCC (generally applicable to all the UCC articles, except where stated to the contrary.... See N.J.S.A. 12A:1-102.

* * *

Certainly, application of the law of fair notice does not conflict with the stated terms of these securities. Publication should not be construed as a stated term, nor as being to the exclusion of fair notice to registered note holders, nor as inconsistent with mailed notice. To expect that the absence of a reference to any of the cited authorities would mean other provisions of law have been ceded to the exclusive discretion of private law-making, i.e., contract law, does not seem logical.... Because I would not construe Article 8 of New Jersey's UCC as limiting review of the fairness of the notice provisions for registered note holders whose names and addresses are readily ascertainable, I see no impediment to applying established principles of law to the notice.

It needs to be emphasized that this appeal does not involve the financial provisions of the notes, the validity or genuineness of the notes, negotiability, or defenses of the issuer.

There is no basis in this record ... to conclude that the Appellate Division's determination in this case of unfair notice to registered note holders would have any adverse effect on the issuance of municipal securities. Indeed, since the January 19, 1990, decision of the Appellate Division, nothing has been brought to the attention of this Court regarding any untoward consequence of that decision on the issuance of tax exempt securities in this state, other than some ipse dixit speculative arguments. It was essentially conceded at arguments before the Appellate Division and this Court that, as a practical matter, what happened in this case would not be repeated because written notice to all holders of registered securities is now the general rule....

The "Preliminary and Final Official Statement" dated May 16, 1984, on which defendants rely to support their claim that there was adequate notice and that plaintiffs individually, as well as all members of the class of registered note holders that they represent, should be bound by the contract, contains a provision somewhat inconsistent with defendants' argument. It provides that the "Official Statement is not to be construed as a contract or an agreement between the Commission and the purchaser or holder of any Notes...."

If the offering statement is not considered to be part of any contract, then all that the purchaser is left with is the "fine print on the back of each note." 238 N.J. Super. at 44, 568 A.2d 1213. The record fails even to disclose whether plaintiffs received the offering statements before the purchase of the securities. See Id. at 49 n. 3, 568 A.2d 1213.

The Law Division judge appeared troubled at oral argument by the fact that First Fidelity Bank (First Fidelity) furnished its own customers with additional notice either by telephone or mail of the calling of the notes. The bank's attorney argued then, and in a post-argument submission, that First Fidelity's trust department was separate and distinct from its investment department, was housed in a separate building, and was merely an "indenture trustee" and not a "common-law trustee." ...

Deposition extracts ... included portions of the testimony of Alex Williams, Executive Vice-president of First Fidelity, to the effect that at some point in 1986 the bank's investment department gave written or oral notice of the call of the notes to its customers whether or not those customers had safe-keeping accounts with the bank, and that this was done prior to the June 23rd call date. He said that First Fidelity felt that it would be "good business" to inform its customers. The reasons given by Williams for First Fidelity's actions were essentially that the bank wanted to sell new bonds to its customers, to continue good customer relations, and its concern that its customers might not receive notice. It is unclear how far in advance First Fidelity commenced notifying its customers of the June 23, 1984, call date....

Charles Hoos, Senior Vice-president of First Fidelity, testified that he was in charge of the corporate trust department and was aware of the fact that First Fidelity elected to give written notice of the redemption of the notes to customers of its investment department.

.... Although the record does not contain the resolution appointing the bank as trustee or any document showing the trustee's actual acceptance of that appointment, it is undisputed that the bank acted not only as indenture trustee, and accepted responsibility under the resolutions, but also acted as a managing underwriter, Paying Agent, Registrar, and eventually Escrow Agent, and was presumably paid for each activity. A September 1, 1985, Escrow Deposit Agreement between the Commission and First Fidelity entered into in connection with First Fidelity being named "in its capacity as trustee" as "Escrow Agent" regarding the defeasance of the lien of the notes is attached as "Exhibit G" to the stipulation of facts.

First Fidelity took the position ... that nothing in the record indicated that the personal notifications given by the investment department of the bank were in any way a result of the bank's position as trustee. It pointed to the deposition testimony of First Fidelity's personnel that the investment department routinely telephones customers with respect to any major developments as to securities it sold. First Fidelity took the position that the deposition testimony demonstrated that a "Chinese wall" existed between the trust department and the investment department that was kept intact during this transaction. It also claimed a narrower scope of responsibility as an indenture trustee as referred to in Meckel v. Continental Resources, [758 F.2d 811, 816 (2d Cir. 1985)] (duties limited to duties set forth in indenture).

However, it was not First Fidelity's trust department that was appointed as trustee, but rather the bank. Indeed, if, as suggested in Meckel, an indenture trustee does not have a trustee's duties of undivided loyalty and "is more like a stakeholder whose duties and obligations are exclusively defined by the terms of the indenture agent," ibid., there is no need for the employment of a trust department and no need to hide behind one side of a "Chinese wall." First Fidelity was not only one of the underwriters, but it was one of the managing underwriters of this issue. It was also the registrar/paying agent, escrow agent, and the indenture trustee for the project notes....

As trustee under the note issue (as well as in the other capacities) First Fidelity presumably received significant fees for its responsibilities, which in part included protecting the rights of note holders. In that capacity, for which it was paid, First Fidelity now says it had no obligation to notify any note holders in any fashion other than by the method of publication as set forth in the Commission's resolution. On the other hand, First Fidelity argues that in its capacity as a bank, its investment department, which also receives fees for its services, including protection of customers, apparently undertook to give special notice to its own customers past and potential, with no obligation to do so.... Thus, First Fidelity argues that it can demand the benefits of both worlds, but without any additional obligations, particularly toward those who did not purchase the notes through it.

Although First Fidelity has a trust department, an investment department, and other departments or functions, it was First Fidelity that was appointed trustee, not one of its departments. It had fiduciary responsibilities under the terms of the resolutions, and those were not negated by federal law or a lesser standard of trusteeship. The bank is charged, or should be charged here, with knowledge of all of the actions of all its departments and subdivisions, whether or not one department had actual contact with another. The fact is that First Fidelity elected to notify selectively its own customers. It acted in a manner that exhibited at best a lack of fair dealing and at worst, bad faith. It should not be allowed to assume duties with one hand and to reject them with the other. This case is a more compelling one to apply the fairness doctrine because First Fidelity knew about the situation with respect to note holders, but acted for only its own customers.... The existence of separate divisions for business purposes does not allow it to act in a disparate manner when it knows the names and addresses of registered note holders who are both customers and non-customers....

The majority opinion chooses to ignore the fact that in the related case of Ellovich v. First Fidelity Bank, N.A., N.J., No. 87-650 (D.N.J.1988), it was established that prior to issuance of the offering statement, First Fidelity's counsel suggested that notice of early redemption be given by mail rather than publication, based on his understanding that that was the usual form of notice to holders of registered securities.... Moreover, the "Stipulation of Facts" submitted in connection with the summary judgment motions stated: "Prior to the publication of the notices, Julie Saloveitch Miller, Administrator of the bond offering at First Fidelity, discussed the notice to be given with Gerald Volpe, Comptroller of the Commission." The Commission insisted on the publication notice....

That a public entity may have participated in what resulted in unfair notice should not be a basis to excuse such action merely because rate payers may be affected. When dealing with the public, "government must 'turn square corners' rather than exploit litigational or bargaining advantages that might otherwise be available to private citizens." W.V. Pangborne & Co. v. New Jersey Dep't of Transp., 116 N.J. 543, 561, 562 A.2d 222 (1989). The government must act fairly and "with compunction and integrity." Id. at 562....

The Appellate Division decision is essentially limited to the notice provisions under the unique circumstances of this case. It does not affect the financial terms of the project notes in any way....

In actuality there is no real burden placed on the securities industry by a requirement that fair notice be given to note holders in the issuance of registered securities. What occurred here was an atypical situation. The limited record before us indicates that with respect to all other issues, and particularly future tax exempt issues, individual notice to the registered security holders is the general practice, encouraged and in effect required by the SEC.

Simply stated, fair dealing should be required....

* * *

Note on Zero Coupon Debt Securities

The next case—Morgan Stanley & Co., Inc. v. Archer Daniels Midland Co.—provides additional guidance on indenture interpretation. It also exposes us to a different type of debt security called a *zero coupon debt security* (referred to as a *"zero"*). Zeroes are securities that pay no annual interest (hence the phrase "zero coupon" in the name). At issuance, however, each security is sold at a significant discount to its face value. Upon maturity, its issuer must pay back the full face value, and thus its holder's compensation is the difference between the zero's face value and the discounted price at which it was originally issued.

Zeroes have an implicit rate of interest associated with them. For example, suppose PNH Corp. issues five-year zeroes with a $1,000 face value for $747.26 each. Using the present value of a lump sum formula (see chapter 3, section 2b(ii)(A)), plug in $1,000 for the future sum, $747.26 for the present value, five years for the time period, and then calculate the discount rate. Using a financial calculator, the implicit rate of interest in this example is 6% assuming annual compounding. Another way of looking at this is to say that $747.26 compounded annually at 6% will grow to $1,000 five years from now.

Although an investor receives no interest payments during the life of a zero, she must recognize the "imputed income" from the zero on her tax return. This means she pays tax on that income even though she receives no cash interest payment from the issuer. Because of this, most investors in zeroes are pension funds, other tax-exempt entities, and individuals buying zeroes for their individual retirement accounts.

A company which cannot afford to pay interest during the term of its outstanding debt securities is a prime candidate for issuing zeroes. While zeroes allow the company to avoid cash outlays in the form of interest payments during the term of the zeroes, the Internal Revenue Code nevertheless permits it to deduct interest expense each year as if it had. For example, suppose PNH Corp. needed $250 million to purchase a large tract of land. It plans on improving that land over a five-year period and then reselling it at a sizeable profit. Because PNH will not receive any return on its investment in the land until it resells it, issuing zeroes makes sense for PNH. Indeed, PNH pays no interest over the five-year period yet deducts interest expense as if it had. When the aggregate face value of the zeroes becomes due at the end of the five-year period, PNH will have the cash necessary to pay investors once it sells the improved land.

More on zero coupon securities can be found on the Securities and Exchange Commission's website (www.sec.gov/answers/zero.htm) and The Bond Market Association's website (www.investinginbonds.com).

Morgan Stanley & Co., Inc. v. Archer Daniels Midland Co.
570 F. Supp. 1529 (S.D.N.Y. 1983)

SAND, District Judge.

This action ... arises out of the planned redemption of $125 million in 16% Sinking Fund Debentures ("the Debentures") by the defendant ADM Midland Company ("ADM") scheduled to take place on Monday, August 1st, 1983. Morgan Stanley & Company, Inc. ("Morgan Stanley") brings this suit under §10(b) of the Securities Exchange Act of 1934 ... §17(a) of the Securities Act of 1933 ... §§323(a) and 316(b) of the Trust Indenture Act of 1939 ... and other state and federal laws, alleging that the proposed redemption plan is barred by the terms of the Indenture, the language of the Debentures, and the Debenture Prospectus. Plaintiff contends, in addition, that the failure on the part of ADM to reveal its intention to redeem the Debentures, as well as its belief that such redemption would be lawful under the terms of the Indenture Agreement, amounts to an intentional, manipulative scheme to defraud in violation of federal and state securities and business laws. Morgan Stanley seeks a preliminary injunction enjoining ADM from consummating the redemption as planned, and, after full consideration on the merits, permanent injunctive relief barring the proposed transaction and damages. Both parties have pursued an expedited discovery schedule and now cross-move for summary judgment.

FACTS

In May, 1981, Archer Daniels issued $125,000,000 of 16% Sinking Fund Debentures due May 15, 2011. The managing underwriters of the Debenture offering were Goldman

Sachs & Co., Kidder Peabody & Co., and Merrill Lynch, Pierce, Fenner & Smith, Inc. The Debentures state in relevant part:

> The Debentures are subject to redemption upon not less than 30 nor more than 60 days' notice by mail, at any time, in whole or in part, at the election of the Company, at the following optional Redemption Price (expressed in percentages of the principal amount), together with accrued interest to the Redemption Date..., all as provided in the Indenture: If redeemed during the twelve-month period beginning May 15 of the years indicated:

Year	Percentage	Year	Percentage
1981	115.500%	1991	107.750%
1982	114.725	1992	106.975
1983	113.950	1993	106.200
1984	113.175	1994	105.425
1985	112.400	1995	104.650
1986	111.625	1996	103.875
1987	110.850	1997	103.100
1988	110.075	1998	102.325
1989	109.300	1999	101.550
1990	108.525	2000	100.775

> and thereafter at 100%; provided, however, that prior to May 15, 1991, the Company may not redeem any of the Debentures pursuant to such option from the proceeds, or in anticipation, of the issuance of any indebtedness for money borrowed by or for the account of the Company or any Subsidiary (as defined in the Indenture) or from the proceeds, or in anticipation of a sale and leaseback transaction (as defined in Section 1008 of the Indenture), if, in either case, the interest cost or interest factor applicable thereto (calculated in accordance with generally accepted financial practice) shall be less than 16.08% per annum.

The May 12, 1981 Prospectus and the Indenture pursuant to which the Debentures were issued contain substantially similar language. The Moody's Bond Survey of April 27, 1981, in reviewing its rating of the Debentures, described the redemption provision in the following manner:

> The 16% sinking fund debentures are nonrefundable with lower cost interest debt before April 15, 1991. Otherwise, they are callable in whole or in part at prices to be determined.

* * *

ADM raised money through public borrowing at interest rates less than 16.08% on at least two occasions subsequent to the issuance of the Debentures. On May 7, 1982, over a year before the announcement of the planned redemption, ADM borrowed $50,555,500 by the issuance of $400,000,000 face amount zero coupon debentures[a] due 2002 and $100,000,000 face amount zero coupon notes due 1992 (the "Zeroes"). The Zeroes bore an effective interest rate of less than 16.08%. On March 10, 1983, ADM raised an additional $86,400,000 by the issuance of $263,232,500 face amount Secured Trust Accrual Receipts, known as "Stars," through a wholly-owned subsidiary, Midland Stars Inc. The Stars carry an effective interest rate of less than 16.08%. The Stars were in

---

a. A description of zero coupon debt securities immediately precedes this case.

the form of notes with varying maturities secured by government securities deposited by ADM with a trustee established for that purpose. There is significant dispute between the parties as to whether the Stars transaction should be treated as an issuance of debt or as a sale of government securities. We assume, for purposes of this motion, that the transaction resulted in the incurring of debt.

In the period since the issuance of the Debentures, ADM also raised money through two common stock offerings. Six million shares of common stock were issued by prospectus dated January 28, 1983, resulting in proceeds of $131,370,000. And by a prospectus supplement dated June 1, 1983, ADM raised an additional $15,450,000 by issuing 600,000 shares of common stock.

Morgan Stanley, the plaintiff in this action, bought $15,518,000 principal amount of the Debentures at $1,252.50 per $1,000 face amount on May 5, 1983, and $500,000 principal amount at $1,200 per $1,000 face amount on May 31, 1983. The next day, June 1, ADM announced that it was calling for the redemption of the 16% Sinking Fund Debentures, effective August 1, 1983. The direct source of funds was to be the two ADM common stock offerings of January and June, 1983. The proceeds of these offerings were delivered to the Indenture Trustee, Morgan Guaranty Trust Company, and deposited in a special account to be applied to the redemption. The amount deposited with the Indenture Trustee is sufficient to fully redeem the Debentures.

Prior to the announcement of the call for redemption, the Debentures were trading at a price in excess of the $1,139.50 call price. At no time prior to the June 1 announcement did ADM indicate in any of its materials filed with the Securities and Exchange Commission or otherwise that it intended to exercise its redemption rights if it felt it was in its self-interest to do so. Nor did it express any contemporaneous opinion as to whether it was entitled under the terms of the Indenture to call the Debentures when it was borrowing funds at an interest rate less than 16.08% if the source of such redemption was other than the issuance of debt.

Plaintiff's allegations can be reduced to two general claims: First, plaintiff contends that the proposed redemption is barred by the express terms of the call provisions of the Debenture and the Indenture Agreement, and that consummation of the plan would violate the Trust Indenture Act of 1939 ... and common law principles of contract law. The plaintiff's claim is founded on the language contained in the Debenture and Trust Indenture that states that the company may not redeem the Debentures "from the proceeds, or in anticipation, of the issuance of any indebtedness ... if ... the interest cost or interest factor ... [is] less than 16.08% per annum." Plaintiff points to the $86,400,000 raised by the Stars transaction within 90 days of the June 1 redemption announcement, and the $50,555,500 raised by the Zeroes transaction in May, 1982—both at interest rates below 16.08%—as proof that the redemption is being funded, at least indirectly, from the proceeds of borrowing in violation of the Debentures and Indenture agreement. The fact that ADM raised sufficient funds to redeem the Debentures entirely through the issuance of common stock is, according to the plaintiffs, an irrelevant "juggling of funds" used to circumvent the protections afforded investors by the redemption provisions of the Debenture. Plaintiff would have the Court interpret the provision as barring redemption during any period when the issuer has borrowing [sic] at a rate lower than that prescribed by the Debentures, regardless of whether the direct source of the funds is the issuance of equity, the sale of assets, or merely cash on hand.

The defendant would have the Court construe the language more narrowly as barring redemption only where the direct or indirect source of the funds is a debt instrument issued at a rate lower than that it is paying on the outstanding Debentures. Where, as here, the defendant can point directly to a non-debt source of funds (the issuance of common stock), the defendant is of the view that the general redemption schedule applies.

DISCUSSION

This Circuit will grant preliminary injunctive relief only upon a showing of (a) irreparable harm *and* (b) either (1) a likelihood of success on the merits or (2) sufficiently serious questions going to the merits to make them a fair ground for litigation and a balance of hardships tipping decidedly toward the party requesting preliminary relief.... Morgan Stanley fails to satisfy these criteria in all respects.

First, plaintiff has failed to present any facts supporting a contention that money damages would be an inadequate remedy should it prevail in this action. Where money damages are available, there can be no finding of irreparable harm....

With respect to the likelihood of success on the merits, defendant's interpretation of the redemption provision seems at least as likely to be in accord with the language of the Debentures, the Indenture, and the available authorities than is the view proffered by the plaintiff. We first note that the one court to directly address this issue chose to construe the language in the manner set forth in this action by the defendant. *Franklin Life Insurance Co.* v. *Commonwealth Edison Co.*, 451 F. Supp. 602 (S.D. Ill. 1978).... While plaintiff is correct in noting that this Circuit is not bound by this decision, and while this case can no doubt be distinguished factually on a number of grounds, none of which we deem to be of major significance, *Franklin* is nevertheless persuasive authority in support of defendant's position.

Defendant's view of the redemption language is also arguably supported by The American Bar Foundation's Commentaries on Model Debenture Indenture Provisions (1977), from which the boilerplate language in question was apparently taken verbatim. In discussing the various types of available redemption provisions, the Commentaries state:

> [I]nstead of an absolute restriction [on redemption], the parties may agree that the borrower may not redeem with funds borrowed at an interest rate lower than the interest rate in the debentures. *Such an arrangement recognizes that funds for redemption may become available from other than borrowing,* but correspondingly recognizes that the debenture holder is entitled to be protected for a while against redemption if interest rates fall and the borrower can borrow funds at a lower rate to pay off the debentures.

Id. at 477 (emphasis added). We read this comment as pointing to the *source* of funds as the dispositive factor in determining the availability of redemption to the issuer—the position advanced by defendant ADM.

Finally, we view the redemption language itself as supporting defendant's position. The redemption provision in the Indenture and the Debentures begins with the broad statement that the Debentures are "subject to redemption ... at any time, in whole or in part, at the election of the company, at the following optional Redemption Price...." Following this language is a table of decreasing redemption percentages keyed to the year in which the redemption occurs. This broad language is then followed by the narrowing provision "provided, however ... the Company may not redeem any of the Debentures pursuant to such option from the proceeds, or in anticipation, of the issuance of any indebtedness" borrowed at rates less than that paid on the Debentures.

While the "plain meaning" of this language is not entirely clear with respect to the question presented in this case, we think the restrictive phrasing of the redemption provision, together with its placement after broad language allowing redemption in all other cases at the election of the company, supports defendant's more restrictive reading.

Morgan Stanley asserts that defendant's view would afford bondholders no protection against redemption through lower-cost borrowing and would result in great uncertainty among holders of bonds containing similar provisions. In its view, the "plain meaning" of the redemption [sic] bondholders of these bonds and the investment community generally, is that the issuer may not redeem when it is contemporaneously engaging in lower-cost borrowing, regardless of the source of the funds for redemption. At the same time, however, the plaintiff does not contend that redemption through equity funding is prohibited for the life of the redemption restriction once the issuer borrows funds at a lower interest rate subsequent to the Debenture's issuance. On the contrary, plaintiff concedes that the legality of the redemption transaction would depend on a factual inquiry into the magnitude of the borrowing relative to the size of the contemplated equity-funded redemption and its proximity in time relative to the date the redemption was to take place. Thus, a $100 million redemption two years after a $1 million short-term debt issue might be allowable, while the same redemption six months after a $20 million long-term debt issue might not be allowable.

This case-by-case approach is problematic in a number of respects. First, it appears keyed to the subjective expectations of the bondholders; if it *appears* that the redemption is funded through lower-cost borrowing, based on the Company's recent or prospective borrowing history, the redemption is deemed unlawful. The approach thus reads a subjective element into what presumably should be an objective determination based on the language appearing in the bond agreement. Second, and most important, this approach would likely cause greater uncertainty among bondholders than a strict "source" rule such as that adopted in *Franklin, supra.*

Plaintiff's fear that bondholders would be left "unprotected" by adoption of the "source" rule also appears rather overstated. The rule proposed by defendant does not, as plaintiff suggests, entail a virtual emasculation of the refunding restrictions. An issuer contemplating redemption would still be required to fund such redemption from a source other than lower-cost borrowing, such as reserves, the sale of assets, or the proceeds of a common stock issue. Bondholders would thus be protected against the type of continuous short-term refunding of debt in times of plummeting interest rates that the language was apparently intended to prohibit. *See Franklin, supra,* 451 F. Supp. at 609. Moreover, this is not an instance where protections against premature redemption are wholly absent from the Debenture. On the contrary, the Debentures and the Indenture explicitly provide for early redemption expressed in declining percentages of the principal amount, depending on the year the redemption is effected.

At this early stage of the proceedings, on the record before us, and for all the reasons outlined above, we find that plaintiff has failed to show a sufficient likelihood of its success on the merits of its contract claims as to entitle it to preliminary injunctive relief.

We turn, finally, to the second, alternative prong of the requirement for preliminary relief. While plaintiff has doubtless presented serious questions going to the merits making a fair ground for litigation, it has made no showing of a balance of hardships tipping decidedly in its favor. Moreover, in this regard, we find quite persuasive the comments of counsel for Morgan Guaranty, the Indenture Trustee. While expressing no position on the merits, counsel urged that the hardships that would result in the event we were to grant preliminary relief at this late date would be incalculable to bondholders other than the plaintiff who already may have made firm business commitments in anticipation of receipt of the redemption funds as of August 1. In this regard, defendant has agreed to treat all bondholders equally after a trial on the merits or other dispositive motions. Defendant has further agreed that it will not contend that there is a waiver of any rights on the part of any of [sic] bondholder who cashes checks issued pursuant to this redemption.

For all of the above reasons, and on the record now before us, plaintiff's application for preliminary injunctive relief is hereby denied.

Decision on the parties' cross-motions for summary judgment is reserved. SO ORDERED.

ON MOTION FOR SUMMARY JUDGMENT

SAND, District Judge.

On July 29, 1983, this Court denied the application of plaintiff Morgan Stanley & Co., Inc. ("Morgan Stanley") for preliminary injunctive relief, reserving decision on the parties' cross-motions for summary judgment. After a thorough review of the record, for the reasons stated in our prior Opinion, and for the reasons stated below, we now grant the motion of defendant Archer Daniels Midland Company ("ADM") for partial summary judgment on the contract claims (Counts VI, X-XII), and deny Morgan Stanley's motion for summary judgment on the federal and state securities and business law claims. We assume familiarity with the facts of this case as set forth in our prior Opinion denying preliminary relief.

Contract Claims

The plaintiff's contract claims arise out of alleged violations of state contract law. Section 113 of the Indenture provides that the Indenture and the Debentures shall be governed by New York law. Under New York law, the terms of the Debentures constitute a contract between ADM and the holders of the Debentures, including Morgan Stanley.... *Van Gemert v. Boeing Co.*, 520 F.2d 1373, 1383 (2d Cir.), *cert. denied*, 423 U.S. 947, 96 S. Ct. 364, 46 L. Ed. 2d 282 (1975), *appeal after remand*, 553 F.2d 812, 813 (2d Cir. 1977) (applying New York law). The relevant contract terms are printed on the Debentures and, by incorporation, in the Indenture.

We note as an initial matter that where, as here, the contract language in dispute is a "boilerplate" provision found in numerous debentures and indenture agreements, the desire to give such language a consistent, uniform interpretation requires that the Court construe the language as a matter of law. *See Sharon Steel Corp. v. Chase Manhattan Bank, N.A.*, 691 F.2d 1039, 1048-49 (2d Cir. 1982) (applying New York law)....

[The court then reviewed the opinion in Franklin Life Insurance Co. v. Commonwealth Edison Co., 451 F. Supp. 602 (S.D. Ill. 1978), *aff'd per curiam on the opinion below*, 598 F.2d 1109 (7th Cir.), *rehearing and rehearing en banc denied*, *id.*, *cert. denied*, 444 U.S. 900, 100 S. Ct. 210, 62 L. Ed. 2d 136 (1979), finding it to be indistinguishable in any meaningful way.]

Morgan Stanley contends nevertheless that Franklin was wrongly decided, as a matter of law, and that a fresh examination of the redemption language in light of the applicable New York cases would lead us to reject the "source" rule. In this regard, Morgan Stanley suggests a number of universal axioms of contract construction intended to guide us in construing the redemption language as a matter of first impression. For example, Morgan counsels that we should construe the contract terms in light of their "plain meaning," and should adopt the interpretation that best accords with all the terms of the contract.... Where several constructions are possible, the court may look to the surrounding facts and circumstances to determine the intent of the parties.... Finally, Morgan Stanley urges that all ambiguities should be resolved against the party that drafted the agreement....

We find these well-accepted and universal principles of contract construction singularly unhelpful in construing the contract language before us. Several factors lead us to this conclusion. First, there is simply no "plain meaning" suggested by the redemption language that would imbue all the contract terms with a significant meaning. Either party's interpretation of the redemption language would dilute the meaning of at least some of the words—either the "indirectly or directly," "in anticipation of" language, were we to adopt defendant's "source" rule, or the "from the proceeds," "as part of a refunding operation" language, were we to adopt the plaintiff's interpretation. Any attempt to divine the "plain meaning" of the redemption language would be disingenuous at best.

Equally fruitless would be an effort to discern the "intent of the parties" under the facts of this case. It may very well be that ADM rejected an absolute no-call provision in its negotiations with the underwriters in favor of language it viewed as providing "greater flexibility." It is also clear, however, that neither the underwriters nor ADM knew whether such "flexibility" encompassed redemption under the facts of this case. The deposition testimony of ADM officials suggesting that they believed at the time they negotiated the Indenture that they could redeem the Debentures at any time except through lower-cost debt merely begs the question. Had ADM management so clearly intended the Indenture to allow refunding under the circumstances of this case, it surely would have considered that option prior to the suggestions of Merrill Lynch, which appears to represent the first time the idea of early redemption funded directly by the proceeds of a stock issue was presented by any of ADM's investment advisors.

Finally, we view this as a most inappropriate case to construe ambiguous contract language against the drafter. The Indenture was negotiated by sophisticated bond counsel on both sides of the bargaining table. There is no suggestion of disparate bargaining power in the drafting of the Indenture, nor could there be. Moreover, even if we were to adopt this rule, it is not at all clear that ADM would be considered the drafter of the Indenture, given the active participation of the managing underwriter. Indeed, it is arguable that the ambiguous language should be construed in favor of ADM....

Not only do the rules of contract construction provide little aid on the facts before us, but we find the equities in this action to be more or less in equilibrium. Morgan Stanley now argues, no doubt in good faith, that the redemption is unlawful under the Indenture. Nevertheless, as we noted in our prior opinion, Morgan Stanley employees were fully aware of the uncertain legal status of an early call at the time they purchased the ADM Debentures. To speak of upsetting Morgan's "settled expectations" would thus be rather misleading under the circumstances. By the same token, however, it is also clear that ADM had no expectations with respect to the availability of an early redemption call until the idea was first suggested by Merrill Lynch.

Because we find equitable rules of contract construction so unhelpful on the facts of this case, the decision in *Franklin* takes on added importance. While it is no doubt true that the decision in that case was a difficult one and in no sense compelled under existing law, we find the reasoning of the court thoroughly convincing given the obvious ambiguity of the language it was asked to construe. We also find the result to be a fair one, primarily for the reasons stated in our prior Opinion denying preliminary relief. Moreover, we note that the decision in Franklin preceded the drafting of the ADM Indenture by several years. We must assume, therefore, that the decision was readily available to bond counsel for all parties. That the parties may not in fact have been aware of the decision at the time the Indenture was negotiated is not dispositive, for the law in force at the time a contract is entered into becomes a part of the contract.... While *Franklin* was decided under Illinois law and is therefore not binding on the New York courts, we cannot ignore the fact that it was the single existing authority on this issue, and was decided on the basis of universal contract principles. Under these circumstances, it was predictable that *Franklin* would affect any subsequent decision under New York law. *Franklin* thus adds an unavoidable gloss to any interpretation of the redemption language.

Finally, we note that to cast aside the holding in *Franklin* would, in effect, result in the very situation the Second Circuit sought to avoid in *Sharon Steel, supra*. In that case, the Court warned that allowing juries to construe boilerplate language as they saw fit would likely result in intolerable uncertainty in the capital markets. To avoid such an outcome, the Court found that the interpretation of boilerplate should be left to the Court as a matter of law. *Sharon Steel, supra*, 691 F.2d at 1048. While the Court in *Sharon Steel* was addressing the issue of varying interpretations by juries rather than by the courts, this distinction does not diminish the uncertainty that would result were we to reject the holding in *Franklin*. Given the paramount interest in uniformly construing boilerplate provisions, and for all the other reasons stated above and in our prior Opinion, we chose to follow the holding in *Franklin*.[4]

Accordingly, we find that the ADM redemption was lawful under the terms of the Debentures and the Indenture, and that therefore defendant's motion for summary judgment on Counts VI and X through XII is hereby granted.

SO ORDERED.

---

4. We note in this regard that the "source" rule adopted in *Franklin* in no sense constitutes a license to violate the refunding provision. The court is still required to make a finding of the true source of the proceeds for redemption. Where the facts indicate that the proposed redemption was indirectly funded by the proceeds of anticipated debt borrowed at a prohibited interest rate, such redemption would be barred regardless of the name of the account from which the funds were withdrawn. Thus, a different case would be before us if ADM, contemporaneously with the redemption, issued new, lower-cost debt and used the proceeds of such debt to repurchase the stock issued in the first instance to finance the original redemption. On those facts, the redemption could arguably be said to have been indirectly funded through the proceeds of anticipated lower-cost debt, since ADM would be in virtually the same financial posture after the transaction as it was before redemption—except that the new debt would be carried at a lower interest rate. Here, by contrast, there is no allegation that ADM intends to repurchase the common stock it issued to fund the redemption. The issuance of stock, with its concomitant effect on the company's debt/equity ratio, is exactly the type of substantive financial transaction the proceeds of which may be used for early redemption.

Moreover, we fail to see how, on the facts of this case, the redemption could be argued to be a refunding from the proceeds of lower-cost debt. The Zeroes transaction occurred over a year before the redemption and appears completely unrelated to it. The proceeds of that transaction were used to purchase government securities that remain in ADM's portfolio. The Stars transaction, while closer in time, similarly is not fairly viewed as the source of the redemption, given that the proceeds of that transaction were applied directly to reducing ADM's short-term debt. To view the redemption as having been funded *indirectly* "from the proceeds" of the Stars transaction would require us to ignore the *direct* source of the refunding, the two ADM common stock issues.

Notes and Questions

1. In Mutual Savings Life Ins. Co. v. James River Corp., 716 So.2d 1172 (Ala. 1998), plaintiff debentureholders alleged that the issuer wrongfully and prematurely called, retired and refunded their debentures with lower-rate debt in violation of the indenture. However, the indenture did not explicitly prohibit or otherwise regulate debenture repurchases, by tender offer or otherwise. The issuer exploited this by conducting a "simultaneous tender and call" (STAC). In a STAC, the issuer makes a tender offer for the debentures priced slightly higher than the call price of the debentures while simultaneously calling the debentures. The tender offer was funded with the proceeds of cheaper debt. Given the higher tender offer price (as compared to the call price), 98% of the debentures were tendered to the issuer. The remaining debentures were redeemed with the proceeds of the sale of a new issue of preferred stock, something the indenture did not prohibit.

Arguing that substance should trump form, the plaintiffs urged the court to collapse the STAC into a single transaction for purposes of the indenture prohibition on refinancing with cheaper debt. The court, however, refused to do so. It placed the burden on the plaintiffs to show specific language from the indenture calling for the collapsing of the two transactions into one. With the plaintiffs failing to meet their burden, the court treated the STAC as two separate transactions, thus placing the tender offer funded with cheaper debt outside the scope of the refunding restriction.

2. In Shenandoah Life Ins. Co. v. Valero Energy Corp., 1988 WL 63491, 14 Del. J. Corp. L. 396 (Del. Ch. 1988), the court, construing language similar to that presented in *Archer Daniels Midland*, held that a redemption of outstanding bonds purportedly from equity did not violate the terms of the indenture even where "new debt was raised contemporaneously with the new equity ... as part of a single integrated transaction," at least where the amount of equity raised was sufficient to redeem the bonds without recourse to the debt.

3. In Harris v. Union Elec. Co., 622 S.W.2d 239 (Mo. App. 1981), the court was faced with a similar limitation on redemption financed by lower cost funds. The provision, however, apparently excepted from this restriction redemptions made from a Maintenance Fund, designed to mandate partial redemption when Union Electric ("UE") failed to devote a specified percentage of annual earnings to maintaining its property, and as to which the source of funds was unrestricted. The issuer borrowed funds at a lower cost than the bonds, deposited most of the proceeds in the Maintenance Fund, and announced a redemption at the "special price" of 100% of par value applicable to Maintenance Fund redemptions thereby circumventing both the limitation on redemption and the redemption premiums.

After UE announced an abandonment of its redemption plans following plaintiffs' initiation of their lawsuit, plaintiffs requested declaratory and injunctive relief prohibiting similar redemptions. Reversing the trial court's holding that redemption was prohibited, the court held that the trial court had erred in considering extrinsic evidence to interpret an unambiguous provision in a contract. The court went on to consider:

> The question ... whether the extrinsic evidence can create an ambiguity and provide another possible interpretation to this otherwise clear language. We believe not. Plaintiffs argue that they thought they were getting "solid" protection against lower interest cost refunding and that UE's top executives were under the same impression. Thus, we should ascribe that meaning to the language. However, plaintiffs' understanding of the redemption protection is

found largely on the fact that special redemptions had never been pursued in the past. And, basically, plaintiffs assumed that they would not be done in the future. UE's executives simply admit that they were not aware of the possibility of a special redemption. It was not until another public utility company announced its plans for a redemption that UE decided to explore the possibility of redemption in a similar manner. These circumstances cannot alter the clear import of the written instrument. If *absolute* protection from lower interest cost redemption for ten years was intended, as plaintiffs contend, the indenture would have been so drafted. Instead, the bonds were merely subject to a limited risk of special redemption—limited in the sense that the amount of bonds redeemable cannot exceed the 1% Improvement Fund deposits and the replacement requirements of the Maintenance Fund. The extrinsic evidence does not convince us that the otherwise unambiguous language is susceptible of any other reasonable interpretation, and we conclude as a matter of law that the Bond Contract's lower interest cost refunding restriction does not apply to special redemptions. To the extent the trial court's decree reflects a contrary view, and it does at various points, it is in error.

Id. at 248, 249. *See also* John Hancock Mut. Life Ins. Co. v. Carolina Power & Light Co., 717 F.2d 664 (2d Cir. 1983) (finding a similar provision unambiguous in favor of the issuer in the face of plaintiffs' argument that general redemptions subject to a refunding limitation were impermissible in years when the issuer had sufficient property credits to avoid making cash deposits into the Maintenance Fund, but nevertheless elected to make such deposits in lieu of using such credits).

4. The bond issue in *Harris* was registered and offered to the public. In *Carolina Power & Light*, the bonds had been privately placed with twenty-three insurance companies. What difference should this make, if any, in the way the court approaches problems of contract interpretation? Should it make a difference that the court does or does not find the provision at issue to be "unambiguous"?

5. Klein, Anderson & McGuiness, The Call Provision of Corporate Bonds: A Standard Form in Need of a Change, 18 J. Corp. Law 653 (1993), describe a device called the "make whole provision," now common in privately placed debt (but rare in publicly issued debt), which is designed to protect lenders from the consequences of refunding redemptions by increasing the redemption price to account for increases in loan values resulting from decreasing interest rates. They undertake an extensive analysis of the economics of call provisions, distinguishing between the appropriate protection of lenders from changes in interest rates and the wisdom of permitting borrowers to benefit, at least to some extent, from decreases in default risk.

6. What is the difference between a liberal approach to contract interpretation, *see*, *e.g.*, Restatement (Second) of Contracts §202 (1981), and fiduciary duty? Tauke, Should Bonds Have More Fun? A Reexamination of the Debate Over Corporate Bondholder Rights, 1989 Colum. Bus. L. Rev. 1, 80, describes the distinction as follows:

> Modern construction of contracts is, of course, a method of determining the meaning of contact [sic] language, not a method, like fiduciary duty, of providing protection to parties presumed incapable of providing their own contractual protection. Modern contract interpretation thus retains the notion that the bondholder-corporation relationship is a bargained one representing a determination by the affected parties as to what is the best way to structure their relationship. The parties thus remain free to provide for the allocation of

risks and the retention of flexibility to act in such a way as to maximize their joint wealth. In particular, the modern approach to contract interpretation avoids the substantial limitation that fiduciary duty would impose on the flexibility of the corporation to exercise discretion in order to maximize corporate wealth in light of constantly changing circumstances. Because the modern mode of contract interpretation is tied to the contract language and surrounding circumstances, it is also likely to give rise to a narrower range of decisions than is the relatively less constrained application by a court of equitable principles in the guise of enforcement of fiduciary duty. Narrowing the possible scope of decisions should have the effect of reducing market uncertainty as to the meaning of contract terms, thereby serving the important goal of providing for predictability of interpretation of contract language.

7. Given these differences (and others that might occur to you), do you agree with the law's treatment of corporate bondholders as contract claimants? For example, against whom should the bond contract be construed? *Compare* Morgan Stanley & Co., Inc. v. Archer Daniels Midland Co., 570 F. Supp. 1529, 1541 (S.D.N.Y. 1983) (suggesting that, in light of the managing underwriter's active participation in drafting, construction of ambiguous language in favor of the debtor might be appropriate) *with* Prescott, Ball & Turban v. LTV Corp., 531 F. Supp. 213, 217 (S.D.N.Y. 1981) (applying New York law requiring contract construction against the drafter to require construction against the issuing corporation); Harris v. Union Elec. Co., 787 F.2d 355, 365 n.7 (8th Cir. 1986), *cert. denied*, 479 U.S. 823 (1986) (applying same rule).

8. Both the court in *Sharon Steel* and the court in *Archer Daniels Midland* were concerned that they were interpreting "boilerplate" language, and assumed, without much analysis, that consistency in interpreting such language was an unqualified good. What *is* "boilerplate"? (One of your editors is particularly incensed by the term, having had, as a new associate, his ears pinned back for using precisely that word during negotiations!) Does the fact that the same (or similar) language is used in many indentures necessarily lead to the conclusion that they are to have the same meanings? What are the disadvantages of treating such language as conclusively (or at least presumptively) having a particular meaning? Is the stockholders' "contract" interpreted in the same way? Shouldn't it be under this reasoning—after all, most corporate charters use the same stylized language.

For extended criticism of *Sharon Steel*, *Harris*, and *Archer Daniels Midland*, see Tauke, Should Bonds Have More Fun? A Reexamination of the Debate Over Corporate Bondholder Rights, 1989 Colum. Bus. L. Rev. 1, 67-99.

---

c. Implied Covenant of Good Faith and Fair Dealing

Katz v. Oak Industries Inc.

508 A.2d 873 (Del. Ch. 1986)

ALLEN, Chancellor.

.... Few words more perfectly illustrate the deceptive dependability of language than the term "coercion" which is at the heart of the theory advanced by plaintiff as entitling him to a preliminary injunction in this case.

Plaintiff is the owner of long-term debt securities issued by Oak Industries, Inc. ("Oak"), a Delaware corporation; in this class action he seeks to enjoin the consummation of an exchange offer and consent solicitation made by Oak to holders of various classes of its long-term debt. As detailed below that offer is an integral part of a series of transactions that together would effect a major reorganization and recapitalization of Oak. The claim asserted is in essence, that the exchange offer is a coercive device and, in the circumstances, constitutes a breach of contract. This is the Court's opinion on plaintiff's pending application for a preliminary injunction.

I

* * *

Through its domestic and foreign subsidiaries and affiliated entities, Oak manufactures and markets component equipments used in consumer, industrial and military products (the "Components Segment"); produces communications equipment for use in cable television systems and satellite television systems (the "Communications Segment") and manufactures and markets laminates and other materials used in printed circuit board applications (the "Materials Segment"). During 1985, the Company has terminated certain other unrelated businesses. As detailed below, it has now entered into an agreement with Allied-Signal, Inc. for the sale of the Materials Segment of its business and is currently seeking a buyer for its Communications Segment.

Even a casual review of Oak's financial results over the last several years shows it unmistakably to be a company in deep trouble. During the period from January 1, 1982 through September 30, 1985, the Company has experienced unremitting losses from operations; on net sales of approximately $1.26 billion during that period ... it has lost over $335 million.... As a result its total stockholders' equity has first shriveled (from $260 million on 12/31/81 to $85 million on 12/31/83) and then disappeared completely (as of 9/30/85 there was a $62 million deficit in its stockholders' equity accounts).... Financial markets, of course, reflected this gloomy history.[2]

Unless Oak can be made profitable within some reasonably short time it will not continue as an operating company. Oak's board of directors, comprised almost entirely of outside directors, has authorized steps to buy the company time. In February, 1985, in order to reduce a burdensome annual cash interest obligation on its $230 million of then outstanding debentures, the Company offered to exchange such debentures for a combination of notes, common stock and warrants. As a result, approximately $180 million principal amount of the then outstanding debentures were exchanged. Since interest on certain of the notes issued in that exchange offer is payable in common stock, the effect of the 1985 exchange offer was to reduce to some extent the cash drain on the Company caused by its significant debt.

About the same time that the 1985 exchange offer was made, the Company announced its intention to discontinue certain of its operations and sell certain of its properties. Taking these steps, while effective to stave off a default and to reduce to some extent the immediate cash drain, did not address Oak's longer-range problems. Therefore, also during 1985 representatives of the Company held informal discussions with several interested parties exploring the possibility of an investment from, combi-

---

2. The price of the company's common stock has fallen from over $30 per share on December 31, 1981 to approximately $2 per share recently.... The debt securities that are the subject of the exchange offer here involved (see note 3 for identification) have traded at substantial discounts.

nation with or acquisition by another company. As a result of these discussions, the Company and Allied-Signal, Inc. entered into two agreements. The first, the Acquisition Agreement, contemplates the sale to Allied-Signal of the Materials Segment for $160 million in cash. The second agreement, the Stock Purchase Agreement, provides for the purchase by Allied-Signal for $15 million cash of 10 million shares of the Company's common stock together with warrants to purchase additional common stock.

The Stock Purchase Agreement provides as a condition to Allied-Signal's obligation that at least 85% of the aggregate principal amount of all of the Company's debt securities shall have tendered and accepted the exchange offers that are the subject of this lawsuit. Oak has six classes of such long term debt.[3] If less than 85% of the aggregate principal amount of such debt accepts the offer, Allied-Signal has an option, but no obligation, to purchase the common stock and warrants contemplated by the Stock Purchase Agreement. An additional condition for the closing of the Stock Purchase Agreement is that the sale of the Company's Materials Segment contemplated by the Acquisition Agreement shall have been concluded.

Thus, as part of the restructuring and recapitalization contemplated by the Acquisition Agreement and the Stock Purchase Agreement, the Company has extended an exchange offer to each of the holders of the six classes of its long-term debt securities. These pending exchange offers include a Common Stock Exchange Offer (available only to holders of the 9⅝% convertible notes) and the Payment Certificate Exchange Offers (available to holders of all six classes of Oak's long-term debt securities). The Common Stock Exchange Offer currently provides for the payment to each tendering noteholder of 407 shares of the Company's common stock in exchange for each $1,000 9⅝% note accepted. The offer is limited to $38.6 million principal amount of notes (out of approximately $83.9 million outstanding).

The Payment Certificate Exchange Offer is an any and all offer. Under its terms, a payment certificate, payable in cash five days after the closing of the sale of the Materials Segment to Allied-Signal, is offered in exchange for debt securities. The cash value of the Payment Certificate will vary depending upon the particular security tendered. In each instance, however, that payment will be less than the face amount of the obligation. The cash payments range in amount, per $1,000 of principal, from $918 to $655. These cash values however appear to represent a premium over the market prices for the Company's debentures as of the time the terms of the transaction were set.

The Payment Certificate Exchange Offer is subject to certain important conditions before Oak has an obligation to accept tenders under it. First, it is necessary that a minimum amount ($38.6 million principal amount out of $83.9 total outstanding principal amount) of the 9⅝% notes be tendered pursuant to the Common Stock Exchange Offer. Secondly, it is necessary that certain minimum amounts of each class of debt securities be tendered, together with consents to amendments to the underlying indentures.[4]

---

3. The three classes of debentures are: 13.65% debentures due April 1, 2001, 10½% convertible subordinated debentures due February 1, 2002, and 11⅞% subordinated debentures due May 15, 1998. In addition, as a result of the 1985 exchange offer the company has three classes of notes which were issued in exchange for debentures that were tendered in that offer. Those are: 13.5% senior notes due May 15, 1990, 9⅝% convertible notes due September 15, 1991 and 11⅝% notes due September 15, 1990.

4. The holders of more than 50% of the principal amount of each of the 13.5% notes, the 9⅝% notes and the 11⅝% notes and at least 66⅔% of the principal amount of the 13.65% debentures, 10½% debentures, and 11⅞% debentures, must validly tender such securities and consent to certain proposed amendments to the indentures governing those securities.

Indeed, under the offer one may not tender securities unless at the same time one consents to the proposed amendments to the relevant indentures.

The condition of the offer that tendering security holders must consent to amendments in the indentures governing the securities gives rise to plaintiff's claim of breach of contract in this case. Those amendments would, if implemented, have the effect of removing significant negotiated protections to holders of the Company's long-term debt including the deletion of all financial covenants. Such modification may have adverse consequences to debt holders who elect not to tender pursuant to either exchange offer.

Allied-Signal apparently was unwilling to commit to the $15 million cash infusion contemplated by the Stock Purchase Agreement, unless Oak's long-term debt is reduced by 85% (at least that is a condition of their obligation to close on that contract). Mathematically, such a reduction may not occur without the Company reducing the principal amount of outstanding debentures (that is the three classes of outstanding notes constitute less than 85% of all long-term debt). But existing indenture covenants ... prohibit the Company, so long as any of its long-term notes are outstanding, from issuing any obligation (including the Payment Certificates) in exchange for any of the debentures. Thus, in this respect, amendment to the indentures is required in order to close the Stock Purchase Agreement as presently structured.

Restrictive covenants in the indentures would appear to interfere with effectuation of the recapitalization in another way. Section 4.07 of the 13.50% Indenture provides that the Company may not "acquire" for value any of the 9⅝% Notes or 11⅞% Notes unless it concurrently "redeems" a proportionate amount of the 13.50% Notes. This covenant, if unamended, would prohibit the disproportionate acquisition of the 9⅝% Notes that may well occur as a result of the Exchange Offers; in addition, it would appear to require the payment of the "redemption" price for the 13.50% Notes rather than the lower, market price offered in the exchange offer.

In sum, the failure to obtain the requisite consents to the proposed amendments would permit Allied-Signal to decline to consummate both the Acquisition Agreement and the Stock Purchase Agreement.

* * *

II

Plaintiff's claim that the Exchange Offers and Consent Solicitation constitutes a threatened wrong to him and other holders of Oak's debt securities[6] appear [sic] to be summarized in paragraph 16 of this Complaint:

> The purpose and effect of the Exchange Offers is [1] to benefit Oak's common
> stockholders at the expense of the Holders of its debt securities, [2] to force
> the exchange of its debt instruments at unfair price and at less than face value
> of the debt instruments [3] pursuant to a rigged vote in which debt Holders
> who exchange, and who therefore have no interest in the vote, must consent to

6. It is worthy of note that a very high percentage of the principal value of Oak's debt securities are owned in substantial amounts by a handful of large financial institutions. Almost 85% of the value of the 13.50% Notes is owned by four such institutions (one investment banker owns 55% of that issue); 69.1% of the 9⅝% Notes are owned by four financial institutions (the same investment banker owning 25% of that issue) and 85% of the 11⅞% Notes are owned by five such institutions. Of the debentures, 89% of the 13.65% debentures are owned by four large banks; and approximately 45% of the two remaining issues is owned by two banks.

the elimination of protective covenants for debt Holders who do not wish to exchange.

[P]laintiff's claim is that no free choice is provided to bondholders by the exchange offer and consent solicitation. Under its terms, a rational bondholder is "forced" to tender and consent. Failure to do so would face a bondholder with the risk of owning a security stripped of all financial covenant protections and for which it is likely that there would be no ready market. A reasonable bondholder, it is suggested, cannot possibly accept those risks and thus such a bondholder is coerced to tender and thus to consent to the proposed indenture amendments.

It is urged this linking of the offer and the consent solicitation constitutes a breach of a contractual obligation that Oak owes to its bondholders to act in good faith. Specifically, plaintiff points to three contractual provisions from which it can be seen that the structuring of the current offer constitutes a breach of good faith. Those provisions (1) establish a requirement that no modification in the term of the various indentures may be effectuated without the consent of a stated percentage of bondholders; (2) restrict Oak from exercising the power to grant such consent with respect to any securities it may hold in its treasury; and (3) establish the price at which and manner in which Oak may force bondholders to submit their securities for redemption.

III

In order to demonstrate an entitlement to the provisional remedy of a preliminary injunction it is essential that a plaintiff show that it is probable that his claim will be upheld after final hearing; that he faces a risk of irreparable injury before final judgment will be reached in the regular course; and that in balancing the equities and competing hardships that preliminary judicial action may cause or prevent, the balance favors plaintiff....

I turn first to an evaluation of the probability of plaintiff's ultimate success on the merits of his claim. I begin that analysis with two preliminary points.... This case does not involve the measurement of corporate or directorial conduct against that high standard of fidelity required of fiduciaries when they act with respect to the interests of the beneficiaries of their trust. Under our law—and the law generally—the relationship between a corporation and the holders of its debt securities, even convertible debt securities, is contractual in nature.... Arrangements among a corporation, the underwriters of its debt, trustees under its indentures and sometimes ultimate investors are typically thoroughly negotiated and massively documented. The rights and obligations of the various parties are or should be spelled out in that documentation. The terms of the contractual relationship agreed to and not broad concepts such as fairness define the corporation's obligation to its bondholders.[7]

Thus, the first aspect of the pending Exchange Offers about which plaintiff complains—that "the purpose and effect of the Exchange Offers is to benefit Oak's common stockholders at the expense of the Holders of its debt"—does not itself appear to allege a cognizable legal wrong. It is the obligation of directors to attempt, within the law, to maximize the long-run interests of the corporation's stockholders; that they may

---

7. To say that the broad duty of loyalty that a director owes to his corporation and ultimately its shareholders is not implicated in this case is not to say, as the discussion below reflects, that as a matter of contract law a corporation owes no duty to bondholders of good faith and fair dealing. See, Restatement of Law, Contracts 2d, §205 [(1981)]. Such a duty, however, is quite different from the congeries of duties that are assumed by a fiduciary....

sometimes do so "at the expense" of others (even assuming that a transaction which one may refuse to enter into can meaningfully be said to be at his expense) does not for that reason constitute a breach of duty. It seems likely that corporate restructurings designed to maximize shareholder values may in some instances have the effect of requiring bondholders to bear greater risk of loss and thus in effect transfer economic value from bondholders to stockholders.... But if courts are to provide protection against such enhanced risk, they will require either legislative direction to do so or the negotiation of indenture provisions designed to afford such protection.

The second preliminary point concerns the limited analytical utility, at least in this context, of the word "coercive" which is central to plaintiff's own articulation of his theory of recovery. If, *pro arguendo*, we are to extend the meaning of the word coercion beyond its core meaning—dealing with the utilization of physical force to overcome the will of another—to reach instances in which the claimed coercion arises from an act designed to affect the will of another party by offering inducements to the act sought to be encouraged or by arranging unpleasant consequences for an alternative sought to be discouraged, then—in order to make the term legally meaningful at all—we must acknowledge that some further refinement is essential. Clearly some "coercion" of this kind is legally unproblematic. Parents may "coerce" a child to study with the threat of withholding an allowance; employers may "coerce" regular attendance at work by either docking wages for time absent or by rewarding with a bonus such regular attendance. Other "coercion" so defined clearly would be legally relevant (to encourage regular attendance by corporal punishment, for example). Thus, for purposes of legal analysis, the term "coercion" itself—covering a multitude of situations—is not very meaningful. For the word to have much meaning for purposes of legal analysis, it is necessary in each case that a normative judgment be attached to the concept ("inappropriately coercive" or "wrongfully coercive," etc.). But, it is then readily seen that what is legally relevant is not the conclusory term "coercion" itself but rather the norm that leads to the adverb modifying it.

In this instance, assuming that the Exchange Offers and Consent Solicitation can meaningfully be regarded as "coercive" (in the sense that Oak has structured it in a way designed—and I assume effectively so—to "force" rational bondholders to tender), the relevant legal norm that will support the judgment whether such "coercion" is wrongful or not will, for the reasons mentioned above, be derived from the law of contracts....

Modern contract law has generally recognized an implied covenant to the effect that each party to a contract will act with good faith towards the other with respect to the subject matter of the contract. *See, Restatement of Law, Contracts 2d*, §205 (1981).... The contractual theory for this implied obligation is well stated in a leading treatise:

> If the purpose of contract law is to enforce the reasonable expectations of parties induced by promises, then at some point it becomes necessary for courts to look to the substance rather than to the form of the agreement, and to hold that substance controls over form. What courts are doing here, whether calling the process "implication" of promises, or interpreting the requirements of "good faith," as the current fashion may be, is but a recognition that the parties occasionally have understandings or expectations that were so fundamental that they did not need to negotiate about those expectations. When the court "implies a promise" or holds that "good faith" requires a party not to violate those expectations, it is recognizing that sometimes silence says more than words, and it is understanding its duty to the spirit of the bargain is higher than its duty to the technicalities of the language. *Corbin on Contracts* (Kaufman Supp. 1984), §570.

It is this obligation to act in good faith and to deal fairly that plaintiff claims is breached by the structure of Oak's coercive exchange offer. Because it is an implied *contractual* obligation that is asserted as the basis for the relief sought, the appropriate legal test is not difficult to deduce. It is this: is it clear from what was expressly agreed upon that the parties who negotiated the express terms of the contract would have agreed to proscribe the act later complained of as a breach of the implied covenant of good faith—had they thought to negotiate with respect to that matter. If the answer to this question is yes, then, in my opinion, a court is justified in concluding that such act constitutes a breach of the implied covenant of good faith....

With this test in mind, I turn now to a review of the specific provisions of the various indentures from which one may be best able to infer whether it is apparent that the contracting parties—had they negotiated with the exchange offer and consent solicitation in mind—would have expressly agreed to prohibit contractually the linking of the giving of consent with the purchase and sale of the security.

IV

Applying the foregoing standard to the exchange offer and consent solicitation, I find first that there is nothing in the indenture provisions granting bondholders power to veto proposed modifications in the relevant indenture that implies that Oak may not offer an inducement to bondholders to consent to such amendments. Such an implication, at least where, as here, the inducement is offered on the same terms to each holder of an affected security, would be wholly inconsistent with the strictly commercial nature of the relationship.

Nor does the second pertinent contractual provision supply a ground to conclude that defendant's conduct violates the reasonable expectations of those who negotiated the indentures on behalf of the bondholders. Under that provision Oak may not vote debt securities held in its treasury. Plaintiff urges that Oak's conditioning of its offer to purchase debt on the giving of consents has the effect of subverting the purpose of that provision; it permits Oak to "dictate" the vote on securities which it could not itself vote.

The evident purpose of the restriction on the voting of treasury securities is to afford protection against the issuer voting as a bondholder in favor of modifications that would benefit it as issuer, even though such changes would be detrimental to bondholders. But the linking of the exchange offer and the consent solicitation does not involve the risk that bondholder interests will be affected by a vote involving anyone with a financial interest in the subject of the vote other than a bondholder's interest. That the consent is to be given concurrently with the transfer of the bond to the issuer does not in any sense create the kind of conflict of interest that the indenture's prohibition on voting treasury securities contemplates. Not only will the proposed consents be granted or withheld only by those with a financial interest to maximize the return on their investment in Oak's bonds, but the incentive to consent is equally available to all members of each class of bondholders. Thus the "vote" implied by the consent solicitation is not affected in any sense of those with a financial conflict of interest.

In these circumstances, while it is clear that Oak has fashioned the exchange offer and consent solicitation in a way designed to encourage consents, I cannot conclude that the offer violates the intendment of any of the express contractual provisions considered or, applying the test set out above, that its structure and timing breaches an implied obligation of good faith and fair dealing.

One further set of contractual provisions should be touched upon: Those granting to Oak a power to redeem the securities here treated at a price set by the relevant indentures. Plaintiff asserts that the attempt to force all bondholders to tender their securities at less than the redemption price constitutes, if not a breach of the redemption provision itself, at least a breach of an implied covenant of good faith and fair dealing associated with it. The flaw, or at least one fatal flaw, in this argument is that the present offer is not the functional equivalent of a redemption which is, of course, an act that the issuer may take unilaterally. In this instance it may happen that Oak will get tenders of a large percentage of its outstanding long-term debt securities. If it does, that fact will, in my judgment, be in major part a function of the merits of the offer (i.e., the price offered in light of the Company's financial position and the market value of its debt). To answer plaintiff's contention that the *structure* of the offer "forces" debt holders to tender, one only has to imagine what responses this offer would receive if the price offered did not reflect a premium over market but rather was, for example, ten percent of market value. The exchange offer's success ultimately depends upon the ability and willingness of the issuer to extend an offer that will be a financially attractive alternative to holders. This process is hardly the functional equivalent of the unilateral election of redemption and thus cannot be said in any sense to constitute a subversion by Oak of the negotiated provisions dealing with redemption of its debt.

Accordingly, I conclude that plaintiff has failed to demonstrate a probability of ultimate success on the theory of liability asserted.

V

An independent ground for the decision to deny the pending motion is supplied by the requirement that a court of equity will not issue the extraordinary remedy of preliminary injunction where to do so threatens the party sought to be enjoined with irreparable injury that, in the circumstances, seems greater than the injury that plaintiff seeks to avoid. *Eastern Shore National Gas Co.* v. *Stauffer Chemical Co.*, Del. Supr., 298 A.2d 322 (1972). That principal has application here.

Oak is in a weak state financially. Its board, comprised of persons of experience and, in some instances, distinction, have [sic] approved the complex and interrelated transactions outlined above. It is not unreasonable to accord weight to the claims of Oak that the reorganization and recapitalization of which the exchange offer is a part may present the last good chance to regain vitality for this enterprise. I have not discussed plaintiff's claim of irreparable injury, although I have considered it. I am satisfied simply to note my conclusion that it is far outweighed by the harm that an improvidently granted injunction would threaten to Oak.

For the foregoing reasons plaintiff's application for a preliminary injunction shall be denied.

IT IS SO ORDERED.

Notes and Questions

1. Why did the plaintiff bring suit? Given Oak's unfortunate financial circumstances, why wasn't he simply happy to be able to cash out? What might he have gained had he succeeded in enjoining the exchange offer and consent solicitation that he was losing in the transaction?

2. In *Katz*, Chancellor Allen notes: "But if courts are to provide protection against … enhanced risk [to bondholders], they will require either legislative direction to do so or the negotiation of indenture provisions designed to afford such protection." Why?

3. In its discussion of the implied covenant of good faith, the court refers to "the reasonable expectations of those who negotiated the indentures on behalf of the bondholders." Who are these people? Can you think of any reasons why their "reasonable expectations" might be different from those of the bondholders? If so, whose expectations should matter? Does the court's use of the ubiquitous modifier "reasonable" solve the problem?

4. In terms of the consent solicitation in *Katz*, is it fair for tendering debtholders who provide their consent to the waiver of financial covenants to influence the treatment of the nontendering debtholders going forward? To use a Titanic analogy, why should the passengers leaving on the ship's life boats have a say as to what music the band plays for those who remain stuck on deck? How would Chancellor Allen respond to this analogy?

5. Footnote 6 of the court's opinion notes the high proportion of Oak's debt held by institutional investors. As a general matter, institutions are the major corporate debtholders in America. Why do you think this is the case? Keep this question in mind as you continue your study of corporate debt. Is the concentration of debt ownership in financial institutions a good, bad, or indifferent phenomenon? How is it affected by the protections available to individual debtholders?

Problem — Coercing Bondholders

Barbary Airlines, Inc. ("Barbary"), negotiated a merger with Montgolfier Airline Corp. ("Montgolfier"), pursuant to which Montgolfier would merge with and into a subsidiary of Barbary, cashing out Montgolfier's stockholders. The merging corporations agreed that, following the merger, the subsidiary ("Montgolfier II") would pay a dividend of $1.75 per share to Barbary, its new parent. However, such a payment required the consent of Montgolfier's bondholders, who would continue to be bondholders of the subsidiary. In order to obtain such consents, Montgolfier has offered to pay each consenting bondholder either $35 in cash, or $125 in Montgolfier Airline ticket vouchers, for each $1,000 face amount of bonds.

Earhart, a Montgolfier bondholder, wants to sue to enjoin the consent proceeding and invalidate any consents already tendered. You are Earhart's counsel. Should Earhart bring this action? On what theories would she bring her case, and what are the likely results? Would the results be different if the economic inducements were offered to some bondholders and not others? If Montgolfier intentionally concealed them from the bondholders to whom they were not offered?

DeMott, The Biggest Deal Ever
Introduction to Symposium: Fundamental Corporate Changes: Causes, Effects, and Legal Responses, 1989 Duke L.J. 1-3

Twenty-five billion dollars buys a lot of Oreos, Winstons, and Milk Bone dog biscuits. In early December 1988, Kohlberg, Kravis, Roberts & Co. (KKR), a firm specializing in leveraged buyouts, won the contest for ownership and control of RJR Nabisco, Inc., a victory that resulted in the largest corporate control transaction in the United States to date. When the LBO was completed in 1989, the nineteenth-largest industrial company in the United States had increased its indebtedness from $5 billion to $20.1 billion. RJR Nabisco's former public shareholders received, in addition to cash, a package of preferred stock and notes convertible into common stock, but immediate control of the company, and its equity, passed to KKR in exchange for a $1.5 billion equity investment. KKR itself provided an estimated 1% of this equity investment, or $15 million, and a pool of funds that KKR gathered from institutional investors provided the remainder.

* * *

On October 19, 1988, F. Ross Johnson, the president and chief executive officer of RJR Nabisco, took the outside directors of his company's board out to dinner in Atlanta on the night before a board meeting. Mr. Johnson told the outside directors that he was considering leading an LBO for the company because the price of its stock had, despite his two-year effort to increase the stock's value by restructuring the company, continued to lag. The directors were stunned but did not object to Mr. Johnson's proposal: "We came to the conclusion that shareholders would be best served by a short-term gain," one of the directors recalled later. At the time of Mr. Johnson's proposal, RJR Nabisco was trading around $55 per share, and thus the stock market's implicit price tag on the entire company was around $13 billion.

Although Mr. Johnson's formal proposal did not emerge until a few weeks later, RJR Nabisco promptly issued a press release announcing that members of its senior management, in association with Shearson Lehman Hutton, would offer $17 billion, or $75 per share, to buy out RJR Nabisco's shareholders. This announcement promptly led to a steep drop in the price of the company's outstanding bonds. As a senior bond trader at Drexel Burnham Lambert ... said, "Bondholders suffer from those sorts of transactions.... It is clear that the industrial bond market cannot benefit from this deal." Indeed, institutional holders of RJR Nabisco bonds eventually sued, alleging that, among other things, the company neglected to disclose that discussions about a prospective LBO had already occurred when the holders bought their bonds in spring 1988.

For popular treatments of the RJR Nabisco leveraged buy-out, see Heylar & Burrough, Barbarians at the Gate (1990); Lampert, True Greed: What Really Happened in the Battle for RJR Nabisco (1990); Sterngold, The Board Room Battle for RJR Nabisco, N.Y. Times, Dec. 5, 1988, at A1.

Metropolitan Life Ins. Co. v. RJR Nabisco, Inc.
716 F. Supp. 1504 (S.D.N.Y. 1989)

WALKER, District Judge:

I. INTRODUCTION

The corporate parties to this action are among the country's most sophisticated financial institutions, as familiar with the Wall Street investment community and the securities market as American consumers are with the Oreo cookies and Winston cigarettes made by defendant RJR Nabisco, Inc. (sometimes "the company" or "RJR Nabisco"). The present action traces its origins to October 20, 1988, when F. Ross Johnson, then the Chief Executive Officer of RJR Nabisco, proposed a $17 billion leveraged buy-out ("LBO") of the company's shareholders, at $75 per share.[1] Within a few days, a bidding war developed among the investment group led by Johnson and the investment firm of Kohlberg Kravis Roberts & Co. ("KKR"), and others. On December 1,1988, a special committee of RJR Nabisco directors, established by the company specifically to consider the competing proposals, recommended that the company accept the KKR proposal, a $24 billion LBO that called for the purchase of the company's outstanding stock at roughly $109 per share.

[T]he bidding war for RJR Nabisco spawned at least eight lawsuits, filed before this Court, charging the company and its former CEO with a variety of securities and common law violations.[2] The Court agreed to hear the present action—filed even before the company accepted the KKR proposal—on an expedited basis, with an eye toward March 1, 1989, when RJR Nabisco was expected to merge with the KKR holding entities created to facilitate the LBO. On that date, RJR Nabisco was also scheduled to assume roughly $19 billion of new debt. After a delay unrelated to the present action, the merger was ultimately completed during the week of April 24, 1989.

Plaintiffs now allege, in short, that RJR Nabisco's actions have drastically impaired the value of bonds previously issued to plaintiffs by, in effect, misappropriating the value of those bonds to help finance the LBO and to distribute an enormous windfall to the company's shareholders. As a result, plaintiffs argue, they have unfairly suffered a multimillion dollar loss in the value of their bonds.[4]

On February 16, 1989, this Court heard oral argument on plaintiffs' motions.... Given plaintiffs' failure to show irreparable harm, the Court denied their request for injunctive relief. This initial ruling, however, left intact plaintiffs' underlying motions, which, together with defendants' cross-motions, now require attention.

The motions and cross-motions are based on plaintiffs' Amended Complaint, which sets forth nine counts.[6] Plaintiffs move for summary judgment pursuant to Fed. R. Civ.

---

1. A leveraged buy-out occurs when a group of investors, usually including members of a company's management team, buy the company under financial arrangements that include little equity and significant new debt. The necessary debt financing typically includes mortgages or high risk/high yield bonds, popularly known as "junk bonds." (Junk bonds are discussed *supra* at sections 2b(ii).) Additionally, a portion of this debt is generally secured by the company's assets. Some of the acquired company's assets are usually sold after the transaction is completed in order to reduce the debt incurred in the acquisition. Leveraged buy-outs are discussed *infra* at section 8a.

2. On December 7, 1989, this Court agreed to accept as related all actions growing out of the RJR Nabisco LBO. On January 4, 1989, the Court consolidated with the present suit an action brought by three KKR affiliates—RJR Holdings Corp., RJR Holdings Group, Inc., and RJR Acquisition Corporation—against the Jefferson-Pilot Life Insurance Company. KKR established those entities to effect the buyout of RJR Nabisco. Throughout this Opinion, these entities and their parent will be referred to collectively as "KKR." ...

4. Agencies like Standard & Poor's and Moody's generally rate bonds in two broad categories: investment grade and speculative grade. Standard & Poor's rates investment grade bonds from "AAA" to "BBB." Moody's rates those bonds from "AAA" to "Baa3." Speculative grade bonds are rated either "BB" and lower, or "Bal" and lower, by Standard & Poor's and Moody's, respectively. *See, e.g., Standard and Poor's Debt Rating Criteria* at 10-11. No one disputes that, subsequent to the announcement of the LBO, the RJR Nabisco bonds lost their "A" ratings.

6. Count I alleges a breach of an implied covenant of good faith and fair dealing (against defendant RJR Nabisco); Count II alleges fraud (against both defendants); Count III alleges violations of Section 10(b) of the Securities Exchange Act of 1934 (against both defendants); Count IV alleges violations of Section 11 of the 1933 Act (on behalf of plaintiff Jefferson-Pilot Life Insurance Company against both defendants); Count V is labeled "In Equity," and is asserted against both defendants; Count VI alleges breach of duties (against defendant Johnson); Count VII alleges tortious interference with property (against Johnson); Count VIII alleges tortious interference with contract

P. 56 against the company on Count I, which alleges a "Breach of Implied Covenant of Good Faith and Fair Dealing," and against both defendants on Count V, which is labeled simply "In Equity."

For its part, RJR Nabisco moves pursuant to Fed. R. Civ. P. 12(c) for judgment on the pleadings on Count I in full; on Count II (fraud) and Count III (violations of §10(b) of the Securities Exchange Act of 1934 and Rule 10b-5 promulgated thereunder) as to most of the securities at issue; and on Count V in full. In the alternative, the company moves for summary judgment on Counts I and V. In addition, RJR Nabisco moves pursuant to Fed. R. Civ. P. 9(b) to dismiss Counts II, III and IX (alleging violations of applicable fraudulent conveyance laws) for an alleged failure to plead fraud with requisite particularity. Johnson has moved to dismiss Counts II, III and V.

Although the numbers involved in this case are large, and the financing necessary to complete the LBO unprecedented,[8] the legal principles nonetheless remain discrete and familiar. Yet while the instant motions thus primarily require the Court to evaluate and apply traditional rules of equity and contract interpretation, plaintiffs do raise issues of first impression in the context of an LBO. At the heart of the present motions lies plaintiffs' claim that RJR Nabisco violated a restrictive covenant—not an explicit covenant found within the four corners of the relevant bond indentures, but rather an *implied* covenant of good faith and fair dealing—not to incur the debt necessary to facilitate the LBO and thereby betray what plaintiffs claim was the fundamental basis of their bargain with the company. The company, plaintiffs assert, consistently reassured its bondholders that it had a "mandate" from its Board of Directors to maintain RJR Nabisco's preferred credit rating. Plaintiffs ask this Court first to imply a covenant of good faith and fair dealing that would prevent the recent transaction, then to hold that this covenant has been breached, and finally to require RJR Nabisco to redeem their bonds.

RJR Nabisco defends the LBO by pointing to express provisions in the bond indentures that, *inter alia*, permit mergers and the assumption of additional debt. These provisions, as well as others that could have been included but were not, were known to the market and to plaintiffs, sophisticated investors who freely bought the bonds and were equally free to sell them at any time. Any attempt by this Court to create contractual terms *post hoc*, defendants contend, not only finds no basis in the controlling law and undisputed facts of this case, but also would constitute an impermissible invasion into the free and open operation of the marketplace.

For the reasons set forth below, this Court agrees with defendants. There being no express covenant between the parties that would restrict the incurrence of new debt, and no perceived direction to that end from covenants that are express, this Court will not imply a covenant to prevent the recent LBO and thereby create an indenture term that, while bargained for in other contexts, was not bargained for here and was not even within the mutual contemplation of the parties.

(against Johnson); and Count IX alleges a violation of the fraudulent conveyance laws (against RJR Nabisco).

8. On February 9, 1989, KKR completed its tender offer for roughly 74 percent of RJR Nabisco's common stock (of which approximately 97% of the outstanding shares were tendered) and all of its Series B Cumulative Preferred Stock (of which approximately 95% of the outstanding shares were tendered). Approximately $18 billion in cash was paid out to these stockholders. KKR acquired the remaining stock in the late April merger through the issuance of roughly $4.1 billion of pay-in-kind exchangeable preferred stock and roughly $1.8 billion in face amount of convertible debentures.

II. BACKGROUND

Summary judgment, of course, is appropriate only where "there is no genuine issue as to any material fact ..." Fed. R. Civ. P. 56(c)....

Both sides now move for summary judgment on Counts I and V.... Having carefully reviewed the submissions before it, the Court agrees with the parties that there is no genuine issue as to any material fact regarding these counts, and given the disposition of the motions as to Counts I and V, the Court, as it must, draws all reasonable inferences in favor of the plaintiffs.

A. *The Parties:*

Metropolitan Life Insurance Co. ("MetLife"), incorporated in New York, is a life insurance company that provides pension benefits for 42 million individuals.... MetLife alleges that it owns $340,542,000 in principal amount of six separate RJR Nabisco debt issues, bonds allegedly purchased between July 1975 and July 1988. Some bonds become due as early as this year, others will not become due until 2017. The bonds bear interest rates of anywhere from 8 to 10.25 percent. MetLife also owned 186,000 shares of RJR Nabisco common stock at the time this suit was filed.

Jefferson-Pilot Life Insurance Co. ("Jefferson-Pilot") is a North Carolina company that has more than $3 billion in total assets, $1.5 billion of which are invested in debt securities. Jefferson-Pilot alleges that it owns $9.34 million in principal amount of three separate RJR Nabisco debt issues, allegedly purchased between June 1978 and June 1988. Those bonds, bearing interest rates of anywhere from 8.45 to 10.75 percent, become due in 1993 and 1998.

RJR Nabisco, a Delaware corporation, is a consumer products holding company that owns some of the country's best known product lines, including LifeSavers candy, Oreo cookies, and Winston cigarettes. The company was formed in 1985, when R.J. Reynolds Industries, Inc. ("R.J. Reynolds") merged with Nabisco Brands, Inc. ("Nabisco Brands"). In 1979, and thus before the R.J. Reynolds-Nabisco Brands merger, R.J. Reynolds acquired the Del Monte Corporation ("Del Monte"), which distributes canned fruits and vegetables. From January 1987 until February 1989, co-defendant Johnson served as the company's CEO. KKR, a private investment firm, organizes funds through which investors provide pools of equity to finance LBOs.

B. *The Indentures:*

The bonds[9] implicated by this suit are governed by long, detailed indentures, which in turn are governed by New York contract law.... [T]hose indentures are often not the product of face-to-face negotiations between the ultimate holders and the issuing company. What remains equally true, however, is that underwriters ordinarily negotiate the terms of the indentures with the issuers. Since the underwriters must then sell or place the bonds, they necessarily negotiate in part with the interests of the buyers in mind.... [S]ophisticated investors like plaintiffs are well aware of the indenture terms and, presumably, review them carefully before lending hundreds of millions of dollars to any company.

Indeed, the prospectuses for the indentures contain a statement relevant to this action:

---

9. For the purposes of this Opinion, the terms "bonds," "debentures," and "notes" will be used interchangeably. Any distinctions among these terms are not relevant to the present motions.

The Indenture contains no restrictions on the creation of unsecured short term debt by [RJR Nabisco] or its subsidiaries, no restriction on the creation of unsecured Funded Debt by [RJR Nabisco] or its subsidiaries which are not Restricted Subsidiaries, and no restriction on the payment of dividends by [RJR Nabisco].[11]

Further, as plaintiffs themselves note, the contracts at issue "[do] not impose debt limits, since debt is assumed to be used for productive purposes."

1. The relevant Articles:

A typical RJR Nabisco indenture contains thirteen Articles. At least four of them are relevant to the present motions and thus merit a brief review.

Article Three delineates the covenants of the issuer. Most important, it first provides for payment of principal and interest. It then addresses various mechanical provisions regarding such matters as payment terms and trustee vacancies. The Article also contains "negative pledge" and related provisions, which restrict mortgages or other liens on the assets of RJR Nabisco or its subsidiaries and seek to protect the bondholders from being subordinated to other debt.

Article Five describes various procedures to remedy defaults and the responsibilities of the Trustee....

Article Nine governs the adoption of supplemental indentures. It provides, *inter alia*, that the Issuer and the Trustee can

add to the covenants of the Issuer such further covenants, restrictions, conditions or provisions as its Board of Directors by Board Resolution and the Trustee shall consider to be for the protection of the holders of Securities, and to make the occurrence, or the occurrence and continuance, of a default in any such additional covenants, restrictions, conditions or provisions an Event of Default permitting the enforcement of all or any of the several remedies provided in this Indenture as herein set forth....

Article Ten addresses a potential "Consolidation, Merger, Sale or Conveyance," and explicitly sets forth the conditions under which the company can consolidate or merge into or with any other corporation. It provides explicitly that RJR Nabisco "may consolidate with, or sell or convey, all or substantially all of its assets to, or merge into or with any other corporation," so long as the new entity is a United States corporation, and so long as it assumes RJR Nabisco's debt. The Article also requires that any such transaction not result in the company's default under any indenture provision....

2. The elimination of restrictive covenants:

In its Amended Complaint, MetLife lists the six debt issues on which it bases its claims. Indentures for two of those issues—the 10.25 percent Notes due in 1990, of which MetLife continues to hold $10 million, and the 8.9 percent Debentures due in 1996, of which MetLife continues to hold $50 million—once contained express

---

11. While nine securities are at issue in this suit, the parties agree—and the Court's review confirms—that the separate indentures mirror one another in all important respects.... Indeed, plaintiffs have submitted a helpful Addendum in which they outline what they term "[t]ypical RJR Nabisco [i]ndenture [t]erms."

Thus, the prospectus statement quoted above has its counterpart in each of the other prospectuses.

covenants that, among other things, restricted the company's ability to incur precisely the sort of debt involved in the recent LBO. In order to eliminate those restrictions, the parties to this action renegotiated the terms of those indentures, first in 1983 and then again in 1985.

MetLife acquired $50 million principal amount of 10.25 percent Notes from Del Monte in July of 1975. To cover the $50 million, MetLife and Del Monte entered into a loan agreement. That agreement restricted Del Monte's ability, among other things, to incur the sort of indebtedness involved in the RJR Nabisco LBO. In 1979, R.J. Reynolds—the corporate predecessor to RJR Nabisco—purchased Del Monte and assumed its indebtedness. Then, in December of 1983, R.J. Reynolds requested MetLife to agree to deletions of those restrictive covenants in exchange for various guarantees from R.J. Reynolds. A few months later MetLife and R.J. Reynolds entered into a guarantee and amendment agreement reflecting those terms. Pursuant to that agreement, and in the words of Robert E. Chappell, Jr., MetLife's Executive Vice President, MetLife thus "gave up the restrictive covenants applicable to the Del Monte debt ... in return for [the parent company's] guarantee and public covenants."

MetLife acquired the 8.9 percent Debentures from R.J. Reynolds in October of 1976 in a private placement. A promissory note evidenced MetLife's $100 million loan. That note, like the Del Monte agreement, contained covenants that restricted R.J. Reynolds' ability to incur new debt. In June of 1985, R.J. Reynolds announced its plans to acquire Nabisco Brands in a $3.6 billion transaction that involved the incurrence of a significant amount of new debt. R.J. Reynolds requested MetLife to waive compliance with these restrictive covenants in light of the Nabisco acquisition.

In exchange for certain benefits, MetLife agreed to exchange its 8.9 percent debentures—which *did* contain explicit debt limitations—for debentures issued under a public indenture—which contain no explicit limits on new debt. An internal MetLife memorandum explained the parties' understanding:

> [MetLife's $100 million financing of the Nabisco Brands purchase] had its origins in discussions with RJR regarding potential covenant violations in the 8.90% Notes. More specifically, *in its acquisition of Nabisco Brands, RJR was slated to incur significant new long-term debt, which would have caused a violation in the funded indebtedness incurrence tests in the 8.90% Notes*. In the discussions regarding [MetLife's] willingness to consent to the additional indebtedness, *it was determined that a mutually beneficial approach to the problem* was to 1) agree on a new financing having a rate and a maturity desirable for [MetLife] and 2) modify the 8.90% Notes. The former was accomplished with agreement on the proposed financing, while the latter was accomplished by [MetLife] agreeing to substitute RJR's public indenture covenants for the covenants in the 8.90% Notes. In addition to the covenant substitution, RJR has agreed to "debenturize" the 8.90% Notes upon [MetLife's] request. This will permit [MetLife] to sell the 8.90% Notes to the public. (emphasis added).

3. The recognition and effect of the LBO trend:

.... At least as early as 1982, MetLife recognized an LBO's effect on bond values.[14] In the spring of that year, MetLife participated in the financing of an LBO of a company

---

14. MetLife itself began investing in LBOs as early as 1980. *See* MetLife Special Projects Memorandum, dated June 17, 1989 ("[MetLife's] history of investing in leveraged buyout transactions dates back to 1980; and through 1984, [MetLife] reviewed a large number of LBO investment

called Reeves Brothers ("Reeves"). At the time of that LBO, MetLife also held bonds in that company. Subsequent to the LBO, as a MetLife memorandum explained, the "Debentures of Reeves were downgraded by Standard & Poor's from BBB to B and by Moody's from Baal to Ba3, thereby lowering the value of the Notes and Debentures held by [MetLife]."

MetLife further recognized its "inability to force any type of payout of the [Reeves'] Notes or the Debentures as a result of the buy-out [which] was somewhat disturbing at the time we considered a participation in the new financing. However," the memorandum continued,

> our concern was tempered since, as a stockholder in [the holding company used to facilitate the transaction], we would benefit from the increased net income attributable to the continued presence of the low coupon indebtedness. The recent downgrading of the Reeves Debentures and the consequent "loss" in value has again raised questions regarding our ability to have forced a payout. *Questions have also been raised about our ability to force payouts in similar future situations, particularly when we would not be participating in the buyout financing.*

Id. (emphasis added). In the memorandum, MetLife sought to answer those very "questions" about how it might force payouts in "similar future situations."

> *A method of closing this apparent "loophole," thereby forcing a payout of [MetLife's] holdings, would be through a covenant dealing with a change in ownership.* Such a covenant is fairly standard in financings with privately held companies.... It provides the lender with an option to end a particular borrowing relationship via some type of special redemption....

Id., at 2 (emphasis added).

A more comprehensive memorandum, prepared in late 1985, evaluated and explained several aspects of the corporate world's increasing use of mergers, takeovers and other debt-financed transactions. That memorandum first reviewed the available protection for lenders such as MetLife:

> Covenants are incorporated into loan documents to ensure that after a lender makes a loan, the creditworthiness of the borrower and the lender's ability to reach the borrower's assets do not deteriorate substantially. *Restrictions on the incurrence of debt,* sale of assets, mergers, dividends, restricted payments and loans and advances to affiliates *are some of the traditional negative covenants that can help protect lenders in the event their obligors become involved in undesirable merger/takeover situations.* (emphasis added).

The memorandum then surveyed market realities:

> Because almost any industrial company is apt to engineer a takeover or be taken over itself, *Business Week* says that investors are beginning to view debt securities of high grade industrial corporations as Wall Street's riskiest investments. In addition, *because public bondholders do not enjoy the protection of any restrictive covenants,* owners of high grade corporates face substantial losses from takeover situations, if not immediately, then when the bond market fi-

---

opportunities presented to us by various investment banking firms and LBO specialists. Over this five-year period, [MetLife] invested, on a direct basis, approximately $430 million to purchase debt and equity securities in 10 such transactions ...").

nally adjusts.... [T]here have been 10-15 merger/takeover/LBO situations where, *due to the lack of covenant protection, [MetLife] has had no choice but to remain a lender to a less creditworthy obligor.* ...

Indeed, MetLife does not dispute that, as a member of a bondholders' association, it received and discussed a proposed model indenture, which included a "comprehensive covenant" entitled "Limitations on Shareholders' Payments."[16] As becomes clear from reading the proposed—but never adopted—provision, it was "intend[ed] to provide protection against all of the types of situations in which shareholders profit at the expense of bondholders." *Id.* The provision dictated that the "[c]orporation will not, and will not permit any [s]ubsidiary to, directly or indirectly, make any [s]hareholder [p]ayment unless ... (1) the aggregate amount of all [s]hareholder payments during the period [at issue] ... shall not exceed [figure left blank]." The term "shareholder payments" is defined to include "restructuring distributions, stock repurchases, debt incurred or guaranteed to finance merger payments to shareholders, etc." *Id.* at i.

Apparently, that provision—or provisions with similar intentions—never went beyond the discussion stage at MetLife. That fact is easily understood; indeed, MetLife's own documents articulate several reasonable, undisputed explanations:

> While it would be possible to broaden the change in ownership covenant to cover any acquisition-oriented transaction, we might well encounter significant resistance in implementation with larger public companies.... With respect to implementation, we would be faced with the task of imposing a non-standard limitation on potential borrowers, *which could be a difficult task in today's highly competitive marketplace. Competitive pressures notwithstanding, it would seem that management of larger public companies would be particularly opposed to such a covenant since its effect would be to increase the cost of an acquisition* (due to an assumed debt repayment), a factor that could well lower the price of any tender offer (thereby impacting shareholders).

(emphasis added). The November 1985 memorandum explained that

> ... public securities do not contain any meaningful covenants, [and therefore] it would be very difficult for [MetLife] to demand takeover protection in public bonds. Such a requirement would effectively take us out of the public industrial market. A recent *Business Week* article does suggest, however, that there is increasing talk among lending institutions about requiring blue chip companies to compensate them for the growing risk of downgradings. *This talk, regarding such protection as restrictions on future debt financings, is met with skepticism by the investment banking community which feels that CFO's are not about to give up the option of adding debt and do not really care if their companies' credit ratings drop a notch or two.* (emphasis added).

The Court quotes these documents at such length not because they represent an "admission" or "waiver" from MetLife, or an "assumption of risk" in any tort sense, or its "consent" to any particular course of conduct—all terms discussed at even greater length in the parties' submissions. Rather, the documents set forth the background to the present action, and highlight the risks inherent in the market itself, for any investor.

---

16. That exhibit is an August 5, 1988 letter from the New York law firm of Kaye, Scholer, Fierman, Hays & Handler. A partner at that firm sent the letter to "Indenture Group Members," including MetLife, who participated in the Institutional Bondholders' Rights Association ("the IBRA"). The "Limitations on Shareholders' Payments" provision appears in a draft IBRA model indenture.

Investors as sophisticated as MetLife and Jefferson-Pilot would be hard-pressed to plead ignorance of these market risks....

* * *

III. DISCUSSION

* * *

The indentures at issue clearly address the eventuality of a merger. They impose certain related restrictions not at issue in this suit, but no restriction that would prevent the recent RJR Nabisco merger transaction.... The indentures also explicitly set forth provisions for the adoption of new covenants, if such a course is deemed appropriate.... [N]o explicit provision either permits or prohibits an LBO....

* * *

A. *Plaintiffs' Case Against the RJR Nabisco LBO*:

1. Count One: The implied covenant:

In their first count, plaintiffs assert that [d]efendant RJR Nabisco owes a continuing duty of good faith and fair dealing in connection with the contract [i.e., the indentures] through which it borrowed money from MetLife, Jefferson-Pilot and other holders of its debt, including a duty not to frustrate the purpose of the contracts to the debtholders or to deprive the debtholders of the intended object of the contracts—purchase of investment-grade securities.

> In the "buy-out," the [c]ompany breaches the duty [or implied covenant] of good faith and fair dealing by, *inter alia*, destroying the investment grade quality of the debt and transferring that value to the "buy-out" proponents and to the shareholders.

In effect, plaintiffs contend that express covenants were not necessary because an *implied* covenant would prevent what defendants have now done.

A plaintiff always can allege a violation of an express covenant. If there has been such a violation, of course, the court need not reach the question of whether or not an *implied* covenant has been violated. That inquiry surfaces where, while the express terms may not have been technically breached, one party has nonetheless effectively deprived the other of those express, explicitly bargained-for benefits. In such a case, a court will read an implied covenant of good faith and fair dealing into a contract to ensure that neither party deprives the other of "the fruits of the agreement." *See, e.g. Greenwich Village Assoc. v. Salle*, 110 A.D.2d 111, 115, 493 N.Y.S.2d 461, 464 (1st Dep't 1985).... Such a covenant is implied only where the implied term "is consistent with other mutually agreed upon terms in the contract." *Sabetay v. Sterling Drug, Inc.*, 69 N.Y.2d 329, 335, 514 N.Y.S.2d 209, 212, 506 N.E.2d 919, 922 (1987). In other words, the implied covenant will only aid and further the explicit terms of the agreement and will never impose an obligation "'which would be inconsistent with other terms of the contractual relationship.'" *Id.* (citation omitted). Viewed another way, the implied covenant of good faith is breached only when one party seeks to prevent the contract's performance or to withhold its benefits. *See Collard v. Incorporated Village of Flower Hill*, 75 A.D.2d 631, 632, 427 N.Y.S.2d 301, 302 (2d Dep't 1980). As a result, it thus ensures that parties to a contract perform the substantive, bargained-for terms of their agreement....

In contracts like bond indentures, "an implied covenant ... derives its substance directly from the language of the Indenture, and 'cannot give the holders of Debentures any rights inconsistent with those set out in the Indenture.' [*Where*] *plaintiffs' contractual rights[have not been] violated, there can have been no breach of an implied covenant.*" *Gardner & Florence Call Cowles Foundation* v. *Empire Inc.*, 589 F. Supp. 669, 673 (S.D.N.Y. 1984) ... (emphasis added).

* * *

The appropriate analysis, then, is first to examine the indentures to determine "the fruits of the agreement" between the parties, and then to decide whether those "fruits" have been spoiled—which is to say, whether plaintiffs' contractual rights have been violated by defendants.

The American Bar Foundation's *Commentaries on Indentures* ("the *Commentaries*"), relied upon and respected by both plaintiffs and defendants, describes the rights and risks generally found in bond indentures like those at issue:

> The most obvious and important characteristic of long-term debt financing is that the holder ordinarily has not bargained for and does not expect any substantial gain in the value of the security to compensate for the risk of loss.... [T]he significant fact, *which accounts in part for the detailed protective provisions of the typical long-term debt financing instrument*, is that *the lender (the purchaser of the debt security) can expect only interest at the prescribed rate plus the eventual return of the principal.* Except for possible increases in the market value of the debt security because of changes in interest rates, the debt security will seldom be worth more than the lender paid for it.... It may, of course, become worth much less. Accordingly, the typical investor in a long-term debt security is primarily interested in every reasonable assurance that the principal and interest will be paid when due.... Short of bankruptcy, *the debt security holder can do nothing to protect himself against actions of the borrower which jeopardize its ability to pay the debt unless he ... establishes his rights through contractual provisions set forth in the debt agreement or indenture.*

Id. at 1-2 (1971) (emphasis added).

A review of the parties' submissions and the indentures themselves satisfies the Court that the substantive "fruits" guaranteed by those contracts and relevant to the present motions include the periodic and regular payment of interest and the eventual repayment of principal. ("The Issuer covenants ... that it will duly and punctually pay ... the principal of, and interest on, each of the Securities ... at the respective times and in the manner provided in such Securities ...."). According to a typical indenture, a default shall occur if the company either (1) fails to pay principal when due; (2) fails to make a timely sinking fund payment; (3) fails to pay within 30 days of the due date thereof any interest on the date; or (4) fails duly to observe or perform any of the express covenants or agreements set forth in the agreement. Plaintiffs' Amended Complaint nowhere alleges that RJR Nabisco has breached these contractual obligations; interest payments continue and there is no reason to believe that the principal will not be paid when due.

It is not necessary to decide that indentures like those at issue could never support a finding of additional benefits, under different circumstances with different parties. Rather, for present purposes, it is sufficient to conclude what obligation is *not* covered, either explicitly or implicitly, by these contracts held by these plaintiffs. Accordingly, this Court holds that the "fruits" of these indentures do not include an implied restrictive covenant that would prevent the incurrence of new debt to facilitate the recent LBO. To hold otherwise would permit these plaintiffs to straightjacket the company in order to guarantee their investment. These plaintiffs do not invoke an implied covenant of good faith to protect a legitimate, mutually contemplated benefit of the indentures; rather, they seek to have this Court create an additional benefit for which they did not bargain.

Although the indentures generally permit mergers and the incurrence of new debt, there admittedly is not an explicit indenture provision to the contrary of what plaintiffs now claim the implied covenant requires. That absence, however, does *not* mean that the Court should imply into those very same indentures a covenant of good faith so broad that it imposes a new, substantive term of enormous scope. This is so particularly where, as here, that very term—a limitation on the incurrence of additional debt—has in other past contexts been expressly bargained for; particularly where the indentures grant the company broad discretion in the management of its affairs, as plaintiffs admit, particularly where the indentures explicitly set forth specific provisions for the adoption of new covenants and restrictions, and *especially* where there has been no breach of the parties' bargained-for contractual rights on which the implied covenant necessarily is based. While the Court stands ready to employ an implied covenant of good faith to ensure that such bargained-for rights are performed and upheld, it will not, however, permit an implied covenant to shoehorn into an indenture additional terms plaintiffs now wish had been included....

Plaintiffs argue in the most general terms that the fundamental basis of all these indentures was that an LBO along the lines of the recent RJR Nabisco transaction would never be undertaken, that indeed *no* action would be taken, intentionally or not, that would significantly deplete the company's assets. Accepting plaintiffs' theory, their fundamental bargain with defendants dictated that nothing would be done to jeopardize the extremely high probability that the company would remain able to make interest payments and repay principal over the 20 to 30 year indenture term—and perhaps by logical extension even included the right to ask a court "to make sure that plaintiffs had made a good investment." *Gardner*, 589 F. Supp. at 674. But as Judge Knapp aptly concluded in *Gardner*, "Defendants ... were under a duty to carry out the terms of the contract, but not to make sure that plaintiffs had made a good investment. The former they have done; the latter we have no jurisdiction over." *Id.* Plaintiffs' submissions and Metlife's previous undisputed internal memoranda remind the Court that a "fundamental basis" or a "fruit of an agreement" is often in the eye of the beholder, whose vision may well change along with the market, and who may, with hindsight, imagine a different bargain than the one he actually and initially accepted with open eyes.

The sort of unbounded and one-sided elasticity urged by plaintiffs would interfere with and destabilize the market. And this Court, like the parties to these contracts, cannot ignore or disavow the marketplace in which the contract is performed. Nor can it ignore the expectations of that market—expectations, for instance, that the terms of an indenture will be upheld, and that a court will not, *sua sponte*, add new substantive terms to that indenture as it sees fit. The Court has no reason to believe that the market, in evaluating bonds such as those at issue here, did not discount for the possibility that any company, even one the size of RJR Nabisco, might engage in an LBO heavily financed by debt. That the bonds did not lose any of their value until the October 20, 1988 announcement of a possible RJR Nabisco LBO only suggests that the market had theretofore evaluated the risks of such a transaction as slight.

The Court recognizes that the market is not a static entity, but instead involves what plaintiffs call "evolving understanding[s]." Just as the growing prevalence of LBO's has helped change certain ground rules and expectations in the field of mergers and acquisitions, so too it has obviously affected the bond market, a fact no one disputes....

To respond to changed market forces, new indenture provisions can be negotiated, such as provisions that were in fact once included in the 8.9 percent and 10.25 percent debentures implicated by this action. New provisions could include special debt restrictions or change-of-control covenants. There is no guarantee, of course, that companies like RJR Nabisco would accept such new covenants; parties retain the freedom to enter into contracts as they choose. But presumably, multi-billion dollar investors like plaintiffs have some say in the terms of the investments they make and continue to hold. And, presumably, companies like RJR Nabisco need the infusions of capital such investors are capable of providing.

Whatever else may be true about this case, it certainly does not present an example of the classic sort of form contract or contract of adhesion often frowned upon by courts. In those cases, what motivates a court is the strikingly inequitable nature of the parties' respective bargaining positions.... Plaintiffs here entered this "liquid trading market," with their eyes open and were free to leave at any time. Instead they remained there notwithstanding its well understood risks.

* * *

In the final analysis, plaintiffs offer no objective or reasonable standard for a court to use in its effort to define the sort of actions their "implied covenant" would permit a corporation to take, and those it would not.[28] Plaintiffs say only that investors like themselves rely upon the "skill" and "good faith" of a company's board and management, and that their covenant would prevent the company from "destroy[ing] ... the legitimate expectations of its long-term bondholders." As is clear from the preceding discussion, however, plaintiffs have failed to convince the Court that by upholding the explicit, bargained-for terms of the indenture, RJR Nabisco has either exhibited bad faith or destroyed plaintiffs' *legitimate*, protected expectations.

.... [The Court] concludes that courts are properly reluctant to imply into an integrated agreement terms that have been and remain subject to specific, explicit provisions, where the parties are sophisticated investors, well versed in the market's assumptions, and do not stand in a fiduciary relationship with one another.

It is also not to say that defendants were free willfully or knowingly to misrepresent or omit material facts to sell their bonds. Relief on claims based on such allegations would of course be available to plaintiffs, if appropriate[29]—but those claims properly sound in fraud, and come with requisite elements. Plaintiffs also remain free to assert their claims based on the fraudulent conveyance laws, which similarly require specific proof.[30] Those burdens cannot be avoided by resorting to an overbroad, superficially appealing, but legally insufficient, implied covenant of good faith and fair dealing.

---

28. Under plaintiffs' theory, bondholders might ask a court to prohibit a company like RJR Nabisco not only from engaging in an LBO, but also from entering a new line of business—with the attendant costs of building new physical plants and hiring new workers—or from acquiring new businesses such as RJR Nabisco did when it acquired Del Monte.

29. The Court, of course, today takes no position on this issue.

30. As noted elsewhere, plaintiffs can also allege violations of express terms of the indentures.

2. Count Five: In Equity:

* * *

In their papers, plaintiffs variously attempt to justify Count V as being based on unjust enrichment, frustration of purpose, an alleged breach of something approaching a fiduciary duty, or a general claim of unconscionability. Each claim fails. First, as even plaintiffs recognize, an unjust enrichment claim requires a court first to find that "the circumstances [are] such that in equity and good conscience the defendant should make restitution." *See, e.g., Chase Manhattan Bank* v. *Banque Intra, S.A.*, 274 F. Supp. 496, 499 (S.D.N.Y. 1967). Plaintiffs have not alleged a violation of a single explicit term of the indentures at issue, and on the facts alleged this Court has determined that an implicit covenant of good faith and fair dealing has not been violated. Under these circumstances, this Court concludes that defendants need not, "in equity and good conscience," make restitution.

Second, in support of their motions plaintiffs claim frustration of purpose. Yet even resolving all ambiguities and drawing all reasonable inferences in plaintiffs' favor, their claim cannot stand. A claim of frustration of purpose has three elements:

> First, the purpose that is frustrated must have been a principal purpose of that party in making the contract.... The object must be so completely the basis of the contract that, as both parties understand, without it the transaction would make little sense. Second, the frustration must be substantial. It is not enough that the transaction has become less profitable for the affected party or even that he will sustain a loss. The frustration must be so severe that it is not fairly to be regarded as within the risks that he assumed under the contract. Third, the non-occurrence of the frustrating event must have been a basic assumption on which the contract was made.

Restatement (Second) of Contracts, 265 comment a (1981).... [T]here is no indication here that an alleged refusal to incur debt to facilitate an LBO was the "essence" or "principal purpose" of the indentures, and no mention of such an alleged restriction is made in the agreements. Further, while plaintiffs' bonds may have lost some of their value, "[d]ischarge under this doctrine has been limited to instances where a virtually cataclysmic, wholly unforeseeable event *renders the contract valueless to one party.*" *United States* v. *General Douglas MacArthur Senior Village, Inc.*, 508 F.2d 377, 381 (2d Cir. 1974) (emphasis added). That is not the case here. Moreover, "the frustration of purpose defense is not available where, as here, the event which allegedly frustrated the purpose of the contract ... was clearly foreseeable." *VJK Productions* v. *Friedman/Meyer Productions*, 565 F. Supp. 916 (S.D.N.Y. 1983) (citation omitted). Faced with MetLife's internal memoranda, plaintiffs cannot but admit that "MetLife has been concerned about 'buy-outs' for several years." Nor do plaintiffs provide any reasonable basis for believing that a party as sophisticated as Jefferson-Pilot was any less cognizant of the market around it.[32]

Third, plaintiffs advance a claim that remains based, their assertions to the contrary notwithstanding, on an alleged breach of a fiduciary duty. Defendants go to great lengths to prove that the law of Delaware, and not New York, governs this question. De-

---

32. At least one of Jefferson-Pilot's directors—Clemmie Dixon Spangler—not only was aware of the possibility of an LBO of a company like RJR Nabisco, but he also in fact *proposed* an LBO of RJR Nabisco *itself*, a fact plaintiffs do not dispute. Spangler apparently never mentioned his unsolicited bid for RJR Nabisco to his fellow Jefferson-Pilot directors.

fendants' attempt to rely on Delaware law is readily explained by even a cursory reading of *Simons v. Cogan*, 549 A.2d 300, 303 (Del. 1988), the recent Delaware Supreme Court ruling which held, *inter alia*, that a corporate bond "represents a contractual entitlement to the repayment of a debt and does not represent an equitable interest in the issuing corporation necessary for the imposition of a trust relationship with concomitant fiduciary duties." Before such a fiduciary duty arises, "an existing property right or equitable interest supporting such a duty must exist." *Id.* at 304. A bondholder, that court concluded, "acquires no equitable interest, and remains a creditor of the corporation whose interests are protected by the contractual terms of the indenture." *Id.* Defendants argue that New York law is not to the contrary, but the single Supreme Court case they cite—a case decided over fifty years ago that was not squarely presented with the issue addressed by the *Simons* court—provides something less than dispositive support. *See Marx v. Merchants' National Properties, Inc.*, 148 Misc. 6, 7, 265 N.Y.S. 163, 165 (1933). For their part, plaintiffs more convincingly demonstrate that New York law applies than that New York law recognizes their claim.[34]

Regardless, this Court finds *Simons* persuasive, and believes that a New York court would agree with that conclusion. In the venerable case of *Meinhard v. Salmon*, 249 N.Y. 458, 164 N.E. 545 (1928), then Chief Judge Cardozo explained the obligations imposed on a fiduciary, and why those obligations are so special and rare:

> Many forms of conduct permissible in a workaday world for those acting at arm's length, are forbidden to those bound by fiduciary ties. A trustee is held to something stricter than the morals of the market place. Not honesty alone, but the punctilio of an honor the most sensitive, is then the standard of behavior. As to this there has developed a tradition that is unbending and inveterate. Uncompromising rigidity has been the attitude of courts of equity when petitioned to undermine the rule of undivided loyalty.... Only thus has the level of conduct for fiduciaries been kept at a level higher than that trodden by the crowd.

Id. at 464 (citation omitted). Before a court recognizes the duty of a "punctilio of an honor the most sensitive," it must be certain that the complainant is entitled to more than the "morals of the market place," and the protections offered by actions based on fraud, state statutes or the panoply of available federal securities laws. This Court has concluded that the plaintiffs presently before it—sophisticated investors who are unsecured creditors—are not entitled to such additional protections.

Equally important, plaintiffs' position on this issue—that "A Company May Not Deliberately Deplete its Assets to the Injury of its Debtholders," provides no reasonable or workable limits, and is thus reminiscent of their implied covenant of good faith. Indeed, many indisputably legitimate corporate transactions would not survive plaintiffs' theory. With no workable limits, plaintiffs' envisioned duty would extend equally to trade creditors, employees, and every other person to whom the defendants are liable in any way. Of all such parties, these informed plaintiffs least require a Court's equitable protection; not only are they willing participants in a largely impersonal market, but they also possess the financial sophistication and size to secure their own protection.

Finally, plaintiffs cannot seriously allege unconscionability, given their sophistication and, at least judging from this action, the sophistication of their legal counsel

---

34. .... Ultimately, the point is academic; as explained below, the Court would grant defendants summary judgment on this count under either New York or Delaware law.

as well. Under the undisputed facts of this case, ... this Court finds no actionable unconscionability.

* * *

III. CONCLUSION

For the reasons set forth above, the Court grants defendants summary judgment on Counts I and V, judgment on the pleadings for certain of the securities at issue in Count III, and dismisses for want of requisite particularity Counts II, III, and IX. All remaining motions made by the parties are denied in all respects. Plaintiffs shall have twenty days to replead.

SO ORDERED.

Denouement

Settlement

On January 24, 1991, RJR Nabisco settled this litigation with Metropolitan Life and Jefferson-Pilot by permitting them to exchange all pre-buyout debt for other securities, including equity and new debt. In addition, RJR Nabisco agreed to pay plaintiffs' legal fees and expenses. Metropolitan Life, claiming to be satisfied with the settlement, said it would offer to purchase the bonds of investors not covered by the settlement at or near par. *See* Hylton, Metropolitan Life Settles Its Bond Dispute With RJR, N.Y. Times, Jan. 25, 1991, at D1.

RJR Nabisco

RJR Nabisco did not perform especially well immediately after the LBO. To reduce the $29.6 billion in LBO debt, RJR Nabisco sold $6.2 billion in assets leading to the termination of more than 46,000 employees. In July of 1990 a floundering junk bond market forced KKR to inject an additional $1.7 billion in equity to refinance its debt and protect RJR Nabisco from insolvency. A cigarette price war with Philip Morris in 1993 triggered a 25% drop in RJR Nabisco's stock price while anti-tobacco pressure from Washington depressed the stock price throughout 1994. To make matters worse, in 1995 RJR Nabisco was named as a defendant in 667 tobacco lawsuits. (The tobacco industry, including RJR Nabisco, settled the tobacco litigation in late 1998 by agreeing to pay $200 billion over 25 years to more than 40 states.) On the bright side, strong sales for Snackwell's, Oreos, and Ritz crackers led to a 1995 public offering of 19.5% of Nabisco Holdings, the food unit of RJR Nabisco. Before the equity offering, debt was divided between RJR and Nabisco, with RJR carrying $31.4 billion and Nabisco carrying $11.8 billion.

In June 1999, due to pressure from corporate raider Carl Icahn and a crippling debt burden, RJR Nabisco split its cigarette and food groups by spinning off R.J. Reynolds Tobacco as a public company, and renaming the remainder Nabisco Group Holdings.[1]

---

1. RJR Nabisco most likely would have separated the food and tobacco groups sooner but for the fear of "fraudulent conveyance" lawsuits threatened by plaintiffs in the on-going tobacco litigation. They accused the company of attempting to put valuable assets beyond the reach of anti-tobacco litigants. This obstacle was overcome by attaching RJR Nabisco's existing liability (from tobacco litigation settlements) to both the tobacco and food groups.

As part of the spin-off, R.J. Reynolds Tobacco retired its LBO debt when it sold its overseas cigarette arm to Japan Tobacco for $7.8 billion. In 2000, Icahn, who was apparently irate about Nabisco Group's stock performance, increased his ownership stake in Nabisco Group to 9.6% and commenced a hostile tender offer. In response, Nabisco Group's board put the entire company up for auction, and (ironically) Philip Morris was finally awarded the food company when it raised its bid to $55 per share. Icahn fared well with the sale, making a 68% gain of $893 million for shares he purchased in RJR Nabisco from late 1995 to mid-2000.

In 2004, R.J. Reynolds Tobacco combined with Brown & Williamson Tobacco Corporation to form the publicly traded Reynolds American Inc.

KKR

Investors who bought into KKR's 1987 buyout fund may be the deal's biggest losers. The fund invested $3.1 billion in RJR Nabisco at $5.62 per share (on a cost adjusted basis). In March 1995, KKR unloaded its remaining stake in RJR Nabisco for about $5.73 per share to Borden Inc., but not for cash but rather for ownership of Borden. The $3.1 billion investment produced single digit annual returns, a far cry from the 25% to 30% annual returns KKR had grown accustomed to in the 1980's. Fortunately, other investments made by the 1987 buyout fund, including the takeover of Duracell Batteries, proved much more profitable. KKR has told investors that the 1987 buyout fund had a compound annual return of more than 10%. *See* Norris, Kolhberg Kravis Readies the Banal Finale to the Greatest Leveraged Buyout on Wall Street, N.Y. Times, July 8, 2004, at C7.

KKR's members fared much better. While the $126 million they personally invested in the deal did not appreciate significantly, KKR collected almost $500 million in fees, including a $75 million transaction fee on the original deal, $60 million in "advisory fees," $2.3 million in directors' fees for KKR partners who served on RJR Nabisco's board, and a 1.5% management fee on the LBO fund yielding $279 million on the RJR deal alone. *See* Lesly, "Barbarians" Revisited: KKR's Buyout of RJR Nabisco Was a Major Fizzle for Investors, Bus. Week, Apr. 3, 1995, at 138.

According to Fortune Magazine, "RJR turned out to be a watershed, a costly and damaging miscue after which KKR went through a period of embarrassing sloppiness—misjudging markets and managements—that eroded its competitive position. Says Kravis: 'Quite frankly, we got sort of arrogant and made some terrible mistakes.'" Loomis, KKR: The Sequel, Fortune, June 13, 2005, at 64.

Since 2000, KKR has experienced a comeback on a global basis. It led the two largest Canadian buyouts—the C$2.5 billion buyout of Shoppers Drug Mart in 2000, and the C$3.1 billion buyout of Yellow Pages Group in 2002. In addition, it led the largest buyout ever in France—the €4.94 billion buyout of Legrand in 2002. Back in the U.S., KKR led the $4.5 billion buyout of PanAmSat Corporation in 2004.

Ross Johnson

Ross Johnson, the RJR CEO who fired the first shot in the takeover war, walked away from the deal with $50 million and an annual pension of $1 million. He divides his time between homes in Florida and Vail. In 2003, he joined the board of directors of Authentidate, Inc. and, in 2005, he became Chairman of that board. Mr. Johnson is also the Chairman and Chief Executive Officer of RJM Group, a management and investment firm.

Notes and Questions

1. What are the distinguishing characteristics between debt and equity that give rise to the disparate legal treatment they receive? Do these differences significantly distinguish debtholders from stockholders? In other words, is the nature of their relationship with the corporation different, and, if so, how?

2. The court in *Metropolitan Life* rejects plaintiffs' argument that an implied covenant of good faith precluded RJR Nabisco from acquiring additional debt to facilitate the leveraged buy-out. What is an implied covenant of good faith? Where does it come from? When is it imposed?

How does an implied covenant of good faith differ from fiduciary duty? *See* Burton, Breach of Contract and the Common Law Duty to Perform in Good Faith, 94 Harv. L. Rev. 369 369-73 (1980):

> A majority of American jurisdictions, the *Restatement (Second) of Contracts*, and the Uniform Commercial Code (U.C.C.) now recognize the duty to perform a contract in good faith as a general principle of contract law. The conduct of virtually any party to any contract accordingly may be vulnerable to claims of breach stemming from this obligation.[4] Yet neither courts nor commentators have articulated an operational standard that distinguishes good faith performance from bad faith performance.[5] The good faith performance doctrine consequently appears as a license for the exercise of judicial or juror intuition,[6] and presumably results in unpredictable and inconsistent applications. Repeated common law adjudication, however, has enriched the concept of good faith performance so that an operational standard now can be articulated and evaluated.
>
> The good faith performance doctrine establishes a standard for contract interpretation and a covenant that is implied in every contract. The good faith question often arises because a contract is an exchange expressed imperfectly and projected into an uncertain future. Contract parties rely on the good faith

---

4. This Article concentrates on claims of bad faith giving rise to a breach of contract rather than on claims of bad faith asserted against a party who concedes the breach but claims to have substantially performed. In the latter case, good faith performance is one of several factors bearing upon substantial performance....

5. *See generally* Farnsworth, *Good Faith Performance and Commercial Reasonableness Under the Uniform Commercial Code*, 30 U. Chi. L. Rev. 666 (1963); Summers, "*Good Faith*" in General Contract Law and the Sales Provisions of the Uniform Commercial Code, 54 Va. L. Rev. 195 (1968). Professor Summers does not purport to identify the criteria that judges use or ought to use in deciding whether particular conduct is in bad faith. Instead, he asserts that

> good faith is an "excluder." It is a phrase without general meaning or (meanings) of its own and serves to exclude a wide range of heterogeneous forms of bad faith. In a particular context the phrase takes on specific meaning but usually this is only by way of contrast with the specific form of bad faith actually or hypothetically ruled out.

Id. at 201. Professor Summers identifies six categories of bad faith in contract performance: evasion of the spirit of the deal, lack of diligence and slacking off, willfully rendering only "substantial" performance, abuse of a power to specify terms, abuse of a power to determine compliance, and interference with or failure to cooperate in the other party's performance. *Id.* at 232-43. He identifies similar categories relating to contract formation and enforcement. *Id.* at 220-32, 243-52. No effort is made to develop a unifying theory that explains what these categories have in common. Indeed, the assertion is made that one cannot or should not do so. *Id.* at 204-07....

6. The question of a contract party's good faith performance generally is one of fact....

of their exchange partners because detailed planning may be ineffectual or inadvisable. Therefore, express contract terms alone are insufficient to determine a party's good faith in performance.

Even so, the courts employ the good faith performance doctrine to effectuate the intentions of parties, or to protect their reasonable expectations. Standards expressed in these terms, however, are of little aid in applying the doctrine. They direct the inquiry away from duties imposed upon the parties irrespective of their assent. But they direct attention to the amorphous totality of the factual circumstances at the time of formation, and fail to distinguish relevant from irrelevant facts with that realm. The analysis would be advanced further by an operational standard that respects the autonomy of contract parties and calls the relevant facts to the foreground of the totality of the circumstances.

This requires a better understanding of the contractual expectation interest. Traditionally, the expectation interest is viewed as comprising the property, services, or money to be received by the promisee. This Article suggests that it also encompasses the expected cost of performance to the promisor. This expected cost consists of alternative opportunities forgone upon entering a particular contract.

The cost perspective is essential to a proper understanding of the good faith performance doctrine, even though it is not necessary when clear express promises are breached. Good faith limits the exercise of discretion in performance conferred on one party by the contract. When a discretion-exercising party may determine aspects of the contract, such as quantity, price, or time, it controls the other's anticipated benefits. Such a party may deprive the other of these anticipated benefits for a legitimate (or good faith) reason. The same act will be a breach of the contract if undertaken for an illegitimate (or bad faith) reason. Therefore, the traditional focus on the benefits due the promisee is inadequate.

Bad faith performance occurs precisely when discretion is used to recapture opportunities forgone upon contracting—when the discretion-exercising party refuses to pay the expected costs of performance. Good faith performance, in turn, occurs when a party's discretion is exercised for any purpose within the reasonable contemplation of the parties at the time of formation—to capture opportunities that were preserved upon entering the contract, interpreted objectively. The good faith performance doctrine therefore directs attention to the opportunities forgone by a discretion-exercising party at formation, and to that party's reasons for exercising discretion during performance.

Also consider Judge Hand's statement in Hotchkiss v. National City Bank of New York, 200 F. 287, 293 (S.D.N.Y. 1911):

.... A contract has, strictly speaking, nothing to do with the personal, or individual, intent of the parties. A contract is an obligation attached by the mere force of law to certain acts of the parties, usually words, which ordinarily accompany and represent a known intent. If, however, it were proved by twenty bishops that either party, when he used the words, intended something else than the usual meaning which the law imposes upon them, he would still be held, unless there were some mutual mistake, or something else of the sort. Of course, if it appear by other words, or acts, of the parties, that they attribute a peculiar meaning to such words as they use in the contract, that meaning will prevail, but only by virtue of the other words, and not because of their unexpressed intent.

And Judge Frank's concurrence in Ricketts v. Pennsylvania R. Co., 153 F.2d 757, 760-62 (2d Cir. 1946):

> In the early days of this century a struggle went on between the respective proponents of two theories of contracts, (a) the "actual intent" theory—or "meeting of the minds" or "will" theory—and (b) the so-called "objective" theory.[2] Without doubt, the first theory had been carried too far: Once a contract has been validly made, the courts attach legal consequences to the relation created by the contract, consequences of which the parties usually never dreamed—as, for instance, where situations arise which the parties had not contemplated. As to such matters, the "actual intent" theory induced much fictional discourse which imputed to the parties intentions they plainly did not have.

> But the objectivists also went too far. They tried (1) to treat virtually all the varieties of contractual arrangements in the same way, and (2), as to all contracts in all their phases, to exclude, as legally irrelevant, consideration of the actual intention of the parties or either of them, as distinguished from the outward manifestation of that intention. The objectivists transferred from the field of torts that stubborn anti-subjectivist, the "reasonable man"; so that, in part at least, advocacy of the "objective" standard in contracts appears to have represented a desire for legal symmetry, legal uniformity, a desire seemingly prompted by aesthetic impulses. Whether (thanks to the "subjectivity" of the jurymen's reactions and other factors) the objectivists' formula, in its practical workings, could yield much actual objectivity, certainty, and uniformity may well be doubted.[6] At any rate, the sponsors of complete "objectivity" in contracts largely won out in the wider generalizations of the Restatement of Contracts and in some judicial pronouncements.

> Influenced by their passion for excessive simplicity and uniformity, many objectivists have failed to give adequate special consideration to releases of claims for personal injuries, and especially to such releases by employees to their employers. Williston, the leader of the objectivists, insists that, as to all contracts, without differentiation, the objective theory is essential because [it is] "founded upon the fundamental principle of the security of business transactions."

> He goes to great lengths to maintain this....

Finally, Chancellor Allen, in a case dealing with preferred stockholders, compared the implied covenant of good faith with fiduciary analysis. In HB Korenvaes Invs., L.P. v.

---

2. .... The "actual intent" theory, said the objectivists, being "subjective" and putting too much stress on unique individual motivations, would destroy that legal certainty and stability which a modern commercial society demands. They depicted the "objective" standard as a necessary adjunct of a "free enterprise" economic system. In passing, it should be noted that they arrived at a sort of paradox. For a "free enterprise" system is, theoretically, founded on "individualism"; but, in the name of economic individualism, the objectivists refused to consider those reactions of actual specific individuals which sponsors of the "meeting-of-the-minds" test purported to cherish. "Economic individualism" thus shows up as hostile to real individualism. This is nothing new: The "economic man" is of course an abstraction, a "fiction." ...

6. .... Perhaps the most fatuous of all notions solemnly voiced by learned men who ought to know better is that when legal rules are "clear and complete" litigation is unlikely to occur.... [T]housands of decisions yearly turn on disputes concerning the facts, i.e., as to whether clear-cut legal rules were in fact violated. It is the uncertainty about the "facts" that creates most of the unpredictability of decisions....

Marriott Corp., [1993 Transfer Binder] Fed. Sec. L. Rep. (CCH) ¶ 97,728 (Del. Ch. June 9, 1993), he held that the dispute at issue was contractual and not fiduciary, and wrote:

> Of course even where a court concludes that contract principles govern the analysis, the need to address questions of ambiguity as to the scope of rights and duties under the certificate of designation may remain. The cognitive limitations of drafters, imperfect information and the nature of language itself assure that in contract law as well as fiduciary law, good faith disagreements about the nature of the duty will arise. Indeed the contract doctrine of an implied covenant of good faith and fair dealing may be thought in some ways to function analogously to the fiduciary concept.

In Katz v. Oak Indus. Inc., *supra* at the beginning of this section 4c, Chancellor Allen described the test for identifying a breach of the duty of good faith: "is it clear from what was expressly agreed upon that the parties who negotiated the express terms of the contract would have agreed to proscribe the act later complained of as a breach of the implied covenant of good faith—had they thought to negotiate with respect to that matter." What does this suggest about the Chancellor's understanding of fiduciary obligation? Is he correct?

3. The court quotes from Gardner & Florence Call Cowles Found. v. Empire Inc.: "'[Where] plaintiffs' contractual rights [have not been] violated, there can have been no breach of an implied covenant.'" What does this tell you about the implied covenant of good faith?

In Hartford Fire Ins. Co. v. Federated Dep't Stores, Inc., 723 F. Supp. 976, 990-93 (S.D.N.Y. 1989), the court dismissed the plaintiffs' causes of action for breach of an implied covenant of good faith and fair dealing. In discussing plaintiffs' contention that defendants had breached their implied covenant of good faith and fair dealing in the indenture by permitting a leveraged takeover of the issuer to occur, the court wrote:

> However, the implied covenant of good faith and fair dealing does not provide a court *carte blanche* to rewrite the parties' agreement. Thus, a court cannot imply a covenant inconsistent with terms expressly set forth in the contract.... In addition, "[t]he mere exercise of one's contractual rights, without more, cannot constitute ... a breach [of the implied covenant of good faith and fair dealing]." [Broad v. Rockwell Int'l Corp., 642 F.2d 929, 957 (5th Cir. 1981)]. Nor can a court imply a covenant to supply additional terms for which the parties did not bargain....
>
> The argument the Plaintiffs urge on this court violates each of these strictures. The Indenture expressly authorized Federated to merge with another company and to incur additional debt. Under the heading "Consolidation, Merger, Sale, or Conveyance," the Indenture provided: "Nothing contained in this Indenture or in any of the Securities shall prevent any consolidation or merger of the Company with or into any other corporation...." Indenture §11.01. The Indenture conditioned this right in three respects ... [, all of which were satisfied by the merger.] The Indenture then reiterated: "Nothing contained in this Indenture or in any of the Securities shall prevent the Company from merging into itself any other corporation (whether or not affiliated with the Company)." Indenture §11.02. The Indenture also expressly permitted Federated to incur additional debt, provided it secured the Notes "equally and ratably" with any new debt guaranteed by Federated's assets. Indenture §4.05.
>
> An implied covenant prohibiting Federated from merging with CRTF [Corporation ("CRTF")] or incurring additional debt for that purpose would

directly contravene these provisions and penalize Federated for exercising its rights under the Indenture. The Plaintiffs counter that this language applies to a "traditional merger," ... and to "debt in the ordinary course of business, for the purpose of expanding, developing and strengthening its business." *Id.* Moreover, permitting courts to weigh the virtues of such transactions on a case-by-case basis threatens to inject an impermissible degree of uncertainty into the bond market....

Implying a term barring Federated's merger with CRTF also would require the court to add a substantive provision for which the parties did not bargain. That is especially troublesome in light of the fact that the Indenture could easily have been drafted to incorporate expressly the terms the Plaintiffs now urge this court to imply. For example, the Indenture could have barred mergers altogether, permitted the Noteholders to participate in a tender offer by making the Notes convertible into stock, or required the Notes to be redeemed in the event of a takeover. It also could have restricted the amount of additional debt Federated could incur or imposed ceilings on the ratios of debt to equity, debt to assets, or earnings to fixed charges....

The fact that these terms appeared nowhere in the Indenture does not mean the court now should imply them to protect the parties' bargain. In fact the opposite appears to be true. Because the risk of a takeover—and the indenture provisions available to limit that risk—were well-known, to imply such provisions could impose on the parties terms they affirmatively excluded from their contract. It also could have broader ramifications. As Judge Walker recently observed:

> The sort of unbounded and one-sided elasticity urged by plaintiffs would interfere with and destabilize the market. And this Court, like the parties to these contracts, cannot ignore or disavow the marketplace in which the contract is performed. Nor can it ignore the expectations of that market—expectations, for instance, that the terms of an indenture will be upheld, and that a court will not, *sua sponte*, add new substantive terms to that indenture as it sees fit. The Court has no reason to believe that the market, in evaluating bonds such as those at issue here, did not discount for the possibility that any company, even one the size of RJR Nabisco, might engage in an LBO heavily financed by debt.

Metropolitan Life [Ins. Co. v. RJR Nabisco, Inc., 716 F. Supp. 1504, 1520 (S.D.N.Y. 1989)].

Could the court have found for plaintiffs without relying on the covenant of good faith?

4. Why does Judge Walker spend so much time analyzing the knowledge, sophistication, and bargaining power of plaintiffs in *Metropolitan Life*? Does he treat these factors as relevant in his legal analysis? If not, of what relevance (if any) are they?

In Geren v. Quantum Chem. Corp., 832 F. Supp. 728 (S.D.N.Y. 1993), Judge Leval rejected plaintiff bondholder's attempt to distinguish *Metropolitan Life* on the basis of the sophistication of the investors in the latter case: "I do not believe Judge Walker contemplated a cause of action that would lie in favor of ordinary investors but not in favor of market professionals.... It is not as if these Bonds were issued on unconscionable terms that duped unsophisticated investors; nor is this a case where the Bonds seemed to carry protections that were contradicted by refinements in the fine print.... The sophistication of the investors in *RJR Nabisco* does not involve a meaningful distinction." *Id.* at 734. Should it?

5. Is the court right to be solicitous of the bond markets? What is the judge's underlying view of the purpose of law, at least as expressed in this case?

6. The cases generally deal with the relationship of debt to the corporation. What theory of the corporation underlies this treatment? Is it meaningful to talk of a relationship to the corporation in this context? Do the particular types of problems for debtholders presented by the cases inform your answer?

7. Does denial of fiduciary rights to debtholders reveal an underlying theory of fiduciary duty? Is it the same in all of the cases? For example, does the philosophy of Judge Walker in *Metropolitan Life* appear to be the same as that of the Delaware Supreme Court as expressed in *Simons*?

8. With which of these approaches to bondholders' rights do you agree? How would you address the problems presented by the cases in this subsection? Does the simple imposition of fiduciary duties on "the corporation" help? On the board? If not, why not? What alternative approaches can you suggest?

9. The court in *Metropolitan Life* notes that significant differences originally existed in the protections provided under RJR's privately negotiated indentures and the indentures for its public debt. Why do you think these differences existed? *See* Moody's Investors Service, Moody's Special Comment: Event Risk: Moody's Amplifies Its Views on Indenture Protection Issues, Jan. 5, 1989 ("Standard covenant protection has deteriorated since the 1960s and the early 1970s"). Should the reason for this distinction influence the outcome of *Metropolitan Life*? The court further notes that public bond indentures "... are often not the product of face-to-face negotiations between the ultimate holders and the issuing company." Rather, negotiations typically occur between the company's management and the bond's underwriters. Obviously, in the *Metropolitan Life* case, plaintiffs' sophistication and market power diminished the likelihood of their demonstrating a fiduciary relationship. Would this be an equally valid conclusion with respect to an individual bondholder?

10. Extra-contractual protection for bondholders *might* not matter if adequate information with respect to bond terms is absorbed by the market and incorporated into bond pricing.[a] Professor Marcel Kahan surveyed the empirical literature examining this "informational efficiency" of the bond market. Kahan, The Qualified Case Against Mandatory Terms in Bonds, 89 Nw. U. L. Rev. 565 (1995). He found that only a limited number of studies examined whether the legal terms of bonds are incorporated into their price at issuance, but noted some inverse correlation between protective covenants and price, which is what one would expect to find if these terms were incorporated in price. From these, and other studies in different contexts, Kahan concludes that "at least some legal terms are priced. Moreover, there is no evidence pointing to particular informational inefficiencies in the market for newly issued bonds. To the contrary, the primary market for newly issued bonds is more informationally efficient than the secondary bond market." *Id.* at 579. However, he goes on to note that these studies do not support the conclusion that legal terms are accurately priced (although they do not support the contrary either). Finally, he notes the possibility that some terms may not be priced at all. He then goes on to argue that the institutional setting in which bonds are issued and priced, especially the very heavy concentration of institutional bond ownership,

---

a. We say "*might* not" because we believe that law serves other values in addition to promoting market efficiency.

the standardization of bond covenants and judicial consistency in the treatment of bond contract analysis, all diminish the effects of any informational inefficiencies that might be present.

11. A possible example of market forces at work is the development of the "friendly put," otherwise known as a "poison put," a bond covenant giving the bondholder the right to sell her bonds back to the issuer at full face value upon the occurrence of certain contingencies, like a tender offer or merger. We say "possible example" of market forces because it is not clear *why* these puts have been included in new debt issues or added to outstanding issues. Douglas Cook and John Easterwood have asserted:

> Event risk covenants or "poison puts" could be included in corporate debt for three reasons. First, poison puts, as the name suggests, could be designed to make firms less attractive as takeover targets and thus provide an additional mechanism for strengthening managerial resistance to hostile bids. This view will be termed the "entrenchment hypothesis." ... Puts and related provisions serve this purpose only if they impose some cost on prospective bidders. Such a cost could be explicit in the form of a put price above par or implicit if it increases the bidder's costs of obtaining additional financing. Prospectuses of bonds with poison puts frequently include statements like:
>
> > Since the events described in this section could be expected to occur in connection with certain forms of takeover attempts, these provisions could deter hostile or friendly acquisitions of the Company where the person attempting the acquisition views itself as unable to finance the purchase of the principal amount of the Notes which may be tendered to the Company upon occurrence of a Designated Event.[1]
>
> The entrenchment hypothesis predicts a negative stock price reaction at the issue announcement of protected bonds. The entrenchment hypothesis has no predicted impact on the value of an issuing firm's outstanding debt.[2]

* * *

> A second potential reason for event risk covenants is to protect bondholders from wealth transfers that allegedly accompany debt-financed takeovers and recapitalization. This would reduce the probability and extent of expropriation of bondholder wealth, rather than protect incumbent managers. This reason will be called the "bondholder protection hypothesis." If puts served this purpose, their inclusion would not reduce the probability of *all* takeovers. They will only protect against takeovers in which wealth transfers are a consideration.
>
> The reaction of the firm's existing bonds under the bondholder protection hypothesis depends on whether or not protection to them has been increased. If event risk covenants extend protection to other bond issues, then these bonds should appreciate in value because risk has been reduced. Poison puts might extend event risk protection if, by themselves, they reduce the probability of wealth-transferring takeovers. Puts might also extend event risk protection to outstanding debt if the outstanding debt requires redemption or con-

---

1. This passage is taken from the prospectus of the 10¾ percent notes issued by Grummon Corporation that mature in 1999.
2. This assumes the firm is currently not in financial distress. In cases of financial distress, a takeover may add value to bondholders by reducing potential bankruptcy costs. This is not the case for any issues in our sample.

sent before payment can be made to the holders of the put bond.[4] If puts and related covenants do not increase the protection of existing debt, then the bondholder protection hypothesis has no implication for the prices of the firm's outstanding debt.

The impact on stock returns reflects the net of two opposite influences. First, takeovers motivated primarily by wealth transfers are hindered, and shareholders lose the potential to receive these transfers. Second, debt with event risk covenants is issued at an interest cost that is lower than unprotected debt. Managers acting in the interests of shareholders would choose to issue bonds with poison puts only if the interest cost savings outweigh the foregone wealth transfers. Thus, the bondholder protection hypothesis predicts a non-negative stock price reaction to issues of protected debt.[5]

* * *

The entrenchment and bondholder protection hypotheses have been presented thus far as mutually exclusive. However, the interests of managers and bondholders may be complementary under some circumstances. Managers undertake actions that protect their positions. By coincidence, these actions could also offer benefits to bondholders. In this case, the interests of managers and bondholders would be aligned in that both wish to guard against hostile, debt-financed takeovers. Consequently, the interests of managers and bondholders would conflict with those of shareholders. This view is termed the "mutual interest hypothesis," and it suggests that stock price reactions could be negative while the price reaction of existing bonds could be positive. In addition, the wealth effects for debt and equity could be negatively correlated because more protective puts would make the stock price response more negative and the price response for existing debt more positive. No previous study has tested the mutual interest hypothesis.

The notion that managers and bondholders have mutual interests is supported by the literature that argues that they have similar claims on the firm. For example, Amihud and Lev (1981) find evidence for their hypothesis that conglomerate acquisitions are motivated by management's desire to reduce the risk associated with their own income by undertaking actions that are inconsistent with shareholder wealth maximization. Since managers and bondholders similarly benefit from risk-reducing activities like decreasing the likelihood of leverage increasing takeovers, the interests of managers and bondholders are aligned against the interests of shareholders.

Cook and Easterwood conclude:

This study finds that the issuance of bonds with poison puts has a negative effect on stockholders and a positive effect on outstanding bondholders, while

---

4. About 15 percent of the prospectuses for our sample specifically mention such covenants in the issuer's other debt. In all but one of these instances, the bond with the poison put is subordinated debt. In some other cases, the other debt is identified as bank loans; in other cases, the other debt is simply described as senior indebtedness.

5. To the extent that factors other than the presence of event risk covenants might cause a negative equity reaction to the announcement of any new bond issue, the bondholder protection hypothesis predicts that the reaction is no more negative for bonds with event risk covenants than bonds without such covenants. The entrenchment hypothesis predicts that bonds with event risk covenants will have a mere negative stock price reaction than bonds without these covenants.

a control sample of straight bond issues without poison puts has no stock price effect. Furthermore, a cross-sectional regression for the put sample explains a significant portion of the outstanding bondholders' returns and indicates a strong negative relation between stock and outstanding bond returns. No such relation exists for the nonput sample. These results are consistent with the mutual interest hypothesis, which suggests that the issuance of poison put bonds protects managers from hostile takeovers and bondholders from event risk, at the expense of stockholders.

Cook & Easterwood, Poison Put Bonds: An Analysis of Their Economic Role, 49 J. of Fin. 1905 (1994).

Professors Kahan and Klausner offer a different evaluation of antitakeover provisions:

Change of control covenants implicate the interests of shareholders, bondholders, and managers. Bondholders value protection against the increased leverage that often accompanies an acquisition or recapitalization. By providing bondholders with such protection, a change of control covenant can reduce a firm's agency cost of debt and thereby increase its value. To the extent that a covenant's protection is reflected in the price of a bond, shareholders reap the benefit of this increased value.

Managers, however, have parochial interests in change of control covenants and substantial control over their terms. Consequently, a corporation's managers may omit management buyouts, other friendly acquisitions and recapitalizations from the scope of a covenant, even though coverage of these transactions would reduce the firm's agency cost of debt. Furthermore, managers may use a change of control covenant to impede hostile control changes, even though these control changes would increase firm value. This overbroad and selective coverage would help insulate managers from the threat of a hostile control change and thereby increase their firm's agency cost of equity.

Empirically, we find that change of control covenants reflect both of these managerial interests. Substantially all bonds issued prior to October 1988—the date the RJR Nabisco buyout was announced—contain Hostile Control Change Covenants,[a] which encumber only hostile takeovers and proxy contests, usually without regard of their effect on bond values. These covenants combine incomplete bondholder protection with strong management entrenchment features. On the other hand, most bonds issued after October 1988 contain Dual Trigger Covenants. These covenants provide significantly more, though incomplete, protection to bondholders, but still contain some management entrenchment features.

We explain this improved protection by factors related to the leveraged buyout of RJR Nabisco. Both before and after the buyout, providing takeover protection to bondholders would have increased firm value. The buyout, however, served as a catalyst for the development of a novel contractual provision. It in-

---

a. Kahan and Klausner divided all covenants into three catagories: Hostile Control Change Covenants—those triggered by takeover related events that occur without the approval of management; Pure Rating Decline Convenants—those triggered by a bond rating decline; and Dual Trigger Covenants—those triggered by takeover related events that coincide with a bond rating decline. [Eds.]

creased the magnitude of the gains to be derived from such a provision and may have enhanced the pricing of bondholder protection. These two effects increased the benefits to shareholders of including protective covenants in bond indentures.

Managers may have accepted the restrictions imposed by Dual Trigger Covenants for two reasons. First, the gains in share value achieved with these covenants may have outweighed management's parochial interest. Second, as our data suggest, these covenants were used predominantly by managers apparently concerned more with becoming targets of hostile takeovers or proxy contests than with the possibility of a management buyout, friendly acquisition, or recapitalization.

The same two factors may also have contributed to the infrequent use of Dual Trigger Covenants in 1991. The decline in takeover activity reduced the gains to be derived from such covenants. Also, the virtual disappearance of hostile acquisitions and the drop in proxy contests reduced managers' interest in fending off hostile control changes relative to their interest in retaining unencumbered discretion to engage in transactions they favor.

Our findings are inconsistent with those commentators who claim that bondholders cannot obtain effective contractual protection. These commentators argue that, because bondholders do not negotiate the contractual terms of a bond, they need extra-contractual protection. We find, however, that bondholders did obtain substantial contractual protection in the wake of the RJR buyout. At that time, the requisite conditions for the inclusion of such protection were present: bondholders were willing to accept lower interest rates in return for protection; protection of bondholders increased share values; and managers were willing to tolerate restrictions on their discretion.

Instead, our analysis identifies two different market failures, the costs of which are borne by shareholders, rather than bondholders. First, parochial managerial interests have led to underinclusive change of control covenants: they fail to cover transactions that management favors. As a result, the agency cost of debt is higher than necessary. Second, parochial managerial interests have caused change of control covenants to be overinclusive: they impede hostile control changes that do not harm bondholders, and they tend to overcompensate bondholders. As a result, the agency cost of equity is higher than necessary. Whether these market failures justify legal intervention, however, is a more complex question that lies beyond the scope of this Article.

Kahan and Klausner, Antitakeover Provisions in Bonds: Bondholder Protection or Management Entrenchment?, 40 UCLA L. Rev. 931, 980-82 (1993).

One commentator has described the way these puts work as follows:

Some companies have issued debt securities that contain put rights in the event of a change of control or upon the occurrence of other events. For example, a holder of Edo Corp.'s 7% convertible subordinated debentures due 2011 has the right to put the debentures back to the company at a premium redemption price in the event that: (i) a person or group acquires a majority of the voting stock of the company; or (ii) the company merges with another company unless the holders of the common stock receive cash consideration equal to the product of the conversion price times the redemption premium; or (iii) without the written consent of a majority of the "independent directors" (i.e., directors who are not employees of the company), the company becomes liable for any debt unless consolidated net tangible assets are at least 150% of consolidated debt.

To explain the nature of the put right more clearly, let's use an example of the event described in clause (ii) above. Assume the current market price of the common stock is $17. The conversion price is $22. The redemption premium applicable in 1987 is 107% and it scales down over time thereafter. The product of $22 and 107% is $23.54. Thus, if the company engaged in a merger in which its stockholders received $21 cash per share, the holders of the debentures would be entitled to put their debentures to the company at a price equal to 107% of the principal amount of their debentures. If the stockholders received $23.54 or more, the debenture holders would not be entitled to put their shares to the company but could exercise their right to convert to common stock at a price of $22 per share.

Another example of a put option would be a requirement that the company offer to acquire a certain percentage of the debt securities in the event that consolidated tangible net worth falls below a specified level.

Clemens, Poison Debt: The New Takeover Defense, 42 Bus. Law. 747, 751 (1987).

Moody's Investors Service, Inc. which, along with Standard & Poor's (a division of McGraw-Hill Companies, Inc.) and Fitch, Inc., constitute the major bond rating agencies (discussed *infra* at section 5c), has indicated that it will give consideration to these friendly or poison puts, as one form of "event risk protection" in rating the investment quality of industrial corporate bonds. Moody's Special Comment, Indenture Protection and Event Risk, November 18, 1988; Moody's Special Comment, Event Risk: Moody's Amplifies Its Views on Indenture Protection Issues, January 5, 1989. Moody's raised some concerns, however, about the efficacy of some forms of this type of protection. For example, one such type of put takes effect upon the acquisition of more than a certain percentage of the issuer's stock without the board's approval. Since, as Moody's points out, most successful hostile takeovers ultimately will be approved by the board, or management will restructure defensively, "the put is never triggered." *Id.* at 6. Another common trigger is a downgrade in bond ratings "within a specified time after the event." But since ratings are meant to be prospective and downgradings typically occur prior to the consummation of the negative event, the puts will not be triggered under this condition either. *Id.* Of course bondholders always can be asked to relinquish wealth themselves. For an example, Ratners Group PLC offered to acquire the stock of Kay Jewelers Inc. conditioned on Kay's bondholders tendering their bonds for consideration equal to $.75 on the dollar, despite event risk protection allowing them to put their bonds to Kay for 100 cents on the dollar. *See* Wallace, Bid for Kay Stirs Bondholders' Ire, The New York Times, July 12, 1990, D2.

In McMahan & Company v. Wherehouse Entertainment, Inc., 900 F.2d 576 (2d Cir. 1990), the court, in a 2-1 decision, reversed the district court's grant of defendants' motion for summary judgment. Plaintiffs were financial institutions owning a significant amount of Wherehouse debentures, the indenture for which provided in part that debenture holders could tender the debentures to Wherehouse upon the occurrence of certain triggering events:

> (a) A person or group shall attain the beneficial ownership of an equity interest representing at least 80% of the voting power unless such attainment has been approved by a majority of the Independent Directors;

> (b) The Company consolidates or merges unless approved by a majority of the Independent Directors;

(c) The Company incurs any Debt excluding Debt which is authorized or ratified by a majority of the Independent Directors, immediately after the incurrence of which the ratio of the Company's Consolidated Total Debt to its Consolidated Capitalization exceeds .65 to 1.0.

This tender right was also described in the prospectus for the debentures.

Eighteen months after plaintiff bought the debentures, Wherehouse merged with another corporation in a leveraged buy-out which "left Wherehouse with a debt approaching 90% of its capitalization and left plaintiffs' debentures valued at only approximately 50% of par." Although plaintiffs tried to tender their debentures, Wherehouse refused on the ground that the merger had been approved by the board of directors (including "Independent Directors").

Plaintiffs sued under Sections 11 and 12(2) of the Securities Act of 1933 and Section 10(b) of the Securities Exchange Act of 1934, alleging that the description of the debentures in the prospectus, as well as oral representations made to them, were materially misleading in that they suggested that the tender right was valuable, when in fact it was worthless. The court agreed that a jury could conclude that the right to tender was presented as a valuable right. It went on to note:

> Although the offering materials explain that the Independent Directors would be chosen from the company's board of directors, the term "Independent Director" implies a special status, some distinction from an "ordinary" director. The term suggests that these directors would be "independent" of management and the normal obligations of board members to act in the interests of shareholders. Thus the restriction could reasonably be understood to mean that in the case of a triggering event, the right to tender would arise *unless* the Independent Directors find the event to be in the interests of the debentureholders. In short, as plaintiffs argue, a reasonable investor could have regarded the right to tender as a valuable right, protected by Independent Directors who would, in situations endangering the security of the debentures, consider debentureholders' interests before approving any waiver of their right.
>
> By thus representing that in a takeover context the Independent Directors would be considering the interests of debentureholders, the defendants implied that the Independent Directors had a duty to protect the debentureholders' interests. Defendants, however, have shown nothing in their corporate charter or by-laws that would have permitted, much less required, these Independent Directors to favor debentureholders over shareholders. Moreover, at the time of the approval of this merger, the Independent Directors constituted all but one of the "ordinary" directors on the board. As ordinary directors, they had a fiduciary duty to protect the interests of shareholders in any takeover situation, regardless of debentureholders' interests or rights. It is inevitable, then, that the so-called Independent Directors had no independence; they would never protect the interests of debentureholders except by coincidence because, as ordinary directors, they were required by law to protect the interests of the shareholders. From this perspective, there is merit in plaintiffs' contentions that the right to tender was illusory and that the representations of it in the offering materials were misleading.

900 F.2d at 580.

12. Another type of protection available to bondholders has been used in the junk bond market. Reset provisions require the issuer periodically to adjust the interest rate

on their outstanding bonds trading below par so that they will trade at par. For example, junk bonds issued to finance KKR's leveraged buy-out of RJR Nabisco contained such a reset provision. The protection is not perfect, however. The reset doesn't actually have to bring the bonds to par in the trading market: rather, all that is required is that two investment bankers opine that at the adjusted interest rate the bonds would have traded at par on a selected day. Obviously such a provision can be expensive for issuers. In RJR's case, the issuer refinanced the bonds rather than make the costly interest rate adjustment. *See* White & Hilder, KKR Said to Raise $1.7 Billion for RJR in Bid to Bolster Firm's Sagging Bonds, Wall St. J., June 13, 1990, at A3.

13. In Geren v. Quantum Chem. Corp., 832 F. Supp. 728 (S.D.N.Y. 1993), Judge Leval rejected plaintiff bondholder's attempt to distinguish the leveraged buyout at issue in *Metropolitan Life* from a special dividend to stockholders of $50 per share. In order to pay the dividend, Quantum allegedly borrowed $1.2 billion, causing stockholders' equity to decrease from $748 million to negative $406 million, thus causing the value of Quantum's outstanding bonds to decline by approximately 50%. In granting defendants' motion to dismiss, the court noted that the indenture contained no prohibition against the corporation incurring additional debt (with the exception of certain secured debt). Because the corporation did not violate any express covenant by the borrowing and the dividend, and did not prevent the bondholders from receiving the benefit of any express indenture term, the court held that no implied covenant of good faith was violated either. There was, in Judge Leval's view, no "significant difference" between the transaction at issue here and the leveraged buyout in *Metropolitan Life*.

Problem—Negotiating and Drafting Event Risk Protection

You are counsel to Junque, Bustup & Co. ("JBC"), an investment banking firm. JBC has been retained by Cash Cow, Inc., a major dairy producer, to underwrite a $50,000,000 issue of twenty-year corporate bonds. JBC's sales force has been canvassing investment managers of its principal clients, insurance companies, and pension funds, to evaluate the probable success of the issue. They have learned that fund managers generally are concerned with the possibility that leveraged buy-outs might seriously increase the riskiness of bonds in their portfolios and damage the market value of those portfolios. Specifically, these investment managers have made clear to JBC that they would not buy long-term bonds of a prime takeover target like Cash Cow without some form of event risk protection. JBC also knows that it will only be able to sell a small portion of the issue at an interest rate acceptable to Cash Cow unless its institutional clients are willing to participate.

1. JBC has asked you to draft language providing event risk protection to bondholders to address its clients' concerns. In drafting this language, be sure to cover: (i) the type of protection to be provided (including financial compensation, if any, to bondholders); (ii) the specific events that will trigger the protection; (iii) the manner in which the triggering events will be determined to have occurred; and (iv) the mechanisms for effectuating the protection.

2. After completing your draft, review it in the role of counsel to Cash Cow. In what respects is it acceptable or unacceptable? What additional suggestions do you have? In responding, be sure to identify specific language that you find problematic and draft alternative language where appropriate.

3. Finally, review the finished product in the role of an analyst employed by a bond rating agency. Do you think that its inclusion in the bond indenture justifies an enhanced rating? Why or why not?

d. The Right to Sue

In our earlier examination of debtholders' rights discussed in section 4a, the principal focus was on whether corporate management owed a fiduciary duty directly to bondholders. As you know from your previous study of corporate law, directors and officers primarily owe their fiduciary obligations to the corporation itself.[1] Typically these duties are broken down into the duty of care and the duty of loyalty, and are enforceable by the corporation (represented by one or more stockholders) through the mechanism of derivative litigation. Occasionally bondholders have sought to enforce these corporate duties or redress their breach. The results are set forth in this subsection.

(i) Derivative Suits

Hoff v. Sprayregan

52 F.R.D. 243 (S.D.N.Y. 1971)

FRANKEL, District Judge.

Plaintiffs, presenting themselves as "stockholders," bring this as a derivative action on behalf of the nominal defendant Technical Tape, Inc. They recount as bases for the suit events beginning in April and extending into August of 1969. The corporation, far from appreciating these efforts ostensibly for its benefit, moves to dismiss the complaint, citing Fed. R. Civ. P. 23.1[a] and asserting that plaintiffs were not, as the Rule requires, shareholders "at the time of the transaction of which" they complain....

On March 11, 1969, the plaintiffs invested $10,000, and on May 27, 1969, another $12,000 in 6% convertible subordinated debentures of Technical Tape due October 1, 1982. Among the rights they thus acquired was the option, expiring July 16, 1969, to convert the debentures into shares of the company's common stock at the conversion price of one share of stock for each seven dollars principal amount of debentures. The plaintiffs exercised this option ... on July 11, 1969.... In opposition to the motion to dismiss their complaint, plaintiffs contend that they were "shareholders" within the

---

1. What theory of the corporation does this formulation suggest? Would other theories equally support this description of management's duties?
   a. "**Rule 23.1 Derivative Actions by Shareholders**
   In a derivative action brought by one or more shareholders or members to enforce a right of a corporation or of an unincorporated association, the corporation or association having failed to enforce a right which may properly be asserted by it, the complaint shall be verified and shall allege (1) that the plaintiff was a shareholder or member at the time of the transaction of which the plaintiff complains or that the plaintiff's share or membership thereafter devolved on the plaintiff by operation of law, and (2) that the action is not a collusive one to confer jurisdiction on a court of the United States which it would not otherwise have. The complaint shall also allege with particularity the efforts, if any, made by the plaintiff to obtain the action the plaintiff desires from the directors or comparable authority and, if necessary, from the shareholders or members, and the reason for the plaintiff's failure to obtain the action or for not making the effort. The derivative action may not be maintained if it appears that the plaintiff does not fairly and adequately represent the interests of the shareholders or members similarly situated in enforcing the right of the corporation or association. The action shall not be dismissed or compromised without the approval of the court, and notice of the proposed dismissal or compromise shall be given to shareholders or members in such manner as the court directs."
   Most states have a similar rule. Compare Revised Model Business Corporation Act §§7.40-7.42 ; ALI Princ. Corp. Gov. §§7.01-7.03, 7.13. [Eds.]

meaning of Rule 23.1 from the time they acquired the convertible debentures, and that, in any event, the wrongs of which they complain continued after mid-July 1969, when there is no question of their status as shareholders in the most conventional and familiar sense. The corporation disputes the contention that plaintiffs were shareholders while they held the debentures. Secondly, ... the corporation argues that the assertedly unlawful transactions giving rise to the complaint had been completely accomplished by the middle of June 1969, and that plaintiffs cannot achieve standing on their theory of "continuing wrongs."

Turning, then, to the charges in the complaint: Plaintiffs ... allege that their action arises under §10(b) of the 1934 Act, 15 U.S.C. §78j(b), S.E.C. Rule 10b-5, 17 CFR 240.10b-5, "and common law principles." As of June 5, 1969, it is alleged, Technical Tape had 2,613,973 shares of common stock outstanding, these being traded on the American Stock Exchange, and each share being entitled to one vote. It is alleged that defendants Gerald Sprayregan and Lawrence N. Hurwitz, at the times in question, were directors of Technical Tape, and, respectively, chairman of the board and president of defendant Sprayregan & Co. On April 16, 1969, the complaint states, Sprayregan & Co. acquired 300,000 shares of Technical Tape common stock and an option to purchase an additional 100,000 shares at a price of nine dollars per share from the widow of the founder of Technical Tape. The shares thus bought, together with those under the option (valid until April 1970), comprise about 17.5% of the outstanding voting stock of Technical Tape. In addition to these, defendant Gerald Sprayregan beneficially owns 15,000 shares. As a result of the foregoing purchase, Sprayregan & Co. came to dominate the Technical Tape board, placing thereon the individual defendants Sprayregan and Hurwitz.

On or about May 28, 1969, it is alleged, "Sprayregan & Co. caused Technical Tape to enter into an agreement with Sprayregan & Co. in which Technical Tape agreed to pay a 5% commission to Sprayregan & Co. in cash for any successful private placement of Technical Tape's notes or securities with SMC Investment Corporation ('SMC') and in addition to issue to Sprayregan & Co. 20,000 warrants to purchase 20,000 shares of common stock of Technical Tape at $9.00 per share for every 1,000,000 of notes and securities so placed." Then, on June 6, 1969, "Sprayregan & Co. caused Technical Tape to enter into an agreement with SMC which provided for the issuance by Technical Tape to SMC of up to $5,000,000 principal amount of 7½% Exchangeable Subordinated Notes due June 6, 1971 (Notes) at a purchase price of $5,000,000. The agreement also provided that the Notes issued to SMC would be exchanged for shares of Series A Exchangeable Preferred Stock (Preferred Stock) if the proposal of Technical Tape to authorize 714,286 shares of said Preferred Stock was approved by the stockholders of Technical Tape. On or about August 8, 1969, the shareholders of Technical Tape authorized the aforesaid shares of Preferred Stock." In addition, on or about August 15, 1969, SMC purchased in a private placement $5,000,000 worth of the preferred stock thus authorized from Technical Tape. As a result of that $5,000,000 purchase and under the agreement of May 28, 1969, Sprayregan & Co. has received $250,000 in cash plus warrants to purchase 100,000 shares of Technical Tape common stock at nine dollars per share. At the time of the May agreement, this common stock was selling at between $11 and $12 per share on the American Stock Exchange so that the warrants were worth over three dollars each, or a total in excess of $300,000. These arrangements gave Sprayregan & Co. compensation which, according to plaintiffs, exceeds customary fees for services of the kind it rendered and is "grossly in excess of the value" of such services. This represents "an unlawful diversion, gift and waste of the assets of Technical Tape for the benefit of Sprayregan & Co." It is charged that the amount of such compensation is in itself "so grossly excessive as to lead to the conclusion that it was not due to an honest error judgment [*sic*] but rather to bad faith and a wilful and reckless disregard of the rights of Technical Tape and its stockholders."

The complaint goes on to allege violations by Sprayregan & Co. and the individual defendants of Section 10(b) of the 1934 Act and Rule 10b-5 thereunder. As assorted specifications under this heading, the complaint charges a failure by Sprayregan & Co. and individual defendants Sprayregan and Hurwitz to disclose to the other Technical Tape directors the excessive character of the compensation agreed to be paid to Sprayregan & Co. The individual defendant directors are charged with failure "to exercise due care, skill and diligence in conducting the business of Technical Tape * * *." It is said that their conduct "has been fraudulent and grossly negligent." There is a demand for compensatory damages "in excess of $450,000," exemplary damages, and other varieties of relief.

.... The only question now presented is whether plaintiffs had the requisite status as shareholders "at the time of the transaction" of which complaint is made.

On this exclusive and narrow subject, the court concludes that plaintiffs should prevail on both branches of the argument they make. While a convertible debenture of the kind in question is obviously a hybrid, the interest of its holder in the corporation's stock is sufficient for our purposes to satisfy the requirement of Rule 23.1. The 1934 Act, implicated by the complaint herein, defines such a debenture as an "equity security," 15 U.S.C. §78c(a)(11), and it is appropriate in cases involving Rule 23.1 to look to the underlying substantive law for a definition of "shareholder." 3B Moore, Federal Practice; ¶23.1.17. The rule may not serve as a barrier to suit by a plaintiff given standing by a substantive federal statute.... On cognate principles, it is appropriate to apply the rule in light of pertinent terms and standards suggested by the statute sued upon. A warrant, defined in §2(a)(35) of the Investment Company Act of 1940, 15 U.S.C. §80a-2(a)(35), so that it resembles a convertible debenture in the definition mentioned above, has been held by this court to confer the status of "shareholder" within the meaning of Rule 23.1, after the court looked to the "broadly remedial" nature of the Act. Entel v. Guilden, 223 F. Supp. 129 (S.D.N.Y. 1963). The court finds the cited decision of Judge Tyler persuasive and a close analogy for the case at hand.

Not always certain whether bad law is more likely to spring from hard or easy cases, the court notes the obvious substantiality of the $22,000 investment made by the plaintiffs in this case well before any of the events about which they sue. It is plain that their interest in the stock of the corporation from the inception of their investment was real and far weightier than that of a holder of, say, 100 shares who would unquestionably be entitled to maintain the action. To allow standing to plaintiffs like these generates no trace of the problems or evils against which Rule 23.1 is directed.

Alternatively, the court would hold, in any event, that the wrongs charged in the complaint continued beyond the point when plaintiffs undisputedly became shareholders, and that this would entitle them to sue even if their requisite status dated only from the middle of July, 1969....

This is not to suggest, of course, any view one way or the other on the merits of this controversy. It is merely to point out that plaintiffs' characterization of their charges as showing "continuing wrongs" seems meritorious.

The motion to dismiss is denied. So ordered.

Notes and Questions

1. Why would the Securities Exchange Act of 1934 include convertible debt securities within the definition of "equity security"? Is it to allow convertible debtholders to bootstrap their way into bringing derivative actions on behalf of issuers? Hint: think about the underlying purpose behind the 1934 Act.

2. With the principal case, compare Brooks v. Weiser, 57 F.R.D. 491 (S.D.N.Y. 1972), in which plaintiffs, holders of debentures issued by National Equipment Rental, Inc. (NER), convertible into the common stock of American Export Industries, Inc. (AEI)[1], brought a derivative action on behalf of NER under state law. (The court did not describe the nature of the state law action.) In granting defendants' motion to dismiss due to plaintiffs' lack of standing, the court distinguished Hoff v. Sprayregan, 52 F.R.D. 243 (S.D.N.Y. 1971), on two grounds: First, Hoff did not hold "that all convertible debentures are shares entitling their holders to sue derivatively." In this case the NER debentures were convertible into AEI stock, whereas in Hoff the debentures were convertible into the stock of the issuing corporation.[2] Thus plaintiffs lacked even a colorable equity interest in NER, and since it was "clear beyond any doubt" that the debentures themselves were not shares, Hoff did not control. Second, the substantive law underlying Hoff was the Securities Exchange Act of 1934, which broadly defined the notion of "shareholder." Here, the underlying substantive law was state law. The court did not decide whether New York law (which governed the debenture indenture) or Delaware law (which was the state in which the issuer was incorporated) applied, holding that both denied the holders shareholder status.

Is Hoff as narrow as Brooks suggests? Need it be read so narrowly?

3. For additional cases and commentary on this issue, see In re Krause, 114 B.R. 582 (Bankr. N.D. Ind. 1988); Starr v. State Mut. Inv., F.2d 375, (6th Cir. 1979); Scharfam, Derivative Suits in Bankruptcy, 10 Stan. J.L. Bus. & Fin. 1 (2004); Larose, Suing in the Right of the Corporation: A Commentary and Proposal for Legislative Reform, 19 Mich. J. L. Reform 499 (1986).

Harff v. Kerkorian
324 A.2d 215 (Del. Ch. 1974)

QUILLEN, Chancellor:

This action is a combined derivative and class action challenging a singular corporate act—the declaration and payment of a $1.75 per share dividend by Metro-Goldwyn-Mayer, Inc., in the late fall of 1973.

Plaintiffs are holders of 5% convertible subordinated debentures due 1993 which were issued by Metro-Goldwyn-Mayer, Inc. (MGM), pursuant to an Indenture Agreement between MGM and The Chase Manhattan Bank (Trustee) dated July 1, 1968. On November 21, 1973, the Board of Directors of MGM declared a cash dividend, the first

---

1. The opinion does not describe the corporate relationship between NER and AEI, stating it to be "unnecessary to the understanding of this motion." Id. at 493.

2. See also Dorfman v. Chemical Bank, 56 F.R.D. 363 (S.D.N.Y. 1972), distinguishing Hoff on this basis on similar relevant facts.

cash dividend since 1969, in the amount of $1.75 per share of common stock. Plaintiffs contend that the dividends were declared improvidently and for the financial benefit of defendant Kerkorian, a member of the Board of Directors as well as the controlling stockholders of MGM. Plaintiffs allege that the declaration of cash dividends (1) damaged MGM by depleting its capital, thereby endangering its future prospects and (2) damaged the debenture holders in that it impaired the value of the conversion feature and caused a decline in the market value of the debentures themselves.

On this basis, plaintiffs are simultaneously maintaining a derivative action on behalf of the corporation as well as a class action on behalf of all holders of MGM's convertible debentures, excluding the members of the Board of Directors. The defendants are the individual directors of MGM and the corporation itself. In connection with the derivative claim, plaintiffs seek to recover from the individual defendants, on behalf of the corporation, the amount of the cash dividends which was paid pursuant to the November 21 declaration and damages for the loss of the use of the funds which were appropriated to make the dividend payments. In addition, plaintiffs request that all damages which may be recovered on the derivative claim be placed in a constructive trust "for the benefit of the class members." With regard to the class action, plaintiffs seek to recover money damages for class members.

Defendants have moved to dismiss the derivative action on the ground that plaintiffs lack standing to maintain an action on behalf of MGM due to the fact that they are not stockholders....

I.
STANDING TO MAINTAIN DERIVATIVE ACTIONS

Defendants ... contend that plaintiffs do not have standing to sue derivatively as they are not stockholders of MGM within the meaning of 8 Del. C. §327, the terms of which are set forth below. Plaintiffs, on the other hand, argue that the convertibility of their debentures into common stock of MGM provides them with the necessary standing to sue on behalf of MGM. Plaintiffs emphasize the fact that they are not suing on behalf of themselves but rather are seeking to enforce a claim which belongs to the corporation which management refused to assert.

The only statutory provision in Delaware dealing with the derivative action is 8 Del. C., §327, which provides as follows:

"In any derivative suit instituted by a stockholder of a corporation, ... it shall be averred in the complaint that the plaintiff was a stockholder of the corporation at the time of the transaction of which he complains or that his stock thereafter devolved upon him by operation of law." ...

It is noted, as plaintiffs have asserted, that when read literally §327 does not provide that only stockholders have standing to sue derivatively.[3] It must be recognized, however, that §327 does not create the right to sue derivatively but rather restricts that right. Section 327 was enacted to eliminate strike suits and other abuses which developed along with the derivative suit.... The purpose behind its enactment in 1945 was to prevent what has been considered to be an evil, namely, the purchasing of shares in order

---

3. Plaintiffs contend that the statutory language "[i]n any derivative suit instituted by a stockholder" indicates that nonstockholders may have standing to sue derivatively since it apparently limits its application to suits brought by stockholders.

to maintain a derivative action designed to attack a transaction which occurred prior to the purchase of stock....

The derivative action was developed by equity to enable stockholders to sue in the corporation's name where those in control of the corporation refused to assert a claim belonging to the corporation. The nature of the derivative suit is two fold: first, it is the equivalent of a suit by the stockholders to compel the corporation to sue; and second, it is a suit by the corporation, asserted by the stockholders in its behalf, against those liable to it.... Suits by stockholders alleging mismanagement on the part of the directors are of course included within the umbrella of a derivative action....

But it has been generally accepted under Delaware law that only one who was a stockholder at the time of the transaction or one whose shares devolved upon him by operation of law may maintain a derivative action.... For purposes of a derivative action, an equitable owner is considered a stockholder.... But Delaware law seems clear that stockholder status at the time of the transaction being attacked and throughout the litigation is essential....

The holder of an option to purchase stock is not an equitable stockholder of the corporation.... Debenture holders are not stockholders and their rights are determined by their contracts.... A holder of a convertible bond "does not become a stockholder, by his contract, in equity any more than at law." Parkinson v. West End St. Ry. Co., 173 Mass. 446, 53 N.E. 891, 892 (1899), an opinion by Justice Holmes.

Plaintiffs conceded at oral argument that creditors generally are not entitled to sue derivatively. Nor does this case involve any statutorily recognized rights where debenture holders are deemed to be stockholders. Compare 8 Del. C., §221.[a] Nevertheless, plaintiffs contend that the convertibility feature of the debentures which they hold sets them apart from other creditors and gives them standing to maintain a derivative suit. Plaintiffs rely on Hoff v. Sprayregan, S.D.N.Y., 52 F.R.D. 243 (1971), wherein it was held that convertible debenture holders had standing to institute a derivative suit. In Hoff, the plaintiffs had alleged a violation of the Securities Exchange Act of 1934, which classifies convertible debentures within the definitional meaning of "equity security." 15 U.S.C.A. §78c(a)(11). On the basis of this definitional section in the Federal Act, the District Court found that the convertible debenture holders were "stockholders" for purposes of bringing the derivative action.

In this case, plaintiffs are not suing under the Federal Act and they do not contend that they are stockholders of MGM. They do, however, argue that the result in Hoff should be followed due to their interest in the stock of the corporation. They also assert that inasmuch as the minority stockholders of MGM received their proportionate share of the dividends complained of, such stockholders are not in as favorable a position as are the plaintiffs to challenge the wrong to the corporation....

Notwithstanding these arguments, the conclusion is inescapable that plaintiffs are creditors of MGM and simply do not have standing to maintain a stockholder's derivative action under Delaware law. The key differences were well noted in a recent New York case, In re Will of Migel, 71 Misc. 2d 640, 336 N.Y.S.2d 376, 379 (Sup. Ct. 1972):

---

a. Del. Gen. Corp. Law §221 authorizes the corporation to grant voting rights to bonds and debentures if, and to the extent that, such rights are specified in the charter. If such rights are granted, bondholders are deemed "stockholders" for purposes of the statute. See 1 Ward, Welch & Turezyn, Folk on the Delaware General Corporation Law §221 (4th ed. 1998 & Supp. 2005-1). What difference would bondholders' voting rights have made in the outcome of this case? What difference should they have made? [Eds.]

"A share of stock is evidence of ownership of corporate assets, ... and not evidence of corporate indebtedness as is a bond. A convertible bond is simply a bond convertible into stock under certain conditions.... From an investor's point of view, a bond is a less speculative investment because it is a secured debt entitled to priority in the event of corporate distribution or dissolution. That a bond is convertible at the sole option of its holder into stock should no more affect its essential quality of being a bond than should the fact that cash is convertible into stock affect the nature of cash. Any bond, or any property, for that matter, is convertible into stock through the intermediate step of converting it to cash.

"Except for cases involving the Securities Exchange Act of 1934, case law indicates that a convertible debenture is a bond and not an equity security until conversion occurs....

"As to the Securities Exchange Act of 1934, 15 U.S.C. Section 78c(a)(11) does define an 'equity security' to include all securities convertible in to stock. However, such definition is *expressly* limited to use within the Securities Exchange Act, and the rationale of the act and the cases interpreting the act do not warrant a broader application." ...

Plaintiffs have been unable to cite any cases decided under state law, Delaware or elsewhere, which allow a creditor of a corporation to enforce a corporate cause of action derivatively....

It is obviously important that the Delaware corporate law have stability and predictability. The novel theory being suggested by the plaintiffs has no support under our law. The plaintiffs simply lack standing to maintain a derivative suit on behalf of MGM. The derivative cause of action is therefore dismissed. IT IS SO ORDERED.

Notes and Questions

1. On appeal the Delaware Supreme Court affirmed the Chancellor's holding as to the debenture holders' standing to maintain a derivative action but reversed the dismissal of the class action on the ground that plaintiffs had stated a colorable claim of fraud. Harff v. Kerkorian, 347 A.2d 133 (Del. 1975), *rev'd on other grounds*, 531 F.2d 1234 (3d Cir. 1976). The Court's affirmance of the dismissal of the derivative action caused some confusion (in our minds, unnecessarily) over whether the Court had meant to completely preclude convertible debenture holders from bringing derivative suits. This confusion was clearly resolved in Simons v. Cogan, 549 A.2d 300 (Del. 1988), *supra* at section 4a.

2. The cases dealing with the right of corporate constituents other than stockholders to bring derivative actions on behalf of the corporation to recover damages for breaches of the duty of care or loyalty generally reject such claims on the ground that the constituent/plaintiff is not an "owner" of the corporation and therefore has no standing to bring an action developed and reserved for owners.

This reasoning is illustrated by the opinion in Kusner v. First Pennsylvania Corp., 395 F. Supp. 276 (E.D. Pa. 1975), *rev'd on other grounds*, 531 F.2d 1234 (3d Cir. 1976).[a]

---

a. *See also* Bangor Punta Operations, Inc. v. Bangor & Aroostook R.R., 417 U.S. 703, 94 S. Ct. 2578, 41 L. Ed. 2d 418 (1974); Del. Gen. Corp. Law §327; 2 Ward, Welch & Turezyn, Folk on the Delaware General Corporation Law §327 (4th ed. 1998 & Supp. 2005-1); N.Y. Bus. Corp. Law §626(b); Rev. Model Bus. Corp. Act §7.40.

Kusner was, in part, a derivative action brought by convertible debenture holders in The First Pennsylvania Mortgage Trust ("Trust"), a Massachusetts business trust organized by First Pennsylvania Corporation, to redress alleged fraud in the form of excessive fees and commissions paid by Trust to certain of its affiliates in violation of federal securities laws and the Investment Advisers Act of 1940. In dismissing the derivative count for plaintiffs' lack of standing Judge Higginbotham, in a detailed opinion, described the reasons underlying the policy of limiting derivative suit standing to shareholders:

> In *Kauffman v. Dreyfus Fund, Inc.*, 434 F.2d 727, 735 (3d Cir. 1970) the Court of Appeals recognized that only a proprietary interest in a business entity invests a party with the requisite legal standing to prosecute a secondary or derivative action. Judge Aldisert was emphatic in his recognition of this well established principle.

> "The timber of sound reason forms the conceptual underpinning of the rule requiring stock ownership in a corporation as the prerequisite for bringing a derivative action in its behalf. Only by virtue of the shareholder's interest, which has been described as 'a proprietary interest in the corporate enterprise which is subject to injury through breaches of trust or duty on the part of the directors,' Ashwander v. Tennessee Valley Authority, 297 U.S. 288, 321, 56 S. Ct. 466, 471, 80 L. Ed. 688 (1936), does equity permit him 'to step into the corporation [sic] shoes and seek in its right the restitution he could not demand on his own.' Standing is justified only by this proprietary interest created by the stockholder relationship and the possible indirect benefits the nominal plaintiff may acquire *qua* stockholder of the corporation which is the real party in interest. Without this relationship, there can be no standing, 'no right in himself to prosecute this suit,' Hawes v. Oakland (Hawes v. Contra Costa Water Co.), 104 U.S. 450, 462, 26 L. Ed. 827...."

* * *

> In contrast, the interest of a mere creditor, although it may constitute a substantial financial stake in the success of the business enterprise, is clearly nonproprietary....

> A debenture is a credit instrument, one which does not devolve upon its holder an equity interest in a business enterprise. But plaintiff urges the court to consider the convertibility feature of his debentures and the attached warrants to purchase shares of beneficial interest as an interest in Trust sufficiently akin to shares that the law should accord him the status of a shareholder in interpreting the scope of Rule 23.1. Entertaining plaintiff's argument requires that I look beyond his complete lack of share ownership and engage in a comparative analysis of his present interest and the interest which he would hold were he the legal or beneficial owner of Trust shares.... [T]he concept of proprietary interest is distorted beyond analytical usefulness when the holder of a mere option to purchase shares who has not yet exercised his option or legally committed himself to the exercise of his option is held a shareholder under Rule 23.1 by virtue of the dollar amount of his financial investment in business enterprise [sic] on behalf of which he seeks to bring suit.[6] In this instance

---

6. I decline to adopt the rationale of *Hoff* v. *Sprayregan*, 52 F.R.D. 243 (S.D.N.Y. 1971). However, it is significant in that case that the warrant holder had exercised his warrants as of the date upon which the complaint was filed.

plaintiff does not hold Trust shares and the interest which he does hold is nonproprietary.

The plaintiff's interest in Trust does not afford him rights or privileges traditionally associated with an ownership interest. He presently owns eighteen $1000 six and three-quarter percent convertible subordinated debentures due September 1, 1991, with attached series B warrants issued by Trust in August 1, 1971 [sic]. These securities do not entitle plaintiff to vote, he is not entitled to participate in Trust profits or distributions,[7] nor is he subject to Trust losses.[8] Plaintiff holds a debt obligation of the Trust upon which he is entitled to receive interest at a rate of six and three-quarter percent per year. These obligations mature September 1, 1991, at their face value but are callable at the option of Trust at an earlier date at a premium price designated by the Trust indenture. The principal amount of the indebtedness is secured by a sinking fund.

The contractual options which he holds in the form of warrants and the convertibility term in his debentures do not alter plaintiff's status. Despite his ownership of the warrants and the convertible debentures his right to participate as a proprietor of Trust is not changed and he does not assume the additional financial risks of a shareholder. The difference between the risk which plaintiff presently assumes as a debenture holder of Trust and the risks which he would assume if he were to exercise his conversion privileges are quite dramatic. If plaintiff were to convert his debentures into shares of beneficial interests, he would lose the security of Trust's contractual obligation to pay interest at designated intervals upon the amount of converted debenture in exchange for the risk of gain or loss realized by Trust's investment portfolio. As a debenture holder, the principal amount of his debt is payable at a time certain, but as a shareholder the value of his shares is completely at the mercy of the market unless, of course, the Trust is liquidated in which case he may or may not realize a full return of his initial investment....

Plaintiff is a creditor, not a shareholder. He receives interest, not dividends. He holds a legally enforceable promise of Trust, not a share in its earnings and losses. Plaintiff has made a loan and he limits his financial risks to a lender's risk, his responsibilities to a lender's responsibility, and justly, his standing to a lender's standing. Despite plaintiff's contention, he remains a creditor until he either converts his debentures or exercises his warrants....

The question this approach raises, of course, is that of the concept of "ownership" underlying the doctrine. It is not clear that stockholders are the only "owners" of a corporation. Recognizing this, Black and Scholes have reversed the traditional concept of corporate ownership to suggest that bondholders actually own a corporation's assets with an option in the stockholders to repurchase the assets by repaying the debt. Black & Scholes, The Pricing of Options and Corporate Liabilities, 81 J. Pol. Econ. 637 (1973).

Even if bondholders' interests are not considered "ownership" interests, does it ineluctably follow that they ought to be precluded from bringing derivative actions? What

---

7. The face of plaintiff's warrants read, in part:
   "Prior to the exercise of any Series B. warrant represented hereby, the holder hereof shall not be entitled to any rights of a Shareholder of the Trust, including without limitation the right to vote or the right to receive distributions...."
8. Plaintiff does not allege that Trust is in default upon its obligations or that it is at this time in any imminent danger of insolvency.

interests of bondholders would support their right to bring such actions? What interests of the corporation support the contrary conclusion? *See* Mitchell, The Fairness Rights of Corporate Bondholders, 65 N.Y.U. L. Rev. 1165 (1990) (arguing that the interest of bondholders in checking breaches of duties of care and loyalty is similar in kind, if not in degree, to that of stockholders).

How does the *Kusner* court reach the conclusion that stockholders are "owners" and bondholders are "creditors"? Is the court's reasoning convincing? Even if convincing, is it complete? Are Black and Scholes any more persuasive?

American Law Institute Principles of Corporate Governance: Analysis and Recommendations

(1994)ᵃ

Section 7.02 Standing to Commence and Maintain a Derivative Action

(a) A holder [§1.22] of an equity security [§1.20]ᵇ has standing to commence and maintain a derivative action if the holder:

(1) Acquired the equity security either (A) before the material facts relating to the alleged wrong were publicly disclosed or were known by, or specifically communicated to, the holder, or (B) by devolution of law, directly or indirectly, from a prior holder who acquired the security as described in the preceding clause (A);

(2) Continues to hold the equity security until the time of judgment, unless the failure to do so is the result of corporate action in which the holder did not acquiesce, and either (A) the derivative action was commenced prior to the corporate action terminating the holder's status, or (B) the court finds that such holder is better able to represent the interests of the shareholders than any other holder who has brought suit;

(3) Has complied with the demand requirement of §7.03 (Exhaustion of Intracorporate Remedies: The Demand Rule) or was excused by its terms; and

(4) Is able to represent fairly and adequately the interests of the shareholders.

(b) On a timely motion, a holder of an equity security should be permitted to intervene in a derivative action, unless the court finds that the interests to be represented by the intervenor are already fairly and adequately represented or that the intervenor is unable to represent fairly and adequately the interests of the shareholders.

(c) A director [§1.13] of a corporation has standing to commence and maintain a derivative action unless the court finds that the director is unable to represent fairly and adequately the interests of the shareholders.

---

a. Copyright 1994 by The American Law Institute. Reprinted with the permission of The American Law Institute.

b. The term "equity security" is defined as follows:
§1.20 Equity Security
"Equity security" means (a) a share in a corporation or similar security, or (b) a security convertible, with or without consideration, into such a security, or carrying a warrant or right to subscribe to or buy such a security if the warrant or right is issued by the issuer of that security.

Comment:

* * *

c. *Ownership requirements.* To have standing under §7.02, a plaintiff must meet three ownership requirements: the plaintiff must hold an equity security; either have acquired it prior to the disclosure of the wrong (or prior to the time at which the wrong had become known by, or had specifically been communicated to, the holder) or have acquired it by operation of law (e.g., bequest or intestate succession) from such a holder; and continued to hold it throughout the litigation....

* * *

Under §7.02(a), a creditor (including a holder of nonconvertible bonds) may not bring a derivative action against a solvent corporation. This traditional rule protects corporate officials from exposure to litigation brought by creditors who would rationally have a far different and more skeptical attitude toward business risks than shareholders, and it is also justified by the greater availability to creditors of contractual mechanisms by which to establish and enforce their rights.

A more difficult problem surrounds the definition of the term "equity security." Cases are divided on the issue of whether the holder of a convertible security can bring a derivative action. See Reporter's Note 2. Although it is recognized that convertible securities are a hybrid, which sometimes approach debt and sometimes equity, depending on individual circumstances, the need for a bright-line test seems clear in order to avoid uncertainty and unnecessary litigation over collateral issues. Therefore, §7.02(a) adopts an inclusive approach by utilizing the term "equity security," which is defined in §1.20 to include securities convertible into equity securities, or carrying a warrant or right to buy such a security, issued by the corporation. However, §7.02(a)(4) subjects such holders to the requirement that they must fairly and adequately represent the interests of the shareholders. If the grievance asserted seems in the court's judgment primarily that of a class of non-equity holders, the court may deny such a holder standing. Section 7.02(a) takes no position on whether the holder of a warrant or right issued by the corporation and not attached to some other security should have standing to bring a derivative action.

* * *

Reporter's Note

* * *

2. *Convertible and debt securities....* Section 7.02 is consistent with modern accounting practice, which classifies a convertible security as a "common stock equivalent" under the most common circumstances.... In contrast, the common law has traditionally denied standing to creditors of a solvent corporation to maintain a derivative action.... Some commentators have strongly criticized this rule. See, e.g., McDaniel, Bondholders and Corporate Governance, 41 Bus. Law. 413 (1986).... As they have pointed out, creditors today often lack contractual covenants protecting them against even obvious risks. However, their proposed remedy of a creditors' derivative suit seems overbroad. On balance, the common law rule is justified because creditor suits based on broad concepts of fiduciary duty might chill the board's willingness to accept desirable business risks. As a generalization, it still remains largely true that substantial creditors in most instances can protect themselves through contractual agreements, whereas the amendment of the corporate charter is a far less feasible protection for shareholders. Further, a common provision in many corporate indentures denies the individual holder of a debt security the ability to sue unless first

joined by a requisite percentage of his fellow holders. The intent of this provision might be nullified if the same holder could commence suit in the corporation's name against corporate officials. Section 7.02 does not address (or restrict) the capacity of a trustee in bankruptcy to hold corporate officials accountable; that topic is outside the scope of Part VII.

* * *

Questions

1. What is the relevance of the Reporter's observation that "substantial creditors ... can protect themselves through contractual agreements, whereas the amendment of the corporate charter is a far less feasible protection for shareholders"?

2. Does the fact that creditors generally are more risk averse than shareholders justify denying the former the important remedy of the derivative suit?

3. What is the relationship between the availability of the derivative suit mechanism and the existence of a corporate fiduciary relationship?

4. Should corporate creditors be permitted to bring derivative suits? If so, would you impose any limitations on this right?

(ii) Contractual Limitations

Problem — Standing to Sue

Shop-O-Rama, Inc. (the "Company") is a corporation engaged in television marketing of a wide variety of consumer products ("it slices, it dices," etc.) and is incorporated in the State of Confusion. Two years ago, the Company issued $150,000,000 of convertible subordinated debentures, underwritten by our ubiquitous underwriter, Junque Bustup & Co. The issue was marketed internationally, in the hope of satisfying the Company's desire to build up its equity market outside of the United States. The indenture provided for conversion into the Company's common stock at a price of $30 per share. At the time of issuance, the stock was trading on the New York Stock Exchange at $25 per share.

A year later, Junque Bustup approached the Company's board and told it that unless the conversion price were reset, it was unlikely that its hopes for a foreign equity market would be realized. The board agreed. Consequently, the Company executed a supplemental indenture resetting the conversion price to the lower of (i) $30 or (ii) 25% of the average of the last reported sales prices of the Company's common stock for the 30 consecutive trading days ending on the day immediately preceding the next. Because the market price of the Company's common stock dropped significantly, the conversion price ultimately was reset at $8 per share, with the result that each $1,000 principal amount of debenture was then convertible into 125 shares in contrast to the 33 shares that would have been issuable under the higher price. Conversion by the debentureholders obviously would significantly dilute the Company's equity, and when the board realized this it became quite upset.

The Company sued Junque Bustup in the State of Agitation, claiming that Junque Bustup (which itself owned a significant amount of the debentures) had fraudulently induced it to reset the conversion price. Simultaneously, the Company issued a press release announcing that it would honor conversions at the reset price but would issue legended shares indicating that those in excess of the number that would have been issued at the original conversion price would be cancelled in the event that the Company's litigation was successful.

Diversified Bond Fund, a mutual fund holding some of the debentures, then sued the Company in the Chancery Court of Confusion, claiming that the Company's legending the shares (which dramatically affected the market price both of the legended shares and the debentures) was a breach of the indenture, and seeking injunctive relief.

You are the chancellor. The relevant indenture provision is as follows:

Section 508.

Notwithstanding any other provision in this Indenture, the Holder of any Debenture shall have the right, which is absolute and unconditional, to receive payment of the principal of (and premium, if any) and interest on such Debenture on the maturity date expressed in such Debenture (or, in the case of redemption at the option of the Company or the Holder, on the redemption date) and to convert such Debenture in accordance with Article Twelve, and to institute suit for the enforcement of any such payment and right to convert, and such rights shall not be impaired without the consent of such Holder.

The indenture also contains a provision (Section 507) limiting the right of debenture holders to sue the Company that is substantially identical to Section 507 of the Model Indenture appearing below.

The Company has moved to dismiss the action on the grounds that (i) plaintiff lacks standing under Section 507 of the indenture, and (ii) the Company has not breached Section 508.

Write your opinion disposing of this motion.

American Bar Foundation Commentaries on Model Debenture Indenture Provisions
(1971)

§5-7 [Section 507]. Limitation on Suits.

No Holder of any Debenture or coupon shall have any right to institute any proceeding, judicial or otherwise, with respect to this Indenture, or for the appointment of a receiver or trustee, or for any other remedy hereunder, unless

(1) such Holder has previously given written notice to the Trustee[a] of a continuing Event of Default;

(2) the Holders of not less than 25% in principal amount of the Outstanding Debentures shall have made written request to the Trustee to institute proceedings in respect of such Event of Default in its own name as Trustee hereunder;

(3) such Holder or Holders have offered to the Trustee reasonable indemnity against the costs, expenses and liabilities to be incurred in compliance with such request;

(4) the Trustee for 60 days after its receipt of such notice, request and offer of indemnity has failed to institute any such proceeding; and

(5) no direction inconsistent with such written request has been given to the Trustee during such 60 day period by the Holders of a majority in principal amount of the Outstanding Debentures;

---

a. For an analysis of the obligations of the Indenture Trustee, see *infra* section 5b.

it being understood and intended that no one or more Holders of Debentures or coupons shall have any right in any manner whatever by virtue of, or by availing of, any provision of this Indenture to affect, disturb or prejudice the rights of any other Holders of Debentures or coupons, or to obtain or seek to obtain priority or preference over any other Holders or to enforce any right under this Indenture, except in the manner herein provided and for the equal and ratable benefit of all the Holders of Debentures and coupons.

The major purpose of this Section is to deter individual debentureholders from bringing independent law suits for unworthy or unjustifiable reasons, causing expense to the Company and diminishing its assets. The theory is that if the suit is worthwhile, 25% of the debentureholders would be willing to join in sponsoring it. The 25% figure is standard. An additional purpose is the expression of the principal of law that would otherwise be implied that all rights and remedies of the indenture are for the equal and ratable benefit of all the holders.

Note that this limitation is only on suits under the indenture—the right of a debentureholder to sue on his debenture for payment when due is absolute and unconditional, as provided in Section 508.

Limitations similar to those contained in Section 507 have been generally upheld by the courts.

* * *

As a practical matter, if an event of default has occurred, the Trustee is obliged to exercise such of the rights and powers vested in it as would a prudent man under the circumstances (Section 601(b)). It is unlikely that the Trustee would refuse to take any action for more than two months after a request to do so by 25% of the debentureholders when an event of default (i.e., a ripened default) has occurred and is continuing.

Of course, any suit by one debentureholder seeking to collect the principal of his debenture might prejudice other holders who do not bring such a suit but this kind of action is an absolute right of the debentureholder under the debenture and Section 508 of the Model Provisions. The reference in the latter part of Section 507 to disturbing or prejudicing rights under the indenture developed from mortgage indenture language in which there is concern over disturbing the lien securing the bonds. One example of how a holder may affect the rights of other holders under a debenture indenture might be a suit for reformation of the indenture.

Simons v. Cogan
549 A.2d 300 (Del. 1988)

[The facts and parts I-III of the opinion are set forth *supra* in section 4a.]

* * *

IV

Finally we consider the Court of Chancery's holding that Simon [sic] is precluded by section 8.08 of the indenture from bringing a claim for breach of indenture against the issuing corporation. Section 8.08 of the indenture provides in part:

No holder of any Debenture shall have any right to institute any action, suit or proceeding at law or in equity for the execution of any trust hereunder or for the appointment of a receiver or for any other remedy hereunder, unless (i) such holder previously shall have given to the Trustee written notice of the happening and continuing of one or more of the Events of Default herein specified, (ii) the holders of 35 percent in principal amount of the Debentures then outstanding shall have requested the Trustee in writing to take action in respect of the matter complained of, and shall have afforded to it a reasonable opportunity either to proceed to exercise the powers herein granted or to institute such action, suit or proceeding in its own name....

The purpose of section 8.08 "is to deter individual debenture-holders from bringing independent law suits for unworthy or unjustifiable reasons, causing expense to the Company and diminishing its assets." American Bar Foundation, *Commentaries on Model Debenture Indenture Provisions* §5-7, at 232 (1971). Such limitations on the bringing of a suit are standard in indenture agreements and have been generally upheld by the courts. Id. at 233.

Thus, under the terms of the indenture the holders of 35 percent in principal amount of debenture must make a written request to the trustee to institute suit before any one of them can bring a claim based on an alleged violation of the indenture. Simons' complaint does not assert that the 35 percent threshold of section 8.08 has been satisfied and Simons tacitly concedes that it has not. Such a concession appears fatal to Simons' claims for breach of indenture.

Simons counters, however, that the Chancellor, in concluding that section 8.08 was controlling, failed to consider the effect of section 8.09 of the indenture which provides:

> No remedy herein conferred upon or reserved to the Trustee or to the holders of Debentures is intended to be exclusive of any other remedy or remedies, and each and every remedy shall be cumulative and shall be in addition to every other remedy given hereunder or now or hereafter existing at law or in equity or by statute.

Simons argues that the thrust of section 8.09 is to allow debenture holders to bring claims for violation of the indenture independent of the procedural provisions of section 8.08. We disagree. Section 8.09 is a general provision providing for cumulative remedies, i.e., the indenture trustee or debenture holders have the right, apart from the indenture, to seek relief for statutory violations or fraud. However, section 8.09 cannot reasonably be read to circumvent the standing restrictions of section 8.08 which specifically restricts enforcement "of any right hereunder." The Chancellor correctly applied the bar of section 8.08 in dismissing the contract claims against the corporation.

* * *

Problem — The Extra-Contractual Rights of Bondholders

Hotsheets Hotel Co. (the "Company") is a closely held corporation. Members of the Adams family own 51 percent of the issued and outstanding common stock (the only class of stock outstanding) and the remaining 49 percent is owned by a relatively small number of key employees. Recently the stock has been appraised at a total of $160,000,000. On August 1, 1995, the Company issued an aggregate amount of $50,000,000 in bonds due August 1, 2005, at an interest rate of 7 percent, as security for which it pledged certain real estate it owns. The Blinders Trust Company ("Blinders") agreed to serve as indenture trustee. The indenture and the bonds provided that two-thirds or more in principal amount of the bonds could agree with the Company to modify and extend the maturity date of the bonds, as long as all of the bonds were equally affected. From the time of issuance, members of the Adams family, who also constituted the Company's board of directors, owned 70 percent in principal amount of the bonds.

On June 1, 2005, those members of the Adams family who were bondholders entered into an agreement with the Company to extend the maturity of the bonds until August 1, 2015, and on that date Blinders executed a supplemental indenture with the Company reflecting that change. In effectuating that change the Adams family, Blinders and the Company complied strictly with the terms of the indenture, and notice of the amendment was given to all bondholders.

John Jones acquired $50,000 principal amount of the bonds on July 1, 2005. In August 2005, he sued the Company, Blinders and the Adams family, all for various breaches of their fiduciary duties, bad faith and fraud, as well as the Company for breach of an implied covenant of good faith in the indenture. All defendants have moved to dismiss.

You are the judge. Write your opinion disposing of defendants' motion.

Rabinowitz v. Kaiser-Frazer Corp.
111 N.Y.S.2d 539 (Sup. Ct. 1952)

HART, Justice.

Defendant Kaiser-Frazer Corporation (hereinafter referred to as Kaiser-Frazer) moves to dismiss the complaint on the grounds that: ... (2) the plaintiff has not legal capacity to sue.

This action was instituted against the three named defendants, Kaiser-Frazer, Bank of America National Trust and Savings Association (hereinafter referred to as Bank of America) and Graham-Paige Motors Corporation (hereinafter referred to as Graham-Paige)....

The plaintiff is the original owner and holder of $10,000 in principal amount of 4% Convertible Debentures of Graham-Paige which were issued under an indenture with the Bank of America as trustee and has brought this action in behalf of himself and all other owners of such debentures similarly situated.

The material facts, as alleged in the complaint, may be summarized as follows: Prior to World War II Graham-Paige was engaged primarily in the production, distribution and sale of automobiles and replacement parts therefor. During the war Graham-Paige was engaged almost entirely in the production of war materials. On August 9, 1945, Joseph W. Frazer, then Chairman of the Board of Directors and President of Graham-Paige, and one Henry J. Kaiser were instrumental in the formation of Kaiser-Frazer. On September 20, 1945, Graham-Paige purchased 250,000 shares of common stock of Kaiser-Frazer. On that same date Graham-Paige and Kaiser-Frazer entered into an agreement for joint use of the former bomber plant at Willow Run in Ypsilanti, Michigan, for the manufacture of automobiles and farm equipment. Under this agreement Graham-Paige was entitled to use one-third of Willow Run's automotive production facilities; Kaiser-Frazer the other two-thirds.

In order to obtain its share of the needed capital to convert the Willow Run plant to automobile production and to obtain other working capital, Graham-Paige issued $11,500,000 of 4% Convertible Debentures due April 1, 1956, under an Indenture with Bank of America as trustee. Behind these debentures were pledged the Graham-Paige plant in Detroit, Michigan and the aforesaid 250,000 shares of Kaiser-Frazer common stock.

Graham-Paige covenanted in said Indenture (Article "Third" relating to "sinking Fund and Redemption of Debentures") that on or before April 1 of each year to and including April 1, 1956, so long as any of the debentures are outstanding, it would pay to the trustee, as and for a Sinking Fund for the retirement of the debentures, an amount in cash equal to 25% of its net earnings for the preceding calendar year.

Article Thirteenth of the Indenture, in so far as applicable herein, also provided:

"§13.01. Nothing in this Indenture shall prevent * * * any sale or conveyance, subject to the lien of this Indenture on the mortgaged and pledged property, of all or substantially all of the property of the corporation (Graham-Paige) to any other corporation * * *; provided, however, and the corporation covenants and agrees, that

"(1) Any such * * * sale or conveyance shall be upon such terms as fully to preserve and in no respect to impair the lien of security of this Indenture * * *, and

"(2) Upon any such * * * sale or conveyance, * * * the corporation to which all or substantially all the property of the Corporation shall be sold or conveyed shall execute with the trustee and record an indenture, satisfactory to the trustee, whereby the successor corporation shall expressly agree to pay duly and punctually the principal of and the interest and premium, if any, on the Debentures according to their tenure, and shall expressly assume the due and punctual performance and observance of all the covenants and conditions of this Indenture to be performed or observed by the Corporation."

"§13.02. Upon any such * * * sale or conveyance * * * such successor corporation shall succeed to and be substituted for the Corporation with the same effect as if it had been named as the party of the first part (Graham-Paige) * * * ."

By a contract dated December 12, 1946, effective February 1, 1947, Graham-Paige agreed to sell to Kaiser-Frazer all of its automotive assets (excluding only such assets as had been acquired for use in the manufacture of farm equipment) in consideration, among other things, of the issue to Graham-Paige of 750,000 shares of common stock of Kaiser-Frazer, of an agreement by Graham-Paige to pay Kaiser-Frazer $3,000,000 and by a debenture payment agreement (subsequently executed on February 10, 1947) between Graham-Paige and Kaiser-Frazer whereunder the latter undertook to pay the interest on and the principal of the debentures of Graham-Paige then outstanding ($8,524,000).

The agreement of December 12, 1946 (Article XI), specifically provides that Kaiser-Frazer shall not be required to pay the principal of any or all said 4% Convertible Debentures of Graham-Paige prior to the maturity date thereof (except for default in the payment of interest) and the debenture payment agreement of February 10, 1947, specifically provided (Article V) that except as therein provided Kaiser-Frazer does not "assume or agree to perform any of the promises, covenants, terms or conditions of the Indenture to be performed by" Graham-Paige and that neither the trustee under the indenture nor any debenture holder shall have any rights by virtue of such agreement and that the undertakings of Kaiser-Frazer are solely for the benefit of Graham-Paige and that they are limited to the making of Graham-Paige of the payments Kaiser-Frazer therein agreed to make.

At this point it is significant to note that by virtue of the foregoing provisions Kaiser-Frazer specifically avoided any undertaking on its part to apply 25% of its annual net profits to the sinking fund of the debentures in accordance with the provisions of Article Third of the Debenture. It is this failure of Kaiser-Frazer to have assumed the obligations of the sinking fund and to have paid 25% of its annual profits into such fund which presents the crux of this case and which forms the basis for the recovery sought herein against Kaiser-Frazer.

The complaint then proceeds to allege that the sale in question to the knowledge of Bank of America and Kaiser-Frazer constituted a conveyance of "all or substantially all" of the property of Graham-Paige and thereby terminated Graham-Paige's manufacturing and other activities in the automotive field; that Bank of America and Kaiser-Frazer knew or should have known that the sale as consummated would have the effect of depriving Graham-Paige of an opportunity to earn any moneys in the immediate or foreseeable future and would result in rendering nugatory the provisions in the indenture requiring Graham-Paige to make deposits in the sinking fund.

It is further alleged that by reason of the said sale Bank of America was under a duty, as trustee, and within its powers under the terms of the indenture, to obtain from Kaiser-Frazer a supplemental indenture satisfactory in form to itself, whereby Kaiser-Frazer would expressly assume the performance of *all* the covenants and conditions of the indenture to be performed by Graham-Paige, particularly those provisions of the indenture (Article Third) relating to the "Sinking Fund and Redemption of Debentures"; that Bank of America failed or refused to perform its duties as trustee in this respect and thereby breached the trust indenture; that by reason of the negligent and wilful misconduct on the part of Bank of America, plaintiff and all other debenture holders similarly situated were deprived, and unless this Court interferes, will be deprived of the benefits of the Sinking Fund provisions of the Indenture to the extent of the automotive assets of Graham-Paige and the earnings of Kaiser-Frazer, to the damage of the debenture holders in the amounts hereinafter set forth, "for which Bank of America is liable." ...

It is also alleged that Kaiser-Frazer is bound by the terms of the trust indenture despite its failure to execute a supplemental indenture to assume expressly the provisions relating to the "Sinking Fund"; that Kaiser-Frazer should have deposited with the trustee each year an amount in cash equal to 25% of its net earnings for the next preceding year; to wit, for the year 1947 the sum of $4,753,889.25 and for the year 1948 the sum of $2,590,524.50, making a total of $7,344,413.75, no part of which has been paid, and that Kaiser-Frazer is further obligated to the trustee for future sinking fund payments as provided in Article "Third" of the Indenture.

As of the date of this complaint there was outstanding $8,524,000 principal amount of the said 4% Convertible Debentures of Graham-Paige.

It is also alleged that Graham-Paige made no deposit with the trustee of any part of its net earnings for the years 1947 and 1948; that there was a net income for the calendar year 1947 of $123,766.73 but for the calendar year 1948 Graham-Paige had a net loss of $3,391,113.36, and that Graham-Paige's manufacturing operations of the farm equipment business were closed early in 1949.

The complaint contains the following allegation: "Thirty-Third: This action and the relief herein sought are not for the remedies provided by the Indenture, this being an action invoking the inherent powers of this Court as a court of equity to declare, protect and preserve the rights of the debenture holders. No demand upon the Trustee to institute or prosecute this action is necessary, nor has such demand been made for the reason that the Trustee is a defendant herein and is liable to the plaintiff and other debenture holders similarly situated, for its own negligent and wilful misconduct with respect to the acts herein complained of, and would be demanding that the Trustee sue itself, and such demand would be entirely useless and futile."[a]

---

a. To compare the concept of demand futility in stockholder derivative suits, see, for New York,

After alleging that he has no adequate remedy at law the plaintiff demands judgment as follows:

"1. Declaring and decreeing that Kaiser-Frazer has assumed the due and punctual performance and observance of all of the covenants and conditions of the Indenture, dated as of April 1, 1946, between Graham-Paige and Bank of America, with the same effect as if Kaiser-Frazer had been named in the Indenture in place and stead of Graham-Paige.

"2. Adjudging and decreeing that Kaiser-Frazer is liable to Bank of America, as Trustee, and shall pay over to Bank of America, as Trustee, or any Successor Trustee, for the benefit of the plaintiff and all other debenture holders similarly situated, the sum of $7,344,413.75, to be held and disposed of by the Trustee, in accordance with Article 'Third' of said Indenture relating to 'Sinking Fund and Redemption of Debentures.'

"3. Declaring and decreeing that so long as any of the said debentures are outstanding, 25% of the net earnings of Kaiser-Frazer, as defined in said Indenture, for each of the calendar years 1949 through 1954 be paid by Kaiser-Frazer to Bank of America, as Trustee, or any Successor Trustee in accordance with said Article 'Third' of said Indenture.

"4. Adjudging and decreeing that Bank of America be directed to account to the plaintiff and all other debenture holders similarly situated for its acts and for its failure to act as Trustee under said Indenture and that it be surcharged and directed to pay to itself as Trustee or to any Successor Trustee any and all damages sustained by the Trust Estate by reason of such acts or failure to act.

"5. Granting such other and further relief as to the Court may seem just and proper together with the costs and disbursements of this action, and reasonable and proper counsel fees to plaintiff's attorneys."

As stated above, plaintiff has instituted this action on behalf of himself and all other bondholders similarly situated. The plaintiff alleges ownership of less than one-eighth of 1% of the outstanding debentures. The objection that plaintiff lacks the legal capacity to sue is predicated on the language of §8.08 of the Indenture which provides in substance that "no holder of any Debenture * * * shall have any right to institute any suit * * * unless such holder previously shall have given to the Trustee written notice of default * * * and unless also the holders of not less than 25% in aggregate principal amount of the Debentures then outstanding shall have made written request upon the Trustee to institute such action and the Trustee * * * shall have neglected or refused to institute any such action * * *."

* * *

The plaintiff, however, urges that notwithstanding the presence of a "no action" clause, an individual bondholder has the right to bring a class action to protect his interests and the interests of all other bondholders of the same issue whenever the Indenture Trustee has acted in such a manner as to put itself in a position where it cannot faithfully and competently discharge its duty as a fiduciary. It seems to me that plaintiff's position is sound and is supported by such cases as Ettlinger v. Persian Rug & Carpet Co., 142 N.Y. 189, 36 N.E. 1055; Campbell v. Hudson & Manhattan R. Co., 277 App. Div. 731, 102 N.Y.S.2d 878, affirmed 302 N.Y. 902, 100 N.E.2d 183; Birn v. Childs Co., Sup., 37 N.Y.S.2d 689; ... Buel v. Baltimore & O. S. Ry. Co., 24 Misc. 646, 53 N.Y.S.

Marks v. Akers, 88 N.Y.2d 189 (N.Y. 1996); Auerbach v. Bennett, 47 N.Y.2d 619 (N.Y. 1979). And for Delaware, see Grobow v. Perot, 539 A.2d 180 (Del. 1988); Aronson v. Lewis, 473 A.2d 805 (Del. 1984); Zapata Corp. v. Maldonado, 430 A.2d 779 (Del. 1981). See also Principles of Corp. Gov. §7.03 (Amer. L. Inst. 1994). [Eds.]

749. In the Ettlinger case, supra, the incompetency of the trustee to act for the bond-holders was predicated upon the trustee's absence from this country and his probable insanity. In the Birn case the trustee's incompetency was based on its unreasonable re-fusal to sue. In the Buel case the incompetency of the trustee was predicated upon its inconsistent position as trustee of conflicting trusts. In the Campbell case, 277 App. Div. 731, 102 N.Y.S.2d 878, where the trustee "renounced" or "abdicated" its function to sue, the Court made the following apposite statement 277 App. Div. at pages 734-37, 102 N.Y.S.2d at page 881: "All of those cases, and others like them, presuppose a trustee competent to act, and exercising its judgment in good faith respecting what is best for the bondholders as a whole concerning the matter in issue. If a trustee under such an indenture acts in bad faith, or, abdicating its function with respect to the point in ques-tion, declines to act at all, bondholders for themselves and others similarly situated may bring a derivative action in the right of the trustee, rather than in their own individual rights as bondholders. In that event they are not subject to the limitations of Article Seventh of the Indenture, which are not imposed on the trustee or on bondholders act-ing in the status of the trustee. This subject was considered lucidly, and the same result reached, by Justice Walter in Birn v. Childs Co., Sup., 37 N.Y.S.2d 689, 696....

Plaintiff's affidavit in opposition to the instant motion sets forth that subsequent to the date of the Indenture, Bank of America made several loans to both Kaiser-Frazer and Gra-ham-Paige which were enmeshed with the sale of the automotive assets of the latter to Kaiser-Frazer. The nature of these transactions was such as to create a conflict in the inter-ests of Bank of America as trustee and Bank of America as a creditor of both Graham-Paige and Kaiser-Frazer. As trustee it was bound to protect the interests of the debenture holders and was charged with the duty of requiring Kaiser-Frazer to assume the sinking fund pro-visions when the latter company acquired the automotive assets of Graham-Paige. On the other hand, as a bank creditor and in its self-interest Bank of America gave its express writ-ten consent to the terms of the Sales Agreement whereby Kaiser-Frazer delimited its under-takings with respect to the debentures so that it did not assume the obligations of the Sink-ing Fund provision of the Indenture. At the same time, in order to protect its own interests, in making a loan of $12,000,000 to Kaiser-Frazer, Bank of America required Kaiser-Frazer to amortize that loan to the extent of 25% of its annual net profits in addition to securing a mortgage on all of Kaiser-Frazer's property as well as on the property of Graham-Paige, the sale of which to Kaiser-Frazer was being contemplated and in the course of negotiation.

It seems to me that when Bank of America consented to Kaiser-Frazer's declination of assuming any of the provisions of the Indenture, including the sinking fund provi-sions, it placed itself in a position which was antagonistic to and in conflict with the in-terests of the debenture holders.

As was stated in Farmers' Loan & Trust Co. v. Northern Pacific R. Co., C.C., 66 F. 169, 176: "A trustee cannot be permitted to assume a position inconsistent with or in opposition to his trust. His duty is single, and he cannot serve two masters with antagonistic interests."

The movant urges that under the circumstances of this case plaintiff's proper remedy is to have a new or substitute trustee appointed but such argument is untenable for the same reasons that the Court in the Ettlinger case rejected a similar contention. There the Court stated at page 193 of 142 N.Y., at page 1056 of 36 N.E.: "But the special term say [sic] that in such event a new trustee should have been appointed. That simply re-produces the same difficulty in another form, for a court would hardly remove a trustee without notice to him, and giving him an opportunity to be heard; and why should a new appointment be made, when any one of the bondholders can equally do the duty of pursuing the foreclosure? The court, in such an action, takes hold of the trust, dictates and controls its performance, distributes the assets as it deems just, and it is not vitally important which of the two possible plaintiffs sets the court in motion. The bondholders are the real parties in interest. It is their right which is to be redressed, and their loss which is to be prevented; and any emergency which makes a demand upon the trustee futile or impossible, and leaves the right of the bondholder without other reasonable means of redress, should justify his appearance as plaintiff in a court of equity for the purpose of a foreclosure."

In view of the foregoing it is my view that the "no action" clause involved in the case at bar is inoperative and inapplicable.

* * *

The other contentions of the movant have been considered and found untenable.

Accordingly, this motion is denied in all respects. Settle order on notice.

Notes and Questions

1. What is the reason for limiting the rights of individual bondholders to bring suit against the issuer for breach of the indenture? Is the limitation more or less justifiable than the preclusion of derivative standing to creditors? Would the same reasons support limiting bondholders' litigation when the rights they seek to assert arise outside of the contract? When they arise under the contract but in the form of implied covenants?

2. Do you agree that it is sufficient for bondholders to be able to sue directly on their bonds rather than have the right to bring action under the indenture? In what circumstances will this right be inadequate? What advantages might the litigation limitation have for bondholders?

3. In Metropolitan Securities v. Occidental Petroleum Corp., 705 F. Supp. 134 (S.D.N.Y. 1989), plaintiffs owned convertible bonds of MidCon Corp. ("MidCon"), which was acquired as a result of a friendly tender offer by Occidental Petroleum Corporation ("Occidental"), to help MidCon avert an unwanted takeover by Coach Acquisition Co. ("Coach"). The debentures were convertible, among other things, upon the consolidation, merger or sale of MidCon with or into another person. Unlike the Coach offer, the Occidental tender offer excluded the debenture holders who were informed by Occidental that they would be required to convert their debentures into stock to take advantage of the offer.

Occidental did not indicate whether the conversion option would continue to apply were the merger successful. This was significant because if it did, debenture holders would do better financially by continuing to hold their debentures, whereas if it did not, debenture holders would have suffered a loss in the value of their debentures if they failed to convert. Ultimately, the conversion option continued to apply, but by the time this was clear plaintiff had converted some of its debentures into stock and sold others on the open market.

Plaintiffs sued under §§14(e) and 10(b) of the Securities Exchange Act of 1934 (respectively, an anti-fraud provision in connection with tender offers and a general anti-fraud provision), alleging that Occidental's statement with respect to the conversion rights was false and misleading because debenture holders did not have to convert to profit from the offer.

The court affirmed the district court's grant of defendant's motion to dismiss. It held that plaintiffs lacked standing under §14(e) because standing under that statute is limited to security holders to whom the offer is made. Furthermore, Metropolitan could not maintain standing as a common stockholder (even though it had converted its debentures) "because the injuries which it alleges arise in connection with its status as a holder of the debentures, not as a holder of common stock."

As to Metropolitan's claim under §10(b), the court held that Occidental's statement was not materially misleading but merely reflected uncertainty with respect to the debentures. Moreover, neither Occidental nor MidCon owed a duty of disclosure to plaintiff that would support a claim under §10(b): "... [w]here the duties of an issuer (and trustee) to debenture holders are circumscribed by the Indenture Agreement, no extraordinary duties will be implied under the federal securities laws." What questions, if any, does this last-quoted statement raise in your mind?

Problem — Collective Action by Bondholders

1. You are counsel to an organization called Debentureholders' Efforts for Free And Unrestricted Litigation Techniques ("DEFAULT"), composed of a number of institutional and individual bondholders. Although your group is somewhat dissatisfied with Section 507 of the Model Indenture, it does not think that it yet has the leverage to discourage issuers from including it in their indentures. Your concern therefore has shifted to the problem of making Section 507 more effective by providing some means of (i) ensuring the flow of sufficient information to permit bondholders to monitor issuers' compliance with their indentures, and (ii) providing for communication among bondholders and mechanisms for collective action to make the 25 percent demand provision of Section 507 effective. DEFAULT's chairperson has asked you to come up with a proposal to achieve these goals and draft language embodying the proposal to be inserted in indentures. When you have completed your draft, write a memorandum to DEFAULT's members and prospective bond issuers explaining what you have done, and why. Recall that the registration and reporting requirements of Sections 12(g) and 13 of the Securities Exchange Act of 1934 apply to publicly-issued bonds.

2. DEFAULT's chairperson has just returned from an extended trip to Europe where she has met with groups of institutional bondholders in a variety of civil law countries. She informs you of some of the differences in approach those countries take to bondholders' rights, and asks you to write a memorandum comparing those approaches with those of American jurisdictions and recommending any changes you think are advisable based upon your comparison. She also asks you to indicate how likely you think it is that American issuers would accept such changes. Finally, she asks you to analyze the American approach from a public policy perspective and suggest whether any legislative changes in that approach might be appropriate.

The duties of the indenture trustee are pursued in more detail *infra* at section 5b.

Section 5
Other Participants in Debt Offerings

a. Underwriter

Consider the role of the underwriter. In addition to its traditional role in placing the debt securities being offered with public investors in return for a commission, to whom does it owe a duty, if anyone? Prospective debtholders? The issuer of the debt securities? No one? If a duty is owed, what type of duty is it? *See* Mitchell, The Fairness Rights of Corporate Bondholders, 65 N.Y.U. L. Rev. 1165 (1990).

Dale Tauke assesses the argument that underwriters functionally, if not legally, protect the interests of public bondholders. He notes that underwriters must sell the bonds to the public in order to profit, and thus have an incentive to negotiate for increased indenture protections that will permit issuance at higher prices. He also observes that underwriters must protect their reputations for effectiveness in selling bonds (often referred to as "reputational capital"), which will lead them to negotiate for greater bondholder protection. *See* Tauke, Should Bonds Have More Fun? A Reexamination of the Debate over Corporate Bondholder Rights, 1989 Colum. Bus. L. Rev. 1, 24-26. *See also* Kahan, The Qualified Case Against Mandatory Terms in Bonds, 89 Nw. U. L. Rev. 565, 591-92 (1995) (making the reputational argument). Additionally, as one of your editors knows from first hand experience, it is counsel to the underwriters that provides the first draft of the financial covenant package for a prospective indenture. This package, after being negotiated with issuer's counsel, is inserted into the indenture.[1]

Despite these incentives, Tauke notes some weaknesses in the argument that underwriters protect bondholders. First, in a "firm commitment" underwriting, underwriters buy the bonds from the issuer and immediately resell them to the public. Thus, underwriters "own" the bonds for only a brief period of time during the distribution process, and thus face little direct risk from inadequate covenant protection. Moreover, the issuer, not the bondholders, selects the underwriter, and the underwriter may not press too hard for bondholder protection for fear of losing future business from that issuer. This future business could include not only the underwriting of additional securities offerings but also advising on lucrative mergers and acquisitions. He also questions the efficacy of bond pricing as a means of controlling underwriters. *But see* Kahan, *supra* at 574-80. Finally, he notes that even if underwriters do have incentives to negotiate for bondholder protective covenants, the limits to foresight may result in bondholder underprotection.

For more critical evaluations of the underwriters' role in protecting bondholders through the imposition of contractual constraints, see Campbell & Zack, Put a Bullet in the Poor Beast. His Leg is Broken and His Use is Past. Conflict of Interest in the Dual Role of Lender and Corporate Indenture Trustee: A Proposal to End it in the Public Interest, 32 Bus. Law. 1705 (1977); Mitchell, The Fairness Rights of Corporate Bondholders, 65 N.Y.U. L. Rev. 1165, 1183 (1990).

b. Indenture Trustee

The Trust Indenture Act of 1939 (TIA) represented yet another congressional attempt to institute control over the securities industry after the stock market collapse of 1929. According to the TIA's legislative history, the primary purposes of the TIA are: (1) to provide full and fair disclosure to debtholders, not only at the time when corporate issuers originally issue debt securities, but also throughout the life of those securi-

---

1. Interestingly, Steven Schwarcz has argued that, in his experience, covenants contained in public bond indentures are weaker than those contained in privately negotiated loan agreements. *See* Schwarcz, Rethinking a Corporation's Obligations to Creditors, 17 Cardozo L. Rev. 647, 660-61 (1996).

ties; (2) to provide a tool whereby debtholders may organize for the protection of their own interests; and (3) to ensure that debtholders will have the services of a disinterested indenture trustee which conforms to the high standards of conduct observed by trust institutions.

In deciding that an implied private cause of action in favor of debtholders existed under the TIA, the Third Circuit provided a brief outline of the structure and background of the TIA:

> .... A study was conducted by the Securities and Exchange Commission (SEC) in 1936 which revealed widespread abuses in the issuance of corporate bonds under indentures.[2] The main problems identified by the study were that the indenture trustee was frequently aligned with the issuer of the debentures and that the debenture holders were widely dispersed, thereby hampering their ability to enforce their rights. Furthermore, courts frequently enforced broad exculpatory terms of the indenture inserted by the issuer, which offered the investors less protection than the traditional standards of fiduciary duty.

> Rather than allow the SEC direct supervision of trustee behavior and thereby provide for a more overt intrusion into capital markets, the Act establishes a standard of behavior indirectly by refashioning the form of the indenture itself. The Act is structured so that before a debt security non-exempted from the Act may be offered to the public, the indenture under which it is issued must be "qualified" by the SEC. The indenture is deemed "qualified" when registration becomes effective. Before registration of the debenture is declared effective it must be qualified under the following conditions: (1) the security has been issued under an indenture; (2) the person designated as trustee is eligible to serve; and (3) the indenture conforms to the requirements of §§ 310-318, 15 U.S.C. §§ 77jjj-77rrr. [The district court] aptly described the operative provisions of the Act, §§ 310-318, as follows.

>> Sections 310 through 318 form the core of the Act in that they outline the substantive duties that the indenture must impose on the trustee. These sections are of three types. The first type is proscriptive in nature, prohibiting certain terms. For example, § 315, 15 U.S.C. § 77ooo (d), prohibits provisions in the indenture which would relieve or exculpate the trustee from liability for negligence. The second type of section is merely permissive in nature. An example of this type of section is § 315(a), 15 U.S.C. § 77ooo(a)(1), which states that the indenture may contain a provision relieving the trustee of liability except for the performance of such duties as are specifically set out in such indenture.

>> The third type of section, and the most important for our purposes, is mandatory and prescriptive in nature. These sections begin with the phrase "indenture to be qualified shall provide" or "shall require." An example of this type of section is § 311, 15 U.S.C. § 77kkk, which states that the indenture shall require the trustee to establish certain accounts for

---

2. See Securities and Exchange Commission Report on the Study and Investigation of the Work, Activities, Personnel and Functions of Protective and Reorganization Committees, Part IV, Trustees Under Indentures (1937); See also Hearings on H.R. 10292 Before a Subcommittee of the Committee on Interstate and Foreign Commerce, 75th Cong., 3d Sess. 20 (1938).

the benefit of bond holders in the event the trustee also becomes a creditor of the issuer and the issuer defaults on the bonds.

473 F. Supp. at 206.

The SEC has no enforcement authority over the terms of the indenture once the registration statement becomes effective, and it cannot issue a stop order for violation of indenture provisions by the indenture trustee. After the effective date of the indenture the SEC's role is limited to general rulemaking and investigation. 15 U.S.C. §§ 77ddd(c), (d), (e); 77eee(a), (c); 77ggg; 77sss; 77ttt. The Act contains criminal liability for certain willful violations and misrepresentations[4] and express civil liability for any omission or misstatement in the filing documents.[5]

Enforcement of the terms of the indenture is left to the parties....

Zeffiro v. First Penn. Banking & Trust Co., 623 F.2d 290 (3d Cir. 1980), *cert. denied,* 456 U.S. 1005 (1982).

The TIA generally applies to the sale by issuers of debt securities and interests in debt securities to the public. The TIA does not apply to debt securities issued in private placements, because transactions which are exempt from the registration requirements of the Securities Act of 1933 are also exempt from the requirements of the TIA. Absent an exemption, any security subject to the TIA must be distributed under an indenture that complies with the TIA. The trust indenture must be filed with the SEC. Moreover, the TIA sets forth the eligibility requirements for indenture trustees. The TIA also sets forth certain statutory duties and obligations for the trustee, such as the issuance of periodic reports to debtholders. Additionally, it grants trustees certain powers such as the right to bring suit against the issuer on behalf of debtholders in the event of a default by the issuer.

Since the TIA's enactment, significant changes have occurred in the U.S. and international debt markets. The types of securities offered have changed along with the method of their distribution. As market developments rendered aspects of the original TIA outdated, the SEC submitted a proposal to Congress in the late 1980s to modernize the TIA to enable it to adapt to current practices and future developments in the public market for debt securities. Congress passed the first extensive revision of the TIA in 1990. This revision, which is known as the Trust Indenture Reform Act of 1990 (TIRA), not only modernized the fifty-year old TIA going forward, but it also applied retroactively to all existing indentures.

Senate Report 101-155 (1989) describes the purpose of TIRA as follows:

> The principal purpose of Title IV is to modernize the Trust Indenture Act of 1939 (Act) which regulates the public issuance of debt securities. In the fifty years since its enactment, the Act has not been amended in any important respect. During the same period, however, the public market for debt securities has undergone significant changes. Innovations in the forms of debt instruments have produced securities, such as collateralized mortgage obligations, which were not contemplated in 1939. Technological developments and regulatory changes have resulted in new distribution methods, including "shelf" offerings, direct placements and "dutch auctions." Finally, public securities markets have been profoundly changed by internationalization. Enactment of Title IV would conform the Act to the present realities of the market and make it adaptable to future developments, while facilitating the administration of the Act.

---

4. Section 325 [15 U.S.C. § 77yyy].
5. Section 323 [15 U.S.C. § 77www].

Title IV would effect four principal revisions to the Act. The procedures for qualifications of indentures under the Act would be simplified and strengthened. Broad exemptive authority would be granted to the Commission to provide flexibility in administration and adaptability to future developments. The determination of conflicts of interest disqualifying a trustee from service would be made at the time of a default under the indenture. Trusteeships by foreign persons would be conditionally permitted in order to encourage continued internationalization of securities markets. The legislation would also effect a number of technical changes to the Act.

Among the most relevant provisions of the TIA for our purposes are those relating to the indenture trustee. Section 310(a)(1) of the Act requires that, as to each indenture, there be one or more indenture trustees meeting a series of threshold qualifications. At least one trustee must be a "corporation organized and doing business under the laws of the United States or of any State or Territory of the District of Columbia...." Section 310 sets forth in great detail the appropriate characteristics of the trustee as well as disqualifying factors. Section 315 of the Act describes the duties and responsibilities of the trustee:

(a) Duties prior to default

The indenture to be qualified shall automatically be deemed (unless it is expressly provided therein that any such provision is excluded) to provide that, prior to default (as such term is defined in such indenture) —

(1) the indenture trustee shall not be liable except for the performance of such duties as are specifically set out in such indenture; and

(2) the indenture trustee may conclusively rely, as to the truth of the statements and the correctness of the opinions expressed therein, in the absence of bad faith on the part of such trustee, upon certificates or opinions conforming to the requirements of the indenture;

but the indenture trustee shall examine the evidence furnished to it pursuant to [section 314] to determine whether or not such evidence conforms to the requirements of the indenture.

(b) Notice of defaults

The indenture trustee shall give to the indenture security holders, in the manner and to the extent provided in subsection (c) of [section 313], notice of all defaults known to the trustee, within ninety days after the occurrence thereof: *provided*, that such indenture shall automatically be deemed (unless it is expressly provided therein that such provision is excluded) to provide that, except in the case of default in the payment of the principal of or interest on any indenture security, or in the payment of any sinking or purchase fund installment, the trustee shall be protected in withholding such notice if and so long as the board of directors, the executive committee, or a trust committee of directors and/or responsible officers, of the trustee in good faith determine that the withholding of such notice is in the interests of the indenture security holders.

(c) Duties of the trustee in case of default

The indenture trustee shall exercise in case of default (as such term is defined in such indenture) such of the rights and powers vested in it by such indenture, and to use the same degree of care and skill in their exercise, as a prudent man would exercise or use under the circumstances in the conduct of his own affairs.

(d) Responsibility of trustee

The indenture to be qualified shall not contain any provisions relieving the indenture trustee from liability for its own negligent action, its own negligent failure to act, or its own willful misconduct, except that—

(1) such indenture shall automatically be deemed (unless it is expressly provided therein that any such provision is excluded) to contain the provisions authorized by paragraphs (1) and (2) of subsection (a) of this section;

(2) such indenture shall automatically be deemed (unless it is expressly provided therein that any such provision is excluded) to contain provisions protecting the indenture trustee from liability for any error of judgment made in good faith by a responsible officer or officers of such trustee, unless it shall be proved that such trustee was negligent in ascertaining the pertinent facts; and

(3) such indenture shall automatically be deemed (unless it is expressly provided therein that any such provision is excluded) to contain provisions protecting the indenture trustee with respect to any action taken or omitted to be taken by it in good faith in accordance with the direction of the holders of not less than a majority in principal amount of the indenture securities at the time outstanding (determined as provided in subsection (a) of [section 316]) relating to the time, method, and place of conducting any proceeding for any remedy available to such trustee, or exercising any trust or power conferred upon such trustee, under such indenture.

(e) Undertaking for costs

The indenture to be qualified shall automatically be deemed (unless it is expressly provided therein that any such provision is excluded) to contain provisions to the effect that all parties thereto, including the indenture security holders, agree that the court may in its discretion require, in any suit for the enforcement of any right or remedy under such indenture, or in any suit against the trustee for any action taken or omitted by it as trustee, the filing by any party litigant in such suit of an undertaking to pay the costs of such suit, and that such court may in its discretion assess reasonable costs, including reasonable attorneys' fees, against any party litigant in such suit, having due regard to the merits and good faith of the claims or defenses made by such party litigant: Provided, That the provisions of this subsection shall not apply to any suit instituted by such trustee, to any suit instituted by any indenture security holder, or group of indenture security holders, holding in the aggregate more than 10 per centum in principal amount of the indenture securities outstanding, or to any suit instituted by any indenture security holder for the enforcement of the payment of the principal of or interest on any indenture security, on or after the respective due dates expressed in such indenture security.

The following cases explore trustee conflicts of interest with bondholders. As you read the cases consider (i) what function does (and should) an indenture trustee perform, and (ii) does the device of an indenture trustee continue to make sense? Reconsider Problem—Collective Action by Bondholders, *supra* at section 4d(ii).

(i) *Trustee as Competing Creditor*

Morris v. Cantor

390 F. Supp. 817 (S.D.N.Y. 1975)

WARD, District Judge.

Plaintiffs Robert G. Morris, Israel Patents Corporation and Patents Management Corporation, calling themselves the "Protective Committee of 4% Convertible Subordinated Debentures of Interstate Department Stores, Inc.," bring this action on behalf of themselves and all others similarly situated ("the bondholders"). The complaint alleges that the several defendants violated provisions of the Trust Indenture Act of 1939, ... ("the Act") and the Securities Act of 1933, ... ("the Securities Act"), and breached their common law fiduciary obligations to the bondholders, in connection with various loans to defendant Interstate Department Stores, Inc. ("the Company") during 1972.

The Bankers Trust Company ("the Bank") which is charged with violations of the Trust Indenture Act and breach of fiduciary obligations, moves pursuant to Rule 12(b), Fed. R. Civ. P., to dismiss the complaint against itself for failure to state a claim upon which relief can be granted. For the reasons discussed below, the motion is denied.

The Company issued $20,000,000 in 4% convertible subordinated debentures under an indenture agreement dated August 1, 1967, in which the Bank was named Trustee. The indenture agreement was duly registered with the Securities and Exchange Commission ("the Commission"), and its terms conformed to the requirements of the Act. The debentures were by their terms unsecured and subordinated to all "senior indebtedness" of the issuer, as that term was defined in the indenture agreement, including any which might be later acquired. The indenture agreement provided that should the indenture trustee be or become a creditor of the issuer, the trustee would be entitled to the benefit of the subordination provisions of the indenture with respect to senior indebtedness to the same extent as any other holder of such indebtedness.

The complaint alleges that the Bank, while Trustee, acted as lead bank in negotiating the extension of a $90,000,000 line of credit to the Company, which qualified as senior indebtedness with respect to the debentures. The Bank thus became a preferred secured creditor of the Company, with priority over the bondholders, in the event of bankruptcy. Plaintiffs concede that the loan was not consummated until after the Bank resigned as Trustee, and in any event, not even negotiated within four months prior to a default in payment of the principal or interest under the indenture. They contend, however, that the Bank's action constituted "willful misconduct" within the meaning of §315(d) of the Act, 15 U.S.C. §77ooo(d).[a]

This Court's jurisdiction of the controversy between plaintiffs and the Bank is based exclusively upon the Trust Indenture Act.... A threshold question therefore is whether the Act by its terms creates any liability for violation of the provisions of indentures qualified thereunder, or more generally for willful misconduct on the part of a trustee appointed according to the Act's provisions. A second question is whether there exists a civil right of action so that the bondholders may enforce such liability. Neither of these questions has yet been decided by the courts. The final question presented to the Court by this motion is whether, assuming it is proven, the conduct alleged constitutes a violation of the Act.

---

a. TIRA amended §315(d) to provide that its terms (set out below in the opinion) are deemed to be included in a qualified indenture, thus making those provisions of the TIA a matter of substantive law. [Eds.]

The unique structure of the Act creates the first question, whether by its terms it imposes any obligations upon the indenture trustee. The Act requires that any indenture agreement under which an issue of over $1,000,000 is offered to the public be registered with the Commission and contain certain terms which the Act carefully specifies. Thus, section after section of the Act begins with the language, "The indenture to be qualified [shall] provide ..." or "shall require ..." or "shall contain provisions requiring ..." and continues with detailed and often technical terms pertaining to the naming of the trustee, qualifications of eligible trustees, required reports to bondholders or from the obligor to the trustee, duties of the trustee both prior to and in the event of default, or in the event of its acquiring conflicting interests. Other sections are permissive in language, substituting the language "... may require ...". The particular section at issue here reads:

> "The indenture to be qualified shall not contain any provisions relieving the indenture trustee from liability for its own negligent action, its own negligent failure to act, or its own willful misconduct ..." 15 U.S.C. §77ooo(d).

Once the indenture is registered, the Commission has no power to enforce its provisions. 15 U.S.C. 77iii(e). While the Act gives the Commission general rule making and investigative authority, it limits that authority to matters involving qualification of the indenture and required reports. 15 U.S.C. §77sss, ttt, and uuu. The only civil liability expressly imposed is for material misstatement or omission in any report filed with the commission pursuant to the Act, in connection with the qualification of the indenture or thereafter. 15 U.S.C. §77www.

Prior to the Act's passage, indenture agreements, as private contracts, had been governed by the common law of contracts and fiduciary obligations, articulated primarily in the state courts.... Of the substantial body of law which had evolved defining rights of bondholders and trustees, some addressed the specific question of what constitutes willful misconduct on the part of the indenture trustee. But trustees under such indenture agreements had developed a widespread practice of contractually limiting their liability for performance of their trust functions, and courts enforced these terms of limitation in many instances.

Thus, the scheme of the Act is to regulate in a limited fashion by taking a type of private contract, requiring that it contain certain terms and be registered with the Commission, and that the parties disclose certain information, and precluding the Commission from enforcing those terms. The Bank argues that the contract itself remains a private contract, enforceable only in the state courts or under the diversity jurisdiction of this Court, and that the only "liability created by the statute" within the meaning of its jurisdiction granting section, 15 U.S.C. §77vvv, is for failure to include the requisite terms in the contract, or for failure to register it as required by the Act, or for material misstatements in connection with that registration, or misrepresentation of the effect of registration. Plaintiffs contend that the Act, albeit indirectly, imposes substantive obligations upon the trustee and therefore creates liability enforceable in this Court for violation of any of the terms of the contract itself which are required under the Act, as well as for those common law obligations of trusteeship which the Act prohibits the contract from abridging.

The legislative history does not speak directly to the question, but upon careful reading persuades the Court that the Act creates substantive liabilities in those areas it specifically addresses.

* * *

The existence of a private right of action follows, *a fortiori*. This is not the situation where Congress has imposed liability but expressly created only criminal or administrative enforcement procedures, and the courts imply a civil right of action. *See, e.g.*, Kardon v. National Gypsum Co., 69 F. Supp. 512 (E.D. Pa. 1946); on the merits, 73 F. Supp. 798 (E.D. Pa. 1947); on requests for additional findings, 83 F. Supp. 613 (E.D. Pa. 1947).... Here, instead, Congress expressly anticipated that any liability indirectly imposed would be enforced by private civil actions, and specifically excluded the Commission from an enforcement role.

* * *

The statutory language itself reflects Congress' intention that there be such a right. 15 U.S.C. §77ooo(e) provides that the indenture may contain terms by which the parties "agree that the court may in its discretion require, in any suit for the enforcement of any right or remedy under such indenture, or in any suit against the trustee for any action taken by it as trustee ...[,]" the filing of an undertaking for costs.

Since this Court has found that the statute was intended to create liability for breach of the indenture provisions, and for breach of fiduciary obligations which it expressly preserved from limitation by contract, and since, consequently, this Court has jurisdiction to enforce such liability, bondholders alleging such a breach may bring their actions in this Court.

The Bank argues that nevertheless, on the facts alleged, plaintiffs have not stated a claim upon which relief can be granted. It contends that the Act addresses the situation of the trustee-creditor in clear terms in 15 U.S.C. §77kkk,[b] and that if a trustee's actions as creditor of the obligor on the bonds do not violate that section, they cannot be considered willful misconduct within the meaning of §77ooo. The parties agree that the Bank's action does not constitute a violation of §77kkk.

The Act requires that qualified indenture agreements contain provisions for disqualification of the institutional trustee upon the occurrence of certain enumerated conflicts of interest, thus in effect prohibiting those conflicts. §77jjj.[c] Its creditor relationship to the obligor on the bonds is not among these conflicts. Rather, the Act requires merely that the indenture provide that the trustee who is also a creditor within four months prior to any default on the bonds, or at any time thereafter, and who receives any preferential payment as a creditor, shall hold the proceeds for distribution to the bondholders. §77kkk. The Bank reads this requirement as an implied permission for it to be simultaneously trustee under the indenture agreement and creditor of the obligor, and further, for it to become even a preferred creditor of the obligor while it is trustee.

The legislative history supports the Bank's interpretation, revealing that Congress explicitly considered the problems of conflicting interest that might arise in such a circumstance. The S.E.C. Report[d] condemned the practice of a bank simultaneously act-

---

b. Also amended in part by TIRA to make the provision mandatory. [Eds.]

c. Also amended in part by TIRA to make the provision mandatory. [Eds.]

d. Securities and Exchange Commission, Report on the Study and Investigation of the Work, Activities, Personnel and Functions of Protective and Reorganization Committees, Part VI, Trustees Under Indentures (1937).

ing as trustee and creditor, Report, e.g. at 84, 90, 98, 107, while, however, noting that the period of greatest danger to the interests of the bondholders was immediately prior to a default. *Id.* at 98. But spokesmen for several banks testified before the House Committee, emphasizing that it was often in the interest of a company and its bond-holders that credit be available to sustain the company as a going concern, and that frequently the bank most familiar with the affairs of the company and most willing to advance credit was also the indenture trustee. *See, e.g.,* Hearings,[e] at 159-60, 170-71, 268-69. Congress determined to protect the interests of the bondholders, without pro-hibiting such a dual relationship, by providing that any preferential collection which the trustee as creditor should make in the four months prior to default, when it should have a clear idea of the precarious position of the company, be held for the benefit of the bondholders....

The Court therefore concludes that the mere existence or creation of a dual relation-ship, as trustee under the indenture and as preferred creditor of the obligor on the bonds, although there may be an inherent conflict of interest, does not of itself consti-tute a violation of §77ooo(d). Congress specifically dealt with this inherent conflict when drafting the bill, in such a way as to permit it, with certain named protections for the interests of the bondholders. Having so prescribed contract terms addressed to this subject, it removed this conduct from the area of residual liability which could not be limited by contract, set forth in §77ooo(d).

That area of residual liability, however, is defined by the common law as it had devel-oped prior to the statute and has developed since. Willful misconduct encompasses knowing, intentional action in flagrant disregard of the interests of the bondholders.... While the mere making of a loan to the Company, protected under §77kkk, cannot be such willful misconduct as the statute contemplates, it is possible that in the circum-stances known to the Bank, to negotiate such a loan did constitute knowing, intentional action in flagrant disregard of the interests of the bondholders. Were these facts devel-oped during discovery and at trial, plaintiffs would have stated a claim upon which re-lief can be granted under the statute. Accordingly, the Court considers it premature to dismiss the complaint.

Defendant Bankers Trust Company's motion to dismiss the complaint is denied.

It is so ordered.

Questions

1. Does TIRA strengthen or weaken the court's conclusion that the TIA imposes sub-stantive obligations on the trustee?

2. Do you agree or disagree with the court's conclusion that the TIA permits a trustee to be a senior lender in conflict with the debenture holders for whom it serves?

3. Does TIRA strengthen or weaken the court's conclusion that the TIA does not pre-empt common law principles?

---

e. Hearings on H.R. 2191 and H.R. 5220 before a Subcommittee of the Committee on Interstate and Foreign Commerce, House of Representatives, 76th Cong., 1st Sess. (1939).

(ii) Breach of Fiduciary Duty under State Law
Broad v. Rockwell International Corporation
642 F.2d 929 (5th Cir. 1981), cert. denied,
454 U.S. 965 (1981)

* * *

.... There remains the question of the Trust Company's liability for breach of fiduciary duty under applicable state law.

The panel relied on *Dabney* v. *Chase National Bank*, 196 F.2d 668 (2d Cir. 1952), and *United States Trust Co.* v. *First National City Bank*, 57 A.D.2d 285, 394 N.Y.S.2d 653 (1st Dep't 1977), aff'd mem., 45 N.Y.2d 869, 382 N.E.2d 1355, 410 N.Y.S.2d 580 (1978), for its conclusion that even in the absence of a default, an indenture trustee is cloaked under New York law with a fiduciary duty to the holders of debentures that may extend beyond its strict obligations under the indenture. Both *Dabney* and *City Bank* involved conflicts of interest in which the trustee put itself in a position of advantage over the beneficiaries of the trust. Arguably, the Trust Company faced a similar conflict of interest in the case at bar when Rockwell threatened to bring a lawsuit, to withdraw other business it had with the Trust Company, and to force the Trust Company's resignation as Trustee if it refused to execute the supplemental indenture necessary for the merger.

Be that as it may, however, there is no actionable wrong in this case. We assume, without deciding, that the panel was correct in concluding that under New York law, the Trust Company's obligations "exceeded the narrow definitions of its duties in the indenture and encompassed fiduciary duties as well." 614 F.2d at 432. And had we agreed with the panel that the Indenture was ambiguous, there would be a real question whether the holders of Debentures had received in the supplemental indenture all that was contractually due them under the Indenture. Were that question answered in the negative, there would have been the further question whether the Trust Company had adequately discharged its duties to the holders of Debentures with the "absolute singleness of purpose" required by New York law. *Dabney*, 196 F.2d at 671. The evidence in the record regarding the advice given the Trust Company by its counsel prior to the execution of the supplemental indenture undoubtedly would have been relevant to the Trust Company's defensive claim that it had acted in good faith and on advice of counsel.

But the question of whether the holders of Debentures received in the supplemental indenture all that was contractually due to them is conclusively answered by our holding in part II of this opinion.... Regardless of the Trust Company's motives, or its prior opinion as to the meaning of the Indenture, there is no question but that the Trust Company's ultimate action—executing the supplemental indenture—fully protected what we have determined to be the legitimate rights of the holders of Debentures under the Indenture. Broad has cited no New York authority for the proposition that an indenture trustee has a duty, fiduciary or otherwise, to seek for the holders of debentures any benefits that are *greater* than those contractually due them; indeed, there is support in the New York cases for the opposite conclusion. *See Hazzard* v. *Chase National Bank*, 159 Misc. 57, 287 N.Y.S. 541 (Sup. Ct. 1936), aff'd mem., 257 A.D. 950, 14 N.Y.S.2d 147 (1st Dep't 1939), aff'd mem., 282 N.Y. 652, 26 N.E.2d 801, cert. denied, 311 U.S. 708, 61 S. Ct. 319, 85 L. Ed. 460 (1940). We hold that the Trust Company had no duty, as a matter of law, to do anything other than that which it in fact did. Thus, there is no question for a jury as to whether there has been a breach of fiduciary duty. Accordingly, we affirm the judgment of the district court with respect to both the state and federal breach of fiduciary duty claims against the Trust Company.

(iii) Pre-Default Duties of a Trustee under the TIA
Elliott Assoc. v. J. Henry Schroder Bank & Tr. Co.
838 F.2d 66 (2d Cir. 1988)

ALTIMARI, Circuit Judge:

This appeal involves an examination of the obligations and duties of a trustee during the performance of its predefault duties under a trust indenture, qualified under the Trust Indenture Act of 1939 ... (the "Act"). The instant action was brought by a debenture holder who sought to represent a class of all debenture holders under the trust indenture. The debenture holder alleged in its complaint that the trustee waived a 50-day notice period prior to the redemption of the debentures and did not consider the impact of the waiver on the financial interests of the debenture holders. The debenture holder alleged further that, had the trustee not waived the full 50-day notice period, the debenture holders would have been entitled to receive an additional $1.2 million in interest from the issuer of the debentures. The debenture holder therefore concludes that the trustee's waiver was improper and constituted a breach of the trustee's duties owed to the debenture holders under the indenture, the Act and state law.

The district court dismissed the debenture holder's action after conducting a bench trial and entered judgment in favor of the defendants. The district court held that the trustee's waiver did not constitute a breach of any duty owed to the debenture holders — under the indenture or otherwise — because, as the court found, a trustee's predefault duties are limited to those duties expressly provided in the indenture. See 655 F. Supp. 1281, 1288-89 (S.D.N.Y. 1987). We agree with the district court that no breach of duty was stated here. Accordingly, we affirm the district court's decision dismissing the action.

FACTS and BACKGROUND

Appellant Elliott Associates ("Elliott") was the holder of $525,000 principal amount of 10% Convertible Subordinated Debentures due June 1, 1990 (the "debentures") which were issued by Centronics Data Computer Corporation ("Centronics") pursuant to an indenture between Centronics and J. Henry Schroder Bank and Trust Company ("Schroder"), as trustee. Elliott's debentures were part of an aggregate debenture offering by Centronics of $40,000,000 under the indenture which was qualified by the Securities Exchange Commission ("SEC") pursuant to the Act.

The indenture and debentures provided, inter alia, that Centronics had the right to redeem the debentures "at any time" at a specified price, plus accrued interest, but the indenture also provided that, during the first two years following the issuance of the debentures, Centronics' right to redeem was subject to certain conditions involving the market price of Centronics' common stock. To facilitate its right to redeem the debentures, Centronics was required to provide written notice of a proposed redemption to the trustee and to the debenture holders. Section 3.01 of the indenture required that Centronics give the trustee 50-day notice of its intention to call its debentures for redemption, "unless a shorter notice shall be satisfactory to the [t]rustee." Section 3.03 of the indenture required Centronics to provide the debenture holders with "[a]t least 15 days but not more than 60 days" notice of a proposed redemption.

At the option of the debenture holders, the debentures were convertible into shares of Centronics' common stock. In the event Centronics called the debentures for redemption, debenture holders could convert their debentures "at any time before the close of business on the last Business Day prior to the redemption date." Subject to certain adjustments, the conversion price was $3.25 per share. The number of shares issuable upon conversion could be determined by dividing the principal amount converted by the conversion price. Upon conversion, however, the debentures provided that "no adjustment for interest or dividends [would] be made."

Debenture holders were to receive interest payments from Centronics semi-annually on June 1 and December 1 of each year. Describing the method of interest payment, each debenture provided that

[t]he Company will pay interest on the Debentures (except defaulted interest) to the persons who are registered Holders of Debentures at the close of business on the November 15 or May 15 next preceding the interest payment date. Holders must surrender Debentures to a Paying Agent to collect principal payments....

In early 1986, Centronics was considering whether to call its outstanding debentures for redemption. On March 12, 1986, Centronics' Treasury Services Manager, Neil R. Gordon, telephoned Schroder's Senior Vice President in charge of the Corporate Trust Department, George R. Sievers, and informed him of Centronics' interest in redeeming the debentures. Gordon told Sievers that Centronics "was contemplating redemption" of all of its outstanding debentures, subject to SEC approval and fluctuations in the market for Centronics' common stock. Specifically addressing the 50-day notice to the trustee requirement in section 3.01 of the indenture, Gordon asked Sievers how much time "Schroder would need once the SEC had Centronics' registration materials and an actual redemption date could therefore be set." Sievers responded that "Schroder would only need [one] week" notice of the redemption. Sievers explained that this shorter notice would satisfy section 3.01 because Centronics was proposing a complete rather than a partial redemption, and because there were relatively few debenture holders. Sievers explained that the shorter notice therefore would provide it with sufficient time to perform its various administrative tasks in connection with the proposed redemption.

Shortly thereafter, on March 20, 1986, Centronics' Board of Directors met and approved a complete redemption of all of its outstanding debentures and designated May 16, 1986 as the redemption date. On April 4, 1986—42 days prior to the redemption—Centronics' President, Robert Stein, wrote Schroder and informed the trustee that "pursuant to the terms of the Indenture, notice is hereby given that the Company will redeem all of its outstanding 10% Convertible Subordinated Debentures due June 1, 1990, on May 16, 1986." Centronics then proceeded to file registration materials with the SEC in order to receive clearance for the redemption. Schroder was furnished with copies of all the materials Centronics had filed with the SEC.

On May 1, 1986, the SEC cleared the proposed redemption. On that same day, pursuant to section 3.03 of the indenture, Centronics gave formal notice of the May 16, 1986 redemption to the debenture holders. In a letter accompanying the Notice of Redemption, Centronics' President explained that, as long as the price of Centronics' common stock exceeded $3.75 per share, debenture holders would receive more value in conversion than in redemption. In the Notice of Redemption, debenture holders were advised, inter alia, that the conversion price of $3.25 per share, when divided into each $1,000 principal amount being converted, would yield 307.69 shares of Centronics common stock. Based upon the April 30, 1986 New York Stock Exchange closing price of $5⅜ per share of Centronics' common stock, each $1,000 principal amount of debenture was convertible into Centronics common stock having an approximate value of $1,653.83. Debenture holders were advised further that failure to elect conversion by May 15, 1986 would result in each $1,000 principal amount debenture being redeemed on May 16 for $1,146.11, which consisted of $1,000 in principal, $100 for the 10% redemption premium, and $46.11 in interest accrued from December 1, 1985 (the last interest payment date) to May 16, 1986 (the redemption date). Finally, the notice of redemption explained that accrued interest was not payable upon conversion....

On May 15, 1986, the last day available for conversion prior to the May 16, 1986 redemption, Centronics' common stock traded at $6⅝ per share. At that price, each $1,000 principal amount of debentures was convertible into Centronics' common stock worth approximately $2,038. Thus, it was clear that conversion at $2,038 was economically more profitable than redemption at $1,146.11. Debenture holders apparently recognized this fact because all the debenture holders converted their debentures into Centronics' common stock prior to the May 16, 1986 redemption.

Elliott filed the instant action on May 12, 1986 and sought an order from the district court enjoining the May 16, 1986 redemption. Elliott alleged in its complaint that Schroder and Centronics conspired to time the redemption in such a manner so as to avoid Centronics' obligation to pay interest on the next interest payment date, i.e., June 1, 1986. This conspiracy allegedly was accomplished by forcing debenture holders to convert prior to the close of business on May 15, 1986. Elliott contended that, as part of this conspiracy, Schroder improperly waived the 50-day notice in section 3.01 of the indenture and thus allowed Centronics to proceed with the redemption as planned. Elliott claimed that Schroder waived the 50-day notice without considering the impact of that waiver on the financial interests of the debenture holders and that the trustee's action in this regard constituted, inter alia, a breach of the trustee's fiduciary duties. Finally, Elliott alleged that, had it not been for the trustee's improper waiver, debenture holders would have been entitled to an additional payment of $1.2 million in interest from Centronics.

* * *

DISCUSSION

The central issue on this appeal is whether the district court properly held that the trustee was not obligated to weigh the financial interests of the debenture holders when it decided on March 12, 1986 to waive Centronics' compliance with section 3.01's 50-day notice requirement. We agree with the district court's conclusion that the trustee was under no such duty. *See* 655 F. Supp. at 1288-89.

At the outset, it is important to sort out those matters not at issue here. First, Elliott does not dispute that Centronics complied in all respects with the indenture's requirement to provide notice of redemption to the debenture holders. Elliott's claim only challenges the sufficiency of the notice to the trustee and the manner in which the trustee decided to waive that notice. Moreover, Elliott does not dispute that Schroder's actions were expressly authorized by section 3.01, which specifically allows the trustee discretion to accept shorter notice of redemption from Centronics if that notice was deemed satisfactory. Finally, except for bald assertions of conflict of interest, Elliott presents no serious claim that Schroder personally benefitted in any way from the waiver, or that, by waiving the notice period, it was taking a position that would harm the interests of the debenture holders and correspondingly inure to the trustee's benefit. Rather, Elliott's claim essentially is that the trustee was under a duty—implied from the indenture, the Act or state law—to secure greater benefits for debenture holders over and above the duties and obligations it undertook in the indenture.

No such implied duty can be found from the provisions of the Act or from its legislative history. Indeed, section 315(a)(1) of the Act allows a provision to be included in indentures (which was incorporated into the indenture at issue here) providing that

> the indenture trustee shall not be liable except for the performance of such duties [prior to an event of default] as are specifically set out in [the] indenture.

See 15 U.S.C. §77ooo (a)(1).[a] Moreover, when the Act was originally introduced in the Senate by Senator Barkley, it provided for the mandatory inclusion of a provision requiring the trustee to perform its pre-default duties and obligations in a manner consistent with that which a "prudent man would assume and perform." ... After extensive hearings on the House and Senate versions of the Act, during which representatives of several financial institutions expressed concern over the imposition of pre-default duties in excess of those duties set forth expressly in the indenture, *see* Hearings on H.R. 2191 and 5220 Before the Subcomm. of the House on Interstate and Foreign Commerce, 76th Cong., 1st Sess. (1939), Congress enacted the present version of section 315 of the Act. Thus, it is clear from the express terms of the Act and its legislative history that no implicit duties, such as those suggested by Elliott, are imposed on the trustee to limit its pre-default conduct.

It is equally well-established under state common law that the duties of an indenture trustee are strictly defined and limited to the terms of the indenture..., although the trustee must nevertheless refrain from engaging in conflicts of interest....

In view of the foregoing, it is no surprise that we have consistently rejected the imposition of additional duties on the trustee in light of the special relationship that the trustee already has with both the issuer and the debenture holders under the indenture.... As we recognized in *Meckel* [v. *Continental Resources Co.*, 785 F.2d 811, 816 (2d Cir. 1985)],

> [a]n indenture trustee is not subject to the ordinary trustee's duty of undivided loyalty. Unlike the ordinary trustee, who has historic common-law duties imposed beyond those in the trust agreement, *an indenture trustee is more like a stakeholder whose duties and obligations are exclusively defined by the terms of the indenture agreement.*

758 F.2d at 816 (citing *Hazzard v. Chase National Bank, supra*) (emphasis added). We therefore conclude that, so long as the trustee fulfills its obligations under the express terms of the indenture, it owes the debenture holders no additional, implicit pre-default duties or obligations except to avoid conflicts of interest.

---

a. Amended by TIRA to make the provision mandatory. [Eds.]

Our analysis here is therefore limited to determining whether the trustee fulfilled its duties under the indenture. As set forth above, section 3.01 requires that, when the company intends to call its debentures for redemption, it must provide the trustee with 50-day notice of the redemption, "unless a shorter notice shall be satisfactory to the [t]rustee." Section 3.02 of the indenture sets forth the manner in which the trustee selects which debentures are to be redeemed when the company calls for a partial redemption. The American Bar Foundation's *Commentaries on Model Debenture Indenture Provisions* (1971) (the "Commentaries") explains that "[n]otice of the Company's election to redeem *all* the debentures need not be given to the Trustee since such a redemption may be effected by the Company without any action on the part of the Trustee...." *Id.* at §11-3, p. 493. Thus, it appears that section 3.01's notice requirement is intended for the trustee's benefit to allow it sufficient time to perform the various administrative tasks in preparation for redemption. While compliance with a full notice period may be necessary in the event of partial redemption, the full notice may not be required in the event of a complete redemption. We find that, although the trustee may reasonably insist on the full 50-day notice in the event of a complete redemption, it nevertheless has the discretion to accept shorter notice when it deems such shorter notice satisfactory.

In his affidavit filed on behalf of Schroder's motion to dismiss, Sievers explained the reasoning behind his decision on behalf of Schroder to waive the notice:

* * *

I know [from] personal knowledge ... that the notice periods are meant to coordinate with the Trustee's own obligation to give notice to debentureholders in a partial redemption. The Trustee must be informed of a partial optional redemption sufficiently in advance of the time for giving such notice to permit it to make the selection of debentures to be redeemed.... If less time is required than the full number of days allowed by the particular indenture, then the trustee can and should waive the unnecessary and unneeded days. This pragmatic consideration is the reason that virtually all indentures modeled after the ABA instrument explicitly provide "unless a shorter notice shall be satisfactory to the Trustee."

In view of the fact that only 23 debentureholders held all of the Company's Debentures, the determination to proceed with a redemption of all the Debentures with a notice of less than 50 days would have been within Schroder's discretion and waiver of the 50 day period would have been consistent with the intent of Section 3.01 of the Indenture.

* * *

When Schroder received Centronics' May 1, 1986, formal letter, it had more than sufficient time to give the required notice to the 23 debentureholders. Accordingly, Schroder did not object because, in the language of the indenture and according to uniform custom, the "shorter notice shall be (and was indeed) satisfactory to the Trustee."

From Siever's affidavit, it is clear that Schroder complied with the letter and spirit of the indenture when it waived compliance with the full 50-day notice. Schroder was given the discretion to waive full notice under appropriate circumstances, and we find that it reasonably exercised that discretion.

To support its argument that Schroder was obligated to consider the impact of the waiver on the interests of the debenture holders, Elliott relies on our decision in *Dabney v. Chase National Bank*, 196 F.2d 668 (2d Cir. 1952), *as suppl'd*, 201 F.2d 635 (2d Cir.), *cert. dismissed per stipulation*, 346 U.S. 863, 74 S. Ct. 102, 98 L. Ed. 374 (1953). *Dabney* provided that

> the duty of a trustee, not to profit at the possible expense of his beneficiary, is the most fundamental of the duties which he accepts when he becomes a trustee. It is a part of his obligation to give his beneficiary his undivided loyalty, free from any conflicting personal interest; an obligation that has been nowhere more jealously and rigidly enforced than in New York where these indentures were executed. "The most fundamental duty owed by the trustee to the beneficiaries of the trust is the duty of loyalty * * * In some relations the fiduciary element is more intense than in others; it is peculiarly intense in the case of a trust." We should be even disposed to say that without this duty there could be no trust at all.

196 F.2d at 670 (footnotes omitted) (citations omitted); *see United States Trust Co. v. First National City Bank*, 57 A.D.2d 285, 394 N.Y.S.2d 653, 660-61 (1st Dept. 1977), *aff'd*, 45 N.Y.2d 869, 410 N.Y.S.2d 580, 382 N.E.2d 1355 (1978) (adopting *Dabney*). *Dabney* arose, however, in an entirely different factual context than the instant case.

The *Dabney* court examined the conduct of a trustee who knew or should have known that the company for whose bonds it served as trustee was insolvent. While possessing knowledge of the company's insolvency, the trustee proceeded to collect loan obligations from the company. The court held that the trustee's conduct in this regard constituted a breach of its obligation not to take an action which might disadvantage the debenture holders while providing itself with a financial advantage, i.e., the trustee engaged in a conflict of interest. *See* 196 F.2d at 673. Thus, while *Dabney* stands for the proposition that a trustee must refrain from engaging in conflicts of interest, it simply does not support the broader proposition that an implied fiduciary duty is imposed on a trustee to advance the financial interests of the debenture holders during the period prior to default. Because no evidence was offered in the instant case to suggest that Schroder benefitted, directly or indirectly, from its decision to waive the 50-day notice, and thus did not engage in a conflict of interest, it is clear that *Dabney* is inapposite to the instant appeal.

Schroder also contends that, even if we were to find that the trustee owed the debenture holders a duty to consider the impact of the waiver, we would nevertheless be compelled to dismiss this action because the debenture holders were not entitled to payment of accrued interest upon conversion. However, since we agree with the district court that the trustee had no duty to consider the impact of the waiver, we do not decide this question.

* * *

Affirmed.

Note

For an additional case that emphatically underscores that, absent a conflict of interest, the duties of an indenture trustee, unlike those of a typical trustee, are defined exclusively by the terms of the indenture, see Lorenz v. CSX Corp., 1 F.3d 1406 (3d Cir. 1993).

(iv) Loyalty to Debtholders

Rabinowitz v. Kaiser-Frazer Corp.
111 N.Y.S.2d 539 (Sup. Ct. 1952)
[Supra at section 4d(ii)]

U.S. Trust Co. of New York v. First Nat'l City Bank
394 N.Y.S.2d 653 (N.Y. App. Div. 1977), *aff'd*,
382 N.E.2d 1355 (N.Y. 1979)

SILVERMAN, Justice.

These are cross-appeals from an order of the Special Term of the Supreme Court granting the motion of defendant to dismiss certain causes of action in the complaint on the ground that they failed to state a cause of action; denying the motion as to other causes of action; and denying plaintiff's motion for partial summary judgment on the ground that there is no defense to its causes of action.

The case arises out of the collapse of Equity Funding Corporation of America ("Equity Funding") reputedly one of the largest and most notorious of modern corporate financial frauds. Although the order appealed from was entered October 23, 1975, the parties did not bring this appeal on for argument for a year and one-half, but in the interim the Plan of Reorganization of Equity Funding was apparently approved by the United States District Court for the Central District of California. The record on this appeal of course does not tell us whether the Plan of Reorganization has any bearing on the dispute involved in this appeal and the rights of the parties with respect thereto.

Plaintiff, United States Trust Company of New York, is the successor Indenture Trustee under an Indenture dated as of December 1, 1971 between Equity Funding and defendant, First National City Bank, Trustee, pursuant to which $38,500,000 of 5½% Convertible Subordinated Debentures due 1991 were issued and are outstanding. Defendant, First National City Bank, was the original Trustee under said Indenture. It gave notice of its resignation as Trustee on April 5, 1973, the date Equity Funding filed a petition for reorganization under Chapter X of the Bankruptcy Act. (U.S. Code, tit. 11, ch. 10.)

In essence the complaint charges that while defendant was Trustee, it favored its own interest as an individual creditor of Equity Funding over the interest of the Debenture holders whose Indenture Trustee the defendant was, and that the defendant is therefore liable for an accounting and for related relief, etc.

* * *

B. *Defendant's Motions*
The Revolving Credit Agreement

The first nine causes of action in the complaint relate to property and monies received by defendant as an individual creditor under a "Revolving Credit Agreement." The Revolving Credit Agreement dated as of June 29, 1972, was entered into by the defendant as agent for itself and three other banks. Under the Revolving Credit Agreement these four banks agreed to make loans to Equity Funding up to a maximum of $75,000,000. Defendant's share of the total lending commitment was about 47%. The Revolving Credit Agreement contained a provision whereby Equity Funding was required to pay a commitment fee of ½% per annum on unused portions of the loan commitment. To the extent that the loan was availed of, Equity Funding was to pay interest at a fluctuating rate equal to or greater than the base rate (also apparently sometimes referred to as the prime rate). Equity Funding had the right to prepay and reborrow. Repayment was required to be made in quarterly installments between September 30, 1976 and June 30, 1980, with provisions under which the lenders could require earlier payments in certain contingencies. The advances under the Revolving Credit Agreement were evidenced by a "grid note," a promissory note on which notations of advances and repayments would be made. On June 29, 1972 the banks advanced $41,000,000 to Equity Funding under the Revolving Credit Agreement. Additional advances of $5,000,000 each were made on or about October 10, 1972 and February 20, 1973, making total advances under the Revolving Credit Agreement of $51,000,000.

* * *

Second, Fourth, Sixth, Seventh, Eighth, and Ninth Causes of Action—Breach of Common Law Fiduciary Duties

The transactions attacked in the First, Third, and Fifth causes of action under §613(a) of the Indenture[a] are also attacked in the Second, Fourth, and Sixth causes of action, respectively, as a breach of the defendant Trustee's fiduciary duty, at a time when defendant knew Equity Funding was in danger of insolvency.

In the Seventh, Eighth, and Ninth causes of action, plaintiff attacks the failure of defendant to declare a default and accelerate the maturity of the Debentures until May 1, 1973, which was more than four months after the collection of collateral interest under the Revolving Credit Agreement on December 31, 1972, thus taking those payments out of the reach of §613(a) of the Indenture. The complaint alleges that the filing by Equity Funding of a petition for reorganization on April 5, 1973 was an "Event of Default" under the Indenture; that thereupon defendant as Trustee could have accelerated the maturity of the Debentures; and that the non-payment of the accelerated principal would have been a default, bringing within the reach of §613(a) of the Indenture all payments made after four months prior thereto. The complaint further alleges that on or about April 3, 1973, defendant delivered to Equity Funding a notice declaring that Events of Default had occurred under the Revolving Credit Agreement and accelerating the maturity of the indebtedness under the Revolving Credit Agreement; but that although the defendant could have similarly accelerated the maturity of the Debentures, it did not do so until May 1, 1973. This failure by defendant is alleged to be a breach of its obligation to use the same degree of care and skill as a prudent man would exercise in the conduct of his own affairs, and willful misconduct or negligence, and a breach of its fiduciary duties to the debenture holders.

* * *

a. Section 613(a) of the Indenture, required by the TIA, 15 U.S.C. §77kkk, "requires that the Trustee hold in a special account for the benefit of the Trustee individually and of the holders of the Debentures any amounts or property received by the Trustee in reduction of amounts owed or as security for the Trustee's individual creditor claim after four months prior to a default under the Indenture." 394 N.Y.S.2d at 656. [Eds.]

Defendant also contends that its duties as Trustee were circumscribed by the Indenture, that they were purely contractual duties, and that the defendant was not really a trustee within the rules imposing fiduciary liability on trustees.

This precise contention was made and rejected in *Dabney v. Chase National Bank*, 196 F.2d 668 (2d Cir. 1952). There the court had before it an indenture executed before the Trust Indenture Act and governed by the preexisting law of New York. The court held in an opinion by Judge Learned Hand that notwithstanding very narrow definitions of the trustee's duties in the indenture, the trustee was still liable for breach of its fiduciary obligation of loyalty. In his opinion, Judge Hand said:

> "[T]he duty of a trustee, not to profit at the possible expense of his beneficiary, is the most fundamental of the duties which he accepts when he becomes a trustee. It is a part of his obligation to give his beneficiary his undivided loyalty, free from any conflicting personal interest; an obligation that has been nowhere more jealously and rigidly enforced than in New York where these indentures were executed." (p. 670)

Speaking of some language in *Hazzard v. Chase National Bank*, 159 Misc. 57, 84, 287 N.Y.S. 541, 570, *aff'd* 257 App. Div. 950, 14 N.Y.S.2d 147, *aff'd* 282 N.Y. 652, 26 N.E.2d 801 (1940), that seemed to suggest that an indenture trustee's rights and duties were defined not by the fiduciary relationship but exclusively by the terms of the agreement, Judge Hand said:

> "That language we read only as criticism of practices that had grown up, and not as asserting that the courts of New York had given any countenance to the notion that, so far as a corporation sees fit to assume the duties of an indenture trustee, it can shake off the loyalty demanded of every trustee, corporate or individual. We can find no warrant for so supposing; and, indeed, a trust for the benefit of a numerous and changing body of bondholders appears to us to be preeminently an occasion for a scruple even greater than ordinary; for such beneficiaries often have too small a stake to follow the fate of their investment and protect their rights." (p. 671)

Defendant argues that the Trust Indenture Act has changed this rule, and that by giving its blessing to a corporate trustee also having the status of an individual creditor, the Act in essence made the rule of the *Dabney* case inapplicable to indentures governed by the Trust Indenture Act. We do not agree. We do not think that the Trust Indenture Act was intended in any way to take away from debenture holders any protections which they had before the Act.

And we think that the language of both the Trust Indenture Act §323(b) (15 U.S.C. §77www) and §510 of the Indenture expressly preserve any rights of the debenture holders under the law prior to the enactment of the Trust Indenture Act. The Trust Indenture Act §323, provides in part:

> "The rights and remedies provided by this subchapter shall be in addition to any and all other rights and remedies that may exist under the Securities Act of 1933, or the Securities Exchange Act of 1934, or the Public Utility Holding Company Act of 1935, or otherwise at law or in equity...."

Section 510 of the Indenture provides in part:

> "No right or remedy herein conferred upon or reserved to the Trustee or to the Holders is intended to be exclusive of any other right or remedy, and every right and remedy shall, to the extent permitted by law, be cumulative and in

addition to every other right and remedy given hereunder or now or hereafter existing at law or in equity or otherwise."

In our view, the motion to dismiss for failure to state a cause of action was ... erroneously granted as to the Seventh, Eighth, and Ninth causes of action....

Harriet & Henderson Yarns, Inc. v. Castle
75 F. Supp.2d 818 (W.D. Tenn. 1999)

DONALD, D.J.:

.... FLR Hosiery ("FLR") and Lora Lee Knitting ("Lora Lee") were two pre-existing Tennessee hosiery companies, both experiencing financial difficulties in early 1995. Both companies were heavily indebted to trade creditors, most of whom supplied them with raw materials. Together they owed approximately $3,000,000, much of it to Plaintiffs [FLR's landlord and various suppliers of yarn or textile services]. Brookfield & Company ("Brookfield"), an investment banking firm, became involved with FLR and Lora Lee, assisting in the two companies' attempt to secure additional financing. Brookfield arranged a deal whereby FLR and Lora Lee would contribute substantially all their combined assets to form a new company, Star. Brookfield arranged for Congress Financial ("Congress") to finance the new company. Brookfield also engaged the Defendant law firm Wolff Ardis, P.C. ("Wolff Ardis") to represent Star during its creation, incorporation, and loan deal from Congress. Defendant Renee Castle ("Castle") was a shareholder in Wolff Ardis, and was the lead attorney for the Star transactions.

In order for Star to obtain financing from Congress, Brookfield advised that much of the pre-existing FLR and Lora Lee debt should be restructured into subordinated, convertible debenture notes ("Debenture Notes"). The Debenture Notes were to be paid by Star over three years. To induce the existing creditors to accept the Debenture Notes, the creditors were granted a second lien in Star's machinery and equipment to secure the Debenture Notes, behind a first lien held by Congress. The creditors were also told that the Star merger and financing plan would improve the likelihood that the current debt would be paid off. As the creditors were informed about the proposed creation of Star, they were asked to sign confidentiality agreements, which prevented the creditors from sharing information or discussing the proposal.

Brookfield had Castle prepare the necessary documents. Castle drafted the Debenture Note based on a form given her by Brookfield. She also drafted the Indenture Agreement, based on a form in the Wolff Ardis computer files. The Debenture Notes provided that Star promised to pay various amounts to the different Debenture holders. They also named Wolff Ardis as trustee. Other relevant parts of the Debenture Notes included the following:

1. *Payment of Principal.* The total obligation of Star to all Debenture Holders is set forth in the Indenture Agreement dated as of December 1, 1995, by and between Star and Wolff Ardis P.C., as Trustee for the Debenture Holders (the "Indenture Agreement")....

5. *Indenture Agreement.* This Debenture is one of several debentures of Star issued pursuant to the Indenture Agreement, the provisions of which are hereby incorporated by reference and made a part of this Debenture. All the Debentures issued pursuant to that Indenture Agreement are equally secured by a second lien and security interest in certain of Star's equipment, as more

fully described in the Indenture Agreement. Reference is hereby made to the Indenture Agreement for a more detailed description of the property in which the Trustee holds a security interest, the nature and extent of the security interest, the rights and obligations of the Debenture Holder and other debenture holders, of Star, and of the Trustee....

The Indenture Agreement stated, in relevant part:

> This Indenture Agreement between Star Hosiery, Inc., a Tennessee corporation (the "Company" or "Star") and Renee E. Castle of Wolff Ardis, P.C.... (the "Trustee"), dated as of this 12th date of December, 1995, is for the benefit of certain holders of Debenture Notes ("Noteholders") who hold Debenture Notes issued pursuant to this Indenture.... The terms of the Debentures include those stated in the Note Debentures and those made part of the Note Debentures by reference to the Trust Indenture Act of 1939 (the "Trust Indenture Act") as in effect on the date of the Debentures....

> *Security.* The Debenture Notes shall be secured by a subordinate lien on all equipment owned by the Company. This lien shall extend on a pro rata basis to each Noteholder. It shall have a second priority (inferior to the liens securing Senior Indebtedness) on all equipment with the exception of the equipment presently encumbered by liens in favor of GECC, Speizman and Nations Bank, in which case the lien shall have a third priority....

> *The Trustee.* The Trustee shall be under no obligation to exercise any of its rights or powers under this Indenture relating to any issue of Debentures at the request of any of the holders thereof, unless they shall have offered to the Trustee security and indemnity satisfactory to it....

The Debenture Notes prepared by Castle were sent to each Plaintiff in November, 1995 by FLR and Lora Lee, each for a varying amount. The Indenture Agreement was presented to Plaintiffs by their debtors as the best chance for them to recover the money owed them, and they were urged by FLR and Lora Lee to sign the Debenture Notes. Each Plaintiff did sign and return its Debenture Note. Once all Notes had been returned, Castle prepared the final Indenture Agreement, which stated that the total sum owed to the holders of the Debenture Notes pursuant to the Notes was $2,322,973.42.

The closing of the transactions occurred on December 12, 1995. At the closing were Defendant Castle and representatives of FLR, Lora Lee, Star, Congress, and Brookfield. None of the Plaintiffs had an attorney or other representative present. After the closing, copies of the signed Debenture Notes were sent to Plaintiffs, and the original Debenture Notes were kept in the offices of Wolff Ardis.

Castle had received instructions from Congress regarding the execution and filing of UCC-1 financing statements to perfect Congress' first lien in Star's equipment. Those financing statements, executed by Star in favor of Congress, were duly recorded with the Tennessee Secretary of State. However, there was never any discussion among any of the parties to the transaction about preparing or filing financing statements in favor of Plaintiffs. No UCC-1 financing statements were prepared, executed, or filed with regard to Plaintiffs' lien in Star's equipment. Because no financing statement was filed, the Debenture holders' lien was never properly perfected under Tennessee law.

Star made the required payments from January to June, 1996. However, it then stopped making payments, and on August 16, 1996, Star filed for Chapter 11 bankruptcy.

Shortly thereafter, Plaintiffs learned that no financing statements had been filed on their behalf. Because the lien was unperfected, each Plaintiff was treated as an unsecured creditor in Star's bankruptcy case. Star's assets were sold in bankruptcy, resulting in full repayment to Congress, but only approximately a 3% dividend to Plaintiffs and other unsecured creditors. Plaintiffs contend that they would have received all or most of the debt owed to them under the Debenture Notes if their security interest in Star's equipment had been properly perfected.

The crux of this suit is Plaintiffs' claim that Defendants had the responsibility to perfect Plaintiffs' security interests, or to ensure that the interests were perfected..... .

[The court first rejected Plaintiffs' claims for professional negligence against the Defendant law firm, finding that no attorney-client relationship existed between them and that Plaintiffs were not intended third-party beneficiaries of the retention agreement between Star and the Defendant law firm. But the cout also refused to grant Defendant law firm's motion for summary judgment on a different theory. Tennessee law allows claims of attorney negligence by non-clients where the attorneys get so "deeply involved" in a transaction that a trier of fact could find that a lawyer represented multiple clients. In this case, the law firm's role as Trustee under the Indenture may have created such a "deep involvement" in the transaction.]

Plaintiffs ... allege that by not perfecting Plaintiffs' security interests, Defendants breached a state common law fiduciary duty owed to Plaintiffs. Defendants filled the role of trustee in this case, and Plaintiffs were the trust beneficiaries. Under Tennessee law, a trustee owes a duty of loyalty to the trust beneficiary. A trustee also has a duty to act in good faith, with due diligence, and with care and skill. Plaintiffs contend that Defendants had a fiduciary duty to ensure that Plaintiffs' interests under the Indenture Agreement and Debenture Notes were protected. Plaintiffs argue that Defendants breached this duty by failing to perfect the liens.

This case does not deal with the duty of an ordinary trustee, but with the obligations of an indenture trustee. In arguing over the scope of those duties, the parties look primarily to case law from the state of New York, out of which most of the important cases on this topic have issued. The leading authorities make clear that, unlike those of an ordinary trustee, the duties of an indenture trustee are generally defined by and limited to the terms of the indenture. *See, e.g., Elliott Assocs. v. J. Henry Schroder Bank & Trust Co.*, 838 F.2d 66, 71 (2nd Cir. 1988)....

That limits are imposed on the duties of an indenture trustee is not arbitrary, but reasonably based on the difference between the role of an indenture trustee and an ordinary trustee. One difference is that the rights and duties of an ordinary trustee arise from the common law, whereas the duties of an indenture trustee arise out of, and thus are limited to, a contract. Another reason for the difference is that an indenture trustee must consider the interests of the issuer of the debenture as well as the beneficiaries. And a third reason is that "the purchaser of such debt is offered, and voluntarily accepts, a security whose myriad terms are highly specified. Broad and abstract requirements of a 'fiduciary' character ordinarily can be expected to have little or no constructive role to play in the governance of such a negotiated, commercial relationship." *Simons v. Cogan*, 542 A.2d 785, 786 (Del. Ch. 1987).

The Indenture Agreement in this case said nothing about a duty of Defendants to perfect Plaintiffs' liens. Courts, however, have found two narrow exceptions to the general rule that the duties of an indenture trustee are strictly defined by the indenture agreement. One of these is that after default, "the loyalties of an indenture trustee no longer are divided between the issuer and the investors, and as a consequence ... the limits on an indenture trustee's duties before an event of default ... do not apply after an event of default ..." *LNC Inv.*, 935 F. Supp at 1347.... This post-default exception does not apply to the case at bar, in which the alleged breach of duty occurred prior to Star's default. Once Star had defaulted, it was already too late for the security interests to be effectively perfected.

Plaintiffs contend that the other exception to the limits of an indenture trustee's duties applies here. That exception is the requirement that even indenture trustees have an obligation to avoid a conflict of interest.... *Elliot*, 838 F.2d at 77 ("So long as the trustee fulfills its obligations under the express terms of the indenture, it owes the debenture holders no additional, implicit pre-default duties or obligations except to avoid conflicts of interests.").

Plaintiffs argue that by assuming the role of trustee, Defendants created a conflict of interest, and thereby breached the fiduciary duty they owed to Plaintiffs. However, the existing legal authority in this area does not support Plaintiffs' argument that this dual role sufficed to impart additional fiduciary duties. In *In re E.F. Hutton*, the Fifth Circuit stated that "heightened fiduciary duties ... are not activated until a conflict arises where it is evident that the indenture trustee may be sacrificing the interests of the beneficiaries in favor of its own financial position. There must be a clear possibility of this evident from the facts of the case, *e.g.*, where the indenture trustee is a general creditor of the obligor, who is in turn in financial straits. A mere hypothetical possibility that the indenture trustee might favor the interests of the issuer merely because the former is an indenture trustee does not suffice." 953 F.2d at 972. Similarly, the Second Circuit found no conflict of interest in *Elliot* when it found that "except for bald assertions of conflict of interest, [the plaintiff] presents no serious claim that [the indenture trustee] personally benefitted [sic] in any way ..." 838 F.2d at 70. In the case before the court, Plaintiffs likewise have done no more than make bald assertions of a conflict of interest.[2]

Plaintiffs accurately point out that many of the cases finding no implied duties for indenture trustees involved indenture agreements containing clauses specifically excusing the trustee of any duty outside of those made explicit in the agreement. This at least suggests that in the absence of such a clause, an indenture trustee could be held to a higher fiduciary standard. There was no such clause in the Indenture Agreement in this case. However, Plaintiffs are unable to direct the court to a single case in which, in the absence of such a disclaimer, a court has found that an indenture trustee has the same fiduciary duty as an ordinary trustee.

Plaintiffs also attempt to distinguish this case by virtue of the fact that the Defendants were the attorneys of the debenture issuer, as opposed to the financial institutions which served as trustees in many of the cited cases. Plaintiffs argue that where the trustees are attorneys of an obligor who will benefit at the expense of the trust beneficiaries, the trustees have a conflict of interest which violates their fiduciary duty. However, Plaintiffs again are unable to produce any legal authority to back their argument,

---

2. The court notes that [earlier in the opinion] it held that Defendants placed themselves in a position of conflict of interest. That the court finds no actual conflict of interest here is not a result of inconsistency, but a function of differing legal standards. Tennessee allows claims of attorney negligence by non-clients where the attorneys get so deeply involved in a transaction "that a trier of fact could find that they were representing multiple interests ..." *Stinson*, 738 S.W.2d at 190. On the other hand, heightened fiduciary duties of an indenture trustee arise only where there is clear evidence that the trustee personally benefitted [sic] from the conflict of interest. *In re E.F. Hutton*, 953 F.2d at 972; *Elliot*, 838 F.2d at 70.

and there is no evidence to suggest that Defendants could have personally benefitted [sic] from the failure to file the financing statements.

Plaintiffs can successfully distinguish this case from any of the other individual cases on the fiduciary duties of indenture trustees. But what Plaintiffs ultimately ask this court to do is to find a new exception to well-settled law. This the court is unwilling to do. As a general rule, the duties of indenture trustees are strictly defined by the indenture agreement. There is no reason in this case not to follow that rule. The governing documents did not impose on the trustees the duty to perfect the security interests. . . .

Plaintiff [also argues] that Defendants' failure to ensure that Plaintiffs' liens were perfected violated a provision of the Trust Indenture Act of 1939 ("Trust Indenture Act"). Before discussing that claim, the court must resolve the preliminary dispute over whether that Act applies to this case at all.

Plaintiffs contend that the Indenture Agreement incorporates by reference the Trust Indenture Act. Indeed, the Indenture Agreement states:

> The terms of the Debentures include those stated in the Note Debentures and those made part of the Note Debentures by reference to the Trust Indenture Act of 1939 (the "Trust Indenture Act") as in effect on the date of the Debentures.

The Debenture Notes, however, make no reference to the Trust Indenture Act. Defendants argue that the Trust Indenture Act therefore was not incorporated. Defendants claim that "the clear meaning" of the Indenture Agreement provision is that "because there are no references to the Indenture Act contained in the debenture notes . . . no Indenture Act provisions were incorporated by reference into the indenture transaction."

Defendants may find the meaning of this provision "clear," but the court does not. The language of a contract is ambiguous if its meaning is susceptible to more than one reasonable interpretation. If the terms are ambiguous, then the intended meaning of the contract becomes a question for the finder of fact. It is also true that where the language of the contract is ambiguous, it will be construed against the party responsible for the drafting (in this case, Defendants).

Despite Defendants' contention to the contrary, the one thing that is clear about this provision is that it is ambiguous. Therefore, at the very least, the meaning should be left to be determined by the finder of fact. However, due to the court's ultimate disposition of this issue on another basis, it is unnecessary to decide this question. Instead, the court will assume *arguendo* that the Trust Indenture Act was incorporated into the Indenture Agreement.

Plaintiffs state that the Trust Indenture Act requires an indenture trustee to review the filing and effectiveness of any lien intended to be created by the Debenture Notes. According to Plaintiffs, this duty is imposed by 15 U.S.C.A. §77nnn(b). Putting it simply, Plaintiffs either misunderstand or misrepresent the duty imposed by that section of the Trust Indenture Act. That section imposes two duties upon Star, the *obligor* of the indenture agreement. Furthermore, the duties imposed are for the benefit of the indenture trustee, i.e. Defendants. And finally, the duty it imposes is not to actually file the indenture, but merely to furnish an opinion of counsel as to whether the indenture has been properly recorded and filed. 15 U.S.C.A. §77nnn(b). This section clearly does not impose a duty on indenture trustees to ensure that liens are perfected for the benefit of the debenture holders. Therefore the question of whether the Trust Indenture Act is incorporated into the Indenture Agreement is irrelevant.

* * *

Notes and Questions

1. Is there a distinction between a trustee who happens to be a lawyer and a lawyer who assumes the role of trustee? Why did the law firm agree to act as trustee under the Indenture?

2. Why was the TIA referenced in this private debt agreement? What is the purpose of the indenture language limiting the Trustee's duty to act?

3. The court also rejected Plaintiffs' breach of contract theory. Why?

4. What do the opinions in *Broad, Elliott Associates, Harriet & Henderson, Rabinowitz* and *U.S. Trust Co.* suggest is the scope of the indenture trustee's fiduciary obligation?

Problem — The Duties of the Indenture Trustee

Your Bondolian clients have asked you to consider the role of the indenture trustee in light of (i) Section 315 of the TIA, as amended, and (ii) the case law dealing with the obligations of the trustee. Draft a memorandum proposing a role for the indenture trustee under Bondolian law and explaining your proposal. In so doing, consider whether the trustee's role should be legislatively mandated or developed as a matter of common law. You might also consider proposing the development of a group of professional trustees who are unaffiliated with financial institutions. What would be the advantages and disadvantages of such an approach?

c. Rating Agencies

The rating agencies are central actors in the public debt and preferred stock market. An issuer of new debt typically will pay a fee to the agency to evaluate the risk on the debt and assign a rating, as well as continue to reevaluate that rating during the life of the debt. The rating assigned "is an assessment of the likelihood of payment, both *when promised* and *in the full amount* promised. Put more simply, a rating assesses the likelihood of *both* prompt *and* full payment."[1] Although ratings are not legally required, they are a practical necessity in the public debt and preferred stock market. Since debt ratings provide a measure of risk (which, as you will recall, is a central factor in valuation), they have a significant effect on an issuer's cost of capital, with the consequence that the issuer ordinarily will want to obtain the highest rating possible.[2] This is particularly the

---

1. Schwarcz, Markell & Broome, Securitization, Structured Finance and Capital Markets § 1.02, at 5 (2004).

2. The desire to obtain a higher rating, and thus a lower cost of capital, helped spur the development of asset-backed securitization, which is discussed *infra* at section 8b.

case in light of the investment limitations of certain regulated institutional investors,[3] as well as self-imposed limitations by non-regulated investors.

How are ratings determined? Van Horne, Financial Management and Policy 296-97 (12th ed. 2002), notes: "The rating agencies look at a number of things before assigning a grade: trends in ratios of liquidity, debt, profitability, and coverage; the firm's business risk, both historically and expected; present and likely future capital requirements; specific features associated with the instrument being issued; the relative proportion of debt; and, perhaps most important, the cash-flow ability to service principal and interest payments."

Moody's and Standard & Poor's provide similar (though not identical) grades to securities. Moody's ratings[4] are as follows:

GRADE	DESCRIPTION
Aaa	Best quality bonds, with least investment risk
Aa	Judged to be of high quality by all standards
A	Upper medium grade obligations
Baa	Medium grade obligations
Ba	Bonds which have speculative elements
B	Generally lack characteristics of desirable investment
Caa	Poor standing; issues may be in default
Ca	Speculative in a high degree; issues often in default
C	Lowest rated class of bonds; extremely poor prospects of attaining investment standing; considered to be in default.

Since 1979, there has been a substantial decline in the number of Aaa-rated American companies. In 1979, there were 61 such companies, in 1992 there were 21, in 2002 there were 9 and, as of April 11, 2005, there were only 7: Automatic Data Processing (ADP), Berkshire Hathaway, ExxonMobil, General Electric, Johnson & Johnson, Pfizer and United Parcel Service (UPS). The major reasons cited for the decline are deregulation, global competition, debt-financed mergers, companies merging out of existence, bad management decisions and, perhaps surprisingly, a growing tolerance for risk among investors. However, some companies clearly have concluded that their optimal debt-to-equity ratio is not one that yields a Aaa rating. There has also been a healthy decline in the number of American companies with Aa and A ratings.[5]

Despite the misgivings of one of your editors,[6] it is clear that ratings agencies *do* provide some protection to investors. Moreover, although it should be clear by now

3. For example, the New York Comptroller, the trustee for New York State Employees' Retirement Funds, is limited by N.Y. Retire. & Soc. Sec. Law §13(b) (McKinney 1973): "[H]e may invest in obligations consisting of notes, bonds, debentures, or equipment trust certificates issued under an indenture, which are the direct obligations of, or in the case of equipment trust certificates are secured direct obligations of, a railroad or industrial corporation, or a corporation engaged directly and primarily in the production, transportation, distribution, or sale of electricity or gas, or the operation of telephone or telegraph systems or waterworks, or in some combination of them; provided the obligor corporation is one which is incorporated under the laws of the United States, or any state thereof, or of the District of Columbia, and *said obligations shall be rated at the time of purchase within the three highest classifications established by at least two standard rating services.*" [Emphasis added.]

4. Taken from Moody's ratings system and definitions set forth on its homepage located at www.moodys.com.

5. *See* Pender, Steep Drop in Triple-A Ratings, San Fran. Chron., Mar. 3, 2002, at G1.

6. Mitchell, The Fairness Rights of Corporate Bondholders, 65 N.Y.U. L. Rev. 1165 (1990).

that boards of directors cannot adopt policies that support debt values without demonstrable benefit to stockholders, at least under some circumstances, Revlon, Inc. v. MacAndrews & Forbes Holdings, Inc., 506 A.2d 173, 182 (Del. 1986), downgradings can adversely affect stockholders such that ratings maintenance appears consistent with directors' fiduciary duties. For example, downgradings can result in negative evaluations of an issuer by stock analysts, who recommend selling the stock with a consequent drop in stock price. More directly, downgradings are likely to raise the cost of capital of new debt issues. Indeed, Standard & Poor's downgrading of the debt securities of General Motors and Ford to junk status in May 2005 reflected its "skepticism about whether management's strategies will be sufficient to address the competitive disadvantages faced by the two automakers." Doyle, S&P downgrades GM and Ford to "Junk" Status, World Markets Analysis (May 6, 2005). *See also* Stertz, Chrysler Financial Faces Tight Credit After Downgrade Despite Record Net, Wall St. J., June 21, 1990, at A5 (quoting chairman of Chrysler Financial Corp. as stating that downgrading "means our borrowing costs are higher and our profits will be lower").

Despite the possible practical protections the rating agencies may provide, they are not complete. Professor Kahan argues that ratings are assigned principally on the basis of credit risk and that the quality of legal protections in the bond indenture has no significant effect on the ratings. Kahan, The Qualified Case Against Mandatory Terms in Bonds, 89 Nw. U. L. Rev. 565, 592 (1995).

Since 1975, the Securities and Exchange Commission (SEC) has increasingly used credit ratings from market-recognized credible rating agencies for distinguishing among grades of creditworthiness in various regulations under the Federal securities laws. By means of no-action letters, the SEC has designated the following four rating agencies as "nationally recognized statistical rating organizations" (NRSROs): Moody's Investors Service, Inc., Standard & Poor's (a division of McGraw-Hill Companies, Inc.), Fitch, Inc., and Dominion Bond Rating Service Limited.

Over the years, the SEC and Congress have reviewed a number of issues regarding credit rating agencies and, in particular, the subject of regulatory oversight of them. In 1994, the SEC solicited public comments on the appropriate role of credit ratings in rules under the Federal securities law, and the need to establish formal procedures for recognizing and monitoring the activities of NRSROs. Comments received led to an SEC rule proposal in 1997 which, among other things, would have defined the term "NRSRO" in the net capital rule applicable to broker-dealers. However, the SEC never acted upon that rule proposal.

After the scandals of Enron, Worldcom and several other corporations came to light in the early 2000s, critics pointed fingers at the rating agencies alleging that they failed to discover the malfeasance before it was too late. *See* Hill, Rating Agencies Behaving Badly: The Case of Enron, 35 Conn. L. Rev. 1145 (2002); Oppel, Enron's Many Strands: The Hearings; Credit Agencies Say Enron Dishonesty Misled Them, N.Y. Times, Mar. 21, 2002, at C6; Stevenson & Gerth, Enron's Collapse: The System; Web of Safeguards Failed as Enron Fell, N.Y. Times, Jan. 20, 2002, Sec. 1, at 11; Morgenson, Market Watch; Post-Enron, All Eyes on Rating Agencies, Dec. 16, 2001, Sec. 3, at 31.

As part of the Sarbanes-Oxley Act of 2002, Congress called for an SEC review of credit rating agencies from top to bottom. The SEC report stemming from that review focused on rating agency disclosures, potential conflicts of interest, alleged anticompetitive practices, barriers to entry into the business and the need for additional oversight. *See* Report on the Role and Function of Credit Rating Agencies in the Operation of the Securities

Markets, As Required by Section 702(b) of the Sarbanes-Oxley Act of 2002, U.S. Securities and Exchange Commission, Jan. 2003. *See also* Rating Agencies and the Use of Credit Ratings under the Federal Securities Law, Securities Act Rel. No. 33-8236 (June 12, 2003). At long last, it appears that the SEC is ready to press ahead with a new regulatory framework that ensures that debt ratings are a result of thorough analysis rather than the credit agencies' desire for larger profits. *See* Morgenson, Wanted: Credit Ratings. Objective Ones, Please, N.Y. Times, Feb. 6, 2005, Sec. 3, at 31.

Questions

Can the ratings agencies provide the protections for bondholders that the law has failed to provide? If so, is this a cause or a consequence of the legal environment? Is it a sufficient answer for judges and legislatures that private industry provides adequate protection?

Section 6
The Bankruptcy Rights of Debtholders

a. Introduction

Although corporate law provides no meaningful protection to the debtholders of a solvent corporation, the situation changes when the corporation approaches insolvency or becomes bankrupt. In these circumstances, the principle of limited liability discussed in chapter 2 produces a stark conflict between creditors and stockholders, as the corporation has insufficient wealth to satisfy the interests of all claimants. Equitable doctrines of corporate law exist to prevent stockholders from taking unfair advantage of creditors, and bankruptcy law provides methods external to corporate governance to help resolve competing claims among creditors and between creditors and stockholders.

b. Operating in the "Vicinity of Insolvency"

Recall that Simons v. Cogan, *supra* at section 4a, highlighted that the rights of debtholders are confined to the terms of their indenture "unless there are special circumstances which affect the rights of the [debt]holders as creditors of the corporation, e.g., fraud, insolvency, or a violation of a statute...." * This subsection explores one such "special circumstance."

Pepper v. Litton
308 U.S. 295 (1939)

Mr. Justice DOUGLAS delivered the opinion of the Court.

The case presents the question of the power of the bankruptcy court to disallow either as a secured or as a general or unsecured claim a judgment obtained by the domi-

---

* 549 A.2d 300, 302 (Del. 1988) (quoting Harff v. Kerkorian, 324 A.2d 215, 222 (Del. Ch. 1974)).

nant and controlling stockholder of the bankrupt corporation on alleged salary claims. The judgment of the District Court disallowing the claim was reversed by the Circuit Court of Appeals (100 F.2d 830). We granted certiorari because of an apparent restriction imposed by that decision on the power of the bankruptcy court[a] to disallow or to subordinate such claims in exercise of its broad equitable powers.

The findings of the District Court, amply supported by the evidence, reveal a scheme to defraud creditors reminiscent of some of the evils with which 13 Eliz. c.5[b] was designed to cope. But for the use of a so-called "one-man" or family corporation, Dixie Splint Coal Company, of which respondent was the dominant and controlling stockholder, that scheme followed an ancient pattern.

[Briefly, the case resulted from an attempt by Litton, the sole stockholder of Dixie Splint Coal Company, to defeat plaintiff's claim through a series of maneuvers by which he established a fraudulent claim for back salary by causing the corporation to confess a judgment, and then placing the corporation in bankruptcy (after effecting a transfer of the corporation's property to another wholly owned corporation) following which he filed a claim in bankruptcy to recover the confessed judgment. Litton then maneuvered to eliminate all other creditors of the corporation, leaving plaintiff "to appear as the only general creditor." Ultimately, the Circuit Court of Appeals reversed the District Court which had disallowed Litton's claim, holding that a state court judgment granting that claim was *res judicata*.]

We think that the Circuit Court of Appeals was in error in reversing the judgment of the District Court.

[The Court then examined and reversed the Court of Appeals' holding that the state court decision was *res judicata* in the bankruptcy court. It also proceeded to establish that bankruptcy courts are courts of equity and, as such, have the power to inquire into the validity of "any claim asserted against the estate and to disallow it if it is ascertained to be without lawful existence." The fact that "a claim has been reduced to judgment does not prevent such an inquiry."]

* * *

That equitable power also exists in passing on claims presented by an officer, director, or stockholder in the bankruptcy proceedings of his corporation. The mere fact that an officer, director, or stockholder has a claim against his bankrupt corporation or that he has reduced that claim to judgment does not mean that the bankruptcy court must accord it *pari passu* treatment with the claims of other creditors. Its disallowance or subordination may be necessitated by certain cardinal principles of equity jurisprudence. A director is a fiduciary. *Twin-Lick Oil Co.* v. *Marbury*, 91 U.S. 587, 588. So is a dominant or controlling stockholder or group of stockholders. *Southern Pacific Co.* v. *Bogert*, 250 U.S. 483, 492. Their powers are powers in trust. See *Jackson* v. *Ludeling*, 21 Wall. 616, 624. Their dealings with the corporation are subjected to rigorous scrutiny and where any of their contracts or engagements with the corpora-

---

a. The court refers both to the bankruptcy court and the district court. These are the same court. Under the Bankruptcy Act in effect at the time of this litigation, the "courts of the United States" were constituted as "courts of bankruptcy." 11 U.S.C. §§1, 11 (1938). [Eds.]

b. 13 Eliz. c.5 was the forerunner of modern fraudulent conveyance statutes, discussed *infra* at section 6e(iv). [Eds.]

tion is challenged the burden is on the director or stockholder not only to prove the good faith of the transaction but also to show its inherent fairness from the viewpoint of the corporation and those interested therein. *Geddes* v. *Anaconda Copper Mining Co.*, 254 U.S. 590, 599. The essence of the test is whether or not under all the circumstances the transaction carries the earmarks of an arm's length bargain.[14] If it does not, equity will set it aside. While normally that fiduciary obligation is enforceable directly by the corporation, or through a stockholder's derivative action, it is, in the event of bankruptcy of the corporation, enforceable by the trustee.[c] For that standard of fiduciary obligation is designed for the protection of the entire community of interests in the corporation—creditors as well as stockholders.

.... [T]hese rules governing the fiduciary responsibilities of directors and stockholders come into play on allowance of their claims in bankruptcy. In the exercise of its equitable jurisdiction the bankruptcy court has the power to sift the circumstances surrounding any claim to see that injustice or unfairness is not done in administration of the bankrupt estate. And its duty so to do is especially clear when the claim seeking allowance accrues to the benefit of an officer, director, or stockholder. That is clearly the power and duty of the bankruptcy courts under the reorganization sections.... [S]alary claims of officers, directors, and stockholders in the bankruptcy of "one-man" or family corporations have been disallowed or subordinated where the courts have been satisfied that allowance of the claims would not be fair or equitable to other creditors. And that result may be reached even though the salary claim has been reduced to judgment. It is reached where the claim asserted is void or voidable because the vote of the interested director or stockholder helped bring it into being or where the history of the corporation shows dominancy and exploitation on the part of the claimant. It is also reached where on the facts the bankrupt has been used merely as a corporate pocket of the dominant stockholder, who, with disregard of the substance or form of corporate management, has treated its affairs as his own. And so-called loans or advances by the dominant or controlling stockholder will be subordinated to claims of other creditors and thus treated in effect as capital contributions by the stockholder not only in the foregoing types of situations but also where the paid-in capital is purely nominal, the capital necessary for the scope and magnitude of the operations of the company being furnished by the stockholder as a loan.

Though disallowance of such claims will be ordered where they are fictitious or a sham, these cases do not turn on the existence or non-existence of the debt. Rather they involve simply the question of order of payment. At times equity has ordered disallowance or subordination by disregarding the corporate entity. That is to say, it has treated the debtor-corporation simply as a part of the stockholder's own enterprise, consistently with the course of conduct of the stockholder. But in that situation as well as in the others to

---

14. This Court said in *Twin-Lick Oil Co.* v. *Marbury, supra,* p. 590: "So, when the lender is a director, charged, with others, with the control and management of the affairs of the corporation, representing in this regard the aggregated interest of all the stockholders, his obligation, if he becomes a party to a contract with the company, to candor and fair dealing, is increased in the precise degree that his representative character has given him power and control derived from the confidence reposed in him by the stockholders who appointed him their agent. If he should be a sole director, or one of a smaller number vested with certain powers, this obligation would be still stronger, and his acts subject to more severe scrutiny, and their validity determined by more rigid principles of morality, and freedom from motives of selfishness."

c. For an overview of corporate reorganization under Chapter 11 of the United States Bankruptcy Code, see *infra* section 6c. [Eds.]

which we have referred, a sufficient consideration may be simply the violation of rules of fair play and good conscience by the claimant; a breach of fiduciary standards of conduct which he owes the corporation, its stockholders and creditors. He who is in such a fiduciary position cannot serve himself first and his *cestuis* second. He cannot manipulate the affairs of his corporation to their detriment and in disregard of the standards of common decency and honesty. He cannot by the intervention of a corporate entity violate the ancient precept against serving two masters.... Where there is a violation of those principles, equity will undo the wrong or intervene to prevent its consummation.

On such a test the action of the District Court in disallowing or subordinating Litton's claim was clearly correct. Litton allowed his salary claims to lie dormant for years and sought to enforce them only when his debtor corporation was in financial difficulty. Then he used them so that the rights of another creditor were impaired. Litton as an insider utilized his strategic position for his own preferment to the damage of Pepper. Litton as the dominant influence over Dixie Splint Coal Company used his power not to deal fairly with the creditors of that company but to manipulate its affairs in such a manner that when one of its creditors came to collect her just debt the bulk of the assets had disappeared into another Litton company. Litton, though a fiduciary, was enabled by astute legal maneuvering to acquire most of the assets of the bankrupt not for cash or other consideration of value to creditors but for bookkeeping entries representing at best merely Litton's appraisal of the worth of Litton's services over the years.

This alone would be a sufficient basis for the exercise by the District Court of its equitable powers in disallowing the Litton claim. But when there is added the existence of a "planned and fraudulent scheme," as found by the District Court, the necessity of equitable relief against that fraud becomes insistent. No matter how technically legal each step in that scheme may have been, once its basic nature was uncovered it was the duty of the bankruptcy court in the exercise of its equity jurisdiction to undo it. Otherwise, the fiduciary duties of dominant or management stockholders would go for naught; exploitation would become a substitute for justice; and equity would be perverted as an instrument for approving what it was designed to thwart.

The fact that Litton perfected his lien more than four months preceding bankruptcy is no obstacle to equitable relief. In the first place, that lien was but a step in a general fraudulent plan which must be viewed in its entirety. The subsequent sale cannot be taken as an isolated step unconnected with the long antecedent events, all designed to defeat creditors. *Buffum* v. *Peter Barceloux Co.*, 289 U.S. 227, 232-33. In the second place, Litton is seeking approval by the bankruptcy court of his claim. The four months' provision of the bankruptcy act is certainly not a statutory limitation on equitable defenses arising out of a breach of fiduciary duties by him who seeks allowance of a claim.

In view of these considerations we do not have occasion to determine the legitimacy of the "one-man" corporation as a bulwark against the claims of creditors.[28]

---

28. On this point the district court said: "An examination of the facts disclosed here shows the history of a deliberate and carefully planned attempt on the part of Scott Litton and Dixie Splint Coal Company to avoid the payment of a just debt. I speak of Litton *and* Dixie Splint Coal Company because they are in reality the same. In all the experience of the law, there has never been a more prolific breeder of fraud than the one-man corporation. It is a favorite device for the escape of personal liability. This case illustrates another frequent use of this fiction of corporate entity, whereby the owner of the corporation, through his complete control over it, undertakes to gather to himself all of its assets to the exclusion of its creditors."

Accordingly the judgment of the Circuit Court of Appeals is reversed and that of the District Court is affirmed.

Reversed.

Notes and Questions

1. What is the holding of Pepper v. Litton? How does Justice Douglas reach the conclusion that Litton owed Pepper a fiduciary duty? What is the relevance of Dixie Splint's insolvency?

Consider Chancellor Allen's now-famous remarks in Credit Lyonnais Bank Nederland, N.V. v. MGM Pathe Communications Co., 1991 WL 277613, at 34 and n.55:

> [W]here a corporation is operating in the vicinity of insolvency, a board of directors is not merely the agent of the residual risk bearers, but owes its duty to the corporate enterprise.... [The management] had an obligation to the community of interests that sustained the corporation, to exercise judgment in an informed, good faith effort to maximize the corporation's long-term wealth creating capacity.

In footnote 55, Chancellor Allen wrote:

> The possibility of insolvency can do curious things to incentives, exposing creditors to risks of opportunistic behavior and creating complexities for directors. Consider, for example, a solvent corporation having a single asset, a judgment for $51 million against a solvent debtor. The judgment is on appeal and thus subject to modification or reversal. Assume that the only liabilities of the company are to bondholders in the amount of $12 million. Assume that the array of probable outcomes of the appeal is as follows:

			Expected Value
25%	chance of affirmance	($51mm)	$12.75
70%	chance of modification	($4mm)	2.8
5%	chance of reversal	($0)	0
	Expected Value of Judgment on Appeal		$15.55

Thus, the best evaluation is that the current value of the equity is $3.55 million. ($15.55 million expected value of judgment on appeal − $12 million liability to bondholders). Now assume an offer to settle at $12.5 million (also consider one at $17.5 million). By what standard do the directors of the company evaluate the fairness of these offers? The creditors of this solvent company would be in favor of accepting either a $12.5 million offer or a $17.5 million offer. In either event they will avoid the 75% risk of insolvency and default. The stockholders, however, will plainly be opposed to acceptance of a $12.5 million settlement (under which they get practically nothing). More importantly, they very well may be opposed to acceptance of the $17.5 million offer under which the residual value of the corporation would increase from $3.5 to $5.5 million. This is so because the litigation alternative, with its 25% probability of a $39 million outcome to them ($51 million − $12 million = $39 million) has an expected value to the residual risk bearer of $9.75 million ($39 million × 25% chance of affirmance), substantially greater than the $5.5 million available to them in the settlement. While in fact the stockholders' preference would reflect their appetite for risk, it is possible (and with diversified shareholders likely) that shareholders would prefer rejection of both settlement offers.

But if we consider the community of interests that the corporation represents it seems apparent that one should in this hypothetical accept the best settlement offer available providing it is greater than $15.55 million, and one below that amount should be rejected. But that result will not be reached by a director who thinks he owes duties directly to shareholders only. It will be reached by directors who are capable of conceiving of the corporation as a legal and economic entity. Such directors will recognize that in managing the business affairs of a solvent corporation in the vicinity of insolvency, circumstances may arise when the right (both the efficient and the fair) course to follow for the corporation may diverge from the choice that the stockholders (or the creditors, or the employees, or any single group interested in the corporation) would make if given the opportunity to act.

For an interesting essay challenging the Chancellor's reasoning, see Morris, Directors' Duties in Nearly Insolvent Corporations: A Comment on Credit Lyonnais, 19 J. Corp. Law 61 (1993).

For a case presenting a fact pattern essentially similar to *Pepper*, and relying on *Credit Lyonnais* to hold that it is the fact of insolvency rather than the commencement of statutory proceedings that triggers fiduciary obligations to creditors, see Geyer v. Ingersoll Publications Co., 621 A. 2d 748 (Del. Ch. 1992).

2. How important to Justice Douglas is the fact that Litton was the sole stockholder of Dixie Splint? What would be the result if Litton merely owned a controlling interest and there were ten other stockholders? If Dixie Splint were a public corporation in which Litton owned working control and there were 5,000 other stockholders?

3. For a further examination of Justice Douglas' views on limited liability, *see* Douglas & Shanks, Insulation from Liability Through Subsidiary Corporations, 39 Yale L.J. 193 (1929).

4. Dixie Splint Coal Company did not file its bankruptcy petition until most of Litton's manipulations had been completed. In fact, the bankruptcy petition seems unimportant in Justice Douglas' extended discussion of fiduciary duty. Compare his obvious indignation with the tone of the Delaware Supreme Court in Simons v. Cogan, *supra* section 4a. For example, Justice Douglas asserts that Litton's ability, as sole stockholder of Dixie Splint, to manipulate its affairs would alone "be a sufficient basis for the exercise by the District Court of its equitable powers in disallowing the Litton claim." Would Pepper have been able to assert personal liability against Litton if the bankruptcy petition hadn't been filed? Would she be able to do so today outside of the bankruptcy context? *See* McDaniel, Bondholders and Stockholders, 1988 J. Corp. Law 205, 267, arguing (in our view, incorrectly) that Pepper v. Litton establishes a corporation's fiduciary duty to its creditors as a general proposition. Is the Court's

holding clear in this respect? If the fiduciary duties applied in *Pepper* are limited to the bankruptcy context, what justifies that result? For recent cases applying *Pepper*, see In re Clarkeies Mkt. L.L.C., 322 B.R. 487 (Bankr. D.N.H. 2005); In re Ames Dep't Stores, Inc., 274 B.R. 600 (Bankr. S.D.N.Y. 2002); In re 1236 Dev. Corp., 188 B.R. 75 (Bankr. D. Mass. 1995); Marquis Theatre Corp. v. Condedo Mini Cinema, 846 F.2d 86 (1st Cir. 1988); In re Giorgio, 862 F.2d 933 (1st Cir. 1988); Matter of C.T.S. TRUSS, Inc., 868 F.2d 146 (5th Cir. 1989); Corcoran v. Frank B. Hall and Co., Inc., 545 N.Y.S.2d 278 (1st Dep't 1989). Reread Simons v. Cogan, *supra* section 4a, to see the Delaware Supreme Court's use of Pepper v. Litton.

5. For additional analysis on the rights of creditors when debtors sink into insolvency, see Schwarcz, Rethinking a Corporation's Obligations to Creditors, 17 Cardozo L. Rev. 647, 665-77 (1996).

---

c. The Options Available to a Financially Troubled Corporation[a]

"What happens to a dream deferred?"[1] Sometimes it winds up insolvent! The issuance of large amounts of debt securities in the 1980s, to finance both corporate acquisitions and corporate development, ultimately resulted in a number of defaults in the payment of interest. Most of the defaults resulted from excessive leverage (too much debt), economic downturns, industry-specific problems (such as high fuel prices in the airline industry), and company-specific problems (such as inept management). When bad times befall a corporation, corporate executives need effective and cost efficient techniques to restructure financially troubled corporations.

A financially troubled corporation (the "debtor") has two basic options: (i) a voluntary, non-bankruptcy restructuring, or (ii) a voluntary bankruptcy reorganization proceeding under Chapter 11 of the U.S. Bankruptcy Code (the "Code"). 11 USC §§101-1532. The debtor also faces the possibility that creditors may file an involuntary bankruptcy petition under Chapter 11 (reorganization) or Chapter 7 (liquidation) of the Code. The costs of a bankruptcy proceeding generally exceed those of a consensual non-bankruptcy proceeding because the legal process surrounding the former can take years to resolve, and the debtor generally pays the fees and expenses of attorneys, accountants, and investment bankers (11 USC §330).

In addition, filing a bankruptcy petition may have an adverse impact on the debtor's customers or suppliers. Suppliers who extend credit to the debtor and customers with long-term contracts are justifiably reluctant to deal with a business undergoing a Chapter 11 reorganization, since only a small percentage of firms emerge successfully from Chapter 11 reorganization. Also, a debtor in bankruptcy may experience more difficulty in attracting and retaining employees than one undergoing a voluntary, non-bankruptcy restructuring.

---

a. The portion of the following note dealing with voluntary non-bankruptcy reorganization is based upon, and adapted from, Weingarten, Consensual Non-Bankruptcy Restructuring of Public Debt Securities, Rev. of Sec. & Com. Reg., Sept. 19, 1990.

1. Langston Hughes, Harlem (1951).

a. Voluntary Non-Bankruptcy Reorganization

In contemplating a restructuring, the debtor's management must identify and assess its operational and financial difficulties. Those operations which are, or can become, profitable must be distinguished from those that should be closed or sold. The debtor may need to pare down operations to reduce expenses, but it must also assess the impact of winding down activities on its ability to preserve tax advantages. The debtor must project its earning ability and its cash needs, which will likely require a reorganization of its capital structure. The debtor must deal with three types of creditors: (i) banks; (ii) trade creditors (suppliers); and (iii) public debtholders. Public debtholders increasingly are forming their own informal committees to negotiate with management and other creditor groups. These committees may retain attorneys and investment bankers (whose fees and expenses are often paid by a debtor in bankruptcy (11 USC §330)) to evaluate the debtor's proposals.

Two basic non-bankruptcy reorganization techniques are used by the debtor: exchange offers and/or consent solicitations. In an exchange offer, the debtor exchanges old debt securities for new debt or equity securities of the debtor or one of its affiliates. As an alternative to, or in conjunction with, an exchange offer, the debtor may solicit debtholders' consent to modify the terms of the old debt securities.

In structuring an exchange offer, the debtor must consider the extent to which debtholders will be willing to sacrifice their interests for the possibility of future gain. The debtor may merely extend the debt's maturity, or it may capture the discount at which its debt trades in the market and tie the offer to the current value of the debt securities.

In formulating an exchange offer, the debtor should pay particular attention to the identity of its creditors and stockholders. Increasingly, debt obligations of financially troubled companies are being purchased by "vulture capitalists" who have purchased the securities on the market at a steep discount (reflecting the debtor's financial woes). Dealing with the vultures has advantages and disadvantages. As sophisticated investors, vultures understand the restructuring process and can realistically assess the alternatives available to the debtor. However, they are tough negotiators who expect a profit and may even have purchased the debt securities specifically for the purpose of acquiring control of the corporation.

The debtor may offer the debtholders incentives to accept its proposal. One such incentive is a package of new debt and equity securities having a greater potential market value on the completion of the restructuring than would the existing debt if the restructuring is not consummated. Other incentives include an equity position in the debtor, a higher interest rate on the new debt, or a senior (secured) creditor position. The debtor may offer securities convertible into equity at a rate which adjusts most favorably from the holder's viewpoint to prevailing market conditions. In addition to (or in lieu of) these positive inducements, a debtor may also use negative incentives to persuade creditors to accept its plan. Examples include the specter of bankruptcy reorganization or, perhaps more severely, liquidation if the exchange offer is not completed, or the threat that debtholders who do not accept the exchange offer will be left in a junior, and potentially less valuable, position in relation to those debtholders who do accept the exchange offer. (Recall Katz v. Oak Industries Inc., *supra* at section 4c.) For example, the debtor may build into the new debt securities covenants restricting the debtor's ability to refinance the old securities not tendered in the exchange offer. However, a bankruptcy court may not uphold the seniority of the new securities.

The debtor must also consider that an exchange offer does not bind non-exchanging debtholders, a significant disadvantage. In contrast to the exchange offer, all of the debtholders in a Chapter 11 proceeding are bound by the plan of reorganization if confirmed. Thus, the identity of the debtholder is critical to the success of an exchange offer. If the old debt securities are widely held, the debtor will face the possibility that a number of debtholders, particularly small holders, may fail to accept the exchange offer.

When a class of creditors does not consent to the plan in a bankruptcy proceeding under Chapter 11, the debtor may request that the court "cram down" a plan on that class if it finds that the non-consenting class will receive as much as it would have received in a liquidation (11 USC §1129(a)(7)(A)), and no junior class obtains any distribution (11 USC §1129(b)). For more on "cram down," see *infra* section 6e(ii).

Generally, a debtor cannot require all debtholders to accept an exchange offer. Exceptions do exist, however, under state law. For example, in Delaware, the certificate of incorporation may contain a provision allowing the Chancery Court to order a meeting of creditors if a compromise or an arrangement is proposed between the corporation and its creditors. If the requisite number of creditors agree to the compromise or arrangement, with court approval, all the creditors or class of creditors are bound (Del. Gen. Corp. Law §102(b)(2)).

The debtor may propose a consent solicitation which seeks to amend the trust indenture relating to the old debt securities. A debtor uses a consent solicitation to modify covenants in the indenture that, if not changed, would conflict with other transactions comprising the financial restructuring, and to remove certain substantive covenants from the indenture, thereby reducing the attractiveness of the old securities to the non-exchanging debtholders. For example, the acceleration clause of a typical indenture requires the debtor, upon default, to immediately pay debtholders the principal amount of the securities and all interest due. If a debtor has or will default, the debtor will typically seek a waiver of the acceleration clause from the debtholders concurrent with a plan to remedy the situation. (Recall, again, Katz v. Oak Industries Inc., *supra* at section 4c.)

A debtor can use the consent technique to modify all indenture provisions. Most trust indentures only require a majority vote of the aggregate amount of the debt securities to consent to the modification of an indenture. Other indentures require the vote of at least two-thirds of the aggregate principal amount of the debt securities. An exception exists for key provisions, such as interest rate, maturity date, and principal amount, modifications of which require unanimous consent of the debtholders.

Unless the indenture specifically prohibits the practice, the debtor can pay cash or other types of consideration to consenting debtholders as a positive incentive to exchange. The debtor must, however, offer the consideration to all debtholders or the payments may be regarded as "voting buying" and thus voidable. The debtor may try to strengthen its bargaining position by combining an exchange offer with a pre-petition solicitation of consent to a Chapter 11 plan of reorganization. This pre-packaged Chapter 11 plan (often referred to as a "pre-pak") often will incorporate the terms of the exchange offer with minor differences. If the debtor is unable to consummate a non-bankruptcy restructuring because of its inability to obtain the requisite acceptance rate by debtholders (typically at least 80%, but sometimes as much as 95%, as specified in the indenture), the debtor will use the vote in favor of the pre-packaged

Chapter 11 plan to satisfy the lower voting requirements of Chapter 11.[2] Under the Code, a class of claims accepts a plan if approved by creditors holding at least two-thirds in amount and more than one-half in number of the allowed claims held by the creditors that have voted on the plan (11 USC §1126(c)). Coupling an exchange offer with a pre-packaged Chapter 11 plan sends a strong signal to debtholders that a debtor is seriously contemplating a Chapter 11 proceeding.

b. Reorganization under Chapter 11 of the Bankruptcy Code

A business reorganization under Chapter 11 of the Code may be voluntary or involuntary.

A debtor commences a voluntary reorganization by filing a petition in a U.S. Bankruptcy Court (11 USC §301), and may do so without regard to its financial condition.[3] A petition may also be filed in the appropriate U.S. District Court (*See* 28 USC §1408(1)).

Involuntary reorganization proceedings under Chapter 11 are commenced when a petition is filed in a bankruptcy court by three or more creditors (11 USC §303(b) or (b)(1)). The petition in an involuntary proceeding must allege either that the debtor generally is not paying its debts as they come due (equitable insolvency), or a non-bankruptcy general receiver, assignee, or custodian (except one appointed to enforce a lien on less than substantially all of the debtor's property) was appointed or authorized to take possession of substantially all of the debtor's property within 120 days before the filing of the petition (11 USC §303(h)(1),(h)(2)).

The debtor may continue to operate its business as if the bankruptcy case had not commenced, unless, upon request of a party in interest, the court appoints an interim trustee to operate the debtor's business (11 USC §§303(f) & (g)). A strong presumption exists in bankruptcy law that the debtor's existing management should continue to run the business. A bankruptcy court will displace management and appoint a trustee only for cause (including fraud, dishonesty, mismanagement or incompetence) or if the court determines that the appointment of a trustee is in the best interests of creditors, equity security holders or other interested parties. Under the Bankruptcy Abuse Prevention and Consumer Protection Act of 2005 (the "2005 Act"), the U.S. Trustee must move for the appointment of a trustee if reasonable grounds exist to suspect corporate executives of fraud, dishonesty or criminal conduct (11 USC §1105(e)).

The debtor's creditors receive notice of the commencement of the bankruptcy proceeding (11 USC §342), based on the information contained in the debtor's list of creditors, schedule of assets and liabilities, and statement of financial affairs (11 USC §521(1)). If a trustee is appointed, the trustee must file such information (11 USC §1106(a)(2)).

Creditors or stockholders of the debtor whose claims or interests are scheduled by the debtor or the trustee need not file a proof of claim or interest unless it is listed as "disputed, contingent or unliquidated" (11 USC §1111(a)). If the claim or interest is

---

2. For a bankruptcy case involving a pre-packaged bankruptcy, see In re Zenith Electronics Corp., 241 B.R. 92 (D. Del. Bankr. 1999), *supra* at section 6e(ii).
3. Collier Bankruptcy Manual ¶ 301.03 (3d rev. ed. 2005).

disputed, contingent or unliquidated, a proof of claim or interest may be filed unless the debtor objects (11 USC §§501(a), 502(a)). If a secured creditor files a claim, the court, upon application of the debtor or the trustee, may determine how much of the claim is secured and how much is unsecured (11 USC §§506(a) & 1111(b)).

After the filing of the requisite financial information, the debtor, creditors and stockholders devote their affairs to facilitating the administration of the proceeding. The unsecured creditors will be organized into a creditors' committee whose members are appointed by the court. The committee will consist of the seven largest unsecured creditors who are willing to serve (11 USC §1102(b)).[4] If the unsecured creditors formed a committee prior to filing the bankruptcy petition, that committee will serve as the official committee provided it "was fairly chosen and is representative of the different kinds of claims to be represented" (11 USC §1102(b)(1)). Additional official committees may be appointed by the court if needed (11 USC §1102(a)(2)).

Once organized, the official creditors' committee proceeds with four tasks: (i) to determine whether the debtor should continue to operate its business; (ii) to determine whether the court should appoint a trustee; (iii) to conduct an investigation of the debtor's acts and financial affairs; and (iv) generally to consult with the debtor or trustee in the administration of the proceeding.

Unless the court orders otherwise, the debtor's management continues to operate the business as a "debtor in possession." However, the creditors may seek appointment of a trustee to assume responsibility for the operation of the business and the formation of a plan of reorganization (11 USC §1104). The court may appoint that trustee, upon the request of a party in interest, either for cause (such as fraud, dishonesty, incompetence, or gross mismanagement before or after the filing of the petition) or in the interests of the creditors and the stockholders (11 USC §1104(a)). If the court determines that a trustee is to be appointed, then the United States trustee, subject to court approval and consultation with the parties in interest, appoints the trustee (11 USC §1104(b)(1)). However, if the creditors elect an eligible, disinterested trustee, the U.S. Trustee must file a report certifying the election and the elected trustee shall be considered appointed (11 USC §1104(b)(2)).

The filing of a bankruptcy petition results in an automatic stay which gives a debtor time to make key operating decisions. Pursuant to the automatic stay, all actions against the debtor, except for governmental actions to enforce police or regulatory powers, are enjoined (11 USC §362(a)). Absent affirmative steps by a secured creditor, the automatic stay continues as long as the debtor has an interest in the property, until vacated by the court, or until the case is closed or dismissed (11 USC §§362(c) & (d)). An automatic stay will also automatically terminate after 30 days if a new case is filed within a year of when an earlier dismissed case was pending because the new case was presumably filed in bad faith. (11 USC §362(c)).

Prior to the confirmation stage of a bankruptcy proceeding under Chapter 11, a plan of reorganization must be prepared and filed. Every plan must divide the creditors into classes, set forth how the creditors will ratify the plan, state which claims are

---

4. Pursuant to the 2005 Act, a small business creditor can petition the court to be added as a special member of the creditors' committee if the debt owed to that creditor is disproportionately large in comparison to the creditor's annual gross revenue (11 USC §1102(a)(4)).

not "impaired" under the plan, and treat each creditor of a class in the same manner (11 USC §§1123(a) & (b)).

A plan of reorganization may be filed with the petition commencing a Chapter 11 case or thereafter. Although the debtor, its creditors, or the trustee (if one is appointed) may file a plan of reorganization, generally the debtor will have an exclusive period of up to 180 days in which to negotiate, file, and seek acceptance of its plan. If a trustee is not appointed, only the debtor can file a plan during the first 120 days of the proceeding (11 USC §1121(b)).[5] The debtor is entitled to an additional 60 days, for a total of 180 days, to obtain the necessary acceptances of the plan (11 USC §1121(c)(3)), and can petition for even more time.[6]

Other parties in interest have two opportunities to reduce the debtor's exclusive period to file a plan. First, such party may file an application with the court to reduce the debtor's exclusive 120 and 180 day periods (11 USC §1121(d)). Second, the debtor's exclusive plan period expires on the appointment of a trustee. Thereafter, any party in interest may file a plan (11 USC §1121(c)). Regardless of who files the plan, the creditors' committee generally plays a significant role in structuring the plan. The plan may alter the rights of the debtor's creditors and/or the stockholders. The plan must divide the creditors' claims into classes, and each claim within a specified class must be "substantially similar" (11 USC §1122(a)).

The bankruptcy court must hold a hearing, giving notice to the parties in interest, on the confirmation of the plan (11 USC §1128). Confirmation of a plan of reorganization turns on four key issues: (i) which classes must affirmatively approve the plan; (ii) what percentage of each class must approve the plan; (iii) what standard protects the dissenting members of an approving class from an unfair business plan; and (iv) what limits exist on the solicitation of acceptances of the plan.

i. Classes Required to Approve the Plan

Generally a plan need not be approved by unsecured creditors or stockholders in two situations:

a) when the plan does not impair the rights of the unsecured creditors or stockholders (11 USC §1126(f)); or

b) when the plan deals with the rights of the unsecured creditors or stockholders but the value of the business is such that, after applying the appropriate creditor priorities, the classes of unsecured creditors or stockholders have no legitimate financial interest in the reorganized business. Thus, if the class receives nothing under the plan, it is deemed to have rejected it (11 USC §1126(g)).

A class of claims or interests is "impaired" unless: (i) the rights of the holder are "unaltered" (i.e., the plan does not adversely change the rights of the holder); (ii) the alteration of rights is the reversal of an acceleration on default by curing the default and reinstating the debt; or (iii) the cash payment on the effective date of the plan to (a) a creditor equals the allowed amount of the claim, or (b) a stockholder equals the greater of the share's redemption price or its liquidation preference (11 USC §1124).

---

5. The 2005 Act has increased this to 180 days for debtors classified as "small businesses."

6. Under the 2005 Act, in no event may the debtor's 120 day period be extended beyond 18 months from the date of the court's order of relief, nor the 180 day period extended beyond 20 months from such date.

Each class of creditors or stockholders must accept the plan if it is fair and equitable and does not discriminate unfairly (11 USC §1129(b)(1)). A plan is fair and equitable to a class of impaired unsecured creditors (and thus the acceptance of the plan by such class is not necessary) if the junior claims and interests neither receive nor retain anything (11 USC §1129(b)(2)(B)(ii)). With respect to the holder of a secured claim, a plan is fair and equitable if the holder of the secured claim retains its lien, and the payments equal at least the amount of the allowed secured claim and the payments have a present value equal to the value of the claim (11 USC §1129(b)(2)(A)(i)).

ii. Requisite Approval by Each Required Class

A class accepts a plan when a majority in number and two-thirds in amount of the allowed claims (or interests) actually voting accept the plan (11 USC §§1126 (c),(d)). The consenting creditors of a class can force the nonconsenting creditors to accept less than full payment of their debt. If any impaired class does not accept the plan, no plan can be confirmed without a judicial determination that the class or interest has no legitimate interest in the reorganization values. Any plan which is not accepted by all impaired classes and interests will result in a judicial determination of the going concern value of the business.

iii. The Financial Standard

The confirmation of a Chapter 11 plan requires that a "best interests" test be applied to the acceptance of the plan by all classes of impaired claims and stockholder interests. The "best interests" test protects a dissenting minority of an accepting class by requiring that all members of the class receive at least what they would have received upon the liquidation of the business in a Chapter 7 proceeding (11 USC §1129(a)(7)(A)).

iv. Solicitation of Acceptances

Before the acceptance of creditors and stockholders may be used to confirm a plan in any Chapter 11 proceeding, the court must find that the solicitation of acceptances was based on disclosure of adequate financial information.

If the acceptances to a plan were solicited prior to filing a Chapter 11 proceeding (in a prepackaged plan), such acceptances may be counted provided that the solicitation was in compliance with an applicable non-bankruptcy law regulating the adequacy of disclosure in connection with such solicitation. If there was no such law, the acceptances may be counted if solicited with adequate disclosure of relevant business information (11 USC §1126(b)).

If the acceptances to a plan were solicited after the filing of a Chapter 11 proceeding, at or before the time of such solicitation, the creditors or stockholders must receive the plan (or a summary of the plan) and a written disclosure statement. The court must certify that the disclosure statement contains "adequate information," including potential material Federal tax consequences to the debtor, successors and any hypothetical investors typical of the holders of claims or interest in the case (11 USC §1125(a)). "Adequate information" is information which is "reasonably practicable" for the debtor to provide to a "hypothetical investor" in order for that investor to make an informed judgment on the plan (11 USC §1125(a)).

Once the plan is confirmed, the plan governs the performance of the debtor's obligations and binds creditors and stockholders (11 USC §1141(a)). Confirmation of a plan operates as a discharge of a debtor's obligations to its creditors regardless of whether the plan deals with such obligations or those creditors participate in the reorganization (11 USC §1141(d)(1)).

v. Tax Aspects

The Internal Revenue Code generally creates incentives for debtors to reorganize within the protection of Chapter 11 of the U.S. Bankruptcy Code rather than to undertake voluntary, non-bankruptcy reorganizations. For example, one tax issue arises from the forgiveness of indebtedness, a common characteristic of reorganizations in which debt with a lower face value is issued by the corporation in exchange for outstanding higher face value debt. Typically the forgiveness of debt is immediately recognized as income. However, if the corporation is reorganizing under Chapter 11, or is insolvent (in the bankruptcy sense) when the debt is discharged (and is not made solvent by the discharge), the recognition of income from the forgiveness of indebtedness is deferred. I.R.C. §108.

Moreover, limitations exist on the extent to which a corporation may use its net operating losses to offset future income if a change in control has occurred. Such a change may well occur if a reorganizing debtor exchanges stock for debt. Section 382 of the I.R.C. exempts corporations in Chapter 11 proceedings from some of these limitations where the pre-control change shareholders and creditors of the debtor own at least 50 percent of the value and voting power of the debtor's stock after the control change.

A number of other significant tax issues exist, some of which apply equally to corporations in and out of Chapter 11. For further discussion of these issues, see Gargotta, Post-Petition Tax Compliance under the Bankrtupcy Code: Can the IRS Enforce Tax Collection after Bankruptcy is Filed?, 11 Am. Bankr. Inst. L. Rev. 113 (2003); Cieri, Heiman, Henze, Jenks, Kirschner, Riley & Sullivan, An Introduction to Legal and Practical Considerations in the Restructuring of Troubled Leveraged Buyouts, 45 Bus. Law. 333, 368-76 (1989); Saggese, Noel & Mohr, A Practitioner's Guide to Exchange Offers and Consent Solicitations, 24 Loy. L.A. L. Rev. 527, 547-48, 552-53 (1991).

---

d. Why Allow a Failed Business to Reorganize?

Roe, Bankruptcy and Debt: A New Model for Corporate Reorganization
83 Colum. L. Rev. 527, 534-36 (1983)[a]

* * *

B. *Feasibility: Plan Viability vs. Firm Viability*

Feasibility in reorganization[21] could mean at least two things: that the plan be viable, i.e., that creditors will get what they have been promised in the plan, or that the firm be viable—or at least as viable as possible—once the plan is in effect.[23]

---

a. Copyright c. 1983 by the Directors of the Columbia Law Review Association, Inc. All rights reserved. This article originally appeared at 83 Colum. L. Rev. 527 (1983). Reprinted by permission.

21. See Bankruptcy Code §1129(a)(1), which Congress intended to carry forward chapter X's requirement that a plan be feasible. S. Rep. No. 989, 95th Cong., 2d Sess. 128 (1978).

23. The conceptual confusion courts may have when grappling with feasibility is illustrated by In re Transvision, Inc., 217 F.2d 243 (2d Cir. 1954), cert. denied, 348 U.S. 952 (1955). The court first stated that feasibility was a test of firm viability: "The feasibility of the arrangement must be examined with a view toward determining whether ... the desired financial recovery will be effected without unduly prejudicing the rights of any interested parties." Id. at 246. A few paragraphs later, however, the court seemed to treat *plan* feasibility as the primary concern, with *firm* viability of

Plan viability is satisfied if the firm is expected to stagger successfully through semi-annual interest coupons, sinking fund payments, and the maturity of principal, even if the resulting cash outflow leaves nothing to maintain a going concern. The two meanings are, of course, not mutually exclusive. In many instances, to conclude that the *plan* is viable indicates some likelihood that the *firm* will also be viable. But some *plans* that are viable will not leave the affected *firms* viable, or at least not as viable as they could have been under some other plan. Thus, the notion of feasibility as firm viability is the standard that bankruptcy courts sometimes do and, perhaps, always should apply in the case of the large public firm. But not all courts apply such a standard.

The Bankruptcy Code arguably adopts a requirement of firm viability. As stated in section 1129(a)(11), as a prerequisite to confirmation of the proposed plan, the bankruptcy court must determine that the plan "is not likely to be followed by the liquidation, or the need for further financial reorganization, of the debtor." The legislative history refers to this section as adopting the old chapter X notion of feasibility, which usually was viewed as a firm-viability standard. No room is left as a formal matter under the statute either for deference to the parties to the reorganization bargain on the question of feasibility or for judicial avoidance of a finding of feasibility.

Although Congress has not stopped liquidation even if satellite interests such as a firm's suppliers, local communities, and employees are harmed, Congress has created a structure to preserve those interests as long as the value of the firm, if it continues to operate, exceeds its liquidation value.[29] Indeed, the reorganization statutes can be seen as arising from a congressional belief that some creditors would, if given the authority to do so, liquidate a viable firm as long as liquidation assured creditors of payment-in-full while maintenance of the going concern presented some risk of nonpayment.

Thus, we approach the problem of debt from the perspective that chapter 11 courts should require that a reorganization plan leave the firm viable. We then will ask what method of reorganization will maximize firm viability and minimize social costs. Does current financial analysis suggest any general rule as to how to do this? Will a standardized capital structure best move reorganization toward these goals?

---

secondary importance. Not only should the arrangement lead to the creditors' being paid, but the shareholder and the firm *might* also benefit as well, if the arrangement works. Id. at 246-47.

29. Obviously, a system could be constructed that in a more formal way recognized values other than those of creditors and shareholders. Some commentators suggest that realistically this is the system today. See, e.g., P. Drucker, Concept of the Corporation 20-21 (rev. ed. 1972):

> Though we have largely abandoned it in legal and political practice, the old crude fiction still lingers on which regards the corporation as nothing but the sum of the property rights of the individual shareholders. Thus, for instance, the president of a company will report to the shareholders on the state of "their" company. In this conventional formula the corporation is seen as transitory and as existing only by virtue of a legal fiction while the shareholder is regarded as permanent and actual. In the social reality of today, however, shareholders are but one of several groups of people who stand in a special relationship to the corporation. The corporation is permanent, the shareholder is transitory. It might even be said without much exaggeration that the corporation is really socially and politically a priori whereas the shareholder's position is derivative and exists only in contemplation of law. This, for instance, is the position taken in our bankruptcy laws which put the maintenance of corporate integrity above the rights of the shareholders. We would not have needed the experience of the Great Depression of 1929-39 to show us that society must insist on the maintenance of the "going concern" and must if necessary sacrifice to it the individual rights of shareholders, creditors, workers, and, in the last analysis, even of consumers.

Baird and Jackson, Corporate Reorganization and the Treatment of Diverse Ownership Interests: A Comment on Adequate Protection of Secured Creditors in Bankruptcy

51 U. Chi. L. Rev. 97, 101-103 (1984)

* * *

I. THE PROBLEM OF DIVERSE OWNERSHIP INTERESTS

Those who have argued that secured creditors should not be given the full value of their rights under state law in bankruptcy often also argue that a bankruptcy proceeding must respond to the greater social problems that attend a business failure. The failure of a firm affects many who do not, under current law, have cognizable ownership interests in the firm outside of bankruptcy. The economy of an entire town can be disrupted when a large factory closes. Many employees may be put out of work. The failure of one firm may lead to the failure of those who supplied it with raw materials and those who acquired its finished products. Some believe that preventing such consequences is worth the costs of trying to keep the firm running and justifies placing burdens on a firm's secured creditors.

We think that this view is, as a matter of bankruptcy policy, fundamentally wrong. Fashioning remedies for all the harm a failing business may bring is difficult and beyond the competence of a bankruptcy court. The wider effects of the failure of a particular enterprise are not easy to assess. A principal characteristic of a market economy is, after all, that some firms fail, and postponing the inevitable or keeping marginal firms alive may do more harm than good. Forcing investors to keep assets in a relatively unproductive enterprise may limit the freedom of the same or different investors to use those assets in a different and more productive one. Keeping a firm in one town from closing may have the indirect effect of keeping a new one in a different town from opening. Moreover, limiting the ability of investors to reclaim their assets may reduce their incentive to invest (rather than consume) in the first instance. Instead of weighing these effects equally, a bankruptcy judge is likely to focus on the demonstrable harms of those who are before him.

But there is a more important reason for denying a bankruptcy judge broad license to protect people in the wake of economic misfortune. The problems brought by business failures are not bankruptcy problems. A bankruptcy proceeding should not be the place to implement a policy that society does not enforce outside of bankruptcy and that is unrelated to the preservation of assets for the firm's investor group. Most businesses fail without a bankruptcy petition ever being filed. If it is a bad policy to protect secured creditors in full while workers remain unpaid, it should not matter whether a bankruptcy petition has been filed. So, too, if a secured creditor should properly share with everyone else in the economic misfortunes of a debtor, he should be required to carry his share of the loss in every instance, not just in the minority of cases in which a bankruptcy petition is filed.

Nonbankruptcy concerns, we believe, should not be addressed by changing bankruptcy policy. Our view derives from two related observations: first, that bankruptcy law is, and should be, concerned with the interests of those (from bondholders to unpaid workers to tort victims to shareholders) who, outside of bankruptcy, have property rights in the assets of the firm filing a petition, and, second, that in analyzing the interests of these parties with property rights, our baseline should be applicable nonbankruptcy law. A collective insolvency proceeding is directed toward reducing the costs associated with diverse ownership interests and encouraging those with interests in a firm's assets to put those assets to the use the group as a whole would favor.

Other problems should be addressed as general problems, not as bankruptcy problems....

Roe, Bankruptcy and Debt: A New Model for Corporate Reorganization
83 Colum. L. Rev. 527, 528-33 (1983)[a]

Two of the core determinations made in a reorganization proceeding under chapter 11 of the Bankruptcy Code are simply stated: Who gets how much? What will the new capital structure be? To resolve these simply stated questions of valuation and recapitalization, bankruptcy courts loosely oversee a lengthy bargaining process that is widely thought to be cumbersome, costly, and complex. The strain of extended financial stress results in lost sales when customers seek a more secure supply source, in consumption of valuable management time spent resolving financial difficulties, and in forgone opportunities to obtain new projects. Additional costs are borne by the employees, customers, and suppliers of the bankrupt company, as well as the communities in which it operates. Furthermore, while contraction of the bankrupt firm is usually in order, parts of the firm may sometimes be liquidated even though liquidation value is less than operational value. Finally, the firm often emerges from reorganization with an unnecessarily complex capital structure. Such a complex capital structure can cause the reorganized firm to adopt poor operational strategies, prevent it from raising new capital, and pose a barrier to a healthy merger.

This overview suggests three principal characteristics desirable for a reorganization mechanism: speed, low cost, and a resulting sound capital structure. Other desirable characteristics are accuracy in valuation and compensation, predictability, and fairness. Accuracy and predictability diminish the uncertainty of the results of bankruptcy reorganizations, facilitating investment in risky but worthwhile enterprises before a bankruptcy occurs. Speed and low cost help diminish the deadweight costs of the bankruptcy when it does occur.

Three general mechanisms might be considered to accomplish reorganization: (1) the bargain among creditors and stakeholders, i.e., a "workout" that occurs outside the bankruptcy court or after the filing of a bankruptcy petition, but even then with minimal court supervision; (2) litigation in which the court imposes a solution and capital structure; and (3) although rarely even noted as a serious possibility, use of the market. Congress preferred that the parties first attempt a bargained-for solution, and if the bargain failed, that a judicial solution be imposed. Congress and the courts have assumed that marketplace valuation for bankrupts is too inaccurate, principally because of a lack of adequately informed buyers, to be a viable alternative. If, however, the bargain fails, courts in the ensuing litigation often hear investment bankers and other experts on the crucial questions of valuation and capital structure. The judicial solution thereby mimics the market, attempting to reach an idealized value of the bankrupt that the court believes would arise if a perfect market were at work. Both the bankruptcy bargain and the litigation mechanisms are slow, costly, and often unpredictable. Could a more direct market based mechanism be better?

This Article examines the intertwined propositions that (1) the goal of a speedy and inexpensive reorganization for the large public firm whose stock is widely traded could best be attained by a general rule requiring that reorganization courts confirm only plans with simplified all-common-stock capital structures; and (2) the reorganization value of the public firm could be found by selling a slice, say 10%, of new common stock into the market, and extrapolating enterprise value from the sale price. Once the corporation were so valued by the market and given an all-common-stock capital structure, claimants and interests would fall into place according to the Bankruptcy Code's absolute priority rule, under which senior claimants are paid in full before juniors receive anything. If this proposal could be successfully implemented, two major tasks of reorganization—valuation and restructuring—could take place not as now occurs over the course of years, but over a much shorter period.

In Part I we shall see that a policy of solely promoting post-reorganization firm viability would ordinarily (and, I believe, perhaps obviously) lead to a generalized requirement of an all-common-equity capital structure. A bargain among creditors and the bankrupt will often, however, not reach this result because of uncertainty, institutional-creditor preferences for debt, and tax considerations. Because of a multiplicity of goals—not only, for example, to promote post-reorganization firm viability, but also to satisfy creditor preferences at the time of reorganization—bankruptcy institutions generally permit "reasonable" levels of debt. Even a court concerned solely with firm viability would, however, be uncertain as to the importance of promoting a generalized all-common-equity rule. Because bargaining deadlocks and the propensity to litigate would not be eliminated, the adoption of an all-common-stock rule would by itself fail to eliminate the crippled capital structure quickly and move the firm through reorganization rapidly. Quick reorganization may be the central viability problem, as may be easily and intuitively understood by those who have observed a reorganization. Indeed, without an objective basis for valuation that would avoid conflict and delay, the adoption of only an all-common-stock rule conceivably might exacerbate reorganization difficulties. A quick, objective method of valuing the firm is therefore a necessary complement to a standardized capital structure. In Parts II and III we shall examine the significant obstacles to adoption of market valuation as such a complement. Though it seems plausible that market valuation in principle could provide an objective valuation of the firm, difficulties in implementation of a market methodology are likely. In Part IV, we shall see that precedent and statute also would present obstacles to use of the market during reorganizations.

Notes and Questions

1. What do you think of Professor Roe's solution to the problem of reorganizations generally? Professor Baird and Dean Jackson suggest that the central issue is identifying the residual owner who then should be left to bargain with the other claimants. Baird & Jackson, Bargaining After the Fall and the Contours of the Absolute Priority Rule, 55 U. Chi. L. Rev. 738 (1988).

2. What are the valuation problems likely to be encountered in a reorganization? As a bankruptcy judge, how would you deal with them? What concerns would you have as counsel to secured creditors? Unsecured creditors? The issuer?

e. Fundamental Bankruptcy Concepts

(i) Automatic Stay and Adequate Protection

Baird and Jackson, Corporate Reorganization and the Treatment of Diverse Ownership Interests: A Comment on Adequate Protection of Secured Creditors in Bankruptcy

51 U. Chi. L. Rev. 97, 98-101 (1984)

The filing of a bankruptcy petition automatically stays creditors from repossessing property of the debtor in which they have a security interest.[4] These creditors, however, can demand that the stay be lifted unless their interests in the debtor's property are "adequately protected."[5] As a matter of statutory illustration, adequate protection is the granting of relief that "will result in the realization by [the holder of the interest] of the indubitable equivalent of such entity's interest in such property."[6] In the context of secured credit, the need for adequate protection, according to the legislative history of the Bankruptcy Code, rests "as much on policy grounds as on constitutional grounds. Secured creditors should not be deprived of the benefit of their bargain."

However clear and simple this statutory command may appear, it has nevertheless come under attack from two distinct directions. Professor Rogers has asserted in a recent article that Congress has given secured creditors too much protection in bankruptcy because it erroneously thought the fifth amendment constrained it from limiting the rights of secured creditors (and presumably others).[8] Bankruptcy judges, moreover, have been asserting with growing frequency that adequate protection for a secured creditor whose collateral is left in the estate during the pendency of the bankruptcy proceeding does not include compensation for the "time value" of their secured claims, but only the cost of physical depreciation—a conclusion with which Professor Rogers and others have concurred. These judges and commentators have assumed both that a central goal of bankruptcy law, embodied in its reorganization provisions, is to help firms in financial straits stay in business and that limiting the rights of secured creditors in this way advances this goal without significantly undercutting any other worthwhile policies.

As others have shown, however, an interpretation of the Bankruptcy Code that denies creditors compensation for the time value of their secured claims is, as a matter of statutory construction, strained, if not clearly wrong. As interesting an inquiry, to which we turn in this article, is whether those who want to limit the rights

---

4. 11 U.S.C. §362(a) (1982) imposes the automatic stay.

5. Section 362(d)(1) of the Bankruptcy Code, 11 U.S.C. §362(d)(1) (1982), expresses the adequate protection rule as follows:

> On request of a party in interest and after notice and a hearing, the court shall grant relief from the stay provided under subsection (a) of this section, such as by terminating, annulling, modifying, or conditioning such stay—(1) for cause, including the lack of adequate protection of an interest in property of such party in interest....

6. 11 U.S.C. §361(3) (1982). *But see In re* Alyucan Interstate Corp., 12 Bankr. 803, 809 (Bankr. D. Utah 1981) ("Indubitable equivalence is not a method; nor does it have substantive content.... At best, it is a semantic substitute for adequate protection and one with dubious, not indubitable, application to the question of relief from the stay.").

8. Rogers, *The Impairment of Secured Creditors' Rights in Reorganization: A Study of the Relationship Between the Fifth Amendment and the Bankruptcy Clause*, 96 Harv. L. Rev. 973, 977-97 (1983).

of secured creditors are correct as a matter of what bankruptcy law *should* be. This normative inquiry must begin with critical questions about why a *bankruptcy* process exists at all—questions that simple statements about the purposes of bankruptcy law do not answer. Consider the "rehabilitation" goal of a Chapter 11 proceeding. No one, to our knowledge, argues that keeping a firm intact is *always* a good thing. Yet as soon as one concedes that a reorganization may not always be desirable, one is faced with the problem of understanding and articulating *why* reorganizations are favored in the first place and *how much* should be given up to facilitate them. Similarly, the observation that Congress, at least if it acted prospectively, *could* deny secured creditors compensation for the time value of their claims does little more than rebut an argument of almost no constitutional currency. Indeed, Congress, acting prospectively, probably could refuse to recognize the rights of secured creditors altogether. But to say this much is not to say that Congress *should* refuse to recognize those rights or that it should refuse to recognize them only in bankruptcy.

In this article, we suggest that bankruptcy law at its core should be designed to keep individual actions against assets, taken to preserve the position of one investor or another, from interfering with the use of those assets favored by the investors as a group.[15] Arguments over the wisdom of many substantive rules are not arguments about the way to implement this goal, and it misperceives the inquiry to focus on the wisdom of such rules as a matter of bankruptcy policy. Bankruptcy law should change a substantive nonbankruptcy rule only when doing so preserves the value of assets for the group of investors holding rights in them. For this reason, bankruptcy law necessarily overrides the remedies of individual investors outside of bankruptcy, for those "grab" rules undermine the very advantages sought in a collective proceeding....

Based upon this view of bankruptcy law, we examine the protection afforded to secured creditors in bankruptcy, asking, first, what exactly the secured creditors' nonbankruptcy rights are and, second, whether any modification of those rights is necessary in order to preserve or enhance the firm's assets for the general benefit of the investor group. What these nonbankruptcy rights should be is a question that is unrelated to whether they should be followed in bankruptcy. We show that protecting the value of a secured creditor's nonbankruptcy rights—whatever they might be—actually reinforces the bankruptcy policy of putting the firm's assets to their best use by placing the costs of trying to keep the assets of a firm together on those who stand to benefit from such an effort. If these parties do not bear these costs, they will have an incentive to place a firm in bankruptcy and to draw out the proceeding, even though doing so does not work to the advantage of those with rights to the firm's assets when their interests are considered as a group.

* * *

15. By "investor" (or "owner"), we mean anyone with rights, however contingent, to the debtor's assets under nonbankruptcy law. By "rights," we mean the right to the income stream generated by the firm's assets, the right to receive payment out of the assets, or the right to the assets upon dissolution. "Rights," so used, is not the same as "interests" as used in 11 U.S.C. §361 (1982) (defining adequate protection) and 11 U.S.C. §362(d) (1982) (grounds on which court may grant relief from the automatic stay). Those with rights include not only secured creditors, but also, for example, shareholders, who, like the other investors, have a right to the firm's assets (subject to the rights of creditors). The creation of "rights" as we speak of them here, moreover, may be voluntary, as in the case of shareholders, bondholders, or trade creditors, or involuntary, as in the case of tort victims and the government (in its capacity as tax collector).

(ii) Absolute Priority Rule and "Cram Down"
Consolidated Rock Products Co. v. Du Bois
312 U.S. 510 (1941)

Mr. Justice DOUGLAS delivered the opinion of the Court.

This case involves questions as to the fairness under §77B of the Bankruptcy Act ... of a plan of reorganization for a parent corporation (Consolidated Rock Products Co.) and its two wholly owned subsidiaries[1]—Union Rock Co. and Consumers Rock and Gravel Co., Inc. The District Court confirmed the plan; the Circuit Court of Appeals reversed. 114 F.2d 102. We granted the petitions for certiorari because of the importance in the administration of the reorganization provisions of the Act of certain principles enunciated by the Circuit Court of Appeals.

The stock of Union and Consumers is held by Consolidated. Union has outstanding in the hands of the public $1,877,000 of 6% bonds secured by an indenture on its property, with accrued and unpaid interest thereon of $403,555—a total mortgage indebtedness of $2,280,555. Consumers has outstanding in the hands of the public $1,137,000 of 6% bonds secured by an indenture on its property, with accrued and unpaid interest thereon of $221,715—a total mortgage indebtedness of $1,358,715. Consolidated has outstanding 285,947 shares of no par value preferred stock[7] and 397,455 shares of no par common stock.

The plan of reorganization calls for the formation of a new corporation to which will be transferred all of the assets of Consolidated, Union,[8] and Consumers free of all claims.[9] The securities of the new corporation are to be distributed as follows:

Union and Consumers bonds held by the public will be exchanged for income bonds[10] and preferred stock[11] of the new company. For 50 per cent of the principal amounts of their claims, those bondholders will receive income bonds secured by a mortgage on all of the property of the new company; for the balance they will receive an equal amount of par value preferred stock. Their claims to accrued interest are to be extinguished, no new securities being issued therefor. Thus Union bondholders for their claims of $2,280,555 will receive income bonds and preferred stock in the face amount of $1,877,000; Consumers bondholders for their claims of $1,358,715 will re-

---

1. The proceedings under §77B were instituted in 1935 by the filing of separate voluntary petitions by Consolidated, Union and Consumers. No trustees have been appointed, Consolidated remaining in possession.

7. With a preference on liquidation of $25 per share plus accrued dividends.

8. Reliance Rock Co. is a wholly owned subsidiary of Union whose properties also were to be transferred to the new company.

9. The claims of general creditors will be paid in full or assumed by the new company.

10. These bonds will mature in 20 years and will bear interest at the rate of 5 per cent if earned. The interest will be cumulative if not paid. The bonds, as well as the preferred stock, to be issued to Union and Consumers bondholders will be in separate series. The net income of the new company is to be divided into two equal parts: each part to be used to pay, with respect to bonds and preferred stock of each series, first, interest and sinking fund payments on the bonds; second, dividends and sinking fund payments on the preferred stock. Income remaining will be available for general corporate purposes.

11. The new preferred stock will have a par value of $50 and will carry a dividend of 5 per cent. It will be noncumulative until the retirement of the bonds of the same series except to the extent that net income is available for dividends. Thereafter it will be cumulative.

ceive income bonds and preferred stock[12] in the face amount of $1,137,000. Each share of new preferred stock will have a warrant for the purchase of two shares of new $2 par value common stock at prices ranging from $2 per share within six months of issuance, to $6 per share during the fifth year after issuance.

Preferred stockholders of Consolidated will receive one share of new common stock ($2 par value) for each share of old preferred or an aggregate of 285,947 shares of new common.

A warrant to purchase one share of new common for $1 within three months of issuance will be given to the common stockholders of Consolidated for each five shares of old common.[13]

The new preferred stock, to be received by the old bondholders, will elect four out of nine directors of the new company; the new common stock will elect the remainder.[14] But on designated delinquencies in payment of interest on the new bonds, the old bondholders would be entitled to elect six of the nine directors.

The bonds of Union and Consumers held by Consolidated, the stock of those companies held by Consolidated, and the intercompany claims (discussed hereafter) will be cancelled.

In 1929 when Consolidated acquired control of these various properties, they were appraised in excess of $16,000,000 and it was estimated that their annual net earnings would be $500,000. In 1931 they were appraised by officers at about $4,400,000, "exclusive of going concern, good will and current assets." The District Court did not find specific values for the separate properties of Consolidated, Union, or Consumers, or for the properties of the enterprise as a unit. The average of the valuations (apparently based on physical factors) given by three witnesses at the hearing before the master were $2,202,733 for Union as against a mortgage indebtedness of $2,280,555; $1,151,033 for Consumers as against a mortgage indebtedness of $1,358,715. Relying on similar testimony, Consolidated argues that the value of its property, to be contributed to the new company, is over $1,359,000, or exclusive of an alleged good will of $500,000, $859,784. These estimated values somewhat conflict with the consolidated balance sheet (as of June 30, 1938) which shows assets of $3,723,738.15 and liabilities (exclusive of capital and surplus) of $4,253,224.41. More important, the earnings record of the enterprise casts grave doubts on the soundness of the estimated values. No dividends were ever paid on Consolidated's common stock; and except for five quarterly dividends in 1929 and 1931, none on its preferred stock. For the eight and a half years from April 1, 1929, to September 30, 1937, Consolidated had a loss of about $1,200,000 before bond interest but after depreciation and depletion. And except for the year 1929, Consolidated had no net operating profit, after bond interest and amortization, depreciation and depletion, in any year down to September 30, 1937. Yet on this record the District Court found that the present fair value of all the assets of the several companies, exclusive of good will and going concern value, was in excess of the total bonded indebtedness, plus accrued and unpaid interest. And it also found that such value, including good will and

---

12. All of the new income bonds and preferred stock are to be issued to the public holders of Union and Consumers bonds.

13. 79,491 shares of new common will be reserved for the exercise of warrants issued to old common stockholders; an additional 60,280 shares of new common, for the exercise of warrants attached to the new preferred.

14. It is apparent that the majority of the new common will be held by the old preferred stockholders even if all warrants are exercised.

going concern value, was insufficient to pay the bonded indebtedness plus accrued and unpaid interest and the liquidation preferences and accrued dividends on Consolidated preferred stock. It further found that the present fair value of the assets admittedly subject to the trust indentures of Union and Consumers was insufficient to pay the face amount, plus accrued and unpaid interest of the respective bond issues. In spite of that finding, the District Court also found that "it would be physically impossible to determine and segregate with any degree of accuracy or fairness properties which originally belonged to the companies separately"; that as a result of unified operation properties of every character "have been commingled and are now in the main held by Consolidated without any way of ascertaining what part, if any thereof, belongs to each or any of the companies separately"; and that, as a consequence, an appraisal "would be of such an indefinite and unsatisfactory nature as to produce further confusion."

The unified operation which resulted in that commingling of assets was pursuant to an operating agreement which Consolidated caused its wholly owned subsidiaries to execute in 1929. Under that agreement the subsidiaries ceased all operating functions and the entire management, operation and financing of the business and properties of the subsidiaries were undertaken by Consolidated. The corporate existence of the subsidiaries, however, was maintained and certain separate accounts were kept. Under this agreement Consolidated undertook, *inter alia*, to pay the subsidiaries the amounts necessary for the interest and sinking fund provisions of the indentures and to credit their current accounts with items of depreciation, depletion, amortization and obsolescence.[19] Upon termination of the agreement the properties were to be returned and a final settlement of accounts made, Consolidated meanwhile to retain all net revenues after its obligations thereunder to the subsidiaries had been met. It was specifically provided that the agreement was made for the benefit of the parties, not "for the benefit of any third person." Consolidated's books as at June 30, 1938, showed a net indebtedness under that agreement to Union and Consumers of somewhat over $5,000,000. That claim was cancelled by the plan of reorganization, no securities being issued to the creditors of the subsidiaries therefor. The District Court made no findings as respects the amount or validity of that intercompany claim; it summarily disposed of it by concluding that any liability under the operating agreement was "not made for the benefit of any third parties and the bondholders are included in that category."

We agree with the Circuit Court of Appeals that it was error to confirm this plan of reorganization.

I. On this record no determination of the fairness of any plan of reorganization could be made. Absent the requisite valuation data, the court was in no position to exercise the "informed, independent judgment" (*National Surety Co.* v. *Coriell*, 289 U.S. 426, 436) which appraisal of the fairness of a plan of reorganization entails. *Case* v. *Los Angeles Lumber Products Co.*, 308 U.S. 106.... There are two aspects of that valuation problem.

In the first place, there must be a determination of what assets are subject to the payment of the respective claims. This obvious requirement was not met. The status of the

---

19. The agreement was modified in 1933 (by two offices acting for each of the four companies) whereby the depreciation to be credited to the subsidiaries should be credited only on termination of the agreement. At that time Consolidated was to have the right, by paying a five per cent penalty, to pay twenty-five per cent of the amount of the depreciation credit in ten annual installments and the balance at the end of ten years from the date of termination. Some question has been raised as to the propriety of that modification, a question on which we express no opinion.

Union and Consumers bondholders emphasizes its necessity and importance. According to the District Court the mortgaged assets are insufficient to pay the mortgage debt. There is no finding, however, as to the extent of the deficiency or the amount of unmortgaged assets and their value. It is plain that the bondholders would have, as against Consolidated and its stockholders, prior recourse against any unmortgaged assets of Union and Consumers. The full and absolute priority rule of *Northern Pacific Ry. Co.* v. *Boyd*, 228 U.S. 482, and *Case* v. *Los Angeles Lumber Products Co.*, *supra*, would preclude participation by the equity interests in any of those assets until the bondholders had been made whole. Here there are some unmortgaged assets, for there is a claim of Union and Consumers against Consolidated—a claim which according to the books of Consolidated is over $5,000,000 in amount. If that claim is valid, or even if it were allowed only to the extent of 25% of its face amount,[21] then the entire assets of Consolidated would be drawn down into the estates of the subsidiaries. In that event Union and Consumers might or might not be solvent in the bankruptcy sense. But certainly it would render untenable the present contention of Consolidated and the preferred stockholders that they are contributing all of the assets of the [sic] Consolidated to the new company in exchange for which they are entitled to new securities. On that theory of the case they would be making a contribution of only such assets of Consolidated, if any, as remained after any deficiency of the bondholders had been wholly satisfied.

There are no barriers to a valuation and enforcement of that claim. If as Consolidated maintains the subsidiaries have no present claim against it, the claim can readily be discounted to present worth. It is provable by trustees of the subsidiaries, for the term "creditors" under §77B(b) includes "holders of claims of whatever character against the debtor or its property, including claims under executory contracts, whether or not such claims would otherwise constitute provable claims under this Act." Consolidated makes some point of the difficulty and expense of determining the extent of its liability under the operating agreement and of the necessity to abide by the technical terms of that agreement[24] in ascertaining that liability. But equity will not permit a holding company, which has dominated and controlled its subsidiaries, to escape or reduce its liability to those subsidiaries by reliance upon self-serving contracts which it has imposed on them. A holding company, as well as others in dominating or controlling positions (*Pepper* v. *Litton*, 308 U.S. 295), has fiduciary duties to security holders of its system which will be strictly enforced. See *Taylor* v. *Standard Gas & Electric Co.*, 306 U.S. 307. In this connection Consolidated cannot defeat or postpone the accounting because of the clause in the operating agreement that it was not made for the benefit of any third person. The question here is not a technical one as to who may sue to enforce that liability. It is merely a question as to the amount by which Consolidated is indebted to the subsidiaries and the proof and allowance of that claim. The subsidiaries need not be sent into state courts to have that liability determined. The bankruptcy court having exclusive jurisdiction over the holding company and the subsidiaries has plenary power to adjudicate all the issues pertaining to the claim. The intimations of Consolidated that there must be foreclosure proceedings and protracted litigation in state courts involve a

---

21. Respondent points out that even on the basis of a $3,300,000 valuation of the properties of Union and Consumers depreciation, depletion and obsolescence charges would be approximately $1,250,000.

24. Thus Consolidated argues that under the operating agreement the machinery for an appraisal provided therein must be employed. Yet assuming *arguendo* that that is true, Consolidated which has been in possession and control throughout cannot rely on the failure to have an appraisal as a reason for blocking or delaying its duty to account.

misconception of the duties and powers of the bankruptcy court. The fact that Consolidated might have a strategic or nuisance value outside of §77B does not detract from or impair the power and duty of the bankruptcy court to require a full accounting as a condition precedent to approval of any plan of reorganization. The fact that the claim might be settled, with the approval of the Court after full disclosure and notice to interested parties, does not justify the concealed compromise effected here through the simple expedient of extinguishing the claim.

So far as the ability of the bondholders of Union and Consumers to reach the assets of Consolidated on claims of the kind covered by the operation agreement is concerned, there is another and more direct route which reaches the same end. There has been a unified operation of those several properties by Consolidated pursuant to the operating agreement. That operation not only resulted in extensive commingling of assets. All management functions of the several companies were assumed by Consolidated. The subsidiaries abdicated. Consolidated operated them as mere departments of its own business. Not even the formalities of separate corporate organizations were observed, except in minor particulars such as the maintenance of certain separate accounts. In view of these facts, Consolidated is in no position to claim that its assets are insulated from such claims of creditors of the subsidiaries. To the contrary, it is well settled that where a holding company directly intervenes in the management of its subsidiaries so as to treat them as mere departments of its own enterprise, it is responsible for the obligations of those subsidiaries incurred or arising during its management.... We are not dealing here with a situation where other creditors of a parent company are competing with creditors of its subsidiaries. If meticulous regard to corporate forms, which Consolidated has long ignored, is now observed, the stockholders of Consolidated may be the direct beneficiaries. Equity will not countenance such a result. A holding company which assumes to treat the properties of its subsidiaries as its own cannot take the benefits of direct management without the burdens.

We have already noted that no adequate finding was made as to the value of the assets of Consolidated. In view of what we have said, it is apparent that a determination of that value must be made so that criteria will be available to determine an appropriate allocation of new securities between bondholders and stockholders in case there is an equity remaining after the bondholders have been made whole.

There is another reason why the failure to ascertain what assets are subject to the payment of the Union and Consumers bonds is fatal. There is a question raised as to the fairness of the plan as respects the bondholders *inter sese*. While the total mortgage debt of Consumers is less than that of Union, the net income of the new company, as we have seen, is to be divided into two equal parts, one to service the new securities issued to Consumers bondholders, the other to service those issued to Union bondholders. That allocation is attacked here by respondent as discriminatory against Union, on the ground that the assets of Union are much greater in volume and in value than those of Consumers. It does not appear from this record that Union and Consumers have individual earnings records. If they do not, some appropriate formula for at least an approximate ascertainment of their respective assets must be designed in spite of the difficulties occasioned by the commingling. Otherwise the issue of fairness of any plan of reorganization as between Union and Consumers bondholders cannot be intelligently resolved.

In the second place, there is the question of the method of valuation. From this record it is apparent that little, if any, effort was made to value the whole enterprise by a capitalization of prospective earnings. The necessity for such an inquiry is emphasized by the poor earnings record of this enterprise in the past. Findings as to the earning capacity of an enterprise are essential to a determination of the feasibility as well as the fairness of a plan of reorganization. Whether or not the earnings may reasonably be expected to meet the interest and dividend requirements of the new securities is a *sine qua non* to a determination of the integrity and practicability of the new capital structure. It is also essential for satisfaction of the absolute priority rule of *Case v. Los Angeles Lumber Products Co., supra*. Unless meticulous regard for earning capacity be had, indefensible participation of junior securities in plans of reorganization may result.

As Mr. Justice Holmes said in *Galveston, H. & S. A. Ry. Co. v. Texas*, 210 U.S. 217, 226, "the commercial value of property consists in the expectation of income from it." ... Such criterion is the appropriate one here, since we are dealing with the issue of solvency arising in connection with reorganization plans involving productive properties. It is plain that valuations for other purposes are not relevant to or helpful in a determination of that issue, except as they may indirectly bear on earning capacity.... The criterion of earning capacity is the essential one if the enterprise is to be freed from the heavy hand of past errors, miscalculations or disaster, and if the allocation of securities among the various claimants is to be fair and equitable.... Since its application requires a prediction as to what will occur in the future, an estimate, as distinguished from mathematical certitude, is all that can be made. But that estimate must be based on an informed judgment which embraces all facts relevant to future earning capacity and hence to present worth, including, of course, the nature and condition of the properties, the past earnings record, and all circumstances which indicate whether or not that record is a reliable criterion of future performance. A sum of values based on physical factors and assigned to separate units of the property without regard to the earning capacity of the whole enterprise is plainly inadequate.... But hardly more than that was done here. The Circuit Court of Appeals correctly left the matter of a formal appraisal to the discretion of the District Court. The extent and method of inquiry necessary for a valuation based on earning capacity are necessarily dependent on the facts of each case.

II. The Circuit Court of Appeals held that the absolute priority rule of *Northern Pacific Ry. Co. v. Boyd, supra*, and *Case v. Los Angeles Lumber Products Co., supra*, applied to reorganizations of solvent as well as insolvent companies. That is true. Whether a company is solvent or insolvent in either the equity or the bankruptcy sense, "any arrangement of the parties by which the subordinate rights and interests of the stockholders are attempted to be secured at the expense of the prior rights" of creditors "comes within judicial denunciation." *Louisville Trust Co. v. Louisville, N.A. & C. Ry. Co.*, 174 U.S. 674, 684. And we indicated in *Case v. Los Angeles Lumber Products Co., supra*, that that rule was not satisfied even though the "relative priorities" of creditors and stockholders were maintained (pp. 119-20).

The instant plan runs afoul of that principle. In the first place, no provision is made for the accrued interest on the bonds. This interest is entitled to the same priority as the principal.... In the second place, and apart from the cancellation of interest, the plan does not satisfy the fixed principle of the *Boyd* case even on the assumption that the enterprise as a whole is solvent in the bankruptcy sense. The bondholders for the principal amount of their 6% bonds receive an equal face amount of new 5% income bonds and preferred stock, while the preferred stockholders receive new common stock. True, the relative priorities are maintained. But the bondholders have not been made whole. They have received an inferior grade of securities, inferior in the sense that the interest rate has been reduced, a contingent return has been substituted for a fixed one, the maturities have been in part extended and in part eliminated by the substitution of preferred stock, and their former strategic position has been weakened. Those lost rights are of value. Full compensatory provision must be made for the entire bundle of rights which the creditors surrender.

The absolute priority rule does not mean that bondholders cannot be given inferior grades of securities, or even securities of the same grade as are received by junior interests. Requirements of feasibility[26] of reorganization plans frequently necessitate it in the interests of simpler and more conservative capital structures. And standards of fairness permit it.... Thus it is plain that while creditors may be given inferior grades of securities, their "superior rights" must be recognized. Clearly, those prior rights are not recognized, in cases where stockholders are participating in the plan, if creditors are given only a face amount of inferior securities equal to the face amount of their claims. They must receive, in addition, compensation for the senior rights which they are to surrender. If they receive less than that full compensatory treatment, some of their property rights will be appropriated for the benefit of stockholders without compensation. That is not permissible. The plan then comes within judicial denunciation because it does not recognize the creditors' "equitable right to be preferred to stockholders against the full value of all property belonging to the debtor corporation." *Kansas City Terminal Ry. Co.* v. *Central Union Trust Co.*, [271 U.S. 445, 454].

Practical adjustments, rather than a rigid formula, are necessary. The method of effecting full compensation for senior claimants will vary from case to case. As indicated in the *Boyd* case (228 U.S. at p. 508) the creditors are entitled to have the full value of the property, whether "present or prospective, for dividends or only for purposes of control," first appropriated to payment of their claims. But whether in case of a solvent company the creditors should be made whole for the change in or loss of their seniority by an increased participation in assets, in earnings or in control, or in any combination thereof, will be dependent on the facts and requirements of each case.[27] So long as the new securities offered are of a value equal to the creditors' claims, the appropriateness of the formula employed rests in the informed discretion of the court.

The Circuit Court of Appeals, however, made certain statements which if taken literally do not comport with the requirements of the absolute priority rule. It apparently ruled that a class of claimants with a lien on specific properties must receive full compensation out of those properties, and that a plan of reorganization is *per se* unfair and inequitable if it substitutes for several old bond issues, separately secured, new securities constituting an interest in all of the properties. That does not follow from *Case* v.

---

26. §77B(f)(1).
27. In view of the condition of the record relative to the value of the properties and the fact that the accrued interest is cancelled by the plan, it is not profitable to attempt a detailed discussion of the deficiencies in the alleged compensatory treatment of the bondholders. It should, however, be noted as respects the warrants issued to the old common stockholders that they admittedly have no equity in the enterprise. Accordingly, it should have been shown that there was a necessity of seeking new money from them and that the participation accorded them was not more than reasonably equivalent to their contribution. *Kansas City Terminal Ry. Co.* v. *Central Union Trust Co., supra; Case* v. *Los Angeles Lumber Products Co., supra*, pp. 121-122. In the latter case we warned against the dilution of creditors' rights by inadequate contributions by stockholders. Here that dilution takes a rather obvious form in view of the lower price at which the stockholders may exercise the warrants. Warrants exercised by them would dilute the value of common stock purchased by bondholders during the same period. Furthermore, on Consolidated's estimate of the equity in the enterprise, the values of the new common would have to increase many fold to reach a value which exceeds the warrant price by the amount of the accrued interest. [The problem of dilution generally is dealt with *infra* at chapter 8, section 5.—Eds.]

Los Angeles Lumber Products Co., supra. If the creditors are adequately compensated for the loss of their prior claims, it is not material out of what assets they are paid. So long as they receive full compensatory treatment and so long as each group shares in the securities of the whole enterprise on an equitable basis, the requirements of "fair and equitable" are satisfied.

Any other standard might well place insuperable obstacles in the way of feasible plans of reorganization. Certainly where unified operations of separate properties are deemed advisable and essential, as they were in this case, the elimination of divisional mortgages may be necessary as well as wise. Moreover, the substitution of a simple, conservative capital structure for a highly complicated one may be a primary requirement of any reorganization plan. There is no necessity to construct the new capital structure on the framework of the old.

Affirmed.

Notes and Questions

1. Case v. Los Angeles Lumber Products Co., Ltd., 308 U.S. 106 (1939), dealt with "the question of the conditions under which stockholders may participate in a plan of reorganization under §77B ... of the Bankruptcy Act where the debtor corporation is insolvent both in the equity and in the bankruptcy sense." *Id.* at 108, 109. As in *Consolidated Rock,* the debtor corporation was at the top of a corporate group consisting of itself and several subsidiaries. The district court had approved a plan of reorganization whereby a new corporation was to be formed, to which the assets of the debtor would be transferred. The bondholders of the old corporation would receive participating preferred stock in the new corporation, and the common stockholders of the old corporation would receive common stock in the new corporation. As Justice Douglas described the district court's action:

> And the court approved it [the Plan] despite the fact that the old stockholders, who have no equity in the assets of the enterprise, are given 23% of the assets and voting power in the new company without making any fresh contribution by way of subscription or assessment. The court, however, justified inclusion of the stockholders in the plan (1) because it apparently felt that the relative priorities of the bondholders and stockholders were maintained by virtue of the preferences accorded the stock which the bondholders were to receive and the fact that the stock going to the bondholders carried 77% of the voting power of all the stock presently to be issued under the plan; and (2) because it was able to find that they had furnished the bondholders certain "compensating advantages" or "consideration."

Id. at 112. Among these "compensating advantages" were the familiarity of the stockholders with the operation of the business, the fact that immediate foreclosure would result in the bondholders' receipt of "substantially less" than the appraised value and the difficulties and expenses of a challenged foreclosure.

Justice Douglas for the Court agreed with plaintiff, a bondholder who had not voted in favor of the plan, that the plan was not "fair and equitable" within the meaning of the bankruptcy act, as a matter of law.

It was not enough that the requisite percentage of security holders had approved the plan since the statute required that, in addition to security holder approval, it be "fair and equitable."

Justice Douglas then went on to interpret the meaning of the phrase "fair and equitable" and apply it to the facts:

The words "fair and equitable" as used in §77B(f) are words of art which prior to the advent of §77B had acquired a fixed meaning through judicial interpretations in the field of equity receivership reorganizations. Hence, as in case of other terms or phrases used in that section, ... we adhere to the familiar rule that where words are employed in an act which had at the time a well known meaning in the law, they are used in that sense unless the context requires the contrary. *Keck v. United States*, 172 U.S. 434, 446.

In equity reorganization law the term "fair and equitable" included, *inter alia*, the rules of law enunciated by this Court in the familiar cases of *Railroad Co. v. Howard*, 7 Wall. 392; *Louisville Trust Co. v. Louisville, N.A. & C. Ry. Co.*, 174 U.S. 674; *Northern Pacific Ry. Co. v. Boyd*, 228 U.S. 482; *Kansas City Terminal Ry. Co. v. Central Union Trust Co.*, 271 U.S. 445. These cases dealt with the precedence to be accorded creditors over stockholders in reorganization plans. In *Louisville Trust Co. v. Louisville, N.A. & C. Ry. Co.*, *supra*, this Court reaffirmed the "familiar rule" that "the stockholder's interest in the property is subordinate to the rights of creditors; first of secured and then of unsecured creditors." And it went on to say that "any arrangement of the parties by which the subordinate rights and interests of stockholders are attempted to be secured at the expense of the prior rights of either class of creditors comes within judicial denunciation" (p. 684). This doctrine is the "fixed principle" according to which *Northern Pacific Ry. Co. v. Boyd*, *supra*, decided that the character of reorganization plans was to be evaluated. And in the latter case this Court added, "If the value of the road justified the issuance of stock in exchange for old shares, the creditors were entitled to the benefit of that value, whether it was present or prospective, for dividends or only for purposes of control. In either event it was right of property out of which the creditors were entitled to be paid before the stockholders could retain it for any purpose whatever." (p. 508.) On the reaffirmation of this "fixed principle" of reorganization law in *Kansas City Terminal Ry. Co. v. Central Union Trust Co.*, *supra*, it was said that "to the extent of their debts creditors are entitled to priority over stockholders against all the property of an insolvent corporation" (p. 455). In application of this rule of full or absolute priority this Court recognized certain practical considerations and made it clear that such rule did not "require the impossible and make it necessary to pay an unsecured creditor in cash as a condition of stockholders retaining an interest in the reorganized company....

Throughout the history of equity reorganizations this familiar rule was properly applied in passing on objections made by various classes of creditors that junior interests were improperly permitted to participate in a plan or were too liberally treated therein. In such adjudications the doctrine of *Northern Pacific Ry. Co. v. Boyd*, *supra*, and related cases, was commonly included in the phrase "fair and equitable" or its equivalent. As we have said, the phrase became a term of art used to indicate that a plan of reorganization fulfilled the necessary standards of fairness. Thus throughout the cases in this earlier chapter of reorganization law, we find the words "equitable and fair," "fair and equitable," "fairly and equitably treated," "adequate and equitable," "just, fair and equitable," and like phrases used to include the "fixed principle" of the *Boyd* case, its antecedents and its successors. Hence, we conclude, as have other courts, that that doctrine is firmly imbedded in §77B.

We come then to the legal question of whether the plan here in issue is fair and equitable within the meaning of that phrase as used in §77B.

We do not believe it is, for the following reasons. Here the court made a finding that the debtor is insolvent not only in the equity sense but also in the bankruptcy sense. Admittedly there are assets not in excess of $900,000, while the claims of the bondholders for principal and interest are approximately $3,800,000. Hence even if all of the assets were turned over to the bondholders they would realize less than 25 percent on their claims. Yet in spite of this fact they will be required under the plan to surrender to the stockholders 23 percent of the value of the enterprise.

True, the relative priorities of the bondholders and the old Class A stockholders are maintained by virtue of the priorities accorded the preferred stock which the bondholders are to receive. But this is not compliance with the principle expressed in *Kansas City Terminal Ry. Co. v. Central Union Trust Co., supra*, that "to the extent of their debts creditors are entitled to priority over stockholders against all the property of an insolvent corporation," for there are not sufficient assets to pay the bondholders the amount of their claims. Nor does this plan recognize the "equitable right" of the bondholders "to be preferred to stockholders against the full value of all property belonging to the debtor corporation," within the meaning of the rule announced in that case, since the full value of that property is not first applied to claims of the bondholders before the stockholders are allowed to participate. Rather it is partially diverted for the benefit of the stockholders even though the bondholders would obtain less than 25% payment if they received it all. Under that theory all classes of security holders could be perpetuated in the new company even though the assets were insufficient to pay— in new bonds or stock—the amount owing senior creditors. Such a result is not tenable.

It is, of course, clear that there are circumstances under which stockholders may participate in a plan of reorganization of an insolvent debtor. This Court, as we have seen, indicated as much in *Northern Pacific Ry. Co. v. Boyd, supra*, and *Kansas City Terminal Ry. Co. v. Central Union Trust Co., supra*. Especially in the latter case did this Court stress the necessity, at times, of seeking new money "essential to the success of the undertaking" from the old stockholders. Where that necessity exists and the old stockholders make a fresh contribution and receive in return a participation reasonably equivalent to their contribution, no objection can be made. But if these conditions are not satisfied the stockholder's participation would run afoul of the ruling of this Court in *Kansas City Terminal Ry. Co. v. Central Union Trust Co., supra*, that "Whenever assessments are demanded, they must be adjusted with the purpose of according to the creditor his full right of priority against the corporate assets, so far as possible in the existing circumstances" (p. 456). If, however, those conditions we have mentioned are satisfied, the creditor cannot complain that he is not accorded "his full right of priority against the corporate assets." If that were not the test, then the creditor's rights could be easily diluted by inadequate contributions by stockholders. To the extent of the inadequacy of their contributions the stockholders would be in precisely the position which this Court said in *Northern Pacific Ry. Co. v. Boyd, supra*, the stockholders there were in, viz., "in the position of a mortgagor buying at his own sale" (p. 504).

In view of these considerations we believe that to accord "the creditor his full right of priority against the corporate assets" where the debtor is insolvent, the stockholder's participation must be based on a contribution in money or in money's worth, reasonably equivalent in view of all the circumstances to the participation of the stockholder.

The alleged consideration furnished by the stockholders in this case falls far short of meeting those requirements.

308 U.S. at 115-22.

2. What is the purpose of bankruptcy law? Why should the law show any solicitude for junior claimants, especially stockholders, in bankruptcy such that, under some circumstances, a creditor's contract rights can be disregarded. See, e.g., 11 U.S.C. 1129(b) (permitting court to force a plan on a dissenting class as long as the dissenters receive compensation equal to the amount of their claim or stake in the enterprise, or the court finds that the value of the firm is too small to reach down to the dissenters' layer in the capital structure). After all, courts generally are unwilling to "supplement" those rights in a solvent corporation to provide greater protection to creditors than their contract requires. What about bankruptcy is different? The relationships at issue? The societal problems raised by the bankruptcy? Or is nothing at all different?

Kham & Nate's Shoes No. 2, Inc. v. First Bank of Whiting
908 F.2d 1351, 1359-63 (7th Cir. 1990)

EASTERBROOK, Circuit Judge.

Kham & Nate's Shoes No. 2, Inc., ran four retail shoe stores in Chicago. It has been in bankruptcy since 1984, operating as a debtor in possession. First Bank of Whiting, one of Kham & Nate's creditors, appeals from the order confirming its plan of reorganization. This order not only reduces the Bank's secured claim to unsecured status but also allows Khamolaw Beard and Nathaniel Parker, the debtor's principals, to retain their equity interests despite the firm's inability to pay its creditors in full. The bankruptcy judge subordinated the Bank's claims after finding that it behaved "inequitably," and he allowed Beard and Parker to retain their interests on the theory that their guarantees of new loans to be made as part of the reorganization are "new value."

I

The Bank first extended credit to the Debtor in July 1981. This $50,000 loan was renewed in December 1981 and repaid in part in July 1982. The balance was rolled over until late 1983, when with interest it came to $42,000. In September 1983 Bank issued several letters of credit in favor of Debtor's customers. Debtor furnished a note to support these letters of credit; the Bank's security interest was limited to the goods the suppliers furnished. In late 1983 Debtor, experiencing serious cash-flow problems, asked for additional capital, which Bank agreed to provide if the loan could be made secure. That was hard to do, for Debtor had lost money the previous two years and owed more than $440,000 to tax collectors; any new loan from Bank would stand behind the back tax liabilities. The parties discussed two ways to make Bank secure: a guarantee by the Small Business Administration, and a bankruptcy petition followed by an order giving a post-petition loan super-priority.

While waiting for the SBA to act on its application, Debtor filed its petition under Chapter 11 of the Bankruptcy Code in January 1984. Judge Toles granted its application for an order under 11 U.S.C. §364(c)(1) giving a loan from Bank priority even over the administrative expenses of the bankruptcy. Debtor and Bank then signed their loan agreement, which opens a $300,000 line of credit. The contract provides for cancellation on five days' notice and adds for good measure that "nothing provided herein shall constitute a waiver of the right of the Bank to terminate financing at any time."

The parties signed the contract on January 23, 1984, and Debtor quickly took about $75,000. Suppliers began to draw on the letters of credit. On February 29 Bank mailed Debtor a letter stating that it would make no additional advances after March 7. Although the note underlying the line of credit required payment on demand, Bank did not make the demand. It continued honoring draws on the letters of credit. Debtor's ultimate indebtedness to Bank was approximately $164,000: $42,000 outstanding on the loan made in 1981, $47,000 on the letters of credit, and $75,000 on the line of credit. Debtor paid $10,000 against the line of credit in April 1985 but has made no further payments....

There matters stood until the spring of 1988, when Debtor proposed its fourth plan of reorganization. Although the previous three plans had called for Bank to be paid in full, the fourth plan proposed to treat Bank's claims as general unsecured debts. This fourth plan also proposed to allow the shareholders to keep their stock, in exchange for guaranteeing new loans to Debtor.

Bankruptcy Judge Coar held an evidentiary hearing and concluded that Bank had behaved inequitably in terminating the line of credit and inducing Debtor's suppliers to draw on the letters of credit. These draws, the judge concluded, converted Bank from an unsecured lender (the position it held before the bankruptcy) to a super-secured lender under Judge Toles' financing order. Judge Coar first vacated the financing order and then subordinated Bank's debt, on the authority of 11 U.S.C. §510(c). Finally, Judge Coar confirmed the plan of reorganization, including the provision allowing the stockholders of Debtor to retain their interests. He found that their guarantees were "new value" equivalent to the worth of the interests they would retain, which the judge thought small. The district judge affirmed, 104 B.R. 909 (N.D. Ill. 1989).

* * *

IV

A plan of reorganization may be confirmed only if each class of impaired creditors votes to accept it. There is one exception to the requirement of approval: 11 U.S.C. §1129(b)(1), provides that a "fair and equitable" plan may be crammed down the throats of objecting creditors. The Code says that a plan treats unsecured creditors fairly and equitably if "the holder of any claim or interest that is junior to the claims of such class will not receive or retain under the plan on account of such junior claim or interest any property." 11 U.S.C. §1129(b)(2)(B)(ii). This is the "absolute priority rule." An objection to the plan may be overridden only if every class lower in priority is wiped out. Priority is "absolute" in the sense that every cent of each class comes ahead of the first dollar of any junior class....

Judge Coar approved a "cram-down" plan in this case. Unsecured creditors (including Bank) will not be paid in full. Bank objected to the plan, and the court overrode its objection after finding that the plan would be "fair and equitable." Yet the court did not extinguish the interests of every class junior to the unsecured creditors. Instead it allowed the stockholders to retain their interests, reasoning that by guaranteeing a $435,000 loan to be made as part of the plan, Beard and Parker contributed "new value" justifying the retention of their stock. The size of the new debt made the risk of the guarantees "substantial," the court found. The risk also exceeded the value of the retained stock, because "given the history of Debtor and the various risks associated with its business," the stock would have only "minimal" value. Beard and Parker thus would contribute more than they would receive, so the court allowed them to keep their stock.

There is something unreal about this calculation. If the stock is worth less than the guarantees, why are Beard and Parker doing it? If the value of the stock is "minimal," why does Bank object to letting Beard and Parker keep it? Is *everyone* acting inconsistently with self-interest, as the court's findings imply? And why, if the business is likely to fail, making the value of the stock "minimal," could the court confirm the plan of reorganization? Confirmation depends on a conclusion that the reorganized firm is likely to succeed, and not relapse into "liquidation, or the need for further financial reorganization." 11 U.S.C. §1129(a)(11). If, as the bankruptcy court found, the plan complies with this requirement, then the equity interest in the firm *must* be worth something— as Beard, Parker, and Bank all appear to believe.

Stock is "property" for purposes of §1129(b)(2)(B)(ii) even if the firm has a negative net worth, *Norwest Bank Worthington v. Ahlers*, 485 U.S. 197 ... (1988). An option to purchase stock also is "property." The bankruptcy judge gave Beard and Parker a no-cost option to buy stock, which they could exercise if they concluded that the shares were worth more than the risk created by the guarantees. Whether we characterize the stock or the option to buy it as the "property," the transaction seems to run afoul of §1129(b)(2)(B)(ii), for it means that although a class of unsecured creditors is not paid in full, a junior class (the stockholders) keeps some "property."

Only the "new value exception" to the absolute priority rule could support this outcome. Dicta in cases predating the 1978 Code said that investors who put up new capital may retain interests equal to or lower in value than that new contribution. These interests are not so much "retained" as purchased for the new value (the "option" characterization of the transaction). Some firms depend for success on the entrepreneurial skills or special knowledge of managers who are also shareholders. If these persons' interests are wiped out, they may leave the firm and reduce its value. If they may contribute new value and retain an interest, this may tie them to the firm and so improve its prospects.

In principle, then, the exchange of stock for new value may make sense. When it does, the creditors should be willing to go along. Creditors effectively own bankrupt firms. They may find it worthwhile, as owners, to sell equity claims to the managers; they may even find it worthwhile to give the equity away in order to induce managers to stay on and work hard. Because the Code allows creditors to consent to a plan that impairs their interests, voluntary transactions of this kind are possible. Only collective action problems could frustrate beneficial arrangements. If there are many creditors, one may hold out, seeking to engross a greater share of the gains. But the Code deals with holdups by allowing half of a class by number (two-thirds by value) to consent to a lower class's retention of an interest. 11 U.S.C. §1126(c). Creditors not acting in good faith do not count toward the one-third required to block approval, §1126(e). When there is value to be gained by allowing a lower class to kick in new value and keep its interest, the creditors should be willing to go along. *Ahlers*, 485 U.S. at 207.... A "new value exception" means a power in the *judge* to "sell" stock to the managers even when the creditors believe that this transaction will *not* augment the value of the firm. To understand whether the Code gives the judge this power (and, if it does, the limits of the power), it is necessary to examine the genesis of the doctrine.

The Bankruptcy Act of 1898 required plans of reorganization to be "fair and equitable" but did not define that phrase. It also allowed creditors to consent to plans that impaired their interests, but the consent had to be unanimous. The absolute priority rule came into being as a cross between the interpretation of "fair and equitable" and a rule of contract law. *Northern Pacific Ry. v. Boyd*, 228 U.S. 482 ... (1913). Because contracts give creditors priority over shareholders, a plan of reorganization had to do the same. But under the 1898 Act bankruptcy also was a branch of equity so it is not surprising that equitable modifications of the doctrine developed. One of these was the "new value exception" to the absolute priority doctrine. So far as the Supreme Court is concerned, however, the development has been 100% dicta.

Kansas City Terminal Ry. v. Central Union Trust Co., 271 U.S. 445 ... (1926), is the genesis of the exception. The Court conceived the absolute priority rule as barring any retention of interest by a shareholder if any layer of creditors is excluded. It used this rule to veto a decision by the secured creditor to allow the shareholder a stake when junior creditors were cut out and objected. Yet the senior creditor, which as a practical matter owned 100% of the firm, must have had a reason to suffer the continued existence of the shareholder. The plan in *Kansas City Ry.* was identical in principle to selling the firm to the secured creditor at auction, and the secured creditor giving some stock to the manager and former shareholder. Only the fact that both steps were rolled into one plan of reorganization gave the junior creditor an opportunity to say no (as a practical matter to hold out for some portion of the gains). The Court said in dicta that this right to object did not give the junior creditor as potent a power as it might, because the judge could modify the strict priority equitably if the shareholder agreed to contribute new value.

Case v. Los Angeles Lumber Products Co., 308 U.S. 106 ... (1939), came next. The bankruptcy judge took the hint in *Kansas City Ry.* and allowed shareholders to retain an interest in exchange for their promise to contribute value in the form of continuity of management, plus financial standing and influence in the community that would enable the debtor to raise new money. It allowed the shareholders to retain their interests even though the class of senior creditors objected (because unanimity could not be achieved)—a dramatic step from the suggestion in *Kansas City Ry.* that new value plus the *consent* of the creditor whose claim exceeded the value of the firm would suffice. The Supreme Court reversed, holding that new value must mean "money or money's worth," 308 U.S. at 121-22.... It did not remark on the difference between consent and objection from the creditors, and it did not really need to given its conclusion that nonmonetary value is insufficient.

Cases in the lower courts proceeded to apply the dicta in *Case* and *Kansas City Ry.* without noticing the difference between consent and objection by the creditors. But see *SEC v. Canandaigua Enterprises Corp.*, 339 F.2d 14, 21 (2d Cir. 1964) (Friendly, J.), questioning the doctrine on this basis; Henry J. Friendly, *Some Comments on the Corporate Reorganization Act*, 48 Harv. L. Rev. 39, 77-78 (1934). Perhaps this distinction was not an essential one in the administration of a common law doctrine, especially not when (a) the unanimity rule made the lack of consent the norm, and (b) bankruptcy was a branch of equity.

Everything changed with the adoption of the Code in 1978. The definition of "fair and equitable" is no longer a matter of common law; §1129(b)(2) defines it expressly. Holdouts that spoiled reorganizations and created much of the motive for having judges "sell" stock to the manager-shareholders no longer are of much concern, now that §1126(c) allows the majority of each class (two-thirds by value) to give consent. And bankruptcy judges no longer have equitable powers to modify contracts to achieve "fair" distributions. Bankruptcy judges enforce entitlements created under state law. *Butner v. United States*, 440 U.S. 48 ... (1979).... "[W]hatever equitable powers remain in the bankruptcy courts must and can only be exercised within the confines of the Bankruptcy Code." *Ahlers*, 485 U.S. at 206....

Whether the "new value exception" to the absolute priority rule survived the codification of that rule in 1978 is a question open in this circuit. *In re Stegall*, 865 F.2d 140, 142 (7th Cir. 1989). The language of the Code strongly suggests that it did not, and we are to take this language seriously even when it alters pre-Code practices.... The legislative history reinforces the implication of the text. The Bankruptcy Commission proposed a modification of the absolute priority rule, and its proposal was not warmly received.... Congress moved in the other direction, enacting the rule in an uncompromising form: "The general principle of the subsection permits confirmation notwithstanding non-acceptance by an impaired class if that class and all below it in priority are treated according to the absolute priority rule. The dissenting class must be paid in full before any junior class may share under the plan." H.R. Rep. No. 95-595, 95th Cong., 1st Sess. 413 (1977), U.S. Code Cong. & Admin. News 1978, pp. 5787, 6369. Neither the report nor any part of the text of the Code suggests a single exception to this blanket rule.

Bank asks us to hold that the new value exception vanished in 1978. We stop short of the precipice, as the Supreme Court did in *Ahlers*, 485 U.S. at 203-04 n.3..., for two reasons: first, the consideration for the shares is insufficient even if the new value exception retains vitality; second, although Bank vigorously argues the merits of the new value exception in this court, it did not make this argument in the bankruptcy court. Despite Bank's failure to preserve its argument, the history and limits of the rule before 1978 are pertinent to our analysis because, as the Court held in *Ahlers*, 485 U.S. at 205-06..., at a minimum the Code forbids any expansion of the exception beyond the limits recognized in *Case*.

Case rejected the argument that continuity of management plus financial standing that would attract new investment is "new value." According to the Court, only an infusion of capital in "money or money's worth" suffices. *Ahlers* reinforces the message, holding that a promise of future labor, coupled with the managers' experience and expertise, also is not new value. It remarked that the promises of the managers in *Case* "[n]o doubt ... had 'value' and would have been of some benefit to any reorganized enterprise. But ultimately, as the Court said..., '[t]hey reflect merely vague hopes or possibilities.' The same is true of respondents' pledge of future labor and management skills." 485 U.S. at 204 ... (citations omitted). The Court observed, *ibid.*, again quoting from *Case*, that the promise was "intangible, inalienable, and, in all likelihood, unenforceable. It 'has no place in the asset column of the balance sheet of the new [entity].'"

Guarantees are no different. They are intangible, inalienable, and unenforceable by the firm. Beard and Parker may revoke their guarantees or render them valueless by disposing of their assets; although a lender may be able to protest the revocation, the debtor cannot compel the guarantor to maintain the pledge in force. Guarantees have "no place in the asset column" of a balance sheet. We do not know whether these guarantees have the slightest value, for the record does not reveal whether Parker could subscribe for shares against a promise of labor, but the firm and Beard have substantial unencumbered assets that the guarantees would put at risk. If Beard and Parker were organizing a new firm in Illinois, they could not issue stock to themselves in exchange for guarantees of loans. Illinois requires the consideration for shares to be money or other property, or "labor or services actually performed for the corporation," Ill. Rev. Stat. ch. 32 ¶ 6.30. So Beard and Parker could subscribe for shares against a promise of labor, but the firm could not issue the shares until the labor had been performed. A guarantee does not fit into any of the statutory categories, and there is no reason why it should. One who pays out on a guarantee becomes the firm's creditor, a priority higher than that of stockholder. A guarantor who has *not* paid has no claim against the firm. Promises inadequate to support the issuance of shares under state law are also inadequate to support the issuance of shares by a bankruptcy judge over the protest of the creditors, the real owners of the firm.

Debtor relies on *In re Potter Material Service, Inc.*, 781 F.2d 99 (7th Cir. 1986), but it does not support the bankruptcy judge's decision. The new value in *Potter* was a combination of $34,800 cash plus a guarantee of a $600,000 loan. If Beard and Parker had contributed substantial cash, we would have a case like *Potter*. They didn't, and we don't. To the extent *Potter* implies that a guarantee alone is "new value," it did not survive *Ahlers*. *Potter* observed that the guarantor took an economic risk, 781 F.2d at 103. *Ahlers* holds that *detriment* to the shareholder does not amount to "value" to the firm; there must be an infusion of new capital.... A guarantee may be costly to the guarantor, but it is not a balance-sheet asset, and it therefore may not be treated as new value. The plan of reorganization should not have been confirmed over Bank's objection.

VACATED AND REMANDED.

In 1999 it appeared that the Supreme Court would finally answer the riddle of whether a "new value" exception existed under modern bankruptcy law. However, watch Justice Souter "punt" this issue with the skill and dexterity of an All-Pro kicker.

Bank of America Nat'l Trust v. 203 N. LaSalle St. Partnership
526 U.S. 434 (1999)

Justice SOUTER delivered the opinion of the Court:

The issue in this Chapter 11 reorganization case is whether a debtor's prebankruptcy equity holders may, over the objection of a senior class of impaired creditors, contribute new capital and receive ownership interests in the reorganized entity, when that opportunity is given exclusively to the old equity holders under a plan adopted without consideration of alternatives. We hold that old equity holders are disqualified from participating in such a "new value" transaction by the terms of 11 U.S.C. §1129(b)(2)(B)(ii), which in such circumstances bars a junior interest holder's receipt of any property on account of his prior interest.

I.

Petitioner, Bank of America National Trust and Savings Association (Bank), is the major creditor of respondent, 203 North LaSalle Street Partnership (Debtor or Partnership), an Illinois real estate limited partnership. The Bank lent the Debtor some $93 million, secured by a nonrecourse first mortgage on the Debtor's principal asset, 15 floors of an office building in downtown Chicago. In January 1995, the Debtor defaulted, and the Bank began foreclosure in a state court.

In March, the Debtor responded with a voluntary petition for relief under Chapter 11 of the Bankruptcy Code, which automatically stayed the foreclosure proceedings. The Debtor's principal objective was to ensure that its partners retained title to the property so as to avoid roughly $20 million in personal tax liabilities, which would fall due if the Bank foreclosed. The Debtor proceeded to propose a reorganization plan during the 120-day period when it alone had the right to do so. The Bankruptcy Court rejected the Bank's motion to terminate the period of exclusivity to make way for a plan of its own to liquidate the property, and instead extended the exclusivity period for cause shown, under §1121(d).

The value of the mortgaged property was less than the balance due the Bank, which elected to divide its undersecured claim into secured and unsecured deficiency claims under §506(a) and §1111(b). Under the plan, the Debtor separately classified the Bank's secured claim, its unsecured deficiency claim, and unsecured trade debt owed to other creditors. See §1122(a). The Bankruptcy Court found that the Debtor's available assets were prepetition rents in a cash account of $3.1 million and the 15 floors of rental property worth $54.5 million. The secured claim was valued at the latter figure, leaving the Bank with an unsecured deficiency of $38.5 million.

So far as we need be concerned here, the Debtor's plan had these further features:

(1) The Bank's $54.5 million secured claim would be paid in full between 7 and 10 years after the original 1995 repayment date.

(2) The Bank's $38.5 million unsecured deficiency claim would be discharged for an estimated 16% of its present value.

(3) The remaining unsecured claims of $90,000, held by the outside trade creditors, would be paid in full, without interest, on the effective date of the plan.

(4) Certain former partners of the Debtor would contribute $6.125 million in new capital over the course of five years (the contribution being worth some $4.1 million in present value), in exchange for the Partnership's entire ownership of the reorganized debtor.

The last condition was an exclusive eligibility provision: the old equity holders were the only ones who could contribute new capital.

The Bank objected and, being the sole member of an impaired class of creditors, thereby blocked confirmation of the plan on a consensual basis. See §1129(a)(8). The Debtor, however, took the alternate route to confirmation of a reorganization plan, forthrightly known as the judicial "cramdown" process for imposing a plan on a dissenting class. §1129(b).

There are two conditions for a cramdown. First, all requirements of §1129(a) must be met (save for the plan's acceptance by each impaired class of claims or interests, see §1129(a)(8)). Critical among them are the conditions that the plan be accepted by at least one class of impaired creditors, see §1129(a)(10), and satisfy the "best-interest-of-creditors" test, see §1129(a)(7). Here, the class of trade creditors with impaired unsecured claims voted for the plan, and there was no issue of best interest. Second, the objection of an impaired creditor class may be overridden only if "the plan does not discriminate unfairly, and is fair and equitable, with respect to each class of claims or interests that is impaired under, and has not accepted, the plan." §1129(b)(1). As to a dissenting class of impaired unsecured creditors, such a plan may be found to be "fair and equitable" only if the allowed value of the claim is to be paid in full, §1129(b)(2)(B)(i), or, in the alternative, if "the holder of any claim or interest that is junior to the claims of such [impaired unsecured] class will not receive or retain under the plan on account of such junior claim or interest any property," §1129(b)(2)(B)(ii). That latter condition is the core of what is known as the "absolute priority rule."

The absolute priority rule was the basis for the Bank's position that the plan could not be confirmed as a cramdown. As the Bank read the rule, the plan was open to objection simply because certain old equity holders in the Debtor Partnership would receive property even though the Bank's unsecured deficiency claim would not be paid in full. The Bankruptcy Court approved the plan nonetheless.... The District Court affirmed, as did the Court of Appeals.

The majority of the Seventh Circuit's divided panel found ambiguity in the language of the statutory absolute priority rule, and looked beyond the text to interpret the phrase "on account of" as permitting recognition of a "new value corollary" to the rule. According to the panel, the corollary, as stated by this Court in *Case v. Los Lumber Products Co.*, 308 U.S. 106 ... (1939), provides that the objection of an impaired senior class does not bar junior claim holders from receiving or retaining property interests in the debtor after reorganization, if they contribute new capital in money or money's worth, reasonably equivalent to the property's value, and necessary for successful reorganization of the restructured enterprise....

We granted certiorari to resolve a Circuit split on the issue.... We do not decide whether the statute includes a new value corollary or exception, but hold that on any reading respondent's proposed plan fails to satisfy the statute, and accordingly reverse.

II.

The terms "absolute priority rule" and "new value corollary" (or "exception") are creatures of law antedating the current Bankruptcy Code, and to understand both those terms and the related but inexact language of the Code some history is helpful. The Bankruptcy Act preceding the Code contained no such provision as subsection (b)(2)(B)(ii), its subject having been addressed by two interpretive rules. The first was a specific gloss on the requirement of §77B (and its successor, Chapter X) of the old Act, that any reorganization plan be "fair and equitable." 11 U.S.C. §205(e) (1934 ed., Supp. I) (repealed 1938) (§77B); 11 U.S.C. §621(2) (1934 ed., Supp. IV) (repealed 1979) (Chapter X). The reason for such a limitation was the danger inherent in any reorganization plan proposed by a debtor, then and now, that the plan will simply turn out to be too good a deal for the debtor's owners. Hence the pre-Code judicial response known as the absolute priority rule....

The second interpretive rule addressed the first. Its classic formulation occurred in *Case v. Los Angeles Lumber Products Co.*, in which the Court spoke through Justice Douglas in this dictum:

> It is, of course, clear that there are circumstances under which stockholders may participate in a plan of reorganization of an insolvent debtor.... Where the necessity [for new capital] exists and the old stockholders make a fresh contribution and receive in return a participation reasonably equivalent to their contribution, no objection can be made....

> We believe that to accord 'the creditor his full right of priority against the corporate assets' where the debtor is insolvent, the stockholder's participation must be based on a contribution in money or in money's worth, reasonably equivalent in view of all the circumstances to the participation of the stockholder.

308 U.S. at 121-122.

Although counsel for one of the parties here has described the Case observation as "'black-letter' principle," it never rose above the technical level of dictum in any opinion of this Court, which last addressed it in *Norwest Bank Worthington v. Ahlers*, 485 U.S. 197 ... (1988), holding that a contribution of "'labor, experience, and expertise'" by a junior interest holder was not in the "'money's worth'" that the Case observation required. 485 U.S. at 203-205.... Nor, prior to the enactment of the current Bankruptcy Code, did any court rely on the Case dictum to approve a plan that gave old equity a property right after reorganization. Hence the controversy over how weighty the *Case* dictum had become....

Enactment of the Bankruptcy Code in place of the prior Act might have resolved the status of new value by a provision bearing its name or at least unmistakably couched in its terms, but the Congress chose not to avail itself of that opportunity.... [After reviewing a variety of legislative history concerning the issue, the Court concluded that] this history does nothing to disparage the possibility apparent in the statutory text, that the absolute priority rule now on the books as subsection (b)(2)(B)(ii) may carry a new value corollary. Although there is no literal reference to "new value" in the phrase "on account of such junior claim," the phrase could arguably carry such an implication in modifying the prohibition against receipt by junior claimants of any interest under a plan while a senior class of unconsenting creditors goes less than fully paid.

III.

Three basic interpretations have been suggested for the "on account of" modifier. The first reading is proposed by the Partnership, that "on account of" harks back to accounting practice and means something like "in exchange for," or "in satisfaction of," On this view, a plan would not violate the absolute priority rule unless the old equity holders received or retained property in exchange for the prior interest, without any significant new contribution; if substantial money passed from them as part of the deal, the prohibition of subsection (b)(2)(B)(ii) would not stand in the way, and whatever issues of fairness and equity there might otherwise be would not implicate the "on account of" modifier.

This position is beset with troubles, the first one being textual. Subsection (b)(2)(B)(ii) forbids not only receipt of property on account of the prior interest but its retention as well. A common instance of the latter would be a debtor's retention of an interest in the insolvent business reorganized under the plan. Yet it would be exceedingly odd to speak of "retaining" property in exchange for the same property interest, and the eccentricity of such a reading is underscored by the fact that elsewhere in the Code the drafters chose to use the very phrase "in exchange for[]"....

The second difficulty is practical: the unlikelihood that Congress meant to impose a condition as manipulable as subsection (b)(2)(B)(ii) would be if "on account of" meant to prohibit merely an exchange unaccompanied by a substantial infusion of new funds but permit one whenever substantial funds changed hands. "Substantial" or "significant" or "considerable" or like characterizations of a monetary contribution would measure it by the Lord Chancellor's foot, and an absolute priority rule so variable would not be much of an absolute. Of course it is true (as already noted) that, even if old equity holders could displace the rule by adding some significant amount of cash to the deal, it would not follow that their plan would be entitled to adoption; a contested plan would still need to satisfy the overriding condition of fairness and equity. But that general fairness and equity criterion would apply in any event, and one comes back to the question why Congress would have bothered to add a separate priority rule without a sharper edge.

Since the "in exchange for" reading merits rejection, the way is open to recognize the more common understanding of "on account of" to mean "because of." This is certainly the usage meant for the phrase at other places in the statute. So, under the common-sense rule that a given phrase is meant to carry a given concept in a single statute, the better reading of subsection (b)(2)(B)(ii) recognizes that a causal relationship between holding the prior claim or interest and receiving or retaining property is what activates the absolute priority rule.

The degree of causation is the final bone of contention. We understand the Government, as amicus curiae, to take the starchy position not only that any degree of causation between earlier interests and retained property will activate the bar to a plan providing for later property, but also that whenever the holders of equity in the Debtor end up with some property there will be some causation; when old equity, and not someone on the street, gets property the reason is *res ipsa loquitur.* An old equity holder simply cannot take property under a plan if creditors are not paid in full.

There are, however, reasons counting against such a reading. If, as is likely, the drafters were treating junior claimants or interest holders as a class at this point then the simple way to have prohibited the old interest holders from receiving anything over objection would have been to omit the "on account of" phrase entirely from subsection (b)(2)(B)(ii). On this assumption, reading the provision as a blanket prohibition would leave "on account of" as a redundancy, contrary to the interpretive obligation to try to give meaning to all the statutory language. One would also have to ask why Congress would have desired to exclude prior equity categorically from the class of potential owners following a cramdown. Although we have some doubt about the Court of Appeals's assumption that prior equity is often the only source of significant capital for reorganizations, old equity may well be in the best position to make a go of the reorganized enterprise and so may be the party most likely to work out an equity-for-value reorganization.

A less absolute statutory prohibition would follow from reading the "on account of" language as intended to reconcile the two recognized policies underlying Chapter 11, of preserving going concerns and maximizing property available to satisfy creditors. Causation between the old equity's holdings and subsequent property substantial enough to disqualify a plan would presumably occur on this view of things whenever old equity's later property would come at a price that failed to provide the greatest possible addition to the bankruptcy estate, and it would always come at a price too low when the equity holders obtained or preserved an ownership interest for less than someone else would have paid. A truly full value transaction, on the other hand, would pose no threat to the bankruptcy estate not posed by any reorganization, provided of course that the contribution be in cash or be realizable money's worth....

IV.

Which of these positions is ultimately entitled to prevail is not to be decided here, however, for even on the latter view the Bank's objection would require rejection of the plan at issue in this case. It is doomed, we can say without necessarily exhausting its flaws, by its provision for vesting equity in the reorganized business in the Debtor's partners without extending an opportunity to anyone else either to compete for that equity or to propose a competing reorganization plan. Although the Debtor's exclusive opportunity to propose a plan under §1121(b) is not itself "property" within the meaning of subsection (b)(2)(B)(ii), the respondent partnership in this case has taken advantage of this opportunity by proposing a plan under which the benefit of equity ownership may be obtained by no one but old equity partners. Upon the court's approval of that plan, the partners were in the same position that they would have enjoyed had they exercised an exclusive option under the plan to buy the equity in the reorganized entity, or contracted to purchase it from a seller who had first agreed to deal with no one else. It is quite true that the escrow of the partners' proposed investment eliminated any formal need to set out an express option or exclusive dealing provision in the plan itself, since the court's approval that created the opportunity and the partners' action to obtain its advantage were simultaneous. But before the Debtor's plan was accepted no one else could propose an alternative one, and after its acceptance no one else could obtain equity in the reorganized entity. At the moment of the plan's approval the Debtor's partners necessarily enjoyed an exclusive opportunity that was in no economic sense distinguishable from the advantage of the exclusively entitled offeror or option holder. This opportunity should, first of all, be treated as an item of property in its own right. Cf.... *Kham & Nate's Shoes No. 2, Inc. v. First Bank*, 908 F.2d 1351, 1360 (CA7 1990).... While it may be argued that the opportunity has no market value, being significant only to old equity holders owing to their potential tax liability, such an argument avails the Debtor nothing, for several reasons. It is to avoid just such arguments that the law is settled that any otherwise cognizable property interest must be treated as sufficiently valuable to be recognized under the Bankruptcy Code. Even aside from that rule, the assumption that no one but the Debtor's partners might pay for such an opportunity would obviously support no inference that it is valueless, let alone that it should not be treated as property. And, finally, the source in the tax law of the opportunity's value to the partners implies in no way that it lacks value to others. It might, indeed, be valuable to another precisely as a way to keep the Debtor from implementing a plan that would avoid a Chapter 7 liquidation.

Given that the opportunity is property of some value, the question arises why old equity alone should obtain it, not to mention at no cost whatever. The closest thing to an answer favorable to the Debtor is that the old equity partners would be given the opportunity in the expectation that in taking advantage of it they would add the stated purchase price to the estate. But this just begs the question why the opportunity should be exclusive to the old equity holders. If the price to be paid for the equity interest is the best obtainable, old equity does not need the protection of exclusiveness (unless to trump an equal offer from someone else); if it is not the best, there is no apparent reason for giving old equity a bargain. There is no reason, that is, unless the very purpose of the whole transaction is, at least in part, to do old equity a favor. And that, of course, is to say that old equity would obtain its opportunity, and the resulting benefit, because of old equity's prior interest within the meaning of subsection (b)(2)(B)(ii). Hence it is that the exclusiveness of the opportunity, with its protection against the market's scrutiny of the purchase price by means of competing bids or even competing plan proposals, renders the partners' right a property interest extended "on account of" the old equity position and therefore subject to an unpaid senior creditor class's objection.

.... Under a plan granting an exclusive right, making no provision for competing bids or competing plans, any determination that the price was top dollar would necessarily be made by a judge in bankruptcy court, whereas the best way to determine value is exposure to a market. This is a point of some significance, since it was, after all, one of the Code's innovations to narrow the occasions for courts to make valuation judgments, as shown by its preference for the supramajoritarian class creditor voting scheme in §1126(c). In the interest of statutory coherence, a like disfavor for decisions untested by competitive choice ought to extend to valuations in administering subsection (b)(2)(B)(ii) when some form of market valuation may be available to test the adequacy of an old equity holder's proposed contribution.

Whether a market test would require an opportunity to offer competing plans or would be satisfied by a right to bid for the same interest sought by old equity, is a question we do not decide here. It is enough to say, assuming a new value corollary, that plans providing junior interest holders with exclusive opportunities free from competition and without benefit of market valuation fall within the prohibition of §1129(b)(2)(B)(ii).

The judgment of the Court of Appeals is accordingly reversed . . . .

Justice THOMAS, with whom Justice SCALIA joins, concurring in the judgment.

I agree with the majority's conclusion that the reorganization plan in this case could not be confirmed. However, I do not see the need for its unnecessary speculations on certain issues and do not share its approach to interpretation of the Bankruptcy Code. I therefore concur only in the judgment.

Our precedents make clear that an analysis of any statute, including the Bankruptcy Code, must not begin with external sources, but with the text itself. The relevant Code provision in this case, 11 U.S.C. §1129(b), does not expressly authorize prepetition equity holders to receive or retain property in a reorganized entity in exchange for an infusion of new capital. Instead, it is cast in general terms and requires that, to be confirmed over the objections of an impaired class of creditors, a reorganization plan be "fair and equitable." §1129(b)(1). With respect to an impaired class of unsecured creditors, a plan can be fair and equitable only if, at a minimum, it "provides that each holder of a claim of such class receive or retain on account of such claim property of a value, as of the effective date of the plan, equal to the allowed amount of such claim," §1129(b)(2)(B)(i), or if "the holder of any claim or interest that is junior to the claims of such class will not receive or retain under the plan on account of such junior claim or interest any property," §1129(b) (2)(B)(ii).

Neither condition is met here. The Bank did not receive property under the reorganization plan equal to the amount of its unsecured deficiency claim. Therefore, the plan could not satisfy the first condition. With respect to the second condition, the prepetition equity holders received at least two forms of property under the plan: the exclusive opportunity to obtain equity, and an equity interest in the reorganized entity. The plan could not be confirmed if the prepetition equity holders received any of this property "on account of" their junior interest.

The meaning of the phrase "on account of" is the central interpretive question presented by this case. This phrase obviously denotes some type of causal relationship between the junior interest and the property received or retained—such an interpretation comports with common understandings of the phrase. It also tracks the use of the phrase elsewhere in the Code. Regardless how direct the causal nexus must be, the prepetition equity holders here undoubtedly received at least one form of property— the exclusive opportunity—"on account of" their prepetition equity interest. Since §1129(b)(2)(B)(ii) prohibits the prepetition equity holders from receiving "any" property under the plan on account of their junior interest, this plan was not "fair and equitable" and could not be confirmed. That conclusion, as the majority recognizes, is sufficient to resolve this case. Thus, its . . . speculations about the desirability of a "market test," are dicta binding neither this Court nor the lower federal courts.

Justice STEVENS, dissenting.

Prior to the enactment of the Bankruptcy Reform Act of 1978, this Court unequivocally stated that there are circumstances under which stockholders may participate in a plan of reorganization of an insolvent debtor if their participation is based on a contribution in money, or in money's worth, reasonably equivalent in view of all the circumstances to their participation.... I believe the Court should now definitively resolve the question and state that a holder of a junior claim or interest does not receive property "on account of" such a claim when its participation in the plan is based on adequate new value.

The Court today wisely rejects the ... position that an old equity holder can never receive an interest in a reorganized venture as a result of a cramdown unless the creditors are first paid in full. Nevertheless, I find the Court's objections to the plan before us unsupported by either the text of 11 U.S.C. §1129(b)(2)(B)(ii) or the record in this case....

Notes

1. Whether the new value exception to the absolute priority rule endures enactment of the 1978 Bankruptcy Code thus remains an open legal question. Courts recognizing the enduring exception have nevertheless whittled it down. They apply stringent tests requiring "new value" to (a) represent a "substantial contribution" compared to claims and debt discharged in the proceeding and (b) at least equal the interest the contributor receives in the new corporation. See Carlson & Williams, The Truth About the New Value Exception to Bankruptcy's Absolute Priority Rule, 21 Cardozo L. Rev. 1303 (2000) (study of 202 Chapter 11 proceedings shows plans containing new value proposals were approved in only five).

2. Section 308 of the Sarbanes-Oxley Act of 2002 creates a "Fair Funds for Investors" provision. The SEC may impose penalties on SEC registrants found to have committed fraud. The estate of a bankrupt registrant facing such penalties may be obliged to allocate payment to the Fund, for shareholders, absorbing assets in the estate otherwise allocable to creditors, including bondholders.

The SEC invoked Section 308 in proposing a settlement of its civil action against WorldCom Inc. The SEC alleged that WorldCom misled investors by overstating its income from early 1999 through the first quarter of 2002 as a result of undisclosed improper accounting practices. The SEC proposed, and the district court approved, a civil penalty of $2.25 billion to be discharged in WorldCom's bankruptcy proceeding by payment of $.75 billion. The funds would be distributed to "victims" of World-Com's fraud, principally its shareholders, in the form of $.5 billion in cash and $.25 billion in the company's new common stock. S.E.C. v. Worldcom, Inc., 273 F. Supp.2d 431 (S.D.N.Y. 2003).

What is the theory of Section 308 when invoked in a bankruptcy proceeding? Two effects seem to follow from its functional reallocation of a bankrupt registrant's assets from bondholders to shareholders: to increase the cost of debt capital relative to equity capital and to increase incentives for debt to monitor registrant activity for the detection and prevention of fraud.

Are bondholders better positioned than shareholders to shoulder the monitoring burden? What is the effect of that burden on the relative cost of debt compared to equity capital? To the extent the managerial incentives to engage in fraudulent financial reporting relate to maintaining a relatively high share price, shareholders may be poor monitors compared to bondholders.

The SEC's proposal in the WorldCom case was subject to approval of the District Court hearing the SEC's claims as well as of the Bankruptcy Court administering WorldCom's estate.

What effect, if any, should a "pre-packaged" plan of reorganization developed by a financially-troubled debtor and its creditors prior to the time the debtor files for bankruptcy have with respect to the application of the absolute priority rule inside of bankruptcy? Consider the following case.

In re Zenith Electronics Corp.

241 B.R. 92 (D. Del. Bankr. 1999)

WALRATH, J.:

This case is before the Court on the request of Zenith Electronics Corporation ("Zenith") for approval of its Disclosure Statement and confirmation of its Pre-Packaged Plan of Reorganization filed August 24, 1999 ("the Plan"). The Plan is supported by Zenith's largest shareholder and creditor, LG Electronics, Inc. ("LGE"), and the holders of a majority of the debentures issued by Zenith pre-petition ("the Bondholders"). The Plan is opposed by the Official Committee of Equity Security Holders ("the Equity Committee") and numerous shareholders, including Nordhoff Investments, Inc. ("Nordhoff") (collectively, "the Objectors"). For the reasons set forth below, we overrule the objections, approve the Disclosure Statement and will confirm the Plan, if modified in accordance with this Opinion.

Zenith has been in business for over 80 years. It was a leader in the design, manufacturing, and marketing of consumer electronics for many years. In recent years it has experienced substantial financial difficulties. It incurred losses in 12 of the last 13 years.

In 1995 Zenith persuaded one of its shareholders, LGE which held approximately 5% of its stock, to invest over $366 million in acquiring a total 57.7% stake in the company. Notwithstanding that investment, and loans and credit support in excess of $340 million provided subsequently by LGE, Zenith's financial condition continued to deteriorate. Zenith suffered net losses in 1996 of $178 million, in 1997 of $299 million and in 1998 of $275 million.

In late 1997, the Asian financial crisis and the continuing losses at Zenith, caused LGE (and Zenith) to question LGE's ability to continue to support Zenith and Zenith's need to reorganize. LGE retained McKinsey & Co. ("McKinsey") to evaluate its investment in Zenith and to suggest improvements Zenith could make in its operations and focus. Zenith hired an investment banking firm, Peter J. Solomon Company ("PJSC") in December, 1997, and a new CEO, Jeff Gannon, in January 1998. Under Mr. Gannon, Zenith made substantial operational changes, including a conversion from manufacturer to a marketing and distribution company which outsourced all manufacturing. Zenith's manufacturing facilities were sold or closed in 1998 and 1999. While those operational changes did have some effect on stemming the losses, they were insufficient to eliminate them. Contemporaneously, PJSC evaluated Zenith's assets on a liquidation and going concern basis.

In early 1998, Zenith also attempted to attract a strategic investor or purchaser of part or all of its business or assets. Because of its financial condition, Zenith was advised that it could not raise money through the issuance of more stock or debt instruments. Zenith's strategy was to identify companies which might have an interest and then to have Zenith's CEO approach the target's CEO to discuss the possibilities. Several meetings were conducted with such entities. No offers were received for a sale of substantial assets or business divisions; nor were any offers of equity investments received.

In April 1998, LGE proposed a possible restructuring of its debt and equity in Zenith, contingent on substantial reduction of the bond debt and elimination of the shareholder interests. Zenith appointed a Special Committee of its Board of Directors to evaluate the restructuring proposal and to conduct negotiations on behalf of Zenith. After agreement was reached with the Special Committee, negotiations proceeded with the Bondholders' Committee. Ultimately the restructuring proposal was reduced to a pre-packaged plan of reorganization.

A Disclosure Statement and Proxy Statement-Prospectus for the solicitation of votes on the Plan was prepared and reviewed by the SEC.... On July 15, 1999, after numerous revisions, the SEC declared the Disclosure Statement effective. On July 20, 1999, Zenith mailed the Plan and Disclosure Statement to the Bondholders and others entitled to vote on the Plan. After voting was completed on August 20, 1999, the Bondholders had voted in favor of the Plan by 98.6% in amount and 97.01% in number of those voting. LGE and Citibank, a secured creditor, had also voted to accept the Plan. Zenith immediately filed its chapter 11 petition on August 24, 1999. At the same time, Zenith filed its Plan and Disclosure Statement and sought prompt approval of both. A combined Disclosure Statement and confirmation hearing was scheduled for September 27 and 28, 1999.

An ad hoc committee of minority shareholders sought a postponement of the confirmation hearing, which was denied. We did, however, grant its motion for appointment of an official committee of equity holders, over the objection of Zenith, LGE and the Bondholders' Committee. We did so to give the equity holders an opportunity to conduct discovery and present their arguments against confirmation of the Plan.

* * *

As an initial matter, the Equity Committee objects to the adequacy of the Disclosure Statement ...

Typically, under [Section 1125(b) of] chapter 11 of the Bankruptcy Code, the court approves the debtor's disclosure statement before it, and the plan of reorganization, are sent to creditors and others entitled to vote on the plan....

However, Congress recognized the validity of votes solicited pre-bankruptcy (a practice which had developed under chapter X of the Bankruptcy Act). Section 1126(b) provides:

> (b) For the purposes of subsections (c) and (d) of this section, a holder of a claim or interest that has accepted or rejected the plan before the commencement of the case under this title is deemed to have accepted or rejected such plan, as the case may be, if:
>
> (1) the solicitation of such acceptance or rejection was in compliance with any applicable nonbankruptcy law, rule, or regulation governing the adequacy of disclosure in connection with such solicitation; or
>
> (2) if there is not any such law, rule, or regulation, such acceptance or rejection was solicited after disclosure to such holder of adequate information, as defined in section 1125(a) of this title.

11 U.S.C. §1126(b).

Zenith asserts that the Disclosure Statement meets both criteria. We agree....

In this case, the SEC was required to approve the Disclosure Statement because the Plan provides for the issuance of new securities to the Bondholders. The SEC did approve the Disclosure Statement on July 15, 1999, as containing adequate information (after 11 months of discussions and numerous amendments).

We conclude that the Disclosure Statement, having been approved by the SEC as containing adequate information, complies with the provisions of section 1126(b)(1).

Even if it did not fit the provisions of section 1126(b)(1), the Disclosure Statement does contain sufficient information to comply with section 1126(b)(2) and 1125(a)....

* * *

The valuation issue in this case is somewhat unique. It is not presented in connection with determining whether the Plan complies with section 1129(a)(7): the Equity Committee concedes that on a liquidation under chapter 7 the shareholders will receive nothing. PJSC estimates the liquidation value of Zenith at $170 million; creditors' claims exceed $545 million.

The value of Zenith as a going concern is, however, disputed and is relevant to the issues of whether the Plan is fair and equitable and proposed in good faith.

PJSC values Zenith as a going concern at $310 million, while the Equity Committee's experts value it at $1.05 billion. The significant difference in the experts' conclusions is the value attributed to the VSB technology developed by Zenith ($155 million according to PJSC, $833 million according to [Ernst & Young ("E&Y")].... [After a thorough analysis, the court then determined that Zenith was worth $310 million as a going concern rather than $1.05 billion.]

* * *

Where a class of creditors or shareholders has not accepted a plan of reorganization, the court shall nonetheless confirm the plan if it "does not discriminate unfairly and is fair and equitable." 11 U.S.C. §1129(b)(1). Fair and equitable treatment with respect to a class of equity interests—the sole non-accepting class in this case—means either the class receives or retains property equal to the value of its interest or no junior interest receives or retains anything under the plan. Id. at §1129(b)(2)(C). [B]oth alternatives are satisfied. No class junior to the common shareholders is receiving or retaining anything under the Plan. Further, based on our conclusion of the value of Zenith as a going concern, the shareholders are receiving the value of their interests under the Plan—nothing.

The Equity Committee asserts, however, that the Plan's treatment of the Bondholders violates the fair and equitable requirements of the Code. Specifically, the Plan provides that if Bondholders do not accept it, they will receive nothing under the Plan and the Plan proponents will seek cramdown pursuant to section 1129(b) as to them. In contrast, if the Bondholders accept the Plan, they will be entitled to a pro rata distribution of $50 million of the new 8.19% Senior Debentures. The Equity Committee asserts that this treatment is unfair because (1) if the Plan proponents are correct in their valuation of Zenith, Bondholders are not entitled to any distribution and offering them something for their vote in favor of the Plan is not appropriate, and (2) the shareholders were not offered a similar deal.

There is no prohibition in the Code against a Plan proponent offering different treatment to a class depending on whether it votes to accept or reject the Plan. One justification for such disparate treatment is that, if the class accepts, the Plan proponent is saved the expense and uncertainty of a cramdown fight. This is in keeping with the Bankruptcy Code's overall policy of fostering consensual plans of reorganization and does not violate the fair and equitable requirement of section 1129(b).

Nor were the votes of the Bondholders solicited in bad faith (and subject to disqualification) as a result of the above provision. See 11 U.S.C. §1126(e). [T]he distribution ...

is going to all creditors in the same class, is being made pursuant to the Plan, and is fully disclosed to all interested parties. Disqualification of the vote of that entire class is not mandated.

There is similarly no prohibition against the Bondholders receiving different (and better) treatment than the shareholders receive under the Plan. In fact, the cramdown provisions of the Code mandate that the Bondholders be treated better than the shareholders. In the absence of the Bondholders receiving payment in full or consenting, the shareholders may not receive anything under the Plan. 11 U.S.C. §1129(b)(2)(B). [I]t is not fundamentally unfair for the Bondholders to have been offered a distribution under the Plan in exchange for their assent to the Plan, while the shareholders were not.

The Equity Committee also asserts that the Plan violates the absolute priority rule, as recently articulated by the United States Supreme Court, by allowing LGE to obtain the stock of Zenith without subjecting it to sale on the open market. *See Bank of America v. 203 North LaSalle Street Partnership*, 526 U.S. 434, 119 S. Ct. 1411, 143 L. Ed. 2d 607 (1999). The *203 North LaSalle* case, however, is distinguishable.... In that case, the plan gave the shareholders the exclusive right to "buy" the equity, without giving creditors a similar right or allowing the market to test the price. The Supreme Court held that because shareholders were receiving the exclusive right to bid for the equity, and creditors were not being paid in full, this violated section 1129(b)(2)(B).

In this case, all creditor classes have accepted the Plan and there is no objection to confirmation by any creditor. Thus, the absolute priority rule embodied in section 1129(b)(2)(B) is not even applicable. Rather, section 1129(b)(2)(C) is the applicable section in this case.

Further, in this case, it is not a shareholder who is being given the right to buy equity ... [I]t is LGE in its capacity as a substantial secured and unsecured creditor who is being given that right. [I]f the Plan were to allow the minority shareholders the right to bid on the equity, as they urge, it would present the same problem as the *203 North LaSalle* plan did. The Supreme Court in *203 North LaSalle* did not say that a plan which allowed a senior secured creditor to buy the equity violated the Code; ... it suggested that the plan in that case violated the absolute priority rule because it did not let the creditor bid on the equity.

It is not appropriate to extend the ruling of the *203 North LaSalle* case beyond the facts of that case. To do so would require in all cases that a debtor be placed "on the market" for sale to the highest bidder. Such a requirement would eliminate the concept of exclusivity contained in section 1121(b) and the broad powers of the debtor to propose a plan in whatever format it desires. For example, section 1123(a)(5) specifically allows a debtor to propose a plan which allows the debtor to retain all or part of its property, to transfer all or part of its property, to merge or consolidate its business with others, to sell all or part of its property (subject to or free of liens), to satisfy or modify liens, and to cancel, modify or issue securities. The restriction on the debtor's right to propose a plan contained in the *203 North LaSalle* case should be limited to the facts of that case—where the absolute priority rule encompassed in section 1129(b)(2)(B) is violated.

The Plan ... does not violate the absolute priority rule articulated in section 1129(b)(2)(B) or (C) because all creditor classes have accepted the Plan and LGE is not retaining any interest because of its shareholder status. LGE is obtaining the equity in Zenith because of its status as a creditor, senior in right to the minority shareholders.

The Equity Committee asserts, however, that LGE's secured and unsecured claims should be disallowed, recharacterized as equity or equitably subordinated. Other than conclusory statements of the "multiplicity of relationships" between LGE and Zenith and how LGE dominated the company, there is little support offered for the Committee's premise.

In order for a claim to be disallowed, there must be no legitimate basis for it. The records of Zenith, its public filings, the Disclosure Statement and the testimony at the confirmation hearing all support the conclusion that LGE has claims against Zenith in excess of $375 million representing funds actually lent by it to Zenith or funds paid by it in satisfaction of its guarantee of Zenith's debts. Further, the Special Committee did review the transactions between LGE and Zenith and concluded that the restructuring provided more value to the company than the pursuit of any actions against LGE. The Equity Committee presents no evidence to refute the claims of LGE. Therefore, there is no basis to disallow those claims.

To recharacterize debt as equity or to equitably subordinate a claim, the creditor must have done something inequitable.... In this case, the Equity Committee has presented no evidence of inequitable conduct. There is nothing inequitable about LGE seeking to restructure its debt position in Zenith, requiring that the restructuring be accomplished in chapter 11, or insisting on 100% of the equity in exchange for forgiveness of $200 million of debt and new funding of $60 million. The valuation and other testimony at the trial confirms the fairness of the conduct of LGE. There is no basis to equitably subordinate its claims.

The Objectors also assert that the Plan cannot be confirmed because it violates the requirement of the Bankruptcy Code that the Plan be "proposed in good faith and not by any means forbidden by law." 11 U.S.C. §1129(a)(3). The good faith standard requires that the plan be "proposed with honesty, good intentions and a basis for expecting that a reorganization can be effected with results consistent with the objectives and purposes of the Bankruptcy Code." *In re Sound Radio, Inc.*, 93 B.R. 849, 853 (Bankr. D.N.J. 1988).

We easily conclude that Zenith's Plan is proposed in good faith under the general requirements of the Bankruptcy Code. It is proposed with the legitimate purpose of restructuring its finances to permit it to reorganize successfully. The fact that Zenith is a financially troubled company cannot be disputed; its substantial losses in the last decade attest to that. Even with its operational restructuring (which significantly reduced the losses), Zenith needs more. Readjustment of its debt structure and forgiveness of a substantial amount of its debt is necessary for it to operate profitably and to position itself in the market to take advantage of the technology it owns. This reorganization is exactly what chapter 11 of the Bankruptcy Code was designed to accomplish.

Both the Equity Committee and Nordhoff argue, however, that the Plan must not only comply with the provisions of the Code, but must meet the standards for approval of such a transaction under Delaware corporate law. We agree that section 1129(a)(3) does incorporate Delaware law (as well as any other applicable nonbankruptcy law).

In evaluating a transaction between a controlling shareholder and its corporation, the Delaware courts require a showing that the transaction is entirely fair....

The initial argument of the Objectors ... that LGE has not met the Delaware standard appears to be premised on the assertion that LGE required that Zenith file bankruptcy in order to take advantage of the Code's cramdown (and other) provisions. However, [it is not 'bad faith' for debtors to file for bankruptcy to take advantage of particular Code provisions].

[W]e do not find that LGE's position as a significant creditor and shareholder unduly influenced the process. Throughout the negotiation of the restructuring, Zenith and LGE had separate counsel and other professionals. Zenith properly appointed a Special Committee of its Board of Directors (which did not include any LGE appointees) to negotiate with LGE. Further, LGE did not object or impede Zenith's efforts to find a different strategic investor or purchaser and, in fact, introduced Zenith to some targets. Finally, any undue influence which LGE might have had over Zenith was countered by the Bondholders participation (through separate professionals) in negotiating the Plan.

[W]e disagree with the Equity Committee's assertion that there was no effort to consider other alternatives. Mr. Gannon testified to his substantial efforts to obtain another investor or buyer. No alternative was forthcoming after eighteen months. [N]one of the Equity Committee's witnesses could identify any concrete offer or alternative to the LGE proposal that would afford creditors or shareholders a better return. The only alternative posited by them was to deny confirmation of the Plan and try to market the company while it is in bankruptcy. Mr. Gannon testified that the company could not survive that process. Given Zenith's efforts pre-bankruptcy, we conclude it would be a futile effort.

The Equity Committee asserts that it is significant that the Special Committee did not obtain an opinion attesting to the fairness of the process. We do not find this to be fatal. The Court is the ultimate arbiter of the fairness of the transaction. The lack of an expert's opinion on this point, while it may be comforting to a Board of Directors, is not dispositive of the issue.

We have already concluded that the disclosure requirements of the Code have been met by the Disclosure Statement issued by Zenith....

[T]he Equity Committee argues that the failure of Zenith or LGE to have any meaningful negotiations with the minority shareholders renders the process unfair. We disagree. Since PJSC determined that there was no equity in the company, asking the minority shareholders for input into the financial restructuring of the company would have been futile. We find no evidence that the minority shareholders were denied information about the company or the process. Again, there is no suggestion that Zenith did not file the periodic reports required of a public company or that those reports were inaccurate. If the minority shareholders had a proposal for restructuring the company, they were free to present it to Zenith or LGE. There is no evidence that a proposal was ever presented to the company or ignored by it.

Consequently, we conclude that the process utilized by Zenith, LGE, and the Bondholders to negotiate a financial restructuring of the company was fair.

With respect to the issue of fair price, we start with the value of Zenith which we found above, $310 million ... premised on the PJSC valuation which properly considered both Zenith's current operations (the consumer electronics business and royalties earned by the tuner technology) as well as its inherent value (the future value of the VSB technology)....

Under the restructuring proposal, LGE is acquiring 100% of the equity of Zenith, which will still owe $67 million to Citibank and $50 million to the Bondholders. The net equity of the company is therefore $193 million ($310 million less the assumed debt of $117 million). In exchange, LGE is relinquishing $200 million of debt, investing up to an additional $60 million in capital funds, and exchanging $175 million in claims for [a plant] (valued at $40 million) plus a note for $135 million paid over time. We conclude that LGE is paying a fair price for the equity in the new Zenith.

This is bolstered by the fact that Zenith was unable to locate any other buyer or investor in the company pre-bankruptcy despite efforts over the last two years....

Finding that the process and the price were fair, we conclude that Zenith and LGE have met the "entirely fair" standard under Delaware law for the approval of the Plan ...

[T]he Plan ... may be confirmed....

Baird and Jackson, Bargaining after the Fall and the Contours of the Absolute Priority Rule

55 U. Chi. L. Rev. 738, 738-47 (1988)

The absolute priority rule provides that in a reorganization senior owners are paid in full before junior owners are paid anything. When a firm owes more than its assets are worth, the shareholders receive nothing unless the creditors consent. Under the 1978 Bankruptcy Code, consent can be given through a classwide vote of creditors. A single uncompromising creditor's objection is not sufficient to prevent the participation of shareholders. Nevertheless, the absolute priority rule and its rhetoric stand in distinct contrast to the distrust of market mechanisms and ex ante bargains that pervades both the practice of bankruptcy and discussions of bankruptcy policy....

Part of the initial bargain among those who contribute capital to a firm is an agreement about how assets of the firm will be divided if there is a day of reckoning on which everyone's ownership interest is valued. In most firms, one set of owners will take before others.[8] Debt will be paid before equity. In many firms, there are multiple layers of ownership. There are, commonly, secured creditors, general creditors, subordinated debenture holders, preferred stockholders, and common stockholders, among others. Why those who contribute capital to a firm choose to structure ownership interests in this fashion is one of the central questions of corporate finance.[9]

Quite apart from the question of why there are multiple layers of ownership, however, are the problems associated with recognizing this hierarchical structure at the time of the reckoning. Sorting out the different ownership layers often is not an easy affair when the firm is to stay intact as a going concern. When some of the old owners are to remain involved with the firm after the accounting, they may be in a position to renegotiate their original bargain. The supplier who is owed money may condition delivery of further supplies on its past debts being paid in full. The manager who agreed to work for the old firm in return for equity may insist on equity in the new firm as well. The shareholder who offers new capital may insist that it have an equity interest in the new firm even though there is not enough cash to pay those senior to it.

To the extent that the junior owners can offer new supplies, expertise, or capital on terms more favorable than anyone else, it is in everyone's interest that they do so. In negotiations involving prior owners who are also future suppliers, striking a deal requires distinguishing between their rights as existing owners of the firm and their ability to provide a new input to the firm on favorable terms. It also requires some mechanism for determining who may bargain on behalf of the firm. Someone must not only set the

---

8. By "owners," we mean those who have some claim to the income stream or assets of the enterprise. As such, it includes creditors and holders of equity interests alike, instead of the conventional equation of ownership with common stock.

9. The seminal article is Modigliani and Miller, The Cost of Capital, Corporation Finance and the Theory of Investment, 48 Am. Econ. Rev. 261 (1958). [The theory presented by Modigliani and Miller in this article is discussed *supra* in the Notes and Questions at the end of section 1.—Eds.]

terms of the bargain, but also guard against the possibility that the old owners are offering something that they are already legally obliged to supply the firm.

* * *

In other cases, the firm, although insolvent, is worth preserving, but the existing owner-managers need to be replaced. In these cases the appropriate course also is to allow the most senior creditor (assuming again it is owed more than the firm is worth) to sell the assets of the firm either to a third party or to itself. The only difference is that the senior creditor should now sell the assets as a unit rather than piece by piece. The junior creditors and the shareholders cannot complain because they have bargained for a position inferior to that of the senior creditor with respect to all the assets being sold. The senior creditor is entitled to be paid in full before anyone junior to it receives anything. Again, there is nothing to bargain over vis-a-vis the existing owners, as none of them have anything to offer the most senior creditor. Indeed, the firm is more valuable without them than with them.

As applied to these cases, the absolute priority rule simply restates the idea of a layered ownership structure in which one owner has bargained for the right to be paid before others. One can look exclusively to the extant agreements among the participants as owners, because none of them bring any special advantages (and hence bargaining strength) relevant to the firm's future. Harder cases, however, arise when the firm, although insolvent, is worth keeping intact as a going concern and an existing owner is a peculiarly well-positioned source of capital, supplies, or expertise to the firm or otherwise has the ability to strike a deal that gives it a better position than its preexisting position in the ownership hierarchy entitles it to. The problem is most stark when the firm is worth less than what the most senior creditor is owed and the senior creditor has reason to recombine with the old shareholder. The effect of the recombination would be to freeze out an intermediate creditor.

It might seem that the intermediate creditor has little to complain about....

Under this view, the senior creditor, having the exclusive right to the firm's assets following foreclosure, should be able to convey an interest in them to anyone it pleases.[17] That it is willing to share those assets with the old shareholder suggests that it sees advantage in doing so.... The old shareholder is acquiring an interest because the senior creditor has concluded doing so is in its interest, not because of the old shareholder's preexisting status. The senior creditor would be as willing to deal with the intermediate creditor, indeed, anyone at all, if the party were willing to contribute capital or provide the needed expertise. The senior creditor, in other words, presumably combines its assets with something new being contributed by the old shareholders, and this transaction thereby violates no rights of the intermediate class....

Given our characterization of this problem, it is not at all clear why passing over an intermediate class is objectionable. We have described any recombination of a senior creditor with the old shareholder as consisting of two separate steps: a foreclosure on the assets by the senior party that is followed by a recombination of those assets with the old shareholder for a reason of the senior creditor's choosing. *Boyd*,[a] however, rests

---

17. The valuation may not be believable. To demonstrate valuations, default rules typically give a debtor the right to force liquidation of the collateral by a secured party. See, e.g., U.C.C. §9-505 (1978). A similar rule may be desirable to protect general creditors from valuation worries. These worries, however, would provoke a response, forced sale procedures, distinct from the one under discussion, simply banning the transaction....

a. Northern Pacific Ry. Co. v. Boyd, 228 U.S. 482 (1918).

on a different description of the transaction: The old shareholder starts with an owner-ship interest in the firm that is subject to the claims of its general creditors. She then strikes a deal with the senior creditor, and immediately finds herself with an ownership interest in the same firm that is free of those claims.

Sharply different initial conclusions follow from this vision of the transaction. The general creditors may not have been entitled to anything if all the firm's assets were con-verted to cash today, but a recapitalization is occurring, not a dismemberment of the firm. Where the firm continues, the general creditors, but for the restructuring, might have something of value that the restructuring takes away and gives to the shareholder. Even though the firm will likely not be able to pay off the secured creditor, the possibil-ity that the firm will do much better than expected makes the general creditors' right to reach the assets of the firm before the shareholders worth something.

The general creditors' objection is not to the senior creditor's right to foreclose and sell the firm as a going concern.... Their objection instead goes to the shareholder's re-capture of an interest in the firm. Under this argument, the general creditors should be able to object if the old shareholder recovers something over which the general creditors have a prior claim and does so by means of a transaction in which the general creditors have no voice.

Viewed this way, the general creditors should be able to prevent the old shareholder from engaging in a transaction that freezes out the interests of the general creditors while leaving something for the old shareholder.... Because this transaction has the ef-fect of allowing the old shareholder to claim an interest in the firm free of the claims of the general creditors, it can be seen as a fraudulent conveyance.

An understanding of the absolute priority rule, then, must turn on choosing be-tween two radically different ways of viewing the same transaction. From one perspec-tive, the transaction is viewed as a proper foreclosure, followed by a recombination be-tween the senior creditor (or other buyer of assets) and the old shareholder (who is making some contribution to the firm that entices the senior creditor, or other buyer, to share its assets with the old shareholders). From the other perspective, the transaction is viewed as a conveyance that, by preferring holders of equity interests over creditors, vi-olates the payout norms implicit in the debtor-creditor relation.

The absolute priority rule, in short, was originally about a three-party transaction where the issue was whether a senior claimant with the right to the entire firm in a liq-uidation could ignore an intermediate party if it chose to include old equity holders in the reorganized firm. This aspect of the rule, the heart of the holding in *Boyd*, has been transported uncritically into the Bankruptcy Code even though its superiority over the competing rule—treating the shareholders as contributing something of value to the reorganized firm and hence permitting the freeze-out—is far from obvious.

* * *

---

11 U.S.C. §1129 (2005)

§1129. Confirmation of plan

(a) The court shall confirm a plan only if all of the following requirements are met:

* * *

(7) With respect to each impaired class of claims or interests—

    (A) each holder of a claim or interest of such class—

        (i) has accepted the plan; or

        (ii) will receive or retain under the plan on account of such claim or interest property of a value, as of the effective date of the plan, that is not less than the amount that such holder would so receive or retain if the debtor were liquidated under chapter 7 of this title on such date....

(8) With respect to each class of claims or interests—

    (A) such class has accepted the plan; or

    (B) such class is not impaired under the plan.

* * *

(10) If a class of claims is impaired under the plan, at least one class of claims that is impaired under the plan has accepted the plan, determined without including any acceptance of the plan by any insider.

(11) Confirmation of the plan is not likely to be followed by the liquidation, or the need for further financial reorganization, of the debtor or any successor to the debtor under the plan, unless such liquidation or reorganization is proposed in the plan....

(b)(1) Notwithstanding section 510(a) of this title, if all of the applicable requirements of subsection (a) of this section other than paragraph (8) are met with respect to a plan, the court, on request of the proponent of the plan, shall confirm the plan notwithstanding the requirements of such paragraph if the plan does not discriminate unfairly, and is fair and equitable, with respect to each class of claims or interests that is impaired under, and has not accepted, the plan....

(2) For the purpose of this subsection, the condition that a plan be fair and equitable with respect to a class includes the following requirements:

(A) With respect to a class of secured claims, the plan provides—

    (i)(I) that the holders of such claims retain the liens securing such claims, whether the property subject to such liens is retained by the debtor or transferred to another entity, to the extent of the allowed amount of such claims; and

    (II) that each holder of a claim of such class receive on account of such claim deferred cash payments totaling at least the allowed amount of such claim, of a value, as of the effective date of the plan, of at least the value of such holder's interest in the estate's interest in such property;

    (ii) for the sale, subject to section 363(k) of this title, of any property that is subject to the liens securing such claims, free and clear of such liens, with such liens to attach to the proceeds of such sale, and the treatment of such liens on proceeds under clause (i) or (iii) of this subparagraph; or

    (iii) for the realization by such holders of the indubitable equivalent of such claims.

(B) With respect to a class of unsecured claims—

    (i) the plan provides that each holder of a claim of such class receive or retain on account of such claim property of a value, as of the effective date of the plan, equal to the allowed amount of such claim; or

(ii) the holder of any claim or interest that is junior to the claims of such class will not receive or retain under the plan on account of such junior claim or interest any property....

(C) With respect to a class of interests—

(i) the plan provides that each holder of an interest of such class receive or retain on account of such interest property of a value, as of the effective date of the plan, equal to the greatest of the allowed amount of any fixed liquidation preference to which such holder is entitled, any fixed redemption price to which such holder is entitled, or the value of such interest; or

(ii) the holder of any interest that is junior to the interests of such class will not receive or retain under the plan on account of such junior interest any property.

(c) Notwithstanding subsections (a) and (b) of this section and except as provided in section 1127(b) of this title, the court may confirm only one plan, unless the order of confirmation in the case has been revoked under section 1144 of this title. If the requirements of subsections (a) and (b) of this section are met with respect to more than one plan, the court shall consider the preferences of creditors and equity security holders in determining which plan to confirm.

(d) Notwithstanding any other provision of this section, on request of a party in interest that is a governmental unit, the court may not confirm a plan if the principal purpose of the plan is the avoidance of taxes or the avoidance of the application of section 5 of the Securities Act of 1933 (15 U.S.C. 77e). In any hearing under this subsection, the governmental unit has the burden of proof on the issue of avoidance.

A Note on the Bankruptcy Abuse Prevention and Consumer Reform Act of 2005

On April 20, 2005, President Bush signed the Bankruptcy Abuse Prevention and Consumer Reform Act (the "2005 Act") which amended Title 11 of the United States Code. The primary purpose of the 2005 Act was to deter individuals from using the bankruptcy laws to avoid paying debts (1.56 million individual bankruptcy cases were filed in 2004). As such, only a limited number of the changes concern corporate insolvency, though it is notable that a corporate Chapter 11 debtor must now file a plan of reorganization within 18 months. However, some of the Title 11 amendments that do not directly relate to corporate insolvency warrant a brief discussion.

Small Businesses

On the creditor side, one of the most important provisions of the 2005 Act for small business cases is Section 1102(a)(4). It allows courts to add a creditor which is a "small business concern"[1] to the committee of creditors, provided that the creditor is owed a debt equal to a disproportionately large percentage of its gross annual revenue. This increased creditor influence should benefit small businesses with respect to bankrupt debtors.

---

1. According to 11 U.S.C. § 1102(a)(4), "small business concern" is defined in Section 3(a)(1) of the Small Business Act. That Act provides that "a small business concern ... shall be deemed to be one which is independently owned and operated and which is not dominant in its field of operation...." 15 U.S.C. § 632(a)(1).

On the debtor side, the 2005 Act generally makes it more difficult for "small business debtors"[2] to reorganize, establish payment plans with creditors, and continue to operate during bankruptcy. In order to prevent "serial" bankruptcy filings, the 2005 Act limits the Section 362 automatic stay period when a small business debtor files for bankruptcy within a year of its first filing. Under the 2005 Act, a small business debtor has only six months to file a plan of reorganization, as opposed to a corporate debtor which has 18 months. In a small business reorganization, only the debtor may file a plan of reorganization. If no plan is filed within 300 days, the debtor loses Chapter 11 protection. The 2005 Act also adds stringent reporting requirements and a "means test" to determine if debt repayment is possible. The 2005 Act subjects the small business debtor to increased supervision by the U.S. Trustee.

New Chapter 15

New Chapter 15 is designed to encourage cooperation between foreign countries and the United States regarding multi-national insolvency cases. Essentially, the chapter seeks to increase the efficiency of these types of cases by streamlining procedural issues such as attaching ancillary cases or authorizations to act in a foreign country. Few provisions deal expressly with corporate issues. Interestingly, though, foreign insurance companies that do business in the United States are eligible for relief under Chapter 15 but foreign banks with branches in the United States are not.

(iii) Equitable Subordination

Taylor v. Standard Gas & Electric Co., 306 U.S. 307 (1939), cited in Pepper v. Litton, 308 U.S. 295 (1939), *supra* at section 6b, involved a challenge by a committee of the debtor's preferred stockholders to the district court's approval of a reorganization plan under §77B of the Bankruptcy Act then in force. U.S.C. Tit. 11, §207. The focus of the challenge was a creditor's claim by Standard Gas & Electric Co. for amounts allegedly owed to it by its subsidiary, Deep Rock Oil Corporation, the debtor in bankruptcy. Deep Rock had been organized by Standard to acquire certain oil properties then owned by C. B. Shaffer. Standard's officers and directors had always constituted a majority of Deep Rock's board of directors, with the balance either selected from Deep Rock's officers and employees and other persons under Standard's control. In addition, Standard maintained complete financial control over Deep Rock's affairs, although Deep Rock's officers were permitted some discretion in the development and operation of its oil properties. As the Court put it: "All of the fiscal affairs of the debtor were wholly controlled by Standard, which was its banker and its only source of financial aid."

Deep Rock constantly was in financial trouble. The Court noted: "From the outset Deep Rock was insufficiently capitalized, was topheavy with debt and was in parlous financial condition. Standard so managed its affairs as always to have a stranglehold upon it." In addition to aggressively financing Deep Rock with debt, Standard caused it to declare substantial dividends on its common stock (which were taken by Standard in common stock while outside minority stockholders were paid in cash) "... in the face of the fact that Deep Rock had not the cash available to pay them and was, at the time, borrowing in large amounts from or through Standard."

---

2. A "small business debtor" is defined as a person or affiliate of such a person that "has aggregated noncontingent liquidated secured and unsecured debts ... in an amount not more than $2,000,000...." 11 U.S.C. §101(51D)(A).

Justice Douglas' description of the facts is detailed, but the foregoing should suffice to convey some flavor of the relationship between Standard and its subsidiary. The plan of reorganization ultimately approved by the district court (and challenged in this case) allowed a compromise claim of $5,000,000 to Standard, as creditor. In holding that the district court abused its discretion in approving the plan, Justice Douglas had this to say:

> Petitioners invoke the so-called instrumentality rule,—under which, they say, Deep Rock is to be regarded as a department or agent of Standard,—to preclude the allowance of Standard's claim in any amount. The rule was much discussed in the opinion below. It is not, properly speaking, a rule, but a convenient way of designating the application in particular circumstances of the broader equitable principle that the doctrine of corporate entity, recognized generally and for most purposes, will not be regarded when so to do would work fraud or injustice. This principle has been applied in appropriate circumstances to give minority stockholders redress against wrongful injury to their interests by a majority stockholder. It must be apparent that the preferred stockholders of Deep Rock assert such injury by Standard as the basis of their attack on the decree below. We need not stop to discuss the remedy which would be available to them if §77B of the Bankruptcy Act had not been adopted for we think that, by that section, the court, in approving a plan, was authorized and required, as a court of equity, to recognize the rights and the status of the preferred stockholders arising out of Standard's wrongful and injurious conduct in the mismanagement of Deep Rock's affairs.
>
> The section contains a provision new in bankruptcy legislation with respect to the standing of stockholders in corporate reorganization. Subsection (b) provides: "A plan of reorganization ... (2) may include provisions modifying or altering the rights of stockholders generally, or of any class of them, either through the issuance of new securities of any character or otherwise; ..." In the present case there remains an equity after satisfaction of the creditors in which only the preferred stockholders and Standard can have an interest. Equity requires the award to preferred stockholders of a superior position in the reorganized company. The District Judge, we think, properly exercised his discretion in refusing to approve the first offer of compromise and concomitant plan because it partly subordinated preferred stockholders to Standard. The same considerations which moved him to reject that plan required the rejection of the new offer and the amended plan.
>
> Deep Rock finds itself bankrupt not only because of the enormous sums it owes Standard but because of the abuses in management due to the paramount interest of interlocking officers and directors in the preservation of Standard's position, as at once proprietor and creditor of Deep Rock. It is impossible to recast Deep Rock's history and experience so as even to approximate what would be its financial condition at this day had it been adequately capitalized and independently managed and had its fiscal affairs been conducted with an eye single to its own interests. In order to remain in undisturbed possession and to prevent the preferred stockholders having a vote and a voice in the management, Standard has caused Deep Rock to pay preferred dividends in large amounts. Whatever may be the fact as to the legality of such dividends judged by the balance sheets and earnings statements of Deep Rock, it is evident that they would not have been paid over a long course of years by a company on the precipice of bankruptcy and in dire need of cash working capital. This is only one of the aspects in which Standard's management and control has operated to the detriment of Deep Rock's

financial condition and ability to function. Others are apparent from what has been said and from a study of the record.

If a reorganization is effected the amount at which Standard's claim is allowed is not important if it is to be represented by stock in the new company, provided the stock to be awarded it is subordinated to that awarded preferred stockholders. No plan ought to be approved which does not accord the preferred stockholders a right of participation in the equity in the Company's assets prior to that of Standard, and at least equal voice with Standard in the management. Anything less would be to remand them to precisely the status which has inflicted serious detriment on them in the past.

Problem — Reorganizing the Troubled Debtor

Master Builder, Inc. (the "Company"), is a publicly held commercial contracting company with operations throughout the eastern United States. Over the years it has come to specialize in the construction of department stores and shopping malls. Its typical practice is to engage in "turnkey" operations, in connection with which it contracts with a purchaser to build and outfit a facility, after which it sells the completed facility in operational condition to the buyer. Although purchasers are required to deposit 10 percent of the purchase price at the time of contracting, no other funds are due the Company until title passes at closing. The consequence of this method of operation is that the Company must carry the cost of construction until completion of the project. Although it relies as much as possible on financing these operations from retained earnings, it generally is required to take on substantial construction loans. Eight years ago ("year 1"), however, during a boom in commercial real estate construction and a rapidly increasing market, it issued $150,000,000 of 10 percent subordinated debentures due in year 20 to the public, with Trusty Bank & Trust Co. as Indenture Trustee (the "Trustee"). The Company's normal time to complete a project from the time of contracting to closing is two years.

At March 31, year 5, the Company's balance sheet was as follows:

Assets (in 000s)	
Cash	$ 10,000
Accounts receivable[1]	50,000
Inventory[2]	160,000
Land, building, and equipment	30,000
(net of accumulated depreciation)	
Total Assets	$250,000
Liabilities (in 000s)	
Accounts payable	$ 20,000
10% Debentures	150,000
Mortgage Debt	30,000
Total Liabilities	$200,000
Equity (in 000s)	
Common stock (5,000,000 shares at $.01 par)	50
Retained earnings	49,950
Total Equity	$ 50,000
Total Liabilities and Equity	$250,000

Notes:
1. Includes land and buildings under contract at current state of completion.
2. Used in Company's operations.

The Company's net after-tax income for the year ended March 31, year 5 was $18,000,000 on sales of $220,000,000.

———————

In the late spring of year 5, the Company contracted to build five new shopping malls in Arlington, Mass., White Plains, N.Y., Trenton, N.J., Easton, Pa., and Nashua, N.H. The total contract price for these projects was $300,000,000, of which $240,000,000 represented anticipated construction costs (including interest on debt). The board of directors was concerned about projections of rising interest rates, but nevertheless was convinced that the prospects for the Company's future were strong, and so committed $8,000,000 of the Company's cash as initial equity (in addition to the $30,000,000 paid by the buyers at the time of contracting). The Company borrowed the remaining $202,000,000 at a rate of 12 percent from a consortium of banks (the "Syndicate") led by Easy Money Bank & Trust Co., secured by the projects themselves, with disbursements to be made as needed over the period of construction. Although Easy Money was concerned about the weakness of the Company's balance sheet, it agreed with the Company's assessment of its prospects. In addition, Goniff, the chairman of Easy Money's lending committee (and the bank's principal advocate for the loans), is the father-in-law of Ibsen, the Company's president.

The Company and the banks were wrong. A recession in year 7 led to a strong downturn in consumer spending affecting retail sales nationwide. The Company's net earnings declined to $12,000,000 in year 6 and $5,000,000 in year 7. The buyers defaulted on each of the Company's five contracts during the fall of year 7, leaving the Company with partially completed construction appraised at a total of $100,000,000, with no potential buyers. Interest expense continued to mount and the Company's losses for the year ended March 31, year 8 were $1,500,000. At this point, the Company ceased to be able to pay interest on any of its indebtedness, and its balance sheet was as follows:

Assets (in 000s)	
Cash	$ 2,000
Accounts receivable[1]	90,000
Inventory	200,000
Land, building, and equipment	40,000
(net of accumulated depreciation)	
Total Assets	$332,000
Liabilities (in 000s)	
Accounts payable	$ 62,000
10% Debentures	150,000
Mortgage Debt	20,000
12% Syndicate Loan	202,000
Total Liabilities	$434,000
Equity (in 000s)	
Common stock (5,000,000 shares at $.01 par)	50
Retained earnings	(102,050)
Total Equity	($102,000)
Total Liabilities and Equity	$332,000

Note 1. The Corporation expects that a high percentage of these receivables will be uncollectible because of the buyers' defaults on the five contracts.

———————

Although the Company's present looks bleak, its future prospects are good. Economists are virtually unanimous in predicting an early end to the recession. There also appears to be a new burst of consumer confidence. The Company's board of directors is convinced that if it can only remain afloat for a year or two, it will be able to dispose of its inventory of projects at a profit and resume interest payments on its debt in an expanding economy.

Ibsen has called a meeting of the Trustee, the Syndicate, and representatives of the Company's major trade creditors. His goal is to reach an agreement on dealing with the Company's problems. At the beginning of the meeting he points out the fact that the Company's liquidation value is insufficient to satisfy its creditors, and would like to come to an arrangement that permits the Company to ride out the balance of the recession and have a chance to restore its profitability. He suggests that all of the Company's creditors agree to accept common stock in lieu of their debt.

A. Assume you are the following:

      (i) counsel to the Company;

      (ii) counsel to the Trustee;

      (iii) counsel to the Syndicate;

      (iv) counsel to the Company's largest trade creditor.

How do you react to the Company's proposal? In evaluating the proposal consider (a) how you would value the Company (and its new common stock) and (b) whether filing a bankruptcy petition for reorganization might be more desirable than the Company's proposal. In so doing, try to develop a plan that is "fair and equitable." In addition, be sure to evaluate your client's priority in bankruptcy and the likelihood that your client's interest will be "impaired."

B. Ibsen owns approximately 1 percent of the Company's common stock. The Syndicate has taken the position that his talents and services are essential to the Company's ultimate success, and would like to ensure his participation in the plan. How may Ibsen participate in a manner that will pass muster in bankruptcy court?

(iv) Fraudulent Conveyance

A fraudulent conveyance occurs when a debtor conveys or transfers funds or assets for the purpose of defrauding its creditors. The third party that receives the funds or assets from the debtor typically provides little or no consideration in return. Both the Bankruptcy Code and state law invalidate these conveyances or transfers.

Section 548(a) of the Bankruptcy Code covers fraudulent conveyances that are either intentionally fraudulent or constructively fraudulent. Actual fraudulent intent is usually established through evidence that demonstrates a close relationship between the transferor and the transferee. When determining whether a transfer was constructively fraudulent, courts examine the adequacy of consideration for the transfer and the financial position of the debtor. A rebuttable presumption arises that a transfer is constructively fraudulent if certain indicia are found to exist. A bankruptcy trustee or the debtor itself (operating as the debtor-in-possession or DIP) has the power under the Bankruptcy Code to recover for the benefit of the debtor's creditors any property fraudulently conveyed to third parties.

Section 544(b) of the Bankruptcy Code permits a bankruptcy trustee or DIP to attack a pre-bankruptcy transfer as fraudulent under state law. In pertinent part, Section 544(b) allows a trustee or DIP to void any transfer of the debtor's property or any obligation incurred by the debtor that is voidable under applicable state law by a creditor holding an unsecured claim. A trustee or DIP who makes a successful claim through Section 544(b) can pursue remedies under applicable state law or the Bankruptcy Code.

State fraudulent transfer laws are modeled after either the Uniform Fraudulent Conveyance Act (1918) (UFCA) or the newer Uniform Fraudulent Transfer Act (1984) (UFTA).

Section 5(a) of UFTA is broad in scope and applies to all transfers of any property by any debtor for any purpose, provided there is either intent on the part of the debtor to defraud a creditor or the debtor receives less than reasonable value for the property. UFTA provides both an actual intent test and a constructive intent test. Section 4(a)(1) of UFTA finds "actual intent" if there is intent to hinder, delay or defraud creditors. Section 4(a)(2) of UFTA finds constructive intent when the seller does not receive reasonably equivalent value for the transferred assets and the seller's remaining assets are unreasonably small in relation to its business. Courts look to the balance sheet of a debtor corporation when determining whether a given transfer was intended to leave the corporation insolvent.

The standards for determining whether a transfer is constructively fraudulent are different under the Bankruptcy Code and UFTA. Therefore, if the debtor is in bankruptcy, consideration must be given to which law is best suited to invalidate a particular transfer. Sections 4 and 5 of the UFTA are set forth below.

Uniform Fraudulent Transfer Act (1984)
Selected Provisions

§ 4. Transfers Fraudulent as to Present and Future Creditors.

(a) A transfer made or obligation incurred by a debtor is fraudulent as to a creditor, whether the creditor's claim arose before or after the transfer was made or the obligation was incurred, if the debtor made the transfer or incurred the obligation:

(1) with actual intent to hinder, delay, or defraud any creditor of the debtor; or

(2) without receiving a reasonably equivalent value in exchange for the transfer or obligation, and the debtor:

(i) was engaged or was about to engage in a business or a transaction for which the remaining assets of the debtor were unreasonably small in relation to the business or transaction; or

(ii) intended to incur, or believed or reasonably should have believed that he [or she] would incur, debts beyond his [or her] ability to pay as they became due.

(b) In determining actual intent under subsection (a)(1), consideration may be given, among other factors, to whether:

(1) the transfer or obligation was to an insider;

(2) the debtor retained possession or control of the property transferred after the transfer;

(3) the transfer or obligation was disclosed or concealed;

(4) before the transfer was made or obligation was incurred, the debtor had been sued or threatened with suit;

(5) the transfer was of substantially all the debtor's assets;

(6) the debtor absconded;

(7) the debtor removed or concealed assets;

(8) the value of the consideration received by the debtor was reasonably equivalent to the value of the asset transferred or the amount of the obligation incurred;

(9) the debtor was insolvent or became insolvent shortly after the transfer was made or the obligation was incurred;

(10) the transfer occurred shortly before or shortly after a substantial debt was incurred; and

(11) the debtor transferred the essential assets of the business to a lienor who transferred the assets to an insider of the debtor.

* * *

§5. Transfers Fraudulent as to Present Creditors.

(a) A transfer made or obligation incurred by a debtor is fraudulent as to a creditor whose claim arose before the transfer was made or the obligation was incurred if the debtor made the transfer or incurred the obligation without receiving a reasonably equivalent value in exchange for the transfer or obligation and the debtor was insolvent at that time or the debtor became insolvent as a result of the transfer or obligation.

(b) A transfer made by a debtor is fraudulent as to a creditor whose claim arose before the transfer was made if the transfer was made to an insider for an antecedent debt, the debtor was insolvent at that time, and the insider had reasonable cause to believe that the debtor was insolvent.

———————————

Section 7
Legislative Responses to the Plight of Debtholders

We are now ready to reevaluate the traditional legal approach to bondholders' rights with which we began this chapter. The materials that follow present several possible approaches. Consider whether these are better, worse, or, ultimately, really any different from the traditional approaches, and further consider whether there are any alternate ways of dealing with bondholders' rights that might be more satisfactory.

Problem — Bondholder Protective Legislation

Consider the following proposed but never adopted legislation which was introduced in the New York State Senate during its 1989-1990 session and referred to its judiciary committee:

§5-1321. Repurchase of bonds under certain circumstances. Unless otherwise expressly provided by contract, no issuer of indebtedness of borrowed money maturing more than two years from the date of issuance and governed by or subject to the law of this state, or any affiliate thereof, shall directly or indirectly enter into or agree to enter into or suffer to occur any transaction or transactions with respect to the acquisition by any person or group of related persons (other than such issuer) of more than fifty per centum of the voting stock, or all or substantially all of the assets of such issuer if the market value of such indebtedness on the thirtieth day after the public announcement of such transaction or transactions or any proposed similar transaction has been reduced by more than ten per centum from the market value of such indebtedness on the day prior to such public announcement solely on account of such transaction or transactions unless the issuer, prior to consummation of any such transaction or transactions, either offers to repurchase such indebtedness at a price equal to the average market value of such indebtedness for the ten business days prior to the date of the public announcement of such transaction or transactions or any proposed similar transaction plus accrued and unpaid interest or makes other adequate provision to compensate the holders of such indebtedness for such reduction. In the absence of market value, "market value" for the purposes of this section shall mean fair value....

Does it resolve the problems of bondholders' rights? What problems of its own does it raise? Are there better solutions (including, of course, the possibility that the current state of affairs is satisfactory)?

In 1989, the state of Wyoming enacted a bondholder protection act that remains in force today. It reads, in relevant part, as follows:

17-18-201 PROTECTION PROVISIONS; APPLICABILITY; DEFINED.—
(a) A qualified corporation may, if its articles of incorporation authorize it to utilize the bondholder protection provisions of this act, utilize any of the provisions set forth in subsection (b) of this section. These protections shall apply only to bonds, debentures or other debt instruments whose original aggregate value at maturity is equal to or greater than five million dollars ($5,000,000.00) and whose original term is two (2) years or greater. Any number of bondholder protection provisions may be in effect at any time.

(b) A qualified corporation may provide bondholder protection by requiring any or all of the following:

(i) Bondholder approval of the replacement of more than twenty-four percent (24%) of the directors in any twelve (12) month period.... If more than twenty-four percent (24%) of the directors are to be replaced, the approval of holders of a majority of the bonds shall be obtained in writing at the meeting where the directors are to be replaced or no more than thirty (30) days prior to the meeting. The consent of the bondholders shall be obtained to exceeding the twenty-four percent (24%) limit rather than to the individual directors to be replaced....

(ii) Bondholder consent to any merger or acquisition which the corporation may be subject to or which the corporation may make, subject to the following:

(A) The notice of bondholder protection shall specify the size of merger or acquisition at or above which the bondholder consent is required. The size may vary depending on whether the company is the acquiring party or is being acquired. In a merger the relative memberships on the board of directors of the surviving corporation may be used to determine whether or not bondholder consent is required;

(B) The term acquisition shall be deemed to include the purchase of more than a specified percentage of the shares entitled to vote for directors by a person or combination of persons under common ownership or control or acting in concert. If a person or combination of persons acquires more than the specified percentage of shares, they shall be entitled to vote only the specified percentage until bondholder consent is acquired. The specified percentage shall be set in the notice of bondholder protection and shall not be less than ten percent (10%);

(C) The bondholder consent shall be to a specific merger or acquisition rather than the general concept of mergers and acquisitions.

(iii) Bondholder consent to the sale or disposal of certain assets, or assets exceeding a certain percentage of the corporation's total assets, or assets exceeding a set total value or any combination of these factors. The specifics of what requires bondholder consent shall be set forth in the notice of bondholder protection. Disposal of assets shall be construed to include the disposition of the assets to the shareholders either directly or through distribution of shares in a new or subsidiary corporation;

(iv) Bondholder consent to the acquisition of debt above a specified percentage of total assets, a specified percentage of the net worth of the corporation, a specific amount, or any combination of these factors. The consent may be required generally or may be required only if the debt is to be used to pay for a merger or acquisition or a distribution to shareholders. The notice of bondholder protection shall specify the conditions under which bondholder consent is required.

* * *

17-18-206 ADDITIONAL BONDHOLDER PROTECTION PROVISIONS ALLOWED.—Any other bondholder protection provisions may be provided in the notice of bondholder protection, and shall be valid unless inconsistent with the [foregoing] provisions ... or other law.

1. You are counsel to the Governor of the State of Grace. The Governor is considering proposing to the state legislature that Grace adopt a bondholder protection act identical to Wyoming's. She asks for your advice. Please write a memo to the Governor evaluating this proposal. In writing your memo, please address separately (i) the need for any bondholder protective legislation, and (ii) assuming the need for such protection, the wisdom of adopting the Wyoming statute. In drafting your memo, please be sure to evaluate these issues in light of financial theory, case law, and legal theory. You should assume that the courts of the State of Grace generally limit bondholders' rights to the terms of their contracts, which the courts strictly construe. Reconsider Problem—Negotiating and Drafting Event Risk Prevention, *supra* section 4c.

2. You are general counsel to the National Association of Bondholders, a bondholders' organization that lobbies for bondholder protection. Please prepare a memorandum addressed to all Wyoming corporations to which the statute applies arguing in favor of their adopting bondholder protections pursuant to Section 17-18-206. Please describe in detail the protective measures you would suggest, and explain why the corporations should adopt them. Remember, you must be reasonable in your requests in order to ensure that these measures are adopted. You should assume that the courts of the state of Wyoming generally limit bondholders' rights to the terms of their contracts, which the courts strictly construe.

The issue of bondholders' rights implicitly raises the question of whether corporate law rights should extend to other corporate constituents such as employees, trade creditors, suppliers, customers, and the community in general. Consider Section 717(b) of the New York Business Corporation Law:

(b) In taking action, including, without limitation, action which may involve or relate to a change or potential change in the control of the corporation, a director shall be entitled to consider, without limitation, (1) both the long-term and the short-term interests of the corporation and its shareholders and (2) the effects that the corporation's actions may have in the short-term or in the long-term upon any of the following:

(i) the prospects for potential growth, development, productivity and profitability of the corporation;

(ii) the corporation's current employees;

(iii) the corporation's retired employees and other beneficiaries receiving or entitled to receive retirement, welfare or similar benefits from or pursuant to any plan sponsored, or agreement entered into, by the corporation;

(iv) the corporation's customers and creditors; and

(v) the ability of the corporation to provide, as a going concern, goods, services, employment opportunities and employment benefits and otherwise to contribute to the communities in which it does business.

Nothing in this paragraph shall create any duties owed by any director to any person or entity to consider or afford any particular weight to any of the foregoing or abrogate any duty of the directors, either statutory or recognized by common law or court decisions.

For purposes of this paragraph, "control" shall mean the possession, directly or indirectly, of the power to direct or cause the direction of the management and policies of the corporation, whether through the ownership of voting stock, by contract, or otherwise.

What do you think of this statute? Is the idea of constituent protection a good one? If so, does this statute adequately provide such protection? What additional problems, if any, does it create?

Constituency statutes now have been adopted in the following thirty states: Ariz. Rev. Stat. Ann. §10-2702 (2004); Conn. Gen. Stat. §33-756 (2004); Fla. Stat. §607.0830 (2005); Ga. Code Ann. §14-2-202(b)(5) (2004); Haw. Rev. Stat. §414-221 (2004); 805 Ill. Comp. Stat. 180/15-15 (2005); Idaho Code §30-1602 (Michie 2005); Ind. Code §23-1-35-1 (Michie 2004); Iowa Code Ann. §491.101B (West 2004); Ky. Rev. Stat. Ann. §271B.12-210 (Michie 2004); La. Rev. Stat. Ann. §12:92 (West 2005); Mass. Gen. L. ch. 156-D §8.30 (West 2005); Me. Rev. State. Ann. tit. 13-C §831 (2005); Minn. Stat. §302A.251 (2004); Miss. Code Ann. §79-4-8.30 (2005); Mo. Rev. Stat. §351.347 (2005); N.J. Rev. Stat. §14-A:6-1 (West 2005); N.M. Stat. Ann. §53-11-35 (Michie 2005); N.Y. Bus. Corp. Law §717 (Consol. 2005); N.D. Cent. Code, §10-19.1-50 (2005); Nev. Rev. Stat. §78.138 (Michie 2004); Ohio Rev. Code Ann. §1702.30 (Anderson 2005); Or. Rev. Stat. §60.357 (2003); 15 Pa. Cons. Stat. §§1715, 1716 (2004); R.I. Gen. Laws §7-5.2-8 (2005); Tenn. Code Ann. §48-103-204 (2004); Wash. Rev. Code Ann. §23B.19.010 (West 2005); Wis. Stat. §180.0827 (2004); Vt. Stat. Ann. Tit. 11A. §8.30 (2004); and Wyo. Stat. Ann. §17-16-830 (Michie 2005).

There is some variation among these statutes. For example, Connecticut, Iowa, Louisiana, Missouri, Oregon, Tennessee, and Rhode Island limit constituency consideration to control transactions. Georgia does not have a constituency statute *per se*, but permits corporations to include constituency promises in their charters. Arizona articulates constituency concerns in light of the long-term and short-term interests of the corporation and its shareholders. Finally, Washington expresses its concern with constituency protection in the preamble to its takeover statute.

For additional views on constituency statutes and constituency protection generally, see McDonnell, Corporate Governance and the Sarbanes-Oxley Act: Corporate Constituency Statutes and Employee Governance, 30 Wm. Mitchell L. Rev. 1227 (2004); Subramanian, The Influence of Antitakeover Statutes on Incorporation Choice: Evidence on the "Race" Debate and Antitakeover Overreaching, 150 U. Pa. L. Rev. 1795 (2002); Braendel, Defeating Poison Pills through Enactment of a State Shareholder Protection Statute, 25 Del. J. Corp. L. 651 (2000); Springer, Corporate Law Corporate Constituency Statutes: Hollow Hopes and False Fears, 1999 Ann. Surv. Am. L. 85; Van Der Weide, Against Fiduciary Duties to Corporate Stakeholders, 21 Del. J. Corp. L. 27 (1996).

Section 8
Advanced Debt Topics

a. Application of Fraudulent Conveyance Statutes to Leveraged Acquisitions

You have been introduced to the concept of fraudulent conveyances in section 6e(iv). Here we address an issue which has mushroomed since the 1980s: the applicability of fraudulent conveyance statutes to leveraged buy-outs. As you read the following problem and materials, consider how these statutes might apply to leveraged buy-outs, and whether such application is appropriate.

Problem — The LBO That Failed

In 1904 Morris, an immigrant from Eastern Europe who had lived in New York for ten years, had an idea. Prices of clothing and household goods had increased substantially and many of the people he knew had trouble making ends meet. One day, while walking in an alley behind a clothing factory, Morris saw several workmen discarding large piles of clothing in the trash. He stopped to ask them what they were doing, and was told that the clothes were no good because some of them were out of fashion, and others had come out the wrong color. To Morris, however, they looked perfectly serviceable. He asked the men to direct him to the factory manager, which they did. Morris asked the manager whether he could buy the piles of discarded clothing, and at what price. The surprised manager thought for a few moments and agreed to sell Morris all of the clothing at 15 percent of cost.

Morris then rented a pushcart from a friend, put the clothes on it, and went into the streets. Within two days he had sold the clothing at a markup of 100 percent, and went back to the factory for more.

Morris' business grew. By 1905 he was able to open a small store, and had contracted with a number of clothing and household goods manufacturers to purchase their excess, outdated, and imperfect items (called "seconds") at a fraction of their cost. By 1906, Morris was ready to open a second store, and it was at that time that he incorporated Mo's Bargain Dry Goods (the "Company"), in the State of Panic.

The business prospered. In 1945, the Company went public under the presidency of Morris' son, Harvey. By 1965, when the family sold its holdings in the Company, it owned over five hundred stores in the Northeast, and had changed its name to Discounters, Inc. By 1981, the Company had 11,000,000 shares of common stock outstanding which were traded on the New York Stock Exchange. It also had outstanding an issue of preferred stock par value $25 per share, and $100,000,000 in principal amount of 8 percent subordinated debentures due 2009 (the "Debentures"), which had been publicly issued in 1979.

Ten years ago, the Company's business had begun to weaken somewhat. The idea of discounting had caught on with the general public, and the Company was faced with a great deal of competition. In addition, inexpensive foreign products diminished the desirability of off-price goods. In that year, United Department Stores, Inc. ("United"), acquired 35 percent of the Company's common stock on the open market, and from that time controlled its board.

United was no more successful with the Company than its previous management had been. In January, seven years ago, the Company was insolvent (in the equitable sense) and its stock was trading at $5. Its per share book value was $7, but its per share net asset value was $14 according to a recent appraisal, largely because of the value of the Company's unencumbered real estate holdings. On February 1 of that same year, DI Acquisition, Inc. ("DIA"), a wholly owned subsidiary of Fashion Stores, Inc. ("FSI"), a holding company owning a number of major department store chains, approached United and the Company's board about making a friendly acquisition of the Company. United and the Company's board (by a unanimous vote) agreed that DIA would make a tender offer for all of the Company's issued and outstanding shares at $12 per share, and United agreed to tender its shares into the offer. Any untendered shares would be merged out following the tender offer for the same cash consideration.

The parties further agreed to a plan of financing. DIA needed $132,000,000 to acquire all of the Company's shares. Because the Company's assets were unencumbered, it was agreed that DIA would borrow the money from Riskophile Bank & Trust Co. (the "Bank"), and would secure the loan with all of the Company's assets, including real estate and accounts receivable. Under the terms of the loan, the Bank was required to approve all dividends, significant sales of assets, significant capital expenditures, and significant alterations in the Company's business policy. In addition, the Bank was given one seat on the Company's board of directors (which consisted of nine directors, four of whom were Company employees).

The transaction was consummated, as a result of which each of the Company's stockholders received $12 per share (giving United a total of $46,200,000). All information that was required to be disclosed by the parties under state or federal law was disclosed. Unfortunately for FSI, it was no better a manager than United had been. Two years ago, the Company filed for reorganization under Chapter 11 of the Bankruptcy Code.

At the time of this filing, all of the Debentures remained outstanding, as did all of the Bank's acquisition debt. In addition, the Company's principal labor union filed a claim for $8,000,000 in unpaid wages, and trade creditors filed claims totaling $20,000,000.

1. The trustee in bankruptcy brought claims against the Company's directors, the Company's public stockholders, United, FSI, and the Bank, alleging (i) that the leveraged tender offer resulted in a fraudulent conveyance to United and the Company's public stockholders, (ii) that the Company's directors breached their fiduciary duty to the Company and its unsecured creditors, (iii) that United, as controlling stockholder, breached its fiduciary duty to the Company's unsecured creditors, and (iv) that the Bank's debt should be equitably subordinated to the claims of the unsecured creditors. You are counsel for the trustee. What arguments would you make in support of these claims? As counsel for the respective defendants, how would you refute each of these arguments?

2. A class of the Debenture holders has brought an action against the Company and its directors alleging breach of an implied covenant of good faith and breach of fiduciary duty to the Debenture holders. You are counsel for the class. What arguments would you make in support of these claims? As counsel for the Company and its directors, how would you refute each of these arguments?

3. You are the bankruptcy judge for the Northern District of Panic. How do you resolve all of these claims, and why?

Pay 'N Pak Stores, Inc. v. Court Square Capital Ltd.
141 F.3d 1178, 1998 WL 133560 (9th Cir. 1998)
(unpublished memorandum opinion)

Before WRIGHT, REAVLEY and KLEINFELD, Circuit Judges:

Citicorp, through separate entities named as defendants, purchased Pay 'N Pak in a leveraged buyout. Four and a half years later, Pay 'N Pak went bankrupt. After a few months in Chapter 11 status, it was liquidated. Unsecured creditors sued the Citicorp entities and others for their losses.

The basic theory of the lawsuit was that the leveraged buyout sucked so much capital out of the business that the business was bound to collapse, leaving the creditors holding the bag. Because the company became insolvent after it paid for its own acquisition, the directors' fiduciary duty ran to the creditors rather than the shareholders, and that duty was breached. The payments to the acquiring shareholders and their lenders were, according to plaintiffs, fraudulent conveyances. The way that the capital got sucked out was that after acquiring Pay 'N Pak, Citicorp used the Pay 'N Pak treasury, as is typical in a leveraged buyout, to pay back the money Citicorp had borrowed to buy the Pay 'N Pak stock. Citicorp had created holding companies that borrowed money, bought the outstanding shares, caused Pay 'N Pak to issue bonds after it was acquired, and caused Pay 'N Pak to use the bond proceeds to pay off the loans. Thus at the end of it all, Pay 'N Pak was out about $262 million for payments to the previous shareholders and to Citicorp for its expenses in buying the stock. In effect, Pay 'N Pak paid for its own acquisition, thereby looting its own treasury so that it could not weather bad times.

Citicorp's theory was that the buyout benefitted [sic] Pay 'N Pak, because Citicorp saved Pay 'N Pak from an unethical raider who was otherwise going to do the same thing, but would loot the treasury instead of carrying on the business. Citicorp preserved high quality management and carried on the business successfully for several years, which was well beyond how long it would have lasted had the leveraged buyout rendered the company insolvent as plaintiff claimed. The leveraged buyout did not make the company insolvent. The reason the company went bankrupt was that its business depended on residential construction, and an unanticipated severe decline in the home building industry in the areas served by Pay 'N Pak stores, as well as intense competition from new entrants to the home improvement market (Eagle, Home Depot, etc.). Some of the creditors represented by plaintiff were large, sophisticated, trade creditors who continued to sell goods to Pay 'N Pak after the leveraged buyout and even after the bankruptcy. Some were buyers of the high interest, high risk bonds used to accomplish the leveraged buyout. Far from being victims, these creditors knew exactly what risks they were taking, for what purpose.

The case went to a jury trial, and the jury returned a verdict for Citicorp. In this appeal, the unsecured creditors' committee asks us to vacate the judgment. We decline to do so....

The creditors had to prove, under the district court's instruction, that "Pay 'N Pak did not receive something of fairly equivalent value in exchange for the transfer." The transfer referred to is the money used to pay off Citicorp's loans and expenses. The court instructed that the jury should consider not only money and property received, "but also all of the surrounding circumstances, including any non-monetary benefits received by Pay 'N Pak as a result of the transaction." The creditors argue that the district court should have instructed that as a matter of law, Pay 'N Pak did not receive fair consideration, instead of leaving the question to the jury. The creditors point out that Pay 'N Pak shoveled out a quarter of a billion dollars, and did not get a nickel's worth of property or money back. Citicorp got the company for next to nothing.

Citicorp argues that the jury would not have even reached this issue if it decided that Pay 'N Pak was solvent and sufficiently capitalized after the takeover, and only collapsed some years later because of a change in the business climate. It is entirely plausible that the jury agreed with that argument, because Pay 'N Pak did not collapse for several years after the money was paid out.

Though it seems probable from the evidence that the jury accepted that argument, the verdict does not establish it. The instructions allowed for the possibility that the jury found for Citicorp even though it decided Pay 'N Pak was insolvent when the leveraged buyout was completed, because it concluded that the consideration was fair. Citicorp's fair consideration theory was basically that Pay 'N Pak got for its money a better owner, preserved its management, and continued as a functioning business, instead of being broken up into pieces. The creditors conceded, at trial and in their briefs on appeal, that "non-monetary benefits may constitute fair consideration," including "an intangible type benefit, such as keeping management in." We therefore have no occasion to decide whether, as a general proposition, a leveraged buyout that quickly leads to bankruptcy subjects those who engineer the takeover liable to creditors. The case turns only on whether the evidence sufficed to establish a jury question.

Much of Citicorp's evidence was an attack on Paul Bilzerian. Pay 'N Pak used Citicorp as a "white knight" to avert a Bilzerian takeover. Citicorp put on evidence that Bilzerian was a "raider," and that "raiders came in and ripped up a company, laid a lot of people off, stopped your expansion and didn't really care about the people." The jury might plausibly have rejected Citicorp's defense, and concluded that Citicorp was no better than Bilzerian would have been. After all, the employees were left jobless and the creditors unpaid despite the "white knight" takeover—what was supposed to happen if the bogeyman of the case, Bilzerian, took over, did happen after Citicorp took over, perhaps a little later. Perhaps Pay 'N Pak would have weathered the storm of the subsequent cyclic industry decline had its treasury not been drained to pay for Citicorp's leveraged buyout.

But Citicorp presented evidence that, after the leveraged buyout, Pay 'N Pak was solvent, kept the same management, employees, expansion and sales programs that it had in place before the buyout, and that it started down the steep hill to failure about three years later only because of increased competition and a recession in the home building industry. The evidence allowed for the conclusion that the company would have fallen apart immediately had Bilzerian bought it, and would have survived and thrived after Citicorp's buyout, but for an unforeseen recession and increase in competition. Powerful evidence supporting Citicorp's theory was that trade creditors were paid in full for the first three years after the buyout. Because a reasonable jury could go either way on the question of "consideration of fairly equivalent value," the district court did not err in giving the instruction and leaving resolution to the jury....

————————

ProtoComm Corp. v. Novell, Inc.
171 F. Supp. 2d 459 (E.D. Pa. 2001)

REED, Senior District Judge:

In or around January, 1993, Novell began investigating the possibility of investing in Fluent. In February, 1993, Novell appeared "positive" toward making such an investment. This investment would go into Fluent's treasury. [A third party, ProtoComm, had meanwhile sued Fluent for breach of contract, which led Novell to suspend negotiations "until the suit was settled."]

On March 19, 1993, David Bradford, Novell's Senior Vice President and General Counsel, sent a draft letter of intent to Cornelius Ferris, Fluent's President; the letter contemplated that the acquisition would take the form of an asset purchase. On April 28, 1993, Bradford sent a letter of intent to Ferris; the letter contemplated that the acquisition would take the form of a stock sale in which Fluent would become a wholly owned subsidiary of Novell. The letter of intent required as a condition precedent to the acquisition that "the lawsuit with ProtoComm be provided for to Novell's satisfaction."

Where the April 28, 1993 letter of intent had included the language that Novell would acquire "all of the business, assets, and obligations of Fluent," the actual agreement, dated June 4, 1993, excluded such language. The agreement did retain language providing that the ProtoComm litigation "shall have been resolved to the satisfaction of Fluent and Novell." The proxy statement furnished to Fluent's stockholders in connection with the solicitation of proxies by Fluent's Board approving the agreement, introduces the acquisition as a "merger" constituting "a liquidation of the Company under the Charter." On July 2, 1993, Paul Desjourdy, Fluent's attorney, sent a letter to Betty Depaola at Novell, detailing the disbursement of payments as a result of the acquisition. The payment included, inter alia, employee bonus payments and noteholder payments. Neither Bradford nor Cameron Read, Fluent's counsel for the transaction, could recall at their depositions why the acquisition evolved into a cash-for-stock transaction.

The ProtoComm I lawsuit was discussed during at least three Board meetings. The files of Read contained the complaint and the underlying agreement, as well as other ProtoComm related documents. Ferris originally testified at his deposition that at the final hours before the deal, Bradford requested that the deal be redone to set aside money for the potential judgment in the ProtoComm I suit. Ferris pleaded with Bradford not to make this change, and Bradford acquiesced. Ferris later recanted this testimony. In June, 1993, Rob Hicks, an associate counsel at Novell, sent a fax to Dan Heist, President of ProtoComm, proposing a settlement in the ProtoComm I litigation. A second proposal was then made by Novell.

On July 7, 1993, the acquisition occurred. Novell paid $18.5 million and assumed $3 million in liabilities. The litigation had not ended at the time of the closing. On August 9, 1993, Ernst & Young sent Novell an asset valuation study of Fluent, in which the assets were valued at $21.55 million Eventually, Fluent's assets, including, inter alia, Fluent's intellectual property and technology patents, as well as Fluent employees, were transferred to Novell. It is unclear to this Court when the transfer began. It seems that at least some employees were transferred onto the Novell payroll soon after the closing. It appears the technology assets were transferred by May, 1994.

ProtoComm's claim is essentially as follows: Although defendants called Novell's acquisition of Fluent a stock purchase, in reality, it was an asset sale designed to leave Fluent an empty shell and ProtoComm holding an uncollectible judgement. Fluent's assets were conveyed to Novell, and the purchase price was paid out ... as a fraudulent conveyances [sic] ... to Fluent's shareholders. Fluent was then left with nothing but obligations to ProtoComm.

The Former Fluent Shareholders essentially contend the following: On July 7, 1993, Novell purchased all of the outstanding stock of Fluent from the Fluent shareholders. After the stock sale occurred, Fluent became a wholly owned subsidiary of Novell and the stock sale ownership of Fluent passed to Novell. It was only after Novell's sales of Fluent's products were deemed disappointing that steps were taken to consolidate Fluent with Novell and to transfer the assets....

The claim for fraudulent conveyances is brought under the Pennsylvania Uniform Fraudulent Conveyances Act ("PAUFCA"). The purpose of fraudulent transfer law is to prevent a debtor from transferring valuable assets for inadequate consideration if such transfer leaves the debtor with insufficient assets to pay honest creditors. The uniform statute was established upon the recognition that debtors often try to avoid payment of legitimate debts by concealing or transferring property. Conveyance is defined by statute as "every payment of money, assignment, release, transfer, lease, mortgage, or pledge of tangible or intangible property, and also the conveyance of any lien or incumbrance." 39 P.S. §351. Stocks are thus absent from this definition. A claim may be brought under this Act by a future creditor, *i.e.*, by a party which has not yet received a judgment on a legal claim at the time of the transfer in question.

In my prior opinion, I concluded, inter alia, that ProtoComm could establish a claim for fraudulent conveyances upon showing that the stock transaction between the Former Fluent Shareholders and Novell was only part of a complex transaction that transferred assets of Fluent to Novell, paid money to the shareholders and left Fluent insolvent. *ProtoComm III*, 55 F. Supp. 2d at 327-28. Analogizing to Leveraged Buyout ("LBO") cases, I concluded that upon such a showing, this Court would be convinced to treat the transactions among the Former Fluent Shareholders, Fluent and Novell as one integrated transaction for the purposes of ProtoComm's claim of fraudulent conveyances. *See id.* at 328.

In *U.S. v. Tabor Court Realty Corp.*, 803 F.2d 1288 (3d Cir. 1986), *cert. denied*, 483 U.S. 1005 (1987), the Court of Appeals for the Third Circuit applied PAUFCA to LBOs for the first time. As articulated by the Court, a typical LBO involves the following:

> A company is sold to a small number of investors, typically including members of the company's management, under financial arrangements in which there is a minimum amount of equity and a maximum amount of debt. The financing typically provides for a substantial return of investment capital by means of mortgages or high risk bonds, popularly known as "junk bonds."

Id. at 1292. *Tabor* involved an incredibly complex LBO in which the court "collapsed" separate transactions for the purposes of the claims brought under PAUFCA. In summary, the President of Raymond Group ("Raymond"), James Durkin ("Durkin"), received an option to buy Raymond from its shareholders for $8.5 million. See id. After failed attempts to secure financing, Durkin and investors incorporated a holding company, Great American, to which the option was assigned. To effectuate the buy-out, Great American, a seemingly empty company, received a loan commitment from Institutional Investors Trust ("ITT") for $8.5 million. The loan was structured to divide Raymond into borrowing companies and guarantor companies and was secured by mortgages on assets of both groups of companies.

The loan arrangement occurred in two stages. "The loan proceeds went from ITT to the borrowing Raymond Group companies, which immediately turned the funds over to Great American, which used the funds for the buy-out." Id. at 1302. The Court in *Tabor* upheld the district court finding that the ITT loan proceeds merely passed through the borrowers to Great American and in the end to the selling stockholders and could not be deemed consideration received by the borrowing companies. Other courts have applied fraudulent conveyance to the LBO context and collapsed the transactions for the purposes of fraudulent conveyance law. *See, e.g. In re Bay Plastics, Inc.*, 187 B.R. 315; *MFS/Sun Life Trust-High Yield Series v. Van Dusen Airport Serv. Co.*, 910 F. Supp. 913 (S.D.N.Y. 1995). In essence, courts look "past the form of a transaction to its substance" and evaluate the transactions on a whole to determine whether a fraudulent conveyance has occurred. *MFS/Sun Life Trust*, 910 F. Supp. at 933. Thus while each transaction in isolation may appear kosher, the full transaction is examined to determine whether fraudulent conveyance law has been violated.

Former Fluent Shareholders argue that no asset sale occurred and that ProtoComm is unable to show that the stock sale was but one occurrence in a series of interdependent steps. ProtoComm counters that genuine issues of material fact exist as to both issues. At the motion to dismiss stage, ProtoComm appeared to rely solely on the collapsing theory. In other words, plaintiff sought to establish that the stock sale and the asset transfer which followed should be viewed as one transaction. Plaintiff now brings forth evidence which it argues raises a genuine dispute as to whether the initial transaction actually constituted an asset transfer. ProtoComm essentially relies on the same evidence for these alternative theories which in reality do not differ significantly because the end result is the same: ProtoComm needs to show that an asset transfer, as opposed to a stock sale, took place.

ProtoComm's expert witness, Michael Pakter ("Pakter"), characterizes the acquisition as an asset sale. In addition to Pakter's expert opinion, ProtoComm points to the following evidence, *inter alia*, to demonstrate that genuine issues of material fact exist concerning what type of transition occurred. According to Novell's 10-K the acquisition cost $21.5 million. Instead of distributing cash on a *pro rata* basis to the Former Fluent

Shareholders, the cash was distributed at the direction of Fluent's Board and included monies for employee bonuses and reimbursements for bridge loans. The Ernst & Young Report, while admittedly conducted after the stock transaction occurred, valued the assets of Fluent at approximately the same price as the acquisition cost. ProtoComm also relies on the fact that early in the negotiations, an asset sale was considered and then the structure changed without explanation. In the backdrop of the transaction was the looming potential judgment from the ProtoComm I litigation. Thus, under Proto-Comm's theory defendants knew that if the deal was in the structure of an asset transfer, they would potentially be liable under fraudulent transfer law. I conclude based on the foregoing that ProtoComm has raised a genuine issue of material fact as to the predicate issue of whether the stock transfer was actually an asset sale. Plaintiff has established evidence under which a reasonable trier of fact could find either that the initial transaction in June, 1993, was actually an asset sale, or, alternatively, that the initial transaction was not complete until the assets were physically transferred.

I now turn to whether plaintiff raises genuine issues of material fact with respect to the specific provisions of PAUFCA. Four sections of the Act detail situations in which a conveyance will be deemed fraudulent. Sections 354 and 355 are the constructive intent provisions of the Act. Both provisions require that the conveyance occur without "fair consideration" which occurs "when property of a fair equivalent is transferred in good faith." *Buncher Co. v. Official Comm. of Unsecured Creditors of GenFarm Ltd. P'ship IV*, 229 F.3d 245, 251 (3d Cir. 2000). "Knowledge of insolvency is a rational interpretation of the statutory language of lack of 'good faith.'" *Tabor*, 803 F.2d at 1296. Section 354 provides that a conveyance is fraudulent where the debtor was left insolvent at the time of the transfer or becomes insolvent thereby. The statute encompasses insolvency both in the bankruptcy sense, i.e., a negative net worth and in the equity sense, i.e., inability to pay existing debt as they mature. Section 355 provides that a conveyance is fraudulent where the debtor was left with unreasonably small capital after the transfer which indicates "a financial condition short of equitable insolvency." *Moody v. Security Pacific Bus. Credit, Inc.*, 971 F.2d 1056, 1064 (3d Cir. 1992). The test is one of "reasonable foreseeability." The main inquiry under the constructive intent provision is "whether there is a link between the challenged conveyance and the debtor's insolvency." *Id.*

If insolvency or unreasonably small capital is established, the burden shifts to the transferees, the Former Fluent Shareholders, to show by clear and convincing evidence either that the transferor was then solvent, not rendered insolvent, not left with unreasonably small capitol or that the assets were transferred for fair consideration. Thus, the first question is whether ProtoComm has raised a genuine issue of material fact as to either Fluent's solvency at the time of the transfer or as a result of the transfer, as required under section 354, or as to whether the transfer left Fluent with unreasonably small capital, as required under section 355. These issues are in large part dependent on how the fact finder characterizes the acquisition. For example, the trier of fact could reasonably find that a legitimate stock-for-cash transaction took place which had no impact on Fluent's assets, or it could reasonably find that an asset sale occurred which was structured to deplete Fluent's treasury. Thus, I conclude that a genuine issue of material fact has been raised as to the required elements of sections 354 and 355.

Sections 356 and 357 are the actual intent provisions of the Act. Section 356 also requires that the conveyance be made without fair consideration; it provides that a conveyance is fraudulent where the debtor intends or believes that it was unable to pay future debts as they became due as a consequence of the transfer. Again, the issue raised by this provision turns in large part on how the fact finder sees the acquisition. For example, if it is found to be a exchange for stock and that Fluent's assets were transferred only after Fluent's products did not reach expectations, then the requisite intent and unfair consideration may be unfounded. If, however, an asset transfer is found, then the structure of the acquisition could reasonably be seen as a transfer made without proper consideration to Fluent's treasury and with the intent or belief that creditors could not be satisfied. Thus, I conclude that a genuine issue of material fact has been raised as to the required elements of section 356.

The final question under PAUFCA concerns section 357 which provides that a conveyance is fraudulent where the conveyance was made with the actual intent to hinder, delay or defraud present or future creditors. Such intent must be proven by clear and convincing evidence.

Thus this Court must ask whether ProtoComm has raised a genuine of material fact in showing by clear and convincing evidence that defendants intentionally structured the acquisition to defraud creditors. This question of fact, though ProtoComm will face a higher burden of proof, overlaps with the aforementioned provisions because under Pennsylvania law, intent may be inferred when transfers are made without fair consideration and where the parties to the transfer have knowledge of the claims of creditors and know that such creditors cannot be paid. [G]enuine disputes remain concerning these questions. Thus, I conclude that ProtoComm has met its burden in raising a triable issue.

I therefore conclude that defendants are not entitled to judgment on the PAUFCA claim as a matter of law....

Notes and Questions

1. The Pennsylvania statute at issue in *ProtoComm* (and also in U.S. v. Tabor Court Realty Corp. referred to therein) was repealed and replaced by 12 Pa.Cons.Stat. §5101 *et. seq.*

2. Given the uncertainty concerning whether fraudulent conveyance statutes should be applied to leveraged buyouts, how sturdy is the *ProtoComm* court's invocation of that theory to the Novell-Fluent transaction? What other theories could have been used?

3. Should fraudulent conveyance statutes be applied to leveraged buy-outs? If so, to which categories of participants in an LBO should they be applied? For cases questioning the applicability of fraudulent conveyance law to leveraged buy-outs, see Credit Managers Assoc. of So. Cal. v. The Federal Co., 629 F. Supp. 175 (C.D. Calif. 1985); In re Knox Kreations, 474 F. Supp. 567, 571 n.4 (E.D. Tenn. 1979), *modified*, 656 F.2d 230 (6th Cir. 1981). For cases applying fraudulent conveyance law to leveraged buy-outs, see Wieboldt Stores, Inc. v. Schottenstein, 94 B.R. 488 (N.D. Ill. 1988); U.S. v. Tabor Court Realty Corp., 803 F.2d 1288 (3d Cir. 1986), *cert. denied*, 483 U.S. 1005 (1987); Roxbury State Bank v. The Clarendon, 129 N.J. Super. 358, 324 A.2d 24 (1974). A good review of the case law is provided in In re Revco D.S., Inc., 118 B.R. 468, 510-13 (Bankr. N.D. Ohio 1990), in which the bankruptcy court joined the majority of courts which have considered the problem in applying fraudulent conveyance law to LBOs.

As an increasing number of LBOs fail, litigation over the applicability of, and interpretation of fraudulent conveyance law with respect to, those transactions continues. Three recent cases illustrate the range of issues, and the manner in which they are being resolved.

In re the O'Day Corporation, 126 B.R. 370 (D. Mass. 1991), involved the post-LBO bankruptcy of a well-known sailboat manufacturer at a time when, unlike the Raymond Group, the debtor was reasonably healthy. The buyout was financed in large part by a series of loans from Meritor Savings Bank. In this action, following O'Day's involuntary bankruptcy, the Trustee sued Meritor under the Uniform Fraudulent Conveyance Act, seeking to avoid its security interests in O'Day's property and to subordinate Meritor's claim to the claims of unsecured creditors. The trustee was successful in both endeavors, with the court ruling that Meritor had violated UFCA §§4 and 5 because the LBO left O'Day both insolvent and without sufficient capital (although not that Meritor had intended to defraud creditors in violation of UFCA §7), and that Meritor's post-LBO conduct justified equitable subordination of its claim to those of O'Day's unsecured creditors.

Although Meritor made available over $9.5 million in loan facilities for the LBO (for which it took security interests in all of O'Day's assets), O'Day retained only $1,343.96 of the proceeds following the transaction. Nevertheless, the business was in reasonably good shape when the LBO occurred, and the bank's projections showed a bright future.

Following the LBO, O'Day's business declined, in part as a result of which, among other things, Meritor pressured O'Day to delay payments to its suppliers. Twenty-two months following the LBO closing, the involuntary bankruptcy petition was filed.

The key to determining whether Meritor had violated UFCA §4 (person rendered insolvent by transaction) and §5 (person left by transaction with unreasonably small capital), was whether Meritor's security interest was obtained for "fair consideration" as defined in UFCA §3.

The court disregarded Meritor's argument that each aspect of the deal should be looked at separately, and collapsed the various parts of the LBO transaction, see also Wieboldt Stores, Inc. v. Schottenstein, 94 B.R. 488 (N.D. Ill. 1988), for the purpose of determining, from the creditors' perspective, whether O'Day had received some direct or indirect economic benefit from the transaction. The court first held that the Meritor loans were not fair consideration to O'Day because all of the proceeds (save $1,300) went to the selling stockholders rather than the corporation. The court then turned to the question of whether the simultaneous cancellation of intercompany debt from O'Day to its former parent was fair consideration, and concluded that it was not, in part because the intercompany loans were part of a corporate structure designed for a previous owner's tax advantage, and in part because they were not treated "scrupulously" as liabilities by the corporation.

The court then turned to the issue of whether O'Day had been rendered insolvent by the deal. The central issue was over whether solvency should be measured on the basis of O'Day's balance sheet or as a going concern. Although the court struggled with the propriety of using a balance sheet test in lieu of a going-concern value test, it ultimately concluded that "... in the context of this case, section 2 of the UFCA requires a balance sheet test—debts must be compared to the value of the assets." Id. at 403.[1] The court found that O'Day would have been insolvent under a balance sheet test whether it accepted the Trustee's evidence or Meritor's evidence.

The court also concluded that the LBO left O'Day with "unreasonably small capital." In the court's view, the determination was to be made at the time of the LBO, and not

---

1. The court noted its displeasure with the cash flow and earnings projections used by Meritor, id., which displeasure is further discussed infra.

based on subsequent events. Consequently, the issue turned on the bank's financial projections for O'Day, and the reasonableness of the underlying assumptions, both of which the court found to be "imprudent." *Id.* at 407.

Finally, the court held that Meritor's post-LBO conduct justified subordinating Meritor's claim to those of O'Day's unsecured creditors. This conduct included (i) assuring payment of its own debt by demanding that O'Day delay payments to other creditors, (ii) demanding that O'Day pay off preexisting debt when it was unable to do so, (iii) demanding principal prepayments to cover a collateral shortfall, and (iv) recording a subsequent mortgage in its favor when O'Day was insolvent. *Id.* at 412. This the court characterized as overreaching, sufficient to warrant equitable subordination.

C-T of Virginia, Inc. f/k/a/ Craddock-Terry Shoe Corporation v. Euroshoe Associates Limited Partnership, 762 F. Supp. 675 (W.D. Va. 1991), involved a suit by the bankrupt corporation on behalf of its creditors against its former shareholders (most of whom were "outsiders") who received cash for the stock in an LBO. The corporation alleged that the cash transfers to its former shareholders were not for "consideration deemed valuable at law" and unjustly enriched these shareholders at its creditors' expense. The court ruled that the corporation had in fact received valuable consideration, following the Virginia requirement that any consideration was sufficient, and that the Bankruptcy Code "reasonably equivalent value" standard did not apply. Finding that the corporation benefitted from new management with a fresh infusion of capital, the court dismissed both aspects of plaintiff's claim.

In Moody v. Security Pacific Business Credit Inc., 127 B.R. 958 (W.D. Pa. 1991), *aff'd* 971 F.2d 1056 (3d Cir. 1992), the trustee in bankruptcy of Jeannette Corporation sued the various participants in a 1981 leveraged buy-out of the company under the Pennsylvania fraudulent conveyance act. The district court, ruling for defendants, held that no intent to defraud existed. Moreover, although the transaction was without fair consideration, the court held that Jeannette was not thereby rendered insolvent, nor was its post-LBO capital unreasonably small. As is becoming common, the district court collapsed the various aspects of the LBO transaction into one. It further found that Jeannette's grant to Security Bank of a security interest in its assets was without fair consideration, because the funds advanced by the bank were for the benefit of the acquiring corporation and not Jeannette itself. The fact that Jeannette was given access to additional funds pursuant to a revolving line of credit obtained by the new management as part of the LBO arrangement was, in the court's view, "woefully inadequate consideration" for Jeannette's new obligations.

Jeanette's pre-LBO solvency was not disputed. The district court found that Jeannette's failure was due to a combination of factors, including a substantial decrease in orders and sales due to increased competition and the effects of a recession, poor management (in part as a result of the illness of a key manager and LBO-investor) and the exacerbation of these failures by the involuntary bankruptcy filing.

As for post-LBO insolvency, in resolving the constructive fraud complaint the district court found that Pennsylvania law looked at the issue of insolvency both in a bankruptcy sense and an equity sense, and in neither case was Jeannette insolvent. As to the value of Jeannette's assets, the court held that they need not have been found to be immediately saleable to have a "present fair saleable value" within the meaning of the act. Rather, the court looked to the "economic realities of the transfer" to determine solvency. Perhaps of greatest importance, the court held that Jeannette's assets had to be valued on a going concern rather than a liquidation basis.

Finally, in examining the question of whether Jeannette was insolvent in an equitable sense, the district court also examined whether it was left with "unreasonably small capital," defending its treatment of the two concepts as substantially equivalent. The court concluded that Jeannette's projections at the time of the LBO were "reasonable and prudent when made," and showed Jeannette as a healthy corporation. The court also found significant the fact that Jeannette had access to cash through the Security Pacific revolving credit, which was adequate to maintain Jeannette's necessary working capital.

In affirming, the Third Circuit agreed with the district court's conclusion that the LBO did not constitute a fraudulent conveyance under the constructive fraud or the intentional fraud provisions of the Uniform Fraudulent Conveyance Act.

4. Consider the following views:

a. Sherwin, Creditors' Rights Against Participants in a Leveraged Buyout, 72 Minn. L. Rev. 449, 472-73, 474-77 (1988):[1]

1. Three-Party Transfers

Courts generally have taken the view that benefits that flow to third parties as a result of a buyout or similar transaction are not fair consideration or reasonably equivalent value for a transfer. Problems of third-party benefit arise in many different ways. One typical example is the case of a controlling shareholder who causes the corporation to pay a personal debt. Another setting is a loan transaction in which a corporation guarantees repayment of a sum advanced to its parent or affiliate.

In either case the corporation's transferee gives up value in an agreed exchange. Under general contract principles, this would be a sufficient consideration for the corporate transfer. In fraudulent conveyance cases, however, the usual view is that a third-party benefit is inadequate consideration. Thus, if any of the financial circumstances specified in the constructive fraud provisions is present, creditors can recover corporate property from the transferee and set aside corporate obligations. The reason given for this result is that in the context of laws designed for the protection of creditors, adequacy of consideration should be assessed from the creditors' point of view. Courts consider whether any benefit actually passed to the corporate transferor and to what extent the three-party transaction depleted the estate available to creditors.

* * *

Most commentary on three-party situations focuses on indirect benefits to the transferor and does not challenge the underlying proposition that value given to third parties is not fair consideration for a transfer. One comment on the subject of intercorporate guaranties, however, suggests a different approach to third-party benefits. The comment proposes that a guaranty should be viewed as a fraudulent conveyance to the obligor whose debt was guaranteed, but not to the lender to whom it was given. The obligor receives benefits from the guaranty because the guaranty enables the obligor to borrow on more favorable terms than it otherwise could obtain. The lender, in contrast, does not benefit from the transaction, because it advances funds equal to the value of the interests it receives. Therefore, the conveyance is not to the lender but to the obligor.

---

1. Reprinted by permission of the University of Minnesota Law Review and the author.

Two bankruptcy decisions suggest another variation from the general approach to three-party situations. Both cases involved transactions among a corporate transferor, an individual in control of the corporation, and a creditor of the individual. In each case the controlling individual caused the corporation to purchase a cashier's check, which the individual remitted to the creditor in payment of his own debt. Both courts held that the primary transferee was not the creditor who received the funds, but rather the controlling individual for whose benefit the transfer was made. The transaction in each case was viewed as two distinct transfers: a fraudulent transfer to the controlling individual and a valid transfer from the individual to the creditor. These cases imply that a transfer in exchange for third-party benefits can be deemed a conveyance to the party who receives the principal benefit of the overall transaction. Rather than following the direct path of the transferor's property, a court using this approach would trace the substantive benefit of the transfer to identify the fraudulent conveyance and to decide which party should be responsible to creditors of the transferor.

An approach that focuses on the substantive distribution of benefits in a three-party transaction has the advantage of making the party who receives the primary benefit of the transaction accountable to creditors of the party whose assets are depleted. On the other hand, it may go too far in relieving the direct transferee of responsibility to creditors. Although the direct transferee in a three-party case receives no net benefit from the transaction, this does not necessarily determine who, as between the transferee and the general creditors, should bear the loss if the primary beneficiary is unavailable to satisfy creditors' claims.

b. Baird and Jackson, Fraudulent Conveyance Law and Its Proper Domain, 38 Vand. L. Rev. 829, 831-36 (1985):[2]

.... The drafters of [the Uniform Fraudulent Conveyance Act] intended to reach some transactions—such as gifts by insolvent debtors—quite apart from whether the debtor could be thought to have harbored any fraudulent intent. They thought that an insolvent debtor who gives 1000 dollars to his mother makes a fraudulent conveyance, even if he has made a similar gift each year in the past and is not motivated in the slightest by a desire to thwart creditors. The drafters deemed these fraudulent not because the transfers were too costly to distinguish from gifts by insolvents made with an intent to defraud, but rather because they found them inherently objectionable. A birthday gift of cash by an insolvent debtor injures creditors just as much when his intentions are innocent as when they are not, and one can presume creditors would ban them if they could.

If fraudulent conveyance law is not limited simply to cases in which the debtor intended—or could be presumed to have intended—to hinder, delay, or defraud his creditors, what are its limits? ...

The issue has become an important one in the 1980s, however. Identifying the precise reach of fraudulent conveyance law is the crucial inquiry in several important legal disputes, such as whether a foreclosure of a debtor's eq-

---

2. Copyright 1985 by the Vanderbilt Law Review. Reprinted by permission of the Vanderbilt Law Review.

uity of redemption or a leveraged buyout is a fraudulent conveyance. These cases are strikingly different from gratuitous transfers or transfers intended to defraud. It is not clear that permitting the debtor to engage in a leveraged buyout, for instance, is against the long-term interests of the creditors as a group. Because fraudulent conveyance law's use of "fair consideration" is not limited solely to cases in which fraudulent intent can be presumed, a view has recently gained currency that suggests the core principle of fraudulent conveyance law is that creditors should be able to set aside transfers by insolvent debtors that harm the creditors as a group. Under such view, this principle, which covers both transfers made with fraudulent intent and gifts, should inform construction of a section such as section 4 of the Uniform Fraudulent Conveyance Act. But, just as a view of section 4 that treats it as a surrogate of section 7's intentional fraud standard is too narrow, we believe this competing principle is too broad.

* * *

Treating transfers by a debtor that make creditors as a group worse off as fraudulent conveyances is overbroad because many ordinary transfers that a debtor makes do this. Like any other creditor remedy, fraudulent conveyance law must have some limits. Indeed, in considering a legal rule such as fraudulent conveyance law, overbroad rules may be more pernicious than underbroad rules. It is easier for creditors to contract into prohibitions on conduct by a debtor than it is to contract out. If fraudulent conveyance law does not cover a certain kind of activity, yet creditors want to prohibit it, it can be prohibited contractually. Myriad restrictions in loan agreements, for example, perform this function. If certain activity is prohibited by a few large creditors, other creditors (including nonconsensual creditors) may be able to profit by the monitoring of the debtor undertaken by those whose contracts do prohibit such activity. Yet, contracting *out* of a rule that prohibits conduct, such as fraudulent conveyance law, is much harder. To be effective, the consent of *all* creditors must be reached. And in the unlikely case that all creditors *did* so agree, the trustee in bankruptcy could still seek to upset the transfer under section 548 of the Bankruptcy Code.

Thus, we believe, one must be careful in deciding where to place the reach of fraudulent conveyance law. In establishing its limits, one must recognize that the debtor-creditor relationship is essentially contractual. A creditor acquires certain rights to control its debtor's actions. The more rights the creditor acquires, the lower its risk and the lower the interest rate it enjoys. Not all the rights that the creditor wants, or that the debtor would agree to give it, however, can be bargained for explicitly. Sometimes these rights (such as priority rights with respect to a debtor's assets) affect third parties as well and should be subject to legal constraints. The ambition of the law governing the debtor-creditor relationship, including fraudulent conveyance law, should provide all the parties with the type of contract that they would have agreed to if they had had the time and money to bargain over all aspects of their deal. Fraudulent conveyance law, in other words, should be viewed as a species of contract law, representing one kind of control that creditors generally would want to impose and that debtors generally would agree to accept.

c. Sherwin, Creditors' Rights Against Participants in a Leveraged Buyout, 72 Minn. L. Rev. 449, 490-95 (1988):[3]

A. The Balance of Interests

This section identifies the interests affected by application of fraudulent conveyance statutes to buyouts and suggests how courts might weigh those interests. Leveraged buyouts and other transactions involving transfers for the benefit of third parties can harm creditors in exactly the way that fraudulent conveyance laws are designed to prevent. The effect of the transfer is to deplete the estate available to pay creditors' claims. If the transferor is left insolvent, creditors lose the ability to collect their claims in full, although they might have done so immediately before the transfer. If the transferor is solvent in the sense of net worth, but is left without sufficient cash or unencumbered assets for its business, the transaction impairs its capacity to generate income to meet debts, leading eventually to the same result. In the case of a buyout, although the corporation may survive under new management, the transaction increases the risks to creditors beyond the point that is acceptable under fraudulent conveyance statutes.

Nevertheless, courts should be sensitive to the character of a buyout as a three-party transaction and the special impact of the fraudulent conveyance remedy in this context. In most cases of constructive fraud, the creditors' remedy against the transferee is restitutionary. A defendant who receives value without consideration from an insolvent transferee, to the detriment of the transferee's creditors, is unjustly enriched. In a buyout or other three-party situation, however, creditors may assert claims against parties who have not been enriched. This does not prevent the application of fraudulent conveyance law, but in cases of this nature courts should consider the role the defendant played in the transaction and the effects of holding the defendant accountable to creditors.

1. Shareholders

Creditors of a corporation acquired in a leveraged buyout may assert fraudulent conveyance claims against buying and selling shareholders in several contexts. The sellers may be direct recipients of corporate transfers if they finance the buyout by accepting notes secured by corporate assets in exchange for their shares. Alternatively, if the direct recipient of corporate transfers is an outside lender, creditors may assert claims against the buyers and sellers as indirect beneficiaries of the transfer.

In either case the principal parties (buyers and sellers) should be responsible to creditors for the assets diverted from the corporation if the buyout violates the financial standards of fraudulent conveyance laws. This is true even though a buyout can be in the best interests of creditors.... A highly leveraged buyout is a gamble. When the transaction exceeds the statutory limits, it is a gamble the principals should take rather than creditors.

2. Independent Lender

Application of fraudulent conveyance laws to an independent lender who finances a buyout is a more difficult question. *United States v. Gleneagles In-*

---

3. Reprinted by permission of the University of Minnesota Law Review and the author.

vestment Co.[174] and *Roxbury State Bank v. The Clarendon*[175] hold that a lender who participates only by its extension of funds is accountable to creditors if it knows the facts of a buyout transaction. In contrast, the *Greenbrook* decision suggests that a lending institution should not be responsible for the use of loan proceeds as long as it advances money to an entity whose obligations it holds.

A compromise position seems more appropriate. An independent lender who finances a buyout should be held responsible to creditors for the economic consequences of the transaction, but only to the extent it can protect itself against liability by a reasonable preliminary review. Beyond this the lender should not be required to relinquish interests and property it negotiates to receive in exchange for an advance of funds.

3. Objectives in Imposing Liability on Lenders

From the creditors' perspective, application of fraudulent conveyance law to set aside the interests of a buyout lender has two advantages. One is that lenders who foresee that transfers to them could be set aside as fraudulent conveyances will evaluate the economic impact of buyouts and will refuse to participate if the buyout appears fraudulent against creditors. Often the buyout will be impossible without outside financing, and the lender's withdrawal will force the parties to adjust their terms or abandon the transaction.

This is a sound objective in applying fraudulent conveyance law. The lender who finances a buyout is in a better position than general creditors to assess and control the financial impact of the transaction on the corporation and its creditors. The lender generally is informed of the use of loan proceeds and the financial circumstances of the borrowing corporation, can influence the terms of the transaction, and has the ultimate option to refuse to advance funds. Other creditors have no voice in the transaction and may be unable to protect themselves effectively against its consequences. Therefore, even an independent lender should not be completely free of responsibility; it is reasonable to impose a duty on the lender to review the buyout for compliance with fraudulent conveyance law.

The other advantage to creditors in holding the lender liable is a source of compensation for loss caused by the buyout.... This is not a sound objective when considered in relation to the lender's role in the transaction. The lender advances funds in return for the obligations and interests it holds and so is not enriched by the transfer of corporate property and obligations. Unjust enrichment is not an essential condition of liability under fraudulent conveyance law, but the absence of enrichment becomes important when considered in light of the lender's commercial position.... Further, the lender has no relationship to the corporation that under traditional principles would give rise to fiduciary responsibilities to the corporation or its creditors.

The possibility that the lender's interest will be set aside in these circumstances injects a substantial risk of loss into transactions that, to the lender, are ordinary business activities. Application of fraudulent conveyance laws to the lender also may discourage legitimate buyout transactions.... When a buyout

---

174. 565 F. Supp. 556 (M.D. Pa. 1983), *aff'd sub nom.* United States v. Tabor Court Realty Corp., 803 F.2d 1288 (3d Cir. 1986), *cert. denied,* 107 S. Ct. 3229 (1987).

175. 129 N.J. Super. 358, 324 A.2d 34 (Super. Ct. App. Div.), *certif. denied,* 66 N.J. 316, 331 A.2d 16 (1974).

leaves the corporation in an unsound financial condition, the risk imposed on creditors outweighs any positive aspects of the transaction. On the other hand, when the borrowing exceeds what a lender would extend on the basis of the buyers' assets, but does not so deplete corporate assets as to impair creditors' prospects of payment, leveraged buyouts can be efficient both for the particular corporation involved and for the liquidity of investments generally....

5. Part of a corporate lawyer's duties include opining on the legalities of a transaction as to her client, for the benefit of other contracting parties. Typically the opinion will include a paragraph indicating that, as to the client, the agreements involved in the deal and executed by the client "have been duly executed and delivered by the Company and are legal, valid and binding obligations of the Company, enforceable against the Company in accordance with their respective terms." Of course court opinions applying fraudulent conveyance laws to leveraged buy-outs suggest that this might be a difficult opinion for counsel to a borrower or guarantor in a leveraged buyout to give to a lender. The standard exception that follows the quoted language above should be sufficient to account for this problem and reads as follows: "except as such enforceability may be limited by applicable bankruptcy, insolvency, fraudulent conveyance, moratorium or similar laws affecting the enforceability of creditors' rights generally and by general of principles of equity (regardless of whether such enforceability is considered in a proceeding in equity or at law)." Furthermore, if the agreements provide for unusual remedies or those clearly subject to equitable discretion, it is prudent specifically to exempt those remedies from the enforceability opinion. *See* Jessen, Third-Party Legal Opinions: An Introduction to "Customary Practice," 35 Creighton L. Rev. 153 (2001); FitzGibbon & Glazer, Rethinking Legal Opinion Letters: Opinions of Counsel in Corporate Transactions, 1989 Colum. Bus. L. Rev. 323 (1989).

FitzGibbon & Glazer, Legal Opinions in Corporate Transactions: The Opinion on Agreements and Instruments, 12 J. Corp. Law 657, 690-91 (1987), note:

> When the lawyer knows of a specific problem that is likely to affect the opinion recipient's rights in a material way, he should disclose it in the opinion even if it is covered by the bankruptcy qualification. An example is the fraudulent conveyance problem presented by upstream guaranties and leveraged buyouts. Under the Uniform Fraudulent Conveyance Act, a conveyance made by a business "without fair consideration" is fraudulent if after the conveyance "unreasonably small capital" remains in the business. Conveyances and obligations also are fraudulent if incurred "with actual intent ... to hinder, delay, or defraud ... creditors." The Act empowers creditors to set aside fraudulent conveyances under various circumstances, depending on whether the purchaser gave adequate consideration and whether he knew of the fraud. Upstream guaranties almost always raise the question whether the subsidiary is receiving "fair consideration." Leveraged buyouts often raise the question whether the acquired company is left with "unreasonably small capital" after its assets and credit are used to finance the acquisition. In these circumstances experienced counsel, as a matter of good practice, include in their opinions an express statement concerning the fraudulent conveyance problem.

It is also well worth noting the Examiner's Preliminary Report in In re Revco D.S., Inc., 118 B.R. 464, 527-28 (N.D. Ohio 1990), in which the Examiner expressed his opinion that Revco "should be able to recover, as fraudulent transfers, fees it paid to professionals, advisors, and others [including those retained by Revco and those which were retained by another entity but paid by Revco] for which it received no benefit."

b. Asset-Backed Securitization

Introduction

Asset-backed securitization ("ABS") is a relatively new structured finance technique that draws elements from many areas of law, including bankruptcy, securities, property, tax and secured transactions. Stated simply, ABS involves a company selling off revenue-generating assets, such as accounts receivables, car loans and credit card receivables, in order to infuse capital into the company at a cost of capital lower than it could otherwise obtain.

The precursor to ABS was "factoring," a common financing technique encountered frequently today. In a factoring transaction, a company sells its accounts receivables to a financial service company called a "factor." The factor pays a discounted price for the accounts receivable and earns the difference between the price paid and the receivables actually collected. The sale, however, is without recourse. Thus, the selling company has no obligation to compensate the factor for any uncollected receivables.

The first modern securitization transaction occurred in 1970 and involved the Government National Mortgage Association (better known as "Ginnie Mae"). Ginnie Mae purchased notes and mortgages from savings and loan associations (referred to as "orginators"). The notes and mortgages were referred to as "packages" because they were similar as to term, interest rate and quality. Ginnie Mae placed these packages into a trust (referred to as a "Special Purpose Entity" or "SPE"). The trust was responsible for collecting the interest and principal payments from the pooled mortgages. To raise the money necessary to purchase the pooled mortgages, the trust sold fractional undivided interests in them to the public. The investors were entitled to receive the interest and principal from the pool of mortgages. In this way, "mortgage pass-through securities" came into being as the payments collected by the trust were then passed through to the investors. Ginnie Mae used the proceeds from the sale of the securities to purchase the packages of notes and mortgages from the savings and loans. The savings and loans, meanwhile, were infused with cash paid over by Ginnie Mae. They were then free to lend money to more customers, and the process would thus start anew.

While securitization may have started out with home mortgages in the 1970s, it has since evolved to encompass a wide range of revenue-producing assets. These include accounts receivable, car loans and credit card receivables. Moreover, in the last 10 years royalties relating to fast food franchises, films and drugs have been securitized. Even David Bowie the singer/songwriter has securitized his music royalties.

The Securitization Decision

Securitization thrives because it provides companies with needed funding at a cost less (often far less) than more traditional means of financing. Because the SPE's low risk assets are more creditworthy than the originator as a whole (if not, the originator would simply borrow directly), the SPE can borrow funds at a lower cost and pass the savings on to the originator.[1] Indeed, potential investors in an SPE's

---

1. As emphasized by Professor Steven Schwarcz, "[S]ecuritization is most valuable when the cost of funds, reflected in the interest rate that is necessary to entice investors to purchase the [SPE's] securities, is less than the cost of the originator's other, direct sources of funding." Schwarcz, The Alchemy of Asset Securitization, 1 Stan. J.L. Bus. & Fin. 133, 136 (1994).

debt securities examine the cash flow from the revenue-generating assets sold to the SPE rather the creditworthiness of the originator. Moreover, originators are not subject to the highly restrictive covenants imposed in bank financings and high-yield bond offerings.

Once the *why* question is answered, the next is *when* should a company pursue traditional financing versus ABS financing? Professor Steven Schwarcz, a leading authority on securitization, provides the following answer:

> To determine whether an originator will achieve an overall cost savings from securitization, one must assess the interest savings possible ... against the costs of the securitization transaction. A company considering securitization should compare (i) the expected differential between interest payable on non-securitized financing and interest payable on securities issued by an applicable [SPE] with (ii) the expected difference in transaction costs between the alternative funding options. Whether or not the originator will achieve a cost savings partially depends on the way in which the originator structures the securitization because ... transaction costs can vary over a wide range.... [2]

The Securitization Process

A company seeking to raise capital through securitization engages in a rather grueling multi-step process. The first step is for the company to separate its low risk revenue-generating assets, such as credit card receivables, from the rest of the higher risk company. To do so, the company as the "originator" will sell a group of revenue-generating assets to a special purpose entity ("SPE").[3] The SPE is also known as the "issuer," as it will be issuing either bonds or notes to the public to raise the funds necessary to purchase the revenue-generating assets from the originator. The SPE may be a corporation, trust or limited-liability company, with the latter two being the most tax efficient.

The originator creates the SPE for the limited purpose of isolating the assets being sold from any risk associated with the originator. This is critical since investors do not want the assets securing their debt securities seized in the event of the originator's insolvency or bankruptcy. Indeed, an ABS transaction typically employs *two* SPE's so as to further isolate the assets from the originator.[4]

The next step in securitization is to establish a plan for servicing the revenue-generating assets. The SPE contracts with a servicer to maintain those assets. The servicer is usually associated with the originator and may very well be the originator itself, thereby becoming a seller-servicer. Because the monies owed on the SPE's assets are owed by customers of the originator, the originator has a continuing desire to keep them satisfied in hopes of generating repeat business. The servicer or seller-servicer administers the assets, collects monies paid on the assets and then distributes the cash to the trustee for payment to the investors in accordance with the terms of their indenture. In essence, the servicer acts and functions as the originator yet it must still deal with the SPE at arm's-length in order to keep the assets isolated.

---

2. *Id.* at 137-38.

3. SPEs are sometimes referred to as "special purpose vehicles" or "SPVs." There is no distinction between the two terms.

4. The first SPE, owned by the originator, will establish the second SPE. This prevents the originator from being deemed the direct owner of the entity which holds the assets and issues the debt securities.

Simultaneously, one or more of the nationally recognized statistical rating organizations, such as Moody's, Standard & Poor's or Fitch, will rate the prospective debt securities. A rating is "an assessment of the likelihood of payment, both *when* promised and *in the full amount* promised."[5] Higher rated debt is perceived to carry lower risk, and thus an issuer generally pays a lower rate of interest. For lower rated debt, the exact opposite is true. Thus, the key to a successful ABS transaction is for the originator to have a collection of revenue-generating assets that, when isolated from the originator, has a better rating than that of the originator as a whole. For more on rating agencies, see *supra* section 5c.

The final step is for the SPE to issue the debt securities to the public. Before doing so, however, a registration statement covering the securities must be filed with, reviewed and declared effective by the Securities and Exchange Commission (SEC). For more on SEC registration, see *Federal Securities Laws* below.

The documentation of an ABS transaction is extremely complex and lawyer-intensive. One unique ABS document is the "pooling and servicing agreement" between the originator, trustee and servicer. The pooling and servicing agreement sets forth the rights and obligations of the parties and governs the transfer of assets. The agreement outlines how the cash flows the assets produce will be distributed in terms of allocation and priority. Cash flows include interest, principal and other payments on the securities, as well as expenses associated with servicing fees, trustee fees and any monies used to support the credit rating of the SPE.

Bankruptcy Remoteness

To succeed, an ABS transaction must be structured so that the SPE's assets will not be threatened by the originator's bankruptcy (a concept referred to as "bankruptcy remoteness").[6] This is important because the investors purchasing the SPE's debt securities need assurance that they will be paid back even if the originator files for bankruptcy. For example, if the originator owns or controls the SPE, it may have the power to force the SPE to file for bankruptcy as well. If this were to occur, payments to SPE noteholders would be stayed during the pendency of the bankruptcy proceedings, and SPE noteholders could lose priority over the SPE's assets to the originator's creditors.

In order to mitigate bankruptcy risk, a SPE's charter will include provisions that substantially limit or preclude a voluntary bankruptcy filing by the SPE. Specifically, the SPE charter will require a requisite number of independent directors of the board to vote in favor of the filing of a bankruptcy petition.[7] An independent director is typically defined as a person who is not a director, officer, employee or holder of 5% or more of the voting securities of the originator or any of the originator's affiliates.

Bankruptcy remoteness does not necessarily mean bankruptcy proof. Therefore, rating agencies require the SPE to limit its activities to the transaction at hand. The SPE also has a limitation on the debt it can incur, and it is prohibited from merging, dissolving, liquidating, consolidating or selling all or substantially all of its assets. Finally, the SPE must maintain sufficient capital in order to avoid bankruptcy.

---

5. Schwarcz, Markell & Broome, Securitization, Structured Finance and Capital Markets §1.02, at 5 (2004).

6. *See* Securitization of Financial Assets §5.01 (Jason H.P. Kravitt ed., 2d ed. 1997).

7. *See* In re Kingston Square Assocs., 214 B.R. 713 (Bankr. S.D.N.Y. 1997).

Bankruptcy remoteness is further achieved if the originator transfers its assets to the SPE in a manner that evinces a true sale.[8] If a true sale has occurred, then the economic and legal links between the originator and the revenue-generating assets have been successfully severed. The SPE is now deemed the "owner" of the assets and the originator neither retains any benefits nor has any control over those assets. Thus, in the event of a bankruptcy of the originator, those assets will not be included in the estate of the originator. Also, a true sale has the effect of improving the overall financial strength of the originator, because the ABS transaction is recorded as an asset sale on its balance sheet as opposed to a secured loan.

If, however, a true sale of the revenue-generating assets has not occurred, a bankruptcy court will treat the ABS transaction as a secured loan or other advance of funds by the SPE to the originator. Within the context of bankruptcy, a finding against a true sale relegates the SPE to the position of a secured creditor vis-à-vis the originator. Under Section 362 of the Bankruptcy Code (11 U.S.C. §362), this means the SPE is automatically stayed from foreclosing on those assets or conducting any further payment collections. Therefore, any potential investor in debt securities issued by the SPE, as well as the rating agencies rating those securities, must pay particular attention to the terms of the sale.

A bankruptcy court determines whether or not a true sale has occurred by looking to state law. Generally, a true sale will be found if the originator has truly severed the economic risks and benefits attendant to the ownership of the assets in question. A court weighs the following factors, among others, when determining whether or not a true sale has occurred: (1) recourse; (2) retained rights to surplus; (3) pricing mechanism; and (4) administration and collection of accounts. These are discussed below.

(1) Recourse

Recourse, in this context, refers to the SPE's ability to seek repayment against the originator if the assets it purchased are not sufficient to pay off the debt securities it issued. If the SPE is able to seek recourse, a bankruptcy court will likely find that a true sale did not occur. Thus, an originator who retains the economic risk of the assets will look more like a secured creditor than a seller of assets in the eyes of the court. A court examining a true sale question will look to the particular facts and circumstances of each case to determine if the risks associated with the transferred assets have shifted from the originator to the SPE. Consider the following case which, although addressing a factoring transaction, has equal relevance to an ABS transaction.

Major's Furniture Mart, Inc. v. Castle Credit Corp., Inc.
602 F.2d 538 (3rd Cir. 1979)

Garth, Circuit Judge:

This appeal requires us to answer the question: "When is a sale not a sale, but rather a secured loan?" The district court held that despite the form of their Agreement, which purported to be, and hence was characterized as, a sale of accounts receivable, the parties' transactions did not constitute sales. *Major's Furniture Mart, Inc. v. Castle Credit Corp.*, 449 F. Supp. 538 (E.D.Pa.1978). No facts are in dispute, and the issue presented on this appeal is purely a legal issue involving the interpretation of relevant sections of

---

8. *See* Hilson & Turner, Asset-Backed Lending: A Practical Guide to Secured Financing §4:6, at 4-11 (5th ed. 2002).

the Uniform Commercial Code as enacted in Pennsylvania, 12A P.S. §1-101 *et seq.* and their proper application to the undisputed facts presented here.

The district court granted plaintiff Major's motion for summary judgment. Castle Credit Corporation appeals from that order. We affirm.

I

Major's is engaged in the retail sale of furniture. Castle is in the business of financing furniture dealers such as Major's. Count I of Major's amended complaint alleged that Major's and Castle had entered into an Agreement dated June 18, 1973 for the financing of Major's accounts receivable; that a large number of transactions pursuant to the Agreement took place between June 1973 and May 1975; that in March and October 1975 Castle declared Major's in default under the Agreement; and that from and after June 1973 Castle was in possession of monies which constituted a surplus over the accounts receivable transferred under the Agreement. Among other relief sought, Major's asked for an accounting of the surplus and all sums received by Castle since June 1, 1976 which had been collected from the Major's accounts receivable transferred under the Agreement.

The provisions of the June 18, 1973 Agreement which are relevant to our discussion provide: that Major's shall from time to time "sell" accounts receivable to Castle and that all accounts so "sold" shall be with full recourse against Major's. Major's was required to warrant that each account receivable was based upon a written order or contract fully performed by Major's.[3] Castle in its sole discretion could refuse to "purchase" any account. The amount paid by Castle to Major's on any particular account was the unpaid face amount of the account exclusive of interest[4] less a fifteen percent "discount"[5] and less another ten percent of the unpaid face amount as a reserve against bad debts.[6]

Under the Agreement the reserve was to be held by Castle without interest and was to indemnify Castle against a customer's failure to pay the full amount of the account (which included interest and insurance premiums), as well as any other charges or losses sustained by Castle for any reason.

In addition, Major's was required to "repurchase" any account "sold" to Castle which was in default for more than 60 days. In such case Major's was obligated to ... repurchase

---

3. The parties do not dispute that their rights are governed by the law of Pennsylvania. The Pennsylvania Uniform Commercial Code, and in particular 12A P.S. §9-105, classifies the accounts receivable which are the subject of the agreement as "chattel paper."

4. According to Major's brief, the "face amount" of its customers' installment payment agreements included (1) the retail cost of the furniture purchased (amount financed), (2) the total amount of interest payable by the customer over the life of the customer's installment payment agreement, and (3) insurance charges.

5. The 15% "discount" was subsequently increased unilaterally by Castle to 18% and thereafter was adjusted monthly to reflect changes in the prime rate.

6. It becomes apparent from a review of the record that the amount which Castle actually paid to Major's on each account transferred was the unpaid face amount exclusive of interest *and* exclusive of insurance premiums less 28% (18% "discount" and 10% Reserve).

In its brief on appeal, Castle sets out the following summary of the transactions that took place over the relevant period. It appears that the face amount of the accounts which were "sold" by Major's to Castle was $439,832.08, to which finance charges totalling $116,350.46 and insurance charges totaling $42,304.03 were added, bringing the total amount "purchased" by Castle to $598,486.57. For these "purchases" Castle paid Major's $316,107. Exclusive of any surplus as determined by the district court Castle has retained $528,176.13 which it has received as a result of customer collections and repurchases by Major's. Collection costs were found by the district court to be $1,627.81.

a defaulted account not for the discounted amount paid to it by Castle, but for a "repurchase" price based on the balance due by the customer, plus any costs incurred by Castle upon default.

* * *

.... The repurchase price was either charged fully to reserve or, as provided in the Agreement, 50% to reserve and 50% by cash payment from Major's. In the event of bankruptcy, default under the agreement or discontinuation of business, Major's was required to repurchase all outstanding accounts immediately. Finally, the Agreement provided that the law of Pennsylvania would govern and that the Agreement could not be modified except in writing signed by all the parties....

Under the Agreement, over 600 accounts were transferred to Castle by Major's of which 73 became delinquent and subject to repurchase by Major's. On March 21, 1975, Castle notified Major's that Major's was in default in failing to repurchase delinquent accounts. Apparently to remedy the default, Major's deposited an additional $10,000 into the reserve. After June 30, 1975, Major's discontinued transferring accounts to Castle. On October 7, 1975 Castle again declared Major's in default.

Major's' action against Castle alleged that the transaction by which Major's transferred its accounts to Castle constituted a financing of accounts receivable and that Castle had collected a surplus of monies to which Major's was entitled. We are thus faced with the question which we posed at the outset of this opinion: did the June 18, 1973 Agreement create a *secured interest* in the accounts, or did the transaction constitute a *true sale* of the accounts? The district court, contrary to Castle's contention, refused to construe the Agreement as one giving rise to the sales of accounts receivable. Rather, it interpreted the Agreement as creating a security interest in the accounts which accordingly was subject to all the provisions of Article 9 of the U.C.C., 12A P.S. §9-101 *et seq.* It thereupon entered its order of June 13, 1977 granting Major's' motion for summary judgment and denying Castle's motion for summary judgment....

Castle on appeal argues (1) that the express language of the Agreement indicates that it was an agreement for the sale of accounts and (2) that the parties' course of performance and course of dealing compel an interpretation of the Agreement as one for the sale of accounts. Castle also asserts that the district court erred in "reforming" the Agreement and in concluding that the transaction was a loan. In substance these contentions do no more than reflect Castle's overall position that the Agreement was for an absolute sale of accounts.

II

Our analysis starts with Article 9 of the Uniform Commercial Code which encompasses both *sales* of accounts and *secured interests* in accounts. Thus, the Pennsylvania counterpart of the Code "applies ... (a) to any transaction (regardless of its form) which is intended to create a security interest in ... accounts ... ; and also (b) to any sale of accounts ..." 12A P.S. §9-102. The official comments to that section make it evident that Article 9 is to govern *all* transactions in accounts. Comment 2 indicates that, because "(commercial) financing on the basis of accounts ... is often so conducted that the distinction between a security transfer and a sale is blurred," that "sales" as well as transactions "intended to create a security interest" are subject to the provisions of Article 9. Moreover, a "security interest" is defined under the Act as "any interest of a buyer of accounts." 12A P.S. §1-201(37). Thus even an outright buyer of accounts, such as Castle claims to be, by definition has a "security interest" in the accounts which it purchases.

.... [T]he distinction between an outright sale and a transaction intended to create a security interest becomes highly significant with respect to certain provisions found in Part 5 of Article 9. That part pertains to default under a "security agreement."[10] 12A P.S. § 9-501, *et seq.*

The default section relevant here, which distinguishes between the consequences that follow on default when the transaction *secures an indebtedness* rather than a *sale*, provides:

> A secured party who by agreement is entitled to charge back uncollected collateral or otherwise to full or limited recourse against the debtor and who undertakes to collect from the account debtors or obligors must proceed in a commercially reasonable manner and may deduct his reasonable expenses of realization from the collections. *If the security agreement secures an indebtedness, the secured party must account to the debtor for any surplus,* and unless otherwise agreed, the debtor is liable for any deficiency. But, *if the underlying transaction was a sale of accounts,* contract rights, or chattel paper, *the debtor is entitled to any surplus* or is liable for any deficiency *only if the security agreement so provides.*

12A P.S. § 9-502(2) (emphasis added).

Thus, if the accounts were transferred to Castle *to secure Major's' indebtedness,* Castle was obligated to account for and pay over the surplus proceeds to Major's under 12A P.S. § 9-502(2), as a debtor's (Major's') right to surplus in such a case cannot be waived even by an express agreement. 12A P.S. § 9-501(3)(a). On the other hand, if a *sale of accounts* had been effected, then Castle was entitled to all proceeds received from all accounts because the June 18, 1973 Agreement does not provide otherwise.

However, while the Code instructs us as to the consequences that ensue as a result of the determination of "secured indebtedness" as contrasted with "sale," the Code does not provide assistance in distinguishing between the character of such transactions. This determination, as to whether a particular assignment constitutes a sale or a transfer for security, is left to the courts for decision. 12A P.S. § 9-502, Comment 4. It is to that task that we now turn.

III

Castle contends that because the June 18, 1973 Agreement expressly refers only to "sales" and "purchases" that the parties intended a true "sale" of accounts and not a security transfer. However, it has been held in Pennsylvania, as it has elsewhere, that

> "Courts will not be controlled by the nomenclature the parties apply to their relationship": Kelter, Tr. v. American Bankers' Finance Co., 306 Pa. 483, 492, 160 A. 127, 130, 82 A.L.R. 999. In Smith-Faris Company v. Jameson Memorial Hospital Association, 313 Pa. 254, 260, 169 A. 233, 235, it was said: "'Neither the form of a contract nor the name given it by the parties controls its interpretation. In determining the real character of a contract courts will always look to its purpose, rather than to the name given it by the parties. * * * The proper construction of a contract is not dependent upon any name given it by the parties, or upon any one provision, but upon the entire body of the contract and its legal effect as a whole.' 6 R.C.L., p. 836 § 226."

---

10. A "security agreement" is "an agreement which creates or provides for a security interest." 12A P.S. § 9-105(1)(h).

Capozzoli v. Stone & Webster Engineering Corporation, 352 Pa. 183, 42 A.2d 524, 525 (1945)....

It thus became the district court's task, as it is now ours, to examine the record developed by the parties in order to determine whether the transactions in question in fact constitute true sales or security interests....

* * *

.... Our examination of that record and the legal principles pertinent to that issue satisfies us that the district court did not err.

IV

The comments to § 9-502(2) (and in particular Comment 4) make clear to us that the presence of recourse in a sale agreement without more will not automatically convert a sale into a security interest. Hence, one of Major's arguments which is predicated on such a *per se* principle attracts us no more than it attracted the district court. The Code comments however are consistent with and reflect the views expressed by courts and commentators that "(t)he determination of whether a particular assignment constitutes a (true) sale or a transfer for security is left to the courts." 12A P.S. § 9-502, Comment 4. The question for the court then is whether the *nature* of the recourse, and the true nature of the transaction, are such that the legal rights and economic consequences of the agreement bear a greater similarity to a financing transaction or to a sale.

In *In re Joseph Kanner Hat Co., Inc.,* 482 F.2d 937 (2d Cir. 1973), Kanner having obtained a loan of $25,000 from a bank executed an assignment to the bank of $25,000 which was due Kanner from the Norwalk Redevelopment Agency and represented compensable moving expense. The assignment reads "That Joseph Kanner Hat Company, Inc.... in consideration of the sum of $25,000.00 ... does hereby sell, assign and transfer ... any and all sums of money due and owing ... the said assignor by ... the Norwalk Redevelopment Agency...." 482 F.2d at 938 n.4. The bank contended that the assignment constituted a transfer of an absolute right to collect whatever monies were due Kanner from the Redevelopment Agency. Kanner's trustee in bankruptcy claimed that the transaction created no more than a security interest under the Connecticut Commercial Code, that the security interest had not been perfected by filing, and that the trustee's interest was entitled to priority over the bank's. The Second Circuit, looking to the true nature of the transaction, did not consider itself restricted by the form of words used by the parties. Noting that the bank regarded and treated the assignment as a method of payment of a loan, the court held that despite the "absolute assignment" of the entire claim, the transaction was no more than an assignment for security.

In *Kelter v. American Bankers' Finance Co.,* 306 Pa. 483, 160 A. 127 (1932), the Integrity Construction Company, a general contractor, had borrowed money from American Bankers' Finance Company. The money was loaned to Integrity in exchange for the transfer of contracts made between independent home owners and Integrity. The contracts of the property owners were "sold, assigned and transferred" by Integrity to American Bankers' by a writing which, among other things, specified that Integrity had completed the work required, and that Integrity guaranteed that all the monies due under the contracts would be promptly paid. Ultimately, Integrity was adjudicated a bankrupt and the trustee of Integrity's estate obtained an order restraining American Bankers' from collecting or applying to its use any of the funds becoming due on the contracts which Integrity had transferred to it. Recognizing that the central question was whether the transaction between Integrity and

American Bankers' constituted a sale of the contracts or merely loans secured by the assignments, the court reviewed the course of dealings between the parties. In holding in favor of the bankruptcy trustee that the transactions were no more than loans secured by the collateral of the assigned contracts, the court (quoting the lower court) stated:

> "It is true that the letters exchanged (which constitute the contracts) speak of 'money advanced' and they provide for 'finance charges' on the money advanced and for 'searches' made in the lender's interest. On profitable contracts a balance was paid by the so-called 'buyer' of the contract to the alleged 'seller.' We cannot reconcile the payment of interest and finance charges, nor of the buyer's expenses in 'searches' with the idea that the contractor had sold his contract to the banker. The parties may call this what they please. It is in fact nothing but a loan upon the collateral of the assigned contract."
>
> In cases of this kind it is more important what parties actually do than what they say they do....

160 A. at 130.

Lyon v. Ty-Wood Corporation, 212 Pa.Super. 69, 239 A.2d 819 (1968), is consistent with the approach taken in *Kanner* and *Kelter*. On the record presented in *Lyon*, the court, "after a long and careful weighing of all of the evidence," held that the assignments constituted a sale rather than a security interest.

Hence it appears that in each of the cases cited, despite the express language of the agreements, the respective courts examined the parties' practices, objectives, business activities and relationships and determined whether the transaction was a sale or a secured loan only after analysis of the evidence as to the true nature of the transaction. We noted earlier that here the parties, satisfied that there was nothing other than the Agreement and documents bearing on their relationship (Part III, *supra*), submitted to the court's determination on an agreed record. The district court thereupon reviewed the Agreement and the documents as they reflected the conduct of the parties to determine whether Castle treated the transactions as sales or transfers of a security interest. In referring to the extremely relevant factor of "recourse"[12] and to the risks allocated, the district court found:

> In the instant case the allocation of risks heavily favors Major's claim to be considered as an assignor with an interest in the collectibility of its accounts. It appears that Castle required Major's to retain all conceivable risks of uncollectibility of these accounts. It required warranties that retail account debtors—e. g., Major's customers—meet the criteria set forth by Castle, that Major's perform the credit check to verify that these criteria were satisfied, and that Major's warrant that the accounts were fully enforceable legally and were "fully and timely collectible." It also imposed an obligation to indemnify Castle

---

12. Gilmore, in commenting on the Code's decision to leave the distinction between a security transfer and a sale to the courts, would place almost controlling significance on the one factor of recourse. He states:

> If there is no right of charge-back or recourse with respect to uncollectible accounts and no right to claim for a deficiency, then the transaction should be held to be a sale, entirely outside the scope of Part 5. If there is a right to charge back uncollectible accounts (a right, as §9-502 puts it, of "full or limited recourse") or a right to claim a deficiency, then the transaction should be held to be for security and thus subject to Part 5 as well as the other Parts of the Article.

II Gilmore, Security Interests in Personal Property, § 44.4 at 1230.

Here, of course, the Agreement provided Castle with full recourse against Major's.

out of a reserve account for losses resulting from a customer's failure to pay, or for any breach of warranty, and an obligation to repurchase any account after the customer was in default for more than 60 days. Castle only assumed the risk that the assignor itself would be unable to fulfill its obligations. Guaranties of quality alone, or even guarantees of collectibility alone, might be consistent with a true sale, but Castle attempted to shift all risks to Major's, and incur none of the risks or obligations of ownership. It strains credulity to believe that this is the type of situation, referred to in Comment 4, in which "there may be a true sale of accounts... although recourse exists." When we turn to the conduct of the parties to seek support for this contention, we find instead that Castle, in fact, treated these transactions as a transfer of a security interest.

449 F. Supp. at 543.

Moreover, in looking to the conduct of the parties, the district court found one of the more significant documents to be an August 31, 1973 letter written by Irving Canter, President of Castle Credit, to Major's. As the district court characterized it, and as we agree:

This letter, in effect, announces the imposition of a floating interest rate on loans under a line of credit of $ 80,000 per month, based upon the fluctuating prime interest rate. The key portion of the letter states:

Accordingly, your volume for the month of September cannot exceed $80,000. Any business above that amount will have to be paid for in October. I think you'll agree that your quota is quite liberal. The surcharge for the month of September will be 3% of the principal amount financed which is based upon a 9½% prime rate. On October 1, and for each month thereafter, the surcharge will be adjusted, based upon the prime rate in effect at that time as it relates to a 6½% base rate....

This unilateral change in the terms of the Agreement makes it obvious that Castle treated the transaction as a line of credit to Major's—i.e., a loan situation. Were this a true sale, as Castle now argues, it would not have been able to impose these new conditions by fiat. Such changes in a sales contract would have modified the price term of the agreement, which could only be done by a writing signed by all the parties.

449 F. Supp. at 543.

It is apparent to us that on this record none of the risks present in a true sale is present here. Nor has the custom of the parties or their relationship, as found by the district court, given rise to more than a debtor/creditor relationship in which Major's' debt was secured by a transfer of Major's' customer accounts to Castle, thereby bringing the transaction within the ambit of 12A P.S. §9-502. To the extent that the district court determined that a surplus existed, Castle was obligated to account to Major's for that surplus and Major's' right to the surplus could not be waived, 12A P.S. §9-502(2). Accordingly, we hold that on this record the district court did not err in determining that the true nature of the transaction between Major's and Castle was a secured loan, not a sale.

* * *

———————

(2) Retained Rights and Right to Surplus

The originator's right to redeem or repurchase transferred assets decreases the likelihood that a court will find a true sale. Similarly, as seen in *Major's Furniture Mart*, an originator may be deemed a secured creditor if it retains the right to receive any surplus the SPE collects on the transferred assets.[1] For example, if the originator is entitled to receive payments on accounts receivables in excess of traditional collection rates, then a court may find that a true has not occurred.

(3) Pricing Mechanism

Courts also look at the pricing mechanism agreed to by the parties when determining whether a true sale has occurred. Specifically, if the price of the revenue-generating assets is linked to a fluctuating rate, this may evidence a loan as opposed to a sale. Similarly, a court may also view the transaction as a loan if the pricing mechanism calls for retroactive adjustment of the price to reflect the actual collection experience of the transferred assets.[2] Most originators avoid this by selling the assets to the SPE at a discounted price in order to account for the perceived risk associated with the inability to collect on some of the assets. A discounted price for the sale of an asset, such as a receivable, that cannot be altered later on is a good indication of a true sale.

(4) Administration and Collection of Assets

For a true sale to be found, the SPE must always retain the authority to control the collection of monies paid on the assets.[3] In many standard securitization agreements, the originator or one if its affiliates serves as the collection agent. However, a contractual agency relationship must exist between the originator and the SPE. In other words, the collection agency must be paid an arm's-length fee for its administration of the assets. Additionally, the SPE should be able to appoint itself or a third party as collection agent in place of the originator if necessary. The SPE can demonstrate its authority if it owns all the books, records and computer records relating to the purchased assets, and retains the right to control the actions of the collection agent in reference to those assets.

Substantive Consolidation and Fraudulent Transfers

Even if a true sale is found, a bankruptcy court may disregard the separateness of the SPE and the originator under the doctrine of substantive consolidation. Substantive consolidation is an equitable doctrine that courts apply on a case-by-case basis. If a court chooses to apply the doctrine to a given case, the SPE's assets will be substantively consolidated into the originator's estate, thus exposing them to bankruptcy risk. In order to avoid substantive consolidation, those structuring and later implementing an ABS transaction avoid the following factors: (1) the commingling of assets and business functions; (2) unity of ownership; (3) difficulty in separating individual liabilities and assets; (4) parental loan guarantees in favor of a subsidiary; (5) the existence of consolidated financial statements; and (6) lack of adherence to corporate formalities during the transfer of assets.[4]

---

1. *See* In re Evergreen Valley Resort, Inc., 23 B.R. 659, 661-62 (Bankr. D. Me. 1982); In re Nixon Mach. Co., 6 B.R. 847, 854 (Bankr. E.D. Tenn. 1980).
2. *See* Home Bond Co. v. McChesney, 239 U.S. 568 (1916); Dorothy v. Commonwealth Commercial Co., 116 N.E. 143 (Ill. 1917).
3. *See* People v. Service Inst., 421 N.Y.S. 2d 325 (N.Y. Sup. Ct. 1979).
4. *See, e.g.,* Franklin v. Compton (In re Bonhman), 229 F.3d 515, 516-517 (2d Cir. 1988); In re Vecco Construction Industries, 4 Bankr. 407, 410 (Bankr. E.D. Va. 1980); 2 Collier On Bankruptcy ¶ 105.09 (Alan Resnick & Henry Sommer, eds., 15th rev. ed. 2003).

Under state law and the Bankruptcy Code, a transfer of assets can be set aside as fraudulent if the exchange is not for "reasonably equivalent value" or if it is entered into at a time when the transferor has "unreasonably small capital." Within the context of an ABS transaction, an originator who sells revenue-generating assets at a price lower than the "reasonably equivalent value" of the payment stream it is selling risks having the sale set aside as a fraudulent transfer. Similarly, if the sale is structured to actually hinder, delay or defraud the originator's creditors, it will be set aside as a fraudulent transfer. A court is more likely to find a transfer fraudulent if the originator effects it at a time when it is in financial distress. For more on fraudulent transfers, see *supra* section 6e(iv).

Federal Securities Laws

Until recently, the SEC has treated asset-backed securities like corporate securities issued by true operating companies. However, asset-backed securities differ from other securities in that the issuer generally has no material business or management to describe. Thus, among other things, there can be no meaningful management's discussion and analysis ("MD&A") of the financial condition of the issuer.[5] Similarly, GAAP financial information about the issuer does not offer any relevant information to investors.[6]

As discussed earlier, potential investors in asset-backed securities pay special attention to the terms of the sale of the underlying assets to the SPE. Important to an investor is the quality and characteristics of the underlying assets, the servicing standards, the timing and receipt of cash flows from the assets, and the structure for distribution of the cash flows.[7]

Information regarding the characteristics and quality of the assets is, therefore, an indication of how the pool of assets will perform. The quality of the servicing of the underlying assets is also important to investors. This information allows investors to gauge the performance of the asset pool as well as the integrity of the allocation and distribution of assets. As discussed earlier, the legal and economic separation of the assets from the originator is essential to investors. Thus, the investors in asset-backed securities require disclosure concerning the legal and structural nature of the transaction.

SEC registration and disclosure requirements existing before late 2004 did not adequately meet the needs of investors in asset-backed securities. Before late 2004, the SEC attempted to meet investors' needs by systematically issuing no-action letters and by working with ABS issuers during the registration process. In late 2004, the SEC adopted new rules for asset-backed securities ("Regulation AB") in order to address the particular needs of asset-backed security offerings as well as to codify the SEC's prior practices involving these offerings.[8]

Regulation AB focuses on four primary areas of regulation: (1) Securities Act of 1933 registration; (2) disclosure; (3) communications during the offering process; and (4) ongoing reporting under the Securities Exchange Act of 1934. The following summary of Regulation AB attempts to highlight certain provisions relevant to our discussion of securitization.

---

5. *See* Asset-Backed Securities, Securities Act Release No. 33-8518 (Dec. 22, 2004).
6. Id.
7. Id.
8. Id.

(1) Securities Act Registration

In Regulation AB, the SEC adopted what it calls a "principles-based definition" of an asset-backed security. The SEC's definition is designed to provide legal certainty to offerings. The SEC defines "asset-backed security" as

> a security that is primarily serviced by the cash flows of a discrete pool of receivables or other revenue-generating assets, either fixed or revolving, that by their terms convert into cash within a finite time period, plus any rights or assets designed to assure the servicing or timely distributions of proceeds to the security holders; provided that in the case of financial assets that are leases, those assets may convert to cash partially by the cash proceeds from the disposition of the physical property underlying such assets.[9]

The new definition captures more lease-backed transactions and excludes certain issuing entities. Issuing entities may not be investment companies under the Investment Company Act of 1940. Moreover, they must restrict their activities to the specific asset-backed securitization transaction. This means the issuing entity must be passive in its owning or holding of the pool of assets, and in its issuing of the asset-backed securities.

The SEC believes that this principles-based definition allows for flexibility regarding the types of assets and structures that should be subject to its alternative disclosure and regulatory scheme for asset-backed securities. According to the SEC, flexibility is important because it promotes new developments in the securitization industry. Conversely, expanding the definition could result in the inclusion of transactions that are better served by its existing regulatory regime.

Currently, asset-backed securities are typically registered using SEC Form S-3 which facilitates shelf registration. As a result, the originator is able to offer securities on a delayed basis (*i.e.,* "off the shelf") in the future. The prospectus requirements for a Form S-3 registration statement include both a "base" prospectus and a "prospectus supplement" (also known as a "wrap around" as it is literally wrapped around the base). The base prospectus explains what general types of asset-backed security offerings may be effected in the future as well as more generic information about the offerings. The prospectus supplement provides detailed information about a specific future offering. The final prospectus, pursuant to Securities Act Rule 424, is filed at the time of the actual offering of any securities taken off the shelf. The final prospectus consists of the base prospectus and the final prospectus supplement describing the current deal. Issuers of asset-backed securities eligible for Form S-3 registration are no longer required to deliver a preliminary prospectus prior to the delivery of a sales confirmation as previously required under Exchange Act Rule 15c2-8(b).

(2) Disclosure

Regulation AB provides detailed guidelines for specific items of disclosure for ABS offerings. However, disclosure is not required if an item is not applicable to the transaction in question. Generally, the new rules require the transacting parties to disclose information according to their role in the transaction.

(a) Sponsor

Under Item 1104 of Regulation AB, the sponsor (defined as the person who organizes and initiates an ABS transaction) must provide a general description of its securitization

---

9. 17 C.F.R. § 229.1101 (2004).

experience with all types of assets, as well as a more detailed description of its experience originating and securitizing the relevant asset type. Defaults on prior securitizations and any actions taken to prevent such events must also be disclosed. Additionally, the sponsor's underwriting criteria (*i.e.*, the criteria used to determine which specific assets are ultimately sold) must be described.[10]

(b) Issuing Entity

Item 1107 of Regulation AB requires basic information from the issuing entity (*i.e.* the SPE). Governing documents for the issuing entity and material agreements related to the asset-backed securities must be filed as exhibits to the registration statement. Legal structural elements of the transaction must also be described in the prospectus. For example, disclosure must be made as to whether the issuing entity is bankruptcy remote or whether its assets could be considered part of the bankruptcy estate of the sponsor. Material risks related to bankruptcy remoteness must be disclosed as risk factors in the prospectus. Regulation AB requires disclosure of the market price of a pool of assets when that pool is composed of securities.[11]

(c) Servicer

The SEC defines "servicer" as an entity that is responsible for managing or collecting pooled assets, or conducting allocations or distributions to investors. Generally, under Item 1108 of Regulation AB, a servicer must provide a general description of its experience servicing all assets types and a specific description of its experience servicing the relevant asset type. Like the originator, it must also disclose any prior defaults as well as any prior material noncompliance while servicing other securitizations. Financial information is required if the servicer deems its financial condition to be a material risk likely to impact the performance of the asset-backed securities. Also, the servicer is required to disclose the size, composition and growth of its overall servicing portfolio for the past three years.[12]

(d) Trustee

Pursuant to Item 1109 of Regulation AB, the trustee is required to describe its prior experience in similar ABS transactions, as well as its duties and responsibilities regarding the asset-backed securities under both the governing documents and applicable law. In addition, a trustee must disclose whether or not it independently checks cash flows (and, if so, to what extent), the activity in transaction accounts, and compliance with transaction covenants.[13]

(e) Originator

Some ABS transactions involve pooled assets that were not originated by the sponsor. The sponsor may have acquired the pooled assets from a separate originator or through one or more intermediaries in the secondary market before securitizing them. If the pooled assets from a single originator or group of affiliated originators reach a certain concentration threshold, information regarding that originator and its own origination program may become relevant.

---

10. *Id.* at § 229.1104.
11. *Id.* at § 229.1107.
12. *Id.* at § 229.1108.
13. *Id.* at § 229.1109.

An originator, apart from the sponsor or its affiliates, must be identified if it has originated more than 10% of the pooled assets. An originator that has originated more than 20% of the pooled assets must additionally disclose its experience with the asset type as well as the size and composition of its portfolio and its underwriting criteria, if it is deemed material.[14]

(3) Communications During the Offering Process

The SEC has adopted new and amended rules under the Securities Act of 1933 regarding communications during the offering process that codify its prior no-action letters. Generally, the rules permit the use of various written materials coupled with the statutory prospectus in an offering of asset-backed securities. The materials can provide data regarding potential pay-outs of the revenue-generating assets, and disclosure of information about the structure of the offering or about the underlying asset pool. The SEC has also adopted rules that provide safe harbors permitting the publication of research reports during the offering process. Publications that come under the safe harbor would not violate the communications restrictions of Section 5 of the Securities Act.

(4) Ongoing Reporting Under the Exchange Act

Regulation AB codifies the modified reporting system for asset-backed securities. Under the new rules, a modified annual report on Form 10-K is required with (1) a servicer's statement of compliance with its servicing obligations; and (2) a report by an independent public accountant regarding compliance with particular servicing criteria. Certain senior executives of an asset-backed issuer are also required to include a certification, under Section 302 of Sarbanes-Oxley Act of 2002, with its Form 10-K.[15] Additionally, the SEC adopted a new Form 10-D to function as the report for periodic distribution of information currently provided by asset-backed issuers on Form 8-K.

New Developments

For many years since 1970, home mortgages were essentially the only assets securitized to any significant degree. Over the last 15 years, however, other traditional assets, like automobile loans and credit card receivables, were subjected to securitization. More exotic assets have supported ABS transactions in recent years. These assets come from the intellectual property arena, and include fast food, music, film and drug royalties.[16] In this regard, consider the following.

---

14. *Id.* at §229.1110.

15. The new form of certification, as modified by the proposal, requires each specified senior executive to certify, among other things, that, based on the person's knowledge: (a) the Exchange Act periodic reports, taken as a whole, do not contain any untrue statement of a material fact or omit to state a material fact necessary to make the statements made, in light of the circumstances under which such statements were made, not misleading with respect to the period covered by the report; and (b) all of the distribution, servicing and other information required to be provided under Form 10-D for the period covered by the report is included in the report.

16. *See* Yarett, U.S. Operating-Asset or Whole Business Securitization: An Effective New Financing Technique, J. Structured Fin. 69-75 (Fall 2004).

"Ziggy Stardust" Plays the Market

In 1997, singer/songwriter David Bowie securitized his future music royalty receivables for more than 250 of his songs.[1] The bonds securitized by those receivables carry a fixed rate of 7.9%, have an average life of ten years and reach maturity at fifteen years.[2] This transaction was significant because it was the first time music sound recording and publishing royalties were securitized. The deal also represented the first securitization of any privately-held intellectual property rights.

The assets that backed the bonds issued in the Bowie transaction were the future royalties to his existing catalog of music copyrights. Thus, the transaction came to fruition only because Bowie, unlike most musicians, had retained the copyrights in his songs. Further, Bowie often worked alone which meant that he was the sole copyright owner of most of his music. The deal netted the artist $55 million.

Key to the Bowie deal, as with any ABS transaction, is a showing of stable and significant cash flow from the transferred assets. Since the transaction took place in 1997 and Bowie had been producing and selling music for the preceding thirty years, investors were able to predict a steady cash flow from the copyrights and sales of his music. Thus, the copyright owned by a "one-hit wonder" would not be a candidate for securitization.

Since 2001, few music-backed bonds have been issued as the recording industry skidded into an extended downturn relating to the loss of revenue from illegal file sharing over the Internet. In fact, David Bowie's bonds fell to Earth when Moody's lowered its rating on them to one rung above "junk," citing lower-than-expected sales for recorded music. In late 2005, however, as for-profit online platforms for file sharing such as iTunes showed promise, investment bankers have begun thinking about a music-backed bond reprise. See Richardson, Bankers Hope for a Reprise of "Bowie Bonds," Wall St. J., Aug. 23, 2005, at C1.

Questions

1. What are the benefits of securitization? What are the costs and risks? In advising a client with revenue-generating assets capable of being securitized, what would you tell her about the desirability of moving forward with an ABS transaction?

2. Can you think of any other assets capable of being securitized? If so, which ones? Do any of the assets present additional problems not presented by assets traditionally subjected to securitization? See Yarett, U.S. Operating-Asset or Whole Business Securitization: An Effective New Financing Technique, J. Structured Fin. 69-75 (Fall 2004).

3. Based on your knowledge of corporate governance, how do you assess the role of the "independent director" of a SPE? What exactly is this role and how does it differ (if at all) from that of a director of a true operating company? Would you agree to serve as an independent director of a SPE? Before answering, read In re Kingston Assocs., 214 B.R. 713 (Bankr. S.D.N.Y. 1997).

---

1. See Adler, David Bowie's $55 Million Haul; Using a Musician's Assets to Structure a Bond Offering, Ent. L. & Fin., Aug. 1997.

2. See id. at 5. The "average life" of a bond is the average weighted maturity based on an amortization schedule, or in other words, a calculation of how long it would take to earn half of the amount of the bond issue; the "maturity" of a bond is the termination of the period that a note or other obligation has to run.

4. Which factors make a SPE more or less bankruptcy remote? Why is bankruptcy remoteness vital to the success of an ABS transaction? At which stage(s) of an ABS transaction do bankruptcy issues arise?

5. Assume your car loan was securitized. Do you still have the same obligation to pay? Whom, exactly, do you pay? If you have a question about your loan, whom do you call?

6. Which other recording artists besides David Bowie would be good candidates to have their music royalties securitized? What specific attributes relating to their royalties must exist to make the securitization work? In advising an artist as to the pros and cons of securitization, what would you tell her? *See* Richardson, Bankers Hope for a Reprise of "Bowie Bonds," Wall St. J., Aug. 23, 2005, at C1.

Chapter 6

The Rights of Contract Claimants — Part 2: Preferred Stock

Preferred stock is a hybrid security partaking of the characteristics of both debt and equity. As to the debt-like characteristics, preferred stock typically has a high par value (usually equal to its liquidation value) and regular, defined dividends, and is senior to common stock in liquidation. Often, preferred stock is redeemable over a period of time, and sometimes is convertible. Preferred stockholders ordinarily do not receive more than their stated dividend and do not share with common stockholders in the corporation's residual assets on liquidation.[1] Although public issues of preferred stock are relatively infrequent today, privately placed convertible preferred stock is often used in the early stages of venture capital financing of small issuers.

As to the equity-like characteristics, the par value of preferred stock does represent an equity interest in the corporation. The payment of dividends, while fixed and regular, is still subject to the board's declaration and payment and to the legal capital rules of the state in which the issuer was incorporated. Preferred stock is also junior to the corporation's debt in liquidation and cannot force the issuer into involuntary bankruptcy. Finally, dividends paid by the issuer are not tax deductible to the issuer, unlike interest payments on debt.[2]

This combination of characteristics has resulted in some ambiguity with respect to preferred stockholders' rights in relation to directors, the corporation and common stockholders. After a closer examination of the characteristics of preferred stock, we will turn to an examination of these rights.

As mentioned previously in chapter 5, we have purposely chosen to provide a full discussion of convertible securities, including the economics underlying them, in a separate chapter. Therefore, to learn about convertible preferred stock, see *infra* chapter 7.

---

1. An exception is "participating" preferred stock. Holders of this type of preferred stock are entitled to receive any common stock dividends as if their shares of preferred stock were shares of common stock. They may also share in the residual assets along with the common stockholders after a certain level of distributions have been made.

2. An exception is Monthly Income Preferred Stock (MIPS), which claims the advantage for the issuer of a tax deduction of the periodic dividend. *See* Klein & Coffee, Business Organization and Finance 302 (9th ed. 2004).

Section 1
The Characteristics of Preferred Stock

Klein and Coffee, Business Organization and Finance
(9th ed. 2004), 302-306

1. **Introduction.** In prevailing thought and practice, common stock (equity) and bonds (debt) are the bulwarks of the financial structure of corporations. They are the classic or pure modes. Everything else tends to be explained by comparison with common stock or bonds, or both. Preferred stock is described as a *hybrid* of the two basic securities. What this seems to mean is that as to some functional attributes it is like debt, as to others like equity, and as to still others, somewhere between the two. These attributes, which will be described below, are prescribed mostly in state corporation codes and in the corporate articles and by-laws. In this respect, preferred stock is like common.

In recent years many variations of preferred stock have appeared. Some of the most important features that are used are convertibility (into common stock) and variable rates, leading to instruments such as a convertible, adjustable rate preferred, or CAP....

* * *

2. **Control.** Preferred shareholders do not participate in the election of directors except ... where dividends have not been paid for some specified period of time.[a]

3. **Return.** The return to preferred stock is in the form of dividends declared by the Board of Directors. The amount of the dividend is fixed. It is often expressed as a percentage of the par value of the shares, but can be expressed simply as a dollar amount per share per year. The decision whether to pay a preferred stock dividend is within the discretion of the board. Failure to pay is not an act of default like the failure to pay interest on a debt. From the perspective of the corporation (or, perhaps more accurately, its managers and common shareholders) this is one of the attractions of preferred stock, as compared with bonds and other debt.

These days, publicly issued preferred stock is almost always cumulative, which means that if dividends are not paid in any year, the obligation accumulates. No common stock dividend can be paid unless the preferred's past unpaid (cumulative) dividends, or arrearages, and current dividends have been paid. Moreover, if preferred stock dividends are not paid, the preferred shareholders may become entitled to representation on the Board of Directors. Typically this control provision is triggered by the failure to pay anywhere from four to eight quarterly dividends. The number of directors that the preferred can then elect depends on state law and private agreement; it may or may not be a majority. In the case of so-called "preferred" stock issued privately, in venture capital situations, the preferred dividend may not be cumulative, but no dividend can be paid on common unless a dividend is paid on the preferred. In such situations, the preferred is almost certain to be convertible into common and is likely to carry a vote, so it resembles a second class of common, with a liquidation preference.

If the preferred stock dividend is not cumulative, then in the absence of a provision shifting control to the preferred, the position of the preferred may become virtually un-

---

a. These voting rights are contractual. Preferred stockholders may also be entitled to vote pursuant to statutory corporate law. *See, e.g.,* Del. Gen. Corp. Law § 242(b)(1) & (2); N.Y. Bus. Corp. Law §§ 803(a) & 804(a).

tenable. The common shareholders can exercise their control to retain all earnings, forgoing dividends themselves and paying nothing to the preferred shareholders for, say, five years. In the sixth year they can then have the corporation pay the annual preferred stock dividend and pay all the retained earnings from earlier years as dividends to themselves. It is somewhat surprising, but nonetheless a fact, that cumulative preferred shareholders ordinarily are not entitled to interest on arrearages.

If the corporation is liquidated voluntarily, the preferred shareholders are entitled to a fixed sum (usually par value) plus any cumulative dividends, to the extent that funds are available, before any distribution can be made to common shareholders.

4. **Risk.** Implicit in the preceding discussion is the proposition that the expected volatility of current returns on preferred stock at any time is less than that on common and greater than that on bonds. The same kind of relationship obtains with respect to default risk. In the event of insolvency, the claim of preferred shareholders is subordinate (junior) to the claims of bondholders and other creditors but prior (senior) to the claims of common shareholders. It should be recalled, however, that the failure to pay preferred stock dividends does not trigger any right on the part of preferred shareholders to demand repayment of their investment. And even if the failure to pay dividends results in the preferred shareholders gaining control of the Board of Directors, ordinarily they cannot force liquidation over the objection of the common shareholders.

Sometimes preferred shareholders are protected by special provisions, such as a limitation on the amount of dividends that can be paid on the common. Sinking fund retirement requirements are also sometimes used to reduce the risks to the preferred....

5. **Duration and Its Consequences.** Ordinarily, the duration of the preferred stock investment is indefinite. Often the preferred stock is callable (redeemable) by the corporation, usually at a modest premium over the amount of the initial investment plus any cumulative dividends. The preferred shareholders have no right, however, to a return of their investment at some definite time in the future. This fact, together with the fact that the failure to pay dividends does not lead to a winding up of the firm, has produced some rather dramatic illustrations of ... conflict between junior and senior claimants....

Suppose that upon its formation, X Corporation raises $200,000 by selling 100,000 shares of common stock for $1 per share and 1,000 shares of cumulative preferred stock for $100 per share. Suppose that the promised dividend on the preferred is $8 per share annually and that upon liquidation the preferred is entitled to $100 plus arrearages. Suppose finally that the $200,000 of initial capital is invested in a business that has not turned out well; that the expected annual earnings of the firm are $5,000; that the liquidation value of the firm (based on these earnings) is $50,000; and that the corporation is not in arrears on preferred stock dividends but in the future will be able to pay such dividends only to the extent of current earnings. Consider the position of the common shareholders.

If the corporation were liquidated, the entire proceeds ($50,000) would go to the preferred; the common would be wiped out. As we have seen, however, the common shareholders are under no obligation to consent to liquidation. They have nothing to lose by insisting that the corporation stay in business. Present liquidation value is not controlling. The present value of the common will depend on the prospects for future returns to the corporation above the amount needed to satisfy the claims of the preferred. This will depend, in turn, on the dispersion of possible outcomes for the corporation. Suppose that the present investment strategy of the corporation yields the following set of probabilities, outcomes, and values:

STRATEGY I

Probability	Outcome (Earnings)	Value
0.2	$4,000	$ 800
0.6	5,000	3,000
0.2	6,000	1,200
1.0		$5,000

As long as the corporation adheres to this strategy, the most it will earn is $6,000 per year. Nothing will ever be available for the common. The common might have some obstructionist or nuisance value, depending on what portion of the Board of Directors it elects, but that value presumably would be small.

Now suppose that the corporation has available to it another investment strategy, to which it can easily shift, with the following characteristics:

STRATEGY II

Probability	Outcome (Earnings)	Value
0.4	$ 0	$ 0
0.2	5,000	1,000
0.4	10,000	4,000
1.0		$5,000

A shift to Strategy II would produce a 40 percent chance of a total return of $10,000, which would leave $2,000 for the common, after meeting the $8,000 obligation to the preferred. The prospective gain to the common from such a shift obviously would be at the expense of the preferred. In Strategy I, the entire expected return of $5,000 is allocable to the preferred; in all three possible outcomes, all the earnings in effect belong to the preferred; to the extent that any earnings are retained, the claim of the preferred rises correspondingly. In Strategy II, the expected return to the preferred is only $4,200.[74] The expected return to the common is $800.

Suppose that the common shareholders elect a majority of the directors. They are then in a position to have the corporation shift to Strategy II. While this might seem unfair to the preferred, remember that the preferred shareholders could have bargained for more control; they could have bargained for the right to compel liquidation in the event of a failure to pay their dividend; they could have made a short-term loan rather than investing as preferred shareholders. And if they had insisted on those protections, the promised rate of return would no doubt have been lower.

The most obvious protection for the preferred in situations of the sort contemplated here would be a provision giving the preferred the right to elect a majority of the board upon failure to pay the full promised dividend. But even that would not constitute complete protection: the common might be able to foresee the decline in the fortunes of the firm and shift strategy before it became necessary to miss paying any preferred stock dividends. Moreover, if there is a provision that shifts control to the preferred, we may wind up with the shoe on the other foot. If the corporation were

---

74. The expected return to the preferred consists of 0.4(0) plus 0.2($5,000) plus 0.4($8,000), or 0 plus $1,000 plus $3,200.

initially embarked on Strategy II and the preferred gained control it would then be in a position to cause a shift to Strategy I, thereby depriving the common of the prospect of any return.

* * *

Notes and Questions

1. Brealey & Myers, Principles of Corporate Finance 320-321 (4th ed. 1991), write:

> The contract which sets out the terms of the preferred stock also imposes restrictions on the company, including some limits on payments to common stockholders either as dividends or through repurchase of the common stock. These restrictions may also stipulate that the company cannot make any payments to common stockholders unless it is able to maintain a minimum level of common equity and a minimum ratio of working capital to debt and preferred. Other clauses typically require that further issues of securities must have the consent of two-thirds of the preferred shareholders unless the ratio of equity to all debt and preferred stock exceeds a specified minimum.

2. Professors Klein and Coffee identify problems which are similar in nature to those faced by bondholders. Unlike bonds, however, preferred stock is an equity security and thus the directors and officers are treated as being in a fiduciary relationship with preferred stockholders more readily than with bondholders. As Klein and Coffee illustrate, however, these fiduciaries must sometimes deal with conflicting interests. What are the parameters of a fiduciary duty that can permit the board to avoid or mediate these conflicts? To the extent that the board fulfills its duty to the common stockholders, is it necessarily breaching its duty to the preferred stockholders, or vice versa? Is there a workable solution to this dilemma? Or is it better to treat preferred stockholders more like bondholders, and focus on the terms of their contract as the source of their rights? Is any fiduciary conflict illusory? Does the nexus of contracts view of the corporation provide an answer?

Problem — Drafting and Negotiating the Preferred Stock Contract

Alex and Chris form a Delaware corporation, Fright, Inc. (the "Company"), to carry on the business of producing low budget horror movies. Each of them is issued 550,000 shares of common stock. Unfortunately, while they have talent and (sick) imaginations sufficient to ensure the quality of their films, they lack money and need $5,500,000 to start the business and see it through their first production. After studying various commercial business publications, they contact a number of venture capitalists. One, Volatile Funds, Inc. ("Volatile"), has agreed to invest the necessary $5,500,000 for a 50 percent interest in the corporation. Because the business is developing, Volatile would like to make its investment in the form of noncumulative preferred stock, convertible into 50 percent of the Company's common stock (on a fully diluted basis). Volatile's representatives have indicated that they might want to sell off pieces of their investment to other venture capital funds in the near future.

Set forth below are the proposed provisions relating to the preferred stock. Please review these provisions from the perspective of (i) Fright, Inc. and (ii) Volatile Funds, Inc. and answer the questions that follow.

(a) *Designation.* The Company is authorized to issue 55,000 shares of preferred stock, par value $100 per share (the "Preferred Stock"). The rights, preferences, and voting powers, with the restrictions and qualifications thereof, are as follows:

(b) *Dividends.* Holders of Preferred Stock are entitled to receive, when and as declared, out of the net profits of the Company, dividends per share in the amount of $8.00 per annum, payable as the board of directors may determine, before any dividends shall be set apart for or paid upon the common stock. The dividends on the Preferred Stock shall not be cumulative.

(c) *Voting Rights.* The holders of Preferred Stock shall have the following voting rights:

(i) Each share of Preferred Stock shall entitle the holder thereof to one vote on all matters submitted to a vote of the Company's stockholders; and

(ii) Except as otherwise provided herein or by law, the holders of Preferred Stock and the holders of Common Stock shall vote together as one class on all matters submitted to a vote of the Company's stockholders.

(d) *Redemption at Option of the Company.* The Company shall have the right to redeem shares of Preferred Stock pursuant to the following provisions:

(i) The Company shall have the right, at its sole option, and election, to redeem the shares of the Preferred Stock, in whole or in part, at any time and from time to time at a redemption price of $100 per share plus an amount equal to all unpaid dividends thereon to the redemption date; and

(ii) If less than all of the Preferred Stock at the time outstanding is to be redeemed, the shares so to be redeemed shall be selected by lot, pro-rata or in such other manner as the Board of Directors may determine to be fair and proper.

(e) *Liquidation, Dissolution, or Winding Up.* Upon any liquidation, dissolution, or winding up of the Company (whether voluntary or involuntary), no distribution shall be made (i) to the holders of stock ranking junior (either as to dividends or upon liquidation, dissolution, or winding up) to the Preferred Stock unless, prior thereto, the holders of Preferred Stock shall have received $100 per share, plus an amount equal to unpaid dividends thereon, including accrued dividends, whether or not declared, to the date of such payment or (ii) to the holders of stock ranking on a parity (either as to dividends or upon liquidation, dissolution, or winding up) with the Preferred Stock, except distributions made ratably on the Preferred Stock and all other such parity stock in proportion to the total amounts to which the holders of all such shares are entitled upon such liquidation, dissolution, or winding up.

Which provisions serve which party's interests? If you represented Fright, Inc., how would you redraft them? If you represented Volatile Funds, Inc., how would you redraft them? Why use noncumulative rather than cumulative preferred stock? What issues are raised by these provisions that need to be addressed by the parties? What issues are not addressed that should be? Try to be reasonable in your evaluation as both parties want to do the deal.

Optional Problem—Valuing Preferred Stock

Redwood owns 18,000 shares of non-participating, non-convertible, non-voting preferred stock with a par value of $100 per share (the "preferred stock") of Sequoia Lumber Prods. Co. ("Sequoia"). The preferred stock has a dividend of 1% per share per year for the first ten years, increasing to 7% per share per year thereafter. Furthermore, Sequoia has the option, after the tenth year, to redeem up to 10% of the preferred stock each year at par value until all of the preferred stock has been reacquired. Redwood acquired the preferred stock in September 2004 as partial consideration for his sale of all of his stock in Clear-Cut Corp.

In July 2006 Redwood learned that Sequoia has agreed to merge into Desert, Inc., and that pursuant to the merger agreement he is to receive $35 cash for each share of preferred stock. He wants to retain you as counsel to bring an appraisal action on his behalf, because he believes that he is entitled to merger consideration equal to par value, or $100 per share. Write a memorandum to Redwood explaining, based on your knowledge of the principles of valuation, the likelihood of his succeeding in the appraisal action.

Section 2
Dividends and Voting

Gutmann v. Illinois Central R. Co.
189 F.2d 927 (2d Cir. 1951)

FRANK, Circuit Judge.

The trial court's findings of facts—which are amply supported by the evidence and unquestionably are not "clearly erroneous"—establish that the directors acted well within their discretion in withholding declarations of dividends on the non-cumulative preferred stock up to the year 1948. In so holding, we assume, *arguendo*, that, as plaintiff insists, the standard of discretion in weighing the propriety of the non-declaration of dividends on such preferred stock is far stricter than in the case of non-declaration of dividends on common stock. For, on the facts as found and on the evidence, we think the directors, in not declaring dividends on the preferred in the years 1937-1947, adopted a reasonable attitude of reluctant but contingent pessimism about the future, an attitude proper, in the circumstances, for persons charged, on behalf of all interests, with the management of this enterprise.[2]

The issue, then, is whether the directors could validly declare a dividend on the common stock in 1950 without directing that there should be paid (in addition to preferred dividends on the preferred for that year) alleged arrears of preferred dividends, the amount of which had been earned in 1942-1947 but remained undeclared and unpaid....

Our lode-star is Wabash Railway Co. v. Barclay, 280 U.S. 197, 50 S. Ct. 106, 74 L. Ed. 368, which dealt with the non-cumulative preferred stock of an Indiana railroad

---

2. That the directors were not acting in the interest of the common stockholders in disregard of the interest of the preferred appears from the following: The Union Pacific Railroad holds about 25% of the outstanding common stock (i.e., 348,700 shares out of a total of 1,357,994) and was therefore pretty obviously in control of the Board of Directors. Yet, that same Railroad holds about 52% of the outstanding preferred shares (i.e., 98,270 out of a total of 186,457). Union Pacific would plainly be better off if the plaintiff were successful in this suit.

The interest of the public was involved in the reduction of funded debt. For railroads with excessive fixed charges, in periods of stress tend to skimp maintenance and not to improve service.

[Is Judge Frank necessarily correct in his evaluation of Union Pacific's interests?—Eds.]

corporation. There were no controlling Indiana decisions or statutes on that subject. The United States Supreme Court was therefore obliged to interpret the contract according to its own notions of what the contract meant. We have a similar problem here, since there are no Illinois decisions or statutory provisions which control or guide us. Absent such decisions and statutes, we must take the Wabash opinion as expressing the correct interpretation of the rights of non-cumulative preferred stockholders of this Illinois company. For the difference between the language of the preferred stock here and that in Wabash seems to us to be of no moment.

In the Wabash case, plaintiffs, holders of non-cumulative preferred stock, sought an injunction preventing the defendant railroad company from paying dividends on the common stock unless it first paid dividends on the non-cumulative preferred to the extent that the company, in previous years, had net earnings available for that payment and that such dividends remained unpaid. The Court decided against the plaintiffs. It spoke of the fact that, in earlier years, "net earnings that could have been used for the payment were expended upon improvements and additions to the property and equipment of the road"; it held that the contract with the preferred meant that "if those profits are justifiably applied by the directors to capital improvements and no dividend is declared within the year, the claim for that year is gone and cannot be asserted at a later date." We take that as a ruling that the directors were left with no discretion ever to pay any such dividend. For if they had had that discretion, it would surely have been an "abuse" to pay dividends on the common while disregarding the asserted claim of the non-cumulative preferred to back dividends....

Plaintiff, however, seeks to limit the effect of the Wabash ruling to instances where the net earnings, for a given year, which could have been paid to the non-cumulative preferred, have once been expended justifiably for "capital improvements" or "additions to the property or equipment." He would have us treat the words "non-cumulative" as if they read "cumulative if earned except only when the earnings are paid out for capital additions." He argues that the Wabash ruling has no application when net earnings for a given year are legitimately retained for any one of a variety of other corporate purposes, and when in a subsequent year it develops that such retention was not necessary. We think the attempted distinction untenable. It ascribes to the Supreme Court a naive over-estimation of the importance of tangibles (because they can be touched and seen) as contrasted with intangibles. Suppose the directors of a corporation justifiably invested the retained earnings for the year 1945 in land which, at the time, seemed essential or highly desirable for the company's future welfare. Suppose that, in 1948, it turned out that the land so purchased was not necessary or useful, and that the directors thereupon caused it to be sold. Plaintiff's position compels the implied concession that the proceeds of such a sale would never be available for payment of so-called arrears of unpaid non-cumulative preferred dividends, and that the directors would forever lack all discretion to pay them.[7] We fail to see any intelligible difference between (1) such a situation[8] and (2) one where annual earnings are properly retained for any appropriate corporate purpose, and where in a later year the retention proves wholly un-

---

7. Were plaintiff to contend that the proceeds of such a sale are available for preferred dividends he would logically be required to contend that reserves for depreciation of capital assets are similarly available. For such reserves constitute, in effect, a repayment of investment in capital.

8. Or one where, in our supposititious case, the corporation, no longer needing the land, could easily sell it at a handsome figure.

necessary.[9] There is no sensible ground for singling out legitimate capital outlays, once made, as the sole cause of the irrevocable destruction of the claims of the preferred. We do not believe that the Supreme Court gave the contract with the preferred such an irrational interpretation. It simply happened that in the Wabash case the earnings had been used for capital additions, and that, accordingly, the court happened to mention that particular purpose. Consequently, we think that the Court, in referring to that fact, did not intend it to have any significance....

Here we are interpreting a contract into which uncoerced men entered. Nothing in the wording of that contract would suggest to an ordinary wayfaring person the existence of a contingent or inchoate right to arrears of dividends.[13] The notion that such a right was promised is, rather, the invention of lawyers or other experts, a notion stemming from considerations of fairness, from a policy of protecting investors in those securities. But the preferred stockholders are not—like sailors or idiots or infants— wards of the judiciary. As courts on occasions have quoted or paraphrased ancient poets, it may not be inappropriate to paraphrase a modern poet, and to say that "a contract is a contract is a contract." To be sure, it is an overstatement that the courts never do more than carry out the intentions of the parties: In the interest of fairness and justice, many a judge-made legal rule does impose, on one of the parties to a contract, obligations which neither party actually contemplated and as to which the language of the contract is silent. But there are limits to the extent to which a court may go in so interpolating rights and obligations which were never in the parties' contemplation. In this case we consider those limits clear.

In sum, we hold that, since the directors did not "abuse" their discretion in withholding dividends on the non-cumulative preferred for any past years, (a) no right survived to have those dividends declared, and (b) the directors had no discretion whatever to declare those dividends subsequently.

From the point of view of the preferred stockholders, the bargain they made may well be of a most undesirable kind. Perhaps the making of such bargains should be prevented. But, if so, the way to prevent them is by legislation, or by prophylactic administrative action authorized by legislation, as in the case of the S.E.C. in respect of securities, including preferred stocks, whether cumulative or non-cumulative, issued by public utility holding companies or their subsidiaries. The courts are not empowered to practice such preventive legal medicine, and must not try to revise, extensively, contracts already outstanding and freely made by adults who are not incompetents.

Affirmed.

---

9. The attempted distinction would also come to this: (a) The noncumulative preferred irrevocably loses all rights to a dividend as of a given year, if the earnings for that year are invested in fixed capital, but (b) has an inchoate right in the form of a sort of contingent credit if those earnings are reasonably retained for future investments which are never made and which thereafter show up as wholly unnecessary. This is to say that the preferred take the risk of loss of a dividend as of a year in which it is earned when there is a reasonable need for a present capital investment, but no such risk if there is a present reasonable likelihood of a need for such an investment in the future, which later appears undesirable. We see no rational basis for such a distinction.

13. Berle, a most brilliant legal commentator on corporate finance, who may be credited with the authorship of plaintiff's basic contention, admitted that "popular interpretation," including that of "investors and businessmen," holds "non-cumulative" to mean "that dividends on non-cumulative preferred stock, once passed or omitted, are 'dead'; can never be made up." See Berle, Non-Cumulative Preferred Stock, 23 Columbia Law Review (1923) 358, 364-365.

Notes and Questions

1. The interpretation of "non-cumulative" in *Gutmann* generally is followed. The courts of New Jersey are the principal exception. In Sanders v. Cuba Railroad Company, 120 A.2d 849, 852 (N.J. 1956), the New Jersey Supreme Court reaffirmed that state's "dividend credit rule" which precludes accruals only for years in which the corporation has no net earnings:

> It may be acknowledged that New Jersey's dividend credit rule has not generally been accepted by the other states or in the federal courts.... In the recent case of Guttman v. Illinois Central R. Co.... Judge Frank expressed the view that nothing in the terms of the ordinary non-cumulative preferred stock contract points to "a contingent or inchoate right to arrears of dividends" and that the contrary notion is an invention "stemming from considerations of fairness, from a policy of protecting investors in those securities." There seems to be little doubt that equitable factors did play a significant part in the development of New Jersey's doctrine. In the Wabash Railway case, [280 U.S. 197], Justice Holmes stated that there was a common understanding that dividends which were passed (though there were profits from which they could have been declared) were forever gone insofar as non-cumulative preferred stock was concerned; but he referred to no supporting materials and there are those who have suggested a diametrically opposite understanding. See Lattin, Non-Cumulative Preferred Stock, 25 Ill. L. Rev. 148, 157 (1930). This much is quite apparent—if the common stockholders, who generally control the corporation and will benefit most by the passing of the dividends on the preferred stock may freely achieve that result without any dividend credit consequences, then the preferred stockholders will be substantially at the mercy of others who will be under temptation to act in their own self-interest.... While such conclusion may sometimes be compelled by the clear contractual arrangements between the parties there is no just reason why our courts should not avoid it whenever the contract is silent or is so general as to leave adequate room for its construction. In any event, New Jersey's doctrine has received wide approval in legal writings and there does not seem to be any present disposition in this court to reject it or limit its sweep in favor of the Supreme Court's approach in the Wabash Railway case....

The New Jersey dividend credit rule is dependent upon statutory and contract interpretation. In Leeds and Lippincott Company v. Nevius, 30 N.J. 281, 153 A.2d 45 (1989), the New Jersey Supreme Court interpreted the following charter provision to permit common stockholders to receive dividends out of current profits after current dividends (but not arrears) had been paid to the preferred, but to preclude payment of further dividends to the common out of surplus until the preferred's arrearages had been paid:

> The dividends on the preferred stock shall be noncumulative; provided, however, that no dividends shall be paid for any year on common stock in excess of the net profits for that year remaining after payment of Two Dollars and Fifty cents ($2.50) per share for such year on the preferred stock, until dividends earned, but unpaid for any prior year or years on the preferred stock, shall have been paid, but in no other respects shall dividends on preferred stock be cumulative.
>
> No dividends shall be paid on common stock in any year, or for any year, until the full dividend of Two Dollars and Fifty Cents ($2.50) per share for

such year has been paid on the preferred stock, and for prior years as set forth in the preceding paragraph. When all dividends as aforesaid have been declared and shall have become payable on the preferred stock, the Board of Directors may declare dividends on the common stock, out of Net Earnings in excess of Seven Hundred Thousand ($700,000.00) Dollars, payable then or thereafter, with limitations as aforesaid.

Id. at 46.

How strong is the protection offered by the dividend credit rule? The dividend credit rule has been adopted by statute in North Carolina for non-cumulative preferred stock issued after 1957 and before 1969. *See* N.C. Stats. §§ 55-1-40(6a) & 55-6-01(d)(5).

2. If the dividend credit rule is applied, or a similar approach is drafted in the preferred stock contract, should it matter whether the earned but unpaid dividends have been retained by the corporation in cash or have been reinvested for legitimate business purposes? The New Jersey Supreme Court's answer in the *Sanders* case was "no."

3. If the directors have discretion to refuse to pay dividends on non-cumulative preferred stock, would it be a breach of fiduciary duty to the common stockholders for a board to declare dividends on the preferred stock in years in which there are sufficient earnings to pay dividends on the preferred but not the common?

4. How should the risk of non-payment of dividends factor into the determination of dividend rates on non-cumulative preferred stock? Is the likely cost of such preferred sufficiently high that it would be more worthwhile for the corporation to issue debt instead? What are the advantages of owning such a preferred stock?

5. In Wouk v. Merin, 283 A.D. 522, 128 N.Y.S.2d 727 (1st Dep't 1954), the court wrote:

> The rights of the preferred stockholders are determined by the precise language of the certificate in question. We think the trial court erred as a matter of law in its construction of the certificate of incorporation as amended. So far as relevant, the amended certificate provides that on dissolution, after payment of debts, the assets and funds of the company are first to be applied to payment of the par value of Preferred Stock with "any arrearage of dividends to which the holders of such preferred stock may be *entitled*." (Italics ours throughout.) But the certificate also provides that preferred stock "shall be *entitled* to cumulative dividends * * * *as and when* declared." The word "cumulative" must be considered in the light of the provisions declaring when the preferred stock is "entitled" to dividends. Under this certificate it is only the dividends to which the preferred becomes "*entitled*" that are cumulative. We construe this certificate to mean that arrearage of preferred dividends on dissolution refers only to declared dividends which were not paid. As to undeclared dividends herein, the preferred stockholders never became "entitled thereto" and they did not accumulate....

* * *

Dissenting in Wouk v. Merin, Peck, C.J., wrote:

> On the law, I am satisfied that the weight of authority, accepted understanding of what the law is and should be and modern corporate practices favor the plaintiff....
>
> I am further persuaded to this view by the like treatment which is accorded by the certificate of incorporation to preferred stockholders in respect

to accumulated dividends on redemption and dissolution. On redemption a preferred stockholder is certainly entitled to the contemplated benefits of a provision for the payment of accumulated dividends and a similar provision in respect to dissolutions can hardly be given a different construction. It is noted that the appellants in this case recognize the force of this analogy and try to argue in their brief that there is some difference in the certificate provisions as to the payment of accumulated dividends on redemption and on dissolution.

It is true that there is for no apparent reason a slight difference in wording in case of redemption and dissolution, but I cannot see that the words have any different meaning. In the case of redemption, the provision is for the payment of the redemption value of the preferred stock "together with any accumulated dividends due thereon," whereas in the case of dissolution it is for the payment of the par value of the preferred stock "with any arrearage of dividends to which the holders of such Preferred Stock may be entitled."

The appellants concede that in the case of redemption the preferred stock-holders would be entitled to accumulated dividends which accrued by the mere lapse of time. The argument that in the case of dissolution, on the contrary, they are restricted to arrearages of dividends—not accumulated dividends—attempts a distinction which to my mind lacks substance and might encourage the use of dissolutions as a device to wipe out dividend rights. I see no difference between "arrearage of dividends" and "accumulated dividends"....

Baron v. Allied Artists Pictures Corporation

337 A.2d 653 (Del. Ch. 1975), *appeal dismissed*, 365 A.2d 136 (Del. 1976)

BROWN, Vice Chancellor.

Plaintiff originally brought suit as a stockholder of the defendant Allied Artists Pictures Corporation, a Delaware corporation, (hereafter "Allied") to have the 1973 election of directors declared illegal and invalid and to have a master appointed to conduct a new election pursuant to 8 Del. C. §§ 225 and 227. He has since filed a second action seeking the same relief as to the 1974 election of directors, and the two causes have been consolidated for decision based upon the cross-motions of the parties for summary judgment. Both sides to the controversy agree that there is no material dispute of fact and that the matter is a proper one for determination by summary judgment.

Plaintiff charges that the present board of directors of Allied has fraudulently perpetuated itself in office by refusing to pay the accumulated dividend arrearages on preferred stock issued by the corporation which, in turn, permits the preferred stockholders to elect a majority of the board of directors at each annual election so long as the dividend arrearage specified by Allied's certificate of incorporation exists. Defendants contend that the recent financial history and condition of the corporation has justified the nonpayment of the preferred dividend arrearages, at least to the present ....

By way of background, Allied was originally started in the mid-1930's as Sterling Pictures Corporation and later changed its name to Monogram Films under which it gained recognition for many B-pictures and western films. In the early 1950's it changed its name to the present one. Around 1953, with the advent of television, it fell upon hard times. Being in need of capital, Allied's certificate of incorporation was amended in 1954 to permit the issuance of 150,000 shares of preferred stock at a par value of

$10.00, with the dividends payable quarterly on a cumulative basis. The amended language of the certificate provides that the preferred shareholders are entitled to receive cash dividends "as and when declared by the Board of Directors, out of funds legally available for the purpose...." The amended certificate further provides that

" ... in case at any time six or more quarterly dividends (whether or not consecutive) on the Preferred Stock shall be in default, in whole or in part, then until all dividends in default on the Preferred Stock shall have been paid or deposited in trust, and the dividend thereon for the current quarterly period shall have been declared and funds for the payment thereof set aside, the holders of the Preferred Stock, voting as a class, shall have the right, at any annual or other meeting for the election of directors, by plurality vote to elect a majority of the Directors of the Corporation."

In addition, the amended certificate requires that a sinking fund be created as to the preferred stock into which an amount equal to ten per cent of the excess of consolidated net earnings over the preferred stock dividend requirements for each fiscal year shall be set aside. From this sinking fund the preferred stock is to be redeemed, by lot, at the rate of $10.50 per share.

Thereafter, as to the preferred stock issued under the 1954 offering, regular quarterly dividends were paid through March 30, 1963. Subsequently, Allied suffered losses which ultimately impaired the capital represented by the preferred stock as a consequence of which the payment of dividends became prohibited by 8 Del. C. § 170. Allied has paid no dividends as to the preferred shares since 1963. By September 1964 the corporation was in default on six quarterly dividends and thus the holders of the preferred stock became entitled to elect a majority of the board of directors. They have done so ever since.

As of December 11, 1973 election of directors, Kalvex, Inc. owned 52 per cent of the outstanding preferred stock while owning only 625 shares of Allied's 1,500,000 shares of common stock. Since the filing of the first action herein Kalvex has taken steps to acquire a substantial number of common shares or securities convertible into the same. Thus unquestionably Kalvex, through its control of the preferred shares, is in control of Allied, although its holdings are said to represent only 7 per cent of the corporation's equity.

Plaintiff points out that the defendant Emanual Wolf, as director, president and chief executive officer of Allied at an annual salary of $100,000, is also president and chief executive officer of Kalvex. Defendant Robert L. Ingis, a director, vice-president and chief financial officer of Allied, is the executive vice-president of Kalvex. Defendants Strauss and Prager, elected as directors by the preferred shareholders, are also vice-presidents of Allied. Of the four directors nominated by management to represent the common stockholders, and duly elected, two serve Allied at salaried positions and two serve as counsel for Allied receiving either directly or through their firms substantial remuneration for their efforts. Plaintiff asserts that for fiscal 1973, the officers and directors of Allied, as a group, received $402,088 in compensation.

Returning briefly to the fortunes of the corporation, in 1964 Allied was assessed a tax deficiency of some $1,400,000 by the Internal Revenue Service. At the end of fiscal 1963, it had a cumulative deficit of over $5,000,000, a negative net worth of over $1,800,000 and in that year had lost more than $2,700,000. As a consequence Allied entered into an agreement with the Internal Revenue Service to pay off the tax deficiency over a period of years subject to the condition that until the deficiency was satisfied Allied would pay no dividends without the consent of Internal Revenue.

Thereafter Allied's fortunes vacillated with varying degrees of success and failure which, defendants say, is both a hazard and a way of life in the motion picture and theatrical industry....

Starting with 1972, Allied's financial condition began to improve substantially. It acquired the rights to, produced and distributed the film "Cabaret," which won eight Academy Awards and became the largest grossing film in Allied's history up to that time. It thereafter took a large gamble and committed itself for $7,000,000 for the production and distribution of the film "Papillon." In his initial litigation plaintiff complained vigorously of this, but he has since abandoned his objection since "Papillon" proved to be even a greater financial success than "Cabaret." For fiscal 1973 Allied had net income in excess of $1,400,000 plus a $2,000,000 tax carry-over remaining from its 1971 losses. Presumably its financial situation did not worsen prior to the December 11, 1974 election of directors although unquestionably it has gone forward with financial commitments as to forthcoming film releases.

Throughout all of the foregoing, however, the Internal Revenue agreement, with its dividend restriction, persisted. Prior to the 1973 election the balance owed was some $249,000 and as of the 1974 election, one final payment was due, which presumably has now been made. Prior to the 1973 election, Allied was in default on forty-three quarterly preferred dividends totalling more than $270,000. By the time of the 1974 election, the arrearages exceeded $280,000.

Without attempting to set forth all of the yearly financial data relied upon by the plaintiff, his position is, quite simply, that for one or more years since the preferred shareholders have been in control of Allied the corporate financial statements show that there was either a net income for the preceding fiscal year or a capital surplus at the end of the preceding fiscal year in an amount larger than the accumulated preferred dividend arrearages, and that consequently the board of directors elected by the preferred shareholders, being only a caretaker board, had a duty to use such funds to pay the dividend arrearage, and also the balance due on the Internal Revenue agreement, if necessary, and to thereupon return control of the corporation to the common stockholders at the next annual election.... Thus, plaintiff seeks the Court to order a new election at which Allied's board of directors will be elected by the common stockholders.

Plaintiff stresses that he is not asking the Court to compel the payment of the dividend arrearages, but only that a new election be held because of the preferred board's allegedly wrongful refusal to do so. Since the certificate of incorporation gives preferred shareholders the contractual right to elect a majority of the directors as long as dividends are six quarters in arrears, plaintiff, in effect, is asking that this contractual right be voided because of the deliberate refusal of the preferred shareholders to see themselves paid as soon as funds became legally available for that purpose.

* * *

... I fail to see how [plaintiff's] relief can be granted without reaching the question of whether the dividend arrearages should have been paid. While preferences attaching to stock are the exception and are to be strictly construed, ... it is well established that the rights of preferred stockholders are contract rights. In Petroleum Rights Corporation v. Midland Royalty Corp., 19 Del. Ch. 334, 167 A. 835 (1933) a somewhat similar provision of the corporate charter extended to preferred shareholders the right to elect a majority of the board when six quarterly dividends became in arrears, which right continued "*so long as the surplus* ... applicable to the payment of dividends shall be insufficient to pay all accrued dividends." The Chancellor there held that as long as there was the prescribed default in dividends and the surplus remained insufficient, the preferred stockholders were entitled to elect a majority of the board. It was argued to him that this right of election and control was limited by the language "so long as the surplus ... shall be insufficient" and that the accumulation of a surplus sufficient to pay all accrued dividends constituted a condition subsequent, the existence of which would forthwith defeat the right to elect control. This view was rejected, on the theory that if accepted it would mean that the sole purpose of such a scheme would be to put the preferred in control to force a payment of passed dividends once a dividend fund became available. The Chancellor concluded that a shift of control should not be made to turn on the personal interests of the preferred shareholders in dividends alone but, in addition, on the consideration that if surplus fell below unpaid dividends the time had arrived to try a new management. 167 A. 837. He also stated as follows at 167 A. 836:

> " ... if the surplus does in fact exceed the six quarterly dividends in arrear and the preference stock should elect a majority of the board and the board should resolve not to pay the dividends, the right of the preference stock to continue to elect a majority of the board would undoubtedly terminate."

I interpret this to mean that the contractual right to elect a majority of the board continues until the dividends can be made current in keeping with proper corporate management, but that it must terminate once a fund becomes clearly available to satisfy the arrearages and the preference board refuses to do so. Plaintiff seeks to limit this requirement to a mere mathematical availability of funds, and indeed the charter language in *Petroleum Rights* may have intended such a result. Here, however, Allied's charter, and thus its contract with its preferred shareholders, does not limit the right merely until such time as a sufficient surplus exists, as it did in *Petroleum Rights*, but rather it entitles the preferred shareholders to their dividends only "as and when declared by the Board of Directors, out of funds legally available for the purpose." This obviously reposes a discretion in Allied's board to declare preferred dividends, whether it be a board elected by the common or by the preferred shareholders.

The general rule applicable to the right to receive corporate dividends was succinctly stated by Justice Holmes in Wabash Ry. Co. v. Barclay, 280 U.S. 197, 203, 50 S. Ct. 106, 107, 74 L. Ed. 368 (1930):

> "When a man buys stock instead of bonds he takes a greater risk in the business. No one suggests that he has a right to dividends if there are no met [sic] earnings. But the investment presupposes that the business is to go on, and therefore even if there are net earnings, the holder of stock, preferred as well as common, is entitled to have a dividend declared only out of such part of them as can be applied to dividends *consistently with a wise administration of a going concern*." (Emphasis added.)

Although one purpose of allowing the preferred to elect a majority of the board may be to bring about a payment of the dividend delinquencies as soon as possible, that should not be the sole justification for the existence of a board of directors so elected. During the time that such a preference board is in control of the policies and business decisions of the corporation, it serves the corporation itself and the common shareholders as well as those by whom it was put in office. Corporate directors stand in a fiduciary relationship to their corporation and its shareholders and their primary duty is to deal fairly and justly with both....

The determination as to when and in what amounts a corporation may prudently distribute its assets by way of dividends rests in the honest discretion of the directors in the performance of this fiduciary duty. Eshleman v. Keenan, 22 Del. Ch. 82, 194 A. 40 (1937), aff'd 23 Del. Ch. 234, 2 A.2d 904.... Before a court will interfere with the judgment of a board of directors in refusing to declare dividends, fraud or gross abuse of discretion must be shown. Moskowitz v. Bantrell, Del. Supr., 41 Del. Ch. 177, 190 A.2d 749 (1963). And this is true even if a fund does exist from which dividends could legally be paid. As stated by the Chancellor in Eshleman v. Keenan, *supra*, at 194 A. 43:

> "That courts have the power in proper cases to compel the directors to declare a dividend, is sustained by respectable authorities. But that they should do so on a mere showing that an asset exists from which a dividend may be declared, has never, I dare say, been asserted anywhere. In such a case a court acts only after a demonstration that the corporation's affairs are in a condition justifying the declaration of the dividend as a matter of prudent business management and that the withholding of it is explicable only on the theory of an oppressive or fraudulent abuse of discretion."

Plaintiff ... asks for a ruling that a board of directors elected by preferred shareholders whose dividends are in arrears has an absolute duty to pay off all preferred dividends due and to return control to the common shareholders as soon as funds become legally available for that purpose, regardless of anything else. Thus, in effect, he would have the court limit the discretion given the board by the certificate of incorporation, and make the decision of pay arrearages mandatory upon the emergence of a lawful financial source even though the corporate charter does not require it (as perhaps it did in *Petroleum Rights*). He has offered no precedent for such a proposition, and I decline to create one.

Plaintiff's attempt to distinguish his action by asserting that he does not seek to compel the payment of the dividend arrearages, but only to return control to the common stockholders, has a hollow ring. In either case the basic question is whether or not the board has wrongfully refused to pay dividends even if funds did exist which could have been used for such purpose. The established test for this is whether the board engaged in fraud or grossly abused its discretion. The mere existence of a legal source from which payment could be made, standing alone, does not prove either.[a]

When the yearly hit-and-miss financial history of Allied from 1964 through 1974 is considered along with the Internal Revenue obligation during the same time span, I cannot conclude, as a matter of law, that Allied's board has been guilty of perpetuating itself in office by wrongfully refusing to apply corporate funds to the liquidation of the preferred dividend arrearages and the accelerated payment of the Internal Revenue debt. Thus I find no basis on the record before me to set aside the 1974 annual election and to order a new one through a master appointed by the court....

It is clear, however, that Allied's present board does have a fiduciary duty to see that the preferred dividends are brought up to date as soon as possible in keeping with prudent business management.... This is particularly true now that the Internal Revenue debt has been satisfied in full and business is prospering. It cannot be permitted indefinitely to plough back all profits in future commitments so as to avoid full satisfaction of the rights of the preferred to their dividends and the otherwise normal right of the common stockholders to elect corporate management. While previous limitations on net income and capital surplus may offer a justification for the past, continued limita-

---

a. The board's role in declaring dividends generally is discussed *infra* at chapter 8, section 2.

tions in a time of greatly increased cash flow could well create new issues in the area of business discretion for the future.

* * *

Plaintiff's motion for summary judgment is denied. Defendants' motion for summary judgment is granted. Order on notice.

Notes and Questions

1. Why does plaintiff insist that he is not seeking to compel the payment of dividends but only asking that a new election be held?

2. Given the nature of Allied's business and its rather volatile history, do you think the directors would have been more justified in paying dividends or plowing back earnings? What legal risks would the directors face if they paid the preferred dividends and the business suddenly suffered heavy losses which impaired its operations?

3. Why would the preferred stock-appointed directors want to stay on the board? Why wouldn't they pay the preferred stock arrearage as soon as possible and then resign?

4. In addition to the limited voting rights granted to them by corporate statute (*see, e.g.,* Del. Gen. Corp. Law §242(b)(1) & (2)), preferred stockholders traditionally receive contractual voting rights similar to those discussed in *Baron.* Thus, whenever a company fails to declare and pay a prescribed number of quarterly dividends (typically six), preferred stockholders are entitled to elect one or more directors to the company's board. As a matter of timing, however, *when* are preferred stockholders entitled to elect these directors—immediately or at the next regularly scheduled annual meeting of stockholders?

This issue arose in FGC Holdings Ltd. v. Teltronics Inc., 2005 Del. Ch. LEXIS 240. Teltronics's Certificate of Designation provided holders of Teltronics's Series B preferred stock with the right to elect one director to Teltronics's board. The original owner of all the shares of Series B preferred stock, however, had chosen not to exercise this right for five years. As a current creditor of Teltronics, the original owner believed a conflict of interest would be created if it elected a director. After the original holder sold the preferred shares to the plaintiff, the plaintiff sought to exercise its power to elect one director immediately. Teltronics refused.

In ruling in favor of the plaintiff, the Delaware Chancery Court noted that the Certificate of Designation controlled the situation. Pursuant to it, the Series B shareholders, voting as a separate class, had "the exclusive and special right at all times to elect one (1) director ..." to Teltronics's five member board. Teltronics had argued that the plaintiff must wait until the next annual election because the board already had a full complement of directors. But that argument was flawed, according to the Court, because embracing it would allow the common stockholders to eliminate the plaintiff's right to elect a director for up to a whole year. The Court also rejected Teltronics's argument that the plaintiff had waived its right to elect a director by failing to do so at the annual meeting held immediately after the plaintiff purchased the shares, but before the plaintiff had notified Teltronics of its status. Indeed, the Court highlighted that the Certificate of Designation unambiguously granted the plaintiff the right to elect a director at any time.

Nevertheless, in order not to overly disrupt Teltronics's corporate governance, the Court did not force the board to accept the plaintiff's representative as a full board member immediately. Instead, the Court ordered the board to provide the plaintiff's representative with board materials and to allow him to attend meetings until such time as Teltronics held an annual meeting, which the Court ordered to be held within the next month and a half.

Section 3
Repurchases, Redemptions, Conversions and Liquidations

Problem — Recapitalizing a Distressed Corporation

Boll Weevil, Inc., a Delaware corporation (the "Company"), is a clothing manufacturer located in North Carolina. In addition to its 20,000,000 shares of common stock traded on the New York Stock Exchange, it has outstanding 1,000,000 shares of $100 cumulative convertible 10 percent preferred stock, redeemable by the Company at $100 per share plus accrued dividends. Foreign competition and increasing unionization has led the Company to hard times during the last several years. Over the past six months, the price of the Company's common stock has dropped from $21 to $14 per share. Furthermore, earnings have dropped dramatically, and the Company has been unable to pay quarterly dividends on the preferred stock for the past three quarters. The Company's board of directors does not think that it will be able to pay preferred dividends on the next quarterly payment date, as a result of which the preferred stockholders will be empowered by the Company's charter to elect a majority of its directors. The Company's balance sheet reflects $70,000,000 in earned surplus in addition to the $100,000,000 of stated capital attributed to the preferred stock and $2,000,000 of stated capital attributed to the common stock.

You represent the Company. The board would like to eliminate both the preferred stock and the arrearages on the preferred. Write a memorandum to the board explaining how it might accomplish this goal. How might a dissident preferred stockholder seek to block your planned strategy? What is the likelihood of the dissident's success?

The De Facto Merger Doctrine

When is a merger a merger? The *de facto* merger doctrine holds that a variety of transactions that effect the same result as a merger will be treated as having the legal consequences of a merger. For example, assume that Greenacres Corporation sells all of its assets (and transfers its liabilities) to Blackacres Corporation. In exchange, Blackacres issues to Greenacres some of its common stock. Greenacres then dissolves, distributing its assets (which now consist only of Blackacres stock) to its own stockholders. Following this transaction, only Blackacres survives, with its common stock held by its own stockholders as well as the former Greenacres stockholders. Note that the same result would have been accomplished by a merger of Greenacres into Blackacres, with the Blackacres common stock issued as merger consideration. The only difference is that in our example the transaction was structured as a sale of assets followed by a dissolution rather than as a merger. In some jurisdictions, different legal consequences follow from the difference in structure. For example, Delaware grants appraisal rights to dissenters from a merger, but not to dissenters from a sale of assets. *See* Del. Gen. Corp. Law § 262 (no appraisal rights for asset sales); Rev. Model Bus. Corp. Act § 13.02(a)(3) (appraisal rights for assets sales provided only if dissenter was entitled to vote on the transaction); Section 12.01(1) (voting rights not provided for sales of all of a corporation's assets occurring in the "usual and regular" course of business).

Should the difference in structure, despite identical results, lead to different legal treatment? The *de facto* merger doctrine says "no." But only a relatively small number of states recognize the *de facto* merger doctrine. *See* Model Bus. Corp. Act Ann. §§ 11.06 & 12.02 (annotations thereto) (3rd ed. 1984 & Supp. 2000/01/02). Perhaps most importantly, Delaware has rejected the *de facto* merger doctrine in favor of its doctrine of independent legal significance, which holds that each provision of the Delaware statute is to be interpreted according to its own terms, regardless of the fact that the same result could have been achieved using other statutory sections.

We introduce this material here because the doctrine of independent legal significance has been a significant tool for corporations to use in avoiding preferences on preferred stock. We start with *de facto* merger cases because these provide the clearest expression of the doctrine and the parameters of the issue. We then go on to cases in which preferred stockholders have argued (usually unsuccessfully) that particular transactions have constituted *de facto* liquidations and redemptions.

In re Sunstates Corp. Shareholders' Litigation
788 A.2d 530 (Del. Ch. 2001)

LAMB, Vice Chancellor:

[This is] a class action on behalf of the owner of shares of Sunstates Corporation $3.75 Preferred Stock. The complaint alleges that, between 1991 and 1993, and in violation of its certificate of incorporation, Sunstates purchased shares of its common and Preferred Stock when it was in arrears on the Preferred Stock dividend.

The defendants have moved for summary judgment on this claim. They concede the existence of the special limitation in the charter. But they deny its applicability because, as a matter of fact, Sunstates, itself, made no share repurchases. Rather, all reacquired shares were purchased by one or more of Sunstates's subsidiary corporations. Because the Sunstates certificate does not prohibit (although it might have) share repurchases by subsidiaries when the parent is in arrears on its Preferred Stock dividend, defendants argue that they are entitled to judgment in their favor as a matter of law.

Plaintiffs respond that it would render the protective provision of the charter nugatory and illusory if I interpreted it literally to apply only to share repurchases by the corporation itself, since the limitation could so easily be avoided. In a similar vein, they argue that the doctrine of good faith and fair dealing in contracts requires that I interpret the special limitation more broadly to reach the activity of Sunstates's subsidiaries. Finally, they suggest that I should ignore the separate corporate existence of the subsidiaries and treat them as mere agents of the parent corporation for this purpose.

The clause at issue clearly and unambiguously applies the special limitation against share repurchases only to Sunstates and not to its subsidiary entities. Construing that clause strictly, as I must, ... it would be impermissible for me to find that the limitation also governs actions by Sunstates's subsidiaries. The result may be, as plaintiffs argue, that Sunstates was able to avoid the restriction by the simple means of channeling the repurchases through its subsidiaries. Nevertheless, no one who studied the certificate of incorporation should ever have had any other expectation. If the special limitation had been meant to apply to the actions of Sunstates's subsidiaries, the certificate of incorporation could easily have said so.[2]

.... Sunstates Corporation is a Delaware corporation having a number of subsidiaries incorporated in various jurisdictions. Article IV, Section 4.3 of the Sunstates certificate of incorporation creates the $3.75 Preferred Stock. Paragraph 3 thereof specifies the dividend rights of that stock and provides that, unless Sunstates is current in its payment of dividends on the Preferred Stock:

> [T]he Corporation shall not (i) declare or pay or set apart for payment any dividends or distributions on any stock ranking as to dividends junior to the $3.75 Preferred Stock (other than dividends paid in shares of such junior stock) or (ii) *make any purchase ... of ... any stock ranking as to dividends junior or pari passu to the $3.75 Preferred Stock ...*

(emphasis added). Paragraph 4(e) of section 4.3 similarly proscribes all non-pro rata purchases of shares of Preferred Stock when dividends are in arrears, as follows:

> In the event that any semiannual dividend payable on the $3.75 Preferred Stock shall be in arrears and until all such dividends in arrears shall have been paid or declared and set apart for payment, the Corporation shall not ... purchase or otherwise acquire any shares of $3.75 Preferred Stock except in accordance with a purchase offer made by the Corporation on the same terms to all holders of record of $3.75 Preferred Stock for the purchase of all outstanding shares thereof.

Article I, section 1.1 of the certificate defines the "Corporation" to mean Sunstates Corporation. Nothing in the certificate expressly provides that the "Corporation" includes anything but Sunstates Corporation.

In 1991, Sunstates fell into arrears in the payment of the Preferred Stock dividend. Over the next two years, subsidiary corporations controlled, directly or indirectly, by Sunstates bought shares of both common stock and Preferred Stock. The Preferred Shares were not acquired in compliance with the "any and all" tender offer requirement of paragraph 4(e). According to plaintiffs' brief, the repurchases of common stock amounted, over a three year period, to nearly 70 percent of the total outstanding common stock. The Preferred Stock repurchased equaled nearly 30 percent of the total number outstanding.

Plaintiffs point to evidence from which it may be inferred that the decisions to make all these purchases were made by a single person, Clyde Engle. Engle is Sunstates's Chairman and also served as the Investment Officer for Coronet Insurance Company, one of Sunstates's indirect, wholly-owned subsidiaries. Engle controls Sunstates through his ownership control over Telco Capital Corporation, the owner, directly or indirectly, of a majority of Sunstates's common stock. Engle conducted the share repurchase program through Crown Casualty Company and Sunstates Equities, Inc., wholly-owned subsidiaries of Coronet Insurance Company, and through Sew Simple Systems, Inc. and National Assurance Indemnitee Corp., indirect, wholly-owned subsidiaries of Sunstates.

---

2. Fifty years ago, the fallacy of plaintiffs' argument was recognized in the seminal law review article by Richard M. Buxbaum, Preferred Stock—Law and Draftsmanship, 42 Cal. L. Rev. 243, 257 (1954). In discussing problems in drafting financial restriction clauses in preferred stock contract, Professor Buxbaum stated as follows: "As to all these clauses, *it is vital that all payments, distributions, acquisitions, etc. include those of the subsidiaries; otherwise the provisions can be totally avoided*" (emphasis added).

* * *

Section 151(a) of the Delaware General Corporation Law allows Delaware corporations to issue stock having such "special rights, and qualifications, limitations or restrictions" relating thereto "as shall be stated and expressed in the certificate of incorporation or of any amendment thereto...." Thus, the law recognizes that the existence and extent of rights of preferred stock must be determined by reference to the certificate of incorporation, those rights being essentially contractual in nature....

* * *

Plaintiffs advance no construction of the certificate of incorporation that would permit me to read the word "Corporation" to refer to any corporation other than Sunstates. This is hardly surprising since the language at issue is clear in its meaning and there is nothing within the four corners of the certificate suggesting a broader or different interpretation. Thus, as a matter of simple contract interpretation, there is no basis on which to apply the special limitation against share repurchases to any entity other than Sunstates.

.... First, [plaintiffs] argue that the subsidiary corporations making the share purchases were acting as mere agents for Sunstates and, for that reason, the court should treat their acts as those of Sunstates. Second, they argue that the repurchases violated the implied covenant of good faith and fair dealing. I will address these now.

Plaintiffs' agency theory is both factually and legally flawed. Factually, the record suggests that the repurchases were made to further the interests of Engle, the person who (through several layers of intermediary corporations) controlled Sunstates, and not Sunstates's own interests....

* * *

The legal flaw in the agency argument is more fundamental. For the purposes of the corporation law, the act of one corporation is not regarded as the act of another merely because the first corporation is a subsidiary of the other, or because the two may be treated as part of a single economic enterprise for some other purpose. Rather, to pierce the corporate veil based on an agency or "alter ego" theory, "the corporation must be a sham and exist for no other purpose than as a vehicle for fraud."[11]

Plaintiffs' brief simply ignores this more difficult standard—offering no record evidence from which I might infer that any of the four corporations making the share repurchases was a sham or existed merely to perpetrate a fraud. On the contrary, the record shows that each of those entities was engaged in substantial business operations and was formed or acquired by Sunstates for purposes relating to the pursuit of normal business operations....

Plaintiffs fare no better in arguing that Sunstates violated the implied covenant of good faith and fair dealing by its subsidiaries' share repurchases. It is true, that, as a general matter, the implied covenant of good faith and fair dealing exists in all contracts. Nevertheless, the circumstances in which it is relied on to find a breach of contract are narrow....

[T]he only evidence of what the parties "expressly agreed" is found in the prohibition against certain conduct by the "Corporation." That does not provide a reasonable basis to infer that "the parties would have proscribed" share purchases by Sunstates's subsidiaries "had they thought to negotiate with respect to the matter."

---

11. *Wallace v. Wood*, Del. Ch., 752 A.2d 1175, 1184 (1999).

On the contrary, the law of this State has clearly stated for many decades that special rights or preferences of preferred stock must be expressed clearly and that nothing will be presumed in their favor. Thus, there is no basis to infer that any person negotiating the terms of the Sunstates certificate of incorporation could have reasonably believed that the limitation of share repurchases found in Article IV, section 4.3, paragraphs 3 and 4, would preclude repurchase activity by any party other than Sunstates. Indeed, it is more readily inferred that whoever negotiated the Sunstates certificate of incorporation knew and understood the scope of the limitations contained therein.

For similar reasons, I am unable to accept plaintiffs' related argument that the duty of good faith and fair dealing precluded Sunstates from doing indirectly through its subsidiaries that which it was prevented from doing directly itself. It is true that this court has recognized the possibility of applying such a theory to the enforcement of both corporate duties and contract terms governing corporate securities. It has been careful, however, to limit the scope of such application to situations where the subsidiary was newly created for the purpose of evading the duty or the restriction....

[P]laintiffs' arguments run counter to both the doctrine of strict construction of special rights, preferences and limitations relating to stock and the doctrine of independent legal significance. The situation is not unlike that confronted in *Rothschild Int'l Corp. v. Liggett Group, Inc.*, 474 A.2d 133 (1984). There, the plaintiffs owned preferred shares that were entitled to a liquidation preference. To avoid paying this preference, the defendant companies structured a combined tender offer and reverse cash-out merger that eliminated the preferred shares for a price substantially lower than the liquidation preference. Construing the charter provision strictly, the Supreme Court concluded that the charter provision only operated in the case of a liquidation and that there had been no liquidation. *Id.* at 135-136. Applying the doctrine of independent legal significance, the Supreme Court reiterated "that 'action taken under one section of [the DGCL] is legally independent, and its validity is not dependent upon, nor to be tested by the requirements of other unrelated sections under which the same final result might be attained by different means.'"[20]

Note

A survey conducted by this casebook's editors indicates that the article the court cites by Richard Buxbaum is the most-frequently cited law review article by the Delaware courts in corporate law cases.

Rauch v. RCA Corp.
861 F.2d 29 (2d Cir. 1988)

MAHONEY, Circuit Judge:

Plaintiff Lillian S. Rauch appeals from a judgment of the United States District Court for the Southern District of New York, John F. Keenan, *Judge*, dismissing her class action complaint challenging the propriety of a merger effected by defendants for failure to state a claim upon which relief can be granted. The district court held that Rauch's action was barred by Delaware's doctrine of independent legal significance. We affirm.

---

20. *Id.* at 136 (quoting Orzeck v. Englehart, Del. Supr. 195 A.2d 375, 378 (1963)).

Background

This case arises from the acquisition of RCA Corporation ("RCA") by General Electric Company ("GE"). On or about December 11, 1985, RCA, GE and Gesub, Inc. ("Gesub"), a wholly owned Delaware subsidiary of GE, entered into an agreement of merger. Pursuant to the terms of the agreement, all common and preferred shares of RCA stock (with one exception) were converted to cash, Gesub was then merged into RCA, and the common stock of Gesub was converted into common stock of RCA. Specifically, the merger agreement provided (subject in each case to the exercise of appraisal rights) that each share of RCA common stock would be converted into $66.50, each share of $3.65 cumulative preference stock would be converted into $42.50, and each share of $3.50 cumulative first preferred stock (the stock held by plaintiff and in issue here, hereinafter the "Preferred Stock") would be converted into $40.00. A series of $4.00 cumulative convertible first preferred stock was called for redemption according to its terms prior to the merger.

On February 27, 1986, plaintiff, a holder of 250 shares of Preferred Stock, commenced this diversity class action on behalf of a class consisting of the holders of Preferred Stock. It is undisputed that this action is governed by the law of Delaware, the state of incorporation of both RCA and Gesub. Plaintiff claimed that the merger constituted a "liquidation or dissolution or winding up of RCA and a redemption of the [Preferred Stock]," as a result of which holders of the Preferred Stock were entitled to $100 per share in accordance with the redemption provisions of RCA's certificate of incorporation,[2] that defendants were in violation of the rights of the holders of Preferred Stock as thus stated; and that defendants thereby wrongfully converted substantial sums of money to their own use. Plaintiff sought damages and injunctive relief.

.... The district court concluded that the transaction at issue was a bona fide merger carried out in accordance with the relevant provisions of the Delaware General Corporation Law. Accordingly, the district court held that plaintiff's action was precluded by Delaware's doctrine of independent legal significance, and dismissed the complaint.

Discussion

* * *

According to RCA's Restated Certificate of Incorporation, the owners of the Preferred Stock were entitled to $100 per share, plus accrued dividends, upon the redemption of such stock at the election of the corporation. Plaintiff contends that the merger agreement, which compelled the holders of Preferred Stock to sell their shares to RCA for $40.00, effected a redemption whose nature is not changed by referring to it as a conversion of stock to cash pursuant to a merger. Plaintiff's argument, however, is not in accord with Delaware law.

It is clear that under the Delaware General Corporation Law, a conversion of shares to cash that is carried out in order to accomplish a merger is legally distinct from a redemption of shares by a corporation. Section 251 of the Delaware General Corporation Law allows two corporations to merge into a single corporation by adoption of an

---

2. RCA's Restated Certificate of Incorporation, paragraph Fourth, Part I, provides in relevant part:

> (c) The First Preferred Stock at any time outstanding *may be redeemed by the Corporation,* in whole or in part, *at its election,* expressed by resolution of the Board of Directors, at any time or times upon not less than sixty (60) days' previous notice to the holders of record of the First Preferred Stock to be redeemed, given as hereinafter provided, at the price of one hundred dollars ($100) per share and all dividends accrued or in arrears ... (emphasis added).

agreement that complies with that section. Del. Code Ann. tit. viii, § 251(c) (1983). The merger agreement in issue called for the conversion of the shares of the constituent corporations into cash. The statute specifically authorizes such a transaction.... Thus, the RCA-GE merger agreement complied fully with the merger provision in question, and plaintiff does not argue to the contrary.

Redemption, on the other hand, is governed by sections 151(b) and 160(a) of the Delaware General Corporation Law. Section 151(b) provides that a corporation may subject its preferred stock to redemption "by the corporation at its option or at the option of the holders of such stock or upon the happening of a specified event." Del. Code Ann. tit. viii, § 151(b) (1983). In this instance, the Preferred Stock was subject to redemption by RCA *at its election. See supra* note 2. Nothing in RCA's certificate of incorporation indicated that the holders of Preferred Stock could initiate a redemption, nor was there provision for any specified event, such as the Gesub-RCA merger, to trigger a redemption.[3]

Plaintiff's contention that the transaction was essentially a redemption rather than a merger must therefore fail. RCA chose to convert its stock to cash to accomplish the desired merger, and in the process chose not to redeem the Preferred Stock. It had every right to do so in accordance with Delaware law....

.... [I]t is well settled under Delaware law that "action taken under one section of [the Delaware General Corporation Law] is legally independent, and its validity is not dependent upon, nor to be tested by the requirements of other unrelated sections under which the same final result might be attained by different means." *Rothschild Int'l Corp. v. Liggett Group,* 474 A.2d 133, 136 (Del. 1984) (quoting *Orzeck v. Englehart,* 41 Del. Ch. 361, 365, 195 A.2d 375, 378 (Del. 1963)). The rationale of the doctrine is that the various provisions of the Delaware General Corporation Law are of equal dignity, and a corporation may resort to one section thereof without having to answer for the consequences that would have arisen from invocation of a different section....

Rothschild Int'l Corp. v. Liggett Group is particularly instructive....

* * *

[T]he [*Rothschild*] Court stated that "[i]t is equally settled under Delaware law that minority stock interests may be eliminated by merger. And, where a merger of corporations is permitted by law, a shareholder's preferential rights are subject to defeasance. Stockholders are charged with knowledge of this possibility at the time they acquire their shares." *Id.* at 136-37 (citing *Federal United Corp. v. Havender,* 24 Del. Ch. 318, 332-34, 11 A.2d 331, 338 (Del. 1940)). Thus, the defendants were entitled to choose the most effective means to achieve the desired reorganization, "subject only to their duty to deal fairly with the minority interest." *Id.* at 136.

.... Plaintiff claims that the Gesub-RCA merger was, in effect, a redemption. However, there was no redemption within the well-defined meaning of that term under Delaware law, just as there had been no liquidation in *Liggett.* Thus, because the merger here was permitted by law, defendants legitimately chose to structure their transaction

---

3. Plaintiff points, however, to Del. Code Ann. tit. viii, § 251(e) (1983), which provides that "[i]n the case of a merger, the certificate of incorporation of the surviving corporation shall automatically be amended to the extent, if any, that changes in the amendment are set forth in the agreement of merger." Plaintiff contends that the agreement of merger "purports to alter or impair existing preferential rights," ... thus requiring a class vote under other provisions of Delaware law. There are a number of problems with this contention, but the decisive threshold difficulty is that no "existing preferential rights" are altered or impaired in any way, since the holders of Preferred Stock never had any right to initiate a redemption.

in the most effective way to achieve the desired corporate reorganization, and were subject only to a similar duty to deal fairly.

We note in this regard that plaintiff's complaint nowhere alleges that the $40.00 per share conversion rate for the Preferred Stock was unfair. Rather, "[p]laintiff is complaining of a breach of *contractual* rights, entirely divorced from the purported 'fairness' of the transaction." Brief for Plaintiff-Appellant at 23.[4] Moreover, as the district court stated: "Delaware provides specific protection to shareholders who believe that they have received insufficient value for their stock as the result of a merger: they may obtain an appraisal under §262 of the General Corporation Law." Plaintiff, however, explicitly disavows any appraisal theory or remedy, consistent with her position that fairness is not the issue.

* * *

Plaintiff invokes *Sharon Steel Corp. v. Chase Manhattan Bank*, 691 F.2d 1039 (2d Cir. 1982), *cert. denied*, 460 U.S. 1012, 103 S. Ct. 1253, 75 L. Ed. 2d 482 (1983), in which case we said:

> Where contractual language seems designed to protect the interests of both parties and where conflicting interpretations are argued, the contract should be construed to sacrifice the principal interests of each party as little as possible. An interpretation which sacrifices a major interest of one of the parties while furthering only a marginal interest of the other should be rejected in favor of an interpretation which sacrifices marginal interest of both parties in order to protect their major concerns.

Id. at 1051.

Plaintiff contends that this general principle should lead us to override the Delaware doctrine of independent legal significance and rule that the holders of Preferred Stock had a "major interest" in its redemption, whereas it was a matter of relatively less importance to defendants whether they redeemed or converted the Preferred Stock.

It is an adequate response to say that this contention has no basis in Delaware law, which we are bound to apply in this diversity litigation. The protection afforded by Delaware law is the "imperative duty to accord to the minority fair and equitable terms of conversion." *Sterling v. Mayflower Hotel Corp.*, 33 Del. Ch. 293, 303, 93 A.2d 107, 113 (Del. 1952). Plaintiff makes no claim of unfairness, and no plausible argument that *Sharon Steel's* general statement concerning contract interpretation should prompt us to disregard a settled and controlling principle of Delaware corporate law.

Conclusion

The judgment of the district court dismissing the complaint is affirmed.

Notes and Questions

1. Rothschild Int'l Corp. v. Liggett Group Inc., 463 A.2d 642 (Del. Ch. 1983), discussed in the principal case, presented a similar set of facts on the basis of which plain-

---

4. In view of this statement, we deem it irrelevant that the merger agreement provides for redemption of a series of $4.00 cumulative convertible first preferred stock, but not for redemption of plaintiff's Preferred Stock. Since the holders of Preferred Stock had no right to initiate a redemption, the only conceivable relevance of the redemption of another class of preferred stock would be to a fairness claim, which plaintiff has forsworn.

tiff preferred stockholders argued that the ultimate merger of Liggett into a subsidiary of Grand Metropolitan following a successful tender offer resulted in a liquidation of the preferred stockholders' interests in Liggett[1] and thus contractually should have occurred at the higher liquidation price rather than the merger price Grand Metropolitan ultimately paid. The court rejected this argument, as described in *Rauch*. However, three additional points are noteworthy.

First, in *Rauch*, the plaintiff's claims were characterized by the court as follows:

> Plaintiff claimed that the merger constituted a "liquidation or dissolution or winding up of RCA and a redemption of the [Preferred Stock]," as a result of which holders of the Preferred Stock were entitled to $100 per share in accordance with the redemption provisions of RCA's certificate of incorporation, that defendants were in violation of the rights of the holders of Preferred Stock as thus stated; and that defendants thereby wrongfully converted substantial sums of money to their own use.

In *Rothschild*, the court described plaintiff's claim as "breach[] [of] a fiduciary duty owed to the 7% Preferred shareholders by not causing them to be paid the full contractual value of their preferred shares." Are these the same causes of action? In each case, were they adequately addressed by the respective court's reliance on the express language of the charters?

Second, does reference to the equal dignity rule appropriately conclude the matter? In other words, is it necessarily sufficient in *Rauch* for the court to note that §251 governs rather than §§151(b) and 160(a), by resort to the contract? Do the directors have additional duties under these provisions that might help to sustain plaintiff's claim?

Third, *Rothschild* involved an issue of preferred stock which "contained certain features which are said to be relatively uncommon in today's market. Specifically, it could not be redeemed; it was not convertible; and it was not subject to call. Moreover, it was senior to the other classes of Liggett stock in the event of a liquidation." 463 A.2d at 643. Should any of these facts have been important in the court's analysis? If so, do they make Rothschild's case more, or less, compelling than Rauch's?

2. The "doctrine of independent legal significance," otherwise known as the "equal dignity rule," has been the bane of preferred stockholders' existence. In Bove v. Community Hotel Corp. of Newport, R.I., 249 A.2d 89 (1969), the board of directors of Community Hotel Corp. organized Newport Hotel Corp. for the sole purpose of effectuating a merger of the former into the latter. Community Hotel Corp. had outstanding a class of preferred stock as well as common stock. Newport had only common stock, which Community's preferred stockholders were to receive on a five for one basis as consideration in the merger. Community's common stockholders were to receive one share of Newport common. The effect of the merger, of course, would be to eliminate the preferences of the preferred shares. The court recognized that such a recapitalization by charter amendment would require unanimity under Rhode Island law but that the merger could be effectuated with only a ⅔ vote of each class.[2] The court held, on the basis of the equal dignity rule, that the effect of the merger was irrelevant,

---

1. This argument, as recast by the court, was not that Liggett itself was liquidated—it wasn't—but that the interests of the preferred stockholders in Liggett were liquidated as a result of their forcibly being cashed-out by the merger. The court found this contention adequately answered by the language of Liggett's charter providing for the higher liquidation price "only in the event of 'any liquidation of *the assets* of the Corporation …'" (emphasis added).

2. The court noted that the Rhode Island merger provision was "substantially" identical to that of Delaware.

since it was authorized by statute and therefore legitimate. In addressing the next issue, the legality of a corporation's canceling a preferred stockholder's right to dividend arrearages and other preferences by a merger, the court reviewed the history of Delaware law on the subject:

> The earliest case in point of time is Keller v. Wilson & Co., 21 Del. Ch. 391, 190 A. 115 (1936). Wilson & Company was formed and its stock was issued in 1925 and the law then in effect protected against charter amendments which might destroy a preferred shareholder's right to accumulated dividends. In 1927 that law was amended so as to permit such destruction, and thereafter the stockholders of Wilson & Company, by the required majorities, voted to cancel the dividends which had by then accrued on its preferred stock. In invalidating that action the rationale of the Delaware court was that the right of a holder of a corporation's cumulative preferred stock to eventual payment of dividend arrearages was a fixed contractual right, that it was a property right in the nature of a debt, that it was vested, and that it could not be destroyed by corporate action taken under legislative authority subsequently conferred, without the consent of all of the shareholders.
>
> Consolidated Film Industries, Inc. v. Johnson, 22 Del. Ch. 407, 197 A. 489 (1937), decided a year later, was an almost precisely similar case. The only difference was that Consolidated Film Industries, Inc. was not created until after the adoption of the 1927 amendment, whereas in the earlier case the statutory amendment upon which Wilson & Company purported to act postdated both its creation and the issuance of its stock. Notwithstanding the *Keller* rationale that an investor should be entitled to rely upon the law in existence at the time the preferred stock was issued, the court in this case was "unable to discover a difference in principle between the two cases." In refusing to allow the proposed reclassification, it reasoned that a shareholder's fixed contractual right to unpaid dividends is of such dignity that it cannot be diminished or eliminated retrospectively even if the authorizing legislation precedes the issuance of its stock.
>
> Two years elapsed before Federal United Corp. v. Havender, supra, was decided. The issue was substantially the same as that in the two cases which preceded. The dissenting stockholders had argued, as might have been expected, that the proposed corporate action, even though styled a "merger," was in effect a *Keller* type recapitalization and was entitled to no different treatment. Notwithstanding that argument, the court did not refer to the preferred stockholder's right as "vested" or as "a property right in the nature of a debt." Neither did it reject the use of *Keller*-type nomenclature as creating "confusion" or as "substitutes for reason and analysis" which are the characterizations used respectively in Davison v. Parke, Austin & Lipscomb, Inc., 285 N.Y. 500, 509, 35 N.E.2d 618, 622.... Instead, it talked about the extent of the corporate power under the merger statute; and it held that the statute in existence when Federal United Corp. was organized had in effect been written into its charter, and that its preferred shareholders had thereby been advised and informed that their rights to accrued dividends might be extinguished by corporate action taken pursuant thereto.
>
> Faced with a question of corporate action adjusting preferred stock dividends, and required to apply Delaware law under Erie R.R. v. Tompkins, 304 U.S. 64, 58 Sup. Ct. 817, 82 L. Ed. 1188, it is understandable that a federal court in Hottenstein v. York Ice Machinery Corp., 3 [sic] Cir., 136 F.2d 944, 950, found *Keller, Johnson* and *Havender* irreconcilable and said,

> "If it is fair to say that the decision of the Supreme Court of Delaware in the
> Keller case astonished the corporate world, it is just to state that the decision
> of the Supreme Court in Havender astounded it, for shorn of rationaliza-
> tion the decision constitutes a repudiation of principles enunciated in the
> Keller case and in Consolidated Film Industries v. Johnson, supra," at 950.

With Keller's back thus broken, *Hottenstein* went on to say that under Delaware
law a parent corporation may merge with a wholly-owned inactive subsidiary
pursuant to a plan canceling preferred stock and the rights of holders thereof
to unpaid accumulated dividends and substituting in lieu thereof stock of the
surviving corporation.

> Only four years intervened between *Keller* and *Havender*, but that was long
> enough for Delaware to have discarded "vested rights" as the test for determin-
> ing the power of a corporation to eliminate a shareholder's right to preferred
> stock dividend accumulation, and to have adopted in its stead a standard call-
> ing for judicial inquiry into whether the proposed interference with a preferred
> stockholder's contract has been authorized by the legislature. The *Havender*
> approach is the one to which we subscribed as being the sounder, and it has
> support in the authorities....

3. Bowman v. Armour & Co., 160 N.E.2d 753 (Ill. 1959), addressed the legality of
amending the corporate charter to alter the rights of preferred stock. The preferred had
a stated value of $100, a redemption price (at the issuer's option) of $115 plus accrued
dividends, and cumulative dividends of $6 per year when and if declared. Finally, each
share of preferred was convertible into six shares of common stock. The proposed
amendment, required to be approved by ⅔ of each class of stock, would permit the
board to redeem the preferred at $120 per share payable in 5 percent subordinated
debentures with a maturity of thirty years, and one warrant to purchase one share of
common stock. After holding that the section of the relevant Business Corporation Act
permitted the alteration of a security holder's rights by charter amendment, the court
went on to hold that this particular amendment was not authorized by the section:

> The amendment, whether it is viewed as effecting a purchase of the prior
> stock with bonds or as a compulsory redemption thereof, obviously contem-
> plates that the fundamental relationship of stockholder as between the holders
> of the prior stock and Armour will be changed and the prior stockholders will
> become mere creditors of the company.

> A share of stock in a corporation is a unit of interest in the corporation and it
> entitles the shareholder to an aliquot part of the property or its proceeds to the
> extent indicated. The interest of a shareholder entitles him to participate in the
> net profits in proportion to the number of his shares, to have a voice in the selec-
> tion of the corporate officers and, upon dissolution or liquidation, to receive his
> portion of the property of the corporation that may remain after payment of its
> debts. A change in preferences, qualifications or relative rights may increase or
> decrease the right to participate in profits, the right to participate in distribution
> of the assets of the corporation on dissolution or liquidation, or other indicia of
> ownership manifest by the ownership of corporate stock. But the change here
> contemplated is more than that; it is a compulsory redemption or a purchase of
> the stock rather than a divestiture of certain rights and privileges.

> The plan of recapitalization here is not a divestiture of rights or privileges or
> an increase or decrease in relative rights of shares but it is, as we have said, a

compulsory redemption or purchase that results in a change of the status of the shareholder from that of a shareholder to that of a creditor. The ownership of some equity in the corporation is not modified or changed leaving some resulting ownership, but it is liquidated and a corporate owner prior to the amendment finds that subsequent to the amendment he is a creditor.

4. You may have encountered the equal dignity rule before. You will meet it again in chapter 9, section 4, as applied to the rights of common stockholders. Consider whether the doctrine is equally justifiable in both cases.

Elliot Associates, L.P. v. Avatex
715 A.2d 843 (Del. 1998)

VEASEY, C.J.:

* * *

Defendant Avatex Corporation ("Avatex") is a Delaware corporation that has outstanding both common and preferred stock. The latter includes two distinct series of outstanding preferred stock: "First Series Preferred" and "Series A Preferred." Plaintiffs in these consolidated cases are all preferred stockholders of defendant Avatex. The individual defendants are all members of the Avatex board of directors.

Avatex created and incorporated Xetava Corporation ("Xetava") as its wholly-owned subsidiary on April 13, 1998, and the following day announced its intention to merge with and into Xetava. Under the terms of the proposed merger, Xetava is to be the surviving corporation. Once the transaction is consummated, Xetava will immediately change its name to Avatex Corporation. The proposed merger would cause a conversion of the preferred stock of Avatex into common stock of Xetava. The merger will effectively eliminate Avatex' certificate of incorporation, which includes the certificate of designations creating the Avatex preferred stock and setting forth its rights and preferences. The terms of the merger do not call for a class vote of these preferred stockholders. Herein lies the heart of the legal issue presented in this case....

Plaintiffs filed suit in the Court of Chancery to enjoin the proposed merger, arguing, among other things, that the transaction required the consent of two-thirds of the holders of the First Series Preferred stock. Defendants responded with a motion for judgment on the pleadings, which the Court of Chancery granted, finding that the provisions governing the rights of the First Series Preferred stockholders do not require such consent.

The plaintiffs allege that, because of Avatex' anemic financial state, "all the value of Avatex is [currently] in the preferred stock." By forcing the conversion of the preferred shares into common stock of the surviving corporation, however, the merger would place current preferred stockholders of Avatex on an even footing with its common stockholders. In fact, the Avatex preferred stockholders will receive in exchange for their preferred stock approximately 73% of Xetava common stock, and the common stockholders of Avatex will receive approximately 27% of the common stock of Xetava.

* * *

The text of the terms governing the voting rights of the First Series Preferred Stock is set forth in the certificate of designations as follows:

> Except as expressly provided hereinafter in this Section (6) or as otherwise ... required by law, the First Series Preferred Stock shall have no voting rights....

So long as any shares of First Series Preferred Stock remain outstanding, the consent of the holders of at least two-thirds of the shares of the First Series Preferred Stock outstanding at the time (voting separately as a class ...) ... shall be necessary to permit, effect or validate any one or more of the following: ...

(b) The amendment, alteration or repeal, whether by merger, consolidation or otherwise, of any of the provisions of the Restated Certificate of Incorporation or of [the certificate of designations] which would materially and adversely affect any right, preference, privilege or voting power of the First Series Preferred Stock or of the holders thereof ....

These are the operative terms of Section 6 of the certificate of designations setting forth the rights and preferences of the First Series Preferred stock that became effective March 18, 1983. On September 14, 1983 a new certificate of designations became effective with respect to the Second Series Preferred stock. There is, however, no Second Series Preferred stock outstanding....

Delaware law permits corporations to create and issue stock that carries no voting power.... The Avatex certificate of incorporation provides that Avatex preferred shares have no right to vote except on matters set forth therein or required by law. This denial of the right to vote is subject to an exception carved out for any "amendment, alteration or repeal" of the certificate "whether by merger, consolidation or otherwise" that "materially and adversely" affects the rights of the preferred stockholders. Such an event requires the consent of two-thirds of the First Series Preferred stockholders voting as a class.

This appeal, then, reduces to a narrow legal question: whether the "amendment, alteration or repeal" of the certificate of incorporation is caused "by merger, consolidation or otherwise" thereby requiring a two-thirds class vote of the First Series Preferred stockholders, it being assumed for purposes of this appeal that their rights would be "materially and adversely" affected....

Relying primarily on *Warner Communications Inc. v. Chris-Craft Industries Inc.*, 583 A.2d 962, the Court of Chancery held that it was only the conversion of the stock as a result of the merger, and not the amendment, alteration or repeal of the certificate, that would adversely affect the preferred stockholders. [T]he terms of the preferred stock in *Warner* were significantly different from those present here, because in *Warner* the phrase "whether by merger, consolidation or otherwise" was not included. The issue here, therefore, is whether the presence of this additional phrase in the Avatex certificate is an outcome-determinative distinction from *Warner*.

In *Warner*, the question was whether the Series B preferred stock of Warner Communications, Inc. had the right to a class vote on a proposed merger of Warner with Time, Inc. (renamed Time Warner Inc.) and TW Sub, its wholly-owned subsidiary.... The Chancellor held that the drafters of the Warner Series B certificate of designations did not intend for two-thirds of the Series B stockholders to have a veto over every merger in which their interest would be adversely affected because the right to vote was conferred expressly (as it must under Delaware law), and "only in narrowly defined circumstances ... not present here." The two provisions in the certificate of designations involved in *Warner* were as follows. Section 3.3 provided:

So long as any shares of Series B Stock shall be outstanding and unless the consent or approval of a greater number of shares shall then be required by law, ... the affirmative vote or written consent of the holders of at least two-thirds of the total number of the then outstanding shares of Series B Stock ... voting as a class, shall be necessary to alter or change any rights, preferences or limitations of the Preferred Stock so as to affect the holders of all such shares adversely. . . .

Section 3.4 provided:

> So long as any shares of Series B Stock shall be outstanding and unless the consent or approval of a greater number of shares shall then be required by law, without first obtaining the consent or approval of the holders of at least two-thirds of the number of shares of the Series B Stock . . . the Corporation shall not (i) amend, alter or repeal any of the provisions of the Certificate of Incorporation or By-laws of the Corporation so as to affect adversely any of the preferences, rights, powers or privileges of the Series B Stock or the holders thereof. . . .

[N]owhere in the Series B certificate of designations was found the phrase "by merger, consolidation or otherwise," which is the key phrase in the present case. Nevertheless, the heart of the *Warner* rationale . . . is that it was not the amendment, alteration or repeal of the Warner certificate that adversely affected the Warner Series B stock. [I]t was only the conversion of [Warner preferred into Time preferred] that caused the adverse effect. . . . Further, the Chancellor held that no contractual protection of the Warner Series B stock provided for a class vote on a merger. The Chancellor summarized his rationale in *Warner* as follows:

> 1. Section 3.4(i) does not create a right to a class vote on the proposed merger despite the fact that Warner's certificate of incorporation is being amended in the merger because, in the circumstances, the amendment itself will not "adversely affect" the Series B Preferred.
>
> 2. The same reasoning that supports the conclusion that the proposed merger does not trigger a class vote under Section 3.4(i) requires an identical conclusion with respect to 3.3(i).
>
> 3. If the amendment of Warner's certificate does not trigger the class vote provisions of either 3.4(i) or 3.3(i), the dispositive question becomes whether the merger itself may trigger that result under the language of Section 3.3(i) [or stated differently] whether the predicate words of Section 3.3(i), "alter or change," are to be read to include "convert pursuant to a merger." I conclude that Section 3.3(i) does not create a right to a class vote on a merger that will convert the Series B Preferred stock into other securities, other property or cash.

In more detail, he continued:

> Section 3.4(i) provides a right to a series vote . . . in the event of a charter amendment that amends, alters or repeals any provision of the certificate of incorporation so as to adversely affect the Series B Preferred or its holders.
>
> Warner will be the surviving corporation in the proposed merger. Its charter will be amended in the merger. . . . Nevertheless, Section 3.4(i) does not, in my opinion, grant a right to a series vote in these circumstances because the adverse effect upon defendants is not caused by an amendment, alteration or repeal of any provision of Warner's certificate of incorporation. Rather it is the conversion of the Warner [preferred] into [the Time preferred] that creates the adverse effect. . . .
>
> This conclusion is further supported by a review of other provisions of the certificate of designation. . . .

Plaintiffs here argue that *Warner* is distinguishable for three reasons: (1) the fact that the words "whether by merger, consolidation or otherwise" were not present in the Warner

Series B certificate; (2) in *Warner*, unlike here, the preferred stockholders did not remain as stockholders of the surviving corporation, whose certificate arguably was amended and on which the preferred stockholders in *Warner* were relying for a right to a class vote; and (3) in *Warner*, unlike here, the merger was not an attempt simply to change the rights of the preferred stock, but rather there was economic and business substance to that transaction beyond an effort to do indirectly what could not be done directly.

In our view, only the first reason is valid in this appeal. The third reason cited is not before us because we do not examine the economic quality of the merger for purposes of this appeal. The second reason strikes us as a distinction without a difference. Here the First Series Preferred stock of Avatex is converted to common stock of the surviving corporation, Xetava, a newly formed corporation admittedly a wholly owned subsidiary of Avatex created for the sole purpose of effecting this merger and eliminating the rights of the Avatex First Series Preferred. In *Warner*, the Warner Series B Preferred also received a new security [Time preferred] a senior security issued by the surviving corporation, Time (renamed Time Warner). [I]t makes no difference for purposes of this analysis (as plaintiffs argue) that in *Warner* there were two distinct acts that operated independently—that the substitution of charters was between Warner and TW Sub and the exchange of shares was between Warner and Time. The operative events here are that the proposed downstream merger of Avatex into Xetava results in the conversion of Avatex stock to Xetava stock and the elimination "by merger" of the certificate protections granted to the Avatex First Series Preferred. Thus, it is both the stock conversion and the repeal of the Avatex certificate that causes the adverse effect to the First Series Preferred. In *Warner*, it was only the stock conversion that caused the adverse effect because the phrase, "whether by merger, consolidation or otherwise" was not present....

Section 251 of the DGCL describes three ways that a merger or consolidation can affect the certificate of a constituent corporation:

> (1) Section 251(b)(3) Amendments. First, the merger agreement may call for amendments to the pre-existing certificate of the surviving corporation.

> (2) Displacement and Substitution by Merger. Second, the merger can designate the certificate of one of the constituent corporations as the certificate of the surviving entity, and thereby render the certificate of every other constituent corporation a legal nullity.

> (3) Displacement and Substitution via Consolidation. Finally, in the case of a consolidation, the certificate of the resulting corporation displaces and renders a legal nullity the certificate of every disappearing constituent corporation.

In speaking of the "amendment, alteration or repeal" of the Avatex certificate by "merger, consolidation or otherwise," the drafters must have been referring to some or all of the events permitted by Section 251. Therefore, Section 251 provides the relevant backdrop for the interpretation of the First Series Preferred voting rights.

Avatex argued below, and the Court of Chancery appears to have agreed, that only a Section 251(b)(3) Amendment to the surviving corporation's charter amounts to an "amendment, alteration or repeal" within the meaning of the provisions defining the voting rights of the preferred stockholders. Accordingly, the argument runs, these provisions would apply only in the circumstance (not present here) where Avatex survives the merger and its certificate is amended thereby. Since the proposed merger with Xetava does not contemplate any such amendments to the disappearing Avatex certificate, the argument goes, the transaction can go forward without a First Series class vote.

The difficulty with this reading is that it fails to account for the word consolidation, which appears in the phrase "by merger, consolidation or otherwise." A consolidation cannot entail a Section 251(b)(3) Amendment because in a consolidation there is no "surviving corporation" whose pre-existing certificate is subject to amendment. The resulting corporation in a consolidation is a completely new entity with a new certificate of incorporation. All the certificates of the constituent corporations simply become legal nullities in a consolidation. In short, Avatex' proposed reading of the relevant provisions would render the word consolidation mere surplusage, and is problematic for that reason.

Although the transaction before us is not a consolidation, the drafters' use of the word consolidation is significant. They must have intended the First Series Preferred stockholders to have the right to vote on at least some mergers or other transactions whereby the Avatex certificate—and indeed, Avatex itself—would simply disappear. Consolidation, by definition, implicates the disappearance of all constituent corporations. Here, Avatex disappears, just as it would in a consolidation. Under the terms of the proposed merger, Xetava will be the surviving entity and, since Avatex will cease its independent existence, its certificate becomes a legal nullity, as defendants concede. In our view, this constitutes a repeal, if not an amendment or alteration. Thus, the proposed merger is potentially within the class of events that trigger First Series Preferred voting rights.

The first question is: What will happen as a result of the merger to the "rights, preferences, privileges or voting power" of the Avatex First Series Preferred stock as set forth in the existing Avatex certificate? They disappear when the preferred stockholders of Avatex become common stockholders of Xetava under its certificate that does not contain those protections. We assume, as did the trial court, that their elimination would affect the First Series Preferred stockholders adversely.

The second question is: What act or event will cause this adverse effect if the merger is consummated? The trial court held that, "as in Warner," the adverse effect on the plaintiffs "will not flow from any 'amendment, alteration or repeal' of the First Series Certificate (however accomplished) but from the conversion into common stock of the First Series Preferred in the Proposed Merger." The Court so held notwithstanding that it had noted the distinguishing language of the certificate here—not present in Warner—"whether by merger, consolidation or otherwise." But the Court dismissed this distinction by concluding that this "language only modifies the phrase 'amendment, alteration and repeal' and does not independently create a right to a class vote in the case of every merger." But that is not the issue here where there is no contention that the First Series Preferred have a right to a class vote on every merger.

The First Series Preferred holders claim to have the right to a class vote only if (a) a transaction effects the "amendment, alteration or repeal" of the rights provided in the certificate, and (b) "any right, preference, privilege or voting power of the First Series Preferred" would thereby be materially and adversely affected. For example, plaintiffs make clear that the First Series Preferred would not have a class vote on mergers where they receive the same security in a new entity or are cashed out. The attributes of the First Series Preferred would be intact but for the merger or might be continued if the certificate of the corporation surviving the merger—Xetava provided for separate classes of stock, guaranteeing to these holders those same attributes. In our view, the Court of Chancery misapplied Warner's holding that "the amendment contemplated [as a "housekeeping" measure post-merger] is necessitated by the merger [and the] amendment, like the conversion, flows from the merger and is not a necessary condition of it." This was the case in Warner, but is not here. The error of the trial court here was in its conclusion that the observation in *Warner* quoted above "is at least equally apposite here, where Avatex is to be merged with and into Xetava and will simply cease to maintain a separate corporate existence as a matter of law, without the necessity of any amendment, alteration or repeal" of the certificate.

In our view, the merger does cause the adverse effect because the merger is the corporate act that renders the Avatex certificate that protects the preferred stockholders a "legal nullity," in defendants' words. That elimination certainly fits within the ambit of one or more of the three terms in the certificate: amendment or alteration or repeal. The word repeal is especially fitting in this context because it contemplates a nullification, which is what defendants concede happens to the Avatex certificate.

Articulation of the rights of preferred stockholders is fundamentally the function of corporate drafters. Construction of the terms of preferred stock is the function of courts. This Court's function is essentially one of contract interpretation against the background of Delaware precedent.... Any rights, preferences and limitations of preferred stock that distinguish that stock from common stock must be expressly and clearly stated, as provided by statute. Therefore, these rights, preferences and limitations will not be presumed or implied....

In our view, the rights of the First Series Preferred are expressly and clearly stated in the Avatex certificate. The drafters of this instrument could not reasonably have intended any consequence other than granting to the First Series Preferred stock the right to consent by a two-thirds class vote to any merger that would result in the elimination of the protections in the Avatex certificate if the rights of the holders of that stock would thereby be adversely affected....

The drafters were navigating around several alternatives. First, all parties agree that pure amendment protection available to the First Series Preferred stockholders as granted by Section 242(b)(2) of the DGCL and Section 4 of the certificate does not—absent the very phrase at issue here—apply to this merger. Although *Warner* was decided after the Avatex certificate of designations became effective, *Warner* clearly supports this view and it continues to be valid precedent for that proposition. Second, all parties agree that if Avatex would have been the survivor, and its certificate were amended in the merger as contemplated by 8 Del. C. §251(c)(3), the First Series Preferred would have the right to consent by two-thirds class vote....

If Section 6 of the certificate does not guarantee a class vote to the First Series Preferred in this merger, what could it conceivably be interpreted to mean? Defendants argue that the certificate can be construed to apply only in the second instance noted above—namely, in the case where Avatex is the survivor and its certificate is amended, altered or repealed, as contemplated by Section 251(b)(3). But, as plaintiffs point out, this cannot be the only outcome the drafters intended because the certificate grants the First Series Preferred this protection in a consolidation where Section 251(b)(3) does not apply....

The Court of Chancery held, and defendants contend on appeal that *Warner* compels a different result from that which we reach because *Warner* held that there it was only the stock conversion, not the amendment that adversely affected the preferred. But the short answer here is that the language of the First Series Preferred stock is materially different from the language in *Warner* because here we have the phrase, "whether by merger, consolidation or otherwise." This provision entirely changes the analysis and compels the result we hold today. Here, the repeal of the certificate and the stock conversion cause the adverse effect.

It is important to place what we decide today in proper perspective. The outcome here continues a coherent and rational approach to corporate finance. The contrary result, in our view, would create an anomaly and could risk the erosion of uniformity in the corporation law.... [C]ourts should avoid creating enduring uncertainties as to the meaning of boilerplate provisions in financial instruments. To be sure, there are some boilerplate aspects to the preferred stock provisions in the Avatex certificate and those found in other cases. But one is struck by the disuniformity of some crucial provisions, such as the differences that exist when one compares the provisions in *Warner* ... with those presented here....

The path for future drafters to follow in articulating class vote provisions is clear. When a certificate (like the *Warner* certificate or the Series A provisions here) grants only the right to vote on an amendment, alteration or repeal, the preferred have no class vote in a merger. When a certificate (like the First Series Preferred certificate here) adds the terms "whether by merger, consolidation or otherwise" and a merger results in an amendment, alteration or repeal that causes an adverse effect on the preferred, there would be a class vote. When a certificate grants the preferred a class vote in any merger or in any merger where the preferred stockholders receive a junior security, such provisions are broader than those involved in the First Series Preferred certificate. We agree with plaintiffs' argument that these results are uniform, predictable and consistent with existing law relating to the unique attributes of preferred stock.

Notes and Questions

1. Does the Chief Justice protest too much in concluding that "The outcome here continues a coherent and rational approach to corporate finance"?

2. "Corporate drafters" (as the Chief Justice put it) spend substantial energy "articulating" the rights of preferred stockholders (and others) and negotiating them. It is possible that just such energy went into including the pivotal words "whether by merger, consolidation or otherwise" in the Avatex charter. Then again, it is also possible that it did not.

3. Is there any better way to do this?

Section 4
The Extra-Contractual Rights
of Preferred Stockholders

Problem—Structuring a Merger

Slick Oil, Inc., has proposed a merger with Crude Co. pursuant to which Crude Co. will merge into a Slick Oil subsidiary. Crude Co. has 20,000,000 shares of common stock outstanding which are trading at around $56 on the New York Stock Exchange, and 5,000,000 shares of $100 cumulative convertible 7 percent preferred stock trading at $74. Slick Oil is willing to pay an aggregate of $2,150,000,000 to acquire Crude, but has left to Crude's board of directors the manner in which this consideration is to be allocated. Rodney, Crude's president, has asked you to represent Crude in its merger negotiations, and calls to ask you what the board's legal obligations are in allocating the merger consideration. Advise him. In doing so, consider the following:

(i) Assume that the preferred stock carries a dividend rate which is low in comparison with prevailing interest rates on similar securities. What is the relevance of this fact?

(ii) What procedures should the directors follow to increase the likelihood of successfully defending a suit by the preferred stockholders for breach of fiduciary duty?

———————

Dalton v. American Investment Co.
490 A.2d 574 (Del. Ch. 1985), aff'd, 501 A.2d 1230 (1985)

BROWN, Chancellor.

This action is brought by certain preferred shareholders of American Investment Company, a Delaware corporation. The suit charges that the individual defendants, in their capacity as the board of directors of American Investment Company (hereafter "AIC"), breached the fiduciary duty owed by them to the plaintiffs during the course of a merger whereby AIC was merged into Leucadia American Corp., a wholly-owned subsidiary of Leucadia, Inc. ("Leucadia"). In that merger, the common shareholders of AIC were eliminated from their equity position in the corporation at a price of $13 per share. However, the preferred shareholders of AIC were not cashed out, but were left as preferred shareholders of the corporation surviving the merger. Plaintiffs contend that AIC's board looked only to the interests of the common shareholders in seeking a merger partner for AIC and, by so doing, unfairly froze the preferred shareholders into the post-merger AIC as completely controlled by Leucadia. Thus, the suit is unusual in that the plaintiff shareholders are complaining about being unfairly frozen in as shareholders as opposed to the more normal shareholder lament that they were unfairly cashed out.

The plaintiffs also contend that the benefit allegedly given to them in the merger—an increase in their preferred dividend percentage plus the creation of a sinking fund and a plan for the mandatory redemption of the preferred shares—was wrongfully accomplished since it was done without their approval. They say that this constituted a change which adversely affected their existing preference rights and that as a consequence they were entitled to vote as a class on the merger proposal. They say that the failure of the defendants to permit them to vote as a class rendered shareholder approval of the merger illegal and wrongfully forced them into their present predicament. Under either theory plaintiffs seek a recovery of money damages against the individual defendants as well as against Leucadia indirectly through its subsidiary, AIC.

This is a decision after trial, the plaintiffs' earlier application for a preliminary injunction to prevent the consummation of the merger having been denied. The background facts relevant to the decision are set forth hereafter.

I.

Plaintiffs own collectively some 220,000 shares of the total of some 280,000 shares of AIC's 5½% Cumulative Preference Stock, Series B. At the time of the events complained of, AIC had outstanding one other series of 5½% preferred stock consisting of some 81,000 shares. Immediately prior to the merger forming the basis for this litigation, AIC had slightly more than 5.5 million common shares outstanding. Thus, at the time of the merger the common stock comprised 94% of AIC's outstanding shares while the preferred stock constituted the remaining 6%.

The Series B preferred stock was issued in 1961 in consideration for AIC's purchase of two insurance companies owned by the plaintiffs or their predecessors in interest. This Series B preferred had a stated redemption and liquidation value of $25 per share. There was no provision for mandatory redemption of this preferred stock, but it carried with it an annual dividend rate of 5½% which was thus payable indefinitely. The prevailing interest rate in 1961 was approximately ½% and thus, at the time, an annual dividend of 5½% guaranteed indefinitely no doubt appeared to be a good bargain. These terms of the Series B preferred were negotiated as a part of the sale to AIC of the two insurance companies.

Aside from operating the insurance companies, AIC was in the business of consumer finance. In essence, it borrowed money wholesale in order to lend it at retail rates through a chain of offices scattered throughout the country. It is my impression that consumer finance was the primary business of AIC during the 1970s.

During the latter part of the 1970s, AIC found its fortunes gradually becoming a victim of the inflationary spiral that was overtaking the nation....

[T]he rising interest rates accompanying inflation began to put the squeeze on AIC. Its less than optimal bond rating hampered its efforts to obtain the long-term loans which it needed to conduct its consumer finance business and its earlier long-range financing procured in the previous days of lower interest rates was being gradually paid off with current funds. It became obvious that AIC needed either a merger or sale of assets to remain a viable company. As a result, ... AIC retained the investment banking firm of Kidder, Peabody & Co., Inc. ("Kidder, Peabody") for the purpose of seeking out a prospective purchaser or merger partner.

Kidder, Peabody sent out many letters and pursued numerous merger candidates. Eventually, in 1978, Household Finance Corporation ("HFC") came forth with an offer to acquire all outstanding shares of AIC. The offer of HFC was $12 per share for the common stock and $25 per share for the two series of preferred stock. At the time Kidder, Peabody had valued AIC's common stock within a range of $9 to $11, and the $12 figure offered by HFC approximated the then book value of the common shares. At the $25 redemption and liquidation value, the price offered for the preferred shares represented their book value also. The preferred shares were trading for about $9 per share at the time.

This offer by HFC was approved as fair by Kidder, Peabody and was accepted by AIC's board. It was also approved overwhelmingly by AIC's shareholders, both common and preferred. However, the United States Department of Justice entered the picture and sought to prohibit the acquisition by HFC on antitrust grounds. Ultimately, the acquisition of AIC by HFC was enjoined by the federal courts and HFC's merger proposal was terminated.

... AIC's board authorized Kidder, Peabody to reactivate its efforts to find a merger partner for the company. This time, however, Kidder, Peabody was not given an exclusive right to do so, but rather the company also reserved the right to seek and entertain potential candidates on its own. In this endeavor the defendant Robert J. Brockmann, president of AIC and a member of its board, took the most active role.

It is significant to this decision to take note of three things in connection with this renewed effort to seek financial help for AIC, all of which necessarily permeated Brockmann's approach to the task. First, the HFC offer, being well known, had tended to establish a range for the cost of acquisition by other interested parties by indicating a price in the vicinity of $12 per share for the common stock and by further indicating a total acquisition price in the vicinity of $75 million. Secondly, the fact that HFC's offer had compared favorably to the book value of AIC's shares provided Brockmann with the opportunity to suggest book value as the basis for any new offer, especially since the book value of AIC's common shares had increased during the interim even though its overall business outlook had continued to worsen. Thirdly, the offer of HFC to cash out the preferred shares at the $25 redemption and liquidation value had understandably come as somewhat of a surprise to the members of AIC's board. Since the preferred stock had been trading at less than $10 per share at the time, HFC's offer to cash out the preferred at $25 per share had been openly viewed by at least some of their number as a "Christmas present" for the preferred shareholders.

Accordingly, in his individual efforts to find a merger partner for AIC Brockmann adopted the approach of alluding to the book value of AIC's common shares as the basis on which an offer should be made. By that time, the book value of the common shares had increased to $13.50 per share. Brockmann was apparently careful to not ask for $13.50, or for any specific amount for the common shares even in his discussions with Leucadia, the eventual purchaser. He does concede, however, that by referring to the book value of AIC's stock he was attempting to establish a "floor" at which a potential purchaser would be inclined to commence its bidding....

* * *

In August, 1980, Leucadia ... offered $13 per share for all outstanding shares of AIC's common stock and offered further to increase the dividend rate on the preferred shares from 5½% to 7%. In addition, ... because of Brockmann's expression of concern for the preferred shareholders, Leucadia added a "sweetner" [sic] in the form of a sinking fund to redeem the preferred shares over a period of 20 years at the rate of 5% each year. Any such redemptions were to continue to be made by lot as provided by AIC's original preference designations, but subject, however, to the added proviso that any market purchases or other acquisitions of preferred shares made during a given year could be credited against the annual 5% redemption requirement.

Kidder, Peabody opined that this offer was fair to AIC and its shareholders, stressing the fairness of the price to the common (AIC was trading for $11 per share on the day prior to the announcement of the approval of the merger in principle) and the safety that the proposal would provide to the rights of the preferred. The board of AIC accepted the offer and, when put to the vote of the shareholders, it was overwhelmingly approved by AIC's common shareholders and was approved unanimously by the holders of the other series of preferred stock. However, the holders of the Series B preferred, including the plaintiffs, voted some 170,000 of the 280,000 Series B shares against the proposal. Nonetheless, with all shares being accorded an equal vote, the plan of merger was adopted and AIC was merged into Leucadia American Corp., the wholly-owned subsidiary of Leucadia, with the name of the surviving corporation being changed to AIC. The former common shareholders of AIC were cashed out at $13 per share. Leucadia became the owner of all of AIC's common stock while the preferred shareholders were continued on as shareholders of AIC, albeit at the increased dividend rate and with the added redemption and sinking fund provisions.

* * *

[T]he defendant directors of AIC were fourteen in number, and all of them, to one degree or another, owned common stock in AIC. Collectively, their holdings comprised some 12% of AIC's outstanding common stock. However, only one of their number, the defendant Basil L. Kaufmann, owned preferred shares, and his were shares of the other series of preferred. At the same time Kaufmann's preferred holdings were substantial since he owned some 40,000 shares, or one-half of the other series of preferred. As a director, Kaufmann voted in favor of the Leucadia plan of merger.

* * *

[I]t is conceded by the plaintiffs that as of the time of the merger the market value of their Series B preferred was something less than $9 per share and there was no trading market for such shares. It is also acknowledged that under the terms of the merger the holders of the preferred shares were entitled to appraisal rights so as to realize the value of their shares if they so chose. The plaintiffs did not seek such appraisal rights. Actually, some or all of their number sought an appraisal initially, but later withdrew their application, presumably in favor of this suit. Against this factual background, I turn to the contention of the parties and the issues thus presented. Other relevant facts will be set forth as needed.

II.

Addressing first the plaintiffs [sic] breach of fiduciary duty claims, it is their contention that the individual defendants, in their capacity as directors, owed a duty of fair dealing to all shareholders of AIC, both the common and the preferred, in negotiating and agreeing to any plan of merger. They say, however, that the defendant directors violated this duty to the extent that it was owed to the preferred shareholders once the HFC proposal had aborted. They charge that the defendants did so following the cancellation of the HFC offer by discreetly seeking to channel the whole of any prospective purchase price toward the payment for the common shares of AIC alone, and to the deliberate exclusion of the preferred shares.

Plaintiffs suggest that what Brockmann and the other directors did was note that HFC had offered to pay a total of $75.7 million to acquire AIC, broken down into components of $66.5 million for the common ($12 per share × roughly 5.5 million shares) and $9.2 million for the total of the two series of preferred ($25 per share × some 361,000 shares). They say that simple arithmetic shows that AIC's 1980 book value of $13.50 for the common shares multiplied by the 5.5 million common shares outstanding worked out to approximately $75 million. Since it was not necessary for a potential acquirer to cash out the preferred shareholders in order to gain control of the company, and since the AIC board viewed the offer of HFC to purchase the preferred shares at their redemption value of $25 per share as having been a potential "Christmas present" to the preferred shareholders anyway, plaintiffs charge that what Brockmann did, with the board's ultimate approval, was to suggest the book value of the common stock as the starting point for any merger offer so as to assure that the whole of any new offer would go totally to the owners of the common shares.

And, say plaintiffs, this is precisely what happened. They point out that Brockmann concedes that he responded to the initial interest of Leucadia, among others, by suggesting the book value of the common shares as the "floor" for any offer. They insinuate that by so doing Brockmann was attempting to tip-toe around the fact that he was actually soliciting an offer from Leucadia at $13.50 for the common stock and nothing for the preferred. Plaintiffs charge that as a direct result of what was actually a solicitation by Brockmann, Leucadia made the offer ultimately accepted by AIC's board of $13 for the common stock, with the nominal increase in the dividend rate and the creation of the sinking [sic] being thrown as a bone to the preferred shareholders solely to lend an arguable color of fairness to the overall transaction.

Plaintiffs say that this was wrong. They argue that even though they were minority preferred shareholders of AIC, they were nonetheless entitled to the protections of the fiduciary duty of fairness imposed upon those who were in a position to guide the fortunes of the corporation.... They contend that the recent decision in *Weinberger v. UOP, Inc.*, Del. Supr., 457 A.2d 701 (1984) makes it clear that they were owed a duty of fair dealing by AIC's board in its search for financial assistance for the company through the merger route. They say that our law is well established that where the real and only purpose of a merger is to promote the interests of one class of shareholders to the detriment, or at the expense, of another class of minority shareholders, the duty to deal fairly with all shareholders is violated and the merger transaction itself is rendered improper....

Plaintiffs contend that the evidence here points to but one conclusion, namely, that the entire motivation of the AIC board commencing with the resolution of the proxy contest in 1977 was to extricate the common shareholders from a deteriorating situation at the maximum price possible, without equal regard for the best interests of the preferred shareholders.... They say this is made clear by the uncontroverted fact that following the HFC offer neither Brockmann nor anyone else on behalf of AIC asked for any price whatever for the preferred shares in any discussion with prospective purchasers. They would have this fact measured against the equally indisputable fact that the defendant directors got $1 per share more for the common stock from Leucadia in 1980 than HFC offered for it in 1978 even though AIC's investment banker, Kidder[,] Peabody, valued the common shares no higher in 1980 than it did in 1978 at the time of the HFC offer. Since AIC's fortunes were worse in 1980 than in 1978 and thus did not justify a higher price for the common shares even in Kidder, Peabody's view, plaintiffs suggest that the only plausible explanation for the Leucadia offer is that the defendant directors managed to engineer a switch to the common shares of the funds that a prospective purchaser, based upon the HFC offer, would have otherwise paid for the preferred.

Plaintiffs further argue that the defendant directors cannot hide behind the protection of the business judgment rule in so doing. They point to the fact that the defendant directors all owned common stock in the corporation—some of them in substantial amounts—and that consequently each of them stood to gain personally by what plaintiffs view as a solicitation by Brockmann which enticed Leucadia to load up its offer in favor of the common shareholders to the exclusion of the preferred shareholders....

* * *

In response, the defendants take the position that the arguments of the plaintiffs ignore the economic and legal realities of the situation. They point out first that the preference rights applicable to the Series B preferred were negotiated in 1961 as a result of arms-length bargaining surrounding the purchase of the two insurance companies of AIC. They suggest that if the original preferred shareholders failed to negotiate for redemption or other rights in the event of a merger or sale of substantial assets, they had nobody to blame but themselves. Defendants suggest that the Series B shareholders were probably unable to get such rights because they traded them off in order to get what was then a highly favorable 5½% dividend rate, guaranteed indefinitely. But, say the defendants, the fact that what had been a good deal in 1961 had turned sour by 1980—when interest rates were hovering near 20%—did not impose a fiduciary duty on AIC's board to get the Series B preferred shareholders out of that deal, or to negotiate a new deal for them.

In short, defendants argue that the rights of preferred shareholders are contract rights and that as against the rights of the common shareholders they are fixed by the contractual terms agreed upon when the class of preferred stock is created.... Since the preferred shareholders had no contractual right to be bought out as part of the acquisition of AIC by Leucadia—either at par value or at any other price—defendants argue that the board of AIC had no fiduciary duty to bargain on their behalf in an effort to obtain a cash-out deal for them also.

Second, defendants argue that the record is completely devoid of any evidence that they actually solicited an offer from Leucadia for the common shares alone. In fact, they take the position that Leucadia's offer was unsolicited. They say that all that Brockmann did with regard to Leucadia was the same that he did with all other interested parties, namely, attempt to establish a "floor" for any offer by referring to the fact that HFC's offer had been for the equivalent of book value. They say that this did not amount to asking Leucadia to allocate the whole of any offering price to the common shares and to leave the preferred shares in place. They say that Leucadia made its own decision for its own reasons in deciding to offer $13 per share for the common stock alone, as the evidence indicates....

Thirdly, defendants point out that the real reason for Leucadia's offer for the common shares only was the fact that as to Leucadia the preferred shares constituted "cheap debt," as Leucadia well appreciated. They point out that the cost of borrowing $9 million at an approximate 20% rate of interest in order to pay the preferred shareholders their liquidation value of $25 per share so as to eliminate a debt of the corporation carrying a 5½% dividend rate would have made little economic sense.

Defendants say that they have no idea as to why HFC made the surprising offer in 1978 to buy out the preferred shares at face value. They speculate that perhaps it was due to the fact that the average prime interest rate for 1978 was 9.07% coupled with the fact that corporate dividends can only be paid after corporate taxes are paid. For a profit-making corporation, like HFC, the 5½% dividend rate must effectively be doubled in order to obtain the real, after-tax cost. Thus, arguably, the cost to HFC of a 5½% dividend (11%) would have been greater than the 1978 average prime rate of 9.07%, and thus it might have represented sound economics for HFC to have purchased the preferred shares, even at their liquidation value. Regardless of this, however, defendants point out that Leucadia was in the position in 1980 of having a tax-loss carry forward, and thus it was not paying any taxes. Consequently, the after-tax cost to Leucadia of a 5½% dividend was 5½%, which was substantially below the 20% peak in the prime interest rate in 1980. Accordingly, to leave the preferred shares in place permitted Leucadia to purchase what for it was "cheap debt" as a part of the acquisition of AIC, and defendants contend that the evidence shows that Leucadia never considered doing otherwise.

Finally, defendants point out that Leucadia's view of the preferred shares as "cheap debt," and the fact that Leucadia was well aware that it could accomplish its goal of acquiring AIC without the need to purchase the preferred shares, left Brockmann and the other members of AIC's board with absolutely no leverage with which to negotiate a pay-out for the preferred. Moreover, had they attempted to do so once Leucadia made its offer, two consequences were possible—both being fraught with danger insofar as AIC's board was concerned.

First, if AIC's board had attempted to persuade Leucadia to reduce its $13 per share for the common by some portion in order that the difference might be used to cash out the preferred shareholders, such conduct could have been viewed as a breach of the fiduciary duty of fair dealing owed to the common shareholders and subjected the board members to suit for this reason. Alternatively, such an effort by the AIC board might have caused Leucadia to believe that it could acquire the common shares for less than $13 per share, in which event Leucadia might have reduced its offer for the common and still offered nothing for the preferred—again subjecting the board to potential suit by the common shareholders. And, of course, there was always the possibility that if AIC's board rejected the proposal for its failure to include a price for the preferred shares, Leucadia could have backed off and gone the tender offer route for the common shares so as to acquire control in that manner and bring about a merger under its own terms at some later date.

Thus, the defendants contend that on the evidence there is nothing to establish that AIC's board breached any fiduciary duty—particularly a duty of fair dealing—owed to AIC's preferred shareholders. To the contrary, given the absence of any bargaining power that they had on behalf of the preferred, defendants contend that the AIC board members did well to get the preferred dividend rate increased from 5½% to 7% (a 27.3% increase) and to secure a means for the gradual redemption of the shares at face value where none existed before....

III.

Having considered the foregoing arguments in light of the evidence, I am satisfied that the answer to the plaintiffs' charges of breach of fiduciary duty lies somewhere between the legal positions advocated by the parties, and that it turns on the factual determination of whether or not Leucadia's offer was made in response to a solicitation by Brockmann and the other directors defendants [sic]. I find on the evidence that it was not, and accordingly I rule in favor of the defendants on this point.

As framed, the issue appears to be a troublesome one on the surface. However, it can be placed in perspective if certain factors are first weeded out. To begin with, I have no doubt that Brockmann and the AIC board were attempting to invite an offer of $13.50 for the common stock while at the same time they were seeking nothing specific for the preferred shares. One could scarcely reach any other conclusion. I am convinced also that they well suspicioned that if a third party offered anything near that amount for the common stock there would be little, if anything, offered for the preferred. I think that the inference to be drawn from the evidence on this point clearly preponderates in favor of the plaintiffs.

I think also that the Hobson's choice defense raised by the defendant directors—i.e., that once Leucadia's offer came in at $13 for the common stock they could not have attempted to divert part of it to the preferred shareholders without running the risk of breaching the fiduciary duty owed by them to the common shareholders—misses the point. A close examination of the plaintiffs' position reveals that they are not complaining about the conduct of the defendant directors once the Leucadia offer was on the table. Rather, they are charging that but for the misconduct of the defendant directors, i.e., inviting an offer for the common shares alone in deliberate disregard of the rights of the preferred, Leucadia's offer would not have gotten on the table in the form that it did in the first place.

This latter distinction is made evident by the plaintiffs' concession in post-trial argument that if Leucadia's offer for the common stock had been unsolicited, and if Leucadia had been unwilling to pay anything for the preference shares notwithstanding the price that it had to pay for the common, then there would have been little that the AIC board could have done for the preferred shareholders. I think that the evidence indicates that this is close to the situation as it existed.

Given that Brockmann's approach of alluding to the book value of the common shares can, in the context of matters, be reasonably interpreted as a solicitation for an offer for the common shares only without a corresponding offer for the preferred, what the plaintiffs proceed to do in their argument is to then assume that the Leucadia offer was made in response to that solicitation and as a direct result of it. Because only if that were so can the plaintiffs establish that the predicament in which they now find themselves was caused by the conduct of the AIC directors, and only then would we reach the legal question of whether or not it was a breach of the fiduciary duty owed by the directors to the preferred shareholders for them to have engaged in such conduct.

I find that we do not have to reach this legal question because the inference of causal connection which the plaintiffs attempt to draw from the sequence of events as they happened is adequately rebutted by the direct evidence offered by Leucadia. When the trimmings of precedent and fiduciary duty are brushed aside, plaintiffs' argument, reduced to its simplest terms, is (1) that between the HFC proposal in 1978 and the Leucadia merger in 1980 the price per share for the common stock was increased from $12 to $13 per share while the preferred shareholders went from $25 per share to no cash consideration whatever, and (2) that during the interval between the two events Brockmann and the AIC board were soliciting offers at book value, or $13.50, for the common shares while seeking nothing for the preferred. From these two premises plaintiffs proceed to the conclusion that the difference between the HFC and Leucadia proposals was necessarily a direct result of the efforts by the AIC board to increase the cash consideration from the common stock with knowledge that such an increase would be at the expense of the preferred shares. Having thus bridged the gap to arrive at this factual conclusion, plaintiffs then plug it into the legal principle which holds that it is improper for those in a fiduciary position to utilize the merger process solely to promote the interests of one class of shareholders to the detriment, and at the expense, of the members of a minority class of shareholders....

The weakness in the plaintiffs' argument, as I see it, is making the factual assumption that because Brockmann's solicitation of an offer from Leucadia and the subsequent Leucadia offer crossed each other, the latter must have been a direct result of the former. It is the "but for" assumption. It is an argument that "but for" Brockmann's solicitation of an offer for the common stock alone with nothing sought for the preferred, Leucadia would likely have followed HFC's lead and proposed a buy-out of both classes of stock at a price of something less than $13 per share for the common and at a price either equating or approaching the liquidation value of the preferred. In addition to being speculative, such a proposition does not comport with the evidence.

The evidence indicates that the Leucadia offer was formulated and put forth by two of Leucadia's principle officers and shareholders, Ian M. Cumming and Joseph S. Steinberg. Steinberg in particular helped to structure the offer price. He has a background and experience in investment banking. The deposition testimony of Steinberg was admitted in evidence. It reveals that when asked how he arrived at the $13 per share figure which resulted in the total $72.2 million offer, Steinberg responded as follows:

> "I reviewed the published financial data of AIC. I looked at the trading activity of the AIC stock. I looked up in the newspaper what other consumer finance companies were selling for. And I added to that my intuitive opinion of

what it was worth. And I put that all into a hat and shook it up, and out came the price which we were eventually willing to pay after negotiating an overall deal with AIC."

As to Leucadia's reasons for not offering to cash out the preferred, the following colloquy appears:

"Q. As the transaction ultimately took shape, a determination was made by Leucadia not to offer to cash out the preference stock of AIC in the merger transaction; is that right?

A. Yes.

Q. Why?

A. We regarded the preference stock as the equivalent of debt and an important consideration for us in being interested in American Investment was being able to leave in place all of the various long-term debt agreements of AIC. And we were advised by our attorneys that none of the provisions of any of the debt agreements or the preference stock agreement required that the stock be redeemed or debts paid off, and we did not see that it was to our advantage to prepay any debt or redeem any preference stock and were not interested in doing so and probably would not have been interested in the transaction at all if we have been required to prepay debt or redeem preference stock."

Concerning the activities of Brockmann on behalf of the preferred shareholders, Steinberg's testimony was as follows:

"Q. From American Investment's side, did they at any time insist that you make an offer for the preference stock even though your lawyers told you you weren't legally obliged to do so?

A. Bob Brockmann at some point told Ian [Cumming] and told me that the written terms of the preference stock did not require it to be redeemed as part of a merger transaction but that the board of directors of AIC felt an obligation to the preference stockholders to attempt through negotiation to improve their position, and he requested, Brockmann requested, that Leucadia improve the terms of the preference stock somewhat, and we thought about his request, and in order to get a deal done that would be approved by both boards of directors, we offered and they accepted a modification of the preference stock whereby the interest rate of the dividend went up, I believe, to seven percent and a sinking fund was established for the preference stock."

Finally, when asked to compare Leucadia's offer with the earlier HFC offer, Steinberg responded as follows:

"A. Well, Household, I believe, was offering twelve dollars, and our offer was for thirteen on the common, and Household was prepared to redeem the preference stock at slightly over $25, and we were offering to increase the interest rate from 5½ to 7 and to establish a sinking fund where there was none before.

Q. Did you ever give consideration to offering twelve dollars for the common stock and redeeming the preference stock?

A. No."

Overall, Steinberg's testimony indicates that Leucadia had its own economic justification for not cashing out the preferred shareholders, that Leucadia was advised by its attorneys that it was not legally necessary that the preferred shares be bought out, and that Leucadia reached its decision to offer to purchase the common shares only for its own reasons and not because of anything said by Brockmann or anyone else on behalf of AIC.

Accordingly, I find on the evidence that Leucadia's offer in the form in which it was put forth was not made in direct response to a veiled solicitation by Brockmann.... Thus, I cannot find that the terms of the merger which left the plaintiffs as continuing preferred shareholders of AIC were brought about as a result of any breach of fiduciary duty on the part of the defendant directors of AIC, even assuming without deciding that the conduct of Brockmann and the AIC board in seeking a merger partner in the manner they did would have constituted a breach of fiduciary duty owed to AIC's preferred shareholders.

IV.

Plaintiffs' alternative theory for relief is purely a legal one. As noted previously, it is their claim that the Series B preferred had a right to vote as a class on the merger proposal because the sinking fund and the redemption rights to be given to the preferred shareholders under the terms of the merger agreement adversely affected the existing preference rights of their shares. The argument proceeds as follows.

Prior to the merger, AIC's certificate of incorporation provided that any particular class of preference shares could be redeemed at any time and at the prices specified in the certificate of designations for the class, but subject to the provision, however, that in the event of a redemption of less than all such shares, the shares to be redeemed had to be chosen by lot in a fair and impartial manner.

As part of the merger agreement between Leucadia and AIC it was proposed that AIC's certificate of incorporation, and particularly the certificate of designations for the preferred stock, be amended to increase the dividend rate and to provide for the sinking fund and mandatory redemption requirements over the 20-year period. It was also proposed by the same amendment that direct purchases or other acquisitions of preferred shares by AIC—which purchases or acquisitions were not required to be by lot or at the stated redemption price—could be "applied as a credit" against AIC's obligation to redeem shares pursuant to the newly created sinking fund requirement.

The statute governing such a proposed amendment of stock preferences granted by a certificate of incorporation is found at 8 *Del. C.* § 242(b)(2). In relevant part the statute provides as follows:

> "The holders of the outstanding shares of a class shall be entitled to vote as a class upon a proposed amendment, whether or not entitled to vote thereon by the certificate of incorporation, if the amendment would ... alter or change the powers, preferences or special rights of the shares of such class so as to affect them adversely."

Plaintiffs contend that the requirement of redemption by lot as it existed prior to the merger was a special right given to the Series B preferred and that the proposed amendment to their Series B stock preferences effectively altered that right to their detriment. Because of this belief, it is their position that they were entitled by § 242(b)(2) to vote as a class on the proposed merger and that the denial to them of such a class vote tainted the legality of the merger itself. Recognizing that it is not feasible to now undo the merger, plaintiffs seek monetary damages for the wrong which they feel was thus inflicted upon them and which, in their view, contributed directly to their presently undesirable, locked-in position.

The key to this, of course, is whether or not the amendment as proposed was one which altered the plaintiffs' existing preference rights so as to adversely affect them. Plaintiffs say that it did so because, in effect, it permitted AIC thereafter to redeem Series B shares without doing so by lot.... Thus, plaintiffs say that the intended purpose of the amendment was to empower AIC to make selected redemptions from individual shareholders, thereby depriving the plaintiffs of their previously existing opportunity to have shares belonging to them redeemed based upon the luck of the draw.

Moreover, plaintiffs argue that the amendment further deleted their previously existing preference rights by enabling AIC to fulfill its redemption obligations through negotiated repurchases from Series B shareholders who would find themselves unhappily locked into a bad investment, and to do so under conditions which would be very favorable to AIC. They say that the sinking fund has given rise to a form of "reverse auction" by means of which the Series B shareholders are forced to bid against themselves in an effort to get something for their stock now as opposed to waiting out a period of years at a 7% dividend rate on the chance that at some point a redemption of their shares might possibly occur. They suggest that this constituted a coercive plan designed to enable AIC to purchase the preferred shares cheaply and to thus get credit for redemptions at prices substantially below the stated redemption values. Thus, they argue that the amendment has further altered their previously existing preference rights by providing a means for AIC to redeem their shares at less than the stated redemption price.

I find, however, that I am not persuaded by plaintiffs' argument on this issue. The original requirement that any redemption of less than all shares of the Series B stock be accomplished by lot was not changed by the merger. That requirement still remains in the certificate of incorporation. Thus, any redemptions as such which are made necessary in order to meet the annual 5% mandate of the sinking fund must still be done by lot.

Moreover, the new provision which gives AIC the right to credit purchases of preferred shares against the annual redemption requirement of the sinking fund did not give AIC any new powers as against the Series B shareholders since it is undisputed that even before the merger AIC had the statutory right to purchase shares from its shareholders in voluntary transactions at negotiated prices. See 8 *Del. C.* § 160(a). Such repurchases then would have served to reduce the shares remaining for possible redemption just as the repurchases under the amendment would do now. This illustrates, I think, the point to be made.

Prior to the merger AIC was not required to redeem any of the preferred shares at any time. If a preferred shareholder desired to sell his shares on the market for their trading value, AIC could buy them and thus reduce the preferred shares remaining. Presumably, it could also have acquired shares at negotiated prices below the stated redemption value. Its only obligation was to redeem the preferred shares by lot in the event that it elected to redeem some, but not all, shares of either of its two classes of preferred.

Following the merger and the consequent amendment of the certificate of incorporation, the only change that was made was that AIC became obligated to redeem up to 5% of the Series B preferred in each year provided that it did not purchase that amount or more through negotiated or market purchases. To the extent that it might purchase or otherwise acquire some, but not all, of the annual 5% requirement, it became obligated to redeem the difference between the two at the stated redemption value. In either event the redemptions had to be made by lot just as before.

Thus, as I see it, what the amendment did was impose upon AIC a new obligation in the form of a conditional requirement to redeem up to a certain amount of preferred shares each year when previously it was under no obligation to redeem any shares at all. Aside from this, the rules of the game were not changed.

.... Because there may be sufficient Series B shareholders each year who opt to sell their shares to AIC at prices substantially below redemption value in order to get out of the economic bind in which they find themselves, the result may be, at least for a period of years, that AIC will always be able to purchase enough shares on an annual basis to avoid the need to redeem any Series B shares at the redemption price. This will effectively deprive the plaintiffs of any opportunity to have shares owned by them redeemed by lot at the stated redemption value, at least for a period of time....

At the same time, the fact that the plaintiffs had no right to have their Series B redeemed prior to the merger would seem to indicate that they are no worse off now following the merger simply because AIC, through private purchases, can possibly avoid redeeming Series B shares in any given year even though it now has a conditional obligation under the newly created sinking fund provision to do so.

It seems to me that the real basis for the plaintiffs discontent is that insofar as the merger with Leucadia may have been touted as providing an immediate redemption benefit to the owners of the Series B preferred, it was, and has proved to be, illusory. This may be true, and perhaps it was designed by Leucadia to work in this fashion from the outset. I would not be at all surprised to find that it was. However, to say that the promise of any immediate redemption benefit was illusory is not to say that the sinking fund and mandatory redemption amendments to the certificate of incorporation altered the prior redemption preferences of the Series B preferred shares so as to affect them adversely, at least not in the sense of depriving the Series B shareholders of redemption rights that they possessed before. For this reason, I conclude that the plaintiffs have also failed to prove a claim on which relief can be granted on their theory that the Section B shareholders were entitled to vote on the approval of the merger as a class.

V.

* * *

For the reasons given, judgment will be entered in favor of the defendants. A form of order may be submitted.

Questions

1. What are the duties that directors owe to preferred stockholders? How do they differ from duties to bondholders? Consider Equity-Linked Investors, L.P. v. Adams, 705 A.2d 1040 (Del. Ch. 1997). In that case, Genta Inc. (Genta) was experiencing severe financial difficulties and was contemplating a bankruptcy filing. At that time the aggregate liquidation preference owed to the preferred stockholders exceeded the net worth of Genta. In order to cut their losses, the preferred stockholders pushed the board to pursue a liquidation in which the preferreds would receive most of Genta's assets. However, the contractual rights of the preferred stock did not give the holders the necessary legal power to force this course of action on Genta.

Rather than liquidate the company, the board of Genta attempted to raise additional capital in order to exploit Genta's intellectual property going forward for the benefit of the common stockholders. Once a loan transaction with Aries Domestic Fund, L.P. was secured and announced by Genta, the preferred stockholders brought a lawsuit seeking to enjoin the transaction. In refusing to grant the requested relief, the court stated:

While the facts out of which this dispute arises indisputably entail the imposition by the board of (or continuation of) economic risks upon the preferred stock which the holders of the preferred stock did not want, and while this board action was taken for the benefit largely of the common stock, those facts do not constitute a breach of duty. While the board in these circumstances could have made a different business judgment, in my opinion, it violated no duty owed to the preferred in not doing so. The special protections offered by the preferred are contractual in nature.... The corporation is, of course, required to respect those legal rights. But ... generally it will be the duty of the board, where discretionary judgment is to be exercised, to prefer the interests of common stock—as the good faith judgment of the board sees them to be—to the interests created by the special rights, preferences, *etc.*, of the preferred stock, where there is a conflict.

Id. at 1042.

2. In the *Dalton* case, Chancellor Brown struggled with the fact that directors owe fiduciary duties to preferred stockholders as well as common stockholders, in contexts where their interests are in conflict. He seems to have resolved the conflict between them in the manner in which he defined the content of those duties. Chancellor Allen's approach, in the following case, in some ways appears to be more traditional in its concept of fiduciary duty. Does it resolve the conflict?

Jedwab v. MGM Grand Hotels, Inc.
509 A.2d 584 (Del. Ch. 1986)

ALLEN, Chancellor.

MGM Grand Hotels, Inc., a Delaware corporation ("MGM Grand" or the "Company") that owns and operates resort hotels and gaming establishments in Las Vegas and Reno, Nevada, has entered into an agreement with Bally Manufacturing Corporation, also a Delaware corporation, ("Bally") contemplating a merger between a Bally subsidiary and the Company. On the effectuation of such merger, all classes of the Company's presently outstanding stock will be converted into the right to receive cash.

Defendant Kerkorian individually and through Tracinda Corporation, which he wholly owns, beneficially owns 69% of MGM Grand's issued and outstanding common stock and 74% of its only other class of stock, its Series A Redeemable Preferred Stock (the "preferred stock" or simply the "preferred"). Mr. Kerkorian took an active part in negotiating the proposed merger with Bally and agreed with Bally to vote his stock in favor of the merger. Since neither the merger agreement nor the Company's charter contains a provision conditioning such a transaction on receipt of approval by a greater than majority vote, Mr. Kerkorian's agreement to vote in favor of the merger assured its approval.

Neither Kerkorian nor any director or officer of MGM Grand is affiliated with Bally either as an owner of its stock, or as an officer or director. Nor, so far as the record discloses, has any such person had a business or social relationship with Bally or any director, officer or controlling person of Bally. Bally—at least prior to its obtaining an option on Kerkorian's shares as part of the negotiation of the agreement of merger—has owned no stock in MGM Grand.

Plaintiff is an owner of the Company's preferred stock. She brings this action as a class action on behalf of all owners of such stock other than Kerkorian and Tracinda and seeks to enjoin preliminarily and permanently the effectuation of the proposed merger. The gist of the theory urged as justifying the relief sought is that the effectuation of the proposed merger would constitute a breach of a duty to deal fairly with the preferred shareholders owed to such shareholders by Kerkorian, as a controlling shareholder of MGM Grand, and by the directors of the Company. The merger is said to constitute a wrong to the preferred shareholders principally in that it allegedly contemplates an unfair apportionment among the Company's shareholders of the total consideration to be paid by Bally upon effectuation of the merger. Pending is plaintiff's motion for a preliminary injunction.

I.

Recitation of the relevant facts, as they appear at this preliminary stage, may helpfully be divided into two parts: the facts relating to the 1982 creation of the preferred stock on whose behalf this action is prosecuted and the more current events that have lead [sic] to the proposed Bally merger, including the terms of that proposed transaction. Under plaintiff's theory, the circumstances surrounding the 1982 creation of the preferred stock are significant because those circumstances help to demonstrate the essential equivalence of the preferred and the common stock.

A. *The Creation of the Preferred Stock*

MGM Grand, through wholly-owned subsidiaries, owns and operates the MGM Grand Hotel-Las Vegas and the MGM Grand Hotel-Reno. Prior to May 30, 1980, the Company had been called Metro-Goldwyn-Mayer, Inc., and included both the present hotel business and a film production business now conducted through unrelated corporations.

The Company entered the hotel business in December, 1973, with the opening of its Las Vegas facility.... The Las Vegas hotel was very profitable from the outset and in May, 1978, the Company opened its Reno hotel which was constructed on a similarly large scale.

In November, 1980, tragedy struck at the MGM Grand Hotel-Las Vegas. That night a fire consumed the 25-story hotel and 84 lives were lost. The fire required the closing of the Las Vegas hotel for over 8 months and required almost total renovation of that facility. It gave rise as well to protracted litigation relating both to the personal injuries sustained in the fire and the loss of property by the Company. Hundreds of suits were brought against the Company seeking, in total, more than $650 million in compensatory damages and more than $2 billion in punitive damages. In addition, the Company was required to sue its property insurance carriers seeking recovery of losses occasioned by the fire.

Following the Las Vegas disaster there was a significant fall-off in the market value of MGM Grand's common stock. Closing the week of November 14, 1980, at 13¼, the price of the Company's common stock closed at 10 the following week and closed the week of December 12 at 7½.

Apparently in response to the reduced price of the Company's stock and to the risks to stockholders' investment represented by the fire-related litigation claims, on April 1, 1982, the Company publicly offered to exchange one share of common stock for one share of a new class of stock, the Series A Redeemable Preferred Stock. The offer extended to a maximum of 10 million shares of the Company's then outstanding 32,500,000 shares. The offering document stated that Mr. Kerkorian (who at that time controlled very slightly in excess of 50% of the issued and outstanding common stock) would tender into the offer that number of shares equal to the total numbered [sic] tendered by all other shareholders, but in no event would he tender less than 5 million shares.

The preferred stock issued in connection with the 1982 exchange offer carries a cumulative $.44 annual dividend (the same dividend paid with respect to the common stock both at the time of the exchange offer and now), is non-convertible, elects no directors unless dividends remain unpaid for six quarters, has a liquidation preference of $20 per share and carries a complex redemption right.

The redemption provisions require the Company to acquire each year a number of preferred shares determined by a formula set forth in the certificate designating the rights, preferences, etc. of the preferred. The Company, however, is required to redeem stock at $20 per share in any year only if it is unable privately to purchase, on the market or through a tender offer, the number of preferred shares required to be "redeemed" that year. In fact, during fiscal years 1982-84 the Company purchased a total of 766,551 shares of preferred stock on the open market at an average cost of $7.92 per share and has been required to redeem no shares at $20 per share.

The offering document explained the reasons for the exchange offer as follows:

> Prior to the announcement of the Exchange Offer, in management's opinion the earnings and possible future performance of MGM Grand were not being adequately reflected in the market price of the Common Stock. Accordingly, management decided that present stockholders should be given an opportunity to liquidate all or a portion of their Common Stock holdings in exchange for Preferred Stock. Assuming continued earnings of MGM Grand which are available for redemption of Preferred Stock, stockholders accepting the Exchange Offer who hold their Preferred Stock until their shares are called for redemption will receive $20 per share, without regard to future market fluctuations in the Common Stock. To the extent that MGM Grand has only minimal future net profits or has net losses, redemptions of Preferred Stock could extend over a significant number of years.... MGM Grand presently intends to satisfy its redemption obligations to the extent possible by acquiring Preferred Stock in the open market or otherwise so long as such stock can be acquired at a price of less than $20 per share. Accordingly, no assurance can be given as to whether any significant number of shares of Preferred Stock will ultimately be redeemed at the $20 per share redemption price.

With respect to the effect of the exchange on the rights of persons accepting the offer, the offering document stated in part:

> An exchange of Common Stock will result in the holder receiving a security which MGM Grand must redeem (as net profits become available ...) at a price substantially above the market price for MGM Grand's Common Stock prior to the announcement of the Exchange Offer.... Since the rate of redemption depends upon several factors, including MGM Grand's future net profits and dividend levels on the Common Stock (increased dividend levels will result in a slower rate of redemption, while decreased dividends will result in a faster rate), exchanging stockholders will have no assurance as to when their Preferred Stock will be redeemed, and such holders will receive no income other than annual dividends of $.44 per share (payable $.11 a quarter when and as declared by the Board of Directors) for the time the Preferred Stock is held.... Furthermore, all or a portion of the Preferred Stock to be redeemed may be acquired through open market or other purchases by MGM Grand at prices which are substantially less than $20 per share.

> MGM Grand's Board of Directors will continue to exercise the discretion it is granted by law in the management of MGM Grand, and MGM Grand is

under no obligation to adhere to or adopt policies which might maximize short-term income and the rate of redemption of the Preferred Stock at the expense of MGM Grand's long range best interests.

Through the exchange offer, 9,315,403 common shares were exchanged, including 5 million shares by Mr. Kerkorian and his corporation, Tracinda.

B. *Negotiation of the Proposed Merger*

On June 6, 1985, Tracinda and Kerkorian announced an intention to pursue a cash-out merger transaction that would eliminate the public common stockholders from the Company at $18 per share, but would leave the preferred stock in place. In response, the board of the Company created a special committee to review and evaluate such a proposal. The committee retained legal counsel and hired Bear Stearns & Co., Inc., to act as its financial advisor. While events mooted the Tracinda offer before Bear Stearns rendered a formal opinion on the proposed deal, its internal documents reflect the fact that its experts had apparently concluded by July 29 that the proposed offer at $18 per share was fair to the common stockholders from a financial point of view.

Plaintiff suggests that Kerkorian did not entertain a serious interest in acquiring the remaining common stock of the Company but rather announced the proposed Tracinda deal in order to stimulate other offers. Be that as it may, shortly after Tracinda made its announcement, it was approached about a possible acquisition of MGM Grand's hotel properties. Kerkorian was receptive to exploring such alternatives, but no actual offer was forthcoming.

In August, 1985, the Drexel Burnham firm was engaged to explore alternatives to the Tracinda offer. That firm made a significant effort to instigate possible alternative deals—apparently some 50 firms were contacted, but the only indication of serious interest it apparently received was from Bally Manufacturing Corp.[2]

In early November, 1985, Kerkorian, Stephen Silbert, his principal legal advisor, and representatives of Drexel Burnham met with Robert Mullane, the chairman and chief executive officer of Bally to discuss Bally's interest. At that meeting Bally apparently ultimately took the position that it thought all of the Company's equity was worth $440 million and said it would be willing to make a cash offer at that price for all the Company's stock—common and preferred.

It seems agreed by all parties that Bally made a total price offer and had no real input into the way in which that consideration would be divided among classes of MGM Grand's stock, although its concurrence was obviously required. Kerkorian and Silbert had, however, discussed that question prior to the meeting, and Kerkorian had expressed the view that the common stock should get $18 a share since Tracinda had already announced an offer at that price.

Kerkorian, after discussions with his lawyer Silbert and with Drexel Burnham apparently determined that $14 was the price that would be paid for the preferred. However, a $14 per share price for the outstanding preferred, when added to an $18 price for all the common stock, would result in a cash price in excess of $440 million for all of the

---

2. Previously, in July, 1985, Bear Stearns had approached Bally and suggested that perhaps Bally might be interested in purchasing MGM Grand common stock at a price of $18 per share. Bally's Chief Financial Officer, Donald Romans, did some calculations and concluded that, " ... the price was too rich at 18 for the common to be of interest to Bally." [References to the record have been deleted throughout.]

Company's stock. To solve this problem, Kerkorian agreed to take $12.24 per share for his common stock together with certain other property, including transfer of the exclusive rights to the name MGM Grand Hotels and certain contingent rights in litigation proceeds.[3] This non-cash property has been the subject of an appraisal and, in part on the basis of that appraisal, Bear Stearns has opined that the total value of the consideration Kerkorian will receive for his common stock is less than $18 per share.

.... On November 14, a special meeting of the MGM Grand board was held to consider the proposed Bally merger. At that meeting Drexel Burnham reported on its efforts to locate parties with an interest in acquiring the Company, the results of its work, and its evaluation of the Bally proposal as negotiated. Although not retained to render an opinion on the fairness of the proposed transaction, Drexel Burnham did report its opinion that the price contemplated by the proposal for the common stock and the preferred stock was fair. The directors were presented with copies of the proposed agreement of merger. After discussing the proposal, the meeting was adjourned without board action. The meeting was reconvened the following morning and, after further discussion, the board approved the transaction. The amended and restated agreement and plan of merger was executed shortly thereafter.

At the time the Company's board authorized the execution of the merger agreement, it had no advice from an independent investment banker as to the fairness of the proposed deal to the minority stockholders of the Company. Thereafter Bear Stearns, who had earlier done some work in evaluating the fairness of an $18 price for the common in connection with the proposed Tracinda deal, was retained to opine on the fairness from a financial point of view of the terms of the merger agreement. The merger agreement, however, contains no condition that would permit the board to abandon the transaction if an acceptable opinion of the company's investment banker was not obtainable.

The opinion that was requested was to reflect Bear Stearns' view of the fairness of the $14 price for the preferred and its view whether the consideration to be received by Kerkorian for his common stock had a value that was less than that to be received by the public common stockholders. Bear Stearns' opinion was rendered on February 11, 1986, and concluded that "the aggregate consideration [to be] received by Tracinda and Mr. Kerkorian for their shares of Common Stock [on a per share basis] is less than the consideration per share to be received by the Public Shareholders of the Company's Common Stock ..." and that "the price to be paid for the Preferred Stock ... is fair from a financial point of view ...".

After receipt of that opinion, the directors authorized distribution of the proxy materials relating to the proposed transaction. At the Company's annual meeting of stockholders, held on March 14, 1986, 17,675,942 shares of the Company's common stock (77.5% of all of the issued and outstanding common stock) voted in favor of the proposed merger and 148,145 shares (7.11% of the voting shares not controlled by Kerkorian) voted against the merger. The preferred stock had not [sic] right to vote on the merger. Only 5,081 preferred shares (less than ½ of 1% of the outstanding preferred shares not controlled by Mr. Kerkorian) have requested an appraisal of their stock in lieu of the consideration offered by the merger.

---

3. Specifically, should the merger be effectuated, Kerkorian would receive a right to any recovery from the property insurance litigation, in excess of $59,500,000. His company Tracinda, however, must guarantee that MGM Grand will recover at least $50 million (plus interest) from those claims and Kerkorian will reimburse MGM Grand certain litigation expenses incurred by MGM Grand following the merger.

II.

* * *

The main argument advanced by plaintiff is premised upon the assertion that the directors of a Delaware corporation have a duty in a merger transaction to negotiate and approve only a merger that apportions the merger consideration fairly among classes of the company's stock. To unfairly favor one class of stock over another is, on this view, a breach of the duty of loyalty that a director owes to the corporation and, by extension, that he owes equally to all of its shareholders. Asserting factually that under all the circumstances the two outstanding classes of MGM Grand's stock represent equivalent values, plaintiff contends that the proposed Bally merger which does not apportion the merger consideration equally breaches this duty.

Several evidentiary factors are pointed to in order to establish the factual predicate of the argument: the equivalency implied in the original one-for-one exchange offer; the fact that the Company's auditors treated the preferred as equivalents for the purpose of stating the Company's per-share earnings; the fact that one possible merger candidate apparently considered making the same offer to both classes of stock; and that Kerkorian himself offered $12 per share for both common and preferred in his 1984 tender offer. Finally it is asserted that the market treated both securities as reflecting equivalent value (a contention that is warmly contested).

Plaintiff thus compares the $18 per share price that the public common stockholders are to receive with the $14 per share into which the preferred stock is to be converted and perceives an unfairness. Plaintiff offers an explanation of why this unfairness to the preferred resulted—an explanation that seems required by the fact that the controlling shareholder owns a greater proportion of the preferred (74%) than of the common stock (69%). That explanation posits that in apportioning the merger consideration, Kerkorian felt compelled to allocate $18 per share to the common in order to protect himself from possible lawsuits arising from persons who had purchased MGM Grand common stock after the market price for that stock had risen in response to Kerkorian's announcement of a forthcoming $18 cash out merger with Tracinda. Abandonment of that deal for another that would yield the common less, it is contended, would have exposed Kerkorian to charges of manipulation and to litigation. Thus, in allotting the proceeds of the merger among the Company's two classes of stock, plaintiff complains that Kerkorian sought to avoid a potential personal liability. Moreover, he was not only self-interested in the allocation as a result but he cannot, it is asserted, meet his burden to establish that the resulting apportionment was fair to the preferred.

Intertwined with this central contention, are a host of other liability theories, including arguments (1) that the board of MGM Grand violated its duty of care in negotiating and approving the merger (relying heavily in that connection on the recent holding of our Supreme Court in *Smith v. Van Gorkom*, Del. Supr., 488 A.2d 858 (1985)); (2) that in instigating the merger at this time and in arrogating to himself the power to negotiate the terms of the merger on behalf of the corporation, Kerkorian (without regard to the specific terms ultimately agreed upon) acted without legal authority and in breach of duties to the preferred; and (3) that the merger constitutes a manipulation of the corporate machinery of the Company in order to avoid paying the preferred a $20 redemption price.

* * *

III.

* * *

For the reasons more fully set forth below, I conclude that plaintiff has failed to demonstrate the requisite probability of ultimate success that is essential [for the issuance of a preliminary injunction]. In summary, I conclude for the limited purpose of determining this motion that plaintiff has not established a legal right of the preferred to equivalent consideration in a merger and that with respect to the distinct right to a fair apportionment of the merger proceeds, plaintiff has not established a reasonable probability that such a right will be transgressed by the effectuation of the Bally merger. Finally, I have concluded that plaintiff has not demonstrated a probability of ultimate success on her theories of liability resting upon (a) an alleged breach of a duty of care; (b) claims that the timing and structure of the merger evidence a lack of fair dealing or (c) that the merger constitutes a manipulation of corporate machinery for an inappropriate purpose—the evasion of a legal duty, at some future time, to redeem the preferred at $20 per share.

IV.

Initially I address two preliminary although critical legal questions: first, whether, in these circumstances, defendants owe any fiduciary duties to the preferred at all and, second, what standard—entire fairness or business judgment—is appropriate to assess the probability of ultimate success.

A.

Issue on the merits of claims alleged is first joined on the fundamental question whether the directors of MGM Grand owe any duty to the holders of the preferred stock other than the duty to accord to such holders the rights, powers and preferences set out in the certificate designating and defining the legal rights of the preferred. As I understand plaintiff's principal theories of liability each is premised upon the existence of a supervening fiduciary duty recognized in equity that requires directors and controlling shareholders to treat shareholders fairly. *See*, *Weinberger v. UOP, Inc.*, Del.Supr., 457 A.2d 701 (1983).... If there is no such duty insofar as preferred stockholders are concerned plaintiff's theories of liability would seem fatally flawed.

Defendants contend there is no broad duty of fidelity owed to preferred stock if that duty is understood to extend beyond the specific contractual terms defining the special rights, preferences or limitations of the preferred. In support of its position on this point defendants cite such cases as *Rothschild International Corp. v. Liggett Group, Inc.*, Del. Supr., 474 A.2d 133 (1984); *Wood v. Coastal States Gas Corp.*, Del. Supr., 401 A.2d 932 (1979).... Broadly speaking these cases apply the rule that "preferential rights are contractual in nature and therefore are governed by the express provisions of a company's certificate of incorporation" *Rothschild, supra*, 474 A.2d at 136. Defendants restate this accepted principle as meaning "all rights of preferred shareholders are contractual in nature."[4] They then go on to argue (analogizing to the wholly contractual rights of bondholders—as to which no "fiduciary" duties extend) that the only duties directors have to preferred shareholders are those necessary to accord the preferred

---

4. Certain language in the cases restating the principle quoted above would support defendants' interpretation. For example, in *Judah v. Delaware Trust Company*, Del. Supr., 378 A.2d 624 (1977) it is said (at p. 628): "Generally, the provisions of the certificate of incorporation govern the rights of preferred shareholders, the certificate ... being interpreted in accordance with the law of contracts, with only those rights which are embodied in the certificate granted to preferred shareholders."

rights set out in their contract, i.e., the document designating the rights, preferences, etc., of their special stock.

The flaw in this argument lies in a failure to distinguish between "preferential" rights (and special limitations) on the one hand and rights associated with all stock on the other. At common law and in the absence of an agreement to the contrary all shares of stock are equal.... Thus preferences and limitations associated with preferred stock exist only by virtue of an express provision (contractual in nature) creating such rights or limitations. But absent negotiated provision [sic] conferring rights on preference stock, it does not follow that no right exists. The point may be conclusively demonstrated by two examples. If a certificate designating rights, preferences, etc. of special stock contains *no* provision dealing with voting rights or *no* provision creating rights upon liquidation, it is not the fact that such stock has no voting rights or no rights upon liquidation. Rather, in such circumstances, the preferred stock has the same voting rights as common stock (8 *Del. C.* § 212(a); *Rice & Hutchins, Inc. v. Triplex Shoe Co.,* Del. Ch., 147 A. 317 (1929) *aff'd.,* 152 A. 342 (1930)) or the same rights to participate in the liquidation of the corporation as has such stock (11 W. Fletcher Cyclopedia of the Law of Private Corporations § 5303 (rev. perm. ed. 1971); *Continental Insurance Company v. Reading Company,* 259 U.S. 156, 42 S. Ct. 540, 66 L. Ed...., 871 (1922)).

Thus, with respect to matters relating to preferences or limitations that distinguish preferred stock from common, the duty of the corporation and its directors is essentially contractual and the scope of the duty is appropriately defined by reference to the specific words evidencing that contract; where however the right asserted is not to a preference as against the common stock but rather a right shared equally with the common, the existence of such right and the scope of the correlative duty may be measured by equitable as well as legal standards.

With this distinction in mind the Delaware cases which frequently analyze rights of and duties towards preferred stock in legal (i.e., contractual) terminology (*e.g., Wood v. Coastal States Gas Corp., supra; Judah v. Delaware Trust Company,* Del. Supr., 378 A.2d 624 (1977); *Rothschild International Corp. v. Liggett Group, Inc., supra*) may be made consistent with those cases that apply fiduciary standards to claims of preferred shareholders (*e.g., David J. Greene & Co. v. Schenley Industries, Inc.,* Del. Ch., 281 A.2d 30 (1971)....

Accordingly, without prejudging the validity of any of plaintiff's liability theories, I conclude that her claim (a) to a "fair" allocation of the proceeds of the merger; (b) to have the defendants exercise appropriate care in negotiating the proposed merger and (c) to be free of overreaching by Mr. Kerkorian (as to the timing of the merger for his benefit) fairly implicate fiduciary duties and ought not be evaluated wholly from the point of view of the contractual terms of the preferred stock designations.[6]

B.

Assuming that plaintiff and the other preferred shareholders have a "right" recognized in equity to a fair apportionment of the merger consideration (and such a right to require directors to exercise appropriate care) it becomes material to know what legal standard is to be used to assess the probability that a violation of that right will

---

6. The claim that the merger constitutes a wrongful attempt to circumvent the $20 redemption provision of the preferred stock, on the other hand, does, in my view, relate to a negotiated preference and must be evaluated strictly as a contract right. On such basis it is clear that plaintiff has demonstrated no reasonable probability of ultimate success. *See, Rothschild International Corp. v. Liggett Group, Inc., supra.*...

ultimately be proven. Plaintiff asserts that the appropriate test is one of entire or intrinsic fairness. That test is the familiar one employed when fiduciaries elect to utilize their power over the corporation to effectuate a transaction in which they have an interest that diverges from that of the corporation or the minority shareholders. *See, Weinberger v. UOP, Inc., supra; Gottlieb v. Heyden Chemical Corp.,* Del. Supr., 91 A.2d 57 (1952).

Our Supreme Court has made it quite clear that the heightened judicial scrutiny called for by the test of intrinsic or entire fairness is not called forth simply by a demonstration that a controlling shareholder fixes the terms of a transaction and, by exercise of voting power or by domination of the board, compels its effectuation. (The apparent situation presented in this action.) It is in each instance essential to show as well that the fiduciary has an interest with respect to the transaction that conflicts with the interests of minority shareholders. *Aronson v. Lewis,* Del. Supr., 473 A.2d 805, 812 (1984). Speaking in the context of a parent dealing with a controlled but not wholly-owned subsidiary our Supreme Court has said:

> A parent does indeed owe a fiduciary duty to its subsidiary when there are parent-subsidiary dealings. However, this alone will not evoke the intrinsic fairness standard. This standard will be applied only when the fiduciary duty is accompanied by self-dealing—the situation when a parent is on both sides of a transaction with its subsidiary. Self-dealing occurs when the parent, by virtue of its domination of the subsidiary, causes the subsidiary to act in such a way that the parent receives something from the subsidiary to the exclusion of, and detriment to, the minority stockholders of the subsidiary.

Sinclair Oil Corporation v. Levien, Del. Supr., 280 A.2d 717, 720 (1971).

As to what appears to be the material element of the negotiation of the Bally merger—the $440,000,000 cash price—Mr. Kerkorian had no conflicting interest of a kind that would support invocation of the intrinsic fairness test. With respect to total price, his interest was to extract the maximum available price. Moreover, as to the apportionment of the merger consideration between the two classes of the Company's stock, Mr. Kerkorian's interest again appears to create no significant bias on his part since his ownership of each class is not only great but substantially equal. Indeed, as indicated, Kerkorian's ownership of the preferred is proportionately somewhat greater.

Thus, had Kerkorian apportioned the merger consideration equally among members of each class of the Company's stockholders (as distinguished from equally between classes of stock on a per share basis), then the fact of his substantially equivalent ownership of each class of stock would have supported invocation of the legal test known as the business judgment rule. *Aronson v. Lewis,* Del. Supr., 473 A.2d 805 (1984). The fact that each class was treated differently would not itself require application of the intrinsic fairness test....

But Kerkorian directed the apportionment of merger consideration in a way that treated himself differently from other holders of common stock. He accorded to himself less cash per common share ($12.24) but, in the License Agreement, arrogated to himself the right to use or designate the use of the MGM Grand name and, under the Price Adjustment Agreement, he is to assume certain obligations and acquire certain rights with respect to pending property insurance claims of the Company.

In according to himself a different form of consideration in the merger, Mr. Kerkorian has created a situation in which the fact of his substantially equivalent ownership of each class of stock does not itself negate the existence of a conflicting interest on his part in making the allocation decision. Do these agreements create the possibility of a substantial conflict that would mandate the enhanced judicial scrutiny contemplated by the intrinsic fairness test? As to the License Agreement, for the reasons set forth in the margin, I am persuaded the answer is no.[7]

The Price Adjustment Agreement deals with an asset of MGM Grand that was doubtlessly difficult for Bally to value—insurance claims arising from the company's losses caused by the 1980 fire. Those claims have been in litigation for some time and apparently are complex. In the Price Adjustment Agreement Kerkorian (through Tracinda) removes the uncertainty that such claims create, by (1) guaranteeing that MGM Grand will recover $50 million on the claims treated, (2) undertaking to continue to supervise the litigation and (3) agreeing to pay one-half of the first $1,000,000 of legal fees incurred by MGM Grand following the merger with respect to the claims and all such costs in excess of $1,000,000. In exchange for these undertakings Kerkorian receives the right to all amounts recovered by the Company on the claims in excess of $59.5 million.

To assess the possible impact of the Price Adjustment Agreement on the negotiation and apportionment process, I find it necessary to dilate on these claims for a moment. The amount of the litigated claims appears to be approximately $55,000,000 plus pre-judgment interest. The record contains no information concerning whether pre-judgment interest is recoverable on such a claim under the applicable law or, if it is, in what amount. Assuming the full claim is ultimately awarded and that interest at a rate of, say 9%, is also awarded, (interest, for the period from the November, 1980 loss to the November, 1985 signing of the merger agreement, would thus amount to $29,624,000) there would be a total recovery of $84,624,000. On these not unreasonable assumptions, the maximum value of the contingent litigation rights (without any discount for probability of success and with no deduction for the actuarial value of the $50,000,000 guaranty) would be approximately $25,000,000 or approximately 80¢ per share, when all shares, common and preferred, are included. I do not regard that amount as *de minimis*.

It cannot be said, in my view, that the Price Adjustment Agreement constitutes an independent deal unrelated to the negotiation of the proposed merger. Just as clearly, the opportunity to participate in recoveries on the Company's property claims is one that the deal fashioned by Mr. Kerkorian denies to all other stockholders. I conclude therefore that, in apportioning that element of consideration wholly to his own shares to the exclusion of others Kerkorian was exercising power of a kind and in circumstances justifying invocation of the heightened standard of judicial review.

V.

I also conclude that, as to the claim of the preferred to an equal or fair share of the merger proceeds, the defendants are likely to meet the burden thus imposed upon

---

7. The reasons are two. First, I regard the subject matter of the license as of *de minimis* value in these circumstances. It was valued at $1.3 million by an independent appraisal firm. In the context of a cash price of $440 million for a company of which Kerkorian owns roughly 70% that amount would not appear to create a material conflict. Secondly, it appears that the right to use the MGM Grand name is being transferred to a new company whose stock will be offered to all current MGM Grand shareholders, both common and preferred,—but only to such persons—on the same basis as available to Kerkorian. Thus, while under the merger agreement Kerkorian has the power to dispose of the MGM Grand name, in fact the disposition he is making is such as to negate the existence of a conflict with respect to that asset.

them. It follows that plaintiff has failed to demonstrate a reasonable probability of success on this issue.

First, it seems elementary that the preferred has no *legal* right to equivalent consideration in the merger. Neither the certificate of incorporation nor the certificate of designation of the preferred stock expressly creates such a right. Nor does it appear that such a right may be fairly implied from those documents when read in the light of the terms of the 1982 Exchange Offer. *Cf., Katz v. Oak Industries, Inc.,* Del. Ch., 508 A.2d 873 (1986). Nor do I perceive any basis to recognize an *equitable* right to mathematically equal consideration based upon the conduct of Kerkorian as a fiduciary. Some of what is said below ... supports this conclusion.

As to a right of the preferred to have the total consideration fairly (as distinguished from equally) apportioned, the current record provides no persuasive basis to conclude that the allocation contemplated by the Bally merger is unfair.

Plaintiff's claim of unfairness in an apportionment of $18 per share to the common stockholders and $14 a share to the preferred, in my opinion, involves a fundamental defect: it rests upon an invalid comparison. The pertinent comparison, if one is treating a right to fair apportionment among classes of stock, is between what those classes receive in the merger, on a per share basis, not between what the class of preferred receive per share and what the public holders of common stock are to receive. As shown below, when the financial value of the appropriate comparison is developed (to the extent the current record permits the development and evaluation of that comparison) it does not appear very great and certainly does not at this stage appear unsustainable in light of the differences in the rights of common and preferred stockholders and the historical treatment of both classes of stock by the market.[8]

The essential right plaintiff asserts is the right of the preferred to be treated as well as the common in the merger. There are now outstanding 22,803,194 common shares and 8,549,000 preferred. Thus, in all, there are 31,352,194 shares of MGM Grand stock. But when the total cash consideration—$440 million—is divided by the total number of shares, common and preferred, outstanding the result is $14.03 per share.

But in addition to cash, some MGM Grand common stockholders (i.e., Kerkorian) will get other non-cash consideration that ought to be considered in comparing the financial treatment of the two classes of stock in the merger. If for these purposes we treat the value of the MGM Grand name as worth $1.3 million (its appraised value) and the value of contingent right to litigation proceeds as worth approximately $25 million

---

8. Judging from the record now available, it appears to be an exaggeration to state that the market has historically accorded equal value to MGM Grand's preferred and common stock. It does appear that for most of the months during the period from issuance (5/82) through announcement of the Tracinda offer (6/85) the common traded at a price less than 130% of the market price of the preferred. Typically, during that period, the common did trade at a higher price than did the preferred. Specifically, it appears that during that 37-month period, in 15 of 37 such months the closing high price for MGM Grand's common stock during the month was within ±10% of its preferred high closing price for the month (in 20 of 37 months its lowest closing price was ±10% of the lowest closing price of its preferred). In 9 of 37 months, its highest monthly closing price was between 10 and 20% greater than the high price of the preferred (in 10 of 37 months, its low price was greater within that range) and in 13 of 37 months the price of common measured at its high price was greater than 120% of the high price of the preferred achieved during that month (in 6 of 37 months, when low prices are so compared). During 7 months in 1983 the price of common ranged from approximately 135% of the price of the preferred to approximately 175% of the preferred when measured by monthly high prices (and from 125% to 145% when measured by the lowest prices to which both stocks fell during each such month)....

(for the reasons described above) then it appears that the total value of the merger consideration is approximately $466.3 million. Dividing that number by 31,352,194 yields an average consideration per share for all stockholders of $14.87. Thus, if each preferred stockholder received the average consideration per share that all shareholders will receive, each preferred share would receive, on the foregoing assumption, not $14.00 but $14.87. In fact, the common stock as a class will not receive the $14.87 average for all shareholders but will receive total consideration (on the foregoing assumption) of $15.20 per share.[9]

Given the fact that the preferred has no prospect for a future increment in dividends, no vote, and has historically tended to trade at a discount from the common[,] ... I cannot conclude that the $14 per share price (which represents a 6% discount from the $14.87 per share average value for all shares) is likely to be found not to be entirely appropriate.

Plaintiff might fairly say that the foregoing analysis does not meet the real thrust of her contention. That is, she would argue that the meaningful difference in the preferred's consideration is not between their $14 per share and the average to be received by all shares ($14.87 on the assumption set out above) but between $14 and $18 to be recovered by the public holders of the common stock. This difference—simply because it is materially larger—would be more difficult to justify.

But it is this comparison that I refer to as invalid. It is true that the common as a class is not getting the average of all shareholders—$14.87 on my assumption concerning the value of the contingent litigation rights—but is getting $15.20 per share on that assumption. That difference ($.33 per share), if it is to be justified, must be justified by reference to the difference in the legal claims and economic prospects of the two classes of stock. As indicated above, I cannot conclude on the present record that that justification is unlikely to be demonstrated.

The further difference—between $15.20 per share for the common as a class and the $18 per share that the public holders of common stock will receive need not be so justified in my opinion; it is clearly being funded entirely by Kerkorian personally. That is, the amount of the total increment to be received by the *public* holders of common stock over the average per share consideration to be received by the common stock as a class (7,064,021 public common shares × ($18.00 − $15.20) = $19,779,259) is supplied by Kerkorian, who has taken less for his common stock, even when the non-cash consideration is considered ($12.24 cash + 1.67 non-cash[10] = $13.91 per share). Thus, the amount per share that Kerkorian has given up ($15.20 − $13.91 = $1.29 per share) when multiplied by his total common stock holdings (15,739,173) equals $20,303,533 and more than fully funds the increment that the public common stockholders will receive over the average per share price to be received by common stockholders as a class.

Thus, if plaintiff is correct that Kerkorian sought to make sure the public common stockholders got $18 per share because he feared some potential liability if they got less, the rejoinder is that, to the extent the public holders of common are to receive more than all common stock as a class, Kerkorian paid for that benefit from his own pocket.

---

9. On those assumptions, they will receive an average of $14.05 cash (i.e., $440 million[,] $119.7 million to be paid to preferred = $320.3 million ÷ 22,803,194 common shares = $14.05 cash per share) + $1.15 non-cash (i.e., $25 million + $1.3 ÷ 22,803,194 = $1.15) = $15.20.

10. That is, $25,000,000 value of contingent recovery + $1,300,000 value of MGM Grand name divided by 15,739,173 common shares owned by Kerkorian.

Assuming for purposes of this motion that plaintiff is correct in asserting that $18 per share is an unjustifiably generous price for the publicly held common stock, plaintiff's claim to equal treatment inescapably involves an implied right to require self-sacrifice from a fiduciary. While the law requires that corporate fiduciaries observe high standards of fidelity and, when self-dealing is involved, places upon them the burden of demonstrating the intrinsic fairness of transactions they authorize, the law does not require more than fairness. Specifically, it does not, absent a showing of culpability, require that directors or controlling shareholders sacrifice their own financial interest in the enterprise for the sake of the corporation or its minority shareholders. It follows that should a controlling shareholder for whatever reason (to avoid entanglement in litigation as plaintiff suggests is here the case or for other personal reasons) elect to sacrifice some part of the value of his stock holdings, the law will not direct him as to how that amount is to be distributed and to whom.

Accordingly, I conclude for purposes of this motion that when the appropriate comparisons are made, the different treatment contemplated by the Bally merger of the two outstanding classes of the Company stock is unlikely—given the different legal claims and economic prospects those classes of stock possess—ultimately to be found to constitute a breach of a duty the defendants may have had in the circumstances to apportion the merger proceeds fairly.

* * *

For the foregoing reasons, plaintiff's application for a preliminary injunction shall be denied. IT IS SO ORDERED.

Questions

1. In what capacity is the board to interpret the preferred stock contract? As a fiduciary for the preferred? For the common? As a neutral arbitrator? How does your answer to this question affect your evaluation of the utility of Chancellor Allen's holding?

2. What difference should it make that the preferred contract presumably was drafted by corporate counsel?

———————

Chancellor Allen had more to say about preferred stock and the allocation of merger consideration in the following opinion:

In re FLS Holdings Inc. Shareholders Litigation
1993 WL 104562 (Del. Ch.)

ALLEN, Chancellor.

The present application is for an order under Chancery Court Rule 23(e) approving the settlement and dismissal of certain stockholder class action claims. The class is comprised of the holders of FLS Holdings, Inc. preferred stock, as of the date of a cash merger between FLS and Kyoei Steel Ltd., an unrelated third party.

The claim asserted on behalf of the preferred is against the members of the board of directors of FLS and certain stockholders. The claim is that the price negotiated with Kyoei was not fairly allocated between the preferred stock and the common stock of FLS. The preferred had no right to vote for directors of FLS nor to vote on the merger....

The proposed settlement offers no additional consideration to the preferred. Rather the proponents of the settlement suggest that their efforts in bringing this suit resulted in some additional disclosures in the merger and resulted in some negotiating positions by the defendants that were more favorable to the preferred than would have been taken otherwise. The only cash involved in the proposal is the contemplated payment of $200,000 to the attorneys who have pursued this matter on behalf of the class representative.

The proposal is objected to by members of the class holding approximately 20% of the preferred's claims. The objectors charge that the defendants breached duties to them in allocating the merger consideration between the common and preferred stock; that the settlement makes no serious effort to compromise those claims and that it should be rejected. Finally they ask that they be permitted to intervene to carry on the adjudication of this matter.

* * *

Those who would seek a court to settle and dismiss claims of absent class members must bear the burden to demonstrate that the proposed settlement is a fair compromise and represents adequate compensation for the claims to be released, considering the apparent strengths and weaknesses of those claims. See Barkan v. Amsted Indus., Inc., Del.Supr., 567 A.2d 1279, 1285 (1989).

What follows is a preliminary description and evaluation of the claims asserted. It is not now possible to assess very closely the likelihood that trial of the central claim would result in a determination that the allocation of the merger consideration was not fair. I am, however, able to determine that at trial defendants would bear the burden to establish that their allocation was fair; that the record contains evidence that would support the claims asserted and that the consideration offered to settle the claim, excluding the cash payment to the attorneys, is, in the circumstances relatively insignificant. Together with objections of very substantial shareholders and the willingness of others to press the claims, these factors lead me to conclude that the proponents of the settlement have not borne their burden on this motion. The motion will therefore be denied.

I.
A. The 1988 Leveraged Buy-Out

FLS was formed in 1988 through a management affiliated leveraged buy-out of Florida Steel Company. The bankers and investors in this transaction were Goldman Sachs & Company, and Citibank, N.A. On August 28, 1988 FLS purchased 84.5% of the outstanding common stock of Florida Steel for cash, through a tender offer at $50 per share.[1]

FLS had three classes of stock, Class A and Class B Common and Preferred Stock. Only the 500,000 shares of Class A common stock had voting rights. The Class A common shares were distributed as follows: Senior management of Florida Steel, 33.78%; Goldman Sachs, 45.56%; other FLS employees, 14.71%, other investors, 1.37%; Citicorp Capital Investors, 4.3%, Citicorp also held all 61,013 shares of Class B common.

The second step of the Florida Steel acquisition was accomplished in November 1988. On November 17, FLS caused Florida Steel to merge with a wholly owned sub-

---

1. To finance the purchase, FLS borrowed $180 million from banks; issued $125 million in 14.5% subordinated debentures; and received $25 million in equity from its common stock owners, roughly $16.63 million in cash and shares of Florida Steel, and $8.33 million consisting of waivers by employees of rights under their employment agreements.

sidiary of FLS, thereby converting each of the remaining publicly held shares of Florida Steel, into the right to receive one share of FLS preferred stock. Approximately 940,000 shares of Preferred Stock were issued in the back-end merger. The preferred stock had a liquidation preference of $53.33 per share, and a 17.5% dividend, payable in kind until February 1994 and in cash thereafter. As a result of the payment of dividends in kind since the buy-out, there are now 1,600,806 preferred shares outstanding, representing, at original issue prices, an investment of $80 million. The liquidation preference of these shares, including accrued but unpaid payable in kind dividends, is $94.7 million.

B. Continuing and Increasing Losses: 1988-1992

This LBO proved to be one of those that did not realize its investors' hopes. Operating results failed to meet expectations; the company incurred heavy losses. After earning net income of $3.04 million in 1990, FLS lost $8.9 million in 1991 and $24.2 million in 1992. By late 1991, FLS was in breach of certain financial covenants in its lending agreement. Its banks entered into agreements with FLS, waiving these breaches and agreeing to defer interest payments until December 1992. In return, FLS agreed to stop paying interest to its bondholders and to restructure the company. In sum, FLS was on the brink of insolvency. FLS management and Goldman Sachs began a world-wide search for potential buyers for the company and began to consider other options, such as filing for bankruptcy protection.

C. Negotiations to Sell FLS to Kyoei Steel, Ltd.

The highest offer obtained through these efforts was that of Kyoei Steel, Ltd., which approached Goldman Sachs informally on May 4, 1992 and proposed buying all of FLS's common stock for $10 per share ($5 million), all of the preferred for $27 per share ($43.2 million), and repaying all FLS debt at 100 cents on the dollar. Goldman Sachs, who had been retained by the board to handle the matter, told Kyoei's negotiator, Peter Offerman of BT Securities, Inc., that Kyoei was being too generous to the preferred stock and not generous enough to the common stock.[2]

On May 12, 1992, Kyoei submitted a written proposal to FLS which doubled the offer for the common stock to $20 per share, ($10 million) while reducing the offer for the preferred stock to $24 per share ($38.4 million). This proposal called for paying all bank debt in full and debentures 95 cents on the dollar. This offer was contingent upon acceptance by 90% of the preferred stock and debenture holders, and apparently contemplated a tender offer for these securities.

Hand-written notes from meetings of the FLS leadership the next day suggest that it was concerned that the allocation between the preferred and common was unfair to the

---

2. Let me add an interpretive observation: The negotiator for the board was in a tricky negotiation posture, given the effect that the negotiation might have on the interests of others not present—debt holders and preferred stock. These others might threaten to impede a transaction through court action. Thus the preferred strategy for a buyer would be to pay as high a proportion of the total selling price as possible, to the absent interest holders. So long as the common stock with whom he was negotiating would agree, then the best chance for a completed transaction is achieved in that way. Thus, a buyer in this position has an incentive to offer more than a fair share to the absent party. I mention this because seeing things in this way permits one to interpret the directors' negotiation positions as quite possibly the behavior of persons acting in a fair way despite the fact they were asking that the common be paid more and the preferred less.

common, and therefore unfair to the directors and their affiliates. The notes state that FLS management discussed the fact that the preferred had "no options" because the common could "decide to sell or not to sell." Notes from an FLS staff meeting on May 14, 1992 reflect concerns that if the transaction is not completed quickly the "preferred will get organized and 'want more.'"

On May 22, at the FLS Board Meeting, the question of the allocation between preferred and common stockholders was discussed and legal counsel reported that the allocation "must be fair." ... At a second board meeting on May 27, the amount of the offer for the equity as a whole was described as inadequate and the split between preferred and common as "not good.".... Representatives of Goldman Sachs proposed that FLS demand from Kyoei $60 million, with $20 million going to the common and $40 million to the preferred.

On June 3, Kyoei extended a third offer to FLS, proposing to pay $12.4 million to the common and $38.4 million to the preferred. This offer contemplated a merger and no vote by the preferred stock would be required to complete the transaction.

Goldman continued to negotiate for a higher price for the common stock, apparently seeking $20 million. Eventually a compromise was negotiated, and on June 26, 1992, both parties agreed to a merger between FLS and a wholly owned subsidiary of Kyoei, in exchange for the payment of 100% of the debts owed to banks and bondholders, $38.4 million to the preferred stock and $15 million to the common stock.

D. The Final Terms of Kyoei's Purchase of FLS

Upon completing its due diligence, however, Kyoei apparently discovered $24 million in higher than expected liabilities for environmental clean-up, settlement of a federal criminal and civil investigation, and additional pension costs. Offerman recommended that Kyoei not seek to reduce the price by the full $24 million. He predicted that if Kyoei attempted to do so, FLS would reject the entire deal and attempt a stand alone restructuring in which, in his estimation, the Preferred Stock would receive a substantial equity stake, worth approximately $40 million, while the common stock would receive an equity stake worth roughly $5-10 million.

FLS offered Kyoei a total price reduction of $12.8 million, with a $7.2 million reduction borne by the preferred and $5.6 borne by the residual risk bearing common stock. Kyoei rejected this offer and demanded a $15 million total reduction to which FLS agreed. The additional $2.2 million was deducted solely from the consideration to be paid to the preferred stock. A final further reduction of $400,000 was later agreed to and this amount was borne exclusively by the common stock.... The final price received by the common stockholders therefore, was $17.998 per share ($9 million) while the preferred received $18.124 per share ($29.013 million).

The common stockholders thus recouped 54% of their cash investment and 36% of their total investment (i.e., including waivers of rights by management to deferred compensation) despite three years of losses that exceeded their equity investment. The preferred stock recouped 62% of the value of the Florida Steel common stock interests they surrendered in the 1988 backend merger. The preferred stockholders had, of course, a legal right to dividends payable in kind at a rate of 17.5%, and payable in cash beginning in 1994. This contracted for return on their investment, which the preferred stockholders earned for over three years, is difficult to value. What is clear, however, is that the proportionate claim of the preferred stock in FLS grew at a 17.5% annual rate, and its investment is greater than that represented by their original $47 million contribution at the time of the merger.

E. Procedural Protections for the Preferred Stock

1. Safeguards Generally Lacking

FLS was represented in its negotiations with Kyoei exclusively by directors who either owned large amounts of common stock, or were affiliates of Goldman Sachs and Citicorp. No independent adviser or independent directors' committee was appointed to represent the interests of the preferred stock who were in a conflict of interest situation with the common.[3] The preferred stock did not have a right to vote on the transaction or on the allocation. An opinion was issued by an investment banker, after the merger agreement had been signed, concluding that the allocation was fair to the preferred.

2. The Salomon Brothers Fairness Opinion

On July 28, 1992, FLS retained Salomon Brothers, Inc. to render an opinion as to the fairness of the Kyoei merger to the preferred stockholders, especially with regard to the fairness of the allocation between the preferred and common stock. FLS paid Salomon Brothers $400,000 for its work. To determine the fairness of the allocation, Salomon examined other transactions in which distressed companies were sold or restructured and the equity value of the company divided between the preferred and common stock. The record does not indicate whether the transactions examined involved arms length bargaining between representatives of the preferred and common, or whether the common stock controlled these transactions, as in the present case.

Salomon's survey of other restructuring transactions showed that the median share of the total consideration paid to equity holders, received by preferred stockholders in restructurings, was 68.7%. The FLS preferred stock received 75.5% of the total consideration received by equity in the sale to Kyoei. Based upon this comparison, Salomon opined that the allocation of consideration between the preferred and common stock was fair to the preferred stock from a financial point of view.

II.

A. The Value of the Claims Proposed to be Settled

In allocating the consideration of this merger, the directors, although they were elected by the common stock, owed fiduciary duties to both the preferred and common stockholders, and were obligated to treat the preferred fairly. See Eisenberg v. Chicago Milwaukee Corp., Del.Ch., 537 A.2d 1051, 1062 (1987); Jedwab v. MGM Grand Hotels, Del.Ch., 509 A.2d 584, 593-94 (1986). That standard is, of course, a somewhat opaque one that, unless procedures are employed that are sufficient in themselves to give reasonable assurance of fairness, may require a reviewing agency to make a highly specific inquiry of the company and the transaction.

In preliminarily assessing plaintiffs' claim, I note first that here no mechanism employing a truly independent agency on the behalf of the preferred was employed before the transaction was formulated. Only the relatively weak procedural protection of an investment banker's ex post opinion, was available to support the position that the final

---

3. A bondholders steering committee represented the interests of debenture holders. Debenture holders were originally offered only 95 cents on the dollar and eventually received payment in full.

allocation was fair. Plaintiffs' expert has also now opined that the allocation was fair to the preferred.

* * *

These opinions, while of some weight, in light of the other facts in the record, would not substantially assist in satisfying defendants' burden of showing that the allocation was fair.[4] Defendants may very well meet their burden later in this litigation. On this motion however, I conclude only that there is a substantial issue that is fairly litigable. If this case proceeds to an adjudication of the merits of plaintiffs' claims, defendants will bear the burden of proving that the allocation was fair to the preferred....

* * *

Questions

1. How would the board of FLS go about proving the fairness of the transaction to the preferred stockholders? Would the board have had to shoulder this burden if they had arranged for independent representation of the preferred?

2. What must the Chancellor be assuming in footnote 2? Based on what you know of preferred stockholders' rights, how valid is this assumption?

3. Consider the following language from the Chancellor's first opinion in HB Korenvaes Investments, L.P. v. Marriott Corporation, 1993 WL 205040, CCH Fed. Sec. L. Rep. para. 97,728 (Del. Ch.):

> Rights of preferred stock are primarily but not exclusively contractual in nature. The special rights, limitations, etc. of preferred stock are created by the corporate charter or a certificate of designation which acts as an amendment to a certificate of incorporation. Thus, to a very large extent, to ask what are the rights of the preferred stock is to ask what are the rights and obligations created contractually by the certificate of designation.... In most instances, given the nature of the acts alleged and the terms of the certificate, this contractual level of analysis will exhaust the judicial review of corporate action challenged as a wrong to preferred stock....

---

4. Salomon's approach of comparing the allocation between the preferred and common in other restructuring transaction with the present case, would appear to have some logical flaws. There is no indication of the relative size of the investments of the preferred and common stockholders in the supposedly comparable restructuring transactions in which the preferred and common stock realized losses. A hypothetical may clarify the importance of this omission. A corporation is formed in which the common stockholders invest $100 million and the preferred $10 million. The corporation loses $30 million in its first year and merges with a buyer for $80 million. A fair allocation of the proceeds of the merger would be much different in this instance than if the amount contributed by the two classes of stock was reversed. In all events the allocation would turn on the company and the rights of its classes of security holders, not on what happened on recapitalization in other firms with different capital structures. Salomon's opinion makes no effort to evaluate the capital structure of the companies in its supposedly comparable transactions. Some were "distressed," but whatever range of problems that phrase is meant to cover I take it that it does not mean that the common stock was practically valueless in each case. Thus the relative structure of the company's balance sheet would be important if one sought guidance from comparable allocation cases. Therefore, I attach little weight, at this time, to Salomon's conclusion that the allocation was fair because, the percentage of the total consideration received by the preferred in the present case was above the median received by the preferred in other restructuring transactions.

But the holder of preferred stock is not a creditor of the corporation. Such a holder has no legal right to annual payments of interest, as long term creditors will have, and most importantly has no maturity date with its prospect of capital repayment or remedies for default. In these respects the holder of preferred stock is in the exposed and vulnerable position vis a vis the board of directors that all stockholders occupy. Thus, it has been recognized that directors may owe duties of loyalty and care to preferred stock. See Porges v. Vadsco Sales Corp., Del.Ch., 32 A.2d 148 (1943); MacFarlane v. North American Cement Corp., Del.Ch., 157 A 396 (1928). For example, in a recent case a corporate board, elected by the common stock exclusively, negotiated and recommended to the common stock a cash merger (the preferred had been held to have no right to a class vote). Holders of preferred sued the directors asserting that the allocation of consideration between the common and the preferred was unfair. On a motion under Rule 23(e) to approve a proposed settlement it was held that, in the circumstances, the board had a burden to demonstrate that the apportionment of consideration that it negotiated and presented to the holders of common stock was not unfair to the preferred stock....

In fact, it is often not analytically helpful to ask the global question whether (or to assert that) the board of directors does or does not owe fiduciary duties of loyalty to the holders of preferred stock. The question (or the claim) may be too broad to be meaningful. In some instances (for example, when the question involves adequacy of disclosures to holders of preferred who have a right to vote) such a duty will exist. In others (for example, the declaration of a dividend designed to eliminate the preferred's right to vote) a duty to act for the good of the preferred does not. Thus, the question whether duties of loyalties are implicated by corporate action affecting preferred stock is a question that demands reference to the particularities of context to fashion a sound reply.

Of course even where a court concludes that contract principles govern the analysis, the need to address questions of ambiguity as to the scope of rights and duties under the certificate of designation may remain. The cognitive limitations of drafters, imperfect information and the nature of language itself assure that in contract law as well as fiduciary law, good faith disagreements about the nature of duty will arise. Indeed the contract doctrine of an implied covenant of good faith and fair dealing may be thought in some ways to function analogously to the fiduciary concept.

* * *

For purposes of this motion to dismiss I accept as true the contention of plaintiffs that the Marriott directors were not in any respect motivated to advance the economic interests of the preferred stock in proposing this transaction to the common stockholders. Beyond that, of course, I accept as true all of the factual allegations of the amended complaint.

Nevertheless, given the terms of the certificate of designation I conclude that the proposed transaction does not implicate or engage the directors' duty of loyalty but must be evaluated under the contractual law governing the special rights and preferences of the preferred. Count I of the amended complaint will therefore be dismissed.

In explaining this conclusion it is only necessary to demonstrate that the tailored terms of the certificate, which define the nature of the property owned, govern the propriety of the proposed transaction. Most important, in this connection, is the fact that the certificate of designation expressly contemplates the payment of a special dividend of the type here involved and supplies a device to protect the preferred stockholders in the event such a dividend is paid....

Thus, the legal obligation of the corporation to the Series A Preferred Stock upon the declaration and payment of an in-kind dividend of securities has been expressly treated and rights created. It is these contractual rights—chiefly the right to convert into common stock now or to gross-up the conversion ratio for future conversions—that the holders of preferred stock possess as protection against the dilution of their shares' economic value through a permissible dividend.

This conclusion reaches each aspect of the claimed fiduciary duty. Thus, in my opinion, plaintiffs' first claim fails to state a claim upon which relief might be granted.

———————

Based on the foregoing, what are you able to conclude about the fiduciary rights of preferred stockholders? Consider closely one of your co-editor's thoughts on this topic as well as his proposed solution.

Mitchell, The Puzzling Paradox of Preferred Stock (And Why We Should Care About It)[a]
51 Bus. Law. 443 (1996)

* * *

[A]ll is not well jurisprudentially with preferred stock. Several recent judicial pronouncements seemingly have clarified the preferred stockholders' relationship to the corporation, its directors, and its common stockholders. But that apparent clarity is an illusion. It is fair to say ... that the position of the preferred stockholder in the corporate firmament, fiduciary rhetoric notwithstanding, is more vulnerable than any other financial participant.[4] The only situation in which courts regularly apply fiduciary standards in evaluating preferred stockholders' rights is when their equity stake in the corporation is threatened by corporate control transactions involving interested directors or a controlling stockholder and even then, only in limited circumstances.[5] By contrast, courts will not apply fairness analysis to protect preferred stockholders' return on their equity. These conclusions, when combined with the reality that most preferred stock is structured in a way that never obligates the corporation to redeem it and thus return equity, suggests that the preferred stockholders can, with impunity, be frozen out of realizing any value from the enterprise.[7] In brief, I shall conclude that the preferred stock-

———————

a. Lawrence Mitchell, The Puzzling Paradox of Preferred Stock (And Why We Should Care About It), published in *The Business Lawyer*, Vol. 51, No. 2, Feb. 1996. Copyright (©) 1996 by the American Bar Association; Lawrence E. Mitchell. Reprinted by Permission.

4. For example, the corporation must eventually pay even the relatively weak unsecured debtholder his principal; the preferred stockholder, never.

5. For example, it does not appear that anything like the Revlon rule, derived from Revlon, Inc. v. MacAndrews & Forbes Holdings, Inc., 506 A.2d 173 (Del. 1986), applies to preferred stock. See, e.g., Jedwab v. MGM Grand Hotels, Inc., 509 A.2d 584, 594 (Del. Ch. 1986) (requiring only "fair" apportionment of merger consideration); Dalton v. American Inv. Co., 490 A.2d 574 (Del. Ch.), aff'd, 501 A.2d 1238 (Del. 1985) (permitting a corporation to accept arguably non-maximizing merger consideration for preferred)....

7. This is particularly so when one realizes the ease with which corporations can avoid paying preferred stock dividends and eliminating arrearages....

holder ought not think of himself or herself as a stockholder at all and should plan to rely exclusively on his or her contract as the source of rights, with all that implies in terms of evaluating the stock's pricing. I will also suggest a practical solution to the problem in the form of a contractual fiduciary duty provision....

* * *

THE PARADOX

Preferred stock is, of course, stock. For our purposes, the most significant consequence of this apparent tautology is that preferred stockholders, like common stockholders, are traditionally regarded as having an ownership interest in the corporation. By virtue of this ownership interest, they constitute a statutorily recognized corporate constituency,[11] and it is thus for their benefit, as well as that of the common stockholders, that a corporation's officers and directors must fulfill their duties. Like common stockholders, preferred stockholders have standing to bring derivative litigation challenging alleged directorial breaches of the duties of care and loyalty. And, like common stockholders, preferred stockholders are legally protected from the opportunistic overreaching of controlling stockholders.

Preferred stockholders are, however, also distinct from common stockholders, and it is in consequence of this distinction that problems arise. Preferred stockholders are preferred precisely to the extent that the corporation's charter gives them an advantage over common stockholders. Most commonly, this advantage is recognized in the preferred's priority to common stock upon liquidation, and in the right to receive dividends, and may also include the right to demand redemption (or to be redeemed by the corporation at a premium), and the like.

These advantages, of course, come at the expense of the common stockholders, for the distribution of corporate wealth at any given point in time is zero sum. Whatever the size of the pie, and however much it grows, whatever one gets is, by definition, unavailable to the other. Thus, to the extent of their preferences, preferred and common stockholders are in direct conflict with one another.

.... When such conflicts occur, to whom do the directors owe their fealty?

* * *

An apparently clear answer was provided by Delaware Chancellor William Allen. In the 1986 case of Jedwab v. MGM Grand Hotels, Inc.,[26] the Chancellor confronted a claim by preferred stockholders that they had been treated unequally with the common stockholders, and thus unfairly, in a negotiated merger between their corporation, MGM Grand, and Bally Manufacturing Corp. Straightforwardly addressing the question of whether MGM's controlling stockholder and director owed any fiduciary duty to the preferred, he concluded:

> Thus, with respect to matters relating to preferences or limitations that distinguish preferred stock from common, the duty of the corporation and its directors is essentially contractual and the scope of the duty is appropriately defined by reference to the specific words evidencing that contract;

---

11. See In re Hawkeye Oil Co., 19 F.2d 151, 152 (D. Del. 1927) (preferred stockholders are stockholders, not creditors); see also Del. Code Ann. tit. 8, § 151 (1989 & Supp. 1994).
26. 509 A.2d 584 (Del. Ch. 1986).

where however the right asserted is not to a preference as against the common stock but rather a right shared equally with the common, the existence of such right and the scope of the correlative duty may be measured by equitable as well as legal standards.[27]

Thus, we have a solution. Preference rights are contractual; ordinary stock rights are fiduciary....

Yet the clarity of the Chancellor's pronouncement, and its utility in resolving the preferred stock problem, is illusory. In fact, it merely creates a paradox more severe than the one with which we began. Before we can apply the Jedwab rule, we must know which rights of the preferred are preferences, and thus contractual, and which are shared, and thus fiduciary. Occasionally this will be clear, as in the case of a preference right to cumulative dividends. But, as will more often be true (and the cases of the 1980s and 1990s illustrate this), corporate directors and their lawyers will be required to interpret the terms of the corporate charter in order to determine exactly the contractual rights of the preferred. In the case of third-party transactions, like those with bondholders, this interpretive requirement is not a problem: because the corporation and its creditors are treated as acting at arm's length, directors can interpret these contracts narrowly and aggressively (of course within the bounds of good faith and reason).

But preferred stockholders are not treated as standing at arm's length to the corporation, at least until the contractual terms are interpreted and defined (and then only to the extent of those contractual terms). In fact, as to the noncontractual terms—the residuum—the directors act as fiduciaries to the preferred stockholders. To the extent that the directors interpret and define the contract, they very much determine the scope of their own fiduciary duties, a role traditionally ... [and properly] left to the courts. The central question left unanswered by Jedwab, and the truly important one, is whether directors are to approach their interpretation of the preferred contract as fiduciaries or at arm's length. If the answer is the former, then Jedwab and almost all of the rest of the cases dealing with preferred stock need to be rethought, and a meaningful fiduciary obligation to preferred stockholders must be defined. If the answer is the latter, then preferred stockholders are in no better position than creditors who incidentally have the right to bring derivative litigation, which generally will be of little benefit to them. Case law shows that the answer does indeed appear to be the latter and to say that preferred stockholders have any meaningful fiduciary rights borders on the fraudulent....

THE NATURE OF THE CONFLICT

[S]ome important distinctions with respect to the kinds of conflict at issue need to be made. The previously described conflict which gives rise to what may be called the preferred stock paradox is between common and preferred stockholders. I have previously referred to this type of conflict as "horizontal" in nature[32] because it occurs between two classes of participants in the corporate capital structure, and is centered around their competing legitimate interests in the corporate pie. Perhaps the clearest

---

27. Id. at 594.

32. In Lawrence E. Mitchell, The Fairness Rights of Corporate Bondholders, 65 N.Y.U. L. REV. 1165, 1189-90 (1990) [hereinafter Fairness Rights], I draw and explain the distinction between vertical and horizontal conflict in greater detail....

example of this type of conflict in fiduciary law is that arising between a controlling and minority stockholder.

Horizontal conflicts (which also occur among various classes of stockholders and bondholders, employees, and other corporate constituencies) contrast with "vertical conflicts," which arise between corporate directors (and officers) and the corporation itself and other corporate constituent groups, typically stockholders, who are subject to their virtually exclusive exercise of corporate power. These vertical conflicts are the source of the duties of care and loyalty, created to ensure that those who wield corporate power do so in a responsible manner. As to these types of conflicts, which ordinarily are enforced in derivative litigation, preferred stockholders (unlike bondholders, for example) do have the benefit of real fiduciary duties.

* * *

.... Far more significant to preferred stockholders, and far more damaging from a financial perspective, are horizontal conflicts where directors, even when acting in apparent good faith and in the absence of a particular financial interest in the transaction, can damage the interests of the preferred by furthering exclusively the interests of the common. To be sure, this is not technically a conflict between the directors and the preferred stockholders, but rather one between the common stockholders, acting through the directors, and the preferred stockholders. But, ... both the doctrine and the structure of modern corporate law mandate that directors always act in the interests of the common. The bulk of the cases on preferred stock rights fit into this category, and it is in this category that the preferred stock paradox arises. The net effect of the laws regulating these conflicts is that when directors, who as directors have no legitimate right to corporate wealth, seek to appropriate that wealth at the expense of the preferred (which will almost always also be at the expense of the common), the preferred stockholders may invoke fiduciary protections. But, when directors, acting without obvious self-interest, disadvantage the preferred to the benefit of the common, preferred stockholders must rely upon their contract.

* * *

The only context in which preferred stockholders are able to invoke fiduciary analysis with anything approaching consistency is that of control transactions. The obligation of directors to ensure that preferred stockholders are offered a fair price for their shares implies the obligation to protect equity. But this is only the case when the preferred stock contract can be read not to prohibit the particular control transaction. Although this phrasing is awkward, it is the most accurate way of presenting the issue because the cases are indisputably clear that the preferred stock contract is to be read literally, or at least quite narrowly. This, when combined with the almost universal application of the equal dignity rule,[51] suggests that, in most cases, the challenged transaction will be read to come within the terms of the preferred stock contract. The posture of the complaints thus puts the preferred at an immediate disadvantage; because the transaction is permitted, there must be palpable unfairness in order for relief to be granted. While this

---

51. The equal dignity rule, or doctrine of independent legal significance, broadly sanctions the structuring of a transaction with identical results under any permissible statutory arrangement, notwithstanding the fact that the same result would invoke different legal consequences if structured under a different contractual or statutory provision. The equal dignity rule has been used to deprive preferred stockholders of, among other things, their accrued dividends, Bove v. Community Hotel Corp., 249 A.2d 89, 98-100 (R.I. 1969), effectively to liquidate the corporation without paying preferred stockholders their liquidation preferences, Rauch v. RCA Corp., 861 F.2d 29, 30-32 (2d Cir. 1988), and to redeem the preferred stock without paying redemption premiums. See id.

may seem like nothing more than a restatement of the established distinction between legal power and the exercise of that power (equally applicable to common stock), with the latter being the province of fiduciary obligation, it is more significant in the case of preferred stockholders than that of common stockholders. The directors' fiduciary duties to the common stockholders have come to mean that directors are to operate the corporation in the common stockholders' best interests, which implies their duty to maximize common stockholder value.

No such conclusion is available in the case of preferred stockholders. Because the preferred's rights are treated as primarily contractual, and thus outside the internal structure of the corporation, and because these contractual rights come at the expense of the common stockholders to whom the directors owe a duty to maximize value, the judicial perspective in adjudication is to evaluate preferred interests narrowly. In fact, this posture and the control transaction context (which typically gives rise to fiduciary analysis) combine to produce a fiduciary obligation only for the protection of the preferred stockholders' contingent right to receive their basic equity and no more....

.... The basic duty to the preferred is to protect its investment. The way in which courts approach the issue of contractual interpretation, however, leaves the definition of "investment" at the mercy of draftsmanship rather than the economic and situational realities of the relationship. In contrast to the directors' duty to maximize the value of the common, they seem to have license to minimize the value of the preferred. The fact that courts invoke the fairness test to protect the preferred only in the extreme situation of control transactions (and then only in cases of egregious and obvious unfairness) supports this conclusion....

OF FIDUCIARY DUTY AND CONTRACT RIGHTS

In order fully to clarify what is at stake, it is important to discuss the significant distinction between fiduciary obligation and contract rights....

* * *

[B]oth fiduciary duty and contractual good faith are judicially imposed concepts.... This, however, is where the similarity ends. The purpose of the good faith doctrine is to prevent a contracting party from opportunistically capitalizing upon the ambiguities of language to defeat the other's legitimate contractual expectations. Contractual good faith ... has been applied in the corporate finance context as a very narrow doctrine, which draws its substance from the terms of the agreement itself. Thus, implied good faith terms must be consistent with the explicit terms of the agreement itself and must further the parties' performance of that explicit agreement.[62] ...

* * *

But every corporate lawyer knows instinctively that there are significant differences between fiduciary obligation and contractual good faith. First, and quite significantly, the sources of the duties are different. Contractual good faith responds to the ambiguities and indeterminacies of language and the general context of contract formation but, importantly, derives from the respect for individual autonomy that underlies our system of contract....

Fiduciary duty, by contrast, arises from a situation that is quite the opposite from the supposed free autonomy underlying contract. It is imposed in situations of significant

---

62. Metropolitan Life Ins. Co. v. RJR Nabisco, Inc., 716 F. Supp. 1504, 1516-18 (S.D.N.Y. 1989).

power disparity, where one party is given responsibility and power over something that matters to another party and that vulnerable party is at the mercy of the power-holding party. Once the relationship has been established, the dominated party effectively loses any control over the subject of the relationship, while the power-holder remains autonomous. The power-holding party, in undertaking his or her responsibilities, accepts a limitation on his autonomy; that is, he acknowledges that the dominated party is entitled to his fidelity in the conduct of these affairs. Of course, it is with the expectation of this fidelity that the dominated party cedes power to the power-holder. These markedly different origins of fiduciary obligation suggest a very different content from that of contractual good faith. In fact, the content is quite different. To the extent that fiduciary duty is contractual, the substance of that contract term is loyalty. Thus, the "contractual expectation" is that the fiduciary will act in the beneficiary's interest. This may entail self-sacrifice on the part of the fiduciary, and sometimes even the defeat of the fiduciary's own contractual expectations. This, then, is the essence of fiduciary obligation, and its relationship to contract is clear: fiduciary duty, where it applies, trumps contract.[74] And if fiduciary duty trumps contract, then it can hardly be the case that it is functionally analogous to a doctrine designed for the limited purpose of ensuring the performance of contracts.

The unfettered loyalty that traditionally characterizes fiduciary obligation has been significantly modified in corporate law. In contrast to undivided loyalty, the standard of corporate fiduciary conduct is fairness. Perhaps the most significant difference between these standards is that fairness, at least as applied between or among persons, is an inherently bilateral concept. In order to determine whether something is fair, one must start with some idea of the entitlements of the parties vis-á-vis each other. In the vertical corporate context, the parties will be the directors and the corporation or the stockholders. In the horizontal context, it will be stockholder versus stockholder. The fairness standard thus acknowledges a legitimate right in each side to some portion of the disputed good. While this is a lesser standard than self-sacrifice and undivided loyalty, it is a significantly higher standard than contractual good faith....

Once it is understood that fiduciary duty trumps contract, the paradox becomes clear: any meaningful assertion that directors owe preferred stockholders fiduciary duties must necessarily be inconsistent with, and legally prior to, the assertion that their obligation to those same security-holders lies in contract. For the contract must be interpreted, in the first instance, by directors in planning corporate transactions. As fiduciaries, they must interpret the contract in a manner consistent with their duties, that is to say, in the preferred stockholders' interests. Because fiduciary duty trumps contract, directors can never interpret the preferred stock contract in an arm's length manner; to do so would be inconsistent with their legally mandated role. To the extent that courts tend strictly to interpret the preferred stock contract and to authorize directors to do the same, they defeat any real notion of preferred stock fiduciary duty.

* * *

---

74. I do not mean to include in this statement certain types of obligations which can be contractually waived, for example, liability for breaches of the duty of care. Del. Code Ann. tit. 8, § 102(b)(7) (1989), in R. Franklin Balotti & Jesse A. Finkelstein, The Delaware Law of Corporations and Business Organizations 34-35 (1993). In such cases, the contractual waiver of such duties (and therefore, presumably, the superiority of contract to such liabilities or duties) has received specific legal sanction and is accompanied by procedural and other protections to attempt to ensure the voluntariness of the waiver....

.... Preferred stockholders, unlike bondholders, almost never have the right to have their capital returned. Redemptions typically are at the option of the corporation, and liquidations (construed literally by courts and evadable by corporations thanks to the equal dignity rule) are rare. Thus, preferred stockholders put their capital permanently in the hands of the corporation's directors and are entirely vulnerable to their decisions. When this is combined with the directors' maximizing obligation to the common stockholders, the protections for the preferred are quite skimpy indeed. At a minimum, a meaningful fiduciary obligation to the preferred would encompass a general rule to protect the integrity of the preferred's equity.[88] What this analysis suggests is that any time a corporate transaction exposes the preferred stockholders to additional risk without a corresponding benefit (including, for argument's sake, the indirect benefit of increased security from the possibility of increased corporate wealth), that transaction breaches the directors' fiduciary duty to the preferred.

* * *

THE SOLUTION

It would be relatively easy to make the argument that preferred stockholders ought to be left to their contract rights. To the extent of their preferences, they are not the ultimate residual claimant and therefore may be more risk averse than common stockholders. The imposition of a duty to the preferred could make management less willing to undertake positive net present value projects, to the ultimate inefficiency of our corporate system. Moreover, preferred stockholders have the opportunity to specify their deal with the common in advance and, like other contracting parties, should be held to the bargain they made.... Finally, although the preferred stockholders may not have had an opportunity to bargain out the terms of the contract face to face, they have no obligation to buy preferred stock, the terms of which they dislike.... Consequently, they ought not complain if the investment they choose to make turns out badly.

.... What is notable is that none of these arguments, nor any of the others that are made to deny a variety of corporate contractual constituents' fiduciary obligations, respond to the real underlying issue of the appropriate set of ground rules. Even if preferred stock is primarily a contractual creature, and even if the preference rights of preferred stockholders ought best be interpreted in terms of contract, that alone does not address the baseline from which contractual interpretation begins. For example, it is one thing to say that preferred stockholders ought to be held to have assumed the risk that a restructuring designed to make the corporation work more efficiently and thus to increase the corporation's wealth could have an adverse effect, at least in the short-term, on the value of the preferred stock, or that survival of the corporation may require the board to skip dividend payments and avoid redemptions it otherwise would be required to make. It is quite another to say that directors can engage the corporation in transactions that create wealth for the common stockholders simply by diverting to them some of the value of the preferred stock. In other words, the incidental adverse effects of wealth creation result from the proper pursuit of the goals of the corporation and thus can be seen as a risk legitimately to be assigned to any corporate contract claimant. The mere transfer of wealth, with no value added and no net gain—theft, in other words—ought not to be part of the ground rules.

---

88. The equity, in this context, ought to be the discounted present value of the dividend payments, with a discount rate equal to the dividend rate, together with any redemption or liquidation premium....

This brings us back to Jedwab. The right that both preferred and common stock-holders possess, besides occasional specific rights like voting, is the right to share in the corporate wealth once the corporation's creditors are paid off. True, the preferred receive their money prior to the common and typically receive a predetermined amount, and thus, it is appropriate to adjust their relative fiduciary rights to account for the different financial risks they take. Unlike creditors and other contract claimants, however, and like common stockholders, the corporation has no obligation to pay the preferred at all, and indeed, if the assets are inadequate, no right to do so either. To a very real extent, then, the preferred and common stockholders are participants in a common enterprise of providing the corporation with its equity cushion. And it is this that gives them more in common than courts typically are willing to allow.[152] Thus, preference rights, contractual though they may be, are contingent in a way that shares more with the common stock than other contractual claimants.

Courts obviously recognize this, although never explicitly. It is the understanding behind Chancellor Allen's opinion in Jedwab, as well as the other cases that acknowledge some fiduciary rights of the preferred. It is the truth that underlies the preferred's right to bring derivative litigation to enforce the corporation's rights to directorial care and loyalty....

This is enough to make it clear that directors ought to owe some meaningful duties to the preferred. As I have acknowledged, courts do impose such duties, certainly in the vertical context and sometimes in the horizontal context. But the pure horizontal context, which is the most important, presents a different problem. This context presents the stark case of stockholder against stockholder. It is a well established principle of corporate law that noncontrolling stockholders do not owe each other fiduciary duties, at least in the absence of particular circumstances. Why should things be different here?

The first point to observe is that the conflict is never really starkly one of common versus preferred stockholder. As corporate law is structured, stockholders cannot initiate any transaction; at best they can approve them. The transactions they approve (when such rights apply) are initiated by the directors. Even in the case of tender offers, which are transactions initiated by third parties and made directly to the stockholders, modern statutory[155] and case law[156] make the board central to the success or failure of the offer. Thus, virtually any transaction that benefits the common at the expense of the preferred is, at a minimum, mediated, and typically initiated, by the board. This involvement of the board gives an unmistakably vertical slant to any horizontal conflict because the preferred are often unable to have any impact on the board's action, and thus, are at least as vulnerable as the common.[157] It is this vulnerability that leads to a strong argument in favor of providing meaningful fiduciary rights to the preferred.

---

152. It is interesting to note that in all of the cases in which courts separate the preferred stock-holders from the corporation, by leaving the preferred to their contract, the courts never acknowledge this critical difference between preferred stockholders and other contractual claimants: the preferred stockholders need never be paid.

155. See, e.g., Del. Code Ann. tit. 8, §203 (1989 & Supp. 1994); N.Y. Bus. Corp. Law §912 (McKinney 1986 & Supp. 1996); Securities Exchange Act of 1934, 15 U.S.C. §§78a-78lll (1994 & West Supp. 1995).

156. Paramount Communications, Inc. v. Time Inc., 571 A.2d 1140 (Del. 1989); Unocal Corp. v. Mesa Petroleum Co., 493 A.2d 946 (Del. 1985).

157. The preferred might have voting rights which would enable them to block the transaction or to oust the board at the next election. Class voting rights, however, are a matter of contract which, as we have seen, tend to be construed narrowly. Also, preferred stock typically constitutes a minority of the outstanding capital stock.... Therefore, to the extent the preferred vote as a class with the commons, they will ordinarily be defeated.

The vulnerability of preferred stockholders is not ameliorated by contract. First, the contract is drafted by the issuer and its underwriter and, thus, is unlikely to be particularly favorable to the preferred. Second, and as I suggested when describing the preferred stock paradox, the contract must be interpreted. It is the board that is the first line of interpretation in planning corporate transactions, and exclusively so in those many deals that are never litigated. To the extent that the board is judicially encouraged to interpret the contract narrowly, it is empowered to take advantage of the preferred's vulnerability to defeat their legitimate expectations that their wealth will not gratuitously be transferred to the common.... Thus, to the extent that preferences are treated exclusively as contractual and contracts are interpreted narrowly, preferred stockholders have no fiduciary rights at all. These rights are absent in a context where, for a variety of reasons, we typically impose them. The case that needs to be made, then, is for the denial to preferred stockholders of fiduciary rights, not their provision....

The biggest problem in establishing meaningful horizontal fiduciary rights for preferred stockholders is one of balance. How, it is often argued, can directors be responsible to two groups of claimants with competing interests? The fact is that they already are. This answer begins to reveal itself when we recall that contemporary corporate fiduciary doctrine in the vertical context speaks in terms of fairness. That is the standard that governs the conduct of directors when one of their number has an interest adverse to the corporation.... If we permit directors to allocate corporate wealth between themselves (who have no intrinsic right to that wealth) and the common stockholders, it does not seem to be much of a stretch to demand that they engage in the same process with respect to the preferred stockholders (who do have an intrinsic right to the corporation's wealth) and the common stockholders.

* * *

Fairness has always been a notoriously difficult concept to specify. The argument for applying it to horizontal corporate conflicts says nothing about how it should be applied. But what I thus far have said should suggest some parameters for its application. Put simply, fairness in the horizontal context means that directors cannot gratuitously harm the interests of preferred stockholders for the benefit of the common stockholders. In other words, if the primary or exclusive purpose of a transaction is to transfer wealth from the preferred to the common, it is inherently unfair. If, on the other hand, it is motivated primarily by business reasons—wealth creation—any incidental harm to the preferred is not unfair. This is an easy standard to guide corporate boards....

The litigation context requires some further procedural refinement. Given the fiduciary nature of the duty, it is appropriate that once the preferred stockholders have demonstrated differential treatment of the preferred and the common, it would be incumbent on the directors to demonstrate the primary business motivation for the transaction. If they succeed, they have breached no duty; if they fail, they have.

It would, for the reasons provided, be a significant improvement over current law to impose some kind of duty, such as the one I describe, on corporate directors in favor of preferred stockholders.... But that result may not happen any time soon. In the meantime, what is a preferred stockholder to do? ...

Perhaps the best interim solution would be a covenant precluding the corporation from behaving in a manner that defeats the preferred's legitimate expectations. Such provisions already are used in the specific context of preferred conversion rights. In effect, such a covenant incorporates the fiduciary concept advocated above into the preferred stock provisions of the certificate of incorporation and would read (crudely drafted) something like this:

> The Corporation shall not in any manner, whether by amendment of the Certificate of Incorporation (including, without limitation, any Certificate of Designation), merger, reorganization, recapitalization, consolidation, sales of assets, sale of stock, tender offer, dissolution or otherwise, take any action, or permit any action to be taken, solely or primarily for the purpose of increasing the value of any class of stock of the Corporation if the effect of such action is to reduce the value or security of the Preferred Stock.

By means of such a provision, the preferred stockholder ought then to be in a position to block transactions designed to expropriate their wealth for the benefit of common stockholders and provide them with some rights to the directors' concern and attention in cases of horizontal conflict.

One objection to such a provision may be that issuers would not accept it. But the propriety of such a provision (indeed of a corresponding fiduciary obligation) is made clear by the objection. On what basis could the issuer object to including a covenant not to steal the preferred stockholders' wealth? The only legitimate basis might be the relative uncertainty it creates in structuring corporate transactions. Of course, this relative uncertainty would induce directors to be more attentive to the concerns of preferred stockholders in structuring the deal in the first place, and to ensure that they are fairly treated. Moreover, to the extent that the planned transaction truly is value-creating (and thus socially desirable) in contrast to a mere wealth transfer, the covenant ought not to impede it. Finally, it solves the Jedwab paradox; fiduciary-like obligations are themselves part of the contractual terms and thus are imposed upon the corporation for the benefit of the preferred stockholders.

Clearly, the solution is not perfect. In particular, it may underprotect the class of preferred stockholders who most need fiduciary protection, the public preferred stockholders, who have no opportunity to negotiate for such a provision. On the other hand, it may be that underwriters could induce issuers to include the provision as a signal of good faith to prospective preferred stockholders, which may in turn lead to a decrease in dividend rates. It does create some uncertainty which will have to be worked out through judicial interpretation. But it is a clear improvement over the current state of affairs, where preferred stock hovers in uncomfortable limbo.

Chapter 7

The Rights of Contract Claimants — Part 3: Convertible Securities

We have thus far examined the question of bondholders' and preferred stockholders' rights without considering the significance of incorporating a convertibility feature into the debt instrument or preferred stock. (We refer to convertible debt securities and convertible preferred stock as "convertible securities" throughout this chapter.) Convertible securities deserve special attention because of the inchoate equity interest held by the owners of such securities.

Briefly, a convertible security (whether debt or preferred stock) is a security which permits the holder, while the security remains outstanding or upon specified occurrences, to "trade-in" the security to the issuing corporation in exchange for shares of a specified class of stock at a price determined by means of a ratio or formula included in the security's contract (either an indenture or a certificate of designation, as the case may be). Of course, this convertibility feature provides the convertible securityholder with the potential of appreciation in her investment's value, a potential not available to holders of straight debt securities or preferred stock (unless they sell the debt or preferred stock and then purchase common stock on the market, which subjects them to transaction costs).

Two major related issues arise in connection with convertible securities. The first is the extent to which the inchoate equity interest in convertible securities gives their holders rights extrinsic to their contract, like the fiduciary duties owed by management to common stockholders. The second is the extent to which the corporation is obligated to protect the securityholders' right to convert. Before these issues are presented and discussed, the economics of convertible securities is addressed.

Section 1
Economics of Convertible Securities

Description

A convertible security, such as a convertible bond or share of convertible preferred stock, is a hybrid security that allows its holder to exchange it for a given number of shares of the company's common stock any time up to and including its maturity or earlier redemption date. A convertible security is the combination of two distinct financial instruments. In the case of a convertible bond, it is the combination of (1) a straight debt instrument (*i.e.*, a nonconvertible bond) with the same coupon rate and maturity as the convertible bond and (2) a conversion right similar in many respects to a warrant to purchase shares of the issuer's common stock.[1] Convertible preferred stock likewise is the combination of two distinct financial instruments, the first of which is straight preferred stock (*i.e.*, nonconvertible preferred stock) and the second of which is the aforementioned conversion right.

The conversion right is similar to a warrant in that it allows its holder to convert her security into shares of the company's common stock at a preset *conversion price*.[2] Thus, like a warrant it provides the securityholder with the upside potential of owning common stock in the company.[3] Moreover, the conversion right, when exercised, increases the number of shares of the company's common stock outstanding and thus dilutes existing common stockholders. While the exercise of a warrant has a similar dilutive effect, a warrant holder must normally use cash to pay the exercise price of the warrant. To exercise the conversion right, by contrast, the convertible securityholder does not pay cash but rather turns in her convertible security.

The initial conversion price of a convertible security is typically set somewhere between 20% and 30% above the per share trading price of the issuer's common stock at the time of issuance.[4] This price is subject to later adjustment based on certain actions that an issuer may take that affect its common stock. These events, which are discussed *infra* at section 3b(ii) and (iii), include, among others, the declaration of stock splits or reverse stock splits.

The discussion that follows primarily addresses convertible debt securities. However, the analysis of convertible debt securities is generally applicable to convertible preferred stock as well.[5]

To illustrate the economics of convertible securities, assume that a given convertible bond has a face value of $1,000, a conversion price of $36 per share and a maturity of 30 years.[6] If a bondholder turns in one bond for conversion, she will receive 27 shares of the issuer's common stock [$1,000 face value ÷ $36 per share conversion price = 27.77 shares].[7] The 0.77 of a share in the calculation is called a *fractional share*. Convertible bond indentures typically provide that fractional shares will be cashed out by the issuer based on the current trading price of the issuer's common stock. *See* discussion *infra* at section 3b(iv) (Section 10.03 of the Revised Model Simplified Indenture).

---

1. The conversion right, unlike a warrant, cannot be separately traded as it is embedded within the bond.

2. The conversion price is like the exercise price of a warrant or the strike price of a call option. For a discussion of call options, see *supra* chapter 4, section 1a.

3. According to John Ritchie, "[n]ew cash offerings of convertibles tend to be greater during periods of rising stock prices.... The right to share in future price rises for the common stock is likely to be most highly valued during a period of bullish expectations for common stocks, allowing corporations to issue convertible securities on favorable terms." Ritchie, The Handbook of Fixed Income Securities 292 (Fabozzi & Fabozzi eds., 4th ed. 1995) (hereinafter "Fixed Income Security Handbook").

4. *See id.* at 291.

5. *See* Van Horne, Financial Management and Policy 619 (2002); Fischer & Jordan, Security Analysis and Portfolio Management 457 (6th ed. 1995); Fixed Income Security Handbook, *supra* note 2, at 291.

6. Convertible bonds typically have maturities of 25 to 30 years. *See* Fixed Income Security Handbook, *supra* note 3, at 291.

7. The number of shares of the issuer's common stock that will be obtained through the surrender of the convertible bond is referred to as the *conversion ratio*. Some convertible contracts specify a conversion price, while others specify a conversion ratio.

Due to the conversion right, the deal between the convertible bondholders and the issuer differs from that between nonconvertible bondholders and the issuer in three significant ways. First and foremost, convertible bonds typically pay a rate of interest lower (anywhere from 250 to 350 basis points) than that paid on comparable, nonconvertible bonds.[8] This lower rate reflects the fact that the conversion right has value. Second, convertible bondholders customarily accept "subordinated" status.[9] Third, the indenture for convertible bonds typically contains less restrictive financial covenants than does an indenture for nonconvertible bonds.[10]

All three of these differences provide the issuer with operational flexibility which, in turn, could enhance the intrinsic value of the conversion right. The lower interest rate makes it easier for the issuer to service the debt obligations relating to the convertible bond. The subordinated status of the convertible bond means that the issuer is in a position to incur additional indebtedness at a senior level. The less restrictive financial covenants allow the issuer to operate more freely and with less concern of triggering a covenant default under the indenture.

Investment Value and Conversion Value

As seen in Figure 7-1, when a convertible bond is issued, the present value of the straight bond component (the *investment* or *straight* value) is worth less than the convertible bond's face value of $1,000 ($850 in the case of Figure 7-1). This stems from the below market coupon rate associated with the convertible bond. When the interest payments and the principal to be received in the future are discounted by the interest rate payable on comparable, *nonconvertible* bonds (which rate is higher than that associated with the convertible bond), the present value is below $1,000. (This is the same notion as a nonconvertible bond with a 5% coupon trading in the secondary market at a discount when interest rates rise above 5%). As the convertible bond's maturity approaches, however, the value of the straight bond component rises up to $1,000 (assuming interest rates and issuer credit quality are held constant), as the issuer is contractually obligated to pay $1,000 to the convertible bondholder at maturity.[11] (*See* Figure 7-1.) The investment value of convertible preferred stock is determined in a similar manner.[12]

---

8. *See* Fixed Income Security Handbook, *supra* note 3, at 291.
9. *See* Van Horne, *supra* note 5, at 620; Fixed Income Security Handbook, *supra* note 3, at 291.
10. *See* Fixed Income Security Handbook, *supra* note 3, at 293.
11. *See* Calamos, Convertible Arbitrage 16 (2003).
12. Since preferred stock is a form of ownership, its life is assumed to be infinite and therefore the present value factor used to find its value is not readily available. The investment value of convertible preferred stock is assumed to equal the present value of the preferred dividends over an infinite life (an annuity) discounted at the yield on *straight* preferred stock. The present value factor for an infinite-lived annuity is, therefore:

$$V = \frac{D}{r}$$

where:

D = dividend on the convertible preferred
r = appropriate discount rate or current yield on *nonconvertible* preferred stock

For example, assume that The A&B Freda Company has just issued 8% convertible preferred stock with a $100 par value. If the company had issued nonconvertible preferred stock, the annual dividend (paid in quarterly installments) would likely have been around 10%. Dividing the annual dividend of $8 (8% of $100) by the yield on nonconvertible preferreds, or 10%, results in an investment value for the preferred stock of $80 (8/.10).

Figure 7-1

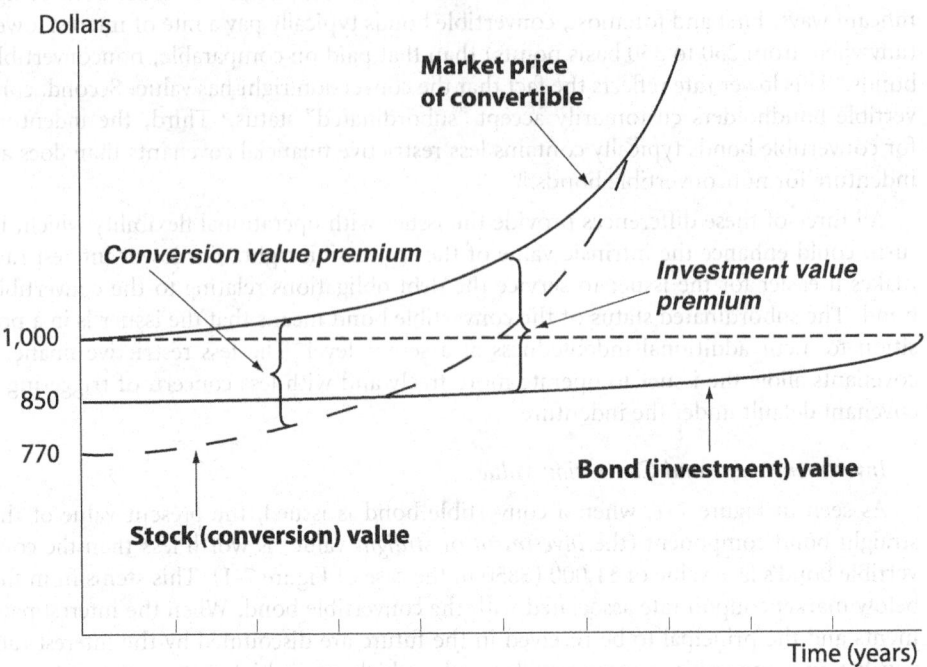

The difference between the convertible bond's $1,000 face value and its present value at issuance is the cost of the conversion right to the convertible bondholder. The value of the conversion right (the *conversion value*) upon issuance of the convertible bond is substantially less than the bond's $1,000 face value, as the conversion right is similar to an "out-of-the-money" call option. For a discussion of call options, see *supra* chapter 4, section 1a.

Figure 7-1 provides an example of a convertible bond with a $1,000 face value and a conversion price of $18.20 per share. At issuance, the issuer's common stock was trading at $14.00 per share; therefore, at that time the conversion value of the convertible bond was only $770. This is calculated by first determining how many shares the bondholder would receive when she converts. The answer (rounded) is 55 shares [$1,000 face value ÷ $18.20 conversion price]. However, if she converted immediately, she would receive 55 shares with a market value of only $14.00 per share. Thus, the conversion value of her convertible bond at issuance is only $770 [55 shares x $14.00 per share].

As seen in Figure 7-1, converting a convertible bond before the issuer's stock price rises up to the conversion price makes no sense. To do so would be to over pay for shares of the issuer's common stock. In the preceding example, why give up your convertible bond to buy stock at $18.20 per share when you can use cash and buy shares in the secondary market for only $14.00 per share? Moreover, converting when the issuer's common stock trading price reaches the conversion price also does not make sense. This is because a convertible bondholder gives up her right to receive the present value of the expected bond payments once she converts, and these payments are valuable. Furthermore, a bondholder who converts gives up her senior status as she is now only a common stockholder.[13]

---

13. The decision on whether to convert could be influenced if the issuer pays dividends (particularly large dividends) on its common stock, as convertible bondholders are not entitled to common stock dividends until such time as they convert.

Figure 7-2

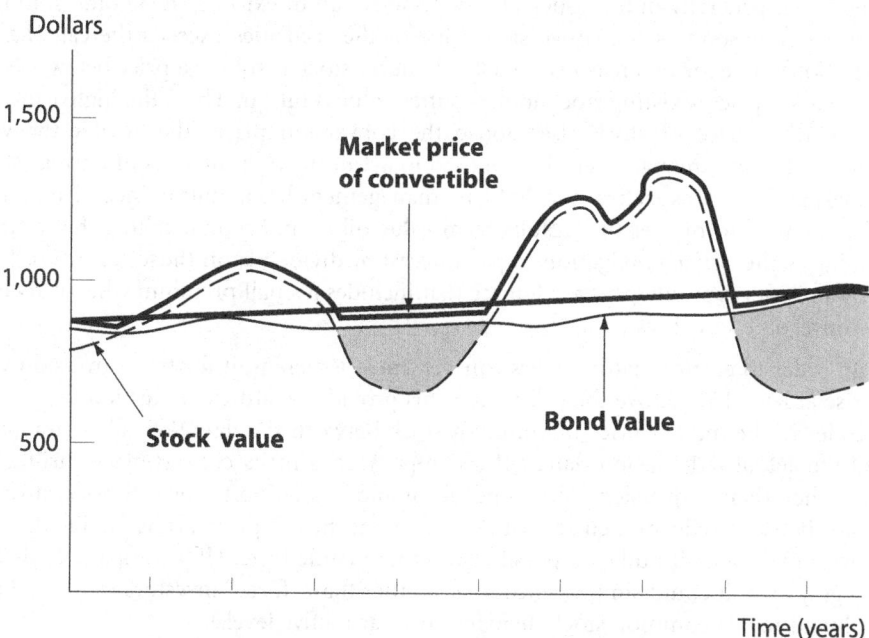

As highlighted by Figure 7-2, the value of a convertible bond will always be the *greater* of its investment (bond) value and its conversion value. At issuance both the investment value and conversion value are less than the convertible bond's $1,000 face value. The difference between the market price of the convertible and the investment value is called the *investment value premium*. The difference between the market price of the convertible and the conversion premium is called the *conversion value premium*. (*See* Figure 7-1). Until the conversion value premium is eliminated, it makes no sense to convert. Because the value of the straight bond is unlikely to rise in any significant way due to its below-market coupon rate, the main way the conversion value premium is eliminated (if at all) is through an increase in the conversion value related to the conversion right. Conversion value, in turn, depends on the value of the issuer's common stock. Increases in the value of the issuer's common stock whittle away at the conversion value premium. At some point after the common stock price rises above the conversion price, the conversion value premium will be eliminated. Convertible bondholders should not convert until this occurs.

Calling the Security

A company typically issues convertible securities expecting that its common stock price will rise above the conversion price, thus resulting in investors exercising their conversion rights. Investors, however, would prefer to continue holding convertible securities even after the conversion right is significantly "in-the money." Indeed, a convertible security's price will continue to rise as the price of the underlying stock increases. Additionally, investors will continue to receive interest or dividend payments along the way and receive the downside protection of being a creditor or preferred stockholder. However, if the company pays a common stock dividend (particularly large ones), investors must factor this into their decision on whether to convert or to continue to hold.

An issuer, however, seeks the optional right to redeem (or "call in") convertible securities.[14] It is generally in the issuer's interest, on behalf of existing stockholders, to force conversion as soon as the conversion value of the securities exceeds the call (*i.e.,* redemption) price for two reasons.[15] First, whenever stock is sold at a price below the current market price, existing stockholders suffer value dilution. Thus, the higher the current market price of stock rises above the conversion price, the greater the value dilution. Because management is supposed to act in the best interests of current stockholders and not prospective stockholders, management has a built in incentive to minimize the wealth transfer that results from value dilution. Second, calling the securities eliminates the issuer's obligation to pay interest or dividends on those securities. However, an issuer typically pays a call price that includes a small premium when it redeems its convertible securities.

In order to ensure that investors convert, most issuers wait for the conversion value to rise at least 15% above the call price. This provides a sufficient cushion for possible declines in the market price of common stock between the date the call is announced and the actual redemption date.[16] If a company calls in its convertible securities at a time when their conversion value is not favorable in relation to the call price, investors could choose to redeem their securities for cash (at the call price), thus forcing the company to make a cash outlay at possibly an inopportune time. (If a company finds itself in a gray area, it could simply "encourage" rather than "force" investors to convert simply by raising its common stock dividend to an attractive level.)

Faced with choosing between a higher conversion value or a lower call price (even one representing a small premium), convertible securityholders opt for the former and convert their convertible securities into shares of the issuer's common stock. Those who forget to do so may pay a very high price for their mistake, as seen *infra* at section 3b(i). According to one study, the median delay before call, once the conversion value exceeds the call price, is only 77 days. However, the median delay is only 20 days when the conversion value rises 20% above the call price.[17]

An example will illustrate the impact of a failure to convert. Assume that Albiera, Inc. issued 7.5% convertible bonds with a face value of $1,000 each and with a conversion price of $50 (and thus each bond can be converted into 20 shares of Albiera common stock). Further assume that the bonds are callable by Albiera at a call price of $1,050 per bond (representing a 5% premium over face value) and that its common stock is now currently trading at $60 per share (and thus the conversion right is "in-the-money"). The conversion value of a bond would be $1,200 (20 shares × $60). If Albiera were to an-

---

14. Issuers often prefer to issue convertible bonds rather than straight debt with warrants attached due to the convertible bonds' call feature.

15. Forced conversion would not make sense if the company's common stock dividend exceeds the after-tax interest expense payable on convertible bonds or the preferred stock dividend payable on convertible preferred stock. On the convertible preferred stock front, Kenneth Dunn and Kenneth Eades found that a substantial number of convertible preferred stockholders did not convert voluntarily when the common dividend income they would realize as common stockholders exceeded the convertible preferred's dividend plus its premium of conversion value over call price. Thus, this would be another instance where a company would choose not to force conversion. *See* Dunn & Eades, Voluntary Conversion of Convertible Securities and the Optimal Call Strategy, J. of Fin. Econ. (Aug. 1989), at 273-301.

16. *See* Van Horne, *supra* note 5, at 622.

17. *See* Asquith, Convertible Bonds Are Not Called Late, J. of Fin. (Sept. 1995), at 1275-89. *See also* Ederington, Canton & Campbell, To Call or Not to Call Convertible Debt, Fin. Mgmt. (Spring 1997), at 22-31.

nounce that it is calling in the bonds for $1,050 each, bondholders would convert their bonds in order to receive stock worth $1,200 rather than opt for $1,050 in cash. Failure to do so would mean unnecessarily forfeiting $150 in value per bond. Those bondholders who prefer cash could simply sell the shares they receive upon conversion.

Section 2
Justifications for Convertible Securities

What motivates investors to purchase convertible securities and issuers to issue them? Why wouldn't an investor interested in capital gains and an appetite for risk simply buy shares of common stock outright? Why wouldn't an investor seeking current income and relative safety of principal buy a higher yielding straight bond?

Investors buying convertible securities apparently are seeking a compromise vehicle. This vehicle blends current income, safety of principal and capital gain potential.[18] Thus, those who buy convertible bonds receive interest on the straight bond component while having the upside potential of common stock. Furthermore, they retain senior securityholder status until such time (if at all) as they convert their convertible bonds into common stock. Even if the issuer's common stock falls in price, the worst-case scenario for a convertible securityholder seeking to sell her convertible security in the secondary market is that the price of that security will only have declined to the point where its yield matches that of a comparable straight bond.[19] (*See* Figure 7-2).

An issuer, by contrast, is often driven to issue convertible securities for two reasons. First, it may view the issuance of convertible securities as deferred common stock financing.[20] In other words, the issuer may desire to raise capital through the sale of common stock rather than straight debt or preferred stock. However, if its management believes its common stock is currently undervalued by the market, issuing additional shares of common stock today is unappealing. By issuing convertible securities instead, the issuer reasons that it is essentially selling its common stock today at a price 20% to 30% higher than the current trading price of its stock. In return for doing so, it must pay interest or dividends to investors until such time, if ever, that it makes economic sense for them to convert their securities.

Second, the issuer may prefer to issue straight bonds or preferred stock but finds it cannot sell them at a reasonable interest or dividend rate due to the issuer's creditworthiness or other factors. In this regard, issuing convertible securities may be better tailored to the issuer's cash flow pattern. The lower coupon or dividend rate associated with convertibles makes it more likely that the company can meet its interest or dividend obligations.

These issuer rationales have been challenged with respect to convertible bonds (although these challenges would apply equally to convertible preferred stock). Thomas Copeland, Fred Weston and Kuldeep Shastri have analyzed the true cost of capital associated with both the straight bond component and the associated conversion right of a convertible bond. They have concluded that, while convertible bonds may represent a

---

18. *See* Fischer & Jordan, Security Analysis and Portfolio Management 462 (6th ed. 1995).
19. *See* Fixed Income Security Handbook, *supra* note 3, at 294.
20. *See* Van Horne, *supra* note 5, at 620.

deferred sale of the company's common stock, that sale is not at an attractive, above-market price. Moreover, based on the convertibles' true cost of capital, they argue that convertible bonds do not represent a form of "cheap debt." Thus, they encourage companies to reexamine why they issue convertible debt securities. *See* Copeland, Weston & Shastri, Financial Theory and Corporate Policy 619-22 (4th ed. 2005).

One potential explanation is the "sequential" or "staged" financing hypothesis of David Mayers. He argues that the issuance of callable convertible bonds provides a firm with the advantages of sequential financing. This, in turn, helps control overinvestment in the firm. Issuance of convertible bonds "precommits" investors into investing in two capital projects. Only if the first project—financed through the initial issuance of the bonds—is successful will the second project receive financing (through the elimination of the debt obligation that occurs upon conversion). If the first project fails, the conversion right of the bonds becomes worthless, the market value of the convertible bonds falls below face value, and the firm has an incentive to repurchase the devalued debt in the open market, thereby returning cash to bondholders. Based on Mayers' hypothesis, firms would be expected to undertake substantial incremental investment and new financing around the time of conversion. Mayers' empirical evidence demonstrated that they, in fact, do. *See* Mayers, Why Firms Issue Convertible Bonds: The Matching of Financial and Real Investment Options, 47 J. of Fin. Econ. 83 (1998).

Along the lines of Copeland, Weston and Shastri, consider Professor Klein's thoughts on this issue:

Klein, The Convertible Bond: A Peculiar Package
123 U. Pa. L. Rev. 547, 558-68 (1975)[a]

[Professor Klein begins this article by questioning why convertible bonds ever are issued or held, noting the existence of several "troublesome characteristics" which "should trigger the flimflam danger signal in one's mind." He first analyzes convertible bonds in terms of the problems inherent in their valuation, analogizing them to bonds with warrants attached, with the additional complicating factor that in the case of convertible bonds, the holder must give up the right to receive fixed interest payments in order to capitalize on the conversion opportunity, a factor he describes as "a rather bizarre kind of gamble on changes in the market rate of interest." In contrast, the holder of the bond and the warrant can retain the bond investment while using cash to exercise the warrant. In other words, in the latter case, the decision to retain the bond and exercise the warrant are separate, whereas in the case of convertible bonds the two decisions necessarily are linked.

From the issuer's perspective, he notes that the price of convertible bonds will be less than the price of warrants and bonds separately issued: "Assuming the separate availability of bonds and options, one would expect that the demand for the package would be significantly lower than the combined demand for the separate elements, which means that the issuer will not maximize its returns, even though few, if any, buyers will obtain a bargain."]

By this point, if not earlier, one should have begun to question why companies ever issue convertible bonds, at least for the purpose of raising new capital. A number of reasons have been suggested, but only two have even enough superficial purely economic

---

a. Copyright 1975 by the University of Pennsylvania Law Review.

rationality to deserve consideration. One reason is associated with the view that a convertible bond is basically debt financing, with the conversion privilege as a "sweetener." The reason for adding the sweetener by issuing a convertible, rather than a straight bond, is to reduce the interest cost or, to put the same idea in slightly different terms, to permit the sale of a bond at an interest cost such that the company's appearance as a good credit risk will not be impaired. What this boils down to is flimflam. The cost of raising the money is not reduced at all, of course; it is just disguised, unless there is only a negligible chance that the price of the common will, in fact, rise to the point where conversion will be attractive to the bondholders. By selling the conversion privilege the company in effect receives a payment for a gamble on the common stock, and uses that payment to reduce the apparent cost of capital. I offer no insight into who is deceived—management, existing shareholders, or purchasers of the bonds, or all of them.

The other most significant reason for issuing convertibles is associated with the view that they are essentially a form of deferred equity financing. The idea behind this view is that management may want to raise equity capital, but it considers that the current market price of the common is too low. Convertible bonds are issued, therefore, with the idea that they will be converted into common when the value of the common rises to a point where the company can force conversion by calling the bond. But if the common looks like such a good buy, why let the purchasers of the convertible bonds in on the expected rise in value? Is it not true that by selling the option, the company's officers are gambling that the stock will not perform as well as the buyers expect? If the market price of the common rises and the bonds are converted, then, to be sure, the company will receive more for the stock than it would have received if it had sold the stock at the time of issuance of the bond, but it will receive less than it would have received for the stock if the bond, with its conversion privilege, had never been issued. For example, assume that the company issues the bond when the price of the common is $20 per share; that the bond is convertible at $25 per share (that is, convertible into forty shares); and that the market value of the conversion element of the bond is $200 or $5 per option share. Ignoring foregone interest, the break-even point for the investor is $25 per share. The buyer must be gambling that the price will rise above $25. Correspondingly, the company must be gambling that the price will not rise above that level—otherwise it would have issued a straight bond and sold common, retiring the bonds, when the price did rise to some point above $25. This seems like a rather peculiar kind of gamble for the corporate managers to be taking, betting against the rise above $25. It might be argued that the managers might not have the option of issuing straight debt because the interest rate might be "too high." But as we have already seen, that cost is not reduced by issuing the convertible, it is merely disguised. It might also be argued that transaction costs are reduced by issuing the convertible bonds, but the harder one thinks about this claim the less sense it seems to make given the possibility, for instance, of raising equity capital at relatively low cost by issuing rights to shareholders.

Professor Klein, in correspondence with one of your editors, has suggested that convertible bonds "may make sense in a certain setting where there may be asymmetric expectations," a suggestion which he has illustrated by means of a "hypothetical conversation between a venture capitalist and an entrepreneur" and which he has permitted us to reprint here:

> VC: So you need $X to expand this business of yours and since you are already borrowed to the hilt you need me to put up equity. That is intriguing, but I'm concerned about risk of loss.

E: Not to worry. There is no risk of loss.

VC: Are you sure?

E: Would I lie to you?

VC: If you're so sure, then you won't mind if we provide that in the event of liquidation I get my money back before you get any.

E: No problem.

VC: I have another problem. My money comes from a fund that requires me to pay interest to my investors.... So I will need a cash flow from you.

E: That's not so good, but I can handle it if we just increase the amount you initially contribute.

VC: Good enough. You understand that you have just agreed to issue me a convertible bond. By the way, I want some elements of control as well, but we can meet my need for that with appropriate covenants.

E: Done.

Questions

1. What, if anything, does the survival of convertible securities in the markets have to say about their desirability or utility?

2. Does modern financial theory offer any help in valuing convertible securities? For a further examination of the problems of pricing and valuing convertible securities, see Brealey, Myers & Allen, Principles of Corporate Finance 684-85 (8th ed. 2006); Copeland, Weston & Shastri, Financial Theory and Corporate Policy 619-22 (4th ed. 2005); Calamos, Convertible Arbitrage 18-20 (2003); Van Horne, Financial Management and Policy 619-28 (2002); Brigham & Houston, Fundamentals of Financial Management 784-88 (8th ed. 1998); Ritchie, The Handbook of Fixed Income Securities 303-05 (Fabozzi & Fabozzi eds., 4th ed. 1995).

3. The American Law Institute has provided for derivative standing for convertible bondholders in its Principles of Corporate Governance. See Principles of Corp. Gov. § 7.02 (Amer. L. Inst. 1994). Do you agree that sufficient differences exist between straight debt and convertible debt that the latter, but not the former, should have standing to bring derivative actions?

Problem — Financing with Convertible Bonds

Poindexter Computer Corporation (the "Company") is a manufacturer of personal computers located in Silicon Valley. After meteoric early success, 4 years ago ("year 1") the Company issued 3,500,000 shares of common stock that has since been trading over-the-counter. Egghead, the Company's founder and president, retained 500,000 shares which he had owned since the Company's creation. At the time the shares were issued at $10, the Company's per share net tangible book value was $1.00. By year 3 the trading price of the shares was $19 and book value had risen to $5. However, the Company began to face increasingly sophisticated competition from abroad and three months ago (in year 5), although book value held steady, the stock's trading price had dropped to $7.

Recently the board met to discuss the Company's problems. Of particular concern was the Company's financial inability to develop a new product designed by its engineers which, the board believed, would make all competitors' products obsolete. The board agreed that it was essential to the Company's survival that the new product be developed. However, the Company needed $35,000,000, and the board then turned to a discussion of financing alternatives. Beancounter, the chief financial officer, presented and commented on several potential financing strategies.

One alternative was to issue common stock. However, the Company's underwriters had informed Beancounter that the highest possible price at which the stock could be marketed was $5.25. Egghead strenuously objected to the dilution this would cause the Company's current stockholders. Beancounter then suggested an issuance of preferred stock, but the lack of dividend deductibility for tax purposes and the problems that would be caused by potential dividend arrearages made this alternative look unattractive. Finally, Beancounter suggested debt. The High-Tech Bank & Trust Co. (the "Bank") had informed Beancounter that it would be willing to syndicate a loan for the entire $35,000,000, at a floating interest rate of prime plus 3 percent. When Beancounter announced this proposal, an audible gasp emanated from the board. But Beancounter went on to say that the Bank was willing to lower its interest rate to a manageable prime plus 1 percent if the Company would issue debt convertible into authorized unissued shares of the Company's common stock at a conversion price of $8.25, with anti-dilution protection satisfactory to the Bank.

What are the advantages and disadvantages, from the Company's perspective, of using convertible debt to meet its financing needs?

Section 3
Obligation of the Corporation to Protect Conversion Rights

Because convertible securityholders give up yield in exchange for their conversion rights, it is crucial to protect the benefits those rights confer. This section first explores whether convertible securityholders are owed fiduciary duties on account of their conversion rights. It then provides a detailed examination of the contractual protections typically granted to convertible securityholders to protect those rights.

a. Fiduciary Duties

Simons v. Cogan, which we have encountered before, is the seminal case addressing whether the expectancy interest created by a conversion right supports the imposition of fiduciary duties under Delaware law.[a]

---

a. *See also* Anadarko Petroleum Corp. v. Panhandle Eastern Corp., 545 A.2d 1171 (Del. 1988) (holding that a corporate parent and the directors of its wholly-owned subsidiary owed no fiduciary duties to prospective stockholders of the subsidiary after the parent declared its intention to spin-off the subsidiary).

Simons v. Cogan
549 A.2d 300 (Del. 1988)

[*Supra* chapter 5, section 4a]

b. Contractual Rights

As Simons v. Cogan makes clear, convertible securityholders must depend on their contract for protection. Special provisions are inserted into the convertible security contract (be it an indenture or a certificate of designation) to protect the value of the convertible securityholders' conversion rights when the company engages in certain voluntary actions that affect its common stock. The goal of these protective provisions is to preserve the benefit of the convertible securityholders' bargain as reflected in their contract.

(i) Notice of Redemption

The convertible security contract often grants the company an optional right of redemption. If the company exercises this right, convertible securityholders cannot convert their securities once the conversion deadline (typically a specified number of days prior to the date of redemption) arrives. If the conversion value of a convertible securityholder's convertible security exceeds the redemption price payable by the company, that securityholder will forfeit the difference between the two if she fails to convert prior to the conversion deadline. Therefore, it is crucial that the company notify the convertible securityholders of its intention to redeem the convertible securities. Consider the following case and accompanying notes.

Van Gemert v. Boeing Co.
520 F.2d 1373 (2d Cir. 1975), *cert. denied*, 423 U.S. 947 (1975)

OAKES, Circuit Judge:

This appeal is from a judgment dismissing the amended complaint in a consolidation class action brought by non-converting holders of The Boeing Company's "4½% Convertible Subordinated Debentures, due July 1, 1980." The complaint was jurisdictionally based on the Securities Exchange Act of 1934 as amended, the Securities Act of 1933 as amended, the Trust Indenture Act of 1939 as amended and the principles of pendent jurisdiction. The gist of the complaint was that the appellants and their class had inadequate and unreasonable notice of Boeing's intention to redeem or "call" the convertible debentures in question and were hence unable to exercise their conversion rights before the deadline in the call of midnight, March 29, 1966. Their damage lay in the fact that the redemption price for each $100 of principal amount of debentures was only $103.25, while under the conversion rate of, at a minimum, two shares of common stock for each $100 of principal amount of debentures, the stock was worth $316.25 on March 29, 1966, the cut-off date for the exercise of conversion privileges, or within 30 days thereafter, $364.00. The named appellants number 56, and the total loss alleged is over $2 million.

The United States District Court for the Southern District of New York, Sylvester J. Ryan, *Judge*, held that Boeing complied with the notice provisions spelled out in the debentures and in the Indenture of Trust Dated July 1, 1958 (the Indenture), between

Boeing and The Chase Manhattan Bank (Chase), Trustee, and that it was required to do no more; that the Trust Indenture Act of 1939, 15 U.S.C. §§77aaa *et seq.*, was not violated; that if Boeing's Listing Agreement with the New York Stock Exchange (NYSE) were violated, it gave appellants no claim for relief; and that even if, as appellants claim, an adjustment in the conversion rate were required, and that failure to make the adjustment gave rise to a cause of action, appellants had no standing to raise the claim since they did not exercise their conversion rights. We reverse and remand on the ground that there was an obligation on Boeing's part to give reasonably adequate notice of the redemption to the debenture holders, which obligation was not fulfilled in this instance....

THE ISSUE OF DEBENTURES

On July 15, 1958, each Boeing shareholder was given [a warrant] to purchase $100 of convertible debentures for each 23 shares of stock then held. The debentures were to pay interest of 4½ per cent per annum and were to be convertible by the debenture-holder into common stock at a rate (subject to adjustment) of two shares per $100 principal amount of debentures. Chase was appointed trustee under the Indenture Agreement, and the debentures, as well as the stock reserved for issuance upon conversion of the debentures, were listed on the NYSE. Application for such listing had been made pursuant to a Listing Agreement between Boeing and the Exchange.

* * *

A number of provisions in the debenture, the Indenture Agreement, the prospectus, the registration statement for the debentures and the Listing Agreement with the NYSE dealt with the possible redemption of the debenture by Boeing and the notice debenture-holders were to receive of a redemption call so that they might timely exercise their right to convert the debentures into common stock rather than have their debentures redeemed at face value.[a] The debentures themselves provided:

> The holder of this Debenture is entitled, at his option, at any time on or before July 1, 1980, or in case this Debenture shall be called for redemption prior to such date, *up to and including but not after the tenth day prior to the redemption date, to convert this Debenture* ... at the principal amount hereof, or such portion hereof, into shares of Capital Stock of the Company....

> The Debentures are *subject to redemption* as a whole or in part, at any time or times, at the option of the Company, *on not less than 30 nor more than 90 days' prior notice, as provided in the Indenture,* at the following redemption prices (expressed in percentages of the principal amount)....

> This Debenture may be registered as to principal upon presentation at the office or agency of the Company, in the Borough of Manhattan, The City of New York, New York....

(Emphasis added.)

The Indenture itself, a 113-page printed booklet, provides in Art. V, §5.02, as follows:

> In case the Company shall desire to exercise the right to redeem all or any part of the debentures, as the case may be, pursuant to Section 5.01, it shall

---

a. Actually, the redemption price of $103.25 represented a 3.25% premium over the $100 face value of the debentures. [Eds.]

publish prior to the date fixed for redemption a notice of such redemption at least twice in an Authorized Newspaper, the first such publication to be not less than 30 days and not more than 90 days before the date fixed for redemption. Such publication shall be in successive weeks but on any day of the week.... [6]

The Indenture also provided that debenture-holders who registered their bonds would receive notice by mail of any redemption call by the Boeing directors.

While the prospectus for the debenture issue did not refer to any registration rights, it did state that redemption could occur "on not less than 30 days' and not more than 90 days' published notice."

The NYSE Listing Agreement dated November 5, 1957, incorporated by reference into the listing application filed by Boeing in respect to the debenture issue, provided in Part III, Paragraph 4, as follows:

4. The Corporation will *publish immediately to the holders* of any of its securities listed on the Exchange *any action taken* by the Corporation *with respect* to dividends or to the allotment of rights to subscribe or *to any rights or benefits pertaining to the ownership of its securities listed on the Exchange*; and will give prompt notice to the Exchange of any such action; and *will afford the holders of its securities listed on the Exchange a proper period within which* to record their interests and *to exercise their rights....*

(Emphasis added.)

Section A10 of the NYSE "Company Manual" specifically defines what is meant by publicity in the Listing Agreement:

Publicity: *The term "publicity,"* as used ... below, and *as used in the listing agreement* in respect of redemption action, *refers to a general news release, and not to the formal notice or advertisement of redemption* sometimes required by provisions of an indenture or charter.

Such news release shall be made as soon as possible after corporate action which will lead to, or which looks toward, redemption is taken ... and shall be made by the fastest available means, i.e., telephone, telegraph or hand-delivery.

To insure coverage which will adequately inform *the public*, the news should be released to at least *one or more newspapers of general circulation in New York City which regularly publish financial news,* or *to one or more of the national news-wire services* (Associated Press, United Press International), in addition to such other release as the company may elect to make.

Section A10 of the Company Manual also provides specifically that when a convertible security is to be redeemed, the news release must include the rate of conversion and the date and time when the conversion privilege expires. It further provides that in addition to the immediate news release the company must give notice immediately to the NYSE itself, so as to enable the NYSE to take any necessary action with respect to further trading in the security.

---

6. An "Authorized Newspaper" is defined as one published at least five days a week and of general circulation in the borough of Manhattan, N.Y. *See* Indenture, Art. I, §1.01.

THE CALL AND ITS CIRCUMSTANCES—HEREIN OF THE NOTICE ACTUALLY GIVEN

On February 28, 1966, the Boeing board of directors *inter alia* authorized the president, vice president-finance or treasurer to call for redemption on a date to be selected by them or any one of them, all of the convertible debentures outstanding under the indenture of July 1, 1958. That same day a news release, headlining 1965 sales and net earnings, and referring to a contemplated stock increase, stock split and post-split dividends, mentioned that "[t]he company's management was also authorized to call for redemption at a future date all of the company's outstanding 4½ percent convertible subordinated debentures." This statement, which did not mention even the tentative dates for redemption and expiration of the conversion rights of debenture holders that had been settled upon, was released by the Boeing "News Bureau" nationally to the financial editors of the New York Times, the New York Herald-Tribune, the Wall Street Journal and other major national newspapers, in addition to the major wire services (Associated Press, United Press International and Dow Jones & Co.).

A short time after the February 28 board meeting, Boeing firmed up the key dates, complied with the indenture notice requirements and communicated to some extent with the Exchange proper. On March 2, 1966, at the home office in Seattle, at a meeting of Boeing officers, bankers and lawyers, it was decided to fix March 8 as the date for the first publication of the formal notice of redemption, April 8 as the redemption date and March 29 as the date for expiration of the conversion privilege. The second date for publication of the formal notice, March 18, was also fixed upon at this March 2 meeting, and Chase was notified to publish the redemption notice on those dates in all editions of the Wall Street Journal. All editions of the Journal carried the formal notices on March 8 and 18; the notices were in due form if not of extensive size. It is conceded by the appellants that the formal requirements of the Indenture were met by the Company and Trustee.

It was not until March 7, the day before the publication of the first formal notice of redemption, that the NYSE was itself notified of the firmed-up dates for redemption, conversion and notice. This was done by a telephone call from Company counsel in Seattle to the Exchange. While the court below found in part that "Boeing did comply with the publicity requirements of the Exchange" and while Company counsel "felt" on the basis of his telephone call "that we had complied with the recommended procedures [of the Stock Exchange Manual]," this finding and feeling are in the face of Boeing's response *admitting* appellants' demand for admission

> That Boeing did not issue any general publicity release, as that term is defined in Section A-10 of the New York Stock Exchange Company manual, concerning the call of the debentures during the period from March 1, through March 24, 1966.

This admission was reconfirmed by counsel for Boeing below and on appeal in the course of an "opening" statement to the court. The original news release of February 28 did not qualify since the dates of conversion and redemption had not been fixed and the Manual requires in the case of convertible securities that the publicity set forth "the rate of conversion and the date and time when the conversion privilege will finally expire" and that if such data are not known at the time publicity is given initially, "similar publicity shall be given immediately it becomes known or determined." The formal notices did not qualify since the Manual refers to a "general news release," and not to the formal notice or advertisement of redemption. In this regard it is interesting to note that a letter dated March 9 from the stock list department of the Exchange to Boeing indicates that "We have noted the recent advertisement advising of the call for redemption" and also asks for a copy of the authorizing resolution.

There was, in short, no general news release as called for by the Listing Agreement as amplified in the Company Manual until on the eve of expiration of the conversion rights, March 25, 1966, it appeared that $10,849,300 face amount of debentures—over one-half of those outstanding at that time—remained unconverted. At that point Boeing issued a press release and then on March 28 the Company republished its earlier advertisement in all editions of the Wall Street Journal (Eastern, Mid-Western, Pacific Coast and South-West) and the New York Times, and additional advertisements were placed. This later action had what the court below termed a "dramatic and widespread rippling effect." Some $9,305,000 of debentures were converted on March 28 and 29. The ripples, however, had not spread to the appellants' class by the midnight deadline on the 29th; they literally went to sleep with $1.5 million of debentures that were worth $4 million if only converted.

It is true, however, and the court did properly find, that in addition to the publication of the two formal indenture notices, notices of the dates of the call and the expiration of the conversion privilege on March 29, 1966, were carried on the following services: NYSE ticker on March 8, 23, 24, 25, 26 and 28, 1966; NYSE Bulletin on March 11, 18 and 25, 1966; The Commercial and Financial Chronicle on March 14, 21 and 28, 1966; Standard & Poor's Bond Outlook on March 19, 1966; Standard & Poor's Called Bond Record on March 9, 11, 18 and 25, 1966; Moody's Industrials on March 11, 1966. Articles about these dates were also carried in the Seattle Post Intelligencer on March 25, 1966; the Seattle Times on March 27, 1966; and the Financial World on March 23, 1966; and the notice was also carried in the Associated Press Bond Tables published on one or more days in at least 30 newspapers published in major cities across the United States. But almost all of these notices or items were in fine print, buried in the multitude of information and data published about the financial markets and scarcely of a kind to attract the eye of the average lay investor or debenture holder. On March 9, 1966, the listing in the New York Times for the convertible debentures read, for example: "Boeing cv 4½ s 80." The change on March 10 was to "Boeing 4½ s 80 cld," giving the investor in Dubuque or Little Rock or Lampasas only 19 days to pick up this change and figure that "cld" meant "called." ...

Because the appellants place some emphasis on the fact, although we do not reach their contention of unreasonable notice based on it, we should mention that Boeing made no attempt to mail notice to the original subscribers (which could have been done at concededly nominal expense), and neither Boeing nor Chase inquired of or gave notice to collecting banks which had tendered for collection coupons bearing the payment dates of July 15, 1965, or January 15, 1966, the last two coupons before the redemption, either of which might have had some beneficial effect.

THE CONTENTIONS OF THE PARTIES

Boeing rests its defense primarily upon the notice specified in the debentures and Indenture, pointing out that in 1958 when the debentures were issued, "the risk that actual notice might not be received by subsequent holders of the debentures was clearly accepted by all even remotely familiar with the nature of such debentures." ... It was "just such a risk" that led Boeing to extend to its stockholders and others who were investing $30 million in these securities the opportunity to register, ... an opportunity availed of by only 7 per cent of the debenture holders. For the proposition that notice by publication provided for here was "standard and conformed with the custom and practice prevailing in the trade in 1958," we are referred by Boeing to *Gampel* v. *Burlington Industries, Inc.*, 43 Misc. 2d 846, 252 N.Y.S.2d 500 (Sup. Ct. 1964), where Justice Korn did not discuss the custom and practice in the trade but did hold that publication in the Wall Street Journal even during a newspaper delivery strike conformed to a provision in the Burlington Industries debentures similar to the one in the case at bar.

* * *

THE INADEQUACY OF THE BOEING NOTICE

The notice Boeing gave, we hold, had two deficiencies. First, Boeing did not adequately apprise the debenture holders what notice would be given of a redemption call. Investors were not informed by the prospectus or by the debentures that they could receive mail notice by registering their debentures, and that otherwise they would have to rely primarily on finding one of the scheduled advertisements in the newspaper or on keeping a constant eye on the bond tables. Second, the newspaper notice given by Boeing was itself inadequate.

The first factor we think highly significant. Many of the debenture holders might well have decided to register their bonds, had the significance of registration, or of the failure to register, been brought home in the materials generally available to the purchasers of the debentures. No detailed information as to notice was given on the face of the debentures, even in the fine print....

There was no indication that registration would mean that a debenture holder would receive mail notice. Nor was there any indication of the extent of newspaper notice to be provided—either as to the papers that would be used or how often the notice would be published. Debenture holders were simply referred by the debenture, as well as by the prospectus, to the 113-page Indenture Agreement, which, to be sure, was available to debenture holders or prospective purchasers upon request, but which was not circulated generally with the warrants or debentures.

We have dwelt at length in the facts on the newspaper notice actually given. While it may have conformed to the requirements of the Indenture it was simply insufficient to give fair and reasonable notice to the debenture holders.

The duty of reasonable notice arises out of the contract between Boeing and the debenture holders, pursuant to which Boeing was exercising its right to redeem the debentures. An issuer of debentures has a duty to give adequate notice either on the face of the debentures ... or in some other way, of the notice to be provided in the event the company decides to redeem the debentures. Absent such advice as to the specific notice agreed upon by the issuer and the trustee for the debenture holders, the debenture holders' reasonable expectations as to notice should be protected.

For less sophisticated investors (it will be recalled that warrants for the purchase of debentures were issued to *all* Boeing shareholders), putting the notice provisions only in the 113-page Indenture Agreement was effectively no notice at all. It was not reasonable for Boeing to expect these investors to send off for, and then to read understandingly, the 113-page Indenture Agreement referred to in both the prospectus and the debentures themselves in order to find out what notice would be provided in the event of redemption.

Boeing could very easily have run more than two advertisements in a single paper prior to the eleventh hour (March 28), at which time it issued its belated news release and advertised for the third time in the Wall Street Journal and for the first time in the New York Times. Moreover, in the same period that the debentures were in the process of being redeemed, Boeing was preparing for its annual meeting (to be held April 24). Proxy materials were being prepared throughout March and were finally mailed some-time between March 24 and March 30. Management could readily have arranged the redemption dates and the proxy mailings so that notice of the redemption dates could have been included in the envelope with the proxy materials. Thus at no extra cost except that of printing brief notices, at least all Boeing shareholders would have received mail notice, and presumably a significant number of the plaintiff class owned Boeing common stock, as well as debentures, in 1966. Had Boeing attempted such mail notice, or mail notice to original subscribers, and also given further newspaper publicity either by appropriate news releases or advertising earlier in the redemption period, we would have a different case and reasonable and sufficient notice might well be found.

* * *

What one buys when purchasing a convertible debenture in addition to the debt obligation of the company incurred thereby is principally the expectation that the stock will increase sufficiently in value that the conversion right will make the debenture worth more than the debt. The debenture holder relies on the opportunity to make a proper conversion on due notice. Any loss occurring to him from failure to convert, as here, is not from a risk inherent in his investment but rather from unsatisfactory notification procedures.... The debenture holders' expectancy is that he will receive reasonable notice and it is his reliance on this expectancy that the courts will protect.... Had there been proper publication, a reasonable investor undoubtedly would have taken action to prevent the loss occurring to him.

Of course, it may be suggested that the appellee corporation itself was not the beneficiary of the appellants' loss; rather, the corporate stockholders benefited by not having their stock watered down by the number of shares necessary to convert appellants' debentures. But an award against Boeing will in effect tend to reduce *pro tanto* the equity of shareholders in the corporation and thus to a large extent those who were benefited, one might almost say unjustly enriched, will be the ones who pay appellants' loss.[23]

Judgment affirmed in part; reversed and remanded in part.

Notes and Questions

1. Why does the *Van Gemert* court protect the bondholders in contrast to the *Simons* court?

2. In *Van Gemert II*, Van Gemert v. The Boeing Co., 553 F.2d 812 (2d Cir. 1977), the court affirmed the district court's award of damages based on the value of Boeing's common stock on March 29, 1966, the cut-off date for the exercise of conversion rights, rather than on April 14, 1966, the date for which plaintiffs argued. On March 29, each $100 of debentures was worth $316.25 in common stock. On April 14 that figure had risen to

---

23. On the remand for a determination of damages, it might be appropriate for the district court to allow Boeing to meet the liability resulting from this case by issuing stock. That is what the plaintiffs would have had if they had received notice of the redemption call, and one of the purposes of the redemption was to enable the company to exchange debt for equity capital. It would thus seem appropriate for Boeing to be able to issue stock to meet all or part of this liability, with, of course, the shares being valued according to their market value at date of issuance.

$364. Applying New York law, which the court found to be controlling, the court rejected the applicability of New York's "fluctuating value" rule applied to stock,[1] as follows:

> The situation presented in the instant case is wholly different from the circumstances existing in ... [the cases relied on by appellants.] Here, appellants never owned any common stock of Boeing and do not claim to have purchased any.... In reality, appellants are asking us to treat them as if they were owners of the stock on the cut-off date, March 29, and to speculate that they would have sold these shares at the highest price reached within a reasonable time thereafter. Such a theory of damages was specifically rejected in *Simon v. Electrospace Corp.*, 28 N.Y.2d 136, 145, 320 N.Y.S.2d 225, 269 N.E.2d (1971).

> In our former opinion we held that appellants' right to damages arose out of their contract with Boeing. *Van Gemert v. Boeing Co., supra*, 520 F.2d at 1383. We are confident that, faced with the facts presented here, the New York courts would apply a breach of contract theory of damages, resulting in the Boeing stock being valued as of the cut-off date, March 29, 1966. In *Simon v. Electrospace Corp., supra*, the defendant breached its contract to deliver shares of stock to the plaintiff for services rendered. The *Simon* court stated:

>> The proper measure of damages for breach of contract is determined by the loss sustained or gain prevented at the time and place of breach.... The rule is precisely the same when the breach of contract is nondelivery of shares of stock.... Plaintiff was never the owner of the stock of Electrospace just because defendant breached its contract to deliver the shares. That breach and the loss caused was fixed and determined in 1967 ... [and that was] the time when the value to him of defendant's performance was to be measured. It was then that plaintiff was to be made whole and not at some future time never specified in the agreement. (Citations omitted).

> *Simon v. Electrospace Corp., supra*, 28 N.Y.2d at 145, 320 N.Y.S.2d 225, 232-33, 269 N.E.2d 21, 26. The cases dealing with converted stock were referred to by the *Simon* court but did not control, because there, as here, the plaintiff did not own the stock. Boeing had the right to call the debentures as of March 29, 1966. However, it breached its contract with the debenture holders by failing to give them reasonably adequate notice of its action, thereby precluding them from participating in the call. We hold that the breach occurred on March 29, 1966; and, for the purpose of computing damages herein, the Boeing stock should be valued as of that date....

3. In Meckel v. Continental Resources Co., 758 F.2d 811 (2d Cir. 1985), the court held that notice given by first class mail in accordance with the indenture was adequate. "In fact, [in *Van Gemert*] we strongly implied that notice by mail would have been adequate." *Id.* at 816. Furthermore, the court held that proof of mailing the notice is sufficient—proof of receipt is unnecessary. But why is proof of receipt unnecessary?

4. Pittsburgh Terminal Corp. v. Baltimore and Ohio R.R. Co., 680 F.2d 933 (3d Cir. 1982), *cert. denied*, 459 U.S. 1056 (1985), produced a riot of theories among three judges resulting in a 2-1 partial reversal of the District Court's opinion holding that the

---

1. Briefly, that rule provides that the measure of damages for conversion of stock is "the cost of replacement within a reasonable period after the discovery of the conversion, regardless of when the conversion may have occurred." *Id.* at 814.

plaintiff's complaint failed to state a claim on which the B & O could be found liable to its bondholders for failing to give adequate opportunity to convert their bonds into common stock and thus participate in a significant dividend.

B & O was a subsidiary corporation of the Chesapeake & Ohio R.R. Co. ("Chessie"), with fourteen common stockholders (including Chessie, which owned 99.63 percent of B & O's common stock) and three outstanding issues of New York Stock Exchange listed convertible debentures. In order to develop its non-rail assets, which federal regulation prohibited ownership of in a railroad corporation, Chessie began hiving off those assets into a separate corporation, which it also did with the non-rail assets of B & O. B & O's non-rail assets were placed in a new corporation, MAC, which was wholly owned by B & O. MAC was then spun off to B & O's stockholders, with Chessie, B & O's controlling stockholder, receiving 99.63 percent of MAC's stock.

In order to do this, however, Chessie had to confront a problem engendered by the Securities Act of 1933. With only fourteen stockholders, the distribution of MAC stock would likely be a private placement under the 1933 Act as to which registration could be avoided. However, B & O had among its three outstanding debt issues two classes of convertible debt. If these debtholders converted their bonds prior to the spin-off, the resulting number of B & O stockholders would necessitate registration of the spin-off under the 1933 Act. To avoid this, Chessie's reorganization committee decided to give the debtholders notice of the distribution only after the record date had passed. As a result, the B & O bondholders lost out on a valuable conversion opportunity.

Judge Gibbons wrote the "Opinion Announcing the Judgment of the Court" which, although not joined by any other judge, resulted in a judgment (joined by Judge Garth) reversing the district court's dismissal of the complaint. He began by setting forth the facts relevant to the conversion feature:

> The convertible debentures also contained a redemption feature which in 1977 called for payment of a premium of 2.5% of their face amount. B & O did not elect to redeem. Conversion privilege features of the indenture oblige B & O to reserve sufficient common stock and to adjust for changes in par value. Conversion rights to the bondholders are protected in the event of merger or sale. Article V, section 12 of the Indenture provides.... [for at least ten days, published notice of any record date for stock dividends.]

> When the convertible debentures were issued in 1956, B & O entered into a listing agreement with the NYSE relating to them, which incorporated by reference B & O's earlier listing agreements. Listing Agreement A-12653 for an earlier bond issue, incorporated by reference in that for the 1956 convertible debenture issue, provides ... [for notice similar to that required by the indenture.]

> In addition to the Listing Agreements, the B & O is bound by the Rules of the NYSE. Section A-2 of its Manual, "Timely Disclosure," provides:

>> A corporation whose securities are listed on the New York Stock Exchange, Inc., is expected to release to the public any news or information which might reasonably be expected to materially affect the market for those securities. This is one of the most important and fundamental purposes of the listing agreement which each corporation enters into with the exchange.

509 F. Supp. at 1008.

In November of 1977, by which time impediments to the payment of dividends on B & O stock in the Convertible Income Bond Debenture and the Refunding and General Mortgage Indenture had been removed, plaintiff Monroe Guttmann[, a holder of common stock and debentures,] wrote to the Secretary of B & O ... [expressing concern that he might not be informed of dividends declared on the common stock in time to convert his debentures to receive the dividend and requesting notice of dividend declarations to give him time to convert.]

To this pointed inquiry the Secretary, on November 17, 1977, replied:

.... You may be assured that if B & O should have any information to announce regarding dividend action on B & O stock, such information will be disseminated promptly to the public at large. Because we cannot prefer you over the public at large advance advice cannot be sent to you, but I will make sure that you get a copy of such press release. We are not in a position to help you with respect to your decision whether or not to convert.

There is no by-law provision relating to the timing of the declaration, record, and payment dates.

By the time of Guttmann's inquiry and the Secretary's reply, the Restructuring Committee's plan to structure the MAC transaction so as to avoid timely notice to the convertible bondholders was well advanced.

Plaintiffs sued, alleging that the Board's action in fixing the record date "violated section 10(b) of the Securities and Exchange Act, the contractual rights of the convertible debenture holders under the provisions of the Indenture, their rights as third party beneficiaries of the NYSE listing agreements, the obligations of B & O under the rules of the NYSE, and the fiduciary duties of directors and of majority stockholders under Maryland law. The District Court, over defendants' objection, held that the convertible debenture holders had standing to make these claims, but rejected each of them."

Judge Gibbons then concluded, as had the district court, that plaintiffs had standing under section 10(b) to maintain this action, after which he turned to the merits:

The Bondholders contend that by fixing the dividend date and the record date of the MAC dividend so as to prevent them from exercising their conversion option in time to participate in that dividend, the defendants violated section 10(b) and SEC Rule 10b-5(a) and (c).... It is undisputed that the defendants made a knowing decision to time the December 13, 1977 transactions so as to prevent the Bondholders from obtaining timely notice of them. Defendants contend that the decision was lawful because they made no affirmative misrepresentation and because they were under no affirmative obligation to speak.

[The court then discussed the "duty" requirement of Chiarella v. United States, 445 U.S. 222, 100 S. Ct. 1108, 63 L. Ed. 2d 348 (1980).]

To put that contention in context, we note that the Bondholders were on December 13, 1977, holders of options to acquire B & O equity securities, while C & O was a majority holder of those securities having voting control of B & O. The convertible debentures were listed on the NYSE, and the listing agreement applicable to them imposed on B & O the affirmative duties (a) to give ten days notice to the Exchange of a record date for a dividend, and (b) to "afford the holders of its securities listed on the Exchange a proper period within which to record their interests and exercise their rights." These requirements of the listing agreement parallel those in SEC Rule 10b-17.

* * *

B & O is the issuer of the convertible debentures, the MAC distribution is a dividend of a security, and that dividend related to the convertible debentures since it was material to a decision about exercising the conversion option. The convertible debentures were not simple debt securities, for which the information about dividends ordinarily would not be material.

Whatever may be the fiduciary duty of majority stockholders and corporate directors under Maryland law to general unsecured creditors, we are here dealing with securities having an equity option feature. Maryland follows the settled rule that a control stockholder owes a fiduciary obligation not to exercise that control to the disadvantage of minority equity participants.... Similarly, Maryland directors must act as fiduciaries to all equity participants.... Although no Maryland case has been called to our attention presenting the precise issue of fiduciary obligations to holders of securities containing stock options, we would be very much surprised if Maryland or any other state would today hold that no such obligations were owed by an issuer of such securities and its directors. Moreover the scope of the obligation of the fiduciary depends upon the nature of the interest of the beneficiary. If the beneficiary of a fiduciary duty needs information in order intelligently to protect that interest, the withholding of it, especially when withholding it confers advantage upon others (in this case C & O and Chessie), is an obvious breach of duty.

The 1956 Indenture under which B & O borrowed the sums evidenced by the convertible debentures was made in New York and the loan transaction completed there. B & O's obligation, therefore, is a New York contract. The law of that state is "that in every contract there is an implied covenant that neither party shall do anything which will have the effect of destroying or injuring the right of the other party to receive the fruits of the contract...." *Kirke La Shelle Co. v. Paul Armstrong Co.*, 263 N.Y. 79, 87, 188 N.E. 163, 167 (1933).... Defendants in this case took steps to prevent the Bondholders from receiving information which they needed in order to receive the fruits of their conversion option should they choose to exercise it. As a matter of New York contract law, B & O had a duty to speak.

In the present context we do not look to the listing agreement, Rule 10b-17, the Maryland law of fiduciary obligations, and the New York law of contracts, as sources of independent causes of action, though they well may be. Rather we look to them as sources of a duty to speak, breach of which under section 10(b) and Rule 10b-5(a) and (c) gives rise to a cause of action for fraud. Those four independent sources of duty to speak in the circumstances of this case amply serve, separately or collectively, to distinguish it from *Chiarella v. United States, supra*. We need not consider other sources of such duty relied on by the Bondholders.

Judge Garth concurred, finding a duty to disclose for rule 10b-5 purposes solely in rule 10b-17. Consequently, he declined to "... reach the question whether the defendants had a duty to disclose under the New York Stock Exchange (NYSE) listing agreement, the Maryland law of fiduciary obligations, or the New York law of contracts."

Judge Adams dissented, concluding that defendants had no duty to speak that could serve to support an action under rule 10b-5. The difficulty arose, in his view, from the unusual legal nature of convertible bonds:

Whatever financial advantages attach to the issuance or purchase of convertible debentures, the legal status of these hybrid securities remains inherently complex. As debt securities, the debentures impose a specific set of obligations on the corporation—namely, the regular payment of interest and the repayment of principal upon maturity. As equity securities, in contrast, the debentures may require a broader range of duties from the issuer. The difficulty lies not in the characterization of the debenture as *either* debt or equity—for it is both—but in determining, in each case, the extent to which the investor is owed rights and remedies beyond those commonly accorded debt holders.[1]

After reviewing the "traditional view" of the rights of convertible bondholders, he noted the expansion of these rights as a result of the enactment of the federal securities laws, which provide convertible bondholders with the same rights as stockholders. Despite this, however, he recognized that the prevailing view continued to be that convertible bondholders' rights are defined by the terms of their contract. Finding nothing in the contract to suggest that defendants' actions were prohibited, he then turned to address Judge Gibbons' other conclusions:

> Apparently mindful of the limited protection afforded to them by the indenture, the plaintiffs maintain that, notwithstanding any lack of an adequate notice provision within the indenture, New York's law of fair dealing required that in any event notice be given prior to the declaration of the MAC dividend. Judge Gibbons credits this argument, concluding that, in failing to give notice, B & O violated the principle "that in every contract there is an implied covenant that neither party shall do anything which will have the effect of destroying or injuring the right of the other party to receive the fruits of the contract...." At 941 (quoting *Kirke La Shelle Co.* v. *Paul Armstrong Co.*, 263 N.Y. 79, 87, 188 N.E. 163, 167 (1933)).

> Such an analysis is clearly inappropriate. By its terms, the principle of fair dealing expressed in *Kirke* and quoted by Judge Gibbons applies only when one party infringes the other's *rights* "to receive the fruits of the contract." Here, under the well-settled *Parkinson* doctrine, Pittsburgh Terminal *had no right*, under the contract, to receive advance notice of the MAC dividend because *no anti-dilution provision to that effect had been included in the indenture.* Thus, the risk of dilution was "inherent in the investment made by the holders of Debentures.... [B & O] did nothing that could be described as 'destroying or injuring the right of the other party to receive the fruits of the contract,' because ... the benefits that the holders of Debentures received were all the rights to which they were contractually entitled." *Broad* v. *Rockwell International Corp., supra* at 958.

> *Van Gemert* ... stands for the narrow proposition that, if the debenture holders are contractually entitled to notice, such notice must be "fair and reasonable." But *Van Gemert* in no way addresses the question posed to us today: namely, whether the B & O debenture holders were entitled to any notice at all.

---

1. *See Green* v. *Hamilton Int'l. Corp.*, No. 76 Civ. 5433 (S.D.N.Y. July 14, 1981) ("If the wrongs alleged in this case impacted upon the securities so as to undermine the debtor-creditor relationship, a contract analysis is appropriate, and plaintiffs ... were owed no special duty outside the bounds of the contract. If the wrongs alleged impinged upon the equity aspects, then the analysis would more properly treat plaintiffs like shareholders to whom the majority shareholders and directors of a corporation owe a duty of 'honesty, loyalty, good faith and fairness.'").

That question, as has already been suggested, can be answered only by reference to the language of the indenture itself.

Finally, he rejected the argument accepted by both Judge Gibbons and Judge Garth (and thus the only argument accepted by a majority of the court) that rule 10b-17 imposed a duty on defendants to make disclosure for plaintiffs' benefit.... [a]

A subsequent panel of the Third Circuit embraced Judge Adams' dissent is the related case of Lorenz v. CSX Corp., 1 F.3d 1406 (3rd Cir. 1993).

(ii) Antidilution

A convertible security contract, as well as a contract for warrants, will typically include antidilution provisions. These provisions protect securityholders against actions that companies voluntarily take that dilute the common stock they receive upon conversion or exercise. Thus, antidilution provisions cover stock splits, stock dividends and the issuance of "cheap stock." Also covered are adjustments for reverse stock splits, although these adjustments protect the company rather than the convertible securityholders.

(A) Stock Splits and Reverse Stock Splits

The convertible securityholders' contract typically adjusts the conversion price whenever the company conducts a stock split (sometimes referred to as a "forward" stock split) or a reverse stock split. The conversion price must be proportionately adjusted so that a given convertible securityholder receives that number of shares of common stock for each convertible security *after* the split in question had she converted that convertible security *immediately prior* to that split. Indeed, this essential proportionate adjustment preserves the parity relationship.

A stock split is an accounting adjustment that does not result in the company transferring assets to its stockholders. A stock split simply increases the number of outstanding common shares. For example, suppose LIF Corporation's common stock is trading at $100 per share. As seen in Table 1, a 3-for-1 stock split would give stockholders three shares of common stock for each share they currently hold. Assuming that LIF had 5 million shares of common stock outstanding, the 3-for-1 stock split will raise the total number of outstanding shares to 15 million [5 million shares × 3]. However, it will also lower the per share trading price to $33.33 [$100 per share ÷ 3].

Current stockholders are not harmed by the price decrease because they are deemed to own three times as many shares as they did previously. The increase in shares held directly offsets the decline in per share trading price. If, for example, a stockholder of LIF held 50 shares worth $100 each (a total of $5,000) before the split, she will own 150 shares worth $33.33 each (a total of $5,000) afterwards.[1]

---

a. In a footnote, Judge Adams further noted his disagreement with Judge Gibbons that the NYSE rules and Maryland's law of fiduciary obligation created any duty to provide notice here.

1. Because the market generally views a forward stock split as a "bullish" or positive sign triggered by the company's management, the company's post-split stock price is often slightly higher than what mathematics would dictate.

Table 1

Calculating Stock Splits

Split	Outstanding Shares After Split	Stock Price After Split
2-for-1	Pre-split shares × 2	Pre-split price ÷ 2
3-for-1	Pre-split shares × 3	Pre-split price ÷ 3
3-for-2	Pre-split shares ÷ 2, then × 3	Pre-split price × 2, then ÷ 3
5-for-4	Pre-split shares ÷ 4, then × 5	Pre-split price × 4, then ÷ 5

A company effects a stock split primarily to make its common stock more affordable on a per share basis to a broader range of investors. Investors prefer buying shares in "round lots," each of which is 100 shares. Many investors, particularly retail investors, cannot afford 100 shares at prices of $100 per share and above (an aggregate price of $10,000 or more). However, they are much more likely to be able to afford 100 shares at $20 per share (an aggregate price of $2,000). Hence, a company will often split its stock when its share price is perceived by management as too high in order to bring that price back down into a more affordable trading range.

In the event of a stock split, the conversion price of convertible securities must be adjusted so that a given convertible securityholder receives that number of shares of common stock for each convertible security *after* the split in question had she converted that convertible security *immediately prior* to that split. Taking our example involving a 3-for-1 common stock split, the conversion price must be divided by 3 in order for each convertible securityholder to retain the benefit of her bargain. Thus, a convertible securityholder will receive three times as many shares of common stock when she converts following the split. This is needed because, after the split, shares of the company's common stock are only one-third as valuable.

As seen in Table 2, when a company declares a reverse stock split, the number of its outstanding shares decreases while the per share trading price increases. For example, suppose PNH Corporation had 100 million shares of common stock outstanding, and that its per share trading price was $1. If PNH declared a 1-for-20 reverse stock split, the number of outstanding shares would decline to 5 million [100 million shares ÷ 20], while the per share trading price of those shares would increase to $20 [$1 per share × 20].

Table 2

Calculating Reverse Stock Splits

Split	Outstanding Shares After Split	Stock Price After Split
1-for-2	Pre-split shares ÷ 2	Pre-split price × 2
1-for-3	Pre-split shares ÷ 3	Pre-split price × 3
2-for-3	Pre-split shares ÷ 3, then × 2	Pre-split price × 3, then ÷ 2
4-for-5	Pre-split shares ÷ 5, then × 4	Pre-split price × 5, then ÷ 4

A company conducts a reverse stock split primarily for one of two reasons. First, a reverse split is used to increase the per share trading price of the company's common stock. In this regard, a public company may find itself in danger of having its shares delisted when its per share trading price drops below the requisite stock exchange listing requirement. A low per share trading price is also unattractive to investors who may come to view the stock as a "penny stock." The company, therefore, conducts a reverse stock split in order to lift its per share trading price back into an acceptable trading range.[2]

Second, a reverse stock split can be used to freeze out a company's minority stockholders. This is usually done at the urging of a controlling stockholder. Assume, for example, that MRH Corporation has 10,000 shares outstanding and that Lucia, the controlling stockholder, owns 5,100 of those shares. If MRH conducts a 1-for-5,100 reverse stock split, with fractional shares converted solely into cash, Lucia will end up owning the one and only share in MRH [her 5,100 shares ÷ 5,100]. All other stockholders end up owning a fraction of one share, and thus will receive cash compensation for their fractional share pursuant to the terms of the reverse stock split. For a case involving a freeze-out via reverse stock split, see Leader v. Hycor, Inc., *supra* at chapter 8, section 6.

Antidilution provisions covering convertible securities handle reverse stock splits the opposite of how they handle forward stock splits. For example, in the case of the 1-for-20 reverse common stock split mentioned above, the conversion price is simply multiplied by 20. Thus, a convertible securityholder receives one-twentieth as many shares of common stock when she converts following the reverse split. This is needed because, after the reverse split, shares of the company's common stock are 20 times as valuable.

Legal mayhem can result when a convertible securityholder's contract does not properly address the possibility of antidilutive actions by the issuer. Consider the following case, which involves warrants and a reverse stock split.

Reiss v. Financial Performance Corp.
764 N.E.2d 958 (N.Y. 2001)

SMITH, J.:

The issue here is whether warrants to purchase shares of stock of defendant corporation must be adjusted in light of a reverse stock split authorized by defendant corporation after plaintiffs received warrants. We answer that question in the negative.

Shortly after September 30, 1993, in partial repayment of a loan, defendant authorized the issuance of warrants enabling plaintiff Rebot Corporation to purchase up to 1,198,904 shares of defendant's common stock for 10 cents per share until September 30, 1998. Defendant also issued warrants to plaintiff Marvin Reiss, in recognition of his services to defendant as a director of the corporation, entitling him to purchase 500,000 shares of common stock at 10 cents per share until August 31, 1998. Although a warrant issued earlier, on September 1, 1993, to Robert S. Trump was accompanied by a warrant agreement providing for a reverse stock split, no other agreement accompanied the authorization of the plaintiffs' warrants. Thus, the warrants given to Rebot and Reiss, unlike the warrants given to Trump, did not incorporate the warrant agreement provisions requiring adjustment in the event of a reverse stock split.

In 1996, defendant's shareholders approved a one-for-five reverse split of its common stock, and, as a consequence, each stockholder owned one-fifth of the original number of shares with the value of each share increased fivefold. In 1998, Rebot and Reiss sought to exercise a portion of their warrants, claiming that in accordance with the terms of the agreement, they were entitled to buy all of the stock specified in the warrants at 10 cents

---

2. Because the market generally views a reverse stock split as a "bearish" or negative sign triggered by the company's management, the company's post-split stock price is often lower (sometimes significantly) than what mathematics would dictate.

per share, without adjustment to reflect the reverse stock split. Defendant rejected the request. Plaintiffs thereafter initiated this action, seeking a declaratory judgment permitting the exercise of their warrants to purchase the full number of shares stated in the warrants at 10 cents a share. Plaintiffs also sought extension of the expiration dates of the warrants.

Supreme Court denied injunctive relief and dismissed the action. A divided Appellate Division modified by declaring judgment in defendant's favor. Relying on *Cofman v. Acton Corp.* (958 F2d 494 [1st Cir 1992]), the Appellate Division held that an essential term of the contract was missing and, according to its determination of the intent of the parties, supplied a term providing for adjustment of the number of shares stated in the warrants. The Appellate Division also found that plaintiffs' claim for reformation of the expiration date to dates in late 2000 was without merit. We now modify to reinstate the first cause of action for declaratory relief.

Duly executed stock warrants are contracts entitling the holder to purchase a specified number of shares of stock for a specific price during a designated time period. Here, the warrants are enforceable according to their terms. They have all the material provisions necessary to make them enforceable contracts, including number of shares, price, and expiration date, and were drafted by sophisticated and counseled business persons....

That the warrants do not address the contingency of a reverse stock split does not, of itself, create an ambiguity.... Even where a contingency has been omitted, we will not necessarily imply a term.

Although defendant claims that to enforce the terms of the warrants creates a windfall for plaintiffs, the record evidences that the parties may have intentionally omitted incorporation of a warrant agreement containing a provision for adjustment for a reverse stock split. For example, one month earlier defendant issued warrant agreements to other investors that did contain specific reference to a reverse split adjustment provision. The Trump warrant agreement is one such agreement, providing that "if at any time or from time to time, the number of outstanding shares of Common Stock of the Corporation is decreased by a reverse split, consolidation or reclassification of shares of Common Stock, or otherwise, then, after the effective date ... each Warrant shall be decreased in proportion to the decrease in outstanding shares and the then applicable Warrant Price shall be appropriately increased."

Further, *Cofman v. Acton Corp. (supra)*, the decision relied upon by the Appellate Division majority, is inapposite here. In *Cofman*, as part of a settlement agreement, a corporation allowed 12 partnerships (Partnerships) to make a one-time demand on the corporation for payment of a sum equal to the price of a share of common stock minus $7 multiplied by 7,500. This provision was a "sweetener," added to the settlement of $120,000, in case the price of a share of stock increased. Later, the corporation executed a reverse stock split, decreasing the number of shares and increasing the price of a share of common stock by a multiple of five. Partnerships sued the corporation for enforcement of the agreement, seeking to use the price of the stock after the reverse split to calculate the settlement. Partnerships argued that the plain language required that the warrants be valued as of the time of their exercise and the defendant corporation assumed the risk of a reverse stock split by not negotiating a different provision. The corporation also relied on the plain language of the warrants, contending that it was entitled to the value of the stock existing when the agreement was signed. The Massachusetts District Court found for the corporation.

Applying Massachusetts law, the First Circuit affirmed the District Court, concluding that Partnerships would not have agreed to a forward stock split because it could have eviscerated the value of the stock. The First Circuit held that the parties had not given any thought to dilution and that an essential term of the contract was missing. Just as Partnerships should not suffer by dilution of the value of the stock, so Acton should not suffer by reverse dilution.

The Appellate Division, applying the *Cofman* analysis, reasoned that, in the event of a forward stock split, supplying a term providing for the proportionate adjustment of the number of shares that could be purchased, and the exercise price, would be necessary to save the warrant holders from having the value of their warrants "eviscerated" (279 AD2d 13, at 18). The Appellate Division then followed Cofman in taking a second step, reasoning that "just as plaintiffs should not suffer from the possibility of dilution of their warrants resulting from a stock split, so too Financial should not suffer from the consolidation of its shares resulting from a declaration of a reverse stock split" (*id.*, at 19). The second step, however, does not necessarily follow from the first, particularly on these facts, where there is evidence that the parties contemplated including an adjustment provision but did not do so.

It may be that Reiss would be entitled to a remedy if Financial performed a forward stock split, on the theory that he "did not intend to acquire nothing" (*Cofman, supra*, 958 F2d, at 497). We should not assume that one party intended to be placed at the mercy of the other (*Wood v. Duff-Gordon*, 222 NY 88, 91 [1917]). It does not follow, however, that Financial should be given a comparable remedy to save it from the consequences of its own agreements and its own decision to perform a reverse stock split.

There remains a remedial problem, which we cannot ignore, although it is not well framed for our review. Plaintiffs' complaint contained two causes of action. The first sought a declaration that they were entitled to exercise the warrants in accordance with their terms, while the second sought to reform the expiration date of the warrants to a date in late 2000—allegedly five years after the warrants were delivered to plaintiffs. Plaintiffs also sought, by order to show cause, an order staying cancellation of the warrants on their stated expiration dates. Supreme Court refused to sign this order and ultimately dismissed both causes of action of the complaint, and the Appellate Division affirmed the dismissal.

Before this Court, plaintiffs have not advocated reinstating the reformation cause of action, which, if granted now, would leave them with nothing more than expired warrants. Rather, they have argued that their attempt to exercise the warrants, together with their motion for an order to show cause, preserved their right to exercise all of the warrants upon the successful conclusion of the litigation. At oral argument plaintiffs suggested, further, that this Court might direct Supreme Court to grant them summary judgment, and that the measure of their damages in that event would be the difference between the price of defendant's stock and the exercise price at the time of their attempted tender, multiplied by the number of shares they were entitled to buy.

We cannot direct Supreme Court to grant plaintiffs summary judgment, as they did not seek it and may not be entitled to it. If Supreme Court determines that plaintiffs are entitled to the declaration they seek on the reinstated cause of action, the Court should also resolve the remaining remedial issues, including the effect of plaintiffs' tender.

Notes and Questions

1. The following is from the Appellate Division opinion in *Reiss*, 715 N.Y.S.2d 29, 33-34:

We find *Cofman* to be dispositive of the issue presented here by force of its logic, albeit not as a matter of stare decisis. In this connection, to accept plaintiffs' interpretation of the contract, namely, that the warrants did not allow for a proportional adjustment to reflect a reverse stock split, would necessarily mean that the warrants also did not allow for a proportional adjustment if there were a stock split. Flowing from that reasoning is the observation that Financial, like the corporation in *Cofman*, could have eviscerated the value of plaintiffs' warrants and escaped its contractual obligations by simply declaring a massive stock split instead of a reverse stock split. Here, as in *Cofman*, it defies all bounds of common sense to believe that plaintiffs could have ever intended such an outcome. This is especially so since, at least with respect to the Rebot warrant, the very purpose of the warrant was to provide satisfaction of a debt that Financial had been unable to pay. Rebot certainly did not intend to enter into an agreement that would permit Financial, if it so chose, to unilaterally extinguish its $187,328.79 debt. We therefore conclude that, just as plaintiffs should not suffer from the possibility of dilution of their warrants resulting from a stock split, so too Financial should not suffer from the consolidation of its shares resulting from a declaration of a reverse stock split (*Cofman v. Acton Corp., supra; cf.,* Restatement [Second] of Contracts §204, comment *c* [1981] [a term can be supplied by logical deduction from the agreed terms and the circumstances of the making of the contract]). Any other conclusion would ignore the plain intent of the parties in issuing and receiving the subject warrants....

Notwithstanding *Cofman (supra)*, plaintiffs and the dissent assert that a literalistic approach to the interpretation of the warrants is compelled as a matter of law. We cannot agree. Surely a court is not required to disregard common sense and slavishly bow to the written word where to do so would plainly ignore the true intentions of the parties in the making of a contract. Such formalistic literalism serves no function but to contravene the essence of proper contract interpretation, which, of course, is to enforce a contract in accordance with the true expectations of the parties in light of the circumstances existing at the time of the formation of the contract....

In any event, to the extent that the warrants may be viewed as not containing an implicit requirement for the proportional adjustment of Financial's stock upon a split or reverse split, it means that the parties omitted what is undeniably an essential term of the agreement. Contrary to the dissent's contention, a provision dealing with this eventuality is essential since it fundamentally affects both the number of shares that may be purchased and the price to be paid. In a circumstance where an essential term is omitted, section 204 of the Restatement (Second) of Contracts is instructive. That section provides:

> When the parties to a bargain sufficiently defined to be a contract have not agreed with respect to a term which is essential to a determination of their rights and duties, a term which is reasonable in the circumstances is supplied by the court.

Here, following the Restatement approach, the only reasonable term would be the one consistent with the self-evident expectations of the parties when the warrants were executed, namely, a term requiring a proportional adjustment of both the number of shares that may be purchased and their price.

A dissenting judge offered tougher justice, 715 N.Y.S.2d at 36-37:

> The law of contracts offers relief from a hard bargain only upon a showing of fraud, duress, mistake, misrepresentation, illegality, impossibility of performance or unconscionability. But, when none of those grounds has been established, and the terms of the agreement under consideration are clearly set forth within the four corners of the document, courts should not alter those terms, even where the alteration achieves a more equitable result. As Judge Cardozo noted:
>
>> "A contract is made. Performance is burdensome and perhaps oppressive. If we were to consider only the individual instance, we might be ready to release the promisor. We look beyond the particular to the universal, and shape our judgment in obedience to the fundamental interest of society that contracts shall be fulfilled." (Cardozo, The Nature of the Judicial Process, at 139-140 [Yale Univ. Press].)
>
> Stock warrants issued by defendant Corporation gave plaintiffs the right to purchase a specified number of shares at a specified price within a defined period. The conflict here arises because a one-for-five reverse stock split, which took place prior to plaintiffs' exercise of the warrants, created a change in the per share value of the Corporation's stock. We are asked to determine whether the stock warrants were actually subject to an implied condition or limitation that the number and price of shares to which the warrants applied would be automatically adjusted in the event of a change in the character of the corporate stock, due to a stock split.

2. The securities in *Cofman* were warrants issued to various partnerships to settle a dispute. The issuer had proposed settling at one figure, the partnerships at another, and they settled for a figure in between coupled with warrants (options to purchase common stock). The warrant agreement provided:

> The Partnership shall be entitled to receive, upon written demand made within the three years following the execution of the Settlement Agreement (the "Exercise Date"), the following one time payment: the sum of "X" times a multiple of 7,500 where "X" equals the "price" of one share of Acton Corporation's common stock on the Exercise Date less $7.00. The "price" on the Exercise Date shall be equal to the average closing price of one share of the common stock of Acton Corporation on the American Stock Exchange for any period, selected by the Partnership, consisting of thirty (30) consecutive trading days prior to the Exercise Date....

Here is the court's report of additional facts and its interpretation of the agreement, *Cofman v. Acton Corp.*, 958 F.2d 494, 497 (1st Cir. 1992) (applying Massachusetts law):

> The manifestly implicit concept, quite apart from the parol evidence, is that if Acton did better, presumably reflected in its stock, it could afford to pay more for the settlement. At the same time, the chances that this would bear much fruit, if any, were not considered large, as Acton was not doing well, and its stock was fluctuating between $1.50 and $3.12. These circumstances are to be considered with the contract language regardless of the parol evidence rule.
>
> About a year after the making of the agreement, Acton's stock not having increased in price, it concluded that there were psychological market advantages in artificially shrinking the number of outstanding shares, and thereby increas-

ing the per share price. It accordingly executed a so-called reverse stock split, as the result of which each stockholder owned one-fifth the original number of shares, with the new shares having five times the par value and, at the outset, approximately five times the immediately preceding price on the Stock Exchange, *viz.*, substantially more than the $7.00 figure in the agreement.

Surprisingly, Acton did not consult Partnerships before engaging in this maneuver; it merely sent a letter explaining that it was of no consequence....

Under Partnerships' interpretation of the agreement the ... Partnerships together are owed $1,218,600 for their abandoned $60,000, based on a per share price of $20.54, although, had the number of shares not been reduced by the reverse split the per share price would have been some $4.11, sparking nothing....

Partnerships' position is simple and straightforward. This is precisely the way the agreement reads; it is unambiguous, and integrated, and even were parol evidence admissible, which they deny, there was no prior discussion suggesting exceptions. The court, taking up this last fact, stated that the agreement "did not address an eventuality such as a reverse stock split," and the very fact that the parties had not considered it supplied the answer.... Finding that the parties had not thought about dilution—a finding that binds Partnerships here—the court found the omission was an ambiguity in the agreement, and resolved it by concluding that the reasonable provision would have been that stock splits would have no effect.

We might turn one of Partnerships' arguments back on them in support of this result. The agreement provided that Partnerships had three years in which to pick a thirty day high price. During the negotiations Partnerships inquired what would happen if, during that period, Acton went private, as a result of which business success would not be reflected on the Exchange. Interestingly enough, while Partnerships are normally hostile to pre-agreement evidence, they narrate this. Acton "refused to give them any protection if Acton went private ... the Partnerships were 'at risk' on that issue." During trial—not subsequently repeated—the court suggested that this indicated Partnerships also took the risk if Acton made a stock split increasing the number of shares. Partnerships assert this implication. If there is any inference, we would draw just the opposite. *Inclusio unius, exclusio alterius.* But certainly this did not mean that Partnerships were accepting any and all defeating actions that Acton might take.

The court ultimately so concluded. "It defies common sense" that Partnerships would have agreed that Acton could effectively escape the specified consequences of a rising market price by increasing the number of shares. And if Partnerships would not suffer from any increasing, it would follow, since a contract must be construed consistently, Acton should not suffer from any decreasing.

No doubt recognizing this symbiosis, when the district court inquired, as later did we, whether Acton could have avoided all liability under the agreement simply by increasing the number of shares, counsel answered affirmatively. The court characterized his proffered concession as "gallant." We can only say that if this particular counsel would have been too gallant to make a claim, surely some less chivalrous could have been found. How could so meaningless an undertaking have been considered a sweetener? It is a fundamental principle that a contract is to be construed as meaningful and not illusory....

It is true that contracts cannot be rewritten simply to "rescue a firm from a sinkhole of its own design." Adding a whole new provision is normally permissible only when additional terms are "essential to a determination." Assuming that rule applicable, which we need not decide, Partnerships contends there was no necessity here; they may have been affirmatively content at the time of contracting to there being no antidilution provision. There are two answers to this. The first is that the court has found the parties gave no thought to dilution, and this finding cannot be said to be plainly wrong. Second, this is precisely a case where to read the contract as meaning that Partnerships should not suffer by dilution—and hence Acton by reverse dilution—is a necessity, or "essential to a determination." There is every reason to presume Partnerships did not intend to acquire nothing,[5] and saving from unenforceability ranks as a necessity.

Whether we reach that result by implying a provision to meet a circumstance not envisaged by the parties, or by construing the word "share" as including following the res, is immaterial ... [T]he rules of construction do not call for Partnership's wooden interpretation.

3. Would any rational investor buy securities convertible, exchangeable or exercisable for other securities at a set ratio without an understanding that should the other securities be sub-divided (split) that a proportionate adjustment in the ratio be made? Would any rational issuer sell such securities without an analogous understanding concerning adjustments if the other securities are combined (reverse split)? If not, what should the law do about this? Should the answer be uniform for splits and reverse splits?

(B) "Cheap" Stock

Antidilution provisions also cover a company's issuance of common stock at prices below that stock's current market price (so-called *cheap stock*).[1] Exceptions, however, typically are made for employee stock options and the conversion of existing securities. Because the issuance of cheap stock dilutes the value of the company's existing common stock, convertible securityholders deserve to receive more shares of the now diluted common stock to make them whole. Thus, a downward adjustment to the conversion price is in order. The following formula illustrates the typical adjustment made to the conversion price when the company issues cheap stock.

$$ACP = CP \times \left[\frac{OCS + \dfrac{(NCS \times OP)}{CMP}}{OCS + NCS} \right]$$

---

5. We do not pause over Partnership's sought analogy to convertible debentures, where the rule is that anti-dilution must be expressly stated.... These are formal, and complicated commercial structures, prepared with care for the general public. Purchasers have the bonds in any event. Here we have a simple agreement between individuals, not even assignable.

1. Depending on the convertible security contract, cheap stock may instead be defined as an issuance of stock below the stated conversion price of the convertible securities.

where:
ACP	=	adjusted conversion price
CP	=	conversion price in effect at the time the adjustment is calculated
OCS	=	number of outstanding shares of common stock
NCS	=	number of new shares of common stock (*i.e.*, the cheap stock) being issued
OP	=	offering price per share of new shares of common stock (*i.e.*, the cheap stock) being issued
CMP	=	current market price per share of common stock (typically based on a 30-day average)

The key to the formula above is the below-market offering price (OP) of the cheap stock essentially being divided by the current market price of the company's common stock (CMP). This results in a number less than one. When this is multiplied by the conversion price (CP), it results in an adjusted conversion price (ACP) that is lower than the conversion price. A lower conversion price, in turn, provides the convertible securityholders with more shares of common stock upon conversion. No adjustment to the conversion price is typically made until a one percent change occurs. Changes affecting the conversion price by an amount less than one percent are carried forward and added to future adjustments when determining whether the one percent threshold has been met.

(C) Distribution of Assets and Evidences of Indebtedness

Adjustments to the conversion price are typically made when the company distributes assets (*e.g.*, shares of a subsidiary distributed as part of a "spin-off") or evidences of indebtedness to its common stockholders. Excluded, however, are cash dividends and warrants or rights covered by other protective provisions typically contained in the convertible security contract. In the event of a distribution, the existing conversion price (CP) is typically adjusted as follows:

$$ACP = CP \times \left(\frac{CMP - D}{CMP} \right)$$

where:
ACP	=	adjusted conversion price
CP	=	conversion price in effect at the time the adjustment is calculated
CMP	=	current market price per share of common stock (typically based on a 30-day average)
D	=	per share value of the distribution being received by common stockholders

The key to the formula above is the subtraction of the per share distribution (D) that common stockholders will receive from the current market price per share of the common stock (CMP). When the difference is then divided by the current market price per share of the company's common stock (CMP), it results in a number less than one. When this is multiplied by the conversion price (CP), it results in an adjusted conversion price (ACP) that is lower than the conversion price. A lower conversion price, in turn, provides the convertible securityholders with more shares of common stock upon conversion. No adjustment to the conversion price is typically made until a one percent change occurs. Changes affecting the conversion price by an amount less than one percent are carried forward and added to future adjustments when determining whether the one percent threshold has been met.

HB Korenvaes Investments, L.P. v. Marriott Corp.

1993 WL 257422, CCH Fed. Sec. L. Rep. para. 97,773 (Del. Ch.)

ALLEN, Chancellor

In this action holders of Series A Cumulative Convertible Preferred Stock of Marriott Corporation seek to enjoin a planned reorganization of the businesses owned by that corporation. The reorganization involves the creation of a new corporate subsidiary, Marriott International, Inc., ("International"), the transfer to International of the greatest part of Marriott's cash-generating businesses, followed by the distribution of the stock of International to all of the holders of Marriott common stock, as a special dividend.

Plaintiffs assert that the proposed special dividend would leave the residual Marriott endangered by a disproportionate debt burden and would deprive them of certain rights created by the certificate of designation that defines the special rights, etc., of the preferred stock. More particularly, they claim: (1) that the proposed transaction, taken together with a recently declared intention to discontinue the payment of dividends on the preferred stock, constitutes coercive action designed wrongfully to force them to exercise their conversion privilege and thus surrender their preference rights; (2) that the planned payment of cash dividends on International's common stock, while plaintiffs' preferred dividend will have been suspended, violates the preferred stock's dividend preference; (3) that the authorization by the directors of Marriott of the spin-off transaction, without the affirmative vote of the holders of preferred stock, violates the voting rights of the preferred conferred by the certificate of designation; and (4) that the distribution of the dividend will violate the provisions of Section 5(e)(iv) of the certificate of designation of the preferred stock. Section 5(e)(iv) is designed to protect the economic interests of the preferred stock in the event of a special dividend. Finally, plaintiffs allege (5) that defendants have made false statements upon which they have relied in buying preferred stock in the market and that defendants are liable for fraud.

The Series A Cumulative Convertible Preferred Stock is Marriott's only outstanding issue of preferred stock. Plaintiffs are four institutional investors who have acquired more than 50% of the preferred stock. They present their case as one involving manipulation, deception and a legalistic interpretation of rights, which, if permitted and generalized will impose a material future cost on the operation of capital markets.

Defendants assert that the reorganization, and more particularly the special dividend, constitutes a valid, good faith attempt to maximize the interests of Marriott's common stockholders. Marriott asserts the right to deal with the preferred stock at arm's length, to afford them their legal rights arising from the certificate of designation, but also to take steps not inconsistent with those rights to maximize the economic position of Marriott's common stock. It claims that this is what the proposed special dividend does. Defendants also deny that they have intentionally misled plaintiffs.

Pending is plaintiffs' motion for a preliminary injunction prohibiting the distribution of the special dividend. It is presently anticipated by defendants that the holders of Marriott's common stock will approve the proposed transaction at the Company's annual meeting now scheduled for July 23, 1993 and that the distribution, if not enjoined, will occur in August or September of this year.

.... [W]here plaintiff shows both a reasonable probability of success on the merits of the claim and the threat of irreparable injury and where the court concludes that granting the remedy threatens less harm to defendant than denying it does to plaintiff, our court will issue a preliminary injunction....

For the reasons that follow, I conclude that plaintiffs have not shown a reasonable likelihood of success with respect to those aspects of their claims that appear to state a claim upon which relief might be granted.... Certain theories plaintiffs advance do not appear to state such a claim and will be dismissed....

I.

Except as otherwise indicated, I take the following background facts to be non-controversial.

(a) The Company

Marriott Corporation, as presently constituted, is in the business (1) of owning and operating hotels, resorts, and retirement homes, (2) of providing institutional food service and facilities management, and (3) of operating restaurants and food, beverage and merchandise concessions at airports, tollway plazas and other facilities. Its common stock has a present market value of approximately $2.6 billion. In December 1991 Marriott issued $200,000,000 face amount of convertible preferred stock bearing an 8¼% cumulative dividend, the stock owned by plaintiffs. Marriott has substantial debt, including Liquid Yield Option Notes ("LYONS") with an accreted value of $228 million;[2] and long-term debt of $2.732 billion. According to its proxy statement, the book value of Marriott's assets is $6.560 billion.

In the fiscal year ending January 1, 1993 Marriott's sales were $8.722 billion; earnings before interest, taxes, depreciation and amortization (EBITDA) was $777 million; earnings before interest and corporate expenses was $496 million; and net income was $85 million.... Each common share has received an annual cash dividend of $0.28 per share and the preferred stock dividends have been paid over its short life.

(b) The terms of the preferred stock in brief

The preferred stock is entitled to an 8¼% cumulative dividend and no more. It ranks prior to the common stock with respect to dividends and distribution of assets. It has in total, a face amount of $200,000,000 and that, plus the amount of any unpaid cumulated dividends, "and no more" is the amount of its liquidation preference. The corporation may, at its option, redeem any or all of the preferred stock after January 15, 1996, at prices set forth in the certificate.

The preferred stock is convertible at the option of the holder into common stock at a conversion price set forth in the certificate. Generally that means that every $50.00 face amount share of preferred stock may be converted into 2.87 shares of common stock. The certificate provides a mechanism to adjust the conversion price "in case the Corporation

---

2. A leading finance text notes that "a liquid yield option note (LYON) is a callable and retractable, convertible zero coupon bond (and you can't get much more complicated than that)." An example set forth in that text explains the security. See Richard A. Brealey and Stewart C. Myers, Principles of Corporate Finance, 4th ed. (1991) at p. 586. [The term LYON is a trademark of Merrill Lynch, which originally designed the instrument.—Eds.]

shall, by dividend ... distribute to all holders of Common Stock ... assets (including securities)...." Certificate of Designation 5(e)(iv).

The value of the right to convert is protected by a notice provision. The certificate provides that "in the event the Corporation shall declare a dividend ... on its Common Stock payable otherwise than in cash or out of retained earnings," the Corporation shall give written notice to the holders of the preferred stock 15 days in advance of the record date....

There are no express restrictions on the payment of dividends other than the requirement that the quarterly dividend on the preferred must be paid prior to the distribution of dividend payments to common stock.

(c) Announcement of the proposed transaction

On October 5, 1993, Marriott announced a radical rearrangement of the legal structure of the Company's businesses. The restructuring was said to be designed to separate Marriott's "ownership of real estate ... and other capital intensive businesses from its management and services businesses." The latter constitute Marriott's most profitable and fastest growing business segments. As indicated above, following this transfer Marriott intends to "spin-off" this new subsidiary by distributing all its stock as a dividend to Marriott's common stockholders.

(d) Marriott International

International is anticipated to be highly profitable from its inception and to be well positioned for future growth. It is expected to pay to its common stockholders the same dividend that has been paid to Marriott's common stock. Marriott's proxy statement describes International's proposed business activities as [owning or operating hotels and other properties under long term contracts].

According to its pro forma balance sheet for the quarter ending March 26, 1993, after the distribution (and assuming the Exchange Offer described below is effectuated ... International will have assets of $3.048 billion, long-term debt of $902 million, and shareholders equity of $375 million....

Had International, with all the assets it will hold, been operated as a separate company in 1992, it would have had sales of $7.787 billion, earnings before interest and corporate expenses of $331 million and net income of $136 million.... Marrriott's adviser, S.G. Warburg & Company, has estimated that in 1993 International will have sales of $8.210 billion, and EBIT of $368 million.

(e) Host Marriott

Marriott's remaining assets will consist of large real estate holdings and Marriott's airport and tollway concession business. Marriott will be renamed Host Marriott ("Host"). The assets retained by Host have a value of several billion dollars but will be burdened with great debt and produce little cash-flow after debt service.

* * *

Assuming the Exchange Offer ... is effectuated,[a] after the special dividend Host will have, according to its pro forma balance sheet as of March 26, 1993, assets of $3.796 billion, long-term debt of [$]2.130 billion and shareholders' equity of $516 million....

---

a. The Exchange Offer is discussed in part I(g) of the opinion. [Eds.]

Host's pro forma income statement for the fiscal year ending January 1, 1993, would reflect sales of $1.209 billion, earnings before corporate expenses and interest of $152 million, interest expense of $196 million, corporate expenses of $46 million, and a net loss of $44 million....

(f) Future operation of Host and International

If the special dividend is distributed, International and Host will formally constitute two separate corporate entities. They will, however, share a large number of relationships.... International will have long-term agreements to manage many of Host's hotel properties and other real estate assets. International will have a right to share in the proceeds of some of Host's asset sales in lieu of receiving base management fees, as well as a right of first refusal in any sale of Host's airport and toll-road concessions....

As discussed below ... International will extend a $630 million line of credit to Host's subsidiary Host Marriott Hospitality, Inc. ("HMH").... For ten years after the special dividend, International will have the right to purchase 20% of Host's common stock if any person acquires more than 20% or announces a tender offer for 30% or more of Host's common stock. The two companies will have common management, as Richard Marriott will be Host's Chairman and J.W. Marriott a director of Host, while both are simultaneously serving as directors of International. There will be a non-competition agreement between the two companies.

(g) Bondholders' suits lead to modified transaction

... Marriott's bondholders reacted strongly against the proposed special dividend. The transaction will of course remove very substantial assets and even more cash flow from their debtor and will, in the circumstances, substantially increase the risk associated with the bondholders' investment, or so it was thought. Ten class-action lawsuits seeking to block the dividend were filed by various classes of bondholders....

On March 11, 1993, Marriott reached a settlement with the bondholder class action plaintiffs. The settlement, if effectuated, would require Marriott to cause the Host subsidiary HMH to offer to exchange for existing bonds new bonds (Exchange Bonds) with a longer average maturity and bearing an interest rate 100 basis points higher than the existing bonds. The Exchange Bonds will include restrictive covenants that greatly limit opportunities for HMH to transfer cash to Host. Host's airport and toll road concession businesses, representing the preponderant part of its operating assets, and 40% of its cash-flow, will be transferred to a subsidiary of HMH. A $630 million credit line will be provided by International to HMH, but it cannot be drawn on to pay preferred dividends. One effect of the Exchange Offer, and the transfers it contemplates, is to restrict further Host's ability, as a practical matter, to pay dividends to the preferred stock. Shortly after the Exchange Offer settlement Marriott announced for the first time that it was intended that, following the special dividend, Host would not pay dividends on its preferred stock....

(h) Plaintiffs' acquisition of preferred stock and short sales of common

Plaintiffs began for the first time to purchase substantial amounts of Marriott's preferred stock following the announcement of the special dividend.

Since the preferred stock is convertible at the option of the holder into 2.87 shares of Marriott common stock and bears a dividend of 8¼% on its stated (liquidation) value of $50 per share, the market value of a share of preferred stock includes two possible components of value: the value of the conversion right and the value of the preferences. The presence of a presently exercisable conversion right will assure that the market value of the preferred will not fall below the market value of the security or property into which the preferred might convert, in this case 2.87 shares of common stock (less transaction costs of the conversion). The stated dividend, the dividend preference and the liquidation preference and other features of the preferred will ordinarily assure that the preferred trades at some premium to the value of the conversion right.

In this instance plaintiffs have acquired a majority of the shares of the preferred stock. Plaintiffs, however, did not simply acquire preferred stock. The record shows that each of the plaintiffs, except one, have hedged their risk by entering short sales contracts with respect to Marriott common stock. In this way plaintiffs have isolated their risk to that part of the preferred stock trading value represented by that stock's preference rights. Any change in the market price of the preferred stock caused by movement in the value of the underlying common stock will in their case be offset by change in the extent of their obligations under the short sales contracts.

(i) Marriott common and preferred stock price changes

The prices of both Marriott common stock and Marriott preferred stock have increased substantially since the announcement of the special dividend. On the last trading day before the announcement of the transaction Marriott's common stock closed at $17.125 per share. The day of the announcement the price increased to $19.25 and by June 4, 1993 it had reached $25.75, for a total increase of approximately 50.3%....

The price of Marriott preferred stock closed on the last trading day before the announcement at $62.75, which represented a premium of $13.54 over the value of the 2.8736 common shares into which each preferred share could convert. The day of the announcement the preferred stock increased to $68.875. On June 4, 1993 the price of the preferred stock closed at $77.00 per share, an increase of 22.8% over the pre-announcement market price. The premium that the preferred stock commanded over the common into which it could convert (i.e., the market value of the preferences) however, had by June 4th, shrunk, to $3.00.

Thus while both common stock and preferred stock have experienced substantial increases in the market value of their securities, because of the impact of their hedging strategy, plaintiffs are in a different position than are non-hedged holders of preferred stock. The reduction of the premium at which the preferred stock trades has resulted in losses on their short sales, leading some plaintiffs, as of June 4, 1993, to net unrealized losses on their investments.

For example, plaintiff, The President and Fellows of Harvard College, ("Harvard") as of June 4, 1993 owned 480,300 shares of preferred stock, which were purchased for $33,580,108 and which had a market value on that day of $37,724,801. Thus, this plaintiff has an unrealized profit of $4,144,693 on its investment in the preferred stock. Harvard also entered into short sales of 1,338,300 shares of Marriott common stock, approximately 2.8 times the number of preferred shares it purchased. It received $30,949,383 on these short sales. The cost to cover these short sales, however, has increased to $34,609,056, or $3,659,673 more than was received on the sales, representing an unrealized loss in that amount. Thus, as of June 4, 1993, although the value of the preferred stock owned by this plaintiff has increased in value by over $4 million, the total value of its investment position has increased by only $485,020....

II.
Plaintifffs' Account

The foregoing set forth much of the factual background of the pending motion as it now appears. It does not set forth those contested facts that form an important part of plaintiffs' account of the case.

Plaintiffs take a dark view. They see themselves being forced by defendants to relinquish their preferences at a time when defendants cannot call or redeem their stock. This coercion is arranged for them, plaintiffs say, because the Marriott family is motivated to assure its continuing control over Host following the spin-off. That such a concern exists is evidenced by certain internal Marriott documents as well as by the existence of certain agreements that will give International the right to purchase 20% of Host's stock in the event that any person (as defined in S.E.C. Rule 13D) acquires 20% or announces a tender offer for 30% of Host's shares....

Working from the premise that control over Host is very important to the Marriott family, plaintiffs point out that after the special dividend (and after the adjustment of the preferred stock conversion rate that it will require) the preferred stock (if none of it is converted before the distribution) would be in a position to convert into more than 50% of the Host common stock. Thus, on this view, given the size of the special dividend, the existence of the conversion right transforms the preferred stock into a threat to Marriott family control of Host. The answer to this problem that plaintiffs say was hit upon was to force the preferred to convert into Marriott common stock before the record date for the special dividend. How could this be done? The principal means, according to plaintiffs, was to announce as early as the filing of Marriott's preliminary proxy on March 15, 1993 that Host would suspend dividends on the preferred stock indefinitely and would not reinstitute payment of the dividend until the Company's "earnings equal or exceed the amount of such dividends." ...

The scheme that plaintiffs detect has other elements (some of which may constitute independent wrongs). For example, in order to make post-distribution conversion less attractive, plaintiffs assert that defendants are intending to deviate from the conversion rate adjustment formula in the certificate of designation.

Plaintiffs' theory has another, more machiavellian aspect. According to plaintiffs, defendants knew in October 1992 that Host would not pay a dividend on its preferred stock, but withheld that information, and even implied the contrary in public statements.... The first question that this assertion raises is the following: If knowledge of the discontinuation of dividends would promote the posited scheme to force conversions, why would defendants in October withhold knowledge of the planned suspension of dividends? This is where the plaintiffs' account gets machiavellian. According to plaintiffs, defendants understood that institutional investors would move into the preferred stock following the October 5 announcement and that these investors would hedge their position by short-selling Marriott common. Investors in this position (who isolate their risk in the preference rights) are, it is said, particularly sensitive to the "coercive" effect of a suspension of dividends. Therefore in delaying the announcement of the preferred dividend suspension defendants intended to cause these especially susceptible holders to move into the preferred stock before they sprang their trap.

III.
Plaintiffs' Legal Theories

Plaintiffs see the planned spin-off and the suspension of Marriott preferred stock dividends that is planned to follow it as constituting wrongs of several sorts.

First, they complain that the proposal violates a fiduciary duty running from the board of directors of Marriott to them as stockholders of the company. For the reasons expressed in an earlier opinion I concluded, with respect to the spin-off transaction, that the Marriott directors owed no fiduciary duty to the holders of preferred stock. See HB Korenvaes Investments, L.P. v. Marriott Corporation, Del.Ch., C.A. No. 12922, Allen, C. (June 9, 1993).

Secondly, plaintiffs assert that the proposed transaction and the suspension of dividends constitute multiple violations of the contractual rights of the preferred stock. The most plausible of these allegations is the claim that the special dividend violates the certificate of designation because it distributes such a large proportion of the value of Marriott that the certificate of designation provision designed to protect the economic value of the preferred, in the face of a special dividend, cannot work.

* * *

IV.
Probability of Success: The Certificate Claims

I turn first to an assessment of the probabilities of success of the claims asserted.... As explained below, in my opinion, the heart of the matter is whether the planned transaction is consistent with the intended functioning of the conversion price adjustment provision contained in the certificate of designation and quoted below. That subject is treated in part V. In this part plaintiffs' other breach of contract theories are addressed.

(a) The claim that the spin-off must be approved by the affirmative vote of 66⅔% of the preferred stock because it creates a class of stock ranking prior to the preferred; and the claim that the planned payment of dividends to International common stockholders, while the Marriott preferred dividend is suspended, violates Sections 1 and 2 of the certificate of designation, both fail to state a claim upon which relief may be granted.

Section 1 of the certificate of designation provides that the preferred shall "rank prior to the Common Stock ... with respect to the payment of dividends and the distribution of assets."

Section 2 restricts the ability of the company to pay dividends on its common stock. It provides in part:

> Unless full cumulative dividends on all outstanding shares of the Convertible Preferred Stock shall have been paid..., no dividend shall be declared upon the Common Stock ... nor shall any Common Stock ... be redeemed, purchased or otherwise acquired ... by the Corporation...."

Section 6 of the certificate of designation provides that except as required by law, the preferred stock shall not have a vote, but, inter alia, the affirmative vote of 66⅔% of all shares of preferred stock shall be necessary:

> to create, authorize or issue ... any shares of any class of stock of the Corporation ranking prior to the Convertible Preferred Stock...." The "Corporation" is defined as Marriott Corporation.

Plaintiffs claim that the special dividend violates Sections 1, 2 and 6 in that once it is effectuated Marriott would be enabled to pay dividends to its common stockholders without first paying the preferred dividend. In addition the transaction would create, it is said, a security ranking prior to the common in terms of dividends, without a class vote of the preferred. In support of these assertions plaintiffs expressly disclaim reliance upon the doctrine that permits a court of equity to ignore the formality of separate legal personality, to "pierce the corporate veil," where the corporate form is used to perpetrate a fraud or other inequitable conduct....

Plaintiffs argue that the size of the special dividend and the close long-term relationships which will exist between Host and International after the special dividend, ... demonstrate that the spin-off has no real purpose other than the avoidance of the rights of bondholders and preferred stockholders. Thus, plaintiffs assert that even accepting the separate legal identity of Host and International, the accomplishment of the planned special dividend would constitute a breach of Sections 1, 2 and 6 of the certificate. They rely upon a principle that courts will prevent contracting parties from evading their obligations by doing indirectly that which their contract forbids them to do directly and in support of this principle plaintiffs cite Shenandoah Life Ins. Co. v. Valero Energy Corp, Del.Ch., C.A. No. 9032, Allen, C. (June 21, 1988).

Such a statement of principle is, in my opinion, too general to be meaningful. The relevant inquiry in contract cases often is what is the contractual obligation. Thus certainly if a contractual duty is breached it ought not to matter that the breach might be said to be the result of indirect action. But that principle does not assist in the identification of the duty owed.

The pertinent foundational inquiry here is whether there is a duty arising from the contract (the certificate) not to transfer substantial assets out of Marriott. The answer clearly is that there is no such duty. The certificate explicitly provides for such special dividends in Section 5. It is impossible to say that the payment of such a dividend is unauthorized. Does the large size of the planned distribution render it an evasion of the rights set forth in Sections 1, 2 or 6? Plainly, in my opinion, it does not. While, as set forth below, the size of the distribution does create an issue under Section 5(e)(iv), if the dividend is consistent with the protections of the preferred there created, then plaintiffs will be afforded all of the protections to which they are entitled.

Only if the distribution of the dividend itself were unauthorized or a violation of the legal rights of plaintiffs could the argument plausibly be advanced that the property held by International after the distribution is equitably the property "of the Corporation," within the meaning of Sections 1, 2 and 6. But if that premise is established, plaintiffs will in all events be entitled to relief. If it is not established then these theories are demonstrably flawed. Thus, it is the predicate fact—the invalidity of the distribution itself—that is legally meaningful. Unless that fact is established, it is perfectly obvious that the common stock of International is not stock "of the Corporation" (Section 6) and dividends paid on it are not paid on "Common Stock" (Sections 1 and 2) as defined in the certificate of designation.... Thus, I conclude that these theories fail to state a claim upon which relief can be granted.

(b) Plaintiffs' claim that defendants are coercing conversion and thus in the process of violating the limitations on Marriott's redemption privilege fails to state a claim for violation of Section 4 of the certificate of designation.

Section 4 of the certificate affords to Marriott an option to redeem the preferred stock at stated prices, after January 15, 1996. The redemption price per share is stated as $52,480 in 1996 and decreases each year thereafter until it is at the stated (liquidation) value of $50,000 per share in the year 2002 and thereafter.

Plaintiffs urge that they are being forced by defendants' suspension of the preferred stock dividend to convert into Marriott common stock and that Section 4 of the certificate grants them "call protection" until January 16, 1996. This aspect of Section 4, they say, constitutes a contractual undertaking by Marriott to permit holders to enjoy the benefits of preferred stock ownership until that date. While plaintiffs concede that Marriott is not now redeeming the preferred stock, it is urged that its actions do violate an implied obligation not to interfere with plaintiffs' enjoyment of their preferred stock until that time. Plaintiffs see the suspension of the preferred dividend (most directly) and the size of the special dividend (less directly) as aimed at forcing them to give up those benefits prematurely.

It is plain that an exercise of the conversion right, whether one accepts that it is "coerced" or not, does not constitute a redemption of that stock. The reasons for this are too obvious and fundamental to require much discussion. Legally, following conversion holders of the preferred stock will remain shareholders of the corporation; were their stock redeemed they would not. Moreover, economically, they will, in this instance, possess far greater value following conversion than the highest stated liquidation value. Redemption and conversion are in all respects fundamentally different actions.

Plaintiffs say they accept that a coerced exercise of their conversion right is not a redemption but they say it does breach another duty contained in Section 4, a duty to respect their "call protection" until 1996. That is, they say the redemption right is a right that becomes exercisable in 1996. Before that time Marriott has no current right to redeem. As a logical consequence of this fact, plaintiffs claim that they have, prior to 1996, a correlative right of some sort (a "no call right") arising from Section 4 to remain as holders of preferred stock.

I need not decide whether such a right exists. Assuming plaintiffs have such an interest it is apparent that the special dividend or the suspension of preferred stock dividends, would not violate it. Any posited contractual right to be free from calls for redemption prior to 1996 plainly could not, for example, create a veto right before that date over mergers that would convert the preferred stock to a right to receive cash; or create a veto right over a corporate dissolution; or the declaration of dividends otherwise authorized. In the preferred stock context, parties who contract with respect to one type of corporate right or action (e.g., redemption) will not be assumed to have intended their contract to affect another corporate right or activity (e.g., declaration of dividend) unless their contract cannot meaningfully be otherwise interpreted. See Waggoner v. Laster, Del.Supr., 581 A.2d 1127 (1990)....

Thus, I conclude that Section 4 of the certificate of designation confers no rights upon plaintiffs that would be violated under the facts alleged in the amended complaint.

(c) Plaintiffs have shown no reasonable probability of prevailing on the claim that the announced suspension of the preferred stock dividends constitutes wrongful coercion regarding plaintiffs' conversion right.

A related claim is that the suspension of dividends constitutes wrongful coercion designed to force plaintiffs to convert to common stock. Plainly the discontinuation of current dividend payments on the preferred stock will tend to make conversion into Marriott common stock prior to the special dividend more attractive. Plaintiffs call the effect coercion and assert that in this context, it is a wrong.

This court has on occasion enjoined as inequitable and inconsistent with an applicable fiduciary duty, corporate action designed principally to coerce stockholders in the exercise of a choice that the applicable certificate of incorporation, bylaws or statute confers upon them. See, e.g., AC Acquisition Corp. v. Anderson, Clayton & Co., supra; Lacos Land Co. v. Arden Group, Inc., Del.Ch., 517 A.2d 271 (1986); Kahn v. U.S. Sugar Co., Del.Ch., C.A. No. 7313, Hartnett, V.C., 11 Del.J.Corp.L. 908 (1986); Eisenberg v. Chicago Milwaukee Corp., 537 A.2d 1051 (1987). These cases are premised upon the existence of a fiduciary duty on the part of the corporate directors with respect to the transaction under review. The last of them involved preferred stockholders to whom a tender offer had been extended by the Company. As an alternative holding this court held that a gratuitous statement by the Company concerning a plan to seek delisting of the preferred, constituted an inappropriate effort to coerce acceptance of the Company's offer. See Eisenberg, 537 A.2d at 1062. Plaintiffs rely upon this precedent to argue that the announcement of the discontinuation of preferred stock dividends has an analogous effect and is analogously a breach of duty.

Plaintiffs are, I believe, incorrect in this. The critical differences between this case as it now appears and Eisenberg are several. First, that case was treated as a fiduciary duty case, not as a case involving, as this one does, the construction and interpretation of rights and duties set forth in the certificate of designation. In this instance Marriott has a right to suspend dividend payments and in the event that should happen, the preferred's protections are in the contract and are several: most importantly, the dividends are cumulative and enjoy a liquidation preference; in addition, the redemption price is adjusted to include unpaid dividends; and prolonged suspension of dividends gives the preferred the right to elect two directors. Finally, the preferred may, in all events, be converted into common stock; and, as I construe the certificate, there is necessarily implied a restriction on the proportion of net worth that may be distributed by special dividend.... These contractual protections are a recognition of the risk that dividends might not be paid currently. These protections are substantial. The correlative of the fact that Marriott has a duty to respect them is the conclusion that it has a right to discontinue dividends when it observes them.

Secondly, unlike Eisenberg it cannot persuasively be urged, at this stage, that the discontinuation of dividends is not itself a prudent, business-driven decision. Thus, assuming that a corporation owes to the holders of its preferred stock the same implied duty of good faith that is present in every contractual relationship, as I believe to be the case, the circumstances as they appear could not be construed as justifying the preliminary conclusion that the suspension of dividend payments is not a good faith business decision. Host is expected to have no net income, even though it will have substantial assets. Plaintiffs' suggestion that Host could, in the circumstances, borrow money to pay preferred dividends presents a classic business judgment issue; that such a possibility may exist does not constitute a persuasive argument that the suspension of dividend payments was itself undertaken in bad faith.

Thus, while the suspension of dividends may exert a powerful influence upon the decision whether holders of preferred stock will exercise rights to convert or not, I can see in that effect, at this time, no violation of any implied right to that degree of good faith that every commercial contractor is entitled to expect from those with whom she contracts.

V.
The Section 5(e)(iv) Claim

I turn now to analysis of that which I regard as the centrally important certificate provision, Section 5(e)(iv). That section affords protection against dilution of the conversion component of the market value of the preferred stock by providing an adjustment to the conversion price when the corporation declares a dividend of assets, including securities. The principle that appears embedded in Section 5(e)(iv) is that when the assets of the firm are depleted through a special distribution to shareholders, the preferred will be protected by the triggering of a conversion price adjustment formula. Under Section 5(e)(iv) the number of shares into which the preferred can convert will be proportionately increased in order to maintain the value of the preferred's conversion feature. The principle seems clear enough; the realization of it will inevitably involve problems.

(a) Section 5(e)(iv) of the certificate of designation requires Marriott, when effectuating a special dividend, to leave sufficient net assets in the corporation to permit that Section to function as intended to protect the pre-disposition value of the preferred stock.

The language of the certificate of designation is as follows:

5. Conversion Rights. The holders of shares of Convertible Preferred Stock shall have the right at their option, to convert such shares into shares of Common Stock on the following terms and conditions:

(a) Shares of Convertible Preferred Stock shall be convertible at any time into fully paid and nonassessable shares of Common Stock at a conversion price of $17.40 per share of Common Stock (the "Conversion Price").

* * *

(e) The conversion Price shall be adjusted from time to time as follows:

(iv) *In case the Corporation shall, by dividend or otherwise, distribute to all holders of its Common Stock ... assets (including securities ...), the Conversion Price shall be adjusted* so that the same shall equal the price determined by multiplying the Conversion Price in effect immediately prior to the close of business on the date fixed for the determination of stockholders entitled to receive such distribution by a fraction of which the numerator shall be the current market price per share (determined as provided in subsection (vi) below) of the Common Stock on the date fixed for such determination less the then fair market value (as determined by the Board of Directors, whose determination shall be conclusive and shall be described in a statement filed with the transfer agent for the Convertible Preferred Stock) of the portion of the evidences of indebtedness or assets so distributed applicable to one share of Common Stock and the denominator shall be such current market price per share of the Common Stock, such adjustment to become effective immediately prior to the opening of business on the day following the date fixed for the determination of stockholders entitled to receive such distribution. (emphasis added).

Thus, stated simply, whenever Marriott distributes assets to its common stockholders this provision protects the value of the preferred conversion right by reducing the conversion price. Protection of this type may be important to the buyer of preferred stock and presumably its inclusion will permit an issuer to arrange the sale of preferred stock on somewhat more advantageous terms than would otherwise be available. What is intuitively apparent is that in a narrow range of extreme cases, a dividend of property may be so large relative to the corporation's net worth, that following the distribution, the firm, while still solvent,[16] will not represent sufficient value to preserve the pre-dividend value of the preferred's conversion right.

---

16. Traditionally preferred stockholders have not been treated as creditors for the amount of the liquidation preference and the preference does not count as a "claim" for fraudulent conveyance

Appended to this opinion are three hypothetical cases in which the Section 5(e)(iv) formula is employed. Case 1 involves a dividend of 40% of the issuing corporation's net asset value. Case 2 is a dividend of 90% of net asset value. Case 3 displays the consequences of a dividend of 95% of asset value. Given the assumptions of the examples (i.e. preferred conversion rights equal 9.1% of total pre-distribution value), only in the last case does the Section 5(e)(iv) formula fail to function.

In light of the mathematical effect demonstrated in the appended examples, a court that must construe Section 5(e)(iv) is required to conclude, in my opinion, that Marriott has voluntarily and effectively bound itself not to declare and distribute special dividends of a proportion that would deprive the preferred stockholders of the protection that provision was intended to afford. In providing a mechanism to maintain pre-distribution value (putting to one side for the moment, how pre-distribution value is determined) the issuer impliedly but unmistakably and necessarily undertook to refrain from declaring a dividend so large that what is left in the corporation is itself worth less than the pre-distribution value of the preferred stock. No other interpretation of the certificate of designation gives the language of Section 5(e)(iv) its intended effect in all circumstances. Thus, were the facts of Case 3 the facts of this case, I would be required to find that the special dividend violated the rights of the preferred stockholders created by the certificate of designation.

Such a holding would not be inconsistent with those cases that hold that rights of preference are to be strictly construed e.g., Waggoner v. Laster, Del.Supr., 581 A.2d 1127, 1134 (1990); Rothschild Int'l Corp. v. Liggett Group Inc., Del.Supr., 474 A.2d 133, 136 (1984); Ellingwood v. Wolf's Head Oil Refining Co., Del.Supr., 38 A.2d 743, 747 (1944). This strict construction perspective on the interpretation of certificates of designation has long been the law of this jurisdiction and others. While that principle does define the court's approach to construction and interpretation of the documents that create preferred stock, that principle does not excuse a court from the duty to interpret the legal meaning of the certificate of designation.... Thus where the necessary implication of the language used is the existence of a right or a duty, a court construing that language is duty bound to recognize the existence of that right or that duty....

(b) Plaintiffs have failed to introduce evidence from which it could be concluded at this time that it is reasonably probable that they will prevail on a claim that the special dividend violates Section 5(e)(iv).

(i) The value that Section 5(e)(iv) intends to protect is the market value of the conversion feature at the time the board authorizes a special dividend transaction.

The determination that Section 5 of the certificate creates by necessary implication an obligation on the part of the corporation to leave sufficient value in the corporation following a special dividend to permit the protections it creates to function with the intended effect, raises the further question, what value does Section 5 intend to protect. Plainly it is the value of the conversion feature, that is what all of Section 5 is about, but measured at what point in time?

On the last day of trading before the announcement of the special dividend, Marriott's common stock closed at $17.125. The preferred's conversion feature, (its right to convert into 11,494,400 common shares) had a value at that time of $196,842,000. Beginning the first trading day after the announcement of the special dividend, Marriott

---

purposes. See Fletcher's Cyc. Corp., § 5293 (Perm. ed. 1986); Compare Model Bus. Corp. Act, § 6.40(c)(2) (Supp.1989).

common stock rose greatly in price. By May 21, 1993, it had increased to approximately $26.00 per share and the value of the preferred's conversion right had increased to $298.5 million....

Plaintiffs' position is that this value, as effected by the prospect of the dividend attacked, is the value that must be left in the corporation.

I cannot accept this interpretation of what good faith adherence to the provisions of the certificate requires of Marriott. Section 5(e)(iv) operates to prevent the confiscation of the value of the preferred conversion right through a special dividend. By necessary implication it limits the board's discretion with respect to the size of special dividends. But that limitation is one that has its effect when it is respected by the board of directors at the time it takes corporate action to declare the dividend. If, when declared, the dividend will leave the corporation with sufficient assets to preserve the conversion value that the preferred possesses at that time, it satisfies the limitation that such a protective provision necessarily implies. That is, Section 5(e)(iv) does not, in my opinion, explicitly or by necessary implication grant the preferred a right to assurance that any increase in the value of their conversion rights following the authorization of a special dividend be maintained.

(ii) Plaintiffs have failed to introduce evidence that establishes a reasonable probability of their proving that the net value remaining in Host after distribution of the special dividend is or is reasonably likely to be insufficient to maintain the pre-distribution value of the preferred's conversion right. In attempting to demonstrate that the special dividend will confiscate some part of their property, plaintiffs rely on the affidavit of Charles R. Wright, a certified public accountant. Mr. Wright states that following the special dividend the value of Host's equity will not exceed $200 million.... This opinion is based upon analyses conducted by Wolfensohn, Inc. in October 1992, concerning the transaction as planned at that time. But the transaction of October 1992 reflected a very different financial structure than that now planned; it contemplated Host bearing substantially more debt than the transaction currently envisioned. Mr. Wright's conclusions are also based upon analyses conducted by S.G. Warburg, but under the assumption that the Exchange Offer ... will not be effectuated. Mr. Wright stated that he did not consider later valuations of the transaction developed by Wolfensohn and S.G. Warburg to be relevant because they were based upon the assumption that the Exchange Offer would close, an assumption plaintiffs regard as unfounded.... I do not accept this premise. For present purposes I assume that the Exchange Offer will close. It is an integral part of the complex transaction that is under review. Any part of that transaction could, in theory, be abandoned or modified. My analysis proceeds on the belief both that preliminary review on this application is nevertheless appropriate and that the transaction now planned is the transaction that forms the basis of that preliminary review.

The later projections by Wolfensohn and S.G. Warburg, provide a different picture of Host's financial status than the earlier ones upon which Mr. Wright relies. On May 7, 1993, Wolfensohn provided Marriott's board with current valuations of Host and International. Wolfensohn concluded that, assuming the Exchange Offer closes, Host will have a total equity value of between $371 million and $556 million....

A discounted cash flow valuation of Host produced by Wolfensohn on April 20, 1993 and based on the assumption that the Exchange Offer will be effectuated, produced a range of values from $270 million (assuming a 14% discount rate; and a multiple of 7 times EBITDA) to $884 million (assuming a 12% discount rate and a multiple of 9 times EBITDA) with a middle case of $567 million (assuming a 13% discount rate and a multiple of 8 times EBITDA.)....

S.G. Warburg's valuation of Host, dated May 6, 1993, estimated the trading value of Host, assuming the Exchange Offer closes, at $1.38 to $2.84 per share or an aggregate of $179 million to $368 million. Warburg also estimated that the summary business value of Host would be in the range of $551 to $830 million or $4.25 to $6.40 per share.

The lower end of S.G. Warburg's estimate of the likely range of trading values for Host stock falls below the $196.8 million that represents the value of plaintiffs' conversion rights prior to the announcement of the distribution. Unspecified assertions by plaintiffs' expert that "major assumptions used in the discounted cash flow analysis are inappropriate" and that companies used for comparison are not comparable to Host, ... do not, however, provide a basis upon which to conclude that it is more likely that Host's common stock will have a value in the lower end of this range of values rather than in the higher part. The mere possibility that this will be the case is not enough to support the grant of a preliminary injunction. I assume the shape of a graph of the probabilities of any of these values in the range being "correct" would form a bell shaped curve. That is to say it is more likely that, upon more exhaustive analysis or with a more definitive valuation technique, the intrinsic value of Host would be the mean number of these ranges rather than either expressed limit of them. These higher probability mean estimates are all in excess of $196 million.

Thus, I am unable to conclude that plaintiffs have shown a sufficient probability of demonstrating that the protective functions of Section 5(e)(iv) will be frustrated by the size of the special dividend to justify the issuance of an injunction preventing the effectuation of the planned reorganization of Marriott.

(c) Plaintiffs have not shown that defendants have breached (or are about to breach) the agreed upon formula for implementing Section 5(e)(iv).

In its June 19, 1993 proxy statement, Marriott described the process that it intends to employ with respect to the operation of Section 5(e)(iv) of the certificate. After paraphrasing the certificate language quoted above..., the proxy statement states:

> The Board currently intends to determine the "fair market value" of the Distribution, for purposes of this calculation, by ascertaining the relative, intrinsic values of Host Marriott and Marriott International (with reference to all factors which it deems relevant) and by designating the allocable portion of the Current Market Price attributable to Marriott International as the fair market value of the Distribution.

In this litigation defendants have amplified their proposed method for determining fair market value of the individual distribution. Marriott intends to first determine "with reference to all relevant factors" the "intrinsic values" of International and Host. Then the fraction of the value of a Marriott share represented by International would be determined by dividing International's "intrinsic value" by the sum of the intrinsic values of International and Host. This fraction would then be multiplied by the current trading value of Marriott to determine the fair market value (per share) of International and thus of the distribution. Therefore, the fair market value of the distribution (i.e., International) is treated by the board's proposed valuation method as fraction of the market value of Marriott prior to the distribution of the dividend.... The premise of this methodology is the assertion that as long as Host common stock trades at some positive value, the fair market value of International for purposes of applying Section

5(e)(iv) must be less than the current market value of Marriott; the whole (Marriott) cannot be less than the sum of its parts (International plus Host).

Defendants claim that this method of determining fair market value is consistent with the certificate and that it reaches a determination of the fair market value of the distribution that can meaningfully be compared to the current market value of Marriott. Indeed, they assert that any alternative technique which yields a value for International that is higher than the market value of Marriott must (as long as Host trades at a positive value) be faulty.

Plaintiffs contend that defendants' approach is inconsistent with the contract language. They say that it is designed to hide the fact that the special dividend is so large that the conversion price adjustment formula cannot work properly with respect to it.

Plaintiffs point out that the conversion price adjustment formula ... requires as a numerator the current per share market price of Marriott (determined over a 30 day period) less the "then fair market value " (expressed as a per share figure) of the assets distributed.[19] This number can be well estimated, it is claimed, by reference to the "when-issued" market which will, for a week or so before the distribution, establish a good proxy for the market value of the assets distributed.[20]

Plaintiffs claim that the method of determining the fair market value of International which defendants propose to employ is an attempt to manipulate Section 5(e)(iv), by artificially limiting the "fair market value" of the assets to be distributed (International's common stock) to a fraction of Marriott's total value despite the fact that Section 5(e)(iv) makes no mention of such a limitation. Plaintiffs rely on the language of the certificate which states explicitly that the board must determine the fair market value of the assets to be distributed, to support their argument that the board is required to determine this value without placing a ceiling on it of the value of Marriott.

* * *

In my opinion, Marriott's proposed technique for determining the values to employ in the contractual formula is one valid way to do what the company is contractually bound to do. It follows that this claim presents no grounds to justify the issuance of a preliminary injunction.

It is, of course, the case that plaintiffs' alternative technique might seem superior to some, in that it looks to a direct market measure of the value of the distribution. While that has appeal, it is also true that the different measuring times that this technique implies ... itself makes it possible that it would cause the adjustment formula to produce a negative number. Given the multiple factors that affect public securities mar-

---

19. I need not express a view as to whether the "then" is best read as (i) the time of the distribution (record date) or (ii) the time period during which the market value of Marriott stock is determined under the formula. In all events the "then fair market" is to be decided "by the Board of Directors, whose determination shall be conclusive," so long as made in good faith I would add.

20. Plaintiffs express the view that it is quite possible that the when issued price for International will be in excess of the market price of Marriott, but if one is assuming contemporaneous measurement and one assumes Host will be solvent (which appears to be the case) it is difficult to see why that would be the case. Marriott common stock captures the full value of International before the distribution plus some additional value of a solvent Host. Thus if Host is solvent it does seem illogical for a market to assign a higher value to International then [sic] to Marriott. The possibility of different measuring periods (the certificate language contemplates that the current market value of Marriott be measured over a thirty day period commencing forty five days before the distribution) would introduce a possibility for the when issued market for International to be higher on any particular day than the value of Marriott common stock over the measuring period.

kets, this could be true, even if far more equity were left in Host than the value of the preferred. Thus, there is good reason to reject plaintiffs' proposal even though it has appealing aspects.

Defendants' intended technique for estimating the "fair market value applicable to one share" would appear to serve the purpose of the section. As explained above, the equation is intended to operate to reduce the conversion price by the same percentage that the total assets of the company are being reduced. Assuming again that Host will have some positive net worth, it is clear that less than 100% of the assets of Marriott are being distributed. Therefore, in such a case the conversion price should be reduced by less than 100%. The method adopted by the company for determining applicable fair market value would, if fairly and competently applied, provide for the adjustment of the conversion price in a manner that effectuates the purposes of the clause. The certificate of course confers broad discretion on Marriott in implementing the formula of Section 5(e)(iv) and makes its choices "conclusive." While that grant may too imply a duty of commercial good faith, the facts adduced do not suggest that the employment of the formula by defendants has been other than in good faith.

Thus, I am unable to conclude that plaintiffs have shown a reasonable probability of success on the merits of their claim that the method of determining the fair market value of the assets to be distributed "applicable to one share of [Marriott] common stock", that defendants have announced they will employ, violates Section 5(e)(iv)....

APPENDIX

The following three hypotheticals demonstrate how Section 5(e)(iv) operates to preserve the economic value of the conversion rights of the preferred when the company's assets are distributed as dividends to the common stockholders, and how at extreme levels it could fail.

CASE I

Assume a company, Corporation Y, with $1 billion in assets and no debts. It has 10 million shares of common stock and 1 million shares of cumulative convertible preferred stock having a face amount and liquidation preference of $100 million. The preferred is convertible into common stock at a price of $100 face amount per common share or into 1 million common shares, in total. The certificate of designation contains a provision identical to Section 5(e)(iv).

Assume further that the capital markets operate efficiently and the common stock trades at price reflecting Corporation Y's asset values on a fully diluted basis.

Under these assumptions at time [T1], Current Market Price ("CMP") is determined as follows:

$$CMP = \$1\,\text{billion} \times \frac{1}{11\,\text{million shares}} = \$90.9091\,\text{per share}$$

Preferred Conversion Value = 1 million shares × $90.9091 = $90,909,100

At time [T2] Corporation Y declares a dividend of assets with a fair market value of $400 million or $40 per outstanding common share, leaving the company with $600 million in assets.

The conversion price would be adjusted by the same formula as applies in Section 5(e)(iv):

$$ACP = CP \times \frac{CMP - FMV}{CMP}$$

Where: ACP = Adjusted Conversion Price;
         CP = Conversion Price;
         FMV = Fair Market Value;
         CMP = Current Market Price common stock

$$ACP = \frac{100 \times \$90.9091 - \$40}{\$90.9091} = \$56.0000$$

The preferred would become convertible into 1,785,710 [sic] common shares,

$$\frac{\$100,000,000 \times 1\,\text{common share}}{\$56.0000} = 1,785,870\ [\text{sic}]\ \text{common shares}$$

with an aggregate value of $90,908,900,

$$\frac{\$600,000,000 \times 1,785,710\ \text{converted shares}}{11,785,710\ \text{common shares}} = \$90,908,900$$

Thus in this case the anti-dilution provision of the certificate would serve to preserve the economic value of the preferred stock despite the diversion of 40% of Corporation Y's net worth out of the company.

CASE II

Now assume alternatively that Corporation Y declares a special dividend to its common stockholders of $900 million of its assets or $90 per outstanding share.

The conversion price adjustment formula would work to adjust the conversion price from $100 to 1.00 per share:

$$ACP = \frac{\$100 \times \$90.0991 - \$90}{\$90.9091} = \$1.0000\ [\text{sic}]$$

The preferred would become convertible into 100,000,000 shares, (91% of all common stock) at [T2].

$$\frac{\$100,000,000 \times 1\,\text{common share}}{1.0000} = 100,000,000\ \text{shares}$$

But the aggregate value of the preferred portion would remain unchanged at $90,909,091:

$$\frac{100,000,000\ \text{converted shares}}{110,000,000\ \text{common shares}} \times \$100,000,000 = \$90,090,091$$

Thus, on these assumptions, even if 90% of Corporation Y's assets are distributed to the common stockholders, the conversion value of the preferred is maintained at its pre-distribution level by the Section 5(e)(iv) gross-up provision.

CASE III

When the special dividend is so large that insufficient equity remains in Corporation Y to maintain the value of the preferred upon conversion the gross up provisions will fail to work.[1] In such a situation the gross-up equation provides for a negative adjusted conversion price and is therefore meaningless.

For example: If Corporation Y declared a dividend of $950 million of its assets, the gross-up equation would give the following result:

$$ACP = \frac{CP \times CMP - FMV}{CMP}$$

$$ACP = \frac{\$100 \times \$90.9091 - \$95.00}{\$90.9091} = -(\$4.499)$$

Thus, a distribution of $950 million leaves only $50 million in assets in the corporation, making it impossible for the preferred to maintain its pre-distribution conversion value of $90.909 million. For that reason it also causes Section 5(e)(iv) to fail to work meaningfully.

————————

Note

In Stephenson v. Plastics Corp. of Amer., Inc., 150 N.W.2d 668 (Minn. 1967), the plaintiff warrant holders were entitled to exercise their warrants for shares in Plastics Corp. of America (Plastics) at an exercise price of $1 per share. In addition, they were entitled to a reduction in the warrants' exercise price that reflected the fair value of any non-cash dividend paid by Plastics to its shareholders. Plastics thereafter sold assets to a newly-formed, wholly owned subsidiary in exchange for all the equity in that subsidiary. Plastics then proposed to distribute the equity of the subsidiary to Plastics' shareholders (i.e., conduct a spin-off of the subsidiary). Plastics gave notice to the warrant holders that required them to exercise their warrants by a certain date or they would not be entitled to shares in the subsidiary (although they would be entitled to a reduction of the warrants' exercise price).

Plaintiffs failed to timely exercise their warrants in order to receive shares of the subsidiary, although they did ultimately exercise their warrants before they expired. Plaintiffs then brought suit demanding the right to receive shares in the spun-off subsidiary or, in the alternative, damages. Plastics defended on the ground that the warrant contract clearly specified what adjustment would be made in the event of a non-cash dividend, such as a spin-off. In reversing and remanding the case, the Minnesota Supreme

————————

1. They may also fail, in the specific case of Section 5(e)(iv) because the measurement period for "current market price" is somewhat historical while the measurement period for "fair market value" of assets distributed is current. Thus, it may happen given the potentials for fluctuating market prices, for a negative number to be generated simply as an artifact of the formula. See supra n. 20.

Court held that a "dividend" under Minnesota law could only be paid out of a company's surplus, paid-in surplus or its net earnings for its current or preceding fiscal year. Based on the limited factual record before it, the court believed it would be premature to rule as a matter of law that the spin-off was intended to be treated as a "dividend" within the meaning of the language of the warrants. *See id.* at 677.

(iii) Antidestruction

Conversion rights are typically drafted to provide the convertible securityholders with a substitute for the company's common stock in the event its common stock is eliminated. A typical "antidestruction provision" will allow a convertible securityholder to convert into the same consideration paid to the company's common stockholders as part of the transaction leading to the elimination of the company's common stock.

For example, suppose WKC Company has shares of convertible preferred stock outstanding that is protected by an antidestruction provision. Currently, each share of preferred stock is convertible into four shares of WKC's common stock based on the current conversion price. Suppose WKC Company agrees to merge with JJH Corp., a subsidiary formed by RHR Co. to effect the merger. WKC will be the surviving company in this reverse triangular merger. Therefore, its convertible preferred stock will remain outstanding. Its common stock, however, will not remain outstanding, as its sole share of common stock will be owned by RHR after the merger. As merger consideration, common stockholders of WKC will receive 1.5 shares of RHR common stock. Accordingly, based on the antidestruction provision, WKC's convertible preferred stockholders will be able to convert each share of their preferred stock into six shares of RHR common stock after the merger [4 × 1.5].

In theory, this is a straight forward exercise. Things get complicated, however, when courts are called up to decide whether an antidestruction clause has been triggered. Consider the following case.

Wood v. Coastal States Gas Corp.
401 A.2d 932 (Del. 1979)

DUFFY, Justice:

This appeal is from an order of the Court of Chancery dismissing the complaints in a consolidated class action filed by the owners of two series of preferred stock[1] in Coastal States Gas Corporation (Coastal), a Delaware corporation. The suit is against Coastal, two of its subsidiaries and its chief executive officer. While this litigation is part of a complex controversy in a mosaic of many persons and disputes, it is entirely between the owners of Coastal's preferred stock and the owners of its common stock.

I

The facts out of which the dispute arises involve the sale and delivery of natural gas to many cities and corporate users in the State of Texas and, although our involvement

---

1. One series is designated, "$1.83 Cumulative Convertible Preferred Stock, Series B," and the other, "$1.19 Cumulative Convertible Preferred Stock, Series A." The certificate of rights and preferences for each series is identical and thus what is said herein of one is applicable to both. We will refer to the stock in the singular as "Series A," or "Series B," or the "preferred stock."

is limited, we must recite some of them to put the appeal into context. For that purpose, the relevant facts are these:

A significant part of Coastal's business is the gathering, transporting and marketing of natural gas, all of which is conducted by a subsidiary, Coastal States Gas Producing Co. (Producing), also a defendant in this action. Producing, in turn, has a subsidiary, Lo-Vaca Gathering Co. (Lo-Vaca), another defendant, which supplies the gas to intrastate customers in Texas, including the Cities of Austin, Brownsville, Corpus Christi and San Antonio.

As a result of several factors associated with the "energy crisis" in the early 1970s, the wellhead price of natural gas increased significantly (from about 20¢ per 1000 cubic feet to about $2.00 for the same quantity) and Lo-Vaca was unable to honor its obligations to deliver gas to its customers at contract prices. In 1973, Lo-Vaca sought and obtained interim permission from the Railroad Commission of Texas (the agency vested with jurisdiction over intrastate utilities in Texas) to increase its rates; that authorization permitted Lo-Vaca to pass to its customers certain of its own cost increases. After the higher rates went into effect, a large number of Lo-Vaca industrial and municipal customers filed suits against Lo-Vaca, Producing, Coastal and Oscar Wyatt (Coastal's chief executive officer, the owner of the single largest block of its common stock and a defendant in this suit) for breach of contract.

In December 1977, the Commission entered a final order denying Lo-Vaca's original petition for rate relief and, in effect, rescinding the interim order which had authorized the increase. The Commission then directed Lo-Vaca to comply with the contract rates and ordered Coastal, Producing and Lo-Vaca to refund the rate increment which had been charged to customers under the 1973 interim order. It is estimated that the refundable amount exceeds $1.6 billion—which is about three times Coastal's net worth.

Given this state of affairs, with its obvious and enormous implications for a large section of Texas, settlement negotiations were undertaken and, eventually, a complex plan evolved. It is unnecessary for us to detail the plan, but the following summary states its substance:

(1) The substantial litigation and disputes between the natural gas sales customers of Lo-Vaca and Coastal, Producing, Lo-Vaca and Wyatt, which developed as a result of the "Lo-Vaca problem," will be settled;

(2) Producing will be renamed "Valero Energy Corporation," restructured into a corporate enterprise and spun off from Coastal; it will consist principally of Producing's present gas utility pipe-line and extraction plant operations, including Lo-Vaca, and a Texas retail gas distribution division of Coastal;

(3) There will be transfers to a trust for the benefit of the customers who adopt the settlement plan ("Settling Customers") of: (a) approximately 1,196,218 shares (or about 5.3%) of the voting securities of Coastal; (b) a one-year interest-bearing promissory note of Valero in the principal amount of $8,000,000; (c) 13.4% of the outstanding shares of the common stock of Valero; and (d) 1,150,000 shares ($115,000,000 aggregate liquidation value) of Valero Preferred Stock, $8.50 Cumulative Series A;

(4) Coastal will issue to Valero approximately 805,130 shares (with approximately $80,513,000 aggregate liquidation value) of Coastal's $8.50 Cumulative Preferred Stock, Series D, $.33⅓ par value (which is a new class of stock);

(5) A long-term program will be established providing for the expenditure of $180,000,000 to $230,000,000 (subject to certain increases or decreases, with a maximum commitment estimated at $495,000,000), by Coastal to find and

develop gas reserves to be made available to the Lo-Vaca System and to be offered for sale by Coastal to Valero at discounted prices and, in turn, resold to
Lo-Vaca (or, in some instances, to third parties) at higher prices, with the net
proceeds (in excess of the cost of gas) received by Valero on such resale to be
paid to the trust for the benefit of certain Settling Customers;

(6) There will be a new gas sales rate structure for Lo-Vaca designed to stabilize it as a viable public utility.

In addition, there will be a distribution by Coastal, in the form of an extraordinary
dividend chargeable to earned surplus, to its common stockholders (except Wyatt) of
the balance (86.6%) of the Valero common stock not transferred to the trust referred to
in (3)(c) above.[2] Shareholders will receive one share of Valero for each share of Coastal
common held at the time of the spin-off. It is this distribution which is at the center of
this litigation between the preferred and common stockholders of Coastal. And
Coastal's dividend history of annual payments to the preferred but none (with one exception) to the common suggests a reason for this. Coastal has paid regular quarterly
dividends of $.2975 per share on the $1.19 Series A and $.4575 per share on the $1.83
Series B since each was issued. Only one dividend of $.075 per share has been paid on
the common in the last twenty years.

Coastal's Board of Directors unanimously approved the settlement and, in August
1978, the Commission gave its approval. The Coastal management then submitted the
plan for approval at a special meeting of its stockholders called for November 10.

Holders of the Series A and Series B preferred stock, (plaintiffs), filed an action in
the Court of Chancery to enjoin the special shareholders meeting. They alleged that the
settlement plan breaches the "Certificate of the Designations, Preferences and Relative,
Participating Optional or other Special Rights" (Certificate) of the Series A and Series B
preferred stock. In essence, plaintiffs say that the plan violates their Certificate rights
because the preferred will not receive any of the Valero shares, that is, the 86.6% to be
distributed entirely to the Coastal common.

After a trial on the merits, the Vice Chancellor entered judgment for defendants and
ordered plaintiffs to pay the costs of giving notice to the members of the class of the
pendency of the action.... The Court determined that the settlement plan and, more
specifically, the spin-off of Producing and the distribution of Valero stock to the common stockholders of Coastal, is not a "recapitalization" within the meaning of the Certificate. (If it is, all parties concede that the preferred is entitled to participate in the
distribution of the Valero shares.) The Vice Chancellor reasoned that a key phrase, "in
lieu of," in the Certificate implies that the existing shares of Coastal common must be
exchanged for something else before there is a "recapitalization" which creates rights in
the preferred. And he found support for that conclusion in another Certificate provision which permits Coastal to pay a dividend to holders of common stock, in other
than its own common, without affecting the rights of the preferred.

The Court also rules that the holders of the preferred stock were not entitled to vote
as a class on the settlement plan, because the requirements of the Certificate for such a
vote had not been met.

Finally, the Court considered plaintiffs' claims that the settlement plan is unfair to
the preferred, unjustly enriched the common and did not have a proper business

---

2. The Valero shares trade on a "when issued" basis at $6.50 to $7.00 per share (against an assumed market value of $6.50 per share).

purpose, and concluded that the rights of the preferred are found, under the circumstances of this case, solely in the Certificate, not in concepts of fairness or fiduciary duty.

On appeal, plaintiffs challenge each of these rulings, as well as the order requiring them to pay the costs of giving notice to the class.

II

* * *

The preferred has a conversion right to exchange for the common on a one-to-one basis. Briefly stated, the preferred argues that a distribution of Valero stock to the common only, and without provision for permitting the preferred to share therein now or at the time of conversion, violates its Certificate rights. We now examine those rights in some detail.

A.

In pertinent part, the Certificate states:

CONVERSION OF ... PREFERRED STOCK INTO COMMON STOCK

(a) Subject to the provisions of this Article..., the holder of record of any ... Preferred Stock shall have the right, at his option, at any time after the issuance of such share(s) to convert each share of ... Preferred Stock into one fully-paid and non-assessable share of Common Stock of the Corporation.

* * *

(c) Conversion of ... Preferred Stock shall be subject to the following additional terms and provisions:

* * *

(4) In the event that the Corporation shall at any time subdivide or combine in a greater or lesser number of shares the outstanding shares of Common Stock, the number of shares of Common Stock issuable upon conversion of the ... Preferred Stock shall be proportionately increased in the case of subdivision or decreased in the case of a combination effective in either case at the close of business on the date when such subdivision or combination shall become effective.

(5) In the event that the Corporation shall be recapitalized, consolidated with or merged into any other corporation, or shall sell or convey to any other corporation all or substantially all of its property as an entirety, provision shall be made as part of the terms of such recapitalization, consolidation, merger, sale or conveyance so that any holder of ... Preferred Stock may thereafter receive in lieu of the Common Stock otherwise issuable to him upon conversion of his ... Preferred Stock, but at the conversion ratio stated in this Article ... which would otherwise be applicable at the time of conversion, the same kind and amount of securities or assets as may be distributable upon such recapitalization, consolidation, merger, sale or conveyance with respect to the Common Stock of the Corporation.

(6) In the event that the Corporation shall at any time pay to the holders of Common Stock a dividend in Common Stock, the number of shares of Common Stock issuable upon conversion of the ... Preferred Stock shall be

proportionately increased, effective at the close of business on the record date for determination of the holders of Common Stock entitled to such dividend.

(7) No adjustment of the conversion ratio shall be made by reason of any declaration or payment to the holders of the Common Stock of the Corporation of a dividend or distribution payable in any property or securities other than Common Stock, any redemption of the Common Stock, any issuance of any securities convertible into Common Stock, or for any other reason, except as expressly provided herein.

(8) The Corporation shall at all times reserve and keep available solely for the purpose of issuance upon conversion of ... Preferred Stock, as herein provided, such number of shares of Common Stock as shall be issuable upon the conversion of all outstanding ... Preferred Stock.

B.

For most purposes, the rights of the preferred shareholders as against the common shareholders are fixed by the contractual terms agreed upon when the class of preferred stock is created.... And, as to the conversion privilege, it has been said that the rights of a preferred shareholder are "least affected by rules of law and most dependent on the share contract." Buxbaum, "Preferred Stock—Law and Draftsmanship," 42 *Cal. L. Rev.* 243, 279 (1954).

Our duty, then, is to construe the contract governing the preferred shares. In so doing, we employ the methods used to interpret contracts generally; that is, we consider the entire instrument and attempt to reconcile all of its provisions "in order to determine the meaning intended to be given to any portion of it." *Ellingwood v. Wolf's Head Oil Refining Co.*, [38 A.2d 743, 747 (Del. 1944)]. More to the point, we must construe the several qualifications of the conversion privilege which are stated in Sections (c)(4)-(7) of the Certificate.

C.

The basic conversion privilege is stated in Section (a) of the Certificate: at the option of the holder, each share of preferred is convertible into one share of common. That is the governing norm, fixing the ratio between the classes. It is the benchmark from which the holder of a preferred share may, at a time of his choice, elect to move from that status to that of a common shareholder. The *right* of the preferred to make the choice is absolute—at least, in contract terms. And the *time* at which the choice may be made is likewise absolute. The *circumstances* under which the choice is made, or may be made, is another matter. The price which the market places upon the respective shares may well be a significant circumstance influencing a decision, to convert or to not convert any given time. In this case, for example, Coastal had not, for some twenty years prior to 1977, paid a dividend on the common stock while the preferred had regularly received the specified dividend. Obviously, the market value of the respective shares reflected that experience. But, assuming silence on the subject in the conversion contract (as here), the preferred has no right to any particular market price ratio between the shares. However, the preferred is ordinarily given (as here) anti-dilution or anti-destruction rights in the conversion contract.

Section (c)(4) in the Coastal Certificate is such an "anti-dilution" clause. It provides for a proportionate change in the conversion ratio in the event of a stock split or a stock combination (that is, a reverse split). In each of those events, the number of outstanding shares of Coastal common would change so, in order to preserve the parity relationship, a proportionate adjustment to the conversion ratio is essential.[4] In brief, (c)(4) prohibits the common from diluting the conversion right by requiring a proportionate adjustment if the number of outstanding shares is increased (and a similar adjustment if there is a decrease resulting from a reverse split).

Section (c)(6) is directed to the same anti-dilution purpose. While (c)(4) applies to subdivisions and combinations (which enlarge or decrease the number of outstanding shares), (c)(6) is directed to a stock dividend, that is, the issuance of Coastal shares to its stockholders as a dividend. That, too, is a circumstance which, by definition, would dilute the prior parity relationship and, to prevent that, the conversion ratio is "proportionately increased" by (c)(6).

Since Coastal is neither splitting nor reverse-splitting its shares, nor distributing them as a dividend, (c)(4) and (6) do not directly apply to this case.

D.

This brings us to (c)(5) which plaintiffs contend is the heart of the matter....

Given the significance of (c)(5) in the dispute, we quote it again, this time omitting the references to consolidations, mergers, sales, and so on, which are not directly germane here. Thus:

> "In the event that the Corporation shall be recapitalized,..., provision shall be made as part of the terms of such recapitalization, ... so that any holder of ... Preferred Stock may thereafter receive in lieu of the Common Stock otherwise issuable to him upon conversion of his ... Preferred Stock, but at the conversion ratio stated in this Article ... which would otherwise be applicable at the time of conversion, the same kind and amount of securities or assets as may be distributable upon such recapitalization, ... with respect to the Common Stock of the Corporation."

After noting that the "recapitalization" has no generally accepted meaning in law or accounting, the Vice Chancellor focused on the phrase, "in lieu of," as it appears in (c)(5) and concluded that, before the Section becomes applicable, the "Common Shares of Coastal must cease to exist and something (must) be given in lieu of them." Since the Coastal shares will continue in being after the spin-off, he concluded that the plan is not a recapitalization within the meaning of the Certificate.

Plaintiffs contend that Section (c)(5) is the key to analysis of the Certificate. They say that the settlement plan constitutes a "recapitalization" of the Coastal, which triggers the adjustment called for in that section.

Relying on the significant changes which the plan will effect in Coastal's capital structure, plaintiffs argue that there will be a recapitalization in fact and law.

Section (c)(5) contains what is typically considered to be "anti-destruction" language. See *Buxbaum, supra* at 287. Transactions listed therein—a merger or consolidation, for example—are the kind of events that will not merely dilute the conversion privilege by altering the number of shares of common but, rather, may destroy

---

4. For example: if the Coastal common were split three for one, the number of outstanding shares would be tripled and, upon conversion thereafter, a preferred stockholder would be entitled to receive three shares of common for each share of preferred surrendered.

the conversion privilege by eliminating the stock into which a preferred share is convertible. We focus, however, on the preferred's claim of right if Coastal "shall be recapitalized."

At trial, both sides offered the testimony of experts as to what "recapitalization" means. Professor Sametz noted that there is not a precise or specific definition, but the term implies a "fundamental realignment of relationships amongst a company's securities" or a "reshuffling of the capital structure." ...

The parties have also cited cases from other jurisdictions, but we are not persuaded that such cases considered language reasonably comparable to that at issue here; so they are of little help. And the same is true of general financial terminology. The point is that we must decide the controversy under the facts in this case and, for present purposes, that means the Certificate language.

We agree with plaintiffs that the changes which the plan will bring to Coastal's financial structure are enormous. And it may be concluded that, collectively, these amount to a "reshuffling of the capital structure" under the general definition to which Professor Sametz testified. But that is not the test. The critical question concerns what is said in the contract.

Section (c)(5) provides that in the event of "recapitalization" one of the provisions shall be that a holder of preferred may "thereafter" receive—something. *When* he may receive it is clear: he may receive it "upon conversion" after the recapitalization has taken place. After that event, he may receive, not what he would have received *before* recapitalization; that was the common stock which was "otherwise issuable to him upon conversion." Certainly this clause is meaningless if the common share remains issuable to him *after* recapitalization. And so is the remainder of the paragraph which requires that the same conversion ratio be retained by distributing to the preferred, upon conversion, the "same kind and amount of securities or assets as may be distributable upon said recapitalization ... with respect to the Common." The "same kind and amount" would be distributable to the common only if the common had been exchanged for something else. This was the situation the draftsman contemplated by the provision that the preferred "may receive" the "same kind and amount" of property "in lieu of the Common Stock."

Since the settlement plan does not include an exchange of the common and, given the added circumstances that the dividend or liquidated [sic] preference of the preferred is not threatened and that earned surplus is ample to support the distribution of the Valero shares to the common, the settlement plan does not include a recapitalization within the meaning of Section (c)(5).

E.

We turn now to (c)(7) which, we think, is related to what is said in (c)(5) and our construction of it; (c)(7) states:

> "No adjustment of the conversion ratio shall be made by reason of any declaration or payment to the holders of the Common Stock of the Corporation of a dividend or distribution payable in any property or securities other than Common Stock, any redemption of the Common Stock, any issuance of any securities convertible into Common Stock, or for any other reason, except as expressly provided herein."

This section, plainly and clearly, lists transactions which do not call for an adjustment to the conversion ratio. Thus an adjustment is not made for:

(1) a dividend payable to holders of the common in property other than Coastal common,

(2) a redemption of the common,

(3) an issuance of securities convertible into common,

(4) "any other reason."

Section (c)(7) concludes with the phrase, "except as expressly provided herein," which creates an ambiguity that must be resolved.

Plaintiffs contend that the phrase relates to all of Section (c), including (c)(5), and thus if a property dividend (the Valero stock) is regarded as a "recapitalization," the latter section controls. It is somewhat difficult to follow that argument but, as we understand it, plaintiffs contend that (c)(7) does not apply here.

In our opinion, the phrase, "except as expressly provided herein," refers to those paragraphs of Section (c) which "expressly ... [provide]" for a change in the conversion ratio. In so doing, the phrase does modify the preceding phrase, "any other reason" (which is all-encompassing). But the transactions referred to are those in (c)(4) and (c)(6), and thus they are the exceptions "expressly [provided]" for. There are no exceptions provided for in (c)(7) and, therefore, the phrase would be meaningless if it were construed as applying to (c)(7).

Section (c)(7) states flatly that an adjustment shall not be made in the conversion ratio in the event any of the three specified events occurs: a dividend in property other than Coastal common, a redemption of the common or the issue of securities convertible into common. And the three specifics are enlarged by the general reference to "any other reason." Given what we believe to be mandatory language ("[n]o adjustment ... shall be made") prohibiting a change in the conversion ratio, we conclude that such a change may be made only if it is "expressly provided" in Section (c), and, as we have said, that means by the anti-dilution provisions of (c)(4) and (c)(6), i.e., by a stock split, reverse split or a stock dividend. It is only in those paragraphs that provisions are found for an *adjustment* in the conversion ratio.[8] Section (c)(5), on the other hand, is not directed merely to an adjustment in the exchange ratio; it is directed toward maintaining parity between the common and the preferred after a specified event has occurred: thus a conversion after recapitalization, merger or consolidation shall be "at the conversion ratio stated in this Article." The "conversion ratio" referred to here is the parity referred to throughout the Article (i.e., the Certificate).[9]

But even if one were to find some inconsistency or contradiction between (c)(5) and (c)(7), then, under familiar and well-settled rules of construction, the specific language of (c)(7) (as applied to the Valero stock) controls over any general language in (c)(5) regarding recapitalization....

F.

We have reviewed Sections (c)(4) through (c)(7) independently but failed to find therein any merit to the contentions which plaintiffs argue. And considering the paragraphs together, *Ellingwood v. Wolf's Head Oil Refining Co., supra*, confirms our conclusion. So viewed, the basic scheme is that parity between the common and preferred is

---

8. The adjustment called for is an increase or decrease, as the case may be, of the number of shares of common to be received for each share of preferred which is converted.

9. Assuming Section (c)(5) could possibly be interpreted to contemplate an adjustment of the conversion ratio, none would be appropriate under our view of these facts since we have concluded that the settlement plan here does not include a recapitalization within the meaning of Section (c)(5).

maintained through any changes in the number of outstanding shares which are unaccompanied by other balance sheet changes: thus a stock split, reverse split or stock dividend changes only the *number of shares* outstanding without any change in corporate assets. Sections (c)(4) and (c)(6) provide for continuing parity by making the appropriate adjustment to the conversion ratio (that is, what will be given for one share of preferred) in such instance. But it appears that a reduction in *assets* by distribution to the common may be made without adjustment to that exchange basis. Thus a cash dividend is permissible under (c)(7), or other corporate assets (stock in a listed company, for example) may be distributed under that paragraph. And if the distribution of assets is in the form of a redemption of the common, that, too, is permissible. In short, dividends and other distribution [sic] of corporate assets are permissible without change in the exchange basis. Speaking generally, such distributions are the ordinary and permissible way in which the holders of common stock share in the earnings of the enterprise. In saying this, we emphasize once more that there is not a charge here that the liquidation preference or the dividend of the preferred is in any way threatened. Nor is fraud involved.

* * *

In summary, we conclude that a distribution of the Valero stock to the holders of the coastal [sic] common is permissible under Section (c)(7) and may be made without adjustment to the conversion ratio; such distribution is not a recapitalization under Section (c)(5).

* * *

IV

Plaintiffs also argue that the settlement plan unjustly enriches the common shareholders at the expense of the preferred shareholders.

There is no contention that Coastal is in arrears on dividends payable to the preferred, nor is the Company in the process of dissolution.[12] After the plan is implemented Coastal will have (according to the pro forma statements) assets of more than $2.2 billion and a net worth of $477 million. But the significant fact is not what Coastal retains nor the extent of the "reshuffling." Any right of the preferred to participate in the Valero distribution must come from the Certificate. Because the contract is the measure of plaintiffs' right, there can be no recovery under an unjust enrichment theory independent of it.

* * *

Affirmed.

Notes and Questions

1. Notwithstanding the court's interpretation of the preferred stock contract, assume that Coastal's board had decided to adjust the preferred's conversion price. If a common

---

12. During oral argument, in response to an inquiry by the Court, plaintiffs acknowledged that after the spin-off of Valero, the preferred would, for balance sheet purposes, be in essentially the same position as before the spin-off. [*Cf.* Anadarko Petroleum Co. v. Panhandle Eastern Co., *infra* at chapter 8, section 4c.—Eds.] We emphasize that plaintiffs do not argue that the plan is in any way fraudulent to them, nor do they say that it jeopardizes their dividend payments or liquidation preferences.

shareholder brought an action against the board for breach of fiduciary duty, what would the result be? Would the action properly be direct or derivative?

2. The court describes the conflict in *Wood* as "entirely between the owners of Coastal's preferred stock and the owners of its common stock." Is this technically correct? What difference does it make?

3. If you represented the preferred stockholders, how would you have argued the case?

4. Notice the contractual evolution that occurred between *Wood* (decided in 1979) and *HB Korenvaes Investments* (decided in 1993), *supra* at section 3b(ii)(C). What specific language in the preferred stock contract involved in *HB Korenvaes Investments* was lacking in the contract involved in *Wood*?

5. In Lohnes v. Level 3 Comm., Inc., 272 F.3d 49 (1st Cir. 2001), plaintiff held a warrant for shares in Level 3 Communications, Inc. (Level 3). The warrant contained a two-paragraph antidilution provision which, upon the occurrence of certain described events, automatically adjusted the number of shares to which the warrantholder would be entitled upon exercise of the warrant. Share adjustments were triggered by the following five separate contingencies, none of which were defined: capital reorganization; reclassification of common stock; merger; consolidation; and sale of all or substantially all the capital stock or assets of Level 3. Conspicuously missing, however, was language covering stock splits.

Later, Level 3 conducted a two-for-one-stock split which was effected in the form of a stock dividend granting shareholders one new share of stock for each share held. After plaintiff's inquiry as to whether the share adjustment provision in the warrant had been triggered was answered in the negative, plaintiff exercised his warrant and sued for breach of the warrant contract. Plaintiff's contention was that the stock split implemented as a stock dividend constituted either a "capital reorganization" or a "reclassification of stock." In justifying its rejection of plaintiff's contention, the First Circuit responded:

> [Does] a stock split entail[] a "substantial change in [a corporation's] capital structure["?] We think not.
>
> First and foremost, the accounting mechanics that accompany a stock split are mere window dressing.... To be sure, a stock split effected through the distribution of shares in the form of a stock dividend results in an increase in the common stock at par account and an offsetting decrease in additional paid-in capital, ... but this subtle set of entries has no effect on the total shareholder equity or on any other substantive aspect of the balance sheet.... Because a stock split does not entail a substantial change in a corporation's capital structure, the unelaborated term "capital reorganization" cannot plausibly include a stock split effected as a stock dividend.

* * *

> We turn next to the phrase "reclassification of stock." ...

* * *

> [T]he sine qua non of a reclassification of stock is the modification of existing shares into something fundamentally different.... [There are] two ways in which a security can be altered fundamentally: (a) by changing the class of stock, or (b) by modifying important rights or preferences linked to stock.
>
> Stock splits effected by stock dividends do not entail any such fundamental alteration of the character of an existing security. For example, Level 3's stock

split in no way altered its shareholders' proportionate ownership interest, varied the class of securities held, or revised any of the attributes associated with the stock. What is more, the stock split did not have a meaningful impact on either the corporation's balance sheet or capital structure. For those reasons, we perceive no principled basis on which to stretch the definition of "reclassification of stock" to encompass a stock split.

* * *

The appellant also makes a conclusory claim that the July 1998 stock split was part and parcel of a comprehensive corporate reorganization (and, thus, animated the warrant's antidilution provision)....

* * *

We reject the appellant's intimation that the stock split is magically transformed into a capital reorganization of stock based upon its inclusion in a long-term business plan that also contains a number of more complex financial maneuvers. Taken to its logical extreme, the appellant's argument invites us to deem any corporate activity engaged in by Level 3 while in the midst of reorganizing its capital structure as a capital reorganization and reclassification of stock. We are unable to perceive any principled basis on which we could accept this invitation.

Id. at 56-59.

6. In the antidestruction context, are convertible securityholders entitled to appraisal rights if the merger in question entitled common stockholders to those rights? Or are they only entitled to the merger consideration received by the common stockholders as per the antidestruction clause? In Aspen Advisors LLC v. United Artists Theatre Co., 861 A.2d 1251 (Del. 2005), the plaintiff warrantholders believed the common stock of United Artists was worth more than the merger consideration being offered. Because the common stockholders were entitled to appraisal rights, the plaintiffs sued for those rights in the hopes of receiving the "fair value" for the stock underlying their warrants rather than the merger consideration. The Delaware Supreme Court, however, denied their request:

[T]he plaintiffs in this case argue that they are entitled to an award of "fair value" as judicially determined through a quasi-appraisal right analogous to a [Del. Gen. Corp. Law] Section 262 proceeding.

In support of that argument, the plaintiffs submit that this Court should draw from our decision in [Continental Airlines Corp. v. American General Corp., 575 A.2d 1160 (Del. 1990),] a "broad lesson which is that warrantholders who are entitled to receive the same *merger consideration* as common stockholders are thereby guaranteed *all* the *rights (contractual, statutory or common law)* that would have belonged to them had they actually converted their warrants into common stock before the merger." Accordingly, the plaintiffs content that, because the statutory right to receive "fair value" through an appraisal proceeding was received by common stockholders of United Artists in connection with the Merger, they have the right to receive "fair value" for their Warrants via a quasi appraisal proceeding....

* * *

A warrantholder is not a stockholder. Warrantholders have paid for an option. They have a choice: whether to take an investment risk or not. A warrantholder only becomes a shareholder by investing something of value that meets the exercise terms of the warrant....

A warrantholder is only entitled to the rights of a shareholder—including statutory appraisal rights—after they make an investment in the corporation in accordance with the terms of the warrant and thereby expose themselves to the risks that are incident to stock ownership.... These Warrantholders did not take that economic risk. Therefore, the Court of Chancery properly determined that the Warrantholders "relegated themselves to the protections afforded them by the Warrants," which "do not include a silent, interstitial right to a remedy akin to statutory appraisal, but lacking the key trade-off inherent in that legislative remedy, the required eschewal of the merger consideration."

Id. at 1262-64.

Problem—Interpreting the Convertible Debenture Contract

Your client, I. M. Litigious, comes to you with a sad story. Litigious owns $10,000 in face value of convertible subordinated debentures ("debentures") issued by Colonial Corp. ("Colonial"). The debentures are convertible into Colonial common stock at $48 per share. When the debentures were issued in 1988, Colonial's stock was trading at $42. The next year, the market price had dropped to $9. Two years ago the stock was trading at $20. A month later, Independence Acquisition Corp. ("Independence"), owned by several members of Colonial's management, entered into a merger agreement with Colonial pursuant to which each Colonial stockholder could exchange her Colonial shares for $27 per share in cash. Following this exchange Independence would be merged into Colonial and each share of Independence stock would be exchanged for one share of Colonial stock. Although each debentureholder was given a chance to convert prior to the merger, none took advantage of this opportunity since the trading price of the debentures exceeded the value upon conversion. The debentureholders were informed that, following the merger, their debentures would remain convertible into Colonial common stock. In order to finance the merger, Independence caused Colonial to assume $1 billion in additional debt, which apparently has not affected the trading price of the debentures.

Litigious is unhappy, and would like to find a way to improve his financial position. The only provision of the indenture that you can find to suggest a cause of action is section 4.05(c) which provides as follows:

In case the company shall ... distribute to all holders of shares of its Common Stock evidences of its indebtedness or securities or assets (excluding cash dividends or cash distributions payable out of consolidated net income or retained earnings of the Company and its consolidated Subsidiaries, or dividends payable in shares of Common Stock) or rights to subscribe therefor ... the conversion price in effect immediately prior to such distribution shall be adjusted.... Such adjustment shall become effective on the date of such distribution retroactively to immediately after the opening of business on the day following the record date for the determination of shareholders entitled to receive such distribution....

Section 4.06 of the indenture provides:

In case of any reclassification or change of outstanding shares of Common Stock deliverable upon conversion of the Debentures (other than a change in par value or from par value to no par value, or from no par value to par value, or as a result of a subdivision or combination), or in case of any consolidation of the Company with one or more other corporations (other than a consolidation in which the Company is the continuing corporation and which does not result in any reclassification or change of outstanding shares of Common Stock issuable upon conversion of the Debentures), or in case of the merger of the Company into another corporation, or in case of any sale or conveyance to another corporation of the property of the Company as an entirety or substantially as an entirety, the Company, or such successor or purchasing corporation, as the case may be, shall execute with the Trustee a supplemental indenture (which shall conform to the Trust Indenture Act of 1939 as in force at the date of the execution of such supplemental indenture) providing that the holder of each Debenture then outstanding shall have ... the right to convert such Debenture into the kind and amount of shares of stock or other securities and property, including cash, receivable upon such reclassification, change, consolidation, merger, sale or conveyance by a holder of the number of shares of Common Stock into which such Debenture might have been converted immediately prior to such reclassification, change, consolidation, merger, sale or conveyance.

Against your better judgment you have agreed to take the case. Write a memorandum to Litigious (i) outlining the arguments you intend to make, and (ii) evaluating the likelihood of their success.

(iv) Contractual Example

The following is an example of typical language used to protect the bargain of convertible securityholders with respect to their conversion rights. Although the provisions are designed for convertible debt securities, substantially similar provisions would be set forth in a certificate of designation for convertible preferred stock.

Revised Model Simplified Indenture[a]

55 Bus. Law. 1115 (2000)

* * *

ARTICLE 10

CONVERSION

Section 10.01. **Conversion Right and Conversion Price.**

A Holder of a Security may convert it into Common Stock at any time during the period stated in paragraph 9 of the Securities. The number of shares issuable upon conversion of a Security is determined as follows: Divide the Principal amount to be converted by the conversion price in effect on the conversion date. Round the result to the nearest 1/100th of a share.

The initial conversion price is stated in paragraph 9 of the Securities. The conversion price is subject to adjustment in accordance with this Article.

A Holder may convert a portion of a Security if the portion is $1000 or a whole multiple of $1000. Provisions of this Indenture that apply to conversion of all of a Security also apply to conversion of a portion of it.

"Common Stock" means the Common Stock of the Company as such Common Stock exists on the date of this Indenture.

* * *

Section 10.03. Fractional Shares.

The Company shall not issue a fractional share of Common Stock upon conversion of a Security. Instead, the Company shall deliver a check for an amount equal to the current market value of the fractional share. The current market value of a fraction of a share shall be determined as follows: Multiply the current market price of a full share by the fraction. Round the result to the nearest cent.

The current market price of a share of Common Stock for purposes of this Section 10.03 shall be the Quoted Price of the Common Stock on the last trading day prior to the conversion date. In the absence of such a quotation, the Board shall determine the current market price in good faith on the basis of such information as it considers reasonably appropriate.

* * *

Section 10.05. Company to Reserve Common Stock.

The Company shall at all times reserve out of its authorized but unissued Common Stock or its Common Stock held in treasury enough shares of Common Stock to permit the conversion of the Securities.

All shares of Common Stock issued upon conversion of the Securities shall be fully paid and non-assessable and free of any preemptive or other similar rights.

The Company shall endeavor to comply with all securities laws regulating the offer and delivery of shares of Common Stock upon conversion of Securities and shall endeavor to list such shares on each national securities exchange on which the Common Stock is listed.

Section 10.06. Adjustment for Change in Capital Stock.

If the Company:

(1) pays a dividend or makes a distribution on its Common Stock in shares of its Common Stock;

(2) subdivides its outstanding shares of Common Stock into a greater number of shares;

(3) combines its outstanding shares of Common Stock into a smaller number of shares;

(4) makes a distribution on its Common Stock in shares of its capital stock other than Common Stock; or

(5) issues by reclassification of its Common Stock any shares of its capital stock, then the conversion privilege and the conversion price in effect immediately prior to such action shall be proportionately adjusted so that the Holder of a Security thereafter converted may receive the aggregate number and kind of shares of capital stock of the Company that the Holder would have owned immediately following such action if the Security had converted immediately prior to such action.

Each adjustment contemplated by this Section 10.06 shall become effective immediately after the record date in the case of a dividend or distribution and immediately after the effective date in the case of a subdivision, combination or reclassification.

If after an adjustment a Holder of a Security upon conversion of it may receive shares of two or more classes of capital stock of the Company, the Board, acting in good faith, shall determine the allocation of the adjusted conversion price among the classes of capital stock. After such allocation, the conversion privilege and the conversion price of each class of capital stock shall thereafter be subject to adjustment on terms comparable to those applicable to Common Stock in this Article. The term "Common Stock" shall thereafter apply to each class of capital stock and the Company shall enter into such supplemental Indenture, if any, as may be necessary to reflect such conversion privilege and conversion price.

The adjustment contemplated by this Section 10.06 shall be made successively whenever any of the events listed above shall occur.

Section 10.07. Adjustment for Rights Issue.

If the Company distributes any rights, options or warrants to all holders of its Common Stock entitling them for a period expiring within 60 days after the record date mentioned below to subscribe for or purchase shares of Common Stock at a price per share less than the current market price per share on that record date, the conversion price shall be adjusted in accordance with the following formula:

$$C' = C \times ((O + N \times P / M) / (O + N))$$

where:

C' = the adjusted conversion price.

C = the current conversion price.

O = the number of shares of Common Stock outstanding on the record date.

N = the number of additional shares of Common Stock subject to such rights, options or warrants.

P = the offering price per share of the additional shares.

M = the current market price per share of Common Stock on the record date.

The adjustment contemplated by this Section 10.07 shall be made successively whenever any such rights, options or warrants are issued and shall become effective immediately after the record date for the determination of stockholders entitled to receive the rights, options or warrants. If at the end of the period during which such rights, options or warrants are exercisable, not all rights, options or warrants shall have been exercised, the conversion price shall immediately be readjusted to what it would have been if "N" in the above formula had been the number of shares actually issued.

Section 10.08. Adjustment for Other Distributions.

If the Company distributes to all holders of its Common Stock any of its assets (including, but not limited to, cash), debt securities or other securities or any rights, options or warrants to purchase assets, debt securities or other securities of the Company, the conversion price shall be adjusted in accordance with the following formula:

$$C' = C \times (M - F) / M$$

where:

    C' = the adjusted conversion price.

    C = the current conversion price.

    M = the current market price per share of Common Stock on the record date mentioned below.

    F = the fair market value on the record date of the assets, securities, rights, options or warrants applicable to one share of Common Stock. Fair market value shall be determined in good faith by the Board, *provided* that the Company shall obtain an appraisal or other valuation opinion in support of the Board's determination from an investment bank or accounting firm of recognized national standing if the aggregate fair market value exceeds $[X] million.

The adjustment contemplated by this Section 10.08 shall be made successively whenever any such distribution is made and shall become effective immediately after the record date for the determination of stockholders entitled to receive the distribution.

This Section 10.08 does not apply to cash dividends or cash distributions paid in any fiscal year out of consolidated net income of the Company for the current fiscal year or the prior fiscal year, as shown on the books of the Company prepared in accordance with generally accepted accounting principles. Also, this Section does not apply to rights, options or warrants referred to in Section 10.07.

Section 10.09. Adjustment for Common Stock Issue.

If the Company issues shares of Common Stock for a consideration per share less than the current market price per share on the date the Company fixes the offering price of such additional shares, the conversion price shall be adjusted in accordance with the following formula:

$$C' = C \times (O + P/M)/A$$

where:

    C' = the adjusted conversion price.

    C = the current conversion price.

    O = the number of shares of Common Stock outstanding on the record date.

    P = the aggregate consideration received for the issuance of such additional shares.

    M = the current market price per share of Common Stock on the record date.

    A = the number of shares of Common Stock outstanding immediately after the issuance of such additional shares.

The adjustment contemplated by this Section 10.09 shall be made successively whenever any such issuance is made and shall become effective immediately after the record date for the determination of stockholders entitled to receive such additional shares of Common Stock.

This Section 10.09 shall not apply to:

    (1) any of the transactions described in Sections 10.07 and 10.08;

    (2) the conversion of the Securities or the conversion or exchange of other securities convertible into or exchangeable for Common Stock;

    (3) the issuance of Common Stock upon the exercise of rights, options or warrants issued to the holders of Common Stock;

(4) the issuance of Common Stock to the Company's employees under bona fide employee benefit plans adopted by the Board, and approved by the holders of Common Stock when required by law, but only to the extent that the aggregate number of shares excluded by this clause (3) and issued after the date of this Indenture shall not exceed 5% of the Common Stock outstanding as of the date of this Indenture;

(5) the issuance of Common Stock to stockholders of any Person that merges into the Company in proportion to their stock holdings of such Person immediately prior to such merger, upon such merger;

(6) the issuance of Common Stock in a bona fide public offering pursuant to a firm commitment underwriting; or

(7) the issuance of Common Stock in a bona fide private placement through a placement agent that is a member firm of the National Association of Securities Dealers, Inc. (except to the extent that any discount from the current market price shall exceed 20% of the then current market price).

Section 10.10. Adjustment for Convertible Securities Issue.

If the Company issues any securities, rights, options or warrants convertible into or exchangeable for Common Stock (other than the Securities or securities issued in transactions described in Sections 10.07, 10.08 and 10.09) for a consideration per share of Common Stock initially deliverable upon conversion or exchange of such securities less than the current market price per share on the date of issuance of such securities, the conversion price shall be adjusted in accordance with the following formula:

$$C' = C \times (O + P / M) / (O + D)$$

where:

C' = the adjusted conversion price.
C = the current conversion price.
O = the number of shares of Common Stock outstanding on the record date.
P = the aggregate consideration received for the issuance of such securities.
M = the current market price per share of Common Stock on the record date.
D = the maximum number of shares of Common Stock deliverable upon conversion or exchange of such securities at the initial conversion or exchange rate.

The adjustment contemplated by this Section 10.10 shall be made successively whenever any such issuance is made and shall become effective immediately after the record date for the determination of stockholders entitled to receive such securities, rights, options or warrants. If at the end of the period during which such securities, rights, options or warrants are convertible into or exchangeable for Common Stock, not all such securities, rights, options or warrants shall have been so converted or exchanged, the conversion price shall immediately be readjusted to what it would have been if "D" in the above formula had been the number of shares actually issued upon conversion or exchange.

This Section 10.10 shall not apply to:

(1) the issuance of convertible securities to stockholders of any Person that merges into the Company, or with a subsidiary of the Company, in proportion to their stock holdings of such Person immediately prior to such merger, upon such merger;

(2) the issuance of convertible securities in a bona fide public offering pursuant to a firm commitment underwriting; or

(3) the issuance of convertible securities in a bona fide private placement through a placement agent that is a member firm of the National Association of Securities Dealers, Inc. (except to the extent that any discount from the current market price shall exceed 20% of the then current market price).

Section 10.11. Current Market Price.

In Sections 10.07, 10.08, 10.09 and 10.10, the current market price per share of Common Stock on any date shall be the average of the Quoted Prices of the Common Stock for the five consecutive trading days selected by the Company commencing not more than 20 trading days before, and ending not later than, the earlier of (i) the date of such determination and (ii) the day before the "ex" date with respect to the issuance or distribution requiring such computation. The "Quoted Price" of a security shall be the last reported sales price of such security as reported by the New York Stock Exchange or, if the security is listed on another securities exchange, the last reported sales price of such security on such exchange which shall be for consolidated trading if applicable to such exchange, or as reported by the Nasdaq National Market System, or, if the security is neither so reported nor listed, the last reported bid price of the security. In the absence of one or more such quotations, the current market price shall be determined in good faith by the Board on the basis of such quotations as it considers reasonably appropriate. For the purposes of this Section 10.11, the term "ex" date, when used with respect to any issuance or distribution, shall mean the first date on which the security trades on such exchange or in such market without the right to receive such issuance or distribution.

Section 10.12. When De Minimis Adjustment May Be Deferred.

No adjustment in the conversion price need be made unless the adjustment would require an increase or decrease of at least 1% in the conversion price. All calculations under this Article shall be made to the nearest cent or to the nearest 1/100th of a share, as the case may be. Any adjustments that are not made shall be carried forward and taken into account in any subsequent adjustment.

Section 10.13. When No Adjustment Required.

No adjustment need be made for a transaction referred to in Sections 10.06, 10.07, 10.08, 10.09 or 10.10 if Securityholders are permitted to participate in the transaction on a basis and with notice that the Board determines to be fair and appropriate in light of the basis and notice on which holders of Common Stock are permitted to participate in the transaction.

No adjustments need be made for rights to purchase Common Stock pursuant to a Company plan for reinvestment of dividends or interest.

No adjustment need be made for a change in the par value or no par value of the Common Stock.

To the extent the Securities become convertible into cash, no adjustment need be made thereafter as to the cash. Interest will not accrue on the cash.

Section 10.14. Notice of Adjustment.

Whenever the conversion price is adjusted, the Company shall promptly mail to Securityholders a notice of the adjustment. The Company shall file with the Trustee a certificate from the Company's independent public accountants briefly stating the facts requiring the adjustment and the manner of computing it. The certificate shall be conclusive evidence that the adjustment is correct, absent mathematical error.

Section 10.15. Voluntary Reduction.

The Company may from time to time reduce the conversion price by any amount for any period of time if the period is at least 20 days and if the reduction is irrevocable during the period; provided, however, that in no event may the conversion price be less than the par value of a share of Common Stock.

Whenever the conversion price is reduced, the Company shall mail to Securityholders a notice of the reduction. The Company shall mail the notice at least 15 days before the date the reduced conversion price takes effect. The notice shall state the reduced conversion price and the period it will be in effect.

A reduction of the conversion price does not change or adjust the conversion price otherwise in effect for purposes of Sections 10.06 through 10.10.

Section 10.16. Notice of Certain Transactions.

If:

(1) the Company takes any action that would require an adjustment in the conversion price pursuant to Section 10.06, 10.07, 10.08, 10.09 or 10.10 and if the Company does not permit Securityholders to participate pursuant to Section 10.13;

(2) the Company takes any action that would require a supplemental indenture pursuant to Section 10.17; or

(3) there is a liquidation or dissolution of the Company,

the Company shall mail to Securityholders a notice stating the proposed record date for a dividend or distribution or the proposed effective date of a subdivision, combination, reclassification, consolidation, merger, transfer, lease, liquidation or dissolution. The Company shall mail the notice at least 20 days before such date. Failure to mail the notice or any defect in it shall not affect the validity of the transaction.

Section 10.17. Reorganization of the Company.

If the Company is a party to a transaction subject to Section 5.01 or a merger that reclassifies or changes its outstanding Common Stock, the Person obligated to deliver securities, cash or other assets upon conversion of Securities shall enter into a supplemental indenture. If the issuer of securities deliverable upon conversion of Securities is an Affiliate of the surviving or transferee corporation, such issuer shall join in the supplemental indenture.

The supplemental indenture shall provide that the Holder of a Security may convert it into the kind and amount of securities, cash or other assets that such holder would have owned immediately after the consolidation, merger or transfer if the Security had been converted immediately before the effective date of the transaction. The supplemental indenture shall provide for adjustments that are as nearly equivalent as practicable to the adjustments provided for in this Article. The successor Company shall mail to Securityholders a notice briefly describing the supplemental indenture.

[If this Section 10.17 applies, Section 10.06 does not apply.]

Section 10.18. Company Determination Final.

Any determination that the Company or the Board must make pursuant to Section 10.03, 10.06, 10.07, 10.08, 10.09, 10.10, 10.11 or 10.13 is conclusive, absent mathematical error. Not later than the date of making any such determination pursuant to Section 10.06, 10.07, 10.08, 10.09, 10.10, 10.11 or 10.13, the Company shall deliver to the Trustee an Officers' Certificate stating the basis upon which such determination was made and, if pursuant to Section 10.06, 10.07, 10.08, 10.09 or 10.10, the calculations by which adjustments under such Sections were made.

* * *

[Commentary]

Section 10.01

1. *Conversion Privilege.* The conversion privilege in the Model Simplified Indenture is similar to that in other indentures: the Principal amount of the Securities is divided by the conversion price in effect on the conversion date, and the conversion price is subject to adjustment. A Security may be converted only in whole multiples of $1000 and into whole shares of Common Stock.

* * *

Section 10.03

1. *Registration of Conversion.* The conversion of debt into equity is exempt from registration under Section 3(a)(9) of the Securities Act, provided the conversion of the debt is exchanged exclusively for another security (such as Common Stock). It is well-established that the Section 3(a)(9) exemption still is available where cash is paid in lieu of fractional shares.... Note, however, that the further disposition of the equity by the Securityholder receiving such equity on conversion may well have to be registered....

2. "Quoted Price." Note the definition of "Quoted Price" in Section 10.11.

Section 10.05

1. *Compliance with Applicable Law and Listing Requirements.* Some indentures allow the Company to prohibit conversions, or at least to postpone delivery of the securities issuable on conversion, if registration or listing requirements are not met. The Model Simplified Indenture, like the [American Bar Foundation's] Indenture Commentaries (at 556), omits any such specific prohibition, and the implication is to the contrary. The parties may negotiate this provision to require either "best efforts" or another standard rather than "endeavor."

Section 10.06

1. *Allocation of Adjustments Among Separate Classes of Securities Issuable Upon Conversion.* The Model Simplified Indenture specifies that, if more than one class of capital stock is issuable upon conversion, adjustment of each class must be effected separately.

2. *Effect of Recapitalization.* The definition of "Common Stock", set forth in Section 10.01, is the Common Stock of the issuer on the date of the Indenture. Nonetheless, Section 10.06 makes clear that after an adjustment which changes the "Common Stock" to another class of capital stock, further adjustments to that class of capital stock, falls under, and are to result in the same adjustments contained in Article 10, as if that capital stock were "Common Stock." See Kaiser Aluminum Corp. v. Matheson, 681 A.2d

392, 396-97 (Del. 1996) (conversion provision used with respect to convertible preferred); see also Section 10.17.

Sections 10.07/10.08/10.09/10.10

1. *Algebraic Equations.* Indentures for convertible debt frequently state anti-dilution formulas in words. Consequently, a user must decipher the text to discern the underlying formulas. The Model Simplified Indenture eliminates that step by stating the formulas as algebraic equations.

2. *Anti-Dilution Formulas Generally.* The Model Simplified Indenture deliberately uses the market price adjustment formula prevalent in recent years in public offerings. Selection of any formula is arbitrary, and often a question of bargaining between the parties to the indenture. The formulas appearing in these Sections reflect the following principle: Securityholders receive stated interest and stockholders receive normal dividends; when stockholders are to receive something more, such as an unusual distribution in kind or in cash, the Securityholders' conversion price should be adjusted. Parties to a proposed indenture may, of course, differ on what constitutes an "unusual" distribution. (It should be noted that these formulas do not make provision for adjustment upon the issuance of other convertible securities, cash dividends paid out of consolidated net income from the prior fiscal year, self-tender offers, or the exercise of other conversion rights.) For a justification of market price adjustment formulas, see generally David L. Ratner, Dilution and Anti-Dilution: A Reply to Professor Kaplan, 33 U. CHI. L. REV. 494 (1965-66). Note that many venture capital investors and other purchasers of private securities prefer a "conversion price" based formula (i.e., protection against issuance of Common Stock for less than the conversion price, even if at above the market price) on the theory that in the absence of a bona fide public market, the "market price" is not a meaningful concept and/or take the position that the securityholders should also be treated like Common Stockholders and therefore either "share" in dividends paid or receive a conversion price adjustment. See Note 4 below.

3. *Applicability and Effect of Conversion Formulas.* Section 10.07 sets out the formula for adjustment of the conversion price in the case of a conventional rights offering, where stockholders are issued rights entitling them for a limited period to subscribe for or purchase, pro rata, additional shares at a discount from the then current market price. Section 10.07 also provides for readjustment in the event that not all such rights, options, or warrants shall have been exercised.

Section 10.08 sets out the formula for adjustment in the case of other rights offerings and other distributions. If Section 10.08 rather than Section 10.07 applies to a rights offering, a greater downward adjustment of the conversion price, favorable to the Securityholders and adverse to the Company, may result because the two formulas do not operate in the same way. In a situation in which the Company has distributed substantial assets to its stockholders (for example, the spin-off of a major subsidiary), the application of Section 10.08 may thereafter materially increase the proportion of equity in the remaining company reserved for the Securityholders....

4. *Optional Adjustments to Conversion Price.* Sections 10.09 and 10.10 were not contained in the [American Bar Association's 1983 Model Simplified Indenture ("1983 MSI")]. Section 10.09 sets out the formula for adjustment of the conversion price in the case of a below market price issuance of additional shares of Common Stock and Section 10.10 sets out the formula for adjustment of the conversion price in the case of an issuance of securities, rights, options or warrants convertible into or exchangeable for

Common Stock. Both Sections except certain below market issuances in an effort to define a list of standard exceptions. Negotiation of these exceptions is appropriate. In many cases, below market issuances should only be treated as an adjustment event if the issuance was to an officer, director or affiliate.

5. *Optional Catch-All Provisions.* This form does not purport to include all conversion or adjustment mechanisms that are alive and well in the market. Indentures often contain other adjustment provisions. Set forth below is an example of an optional catch-all adjustment provision that may be appropriate in certain transactions and may properly be the subject of negotiation.

No Dilution or Impairment. (a) If any event shall occur as to which the provisions of this Article 10 are not strictly applicable but the failure to make any adjustment would adversely affect the rights represented by this Indenture and the Securities in accordance with the essential intent and principles of this Article 10, then, in each such case, the Company shall appoint an investment banking firm of recognized national standing, or any other financial expert that does not (or whose directors, officers, employees, affiliates or stockholders do not) have a material direct or indirect financial interest in the Company or any of its subsidiaries, that has not been, and, at the time it is called upon to give independent financial advice to the Company, is not (and none of the directors, officers, employees, affiliates or stockholders of which are not) a promoter, director or officer of the Company or any of its subsidiaries, which investment banking firm shall give its opinion upon the adjustment, if any, that should be implemented in order to preserve, without dilution, the purchase rights represented by this Indenture and the Securities. Upon receipt of such opinion, the Company shall promptly mail a copy thereof to the holders of the Securities and shall make the adjustments described therein and in this Indenture.

(b) The Company shall not, by amendment of its certificate of incorporation or through any consolidation, merger, reorganization, transfer of assets, dissolution, issue or sale of securities or any other voluntary action, avoid or seek to avoid the observance or performance of any of the terms of this Indenture, but will at all times in good faith assist in the carrying out of all such terms and in the taking of all such action as may be necessary or appropriate in order to protect the rights of the holders of the Securities against dilution or other impairment. Without limiting the generality of the foregoing, the Company (1) will take all such action as may be necessary or appropriate in order that the Company may validly and legally issue fully paid and nonassessable shares of Common Stock that are free of preemptive and other similar rights upon the conversion of the Securities from time to time outstanding and (2) will not take any action that would result in an adjustment of the conversion price if the total number of shares of Common Stock issuable after the conversion of all of the Securities would exceed the total number of shares of Common Stock then authorized by the Company's certificate of incorporation and available for the purpose of issue upon such conversion.

* * *

Section 10.11

1. *Determination of Current Market Price.* Section 10.11 sets forth the method and manner of determining the current market price per share of Common Stock for purposes of Sections 10.07, 10.08, 10.09 and 10.10. Section 10.11 provides for an averaging period of the minimum length reasonably required to prevent aberrations and manipulation of the market price, and permits the averaging period to terminate on the record date or, if earlier, the day prior to the "ex" date. This gives the Company the flexibility to deter-

mine a starting date that will produce an acceptable current market price that accurately reflects the value of the issuance or the distribution. Section 10.11 (formerly Section 10.09 in the 1983 MSI) has been revised to prevent a circumstance where the current market price is less than the fair market value of the issuance or distribution, thus resulting in a negative adjusted conversion price, as discussed in Harcourt Brace Jovanovich, Inc. v. Sun Bank National Ass'n, No. 87-3985 (Fla. Cir. Ct. June 5, 1987), available in part in Mutual Shares Corp. et al., Amendment No. 1 to Schedule 13D Concerning Harcourt Brace Jovanovich, Inc. (July 8, 1987). For a further discussion of Harcourt Brace Jovanovich and a review of convertible indenture provisions providing for limitations on downward adjustment of the conversion price below a "reference market price," see generally Martin Riger, A Conversion Paradox: Negative Anti-Dilution, 44 BUS. LAW. 1243 (1989).

2. *Determination Where No Public Market.* In a situation where there is no active public market, the Board of Directors is to determine a current market price in good faith. Additional requirements applicable to such a determination may be appropriate. For example, the Board of Directors may be required to obtain a quotation from specified investment banks or accounting firms (see, e.g., Section 10.08) or to obtain at least a specified number of quotations.

Section 10.13

1. *Participation in Transactions Otherwise Requiring Adjustment.* This Section provides for no adjustment of the conversion price if Securityholders are given notice of and allowed to participate in the transaction that would otherwise result in the adjustment. It is an approach that is different from those discussed in the ABF Indenture Commentaries, and was adapted by the 1983 MSI from institutional instruments and some convertible preferred stock provisions. In any circumstances, the tax implications of such participation will require careful exploration.

2. *Dividend Reinvestment Plans.* A dividend reinvestment plan where new shares are sold by the Company at a discount might be viewed as a continuous rights offering. However, this Section specifies that no adjustment is required for such a plan since, unlike a conventional rights offering, the right to participate in the plan is not transferable and has little or no independent or realizable value.

Section 10.14

1. *Computation of Adjustment.* Like the ABF Indenture Commentaries and the 1983 MSI, the Model Simplified Indenture requires an accountant's computation. Some indentures permit the Company itself to calculate any adjustment in the conversion price. In addition, under the Model Simplified Indenture, when there is an adjustment under Section 10.08 and the aggregate fair market value on the record date of the assets, securities, rights, or warrants being distributed exceeds $[X] million, the Company must obtain an appraisal or other valuation opinion in support of the Board of Directors' determination of fair market value from an investment bank or accounting firm of national standing.

2. *Publication of Notice.* In line with current practice (arising, presumably, from the Boeing case cited in Note 1 to Section 10.16), the Model Simplified Indenture requires notice of conversion price adjustments to be mailed to all Securityholders of record rather than simply to be published. See Note 2 to Section 3.03.

Section 10.15

1. *Voluntary Reduction.* In this Section, the Model Simplified Indenture formalizes, and places limits on, a privilege occasionally utilized by issuers. Notice of the reduc-

tion in the conversion price, and of the period of its effectiveness, must be given to Securityholders.

2. *Applicability; Limitations.* A voluntary, if temporary, reduction in conversion price may be considered by the Company when it desires to stimulate conversions but is unwilling or unable to undergo the optional redemption procedure. It may also be considered in connection with a call for redemption, but in that case the requirement in this Section for a period of at least 20 days could inhibit a multi-step, gradual reduction intended to reduce the conversion price only as far as necessary to induce the desired amount of conversions. For that reason, users may wish to consider deleting the 20-day limitation and reserving the right to make further reductions at any time during a period when a reduced conversion price is in effect.

3. *Relationship to Sections 10.06, 10.07, 10.08, 10.09 and 10.10.* Any reduced conversion price resulting under this Section is not subject to further adjustment, except voluntarily by the Company. The third paragraph of this Section is intended to cause the Company to continue to calculate adjustments from the pre-reduction price, and always to keep in effect the lower of (i) the reduced price, while it is in effect, or (ii) the adjusted pre-reduction price.

Section 10.16

1. *Notices.* The underlying purpose of the notice requirements of Section 10.16 is to afford Securityholders the opportunity to convert and participate in the distribution, combination or liquidation as stockholders rather than to continue to hold their Securities and receive a conversion price adjustment. No notice is required under this Section (i) if the Company elects under Section 10.13 to let Securityholders participate in the transaction, or (ii) if the transaction is so minor that any adjustment may be deferred under Section 10.12; notice is, however, required in the case of a stock dividend or a stock split. The Company may also be subject to notice requirements arising under SEC rules (such as Rules 10b-5 and 10b-17), under stock exchange and NASD policies (see NYSE Listed Co. Manual ¶ 204.12 and NAT'L ASS'N SEC. DEALERS' MANUAL (CCH) 1143-43.2) and under legal and equitable principles of general applicability. See Pittsburgh Terminal Corp. v. Baltimore & Ohio R.R. Co., 680 F.2d 933 (3d Cir. 1982) (failure to notify holders of convertible debentures of a proposed spin-off of shares of subsidiary); Van Gemert v. Boeing Co., 520 F.2d 1373 (2d Cir. 1975) (failure to give adequate notice to holders of convertible debentures in bearer form of call for redemption).... If the Company has prepared a proxy or information statement for stockholders describing the forthcoming transaction, it should consider sending that statement to Securityholders along with the notice required by this Section.

Section 10.17

1. *Triangular Transactions.* The "person obligated to deliver" upon conversion may be the parent of the new obligor upon the remainder of the Company's obligations under the Indenture. See Note 4 to Section 5.01. If the parent is not that "person" but is the issuer of the securities deliverable upon further conversions, the parent is required by the second sentence of this Section to join in the supplemental indenture for the protection of Securityholders.

2. *Cash Mergers.* Conversion into cash is specifically contemplated by this Section. The fourth paragraph of Section 10.13 provides that interest will not be accrued nor will

subsequent adjustments be made after the cash merger date. See also Note 2 to Section 10.01. Note that in a cash merger, the holders of convertible securities lose their potential option premium. In light of the expectation of stock price appreciation, this provision can work an injustice, particularly for securities with a long remaining life.

* * *

Chapter 8

The Rights of Ownership Claimants — Part 1: General Concepts

When we turn to the rights of ownership claimants, here limited to common stockholders, we return to the familiar principle of fiduciary duty as the fabric binding the corporate structure. State corporation statutes rarely resolve the difficult problems that arise within the context of the relationships of power and dependency created by internal corporate structure. Thus, while most such problems stem, in the first instance, from the use (or non-use) of a particular power granted by statute, it is through the application by courts of broad fiduciary principles that disputes are settled. These fiduciary principles are also an important tool of the counselor, seeking to prevent intracorporate disputes from reaching court, facilitating negotiation of the settlement of disputes among participants or the structuring of transactions to avoid legal problems.

Obviously, to say that the application of fiduciary principles resolves these disputes is to say relatively little. Although once applied as a strict prophylactic in corporate law,[1] the tugs of pragmatism and efficiency have diluted their sting such that the principles have spawned a series of sanitizing enabling rules,[2] leaving only limited proscriptions to be applied in traditional equitable fashion. Thus, a complete understanding of fiduciary duty is best developed both abstractly and contextually.

Of course, the fiduciary concept has been borrowed by corporate law from the law of trusts. Thus, the applicability of the principle was determined in conjunction with the traditional understanding of the nature of the corporation. It may well be that different theories of the corporation result in different approaches to fiduciary duty.[3] Even a traditional approach to fiduciary duty might lead to different understandings of the concept in different types of corporations, for example, in close and public corporations.

Finally, fiduciary duty is one of the most moralistic of our legal principles. Contained within the concept is a vision of the way in which society ought to operate. Of course social visions may change, and with them may occur subtle changes in fiduciary ideology. Much of corporate law has been a progression, sometimes conscious and

---

1. Marsh, Are Directors Trustees? — Conflict of Interest and Corporate Reality, 22 Bus. Law 35 (1966).
2. *Id.*; Brudney, Fiduciary Ideology in Transactions Affecting Corporate Control, 65 Mich. L. Rev. 259 (1966); Mitchell, The Death of Fiduciary Duty in Close Corporations, 138 U. Pa. L Rev. 1675 (1990).
3. For an excellent and thought-provoking examination of the nature and meaning of the corporation, see Johnson, The Delaware Judiciary and the Meaning of Corporate Life and Corporate Law, 68 Tex. L. Rev. 865 (1990).

sometimes not, of fiduciary principles from the traditional prophylactic role to more of a remedial device to compensate for fault-based harm.

This chapter begins with some abstract thoughts on the nature and content of fiduciary principles. It then proceeds to examine other general principles applicable to common stockholders in certain contexts. Special issues relating to mergers and acquisitions are addressed separately in chapter 9.

Section 1
The Nature of Fiduciary Duty

Easterbrook & Fischel, Corporate Control Transactions
91 Yale L.J. 698, 700-703 (1982)[a]

1. The Function of Fiduciary Duties

Corporate directors and other managers are said to be fiduciaries, who must behave in certain upright ways toward the beneficiaries of fiduciary duties. Yet, as Justice Frankfurter put it, "to say that a man is a fiduciary only begins analysis; it gives direction to further inquiry. To whom is he a fiduciary? What obligations does he owe as a fiduciary?" In this section we provide a framework for analyzing the meaning and scope of the duty owed by corporate managers.

Fiduciary principles govern agency relationships. An agency relationship is an agreement in which one or more persons (the principal) delegates authority to another person (the agent) to perform some service on the principal's behalf. The entire corporate structure is a web of agency relationships. Investors delegate authority to directors, who subdelegate to upper managers, and so on. Delegation of authority enables skilled managers to run enterprises even though they lack personal wealth, and it enables wealthy people to invest even though they lack managerial skills. It reduces the risks that investors must incur, because it enables them to spread investments among many enterprises. Delegation also helps managers to pool enough capital to take advantage of available economies of scale in production, to reduce the costs of bargaining and contracting, and to obtain the benefits of productive information that must be used in secret or not at all.

Delegation—including the "separation of ownership and control"—exists because both principal and agent share in the benefits of agency relationships. Nonetheless, the interests of agents may diverge from the interests of principals after the delegation has occurred....

This divergence of interests between principals and agents may be controlled by the operation of the employment market....

Although these market mechanisms automatically reduce the divergence of interests between agents and principals, they do not eliminate the costs of the agency rela-

---

a. Reprinted by permission of The Yale Law Journal Company and Fred B. Rothman & Company from *The Yale Law Journal*, Vol. 91, pp. 698-737.

tionship. They do not work without extensive, and costly, monitoring, so that principals and others know how well the agents perform. And the mechanisms may be inadequate to deal with one-time defalcations, when the agent concludes that the opportunities of the moment exceed any subsequent penalties in the employment market....

The fiduciary principle is an alternative to direct monitoring. It replaces prior supervision with deterrence, much as the criminal law uses penalties for bank robbery rather than pat-down searches of everyone entering banks. Acting as a standard-form penalty clause in every agency contract, the elastic contours of the fiduciary principle reflect the difficulty that contracting parties have in anticipating when and how their interests may diverge.

Socially optimal fiduciary rules approximate the bargain that investors and agents would strike if they were able to dicker at no cost. Such rules preserve the gains resulting from the delegation of authority and the division of labor while limiting the ability of agents to further their own interests at the expense of investors. The existence of such "off-the-rack" rules reduces the costs of transacting and of enforcing restrictions on the agent's powers. It also reduces the risk that managers will manipulate the articles of incorporation to their advantage once they assume control.

Fiduciary principles contain anti-theft directives, constraints on conflict of interest, and other restrictions on the ability of managers to line their own pockets at the expense of shareholders. But these principles have limits that reflect the distinction between managerial practices that harm investors' interests and practices that simultaneously benefit managers and investors. For example, managers of a corporation are free to funnel business to another corporation in which they have an interest if the transaction is approved by disinterested directors or is "fair" (advantageous) to the firm.

Because the fiduciary principle is fundamentally a standard term in a contract to which investors are parties, it makes little sense to say that managers may, consistent with the fiduciary principle, sacrifice the interests of investors to other ends, so long as investors are not hurt "too much." Presumably "too much" in this context means "by so much that investors start contracting around the rule." Such re-contracting may be exceedingly costly, however, because once a firm has been established shareholders have no practical way of revising the articles on their own to overcome intervening legal surprises. To use the fiduciary principle for any purpose other than maximizing the welfare of investors subverts its function by turning the high costs of direct monitoring—the reason fiduciary principles are needed—into a shield that prevents investors from controlling their agents' conduct.[5]

---

5. In saying this we do not necessarily rule out arguments that directors owe fiduciary duties to employees and other groups. Under some circumstances employees are investors in the firm; they invest their human capital, to the extent that they become specialists and obtain skills that are less valuable to other employers. Firms recognize this investment with long term contracts, pension plans, severance payments, and other devices for "repaying" human capital once it is withdrawn from the firm. But fiduciary duties to employees, like fiduciary duties to other investors, are implied contractual terms; there is little warrant for manipulating fiduciary principles to override explicit contractual terms or for using them to achieve ends other than the probable result of cost-free bargaining. We need not pursue the point. The corporate control transactions we discuss in this article involve conflicts among shareholders, not divergences of interest between employees and shareholders, consumers and shareholders, or any other conflict.

Mitchell, The Death of Fiduciary Duty in Close Corporations
138 U. Pa. L. Rev. 1675, 1684-87 (1990)[a]

A fiduciary relationship is a relationship of power and dependency in which the dependent party relies upon the power holder to conduct some aspect of a dependent's life over which the power holder has been given and accepted responsibility. The dependent, for a variety of reasons, has limited (or had limited for her) control over one or more aspects of her personal or economic life. The power holder is charged with assuming the power abdicated by (or not granted to) the dependent in the manner she deems will best fulfill her responsibility. The power holder has, in some cases, voluntarily undertaken the responsibilities with which she has been charged. The dependent's reliance upon the power holder or, not quite conversely, the power holder's service as a surrogate for the dependent, characterizes the fiduciary relationship.

The power holder must do for the dependent what the latter cannot, or will not, do for herself. Although this statement, shorn of context-specific labels, describes all economic and many legal relationships, two principal aspects of the fiduciary relationship are distinctive. First, a great deal of discretion is vested in the power holder. Except for the broad requirements of care and loyalty that set the parameters of the power holder's authority (and, in part, define the scope of her duty), the power holder has complete freedom to conduct that segment of the dependent's life over which she has been given responsibility. Second, not only will the power holder have responsibility over a specific aspect of the dependent's life, but in the typical fiduciary relationship, the dependent will be precluded from exercising any control over that area.

These central components of the fiduciary relationship give rise to certain duties. Because the dependent (or a third party intending to benefit the dependent) is the source of the fiduciary's power, and because the relationship permits the power holder to control an aspect of the dependent's life, the power holder is obligated to act in the dependent's interest, and not her own, in exercising that power.

The obligation of the power holder to act in the dependent's best interests suggests an underlying assumption of fiduciary law, that the power holder is *able* to act in the dependent's best interests. Fiduciary principles are based on the assumption that the power holder can put aside any personal interests in a given situation and adopt a course of conduct designed exclusively to serve the best interests of the dependent. These principles are based upon the further assumption that such persons will, in fact, do so. Without these assumptions, the prophylactic function of fiduciary duty becomes impractical, and the enforcement of fiduciary duties is doomed to regular litigation. Instead, the law assumes a high degree of altruism on the part of the fiduciary.

When the fiduciary and the beneficiary share ownership interests in the property around which the relationship centers, this basic assumption becomes strained. Of course, conflicts of interest will often exist between individuals, and there is no reason to suspect that this will change simply because a relationship is denominated as fiduciary. The traditional solution of fiduciary analysis has been to disqualify the fiduciary from receiving any benefits from the relationship. This relieves the fiduciary of having to balance her own interests against those of her beneficiary and simplifies judicial analysis. This solution reflects the view that requiring self-denial from the fiduciary is a social good. The price of enforcing this standard, however, is some loss of efficiency, a

---

consequence which may explain the general trend in corporate law away from strict fiduciary standards to more permissive rules.

Questions

1. What purpose or purposes does fiduciary duty serve? Do the excerpts agree on its purpose? How, and why, are they different?

2. What is fiduciary duty? How is your answer affected by the conclusions that you've reached with respect to the rights of bondholders and preferred stockholders? How elastic should the contours of fiduciary duty be? How elastic can they be and still serve the purposes that are served by fiduciary duty?

3. Does your approach to fiduciary duty depend upon your theory of the corporation? Your notion of corporate purpose? How, if at all, must your approach be altered to accommodate competing theories?

4. What are the fundamental differences between fiduciary duty and the various contract doctrines designed to prevent overreaching?

Section 2
The Declaration and Payment of Dividends

As you have seen, the limited liability of corporations has set the stage for conflict between the corporation's fixed claimants like bondholders and, to a lesser extent, preferred stockholders, and its residual claimants, the common stockholders. To the extent that the corporation is obligated to satisfy its fixed claims, the remaining assets available for distribution to common stockholders is diminished. Conversely, to the extent that the corporation is permitted to distribute assets to its common stockholders, the risk that fixed claimants will not be paid is increased.

These circumstances created by the feature of limited liability, combined with the legal treatment of fixed claimants, have led these claimants to develop contractual means of limiting distributions to common stockholders while their claims remain unsatisfied. But some statutory limitations exist as well. Commonly known as the legal capital rules, these statutory provisions are meant to cabin the otherwise (almost) unlimited discretion of directors to declare and pay dividends by restricting the sources out of which they may be paid and the circumstances under which their payment is forbidden.

Once important protections to creditors, these legal capital rules evolved along with the principle of limited liability throughout the nineteenth century.[1] But these devices have diminished dramatically in significance since the advent of no-par and low-par value stock, culminating in the dramatic (but different) simplifications of the Revised Model Business Corporation Act and the California Corporations Code. Nevertheless,

---

1. For extended studies of these developments, see Blumberg, Limited Liability and Corporate Groups, 11 J. Corp. Law 573 (1986); Dodd, American Business Corporations Until 1860, 364-437 (1954).

legal capital rules exist in all jurisdictions in different forms. Consequently, we offer a brief overview of the various types of statutory approaches to restricting the payment of dividends before we present other materials relating to dividends.

a. Legal Capital Rules

What is legal capital? Mel Eisenberg offers this answer to this fundamental question:

> Originally, it was the aggregate par value of issued stock. In a bygone era, all shares had a par value and most probably were issued at a price equal to par value. In that era, the concept of legal capital had a certain economic signifi-cance: legal capital was conventionally more or less equal to the economic cap-ital created by the issue of stock. Modern statutes, however, do not require that shares have a par value, and even shares that have a par value may carry a par value much lower than the price at which they are issued. Accordingly, the *eco-nomic capital* generated by the issue of stock may be much greater than the cor-poration's *legal capital*, which has become a mere legal construct determined in a wholly arbitrary manner.

Eisenberg, The Modernization of Corporate Law: An Essay for Bill Cary, 37 U. Miami L. Rev. 187, 199-202 (1983).

Armed with this information, we now turn to the basic statutory approaches to legal capital.

Insolvency Test

The fundamental restriction is the insolvency test, prohibiting the corporation from making distributions that would render the corporation unable to pay its debts as they become due. It is this test which survives as one of the two restrictions in the Revised Model Business Corporation Act, the other being the balance sheet test which forbids distributions that would reduce the corporation's assets to an amount less than its liabil-ities plus the dissolution preferences of preferred stockholders. By adopting these re-strictions, the Revised Model Act eliminated the elaborate accounting concepts that formed the basis for other tests, such as the balance sheet surplus test, the earned sur-plus test, and the ratio/assets surplus test discussed below.

Balance Sheet Surplus Test

The balance sheet surplus test, now also embodied in New York Business Corpora-tion Law § 510(b), restricts dividends to the corporation's assets in excess of its liabili-ties and stated capital. The stated capital concept derives from the practice of assign-ing par value to shares, and consists of the portion of the consideration received for the shares that is equal to their par value. The balance of the consideration is allocated to capital surplus. If the shares are issued without par value, the corporation's stated capital is an amount of the total consideration determined by the directors to be stated capital. Obviously, when the par value of stock is low in relation to the issue price, the prohibition on dividends from stated capital offers creditors little protec-tion. Equally obvious, as to no par shares, the dividend restriction combined with the discretion of the directors to determine the stated capital results in a low level of cred-itor protection.

Earned Surplus Test

The earned surplus test was designed to ensure that dividends were paid from the corporation's earnings, rather than from its capital. Earned surplus represents the retained earnings of the corporation over the life of the corporation until the dividend is declared, rather than any amount of the consideration received for the stock (broken into stated capital and capital surplus). Consequently, dividends paid from earned surplus properly reflect a return *on* capital rather than a return *of* capital. This was the basic approach of the Model Business Corporation Act prior to its revision.

The Ratio/Assets Surplus Test

The ratio/assets surplus test was pioneered in California and reflects a triumph of financial principles over the accounting principles underlying the balance sheet test, the balance sheet surplus test, and the earned surplus test. Under the ratio/assets surplus approach adopted by California, dividends may be paid freely out of retained earnings (equivalent to earned surplus). If retained earnings are insufficient, the corporation may pay dividends out of capital if, following the distribution, the corporation's ratio of assets to liabilities exceeds 1.25:1, and its current (liquid) assets at least equal its current liabilities. In neither case may dividends be paid if the corporation is, or by virtue of such payment is likely to be rendered, insolvent.

Delaware Legal Capital Rule

Delaware's legal capital rule is found in Delaware General Corporation Law § 170(a). It provides that corporate directors may declare and pay dividends upon the shares of its capital stock (*e.g.*, common and preferred stock) either (1) out of its surplus (as defined in and computed in accordance with Del. Gen. Corp. Law §§ 154, 242 and 244), or (2) if there is no surplus, out of its net profits for the fiscal year in which the dividend is declared and/or the preceding fiscal year. The first prong of Delaware's rule is essentially the same as the balance sheet surplus test discussed above. Surplus thus equals total assets less total liabilities less capital. However, the second prong allows a company with no surplus to nevertheless pay a dividend so long as the company has net profits in the current and/or previous fiscal year. Because of this, the second prong is pro-stockholder and anti-creditor. Even if the company has a history of losing money, it nevertheless can pay a dividend to its stockholders so long as it was fortuitous enough to have a net profit in the current fiscal year and/or the previous fiscal year.

The Delaware Supreme Court has held that the numbers on a company's balance sheet are not the "be all, end all" when it comes to determining surplus. In *Klang v. Smith's Food & Drug Centers, Inc.*, 702 A.2d 150 (Del. 1997), the court stated:

> Balance sheets are not ... conclusive indicators of surplus or the lack thereof. Corporations may revalue assets to show surplus, but perfection in the process is not required. Directors have reasonable latitude to depart from the balance sheet to calculate surplus, so long as they evaluate assets and liabilities in good faith, on the basis of acceptable data, by methods they reasonably believe reflect present value, and arrive at a determination of the surplus that is not so far off the mark as to constitute actual or constructive fraud.

Id. at 152.

These, then, are the basic approaches to legal capital. For further study of the legal capital rules, we recommend Manning and Hanks, Legal Capital (3d ed. 1990).

Problem — Legal Restrictions on Dividends

1. Assume that Melville, Poe, and Whitman invested $100,000 in Merry Mount, Inc. and received 1,000 shares of common stock, the only stock the company issued. The company's balance sheet is set forth below. The company has also issued a ten-year note in the amount of $50,000 to each of Emerson and Thoreau that appears on the balance sheet as a long-term liability. The company made $5,000 in profit from its first year operations.

Assets		Liabilities and Shareholders' Equity	
Assets		*Liabilities*	
Current Assets		*Current Liabilities*	
Cash	$ 40,000	Accounts Payable	$50,000
		Notes Payable	
Accounts Receivable	35,000	(current portion)	10,000
		Accrued Expenses	
Inventory	100,000	Payable	15,000
Total Current Assets	$175,000	Total Current Liabilities	$75,000
Fixed Assets		*Long-Term Liabilities*	
Land and Building	95,000	Mortgage	50,000
Machinery and Equipment	130,000	Notes Payable	100,000
Furniture and Fixtures	10,000	Total Long-Term	
Less: Accumulated		Liabilities	150,000
Depreciation	(90,000)		
Net Fixed Assets	145,000	*Total Liabilities*	$225,000
Other Assets		*Shareholders' Equity*	
		Common stock (1000 shs.)	100,000
Prepaid Items	10,000	Earned Surplus	5,000
		Total Liabilities and	
Total Assets	$330,000	*Shareholders'Equity*	$330,000

a. Can Merry Mount, Inc. pay a dividend to its shareholders in the amount of $10,000 at this time (during its second year of operations)?

Assume (alternatively) that:

(i) The corporation is incorporated in Delaware and the par value of the common stock is $100 per share.

(ii) The corporation is incorporated in Delaware and the par value of the common stock is $10.

(iii) The corporation is incorporated under the Model Business Corporation Act.

(iv) The corporation is incorporated under the Revised Model Business Corporation Act.

Consider Del. Gen. Corp. Law §§ 160, 170 and 244; Model Business Corporation Act §§ 6 and 45; and Revised Model Business Corporation Act § 6.40.

b. Suppose the balance sheet shown above is for a date three years after the corporation was formed, and no dividends have been paid and no stock has been repurchased. Melville and Poe, the owners of an aggregate ⅔ of the shares, draw salaries from the business in compensation for their services, but Whitman, who is a retired private investor, does not. Management has been talking with one of its suppliers for two years about buying the supplier's business, but they have been constantly rebuffed. Whitman has been demanding a dividend to be paid in the amount of $30,000, but the other directors have opposed it. What is the likelihood that Whitman would succeed in a suit to compel the payment of the dividend he seeks? What additional information would you like to have? What other courses of action might Whitman pursue?

2. Your Bondolian clients have become somewhat concerned. Now that you have educated them in the intricacies of limited liability and the American approach to creditors' rights, they would like to explore the possibility of providing some measure of creditor protection in their corporations act. After all, the switch from communism to free market capitalism is a big one, and they are uncomfortable with the idea of leaving creditors entirely on their own. Write a memorandum exploring the possible ways in which the Bondolian corporations code might mitigate the effects of limited liability. What are the advantages and disadvantages of each approach? Which would you recommend, and why? In writing your memo, reconsider your answers to Problem—The Term Sheet, *supra* at chapter 2, section 1, and Problem—The Policy of Limited Liability, *supra* at chapter 2, section 2.

1 Revised Model Business Corporation Act Annotated
(3d ed. 1984)[a]

§ 6.40 DISTRIBUTION TO SHAREHOLDERS

(a) A board of directors may authorize and the corporation may make distributions to its shareholders subject to restriction by the articles of incorporation and the limitation in subsection (c).

(b) If the board of directors does not fix the record date for determining shareholders entitled to a distribution (other than one involving a purchase, redemption, or other acquisition of the corporation's shares), it is the date the board of directors authorizes the distribution.

(c) No distribution may be made if, after giving it effect:

(1) the corporation would not be able to pay its debts as they become due in the usual course of business; or

(2) the corporation's total assets would be less than the sum of its total liabilities plus (unless the articles of incorporation permit otherwise) the amount that would be needed, if the corporation were to be dissolved at the time of the distribution, to satisfy the preferential rights upon dissolution of shareholders whose preferential rights are superior to those receiving the distribution.

(d) The board of directors may base a determination that a distribution is not prohibited under subsection (c) either on financial statements prepared on the basis of accounting practices and principles that are reasonable in the circumstances or on a fair valuation or other method that is reasonable in the circumstances.

a. Reprinted with the permission of Prentice Hall Law & Business.

(e) Except as provided in subsection (g), the effect of a distribution under subsection (c) is measured:

(1) in the case of distribution by purchase, redemption, or other acquisition of the corporation's shares, as of the earlier of (i) the date money or other property is transferred or debt incurred by the corporation or (ii) the date the shareholder ceases to be a shareholder with respect to the acquired shares;

(2) in the case of any other distribution of indebtedness, as of the date the indebtedness is distributed; and

(3) in all other cases, as of (i) the date the distribution is authorized if the payment occurs within 120 days after the date of authorization or (ii) the date the payment is made if it occurs more than 120 days after the date of authorization.

(f) A corporation's indebtedness to a shareholder incurred by reason of a distribution made in accordance with this section is at parity with the corporation's indebtedness to its general, unsecured creditors except to the extent subordinated by agreement.

(g) Indebtedness of a corporation, including indebtedness issued as a distribution, is not considered a liability for purposes of determinations under subsection (c) if its terms provide that payment of principal and interest are made only if and to the extent that payment of a distribution to shareholders could then be made under this section. If the indebtedness is issued as a distribution, each payment of principal or interest is treated as a distribution, the effect of which is measured on the date the payment is actually made.

* * *

OFFICIAL COMMENT

.... It has long been recognized that the traditional "par value" and "stated capital" statutes do not provide significant protection against distributions of capital to shareholders. While most of these statutes contained elaborate provisions establishing "stated capital," "capital surplus," and "earned surplus" (and often other types of surplus as well), the net effect of most statutes was to permit the distribution to shareholders of most or all of the corporation's net assets—its capital along with its earnings—if the shareholders wished this to be done. However, statutes also generally imposed an equity insolvency test on distributions that prohibited distributions of assets if the corporation was insolvent or if the distribution had the effect of making the corporation insolvent or unable to meet its obligations as they were projected to arise.

The financial provisions of the revised Model Act, which are based on the 1980 amendments, sweep away all the distinctions among the various types of surplus but retain restrictions on distributions built around both the traditional equity insolvency and balance sheet tests of earlier statutes.

1. THE SCOPE OF SECTION 6.40

Section 1.40 defines "distribution" to include virtually all transfers of money, indebtedness of the corporation or other property to a shareholder in respect of the corporation's shares. It thus includes cash or property dividends, payments by a corporation to purchase its own shares, distributions of promissory notes or indebtedness, and distributions in partial or complete liquidation or voluntary or involuntary dissolution. Section 1.40 excludes from the definition of "distribution" transactions by the corporation in which only its own shares are distributed to its shareholders. These transactions are called "share dividends"....

Section 6.40 imposes a single, uniform test on all distributions. Many of the old "par value" and "stated capital" statutes provided tests that varied with the type of distribution under consideration or did not cover certain types of distributions at all.

2. EQUITY INSOLVENCY TEST

As noted above, older statutes prohibited payments of dividends if the corporation was, or as a result of the payment would be, insolvent in the equity sense. This test is retained, appearing in section 6.40(c)(1).

.... While neither a balance sheet nor an income statement can be conclusive as to this test, the existence of significant shareholders' equity and normal operating conditions are of themselves a strong indication that no issue should arise under that test. Indeed, in the case of a corporation having regularly audited financial statements, the absence of any qualification in the most recent auditor's opinion as to the corporation's status as a "going concern," coupled with a lack of subsequent adverse events, would normally be decisive.

It is only when circumstances indicate that the corporation is encountering difficulties or is in an uncertain position concerning its liquidity and operations that the board of directors or, more commonly, the officers or others upon whom they may place reliance under section 8.30(b), may need to address the issue. Because of the overall judgment required in evaluating the equity insolvency test, no one or more "bright line" tests can be employed. However, in determining whether the equity insolvency test has been met, certain judgments or assumptions as to the future course of the corporation's business are customarily justified, absent clear evidence to the contrary. These include the likelihood that (a) based on existing and contemplated demand for the corporation's products or services, it will be able to generate funds over a period of time sufficient to satisfy its existing and reasonably anticipated obligations as they mature, and (b) indebtedness which matures in the near-term will be refinanced where, on the basis of the corporation's financial condition and future prospects and the general availability of credit to businesses similarly situated, it is reasonable to assume that such refinancing may be accomplished. To the extent that the corporation may be subject to asserted or unasserted contingent liabilities, reasonable judgments as to the likelihood, amount, and time of any recovery against the corporation, after giving consideration to the extent to which the corporation is insured or otherwise protected against loss, may be utilized....

In exercising their judgment, the directors are entitled to rely, under section 8.30(b) as noted above, on information, opinions, reports, and statements prepared by others. Ordinarily, they should not be expected to become involved in the details of the various analyses or market or economic projections that may be relevant. Judgments must of necessity be made on the basis of information in the hands of the directors when a distribution is authorized. They should not, of course, be held responsible as a matter of hindsight for unforeseen developments.

3. RELATIONSHIP TO THE FEDERAL BANKRUPTCY ACT AND OTHER FRAUDULENT CONVEYANCE STATUTES

The revised Model Act establishes the validity of distributions from the corporate law standpoint under section 6.40 and determines the potential liability of directors for improper distributions under sections 8.30 and 8.33. The federal Bankruptcy Act and state fraudulent conveyance statutes, on the other hand, are designed to enable the trustee or other representative to recapture for the benefit of creditors funds distributed to others in some circumstances. In light of these diverse purposes, it was not thought necessary to make the tests of section 6.40 identical to the tests for insolvency under these various statutes.

4. BALANCE SHEET TEST

Section 6.40(c)(2) requires that, after giving effect to any distribution, the corporation's assets equal or exceed its liabilities plus (with some exceptions) the dissolution preferences of senior equity securities. Section 6.40(d) authorizes asset and liability determinations to be made for this purpose on the basis of either (1) financial statements prepared on the basis of accounting practices and principles that are reasonable in the circumstances or (2) a fair valuation or other method that is reasonable in the circumstances....

Section 6.40 does not utilize particular accounting terminology of a technical nature or specify particular accounting concepts. In making determinations under this section, the board of directors may make judgments about accounting matters, giving full effect to its right to rely upon professional or expert opinion.

In a corporation with subsidiaries, the board of directors may rely on unconsolidated statements prepared on the basis of the equity method of accounting (see American Institute of Certified Public Accountants, APB Opinion No. 18 (1971)) as to the corporation's investee corporations, including corporate joint ventures and subsidiaries, although other evidence would be relevant in the total determination.

a. Generally accepted accounting principles

The board of directors should in all circumstances be entitled to rely upon reasonably current financial statements prepared on the basis of generally accepted accounting principles in determining whether or not the balance sheet test of section 6.40(c)(2) has been met, unless the board is then aware that it would be unreasonable to rely on the financial statements because of newly-discovered or subsequently arising facts or circumstances. But section 6.40 does not mandate the use of generally accepted accounting principles; it only requires the use of accounting practices and principles that are reasonable in the circumstances. While publicly-owned corporations subject to registration under the Securities Exchange Act of 1934 must, and many other corporations in fact do, utilize financial statements prepared on the basis of generally accepted accounting principles, a great number of smaller or closely-held corporations do not.... Accordingly, the revised Model Act contemplates that generally acceptable accounting principles are always "reasonable in the circumstances" and that other accounting principles may be perfectly acceptable, under a general standard of reasonableness, even if they do not involve the "fair value" or "current value" concepts that are also contemplated by section 6.40(d).

b. Other principles

Section 6.40(d) specifically permits determinations to be made under section 6.40(c)(2) on the basis of a fair valuation or other method that is reasonable in the circumstances. Thus the statute authorizes departures from historical cost accounting and sanctions the use of appraisal and current value methods to determine the amount available for distribution. No particular method of valuation is prescribed in the statute, since different methods may have validity depending upon the circumstances, including the type of enterprise and the purpose for which the determination is made....

Ordinarily a corporation should not selectively revalue assets. It should consider the value of all of its material assets, whether or not reflected in the financial statements (e.g., a valuable executory contract). Likewise, all of a corporation's material obligations should be considered and revalued to the extent appropriate and possible. In any event, section 6.40(d) calls for the application under section 6.40(c)(2) of a method of determining the aggregate amount of assets and liabilities that is reasonable in the circumstances.

Section 6.40(d) also refers to some "other method that is reasonable in the circumstances." This phrase is intended to comprehend within section 6.40(c)(2) the wide variety of possibilities that might not be considered to fall under a "fair valuation" or "current value" method but might be reasonable in the circumstances of a particular case.

* * *

6. TIME OF MEASUREMENT

Section 6.40(e)(3) provides that the time for measuring the effect of a distribution for compliance with the equity insolvency and balance sheet tests for all distributions not involving the reacquisition of shares or the distribution of indebtedness is the date of authorization, if the payment occurs within 120 days following the authorization; if the payment occurs more than 120 days after the authorization, however, the date of payment must be used. If the corporation elects to make a distribution in the form of its own indebtedness, under section 6.40(e)(2) the validity of that distribution must be measured as of the time of distribution, unless the indebtedness qualifies under section 6.40(g).

Section 6.40(e)(1) provides a different rule for the time of measurement when the distribution involves a reacquisition of shares....

Note

A typically concise overview of the legal capital rules contained in the Revised Model Business Corporation Act is provided by Bayless Manning in Manning, Assets In and Assets Out: Chapter VI of the Revised Model Business Corporation Act, 63 Tex. L. Rev. 1527 (1985).

---

b. A Board's Ability to Declare a Dividend

Gabelli & Co. v. Liggett Group, Inc.
444 A.2d 261 (Del. Ch. 1982), *affd*, 479 A.2d 276 (Del. 1984)

HARNETT, Vice Chancellor.

Defendants-Liggett Group, Inc. ("Liggett") and GM Sub Corporation ("GM Sub") moved to dismiss this action claiming that the complaint fails to state a claim upon which relief may be granted. The gravamen of the suit is whether, under the circumstances, a minority stockholder of a subsidiary corporation—faced with being cashed out by a merger orchestrated by the majority stockholder—may compel payment of a dividend where he alleges breach of fiduciary duty by the parent corporation. For the reasons set forth, I hold that the complaint does not now state a cause of action and therefore grant defendants' motion to dismiss, subject, however to a possible amendment of the complaint.

* * *

II

As alleged in the complaint, the facts are: the plaintiff-Gabelli & Co., Inc. Profit Sharing Plan ("Gabelli") owned 800 shares of Liggett's approximately 8.4 million issued and outstanding common shares before a merger which occurred in August of 1980. Gabelli brought this action just before the merger was to be consummated on its own behalf and on behalf of a class consisting of all persons—other than the defendant— who owned Liggett common stock prior to the merger.

Defendant-Liggett, a Delaware corporation, is a major producer of cigarettes. Defendant-GM Sub, also a Delaware corporation, is an indirect wholly-owned subsidiary of defendant-Grand Metropolitan Limited ("Grand Met"), an English corporation.

GM Sub was formed in March of 1980 for the purpose of purchasing shares of Liggett on Grand Met's behalf by way of a tender offer.... [A]pproximately 85% of Liggett's shareholders accepted the tender offer [price of $69 per share] and tendered their shares to GM Sub in the spring of 1980.

After the tender offer was completed, Grand Met—through its newly acquired majority position—proposed a plan of merger in which Liggett would be merged into either Grand Met or a wholly-owned subsidiary. The minority shareholders were to be cashed out at $69 per share—the amount of the earlier tender offer. The merger date was set for early in August of 1980.

At this time, Liggett was nearing the time period when it had customarily declared a regular quarterly dividend of $.625 per share. For the past sixteen years the Board of Directors had declared a dividend in late July, set an early August record date, and made payment in late August or early September. In July of 1980, however, the dividend was not declared. On July 16, 1980, the plaintiff brought this action asking this Court to compel Liggett's Board to declare the traditional dividend. Shortly thereafter—on August 7, 1980—the minority shareholders were cashed out of their equity interest in Liggett by the merger. Significantly, the complaint did not request an injunction against the consummation of the merger nor attack the adequacy of the price offered. Nor has plaintiff sought to do so—even after defendants have pointed out the omission.

III

.... The critical allegations of the complaint are:

"19. Grand Met, by reason of its majority and controlling position in Liggett, owes a fiduciary duty to Liggett's minority shareholders.

20. Grand Met is breaching its fiduciary duty to Liggett's minority shareholders by causing Liggett to eliminate its regular dividend to enable Grand Met to obtain the Liggett dividend money for itself upon the merger of Liggett and Grand Met."

Defendants, on the other hand, contend that the complaint fails to state a cause of action because the decision to declare a dividend is a matter within the discretion of the Board of Directors and that this decision cannot be judicially interfered with in the absence of a showing of oppressive or fraudulent abuse of discretion. Defendants assert that plaintiff has failed to allege such an abuse of discretion and therefore the complaint must be dismissed.

Moreover, defendants contend that Liggett's decision not to declare a dividend was in essence a routine business decision insulated by the business judgment rule. According to the defendants, the complaint fails to make such allegations as would preclude the business judgment rule applying and thus permit a judicial review of the transaction.

IV

A decision to declare a dividend is a matter ordinarily addressed to the discretion of the Board of Directors invoking, as it does, important business considerations. Prior Delaware cases have permitted directors wide latitude in making this decision and the declaring of a dividend is considered a routine matter which enjoys a presumption of sound business judgment which will not be disturbed by a court in the absence of a disabling factor. *Eshleman v. Keenan*, Del. Ch., 194 A. 40 (1937); *affd.*, 2 A.2d 904 (1938). *Moskowitz v. Bantrell*, Del. Supr. 190 A.2d 749 (1963); and *Baron v. Allied Artists Pictures Corp.*, Del. Ch., 337 A.2d 653 (1975).

The decision to declare a dividend is also within the ambit ... [of 8 *Del. C.*§ 170(a) (Delaware's legal capital rule[a])].... It is assumed for present purposes that Liggett possesses a sufficient capital surplus from which to declare a dividend. Plaintiff, therefore, must allege facts which, if true, would overcome the protection of the business judgment rule so that the transaction might be tested against the intrinsic fairness test which shifts the burden of persuasion to the defendant to show the intrinsic fairness of the entire transaction....

V

The threshold inquiry, therefore, is whether there are allegations in the complaint which, if true, would permit the transaction to be tested against the intrinsic fairness test.

As previously noted, the complaint alleged that Grand Met—through its wholly-owned subsidiary—acquired approximately 85% of the issued and outstanding common stock of Liggett. Grand Met was therefore the majority shareholder or parent corporation at the time of the disputed transaction. The law is settled in this State that such status carries with it a fiduciary duty with respect to the minority shareholders of the subsidiary corporation.... The mere existence of this relationship, however, does not by itself invoke the intrinsic fairness test. The fiduciary relationship must be accompanied by a showing of self-dealing or some other disabling factor before the stricter test is warranted. Thus, within the context of parent-subsidiary dealings there must be a showing that as a result of its control and domination the parent caused the subsidiary to act in such a way that the parent usurped something of value to the exclusion of, and detriment to, the minority shareholders of the subsidiary. *Sinclair Oil Corp. v. Levien*, Del. Supr., 280 A.2d 717 (1971).

* * *

---

a. For Delaware's legal capital rule, see *supra* section 2a.

VI

The defendants' argument that the intrinsic fairness test is not applicable because Grand Met did not cause Liggett to act is based on the earlier cited general principle that a director's decision to declare a dividend is a discretionary determination usually deferred to by the courts. However, this principle does not stand for the proposition that director inaction is never judicially reviewable. In the arena of corporation decision making, a decision not to act is as much a decision as an affirmative decision to enter into a specific transaction. The decision not to declare a dividend is a business decision which should not be motivated by self-interest. Thus, if as alleged, Grand Met— through its dominant position—caused Liggett not to declare a dividend solely for Grand Met's pecuniary gain, then the transaction would not be shielded by the business judgment rule but rather should be tested for intrinsic fairness.

VII

Defendants' next argument is that the intrinsic fairness test is not applicable because Grand Met could not have received anything of value to the exclusion of the plaintiff. The absence of this element was dispositive after trial in *Sinclair Oil Corp. v. Levien, supra....*

[I]n order to invoke the intrinsic fairness test, the plaintiff must at least allege the presence of self-dealing—that is, that Grand Met usurped something of value to the exclusion of the minority stockholders. Plaintiff attempts to show that this essential element is covered by the allegations in the complaint by claiming that the present transaction must be viewed in its entirety. In other words, plaintiff claims that the failure to declare a dividend and the decision to effect a cash out merger must be considered as one transaction. Thus it is claimed the merger, in effect, was the mechanism through which the defendants benefitted at the expense of the minority stockholders. Otherwise, the rationale of *Sinclair* would apply since a decision not to declare a dividend would also impact equally on all the stockholders on a share-for-share basis.

In order for the plaintiff to state a cause of action, therefore, it must allege the existence of two mutually dependent factors. The first is the plaintiff's right to the dividend in question. If such a cognizable right or entitlement exists, however, plaintiff must also necessarily claim, if a cause of action is to be stated, that the impending merger and the consideration being offered did not account for the value of the dividend which would have been forthcoming if the merger had not taken place.

As to the first factor, it is settled law in Delaware that the Court of Chancery will not compel payment of a dividend unless the corporation is in the proper business and financial posture to do so, and if the failure to declare the dividend is the result of an "oppressive or fraudulent abuse of discretion." *Eshleman v. Keenan, supra....* This standard has also been stated in terms of "oppression or bad faith." Folk, The Delaware General Corporation Law, Little, Brown (1972) § 170 p. 188.

Because plaintiff's complaint fails to plead with particularity any fraudulent conduct as required by Chancery Rule 9(b), the plaintiff cannot claim a fraudulent abuse of discretion.

It would appear, however, that plaintiff has stated a legally cognizable right to the dividend based on oppression or bad faith subject, however, to a contingency. Thus, assuming as this Court must, the correctness of the allegations of the complaint, a decision motivated by self-interest to forego a regular dividend immediately prior to a cash out merger might well be oppressive or done in bad faith if the terms of the merger were unfair. The unfairness of the merger is a necessary prerequisite because if the merger price included the value of the dividend which was foregone because of an improper motive, then the plaintiff has suffered no loss nor has the defendant received any benefit.

It follows, therefore, that plaintiff's legal theory and thus its cause of action are inexorably tied to the question of whether the merger price was fair and therefore accounted for the value of the otherwise forthcoming dividend. This points up the fallacy of the complaint. Because plaintiff has never challenged the merger, the complaint does not presently state a claim upon which relief can be granted....

.... The merger itself must necessarily be challenged in order to determine the relevant factors which bear on value and thus fairness. In the present case the only proper inference which can be drawn from the allegations in the complaint concerning the merger price was that it was the same as an earlier tender offer which was apparently inflated as a result of a competing offer. This is not a sufficient allegation to state a cause of action which challenges the fairness of a merger because it does not necessarily follow that the merger price is unfair just because it is the same price as the tender offer price. The tender offer price may have been artificially inflated due to spirited bidding and thus the merger price may have been fair even though it included a value for the passed dividend and even if it was the same as the tender offer price.

* * *

Here the plaintiff has thus far chosen to avoid directly attacking the merger—perhaps because it has accepted the benefits of the merger and thus fears a challenge to its standing to maintain a suit....

... [T]he refusal of the plaintiff to directly attack the merger is fatal because plaintiff has not alleged any basis from which an inference of oppression or bad faith or an inference of breach of fiduciary duty due to self-dealing can be drawn. As a result, there is no present basis upon which to predicate a judicial review of the transaction under the intrinsic fairness test.

Defendants' motion to dismiss for failure to state a claim upon which relief can be granted is therefore granted. Because plaintiff, however, has alleged facts which, if true, would state a claim upon which relief could be granted if the merger can be challenged, plaintiff is given 20 days in which to decide if it desires to seek to amend its complaint so as to supply the missing essential allegation. IT IS SO ORDERED.

Questions

1. Do you agree with the court's assumption that the merger price would be unfair if it failed to account for the upcoming regular dividend? Does a dividend, when regularly paid, become the kind of expectation that rises to the level of a property right?

2. Why did Gabelli care about the missed dividend? It only owned 800 shares worth $55,200 at the cash out merger price of $69 per share. The regular quarterly dividend of $.625 would have only netted it $500.

3. The court in *Gabelli* noted that "it is settled law in Delaware that the Court of Chancery will not compel payment of a dividend unless the corporation is in the proper business and financial posture to do so...." The basic Delaware test is set out in § 170 of the Delaware General Corporation Law, which is quoted in *Gabelli*. Section 6.40 of the Revised Model Business Corporation Act, *supra* at section 2a, has been designed to simplify the legal tests for the declaration of dividends.[1]

---

1. Although our concern here is with dividends, § 6.40 actually is much broader and is meant to deal with *all* corporate distributions to stockholders.

4. The court in *Gabelli* was quite clear about the ordinary prerogative of the board with respect to the declaration of dividends. What is the remedy of a shareholder when the board has declared a dividend but refuses to pay it? In Mann-Paller Foundation v. Econometric Research, Inc., 644 F. Supp. 92, 95 (D.C. Cir. 1986), the court stated the law as follows:

> ERI is incorporated in Delaware, so the substantive law of Delaware governs the Court's disposition of plaintiff's common law claims.... The law of Delaware (like the law of other jurisdictions), is that
>
> > upon the declaration of a lawful dividend by a Board of Directors ... the relation of debtor and creditor is set up between the corporation and the stockholder.... [T]he declaration of the lawful dividend creates an obligation of the corporation and there exists a right of action on the part of the stockholder to enforce its payment. The right is in the nature of a contract and grows out of the declaration of a lawful dividend.
>
> *Selly* v. *Fleming Coal Co.*, 37 Del. 34, 180 A. 326, 328 (Del. Super. 1935); 11 W. Fletcher, Cyclopedia of the Law of Private Corporations § 5365 (rev. perm. ed. 1986).... The action brought in such a situation is an action at law. 11 W. Fletcher, *supra*. Also, a wrongful withholding of dividends is the type of harm which may be remedied on an individual basis because it is a wrong inflicted on the stockholder alone, rather than the corporation. Therefore, the action properly would be brought as an individual cause of action....

5. In Caleb & Co. v. E.I. DuPont de Nemours & Co., 615 F. Supp. 96 (S.D.N.Y. 1985), DuPont mounted a successful tender offer for Conoco, purchasing the tendered shares on August 5 but failing to pay for them until after August 14. On July 31, the Conoco board declared a dividend of $0.65 per share, payable to stockholders of record on August 14. By virtue of its August 5 purchases, DuPont became entitled to receive the dividend as the record owner of the shares. Plaintiff sued, among others, DuPont and First Jersey National Bank, DuPont's exchange agent, alleging that the premature transfer of shares to DuPont was a breach of contractual and fiduciary duties.

The court granted defendants' motions to dismiss the complaint, holding that (i) DuPont's acceptance of the shares on August 5 made it the record owner on the August 14 record date although payment occurred thereafter, and (ii) DuPont, as the purchaser of shares after dividends were declared but prior to the record date, was entitled to receive the dividend.

As to the first point, the court, 615 F. Supp. at 104, relied heavily on Professor Williston:

> The uniform statutes, in force in all of the states in one form or another, definitely provide ... that legal title to stock passes to the buyer upon delivery of the certificate in proper form. But the passing of legal title may, or may not, be coterminous with the passing of the risks, and the rights of ownership, in the shares. Moreover, all of the rights, or obligations, of ownership may not pass at the same time. Thus, the purchaser of shares, absent any agreement to the contrary, is generally entitled to dividends, rights and all the privileges of a shareholder, except voting power, from the time he makes the purchase contract, *whether or not he has made payment*, has taken legal title or has been registered on the corporation records as a shareholder.

8 Williston on Contracts § 953 at 320-21 (1964) (footnotes omitted) (emphasis added).

As to the second point, the court reviewed Delaware precedent to the effect that although the declaration of a dividend creates a debt from the corporation to the stockholder, the holder of record on the record date is entitled to receive the dividend in order to enable the corporation to determine the persons to whom the dividend is to be paid. The court also looked to section 213 of the Delaware General Corporation Law:

> The Delaware Code also establishes the supremacy of the record date over the declaration date for the establishment of shareholders rights:
>
> (a) In order that the corporation may determine the stockholders entitled to notice of or to vote at any meeting of stockholders or any adjournment thereof, or to express consent to corporate action in writing without a meeting, or entitled to receive payment of any dividend or other distribution or allotment of any rights, or entitled to exercise any rights in respect of any change, conversion or exchange of stock or for the purpose of any other lawful action, the board of directors may fix, in advance, a record date, which shall not be more than 60 nor less than 10 days before the date of such meeting, nor more than 60 days prior to any other action.

615 F. Supp. at 105.

Finally, the court concluded:

> Even though neither *Wilmington Trust, supra,* nor the Delaware Code section cited above, directly resolve the confrontation here, I conclude that their clear implication is that the owner as of the record date is the proper recipient of the dividend. Caleb's final cause of action is therefore dismissed.

615 F. Supp. at 106.

Do you agree with the court's conclusion as a matter of policy?

6. Should courts be equally reluctant to interfere with the dividend decisions of close corporations as they are for public corporations? If you conclude that courts should have greater latitude to interfere with the dividend decisions of close corporations, what guidelines should courts use in evaluating those decisions? Fashioning remedies?

The board's discretion in paying dividends and the legal capital rules applicable thereto apply not only to the declaration and payment of common stock dividends but also to preferred stock dividends. Consider the following case.

Baron v. Allied Artists Pictures Corp.
337 A.2d 653 (Del. Ch. 1975),
appeal dismissed, 365 A.2d 136 (Del. 1976)
[*Supra at chapter 6, section 2*]

Section 3
Dividend Policy

Recall from chapter 3, section 3b(iii)(A), that the expected return on a share of common stock under the dividend discount model (the DDM) consists solely of the expected cash dividends to be paid in perpetuity. Recall also that the DDM was presented as a valuation technique alternative to such income statement-based valuation techniques as the capitalization of earnings and measures such as the P/E ratio. We emphasized the perceived superiority of the DDM approach to valuation over the earnings-based approach on several grounds, including the fact that earnings-based approaches are constrained by potentially artificial accounting conventions. From these propositions, we developed a formula under the DDM which holds that the value of a share of common stock is equal to D / k − g, or in words, expected cash dividends divided by the discount rate less the expected growth rate.

From this formula, one can see that the value of the stock will be higher if D is higher. For purposes of dividend policy, therefore, one might prescribe paying the maximum possible dividends to maximize share value. However, setting aside for the moment the possibility of borrowing funds or selling new shares, a company that pays the maximum possible amount out in dividends will have nothing left over to reinvest in growth. As a result, the term g in the foregoing formula would decline as D increases and this has the effect of reducing share value. The challenge, therefore, is to define a dividend policy that maximizes share value by an appropriate level of D and a consequent appropriate level of g. This objective is easier to announce than to implement. In this section, we explore theoretical and practical issues raised by this challenge, using the following problem as a vehicle for analysis and discussion. We also examine the legal context in which these theoretical and practical issues play out.

Problem — Walton Sporting Goods[a]

Walton is an engineer by training but was much more enamored of his principal hobby, fly fishing. Walton progressed from using commercially manufactured equipment in his hobby, to tying his own flies, and, finally, to crafting his own bamboo rods. Streamside companions, and members of Walton's local fishing club, were impressed with his homemade equipment and began to pay him to make equipment for them. When Walton turned forty, personal introspection led him to cast about for other ways to make a living than engineering and he hit upon the idea of forming a corporation (of which he would be the sole stockholder) to make fishing equipment. He had enough money saved up to acquire adequate equipment, and was able to persuade his local bank to give him a second mortgage loan on his house to hire an employee and pay professional advisors.

Walton started by selling his products through a catalogue he produced at home but as word of his products spread, he had so many orders that he was unable to fill them fast enough. Using his retained earnings, he purchased a small factory building and began to increase production. His company, Walton Sporting Goods, Inc. (the "Company"), was a stunning success. In addition to catalogue sales, the Company sold its increasingly wide variety of products through its website and to sporting goods stores throughout the country. After ten years in business, Walton decided to branch out. Still the sole stockholder of the Company, he caused it to conduct a public offering of common stock which, after issuance, constituted 49% of the Company. The Company used the proceeds to purchase other, smaller corporations which produced sporting goods, including manufacturers of tennis equipment, golf equipment, and athletic shoes. Six years ago, he used a new issue of the Company's common stock to acquire Pump-Up, Inc., a publicly held manufacturer of home exercise equipment, reducing Walton's ownership to 32%.

---

a. Based on E. Brigham & L. Gapenski, Cases in Financial Management Module A 912 (1990).

Walton had positioned the Company well for the past decade's health and fitness boom. Profits soared and stock prices rapidly increased. (Originally issued at $12 per share ten years ago, by last summer the stock was trading over-the-counter at $937 per share, reflecting both the Company's prospects and its substantial retained earnings.) Walton's conservative business practices had left the Company with a "clean" balance sheet—no long-term third party debt other than a purchase money mortgage on one of several factories the Company owned. He was able to achieve this by financing the Company's operations almost exclusively from retained earnings and by refusing steadfastly to pay dividends.

With the Company's growth had come the professionalization of its management. Walton, now 60 years old, was chairman of the board. The Company's president was Iago, a young, ambitious MBA who had risen rapidly in the business world and whose secret ambition was to use the Company to build a conglomerate empire for himself. Walton's son, Ichthy, was chief financial officer, and Walton had hopes that Ichthy could grow with the business and maintain family control over it.

The sound of distant thunder reached Walton's ears earlier this year. Although corporate takeovers had fallen off, interest rates were decreasing and acquisition talk was in the air. Moreover, Fritz, the former controlling stockholder of Pump-Up, Inc., and now the Company's second largest stockholder and a member of its board, had been complaining about the lack of dividends. Iago had secretly talked to Fritz about a management buy-out (excluding Walton and Ichthy) to take the Company private and maximize share values, at least if Walton didn't agree to a change in dividend policy.

Iago has whispered into Walton's ear of the need to at least consider paying dividends, and has told him that Fritz is considering a takeover. Although Walton's first instinct was to buy Fritz out, he has decided to place the issue of dividend policy on the agenda for the next board meeting. Although you are a lawyer, and not an investment banker, Walton respects your judgment and has asked you to outline for him the various dividend policies—including maintaining the existing policy—available to maximize share values. He will use the outline as a basis for making a presentation at the next board meeting.

In addition to specific consideration of each of the alternatives set forth below, your outline should also consider the theoretical, practical, and legal issues raised by the general question of dividend policy and how, if at all, any dividend policy will affect the Company's ability to continue to finance its growth. Consider the following alternatives for Walton's outline:

(1) Maintaining the existing policy of paying no dividends;

(2) Declaring and paying a one-time cash dividend; or

(3) Establishing and announcing a permanent cash dividend policy.

Do you need additional information to advise Walton? If so, what?

a. Theories of Dividend Policy

Before proceeding to discuss factors in setting dividend policy, it is necessary to consider the relationship between earnings and dividends, touched on in our discussion of valuation techniques in chapter 3, section 3. We left open in that discussion full treatment of the relevance to dividend valuation of the role of earnings. There are two possibilities. One school of thought holds that future earnings are the chief determinant of a company's ability to pay future dividends. *E.g.*, Cottle, Murray & Block, Graham &

Dodd's Security Analysis 557 (5th ed. 1988) [hereinafter, Graham & Dodd]. Devotees of this school believe that estimates of "future earning power and future dividend-paying capacity are indistinguishable" on the grounds that "earnings are the source of dividends and since the dividend payout rate (the earnings retention rate) must be considered in predicting the growth of earnings, appraisal and prediction of the dividend-paying capacity of a corporation must be an integral part of a careful and thorough estimation of a corporation's earning power." *Id.*

The other school of thought emphasizes the technical inaccuracy of the proposition that earnings are a source of dividends. *E.g.*, Klein & Coffee, Business Organization and Finance 381 (9th ed. 2004). Since cash dividends must by definition be paid in cash but accounting earnings are not reported in terms of cash, earnings cannot be a source of dividends. For example, earnings may be extraordinarly high in a particular year because of record-breaking sales levels but if most sales were made on credit, they will have made no contribution to the company's cash position. Contrariwise, sales and earnings may plummet in the next year but if the debtors paid up for their prior-year's purchases then the company's coffers will be flush with cash. As a practical matter, however, there is usually *some* correlation between high earnings and high cash flows. Therefore, there is *some* correlation between earnings and cash dividend paying ability. But it remains technically incorrect to draw any precise relationship between the two.

The Optimal Payout Ratio. Whatever the source of potential dividends—earnings or cash flow—the crucial issue is what portion of cash available to pay dividends should be paid to stockholders in dividends or reinvested in the business. In other words, the issue is the appropriate payout ratio. A simple answer is in terms of the same set of principles that govern capital budgeting decisions discussed in chapter 3, section 3c: a company should accept and pursue all investment opportunities which have a positive net present value—that is, all opportunities where the expected rate of return exceeds the company's cost of capital. A series of theoretical views of dividend policy exist to evaluate this proposition.

The Traditional Theory. The traditional theory of dividend policy holds that investors prefer a stable and generous dividend over time. It is supported by Graham and Dodd, *supra*. This perceived preference is based preliminarily on the dual grounds that cash is king and that investors deserve a return on their investment in cash. The position is bolstered by the proposition that a stable and generous dividend reduces the variability of returns on stocks and will be expected to be so valued in the market. The traditional theory is also supported by the proposition that investors are skeptical of the extent to which retained earnings will be deployed in ways more beneficial than the ways in which a stockholder could deploy a cash dividend. In part this skepticism may be based on the recognition that earnings retained for plowback remain at risk in the firm and even management's best-laid plans may not in fact meet management's most noble expectations.

The traditional theory of dividend policy contains a prescriptive component that turns on how a stock performs in terms of growth. It follows directly from the foregoing proposition about linking the dividend payout ratio to the capital budgeting decision. Companies with relatively high returns on equity (ROE) should retain a greater portion of earnings, whereas companies with relatively low ROEs should retain a smaller portion. Thus Graham and Dodd conclude as follows:

> The higher the ROE for a company (which will be reflected in the average mul-
> tiplier of earnings) the greater the proportion of earnings that should be re-

tained. Presumably the rate of return on reinvestment will substantially exceed, in the typical case, what the stockholder could earn on the same money received in dividends. A good corporate earnings picture and opportunities for profitable expansion generally go together. For such companies, particularly those in technological fields, in theory at least, low dividends and high reinvestment would appear the best policy for the stockholders. Carried to its logical conclusion, this analysis would suggest that nearly all really successful companies should follow a program of substantial reinvestment of profits, and that cash dividends should be paid only to the extent that opportunities for profitable expansion or diversification are not present....

Id.

An investor preference for cash does not negate this proposition with respect to companies with high ROEs. Any such investor can generate cash by selling his shares and need not rely on dividend payments to satisfy that preference. On this point, Graham and Dodd conclude:

The fact that some owners need cash income from their shares is not a valid argument against complete reinvestment of profits, for presumably these dollars will have a premium value in the market when reinvested. Hence shareholders will fare better by selling off corresponding amounts of their holdings than by receiving the money in dividends. Such cashing in where needed could be readily facilitated by the company through paying periodic small stock dividends to represent the profits plowed back....

Id.

The Irrelevance Theory. In a famous paper, Modigliani and Miller challenged the traditional theory of dividend policy. They argued that once the company has made and disclosed its investment policy to investors, the payout ratio makes no difference for purposes of share values. Miller and Modigliani, Dividend Policy, Growth and the Valuation of Shares, 34 J. Bus. 411-33 (1961). Characterizing the traditional view somewhat derisively as the "bird in the hand theory," Miller and Modigliani contended that share value depended entirely on the earning power of a company's assets. This power, they argued, is unaffected by how operations are financed—whether out of retained earnings or through additional borrowings or stock offerings. In other words, the traditional view implicitly assumes a fixed capital structure and a trade off between paying dividends and reinvesting. But this assumption fails to recognize that it is possible to do both through reconfiguring the capital structure with borrowings or new equity issues.

Miller and Modigliani characterized the traditional view as the bird in the hand theory to refute the claim of its proponents that investors prefer (and therefore value more) a cash dividend paid to them of any amount to the same amount reinvested by the company—that the $1 in hand is less risky than $1 remaining at risk through reinvestment in the company. They disposed of that claim by arguing that most investors would reinvest the $1 in cash in the same or similar firms anyway and that the risk of reinvestment in any firm arises from risk with respect to a company's cash flows and not risk with respect to the future payment of dividends.

The Tax Preference Theory. A third theory of dividend policy recognizes features of tax law that create incentives for earnings retention and accumulation over dividend payment that may lead investors to prefer smaller or no dividends, all other things being equal. The first feature was the more favorable tax rates imposed prior to 1987 on long-term capital gains than on ordinary income. That differential led stockholders to prefer to realize gains on the sale of their stock rather than through dividends taxed as ordinary income. While the Tax Reform Act of 1986 abolished any capital gains preference, dividends remained taxable as ordinary income at each individual investor's personal income tax rate. In May 2003, Congress changed the Internal Revenue Code so that the maximum individual tax rate on corporate dividends is now 15 percent, rather than an investor's personal income tax rate. Moreover, Congress also lowered the capital gains tax on investments held more than one year from 20 percent to 15 percent.[a]

The second tax incentive arises from the corporation's ability to invest earnings that would otherwise have been used to pay taxes at the shareholder level. If a shareholder receives $100 as a dividend, that shareholder can only invest the net after tax (and transaction cost) distribution. If the same earnings are not distributed, but instead are reinvested in the corporation, the full $100 is available for later distribution or to increase share prices through deployment of retained earnings. The potential loss in tax revenues due to the accumulation of earnings led Congress to enact tax penalties to prevent such tax avoidance, including the accumulated earnings tax.[1] The accumulated earnings tax applies to every corporation (with a few exceptions) "formed or availed of for the purpose of avoiding the income tax with respect to its shareholders or the shareholders of any other corporation, by permitting earnings and profits to accumulate instead of being divided or distributed."[2] This improper motive of tax avoidance will be presumed if the earnings of the corporation "accumulate beyond the reasonable needs of the business ... unless the corporation by the preponderance of the evidence shall prove to the contrary."[3] The regulations promulgated by the Treasury Department under the Internal Revenue Code provide some guidance as to what is considered beyond the reasonable needs of a business:

> An accumulation of the earnings and profits (including the undistributed earnings and profits of prior years) is in excess of the reasonable needs of the business if it exceeds the amount that a prudent businessman would consider appropriate for the present business purposes and for the reasonably anticipated future needs of the business.... In order for a corporation to justify an accumulation of earnings and profits for reasonably anticipated future needs, there must be an indication that the future needs of the business required such accumulation, and the corporation must have specific, definite, and feasible plans for the use of such accumulation.[4]

---

a. Although it is unclear what the ultimate effect the new dividend tax rates will have on the dividend policies of public companies, it is certain to cause most to reexamine their dividend policy. An example of a company favoring payout over retention (albeit very reluctantly) is Microsoft. In 2004, Microsoft, having more that $50 billion in cash reserves, declared a $3 per share dividend which amounted to $32 billion in the aggregate. The payout, which personally netted founder and Chairman Bill Gates about $3 billion, is far and away the largest single dividend payout in corporate history. However, one must also consider that, aside from the beneficial dividend tax provisions passed in 2003, Microsoft was so cash rich (at the time the company was generating $1 billion a month in extra cash) that it simply had too much cash with which to reinvest productively—a rare situation indeed. For a discussion of the new dividend tax rates and their possible implications, see Bratton, The New Dividend Puzzle, 93 Geo. L. J. 845 (2005).

1. I.R.C. §§ 531-37.
2. I.R.C. § 532.
3. I.R.C. § 533.
4. Regs. § 1.537-1(a) & (b). The regulations also provide specific examples of what is considered a reasonable accumulation of earnings and what may be considered unreasonable. See Regs. § 1.537-2.

The accumulated earnings tax is imposed on what the Internal Revenue Code defines as accumulated taxable income.[5] A 28% tax is then applied to the accumulated taxable income of the corporation.[6]

Subject to the accumulated earnings rules, two other tax incentives also favor retention over payout. One is that dividends are taxed as received, whereas capital gains are only taxed upon disposition of the asset. The other is that capital assets upon transfer at death are not subject to capital gains taxes at all, but rather the beneficiaries get a so-called stepped-up basis. That is, they take the current value of the stock on the grantor's death as the starting point for measuring capital gains or losses on the asset.

Empirical Testing. Debates about the validity of any of the foregoing theories of dividend policy have been one of the most provocative and intense in financial economics in the past couple of decades. The tests seek to evaluate stock price effects that result from various dividend policies. A chief problem with any such tests is that they necessarily assume we are dealing with efficient capital markets. *See* chapter 3, section 5c. Even setting that not insignificant issue aside, the tests have been inconclusive. The results variably support a range of theoretical possibilities, from concluding that all the theories are right to concluding that all the theories are wrong.

Notes and Questions

1. Under the traditional theory offered by Graham and Dodd, does it matter whether the investment opportunities open to a shareholder are the same as those of the corporation? If a General Motors shareholder has an opportunity to invest in IBM and so does General Motors Corporation, what difference should it make whether the investment is made by the shareholder or by General Motors? *See* Klein & Coffee, *supra.* Does it make a difference whether the two companies are in the same industry? Or is it enough to recognize that shareholders want managers to make business and management decisions with respect to the assets under their direct charge rather than in the assets under the direct charge of another group of managers?

2. Miller and Modigliani's irrelevance theory makes and depends on a series of assumptions about capital markets similar to those on which the efficient capital market hypothesis and the capital asset pricing model are based. *See* chapter 3, sections 5b & c. They observed, in this respect, that "from the standpoint of dividend policy, what counts is not imperfection per se but only imperfection that might lead an investor to have a systematic preference as between a dollar of current dividends and a dollar of current capital gains...." Miller and Modigliani, *supra.*

3. How does Miller and Modigliani's conclusion that a decrease in dividends corresponds with an equivalent increase in retained earnings (and therefore market price) compare with how Graham and Dodd's traditional theory views retained earnings? Is a $1 increase in retained earnings worth as much as $1 paid out in cash dividends? If not, how does this affect Modigliani and Miller's theory? *See* Gordon, Dividends, Earnings and Stock Prices, 41 Rev. Econ. & Stat. 99 (1959).

4. Miller and Modigliani also argue that the presence of debt in a corporation's capital structure does not alter their conclusion that the distribution of corporate wealth between dividends and retained earnings is irrelevant. Does the argument hold if the debt

---

5. I.R.C. §535.
6. I.R.C. §531.

is convertible debt? Mehta notes that, because decreased dividends will result in stock price growth—which in turn will be shared by common stockholders and convertible bondholders—stockholders will not be indifferent to the dividend decision and will prefer higher dividends and lower retained earnings when convertible bonds are outstanding. Mehta, The Impact of Outstanding Convertible Bonds on Corporate Dividend Policy, 31 J. Fin. 489 (1976). Do you see how this proposition works in terms of the formula $V = D / k - g$ (from chapter 3, section 3b(iii)(A))? Mehta goes on to examine the optimal dividend policy for a corporation that has convertible bonds outstanding and concludes:

> [O]ptimal dividend policy when convertible bonds are outstanding [is] influenced by the different motives in issuing the [convertible bonds] in the first place.... [I]f generally observed dividend policies are rational, the motive of "convertible bonds for reducing interest costs" is found seriously questionable.... On the other hand, the motive of "convertible bonds for raising tomorrow's equity today" leads to normative dividend policies that are generally acceptable to management. Since the empirical evidence indicates that management generally endorses the motive of delayed equity for issuing convertible bonds and also likes to raise (rather than curtail) dividends over time, management is rational and consistent in its actions under the assumptions of the model presented here.

> The model rests on two empirically observable premises. First, when convertible bonds are outstanding, management is reluctant or unable to resort to any additional external long term financing. Consequently, growth is financed internally, and the dividend policy becomes a crucial element in the financial strategy formulation. This premise enables us to sidestep the controversy about the role of dividends in influencing the share price. Thus, a more general approach involving additional external financing and the related changes in the conversion privileges is not only desirable in itself but also in shedding light on this ongoing controversy of relevance of dividends.

> The second premise is the phenomenon of *gradual voluntary* conversion of convertible bonds. It is linked with uncertainty and the share price change through market imperfections. Its interrelationships with the firm's dividend policy is traced via the firm's cash flow and profitability characteristics.... Needless to say, however, the phenomenon of voluntary conversion has not been explained rigorously in this paper. Hitherto little attention in the literature to its mere existence and a lack of adequate data for systematic investigation are responsible for the suggested tentative linkage between voluntary conversion and share price change. Nevertheless, available data do indicate that the explanation provided here represents a significant class of situations....

5. Van Horne and McDonald studied the effect of dividend policy and new equity financing together on the value of a corporation's common stock. Van Horne & McDonald, Dividend Policy and New Equity Financing, 26 J. Fin. 507 (1971). They concluded that, although companies paying dividends and financing with new equity did not appreciably differ in value from those that did not pay dividends and financed their investments with retained earnings, this suggested an investor preference for dividends given the transaction costs of new equity financing. Is this necessarily a correct conclusion? What if the transaction costs of new issues were arguably equal to the aggregate transaction costs of stockholders of non-dividend payers who had to sell their shares to realize any return? *Cf.* Booth, Junk Bonds, The Relevance of Dividends, and the Limits of

Managerial Discretion, 1987 Colum. Bus. L. Rev. 553, 560-61 (noting that the magnitude of transaction costs for stock flotation and stockholder selling is similar); 562 (noting that modest brokerage fees diminish the likelihood of a strong clientele effect, discussed below); 567 (noting that significant sales by stockholders will reduce price and preclude new stockholders from selling to obtain a return); Stiglitz, On the Irrelevance of Corporate Financial Policy, 64 Am. Econ. Rev. 851, 852 (1979) (distinguishing between firm specific and economy-wide approaches to assessments of financial policy).

6. If stockholders do prefer cash dividends to the reinvestment of earnings, should the law presume a norm of regular dividend payment?

7. For more on the dividend payout debate, see Brealey, Myers, & Allen, Principles of Corporate Finance 418-19, 422-37 (8th ed. 2006).

b. Practical Issues in Dividend Policy

The inconclusiveness of the empirical testing of the competing theories of dividend policy requires a further focus on some of the practical issues in setting dividend policy. A complex set of practical factors beyond these theoretical accounts of the optimal go into the decision. Among these are the following.

Cash Flows Issues. In addition to the factors discussed in the theoretical literature— the relative profitability of the retention versus payout and the impact that decision has on growth rates or financing decisions—an obvious point is the question of proper management of cash flows in light of liquidity needs over time. In the same way that the question of profitability relates to the capital budgeting decision, the question of liquidity relates to the cash budgeting decision. Consider Shepherd and Scott, Corporate Dividend Policy: Some Legal and Financial Aspects, 13 Am. Bus. Law J. 199, 204-10, 222-23 (1975):

> Dividend policy must also be related to the company's cash budget; this is the formal control and planning device that most firms use to project whether sufficient funds will be on hand at specific times to meet the firm's cash needs. As the dividend payment can be a major cash outflow, the greater the firm's cash and liquidity position, the greater its ability to pay the dividend. This liquidity factor also relates to the rate of growth of the firm. It is not unusual to find the firm which is experiencing above normal growth to be short of cash and other aspects of working capital. For such enterprises, dividend payments can be quite small. This is consistent, however, with the firm taking advantage of favorable short-term growth prospects in anticipation of longer run, high earnings potential. Low dividend payments, or their complete absence, *can* be evidence of prudent business policy.

Role of Control. Dividend policy may also be influenced by a company's shareholder profile. For example, the desired payout ratio could vary depending on whether a company's stockholders are widely dispersed and each is a relatively small holder or whether significant blocks of shares are held by one or more shareholders. In other words, the structure of corporate control may bear on the desired dividend policy. The many contours of this issue of control are summarized by Shepard and Scott, *supra*:

> The factor of control is a two-edged sword as it influences dividend policy. If the current equity owners are firmly in control of the affairs of the organization,

then low payout ratios are likely to result. In such a case, the tendency is to finance all corporate expansion with internally generated funds. To sell stock would obviously dilute the control of the existing owners, and to sell debt would act to mitigate the control factor by way of restrictive covenants in bond issues and other debt-type contracts. On the other hand, for short periods of time it is possible that owners whose control position is not so firmly entrenched might act differently. If control of the firm is being desired by an outside group, then the existing owners and their management team could raise the dividend payout in order to look good to a majority of the existing stockholders.

Signaling Effect. Higher dividends, higher payout ratios, or increases in either may constitute a signal by management to shareholders of a belief in increased cash flows or earning capacity or generally favorable financial forecasts. Backed up by cash, this signal can be expected to have substantial credibility with investors. Shepherd and Scott, *supra*, have this to say about the signaling effect of dividend policy:

> The informational content of dividends is an extremely interesting facet of this area of overall business policy. It can be phrased in the form of a question, to wit: Apart from the current financial impact, just what does a change in the dividend policy of the firm convey to investors? It is likely that an increase in the dividend payout could be interpreted by the market as an indication that the firm's management anticipates that the organization is about to enter a period of satisfactory cash flow. If the firm has maintained a relatively stable dividend payout ratio over time, and this ratio is increased by management, it is possible that some investors will react to the change in dividend policy as a management signal that the future profitability of the firm will be enhanced. This very tendency on the part of investors to weigh the informational content of dividends also helps explain why corporate managements are reluctant to cut dividend payments—even when such action might realistically be called for. Should the firm have available to it an unusually large number of attractive investment opportunities, and the inability to raise funds externally, then cutting the dividend to finance the projects internally makes economic sense. This situation actually could be reflective of company strength, but could be interpreted in the opposite fashion by the investment community. The dividend cut might signal the inability of the firm to maintain its established dividend payout, and unfavorable price movements with respect to the firm's common stock could follow. The real reason for the dividend cut would likely be missed by the market, unless a well-designed public relations plan has been carried out by company management.

Miller and Modigliani, *supra*, detected some misunderstandings about their irrelevance theory in light of observed changes in market price that follow from announced changes in dividend policy. They sought to clear up the misunderstanding by interpreting the signaling effect of dividend policy in the following terms:

> Such a phenomenon would not be incompatible with irrelevance to the extent that it was merely a reflection of what might be called the "information content" of dividends, an attribute of particular dividend payments hitherto excluded by assumption from the discussion and proofs. That is, where a firm has adopted a policy of dividend stabilization with a long-established and generally appreciated "target payout ratio," investors are likely to (and have good reason to) interpret a change in the dividend rate as a change in management's

views of future profit prospects for the firm. The dividend change, in other words, provides the occasion for the price change though not its cause, the price still being solely a reflection of future earnings and growth opportunities. In any particular instance, of course, the investors might well be mistaken in placing this interpretation on the dividend change, since the management might really only be changing its payout target or possibly even attempting to "manipulate" the price. But this would involve no particular conflict with the irrelevance proposition, unless, of course, the price changes in such cases were not reversed when the unfolding of events had made clear the true nature of the situation.

Clientele Effect. Another effect facilitated by the payment of dividends is the possibility of investment by certain types of institutional investors, an effect noted by Shepherd and Scott, *supra*:

> Further incentive for management to establish a dividend distribution rate that can be maintained during all phases of the business cycle, and also strengthening the bias against ever cutting dividends or omitting them entirely, is the existence of legal lists. In many states, financial institutions are regulated with respect to the purchase of common stocks. The state of New Jersey, for example, requires that the corporation must have paid dividends for the last five years before an insurance company operating in the state can purchase the common stock of that firm for its investment portfolio. As corporate managements desire to maintain broad markets and thus demand for their common shares, an effort is made to maintain an unbroken record of dividends. Even though the liquidity position of the company might dictate that the dividend be cut or omitted, such concern over the legal list requirement might cause the firm's management to risk the continuation of the payout.

See also Black & Scholes, The Effects of Dividend Yield and Dividend Policy on Common Stock Prices and Returns, 1 J. Fin. Econ. 1 (1974). In addressing assumptions of perfect markets on which their irrelevance theory was based, Miller and Modigliani, *supra*, added the following points about the clientele effect:

> [E]ven where we do find imperfections that bias individual preferences — such as the existence of brokerage fees which tend to make young "accumulators" prefer low-payout shares and retired persons lean toward "income stocks" — such imperfections are at best only necessary but not sufficient conditions for certain payout policies to command a permanent premium in the market. If, for example, the frequency distribution of corporate payout ratios happened to correspond exactly with the distribution of investor preferences for payout ratios, then the existence of these preferences would clearly lead ultimately to a situation whose implications were different in no fundamental respect from the perfect market case. Each corporation would tend to attract to itself a "clientele" consisting of those preferring its particular payout ratio, but one clientele would be entirely as good as another in terms of the valuation it would imply for the firm. Nor, of course, is it necessary for the distributions to match exactly for this result to occur. Even if there were a "shortage" of some particular payout ratio, investors would still normally have the option of achieving their particular saving objectives without paying a premium for the stocks in short supply simply by buying appropriately weighted combinations of the more plentiful payout ratios. In fact, given the great range of corporate payout ratios known to be available,

this process would fail to eliminate permanent premiums and discounts only if the distribution of investor preferences were heavily concentrated at either of the extreme ends of the payout scale.

Agency Cost Control. Judge Easterbrook has offered a further twist on setting and evaluating dividend policy as a matter of reducing agency costs. He argues that dividends reduce agency costs in two ways: (i) by keeping firms in the capital markets (by creating the need for external financing) where they are subjected to relatively efficient investigation and monitoring by new investors with information verified by underwriters and large lenders, and (ii) by adjusting risk levels taken by managers and other types of investors by reducing equity and raising debt or simply by reducing equity, in each case adjusting the debt/equity ratio. Easterbrook, Two Agency-Cost Explanations of Dividends, 74 Amer. Econ. Rev. 650 (1984).

Notes and Questions

1. The signaling effect of dividends implies "that dividends convey to investors valuable information in addition to that contained in contemporaneous information sources. Further, the benefits of this information appear to outweigh any costs associated with paying dividends." Asquith & Mullins, The Impact of Initiating Dividend Payments on Shareholders' Wealth, 56 J. Bus. 77, 81 (1983). As a consequence, "initiating dividends increases shareholders' wealth. The same is true of subsequent dividend increases." *Id.* at 93-94. If true, does this mean that directors should be *compelled* to pay dividends? Is withholding dividends tantamount to withholding valuable information which inhibits the market and stockholders in their monitoring of management? Asquith & Mullins conclude:

> Dividend policy has several attractive aspects as an information transmission mechanism. Unlike the detailed focus of other announcements, dividends can be used as a simple, comprehensive signal of management's interpretation of the firm's recent performance and its future prospects. Unlike most announcements, dividend announcements must be backed with hard cold cash. The firm must either generate this cash or convince the capital markets to supply it. In addition to the credibility of cash signals, dividends are also highly visible compared with other announcements.

Id. at 94; *See also* Brealey, Myers, & Allen, Principles of Corporate Finance 419-21 (8th ed. 2006).

2. With respect to the clientele effect, in light of the increasing concentration of equity ownership by institutional investors and the arguably positive effect this has on controlling managerial discretion by enhancing monitoring and increasing the possibility of changes in control, is it reasonable to argue that withholding dividends when a corporation is able financially to pay them is a management entrenchment device that should be scrutinized in a manner other than under the business judgment rule?

3. At the intersection between the theoretical and practical issues in dividend policy, consider also Ang, Dividend Policy: Informational Content or Partial Adjustment, 5 Rev. Econ. and Stat. 65, 65-66, 69 (1975), which focused on the issue of "intertemporal change of dividends." Ang distinguished between the informational content of dividends and the "partial adjustment hypothesis." The partial adjustment hypothesis is that firms recognize the variability of earnings and adjust dividend policy in terms of current earnings only gradually over time, rather than in direct proportion to changes in

earnings levels. In particular, if earnings increase, dividend levels will not increase pro-portionately unless there is reason to believe that a higher level of dividends is sustain-able; and if earnings decrease, management will resist cutting dividend levels. As a re-sult, changes in the level of dividends will be slow and gradual.

In tension with this story is Miller and Modigliani's thesis that dividends are changed in response to changing managerial expectations about long-term earnings. Under that thesis, increased dividend levels imply confidence in long-term earnings and cash genera-tion, and decreased dividend levels imply pessimism about both. And if earnings fall, management can signal its unyielding confidence in future earnings and cash flows by maintaining current dividend levels. So not only will there be no lag between earnings level changes and dividend level changes, but dividends may be changing ahead of changes in earnings. Based on these perspectives on these two alternative dividend mod-els, Ang then posited that a firm could analyze its reported or expected earnings and di-vide them into three categories (long-term, medium-term, and short-term) and set divi-dend policy as a function of these three categories. Ang then draws the following insights:

> [I]f a firm follows the partial adjustment process in its approach to dividend payouts, it is more likely to change its dividends fully if it is determined that part of the earnings change is relatively long run, and only partially if the earn-ings change is more or less short term. Thus, the lags will be greater for the shorter-run components. In contrast, a firm that attempts to convey informa-tion to the market via dividend payouts will change its dividends anticipating an earnings change (i.e., dividends lead earnings). It is generally argued that it is the change in long-run earnings that the firm is attempting to forecast.... This suggests that dividends are expected to lead earnings in the long run and the lead diminishes in the shorter run....

Ang's position on the informational content of dividends compared to the partial ad-justment process calls for an empirical assessment of dividend policy as it relates to lev-els of earnings changes over time.

4. Should directors have this almost unconstrained discretion provided by current law to determine whether, when, and in what amounts to pay dividends? On this issue, Victor Brudney, in Dividends, Discretion, and Disclosure, 66 Va. L. Rev. 85, 97–103 (1980), has asserted:

> .... [Court] opinions rarely speak of the relationship of dividends to share prices. The context in which the legal problem generally arises (stockholders' efforts to force dividend payments on the ground that management has re-tained more than is needed by "the business") focuses judicial attention on management's right to retain earnings to meet the needs of the business and maximize profits rather than on any obligation to satisfy the varying prefer-ences of individual stockholders for dividends or share price increases. The accent is on the needs of the enterprise in order to enhance or protect earning power or enterprise value; only when funds are superfluous to such "needs" is consideration given to whether the funds are distributable.... The basis gener-ally expressed in the opinions and treatises for forcing a payout, however, is the "wrongful" or "unreasonable" retention of funds; invariably, "wrongful" or "unreasonable" is defined in terms of favoring insiders to the detriment of outside investors. Thus, while the case law does not deal squarely with the problem at hand, its rationale is unequivocal in emphasizing that manage-ment's role is to focus on enterprise values. If dividend policy affects share

values independently of enterprise value, that has not yet been a matter to which the law has forced management to direct its attention—and the law is not likely to, when to have done so would have been at the expense of enterprise value.

If each shareholder's wealth is seen as maximized by the same dividend policy that maximizes other shareholders' wealth, management's dividend decisions become matters of business judgment (except as management itself has interests that diverge from shareholders' interests) that affect all shareholders equally. Resolution of the question of dividend policy's independent impact on share values is thus addressed to the proper business policy to be adopted by management.[53] If, however, shareholders differ over dividend policy (because of personal tax positions, transaction costs, a near-term focus, or other personal considerations), management is faced with the problem of the relationship of its duty to the enterprise and its duty, if any, to individual shareholders. If individual preferences were the determinants for management, the question whether dividend policy has an independent impact on share values would assume larger significance in defining management's duties.

Both economics and law suggest, however, that corporate management's obligation is the collective good of the enterprise rather than the preferences of individual shareholders that are independent of that collective good. As an economic matter,

> the likelihood that any single dividend policy can serve *all* [stockholder] interests is infinitesimal. Perhaps the best that can be done is for management to take those actions—dividend and otherwise—that are most favorable to the longer-run investment value of the stock. If the stock value is maintained in the market, it follows that stockholders whose preferences are being neglected can reshape their own portfolios without great penalty.[54]

As a legal matter, although the question is not often raised and appears never to have been answered squarely, the received learning leaves little doubt that dividend policy is a matter for managerial rather than stockholder decision and suggests that management's duty is to attend more to the collective good reflected in enhancing enterprise values than to the varying and often conflicting preferences of individual stockholders.

c. Dividends of Property and Securities

Besides paying cash dividends, corporations are also statutorily authorized to issue dividends in the form of property and securities.[1] Stock dividends are dividends that are

---

53. Arguably, if the dividend decision is an unbiased managerial judgment regarding the relative profitability of investment projects as against the current rate of return, managerial failure to produce more profitable results from reinvestment would establish a managerial judgment error. The impossibility of visiting legal sanctions on management for such business "errors" suggests that disciplining management would best be left to the marketplace or to stockholders' votes.

54. *See* J. Walter, Dividend Policy and Enterprise Valuation (1967), at 5 (emphasis in original).

1. *See, e.g.,* Del. Gen. Corp. Law § 173; N.Y. Bus. Corp. Law § 510(a); Rev. Bus. Corp. Act § 1.40 (definition of "distribution").

paid to stockholders in the form of stock rather than cash. The stock a company distributes may be shares of its own stock. In that case, the dividend is usually expressed as a percentage of the shares held by stockholders. For example, a company that pays a 10% stock dividend issues one additional share of stock to its stockholders for every 10 shares of common stock they own.

There are several reasons why companies declare dividends in shares of their own stock. First, stock dividends conserve cash needed to run the business. Second, stock dividends give the investor the ability to sell the shares she receives and generate cash from the sale. Thus, a stock dividend provides the investor with the option of timing her cash income. Third, shares received as a dividend are taxed only when those shares are sold, whereas a cash dividend is declarable as income the year in which it is received.

Finally, a corporation may declare a stock dividend for the purpose of lowering its stock price into a more desirable trading range. Because the issuance of a large number of shares reduces the percentage ownership that each outstanding share represents, the trading value of each share declines. Stockholders receiving the dividend, however, are not hurt because the price decline is offset by their receipt of additional shares. This concept unfolds more dramatically in the context of stock splits and reverse stock splits. *See supra* chapter 7, section 3b(ii)(A).

From an investor's standpoint, a stock dividend in shares of the company's own stock serves as a virtually costless method of reinvesting returns. If a company distributes a cash dividend, an investor seeking to reinvest in the company must use the dividend to buy additional shares in the open market. A stock dividend, by contrast, allows the investor to postpone recognition of tax liabilities and avoid broker expenses and other transaction costs associated with a cash purchase of stock.

A company's issuance of a stock dividend in shares of its own stock is only an accounting transaction, as the company does not transfer any physical assets to its stockholders (unlike in the case of a cash dividend). The stock dividend is charged to a company's retained earnings (earned surplus) account on its balance sheet. The dividend results in a transfer of the aggregate par value of the distributed shares (or, in the case of no par stock, an amount determined by the board) from the retained earnings (earned surplus) account to the common stock account on the balance sheet. The accounting treatment for a stock dividend is one of the ways a stock dividend is distinguished from a stock split.

The stock a company distributes may also be shares in a subsidiary owned by that company. If the company distributes all the subsidiary's shares in the form of a stock dividend, the distribution is called a *spin-off*.[2] A spin-off is an excellent way to unload an unwanted business when an outright sale of that business is not possible on advantageous terms.[3] The subsidiary, which was indirectly owned by the parent company's stockholders prior to the spin-off, becomes directly owned by those stockholders thereafter. If the company distributes only a portion of those shares, the distribution is called a *carve-out*. In this case, the parent company continues to own a large portion (typically 80%) of the subsidiary's shares.

---

2. I.R.C. §355 sets forth the requirements which must be met to ensure that a spin-off is tax-free.

3. Often the business to be spun-off will already exist as a separate corporation. Thus, all that the parent needs to do is distribute the subsidiary's stock. Sometimes, however, the business will exist as an internal division of the parent or another subsidiary. In such a case, the parent must first create another corporation and transfer to it the assets of the business to be spun-off.

Spin-offs can also be used to defend against unwanted takeovers. 1 Lipton & Steinberger, Takeovers & Freezeouts § 6.06[3][c] (perm. ed., rev. vol. 2004). Lipton and Steinberger suggest the possibility of placing a corporation's most valued assets in a separate subsidiary which could then be spun-off to the parent's stockholders. They also suggest using this technique as a method of increasing the parent's stock price by distributing assets that no longer fit the corporation's business plans and that might be valued more highly by the market as an independent entity.

The following case addresses the obligation of the parent's directors to maintain the value of a wholly-owned subsidiary prior to a contemplated spin-off.

Anadarko Petroleum Co. v. Panhandle Eastern Corporation
545 A.2d 1171 (Del. 1988)

WALSH, Justice:

This is an appeal from a decision of the Court of Chancery granting summary judgment against Anadarko Petroleum Corporation ("Anadarko") in its suit against three of its former directors and its former parent, Panhandle Eastern Corporation ("Panhandle"), for an alleged breach of fiduciary duty in modifying certain contracts, the so-called disputed agreements, between Anadarko and Panhandle. The lawsuit arises from a spin-off of Panhandle's wholly-owned subsidiary, Anadarko, through a stock dividend. After the stock dividend was declared but prior to the date of distribution, Panhandle and the Anadarko board of directors approved the disputed agreements. Anadarko argues that the disputed agreements are voidable because they are unfair and were approved in violation of fiduciary duties owed to the prospective stockholders of Anadarko. The Court of Chancery ruled as a matter of law that the former directors of Anadarko owed a fiduciary duty only to the parent corporation, Panhandle, at the time the disputed agreements were approved. Further, because Anadarko's claims with respect to the validity of the disputed agreements were premised on the existence of a fiduciary duty owed to the prospective stockholders of Anadarko, the court granted summary judgment against Anadarko.

This appeal presents a novel issue: whether a corporate parent and directors of a wholly-owned subsidiary owe fiduciary duties to the prospective stockholders of the subsidiary after the parent declares its intention to spin-off the subsidiary. We conclude that prior to the date of distribution the interests held by Anadarko's prospective stockholders were insufficient to impose fiduciary obligations on the parent and the subsidiary's directors. Accordingly, we affirm the decision of the Court of Chancery.

I

Panhandle, through its subsidiaries, Panhandle Eastern Pipeline Company ("Pipeline") and Trunkline Gas Company ("Trunkline"), is engaged in the pipeline transportation of natural gas. Prior to September, 1986, another Panhandle subsidiary Anadarko Production Company ("Production") through its subsidiary Anadarko was engaged in the exploration and production of crude oil and natural gas.

On August 20, 1986, Panhandle's board of directors voted unanimously to effect a spin-off of Panhandle's production and exploration assets by distributing one share of Anadarko common stock for each issued and outstanding share of Panhandle stock held of record on September 12, 1986. The date for distribution of the stock dividend was set at October 1, 1986. To advise Panhandle's shareholders and the market place of the impending spin-off, Panhandle and Anadarko issued an Information Statement for Anadarko Common Stock ("Information Statement") dated August 29, 1986. Further, on September 18, 1986, Panhandle furnished a list of its stockholders of record as of September 12, to Anadarko's transfer agent to facilitate the distribution of the stock dividend.

In order to enhance the value of the spin-off, representatives of Panhandle and Anadarko met with representatives of the New York Stock Exchange for the avowed purpose of creating a market for Anadarko stock prior to the date of distribution. The New York Stock Exchange approved the application and trading began in Anadarko stock on September 8, 1986. From September 8, 1986, to October 1, 1986, Panhandle and Anadarko stock were traded in essentially three forms. First, Panhandle's stock was traded the "regular way" reflecting the combined value of Panhandle and Anadarko. A share of Panhandle traded the regular way included a due bill which required the seller to deliver to the buyer the Anadarko stock dividend if and when it was distributed. Second, Panhandle stock was traded "ex-distribution." This form of trading reflected only the value of Panhandle, with the seller retaining the right to the Anadarko stock dividend. Finally, trading in Anadarko stock was effected on a "when-issued" basis, reflecting the value of Anadarko as an independent entity. Between September 8 and October 1, approximately three million shares of Anadarko shares were traded on a when-issued basis; one million of Panhandle shares were sold on an ex-distribution basis; and more than five million shares of Panhandle were traded the regular way.

Following board approval of the spin-off dividend, Panhandle began restructuring existing contracts between Panhandle and Anadarko. Initially an effort was made to modify the existing contracts through negotiations between the operating staffs of Anadarko and Panhandle. On September 11, Anadarko's board approved modifications to a prior "take or pay" agreement, requiring Anadarko to reduce the advance price of gas sold to Panhandle on a short term basis.[a] After failing to modify the remaining agreements through negotiations, on September 30, 1986, Anadarko's board of directors met to resolve all the outstanding impasse issues relating to the spin-off.

Five of the then seven Anadarko directors participated in the September 30 board meeting. Only one director, James T. Rodgers ("Rodgers"), was not affiliated with Panhandle or one of its subsidiaries. At the meeting Rodgers was joined by Robert J. Allison, Jr., ("Allison") a director of both Anadarko and Panhandle, in protesting the terms of the disputed agreements as being unfair to Anadarko. Further, the board was advised by Anadarko's General Counsel that it owed a fiduciary duty to Anadarko's prospective stockholders which would be breached if the board approved the unfair contracts.

The disputed agreements were approved by Anadarko's board by a 3-2 vote. (Rodgers voted against all of the modifications and Allison voted against five and abstained on one). Following the approval of the agreements the three inside directors resigned, effective October 1, 1986, and were replaced by four new directors. The newly constituted board reviewed the disputed agreements and based on an opinion by outside counsel that the contracts were unfair and voidable, the board voted unanimously to rescind the agreements.

---

a. Take-or-pay agreements are commonly used in the purchase and sale of energy products to allocate risks of production of supply to the seller and the risk of market demand to the buyer, by obligating the seller to supply a minimum quantity without regard to production and obligating the buyer to pay for a minimum quantity without regard to demand. *See* Murray & Murray, Corbin on Contracts § 1085A (Supp. 2004).

II

The linchpin of Anadarko's attack on the terms of the disputed agreements is the claim that the agreements were crafted adversely to Anadarko's interests by entities who were in a fiduciary relationship to Anadarko's prospective shareholders. This assertion assumes significance because if such a relationship exists Panhandle and its designated directors are required to demonstrate the entire fairness of the disputed agreements. *See Sinclair Oil Corporation v. Levien*, Del. Supr., 280 A.2d 717, 720 (1971)....

It is a basic principle of Delaware General Corporation Law that directors are subject to the fundamental fiduciary duties of loyalty and disinterestedness. Specifically, directors cannot stand on both sides of the transaction nor derive any personal benefit through self-dealing. *Guth v. Loft, Inc.*, Del. Supr., 5 A.2d 503 (1939).... However, in a parent and wholly-owned subsidiary context, the directors of the subsidiary are obligated only to manage the affairs of the subsidiary in the best interests of the parent and its shareholders. *See Sinclair Oil Corporation v. Levien*, 280 A.2d at 720....

Anadarko acknowledges that a parent does not owe a fiduciary duty to its wholly owned subsidiary. However, Anadarko argues that Panhandle's actions relating to the spin-off have established a class of stockholders to whom fiduciary duties are owed. Specifically Anadarko contends that by setting a record date for the dividend distribution and by establishing a market for Anadarko shares to be traded on a when-issued basis, Panhandle has created a fiduciary relationship with the prospective shareholders of Anadarko. As a result, Panhandle and the inside directors of Anadarko have assumed responsibility for demonstrating that the agreements are entirely fair to Anadarko's new shareholders—a formidable burden in view of the obvious one-sidedness of the agreements.

Anadarko first argues that record ownership passed to Anadarko's prospective stockholders as of September 12, the record date for the stock dividend. The argument follows that as record owners, the prospective stockholders of Anadarko were owed fiduciary duties by Panhandle and Anadarko's former directors. In support of this argument, Anadarko relies on the fact that the disputed agreements were approved after the record date and that a stock ledger had been prepared and delivered to a transfer agent. We do not view the passing of the record date and preparation of a stock ledger as determinative of the nature of the relationship.

Anadarko correctly states that Delaware law provides that the "stock ledger shall be the only evidence as to who are the stockholders entitled to examine the stockledger, ... or the books of the corporation, or to vote in person or by proxy at any meeting of the stockholders." 8 *Del. C.* §219(c).... The stock ledger referred to in section 219 and in the cases interpreting it, refer to a listing of present stockholders of existing entities. In this case the stock ledger relied on by Anadarko was not a list of Anadarko stockholders but was instead a list of Panhandle stockholders as of September 12. As the Chancery Court noted, the preparation of the stock list and the subsequent delivery to the transfer agent was done merely to facilitate the stock distribution plan for October 1, 1986 and did not serve to pass record ownership to Panhandle's stockholders. Thus, the existence of a stock ledger containing the names of Panhandle's stockholders as of September 12, who had an expectation of becoming Anadarko shareholders at a future specified date, does not provide a valid basis to impose fiduciary duties on Panhandle and Anadarko's former directors.

Anadarko's next argument presents a more substantial issue, i.e., whether beneficial ownership of Anadarko stock passed to Panhandle's stockholders of record and to those who purchased Anadarko stock on a when-issued basis. Anadarko relies on two assertions in support of its beneficial ownership argument; first, Panhandle's stockholders of record had a vested contractual right to the dividend of Anadarko stock; and second, the trading in Anadarko stock prior to the date of distribution created a beneficial interest distinct from Panhandle's legal interest in Anadarko.[3]

The general rule regarding the vesting of cash dividends is that a contractual right of the stockholder to the dividend becomes fixed upon the declaration of the dividend. Thus, upon a valid declaration of a dividend the corporation becomes indebted to the stockholder, and the stockholder may recover the declared amount in an action, *ex contractu*, against the corporation. *See Wilmington Trust Co. v. Wilmington Trust Co.*, Del. Ch., 15 A.2d 665 (1940).... However, the same rule does not extend to stock dividends.

In the context of a stock dividend, the nature of the res distributed and the shareholders' right to and interest in the dividend are less certain. The value of the underlying asset to be distributed, i.e., a proportionate interest in the equity of the corporation, may fluctuate between the date of declaration and date of distribution as a result of market forces and/or management decisions. Thus, the corresponding right to the stock dividend is not compromised by foreseeable changes in the inherent value of the underlying corporation. Given the inherent risk of possible change in equity value, the stock interest held by Anadarko's prospective stockholders does not support the conclusion that a separate class of beneficial stockholders has been created by the declaration of the spin-off dividend.

Andarko [sic] next argues that a distinct beneficial interest was created in Anadarko stock as a result of trading on the New York Stock Exchange in Anadarko and Panhandle stock. Anadarko contends that individuals who bought Anadarko stock on a when-issued basis acquired an interest in Anadarko and not in Panhandle. Similarly, individuals who sold their Panhandle stock on an ex-distribution basis relinquished ownership of Panhandle but retained an interest in Anadarko. The result, as Anadarko contends, is that a beneficial interest in Anadarko was created that was distinct from Panhandle's stockholders' interest in Panhandle individually and as the parent corporation of Anadarko. While we agree that a distinct interest was created by providing a market for Anadarko stock prior to distribution, we conclude that the interest does not rise to the level of a beneficial interest for purposes of imposing fiduciary duties on Panhandle and Anadarko's former directors.

The concept of "beneficial ownership" of stock, though somewhat inexact, is contextually defined, and has become a term of art for purposes of establishing fiduciary duties under Delaware law.... As applied in this case, beneficial ownership contemplates a separation of legal and equitable ownership. Under this concept, the equitable or beneficial owner possesses an economic interest in the subject property distinct from legal ownership or control....

The separation of legal and equitable ownership is lacking in this case. Until the date of distribution, both legal and equitable title remained with Panhandle as the parent of a wholly owned subsidiary. As noted by the Vice Chancellor, Panhandle continued as Anadarko's record owner and, as such, had voting control of Anadarko stock

---

3. In support of its argument that Anadarko's prospective stockholders were beneficial owners, Anadarko also relies, by analogy, on section 16(a) of the Securities Exchange Act of 1934, under which the Securities and Exchange Commission has ruled that beneficial ownership of a dividend stock is acquired on the record date. We are not persuaded by this argument. The definition of "beneficial ownership" under the 1934 act facilitates the broad disclosure function of section 16(a). This expansive definition does not comport with the rationale and purpose of establishing fiduciary duties under Delaware corporate law, and thus will not be adopted in this case.

until the date of distribution. The question of beneficial ownership, however, is less clear and requires an examination of the expectancy interest held by Anadarko's prospective stockholders.

The nature and scope of the expectancy interest held by Anadarko's prospective stockholders is addressed in the Information Statement issued prior to the spin-off of Anadarko. Regarding Panhandle's relationship with Anadarko the Information Statement clearly states that it can be expected that the companies will enter into agreements concluding long-term negotiations providing for adjustments to the terms of certain gas purchase and related contracts....

Significantly, the Information Statement concludes that the adjusted gas purchase agreements will likely result in "contractual terms as to price, 'take or pay' obligations and other matters" which are not as favorable to Anadarko as the terms of its present contracts with Panhandle.

Through the Information Statement, Anadarko's prospective stockholders were thus on notice that Panhandle continued to exercise both legal and equitable ownership of Anadarko and that this ownership would be used to effect contractual arrangements between the two companies. Indeed the contractual modifications complained of in this case were the subject of specific comment in the Information Statement. Panhandle's stockholders and those who purchased Anadarko stock on a when-issued basis could not reasonably expect a continuation of the status quo nor did they have any assurance of a protected financial interest in Anadarko prior to the date of distribution. It cannot be claimed, therefore, that Panhandle purported to act in a fiduciary role to protect Anadarko's prospective stockholders from the risk that changes would occur prior to the distribution date.

Finally, Anadarko argues that as of the record date for distribution, September 12, 1986, Panhandle and Anadarko's directors held Anadarko stock in trust for the prospective stockholders of Anadarko. Specifically, Anadarko contends that as trustees, Panhandle and the Anadarko board had a general fiduciary duty to preserve the value of the corpus of the trust, i.e., the Anadarko stock.... In support of its argument, Anadarko relies on *Sherry v. Union Gas Utilities, Inc.*, Del. Ch., 171 A. 188, 190 (1934) which states: "[w]hen a dividend has been declared and moneys deposited for its payment, it has been determined that such deposit ... is affected with a trust in favor of stockholders."[4] This argument which, again, proceeds on a cash dividend analogy is not persuasive.

In order for a trust relationship to exist there must be evidence of an intention on the part of the grantor to separate legal and equitable title to the subject of the trust.... As previously discussed, this division of interests does not exist in this case. To the contrary, Panhandle, through its actions and public disclosures in the Information Statement, has indicated its intention that Anadarko would continue to be its wholly owned subsidiary until the date of distribution.

The holding in *Sherry v. Union Gas Utilities, Inc.* relied on by Anadarko in support of its trust argument turns upon the intent of the corporation in depositing funds payable to bondholders. This evidence of intent to separate legal and equitable title is lacking in this case since there is no indication that Anadarko shares were deposited or set aside

---

4. In *Sherry* the Court of Chancery resolved a dispute over interest payments on corporate bonds by adopting an analogous theory which imposed a trust on dividends deposited for payment in favor of the record date stockholders.

prior to the date of distribution. The absence of evidence of intent to separate legal and equitable title to Anadarko precludes any implication of a trust relationship in this case.

We hold, therefore, that the Court of Chancery properly concluded that a fiduciary relationship did not exist between Panhandle and Anadarko's prospective stockholders. Accordingly, the decision granting summary judgment is AFFIRMED.

ON MOTION FOR REARGUMENT OR REHEARING EN BANC
Submitted: July 8, 1988

Anadarko seeks reargument on related contentions. First, Anadarko argues that by relying on the Information Statement to support the conclusion that a fiduciary relationship did not exist between Anadarko's directors and its prospective stockholders, this Court has implicitly recognized the proposition that disclosure can relieve a director of the duty of loyalty. Second, Anadarko contends that if disclosure can relieve a director of the duty of loyalty, it is important for this Court, upon reconsideration, to establish a clear test for adequacy of disclosure. Finally, Anadarko seeks the opportunity to litigate the factual adequacy of disclosure upon remand to the Court of Chancery.

Contrary to Anadarko's claims, the ruling in the principal opinion, when confined to its specific facts, is not inconsistent with a director's duty of loyalty nor does it stand for the proposition that disclosure is a substitute for loyalty. As the opinion makes clear, under the circumstances of this case the corporate parent's ownership interest was not legally divisible before the date of distribution for purposes of imposing fiduciary duties on Anadarko's former directors. The relevant inquiry is thus twofold: to whom is the fiduciary duty owed and at what time. Our ruling is specifically confined to Anadarko's claim that, under Delaware corporate law, a fiduciary relationship existed between Anadarko's board and its prospective stockholders prior to the issue date of the expected shares. We have concluded that the duty of loyalty arises only upon establishment of the underlying relationship.

Finally, we note that the viability of Anadarko's claim of nondisclosure, assertable as a federal cause of action, is not before us. Our ruling is confined to claims against corporate directors arising out of an alleged fiduciary relationship.

Given the narrow confines of our holding we find no basis for reargument. Accordingly, the motion for reargument is DENIED.

Notes and Questions

1. In footnote 3 the court rejects plaintiff's argument based on analogy to § 16(a) of the Securities Exchange Act of 1934 as "not comport[ing] with the rationale and purpose of establishing fiduciary duties under Delaware corporate law...." What does the court understand that "rationale and purpose" to be?

2. Does *Anadarko* suggest *when* fiduciary duties will be imposed? How (and if) they might be disclaimed? What is the purpose of the court's discussion of the "expectancy interests" of the Anadarko stockholders-to-be? *See* Easterbrook & Fischel, Corporate Control Transactions, 91 Yale L.J. 698, 700-703 (1982). *But see* Mitchell, A Parable for the '80s: Anadarko Petroleum Co. v. Panhandle Eastern Co., 53 Alb. L. Rev. 655 (1990). Does it have anything to do with fiduciary duty? How has this expectancy interest been created? Does the way in which the expectancy interest is created suggest anything with respect to the propriety of applying the concept of fiduciary duty?

3. In 1996, General Motors effected a split-off of its wholly-owned subsidiary, Electronic Data Systems Holding Corporation (EDS). Unlike in the traditional spin-off situation where parent shareholders have no direct equity stake in a parent's wholly-owned subsidiary prior to the spin-off, GM had previously issued shares of a class of parent company common stock (GM Class E common stock) the attributes of which were linked to the financial performance of EDS as opposed to all of GM. This type of stock is referred to as "tracking stock." (For a discussion of tracking stock, see *infra* the end of this section 3c.) Thus, unlike the shareholders in *Anadarko*, a class of GM equity holders had a strong contractual interest in GM's treatment of EDS *prior* to the split-off.

To effect the split-off, GM exchanged Class E shares (the tracking stock) for real shares in EDS. Prior to doing so, GM caused EDS to enter into new information technology service agreements (including a new master services agreement), as GM would continue to need EDS's services going forward. Moreover, GM caused EDS to make a $500 million lump sum cash transfer payment to GM. Because GM needed to amend its charter in connection with the split-off (to eliminate the Class E shares as well as redefine the two remaining classes of GM common stock), various shareholder votes were required, including a separate class vote of the Class E shareholders. All required votes, including the separate class vote of the Class E shareholders, was obtained.

Plaintiff Class E shareholders challenged the fairness of the terms of the master services agreement as well as the $500 million cash transfer payment, which they referred to as a "freedom payment." In Solomon v. Armstrong, 747 A.2d 1098 (Del. Ch. 1999), *aff'd*, 746 A.2d 277 (Del. 2000), the court held that the decisions made by the defendant GM directors were protected by the business judgment rule. The court noted that "so long as a shareholder vote to approve or disapprove the transaction was made on a fully-informed, non-coerced basis, that vote operates *ex proprio vigore* as an independent foundation for the application of the business judgment rule." *Id.* at 1127. The court also discounted the plaintiffs' allegation that the defendant directors had been motivated to favor GM over EDS in the split-off negotiations because of their disproportionate equity stakes in regular GM common stock as opposed to the Class E stock. Indeed, the court held that for the business judgment rule to be disabled because of self-interest the plaintiffs would have to show that each director's interest in regular GM common stock was "material" to that director, something the plaintiffs failed to do. *Id.* at 1118.

Isquith v. Caremark International, Inc.
136 F.3d 531 (7th Cir. 1998)

POSNER, C.J.:

This is a class action suit under Rule 10b-5 of the SEC and other antifraud provisions of federal securities law, with supplemental claims under state corporation law. The suit, against Baxter International (the pharmaceutical manufacturer) and a spun-off former wholly owned subsidiary of Baxter called Caremark, charges that Baxter submitted a fraudulent statement to the Securities and Exchange Commission in connection with the spinoff....

The complaint alleges that in 1991, when Caremark was still part of Baxter, the government began investigating Caremark for suspected Medicare and Medicaid fraud.... [A]ccording to the complaint (the only source of factual allegations in the case), Baxter decided to try to insulate itself from any potential liability by spinning off Caremark, that is, by transferring the ownership of the subsidiary from Baxter to Baxter's shareholders, each to receive shares of Caremark proportional to their shares in Baxter, with the result that Caremark would no longer be a subsidiary of Baxter but an independent company. In order to avoid having to register the new security created to effectuate the spinoff—for the shares of Caremark, as of Baxter, were to be publicly traded—Baxter needed a "no action" letter from the [Securities and Exchange Commission]. The Commission issued the letter upon Baxter's agreeing to file an "information statement," *see* 17 C.F.R. § 240.14c-2, that would among other things disclose the purpose of the spinoff. The statement said that the purpose of the spinoff was to avoid a looming competitive conflict between Caremark and other lines of Baxter's business. That, according to the complaint, was a lie; the purpose of the spinoff was to minimize the liability of Baxter's shareholders for Caremark's fraud. But because the SEC issued the requested "no action" letter, the spinoff—which did not require the consent of the shareholders—went through, and Baxter shareholders found themselves holding Baxter plus Caremark shares (one of the latter for every four of the former) rather than just Baxter shares.

The immediate effect of the transaction was to reduce the market value of Baxter stock because the spinoff had diminished Baxter's assets. But the market value of Baxter and Caremark stock—the only thing investors would care about—exceeded the value of Baxter stock before the spinoff. Eventually, however, the investing public got wind of Caremark's troubles, and the market value of its shares headed south. In 1995 Caremark pleaded guilty to criminal charges of fraud based on conduct going back to 1986 and paid the government $160 million.

The plaintiff class consists of the owners of Baxter shares at the time of the spinoff. The claim is that the spinoff constituted a forced "sale" of Caremark shares to them and that the sale was effected by fraud because, had the true purpose of the spinoff been revealed, owners of Baxter shares could have gotten the courts to block it; Baxter would then have been kept intact and Baxter stock would, they claim, today be worth more than the current combined value of Baxter and Caremark stock. It is difficult to see why, since Baxter's Caremark subsidiary, as it would have remained, would still have had to pony up the $160 million to the government. But the plaintiff argues, and in the posture of the case we must, though skeptical, accept, that the spinoff destroyed valuable synergies between Baxter and its Caremark subsidiary. If, however, whether on this or some other basis, the plaintiff could have gotten the spinoff enjoined, this implies that she can still sue for damages—as she has done, in the supplemental state law claim now pending in state court. So it is very difficult to see how Baxter's coyness about the purpose of the suit hurt her or the other members of the class....

The plaintiff hints that the SEC, too, would have blocked, or at least delayed, the spinoff had it learned of Caremark's illegalities. Yet she points to nothing in the laws administered by the SEC that would have authorized the Commission to impede the transaction had Baxter confessed that its motivation was to lighten its liabilities. That is not an improper motivation, and anyway the Commission's concern is with the completeness and accuracy of information provided to investors rather than with what the information reveals about the soundness or even morality of the investment. So if Baxter had come clean, the SEC would still have had no grounds for refusing to issue a no-action letter. And, at worst, Baxter would then have had to register the Caremark stock.

There is a lot more that is wrong with this suit. Suppose Baxter had been candid with the SEC—and hence the public, because both the information statement and the no-action letter were public documents, and the statement, at least, was mailed to the shareholders—about Caremark's liability. Then the market value of Baxter's shares would have fallen immediately, discounting any anticipated losses resulting from that liability, and the plaintiff class would have taken its hit then—before they could do anything about it—rather than later. Although investors who bought stock in Baxter or Caremark after the spinoff and in reliance on the stated purpose might have been hurt by Baxter's lack of candor, they are not members of the class. They have their own suit. The class in the present suit is limited to owners of Baxter shares at the time of the spinoff. If we assume with the plaintiff that Baxter would have been liable for its subsidiary's fraud, the spinoff shifted that liability to Caremark. Without the spinoff, it would have remained with Baxter. Since the members of the class owned both companies, the spinoff merely shifted liability from one pocket of their trousers to another. As for the loss of synergy, that has nothing to do with fraud....

The biggest problem with the suit is not the difficulty we're having figuring out how the members of the class could have been hurt by the alleged fraud in concealing the true purpose of the spinoff; for it is too early in the litigation to decide that this puzzle cannot be solved. Rather, it is the absence of other elements of federal securities fraud, such as that there have been a sale (or purchase—but for every purchase there is a sale). *Blue Chip Stamps v. Manor Drug Stores*, 421 U.S. 723, 44 L. Ed. 2d 539, 95 S. Ct. 1917 (1975).... The members of the class did not buy or sell shares in Baxter. They did not buy or sell shares in Caremark. They simply received one share of Caremark stock for every four shares they owned of Baxter. They no more "bought" Caremark stock than the recipient of a stock dividend—which the plaintiff concedes the distribution of the Caremark stock was—buys the stock that he receives as a dividend.

Words are protean in the hands of lawyers, so it can be argued that the Baxter shareholders were forced in effect to "buy" Caremark shares, "paying" for them by the reduction in the value of their Baxter shares as a result of the diminution in Baxter's assets that was brought about by the spinoff. But to accept this argument we would have to have a reason for wanting to play with words in this way, and we cannot think of any that advances the purposes of the securities laws.... The members of the class in this case had no choice. They made no investment decision. They therefore cannot have been induced by the alleged fraud to buy or sell any securities even if the spinoff can somehow be thought of as effecting a sale of their shares in Baxter.

"The members of the class in this case had no choice...." No investment choice, that is. They could have sued to try to stop the spinoff. *Goldberg v. Meridor*, 567 F.2d 209, 218-21 (2d Cir. 1977) (Friendly, J.), holds that this option is enough to establish the materiality of a misleading statement to investors. *See also Field v. Trump*, 850 F.2d 938, 946-48 (2d Cir. 1988). But ... it is not good law in this circuit. *Goldberg* would allow every complaint about the mismanagement of a corporation that issues securities subject to federal securities law to be shoehorned into federal court on the theory that management had defrauded the shareholders by concealing the mismanagement. This would carry the securities laws far outside their intended domain. And it would violate the principle that the only loss of which complaint is possible under the antifraud provisions of those laws is a loss that candor would have averted. Candor would not have averted the consequences of whatever mismanagement or misfortune resulted in Care-mark's scrape with the federal government. Even a successful suit to block the spinoff would not have eliminated the liability to the government that is the ultimate cause of the harm for which the plaintiff seeks redress. . . .

This is a bit overstated; that scrape was the major cause of the loss in value, but there are also those synergies allegedly lost because the spinoff was not enjoined. If we as-sume that a damages suit is somehow blocked, or that the value of those lost synergies could somehow not be quantified (in which event the damages remedy would be inade-quate)—and if we ignore the fact that if this is so, the plaintiff cannot obtain damages, the only relief sought, in the present suit either—then it would be the case that the fraud in the information statement filed with the SEC had caused a loss to the plaintiff. But . . . it would not be a loss that a suit under the antifraud provisions of the securities laws can be based on. For it would not be a loss of the kind that these laws are con-cerned with, namely a loss of investment value as a consequence of the concealment or distortion of the truth. In the lingo of securities law, the plaintiff would have shown "transaction causation" (the transaction, here the spinoff and resulting change in the form of the plaintiff's holdings, would not have occurred but for the fraud) but not "loss causation" (a loss produced by a discrepancy between the actual market value of a stock and what that value would have been had there been no misrepresentation). . . .

The plaintiff directs us to another esoteric and dubious judge-made doctrine, called the "fundamental change" doctrine. It began life as the "forced seller" doctrine of *Vine v. Beneficial Finance Co.*, 374 F.2d 627, 634-35 (2d Cir. 1967). Vine, a minority share-holder squeezed out by the majority, was allowed to characterize the transaction as a sale. Which in a sense it was, as he was forced to exchange stock for cash; that is what a squeeze-out does. But precisely because it was a forced sale, the plaintiff had not been induced to make it by a misrepresentation or misleading omission. There was no induc-ing; there was compulsion. And exactly the same thing is true here. The members of the class were not given a choice about whether to receive Caremark shares.

The doctrine of the *Vine* decision was limited in [*Rathborne v. Rathborne*, 683 F.2d 914 (5th Cir. 1982)]. That case involved a spinoff, just like the present one, and the court held that the spinoff was not a sale of securities, since it did not effect a "fundamental change" in the plaintiff's holding. . . . When *Vine* is read in light of these and other cases, such as *Sargent v. Genesco, Inc.*, 492 F.2d 750, 764-65 (5th Cir. 1974), and also in light of the Supreme Court's decision in *Blue Chip Stamps*, which made clear that the relevant provi-sions of the securities laws are limited to purchases and sales, the "forced seller" doctrine is seen to be limited to situations in which the nature of the investor's holding is so far al-tered as to allow the alteration to be characterized as a sale, as in the exchange of stock for cash in *Vine* itself. A change in form will not count as a sale and so will not be actionable; the change must be in some sense "fundamental" rather than nominal; hence the renam-ing of the doctrine. The distinction is critical in this case. In a squeeze-out, stock is ex-changed for cash; the person squeezed out no longer has any interest in the corporation; that is unquestionably a change in his bundle of property rights. In a spinoff there is no exchange, no forced exit from the corporation, but merely the receipt by the corpora-tion's shareholders of additional stock. Only the form in which the members of the class owned Baxter's assets was changed; it was changed from stock in one corporation to stock in two corporations. After the change the class members owned the same propor-tion, carrying the same rights, of the same pool of assets. Before, their ownership interest was denominated in shares of Baxter; after, in shares of Baxter and Caremark; the interest itself—the amount of assets owned by the members of the class-was unchanged.

So the fundamental-change doctrine, successor to the defunct forced-seller doctrine, is inapplicable to this case. And anyway we very much doubt that the doctrine retains any validity in any class of case, even in squeeze-out cases. In *Santa Fe Industries, Inc. v. Green, supra*, 430 U.S. at 473-77, decided after *Vine*, the Supreme Court made clear for the first time that securities fraud does not include the oppression of minority share-holders, which is what the plaintiff in *Vine* was complaining about. No more does secu-rities fraud include unsound or oppressive corporate reorganizations, which is the es-sential complaint of the plaintiff class in this case....

This is implicit in the requirement that the plaintiff, to maintain his suit, have relied on the fraud, *e.g., Basic Inc. v. Levinson*, 485 U.S. 224, 243, 99 L. Ed. 2d 194, 108 S. Ct. 978 (1988), meaning that he changed his position because of it. It is implicit in the decisions that hold that there can be no suit under the securities laws by someone who has not made an investment decision, that is, who has not made a choice, a voluntary decision albeit one induced by the fraud, to buy or sell securities. There was no investment decision in *Vine....*

.... And similarly in this case, the fraud by which Baxter allegedly obtained swift ap-proval of the spinoff did not induce the members of the plaintiff class to buy or sell Baxter shares. It just made them vulnerable to what was neither a misrepresentation nor a purchase or sale of securities, but merely an involuntary change in the form of their holdings.... But even if, as we greatly doubt, the [fundamental-change] doctrine is good law, it is, as we have explained, inapplicable to this case. To recapitulate: there was no forced sale, because only the form of the plaintiff's investment was changed; and anyway there was no reliance, no investment decision, because the plaintiff did not have a choice whether or not to accept the new stock.

Note on Tracking Stock: The "Internal Spin-Off"

Managers of public corporations engaged in multiple businesses (often referred to as "conglomerates") sometimes believe that the price at which the company's shares trade in the stock market fails to reflect the real value of the company. This can happen, for example, where an old-fashioned industrial company also operates a high-technology or Internet business but the market does not seem to give it credit for the latter. Say its stock trades at around $100 per share but a manager believes that if the two businesses were seen as separate, the old-industrial business might trade at around $75 and the new-technology business at around $50, for a total of $125.

To "unlock" this hidden value within conglomerates, investment banks developed "tracking stock" and pitched it to their corporate clientele. A tracking stock is a separate class of common stock defined in the corporation's charter as linked to the performance of a particular business of the corporation (referred to as a "business group"). By defini-tion, a corporation with a tracking stock equity structure has at least two classes of com-mon stock, each of which is linked to the performance of a distinct business group.

Tracking stocks are usually created by amending a charter to create the multiple classes of common stock. Existing common stock is reclassified as one class of track-ing stock, while shares of new classes are distributed to existing shareholders through a stock dividend. Charter amendments adopting a tracking stock equity structure specify the dividend, voting and liquidation rights of each class of tracking stock. Dividends on each class are payable from the cash flow of the particular busi-ness group to which that class is linked. Voting and liquidation rights set forth in the charter typically provide for annual readjustment based on the relative market capitalizations of each business group.

Transactions between business groups, such as inter-group loans, and allocations of general corporate overhead expenses are governed by managerial policies the board of directors establishes when the corporation adopts a tracking stock structure. These policies are subject to change at the board's discretion. Otherwise, there is no legal separation in the business groups for purposes of corporate law. All shareholders, regardless of the business group their shares track, remain shareholders of the corporation. So all creditors and holders of preferred stock in the corporation retain claims on the entire corporation's assets that rank ahead of all the shareholders. Managers retain legal control over the entire corporation and not of discrete tracked businesses.

So the only thing that really seems to change in these structures is the appearance. Stocks are traded separately, each business group is reported on separately, and the performances of both are followed by the investment community separately. That may produce a desirable increase in the transparency of business performance of the different business groups. It could cause other problems, however. Most strikingly, it can create conflicts of interest between groups of shareholders. Accordingly, it is questionable whether this use of capital structure to promote transparency is superior to more modest yet direct efforts such as clearer reporting of the performance of different business segments in a company's consolidated financial statements.

For a thorough analysis of tracking stock equity structures and some of the additional problems they pose for corporate governance, see Haas, Directorial Fiduciary Duties in a Tracking Stock Equity Structure: The Need for a Duty of Fairness, 94 Mich. L. Rev. 2089 (1996).

Section 4
Redemptions and Repurchases

Dividends are one way in which stockholders receive a return on their investment. One disadvantage they pose, however, is that all shares of the class on which dividends are paid must be treated equally. As noted in section 3b *supra*, moreover, management cannot be sure that any dividend policy that it establishes, or any change to a preexisting dividend policy, will be accurately understood by its investors. Accordingly, the use of dividends as a means of providing a return on investment is an imperfect device.

In this section, we consider two other ways to provide returns to stockholders: redemptions and repurchases. These two terms both refer to a corporation buying back some of its previously issued shares. However, there are two technical distinctions between the sorts of transactions each term is used to define. First, redemptions are usually effected pursuant to a preexisting agreement, which may be set forth in the corporation's charter or in a shareholders' agreement. Repurchases, by contrast, are made upon a decision of the board of directors, not pursuant to any preexisting agreement. Second, repurchases may be accomplished on the open market or through an issuer tender offer, while partial redemptions may, under some circumstances, be accomplished selectively, although the following materials suggest some limitations on this technique.

a. Statutory Treatment

As a financial matter, redemptions and repurchases diminish corporate assets. Assuming the price paid by the corporation adequately reflects the value of redeemed or repurchased shares, this should not bother the remaining stockholders since their *pro rata* share of the assets that remain is not reduced. Creditors, however, will be disturbed by corporate redemptions or repurchases of stock, because the overall value of assets available to satisfy their claims *is* reduced. Consequently, redemptions and repurchases are considered to be distributions to stockholders, like dividends, and are subject to many of the same statutory limitations. For example, section 1.40 of the Revised Model Business Corporation Act includes within the definition of "distribution" the corporation's redemption or purchase of its own shares, which then subjects it to the RMBCA's legal capital rule (section 6.40) discussed *supra* in section 2a.

Delaware law permits corporations to redeem or repurchase their shares unless the corporation's capital is "impaired" or would become so as a result. Del. Gen. Corp. Law § 160(a)(1). In Klang v. Smith's Food & Drug Centers, Inc., 702 A.2d 150 (Del. 1997), plaintiff challenged the corporation's repurchase of shares on the basis that it violated the statutory provision against the impairment of capital. Indeed, the balance sheet would show a negative net worth following the repurchase, as the defendant board members readily admitted. Those members, however, had looked beyond the balance sheet and had restated the value of assets and liabilities thus leading to a positive surplus after the share repurchase. The Delaware Supreme Court upheld the board's right to depart from the balance sheet when calculating surplus. However, the court held that when the directors do so, they must evaluate assets and liabilities in good faith, on the basis of acceptable data, and by methods they reasonable believe reflect present value. They also must arrive at a determination of the surplus that is not so far off the mark as to constitute actual or constructive fraud.

New York, similarly, permits redemptions and repurchases out of surplus except when the corporation is insolvent or would be made so by the repurchase, and further permits redemptions or repurchases out of stated capital (subject to the insolvency limitations) for certain limited purposes (including the satisfaction of appraisal rights). N.Y. Bus. Corp. Law § 513.

Ordinarily, shares reacquired through a redemption or repurchase are treated by the corporation as treasury shares (which are issued but not outstanding). Consequently, although surplus may be reduced, stated capital generally is not changed unless and until the shares are retired. Some statutes, like the Revised Model Business Corporation Act § 6.31 and the California Corporations Code § 510, have, consistent with their simplifications of the legal capital rules, eliminated the concept of treasury shares and simply restore the reacquired shares to the status of authorized but unissued shares.

b. Purpose

If share repurchases serve the same purpose as corporate dividends, why would a given company prefer to repurchase shares as opposed to paying dividends? The primary reason relates to firm flexibility. A company must always pay dividends to shareholders holding the same class of shares on a pro rata basis.[1] By contrast, a company may repurchase shares from only some of its shareholders. However, doing so could lead to an allegation of unfairness from those shareholders whose shares were not repurchased—an allegation that particularly stings in the closely held corporation context.[2]

Additionally, companies seek to avoid the negative signalling effect that a dividend cut would have in the marketplace. Indeed, they generally increase dividend payout only when they believe the increase is sustainable. Therefore, dividends are viewed as a permanent commitment requiring reliable and steady cash flows. Repurchases, by contrast, can be made from cash flows that companies view as temporary. The marketplace does not view repurchases as permanent. Not surprisingly, repurchases tend to increase during boom periods and decrease significantly during periods of economic decline.[3]

A closely held company primarily repurchases shares to facilitate a shareholder's exit from the company (often done pursuant to a contractual arrangement). A public company, by contrast, typically decides to repurchase its own shares when its board of directors views the company's shares as undervalued in the marketplace. In other words, the board decides that the best investment for the company's surplus funds is the company's own stock. Because of the "bullish" or positive signal this conveys, the company's stock price typically rises when the company announces a stock repurchase program.[4] The repurchase also has the effect of reducing the supply of shares in the market thus further buoying the market price of the company's stock as earnings going forward are spread out over fewer shares.

One unfortunate side effect that plagues repurchases but not dividends is the impact that repurchases have on a company's capital structure. While both dividends and repurchases deplete a company's cash, repurchases also reduce a company's equity capital. This leads to an increase in the company's debt-to-equity ratio. The larger the number of shares repurchased, the more highly leveraged a company becomes. Thus, repurchases arguably transfer wealth from existing creditors to a company's stockholders, which is why repurchases are normally subject to the legal capital rules.[5]

c. Federal Regulation

Stock repurchases by public companies have the potential for abuse, as management is in a position to exploit its informational advantage over public shareholders. In

---

1. *See* 11 Fletcher et al., Fletcher Cyclopedia of the Law of Private Corporations § 5352 (perm. ed., rev. vol. 1999 & Supp. 2004).

2. *See, e.g.,* Toner v. Biltmore Envelope Co., 498 A.2d 642 (Md. 1985); Donahue v. Rodd Electrotype Co. of New England, 328 N.E.2d 505 (Mass. 1975), *modified by* Wilkes v. Springside Nursing Home, Inc., 353 N.E.2d 657 (Mass. 1976); Brudney, A Note on "Going Private," 61 Va. L. Rev. 1019, 1047-48 (1975).

3. *See* Guay & Harford, The Cash-Flow Permanence and Information Content of Dividend Increases Versus Repurchases, 57 J. Fin. Econ. 385 (2000).

4. *See* Ikenberry, Lakonishok & Vermaelen, Market Underreaction to Open-Market Share Repurchases, 39 J. Fin. Econ. 181 (1995) (demonstrating positive abnormal returns for the four-year period after the announcement of a repurchase program).

5. *See* Dittmar, Why Do Firms Repurchase Stock?, 73 J. Bus. 331 (2000).

addition, management could use repurchases to manipulate its company's stock price. Moreover, during the 1980s many public companies repurchased shares from hostile bidders or potential hostile bidders in order to induce these bidders to leave them alone. These repurchases were typically made at premium prices, and thus were referred to as *greenmail*. (Greenmail is discussed *infra* at chapter 9, section 2b(iii).) Because of the potential for abuse, the federal government decided to police stock repurchases by public companies.

(i) Open Market Repurchases

Because ordinary stock repurchases that public companies conduct are designed to increase their stock price, they represent a form of stock price manipulation. If not disclosed to the public, they could violate sections 10(b) and 9(a)(2) of the Securities Exchange Act of 1934 (Exchange Act). *See* Halsey, Stuart & Co., Inc., 30 S.E.C. 106, 110-112 (1949). In 1984, the SEC promulgated Exchange Act Rule 10b-18, which operates as a safe harbor for open market repurchase programs conducted by public companies. Rule 10b-18, however, makes clear that it is not the exclusive means to effect issuer repurchases, as no presumption arises that a company violates the Exchange Act if purchases do not meet the conditions of the rule.

(ii) Self-Tender Offers

A corporation may also make a tender offer for its own shares (a so-called "self-tender offer"). Self-tenders, in turn, can be broken down into *issuer tender offers* and *going private transactions*. The Exchange Act and SEC rules govern disclosure and procedures involved in self-tenders.

(A) Issuer Tender Offers

An issuer tender offer is any self-tender other than a going private transaction. Thus, an issuer tender offer is a partial tender offer in which the issuer seeks to repurchase less than all the outstanding shares of a class of equity security held by the public. After an issuer tender offer, the issuer has fewer shares outstanding yet typically remains a public company.

A tender offer by an issuer for its own equity securities is governed by Exchange Act Rule 13e-4. Importantly, that rule essentially requires issuers to follow the same disclosure and timing requirements applicable to third party tender offer. Thus, an issuer must file a disclosure document on Schedule TO with the SEC, publish a summary ad in a national newspaper and send its Offer to Purchase to its stockholders. In addition, like third party bidders, an issuer engaging in an issuer tender offer must comply with the antifraud requirements of Section 14(e) of the Exchange Act and Regulation 14E promulgated thereunder.

An issuer tender offer should be contrasted with issuer repurchases of its own equity securities during the pendency of a third party tender offer. Under Exchange Act Rule 13e-1, an issuer that has received notice of a third party tender offer for the issuer's shares cannot buy back any of its own shares unless it files a "13e-1 statement" with the SEC. Within that statement, an issuer must disclose, among other things, the venue and terms of its purchases, the purpose of its purchases, its plans for the repurchased securities (*e.g.*, retire them, hold them in treasury, resell them at a later date), and the source and amount of funds used to make the purchases.

(B) "Going Private" Transactions

A *going private transaction* is a self-tender by an issuer, the purpose of which is to convert a public company back into a private company. Because this is accomplished by the issuer repurchasing its outstanding stock held by the public, a going private transaction can be thought of as a "reverse initial public offering." Once all the stock has been repurchased from public stockholders, the issuer should no longer qualify as a reporting company under the Exchange Act and, therefore, should be considered a private company.

Going private transactions are led by management of the issuer either alone or in connection with a handful of outside investors. The consideration used to buy out public stockholders is usually cash, debt securities of the issuer (thus turning the former stockholders into creditors) or a combination of the two. Cash consideration is sometimes raised through the issuance of debt securities by or through a leveraged buy-out firm.

Going private transactions involve tremendous conflicts of interest. When current management offers to buy out public stockholders and establishes the price at which to do so, the interests of management and stockholders diverge. Accordingly, the SEC promulgated Exchange Act Rule 13e-3 and Schedule 13E-3 to address going private transactions.

Two major differences exist between Schedule 13E-3 disclosure and Schedule TO disclosure that reflect these conflicts. First, Schedule 13E-3 requires an elaborate statement of the fairness of a going-private transaction with supporting rationale. All material factors behind the statement must be itemized and disclosed. The issuer, therefore, is liable under the antifraud provisions for any false and misleading statements in this regard.

Second, Schedule 13E-3 requires disclosure of all reports and appraisals that the issuer received from outside parties (*e.g.*, an investment bank) "materially relating" to the fairness of the offer. Thus, the issuer must disclose all valuation information it has received. It simply cannot cherry pick the best valuation opinion (in this case the one giving the lowest possible valuation) of several it may have received. For a court's take on "going private" disclosure, see Howing Co. v. Nationwide Corp., 826 F.2d 1470 (6th Cir. 1987), *cert. denied*, 486 U.S. 1059 (1988).

d. Fiduciary Duties

Kahn v. U.S. Sugar Corp.
1985 WL 4449, 11 Del. J. Corp. L. 908 (Del. Ch. 1985)

This suit was brought as a class action challenging a leveraged cash tender offer made by United States Sugar Corporation ("U. S. Sugar") and a trust existing under its Employee Stock Ownership Plan (the "ESOP") to the corporation's stockholders. [O]n October 18, 1983, an application for a preliminary injunction enjoining the consummation of the offer was denied....

I find from all the properly admissible evidence that there was a breach of fiduciary duty by the defendants because the disclosures made in the tender offer solicitation materials did not disclose with complete candor all the material facts a stockholder needed to make a fully informed decision as to whether to accept the tender offer. I also conclude that the tender offer was coercive. I further find that it would be impossible to rescind the transaction and that, therefore, an award of damages is the only possible remedy. I find that the amount of damage is $4 per share.

I

.... The named plaintiffs represent the class of minority, public shareholders of U. S. Sugar who tendered their shares in response to the tender offer by U. S. Sugar and the ESOP. Defendants are U. S. Sugar, the ESOP, and the members of the Board of Directors of U. S. Sugar.

At the time of the tender offer U. S. Sugar was a public company with almost 5 million shares outstanding and its shares were held of record by more than 2,000 shareholders. The shares traded on the over-the-counter market, but only 28% of the outstanding shares were held by the public. The other 72% were owned either by charitable organizations established by Charles Stewart Mott, the founder of U. S. Sugar, or by members of the Mott family (collectively, the "Mott Interests"). The Board of Directors consisted of 14 persons of whom eight were either members of the Mott family or trustees of Mott charities or family trusts. Three were part of management.

* * *

The tender offer came about because the Mott Interests wished to reduce their holdings in U. S. Sugar but did not wish to relinquish their aggregated ability to exercise majority control over the company. The market price for U. S. Sugar stock was already considered to be depressed due to the world sugar glut and the sale of a substantial block of stock would have likely depressed it still further. It was therefore decided that a leveraged tender offer for 75% of the outstanding shares (over 3.5 million shares) was the best means of facilitating the wishes of the Mott Interests, while not depressing the market. Additionally, this tender offer would allow public shareholders to share in the tender offer and thus take advantage of a premium above market price.

Because the Mott Interests planned to tender a substantial number of shares while still retaining majority control, they had competing desires to both receive the highest possible tender offer price and still leave U. S. Sugar as a viable company not unduly burdened with debt. It is asserted by the defendants that these competing interests would tend to assure that those public shareholders who tendered their shares in response to the tender offer would receive as high a price as feasible for their shares, while also assuring that shareholders who did not choose to tender would not be locked into an overburdened corporation. Be that as it may, although more than 93% of the publicly held shares were tendered, more than 42% of the 2,000 shareholders chose not to be completely cashed out but elected to retain some portion of their holdings.

The ESOP was formed as a part of the tender offer plan. It purchased over one million shares at $68 per share with funds borrowed from U. S. Sugar. It was planned that the ESOP would repay U. S. Sugar from the annual tax deductible contributions made to the ESOP by the company.

There being no independent directors on U. S. Sugar's Board, no independent committee of directors could be appointed to review the tender offer and to negotiate on behalf of the public shareholders. However, the existence of the conflicts of interest was disclosed in the tender offer statement.

The tender offer was not intended to be merely the first step of a two-step elimination of public shareholders because those shareholders who did not tender their shares were not to be cashed out in a merger following the tender offer. A substantial number of shares are presently outstanding and held by public shareholders, and there continues to be a market for the trading of U. S. Sugar shares, although it has been trading at a lesser price than it did before the tender offer.

Prior to the challenged transaction, U. S. Sugar was virtually debt free. Chemical Bank, the corporation's traditional bank, was approached and was requested to advance $300 million, $250 million of which was to be used to finance the tender offer while the remaining $50 million would be used for working capital. Chemical Bank determined that U. S. Sugar would generate sufficient cash flow to service such a loan and that its assets would be sufficient to repay the loan in the event a foreclosure became necessary.... The bank further determined that on a "worse case" basis, assuming a foreclosure sale, the assets would be worth at least $369 million (approximately $75 per share.) Chemical Bank, for its loan purposes, concluded that the current market value of U. S. Sugar's assets indicated a real net worth of more than $400 million (more than $80 per share). The replacement cost of U. S. Sugar's assets was estimated by the corporation in 1983 to be over $631 million ($130 per share).

Plaintiffs assert that U. S. Sugar's management disregarded information it had as to the value of its assets and instead arrived at the proposed tender offer price by considering only the price range which could be paid off by a projected cash flow over ten years. This range was $60 to $70 per share.

While consideration of the tender offer price range was still taking place, U. S. Sugar retained First Boston Corporation ("First Boston") to render a fairness opinion on the offering price. It was paid $650,000 for its three weeks of work. Initially First Boston was only informed of the range being considered for the tender offer by the corporation and was not informed of the actual tender offer price of $68 until the Friday before it delivered its opinion on Tuesday, September 13, 1983. In the fairness opinion issued by First Boston it opined that the $68 per share was fair to the public shareholders from a financial point of view.

First Boston was originally engaged to represent the public shareholders, as well as to give an opinion as to fairness. Its representative role was never carried out: it was not asked to recommend an independently arrived at fair price; it did not engage in any negotiations over the offering price with U. S. Sugar; it did not consult with any representatives of the minority shareholders; nor did it solicit outside offers to purchase.

Bear, Stearns & Co. ("Bear, Stearns") was retained to represent the ESOP and U. S. Sugar. It was asked to opine that the price to be offered in the tender offer was reasonable to the ESOP. It was also asked to determine whether after the proposed transaction the fair market value of U. S. Sugar's assets would exceed its liabilities by at least $50 million.

The determination that the corporation's assets had a fair market value which would exceed liabilities by at least $50 million after the tender offer was completed was necessary to allow the Board to make a finding that U. S. Sugar's capital would not be impaired, a finding required by Delaware law. This determination was called for because the distribution to be made under the tender offer would be greater than the net book value of the corporation's assets.

Bear, Stearns did negotiate on behalf of the ESOP. It was responsible for the setting of the offering price at $68 rather than the $70 which the officers of U. S. Sugar had originally determined should be the offering price. The $68 price followed Bear, Stearns' decision that the fair price range was between $62 and $68 per share and that any higher price would be unfair to the ESOP.

The Offer to Purchase ("Tender Offering Statement") was sent to the stockholders by U. S. Sugar and the ESOP about September 20, 1983. In response, 1,288,210 shares were tendered by public stockholders. Of the then outstanding publicly held shares only 89,108 were not tendered.

* * *

II

Plaintiffs contend that the Tender Offering Statement was misleading or coercive and concealed or buried facts which, if disclosed, might have led stockholders to conclude that the $68 price was inadequate....

Plaintiffs also claim that facts were emphasized in the Tender Offering Statement which would lead the shareholders to conclude that the $68 price was fair, while facts to the contrary were omitted or buried....

In addition, plaintiffs find fault with the prominent representations as to Bear, Stearns' finding that the fair market value of U. S. Sugar's assets would exceed stated liabilities by at least $50 million after the transaction. They assert that it created the impression that Bear, Stearns had performed a valuation of the fair market value of the assets when in fact it did not but instead relied upon pre-existing findings of value....

Plaintiffs also assert that the Tender Offering Statement contained disclosures which created the impression that U. S. Sugar's management had arrived at the $68 price based mainly upon the independent valuation opinion of First Boston, that First Boston had been allowed to do a thorough valuation study with no restraints placed upon it, and that the interests of the public shareholders had been adequately represented by First Boston in the process of determining the terms of the offer. These disclosures are claimed to be false and misleading because certain alleged facts were omitted: (1) that U. S. Sugar's management, and not First Boston's, had arrived at the $68 price and that First Boston had never suggested a price which it felt was fair but merely opined as to the fairness of the price suggested by management; (2) that the $68 price was derived from a consideration of the amount which could comfortably be borrowed and repaid rather than from any evaluation of U. S. Sugar's true worth; (3) that management would have paid up to $70 per share if Bear, Stearns had not represented that no price above $68 would be reasonable for the ESOP to pay; (4) that First Boston had accepted a representation that the sale of U. S. Sugar to a third party would not be considered and therefore had made no attempt to solicit outside offers; and (5) that after the meeting of the Board of Directors at which it was unanimously determined that $68 per share was a fair price, Stewart Mott, a director and son of the founder of U. S. Sugar, decided not to tender any of the shares registered in his name.

The tender offer and the disclosures in the Tender Offering Statement are further asserted by the plaintiffs to have been coercive because the shareholders were told that they had a choice between tendering at $68 per share or retaining their stock, which after the transaction would no longer be listed on any exchange, would yield no dividends for a minimum of three years, and would represent ownership in a company burdened by substantial debt.

Plaintiffs claim that the fair value of U. S. Sugar at the time of the tender offer was $122 per share which they claim was the liquidation value of the assets. They request that the Court find that the defendants breached their fiduciary duties by not disclosing all germane facts with complete candor and by structuring a coercive tender offer. They claim that the appropriate remedy is an award of money damages measured by the difference between the $68 tender offering price and $122 which they claim was the true value of the shares at the time of the tender offer, plus prejudgment interest.

On the other hand, defendants [deny the plaintiffs' claim in its entirety and argue that] ... U.S. Sugar was under no duty to offer any particular price since the shareholders had all the information necessary to make an informed decision whether to accept or to reject the offer....

III

I find, from the facts adduced at trial, that the disclosures in the Tender Offer Statement did not fully comply with the requirements for disclosure with complete candor which are mandated by Delaware law. *Singer v. Magnavox Co., Del. Supr., 380 A.2d 969 (1977); Smith v. Van Gorkom, Del. Supr., 488 A.2d 858 (1985);* and *Rosenblatt v. Getty Oil Company, Del. Supr., 493 A.2d 929 (1985).*

There was a failure to clearly indicate in the proxy materials that the book value of the land, which was the principal asset of U. S. Sugar, was based primarily on the 1931 acquisition costs of the land and that in 1982 the internal real estate department of the corporation had rendered an informal opinion to management that the fee simple holdings of land was in excess of $408 million ($83 per share). The tender offer proxy materials also failed to adequately disclose that a Cash Flow Terminal Value Study prepared by First Boston had shown estimated values as high as $100.50 per share; that Bear, Stearns had made some estimates of value of up to $78 per share; and that First Boston did not actually prepare a thorough valuation study without restraints.

I also find that there was a failure to adequately disclose the methods used to arrive at the $68 tender offer price, especially because it was, for all practical purposes, chosen because that is what the ESOP and the corporation could afford to pay to service the loan obtained to finance the tender offer.

I also find that the method used to select the tender offer price was not likely to assure that the public minority stockholders would receive the true value of their shares and, as will be seen, they did not. The tender offer price, unfortunately, was, in essence, arrived at by determining how much debt the corporation could safely and prudently assume. The public stockholders had to either accept this price and tender their shares or to hold on to their shares only to find, because of the large loan which was to be used to pay for the shares tendered, that their shares would dramatically decline in value with no prospects for any dividends for at least three years.

In some circumstances a corporation is under no obligation to offer a particular tender offer price. *Joseph v. Shell Oil Co., Del. Ch., 482 A.2d 335 (1984).* Here, however, because of the highly leveraged nature of the transaction it was coercive and therefore defendants had an obligation to offer a fair price.

I acknowledge that the directors of U. S. Sugar were faced with a most difficult scenario because the majority shareholders desired to sell a substantial portion of their shares and yet insisted on retaining control of the corporation. The only feasible way to accomplish this was for the corporation to buy its own shares by the means of a leveraged tender offer. If the price offered had been fair there would not be any problem. The price offered, however, was not fair and it should have been selected with a greater emphasis on the true value of the corporation.

I do not, however, find the statements in the proxy statement setting forth the results which would likely occur if a stockholder did not tender to have been inadequate, improper or coercive. The proxy materials merely set forth that which was obvious: the minority stockholders who did not tender their shares would end up owning shares with a greatly diminished value because of the large debt being created to finance the tender offer....

Having found that there was a breach of fiduciary duty, I must now find a remedy.

IV

Plaintiffs seek, as damages, the difference between the fair value of the shares and the $68 offering price, plus prejudgment interest. They correctly point out that it would be impossible now to rescind the transaction.

* * *

After considering and weighing all the conflicting testimony,[a] the many value judgments and assumptions (some of which were invalid), and the credentials and demeanor of the witnesses, I conclude that the fair value of the assets of U. S. Sugar at the time of the tender offer was $72 per share. The damages, therefore, are equal to $4 per share ($72 less the $68 tender offer price).

* * *

Grobow v. Perot
539 A.2d 180 (Del. 1988)

HORSEY, Justice

[P]laintiffs-shareholders appeal the Court of Chancery's dismissal of their suits for failure of plaintiffs to make presuit demand under Court of Chancery Rule 23.1. The Court of Chancery held that plaintiffs' complaints as amended failed to allege particularized facts which, if taken as true, would excuse demand under the demand futility test of Aronson v. Lewis, Del.Supr., 473 A.2d 805 (1984)....

I

* * *

A.

In 1984, General Motors Corporation ("GM") acquired 100 percent of Electronic Data Systems' ("EDS") stock. Under the terms of the merger, H. Ross Perot, founder, chairman and largest stockholder of EDS, exchanged his EDS stock for GM Class E stock and contingent notes. Perot became GM's largest shareholder, holding 0.8 percent

---

a. Vice Chancellor Hartnett's frustrations with the use of expert testimony in this case are set forth in note 3 following Le Beau v. M.G. Bancorporation, Inc., *supra* chapter 3, section 4a(i)(B).

of GM voting stock. Perot was also elected to GM's Board of Directors (the "Board") while remaining chairman of EDS.

The merger proved mutually beneficial to both corporations and was largely a success. However, management differences developed between Perot and the other officers and directors of GM's Board over the way GM was running EDS, and Perot became increasingly vocal in his criticism of GM management. By mid-1986, Perot announced to GM that he could no longer be a "company man." Perot demanded that GM allow him to run EDS as he saw fit or that GM buy him out. Perot then began publicly criticizing GM management with such statements as: "Until you nuke the old GM system, you'll never tap the full potential of your people"; and "GM cannot become a world-class and cost-competitive company simply by throwing technology and money at its problems." ...

By late fall of 1986, Perot, anxious, for tax reasons, for a definitive decision before year-end, offered to sell his entire interest in GM. GM responded with a purchase proposal. Perot replied, suggesting additional terms, which Perot characterized as "a giant premium." When a definitive agreement was reached, the Board designated a three-member Special Review Committee ("SRC"), chaired by one of the Board's outside directors to review its terms. The SRC met on November 30, 1986 to consider the repurchase proposal and unanimously recommended that GM's Board approve its terms. The following day, December 1, 1986, the GM Board of Directors met and approved the repurchase agreement.

Under the terms of the repurchase, GM acquired all of Perot's GM Class E stock and contingent notes and those of his close EDS associates for nearly $745,000,000. GM also received certain commitments, termed "covenants," from Perot. In addition to resigning immediately from GM's Board and as Chairman of EDS, Perot further agreed: (1) to stop criticizing GM management, in default of which Perot agreed to pay GM damages in a liquidated sum of up to $7.5 million;[3] (2) not to purchase GM stock or engage in a proxy contest against the Board for five years; and (3) not to compete with EDS for three years or recruit EDS executives for eighteen months.

At all relevant times, a majority of the GM Board of Directors consisted of outside directors. The exact number and composition of the GM Board at the time is not clear. However, from the limited record, it appears that the Board was comprised of twenty-six directors (excluding Perot), of whom eighteen were outside directors.

The GM repurchase came at a time when GM was experiencing financial difficulty and was engaged in cost cutting. Public reaction to the announcement ranged from mixed to adverse. The repurchase was sharply criticized by industry analysts and by members within GM's management ranks as well. The criticism focused on two features of the repurchase: (1) the size of the premium over the then market price of GM class E stock;[4] and (2) the hush mail provision.

---

3. This commitment by Perot would later be characterized as the "hush mail" feature of the agreement. The colloquial term is not defined in the pleadings but is assumed by this Court to combine the terms "green mail" and "hush money" to connote a variation on an unlawful and secret payment to assure silence. Here, the commitment is cast in the form of an explicit liquidated damage clause for future breach of contract. See infra section III B.

4. Plaintiffs allege that the total repurchase price per share [($61.90)] was double the market price of the GM class E stock on the last day of trading before consummation of the repurchase [($31.375)]. However, the extent of premium over market cannot be mathematically calculated with any precision without disregarding the value of the contingent notes. The total repurchase price per share includes not only the price paid for the class E stock, but also the price paid for the contingent notes and the value of the special interest federal tax compensation. See infra note 7.

B.

Plaintiffs filed separate derivative actions (later consolidated) against GM, EDS, GM's directors, H. Ross Perot, and three of Perot's EDS associates. The suits collectively allege: (i) that the GM director defendants breached their fiduciary duties to GM and EDS by paying a grossly excessive price for the repurchase of Perot's and the EDS associates' Class E stock of GM; (ii) that the repurchase included a unique hush mail feature to buy not only Perot's resignation, but his silence, and that such a condition lacked any valid business purpose and was a waste of GM assets; and (iii) that the repurchase was entrenchment motivated and was carried out principally to save GM's Board from further public embarrassment by Perot. The complaints charge the individual defendants with acting out of self-interest and with breaching their duties of loyalty and due care to GM and EDS.

* * *

III

* * *

As previously noted, the business judgment rule is but a presumption that directors making a business decision, not involving self-interest, act on an informed basis, in good faith and in the honest belief that their actions are in the corporation's best interest.... Thus, good faith and the absence of self-dealing are threshold requirements for invoking the rule.... Assuming the presumptions of director good faith and lack of self-dealing are not rebutted by well-pleaded facts, a shareholder derivative complainant must then allege further facts with particularity which, "taken as true, support a reasonable doubt that the challenged transaction was [in fact] the product of a valid exercise of business judgment." [Aronson v. Lewis, 473 A.2d 805, 815 (Del. 1984)].... The complaints as amended do not even purport to plead a claim of fraud, bad faith, or self-dealing in the usual sense of personal profit or betterment.... Therefore, we must presume that the GM directors reached their repurchase decision in good faith....

* * *

A. Disinterest and Independence

* * *

Having failed to plead financial interest with any particularity, plaintiffs' complaints must raise a reasonable doubt of director disinterest based on entrenchment. Plaintiffs attempt to do so mainly through reliance on Unocal Corp. v. Mesa Petroleum Co., Del.Supr., 493 A.2d 946 (1985); Unocal, however, is distinguishable. The enhanced duty of care that the Unocal directors were found to be under was triggered by a struggle for corporate control and the inherent presumption of director self-interest associated with such a contest. See id. at 954-55. Here there was no outside threat to corporate policy of GM sufficient to raise a Unocal issue of whether the directors' response was reasonable to the threat posed. Id. at 955.

Plaintiffs also do not plead any facts tending to show that the GM directors' positions were actually threatened by Perot, who owned only 0.8 percent of GM's voting stock, nor do plaintiffs allege that the repurchase was motivated and reasonably related to the directors' retention of their positions on the Board.... Plaintiffs merely argue that Perot's public criticism of GM management could cause the directors embarrassment sufficient to lead to their removal from office. Such allegations are tenuous at best and are too speculative to raise a reasonable doubt of director disinterest. Speculation on motives for undertaking corporate action are wholly insufficient to establish a case of demand excusal.... Therefore, we agree with the Vice Chancellor that plaintiffs' entrenchment theory is based largely on supposition rather than fact.

Plaintiffs' remaining allegations bearing on the issue of entrenchment are: the rushed nature of the transaction during a period of GM financial difficulty; the giant premium paid;[7] and the criticism (after the fact) of the repurchase by industry analysts and top GM management. Plaintiffs argue that these allegations are sufficient to raise a reasonable doubt of director disinterest. We cannot agree. Not one of the asserted grounds would support a reasonable belief of entrenchment based on director self-interest. The relevance of these averments goes largely to the issue of due care, next discussed. Such allegations are patently insufficient to raise a reasonable doubt as to the ability of the GM Board to act with disinterest. Thus, we find plaintiffs' entrenchment claim to be essentially conclusory and lacking in factual support sufficient to establish excusal [of demand] based on director interest.

* * *

B. Director Due Care

Having concluded that plaintiffs have failed to plead a claim of financial interest or entrenchment sufficient to excuse presuit demand, we examine the complaints as amended to determine whether they raise a reasonable doubt that the directors exercised proper business judgment in the transaction. By proper business judgment we mean both substantive due care (purchase terms), see Saxe v. Brady, Del.Ch., 184 A.2d 602, 610 (1962), and procedural due care (an informed decision), see Smith v. Van Gorkom, Del.Supr., 488 A.2d 858, 872-73 (1985).

With regard to the nature of the transactions and the terms of repurchase, especially price, plaintiffs allege that the premium paid Perot constituted a prima facie waste of GM's assets. Plaintiffs argue that the transaction, on its face, was "so egregious as to be afforded no presumption of business judgment protection."...

The law of Delaware is well established that, in the absence of evidence of fraud or unfairness, a corporation's repurchase of its capital stock at a premium over market from a dissident shareholder is entitled to the protection of the business judgment rule.... We have already determined that plaintiffs have not stated a claim of financial interest or entrenchment as the compelling motive for the repurchase, and it is equally clear that the complaints as amended do not allege a claim of fraud. They allege, at most, a claim of waste based on the assertion that GM's Board paid such a premium for the Perot holdings as to shock the conscience of the ordinary person.

Thus, the issue becomes whether the complaints state a claim of waste of assets, i.e., whether "what the corporation has received is so inadequate in value that no person of ordinary, sound business judgment would deem it worth that which the corporation has paid." Saxe, 184 A.2d at 610. By way of reinforcing their claim of waste, plaintiffs seize upon the hush-mail feature of the repurchase as being the motivating reason for the "giant premium" approved by the GM Board. Plaintiffs then argue that buying the silence of a dissident within management constitutes an invalid business purpose. Ergo,

---

7. The formula plaintiffs use to establish the existence of a "giant premium" is ambiguous, making the allegation conclusory. The total repurchase price includes not only the price paid for the class E stock, but also the price paid for the contingent notes and the value of the tax compensation. Ambiguity is caused when these items are factored in, especially the contingent note discounts....

plaintiffs argue that a claim of waste of corporate assets evidencing lack of director due care has been well pleaded.

The Vice Chancellor was not persuaded by this reasoning to reach such a conclusion and neither are we. Plaintiffs' assertions by way of argument go well beyond their factual allegations, and it is the latter which are controlling. Plaintiffs' complaints as amended fail to plead with particularity any facts supporting a conclusion that the primary or motivating purpose of the Board's payment of a "giant premium" for the Perot holdings was to buy Perot's silence rather than simply to buy him out and remove him from GM's management team. To the contrary, plaintiffs themselves state in their complaints as amended several legitimate business purposes for the GM Board's decision to sever its relationship with Perot: (1) the Board's determination that it would be in GM's best interest to retain control over its wholly-owned subsidiary, EDS; and (2) the decision to rid itself of the principal cause of the growing internal policy dispute over EDS' management and direction.

* * *

In addition to regaining control over the management affairs of EDS, GM also secured, through the complex repurchase agreement, significant covenants from Perot, of which the hush-mail provision was but one of many features and multiple considerations of the repurchase. Quite aside from whatever consideration could be attributed to buying Perot's silence, GM's Board received for the $742.8 million paid: all the class E stock and contingent notes of Perot and his fellow EDS directors; Perot's covenant not to compete or hire EDS employees; his promise not to purchase GM stock or engage in proxy contests; Perot's agreement to stay out of and away from GM's and EDS' affairs, plus the liquidated damages provision should Perot breach his no-criticism covenant.

Plaintiffs' effort to quantify the size of the premium paid by GM is flawed, as we have already noted, by their inability to place a dollar value on the various promises made by Perot, particularly his covenant not to compete with EDS or to attempt to hire away EDS employees.... Thus, viewing the transaction in its entirety, we must agree with the Court of Chancery that plaintiffs have failed to plead with particularity facts sufficient to create a reasonable doubt that the substantive terms of the repurchase fall within the protection of the business judgment rule....

* * *

[The court also rejected plaintiff's claim that the directors did not make an informed decision.]

IV. Conclusion

Apart from whether the Board of Directors may be subject to criticism for the premium paid Perot and his associates for the repurchase of their entire interest in GM, on the present record the repurchase of dissident Perot's interests can only be viewed legally as representing an exercise of business judgment by the General Motors Board with which a court may not interfere. Only through a considerable stretch of the imagination could one reasonably believe this Board of Directors to be "interested" in a self-dealing sense in Perot's ouster from GM's management. We view a board of directors with a majority of outside directors, such as this Board, as being in the nature of overseers of management. So viewed, the Board's exercise of judgment in resolving an internal rift in management of serious proportions and at the highest executive level should be accorded the protection of the business judgment rule absent well-pleaded averments implicating financial self-interest, entrenchment, or lack of due care. These complaints fall far short of stating a claim for demand excusal.

.... We hold that the complaints as amended fail to allege facts sufficient to create a reasonable doubt that the GM Board-approved repurchase transaction is not within the protection of the business judgment rule; thus, the plaintiffs have failed to establish the futility of demand required under Aronson and Pogostin for casting reasonable doubt thereon. The Trial Court, therefore, correctly dismissed the suits under Del.Ch.Ct.R. 23.1 for failure of plaintiffs to make presuit demand upon the GM Board.

Affirmed.

Note and Questions

1. When a company's board of directors privately negotiates a stock repurchase that would involve a change of control, should the court review the transaction under the heightened *Unocal* standard or the ordinary business judgment rule? In Kahn v. Roberts, 679 A.2d 460 (Del. 1996), the Delaware Supreme Court considered the matter a purely factual one. The dispute involved the repurchase of Class A voting stock of DeKalb Genetics Corp. Collectively, the Roberts family owned 1/3 of the A shares. After members of the family had been denied any executive position in the firm, they hinted that they "would 'rethink' [their] position as large DeKalb stockholders." *Id* at 462. In response, the board formed an independent, special committee tasked with negotiating the repurchase of the Class A shares from the family. The committee consulted with an investment banker and ultimately repurchased the shares at $40 per share.

The plaintiff shareholder argued that the repurchase was a defensive measure taken by the board to prevent losing control of the company; thus, the appropriate standard of review was the heightened scrutiny of *Unocal*. The court disagreed, stating that the *Unocal* standard would only apply if the DeKalb directors had initiated the repurchase program as a response to a threat to a corporate policy that involves a potential change in control.

The court saw no evidence that the board instituted the repurchase program as a defensive measure, noting that:

> .... This is not the case where one-third of the outstanding shares are being sought by a third party, or a self-tender for those shares was made in the face of a third party bid for control....
>
> Absent an actual threat to corporate control or action substantially taken for the purpose of entrenchment, the actions of the board are judged under the business judgment rule....

The court further found that DeKalb's procedures, namely establishing an independent committee that hired and met with legal and financial advisors to discuss the repurchase plan, satisfied the duty of care required by Smith v. Van Gorkom, 488 A.2d 858 (Del. 1985), discussed *infra* at chapter 9, section 1a. Therefore, the repurchase plan was an acceptable exercise of business judgment.

Do you agree with the court's assessment that the potential sale of a controlling block of stock is not a threat to the board's control of the company? If such a sale is a threat, does the repurchase plan constitute a proportional defensive measure?

The court states "We have repeatedly ruled that a board may repurchase the stock of a dissatisfied shareholder without implicating heightened scrutiny. *Grobow v. Perot*, Del. Supr., 539 A.2d 180, 188 (1988)." *Id.* at 466 n.6. *Grobow*, however, involved a shareholder selling only a 0.8% block of voting stock. Do you agree that repurchases of a substantial block of voting stock, as seen in *Roberts*, should be evaluated in the same way?

2. Should a state's distribution and share repurchase statutes apply to a leveraged buy-out? In Matter of Munford, Inc., 97 F.3d 456 (11th Cir. 1996), the First Circuit affirmed the trial court's denial of the defendant directors' motion for summary judgment in an action brought by the plaintiff debtor. The debtor alleged that the defendants violated legal restrictions under Georgia's distribution and share repurchase statutes in approving a leveraged buy-out of the debtor, claiming that the LBO left the debtor insolvent. The defendant directors argued that these statutes only applied in circumstances where the directors take assets of the corporation and either distribute them to shareholders or use them to repurchase shares. In both cases, the directors asserted, control of the company does not change hands and the directors determine the source of the assets used. They urged the court to hold that only Georgia's merger statutes applied to the transaction at hand.

In upholding the denial of the directors' motion for summary judgment, the First Circuit (as did the district court below it) adopted the reasoning of the bankruptcy court which had specifically found:

> (1) the directors "approved or assented to the underlying merger agreement which structured and required payment to the shareholders"; (2) the merger agreement contemplated [the acquiror's] pledging of "virtually all of [debtor's] assets as collateral" for the loan that funded the LBO payments made to the shareholders; and (3) the directors knew or should have known "the source, purpose, or use of" [debtor's] assets prior to or at the time the directors approved the merger plan.

Id. at 459. Based on these findings, the bankruptcy court concluded that a reasonable jury could conclude that the merger rendered the debtor insolvent in violation of Georgia's distribution and stock repurchase statutes.

The First Circuit agreed with the denial of the directors' motion for summary judgment. However, it highlighted that the merger in question was not a merger of two separate operating companies into one combined entity. Rather, the LBO transaction represented a "paper merger" of the debtor and a shell corporation with very little assets of its own that had been formed by the acquiror to effect the merger. Presumably, a "real" merger between two operating companies would lead to a different result.

For a case taking a view contrary to that of Munford, see C-T of Virginia, Inc. v. Barrett, 958 F.2d 606 (4th Cir. 1992) (holding that Virginia's share repurchase and distribution statutes were not intended to obstruct an arms'-length acquisition of an enterprise by new owners who have their own plans for commercial success).

Lowenstein, Management Buyouts
85 Colum. L. Rev. 730, 776-778, 779 (1985)

B. *The Case for a Categorical Prohibition*

Ten years of increasing familiarity with buyouts have bred a degree of acquiescence....

No change in social acceptance can mask, however, the potentially raw breach of loyalty when the management of a corporation undertakes to buy the business from its owners at a time, and where possible at a price, of its own choosing. It matters little whether the management will own all or only a significant portion of the newco shares. They will look on the newco side of the bread for much of the butter and surely all of the jam.

Much can be said, therefore, in favor of a strict, prophylactic rule of prohibition. The effort to find a pragmatic rather than a principled solution has not been successful. Our pragmatism has tended to dilute our standards. This has naturally led to the "judicial process becoming ... a sort of arbitration process, a process in which law and principle are largely discarded." What we have seen in Delaware is about what one would expect from such a process: "[p]rocedural laws and principles might thus remain, but substantive ones ... largely disappear." ... Courts eager not to seem rigid and also not to grasp the nettles of determining fair price fall back on a procedural concept of fair dealing in which a fair price is, mirabile dictu, irrelevant.

We live in an era that shies away from strict rules or moral precepts. Not just for the courts, but for commentators as well, the categorical prohibition is "too extreme a solution." Accordingly, commentators have proposed or considered a wide variety of other solutions, such as allowing public company shareholders the benefit of seeing the newco financial statements a year or so after the buyout, allowing them to share in the gain if the newco itself is sold or goes public within some period of time after the buyout, or requiring that the buyout remain open for a period of time to give others a chance to bid. Of course, for economists who "equate utility maximization ... on the part of corporate managers with the maximization of the present value of the firm," it is but a short step from the invisible hand theorem to the laissez faire conclusion, devoid of moral content, that if managers are taking too much, it may be good to let them do the taking once and for all and have done with it, or at least that there is not much harm in such a process.

Utterly ignored in all of these alternatives is the hortatory effect of a simple, "rigid" rule that says buyouts are forbidden. Corporate executives do not often read law review articles, not even the signed reprints sent to them personally. Living in a competitive environment, trained to look for opportunities first and obstacles second, they rely mostly on counsel to instruct them as to what is permitted and what is not. Lawyers who emphasize solutions to problems are more prized than those who see only the problem. There is a good deal to be said, therefore, for a principled solution to the MBO problem. The message for those in a position of trust that some attractive opportunities are not for the taking needs to be stated simply and directly if it is to have effect. While the educational or deterrent effect of law may not be much in vogue, those who inhabit the boardroom and executive suite will be more sensitive than most, if only the message is clear. They have more and better trained advisers plus the institutional instinct to comply....

C. The Preferred Reform: Mandated Auctions

The major drawback of a rigid rule against MBOs is that once a company has been "put into play" by someone else, the shareholders may be better served by the higher bid that a management group is prepared to make. One bidder's money is as good as another's. Despite the conflict of interest, it may be better to let the officers bid than to risk tempting them to sell off good businesses or buy bad ones in order to save their skins. Open the bidding, therefore, to insiders as well as outsiders. Ideally, the managers would not be free to bid unless others were already bidding, but that is a manifestly unworkable distinction. Thus, like all good pragmatists, we fall back on the next best solution: management can initiate the bidding, but others should be allowed to participate on as nearly equal terms as possible. Such a rule at least assumes that management, while wearing its shareholder-representative hat, has concluded that for whatever reason the business ought to be sold.

A rule of open bidding attempts to separate the decision to sell from the selection of the buyer. Accordingly, any reasonable formulation of the rule would require that the decision to sell be irrevocable, subject only to an upset price, terms of payment, or other conditions applicable to all buyers. If the bidding is to be on equal terms, the rule would also require that the information needed to bid, and the time to do so, be made available to all or at least to a group of responsible bidders, with exceptions where, for example, confidential business information is a concern. If recent market activity is indicative, we could expect active and competitive bidding under such a rule, at least if management is barred from using lockups or other such devices.

Section 5
Preemptive Rights and Dilution

Introductory Note and Problem

Assume that Sheridan Corp. (the "Company") is a close corporation formed by Longstreet, Jackson, and Beauregard, each of whom purchased for $10 per share 1,000 shares of its 10,000 authorized shares of common stock, $.01 par value. The Company has not been doing well. After several years of operation the three stockholders (who are also the directors) agree that the best way of raising needed capital is to issue more common stock. Longstreet is willing to invest more but neither Jackson nor Beauregard wants Longstreet to own a greater number of shares. The trouble is, neither of them has available funds to invest. Jackson's friend Ruffin (who is also friendly with Beauregard) is willing to invest an additional $10,000, but does not believe the stock is worth more than $8 per share. Although Jackson and Beauregard vote in favor of the issuance to Ruffin of 1,250 shares at $8 each, Longstreet objects. Why does Longstreet object?

To simplify the problem, assume that the Company's balance sheet remains unchanged from its original formation. It will look like this:

Assets		Liabilities	
Cash	$30,000	None	$0
		Equity	
		Common Stock	
		(3,000 shares, par value	
		$.01 per share)	30
		Additional Paid in Capital	29,970
		Total Liabilities &	
Total Assets	$30,000	Stockholders' Equity	$30,000

This balance sheet shows that the book value of each share is $10 ($30,000 divided by 3,000 shares), which is what the three original stockholders paid. If Ruffin buys the proposed new shares at $8 per share, the balance sheet would look like this:

Assets		Liabilities	
Cash	$40,000	None	$0
		Equity	
		Common Stock (4,250 shares, par value $.01 per share)	42.50
		Additional Paid in Capital	39,957.50
Total Assets	$40,000	Total Liabilities & Stockholders' Equity	$40,000

This balance sheet shows that the book value of each share is equal to $9.41 (40,000 divided by 4,250 shares). As a result of the share issuance to Ruffin, each of the three original stockholders would have suffered a reduction in the per share book value of their investment of $.59, and Ruffin would have enjoyed in effect an increase in the book value per share of his investment of $1.41.[1] Should Longstreet care and what, if anything, can he do about it?

The original legal solution to this dilution of book value per share from a new issuance of shares was the concept of preemptive rights, which give each existing stockholder the right to purchase his *pro rata* share of the new issue at the new issue price. Although this obviously requires an additional investment by a stockholder seeking to maintain his position in the corporation, it also precludes the corporation from altering that position against the shareholder's will, and permits the shareholder at least to share in a portion of the dilutive investment.

Although dilution in the book value per share of common stock may be undesirable to some stockholders, it is also important to recognize that the value of a business is not a function solely of its book value, or of its book value per share. Instead, as you will recall from chapter 3, the value of a business enterprise is also a function of what the business can generate in earnings over time or in cash flows over time. A temporary reduction in the book value per share that creates earnings-generating power or cash-flow-generating power may therefore increase the value of the business and make the Longstreets of the world happy.

On the other hand, the Longstreets of the world must still worry about the dilutive effect that new share issuances have on their voting power. Before the proposed issuance of new shares to Ruffin, each of the three original shareholders of Sheridan owned 33%

---

1. In the next chapter we will examine the use of "poison pills" as a defensive strategy to a hostile takeover. What makes poison pills so effective is their potentially dilutive effect if triggered. *See infra* chapter 9, section 2b(ii).

of the Company's stock. After the proposed issuance, Ruffin would own about 29% and each of the three original shareholders would own just less than 24% of the Company's stock. In other words, the proposed issuance would dilute each original shareholder's percentage ownership interest in the Company from 33% each to 24% each. The new ownership distribution substantially changes the allocation of majority voting power: before the issuance, any two of the original shareholders could exert control, but afterwards control could be exerted either (a) by all three of them acting together (b) or by any one of them acting only with Ruffin.

Preemptive rights are designed principally to protect existing stockholders from the dilution in voting control attendant upon the issuance of new stock. Although preemptive rights protect both value dilution and voting dilution in the case of a corporation like Sheridan, which has only one class of shares outstanding, the primacy of voting dilution protection is recognized by the Revised Model Business Corporation Act which prohibits preemptive rights for non-voting preferred shares. Rev. Model Bus. Corp. Act § 6.30(b)(4). *See also* Rev. Model Bus. Corp. Act § 6.30(b)(5) (common stock has no preemptive right to non-convertible preferred stock).

Both Delaware law (Del. Gen. Corp. Law § 102(b)(3)) and the Revised Model Business Corporation Act (§ 6.30(a)) treat preemptive rights as optional to the corporation in the sense that preemptive rights do not exist unless specified in the corporation's charter. Both the Delaware and Revised Model Act approaches provide for the elaboration of the terms of preemptive rights in the corporation's charter, but the Revised Model Act goes further and sets out certain statutory terms which define the scope of preemptive rights. The Revised Model Business Corporation Act also categorizes the various jurisdictions according to two different approaches each has taken to the question of preemptive rights: 33 jurisdictions (including California, Illinois, Massachusetts, New Jersey and New York) followed the Delaware and Revised Model Act approaches of denying preemptive rights unless they are specified in the charter; 19 jurisdictions (including Texas), either directly or by implication, took the opposite approach of statutorily providing preemptive rights except where they are expressly denied in the charter. In addition, 41 jurisdictions provide specific statutory instances in which preemptive rights would not apply in any event (e.g., shares issued to officers and employees under stockholder-approved stock option plans). *See* Model Bus. Corp. Act Ann. § 6.30, Statutory Comparison (3rd ed. 1984 & Supp. 2000/01/02).

As you read the materials that follow, also consider the following:

(i) What alternatives in addition (or in preference) to preemptive rights could have been used to protect the Company's stockholders?

(ii) How should the government of Bondolia handle preemptive rights in its new corporations code?

(iii) Should certain stock issuances be carved-out from a preemptive rights provision? For example, how should shares issued as merger consideration be treated under such a provision? Or shares delivered to employees when they exercise stock options?

Katzowitz v. Sidler
24 N.Y.2d 512, 249 N.E.2d 359, 301 N.Y.S.2d 470 (1969)

KEATING, Judge.

Isador Katzowitz is a director and stockholder of a close corporation. Two other persons, Jacob Sidler and Max Lasker, own the remaining securities and, with Katzowitz, comprise Sulburn Holding Corp.'s board of directors. Sulburn was organized in 1955 to supply propane gas to three other corporations controlled by these men. Sulburn's certificate of incorporation authorized it to issue 1,000 shares of no par value stock for which the incorporators established a $100 selling price. Katzowitz, Sidler and Lasker each invested $500 and received five shares of the corporation's stock.

The three men had been jointly engaged in several corporate ventures for more than 25 years. In this period they had always been equal partners and received identical compensation from the corporations they controlled. Though all the corporations controlled by these three men prospered, disenchantment with their inter-personal relationship flared into the open in 1956. At this time, Sidler and Lasker joined forces to oust Katzowitz from any role in managing the corporations. They first voted to replace Katzowitz as a director of Sullivan County Gas Company with the corporation's private counsel. Notice of directors' meetings was then caused to be sent out by Lasker and Sidler for Burnwell Gas Corporation. Sidler and Lasker advised Katzowitz that they intended to vote for a new board of directors. Katzowitz at this time held the position of manager of the Burnwell facility.

Katzowitz sought a temporary injunction to prevent the meeting until his rights could be judicially determined. A temporary injunction was granted to maintain the status quo until trial. The order was affirmed by the Appellate Division (*Katzowitz v. Sidler*, 8 A.D.2d 726, 187 N.Y.S.2d 986).

Before the issue could be tried, the three men entered into a stipulation in 1959 whereby Katzowitz withdrew from active participation in the day-to-day operations of the business. The agreement provided that he would remain on the boards of all the corporations, and each board would be limited to three members composed of the three stockholders or their designees. Katzowitz was to receive the same compensation and other fringe benefits which the controlled corporations paid Lasker and Sidler. The stipulation also provided that Katzowitz, Sidler and Lasker were "equal stockholders and each of said parties now owns the same number of shares of stock in each of the defendant corporations and that such shares of stock shall continue to be in full force and effect and unaffected by this stipulation, except as hereby otherwise expressly provided." The stipulation contained no other provision affecting equal stock interests.

The business relationship established by the stipulation was fully complied with. Sidler and Lasker, however, were still interested in disassociating themselves from Katzowitz.... In December of 1961 Sulburn was indebted to each stockholder to the extent of $2,500 for fees and commissions earned up until September, 1961. Instead of paying this debt, Sidler and Lasker wanted Sulburn to loan the money to another corporation which all three men controlled. Sidler and Lasker called a meeting of the board of directors to propose that additional securities be offered at $100 per share to substitute for the money owed to the directors. The notice of meeting for October 30, 1961 had on its agenda "a proposition that the corporation issue common stock of its unissued common capital stock, *the total par value which shall equal the total sum of the fees and commissions now owing by the corporation to its ... directors.*" (Emphasis added.) Katzowitz made it quite clear at the meeting that he would not invest any additional funds in Sulburn in order for it to make a loan to this other corporation. The only resolution passed at the meeting was that the corporation would pay the sum of $2,500 to each director.

With full knowledge that Katzowitz expected to be paid his fees and commissions and that he did not want to participate in any new stock issuance, the other two directors called a special meeting of the board on December 1, 1961. The only item on the agenda for this special meeting was the issuance of 75 shares of the corporation's common stock at $100 per share. The offer was to be made to stockholders in "accordance with their respective preemptive rights for the purpose of acquiring additional working capital." The amount to be raised was the exact amount owed by the corporation to its shareholders. The offering price for the securities was 1/18 the book value of the stock. Only Sidler and Lasker attended the special board meeting. They approved the issuance of the 75 shares.

Notice was mailed to each stockholder that they had the right to purchase 25 shares of the corporation's stock at $100 a share. The offer was to expire on December 27, 1961. Failure to act by that date was stated to constitute a waiver. At about the same time Katzowitz received the notice, he received a check for $2,500 from the corporation for his fees and commissions. Katzowitz did not exercise his option to buy the additional shares. Sidler and Lasker purchased their full complement, 25 shares each. This purchase by Sidler and Lasker caused an immediate dilution of the book value of the outstanding securities.

On August 25, 1962 the principal asset of Sulburn, a tractor trailer truck, was destroyed. On August 31, 1962 the directors unanimously voted to dissolve the corporation. Upon dissolution, Sidler and Lasker each received $18,885.52 but Katzowitz only received $3,147.59.

The plaintiff instituted a declaratory judgment action to establish his right to the proportional interest in the assets of Sulburn in liquidation less the $5,000 which Sidler and Lasker used to purchase their shares in December, 1961.

Special Term (Westchester County) found the book value of the corporation's securities on the day the stock was offered at $100 to be worth $1,800. The court also found that "the individual defendants * * * decided that in lieu of taking that sum in cash (the commissions and fees due the stockholders), they preferred to add to their investment by having the corporate defendant make available and offer each stockholder an additional twenty-five shares of unissued stock." The court reasoned that Katzowitz waived his right to purchase the stock or object to its sale to Lasker and Sidler by failing to exercise his pre-emptive right and found his protest at the time of dissolution untimely.

The Appellate Division (Second Department), two Justices, dissenting, modified the order of Special Term 29 A.D.2d 955, 289 N.Y.S.2d 324. The modification was procedural.... The majority agreed that the book value of the corporation's stock at the time of the stock offering was $1,800. The Appellate Division reasoned, however, that showing a disparity between book value and offering price was insufficient without also showing fraud or overreaching. Disparity in price by itself was not enough to prove fraud. The Appellate Division also found that the plaintiff had waived his right to object to his recovery in dissolution by failing to either exercise his pre-emptive rights or take steps to prevent the sale of the stock.

The concept of pre-emptive rights was fashioned by the judiciary to safeguard two distinct interests of stockholders—the right to protection against dilution of their equity in the corporation and protection against dilution of their proportionate voting control.... [L]egislation fixed the right enunciated with respect to proportionate voting but left to the judiciary the role of protecting existing shareholders from the dilution of their equity (e.g., Stock Corporation Law, § 39, now Business Corporation Law, Consol. Laws, c. 4, § 622....

It is clear that directors of a corporation have no discretion in the choice of those to whom the earnings and assets of the corporation should be distributed. Directors, being fiduciaries of the corporation, must, in issuing new stock, treat existing shareholders fairly.... Though there is very little statutory control over the price which a corporation must receive for new shares[,] ... the power to determine price must be exercised for the benefit of the corporation and in the interest of all the stockholders....

Issuing stock for less than fair value can injure existing shareholders by diluting their interest in the corporation's surplus, in current and future earnings and in the assets upon liquidation. Normally, a stockholder is protected from the loss of his equity from dilution, even though the stock is being offered at less than fair value, because the shareholder receives rights which he may either exercise or sell. If he exercises, he has protected his interest and, if not, he can sell the rights, thereby compensating himself for the dilution of his remaining shares in the equity of the corporation.... [2]

When new shares are issued, however, at prices far below fair value in a close corporation or a corporation with only a limited market for its shares, existing stockholders, who do not want to invest or do not have the capacity to invest additional funds, can have their equity interest in the corporation diluted to the vanishing point....

The protection afforded by stock rights is illusory in close corporations. Even if a buyer could be found for the rights, they would have to be sold at an inadequate price because of the nature of a close corporation. Outsiders are normally discouraged from acquiring minority interests after a close corporation has been organized....

Though it is difficult to determine fair value for a corporation's securities and courts are therefore reluctant to get into the thicket, when the issuing price is shown to be markedly below book value in a close corporation and when the remaining shareholder-directors benefit from the issuance, a case for judicial relief has been established. In that instance, the corporation's directors must show that the issuing price falls within some range which can be justified on the basis of valid business reasons.... If no such showing is made by the directors, there is no reason for the judiciary to abdicate its function to a majority of the board or stockholders who have not seen fit to come forward and justify the propriety of diverting property from the corporation and allow the issuance of securities to become an oppressive device permitting the dilution of the equity of dissident stockholders.

The defendant directors here make no claim that the price set was a fair one. No business justification is offered to sustain it.... Admittedly, the stock was sold at less than book value. The defendants simply contend that, as long as all stockholders were given an equal opportunity to purchase additional shares, no stockholder can complain simply because the offering dilutes his interest in the corporation.

The defendants' argument is fallacious.

---

2. There is little justification for issuing stock far below its fair value. The only reason ... exists in publicly held corporations where the problem of floating new issues through subscription is concerned. The reasons advanced in this situation is that it insures the success of the issue or that it has the same psychological effect as a dividend (Guthman and Dagell, Corporate Financial Policy (3d ed., 1955), p. 369). On rare occasions stock will be issued below book value because this indicia of value is not reflective of the actual worth of the corporation. The book value of the corporation's assets may be inflated or the company may not be glamorous to the public because it is in a declining industry or the company may be under the direction of poor management. In these circumstances there may be a business justification for a major disparity in issuing price and book value in order to inject new capital into the corporation....

The corollary of a stockholder's right to maintain his proportionate equity in a corporation by purchasing additional shares is the right not to purchase additional shares without being confronted with dilution of his existing equity if no valid business justification exists for the dilution....

A stockholder's right not to purchase is seriously undermined if the stock offered is worth substantially more than the offering price. Any purchase at this price dilutes his interest and impairs the value of his original holding.... Judicial review in this area is limited to whether under all the circumstances, including the disparity between issuing price of the stock and its true value, the nature of the corporation, the business necessity for establishing an offering price at a certain amount to facilitate raising new capital, and the ability of stockholders to sell rights, the additional offering of securities should be condemned because the directors in establishing the sale price did not fix it with reference to financial considerations with respect to the ready disposition of securities.

Here the obvious disparity in selling price and book value was calculated to force the dissident stockholder into investing additional sums. No valid business justification was advanced for the disparity in price, and the only beneficiaries of the disparity were the two director-stockholders who were eager to have additional capital in the business.

It is no answer to Katzowitz' action that he was also given a chance to purchase additional shares at this bargain rate. The price was not so much a bargain as it was a tactic, conscious or unconscious on the part of the directors, to place Katzowitz in a compromising situation. The price was so fixed to make the failure to invest costly. However, Katzowitz at the time might not have been aware of the dilution because no notice of the effect of the issuance of the new shares on the already outstanding shares was disclosed....

No reason exists at this time to permit Sidler and Lasker to benefit from their course of conduct. Katzowitz' delay in commencing the action did not prejudice the defendants. By permitting the defendants to recover their additional investment in Sulburn before the remaining assets of Sulburn are distributed to the stockholders upon dissolution, all the stockholders will be treated equitably. Katzowitz, therefore, should receive his aliquot share of the assets of Sulburn less the amount invested by Sidler and Lasker for their purchase of stock on December 27, 1961.

Accordingly, the order of the Appellate Division should be reversed, with costs, and judgment granted in favor of the plaintiff against the individual defendants.

* * *

Order reversed, with costs, and case remitted to Special Term for further proceedings in accordance with the opinion herein.

Note and Question

1. The court repeatedly uses the phrase "fair value." What does it mean by this? Do you agree with this valuation approach in this context?

2. In chapter 9, section 2b(ii), we will examine the use of "poison pills" as a defensive strategy to a hostile takeover. What makes poison pills so effective is their potentially dilutive effect if triggered.

———

Katzowitz involved a closely held corporation. As you read the cases that follow, consider the extent to which the public corporation context makes a difference.

Frantz Mfg. Co. v. EAC Industries

501 A.2d 401 (Del. Super. Ct. 1985)

CHRISTIE, Chief Justice:

The issues in this case focus on the fiduciary duties of the boards of directors of both a target corporation, Frantz Manufacturing Company ("Frantz"), and an acquiring corporation, EAC Industries ("EAC"), after the acquirer has taken control of the target corporation by use of the shareholder consent procedure of 8 *Del. C.* § 228.[1]

EAC sought a preliminary injunction in the Court of Chancery to nullify the actions taken by the Frantz board to regain control of the corporation. The Frantz board had tried to dilute EAC's newly acquired control of 51% of the voting stock of Frantz after EAC had taken steps to assert its control of Frantz. To do this, the Frantz board had transferred 125,000 of its treasury shares to an Employee Stock Ownership Plan ("ESOP") four days after EAC had tendered shareholder consents to Frantz, pursuant to 8 *Del. C.* § 228, by which EAC had altered the Frantz bylaws and placed EAC's president on Frantz' board of directors. The amendments to the Frantz bylaws required, among other things, that all directors be present for a quorum at a board meeting and that a unanimous vote of directors is necessary for all action taken by the board and its committees.

In the Court of Chancery, EAC sought a declaration that the shareholder consents amending the Frantz bylaws were legally effective, and that the subsequent reaction of Frantz management in attempting to deprive EAC of control of Frantz by issuing stock to others was ineffective. Frantz counterclaimed and sought a determination that EAC's bylaw amendments were invalid because the ESOP had been properly created and funded, and the stock issued to the ESOP diluted EAC's purported control of Frantz.

The Court of Chancery concluded that the injunction should issue because the actions of the Frantz board to regain control of the corporation were: (a) not informed, (b) a retrospective defensive maneuver not protected under the business judgment rule, and (c) inequitable conduct undertaken to entrench Frantz management. Frantz then sought review in this Court.

On August 19, 1985, we affirmed the order of the Court of Chancery and found that the EAC consents effectively changed the Frantz bylaws and declared the dilution of EAC's controlling stock ownership by Frantz' funding of an ESOP to be void. This opinion constitutes a further explanation of the rulings announced.

---

1. 8 *Del. C.* § 228(a) states in pertinent part:

Unless otherwise provided in the certificate of incorporation, any action required by this chapter to be taken at any annual or special meeting of stockholders of a corporation, or any action which may be taken at any annual or special meeting of such stockholders, may be taken without a meeting, without prior notice and without a vote, if a consent in writing, setting forth the action so taken, shall be signed by the holders of outstanding stock having not less than the minimum number of votes that would be necessary to authorize or take such action at a meeting at which all shares entitled to vote thereon were present and voted.

* * *

II.

Frantz is a small manufacturing company with more than $7 million in cash reserves. Although Frantz' shares are publicly traded on the American Stock Exchange, prior to recent events it had only about 700 stockholders, and most of its stock was held by the corporation's founding families or in trust for those families. Prior to April 17, 1985, the board was composed of six directors serving staggered terms. All but one of the directors were closely related to the Frantz corporation.[2]

The struggle for control of Frantz began in the spring of 1984 when Snyder, McAlaine & Castle ("SMC"), a Philadelphia-based investment firm, sought to acquire a position in Frantz stock. By May, 1984, SMC held 6.9% of the outstanding shares. In the following months, SMC discussed the possibility of taking Frantz private through a leveraged buyout with the Frantz management.

Negotiations between Frantz and SMC were unsuccessful, however, and Frantz management began to explore the feasibility of taking the company private without SMC. One option for taking the company private involved establishing an Employee Stock Ownership Plan ("ESOP") which would hold 100,000 shares of Frantz stock.

When Frantz began formulating a management-sponsored leveraged buyout, there were approximately 771,902 Frantz shares outstanding, with an additional 285,674 shares held in the company treasury. The largest single block of shares was held in trust and controlled by the Northern Trust Company of Chicago ("Northern") for the benefit of the Wyne family. In addition, the Wyne Foundation, a family trust controlled by Thomas Rosenow and his wife, controlled 44,000 shares.

Musgrove, Frantz' president and chief executive officer, began discussions with Northern in an attempt to acquire the Northern holdings, along with the shares of SMC, the Rosenows, and the Wyne Foundation. The shares to be issued to the ESOP were important to Frantz' plan to take the company private because Frantz without them would be short of a majority after acquiring the shares held by Northern, SMC, the Wyne Foundation, and Rosenow.

In the summer of 1984, Musgrove prepared several documents which analyzed some of the financial considerations for taking the company private. At the Frantz board meeting on August 17, 1984, Musgrove presented his proposals for a management-led leveraged buyout. The board discussed the mechanics of taking the company private and some specific features of the proposed ESOP. The board began to consider having the company purchase 339,000 shares held by Northern, SMC, the Wyne Foundation, and Rosenow and establishing an ESOP with 100,000 of these shares. The board authorized James Collins, the company's lawyer and a member of the board, to begin drafting the necessary documents to create an ESOP and to locate an investment firm to do a

---

2. Thomas Rosenow, the chairman of the board, was the former president of the company. H. Barrett Musgrove was the current president and chief executive officer. James W. Collins was a partner in the law firm retained by Frantz. Bernard U. Bivin and John H. Rutt were former long-time employees of Frantz. Charles R. Bickel was a bank officer in Frantz' principal place of business.

Thomas Rosenow's health was impaired by a series of strokes which limited his speech, memory, and ability to read. Because of his failing health, Mr. Rosenow retired on March 31, 1985. The Board's minutes of February 22, 1985 reflect that the Board was well aware of Rosenow's condition and imminent retirement.

valuation of the company's stock. For this valuation, Frantz retained the investment banking firm of Bacon, Stifel, and Nicholas ("Bacon, Stifel").

Between October, 1984, and February, 1985, Frantz attempted to acquire the shares of Northern and SMC, but the offers were rejected. In early February, 1985, Northern and SMC agreed among themselves to vote and sell their Frantz stock together so that they could both get the highest price possible for their shares. Prior to a Frantz Board Meeting on February 22, 1985, SMC informed Musgrove of the arrangement between SMC and Northern. Thus, at that time about 44%, including the Rosenow and Wyne Foundation shares, of the company's issued and outstanding stock was for sale to the highest bidder.

In preparation for the February 22 board meeting, Musgrove asked the company treasurer, John McCormick, to prepare financial projections of the impact on the company's book value per share and earnings per share of purchasing 339,000 shares of Frantz stock under two different plans. The first plan assumed that Frantz would purchase the stock at $40 per share and retire the shares to the company treasury. The second plan assumed that Frantz and an ESOP would purchase the blocks of stock together, with the ESOP acquiring 100,000 shares, and Frantz retiring 239,000 shares. No analysis was prepared considering Frantz selling treasury shares to an ESOP in a stand-alone transaction.

At the February 22 meeting, the board of directors discussed possible sources of funding for a tender offer and leveraged buyout. The board discussed McCormick's financial projections in two plans for taking the company private and considered funding an ESOP with previously issued and outstanding stock which would be purchased from Northern. The board may have discussed funding an ESOP with treasury stock or authorized but unissued stock, but this source of funding had not been part of any analysis presented to the board. Since Musgrove and Collins had determined that the proposed ESOP would receive IRS clearance without shareholder approval, the board passed a resolution directing the officers to set up an ESOP without requiring shareholder approval.

Between the February 22 board meeting and the next scheduled meeting in mid-April, Musgrove and McCormick set up financing for purchasing shares for the ESOP. Because of favorable tax treatment of interest paid on ESOP loans, the loan commitments sought involved direct loans of $4.5 million to the ESOP, guaranteed by Frantz, with interest rates at 80 to 89% of prime. Frantz received commitments for the necessary loans.

By this time, EAC, a diversified manufacturer of hardware and aircraft products, had begun its quest for control of Frantz. EAC had been contacted by SMC in its efforts to sell the SMC block of Frantz stock and in January 1985, EAC began confidential negotiations with the holders of all of the large blocks of Frantz stock. Between February 12 and April 8, 1985, EAC made market purchases of 17,665 shares (about 2.3% of the outstanding shares of Frantz) in street name. Eventually, Northern was brought into the negotiations with EAC, and through Northern, Rosenow's shares and the shares held by the Wyne Trust were considered for the EAC purchase plan.

After weeks of negotiations, EAC reached an agreement with SMC, Northern, Rosenow, and the Wyne Trust to purchase all of their shares. Because EAC was already highly leveraged, it had difficulty in arranging financing for the purchase of these shares, but by April 15, 1985, EAC was able to secure financing.

Two days later, EAC simultaneously bought the SMC, Northern, Rosenow, and Wyne Trust stock. EAC also purchased a block of shares from Pioneer III, Inc. to accumulate approximately 51% of Frantz' outstanding shares. On April 18, 1985, EAC's president (Peter

Fritzsche) traveled to Frantz' headquarters to assert control through shareholder consents from the owners of 51% of the stock. In addition, Fritzsche presented Rosenow's resignation from the Frantz board and was elected to the Frantz board by the shareholder consents.

The consents also made changes in the bylaws which required: (a) all directors to be present for a quorum; (b) unanimous vote of directors for any board action; (c) unanimous approval for ratification of all committee action; (d) one class of directors; and (e) stockholder approval for indemnification of directors. After a preliminary discussion with Collins, it became clear to Musgrove that if the consents were effective, further action by the Frantz board would be invalid without Fritzsche's approval.

Musgrove acted promptly to try to regain control for Frantz management....

On Monday, April 22, Frantz asked Bacon, Stifel to complete the interrupted valuation study so that the Frantz ESOP could be funded that day. Musgrove called a meeting of the ESOP trustees for that afternoon,[5] and told the other trustees that since the Frantz board had authorized funding the ESOP at its February 22 meeting, they had an obligation to fund the ESOP. Although the resolution by the board had authorized issuance of 100,000 to 125,000 shares to fund the ESOP, at the meeting the trustees only considered purchasing 125,000 shares from the Frantz treasury to fund the ESOP. Musgrove told the other trustees to accept Bacon, Stifel's valuation of $34 per share, and to finance this $4.25 million stock purchase with a loan from Frantz at prime rate rather than through a guaranteed bank loan at less than prime because the EAC bylaw amendments requiring unanimous director approval for board action might prevent board approval to guarantee the ESOP loan.

Next, Musgrove called a directors meeting for April 24. As a "courtesy," Musgrove invited Fritzsche to the meeting, but Fritzsche was invited to participate only as an observer....

Musgrove, conducted the April 24 directors meeting[6] according to a prepared script, and the board mechanically adopted bylaw amendments that restricted the use of the consent procedure,[7] established an executive committee,[8] and approved the funding of the ESOP. If the issuance of treasury shares to the ESOP was effective, EAC then lost its control of a majority of Frantz shares.

It is at this point that EAC sought a preliminary injunction in the Court of Chancery to nullify the actions taken by the Frantz board to deprive it of control, and Frantz, in turn, counterclaimed, seeking a determination that the bylaw amendments imposed on Frantz by EAC were invalid. The Court of Chancery issued an injunction on June 28, 1985, granting relief to EAC Industries against Frantz and its directors....

III.

Frantz has conceded that EAC complied with the mechanics of the consent procedure of 8 *Del. C.* § 228, which permits majority shareholders to obtain immediate action from corporate officials without review or delay.... Therefore, the issues which this Court must address are: (A) whether the EAC amendments enacted by shareholder consents during a

---

5. The trustees of the ESOP were Musgrove and two officers of Frantz: McCormick, the company treasurer, and Froelinger, Frantz' controller.

6. All of Frantz' directors except Rosenow attended. Fritzsche and his attorney attended the meeting, but Fritzsche was not permitted to participate as a director or vote.

7. Frantz' bylaw amendment prohibited use of the 8 *Del. C.* § 228 consent procedure unless the shareholder had given twenty days notice to other shareholders.

8. The executive committee was vested with the authority to discharge the responsibilities of the board, including the power to declare dividends and issue stock, including treasury shares.

change in control of the corporation were illegal and unfair in operation; (B) whether EAC effectively established and retained its majority position because Frantz' funding of the ESOP was invalid; and (C) whether Rosenow breached his fiduciary duty to the corporation and its shareholders by selling his stock and tendering his resignation to EAC.

* * *

B.

The directors of Frantz argue that the February 22, 1985 board resolution empowered the Frantz board to fund the ESOP with treasury shares after the board had learned of EAC's acquisition of a majority of Frantz shares and EAC's other actions to consolidate its position. If the ESOP plan had been carried out as it had been presented to the board on February 22, the incidental dilution of EAC's holdings might have withstood attack. However, whatever the intentions of the Frantz directors may have been on February 22 in authorizing an ESOP, the Court of Chancery found that the board never considered funding an ESOP as a takeover defense by increasing the number of outstanding shares and thereby diluting majority status of an existing stockholder. The board had considered the funding of an ESOP only in connection with taking the company private, where the plan would have decreased the number of outstanding Frantz shares.

Funding the ESOP in the manner it was done prior to the meeting of the board on April 24, 1985, was unauthorized. Furthermore, when the directors ratified the unauthorized funding of the ESOP at the April 24 meeting of the Frantz directors, they were without power to do so by less than unanimous vote. By that time EAC had effectively changed the Frantz bylaws. Since the EAC amendments to the bylaws were valid, such bylaws prevented the Frantz board from ratifying the funding of the ESOP without Fritzsche's consent.

This Court has often held that when a board acts for the sole or primary purpose of perpetuating its own control, this improper motive overrides the ordinary protection of the business judgment rule. See Unocal Corp. v. Mesa Petroleum Co., Del. Supr., 493 A.2d 946 (1985).... The Court of Chancery held that the primary purpose of the Frantz board in agreeing to the funding of the ESOP and in adopting the defensive actions taken between April 18 and 24 was to perpetuate their control of the company. Following the proper standard of review, this Court must agree that the evidence supports a finding that the primary purpose of funding the ESOP at the time the Frantz directors attempted to fund it was to perpetuate their control of the company.

[C]orporate action which seeks to undo a takeover bid *after* control has already passed to another group is not protected by the business judgment rule. Therefore, the measures here taken constituted inequitable conduct. See Moran v. Household International, Inc., Del. Ch., 490 A.2d 1059 (1985), *aff'd* 500 A.2d 1346 (1985).... In Unocal, this Court did not address the issue of whether a board of directors could take retrospective defensive measures against a majority stockholder by divesting the majority stockholder of his statutory right of control. Unocal dealt with the duty of care owed by directors in addressing a possible or a pending takeover of a corporation, not an accomplished takeover. Here, Frantz' activities after April 18 were attempts to defeat the accomplished takeover.

C.

* * *

Frantz asserts that EAC and Thomas Rosenow acted improperly when Rosenow's shares were sold to EAC and at the same time Rosenow submitted his resignation to EAC. It is clear of course that as a director, Mr. Rosenow was in a fiduciary relationship with the corporation and its shareholders. However, it is also clear that directors have the right to deal freely with their shares of stock and to dispose of them at the best price they are able to obtain, so long as they are acting in good faith.... As a general rule, a director has no duty to disclose his stock dealings to the corporation, nor does he have a duty to offer his shares to the corporation before selling them to another.... Directors are also free to resign.

We find no reason to upset the Court of Chancery's finding that Thomas Rosenow did not breach his fiduciary duty to the Frantz stockholders when he resigned his directorship and sold his shares to EAC. We find no merit in Frantz' contentions that Rosenow breached the fiduciary duties set out by this Court in *Unocal*.

IV.

To summarize, we hold ... that funding an ESOP in response to a shift in ownership of a corporation is not valid because the directors' action was not taken under the provision of the then valid bylaws. Finally, we find that a director of a corporation whose imminent retirement is known to the other members of the board does not violate his fiduciary duties to the corporation and its shareholders by tendering his resignation at the same time he sells his stock in the corporation.

For the reasons stated, we agreed with the conclusions of the Court of Chancery and, therefore, issued an order affirming that court.

Notes and Questions

1. Why were the bylaw amendments adopted by means of stockholder consents?

2. How does the court respond to the defendants' argument that the funding of the ESOP was protected by the business judgment rule? Do you agree with the court's reasoning?

3. Why should the Frantz board's action be seen as wrongful?

4. In Condec Corp. v. Lunkenheimer Company, 230 A.2d 769 (Del. Ch. 1967), Condec had made unwanted overtures to take over Lunkenheimer. In response, Lunkenheimer entered into an agreement with U.S. Industries, Inc., to sell its assets to U.S.I. in exchange for U.S.I. preferred stock. To ensure that Condec, which owned sufficient shares of Lunkenheimer stock to prevent the necessary ⅔ vote, could not impede the deal, Lunkenheimer issued 75,000 shares of common stock to U.S.I. in exchange for 75,000 of the same U.S.I. preferred stock to be issued in consideration for Lunkenheimer's assets. In invalidating this issuance the vice-chancellor wrote:

> ... I am persuaded on the basis of the evidence adduced at trial that the transaction here attacked unlike situations involving the purchase of stock with corporate funds was clearly unwarranted[.] ... [I]t unjustifiably strikes at the very heart of the corporate representation by causing a stockholder with an equitable right to a majority of corporate stock to have his right to a proportionate voice and influence in corporate affairs to be diminished by the simple act of an exchange of stock which brought no money into the Lunkenheimer treasury, was not connected with a stock option plan or other proper corporate purpose, and which was obviously designed for the primary purpose of reducing Condec's stock holdings in Lunkenheimer below a majority.

Id. at 777.

A more modern tactic is the issuance by an incumbent board of large blocks of voting stock to an Employee Stock Option Plan. In Norlin Corporation v. Rooney Pace Inc., 744 F.2d 255 (2d Cir. 1984), Norlin "issued new common and voting preferred stock to a wholly owned subsidiary and a newly created employee stock option plan" for the purpose of fending off an unwanted takeover attempt by Piezo Electric Products, Inc. and Rooney Pace by concentrating control in Norlin's board. The court affirmed the district court's preliminary injunction on several grounds.

Ziegler v. American Maize-Products Co.
658 A.2d 219 (Me. 1995)

WATHEN, C.J.

* * *

The relevant facts may be briefly summarized as follows: Plaintiff Ziegler is Chairman of the Board of Directors of American Maize, a Maine corporation with principal divisions in corn and tobacco products. Plaintiff Fidelity is co-trustee with Ziegler of two trusts whose assets include a significant portion of American Maize Class B stock. Plaintiffs seek to enjoin the Directors of American Maize from issuing additional shares of American Maize Class B stock to Eridania Beghin-Say (EBS), a French corporation, pursuant to a stock purchase agreement, that will allow EBS to accumulate, over their opposition, enough votes to approve a merger of American Maize and EBS.

American Maize has two classes of stock whose affirmative vote is required for approval of the merger plan: Class A and Class B. GIH Corporation (GIH) is a Delaware corporation whose principle asset is stock in American Maize. GIH holds 47.3% of the presently outstanding shares of Class B stock. As a result of an agreement reached by the GIH stockholders, Ziegler is in a position to prevent GIH from affirmatively voting its shares of American Maize.[3] In addition to having blocking control of GIH's Class B stock, Ziegler individually and beneficially owns 7.2% of Class B shares and thus effectively controls a 54.5% majority of American Maize Class B stock.

On February 22, 1995, the American Maize Directors approved a Merger Agreement with EBS. As a result of plaintiffs' opposition, the Directors agreed to issue authorized, but previously unissued, Class B shares of American Maize with a pre-emptive rights offer to existing Class B shareholders to be exercised by 5:00 p.m. on Monday, April 10, 1995. The agreement between the shareholders of GIH requiring an affirmative vote of three directors effectively prevents GIH from exercising its pre-emptive rights, and thus EBS would be in a position to purchase the shares and accumulate enough votes to

---

3. Although the New York Ziegler Trust, of which Ziegler and Fidelity are co-trustees, appears to control one more share of GIH stock than the New York Steinkraus Trust, a stockholders agreement requires the affirmative vote of three directors to authorize a vote by GIH. The four directors of GIH are Ziegler, his son William Ziegler, Helen Steinkraus, and her son Eric Steinkraus. Although the Steinkrauses favor the merger and have intervened in this action as a defendant, Zieglers' opposition deadlocks the GIH board and insures that GIH will not vote affirmatively on the merger.

approve the merger. The merger agreement and related stock purchase agreement permit EBS thereafter to acquire American Maize through a tender offer and "cash-out" merger of $40 per share.

Plaintiffs sought preliminary injunctive relief in the Superior Court. The court denied their motion, observing that Maine law is unsettled regarding the authority of a board of directors to issue additional shares of stock for the purpose of permitting a merger without the approval of the current holders of voting stock. Consequently, the court held that plaintiffs had not carried their burden of demonstrating a likelihood of success on the merits.

On appeal, defendants contend as an initial matter that plaintiffs have failed to demonstrate that they control American Maize and consequently they lack standing to petition this Court for the protection of their rights as controlling shareholders. Defendants concede that, but for the issuance of the additional shares, plaintiffs Ziegler and Fidelity would have the power to prevent approval of the proposed merger. Both Ziegler and Fidelity oppose the merger. The board of GIH is therefore deadlocked, and will not vote its Class B shares on the merger. Section 902(3) [13-A M.R.S.A. § 902(3)] requires an affirmative vote by a majority of the stockholders and failure to vote equals a negative vote. The combined effect of Ziegler's "no" votes and GIH's failure to vote would result in the defeat of the merger. Under these circumstances, blocking power equals control, and plaintiffs Ziegler and Fidelity have standing to bring this action. *See Allegheny Corp. v. Breswick*, 353 U.S. 151, 160 (1957) (loss of corporate control engendered by a dilutive stock issuance is a particular injury that compels a direct action).

Turning to the merits, we must determine whether an issuance of stock made solely for the purpose of avoiding an unfavorable vote on a proposed merger is proscribed by section 902(3).

In construing statutes, we have stated that specific statutory provisions take precedence over general provisions.... Defendants in this case rely on 13-A M.R.S.A. § 507(1) to support the legality of the issuance of new voting shares of American Maize stock to facilitate the EBS merger. Section 507(1) is part of the "Corporate Finance" chapter of the Maine Business Corporation Act (MBCA) which deals with the attributes of authorized shares, subscriptions for shares, the issuance of shares, when shares are fully paid and nonassessable, dividends on shares, and similar matters of corporate finance. 13-A M.R.S.A. §§ 501-525. Chapter 9, "Mergers and Consolidations" contains section 902(3) and establishes a comprehensive set of rules governing the circumstances in which corporations can merge, the procedural requirements for mergers, the effects of mergers, dissenters' rights in mergers, and related matters. 13-A M.R.S.A. §§ 901-910.

Section 902(3) specifically addresses the merger at issue in the present case, whereas section 507(1) deals generally with stock issues, without regard to whether the stock issue is an integral part of a merger. When there is in the same statute a specific provision and also a general one, which in its most comprehensive sense would include matters embraced in the specific provision, the general provision must be understood to effect only those cases within its general language that are not within the provisions of the specific provision. The result is that the specific provision controls....

Our decision is also influenced by the principle that a statute in derogation of the common law must be strictly construed.... At common law, no merger could take place without the unanimous consent of the stockholders.... That strict rule long ago abated, and Maine corporations are now permitted to enter into mergers with the affirmative vote of a majority of the shareholders entitled to vote thereon. 13-A M.R.S.A. § 902(3).

Nevertheless, the legislative pronouncement embodied in section 902(3) alters common law only to the extent that the Legislature has made that purpose clear....

In determining the scope and effect of the two sections at issue, we read them together as a single piece of legislation to reach the harmonious result presumably intended by the Legislature.... If the section pertaining to the issuance of stock is construed to authorize issuance in circumstances such as these, directors could overcome the requirement for a bona fide shareholder vote under section 902(3) by the simple expedient of issuing shares to a party certain to vote for the merger. The plan of merger in the present case, rather than calling for the vote of the existing shareholders, included as a first step the issuance of shares for the purpose of creating a favorable majority. As a practical matter, this would allow the directors to stuff the corporate ballot box. We conclude that the Legislature did not Intend to provide, in the same act, a requirement for shareholder approval of a plan of merger, and a ready method of evading such a requirement. *See Rath v. Rath Packing Co.*, 257 Iowa 1277, 136 N.W.2d 410, 417 (Iowa 1965).

We have held that a merger that fails to comply with the specific requirements of the governing merger statute is illegal and invalid. *Marcou v. Federal Trust Co.*, 268 A.2d 629, 634-35 (Me. 1970). In *Marcou* we enjoined a merger where a bank holding company attempted to circumvent the statutory requirements of the Maine Bank Merger statute. We held that the series of steps in the proposed merger, although individually complying with the statutory requirements "for no more than a twinkling of an eye," in fact violated the statute because they actually formed one transaction whose purpose was to compel the stockholder to give up a right that was specifically provided for in the merger statute. *Id.* at 635.

We confront a similar situation in the present case. It is undisputed that the proposed issuance of additional shares of stock, although generally authorized by section 507(1), is designed and intended to permit the merger without the approval of a majority of holders of the stock as required by section 902(3). Under these circumstances, the issuance of the additional shares of stock is precluded by the specific provisions of section 902(3).

[Vacated and remanded for the entry of a permanent injunction against issuing stock pursuant to the stock purchase agreement and from enforcing the deadline for Class B shareholders of American Maize-Products Company to exercise their pre-emptive rights.]

Section 6
Recapitalizations and Restructurings

Problem — Restructuring and the Minority Stockholder

One morning, while digging out a root cellar in his backyard in Hooter Hollow, Billy Joe discovered oil. Instead of simply selling the property and moving to Beverly Hills, as former neighbors of his had done, Billy Joe was ambitious enough to form a corporation for the purpose of drilling the oil and selling it to refineries. Initially, the stockholders were Billy Joe, who owned 51 percent of the 1,000 outstanding shares of common stock, Bo, Billy Joe's nephew, who owned 29 percent, Emmie, Billy Joe's mother, who owned 10 percent, and Sally Jo, Billy Joe's daughter, who owned 10 percent. The board consisted of all four stockholders, and the officers were Billy Joe—president; Bo—vice-president; Emmie—secretary; and Sally Jo—treasurer. Although the stockholders have no voting agreement, they annually have re-elected this board and the board annually has reappointed these officers without controversy. The corporation, Billy Joe Oil Co. (the "Company"), was incorporated in the State of Confusion and commenced business on the day of incorporation.

Things went well for the Company. First year earnings were $10,000,000, and the board declared a dividend of $5,000,000, retaining $5,000,000 in the business. The next year's earnings totaled $20,000,000, and the board declared a dividend of $10,000,000. After the second year of operations, the stock was valued by an independent appraiser at $50,000 per share.

All is not well on the Company's board, however. Billy Joe is getting tired of the responsibilities of having control and, in addition, is getting annoyed with his co-directors. Bo is not very bright and interrupts meetings with stupid questions. Emmie misses most board meetings since she prefers spending her time settin' out on the porch. And Sally Jo insists on bringing her pet hog into board meetings and the Company's offices. Billy Joe would like the opportunity to get out of the business and diversify his investments.

Early in the third year of operations Billy Joe came up with a plan. He formed a new corporation, Billy Joe Holdings, Inc. ("Holdings"), and purchased all of its common stock (which consists of 5,100,000 shares of common stock) in exchange for his 510 shares of the stock of the Company (at a ratio of 10,000 to 1.) The board of Holdings consists of Billy Joe and two of his friends. The consequence of this is that the Company became a partly owned subsidiary of Holdings, which is the Company's controlling stockholder. Next, Billy Joe caused Holdings to file a registration statement with the Securities and Exchange Commission enabling Billy Joe to sell 2,549,999 of his shares of Holdings to the public, which he did for $10 per share. At the same time, Billy Joe caused Holdings to borrow $25,500,010 from Hooter Hollow National Bank, as security for which Holdings pledged its stock in the Company. In addition, as part of the loan agreement, Holdings agreed to continue to use its control to cause the Company to pay sufficient dividends to enable Holdings to pay principal and interest on the loan when due. After these transactions, Billy Joe walked away with $25,499,990, and 2,550,001 shares of a somewhat diversified publicly held company (with the potential for greater diversification) leaving the Company controlled by a publicly held corporation.

Emmie, Bo, and Sally Jo sue Billy Joe for breach of fiduciary duty in the trial court of the State of Confusion.

1. Assume you represent Billy Joe. How would you present your case?

2. You are the judge. The case is one of first impression. How do you rule, and why?

Jones v. H. F. Ahmanson & Co.
1 Cal. 3d 93, 81 Cal. Rptr. 592, 460 P.2d 464 (1969)

TRAYNOR, Chief Justice.

June K. Jones, the owner of 25 shares of the capital stock of United Savings and Loan Association of California brings this action on behalf of herself individually and of all similarly situated minority stockholders of the Association. The defendants are United Financial Corporation of California, fifteen individuals, and four corporations, all of whom are present or former stockholders or officers of the Association. Plaintiff seeks damages and other relief for losses allegedly suffered by the minority stockholders of the Association because of claimed breaches of fiduciary responsibility by defendants in the creation and operation of United Financial, a Delaware holding company that owns 87 percent of the outstanding Association stock.

Plaintiff appeals ... an order sustaining defendants' general and special demurrers.... Defendants have filed a protective cross-appeal. We have concluded that the allegations of the complaint and certain stipulated facts sufficiently state a cause of action and that the judgment must therefore be reversed.

The following facts appear from the allegations of the complaint and stipulation.

[The Association, formerly a depositor-owned institution, was incorporated in April 1956, issuing 6,568 shares of stock, 14.8 percent of which were bought by former depositors (including plaintiff). From 1959 to 1966, the per share book value of Association stock increased from $1,131 to $4,143.70, largely because of its policy of retaining most of its earnings in tax-free reserves. In May 1958, H. F. Ahmanson & Co. acquired a majority of the Association's shares. Due to these factors, among others, the shares were not actively traded, and such trades as occurred were principally among existing stockholders.

Because of the high book value of the stock and the Association's closely held nature, the Association was left behind in the bull market for public savings and loan stocks that took place in the late 1950s and early 1960s. To remedy this, defendants incorporated United Financial, and exchanged their Association stock for United Financial stock at a ratio of 1 for 250. This made the Association an 85 percent owned subsidiary of United Financial. Defendants (the Association's former majority shareholders) did not give the minority shareholders an opportunity to participate in the exchange.

United Financial stock was publicly offered in 1960, in an offering of 60,000 units consisting of two shares of United Financial stock and one $100 principal amount 5 percent subordinated, convertible debenture. Under the terms of the offering, $6,200,000 of the $7,200,000 anticipated proceeds were to be returned to United Financial's original shareholders as a return of capital (equal to $927.50 on each "derived block" of 250 United Financial shares, or, to put it differently, on each Association share). United Financial promised to liquidate or encumber assets of the Association, the proceeds of which would be distributed to United Financial to service the debentures.

An additional offering of United Financial shares (together with an offering by defendants) was made in 1961. As a consequence, market activity in United Financial stock increased, and such trading as existed in Association stock dried up, with United Financial acquiring most Association shares that were sold in an offer directed to Association stockholders (at a price substantially less than both the book value of Association shares and the trading price of derived blocks of 250 United Financial shares).

In 1960, following United Financial's purchase of additional Association shares, defendants caused the Association's president to announce the discontinuation of special dividends to Association stockholders, following which defendants proposed an exchange of United Financial shares for Association stock at a price dramatically lower than the trading price of derived blocks of United Financial shares. After plaintiffs and other minority shareholders objected, defendants abandoned the plan.]

Plaintiff contends that in following this course of conduct defendants breached the fiduciary duty owed by majority or controlling shareholders to minority shareholders.

She alleges that they used their control of the Association for their own advantage to the detriment of the minority when they created United Financial, made a public market for its shares that rendered Association stock unmarketable except to United Financial, and then refused either to purchase plaintiff's Association stock at a fair price or exchange the stock on the same basis afforded to the majority. She further alleges that they also created a conflict of interest that might have been avoided had they offered all Association stockholders the opportunity to participate in the initial exchange of shares....

* * *

II
Majority Shareholders' Fiduciary Responsibility

Defendants take the position that as shareholders they owe no fiduciary obligation to other shareholders, absent reliance on inside information, use of corporate assets, or fraud. This view has long been repudiated in California. The Courts of ... Appeal have often recognized that majority shareholders, either singly or acting in concert to accomplish a joint purpose, have a fiduciary responsibility to the minority and to the corporation to use their ability to control the corporation in a fair, just, and equitable manner. Majority shareholders may not use their power to control corporate activities to benefit themselves alone or in a manner detrimental to the minority. Any use to which they put the corporation or their power to control the corporation must benefit all shareholders proportionately and must not conflict with the proper conduct of the corporation's business.

* * *

Defendants assert, however, that in the use of their own shares they owed no fiduciary duty to the minority stockholders of the Association. They maintain that they made full disclosure of the circumstances surrounding the formation of United Financial, that the creation of United Financial and its share offers in no way affected the control of the Association, that plaintiff's proportionate interest in the Association was not affected, that the Association was not harmed, and that the market for Association stock was not affected. Therefore, they conclude, they have breached no fiduciary duty to plaintiff and the other minority stockholders.

.... In essence defendants suggest that we reaffirm the so-called "majority" rule reflected in our early decisions. This rule, exemplified by the decision in Ryder v. Bamberger, 172 Cal. 791, 158 P. 753 but since severely limited, recognized the "perfect right [of majority shareholders] to dispose of their stock * * * without the slightest regard to the wishes and desires or knowledge of the minority stockholders; * * *" (p. 806, 158 P. p. 759) and held that such fiduciary duty as did exist in officers and directors was to the corporation only. The duty of shareholders as such was not recognized unless they, like officers and directors, by virtue of their position were possessed of information relative to the value of the corporation's shares that was not available to outside shareholders. In such case the existence of special facts permitted a finding that a fiduciary relationship to the corporation and other shareholders existed....

.... [However, the] rule that has developed in California is a comprehensive rule of "inherent fairness from the viewpoint of the corporation and those interested therein." ... The rule applies alike to officers, directors, and controlling shareholders in the exercise of powers that are theirs by virtue of their position and to transactions wherein controlling shareholders seek to gain an advantage in the sale or transfer or use of their controlling block of shares. Thus we held in In re Security Finance, *supra*, 49 Cal. 2d 370, 317 P.2d 1, that majority shareholders do not have an absolute right to dissolve a corporation, although ostensibly permitted to do so by Corporations Code, section 4600, because their statutory power is subject to equitable limitations in favor of the minority. We recognized that the majority had the right to dissolve the corporation to protect their investment *if* no alternative means were available *and* no advantage was secured over other shareholders, and noted that "there is nothing sacred in the life of a corporation that transcends the interests of its shareholders, but because dissolution falls with such finality on those interests, above all corporate powers it is subject to equitable limitations." (49 Cal. 2d 370, 377, 317 P.2d 1, 5.)

* * *

The increasingly complex transactions of the business and financial communities demonstrate the inadequacy of the traditional theories of fiduciary obligation as tests of majority shareholder responsibility to the minority. These theories have failed to afford adequate protection to minority shareholders and particularly to those in closely held corporations whose disadvantageous and often precarious position renders them particularly vulnerable to the vagaries of the majority. Although courts have recognized the potential for abuse or unfair advantage when a controlling shareholder sells his shares at a premium over investment value (Perlman v. Feldmann, 219 F.2d 173, 50 A.L.R.2d 1134 [premium paid for control over allocation of production in time of shortage]; Gerdes v. Reynolds, Sup., 28 N.Y.S.2d 622 [sale of control to looters or incompetents]; Porter v. Healy, 244 Pa. 427, 91 A. 428; Brown v. Halbert, *supra*, 271 A.C.A. 307, 76 Cal. Rptr. 781 [sale of only controlling shareholder's shares to purchaser offering to buy assets of corporation or all shares]) or in a controlling shareholder's use of control to avoid equitable distribution of corporate assets (Zahn v. Transamerica Corporation (3rd Cir. 1946) 162 F.2d 36, 172 A.L.R. 495 [use of control to cause subsidiary to redeem stock prior to liquidation and distribution of assets]), no comprehensive rule has emerged in other jurisdictions. Nor have most commentators approached the problem from a perspective other than that of the advantage gained in the sale of control....

.... The case before us, in which no sale or transfer of actual control is directly involved, demonstrates that the injury [to minority shareholders] ... can be inflicted with impunity under the traditional rules and supports our conclusion that the comprehensive rule of good faith and inherent fairness to the minority in any transaction where control of the corporation is material properly governs controlling shareholders in this state.

We turn now to defendants' conduct to ascertain whether this test is met.

III
Formation of United Financial and Marketing Its Shares

Defendants created United Financial during a period of unusual investor interest in the stock of savings and loan associations. They then owned a majority of the outstanding stock of the Association. This stock was not readily marketable owing to a high book value, lack of investor information and facilities, and the closely held nature of the Association. The management of the Association had made no effort to create a market for the stock or to split the shares and reduce their market price to a more attractive level. Two courses were available to defendants in their effort to exploit the bull market in savings and loan stock. Both were made possible by defendants' status as controlling stockholders. The first was either to cause the Association to effect a stock split (Corp. Code, § 1507) and create a market for the Association stock or to create a holding company for Association shares and permit all stockholders to exchange their shares before offering holding company shares to the public. All stockholders would have benefited alike had this been done, but in realizing their gain on the sale of their stock the majority stockholders would of necessity have had to relinquish some of their control shares. Because a public market would have been created, however, the minority stockholders would have been able to extricate themselves without sacrificing their investment had they elected not to remain with the new management.

The second course was that taken by defendants. A new corporation was formed whose major asset was to be the control block of Association stock owned by defendants, but from which minority shareholders were to be excluded. The unmarketable Association stock held by the majority was transferred to the newly formed corporation at an exchange rate equivalent to a 250 for 1 stock split. The new corporation thereupon set out to create a market for its own shares. Association stock constituted 85 percent of the holding company's assets and produced an equivalent proportion of its income. The same individuals controlled both corporations. It appears therefrom that the market created by defendants for United Financial shares was a market that would have been available for Association stock had defendants taken the first course of action.

After United Financial shares became available to the public it became a virtual certainty that no equivalent market could or would be created for Association stock. United Financial had become the controlling stockholder and neither it nor the other defendants would benefit from public trading in Association stock in competition with United Financial shares. Investors afforded an opportunity to acquire United Financial shares would not be likely to choose the less marketable and expensive Association stock in preference. Thus defendants chose a course of action in which they used their control of the Association to obtain an advantage not made available to all stockholders. They did so without regard to the resulting detriment to the minority stockholders and in the absence of any compelling business purpose. Such conduct is not consistent with their duty of good faith and inherent fairness to the minority stockholders. Had defendants afforded the minority an opportunity to exchange their stock on the same basis or offered to purchase them at a price arrived at by independent appraisal, their burden of establishing good faith and inherent fairness would have been much less. At the trial they may present evidence tending to show such good faith or compelling business purpose that would render their action fair under the circumstances. On appeal from the judgment of dismissal after the defendants' demurrer was sustained we decide only that the complaint states a cause of action entitling plaintiff to relief.

Defendants gained an additional advantage for themselves through their use of control of the Association when they pledged that control over the Association's assets and earnings to secure the holding company's debt, a debt that had been incurred for their own benefit.[10] In so doing the defendants breached their fiduciary obligation to the minority once again and caused United Financial and its controlling shareholders to be-

---

10. Should it become necessary to encumber or liquidate Association assets to service this debt or to depart from a dividend policy consistent with the business needs of the Association, damage to the Association itself may occur. We need not resolve here, but note with some concern, the problem facing United Financial, which owes the same fiduciary duty to its own shareholders as to those of the Association. Any decision regarding use of Association assets and earnings to service the holding company debt must be made in the context of these potentially conflicting interests.

come inextricably wedded to a conflict of interest between the minority stockholders of each corporation....

In so holding we do not suggest that the duties of corporate fiduciaries include in all cases an obligation to make a market for and to facilitate public trading in the stock of the corporation. But when, as here, no market exists, the controlling shareholders may not use their power to control the corporation for the purpose of promoting a marketing scheme that benefits themselves alone to the detriment of the minority. Nor do we suggest that a control block of shares may not be sold or transferred to a holding company. We decide only that the circumstances of any transfer of controlling shares will be subject to judicial scrutiny when it appears that the controlling shareholders may have breached their fiduciary obligation to the corporation or the remaining shareholders.

IV
Damages

Plaintiff contends that she should have been afforded the opportunity to exchange her stock for United Financial shares at the time of and on the same basis as the majority exchange. She therefore proposes that upon tender of her Association stock to the defendants she be awarded the fair market value of a derived block of United Financial shares during 1960-1962 plus interest from the date of her action as well as a return of capital of $927.50 plus interest from the date the same was made to the former majority shareholders....

Defendants, on the other hand, claim that plaintiff seeks a "free ride" after they have taken all of the risks in creating United Financial and marketing its stock....

From the perspective of the minority stockholders of the Association, the transfer of control under these circumstances to another corporation and the resulting impact on their position as minority stockholders accomplished a fundamental corporate change as to them....

The more familiar fundamental corporate changes, merger, consolidation, and dissolution, are accompanied by statutory and judicial safeguards established to protect minority shareholders. (Corp. Code, §§ 4100-4124, 4600-4693.) Shareholders dissenting from a merger of their corporation into another may demand that the corporation purchase their shares at the fair market value. (Corp. Code, § 4300.) ... Protection of shareholder interests is achieved in voluntary corporate dissolution by judicial supervision to assure equitable settlement of the corporation's affairs. (Corp. Code, § 4607; In re Security Finance Co., *supra*, 49 Cal. 2d 370, 317 P.2d 1.)

Judicial protection has also been afforded the shareholder who is the victim of a "de-facto merger" to which he objects....

Appraisal rights protect the dissenting minority shareholder against being forced to either remain an investor in an enterprise fundamentally different than that in which he invested or sacrifice his investment by sale of his shares at less than a fair value. (O'Neal and Derwin, Expulsion or Oppression of Business Associates (1961), *supra*, 62.) Plaintiff here was entitled to no less. But she was entitled to more. In the circumstances of this case she should have been accorded the same opportunity to exchange her Association stock for that of United Financial accorded the majority.

Although a controlling shareholder who sells or exchanges his shares is not under an obligation to obtain for the minority the consideration that he receives in all cases, when he does sell or exchange his shares the transaction is subject to close scrutiny. When the majority receives a premium over market value for its shares, the consideration for which that premium is paid will be examined. If it reflects payment for that which is properly a corporate asset all shareholders may demand to share proportionately.... Here the exchange was an integral part of a scheme that the defendants could reasonably foresee would have as an incidental effect the destruction of the potential public market for Association stock. The remaining stockholders would thus be deprived of the opportunity to realize a profit from those intangible characteristics that attach to publicly marketed stock and enhance its value above book value. Receipt of an appraised value reflecting book value and earnings alone could not compensate the minority shareholders for the loss of this potential. Since the damage is real, although the amount is speculative, equity demands that the minority stockholders be placed in a position at least as favorable as that the majority created for themselves.

If, after trial of the cause, plaintiff has established facts in conformity with the allegations of the complaint and stipulation, then upon tender of her Association stock to defendants she will be entitled to receive at her election either the appraised value of her shares on the date of the exchange, May 14, 1959, with interest at 7 percent a year from the date of this action or a sum equivalent to the fair market value of a "derived block" of United Financial stock on the date of this action with interest thereon from that date, and the sum of $927.50 (the return of capital paid to the original United Financial shareholders) with interest thereon from the date United Financial first made such payments to its original shareholders, for each share tendered. The appraised or fair market value shall be reduced, however, by the amount by which dividends paid on Association shares during the period from May 14, 1959 to the present exceeds the dividends paid on a corresponding block of United Financial shares during the same period.

* * *

Questions

1. What does Judge Traynor's theory of the corporation appear to be? What are the costs and benefits of his approach?

2. Defendants argued that they fully disclosed "the circumstances surrounding the formation of United Financial...," and that their actions had no effect on the internal control relationships or proportionate ownership of the corporation, an argument the court rejected. What, if any, relevance do these facts have to the existence and scope of fiduciary duty?

3. At several points in the opinion the court appears to treat the Association as a close corporation. In what respects is it a close corporation? How, if at all, would this make a difference in assessing the scope of fiduciary duty?

4. What was the relevance of the defendants pledging their control over the Association's assets and earnings to secure United Financial's debt?

5. Can you think of any business or financial reason why the minority should have been excluded from the recapitalization?

6. Is the remedy provided by the court appropriate? Are there other remedies that would serve plaintiff better?

Leader v. Hycor, Inc.

395 Mass. 215, 479 N.E.2d 173 (1985)

NOLAN, Justice.

The plaintiffs, former minority shareholders of the defendant corporation, appeal from a judgment entered against them after a trial before a judge of the Superior Court. Their suit challenged actions taken by the five majority shareholders, who also were named as defendants, which resulted in the forced redemption of all minority stock. On appeal, the plaintiffs argue that (1) the trial judge erred in ruling that the five majority shareholders, who also constituted the entire board of directors of Hycor, Inc., did not violate their fiduciary duty of loyalty to the minority shareholders when they effectuated a "recapitalization" of the corporation; and (2) the trial judge erred in ruling that the five dollar per share price, paid to former minority shareholders for their stock, was "consistent with various indicia used to determine the value of closely-held stock." For the reasons set forth below, we reverse and remand the case for further consideration of the price issue.

The relevant facts may be summarized as follows. Hycor, Inc. (Hycor), is a Massachusetts corporation that was organized in 1967 by the five individual defendants (the majority shareholders). Each of the majority shareholders has been a member of Hycor's board of directors, and an employee of the corporation, since its organization....

The majority shareholders and their family members owned all of Hycor's stock from May, 1967, when the corporation was organized, until February, 1969. At that time, Hycor made a public offering of 75,000 shares of stock, at four dollars a share, in an effort to raise capital. After the public offering, there were 525,000 shares of stock issued and outstanding. The majority shareholders and their families owned approximately 440,000 shares, or eighty-five percent, of the outstanding stock. The stock owned by the majority shareholders was not registered under the Federal Securities Act of 1933, and therefore, sale of this stock was restricted....

.... In June of 1979, discussions took place between some of the majority shareholders and Hycor's corporate counsel. These discussions concerned the possibility of the defendants' acquiring 100 per cent ownership of the Hycor stock. On February 4, 1980, the majority shareholders, acting as directors of Hycor, mailed a written "Notice of Special Meeting of Stockholders" to be held at Hycor's offices on February 13, 1980. The notice stated that the purpose of the meeting was to vote on a recapitalization proposal. Under the terms of this proposal, Hycor's articles of organization would be amended to reduce the authorized capital stock from two million shares with a par value of one cent, to five hundred shares, with a par value of forty dollars. In effect, each "old" share would be reduced to 1/4,000 of a "new" share. Furthermore, no fractional shares of Hycor stock would be recognized after the recapitalization. Each holder of a fractional share would receive five dollars upon surrender of each "old" share certificate.

A letter from defendant Hyman, as president of Hycor, accompanied this notice. Hyman stated the reasons for the proposed recapitalization to be "the somewhat disappointing market history of the stock" and that "dividends ... have not represented a significant return on a $4.00 investment." He indicated that the board of directors had no plans to increase dividends. Hyman also noted that there had been very limited trading in the stock.

On February 13, 1980, there were 517,000 shares of Hycor stock issued and outstanding. Approximately 81 per cent of these shares were owned by the majority shareholders and their families. The remaining shares were owned by 331 shareholders (the minority shareholders). Each minority shareholder owned less than 4,000 shares of stock. The special meeting of shareholders was held on this date. The four plaintiffs and one other minority shareholder appeared at the meeting and objected to the recapitalization proposal and the offer price of five dollars per share. Each of the named plaintiffs voted against the proposed recapitalization. The majority shareholders voted in favor of the plan; therefore, the change in the articles of organization was approved.

On April 24, 1980, the minority shareholders commenced this action. They alleged that the defendants had acted fraudulently, and had misrepresented the basis for the proposed amendment to the articles of organization in order to induce the plaintiffs to approve the change. The plaintiffs also alleged that the actions of the defendants constituted a breach of the fiduciary duty that the defendants owed to the corporation's minority shareholders, and that the defendants failed to give proper notice to the minority shareholders as required by G.L. c. 156B, §87. The plaintiffs sought an appraisal of the fair market value of their shares in Hycor on the date that the amendments to the Articles of Organization became effective....

.... A judge of the Superior Court denied the defendants' motion to dismiss and motion for summary judgment. He granted the plaintiffs' motion for class action certification, except as to the count in the plaintiffs' complaint seeking an independent appraisal of the stock's value under G.L. c. 156B. He noted that only those stockholders who did not vote in favor of the proposal would be proper plaintiffs in such an action. He stated that this number was too small to warrant certification on this count....

After trial, the judge ordered judgment entered for the defendants. He refused to find that "[t]here was no legitimate business purpose for the recapitalization," characterizing the plaintiffs' assertions to this effect as "[u]nsubstantiated by the evidence." The judge denied the plaintiffs' request for findings that the procedure used by the majority shareholders to effectuate the recapitalization was "unfair and a clear abuse of corporate power and control." Furthermore, he was not persuaded that "[a]ny arguable business purpose for the recapitalization could have been achieved by less drastic alternatives." Finally, he ruled that the five dollars per share price offered to the minority shareholders "was fair and reasonable and consistent with various indicia used to determine the value of closely held stock."

1. *Validity of the recapitalization.* The plaintiffs claim that the judge implicitly ruled that, as a matter of law, the recapitalization was fair and not an abuse of corporate power. They challenge this ruling.... Additionally, the plaintiffs argue that the ruling implies that the recapitalization was not a "freezing-out" of minority interests. The plaintiffs conclude that the judge's ruling was "manifest error."

A. *Statutory basis for recapitalization.* The minority shareholders characterize the actions of the majority shareholders as a "freeze out" of minority shareholders which lacked a legitimate business purpose. We turn first to the statutory provisions cited by the majority shareholders as authorizing the transaction at issue. General Laws c. 156B, §71, as appearing in St. 1981, c. 298, §1, provides, in relevant part, that "[a] corporation may ... authorize, at a meeting duly called for the purpose, by vote of two-thirds of each class of stock outstanding and entitled to vote thereon or, if the articles of organization so provide, by vote of a lesser proportion but not less than a majority of each class of stock outstanding and entitled to vote thereon, any amendment of its articles of organization; provided, only, that any provision added to or changes made in its articles of organization by such amendment could have been included in, and any provision deleted thereby could have been omitted from, original articles of organization filed at the time of such meeting." Section 28 of that chapter permits a corporation to issue fractional shares of stock. The statute also authorizes the payment of cash in lieu of fractional share interests.

Pursuant to these statutory provisions, the majority shareholders amended the corporation's articles of organization, effectuating a recapitalization of Hycor and authorizing the payment of cash in exchange for fractional shares. This type of transaction, commonly described as a "reverse stock split," is one method employed by majority shareholders to eliminate public ownership in a company....

The defendants argue that they proceeded in accordance with the applicable corporate statutes in their attempt to return Hycor to private status. In *Teschner v. Chicago Title & Trust Co.*, 59 Ill. 2d 452, 457, 322 N.E.2d 54 (1974), appeal dismissed, 422 U.S. 1002, 95 S. Ct. 2623, 45 L. Ed. 2d 666 (1975), the Illinois Supreme Court considered whether the defendants had proceeded under the provisions of the Illinois Business Corporation Act in amending its articles of incorporation and reclassifying stock for the purpose of eliminating fractional shares. That court accepted the defendants' interpretation of the relevant statutory provisions as authorizing their actions. The court stated that "[a]t common law the unanimous consent of the stockholders of a corporation was required to make fundamental changes in the corporation. To provide needed flexibility and to remove what was in effect a power of veto held by a dissenting minority, legislatures authorized the making of corporate changes by majority vote." *Id.*, 59 Ill. 2d at 456, 322 N.E.2d 54. The court concluded that as a general rule, absent fraud, "interests of minority shareholders can be terminated" under Illinois law. *Id.* We agree with the rationale underlying this conclusion. Setting aside the issues of fairness of price and lack of corporate purpose, which we discuss below, we decide that the majority shareholders acted in compliance with the relevant portions of the Massachusetts corporation law when they effectuated the transaction at issue.

B. *Judicial review of the transaction.* Having decided that the transaction, on its face, was permissible under the provisions of the statute governing Massachusetts corporations, we turn to the plaintiffs' claims of breach of fiduciary duty and unfairness. Despite apparent compliance with statutory requirements, a transaction such as the one at issue is still subject to judicial scrutiny on these grounds.... At this point, however, it is not enough for those challenging such a transaction merely to label it a "freezeout." See *Tanzer Economic Assocs. v. Universal Food Specialties, Inc.*, 87 Misc. 2d 167, 175, 383 N.Y.S.2d 472 (N.Y. Sup. Ct. 1976). "Freezeouts, by definition, are coercive: minority shareholders are bound by majority rule to accept cash or debt in exchange for their common shares, even though the price they receive may be less than the value they assign to these shares. But this alone does not render freezeouts objectionable." Brudney and Chirelstein, A Restatement of Corporate Freezeouts, 87 Yale L.J. 1354, 1357 (1978). At the same time, however, we recognize that courts must avoid an "automatic stamp of approval of that which is manifestly inequitable." *Tanzer, supra.*

We begin our analysis by considering the nature of the duty that the defendants owed to the plaintiffs under these circumstances. The plaintiffs contend that Hycor was a close corporation, and thus the defendants, as directors and majority shareholders, owed the plaintiffs a duty of "utmost good faith and loyalty." *Donahue v. Rodd Electrotype Co. of New England, Inc.*, 367 Mass. 578, 593, 328 N.E.2d 505 (1975). The defendants argue that Hycor was not a close corporation, and suggest that the defendants, as directors and stockholders of Hycor, were required to act in good faith and with inherent fairness....

In ruling on the fairness of the price that the defendants offered to the plaintiffs in exchange for their shares of stock, the judge referred to "indicia used to determine the value of closely held stock." It appears, therefore, that he considered Hycor to be a close corporation. We need not decide this issue.

In *Donahue v. Rodd Electrotype Co. of New England, Inc.*, *supra* at 593, we held that stockholders in a close corporation owe one another a duty of "utmost good faith and loyalty." The test to be applied when minority shareholders in a close corporation bring suit against the majority alleging a breach of the strict faith duty owed to them by the majority is "whether the controlling group can demonstrate a legitimate business purpose for its action." *Wilkes v. Springside Nursing Home, Inc.*, 370 Mass. 842, 851, 353 N.E.2d 657 (1976). Once the majority advances such a purpose, it is incumbent upon the minority shareholders to establish that the majority could have achieved the same legitimate objective through an alternative course of action less harmful to the minority's interest. *Id.* at 851-852, 353 N.E.2d 657. In *Wilkes*, however, we expressed our concern that "untempered application of the strict good faith standard enunciated in *Donahue* [in some instances] will result in the imposition of limitations on legitimate action by the controlling group in a close corporation which will unduly hamper its effectiveness in managing the corporation in the best interests of all concerned." *Id.* at 850, 353 N.E.2d 657.

In the case before us, the judge ruled that the evidence fell short of substantiating the plaintiffs' claim that the recapitalization was not designed to achieve a legitimate business purpose. We find no error in this ruling. The evidence presented by the defendants on this issue included the testimony of Hycor's president, Hyman, and its corporate counsel, Mr. Butterworth. Hyman testified that the main reason behind the recapitalization was not to eliminate all the public stockholders, but was related to the "dreadful market history of the stock." He stated that, while Hycor had the responsibilities of a public company, it did not enjoy the benefits of such status. Specifically, he noted the lack of a ready market for Hycor stock. Mr. Butterworth's testimony supported these assertions. We are satisfied that, based upon the evidence before him, the judge's decision was proper.

In the judge's opinion, the plaintiffs failed to establish that "[a]ny arguable business purpose for the recapitalization could have been achieved by less drastic alternatives." On appeal, the plaintiffs suggest that the "business purpose" at issue was avoiding the annoyance of telephone calls directed to the company's president concerning the purchase and sale of Hycor stock. They argue that less drastic means existed to eliminate this problem. However, the plaintiffs' argument ignores evidence that Hycor's status as a public company required the company to comply with various statutory duties, yet the company did not enjoy a ready market for its stock. We agree that the plaintiffs failed to carry their burden of establishing that less drastic alternatives were available to effectuate the defendants' legitimate business purpose.

* * *

We remand the case, solely with respect to the fairness of the price, for proceedings consistent with this opinion.

So ordered.

Notes and Questions

1. Stock splits (sometimes referred to as "forward" stock splits), and their opposite, reverse stock splits, are legal accounting techniques whereby a change in the number of

shares of a class outstanding can be altered without any change in the corporation's actual wealth. A stock split simply reduces the par value and increases the number of shares by a proportionate amount. For example, if Greenacres Corporation has an outstanding class of common stock consisting of one share with a par value of $1.00, a 2-for-1 stock split will result in a reduction of par value to $.50 and an increase in outstanding shares to two. Conversely, a reverse 1-for-2 stock split of our newly recapitalized Greenacres would result in an increase in par value from $.50 to $1.00 and a decrease in outstanding shares from 2-to-1. Obviously for stock with no par value the number of shares is simply increased or decreased and no balance sheet adjustment is required.

If the stock has a par value, then a charter amendment is necessary to change the par value to reflect the split. Even if the stock lacks a par value, a charter amendment may be necessary to provide sufficient authorized shares to accomplish the split. (Obviously this latter action is unnecessary in the case of a reverse stock split.) *But see* California Corp. Code § 188 (requiring amendment of charter to effectuate stock split notwithstanding the existence of sufficient authorized shares); Model Bus. Corp. Act Ann. § 6.23, Official Comment (3rd ed. 1984 & Supp. 2000/01/02) (reverse stock split requires amendment of charter to reduce number of authorized shares).

The ultimate elimination of minority stockholders through reverse splits is accomplished by choosing a sufficiently high ratio to result in all minority shares becoming fractional shares, as was the case in *Leader.* Then the corporation simply purchases those shares for cash consistent with statutory authority. *See* N.Y. Bus. Corp. Law § 509 (a corporation may issue fractional shares or, alternatively, may pay the fair value of such shares in cash); Rev. Model Bus. Corp. Act § 6.04 (similar); Del. Gen. Corp. Law § 155 (similar).

Stock splits are related to stock dividends, which are virtually identical in effect, but typically are of smaller size. The only noticeable difference is the legal accounting convention; stock dividends are chargeable to surplus whereas stock splits are chargeable to capital. *See* Manning & Hanks, A Concise Textbook on Legal Capital, 127-28, 130-31 (3d ed. 1990). Even this distinction is eliminated by the Revised Model Business Corporation Act, which has abolished the concept of par value, as a consequence of which the treatment of stock splits and stock dividends is identical. Rev. Model Bus. Corp. Act § 6.23.

Finally, it should be noted that, unlike cash dividends, the declaration of a stock dividend does not create a debt of the corporation to its stockholders. *Compare* Caleb & Co. v. E. I. DuPont de Nemours & Co., 615 F. Supp. 96 (S.D.N.Y. 1985) (applying Delaware law), *with* Anadarko Petroleum Corp. v. Panhandle Eastern Corp., 545 A.2d 1171 (Del. 1988), *supra* at section 3c.

The economic consequence of a stock split (or reverse split) should be an immediate decrease (or increase) in the market price or value of each share, and, typically, a corresponding adjustment in dividend rate. *See* Hamilton, Fundamentals of Modern Business § 16.9 (1989 & Supp. 2004).

By far the best (and most readable) treatment of the technical aspects of stock splits and dividends, and indeed legal accounting generally, is Manning & Hanks, *supra. See also* 11 Fletcher et al., Fletcher Cyclopedia of the Law of Private Corporations § 5362 (perm. ed., rev. vol. 2003). For more on stock splits and reverse stock splits, see *supra* chapter 7, section 3b(ii)(A).

2. As noted by the court in *Leader*, reverse stock splits are often used as a freeze-out technique. Reverse stock splits resulting in the creation of fractional shares may result in

the availability of appraisal rights to the fractional stockholder. *See, e.g.,* Rev. Model Bus. Corp. Act § 13.02(a)(4) (dissenter's rights where charter amendment creates fractional shares which are to be acquired for cash). *But see* Del. Gen. Corp. Law § 262(c) (providing appraisal rights for charter amendments only if, and to the extent, provided in the charter); N.Y. Bus. Corp. Law § 806(b)(6) (limiting circumstances under which appraisal rights are available for charter amendments, apparently not including reverse splits).

3. In Lerner v. Lerner, 306 Md. 771, 511 A.2d 501 (1986), the Maryland Court of Appeals rejected, in dictum, the application of a *per se* rule prohibiting freeze-outs by reverse stock splits in closely held corporations, while preliminarily enjoining the specific transaction at issue. In Clark v. Pattern Analysis and Recognition Corporation, 87 Misc. 2d 385, 384 N.Y.S.2d 660 (1976), the court granted plaintiffs' motion for a preliminary injunction against a 4,000 to 1 reverse stock split by which they would have been eliminated, undertaken by the controlling stockholders for the admitted purpose of removing plaintiffs as stockholders. *See also* Edick v. Contran Corporation, Slip Op. No. 7662 (Del. Ch. March 18, 1986) (refusing to dismiss complaint challenging that manner in which reverse split was effectuated and alleging material nondisclosure on the ground that allegations sufficed to state claim for breach of fiduciary duty notwithstanding grant of appraisal rights by charter); Teschner v. Chicago Title and Trust Company, 59 Ill. 2d 452, 322 N.E.2d 54 (1975), *appeal dismissed,* 422 U.S. 1002 (1975) (reverse stock split designed to eliminate minority holding 1/10 of 1 percent of outstanding stock held to be valid in the absence of fraud); Goldman v. Union Bank and Trust, 765 P.2d 638 (Colo. Ct. App. 1988) (affirming grant of summary judgment to defendants, holding that elimination of minority by reverse stock split was statutorily permitted, and noting that, while "courts which have considered the matter [generally] have required a showing of valid business purpose, plaintiffs could not raise this issue for the first time on appeal.").

4. For more on reverse stock splits as a means of going private, see Murdock, Squeeze-outs, Freeze-outs, and Discounts: Why Is Illinois in the Minority in Protecting Shareholder Interests?, 35 Loy. U. Chi. L.J. 737 (2004); Kaplan & Young, Corporate "Eminent Domain": Stock Redemption and Reverse Stock Splits, 57 UMKC L. Rev. 67 (1988); Dykstra, The Reverse Stock Split—That Other Means of Going Private, 53 Chi.-Kent. L. Rev. 1 (1976); Lawson, Reverse Stock Splits: The Fiduciary's Obligations Under State Law, 63 Calif. L. Rev. 1226 (1975).

Note: The One Share, One Vote Debate

An exchange recapitalization plan also can be designed to reallocate voting control from a disaggregated group of public shareholders and consolidate voting control in the hands of management. A typical strategy is to amend the charter to recapitalize the company's existing common stock into two classes. One of the classes would be given super-voting rights, usually ten votes per share, and the other class would have one vote per share. The super-voting class would usually be entitled to dividends only in an amount equal to a fraction (usually 90%) of the cash dividends paid on the one share stock. The holder of each outstanding share prior to the recapitalization would be entitled to choose which class of stock following the recap it would have. Given the dividend sweetener, it is expected that public shareholders will opt for the one-vote, higher dividend stock, and management will opt for the super-voting, lower dividend stock. The result is to consolidate voting control in the management group.

Proposals for dual class recaps attracted great attention and stirred substantial controversy during the 1980s. Up until that time, New York Stock Exchange rules prohibited the listing of stock of company's with such dual class voting capital structures. But in response to requests from a number of its listed companies, beginning with General Motors, the New York Stock Exchange abandoned its longstanding one-share, one-vote listing rule. According to the Securities and Exchange Commission, as of June 1, 1988, the NYSE had 55 listed companies that had either issued stock with disparate voting rights or amended their charters to limit the voting power of large shareholders (capped voting rights plans) or holders of recently purchased shares (tenured or time phased voting plans[1]). In response to this action, the Securities and Exchange Commission proposed a rule, Rule 19c-4, that would prohibit corporations with listed securities from implementing any such dual class recap. See Release Nos. 34-25891 and 34-25891A, Voting Rights Listing Standards Disenfranchisement Rules (July 7 and 13, 1988).

The Rule was intended as a mechanism to ensure management accountability, to protect shareholder interests in connection with contests for corporate control, and to protect the shareholder voting franchise. A number of commentators believed that shareholder approval of disparate voting rights plans was insufficient to prevent abuses because of the coercive influence management can exert on shareholder voting, such as through its control of the proxy agenda, and through the perceived coercion that the dividend sweetener created. Opponents of the rule argued either that these concerns were overstated, or that a remedy for any such concerns should be provided through state corporate law, rather than through the SEC and federal securities law. In particular, some opponents argued, the SEC lacked statutory authority to enact the Rule, since it dealt with the substantive state law issue of a corporation's capital structure, exceeding the SEC's statutory grant of power to regulate matters of proxy procedure and disclosure.

Soon after the SEC adopted the Rule, the Business Roundtable, a lobbying group comprised of about 200 CEOs of major industrial corporations, challenged the SEC's authority to adopt it. A panel of the D.C. Circuit agreed with the Business Roundtable, and vacated the Rule as exceeding the Commission's delegated authority. *The Business Roundtable v. Securities and Exchange Commission*, 905 F.2d 406 (D.C. Cir. 1990). The opinion is perhaps more interesting for its administrative law aspects than for any corporate law concerns, the court making it clear that it was not opining on the merits of the substantive debate: "Neither the wisdom of the requirement, nor of its being imposed at the federal level, is here in question." *Id.* at 407.

Following the *Business Roundtable* decision, the New York Stock Exchange and other exchanges nevertheless adopted (and the SEC approved) a listing rule of their own, patterned on the SEC's stillborn Rule 19c-4. See Release No. 34-35121 (Dec. 19, 1994), 59 Fed. Reg. 66570 (Dec. 27, 1994). The existing listing standards prohibit dual class recaps of listed stock, although they permit listing of the stock of corporations that contain disparate voting rights upon initial issuance. The basis for this distinction is the belief that the offering price for dual class arrangements for stock as initially issued will reflect limited (or no) voting rights. For analysis of the existing

---

1. For a detailed discussion of a tenured voting plan, see Williams v. Geier, 671 A.2d 1368 (Del. 1996).

listing standards, *see* Lang, Shareholder Voting Rights: The New Uniform Listing Standards, Insights (Feb. 1994), at 4; Bainbridge, Revisiting the One Share/One Vote Controversy, The Exchanges' Uniform Voting Rights Policy, 22 Sec. Reg. L.J. 175 (1994).

To crystalize your thinking on the one share, one vote debate, consider the following questions: Why would a stockholder be willing to accept shares with diminished voting rights? What are the values inherent in "universal" corporate suffrage? Should stockholders be prevented from bargaining it away, even if it is economically desirable to do so? Does the ability of management to consolidate control through dual class recapitalizations undermine the legitimacy of the prevailing corporate legal structure? If other goals or values are served by broad-based stockholder democracy, how would you answer the efficiency arguments? Do you favor permitting the initial issuance of stock with disparate voting rights or should dual class capitalizations be prohibited at all stages? Do you think this is appropriately a matter for federal regulation or is it properly left to the states?

Section 7
Fiduciary Duty and Corporate Democracy

There are two sorts of mechanisms through which to obtain control of a public corporation. One is the acquisition of at least a majority of a corporation's voting capital stock, by open market purchases, tender offer, or otherwise. This is addressed more fully in chapter 9. The alternative mechanism is to elect a majority of directors to the board, by persuading existing shareholders to vote for a proposed slate of directors through the proxy solicitation process. From a financing perspective, effecting a change in corporate control by electing nominees to the board in a proxy solicitation is significantly cheaper than acquiring the corporation's capital stock. Proxy contests are far less dependent on market conditions and the vagaries of financing, and are sometimes used when financing falls through (although they also may be used as a prelude to gaining control through the acquisition of stock).

From a legal perspective, the central question in addressing these two sorts of control-seeking strategies is the same: How should we define the duties of the incumbent board of directors in responding to a quest for control given the specter of managerial entrenchment and exacerbation of the gulf between ownership and control? In both contexts, those concerns are addressed by discarding the business judgment rule and subjecting directorial actions to judicial scrutiny.

A central legal issue that distinguishes quests for control fought through the proxy solicitation process from those fought through the acquisition of stock is that proxy contests implicate the shareholder franchise. Under all state corporate statutes, the business and affairs of the corporation are to be managed by or under the control of the board of directors and the circumstances in which shareholders have a voice are very limited. To protect the governance structure thus erected, the shareholder vote concerning who the directors shall be is crucial. As a result, courts have extended substantial protection to the shareholder franchise and imposed significant limits on a board's power to interfere with the electoral process. This solicitude and its theoretical underpinnings are explored, in different ways, in the cases that follow.

Blasius Industries, Inc. v. Atlas Corporation
564 A.2d 651 (Del. Ch. 1988)

Allen, Chancellor.

Two cases pitting the directors of Atlas Corporation against that company's largest (9.1%) shareholder, Blasius Industries, have been consolidated and tried together. Together, these cases ultimately require the court to determine who is entitled to sit on Atlas' board of directors. Each, however, presents discrete and important legal issues.

The first of the cases ... challenges the validity of board action taken at a telephone meeting of December 31, 1987 that added two new members to Atlas' seven member board. That action was taken as an immediate response to the delivery to Atlas by Blasius the previous day of a form of stockholder consent that, if joined in by holders of a majority of Atlas' stock, would have increased the board of Atlas from seven to fifteen members and would have elected eight new members nominated by Blasius.

As I find the facts of this first case, they present the question whether a board acts consistently with its fiduciary duty when it acts, in good faith and with appropriate care, for the primary purpose of preventing or impeding an unaffiliated majority of shareholders from expanding the board and electing a new majority. For the reasons that follow, I conclude that, even though defendants here acted on their view of the corporation's interest and not selfishly, their December 31 action constituted an offense to the relationship between corporate directors and shareholders that has traditionally been protected in courts of equity. As a consequence, I conclude that the board action taken on December 31 was invalid and must be voided....

I.

Blasius Acquires a 9% Stake in Atlas.

Blasius is a new stockholder of Atlas. It began to accumulate Atlas shares for the first time in July, 1987. On October 29, it filed a Schedule 13D with the Securities Exchange Commission disclosing that, with affiliates, it then owed 9.1% of Atlas' common stock. It stated in that filing that it intended to encourage management of Atlas to consider a restructuring of the Company or other transaction to enhance shareholder values. It also disclosed that Blasius was exploring the feasibility of obtaining control of Atlas, including instituting a tender offer or seeking "appropriate" representation on the Atlas board of directors.

* * *

The prospect [of Blasius' controlling shareholders] involving themselves in Atlas' affairs, was not a development welcomed by Atlas' management. Atlas had a new CEO, defendant Weaver, who had, over the course of the past year or so, overseen a business restructuring of a sort. Atlas had sold three of its five divisions. It had just announced (September 1, 1987) that it would close its once important domestic uranium operation. The goal was to focus the Company on its gold mining business. By October, 1987, the structural changes to do this had been largely accomplished. Mr. Weaver was perhaps thinking that the restructuring that had occurred should be given a chance to produce benefit before another restructuring (such as Blasius had alluded to in its Schedule 13D filing) was attempted....

The Blasius Proposal of A Leverage Recapitalization Or Sale.

* * *

[At a December 2, 1987 meeting with Atlas' top officers, counsel, and investment bankers, Blasius' representatives] suggested that Atlas engage in a leveraged restructuring and distribute cash to shareholders. In such a transaction, which is by this date a commonplace form of transaction, a corporation typically raises cash by sale of assets and significant borrowings and makes a large one time cash distribution to shareholders. The shareholders are typically left with cash and an equity interest in a smaller, more highly leveraged enterprise....

* * *

Atlas Asks Its Investment Banker to Study the Proposal.

This written proposal was distributed to the Atlas board on December 9 and Goldman Sachs was directed to review and analyze it.

The proposal met with a cool reception from management. On December 9, Mr. Weaver issued a press release expressing surprise that Blasius would suggest using debt to accomplish what he characterized as a substantial liquidation of Atlas at a time when Atlas' future prospects were promising. He noted that the Blasius proposal recommended that Atlas incur a high debt burden in order to pay a substantial one time dividend consisting of $ 35 million in cash and $ 125 million in subordinated debentures. Mr. Weaver also questioned the wisdom of incurring an enormous debt burden amidst the uncertainty in the financial markets that existed in the aftermath of the October [1987 stock market] crash.

Blasius attempted on December 14 and December 22 to arrange a further meeting with the Atlas management without success. During this period, Atlas provided Goldman Sachs with projections for the Company. Lubin was told that a further meeting would await completion of Goldman's analysis. A meeting after the first of the year was proposed.

The Delivery of Blasius' Consent Statement.

On December 30, 1987, Blasius caused Cede & Co. (the registered owner of its Atlas stock) to deliver to Atlas a signed written consent (1) adopting a precatory resolution recommending that the board develop and implement a restructuring proposal, (2) amending the Atlas bylaws to, among other things, expand the size of the board from seven to fifteen members—the maximum number under Atlas' charter, and (3) electing eight named persons to fill the new directorships....

The reaction was immediate. Mr. Weaver conferred with Mr. Masinter, the Company's outside counsel and a director, who viewed the consent as an attempt to take control of the Company. They decided to call an emergency meeting of the board, even though a regularly scheduled meeting was to occur only one week hence, on January 6, 1988. The point of the emergency meeting was to act on their conclusion (or to seek to have the board act on their conclusion) "that we should add at least one and probably two directors to the board ...". ... At that meeting, the board voted to amend the bylaws to increase the size of the board from seven to nine and appointed John M. Devaney and Harry J. Winters, Jr. to fill those newly created positions. Atlas' Certificate of Incorporation creates staggered terms for directors; the terms to which Messrs. Devaney and Winters were appointed would expire in 1988 and 1990, respectively.

The Motivation of the Incumbent Board In Expanding the Board and Appointing New Members.

In increasing the size of Atlas' board by two and filling the newly created positions, the members of the board realized that they were thereby precluding the holders of a majority of the Company's shares from placing a majority of new directors on the board through Blasius' consent solicitation, should they want to do so. Indeed the evidence establishes that that was the principal motivation in so acting.

.... If the board in fact was not so motivated, but rather had taken action completely independently of the consent solicitation, which merely had an incidental impact upon the possible effectuation of any action authorized by the shareholders, it is very unlikely that such action would be subject to judicial nullification. *See, e.g., Frantz Manufacturing Company v. EAC Industries,* Del.Supr., 501 A.2d 401, 407 (1985).... The board, as a general matter, is under no fiduciary obligation to suspend its active management of the firm while the consent solicitation process goes forward.

There is testimony in the record to support the proposition that, in acting on December 31, the board was principally motivated simply to implement a plan to expand the Atlas board that preexisted the September, 1987 emergence of Blasius as an active shareholder. I have no doubt that the addition of Mr. Winters, an expert in mining economics, and Mr. Devaney, a financial expert employed by the Company, strengthened the Atlas board and, should anyone ever have reason to review the wisdom of those choices, they would be found to be sensible and prudent. I cannot conclude, however, that the strengthening of the board by the addition of these men was the principal motive for the December 31 action....

* * *

It is difficult to consider the timing of the activation of the interest in adding Mr. Winters to the board in December as simply coincidental with the pressure that Blasius was applying. The connection between the two events, however, becomes unmistakably clear when the later events of December 30 and 31 are focused upon. As noted above, on the 30th, Atlas received the Blasius consent which proposed to shareholders that they expand the board from seven to fifteen and add eight new members identified in the consent. It also proposed the adoption of a precatory resolution encouraging restructuring or sale of the Company. Mr. Weaver immediately met with Mr. Masinter. In addition to receiving the consent, Atlas was informed it had been sued in this court, but it did not yet know the thrust of that action.... They decided to add two board members and to hold an emergency board meeting that very day to do so. It is clear that the reason that Mr. Masinter advised taking this step immediately rather than waiting for the January 6 meeting was that he feared that the Court of Chancery might issue a temporary restraining order prohibiting the board from increasing its membership, since the consent solicitation had commenced. It is admitted that there was no fear that Blasius would be in a position to complete a public solicitation for consents prior to the January 6 board meeting.

In this setting, I conclude that, while the addition of these qualified men would, under other circumstances, be clearly appropriate as an independent step, such a step was in fact taken in order to impede or preclude a majority of the shareholders from effectively adopting the course proposed by Blasius. Indeed, while defendants never forsake the factual argument that that action was simply a continuation of business as usual, they, in effect, admit from time to time this overriding purpose....

.... As explained below, I conclude that, in so acting, the board was not selfishly motivated simply to retain power....

The January 6 Rejection of the Blasius Proposal.

On January 6, the board convened for its scheduled meeting. At that time, it heard a full report from its financial advisor concerning the feasibility of the Blasius restructuring proposal. The Goldman Sachs presentation included a summary of five year cumulative cash flows measured against a base case and the Blasius proposal, an analysis of Atlas' debt repayment capacity under the Blasius proposal, and pro forma income and cash flow statements for a base case and the Blasius proposal, assuming prices of $375, $475 and $575 per ounce of gold.

After completing that presentation, Goldman Sachs concluded with its view that ... [implementation of Blasius' restructuring proposal would be severely detrimental to Atlas].

The board then voted to reject the Blasius proposal. Blasius was informed of that action. The next day, Blasius caused a second, modified consent to be delivered to Atlas. A contest then ensued between the Company and Blasius for the votes of Atlas' shareholders....

II.

Plaintiff attacks the December 31 board action as a selfishly motivated effort to protect the incumbent board from a perceived threat to its control of Atlas. Their conduct is said to constitute a violation of the principle, applied in such cases as *Schnell v. Chris Craft Industries, Del.Supr., 285 A.2d 437 (1971),* that directors hold legal powers subjected to a supervening duty to exercise such powers in good faith pursuit of what they reasonably believe to be in the corporation's interest. The December 31 action is also said to have been taken in a grossly negligent manner, since it was designed to preclude the recapitalization from being pursued, and the board had no basis at that time to make a prudent determination about the wisdom of that proposal, nor was there any emergency that required it to act in any respect regarding that proposal before putting itself in a position to do so advisedly.

Defendants, of course, contest every aspect of plaintiffs' claims. They claim the formidable protections of the business judgment rule....

They say that, in creating two new board positions and filling them on December 31, they acted without a conflicting interest (since the Blasius proposal did not, in any event, challenge *their* places on the board), they acted with due care (since they well knew the persons they put on the board and did not thereby preclude later consideration of the recapitalization), and they acted in good faith (since they were motivated, they say, to protect the shareholders from the threat of having an impractical, indeed a dangerous, recapitalization program foisted upon them)....

Moreover, defendants say that their action was fair, measured and appropriate, in light of the circumstances. Therefore, even should the court conclude that some level of substantive review of it is appropriate under a legal test of fairness, or under the intermediate level of review authorized by *Unocal Corp. v. Mesa Petroleum Co., Del.Supr., 493 A.2d 946 (1985),* defendants assert that the board's decision must be sustained as valid in both law and equity.

III.

... [P]laintiffs say that the evidence shows there was no policy dispute or issue that really motivated this action, but that asserted policy differences were pretexts for entrenchment for selfish reasons. If this were found to be factually true, one would not need to inquire further. The action taken would constitute a breach of duty. *Schnell v. Chris Craft Industries,* Del.Supr., 285 A.2d 437 (1971)....

* * *

While I am satisfied that the evidence is powerful, indeed compelling, that the board was chiefly motivated on December 31 to forestall or preclude the possibility that a majority of shareholders might place on the Atlas board eight new members sympathetic to the Blasius proposal, it is less clear with respect to the more subtle motivational question: whether the existing members of the board did so because they held a good faith belief that such shareholder action would be self-injurious and shareholders needed to be protected from their own judgment.

On balance, I cannot conclude that the board was acting out of a self-interested motive in any important respect on December 31. I conclude rather that the board saw the "threat" of the Blasius recapitalization proposal as posing vital policy differences between itself and Blasius. It acted, I conclude, in a good faith effort to protect its incumbency, not selfishly, but in order to thwart implementation of the recapitalization that it feared, reasonably, would cause great injury to the Company.

The real question the case presents, to my mind, is whether, in these circumstances, the board, even if it *is* acting with subjective good faith (which will typically, if not always, be a contestable or debatable judicial conclusion), may validly act for the principal purpose of preventing the shareholders from electing a majority of new directors. The question thus posed is not one of intentional wrong (or even negligence), but one of authority *as between the fiduciary and the beneficiary....*

IV.

It is established in our law that a board may take certain steps—such as the purchase by the corporation of its own stock—that have the effect of defeating a threatened change in corporate control, when those steps are taken advisedly, in good faith pursuit of a corporate interest, and are reasonable in relation to a threat to legitimate corporate interests posed by the proposed change in control. *See Unocal Corp. v. Mesa Petroleum Co.,* Del.Supr., 493 A.2d 946 (1985); *Kors v. Carey,* Del.Ch., 39 Del. Ch. 47, 158 A.2d 136 (1960); *Cheff v. Mathes,* Del.Supr., 41 Del. Ch. 494, 199 A.2d 548 (1964).... Does this rule—that the reasonable exercise of good faith and due care generally validates, in equity, the exercise of legal authority even if the act has an entrenchment effect—apply to action designed for the primary purpose of interfering with the effectiveness of a stockholder vote? Our authorities, as well as sound principles, suggest that the central importance of the franchise to the scheme of corporate governance, requires that, in this setting, that rule not be applied and that closer scrutiny be accorded to such transaction.

1. *Why the deferential business judgment rule does not apply to board acts taken for the primary purpose of interfering with a stockholder's vote, even if taken advisedly and in good faith.*

A. *The question of legitimacy.*

The shareholder franchise is the ideological underpinning upon which the legitimacy of directorial power rests. Generally, shareholders have only two protections against perceived inadequate business performance. They may sell their stock (which, if done in sufficient numbers, may so affect security prices as to create an incentive for altered managerial performance), or they may vote to replace incumbent board members.

It has, for a long time, been conventional to dismiss the stockholder vote as a vestige or ritual of little practical importance. It may be that we are now witnessing the emergence of new institutional voices and arrangements that will make the stockholder vote a less predictable affair than it has been. Be that as it may, however, whether the vote is seen functionally as an unimportant formalism, or as an important tool of discipline, it is clear that it is critical to the theory that legitimates the exercise of power by some (directors and officers) over vast aggregations of property that they do not own. Thus, when viewed from a broad, institutional perspective, it can be seen that matters involving the integrity of the shareholder voting process involve consideration not present in any other context in which directors exercise delegated power.

B. *Questions of this type raise issues of the allocation of authority as between the board and the shareholders.*

The distinctive nature of the shareholder franchise context also appears when the matter is viewed from a less generalized, doctrinal point of view. From this point of view, as well, it appears that the ordinary considerations to which the business judgment rule originally responded are simply not present in the shareholder voting context.[2] That is, a decision by the board to act for the primary purpose of preventing the effectiveness of a shareholder vote inevitably involves the question who, as between the principal and the agent, has authority with respect to a matter of internal corporate governance.... A board's decision to act to prevent the shareholders from creating a majority of new board positions and filling them does not involve the exercise of *the corporation's power* over its property, or with respect to *its* rights or obligations; rather, it involves allocation, between shareholders as a class and the board, of effective power with respect to governance of the corporation. This need not be the case with respect to other forms of corporate action that may have an entrenchment effect—such as the stock buybacks present in *Unocal, Cheff* or *Kors v. Carey.* Action designed principally to interfere with the effectiveness of a vote inevitably involves a conflict between the board and a shareholder majority. Judicial review of such action

---

2. Delaware courts have long exercised a most sensitive and protective regard for the free and effective exercise of voting rights. This concern suffuses our law, manifesting itself in various settings. For example, the perceived importance of the franchise explains the cases that hold that a director's fiduciary duty requires disclosure to shareholders asked to authorize a transaction of all material information in the corporation's possession, even if the transaction is not a self-dealing one. *See, e.g., Smith v. Van Gorkom, Del.Supr.,* 488 A.2d 858 (1985)....

A similar concern, for credible corporate democracy, underlies those cases that strike down board action that sets or moves an annual meeting date upon a finding that such action was intended to thwart a shareholder group from effectively mounting an election campaign. *See, e.g., Schnell v. Chris Craft, supra....*

The cases invalidating stock issued for the primary purpose of diluting the voting power of a control block also reflect the law's concern that a credible form of corporate democracy be maintained. *See Canada Southern Oils, Ltd. v. Manabi Exploration Co., Inc., Del.Ch.,* 33 Del. Ch. 537, 96 A.2d 810 (1953)....

Similarly, a concern for corporate democracy is reflected (1) in our statutory requirement of annual meetings (8 Del. C. §211), and in the cases that aggressively and summarily enforce that right. *See, e.g., Coaxial Communications, Inc. v. CNA Financial Corp., Del.Supr.,* 367 A.2d 994 (1976)..., and (2) in our consent statute (8 Del. C. §228) and the interpretation it has been accorded. *See Datapoint Corp. v. Plaza Securities Co., Del.Supr.,* 496 A.2d 1031 (1985) (order)....

involves a determination of the legal and equitable obligations of an agent towards his principal. This is not, in my opinion, a question that a court may leave to the agent finally to decide so long as he does so honestly and competently; that is, it may not be left to the agent's business judgment.

2. *What rule does apply: per se invalidity of corporate acts intended primarily to thwart effective exercise of the franchise or is there an intermediate standard?*

Plaintiff argues for a rule of *per se* invalidity once a plaintiff has established that a board has acted for the primary purpose of thwarting the exercise of a shareholder vote....

* * *

.... A *per se* rule that would strike down, in equity, any board action taken for the primary purpose of interfering with the effectiveness of a corporate vote would have the advantage of relative clarity and predictability.[4] It also has the advantage of most vigorously enforcing the concept of corporate democracy. The disadvantage it brings along is, of course, the disadvantage a *per se* rule always has: it may sweep too broadly.

In two recent cases dealing with shareholder votes, this court struck down board acts done for the primary purpose of impeding the exercise of stockholder voting power. In doing so, a *per se* rule was not applied. Rather, it was said that, in such a case, the board bears the heavy burden of demonstrating a compelling justification for such action.

* * *

In my view, our inability to foresee now all of the future settings in which a board might, in good faith, paternalistically seek to thwart a shareholder vote, counsels against the adoption of a *per se* rule invalidating, in equity, every board action taken for the sole or primary purpose of thwarting a shareholder vote, even though I recognize the transcending significance of the franchise to the claims to legitimacy of our scheme of corporate governance. It may be that some set of facts would justify such extreme action. This, however, is not such a case.

3. *Defendants have demonstrated no sufficient justification for the action of December 31 which was intended to prevent an unaffiliated majority of shareholders from effectively exercising their right to elect eight new directors.*

The board was not faced with a coercive action taken by a powerful shareholder against the interests of a distinct shareholder constituency (such as a public minority). It was presented with a consent solicitation by a 9% shareholder. Moreover, here it had time (and understood that it had time) to inform the shareholders of its views on the merits of the proposal subject to stockholder vote. The only justification that can, in such a situation, be offered for the action taken is that the board knows better than do the shareholders what is in the corporation's best interest. While that premise is no doubt true for any number of matters, it is irrelevant (except insofar as the shareholders wish to be guided by the board's recommendation) when the question is who should comprise the board of directors. The theory of our corporation law confers power upon directors as the agents of the shareholders; it does not create Platonic masters. It may be that the Blasius restructuring proposal was or is unrealistic and would lead to injury to

---

4. While it must be admitted that any rule that requires for its invocation the finding of a subjective mental state (*i.e.*, a primary purpose) necessarily will lead to controversy concerning whether it applies or not, nevertheless, once it is determined to apply, this *per se* rule would be clearer than the alternative discussed below.

836 THE RIGHTS OF OWNERSHIP CLAIMANTS—PART 1: GENERAL CONCEPTS

the corporation and its shareholders if pursued. Having heard the evidence, I am inclined to think it was not a sound proposal. The board certainly viewed it that way, and
that view, held in good faith, entitled the board to take certain steps to evade the risk it
perceived. It could, for example, expend corporate funds to inform shareholders and
seek to bring them to a similar point of view.... But there is a vast difference between
expending corporate funds to inform the electorate and exercising power for the primary purpose of foreclosing effective shareholder action. A majority of the shareholders, who were not dominated in any respect, could view the matter differently than did
the board. If they do, or did, they are entitled to employ the mechanisms provided by
the corporation law and the Atlas certificate of incorporation to advance that view.
They are also entitled, in my opinion, to restrain their agents, the board, from acting
for the principal purpose of thwarting that action.

I therefore conclude that, even finding the action taken was taken in good faith, it
constituted an unintended violation of the duty of loyalty that the board owed to the
shareholders.... That action will, therefore, be set aside by order of this court.

* * *

Notes and Questions

1. Chancellor Allen identifies the stockholder's ability to sell her stock and to vote as
the two ways in which she can protect against poor business performance. What is the
legal justification for permitting a board to interfere with the market for corporate control but prohibiting a board from interfering with the electoral process? *Compare* Del.
Gen. Corp. Law §§212 & 223 (putting electoral decisions squarely in the hands of
stockholders) *with* Unocal Corp. v. Mesa Petroleum Co., 493 A.2d 946, 953-54 (Del.
1985) (noting that sales of stock by stockholders are not directly statutorily regulated).
Is that legal justification defensible on policy grounds?

2. What theory of the corporation is reflected in *Blasius*? Is it consistent with Chancellor Allen's description of directors as agents of the stockholders?

3. At the conclusion of *Blasius* Chancellor Allen notes "that the concept of an unintended breach of the duty of loyalty is unusual but not novel." What does that mean?
What does it imply about fiduciary duty in corporate law?

4. Chancellor Allen suggests that "the emergence of new institutional voices and
arrangements" may infuse new vitality into the stockholder voting process. The reference is to the change in the composition of shareholders of public corporations that occurred in the United States beginning in the early 1980s. Before that time, individual investors typically invested directly in publicly traded securities of individual companies,
chiefly through stockbrokers, and approximately 90% of all such securities were owned
by individual investors. Since that time, individual investors have shifted to investing in
intermediaries, such as mutual funds and pension plans, that manage aggregated individual investments, and approximately 50% of all publicly traded equity securities are
now owned by such institutional investors.

Chancellor Allen's suggestion that the increase in holdings through institutional investors may revitalize the stockholder voting process echoes the views of some observers
that institutional investors are more capable than individual investors of overcoming
collective action problems that afflict shareholders as a group. As such, they may be
more active and effective monitors of corporate performance and thereby make more
meaningful the shareholder franchise.

There is substantial uncertainty about whether institutional investors do or will provide that revitalization or, even if they do, whether that will be more beneficial to individual investors than other techniques that have been used historically to bridge the separation of ownership from control. In particular, the "voice" to be exercised by institutional investors is by no means unitary. Institutional investors are a heterogeneous group, composed not only of thousands of mutual funds and pensions plans, but also thousands of insurance companies, bank trusts, and foundations. Legal and practical limits on the degree of investment concentration any single institutional investor can maintain may also make it difficult for particular institutional investors to exert meaningful control with respect to a particular investee corporation. Note, however, that Chancellor Allen also emphasizes that the shareholder franchise is a crucial foundational principle of corporate governance whether or not institutional investors do make that franchise more meaningful as a practical matter.

A vast literature has emerged that evaluates the significant change in the demography of the shareholder profile and whether it is or can become meaningful for the structure of corporate law and corporate governance. A sampling includes the following:

Camara, Classifying Institutional Investors, 30 Iowa J. Corp. L. 219 (2005); Hannes, Corporate Stagnation: Discussion and Reform Proposal, 30 Iowa J. Corp. L. 51 (2004); Boot & Macey, Monitoring Corporate Performance: The Role Of Objectivity, Proximity, and Adaptability In Corporate Governance, 89 Cornell L. Rev. 356 (2004); Klausner, Investors' Choices: Institutional Shareholders, Private Equity, and Antitakeover Protection at the IPO Stage, 152 U. Pa. L. Rev. 755 (2003); Bainbridge, Director Primacy: The Means and Ends of Corporate Governance, 97 NW. U.L. Rev. 547 (2003); Smith, Institutions and Entrepreneurs in American Corporate Finance, 85 Calif. L. Rev. 1 (1997).

5. What is the proper test to be applied to directors' actions to forestall a proxy contest designed to result in the ultimate sale of the corporation? In Stahl v. Apple Bancorp, Inc., 579 A.2d 1115 (Del. Ch. 1990), Stahl had acquired approximately 30 percent of Bancorp's outstanding stock by mid-November 1990. Shortly thereafter, Bancorp's board met to consider the Stahl "threat." The result of this meeting was the adoption of a rights plan designed to protect Bancorp from an unwanted takeover. In response, Stahl submitted a stockholder proposal to be submitted at Bancorp's next annual meeting, pursuant to which the size of the board would be increased from twelve to twenty-one, and Stahl's nominees would be elected to fill the newly created vacancies. This, combined with the four seats on Bancorp's staggered board up for election, would give Stahl control. Stahl further disclosed that, if his proposal succeeded, he would recommend that the board redeem the rights plan as well as evaluate the performance of current management.

On March 19, 1990, the board set a record date of April 17 for its annual meeting, with the intent of holding the meeting in May. Under Delaware law, with a record date of April 17 the meeting could be held no later than June 16. On March 28, Stahl announced a tender offer for any and all shares, conditioned upon the success of Stahl's proposal to increase the size of the board and elect his nominees, as well as the redemption or invalidity of the rights plan. Finally, Stahl expressed his intent (although not his promise) to cash out non-tendering stockholders in a second-step merger.

The Bancorp board met on April 9 and 10, where it was told by its proxy solicitor that Stahl was likely to succeed in the absence of an alternative plan, and by its financial advisors that Stahl's offering price was "inadequate and unfair" to the stockholders, and that finding alternatives would take time. In accordance with this advice, the board withdrew the April 17 record date for the annual meeting to give itself time to seek alternatives. Stahl sued to enjoin Bancorp to hold its annual meeting.

The court first addressed the issue of the appropriate test to apply. As the Chancellor saw it, two possibilities existed: the *Blasius*-type test applied to board action designed to affect stockholder voting, and the *Unocal* test. He chose the latter, upholding the board's action as a good faith and proportional response to an inadequate hostile tender offer. The former test looks to whether the board's action was designed to impair or impede "the effective exercise of the corporate franchise." This was inapplicable, concluded the Chancellor, because the board's action did not in fact impair the exercise of the stockholders' franchise, at least not in the manner employed in prior cases in which a board's action either effectively precluded stockholder voting or "snatch[ed] victory from an insurgent slate on the eve of the noticed meeting." The Chancellor recognized that this approach could be attacked as placing too much significance on the formality of setting a meeting date, but claimed that such an act was of "some dignity and significance."

Applying *Unocal*, then, the court concluded that both prongs of the test were satisfied, and that no injunction should therefore issue. The threat reasonably perceived was the stockholders' lack of information with respect to alternatives to the Stahl transaction. "Here the response to the threat was extremely mild." However, the Chancellor noted that as one moved closer to a meeting date or a contested election, the greater the threat that would have to be demonstrated to satisfy *Unocal*.

Stahl won the war. On October 2, 1990, Stahl acquired the stock of Apple Bancorp for $38 per share (*see* Steinmetz, Long War for Apple Ends with Takeover, Newsday, Oct. 3, 1990, at 45), his original offer price (*see* Apple Bancorp Acquired by Realty Investor, Amer. Banker, Oct. 3, 1990, at 2).

6. Given the functional similarities of takeovers and proxy contests in the market for corporate control, should the same test be applied in evaluating protective measures adopted by the board? Are the two processes legally similar? Even if the two processes are, in some respects, functionally similar, are there sufficient distinctions to warrant different treatment?

7. Is there a danger that permitting the board to intervene in the voting process in proxy contests will lead to dilution of stockholder voting rights in other contexts? Does the widespread adoption of constituency legislation discussed *supra* at chapter 9, section 3, suggest good reasons to permit the board to intervene in this process?

8. By this point you have read and should have thought about the idea advanced by a number of corporate law scholars that a corporate charter or bylaws is some form of contract. In fact, in ER Holdings, Inc. v. Norton, 735 F. Supp. 1094 (D. Mass. 1990), the court appears to take that image literally. As a result, it applies contract law principles to a corporate law dispute, holding that the bylaws of the public corporation in question were a "bargained-for agreement". *Id.* at 1097. If this is true, who are the parties to this contract? (The *ER Holdings* court stated that the contract was between the shareholders and the directors. *Id.*) Are there any third-party beneficiaries of any such contract (*e.g.*, the company's employees, suppliers, and customers)? Is it sensible to speak of the intentions of the parties to any such contract? How would constituency legislation inform the "interpretation" of such a contract with respect to the third party beneficiaries question?

Chapter 9

The Rights of Ownership Claimants — Part 2: Mergers and Acquisitions

This chapter focuses on mergers and acquisitions, in general, and board fiduciary duties implicated when an acquiror is pursuing a target company or a target company is repelling an acquiror, in particular. Because many states follow the lead of the Delaware courts in this regard, we will focus primarily on Delaware case law in this chapter. When reading the cases that follow, try to discern when the courts evaluate directorial action under the business judgment rule and when they apply heightened scrutiny. Which factual scenarios give rise to which type of judicial review?

As Delaware case law becomes more and more complex, some states are starting to blaze their own jurisprudential trail in this substantive area of law. Accordingly, as you read the cases below, consider alternatives to Delaware's approach. Are these alternatives better or worse? Be ready to support your position.

Section 1
The Duty of Care and the Business Judgment Rule

a. A Board's Decision to Sell the Company

One of the most important decisions a board of directors can make is an affirmative one to sell the company. After all, the board can only sell the company once and collect a control premium for its stockholders at that time. In deciding whether to sell the company, the board must comply with its duty of care. The seminal Delaware case on point is Smith v. Van Gorkom, 488 A.2d 858 (Del. 1985), which most students read in the basic corporations or business associations class.

Van Gorkom involved a cash-out merger that would result in the sale of Trans Union Corporation ("Trans Union") to the Marmon Group, Inc. ("Marmon"), a company controlled by the takeover "artist" Jay Pritzker. To accomplish this, Trans Union stockholders were asked to approve (and did approve) a merger of Trans Union with and into a wholly-owned subsidiary of Marmon. The merger was recommended to the stockholders by the board of Trans Union. As a result of the merger, Trans Union stockholders were cashed out at $55 per share.

Plaintiff stockholders of Trans Union alleged that the Trans Union directors had acted negligently when approving the cash-out merger. Under Delaware law, the standard of negligence applicable to a director's duty of care is gross negligence. *Id.* at 873. According to the court, "[t]he determination of whether a business judgment is an informed one turns on whether the directors have informed themselves 'prior to making a business decision, of all material information reasonably available to them.'" *Id.* at 872 (quoting Aronson v. Lewis, 473 A.2d 805, 812 (Del. 1984)). In the specific context of a merger, the court added:

> a director has a duty under 8 *Del.C.* § 251(b), along with his fellow directors, to act in an informed and deliberate manner in determining whether to approve an agreement of merger before submitting the proposal to the stockholders. Certainly in a merger context, a director may not abdicate that duty by leaving to the shareholders the decision to approve or disapprove the agreement.

Id. at 873.

The court determined that the Trans Union directors did not satisfy their duty to make an informed business decision and had acted with gross negligence. The court's reasons included:

> The directors (1) did not adequately inform themselves as to Van Gorkom's [Trans Union's CEO] role in forcing the "sale" of the Company and in establishing the per share purchase price; (2) were uninformed as to the intrinsic value of the Company; and (3) given these circumstances, at a minimum, were grossly negligent in approving the "sale" of the Company [at a hastily called board meeting] upon two hours' consideration, without prior notice [about the meeting's purpose], and without the exigency of a crisis or emergency.

> * * *

> Without any documents before them concerning the proposed transaction, the members of the Board were required to rely entirely upon Van Gorkom's 20-minute oral presentation of the proposal. No written summary of the terms of the merger was presented; the directors were given no documentation to support the adequacy of $55 price per share for sale of the Company; and the Board had before it nothing more than Van Gorkom's statement of his understanding of the substance of [a merger agreement] which he admittedly had never read, nor which any member of the Board had ever seen.

Id. at 874.

By highlighting that the directors were uninformed as to the intrinsic value of Trans Union, the court underscored that the board could not determine whether the price Pritzker was offering was fair. The court, however, stopped short of requiring the board to obtain a "fairness opinion" from an investment bank. Such an opinion tells directors that the price being offered "is fair from a financial point of view" based on the bank's valuation of the business. Nevertheless, the court does say that a valuation is needed in order to determine whether the price being offered makes sense:

> We do not imply that an outside valuation study is essential to support an informed business judgment; nor do we state that fairness opinions by independent investment bankers are required as a matter of law. Often insiders familiar with the business of a going concern are in a better position than are outsiders to gather relevant information; and under appropriate circumstances, such directors may be fully protected in relying in good faith upon the valuation reports of their management. See 8 *Del.C.* § 141(e).

Id. at 876-77.

Nor did the court demand as a matter of law that directors read every word of a material agreement before they approve it:

> We do not suggest that a board must read *in haec verba* every contract or legal document which it approves, but if it is to successfully absolve itself from charges of the type made here, there must be some credible contemporary evidence demonstrating that the directors knew what they were doing, and ensured that their purposed action was given effect. That is the consistent failure which cast this Board upon its unredeemable course.

Id. at 883 n. 25.

The defendant directors also argued that the "overwhelming vote" of Trans Union's stockholders in favor of the merger should legally cure any failure of the board to reach an informed business judgment. On this point, the court stated:

> .... [T]he merger can be sustained, notwithstanding the infirmity of the Board's action, if its approval by majority vote of the shareholders is found to have been based on an informed electorate.
>
> * * *
>
> The settled rule in Delaware is that "where a majority of fully informed stockholders ratify action of even interested directors, an attack on the ratified transaction normally must fail." ... The question of whether shareholders have been fully informed such that their vote can be said to ratify director action, "turns on the fairness and completeness of the proxy materials submitted by the management to the ... shareholders." ...
>
> [C]orporate directors owe to their stockholders a fiduciary duty to disclose all facts germane to the transaction at issue in an atmosphere of complete candor. We defined "germane" in the tender offer context as all "information such as a reasonable stockholder would consider important in deciding whether to sell or retain stock." ... In reality, "germane" means material facts.
>
> Applying this standard to the record before us, we find that Trans Union's stockholders were not fully informed of all facts material to their vote on the Pritzker Merger and that the Trial Court's ruling to the contrary is clearly erroneous.

Id. at 889-90.

The *Van Gorkom* decision caused a panic among many directors of public companies. No doubt a great many of them thought it impossible to incur personal liability due to the gross negligence standard employed by Delaware. *Van Gorkom*, however, changed their viewpoint. Many directors resigned as a result, and directors' and officers' (D&O) insurance increased twelve-fold the year *Van Gorkom* was decided. *See* Bradley & Schipani, The Relevance of the Duty of Care Standard in Corporate Governance, 75 Iowa L. Rev. 1, 73 (1989).

The Delaware legislature, seeking to maintain Delaware's preeminence in corporate law, passed Del. Gen. Corp. Law § 102(b)(7) as a result of *Van Gorkom. Cf.* Model Bus. Corp. Act Ann. §2.02(b)(4) (3rd ed. 1984 & Supp. 2000/01/02) (providing for even stronger directorial protection than Delaware's provision). Delaware's provision allows a Delaware corporation to adopt an exculpatory charter provision that essentially relieves directors from personal liability for most breaches of the duty of care (but not the duty of loyalty). Many did just that. Apparently such provisions work, as the Delaware courts have held that an exculpatory charter provision provides an adequate independent ground for dismissing a due care claim. *See* Arnold v. Society for Savings Bancorp, Inc., 650 A.2d 1270 (Del. 1994); Ash v. McCall, 2000 WL 13703341 (Del. Ch. 2000), *infra* at section 1b. However, as an exculpatory charter provision is an affirmative defense, the defendant directors have the burden of establishing each of its elements, including the negation of all specifically carved-out conduct (*e.g.*, breaches of the duty of loyalty). *See* Emerald Partners v. Berlin, 726 A.2d 1215 (Del. 1999).

A breach of the duty of care, as happened in *Van Gorkom*, rebuts the business judgment rule's presumption in favor of directors. The burden of proof then shifts to the directors to prove that the transaction they approved was entirely fair. In that regard, consider the following two cases involving Ronald Perelman's acquisition of Technicolor, Inc.

Cede & Co. v. Technicolor, Inc.[a]
634 A.2d 345 (Del. 1993)

HORSEY, Justice:

* * *

.... The actions stem from a 1982-83 cash-out merger in which Technicolor, Incorporated ("Technicolor"), a Delaware corporation, was acquired by MacAndrews & Forbes Group, Incorporated ("MAF"), a Delaware corporation, through a merger with Macanfor Corporation ("Macanfor"), a wholly-owned subsidiary of MAF.[1] Under the terms of the tender offer and later cash-out merger, each shareholder of Technicolor (excluding MAF and its subsidiaries) was offered $23 cash per share.

Plaintiff Cinerama[, Inc. a New York corporation,] was at all times the owner of 201,200 shares of the common stock of Technicolor, representing 4.405 percent of the total shares outstanding. Cinerama did not tender its stock in the first leg of the MAF acquisition commencing November 4, 1982; and Cinerama dissented from the second stage merger, which was completed on January 24, 1983. After dissenting, Cinerama, in March 1983, petitioned the Court of Chancery for appraisal of its shares pursuant to 8 *Del.C.* § 262. In pretrial discovery during the appraisal proceedings, Cinerama obtained testimony leading it to believe that director misconduct had occurred in the sale of the company. In January 1986, Cinerama filed a second suit in the Court of Chancery against Technicolor, seven of the nine members of the Technicolor board at the time of the merger, MAF, Macanfor and Ronald O. Perelman ("Perelman"), MAF's Chairman and controlling shareholder. Cinerama's personal liability action encompassed claims for fraud, breach of fiduciary duty and unfair dealing, and included a claim for rescissory damages, among other relief. Cinerama also claimed that the merger was void *ab initio* for lack of unanimous director approval of repeal of a supermajority provision of Technicolor's charter.

* * *

.... In June 1991, the [trial] court, in a[n] ... unreported decision (the "Personal Liability Opinion"), 1991 WL 111134, found pervasive and persuasive evidence of the de-

---

a. This case is commonly referred to as "*Cede II.*"

1. Hereafter we refer to MAF and Macanfor, also a Delaware corporation, collectively as "MAF."

fendant directors' breach of their fiduciary duties,[b] but concluded that Cinerama had not met its burden of proof. On that ground, the Chancellor entered judgment for the defendants....

* * *

The pivotal question in this case is whether the Technicolor board's decision of October 29 to approve the plan of merger with MAF was protected by the business judgment rule or should be subject to judicial review for its entire fairness.

* * *

[T]he [trial] court ruled that it was not sufficient for Cinerama to prove that the defendant directors had collectively, as a board, breached their duty of care. Cinerama was required to prove that it had suffered a monetary loss from such breach and to quantify that loss. The court expressed "grave doubts" that the Technicolor board "as a whole" had met that duty in approving the terms of the merger/sale of the company. The court, in effect, read into the business judgment presumption of due care the legal maxim that proof of negligence without proof of injury is not actionable. The court also reasoned that a judicial finding of director good faith and loyalty in a third-party, arms-length transaction should minimize the consequences of a board's *found* failure to exercise due care in a sale of a company. The Chancellor's rationale for subordinating the due care element of the business judgment rule, as applied to an arms-length, third-party transaction, was a belief that the rule, unless modified, would lead to draconian results. The Chancellor left no doubt that he was referring to this Court's decision in *Smith v. Van Gorkom*, Del.Supr., 488 A.2d 858 (1985). He stated, "In all, plaintiff contends that this case presents a compelling case for another administration of the discipline applied by the Delaware Supreme Court in *Smith v. Van Gorkom*, Del.Supr., 488 A.2d 858 (1985)."...

* * *

.... The Chancellor's restatement of the rule—to require Cinerama to prove a proximate cause relationship between the Technicolor board's presumed breach of its duty of care *and* the shareholder's resultant loss—is contrary to well-established Delaware precedent, irreconcilable with *Van Gorkom*, and contrary to the tenets of *Unocal* and *Revlon, Inc. v. MacAndrews & Forbes Holdings*, Del.Supr., 506 A.2d 173 (1986). More importantly, we think the court's restatement of the rule would lead to most unfortunate results, detrimental to goals of heightened and enlightened standards for corporate governance of Delaware corporations.

* * *

The [trial] court found authority for its requirement of proof of injury in a seventy-year-old decision that none of the parties had relied on or felt pertinent. The trial court ruled:

> because the board as a deliberative body was disinterested in the transaction and operating in good faith, plaintiff bears the burden to show that any such innocent, though regrettable, lapse was likely to have injured it. *See, e.g., Barnes v. Andrews*, 298 F. 614 (S.D.N.Y.1924)....

In the absence of plaintiff's proof of injury, the court held that defendants were entitled to judgment "on all claims." The Chancellor concluded that the "fatal weakness in

---

b. Outside directors, based on an arguendo assumption of the trial court, were found grossly negligent for not having "shopped" Technicolor around before agreeing to its sale and for not affording some of the directors adequate time to prepare for the meeting at which the sale was considered and approved.

plaintiff's case" was plaintiff's failure to prove that it had been injured as a result of the defendant's negligence. The court put it this way:

> It is not the case, in my opinion, that *in an arms-length, third party merger* proof of a breach of the board's duty of care itself *entitles plaintiff to judgment.* Rather, in such a case, as in any case in which the gist of the claim is negligence, plaintiff bears the burden to establish that the negligence shown was the proximate cause of some injury to it and what that injury was. *See Barnes v. Andrews,* 298 F. 614, 616-18 (S.D.N.Y.1924)....

On appeal, Cinerama contends ... that the Chancellor erred as a matter of law in invoking the tort principles implemented in *Barnes v. Andrews,* S.D.N.Y., 298 F. 614, 616-18 (1924), to grant defendants judgment on the record before the court. Cinerama's contentions are well taken, factually supported by the record and correct as a matter of law.

* * *

We adopt, as clearly supported by the record, the Chancellor's presumed findings of the directors' failure to reach an informed decision in approving the sale of the company. We disagree with the Chancellor's imposition on Cinerama of an additional burden, for overcoming the rule, of proving that the board's gross negligence caused any monetary loss to Cinerama....

To inject a requirement of proof of injury into the rule's formulation for burden shifting purposes is to lose sight of the underlying purpose of the rule. Burden shifting does not create *per se* liability on the part of the directors; rather, it is a procedure by which Delaware courts of equity determine under what standard of review director liability is to be judged. To require proof of injury as a component of the proof necessary to rebut the business judgment presumption would be to convert the burden shifting process from a threshold determination of the appropriate standard of review to a dispositive adjudication on the merits.

This Court has consistently held that the breach of the duty of care, without any requirement of proof of injury, is sufficient to rebut the business judgment rule. *See Mills,* 559 A.2d at 1280-81; *Van Gorkom,* 488 A.2d at 893. In *Van Gorkom,* we held that although there was no breach of the duty of loyalty, the failure of the members of the board to adequately inform themselves represented a breach of the duty of care, which of itself was sufficient to rebut the presumption of the business judgment rule. *Van Gorkom,* 488 A.2d 858. A breach of either the duty of loyalty or the duty of care rebuts the presumption that the directors have acted in the best interests of the shareholders, and requires the directors to prove that the transaction was entirely fair. *Id.* at 893.... Cinerama clearly met its burden of proof for the purpose of rebutting the rule's presumption by showing that the defendant directors of Technicolor failed to inform themselves fully concerning all material information reasonably available prior to approving the merger agreement. Our basis for this conclusion is the Chancellor's own findings, enumerated above.

In sum, we find the Court of Chancery to have committed fundamental error in rewriting the Delaware business judgment rule's requirement of due care. The court has erroneously subordinated the due care element of the rule to the duty of loyalty element. The court has then injected into the duty of care element a burden of proof of resultant injury or loss. In this regard, we emphasize that the measure of any recoverable loss by Cinerama under an entire fairness standard of review is not necessarily limited to the difference between the price offered and the "true" value as determined under appraisal proceedings. Under *Weinberger,* the Chancellor may "fashion any form of equitable and monetary relief as may be appropriate, including rescissory damages." 457 A.2d at 714. The Chancellor may incorporate elements of rescissory damages into his determination of fair price, if he considers such elements: (1) susceptible to proof; and (2) appropriate under the circumstances. *Id.* Thus, we must reverse and remand the case to the trial court with directions to apply the entire fairness standard of review to the challenged transaction....

* * *

Cinerama, Inc. v. Technicolor, Inc.[a]
663 A.2d 1156 (Del. 1995)

HOLLAND, Justice:

Today's opinion completes a trilogy of decisions by this Court....

* * *

The business judgment rule "operates as *both* a procedural guide for litigants and a substantive rule of law." [*Cede & Co. v. Technicolor, Inc.*, 634 A.2d 345, 360 (Del. 1993) ("CEDE II")].... As a *procedural* guide the business judgment presumption is a *rule of evidence* that places the initial burden of proof on the plaintiff. In *Cede II*, this Court described the rule's evidentiary, or procedural, operation as follows:

> If a shareholder plaintiff fails to meet this evidentiary burden, the business judgment rule attaches to protect corporate officers and directors and the decisions they make, and our courts will not second-guess these business judgments.... If the rule is rebutted, the burden shifts to the defendant directors, the proponents of the challenged transaction, to prove to the trier of fact the "entire fairness" of the transaction to the shareholder plaintiff....

Burden shifting does not create *per se* liability on the part of the directors. *Id.* at 371. Rather, it "is a procedure by which Delaware courts of equity determine under what standard of review director liability is to be judged." *Id.* In remanding this case for review under the entire fairness standard, this Court expressly acknowledged that its holding in *Cede II* did *not* establish liability. *Id.*...

Where, as in this case, the presumption of the business judgment rule has been rebutted, the board of directors' action is examined under the entire fairness standard.... This Court has described the dual aspects of entire fairness, as follows:

> The concept of fairness has two basic aspects: fair dealing and fair price. The former embraces questions of when the transaction was timed, how it was initiated, structured, negotiated, disclosed to the directors, and how the approvals of the directors and the stockholders were obtained. The latter aspect of fairness relates to the economic and financial considerations of the proposed merger, including all relevent factors: assets, market value, earnings, future prospects, and any other elements that affect the intrinsic or inhereht value of a company's stock.... However, the test for fairness is not a bifurcated on as between fair dealing and price. All aspects of the issue must be examined as a whole since the question is one of entire fairness.

---

a. This case is commonly referred to as "*Cede III*."

Weinberger v. UOP, Inc., 457 A.2d [701, 711 (Del. 1989)]. Thus, the entire fairness standard requires the board of directors to establish "to the court's satisfaction that the transaction was the product of both fair dealing and fair price." *Cede II,* 634 A.2d at 361. In this case, because the contested action is the sale of a company, the "fair price" aspect of an entire fairness analysis requires the board of directors to demonstrate "that the price offered was the highest value reasonably available under the circumstances." *Id.*

Because the decision that the procedural presumption of the business judgment rule has been rebutted does not establish substantive liability under the entire fairness standard, such a ruling does not necessarily present an insurmountable obstacle for a board of directors to overcome. Thus, an initial judicial determination that a given breach of a board's fiduciary duties has rebutted the presumption of the business judgment rule does not preclude a subsequent judicial determination that the board action was entirely fair, and is, therefore, not outcome-determinative *per se. Id.* at 371.... To avoid substantive liability, *notwithstanding* the quantum of adverse evidence that has defeated the business judgment rule's protective procedural presumption, the board will have to demonstrate entire fairness by presenting evidence of the cumulative manner by which it otherwise discharged all of its fiduciary duties.

Although the *procedural* decision to shift the evidentiary burden to the board of directors to show entire fairness does not create liability *per se,* the aspect of fair dealing to which *Weinberger* devoted the most attention—*disclosure*—has a unique position in a *substantive* entire fairness analysis.... A combination of the fiduciary duties of care and loyalty gives rise to the requirement that "a director disclose to shareholders all material facts bearing upon a merger vote...." *Zirn v. VLI Corp.,* Del. Supr., 621 A.2d 773, 778 (1993). Moreover, in Delaware, "existing law and policy have evolved into a virtual *per se* rule of [awarding] damages for breach of the fiduciary duty of disclosure." *In re Tri-Star Pictures, Inc. Litig.,* 634 A.2d [319, 333 (Del. 1993)].

* * *

Evidence regarding the manner in which the board otherwise discharged all three of its primary fiduciary duties has probative *substantive* significance throughout an entire fairness analysis,[15] and by necessity must permeate the analysis, for two reasons. First, since the evidence that defeated the *procedural* presumption of the business judgment rule does not establish liability *per se,* a *substantive* finding of entire fairness is only possible after examining and balancing the nature of the duty or duties the board breached *vis-a-vis* the manner in which the board properly discharged its other fiduciary duties. Second, the determination that a board has failed to demonstrate entire fairness will be the basis for a finding of *substantive* liability. The Court of Chancery must identify the breach or breaches of fiduciary duty upon which that liability will be predicated in the *ratio decidendi* of its determination that entire fairness has not been established.[16]

* * *

_____

15. In *Rabkin v. Philip A. Hunt Chem. Corp.,* Del. Supr., 498 A.2d 1099 (1985), this Court explicitly rejected a limiting interpretation of fair dealing....

16. If the board fails to demonstrate entire fairness, the particular breach or breaches of fiduciary duty upon which substantive liability is based currently has great significance because of the provisions for eliminating or limiting liability set forth in 8 Del C. § 102(b)(7). *See Arnold v. Society for Savings Bancorp, Inc.,* Del. Supr., 650 A.2d 1270, 1287 (1994)....

In *Van Gorkom*, this Court concluded that the board of directors' failure to inform itself before recommending a merger to the stockholders constituted a breach of the fiduciary duty of care and rebutted the presumptive protection of the business judgment rule.... In *Van Gorkom*, this Court *also* concluded that the directors had violated the *duty of disclosure*. This Court then held that the directors were liable for damages, since the record after trial reflected that the compound breaches of the duties of care and *disclosure* could not withstand an entire fairness analysis.[18] ... Consequently, because this Court had decided the *substantive* entire fairness issue adversely to the board in *Van Gorkom*, the only issue to remand was the amount of damages the Court of Chancery should assess in accordance with *Weinberger*.

* * *

This Court will now review the entire fairness analysis by the Court of Chancery on remand. The Court of Chancery applied the unified approach to entire fairness mandated by established Delaware law. *Kahn v. Lynch Communication Systems, Inc.*, Del. Supr., 638 A.2d 1110, 1115 (1994).... The Court of Chancery also was cognizant that an entire fairness analysis required it to consider carefully how the *board* of directors discharged all of its fiduciary duties with regard to each aspect of the nonbifurcated components of entire fairness: fair dealing and fair price.

* * *

The fair dealing aspect of entire fairness embraces the question "of when the transaction was timed." *Weinberger v. UOP, Inc.*, 457 A.2d at 711. Cinerama has raised no unfair timing issues in its opening brief in this appeal.... It has, therefore, waived its right to contest that issue on appeal, even if the issue was otherwise previously preserved in the Court of Chancery.... In any event, the record reflects that the case subjudice is not similar to one in which a fiduciary manipulated the timing of a transaction to benefit itself at the stockholder's expense....

* * *

The fair dealing aspect of entire fairness also "embraces questions of ... how [the transaction] was initiated." *Weinberger v. UOP, Inc.*, 457 A.2d at 711. The Court of Chancery found that Technicolor was well-equipped to defend itself against any hostile effort to gain control over it. The record reflects that Perelman "recognized that any deal he might pursue would have to be on friendly terms." ... Consequently, the Court of Chancery determined that MAF was an independent third party with no power to force the initiation of a deal. Accordingly, the Court of Chancery concluded there was no basis for a finding that the MAF transaction was unfairly initiated.

* * *

This Court has held that arm's-length negotiation provides "strong evidence that the transaction meets the test of fairness." *Weinberger v. UOP. Inc.*, 457 A.2d at 709-10 n.7.... The Court of Chancery's finding that the MAF transaction was the result of "true, arm's-length negotiation," was undisturbed on appeal in *Cede II*. That finding is the law of the case.

The Court of Chancery focused on "the evidence ... relating to the course of negotiations." It noted that the Technicolor negotiators had effectively bargained with MAF to

---

18. In *Van Gorkom*, it was unnecessary for this Court to state whether the disclosure violation constituted a breach of the duty of care or loyalty or was a combined breach of both since 8 *Del. C.* § 102(b)(7) had not yet been enacted. The statute was, in fact, a legislative response to this Court's liability holding in *Van Gorkom*....

raise its offer price from an initial $ 15 per share to $ 23 per share. Furthermore, the Court of Chancery found that:

> While the board's failure to adequately canvass the market may arguably be consistent with the idea that they were committed, out of self-interest, to the transaction with Perelman, I do not make this inference. First of all it makes no economic sense given the stockholdings of Mr. Kamerman and Bjorkman. Moreover, the board made this decision on the advice of experienced corporate counsel. They thought they had negotiated a good transaction for the shareholders, and did not want to take steps which might jeopardize it. No improper motive, insofar as the evidence suggests, underlay this decision. In my opinion, the record strongly supports a finding that the directors were motivated by the best interests of the shareholders in negotiating the transaction with MAF.

Cinerama, 663 A.2d at 1150 (footnotes omitted). The Court of Chancery concluded "there is no cogent evidence that the Technicolor Board, in any material respect, put their interests ahead of the shareholders in negotiating the sale of the company." *Id.* at 1150.

The "board approval" aspect of the Court of Chancery's entire fairness analysis, discussed hereafter, also took into consideration that the MAF transaction was not one that involved a board of directors that was dominated by a majority with a financial interest in the transaction, nor a majority with interests in conflict with the corporation's shareholders, nor dominated nor manipulated by a *person* with such interests.[26] The independence of the bargaining parties is a well-recognized touchstone of fair dealing. *See Kahn v. Lynch Communication Systems, Inc.,* Del. Supr., 638 A.2d 1110 (1994). Accordingly, the Court of Chancery's finding that the Technicolor stockholders had the benefit of an independent and disinterested board is particularly probative evidence with respect to the "negotiation" of the MAF transaction as one aspect of the fair dealing component of entire fairness....

* * *

The Court of Chancery carefully examined the structure of the transaction. Cinerama argues that the MAF transaction was unfairly structured because it "unquestionably 'inhibited ... alternative bids.'" It contends that the transaction was locked up, included a no-shop provision, and gave Technicolor no "out," *i.e.,* no right to terminate. Cinerama's contention that the merger agreement left Technicolor with "no out" is contradicted by the testimony of Technicolor's special legal counsel....

Technicolor's negotiation of these structural concessions demonstrates that the directors did not seek to foreclose competing bids. Cinerama's assertion that the merger agreement included a "no-shop" clause that "inhibit[ed] [the] board's 'ability to negotiate with other potential bidders'" is not supported by the record. Although it is true that Technicolor could not "shop" for competing bids, it successfully preserved its right to provide information to, and engage in discussions with, competing bidders.[27]

---

26. The Court of Chancery noted that "Sullivan, the only director with a found, material conflict, fully disclosed that interest to the disinterested members of the board and the contract was thereafter approved by them." *Cinerama,* 663 A.2d at 1141.

27. Technicolor's legal counsel testified at trial that:

> The draft served up by counsel for MacAndrews had a prohibition not only against Technicolor approving or recommending or soliciting any competing proposal but also against Technicolor engaging in discussions with anyone else or furnishing information to anyone else. Those last two points were negotiated out. We said that if another proposal comes along at a better price, even if we can't solicit such a proposal, we should be free to negotiate—excuse me. We should be free to furnish information and engage ... rather than solicit discussions with another prospective purchaser.

The Court of Chancery concluded on remand that the MAF transaction was not "locked up" by any device except its very high price.... The Court of Chancery's conclusion is supported by several scenarios subsequently reported in this Court's jurisprudence regarding contests for corporate control. *See, e.g., Paramount Communications, Inc. v. QVC Network, Inc.*, Del. Supr., 637 A.2d 34, 39 (1994) (QVC made a competing bid, supported by a successful injunctive suit, despite Viacom/Paramount "no-shop" clause, a $100 million termination fee, and an option agreement); *Paramount Communications, Inc. v. Time, Inc.*, Del. Supr., 571 A.2d 1140, 1146-47 (1990) (share exchange agreement, "dry up" agreement and no-shop clause did not prevent Paramount's hostile bid).

* * *

Cinerama contends that the non-disclosure to the *directors* of the Sullivan fee's origination at Bear Stearns (MAF's investment banker) and Sullivan's meetings with Perelman constituted a breach of fiduciary duty. When it considered the non-disclosure of those same two matters to the shareholders, the Court of Chancery found: first, that the original source of Sullivan's fee was immaterial under the standard this Court articulated in *Rosenblatt v. Getty Oil Co.*, Del. Supr., 493 A.2d 929 (1985); and, second, that the record did not support Cinerama's contention that Sullivan was Perelman's "inside man." These rulings were affirmed in *Cede II*. They are now the law of the case.

* * *

With respect to Ryan's assumed interest, which was not disclosed, the Court of Chancery held that "it is clear under the language of the statute, that the alleged hope of better employment opportunities does not constitute the kind of interest covered by [8 *Del. C.*] Section 144." *Cinerama*, 663 A.2d at 1154. In other words, Ryan's inchoate hope of improved job circumstances was not the type of self-dealing transaction contemplated by Section 144. We agree. Just as Ryan's undisclosed assumed interest was not "material" under an analogy to Section 144(a)(2), it was not material under an analogy to Section 144(a)(1)....

* * *

The Court of Chancery properly took into consideration its previous factual finding that "the predominant majority of the board was, in approving the MAF proposal, motivated in good faith to achieve a transaction that was the best available transaction for the benefit of the Technicolor shareholders." *Cinerama*, 663 A.2d at 1138. That finding was not contested in the prior appeal. *Cede II, 634* A.2d at 359. It is now the law of the case.

The Court of Chancery acknowledged that the Technicolor board relied heavily upon the advice of Kamerman, the CEO. The Court of Chancery also recognized that the directors "may not blindly rely upon a strong CEO without risk." *Cinerama*, 663 A.2d at 1141. It then noted that the board of directors also relied upon reports by Goldman Sachs and Debevoise & Plimpton, two firms the Court of Chancery described as highly regarded in the financial community.

In addition, the Court of Chancery found "the Technicolor board's reliance upon experienced counsel to evidence good faith and the overall fairness of the process." *Id.* at 1142.... The Court of Chancery ultimately found the fact that "the directors were acting, and their advisors were guiding them, according to the duties known to them in 1982" was a "relevant but not dominant consideration" in determining fairness. *Id.* at 1141. We agree that the Court of Chancery could properly consider the Technicolor directors' reliance on special legal counsel as a factor supporting fair dealing in an entire fairness analysis.

According to the Court of Chancery, it also weighed "the process of board consideration and approval ..." in determining entire fairness. The degree of procedural due care a board of directors exercises has been recognized as a continuing component of an entire fairness analysis.... Even after evidence of a breach of the duty of due care has rebutted the procedural presumption of the business judgment rule, the degree of care that the board actually exercised remains relevant, not because it entitles the board's decision to *deference*, but rather because, in determining the directors' liability if the substantive entire fairness standard is not satisfied, the Court of Chancery must identify the deficiency in the board's "actual conduct" in discharging one or more of its fiduciary duties....

The Court of Chancery properly considered that the Technicolor board's now undisputed lack of care in making a market check was a flaw in its approval process.[30] However, the Court of Chancery also considered that the Technicolor board: had carefully focused on whether the MAF bid offered the best price available in a sale of the company; had considered whether to shop the company and the risks that course would entail; possessed a substantial amount of prior knowledge pertinent to the decision to sell; and relied on the reports of Kamerman, Goldman Sachs and its outside legal counsel. Under these circumstances, in light of the board's good faith and the arm's-length negotiations, the Court of Chancery determined the decision to approve the MAF proposal without making a market check, while clearly deficient, did not preclude a finding of entire fairness. *Cinerama*, 663 A.2d at 1144-45; *see also Barkan v. Amsted Indus., Inc.*, Del. Supr., 567 A.2d 1279, 1287 (1989);[31] *accord Shamrock Holdings, Inc. v. Polaroid Corp.*, Del. Ch. 559 A.2d 257, 271 (1989).

In its initial personal liability decision, the Court of Chancery found, after trial, that the majority of Technicolor directors were motivated in the transaction, appropriately, to promote the best interests of the shareholders. On remand, the Court of Chancery again concluded "that neither the board nor its deliberations were dominated or manipulated by a person with a material conflicting interest or otherwise lacked independence." *Cinerama*, 663 A.2d at 1139. The Court of Chancery found: the record contained "no persuasive evidence that any of the directors were, in fact, materially influenced in their negotiations by any self-interest they may have had," *id.* at 1149; only one director, Sullivan, had a material conflict; and, no director dominated the process. The Court of Chancery concluded that the record reflected that the Technicolor *board's* approval was untainted by conflicts....

* * *

Another well-recognized aspect of fair dealing is the board of directors duty of disclosure to the shareholders. *Weinberger v. UOP, Inc.*, 457 A.2d at 711. In its original post-trial personal liability opinion, the Court of Chancery concluded there was no merit in any of Cinerama's disclosure claims....

* * *

The Court of Chancery's conclusion that the directors had complied with the disclosure duty is not, in and of itself, determinative of entire fairness, but it does have per-

---

30. Although the flaw in this proceeding was the failure to make a market check, there is "no single blueprint" under Delaware law that a board of directors must follow to fulfill its obligation to seek the best value reasonably available to the stockholders. *Paramount Communications, Inc. v. QVC Network, Inc.*, Del. Supr., 637 A.2d 34, 44 (1994) (quoting *Barkan v. Amsted Indus., Inc.*, Del. Supr., 567 A.2d 1279, 1286-87 (1989)).

31. In *Barkan*, an appeal from a Court of Chancery approval of a settlement, this Court noted that the board of directors might accept a single offer without a canvass of the market, if it has a reliable "body of evidence with which to evaluate the fairness of the transaction." *Barkan v. Amsted Indus., Inc.*, 567 A.2d at 1287.

suasive *substantive* significance.... First, it removes this case from the "virtual *per se* rule of damages for breach of the fiduciary duty of disclosure" this Court recognized in In re *Tri-Star Pictures, Inc. Litig.*, Del. Supr., 634 A.2d 319, 333 (1993). Second, it bears directly upon "how the approval of the ... stockholders [was] obtained." *Weinberger v. UOP, Inc.*, 457 A.2d at 711. Third, it places this case into the category of a "non-fraudulent transaction," wherein this Court recognizes "that price may be the preponderant consideration outweighing other features of the merger." *Id.*

* * *

The record reflects that "more than seventy-five percent of [Technicolor's] shares were tendered in the transaction" to MAF. Cinerama was the *only* stockholder to pursue appraisal rights. Generally, "where a majority of fully informed stockholders ratify action of even interested directors, an attack on the ratified transaction normally must fail." *See Smith v. Van Gorkom*, Del. Supr., 488 A.2d 858, 890 (1985). Accordingly, in the absence of a disclosure violation, the Court of Chancery properly found the tender by an overwhelming majority of Technicolor's stockholders to be tacit approval and, therefore, constituted substantial evidence of fairness....

* * *

In addition to fair dealing, the other major component of the non-bifurcated entire fairness standard is fair price. The Court of Chancery found "numerous reliable sources [that] indicate that the $23 per share received constituted the highest value reasonably available to the Technicolor shareholders." *Cinerama*, 663 A.2d at 1142. First, MAF paid a 109% "one-month deal premium" over the market price. This constituted the fourth highest premium paid over market price in transactions involving comparably sized companies, according to the "Alcar Comparable Deal Analysis" performed by the defendants' primary valuation expert. In fact, with regard to sixty-one other transactions, that analysis demonstrated that the price MAF paid was more than double the average fifty-one percent premium paid over market price and represented a premium of 116% relative to Technicolor's market price one month prior to the MAF tender offer. Within Technicolor's industry specifically, the premium over market price MAF paid was the highest for an acquisition in the 1981-84 period, and four times the average premium (26.55%). Second, Technicolor's senior management accepted MAF's bid and declined to pursue a competing buy-out. Third, the Court of Chancery found the "fact that major shareholders, including Kamerman and Bjorkman who had the greatest insight into the value of the company, sold their stock to MAF at the same price paid to the remaining shareholders also powerfully implies that the price received was fair." *Id.* at 1143-44. If Technicolor was worth more than $62 per share, as Cinerama contends, Kamerman (with 128,874 shares) and Bjorkman (with 409,406 shares) would have lost more than $5 million and $16 million respectively by tendering their shares to MAF for $23 per share. Fourth, "experts in the marketplace," including Goldman Sachs, indicated "explicitly and implicitly" that the price was fair. *Id.*[32] Fifth, the Court of Chancery noted in its original liability opinion that there was no persuasive evidence that

---

32. The Court of Chancery found that Goldman Sachs "opined that the price was fair after performing a number of different analyses, all of which are acceptable valuation bases. Goldman did conclude that a marginally higher price might be arranged for an MBO but even if one assumes that to be the case and infers from that that some buyer other than Perelman or management might have been able to pay such a price, such an inference would be supportive of the conclusion that $23 per share was an entirely fair price." Cinerama, 663 A.2d at 1143. Goldman Sachs made an oral presentation based upon a 78-page "board book." *Cede II*, 634 A.2d at 357.

Technicolor's "private market" or public sale value was greater than $23 per share. *Id.* at 1143-44. Similarly, on remand, the Court of Chancery again noted that Cinerama "offered meager [rebuttal] evidence to support a finding that $23 per share constituted an unfair price."

Cinerama argues that if Technicolor had been "shopped," a "cash rich" purchaser would have come forward and offered a higher price. The Court of Chancery concluded, however, that Cinerama had offered no credible evidence to support that proposition in rebuttal to Technicolor's "fair price" evidence.... Cinerama's only direct evidence relating to price fairness came through its valuation expert, John Torkelsen, whose methodology and conclusions the Court of Chancery found to be "troubling" and "too strikingly odd" to be accepted. *Cinerama,* 663 A.2d at 1144.

This Court has observed that "when it is widely known that some change in control is in the offing and no rival bidders are forthcoming over an extended period of time, that fact is supportive of the board's decision to proceed." *Barkan v. Amsted Indus., Inc.,* Del. Supr., 567 A.2d 1279, 1287 (1989). In *Barkan,* this Court also noted that various other apparent obstacles have not prevented "rival bidders from expressing their interest in acquiring a corporation." *Id....* In this case, the record reflects that no rival bidder came forward even though the MAF transaction did not close for several months after it was announced. *See Cede II,* 634 A.2d at 357-58.

The Court of Chancery concluded that the $23 per share offer "was the highest value reasonably achievable." *Cinerama,* 663 A.2d at 1144 (citing *Paramount Communications, Inc. v. QVC Network, Inc.,* Del. Supr., 637 A.2d 34 (1994)). Substantial record evidence supports the Court of Chancery's finding that the $23 deal price was the highest price reasonably available. That conclusion is the result of an orderly and logical deductive process.

* * *

Over the course of forty-seven days, the Court of Chancery heard more than forty-one days of live testimony, including twenty-six days of expert testimony.[33] It was ultimately called upon to assess the demeanor and credibility of twenty-two witnesses, four of whom were director defendants. According to the Court of Chancery, its entire fairness determination was based, in part, on its conclusions that:

> (1) CEO Kamerman consistently sought the highest price that Perelman would pay; (2) Kamerman was better informed about the strengths and weaknesses of Technicolor as a business than anyone else; he was an active and experienced CEO who had designed and implemented a cost reduction program that was very beneficial and knew the businesses in which Technicolor operated; (3) Kamerman and later the board were advised by firms who were among the best in the country; (4) the negotiations lead to a price that was very high when compared to the prior market price of the stock (about a 100% premium over unaffected market price) or when compared to premiums paid in more or less comparable transactions during the period; (5) while the company was not shopped, there is no indication in the record that more money was possible from Mr. Perelman or likely from anyone else; management declined to do an MBO transaction at a higher price and while I did conclude that the deal was

---

33. This may have been the longest trial in the illustrious two hundred and three year history of the Delaware Court of Chancery....

"probably locked up," if the value of the company at that time was or appeared to be remotely close to the value Cinerama claimed at trial, any "lock-up" arrangement present would not have created an insuperable financial or legal obstacle to an alternative buyer. Indeed the conclusion that the transaction was probably locked up was logically and actually premised upon the belief that the $23 price was high.

Cinerama, 663 A.2d at 1140-41. After considering all of the "admissible credible evidence," following a lengthy trial and this Court's remand, the Court of Chancery concluded that the defendants had met their burden of establishing entire fairness:

* * *

[W]hile I conclude that the process followed by the board in authorizing the corporation to enter into the MAF transaction was flawed in that, as found by the Supreme Court, the board was insufficiently informed to make a judgment worthy of [procedural] presumptive deference, nevertheless considering the whole course of events, including the process that was followed, the price that was achieved and the honest motivation of the board to achieve the most financially beneficial transaction available, I conclude that the defendants have introduced sufficient evidence to support a conclusion that, and I do conclude that, the merger in which plaintiff was cashed out, as well as the tender offer in which MAF acquired the stock interest that enabled MAF to cash out plaintiff were [substantively entirely] fair transactions in all respects to Cinerama.

Id. at 1143-44.

* * *

In Cede II, this Court emphasized that the entire fairness standard is exacting and requires the board of directors to "establish to the *court's* satisfaction that the transaction was the product of both fair dealing *and* fair price." *Cede II*, 634 A.2d at 361. On remand, the Court of Chancery reevaluated the full record regarding the Technicolor board's conduct, in view of this Court's ruling that the directors were grossly negligent in failing to provide for a market test. In its entire fairness analysis, the Court of Chancery weighed that omission in the board process against its other findings of fact concerning the board's proper conduct. The Court of Chancery found itself "unable to conclude that the MAF tender offer/merger was not a completely fair transaction." *Cinerama*, 663 A.2d at 1178.

A finding of perfection is not a *sine qua non* in an entire fairness analysis. That is because the entire fairness standard is not even applied unless the presumption of the business judgment rule has been rebutted by evidence that the "directors ... breached any *one* of the *triads* of their fiduciary duty—good faith, loyalty, or due care." *Cede II*, 634 A.2d at 361. Thus, "perfection is not possible, or expected" as a condition precedent to a judicial determination of entire fairness. *Weinberger v. UOP, Inc.*, Del. Supr., 457 A.2d 701, 709 n.7 (1983).

The standard of entire fairness is also not in the nature of a litmus test that "lends itself to bright line precision or rigid doctrine." *Nixon v. Blackwell*, Del. Supr., 626 A.2d 1366, 1381 (1993). Conversely, in *Nixon*, this Court also stated that entire fairness cannot be ascertained by an unstructured or visceral process. *Id.* at 1378. Rather, it is a standard by which the Court of Chancery must carefully analyze the factual circumstances, apply a disciplined balancing test to its findings, and articulate the bases upon which it decides the ultimate question of entire fairness. *Id.* at 1373, 1378....

The record reflects that the Court of Chancery applied a "disciplined balancing test," taking into account all relevant factors. *See Nixon v. Blackwell*, 626 A.2d at 1373. The Court of Chancery meticulously considered and weighed each aspect of fair dealing and fair price that the Technicolor board had properly discharged, in accordance with its fiduciary duties, against the Technicolor board's failure to test the market. After finding that the price obtained was the highest price reasonably available, the Court of Chancery concluded that the MAF transaction was entirely fair....

That entire fairness determination, incorporating questions of credibility and based on more than forty-one days of live testimony and extensive expert witness presentations, must be accorded substantial deference on appellate review. *Rosenblatt v. Getty Oil Co.*, 493 A.2d at 937. The record supports the Court of Chancery's entire fairness determination. *Id.* The Court of Chancery's determination is also the product of an orderly and logical deductive process. *Id.* Accordingly, this Court affirms the Court of Chancery's holding that the MAF transaction was entirely fair to the Technicolor shareholders.

* * *

On remand, the Court of Chancery properly addressed each of the issues identified by this Court in its mandate. The judgment of the Court of Chancery, in favor of the defendants, is AFFIRMED.

Notes and Questions

1. In *Cede II*, what distinguishes a director's breach of the duty of care from tortious acts of ordinary or even gross negligence? Is the court right in eliminating a plaintiff's need to prove actual harm due to directorial misconduct?

2. To learn more about how *Technicolor* has impacted the Delaware courts' jurisprudence, see Roth, Entire Fairness Review for a "Pure" Breach of the Duty of Care: Sensible Approach or Technicolor Flop?, 3 Del. L. Rev. 145 (2000).

b. A Board's Decision to Purchase a Company

Another important decision a corporate director can make is a decision to acquire another company. Acquisitions are often expensive and almost always time consuming. The main concern is that directors will overpay for the target company thereby diminishing the value of their stockholders' securities. While lawsuits for overpayment or corporate "waste" are less frequent than those involving alleged breaches of fiduciary duties by the boards of acquired companies, they do occur. Consider the following case.

Ash v. McCall
2000 WL 1370341 (Del. Ch. 2000) (unpublished opinion)

CHANDLER, Chancellor:

Shareholder plaintiffs ... assert derivative claims on behalf of McKesson HBOC, Inc. ("McKesson HBOC" or the "Company"), a Delaware corporation, which was formed through the merger of McKesson Corporation ("McKesson") and HBOC & Co. ("HBOC") on January 12, 1999. Approximately 3 1/2 months after McKesson's acquisition of HBOC became effective, McKesson HBOC issued the first of what appears to be three downward revisions of revenues, earnings, net income, and other financial information, for financial years 1996-1998. The complaint generally asserts claims related to these revisions. Pending before me is defendants' motion to dismiss....

* * *

After the merger, six directors from each pre-merger company comprised the combined Company's board of directors....

* * *

B. McKesson HBOC's Accounting Restatements

On April 28, 1999, McKesson HBOC announced that in connection with its year-end audit, DeLoitte & Touche ("DeLoitte"), the Company's auditor, discovered improperly recorded revenue for the financial year ending March 31, 1999.... McKesson HBOC's share price fell by over $31, nearly half of its value, on the afternoon of the announcement.

In May 1999, the Company announced that more revisions would be made to earnings. Two months later, with its internal investigations concluded, the Company announced that it would have to make a further restatement covering the two previous financial years to correct for improperly recorded revenue. In all, McKesson HBOC had to disallow $327.4 million of revenue and $191.5 million of operating income.

All of the earnings overstatements, disclosed by the Company between April and July 1999, are attributable to HBOC. It appears that HBOC began overstating earnings in 1996 and continued to do so until shortly before the board of the combined McKesson HBOC first disclosed such overstatements on April 28, 1999, approximately 3 1/2 months after the McKesson/HBOC merger closed on January 12, 1999.

The bulk of the accounting irregularities, according to the complaint, stem from the decision of HBOC senior executives (and their subordinates) to book contingent sales as final sales, both before and after the merger with McKesson. These sales remained contingent, say plaintiffs, because they were made containing "side letters" providing for rights of return and, thus, not properly booked as revenue under applicable accounting standards. The complaint also alleges that senior HBOC executives (and their subordinates) backdated sales contracts so that revenues could be falsely reported as having occurred in an earlier period.

* * *

On June 21, 1999, McKesson HBOC announced that its board of directors would fire defendant McCall and remove him as chairman, and that defendant Pulido would tender his resignation as president, director, and CEO. The Company also announced the resignation of defendant Richard H. Hawkins, executive vice president and chief financial officer. Pulido's and Hawkins' resignations became effective July 15, 1999.

The board of directors also fired several senior executives of the Company's information technology subsidiary (formerly HBOC)....

D. The "Red Flags"

Plaintiffs' overarching litigation theory ... is that "the directors of McKesson, HBOC and McKesson HBOC failed to institute and maintain appropriate financial controls and recommended the merger based upon a recklessly inadequate investigation in the face of clear warnings of accounting improprieties at HBOC."

These "clear warnings" or "red flags" are the linchpin of plaintiffs' liability theory. Plaintiffs point to four "red flags" that HBOC senior officers and directors, and McKesson's board and management team (presumably in the course of due diligence), allegedly disregarded with some degree of culpability ranging from inattention to actual knowledge.

The first of these "red flags" occurred in January 1997 when *Bloomberg*, a financial news company, published a short article questioning HBOC's accounts receivable and near-term growth. Nothing more is alleged about this article.

The second "red flag" occurred three months later in April 1997 when the Center for Financial Research & Analysis, Inc. ("CFRA"), an organization that researches and publishes reports (primarily for institutional investors) relating to financial and accounting issues of public corporations, issued a report on HBOC observing, among other things, that its balance of receivables had surged upward in recent periods. The report was mailed to CFRA clients on or about April 15, 1997.

On April 17 and 18, 1997, *The Atlanta Constitution* reported that on April 15, HBOC's stock price had declined nearly 8% on market speculation that the CFRA report criticized HBOC's accounting practices. *The Atlanta Constitution* also reported that several industry analysts, who publicly commented on the CFRA report, expressed doubt that it had identified any significant problem at HBOC, citing the Company's "strong fundamentals."

Several analysts took the extraordinary step of publishing special reports contesting the CFRA analysis point by point. An HBOC spokesperson stated that the report "doesn't warrant comment." Following these reassurances, HBOC's stock price rebounded to nearly pre-CFRA report levels.

Indefatigable (and apparently correct), on August 19, 1998, CFRA issued a second report critical of HBOC's revenue recognition procedures. CFRA published this report, the third "red flag," approximately sixteen months after the first report and two months before McKesson and HBOC signed their merger agreement. Based upon a review of HBOC's public filings, CFRA reported, among other things, that HBOC's operations "may be deteriorating, as partially evidenced by a high and generally growing level of receivables relative to revenue." ...

The final alleged "red flag" flew on or around November 13, 1998, when HBOC announced that Jay Gilbertson, chief financial officer, president, and chief operating officer, would leave the company. Plaintiffs argue that "despite this clear signal of financial impropriety neither HBOC, McKesson, nor McKesson HBOC discovered and/or reported the fundamental accounting irregularities that were overstating HBOC's (and thereafter McKesson HBOC's) sales and revenue."

II. CONTENTIONS OF THE PARTIES

* * *

Plaintiffs' first two claims can be distilled into a due care claim and a waste claim. The due care claim alleges that the directors of McKesson and the directors of HBOC breached their duty of care by failing to ... detect HBOC's accounting irregularities during the course of due diligence investigations performed in connection with the merger. Although this claim more logically applies to the McKesson directors, plaintiffs seem to insist that it is equally applicable to the HBOC directors.

Plaintiffs assert their waste claim against the McKesson directors. They contend that the McKesson directors' desision ... to exchange properly valued McKesson shares for over valued HBOC shares amounts to waste.

.... Plaintiffs [also] maintain that the directors of McKesson HBOC failed to monitor adequately the company's financial reporting in order to ensure compliance with applicable federal laws and regulations for a three-and-one-half-month period after the merger (the "Second Oversight Claim")....

Defendants argue that this action must be dismissed for two reasons. First, and primarily, defendants seek dismissal under Chancery Rule 23.1 on the ground that plaintiffs have not made a pre-suit demand on the board of directors and have not alleged particularized facts establishing that demand would be futile....

* * *

2. Is There a Reasonable Doubt that Approval of the Merger was the Product of a Valid Exercise of Business Judgment?

[With respect to their waste claim, plaintiffs] quote an analyst from Warburg Dillon Read, an investment bank, who shortly after the Company's first round of corrective disclosures, purportedly stated that 'the marketplace is basically valuing HBOC as zero.' On the strength of one analyst's hyperbole, made in some undisclosed and uncited medium, plaintiffs argue that McKesson paid $14 billion for something (*i.e.*, HBOC before disclosure of accounting irregularities) that was really worth nothing (*i.e.*, HBOC after disclosure of accounting irregularities). This, argue plaintiffs, constitutes waste. I disagree.

When McKesson exchanged approximately $14 billion of its stock for all of HBOC's outstanding stock, the market valued HBOC stock at or around that price. That is, the merger did not appear wasteful when it was entered into, put to a shareholder vote, and approved. The fact that the merger turned out badly or, indeed, abominably for McKesson simply does not and cannot mean that approval of the merger was an act of corporate waste *at the time* the McKesson board entered into it. The facts alleged by plaintiffs do not make out a waste claim and do not demonstrate that the merger was other than a good faith effort to advance corporate interests or the product of a valid business judgment, at the time the board approved the transaction.

In any event, plaintiffs' argument, in my opinion, fundamentally misapprehends the nature of a waste claim. If Company A exchanges $100 for an asset from Company B that Company A believes is worth $100, it is not "waste" if it later turns out that Company B's asset was worth only $10. Company B may have perpetrated a fraud on Company A or, perhaps, Company A's directors breached their duty of care, but Company A or its directors did not commit "waste."

Plaintiffs are examining a corporate transaction with perfect 20/20 hindsight and declaring that it turned out horribly for McKesson, so horribly that it must be a waste of corporate assets. But the relevant time to measure whether the McKesson board committed "waste" is at the time they entered into and approved the transaction. To analyze this claim under the waste standard confuses the due care standard with substantive due care—a concept that is foreign to the business judgment rule. Due care in the decision making context is process due care—whether the board was reasonably informed of all material information reasonably available at the time it made its decision. That is the true nature of plaintiffs' attack on McKesson's board, to which I turn next.

* * *

Here lies the heart of the lawsuit against former McKesson directors and, to a lesser extent, former HBOC directors.[21] Plaintiffs contend that the directors missed several "red flags" that should have alerted them to the accounting problems, in the course of full-scale due diligence, before they approved the merger. Plaintiffs then allege that the directors failed to identify the accounting defects, with some degree of mental culpability ranging from actual knowledge to gross recklessness, reckless disregard, just plain recklessness and, finally, gross negligence.

The notion that McKesson directors had actual knowledge of HBOC's earnings overstatements and nonetheless proceeded with the merger finds no support in the amended complaint. Moreover, it is simply illogical to presume that McKesson directors would *knowingly* cause McKesson to acquire a company with significant, undisclosed earnings misstatements. Nothing in the pleadings remotely suggests a reason why McKesson would purposefully buy such a company; nor do the pleadings offer anything by way of explanation—not a single fact or theory that could possibly support such a conclusion.

Taking all the facts in the complaint as true, and reading every conceivable inference in plaintiffs' favor, inexorably leads to the conclusion that plaintiffs' claims sound in negligence, at most. The McKesson board determined that it was in McKesson's strategic interests to enter the healthcare information technology business. It then acted on that objective by pursuing a business combination with HBOC—one of the leading companies in the field. It hired expert accounting and financial advisors to perform due diligence on HBOC—DeLoitte & Touche and Bear Stearns, respectively. After DeLoitte and Bear Stearns completed their due diligence reviews, with the participation of McKesson management, they waived "green flags" to the McKesson board, in effect saying, "This merger is financially and strategically sound." The McKesson directors approved the merger.

Defendants characterize the "red flags" that plaintiffs make so much of as "dated," "obscure," and "inconsequential" relative to the prominent "green flags" given to the directors by the accounting and financial experts who conducted due diligence reviews in advance of the merger. When plaintiffs' "red flags" are juxtaposed with the clean bill of health given by DeLoitte and Bear Stearns after due diligence reviews, the complaint permits one conclusion: that the McKesson directors' reliance on the views expressed by their advisors was in good faith. What would plaintiffs have the McKesson board do in the course of making an acquisition other than hire a national accounting firm and investment bank to examine the books and records of the target company? Nothing in the pleadings otherwise casts doubt on the good faith of the McKesson directors.[23]

Undaunted by the facts alleged in their own complaint, plaintiffs contend that "there is no authority for defendants' argument that the directors here are entitled to abdicate

---

21. I characterize this claim as primarily directed against the McKesson directors because the merger represented something of a windfall to the HBOC shareholders to the extent that the losses borne by HBOC shareholders in connection with the accounting irregularities were serendipitously halved (or thereabout) by virtue of the merger. In other words, because HBOC shareholders received properly valued McKesson stock for their own improperly or, rather, overvalued HBOC stock, and held only a 60% interest in the combined company, as opposed to all of it when the irregularities were disclosed and the stock price plummeted, HBOC shareholders bore only 60% of whatever losses accrued from the accounting irregularities, as opposed to 100%. Former McKesson shareholders, undoubtedly to their chagrin, bore the remaining 40% of the losses....

23. If these facts demonstrate anything, it is merely that DeLoitte, Bear Stearns, and McKesson management performed shoddy due diligence. Plaintiffs have not brought claims against any of these parties.

their duties to their experts." It is, in reality, plaintiffs' argument that is without basis in fact or law. Directors of Delaware corporations quite properly *delegate* responsibility to qualified experts in a host of circumstances. One circumstance is surely due diligence review of a target company's books and records. To delegate this assignment is not an "abdication" of duty.

.... [T]he question becomes whether such directors are to be "fully protected" on the basis that they relied in good faith on qualified experts under 8 Del. C. § 141(e). The McKesson board is entitled to the presumption that it exercised proper business judgment, including proper reliance on experts. Plaintiffs have not rebutted the presumption with particularized facts ... (in contrast with conclusions) that, if proved, would show that (1) the directors in fact did not rely on the expert, or (2) that their reliance was not in good faith, or (3) that they did not reasonably believe that the experts' advice was within the experts' professional competence, or (4) that the directors were at fault for not selecting experts with reasonable care, or (5) that the issue (here, alleged accounting deficiencies in HBOC's financial records) was so obvious that the board's failure to detect it was grossly negligent regardless of the experts' advice, or (6) that the board's decision was so unconscionable as to constitute waste or fraud. This complaint is devoid of particularized allegations along these lines and is, therefore, incapable of surviving a motion to dismiss.

In determining whether the complaint creates any doubt that the McKesson directors used due care in approving the merger, the Court considers whether the directors: (i) informed themselves of available critical information before approving the transaction; (ii) considered expert opinion; (iii) provided all Board members with adequate and timely notice of the [transaction] before the full Board meeting and of its purpose; or (iv) inquired adequately into the reasons for or terms of [the transaction]....

Plaintiffs have not alleged facts creating a reasonable doubt that the McKesson directors did not act in accordance with any of these guidelines. Plaintiffs' allegations that directors were less than fully informed of reasonably available material information or that they considered the merger in any other procedurally unsound manner relies entirely on the wisdom of hindsight....

Defendants have also directed the Court's attention to exculpatory charter provisions, enacted under 8 Del. C. § 102(b)(7), in McKesson's and the combined McKesson HBOC's articles of incorporation. Although the exculpatory provisions serve as adequate independent grounds for dismissing the due care claim, I principally rely on plaintiffs' failure to allege particularized, facts creating a reasonable doubt that the merger, at the time it was entered into, was other than a valid exercise of business judgment.

* * *

[D]efendants attack the Second Oversight Claim straightforwardly. They argue that the McKesson HBOC board's failure to detect and cure accounting irregularities for a mere 3 1/2 months (from the merger date in January 1999 until the disclosures of accounting irregularities in April 1999) could not possibly constitute oversight violations under the high liability standards set forth in *Graham v. Allis-Chalmers Mfg. Co.*[, 188 A.2d 125 (1963),] or *In re Caremark Int'l Inc. Derivative Litigation,* [698 A.2d 959 (1996),] the seminal Delaware cases addressing directors' oversight duties....

* * *

Within three months of the McKesson board's recommendation and McKesson shareholders' approval of the merger, the combined Company's auditor, DeLoitte &

Touche, informed the board of HBOC Sub's accounting irregularities. The McKesson HBOC board, comprised of six former McKesson directors and six former HBOC directors, responded to this information by initiating an internal investigation that culminated in a series of sweeping earnings restatements. In addition, the board made sweeping management changes, firing several senior managers and creating a new executive management structure.

In light of these facts, drawn directly from plaintiffs' complaint, it seems ineluctable that McKesson directors became aware of the accounting improprieties after the merger was consummated and immediately took decisive steps to disclose and cure them. These actions do not bespeak faithless or imprudent fiduciaries.

The role played by the six former HBOC directors on the combined Company's board in connection with the disclosure of the accounting irregularities remains somewhat unclear. A modicum of well-pled facts, sprinkled throughout the complaint, could lead to an inference that the HBOC directors might have had knowledge of suspect accounting practices and, therefore, *potential* accounting irregularities, in advance of the DeLoitte report....

* * *

.... If plaintiffs can allege particularized facts that might enable this Court to infer that HBOC directors (or perhaps members of HBOC's audit committee) did possess knowledge of facts suggesting potential accounting improprieties (such as knowledge of the CFRA reports) and took no action to respond to them until they were confronted (three months after the merger) with DeLoitte's audit report, one could argue that the HBOC directors (or the audit committee members) failed to act in good faith.[57] As a result, demand might in turn be excused.

This result presents an awkward circumstance. If HBOC directors possessed knowledge of suspect accounting practices at HBOC *before* the merger, one would think such knowledge might give rise to colorable claims that McKesson, as an acquiror, could assert against HBOC under fraud-based theories or perhaps for breaches of provisions in the parties' merger agreement. McKesson, however, is not asserting such claims.

Although one may speculate as to the reasons behind McKesson's disinclination to take legal action against HBOC and its officers and directors, such speculation is completely idle absent nonconclusory allegations of fact.[58] Nonetheless, if plaintiffs can allege

---

57. Plaintiffs allege that HBOC had an audit committee in place. In light of the known facts, one would be hard pressed to say that it performed particularly well. Nevertheless, the existence of an audit committee, together with HBOC's retention of Arthur Anderson as its outside auditor to conduct annual audits of the company's financial reporting, is some evidence that a monitoring and compliance system was in place at HBOC pre-merger....

58. Plaintiffs have alleged, in a single conclusory paragraph, that demand was futile because the McKesson HBOC board was faced with an "inherent conflict" that made it unable to respond to the disaster or to bring suit against HBOC for fraud or breach of contract.... According to the amended complaint, the McKesson HBOC board is evenly split—consisting of six former McKesson directors and six former HBOC directors. As a result, when the accounting improprieties came to light, "one half of the Board's blame was the other half of the Board's cover." ... The notion of a paralyzed board is belied somewhat by the aggressive steps to disclose the problem and to remove certain senior managers. On the other hand, the current board's failure or refusal to pursue potential claims against HBOC's former directors and managers, or against those firms that performed the due diligence, supports the notion of an incapacitated board. But I need not address this issue now, given that plaintiffs will be afforded an opportunity to plead more particular facts about what the HBOC directors knew concerning the accounting improprieties, and when they knew it, in the context of either a direct attack on the current board's failure to pursue the claim or in a double derivative action, as mentioned earlier. Such facts, together with additional facts regarding the board's composi-

with some particularity facts indicating that HBOC directors had actual knowledge of accounting irregularities, or knowledge of facts indicating potential accounting irregularities, and took no action until confronted with the DeLoitte audit report in early 1999 (after the merger), such facts, to my mind, could possibly excuse demand as to the Second Oversight Claim. In addition ... such facts could give rise to claims that McKesson might bring directly attacking the merger seeking rescission or rescissory damages; or, if McKesson HBOC was unwilling to assert contract-based claims, shareholders might endeavor to bring those claims derivatively on behalf of McKesson HBOC.

* * *

Note

A "failure of oversight," as discussed in *Ash*, is essentially a duty of care violation. The court found none, and even praised the board for responding quickly to the information provided by its accountants. Indeed, the board conducted an internal investigation that culminated in sweeping earnings restatements and a major shake up in management. Moreover, the court found that the directors easily met Delaware's oversight standard espoused in In re Caremark Int'l Inc. Derivative Litigation, 698 A.2d 959 (Del. 1996). In order to be held liable under that standard, directors must be found to have "utterly failed to attempt to assure [that] a reasonable reporting system exists" or exhibited a "sustained and systematic failure to exercise reasonable oversight." *Id.* at 971.

In addition to the need to be careful in making acquisitions, another issue arising in the merger context is the ability of management to engage in actions designed to achieve a favorable shareholder vote. Some actions are both necessary and innocuous, such as promptly preparing and distributing proxy materials. Other actions, however, are more suspect. Consider the following case.

Hewlett v. Hewlett-Packard Co.
2002 WL 549137 (Del. Ch. 2002) (unpublished opinion)

CHANDLER, Chancellor.

This lawsuit challenges certain actions taken in connection with a hotly contested shareholder vote on a proposed merger. The merger would combine Hewlett-Packard Company ("HP") and Compaq Computer Corporation, the second and third largest computer makers in the United States. HP's management strongly supported the merger. Plaintiffs, Walter B. Hewlett, Edwin E. van Bronkhorst, and the William R. Hewlett Revocable Trust (collectively, "the Hewlett Parties"), opposed the merger and waged a vigorous proxy contest against it. On March 19, 2002, HP held its special meeting of stockholders to vote on the proposed combination. Following the meeting, HP announced that the proposed merger had been approved by a slim, but sufficient, margin of votes....

[T]he Hewlett Parties filed this action, pursuant to 8 Del. C. §225(b), seeking a declaration that the merger was not validly approved. They attack the merger vote on two

---

tion, would assist a court in determining whether the board is structurally unable to make an independent and disinterested judgment regarding the potential claim against HBOC.

fronts. First, they allege that a large number of votes were cast in favor of the merger by a stockholder whose approval was obtained through coercion, intimidation, or enticement by HP management. Second, they assert that HP management procured its proxies in favor of the merger by knowingly making material misrepresentations about key financial numbers at the center of HP's proxy campaign.

... HP moved to dismiss the complaint....

* * *

HP and Compaq are each publicly traded Delaware corporations and global providers of computers and computer-related products and services. Hewlett and van Bronkhorst are co-trustees of The William R. Hewlett Revocable Trust (the "Trust"), which owns 72,802,148 shares representing approximately 3.75% of HP's outstanding stock. The Hewlett Parties beneficially own 75,748,594 shares of HP representing approximately 3.90% of HP's outstanding stock.[2]

On September 4, 2001, HP and Compaq entered into an agreement by which the two companies would be combined. Under the terms of this proposed merger, Compaq stockholders would be issued 0.6325 of a share of HP common stock for each share of Compaq stock they owned, representing in the aggregate approximately 35.7% of the combined company. HP stockholders would continue to hold the same number of shares they owned before the merger but, because of the new HP shares issued to former Compaq shareholders, the equity ownership percentage of the existing HP stockholders would be considerably diluted. Consummation of the proposed merger required a majority vote of HP stockholders voting at a meeting where a majority of the outstanding HP shares were present and properly approved the issuance of HP stock to Compaq stockholders.

Immediately following the announcement of the proposed merger, HP's stock price dropped 18.7% from $23.21 to $18.87 (representing an aggregate loss of approximately $8.5 billion in stockholder value). By early November 2001, the price of HP's shares had dropped 27.2%. This continued decline in share price contrasts with a 9.9% gain in share value realized by an index of comparable companies.

On November 6, 2001, in reaction to this decline in value that Hewlett believed confirmed his concerns over the proposed merger, Hewlett publicly announced that he, the Trust, the William and Flora Hewlett Foundation, and his two sisters would all vote against the proposed merger. That same day, David Woodley Packard, son of HP's other founder, announced that he would also vote against the transaction. Later the Packard Foundation also announced its shares would be voted against the proposed merger. The Hewlett Parties, the William and Flora Hewlett Foundation, Hewlett's two sisters, David Packard, and the Packard Foundation collectively represent approximately 18% of HP's voting shares. By a definitive proxy statement dated February 5, 2002, the Hewlett Parties solicited proxies in opposition to the proposed merger.

On March 19, 2002, HP held a stockholders meeting to vote on the proposed transaction. After the meeting, HP publicly claimed that the proposed merger was approved by a slim margin. The independent inspector responsible for certifying the vote, however, has not informed either party of any preliminary results of the voting.

---

2. Hewlett has also been a director of HP for approximately 15 years and is the son of the late William R. Hewlett, one of HP's founders.

A. The Vote-Buying Claim

The Hewlett Parties' allegation with regard to proxies cast in favor of the proposed merger by Deutsche Bank is essentially, although not captioned as such in the complaint, a vote-buying claim. Deutsche Bank holds at least 25 million shares of HP. The plaintiffs allege that Deutsche Bank's last-minute switch from voting 17 million of its shares against the merger to voting those shares for the merger was the result of a combination of inducement and coercion, orchestrated by HP's management, which caused Deutsche Bank to vote in favor of the proposed merger for reasons other than those based upon the merits of the transaction.[4] The Hewlett Parties' allegations in support of this claim focus on actions taken during the four days before and the morning of the special meeting.

* * *

HP responds to these allegations by contending that a claim of vote-buying is disfavored in Delaware as a basis upon which to disenfranchise stockholders and overturn a vote. HP contends that it is the plaintiffs who are, in fact, seeking to disenfranchise shareholders through their prayer for a declaration from this Court that Deutsche Bank's proxies are invalid. Finally, HP argues that the Hewlett Parties have failed to plead adequately a vote-buying claim (assuming that such a claim is still cognizable) because there was not a binding voting agreement governing Deutsche Bank's stock and because a majority of HP stock was not obligated to vote in favor of the transaction.

1. Legal Standard for a Vote-Buying Claim

This Court has, on several earlier occasions, addressed so-called "vote-buying" allegations. In some instances the claims were successful and in others they were not. There does not, however, appear to be an obvious predisposition on the part of the Court one way or another toward vote-buying claims.

* * *

The appropriate standard for evaluating vote-buying claims is articulated in *Schreiber v. Carney*[, 447 A.2d 19 (Del. Ch. 1982)]. *Schreiber* indicates that vote-buying is illegal *per se* if "the object or purpose is to defraud or in some way disenfranchise the other stockholders." *Schreiber* also notes, absent these deleterious purposes, that "because vote-buying is so easily susceptible of abuse it must be viewed as a voidable transaction subject to a test for intrinsic fairness." At first blush this proposition seems difficult to reconcile with the General Assembly's explicit validation of shareholder voting agreements in §218(c).[9] Significantly, however, it was the management of the defendant corporation that was buying votes in favor of a corporate reorganization in *Schreiber*. Shareholders are free to do whatever they want with their votes, including selling them to the highest bidder. Management, on the other hand, may not use corporate assets to buy votes in a hotly contested proxy contest about an extraordinary transaction that would significantly transform the corporation, unless it can be demonstrated, as it was

---

4. Presumably if only 17 million of Deutsche Bank's 25 million shares were switched from voting against to voting for the merger, Deutsche Bank still voted 8 million (or approximately 1/3) of its shares against the merger.

9. Section 218(c) provides:

   (c) An agreement between 2 or more stockholders, if in writing and signed by the parties thereto, may provide that in exercising any voting rights, the shares held by them shall be voted as provided by the agreement, or as the parties may agree, or as determined in accordance with a procedure agreed upon by them.

in *Schreiber*, that management's vote-buying activity does not have a deleterious effect on the corporate franchise.[10]

I am not persuaded by HP's contention that, as a threshold matter, a plaintiff cannot state a cognizable claim unless he establishes that there was a binding obligation to vote a specific way, in the nature of a contract, on the part of the shareholder whose vote is challenged. Of course there must be *some* kind of agreement with regard to how the challenged shares are to be voted for the issue to arise in the first place. I am not convinced, however, by the argument that such agreement must rise to something akin to a contractual obligation to vote shares according to the wishes of another before a cognizable claim may be stated. It is more logical to tie cognizability of a vote-buying claim to actual voting in accordance with a purportedly illegal agreement. Protection of unsuspecting shareholders who are at risk of being defrauded or disenfranchised should be the focus of the Court, not whether the allegedly bad actors were contractually obligated to each other. I conclude, therefore, that a contractually binding obligation between parties to an agreement to vote shares in a particular manner is not a prerequisite to a vote-buying claim. The threshold showing required of a plaintiff is that he plead facts from which it is reasonable to infer that in exchange for "consideration personal to the stockholder," a stockholder has agreed to vote, or has in fact voted, his shares as directed by another.

I also disagree with HP's assertion that to establish the invalidity of a vote-buying agreement, a plaintiff must show that a majority of all outstanding shares was obligated to vote in favor of the transaction as a result of the vote-buying. Again, the focus of the Court's analysis should be on possible deleterious effects of a challenged vote-buying agreement on shareholders. Less than a majority of votes can be decisive in tipping the results of an election one way or another. If voiding the votes cast in accordance with a fraudulent vote-buying agreement with corporate management is sufficient to change the result of a vote, I am again of the opinion that the defrauded or disenfranchised shareholders should not be prevented from bringing a vote-buying claim.

2. Analysis of the Vote-Buying Claim

* * *

Initially, I believe the facts as alleged in the complaint support a reasonable inference that the switch of Deutsche Bank's vote of 17 million shares to favor the merger was the result of the enticement or coercion of Deutsche Bank by HP management. The Hewlett Parties allege that just four days before the stockholders meeting Deutsche Bank was named as a co-arranger of a multi-billion dollar credit facility. That same day (March 15), Deutsche Bank had submitted all of its proxies and voted 25 million shares against the merger. On Monday, March 18, it is alleged that Deutsche Bank expressed fear over losing future business as a result of HP's negative reaction to Deutsche Bank's vote against the HP management-sponsored merger. Finally, the complaint alleges that, on March 19, the date of the special stockholder meeting, HP delayed the meeting while HP management was involved in a purportedly coercive telephone conference and then closed the polls immediately after Deutsche Bank switched 17 million of its votes as a result of the understanding arrived at during that call. As stated above, however, a vote-

---

10. Significantly, the vote-buying at issue in *Schreiber* was ratified in an independent and fully informed vote of the disinterested shareholders. Such ratification carries substantial weight when the Court is determining whether a vote-buying arrangement has a deleterious effect on the shareholder franchise, even if the vote-buying transaction is subject to a test of intrinsic fairness.

buying agreement is not illegal *per se,* even when company management is buying votes. The more difficult question is whether or not the facts alleged support a reasonable inference that the agreement had a materially adverse effect on the franchise of the other HP shareholders.

The Hewlett Parties' primary argument as to why the alleged vote-buying agreement between HP and Deutsche Bank is illegal is that HP management used corporate funds (in essence, funds in which all of HP shareholders have a common interest as owners of HP) to purchase votes in favor of a transaction favored by management that management was required to put to a shareholder vote. Furthermore, HP management failed to use any devices, such as a ratifying vote of independent shareholders, which would protect the integrity of the vote on the proposed merger.

The allegations of the Hewlett Parties, if true, are particularly troubling. The extraordinary transaction at issue in this case is one of the limited types of transactions a corporate board cannot unilaterally cause its corporation to consummate. Because the transaction would have a fundamental impact on the ownership interests of a company's shareholders, the board must present the proposal to the shareholders for approval. If the allegations of the Hewlett Parties are true, the implication is that HP management was concerned that the proposed merger, which *they* supported, would not be supported by a majority of HP's shareholders. Despite the fact that it was for the shareholders to make the ultimate determination of whether to approve the proposed merger, HP management purportedly used the shareholders' own money (in the form of corporate funds) to buy votes in opposition to HP shareholders who did not favor the merger. These actions, if they in fact were taken impermissibly, tipped the balance in favor of HP management's view of how the vote should turn out and made it proportionally more difficult for shareholders opposing the merger to defeat the transaction. In my opinion, that is an improper use of corporate assets by a board to interfere with the shareholder franchise. [I]t was the right of the shareholders to cast their votes on the proposed merger without impermissible interference from HP management.

Schreiber is instructive in demonstrating how a vote-buying agreement in which a board expends corporate assets to purchase votes in support of a board-favored transaction may be validly consummated. There, a vote-buying agreement was being contemplated in which corporate assets were to be loaned to a 35% shareholder on favorable terms as consideration for that shareholder's agreement to vote in favor of a management-endorsed merger. The company formed a special committee to consider the merger and also the advisability of entering into the vote-buying agreement. The special committee hired independent counsel and then determined that both the merger and the shareholder agreement would be in the best interests of the company and its shareholders. After arm's-length bargaining with the 35% shareholder, the parties arrived at agreeable terms for the loan and the special committee recommended the shareholder agreement to the full board. The board of directors unanimously approved the agreement as proposed and submitted the vote-buying proposal to the shareholders for a separate vote—in effect a vote on vote-buying in that particular setting. As a condition for passage of the vote-buying proposal, a majority of outstanding shares, as well as a majority of the shares neither participating in the agreement nor owned by directors and officers of the company, had to be voted in favor of the proposal. After distribution of a proxy statement that fully disclosed the terms of the agreement, the vote-buying proposal was easily approved by the shareholders.

The *Schreiber* Court noted all of these protective measures and ultimately held that "the subsequent ratification of the [shareholder agreement] by a majority of the independent stockholders, after a full disclosure of all germane facts with complete candor precludes any further judicial inquiry." I agree with the well-reasoned opinion by then-Vice Chancellor Hartnett in *Schreiber*. Absent measures protective of the shareholder franchise like those taken in *Schreiber*, this Court should closely scrutinize transactions in which a board uses corporate assets to procure a voting agreement. This is not to say that all of the protective measures taken in *Schreiber* must be present before the Court will validate vote-buying by management using company assets. Each case must be evaluated on its own merits....

Because the Hewlett Parties successfully have alleged that HP bought votes from Deutsche Bank with corporate assets and because no steps were taken to ensure that the shareholder franchise was protected, HP's motion to dismiss the plaintiffs' vote-buying claim is denied. At trial, the plaintiffs will have the significant burden of presenting sufficient evidence for me to find that Deutsche Bank was coerced by HP management during their March 19, 2002 telephone conference into voting 17 million shares in favor of the proposed merger and that the switch of those votes was not made by Deutsche Bank for independent business reasons.

B. The Disclosure Claim

The Hewlett Parties' second claim is that in soliciting proxies in favor of the proposed merger, HP management knowingly made numerous materially false and misleading public statements with regard to the integration of HP and Compaq. Those statements purportedly convinced Institutional Shareholder Services ("ISS") to recommend to its subscribers that they vote in favor of the proposed merger.[15] That recommendation caused at least one of HP's largest shareholders, Barclays Global Investors ("Barclays"), to vote for the proposed merger.[16] Because of the extremely narrow margin of victory claimed by HP management, the vote by Barclays of more than 60 million shares (representing 3.1% of HP's voting shares) in favor of the proposed merger was likely outcome determinative.

To support this claim, the Hewlett Parties allege that in the months leading up to the stockholder vote, HP management repeatedly said, at investor and analyst conferences, to the media, and elsewhere, that HP's efforts to integrate its business with that of Compaq were progressing at least as well as planned. HP management gave assurances that HP was going to achieve at least $2.5 billion in cost savings in the first two years after the merger while losing no more than 5% of revenue, and having to lay off only 15,000 employees.

* * *

In contrast to the public statements made by HP management, plaintiffs allege that at the time those statements were made, management knew that the integration plan was not on track, that projected cost savings and revenue losses were not what investors expected, and that the reality of the integration meant that HP was going to have to have higher revenues, to cut other costs, or to lay off 24,000, not 15,000, HP employees.

* * *

---

15. ISS is a subscription service that "helps institutional investors research the financial implications of proxy proposals and cast votes that will protect and enhance shareholder returns." *See* http://www.issproxy.com/services/index.html. The ISS recommendation to vote for the proposed merger was subscribed to by institutional stockholders holding as much as 23% of HP shares....

16. Before ISS had issued its recommendation to vote for the proposed merger, Barclays had stated that it would unconditionally vote its shares in accordance with the ISS recommendation.

HP responds that the plaintiffs fail to state a disclosure claim because HP share-holders were fully informed of the competing positions and reservations with regard to the proposed merger through the proxy contest, which the Hewlett Parties them-selves characterize as "unique in recent corporate history" and the "most intensive proxy contest in recent years." HP contends that all aspects of the integration issue were thoroughly debated, analyzed, and scrutinized, not only by Hewlett, but also nu-merous sophisticated institutional investors. HP invites the Court to take judicial no-tice of press releases personally issued by Hewlett, as well as of the other extensive cov-erage of the integration issue. HP contends that these sources reveal that the very integration issues the Hewlett Parties claim were presented inaccurately to HP share-holders (projections concerning revenue and the risks of integration with Compaq) were in fact disclosed.

* * *

2. Legal Standard for a Disclosure Claim

In a proceeding under § 225(b), the Court is permitted to "hear and determine the result of any vote of stockholders ... upon matters other than the election of direc-tors."[19] Part of that power includes the power to determine the validity of votes cast. To the extent that HP management procured proxies by disclosing material information that it knew to be false, therefore, the plaintiffs' disclosure claim is cognizable in a pro-ceeding under § 225(b). To be actionable in this context, false or misleading statements must be material to those receiving the statements, which means that there must be a "substantial likelihood that the disclosure of the [the additional information] would have been viewed by the reasonable investor as having significantly altered the 'total mix' of information made available" to the shareholders.

* * *

[A]t this stage of the litigation, it would be impossible for me to hold, as a matter of law, that the Hewlett Parties failed to state a cognizable disclosure claim in this § 225 action.[24]

* * *

---

19. Section 225(b) provides in full:
   (b) Upon application of any stockholder or any member of a corporation without capital stock, the Court of Chancery may hear and determine the result of any vote of stockhold-ers or members, as the case may be, upon matters other than the election of directors, of-ficers or members of the governing body. Service of the application upon the registered agent of the corporation shall be deemed to be service upon the corporation, and no other party need be joined in order for the Court to adjudicate the result of the vote. The Court may make such order respecting notice of the application as it deems proper under the circumstances.

24. I reiterate that the plaintiffs in this case have done more than just allege in conclusory form that they thought the defendant was lying. Such a bare-bones allegation would not be sufficient to invoke § 225 after a party lost a proxy contest. The plaintiffs here have specifically identified reports to management by the integration team that can be verified and that would, accepting the alleged facts as true, prove the bad faith of HP management. The credibility of these allegations, made pri-marily upon information and belief, is bolstered by the fact that one of the plaintiffs, Walter Hewlett, is a director of the defendant corporation and as such has access to confidential company documents. Finally, the alleged misstatements pertain to integration, an issue that was particularly important to ISS, an institution that was effectively able to dictate the vote of a block of shares that we now know was likely outcome determinative. It is in light of all of these factors that I conclude that the plaintiffs may proceed with this challenge under § 225.

Notes and Questions

1. The plaintiffs' "victory" in *Hewlett-Packard* was short lived. The Delaware Chancery Court, after a trial on the merits, concluded:

> Based on all of the testimony and exhibits and for the reasons set forth above, I conclude that plaintiffs have failed to prove that HP disseminated materially false information about its integration efforts or about the financial data provided to its shareholders. In addition, I conclude that plaintiffs have failed to prove that HP management improperly enticed or coerced Deutsche Bank into voting in favor of the merger. Accordingly, I will enter judgment in favor of HP and dismiss the plaintiffs' complaint.

Hewlett v. Hewlett-Packard Co., 2002 WL 818091 (Del. Ch. 2002) (unpublished opinion).

Not surprisingly, Walter Hewlett was dropped from the board as a result of his activism. However, he scored a small measure of revenge when the operational results from the merger were less than rosy. Carly Fiorina—Chairman and CEO of HP, the most vocal supporter of the merger, and Walter Hewitt's personal nemesis—was shown the exit about two and one-half years following the merger. She received a $21 million going away present.

Following the court battle, the SEC conducted an investigation into the alleged HP/Deutsche Bank shenanigans. As a result, Deutsche Bank agreed to pay a $750,000 settlement for failing to disclose conflicts of interest when it voted its clients' proxies as required by law.[1] During the investigation, it was discovered that Fiorina had left the following voicemail message for Robert Waymann, an HP executive, near the end of the proxy battle against Walter Hewlett: "We may have to do something extraordinary for (Deutsche Bank) to bring'em over the line here."[2] Ah, the smoking gun was discovered too late for poor Walter!

2. Worried that Paramount Communications' enticing all-cash tender offer for shares of Time, Inc. would cause Time's stockholders to vote against Time's proposed merger with Warner Brothers, Time restructured the merger into an outright acquisition of Warner. This avoided the necessity of a stockholder vote. *See* Paramount Comm., Inc. v. Time, Inc. 571 A.2d 1140 (Del. 1990). Does this motivation comport with the fulfillment of fiduciary duties to stockholders by Time's board? Should it?

Section 2
The Duty of Loyalty

a. A Board's Decision to Sell the Company

In Revlon, Inc. v. MacAndrews & Forbes Holdings, Inc., 506 A.2d 173 (Del. 1986), the Delaware Supreme Court analyzed the legality of lock-up options designed to favor

---

1. *See* Deutsche Bank Settles Proxy-Votes Case, N.Y. Times, Aug. 20, 2002, at C3.
2. Markoff, U.S. Agencies Looking into Hewlett Vote, N.Y. Times, Apr. 16, 2002, at C1 (quoting Carly Fiorina).

one bidder over another in the context of competing tender offers.[1] Although the court analyzed the initial adoption of these (and other defensive measures) under test of Unocal Corp. v. Mesa Petroleum Co., 493 A.2d 946 (Del. 1985), it noted that a point occurred in the bidding at which the board's duties changed:

> However, when Pantry Pride increased its offer to $50 per share, and then to $53, it became apparent to all that the break-up of the company was inevitable. The Revlon board's authorization permitting management to negotiate a merger or buyout with a third party was a recognition that the company was for sale. The duty of the board had thus changed from the preservation of Revlon as a corporate entity to the maximization of the company's value at a sale for the stockholders' benefit. This significantly altered the board's responsibilities under the *Unocal* standards. It no longer faced threats to corporate policy and effectiveness, or to the stockholders' interests, from a grossly inadequate bid. The whole question of defensive measures became moot. The directors' role changed from defenders of the corporate bastion to auctioneers charged with getting the best price for the stockholders at a sale of the company.

Id. at 182.

In Mills Acquisition Co. v. MacMillan, Inc., 559 A.2d 1261, 1286-88 (Del. 1989), the court explained the relationship between a board's "*Revlon* duties" and its "*Unocal* duties":

> Directors are not required by Delaware law to conduct an auction according to some standard formula, only that they observe the significant requirement of fairness for the purpose of enhancing general shareholder interests. That does not preclude differing treatment of bidders when necessary to advance those interests. Variables may occur which necessitate such treatment.[38] However, the board's primary objective, and essential purpose, must remain the enhancement of the bidding process for the benefit of the stockholders.
>
> In the absence of self-interest, and upon meeting the enhanced duty mandated by *Unocal*, the actions of an independent board of directors in designing and conducting a corporate auction are protected by the business judgment rule.... *Unocal*, 493 A.2d at 954.... Thus, like any other business decision, the board has a duty in the design and conduct of an auction to act in "the best interests of the corporation and its shareholders." *Unocal*, 493 A.2d at 954-56....
>
> However, as we recognized in *Unocal*, where issues of corporate control are at stake, there exists "the omnipresent specter that a board may be acting primarily

---

1. A lock-up option is a defensive device used by a target to ward off hostile bidders. In a stock lock-up, a friendly bidder will purchase an option to buy authorized but unissued shares in the target; in the event the hostile bidder continues the attempted takeover, the friendly bidder may exercise the option. Because the exercise price of the option typically is significantly below the hostile bidder's offering price, the exercise of the option has the dual effect of diluting the value of shares purchased by the hostile bidder and compensating the friendly bidder for its efforts. Depending on how the option is structured, it could even thwart the hostile takeover. In an asset lock-up, the target grants a friendly bidder the option to purchase an especially desirable asset, or crown jewel, at an attractive price. Crown jewel lock-ups often discourage hostile bidders because the potential loss of the asset significantly detracts from the target's value.

38. For example, this Court has upheld actions of directors when a board is confronted with a coercive "two-tiered" bust-up tender offer. *See Unocal*, 493 A.2d at 956.... *Compare Revlon*, 506 A.2d at 184.

in its own interests, rather than those of the corporation and its shareholders." *Unocal*, 493 A.2d at 954. For that reason, an "enhanced duty" must be met at the threshold before the board receives the normal protections of the business judgement rule. *Id.* Directors may not act out of a sole or primary desire to "perpetuate themselves in office." *Id.* at 955....

As we held in *Revlon*, when management of a target company determines that the company is for sale, the board's *responsibilities* under the enhanced *Unocal* standards are significantly altered. *Revlon*, 506 A.2d at 182. Although the board's *responsibilities* under *Unocal* are far different, the enhanced *duties* of the directors in responding to a potential shift in control, recognized in *Unocal*, remain unchanged. This principle pervades *Revlon*,[39] and when directors conclude that an auction is appropriate, the standard by which their ensuing actions will be judged continues to be the enhanced duty imposed by this Court in *Unocal*.

* * *

When *Revlon* duties devolve upon directors, this Court will continue to exact an enhanced judicial scrutiny at the threshold, as in *Unocal*, before the normal presumptions of the business judgment rule will apply. However, as we recognized in *Revlon*, the two part threshold test, of necessity, is slightly different. *Revlon*, 506 A.2d at 182.

At the outset, the plaintiff must show, and the trial court must find, that the directors of the target company treated one or more of the respective bidders on unequal terms. It is only then that the two-part threshold requirement of *Unocal* is truly invoked, for in *Revlon* we held that "[f]avoritism for a white knight to the total exclusion of a hostile bidder might be justifiable when the latter's offer adversely affects shareholder interests, but ... the directors cannot fulfill their enhanced *Unocal* duties by playing favorites with the contending factions." *Id.* 506 A.2d at 184.

In the face of disparate treatment, the trial court must first examine whether the directors properly perceived that shareholder interests were enhanced. In any event the board's action must be reasonable in relation to the advantage sought to be achieved, or conversely, to the threat which a particular bid allegedly poses to stockholder interests. *Unocal*, 493 A.2d at 955.

If on the basis of this enhanced *Unocal* scrutiny the trial court is satisfied that the test has been met, then the directors' actions necessarily are entitled to the protections of the business judgment rule. The latitude a board will have in responding to differing bids will vary according to the degree of benefit or detriment to the shareholders' general interests that the amount or terms of the bids pose. We stated in *Revlon*, and again here, that in a sale of corporate control the responsibility of the directors is to get the highest value reasonably attainable for the shareholders. *Revlon*, 506 A.2d at 182. Beyond that, there are no special and distinct "Revlon duties." Once a finding has been made by a

---

39. *See e.g. Revlon*, 506 A.2d at 184 ("Thus, when a board ends an intense bidding contest on an insubstantial basis, and where a significant by-product of that action is to protect the directors against a perceived threat of personal liability ... the action cannot withstand the enhanced scrutiny which *Unocal* requires of director conduct."). Further, "when bidders make relatively similar offers, or dissolution of the company becomes inevitable, the directors cannot fulfill their enhanced *Unocal* duties by playing favorites with the contending factions." *Id.*

court that the directors have fulfilled their fundamental duties of care and loyalty under the foregoing standards, there is no further judicial inquiry into the matter....

See also Gilson & Kraakman, Delaware's Intermediate Standard for Defensive Tactics: Is There Substance to Proportionality Review?, 44 Bus. Law. 247, 274 (1989) (suggesting the development of the proportionality test as a regulatory, rather than a threshold, test applied to diminish the risk of "substantive coercion: the prospect that shareholders who mistakenly disbelieve well-intentioned manager's representations about future value ... may be led to tender to a hostile bidder against their own best interests"); City Capital Assocs. LP. v. Interco Inc., 551 A.2d 787, 798 (Del. Ch. 1988), *appeal dismissed*, 556 A.2d 1070 (Del. 1988) (the "threat" which, for *Unocal* purposes, in Gilson-Kraakman terms poses the risk that stockholders will disbelieve the board's good faith valuation of the corporation, is insufficient to permit board to block third party offer and deprive stockholders of choice).

Paramount Communications Inc. v. QVC Network Inc.
637 A.2d 34 (Del. 1994)

VEASEY, Chief Justice.

In this appeal we review an order of the Court of Chancery dated November 24, 1993 (the "November 24 Order"), preliminarily enjoining certain defensive measures designed to facilitate a so-called strategic alliance between Viacom Inc. ("Viacom") and Paramount Communications Inc. ("Paramount") approved by the board of directors of Paramount (the "Paramount Board" or the "Paramount directors") and to thwart an unsolicited, more valuable, tender offer by QVC Network Inc. ("QVC"). In affirming, we hold that the sale of control in this case, which is at the heart of the proposed strategic alliance, implicates enhanced judicial scrutiny of the conduct of the Paramount Board under *Unocal Corp. v. Mesa Petroleum Co.*, Del. Supr. 493 A.2d 946 (1985), and *Revlon, Inc. v. MacAndrews & Forbes Holdings, Inc.*, Del. Supr., 506 A.2d 173 (1986). We further hold that the conduct of the Paramount Board was not reasonable as to process or result.

* * *

The Court of Chancery found that the Paramount directors violated their fiduciary duties by favoring the Paramount-Viacom transaction over the more valuable unsolicited offer of QVC. The Court of Chancery preliminarily enjoined Paramount and the individual defendants (the "Paramount defendants") from amending or modifying Paramount's stockholder rights agreement (the "Rights Agreement"), including the redemption of the Rights, or taking other action to facilitate the consummation of the pending tender offer by Viacom or any proposed second-step merger, including the Merger Agreement between Paramount and Viacom dated September 12, 1993 (the "Original Merger Agreement"), as amended on October 24, 1993 (the "Amended Merger Agreement"). Viacom and the Paramount defendants were enjoined from taking any action to exercise any provision of the Stock Option Agreement between Paramount and Viacom dated September 12, 1993 (the "Stock Option Agreement"), as amended on October 24, 1993. The Court of Chancery did not grant preliminary injunctive relief as to the termination fee provided for the benefit of Viacom in Section 8.05 of the Original Merger Agreement and the Amended Merger Agreement (the "Termination Fee").

Under the circumstances of this case, the pending sale of control implicated in the Paramount-Viacom transaction required the Paramount Board to act on an informed basis to secure the best value reasonably available to the stockholders. Since we agree with the Court of Chancery that the Paramount directors violated their fiduciary duties, we have AFFIRMED the entry of the order of the Vice Chancellor granting the preliminary injunction and have REMANDED these proceedings to the Court of Chancery for proceedings consistent herewith.

* * *

I. FACTS

* * *

Paramount is a Delaware corporation with its principal offices in New York City. Approximately 118 million shares of Paramount's common stock are outstanding and traded on the New York Stock Exchange. The majority of Paramount's stock is publicly held by numerous unaffiliated investors. Paramount owns and operates a diverse group of entertainment businesses, including motion picture and television studios, book publishers, professional sports teams and amusement parks.

There are 15 persons serving on the Paramount Board. Four directors are officer-employees of Paramount: Martin S. Davis ("Davis"), Paramount's Chairman and Chief Executive Officer since 1983; Donald Oresman ("Oresman"), Executive Vice-President, Chief Administrative Officer, and General Counsel; Stanley R. Jaffe, President and Chief Operating Officer; and Ronald L. Nelson, Executive Vice President and Chief Financial Officer. Paramount's 11 outside directors are distinguished and experienced business persons who are present or former senior executives of public corporations or financial institutions.

Viacom is a Delaware corporation with its headquarters in Massachusetts. Viacom is controlled by Sumner M. Redstone ("Redstone"), its Chairman and Chief Executive Officer, who owns indirectly approximately 85.2 percent of Viacom's voting Class A stock and approximately 69.2 percent of Viacom's nonvoting Class B stock through National Amusements, Inc. ("NAI"), an entity 91.7 percent owned by Redstone. Viacom has a wide range of entertainment operations, including a number of well-known cable television channels such as MTV, Nickelodeon, Showtime, and The Movie Channel. Viacom's equity co-investors in the Paramount-Viacom transaction include NYNEX Corporation and Blockbuster Entertainment Corporation.

QVC is a Delaware corporation with its headquarters in West Chester, Pennsylvania. QVC has several large stockholders, including Liberty Media Corporation, Comcast Corporation, Advance Publications, Inc., and Cox Enterprises Inc. Barry Diller ("Diller"), the Chairman and Chief Executive Officer of QVC, is also a substantial stockholder. QVC sells a variety of merchandise through a televised shopping channel. QVC has several equity co-investors in its proposed combination with Paramount including BellSouth Corporation and Comcast Corporation.

Beginning in the late 1980s, Paramount investigated the possibility of acquiring or merging with other companies in the entertainment, media, or communications industry. Paramount considered such transactions to be desirable, and perhaps necessary, in order to keep pace with competitors in the rapidly evolving field of entertainment and communications. Consistent with its goal of strategic expansion, Paramount made a tender offer for Time Inc. in 1989, but was ultimately unsuccessful. *See Paramount Communications, Inc. v. Time Inc.*, Del. Supr., 571 A.2d 1140 (1990) ("Time-Warner").

Although Paramount had considered a possible combination of Paramount and Viacom as early as 1990, recent efforts to explore such a transaction began at a dinner meeting between Redstone and Davis on April 20, 1993. Robert Greenhill ("Greenhill"), Chairman of Smith Barney Shearson Inc. ("Smith Barney"), attended and helped facilitate this meeting. After several more meetings between Redstone and Davis, serious negotiations began taking place in early July.

It was tentatively agreed that Davis would be the chief executive officer and Redstone would be the controlling stockholder of the combined company, but the parties could not reach agreement on the merger price and the terms of a stock option to be granted to Viacom. With respect to price, Viacom offered a package of cash and stock (primarily Viacom Class B nonvoting stock) with a market value of approximately $61 per share, but Paramount wanted at least $70 per share.

Shortly after negotiations broke down in July 1993, two notable events occurred. First, Davis apparently learned of QVC's potential interest in Paramount, and told Diller over lunch on July 21, 1993, that Paramount was not for sale. Second, the market value of Viacom's Class B nonvoting stock increased from $46.875 on July 6 to $57.25 on August 20. QVC claims (and Viacom disputes) that this price increase was caused by open market purchases of such stock by Redstone or entities controlled by him.

On August 20, 1993, discussions between Paramount and Viacom resumed when Greenhill arranged another meeting between Davis and Redstone. After a short hiatus, the parties negotiated in earnest in early September, and performed due diligence with the assistance of their financial advisors, Lazard Freres & Co. ("Lazard") for Paramount and Smith Barney for Viacom. On September 9, 1993, the Paramount Board was informed about the status of the negotiations and was provided information by Lazard, including an analysis of the proposed transaction.

On September 12, 1993, the Paramount Board met again and unanimously approved the Original Merger Agreement whereby Paramount would merge with and into Viacom. The terms of the merger provided that each share of Paramount common stock would be converted into 0.10 shares of Viacom Class A voting stock, 0.90 shares of Viacom Class B nonvoting stock, and $9.10 in cash. In addition, the Paramount Board agreed to amend its "poison pill" Rights Agreement to exempt the proposed merger with Viacom. The Original Merger Agreement also contained several provisions designed to make it more difficult for a potential competing bid to succeed. We focus, as did the Court of Chancery, on three of these defensive provisions: a "no-shop" provision (the "No-Shop Provision"), the Termination Fee, and the Stock Option Agreement.

First, under the No-Shop Provision, the Paramount Board agreed that Paramount would not solicit, encourage, discuss, negotiate, or endorse any competing transaction unless: (a) a third party "makes an unsolicited written, bona fide proposal, which is not subject to any material contingencies relating to financing"; and (b) the Paramount Board determines that discussions or negotiations with the third party are necessary for the Paramount Board to comply with its fiduciary duties.

Second, under the Termination Fee provision, Viacom would receive a $100 million termination fee if: (a) Paramount terminated the Original Merger Agreement because of a competing transaction; (b) Paramount's stockholders did not approve the merger; or (c) the Paramount Board recommended a competing transaction.

The third and most significant deterrent device was the Stock Option Agreement, which granted to Viacom an option to purchase approximately 19.9 percent (23,699,000 shares) of Paramount's outstanding common stock at $69.14 per share if any of the triggering events for the Termination Fee occurred. In addition to the customary terms that are normally associated with a stock option, the Stock Option Agreement contained two provisions that were both unusual and highly beneficial to Viacom: (a) Viacom was permitted to pay for the shares with a senior subordinated note of questionable marketability instead of cash, thereby avoiding the need to raise the $1.6 billion purchase price (the "Note Feature"); and (b) Viacom could elect to require Paramount to pay Viacom in cash a sum equal to the difference between the purchase price and the market price of Paramount's stock (the "Put Feature"). Because the Stock Option Agreement was not "capped" to limit its maximum dollar value, it had the potential to reach (and in this case did reach) unreasonable levels.

After the execution of the Original Merger Agreement and the Stock Option Agreement on September 12, 1993, Paramount and Viacom announced their proposed merger....

... Diller sent a letter to Davis on September 20, 1993, proposing a merger in which QVC would acquire Paramount for approximately $80 per share, consisting of 0.893 shares of QVC common stock and $30 in cash. QVC also expressed its eagerness to meet with Paramount to negotiate the details of a transaction. When the Paramount Board met on September 27, it was advised by Davis that the Original Merger Agreement prohibited Paramount from having discussions with QVC (or anyone else) unless certain conditions were satisfied. In particular, QVC had to supply evidence that its proposal was not subject to financing contingencies. The Paramount Board was also provided information from Lazard describing QVC and its proposal.

On October 5, 1993, QVC provided Paramount with evidence of QVC's financing. The Paramount Board then held another meeting on October 11, and decided to authorize management to meet with QVC. Davis also informed the Paramount Board that Booz-Allen & Hamilton ("Booz-Allen"), a management consulting firm, had been retained to assess, inter alia, the incremental earnings potential from a Paramount-Viacom merger and a Paramount-QVC merger. Discussions proceeded slowly....

On October 21, 1993, QVC filed this action and publicly announced an $80 cash tender offer for 51 percent of Paramount's outstanding shares (the "QVC tender offer"). Each remaining share of Paramount common stock would be converted into 1.42857 shares of QVC common stock in a second-step merger. The tender offer was conditioned on, among other things, the invalidation of the Stock Option Agreement, which was worth over $200 million by that point.[5] QVC contends that it had to commence a tender offer because of the slow pace of the merger discussions and the need to begin seeking clearance under federal antitrust laws.

Confronted by QVC's hostile bid, which on its face offered over $10 per share more than the consideration provided by the Original Merger Agreement, Viacom realized that it would need to raise its bid in order to remain competitive. Within hours after QVC's tender offer was announced, Viacom entered into discussions with Paramount concerning a revised transaction. These discussions led to serious negotiations concerning a comprehensive amendment to the original Paramount-Viacom transaction. In effect, the opportunity for a "new deal" with Viacom was at hand for the Paramount Board. With the QVC hostile bid offering greater value to the Paramount stockholders, the Paramount Board had considerable leverage with Viacom.

At a special meeting on October 24, 1993, the Paramount Board approved the Amended Merger Agreement and an amendment to the Stock Option Agreement. The

---

5. By November 15, 1993, the value of the Stock Option Agreement had increased to nearly $500 million based on the $90 QVC bid....

Amended Merger Agreement was, however, essentially the same as the Original Merger Agreement, except that it included a few new provisions. One provision related to an $80 per share cash tender offer by Viacom for 51 percent of Paramount's stock, and another changed the merger consideration so that each share of Paramount would be converted into 0.20408 shares of Viacom Class A voting stock, 1.08317 shares of Viacom Class B nonvoting stock, and 0.20408 shares of a new series of Viacom convertible preferred stock. The Amended Merger Agreement also added a provision giving Paramount the right not to amend its Rights Agreement to exempt Viacom if the Paramount Board determined that such an amendment would be inconsistent with its fiduciary duties because another offer constituted a "better alternative."[6] Finally, the Paramount Board was given the power to terminate the Amended Merger Agreement if it withdrew its recommendation of the Viacom transaction or recommended a competing transaction.

Although the Amended Merger Agreement offered more consideration to the Paramount stockholders and somewhat more flexibility to the Paramount Board than did the Original Merger Agreement, the defensive measures designed to make a competing bid more difficult were not removed or modified. In particular, there is no evidence in the record that Paramount sought to use its newly-acquired leverage to eliminate or modify the No-Shop Provision, the Termination Fee, or the Stock Option Agreement when the subject of amending the Original Merger Agreement was on the table.

Viacom's tender offer commenced on October 25, 1993, and QVC's tender offer was formally launched on October 27, 1993. Diller sent a letter to the Paramount Board on October 28 requesting an opportunity to negotiate with Paramount, and Oresman responded the following day by agreeing to meet. The meeting, held on November 1, was not very fruitful, however, after QVC's proposed guidelines for a "fair bidding process" were rejected by Paramount on the ground that "auction procedures" were inappropriate and contrary to Paramount's contractual obligations to Viacom.

On November 6, 1993, Viacom unilaterally raised its tender offer price to $85 per share in cash and offered a comparable increase in the value of the securities being proposed in the second-step merger. At a telephonic meeting held later that day, the Paramount Board agreed to recommend Viacom's higher bid to Paramount's stockholders.

QVC responded to Viacom's higher bid on November 12 by increasing its tender offer to $90 per share and by increasing the securities for its second-step merger by a similar amount. In response to QVC's latest offer, the Paramount Board scheduled a meeting for November 15, 1993. Prior to the meeting, Oresman sent the members of the Paramount Board a document summarizing the "conditions and uncertainties" of QVC's offer. One director testified that this document gave him a very negative impression of the QVC bid.

At its meeting on November 15, 1993, the Paramount Board determined that the new QVC offer was not in the best interests of the stockholders. The purported basis for this conclusion was that QVC's bid was excessively conditional. The Paramount Board did not communicate with QVC regarding the status of the conditions because it believed that the No-Shop Provision prevented such communication in the absence of firm financing. Several Paramount directors also testified that they believed the Viacom

---

6. Under the Amended Merger Agreement and the Paramount Board's resolutions approving it, no further action of the Paramount Board would be required in order for Paramount's Rights Agreement to be amended. As a result, the proper officers of the company were authorized to implement the amendment unless they were instructed otherwise by the Paramount Board.

transaction would be more advantageous to Paramount's future business prospects than a QVC transaction.[7] ...

The preliminary injunction hearing in this case took place on November 16, 1993. On November 19, Diller wrote to the Paramount Board to inform it that QVC had obtained financing commitments for its tender offer and that there was no antitrust obstacle to the offer. On November 24, 1993, the Court of Chancery issued its decision granting a preliminary injunction in favor of QVC and the plaintiff stockholders. This appeal followed.

II. APPLICABLE PRINCIPLES OF ESTABLISHED DELAWARE LAW

* * *

[T]here are rare situations which mandate that a court take a more direct and active role in overseeing the decisions made and actions taken by directors. In these situations, a court subjects the directors' conduct to enhanced scrutiny to ensure that it is reasonable.[9] ... The case at bar implicates two such circumstances: (1) the approval of a transaction resulting in a sale of control, and (2) the adoption of defensive measures in response to a threat to corporate control.

A. The Significance of a Sale or Change[10] of Control

When a majority of a corporation's voting shares are acquired by a single person or entity, or by a cohesive group acting together, there is a significant diminution in the voting power of those who thereby become minority stockholders....

.... Absent effective protective provisions, minority stockholders must rely for protection solely on the fiduciary duties owed to them by the directors and the majority stockholder, since the minority stockholders have lost the power to influence corporate direction through the ballot. The acquisition of majority status and the consequent privilege of exerting the powers of majority ownership come at a price. That price is usually a control premium which recognizes not only the value of a control block of shares, but also compensates the minority stockholders for their resulting loss of voting power.

In the case before us, the public stockholders (in the aggregate) currently own a majority of Paramount's voting stock. Control of the corporation is not vested in a single person, entity, or group, but vested in the fluid aggregation of unaffiliated stockholders. In the event the Paramount-Viacom transaction is consummated, the public stockholders will receive cash and a minority equity voting position in the surviving corporation. Following such consummation, there will be a controlling stockholder who will have the voting power to: (a) elect directors; (b) cause a break-up of the corporation: (c) merge it with another company; (d) cash-out the public stockholders: (e) amend the certificate of incorporation; (f) sell all or substantially all of the corporate assets; or (g)

---

7. This belief may have been based on a report prepared by Booz-Allen and distributed to the Paramount Board at its October 24 meeting. The report, which relied on public information regarding QVC, concluded that the synergies of a Paramount-Viacom merger were significantly superior to those of a Paramount-QVC merger. QVC has labelled the Booz-Allen report as a "joke."

9. Where actual self-interest is present and affects a majority of the directors approving a transaction, a court will apply even more exacting scrutiny to determine whether the transaction is entirely fair to the stockholders. E.g., Weinberger v. UOP, Inc., Del. Supr., 457 A.2d 701, 710-11 (1983); Nixon v. Blackwell, Del. Supr., 626 A.2d 1366, 1376 (1993).

10. For purposes of our December 9 Order and this Opinion, we have used the terms "sale of control" and "change of control" interchangeably without intending any doctrinal distinction.

otherwise alter materially the nature of the corporation and the public stockholders' interests. Irrespective of the present Paramount Board's vision of a long-term strategic alliance with Viacom, the proposed sale of control would provide the new controlling stockholder with the power to alter that vision.

Because of the intended sale of control, the Paramount-Viacom transaction has economic consequences of considerable significance to the Paramount stockholders. Once control has shifted, the current Paramount stockholders will have no leverage in the future to demand another control premium. As a result, the Paramount stockholders are entitled to receive, and should receive, a control premium and/or protective devices of significant value. There being no such protective provisions in the Viacom-Paramount transaction, the Paramount directors had an obligation to take the maximum advantage of the current opportunity to realize for the stockholders the best value reasonably available.

B. The Obligations of Directors in a Sale or Change of Control Transaction

The consequences of a sale of control impose special obligations on the directors of a corporation.[13] In particular, they have the obligation of acting reasonably to seek the transaction offering the best value reasonably available to the stockholders. The courts will apply enhanced scrutiny to ensure that the directors have acted reasonably....

In the sale of control context, the directors must focus on one primary objective—to secure the transaction offering the best value reasonably available for the stockholders—and they must exercise their fiduciary duties to further that end. The decisions of this Court have consistently emphasized this goal. *Revlon*, 506 A.2d at 182 ("The duty of the board ... [is] the maximization of the company's value at a sale for the stockholders' benefit."); [*Mills Acquisition Co. v. Macmillan, Inc.*, 559 A.2d 1261, 1288 (Del. 1989)] ("In a sale of corporate control the responsibility of the directors is to get the highest value reasonably attainable for the shareholders."); [*Barkan v. Amsted Indus. Inc.*, 567 A.2d 1279, 1286 (Del. 1989)] ("The board must act in a neutral manner to encourage the highest possible price for shareholders."). See also *Wilmington Trust Co. v. Coulter*, Del. Supr., 41 Del. Ch. 548, 200 A.2d 441, 448 (1964) (in the context of the duty of a trustee, "when all is equal ... it is plain that the Trustee is bound to obtain the best price obtainable").

In pursuing this objective, the directors must be especially diligent. See *Citron v. Fairchild Camera and Instrument Corp.*, Del. Supr., 569 A.2d 53, 66 (1989) (discussing "a board's active and direct role in the sale process"). In particular, this Court has stressed the importance of the board being adequately informed in negotiating a sale of control: "The need for adequate information is central to the enlightened evaluation of a transaction that a board must make." *Barkan*, 567 A.2d at 1287. This requirement is consistent with the general principle that "directors have a duty to

---

13. We express no opinion on any scenario except the actual facts before the Court, and our precise holding herein. Unsolicited tender offers in other contexts may be governed by different precedent. For example, where a potential sale of control by a corporation is not the consequence of a board's action, this Court has recognized the prerogative of a board of directors to resist a third party's unsolicited acquisition proposal or offer. See *Pogostin*, 480 A.2d at 627; *Time-Warner*, 571 A.2d at 1152; *Bershad v. Curtiss-Wright Corp.*, Del. Supr., 535 A.2d 840, 845 (1987); *Macmillan*, 559 A.2d at 1285 n. 35. The decision of a board to resist such an acquisition, like all decisions of a properly-functioning board, must be informed, *Unocal*, 493 A.2d at 954-55, and the circumstances of each particular case will determine the steps that a board must take to inform itself, and what other action, if any, is required as a matter of fiduciary duty.

inform themselves, prior to making a business decision, of all material information reasonably available to them." [*Aronson v. Lewis*, 473 A.2d 805, 812 (Del. 1984)].... Moreover, the role of outside, independent directors becomes particularly important because of the magnitude of a sale of control transaction and the possibility, in certain cases, that management may not necessarily be impartial. *See Macmillan*, 559 A.2d at 1285 (requiring "the intense scrutiny and participation of the independent directors").

Barkan teaches some of the methods by which a board can fulfill its obligation to seek the best value reasonably available to the stockholders. 567 A.2d at 1286-87. These methods are designed to determine the existence and viability of possible alternatives. They include conducting an auction, canvassing the market, etc. Delaware law recognizes that there is "no single blueprint" that directors must follow. *Id.* at 1286-87....

In determining which alternative provides the best value for the stockholders, a board of directors is not limited to considering only the amount of cash involved, and is not required to ignore totally its view of the future value of a strategic alliance. *See Macmillan*, 559 A.2d at 1282 n. 29. Instead, the directors should analyze the entire situation and evaluate in a disciplined manner the consideration being offered. Where stock or other non-cash consideration is involved, the board should try to quantify its value, if feasible, to achieve an objective comparison of the alternatives. In addition, the board may assess a variety of practical considerations relating to each alternative including:

> [an offer's] fairness and feasibility; the proposed or actual financing for the offer, and the consequences of that financing; questions of illegality; ... the risk of non-consummation; ... the bidder's identity, prior background and other business venture experiences; and the bidder's business plans for the corporation and their effects on stockholder interests.

Macmillan, 559 A.2d at 1282 n. 29. These considerations are important because the selection of one alternative may permanently foreclose other opportunities. While the assessment of these factors may be complex, the board's goal is straightforward: Having informed themselves of all material information reasonably available, the directors must decide which alternative is most likely to offer the best value reasonably available to the stockholders.

C. Enhanced Judicial Scrutiny of a Sale or Change of Control Transaction

Board action in the circumstances presented here is subject to enhanced scrutiny. Such scrutiny is mandated by: (a) the threatened diminution of the current stockholders' voting power; (b) the fact that an asset belonging to public stockholders (a control premium) is being sold and may never be available again: and (c) the traditional concern of Delaware courts for actions which impair or impede stockholder voting rights.... In *Macmillan*, this Court held:

> When *Revlon* duties devolve upon directors, this Court will continue to exact an enhanced judicial scrutiny at the threshold, as in *Unocal*, before the normal presumptions of the business judgment rule will apply.

559 A.2d at 1288. The *Macmillan* decision articulates a specific two-part test for analyzing board action where competing bidders are not treated equally:

> In the face of disparate treatment, the trial court must first examine whether the directors properly perceived that shareholder interests were enhanced. In any event the board's action must be reasonable in relation to the

advantage sought to be achieved, or conversely, to the threat which a particular bid allegedly poses to stockholder interests.

Id. See also Roberts v. General Instrument Corp., Del. Ch., C.A. No. 11639, Allen, C. (Aug. 13, 1990), reprinted at 16 Del. J. Corp. L. 1540, 1554 ("This enhanced test requires a judicial judgment of reasonableness in the circumstances.").

The key features of an enhanced scrutiny test are: (a) a judicial determination regarding the adequacy of the decisionmaking process employed by the directors, including the information on which the directors based their decision; and (b) a judicial examination of the reasonableness of the directors' action in light of the circumstances then existing. The directors have the burden of proving that they were adequately informed and acted reasonably.

Although an enhanced scrutiny test involves a review of the reasonableness of the substantive merits of a board's actions, a court should not ignore the complexity of the directors' task in a sale of control. There are many business and financial considerations implicated in investigating and selecting the best value reasonably available. The board of directors is the corporate decisionmaking body best equipped to make these judgments. Accordingly, a court applying enhanced judicial scrutiny should be deciding whether the directors made a reasonable decision, not a perfect decision. If a board selected one of several reasonable alternatives, a court should not second-guess that choice even though it might have decided otherwise or subsequent events may have cast doubt on the board's determination....

D. *Revlon* and *Time-Warner* Distinguished

The Paramount defendants and Viacom assert that the fiduciary obligations and the enhanced judicial scrutiny discussed above are not implicated in this case in the absence of a "break-up" of the corporation, and that the order granting the preliminary injunction should be reversed. This argument is based on their erroneous interpretation of our decisions in *Revlon* and *Time-Warner*.

.... Based on the facts and circumstances present in Revlon, we held that "the directors' role changed from defenders of the corporate bastion to auctioneers charged with getting the best price for the stockholders at a sale of the company." 506 A.2d at 182. We further held that "when a board ends an intense bidding contest on an insubstantial basis, ... [that] action cannot withstand the enhanced scrutiny which Unocal requires of director conduct." *Id.* at 184.

It is true that one of the circumstances bearing on these holdings was the fact that "the break-up of the company ... had become a reality which even the directors embraced." Id at 182. It does not follow, however, that a "break-up" must be present and "inevitable" before directors are subject to enhanced judicial scrutiny and are required to pursue a transaction that is calculated to produce the best value reasonably available to the stockholders. In fact, we stated in *Revlon* that "when bidders make relatively similar offers, or dissolution of the company becomes inevitable, the directors cannot fulfill their enhanced Unocal duties by playing favorites with the contending factions." *Id.* at 184 (emphasis added). *Revlon* thus does not hold that an inevitable dissolution or "break-up" is necessary.

* * *

[T]he Paramount defendants have interpreted our decision in *Time-Warner* as requiring a corporate break-up in order for that obligation to apply. The facts in *Time-Warner*, however, were quite different from the facts of this case, and refute Paramount's position here. In *Time-Warner*, the Chancellor held that there was no change of control in the original stock-for-stock merger between Time and Warner because Time would be owned by a fluid aggregation of unaffiliated stockholders both before and after the merger.... [*See*] Paramount Communications Inc. v. Time Inc., Del. Ch., No. 10866, Allen, C. (July 17, 1989), reprinted at 15 Del. J. Corp. L. 700, 739.... Moreover, the transaction actually consummated in *Time-Warner* was not a merger, as originally planned, but a sale of Warner's stock to Time.

In our affirmance of the Court of Chancery's well-reasoned decision, this Court held that "The Chancellor's findings of fact are supported by the record and his conclusion is correct as a matter of law." 571 A.2d at 1150 (emphasis added). Nevertheless, the Paramount defendants here have argued that a break-up is a requirement and have focused on the following language in our *Time-Warner* decision:

> However, we premise our rejection of plaintiffs' *Revlon* claim on different grounds, namely, the absence of any substantial evidence to conclude that Time's board, in negotiating with Warner, made the dissolution or break-up of the corporate entity inevitable, as was the case in *Revlon*.

> Under Delaware law there are, generally speaking and without excluding other possibilities, two circumstances which may implicate *Revlon* duties. The first, and clearer one, is when a corporation initiates an active bidding process seeking to sell itself or to effect a business reorganization involving a clear breakup of the company. However, *Revlon* duties may also be triggered where, in response to a bidder's offer, a target abandons its long-term strategy and seeks an alternative transaction involving the breakup of the company.

Id. at 1150 (emphasis added) (citation and footnote omitted).

The Paramount defendants have misread the holding of *Time-Warner*. Contrary to their argument, our decision in *Time-Warner* expressly states that the two general scenarios discussed in the above-quoted paragraph are not the only instances where "*Revlon* duties" may be implicated. The Paramount defendants' argument totally ignores the phrase "without excluding other possibilities." Moreover, the instant case is clearly within the first general scenario set forth in *Time-Warner*. The Paramount Board, albeit unintentionally, had "initiated an active bidding process seeking to sell itself" by agreeing to sell control of the corporation to Viacom in circumstances where another potential acquiror (QVC) was equally interested in being a bidder.

The Paramount defendants' position that both a change of control and a break-up are required must be rejected....

Accordingly, when a corporation undertakes a transaction which will cause: (a) a change in corporate control; or (b) a break-up of the corporate entity, the directors' obligation is to seek the best value reasonably available to the stockholders. This obligation arises because the effect of the Viacom-Paramount transaction, if consummated, is to shift control of Paramount from the public stockholders to a controlling stockholder, Viacom. Neither *Time-Warner* nor any other decision of this Court holds that a "break-up" of the company is essential to give rise to this obligation where there is a sale of control.

III. BREACH OF FIDUCIARY DUTIES BY PARAMOUNT BOARD

We now turn to duties of the Paramount Board under the facts of this case and our conclusions as to the breaches of those duties which warrant injunctive relief.

A. The Specific Obligations of the Paramount Board

Under the facts of this case, the Paramount directors had the obligation: (a) to be diligent and vigilant in examining critically the Paramount-Viacom transaction and the QVC tender offers; (b) to act in good faith; (c) to obtain, and act with due care on, all material information reasonably available, including information necessary to compare the two offers to determine which of these transactions, or an alternative course of action, would provide the best value reasonably available to the stockholders; and (d) to negotiate actively and in good faith with both Viacom and QVC to that end.

Having decided to sell control of the corporation, the Paramount directors were required to evaluate critically whether or not all material aspects of the Paramount-Viacom transaction (separately and in the aggregate) were reasonable and in the best interests of the Paramount stockholders in light of current circumstances, including: the change of control premium, the Stock Option Agreement, the Termination Fee, the coercive nature of both the Viacom and QVC tender offers,[18] the No-Shop Provision, and the proposed disparate use of the Rights Agreement as to the Viacom and QVC tender offers, respectively.

These obligations necessarily implicated various issues, including the questions of whether or not those provisions and other aspects of the Paramount-Viacom transaction (separately and in the aggregate): (a) adversely affected the value provided to the Paramount stockholders; (b) inhibited or encouraged alternative bids; (c) were enforceable contractual obligations in light of the directors' fiduciary duties; and (d) in the end would advance or retard the Paramount directors' obligation to secure for the Paramount stockholders the best value reasonably available under the circumstances.

The Paramount defendants contend that they were precluded by certain contractual provisions including the No-Shop Provision, from negotiating with QVC or seeking alternatives. Such provisions, whether or not they are presumptively valid in the abstract, may not validly define or limit the directors' fiduciary duties under Delaware law or prevent the Paramount directors from carrying out their fiduciary duties under Delaware law. To the extent such provisions are inconsistent with those duties, they are invalid and unenforceable. *See Revlon*, 506 A.2d at 184-85.

Since the Paramount directors had already decided to sell control, they had an obligation to continue their search for the best value reasonably available to the stockholders. This continuing obligation included the responsibility, at the October 24 board meeting and thereafter, to evaluate critically both the QVC tender offers and the Paramount-Viacom transaction to determine if: (a) the QVC tender offer was, or would continue to be, conditional; (b) the QVC tender offer could be improved; (c) the Viacom tender offer or other aspects of the Paramount-Viacom transaction could be improved; (d) each of the respective offers would be reasonably likely to come to closure, and under what circumstances; (e) other material information was reasonably available for consideration by the Paramount directors; (f) there were viable and realistic alternative courses of action; and (g) the timing constraints could be managed so the directors could consider these matters carefully and deliberately.

---

18. Both the Viacom and the QVC tender offers were for 51 percent cash and a "back-end" of various securities, the value of each of which depended on the fluctuating value of Viacom and QVC stock at any given time. Thus, both tender offers were two-tiered, front-end loaded, and coercive. Such coercive offers are inherently problematic and should be expected to receive particularly careful analysis by a target board. *See Unocal*, 493 A.2d at 956.

B. The Breaches of Fiduciary Duty by the Paramount Board

The Paramount directors made the decision on September 12, 1993, that, in their judgment, a strategic merger with Viacom on the economic terms of the Original Merger Agreement was in the best interests of Paramount and its stockholders. Those terms provided a modest change of control premium to the stockholders. The directors also decided at that time that it was appropriate to agree to certain defensive measures (the Stock Option Agreement, the Termination Fee, and the No-Shop Provision) insisted upon by Viacom as part of that economic transaction. Those defensive measures, coupled with the sale of control and subsequent disparate treatment of competing bidders, implicated the judicial scrutiny of *Unocal, Revlon, Macmillan*, and their progeny. We conclude that the Paramount directors' process was not reasonable, and the result achieved for the stockholders was not reasonable under the circumstances.

When entering into the Original Merger Agreement, and thereafter, the Paramount Board clearly gave insufficient attention to the potential consequences of the defensive measures demanded by Viacom. The Stock Option Agreement had a number of unusual and potentially "draconian"[19] provisions, including the Note Feature and the Put Feature. Furthermore, the Termination Fee, whether or not unreasonable by itself, clearly made Paramount less attractive to other bidders, when coupled with the Stock Option Agreement. Finally, the No-Shop Provision inhibited the Paramount Board's ability to negotiate with other potential bidders, particularly QVC which had already expressed an interest in Paramount.[20]

Throughout the applicable time period, and especially from the first QVC merger proposal on September 20 through the Paramount Board meeting on November 15, QVC's interest in Paramount provided the opportunity for the Paramount Board to seek significantly higher value for the Paramount stockholders than that being offered by Viacom. QVC persistently demonstrated its intention to meet and exceed the Viacom offers, and frequently expressed its willingness to negotiate possible further increases.

The Paramount directors had the opportunity in the October 23-24 time frame, when the Original Merger Agreement was renegotiated, to take appropriate action to modify the improper defensive measures as well as to improve the economic terms of the Paramount-Viacom transaction. Under the circumstances existing at that time, it should have been clear to the Paramount Board that the Stock Option Agreement, cou-

---

19. The Vice Chancellor so characterized the Stock Option Agreement. Court of Chancery Opinion, 635 A.2d at 1272. We express no opinion whether a stock option agreement of essentially this magnitude, but with a reasonable "cap" and without the Note and Put Features, would be valid or invalid under other circumstances. *See Hecco Ventures v. Sea-Land Corp.*, Del. Ch., C.A. No. 8486, Jacobs, V.C. (May 19, 1986) (21.7 percent stock option); *In re Vitalink Communications Corp. Shareholders Litig.*, Del. Ch., C.A. No. 12085, Chandler, V.C. (May 16, 1990) (19.9 percent stock option).

20. We express no opinion whether certain aspects of the No-Shop Provision here could be valid in another context. Whether or not it could validly have operated here at an early stage solely to prevent Paramount from actively "shopping" the company, it could not prevent the Paramount directors from carrying out their fiduciary duties in considering unsolicited bids or in negotiating for the best value reasonably available to the stockholders. *Macmillan*, 559 A.2d at 1287. As we said in *Barkan*: "Where a board has no reasonable basis upon which to judge the adequacy of a contemplated transaction, a no-shop restriction gives rise to the inference that the board seeks to forestall competing bids." 567 A.2d at 1288. *See also Revlon*, 506 A.2d at 184 (holding that "the no-shop provision, like the lock-up option, while not per se illegal, is impermissible under the *Unocal* standards when a board's primary duty becomes that of an auctioneer responsible for selling the company to the highest bidder").

pled with the Termination Fee and the No-Shop Clause, were impeding the realization of the best value reasonably available to the Paramount stockholders. Nevertheless, the Paramount Board made no effort to eliminate or modify these counterproductive devices, and instead continued to cling to its vision of a strategic alliance with Viacom. Moreover, based on advice from the Paramount management, the Paramount directors considered the QVC offer to be "conditional" and asserted that they were precluded by the No-Shop Provision from seeking more information from, or negotiating with, QVC.

By November 12, 1993, the value of the revised QVC offer on its face exceeded that of the Viacom offer by over $1 billion at then current values. This significant disparity of value cannot be justified on the basis of the directors' vision of future strategy, primarily because the change of control would supplant the authority of the current Paramount Board to continue to hold and implement their strategic vision in any meaningful way. Moreover, their uninformed process had deprived their strategic vision of much of its credibility....

When the Paramount directors met on November 15 to consider QVC's increased tender offer, they remained prisoners of their own misconceptions and missed opportunities to eliminate the restrictions they had imposed on themselves. Yet, it was not "too late" to reconsider negotiating with QVC. The circumstances existing on November 15 made it clear that the defensive measures, taken as a whole, were problematic: (a) the No-Shop Provision could not define or limit their fiduciary duties; (b) the Stock Option Agreement had become "draconian"; and (c) the Termination Fee, in context with all the circumstances, was similarly deterring the realization of possibly higher bids. Nevertheless, the Paramount directors remained paralyzed by their uninformed belief that the QVC offer was "illusory." This final opportunity to negotiate on the stockholders' behalf and to fulfill their obligation to seek the best value reasonably available was thereby squandered.

IV. VIACOM'S CLAIM OF VESTED CONTRACT RIGHTS

Viacom argues that it had certain "vested" contract rights with respect to the No-Shop Provision and the Stock Option Agreement. In effect, Viacom's argument is that the Paramount directors could enter into an agreement in violation of their fiduciary duties and then render Paramount, and ultimately its stockholders, liable for failing to carry out an agreement in violation of those duties. Viacom's protestations about vested rights are without merit. This Court has found that those defensive measures were improperly designed to deter potential bidders, and that such measures do not meet the reasonableness test to which they must be subjected. They are consequently invalid and unenforceable under the facts of this case.

The No-Shop Provision could not validly define or limit the fiduciary duties of the Paramount directors. To the extent that a contract, or a provision thereof, purports to require a board to act or not act in such a fashion as to limit the exercise of fiduciary duties, it is invalid and unenforceable. Cf. Wilmington Trust v. Coulter, 200 A.2d at 452-54. Despite the arguments of Paramount and Viacom to the contrary, the Paramount directors could not contract away their fiduciary obligations. Since the No-Shop Provision was invalid, Viacom never had any vested contract rights in the provision.

As discussed previously, the Stock Option Agreement contained several "draconian" aspects, including the Note Feature and the Put Feature. While we have held that lockup options are not per se illegal, see Revlon, 506 A.2d at 183, no options with similar features have ever been upheld by this Court. Under the circumstances of this case, the

Stock Option Agreement clearly is invalid. Accordingly, Viacom never had any vested contract rights in that Agreement.

Viacom, a sophisticated party with experienced legal and financial advisors, knew of (and in fact demanded) the unreasonable features of the Stock Option Agreement. It cannot be now heard to argue that it obtained vested contract rights by negotiating and obtaining contractual provisions from a board acting in violation of its fiduciary duties....

V. CONCLUSION

The realization of the best value reasonably available to the stockholders became the Paramount directors' primary obligation under these facts in light of the change of control. That obligation was not satisfied, and the Paramount Board's process was deficient. The directors' initial hope and expectation for a strategic alliance with Viacom was allowed to dominate their decisionmaking process to the point where the arsenal of defensive measures established at the outset was perpetuated (not modified or eliminated) when the situation was dramatically altered. QVC's unsolicited bid presented the opportunity for significantly greater value for the stockholders and enhanced negotiating leverage for the directors. Rather than seizing those opportunities, the Paramount directors chose to wall themselves off from material information which was reasonably available and to hide behind the defensive measures as a rationalization for refusing to negotiate with QVC or seeking other alternatives. Their view of the strategic alliance likewise became an empty rationalization as the opportunities for higher value for the stockholders continued to develop.

It is the nature of the judicial process that we decide only the case before us—a case which, on its facts, is clearly controlled by established Delaware law. Here, the proposed change of control and the implications thereof were crystal clear. In other cases they may be less clear. The holding of this case on its facts, coupled with the holdings of the principal cases discussed herein where the issue of sale of control is implicated, should provide a workable precedent against which to measure future cases.

[Affirmed and Remanded.]

Notes and Questions

1. What circumstances in QVC led the court to apply enhanced scrutiny review? Would "adoption of defensive measures in response to a threat to corporate control" alone have led the court to apply that standard? Would "the approval of a transaction resulting in sale of control" alone have? What about the reduction in voting power and alteration of voting rights? Does the particular sort of circumstance that triggers enhanced scrutiny review dictate the standard of analysis or is the standard of analysis the same without regard to what triggers it?

2. Notice that the phrase "Revlon duties" is almost completely absent from the QVC opinion. Do you read the opinion to imply that it is not meaningful to speak of a concept of "Revlon duties" under Delaware law? For such an interpretation and an examination of its practical consequences, see Cunningham & Yablon, Delaware Fiduciary Duty Law After QVC and Technicolor: A Unified Standard (and the End of Revlon Duties?), 49 Bus. Law. 1593 (1994) (consult also the charts at the end of this article for a graphical depiction of the structure of Delaware fiduciary duty law before and after QVC and Technicolor).

3. Does *QVC* embrace a shareholder primacy model? What consideration, if any, may a board give to the interests of nonshareholder constituencies in circumstances like those in *QVC*?

4. There is a vast body of literature dealing with a variety of issues raised by tender offers and related restructurings that have been a prominent feature of the corporate landscape in recent decades. A sampling of the literature focused on the law in Delaware includes: Bainbridge, The Business Judgment Rule as Abstention Doctrine, 57 Vand. L. Rev. 83 (2004); Cannon, Augmenting the Duties of Directors to Protect Minority Shareholders in the Context of Going-Private Transactions: The Case for Obligating Directors to Express a Valuation Opinion In Unilateral Tender Offers After Siliconix, Aquila and Pure Resources, 2003 Colum. Bus. L. Rev. 191; Campbell, The Impact of Modern Finance Theory In Acquisition Cases, 53 Syracuse L. Rev. 1 (2003); Hanewicz, When Silence is Golden: Why the Business Judgment Rule Should Apply to No-Shops in Stock-for-Stock Merger Agreements, 28 Iowa J. Corp. L. 205 (2003); Loewenstein, Unocal Revisited: No Tiger in the Tank, 27 J. Corp. L. 1 (2001); Gilson, Unocal Fifteen Years Later (And What We Can Do About It), 26 Del. J. Corp. L. 491 (2001).

A sampling of general treatments includes: Carney, The Illusory Protections of the Poison Pill, 79 Notre Dame L. Rev. 179 (2003); Bebchuk, Coates & Subramanian, The Powerful Antitakeover Force of Staggered Boards: Theory, Evidence, and Policy, 54 Stan. L. Rev. 887 (2002); Stern, A General Model for Corporate Acquisition Law, 26 J. Corp. L. 675 (2001).

b. A Board's Ability to Adopt Defensive Strategies

As you will see throughout this subsection, existing case law gives directors a great deal of discretion in responding to threatened tender offers. That directors should have such a role at all is not intuitively obvious. After all, technically, a tender offer is nothing more than the offer by a bidder to acquire the shares of a corporation from each of its stockholders. The practical consequence of a successful tender offer is, however, far more than the purchase of shares: It effects a wholesale change in control of the corporation. These transactions, then, are of great consequence to the future conduct of the corporation's business, and the involvement of directors at some level seems entirely appropriate.

The problem with providing a role for directors in responding to a tender offer is that the prospect of a change in control creates an inherent conflict of interest. A new owner may well want new management, and directors thus are presented with the spectre of losing their jobs. The fundamental problem presented, then, is that of determining when a board is acting in the interests of the corporation and when it is acting out of self-interest.

Stating the issue this starkly oversimplifies it somewhat. There may be a variety of reasons beyond naked self-interest for a board to erect obstacles to the completion of an unwanted takeover, no matter how financially attractive it is to the stockholders. In states that have adopted constituency statutes discussed *supra* at chapter 5, section 7, it is possible that directors have some obligation to look out for the interests of a wide variety of constituents who may be adversely affected by the offer. Even in Delaware, which has not adopted any constituency statute, the directors may believe in good faith that their long-term business plans are likely to produce higher long-term values for the stockholders, who may nevertheless be tempted by the short-term prospect of receiving a substantial premium over the market price of their shares. State anti-takeover statutes, discussed later in this chapter, have been adopted by a majority of jurisdictions to supplement the common law role of directors in responding to unwanted takeover attempts.

Notwithstanding these possibilities, some commentators have recognized the market for corporate control as an important method of monitoring management, and have suggested that the board should have no right (or at least limited rights) to interfere with the process. It is significant to note that institutional investors have been especially active in opposing managements' attempts to erect barriers to takeovers and have also opposed takeover legislation.

Takeover defenses, then, raise some of the most fundamental issues in corporate law, not the least of which are the nature and purpose of the corporation and the division of rights and duties among constituent groups and directors in corporate governance. A variety of defensive responses to unwanted takeover overtures have been developed since the early 1980s. The judicial response to the adoption of takeover defenses is explored immediately after the following problem.

(i) General Standard

Problem — Repelling the Hostile Tender Offer

Shylock is a wealthy businessman. He originally made his fortune by manufacturing venetian blinds, a business now carried on through Shylock's Shades, Inc. (the "Company"), a Delaware corporation in which he owns 40 percent of the common stock (the only authorized class of stock). The balance of the Company's stock is publicly held and is traded on the New York Stock Exchange. Shylock is chairman of the board and a director of the Company. The rest of the board consists of Shylock's daughter Jessica; Tubal, a partner in the investment banking firm of Tubal & Co.; Launcelot Gobbo, the Duke of Venice Professor of Banking Law at the University of Venice Law School; and Lorenzo, a partner in the law firm of Lorenzo Associates, longtime counsel to Shylock and the Company.

Shylock was getting a little bored of window treatments. To assuage his ennui, he became interested in acquiring another business. The business he targeted was Elsinore Bakery, Inc. ("Elsinore"), a manufacturer of Danish pastries. Elsinore, also a Delaware corporation, is a publicly held corporation whose shares are traded on the New York Stock Exchange. As he considered his acquisition, Shylock conceived a plan whereby he would create a conglomerate of corporations in businesses that intrigued him. The acquisition of Elsinore would merely be the first step.

One day, when Shylock was in the Company's counting room, he confided his dream to Jessica. Jessica encouraged him to pursue this plan.

Bolstered by Jessica's support, Shylock scheduled a meeting with Lorenzo, the Company's lawyer, and Tubal, its investment banker. They agreed that the plan was feasible and set out to structure it. The problems of making the Company the holding company of a conglomerate were deemed insurmountable, so they decided upon a reorganization whereby Shylock would set up a new Delaware corporation, Portia Holdings, Inc. ("Portia"), to which he would contribute his stock in the Company for 91 percent of the stock of Portia. Jessica, it was agreed, would contribute to Portia the 5 percent of the Company she owned in exchange for 9 percent of Portia's shares. Thus the Company would become a partially owned subsidiary of Portia, which in turn would be wholly owned by Shylock and Jessica. After this reorganization was completed, Portia would organize a new Delaware subsidiary, Claudius Holdings, Inc., to which Shylock (through Portia) would contribute sufficient cash to purchase 10 percent of the outstanding shares of Elsinore. The rest of the purchase price for Elsinore would be financed by Claudius through its issue of junk bonds underwritten by Tubal & Co. Claudius would make a tender offer for all of the outstanding shares of Elsinore, and would acquire any shares not tendered through a subsequent merger of Elsinore into Claudius. Claudius would then change its name to Elsinore Bakery, Inc. After these transactions were completed, the directors of the Company would also serve as the directors of Portia and Claudius.

Unbeknownst to Shylock, Elsinore's board of directors (consisting of four inside directors and five outside directors) had, at the urging of its president, Hamlet, recently decided upon a plan whereby Elsinore would diversify its business. After several months of discussion among the board, Elsinore's senior executives, Polonius & Co., Elsinore's investment banking firm (represented by Polonius, a partner in the firm), and Rosencrantz of Rosencrantz & Guildenstern, Elsinore's outside counsel, the board met to discuss the alternatives. Polonius presented an oral report to the board detailing his firm's efforts to find a suitable merger partner and elicit interest in a business combination with Elsinore. He concluded that only two alternatives were realistic: Macbeth, Inc. ("Macbeth"), a publicly held manufacturer of high quality cutlery, and Oberon, Inc. ("Oberon"), a publicly held manufacturer of men's underwear. Polonius presented financial, operating, and other information about both corporations, as well as his firm's assessment of the likely cost of acquisition and growth possibilities of each. He was very pessimistic about the prospects for the men's underwear market and, conversely, highly optimistic about the prospects for the cutlery market. Hamlet, who had also studied both corporations, opined that the corporate culture of Macbeth made it a better fit with Elsinore than Oberon, since, in part, the management and employees of Macbeth were far more dedicated to quality manufacturing than those of Oberon. At the conclusion of this meeting (which lasted five hours), the board unanimously authorized Hamlet to begin negotiations for a merger with Macbeth, with consideration for the merger to be one share of Elsinore Class A Convertible Preferred Stock (convertible, after two years, into two shares of Elsinore common stock). If all of the Class A Stock were converted at the end of the two-year period, the former Macbeth stockholders would own 50 percent of Elsinore.

Following his board's authorization, Shylock approached Hamlet. He proposed that Portia, through Claudius, make a friendly tender offer for all of the outstanding shares of Elsinore. Elsinore common was trading at $20 per share, and Shylock proposed to pay $30 per share in the tender offer, a substantial premium over market price. (Shylock's own projections, based on publicly available information of Elsinore, would permit him to pay up to $35 per share, a fact which he did not disclose to Hamlet.) He also indicated that Hamlet and the board would be expected to resign. Hamlet was not particularly receptive. He informed Shylock that Elsinore was not for sale, and in fact had other long-term business plans which it was more interested in pursuing (although he mentioned no details). Furthermore, Hamlet was very comfortable in his position with Elsinore, and was more than a little reluctant to give it up. He also had heard rumors that Shylock was interested in getting into the greenmail business, and doubted his management abilities. Shylock tried to persuade Hamlet, telling him about his great conglomeration plans.

The next morning, Shylock attended a board meeting at the Company and announced his plans to the board. He described his conversations with Hamlet, and insisted that the reorganization take place and that a hostile tender offer be made for Elsinore through Claudius. He explained that $35 per share would be affordable, but thought that $30 per share would also work and, obviously, would be a better deal for Portia. The board approved the making of the offer, and the lawyers and investment bankers went to work.

Following the formation of Portia and Claudius, the offer for any and all shares of Elsinore at $30 cash per share was begun. The Schedule TO filed by Claudius with the Securities and Exchange Commission announced its intent to acquire any untendered shares of Elsinore through a subsequent merger at $30 cash per share.

The Elsinore board met the next day. Hamlet made a two-hour presentation to the board. First, he reaffirmed his belief that the long-term success of Elsinore would be better served by a merger with Macbeth, and that Elsinore was not for sale. He also im- pugned Shylock's character to the board and informed it of his belief that $30 per share was grossly inadequate. Polonius concurred, and opined that a fair range of prices would be $34 to $40 per share. What neither Hamlet nor Polonius told the board (none of whom asked) was that neither of them had yet approached Macbeth to discuss a deal, although both felt confident, due to their friendship with Lady Macbeth (Macbeth's president), that a deal could be arranged. The board, after some discussion, adopted a plan pursuant to which it entered into a revolving credit agreement for a $2 billion loan with a syndicate of banks pursuant to which an event of default (and acceleration of the loan) would be declared if any third party acquired more than 49 percent of Elsinore's stock. In addition, it contributed 25 percent of Elsinore's common stock to a pre-exist- ing ESOP (bringing the ESOP's ownership to 35 percent) for which members of the Elsinore board served as trustees.

Portia, stymied by these measures, negotiated a friendly deal with Elsinore, predi- cated upon retaining Hamlet and Elsinore's senior management in their current posi- tions for five years, and an increase in price to $35 per share. The board issued a press release and filed a Schedule 14D-9 stating its belief that the corporation had gotten all it could out of baked goods and that the stockholders would receive the best value for their stock by selling into the Portia tender offer.

After Portia's tender offer statement was amended to reflect the terms of the friendly deal and the board's Schedule 14D-9 was filed, but before the tender offer's termination date, Oberon, Inc., announced its own offer for any and all shares of Elsi- nore's stock in exchange for preferred stock of Oberon which it valued at $38 per share. The day after this announcement, the Elsinore board met (at a meeting at which all of the directors were present and voting). The meeting lasted for eight hours, and included a lengthy presentation both by Rosencrantz, Elsinore's regular counsel, and Polonius, who appraised the value of Oberon's offer at $35 (based on public docu- ments issued by Oberon, including its tender offer statement). At the conclusion of the meeting, the board, voting 8 to 1, decided to recommend that the stockholders reject the Oberon deal. (The one dissenting director was one of the outside directors.) Con- sequently, the Elsinore board amended the loan agreement to permit only the Portia acquisition and agreed to vote the ESOP shares in favor of Portia, and the Portia deal was consummated.

Prior to the completion of Portia's tender offer, Ophelia, a minority stockholder of Elsinore, sued in Delaware Chancery Court to enjoin the Elsinore board from blocking the Oberon offer and accepting the Portia offer.

1. You are counsel for Ophelia. What arguments would you present?

2. You are counsel for the defendants. What arguments would you present?

3. You are the chancellor. How do you rule and why?

Unocal Corp. v. Mesa Petroleum Co.
493 A.2d 946 (Del. 1985)

MOORE, Justice.

We confront an issue of first impression in Delaware—the validity of a corporation's self-tender for its own shares which excludes from participation a stockholder making a hostile tender offer for the company's stock.

The Court of Chancery granted a preliminary injunction to the plaintiffs, Mesa Petroleum Co., Mesa Asset Co., Mesa Partners II, and Mesa Eastern, Inc. (collectively "Mesa"),[1] enjoining an exchange offer of the defendant, Unocal Corporation (Unocal) for its own stock. The trial court concluded that a selective exchange offer, excluding Mesa, was legally impermissible. We cannot agree with such a blanket rule. The factual findings of the Vice Chancellor, fully supported by the record, establish that Unocal's board, consisting of a majority of independent directors, acted in good faith, and after reasonable investigation found that Mesa's tender offer was both inadequate and coercive. Under the circumstances the board had both the power and duty to oppose a bid it perceived to be harmful to the corporate enterprise. On this record we are satisfied that the device Unocal adopted is reasonable in relation to the threat posed, and that the board acted in the proper exercise of sound business judgment. We will not substitute our views for those of the board if the latter's decision can be "attributed to any rational business purpose." *Sinclair Oil Corp. v. Levien*, Del. Supr., 280 A.2d 717, 720 (1971). Accordingly, we reverse the decision of the Court of Chancery and order the preliminary injunction vacated.

I.

The factual background of this matter bears a significant relationship to its ultimate outcome.

On April 8, 1985, Mesa, the owner of approximately 13% of Unocal's stock, commenced a two-tier "front loaded" cash tender offer for 64 million shares, or approximately 37%, of Unocal's outstanding stock at a price of $54 per share. The "back-end" was designed to eliminate the remaining publicly held shares by an exchange of securities purportedly worth $54 per share. However, ... Mesa issued a supplemental proxy statement to Unocal's stockholders disclosing that the securities offered in the second-step merger would be highly subordinated, and that Unocal's capitalization would differ significantly from its present structure. Unocal has rather aptly termed such securities "junk bonds."

Unocal's board consists of eight independent outside directors and six insiders. It met on April 13, 1985, to consider the Mesa tender offer. Thirteen directors were present, and the meeting lasted nine and one-half hours. The directors were given no agenda or written materials prior to the session. However, detailed presentations were

---

1. T. Boone Pickens, Jr., is President and Chairman of the Board of Mesa Petroleum and President of Mesa Asset and controls the related Mesa entities.

made by legal counsel regarding the board's obligations under both Delaware corporate law and the federal securities laws. The board then received a presentation from Peter Sachs on behalf of Goldman Sachs & Co. (Goldman Sachs) and Dillon, Read & Co. (Dillon Read) discussing the bases for their opinions that the Mesa proposal was wholly inadequate. Mr. Sachs opined that the minimum cash value that could be expected from a sale or orderly liquidation for 100% of Unocal's stock was in excess of $60 per share. In making his presentation, Mr. Sachs showed slides outlining the valuation techniques used by the financial advisors, and others, depicting recent business combinations in the oil and gas industry....

Mr. Sachs also presented various defensive strategies available to the board if it concluded that Mesa's two-step tender offer was inadequate and should be opposed. One of the devices outlined was a self-tender by Unocal for its own stock with a reasonable price range of $70 to $75 per share. The cost of such a proposal would cause the company to incur $6.1-6.5 billion of additional debt, and a presentation was made informing the board of Unocal's ability to handle it. The directors were told that the primary effect of this obligation would be to reduce exploratory drilling, but that the company would nonetheless remain a viable entity.

The eight outside directors, comprising a clear majority of the thirteen members present, then met separately with Unocal's financial advisors and attorneys. Thereafter, they unanimously agreed to advise the board that it should reject Mesa's tender offer as inadequate, and that Unocal should pursue a self-tender to provide the stockholders with a fairly priced alternative to the Mesa proposal. The board then reconvened and unanimously adopted a resolution rejecting as grossly inadequate Mesa's tender offer. Despite the nine and one-half hour length of the meeting, no formal decision was made on the proposed defensive self-tender.

On April 15, the board met again with four of the directors present by telephone and one member still absent. This session lasted two hours. Unocal's Vice President of Finance and its Assistant General Counsel made a detailed presentation of the proposed terms of the exchange offer. A price range between $70 and $80 per share was considered, and ultimately the directors agreed upon $72. The board was also advised about the debt securities that would be issued, and the necessity of placing restrictive covenants upon certain corporate activities until the obligations were paid. The board's decisions were made in reliance on the advice of its investment bankers, including the terms and conditions upon which the securities were to be issued. Based upon this advice, and the board's own deliberations, the directors unanimously approved the exchange offer. Their resolution provided that if Mesa acquired 64 million shares of Unocal stock through its own offer (the Mesa Purchase Condition), Unocal would buy the remaining 49% outstanding for an exchange of debt securities having an aggregate par value of $72 per share. The board resolution also stated that the offer would be subject to other conditions..., including the exclusion of Mesa from the proposal (the Mesa exclusion)....

Unocal's exchange offer was commenced on April 17, 1985, and Mesa promptly challenged it by filing this suit in the Court of Chancery. On April 22, the Unocal board met again....

[At the meeting, legal] counsel advised that under Delaware law Mesa could only be excluded [from Unocal's exchange offer] for what the directors reasonably believed to be a valid corporate purpose. The directors' discussion centered on the objective of adequately compensating shareholders at the "back-end" of Mesa's proposal, which the latter would finance with "junk bonds." To include Mesa would defeat that goal, because under the proration aspect of the exchange offer (49%) every Mesa share accepted by Unocal would displace one held by another stockholder. Further, if Mesa were permitted to tender to Unocal, the latter would in effect be financing Mesa's own inadequate proposal.

* * *

Meanwhile, on April 22, 1985, Mesa amended its complaint in this action to challenge the Mesa exclusion. . . .

On April 29, 1985, the Vice Chancellor temporarily restrained Unocal from proceeding with the exchange offer unless it included Mesa. The trial court recognized that directors could oppose, and attempt to defeat, a hostile takeover which they considered adverse to the best interests of the corporation. However, the Vice Chancellor decided that in a selective purchase of the company's stock, the corporation bears the burden of showing: (1) a valid corporate purpose, and (2) that the transaction was fair to all of the stockholders, including those excluded.

* * *

II.

The issues we address involve these fundamental questions: Did the Unocal board have the power and duty to oppose a takeover threat it reasonably perceived to be harmful to the corporate enterprise, and if so, is its action here entitled to the protection of the business judgment rule?

Mesa contends that the discriminatory exchange offer violates the fiduciary duties Unocal owes it. Mesa argues that because of the Mesa exclusion the business judgment rule is inapplicable, because the directors by tendering their own shares will derive a financial benefit that is not available to *all* Unocal stockholders. Thus, it is Mesa's ultimate contention that Unocal cannot establish that the exchange offer is fair to *all* shareholders, and argues that the Court of Chancery was correct in concluding that Unocal was unable to meet this burden.

Unocal answers that it does not owe a duty of "fairness" to Mesa, given the facts here. Specifically, Unocal contends that its board of directors reasonably and in good faith concluded that Mesa's $54 two-tier tender offer was coercive and inadequate, and that Mesa sought selective treatment for itself. Furthermore, Unocal argues that the board's approval of the exchange offer was made in good faith, on an informed basis, and in the exercise of due care. Under these circumstances, Unocal contends that its directors properly employed this device to protect the company and its stockholders from Mesa's harmful tactics.

III.

We begin with the basic issue of the power of a board of directors of a Delaware corporation to adopt a defensive measure of this type. Absent such authority, all other questions are moot. . . .

The board has a large reservoir of authority upon which to draw. Its duties and responsibilities proceed from the inherent powers conferred by 8 *Del. C.* §141(a), respecting management of the corporation's "business and affairs."[6] Additionally, the powers

---

6. The general grant of power to a board of directors is conferred by 8 *Del. C.* §141(a), which provides:

(a) The business *and affairs* of every corporation organized under this chapter shall be

here being exercised derive from 8 *Del. C.* §160(a), conferring broad authority upon a corporation to deal in its own stock.[7] From this it is now well established that in the acquisition of its shares a Delaware corporation may deal selectively with its stockholders, provided the directors have not acted out of a sole or primary purpose to entrench themselves in office....

Finally, the board's power to act derives from its fundamental duty and obligation to protect the corporate enterprise, which includes stockholders, from harm reasonably perceived, irrespective of its source.... Thus, we are satisfied that in the broad context of corporate governance, including issues of fundamental corporate change, a board of directors is not a passive instrumentality.

Given the foregoing principles, we turn to the standards by which director action is to be measured. In *Pogostin v. Rice*, Del. Supr., 480 A.2d 619 (1984), we held that the business judgment rule, including the standards by which director conduct is judged, is applicable in the context of a takeover. *Id.* at 627. The business judgment rule is a "presumption that in making a business decision the directors of a corporation acted on an informed basis, in good faith and in the honest belief that the action taken was in the best interests of the company." *Aronson v. Lewis*, Del. Supr., 473 A.2d 805, 812 (1984) (citations omitted). A hallmark of the business judgment rule is that a court will not substitute its judgment for that of the board if the latter's decision can be "attributed to any rational business purpose." *Sinclair Oil Corp. v. Levien*, Del. Supr., 280 A.2d 717, 720 (1971).

When a board addresses a pending takeover bid it has an obligation to determine whether the offer is in the best interests of the corporation and its shareholders. In that respect a board's duty is no different from any other responsibility it shoulders, and its decisions should be no less entitled to the respect they otherwise would be accorded in the realm of business judgment.[9] ... There are, however, certain caveats to a proper exercise of this function. Because of the omnipresent specter that a board may be acting primarily in its own interests, rather than those of the corporation and its shareholders, there is an enhanced duty which calls for judicial examination at the threshold before the protections of the business judgment rule may be conferred.

This Court has long recognized that:

> We must bear in mind the inherent danger in the purchase of shares with corporate funds to remove a threat to corporate policy when a threat to control is

---

managed by or under the direction of a board of directors, except as may be otherwise provided in this chapter or in its certificate of incorporation. If any such provision is made in the certificate of incorporation, the powers and duties conferred or imposed upon the board of directors by this chapter shall be exercised or performed to such extent and by such person or persons as shall be provided in the certificate of incorporation. (Emphasis added)

7. This power under 8 *Del. C.* §160(a), with certain exceptions not pertinent here, is as follows: (a) Every corporation may purchase, redeem, receive, take or otherwise acquire, own and hold, sell, lend, exchange, transfer or otherwise dispose of, pledge, use and otherwise deal in and with its own shares;....

9. This is a subject of intense debate among practicing members of the bar and legal scholars. Excellent examples of these contending views are: Block & Miller, *The Responsibilities and Obligations of Corporate Directors in Takeover Contests*, 11 Sec. Reg. L.J. 44 (1983); Easterbrook & Fischel, *Takeover Bids, Defensive Tactics, and Shareholders' Welfare*, 36 Bus. Law. 1733 (1981); Easterbrook & Fischel, *The Proper Role of a Target's Management In Responding to a Tender Offer*, 94 Harv. L. Rev. 1161 (1981). Herzel, Schmidt & Davis, *Why Corporate Directors Have a Right To Resist Tender Offers*, 3 Corp. L. Rev. 107 (1980); Lipton, *Takeover Bids in the Target's Boardroom*, 35 Bus. Law. 101 (1979).

involved. The directors are of necessity confronted with a conflict of interest, and an objective decision is difficult.

Bennett v. Propp, Del. Supr., 187 A.2d 405, 409 (1962). In the face of this inherent conflict directors must show that they had reasonable grounds for believing that a danger to corporate policy and effectiveness existed because of another person's stock ownership. *Cheff v. Mathes*, 199 A.2d [548, 554-55 (Del. 1964)]. However, they satisfy that burden "by showing good faith and reasonable investigation...." *Id.* at 555. Furthermore, such proof is materially enhanced, as here, by the approval of a board comprised of a majority of outside independent directors who have acted in accordance with the foregoing standards....

IV.

A.

In the board's exercise of corporate power to forestall a takeover bid our analysis begins with the basic principle that corporate directors have a fiduciary duty to act in the best interests of the corporation's stockholders.... As we have noted, their duty of care extends to protecting the corporation and its owners from perceived harm whether a threat originates from third parties or other shareholders.[10] But such powers are not absolute. A corporation does not have unbridled discretion to defeat any perceived threat by any Draconian means available.

The restriction placed upon a selective stock repurchase is that the directors may not have acted solely or primarily out of a desire to perpetuate themselves in office. *See Cheff v. Mathes*, 199 A.2d at 556; *Kors v. Carey*, 158 A.2d at 140. Of course, to this is added the further caveat that inequitable action may not be taken under the guise of law. *Schnell v. Chris-Craft Industries, Inc.*, Del. Supr., 285 A.2d 437, 439 (1971). The standard of proof established in *Cheff v. Mathes* ... is designed to ensure that a defensive measure to thwart or impede a takeover is indeed motivated by a good faith concern for the welfare of the corporation and its stockholders, which in all circumstances must be free of any fraud or other misconduct. *Cheff v. Mathes*, 199 A.2d at 554-55. However, this does not end the inquiry.

B.

A further aspect is the element of balance. If a defensive measure is to come within the ambit of the business judgment rule, it must be reasonable in relation to the threat posed. This entails an analysis by the directors of the nature of the takeover bid and its effect on the corporate enterprise. Examples of such concerns may include: inadequacy of the price offered, nature and timing of the offer, questions of illegality, the impact on "constituencies" other than shareholders (i.e., creditors, customers, employees, and perhaps even the community generally), the risk of nonconsummation, and the quality of securities being offered in the exchange. *See* Lipton and Brownstein, *Takeover Responses and Directors' Responsibilities: An Update*, p. 7, ABA National Institute on the Dynamics of Corporate Control (December 8, 1983). While not a controlling factor, it also seems to us that a board may reasonably consider the basic stockholder interests at stake, including those of short term speculators, whose actions may have fueled the

---

10. It has been suggested that a board's response to a takeover threat should be a passive one. Easterbrook & Fischel, *supra*, 36 Bus. Law. at 1750. However, that clearly is not the law of Delaware, and as the proponents of this rule of passivity readily concede, it has not been adopted either by courts or state legislatures. Easterbrook & Fischel, *supra*, 94 Harv. L. Rev. at 1194.

coercive aspect of the offer at the expense of the long term investor.[11] Here, the threat posed was viewed by the Unocal board as a grossly inadequate two-tier coercive tender offer coupled with the threat of greenmail.

Specifically, the Unocal directors had concluded that the value of Unocal was substantially above the $54 per share offered in cash at the front end. Furthermore, they determined that the subordinated securities to be exchanged in Mesa's announced squeeze out of the remaining shareholders in the "back-end" merger were "junk bonds" worth far less than $54. It is now well recognized that such offers are a classic coercive measure designed to stampede shareholders into tendering at the first tier, even if the price is inadequate, out of fear of what they will receive at the back end of the transaction. Wholly beyond the coercive aspect of an inadequate two-tier tender offer, the threat was posed by a corporate raider with a national reputation as a "greenmailer."[13]

In adopting the selective exchange offer, the board stated that its objective was either to defeat the inadequate Mesa offer or, should the offer still succeed, provide the 49% of its stockholders, who would otherwise be forced to accept "junk bonds," with $72 worth of senior debt. We find that both purposes are valid.

However, such efforts would have been thwarted by Mesa's participation in the exchange offer. First, if Mesa could tender its shares, Unocal would effectively be subsidizing the former's continuing effort to buy Unocal stock at $54 per share. Second, Mesa could not, by definition, fit within the class of shareholders being protected from its own coercive and inadequate tender offer.

Thus, we are satisfied that the selective exchange offer is reasonably related to the threats posed. It is consistent with the principle that "the minority stockholder shall receive the substantial equivalent in value of what he had before." *Sterling v. Mayflower Hotel Corp.*, Del. Supr., 93 A.2d 107, 114 (1952). *See also Rosenblatt v. Getty Oil Co.*, Del. Supr., 493 A.2d 929, 940 (1985). This concept of fairness, while stated in the merger context, is also relevant in the area of tender offer law. Thus, the board's decision to offer what it determined to be the fair value of the corporation to the 49% of its shareholders, who would otherwise be forced to accept highly subordinated "junk bonds", is reasonable and consistent with the directors' duty to ensure that the minority stockholders receive equal value for their shares.

---

11. There has been much debate respecting such stockholder interests. One rather impressive study indicates that the stock of over 50 percent of target companies, who resisted hostile takeovers, later traded at higher market prices than the rejected offer price, or were acquired after the tender offer was defeated by another company at a price higher than the offer price. *See* Lipton, *supra* 35 Bus. Law. at 106-109, 132-133. Moreover, an update by Kidder Peabody & Company of this study, involving the stock prices of target companies that have defeated hostile tender offers during the period from 1973 to 1982 demonstrates that in a majority of cases the target's shareholders benefited from the defeat. The stock of 81% of the targets studied has, since the tender offer, sold at prices higher than the tender offer price. When adjusted for the time value of money, the figure is 64%. *See* Lipton & Brownstein, *supra* ABA Institute at 10. The thesis being that this strongly supports application of the business judgment rule in response to takeover threats. There is, however, a rather vehement contrary view. *See* Easterbrook & Fischel, *supra* 36 Bus. Law. at 1739-1745.

13. The term "greenmail" refers to the practice of buying out a takeover bidder's stock at a premium that is not available to other shareholders in order to prevent the takeover. The Chancery Court noted that "Mesa has made tremendous profits from its takeover activities although in the past few years it has not been successful in acquiring any of the target companies on an unfriendly basis." Moreover, the trial court specifically found that the actions of the Unocal board were taken in good faith to eliminate both the inadequacies of the tender offer and to forestall the payment of "greenmail."

V.

Mesa contends that it is unlawful, and the trial court agreed, for a corporation to discriminate in this fashion against one shareholder. It argues correctly that no case has ever sanctioned a device that precludes a raider from sharing in a benefit available to all other stockholders. However, as we have noted earlier, the principle of selective stock repurchases by a Delaware corporation is neither unknown nor unauthorized.... The only difference is that heretofore the approved transaction was the payment of "greenmail" to a raider or dissident posing a threat to the corporate enterprise. All other stockholders were denied such favored treatment, and given Mesa's past history of greenmail, its claims here are rather ironic.

* * *

Thus, while the exchange offer is a form of selective treatment, given the nature of the threat posed here the response is neither unlawful nor unreasonable. If the board of directors is disinterested, has acted in good faith and with due care, its decision in the absence of an abuse of discretion will be upheld as a proper exercise of business judgment.

To this Mesa responds that the board is not disinterested, because the directors are receiving a benefit from the tender of their own shares, which because of the Mesa exclusion, does not devolve upon all stockholders equally. See *Aronson v. Lewis*, Del. Supr., 473 A.2d 805, 812 (1984). However, Mesa concedes that if the exclusion is valid, then the directors and all other stockholders share the same benefit. The answer of course is that the exclusion is valid, and the directors' participation in the exchange offer does not rise to the level of a disqualifying interest....

Nor does this become an "interested" director transaction merely because certain board members are large stockholders. As this Court has previously noted, that fact alone does not create a disqualifying "personal pecuniary interest" to defeat the operation of the business judgment rule. *Cheff v. Mathes*, 199 A.2d at 554.

Mesa also argues that the exclusion permits the directors to abdicate the fiduciary duties they owe it. However, that is not so. The board continues to owe Mesa the duties of due care and loyalty. But in the face of the destructive threat Mesa's tender offer was perceived to pose, the board had a supervening duty to protect the corporate enterprise, which includes the other shareholders, from threatened harm.

Mesa contends that the basis of this action is punitive, and solely in response to the exercise of its rights of corporate democracy. Nothing precludes Mesa, as a stockholder, from acting in its own self-interest.... However, Mesa, while pursuing its own interests, has acted in a manner which a board consisting of a majority of independent directors has reasonably determined to be contrary to the best interests of Unocal and its other shareholders. In this situation, there is no support in Delaware law for the proposition that, when responding to a perceived harm, a corporation must guarantee a benefit to a stockholder who is deliberately provoking the danger being addressed. There is no obligation of self-sacrifice by a corporation and its shareholders in the face of such a challenge.

Here, the Court of Chancery specifically found that the "directors' decision [to oppose the Mesa tender offer] was made in the good faith belief that the Mesa tender offer is inadequate." Given our standard of review under *Levitt v. Bouvier*, Del. Supr., 287 A.2d 671, 673 (1972), and *Application of Delaware Racing Association*, Del. Supr., 213 A.2d 203, 207 (1965), we are satisfied that Unocal's board has met its burden of proof. *Cheff v. Mathes*, 199 A.2d at 555.

VI.

In conclusion, there was directorial power to oppose the Mesa tender offer, and to undertake a selective stock exchange made in good faith and upon a reasonable investigation pursuant to a clear duty to protect the corporate enterprise. Further, the selective stock repurchase plan chosen by Unocal is reasonable in relation to the threat that the board rationally and reasonably believed was posed by Mesa's inadequate and coercive two-tier tender offer. Under those circumstances the board's action is entitled to be measured by the standards of the business judgment rule. Thus, unless it is shown by a preponderance of the evidence that the directors' decisions were primarily based on perpetuating themselves in office, or some other breach of fiduciary duty such as fraud, overreaching, lack of good faith, or being uninformed, a Court will not substitute its judgment for that of the board.

In this case that protection is not lost merely because Unocal's directors have tendered their shares in the exchange offer. Given the validity of the Mesa exclusion, they are receiving a benefit shared generally by all other stockholders except Mesa. In this circumstance the test of *Aronson v. Lewis*, 473 A.2d at 812, is satisfied. *See also Cheff v. Mathes*, 199 A.2d at 554. If the stockholders are displeased with the action of their elected representatives, the powers of corporate democracy are at their disposal to turn the board out. *Aronson v. Lewis*, Del. Supr., 473 A.2d 805, 811 (1984). *See also* 8 *Del. C.* §§141(k) and 211(b).

With the Court of Chancery's findings that the exchange offer was based on the board's good faith belief that the Mesa offer was inadequate, that the board's action was informed and taken with due care, that Mesa's prior activities justify a reasonable inference that its principle objective was greenmail, and implicitly, that the substance of the offer itself was reasonable and fair to the corporation and its stockholders if Mesa were included, we cannot say that the Unocal directors have acted in such a manner as to have passed an "unintelligent and unadvised judgment." *Mitchell v. Highland-Western Glass Co.*, Del.Ch., 167 A. 831, 833 (1933). The decision of the Court of Chancery is therefore REVERSED, and the preliminary injunction is VACATED.

Federal law now prohibits public companies from engaging in exclusionary tender or exchange offers like the one described in *Unocal*. Under Securities Exchange Act Rule 14d-10(a)(1) (known as the "all holders rule"), a bidder must accept tenders of shares from all holders of the class of equity securities being sought by the bidder. *Unocal's* basic standard of review of defensive measures, however, remains substantially in tact.

Notes and Questions

1. If the duty of directors is to maximize stockholder value, why do they have any power at all to interfere with control transactions? Why not allow the market to perform its role in an unfettered manner?

2. At several points in the *Unocal* opinion, the court stresses the fact that a majority of the directors were "outside" or "independent." In recent decades, the Delaware Supreme Court, particularly in tender offer cases, increasingly came to rely upon an independent board as a significant, if not determinative, factor in legitimating board action that might otherwise be suspect as self-interested. *See, e.g.,* In re The MONY

Group Inc. Shareholder Litigation, 853 A.2d 661, 666-67 (Del. Ch. 2004) ("[T]he court finds that a disinterested and independent majority of the defendant directors acted in accordance with their fiduciary duties.... Because that decision ... permits a full and fair vote, the court will review it under the business judgment rule."); Paramount Comm. Inc. v. QVC Network, Inc., 637 A.2d 34, 31 (1994) ("[T]he role of outside, independent directors becomes particularly important because of the magnitude of a sale of control transaction and the possibility, in certain cases, that management may not necessarily be impartial."); Solomon v. Armstrong, 747 A.2d 1098, 1113 (Del. Ch. 1999) ("[T]he director defendants must prove that the disputed transaction is entirely fair. The burden of proof, however, can be shifted to the plaintiffs to the extent that the board of directors can establish that it was able to construct a fair process. This showing can be achieved, for example, through the board's use of a well-functioning committee of independent directors."); Nixon v. Blackwell, 626 A.2d 1366, 1375 (Del. 1992) ("In business judgment rule cases, an essential element is the fact that there has been a business decision made by a disinterested and independent corporate decisionmaker."); Mills Acquisition Co. v. MacMillan, Inc., 559 A.2d 1261, 1287 (Del. 1988) ("In the absence of self-interest, and upon meeting the enhanced duty mandated by *Unocal*, the actions of an independent board of directors in designing and conducting a corporate auction are protected by the business judgment rule. [citations omitted]"); Ivanhoe Partners v. Newmont Mining Corp., 535 A.2d 1334, 1343 (Del. 1987) (noting that proof that board satisfied first prong of *Unocal* test is "materially enhanced" where majority of directors were independent).

Chancellor Allen has discussed the importance of independent directors to maintaining transactional integrity, and has evaluated the likelihood that independent directors could truly be effective, particularly in light of some glaring failed cases and a wide spectrum of academic views doubting the true independence of the so-called independent director. He concluded as follows:

> Thus, in the sale context, the Delaware cases suggest that it *is* possible for "outside" directors to function independently, in a way that at least at a preliminary injunction stage, satisfies the standards of a dispassionate and experienced reviewing court.
>
> But those cases demonstrate as well that not every decision by an apparently disinterested special committee deserves or will be accorded that respect.
>
> The factor that distinguishes those circumstances in which the decision of a committee of outside directors has been accorded respect and those in which its decision has not, is not mysterious. The court's own implicit evaluation of the integrity of the special committee's process marks that process as deserving respect or condemns it to be ignored. When a special committee's process is perceived as reflecting a good faith, informed attempt to approximate aggressive, arm's-length bargaining, it will be accorded substantial importance by the court. When, on the other hand, it appears as artifice, ruse or charade, or when the board unduly limits the committee or when the committee fails to correctly perceive its mission—then one can expect that its decision will be accorded no respect.
>
> But how likely is it that these outside directors who have had feelings of solidarity with and to some extent dependency upon management will pursue a process that will be later seen as having integrity?
>
> Consider the outside director who is asked to serve on a special committee to preside over a sale of the company. While he may receive some modest special

remuneration for this service, he and his fellow committee members are likely to be the only persons intensely involved in the process who do not entertain the fervent hope of either making a killing or earning a princely fee. Couple that with the pressure that the seriousness and urgency of the assignment generate, the unpleasantness that may be required if the job is done right, and the fact that no matter what the director does he will probably be sued for it, and you have, I think, a fairly unappetizing assignment.

Combine these factors with those mentioned earlier that create feelings of solidarity with management directors, particularly the corporation's CEO, and it becomes, I would think, quite easy to understand how some special committees appear as no more than, in T.S. Eliot's phrase, "an easy tool, deferential, glad to be of use."[28]

Only one factor stands against these pressures towards accommodation of the CEO: that is a sense of duty.[29] When special committees have appeared to push and resist their colleagues, it has been, I submit, because the men and women who comprised the committee have understood that as a result of accepting this special assignment, they have a new duty and stand in a new and different relationship to the firm's management or its controlling shareholder. When, as in *Mills v. Macmillan*, a special committee has appeared to perform this special assignment badly, it is probably because its members have been ill served by their advisors and, as a result, have failed to understand or to accept the radical change in that relationship that had occurred.

I fully appreciate that corrupt conduct does occur. But I believe—especially in the context of the larger public companies—that when outside directors serving on a special committee fail to meet our expectations, it is likely that they fail because they have not understood what was expected of them. Directors must know what is right before courts can expect them to do what is right.

Thus, I come to the role of the committee's advisors—the lawyers and investment bankers who guide the committee through the process of the sale of a public company. I regard the role of the advisors in establishing the integrity of this process as absolutely crucial. Indeed, the motives and performance of the lawyers and bankers who specialize in the field of mergers and acquisitions is to my mind the great, largely unexamined variable in the process. In all events, it is plain that quite often the special committee relies upon the advisors almost totally. It is understandable why. Frequently, the outside directors who find themselves in control of a corporate sale process have had little or no experience in the sale of a public company. They are in *terra incognito*. Naturally, they turn for guidance to their specialist advisors who will typically have had a great deal of relevant experience.

Thus, in my opinion, if the special committee process is to have integrity, it falls in the first instance to the lawyers to unwrap the bindings that have joined the directors into a single board; to instill in the committee a clear understanding of the radically altered state in which it finds itself and to lead the committee to a full understanding of its new duty.

---

28. T. S. Eliot, "The Love Song of J. Alfred Prufrock" in *Collected Poems 1909-1962* (Harcourt, Brace & World 1970) at 6.

29. The concept of sense of duty seems underutilized if not ignored in the academic study and criticism of law. *But see* A. Etzioni, *The Moral Dimension: Towards a New Economics* (1988).

Much, of course, will turn on the court's evaluation of the integrity of the special committee's process. In reaching that evaluation, the court will be mindful—and the lawyers advising the committee need to be mindful as well—that the committee, if respected, holds the shareholders' welfare in its hands; the court will be mindful that claims of so-called structural bias in the process are plausible and that the court's own power of perception is limited. Thus, in a sale context, counsel for a special committee must accept from the outset that as a practical matter she will have to demonstrate that the special committee's process had integrity; that the committee was informed, energetic and committed in this transaction to the single goal of maximizing the shareholders' interest.

Allen, Independent Directors in MBO Transactions: Are They Fact or Fantasy, University of California, San Diego Seventeenth Annual Securities Regulation Institute, published at 45 Bus. Law. 2055 (1990).

Cf. Langevoort, The Human Nature of Corporate Boards: Law, Norms, and the Unintended Consequences of Independence and Accountability, 89 Geo. L.J. 797 (2001); Lin, The Effectiveness of Outside Directors as a Corporate Governance Mechanism: Theories and Evidence, 90 Nw. U.L. Rev. 898 (1996); Cox, The ALI, Institutionalization, and Disclosure: The Quest for the Outside Director's Spine, 61 Geo. Wash. L. Rev. 1233 (1993); Palmiter, Reshaping the Corporate Fiduciary Model: A Director's Duty of Independence, 67 Tex. L. Rev. 1351, 1436-64 (1989).

3. A number of scholars have challenged the idea that outside directors, as they currently are thought of and elected, can provide effective monitoring services. Gilson & Kraakman, Reinventing the Outside Director: An Agenda for Institutional Investors, 43 Stan. L. Rev. 863 (1991), identifies the following problems:

(i) outside directors are nominated by management and therefore are dependent upon management for retention;

(ii) most outside directors share the view of management as to the intensity of appropriate monitoring by outside directors (noting that 63 percent of public corporation outside directors are themselves chief executive officers of public companies);

(iii) outside directors tend to be social peers and friends of management; and

(iv) lack of significant remuneration, time, and staff diminish outside directors' incentives and abilities to monitor effectively.

As an alternative, Gilson and Kraakman suggest the creation of a professional corps of outside directors who would serve on a number of different boards, be adequately compensated (in the aggregate) by fees from those corporations on whose boards they serve, and be electable through the concerted efforts of institutional investor groups. Professor Weiss had previously argued for the creation of a National Directors Corps, whose members would be appointed by the President with the advice and consent of the Senate, and 2/3 of the members of the boards of all large corporations would have to be drawn from the Corps. Weiss, Social Regulation of Business Activity: Reforming the Corporate Governance System to Resolve an Institutional Impasse, 28 U.C.L.A. L. Rev. 343 (1981).

What advantages and disadvantages are posed by such proposals for a professional corps of directors? Would they be more or less effective than other alternatives you might imagine? What additional problems would adoption of such proposals create? How could they be addressed?

4. Do objective tests as a mode of evaluating directors' conduct serve as adequate protection of stockholder (or other) interests? Could a subjective test be fashioned which adequately protects stockholder (or other) interests without unduly interfering with the board's managerial prerogatives?

5. In Unitrin, Inc. v. American General Corp., 651 A.2d 1361 (Del. 1995), American General announced an all cash/all shares tender offer for Unitrin stock at a 30% premium over market. Members of Unitrin's board at that time controlled 23% of its outstanding stock and Unitrin's charter required a 75% vote to approve business combinations with any holder of more than 15% of its stock. Unitrin's board responded to the hostile bid in part by adopting a stock repurchase program in which the shareholder-directors would not participate and as a result the board's collective ownership interest would increase to 28%. American General argued that the 75% charter provision coupled with the board's post-repurchase 28% ownership position gave the board a veto mechanism and therefore sought to enjoin the repurchase program.

The Chancery Court drew on *Unocal* to enjoin the stock repurchase program on the grounds that it was not a reasonable response to a perceived threat because it would in effect give the board veto power over American General's takeover effort. The Delaware Supreme Court reversed in an opinion described by a senior partner in a major national law firm not involved in the litigation as "rambling, incoherent and confusing." In particular, the Supreme Court disagreed that the effect of the charter provision and the repurchase program would be a board veto power. The Chancery Court had written:

> It seems highly improbable that American General (or any other bidder) would view a proxy contest as a rational alternative once the repurchase program is completed. The repurchase program further reduces American General's incentive to undertake a proxy contest because a successful election will not provide American General with the power to combine the two companies. American General's directors will then control the company, but they still cannot implement a merger agreement without the consent of the former director stockholders.

Counsel promptly sent a letter to the Court of Chancery claiming that the opinion was technically incorrect, explaining as follows:

> If American General were to pursue and succeed in such a proxy contest when it owned less than 15% of Unitrin's stock, which, as the Court noted, are unrealistic assumptions, and the American General directors were then to approve a merger proposal, the supermajority provision would not apply.

The Court of Chancery acknowledged its technical mistake, and issued two corrected pages from its original opinion. Even so, however, the Delaware Supreme Court found that the Court of Chancery continued to misunderstand the dynamics of the bidding situation. The Supreme Court claimed that the Court of Chancery was mistaken as to what it called its "sua sponte" and "subjective premise" that Unitrin's board "would not vote like other stockholders in a proxy contest, i.e., in their own best economic interests." At the bid price, the Court explained, the target's outside directors held target stock worth more than $450 million. Therefore, argued Unitrin, "the stockholder directors had the same interest as other ... stockholders generally, when voting in a proxy contest, to wit: the maximization of the value of their investments."

The Delaware Supreme Court continued:

In rejecting Unitrin's argument, the Court of Chancery stated that the stockholder directors would be "subconsciously" motivated in a proxy contest to vote against otherwise excellent offers which did not include a "price parameter" to compensate them for the loss of the "prestige and perquisites" of membership on Unitrin's Board. The Court of Chancery's subjective determination that the stockholder directors of Unitrin would reject an "excellent offer," unless it compensated them for giving up the "prestige and perquisites" of directorship, appears to be subjective and without record support. It cannot be presumed ... that the prestige and perquisites of holding a director's office or a motive to strengthen collective power prevails over a stockholder-director's economic interest. Even the shareholder-plaintiffs in this case agree with the legal proposition Unitrin advocates on appeal: stockholders are presumed to act in their own best economic interests when they vote in a proxy contest.

Id. (Do you agree that there is a "legal presumption" that stockholders "act in their own best economic interests when they vote in a proxy contest"?) In considering the "substantive coercion" of the hostile bid, the Delaware Supreme Court continued:

The Unitrin Board did not have unlimited discretion to defeat the threat it perceived from the American General Offer by any draconian means available. *See Unocal*, 493 A.2d at 955. Pursuant to the *Unocal* proportionality test, the nature of the threat associated with a particular hostile offer sets the parameters for the range of permissible defensive tactics. Accordingly, the purpose of enhanced judicial scrutiny is to determine whether the Board acted reasonably in "relation ... to the threat which a particular bid allegedly poses to stockholder interests." *Mills Acquisition Co. v. Macmillan, Inc.*, Del. Supr., 559 A.2d 1261, 1288 (1989)....

The record reflects that the Unitrin Board perceived the threat from American General's Offer to be a form of substantive coercion. The Board noted that Unitrin's stock price had moved up, on higher than normal trading volume, to a level slightly below the price in American General's Offer. The Board also noted that some Unitrin shareholders had publicly expressed interest in selling at or near the price in the Offer. The Board determined that Unitrin's stock was undervalued by the market at current levels and that the Board considered Unitrin's stock to be a good long-term investment. The Board also discussed the speculative and unsettled market conditions for Unitrin stock caused by American General's public disclosure. The Board concluded that a Repurchase Program would provide additional liquidity to those stockholders who wished to realize short-term gain, and would provide enhanced value to those stockholders who wished to maintain a long-term investment. Accordingly, the Board voted to authorize the Repurchase Program for up to ten million shares of its outstanding stock on the open market.

... Unitrin's Board deemed three of the concerns exemplified in *Unocal* relevant in deciding to authorize the Repurchase Program: first, the inadequacy of the price offered; second, the nature and timing of American General's Offer; and third, the basic stockholder interests at stake, including those of short-term speculators whose actions may have fueled the coercive aspect of the Offer at the expense of the long-term investor. *Unocal*, 493 A.2d at 955-56. *Accord* Ivanhoe Partners v. Newmont Mining Corp., Del. Supr., 535 A.2d 1334, 1341-42 (1987).

The Court concluded that the Unitrin board's actions had been within the range of reasonableness established by *Unocal* and those directors had met the "proper proportionality burden." In particular, it held that the "Court of Chancery applied an incorrect legal standard when it ruled that the Unitrin decision to authorize the Repurchase Program was disproportionate because it was 'unnecessary'" in light of Unitrin's poison pill. Thus it was not necessary for directors to show that action they took was necessary in response to a perceived threat, but only that it was "within a range of reasonableness."

Problem—Defensive Repurchases

Uncas, Inc., a Delaware corporation (the "Company"), is the last of a dying breed of diversified conglomerates. Its principal assets consist of Leatherstocking, Inc., a well-known manufacturer of leather goods, Chingachgook Co., a corporation engaged in processing and selling seafood products, and Mahican, Inc., an international charter tour operator. During the last several years, the Company has sold off a number of its other subsidiaries to eliminate losses from unprofitable operations. As a consequence, and because the cash flow of its three remaining subsidiaries is quite strong, the Company shows substantial retained earnings on its balance sheet. However, recent events, including the increasingly strong protests of animal rights advocates and the fear of international terrorism, have reduced significantly the profitability of the Company's operating subsidiaries. The Company's capital structure consists of 25,000,000 shares of common stock listed on the New York Stock Exchange and trading at $28, from a high of $35 a year ago. The common stock has a book value of $42. The Company has no significant debt at the parent level, and debt capitalization in each of the operating subsidiaries is modest.

T. Bone Pearlstein has filed a Schedule 13D with the Securities and Exchange Commission, reflecting his acquisition through his investment partnership, Plateau Partners, of 12.5 percent of the Company's stock through open market purchases. Pearlstein has a history of acquiring cash-rich companies through the use of cash and junk bonds, the latter of which he typically issues as consideration in second-step mergers designed to eliminate non-tendering stockholders after he has acquired control. Not infrequently, Pearlstein's tender offers have been defeated by higher bidders, and Pearlstein has succeeded in profiting handsomely from the sale of his stock to these bidders.

Cooper, the Company's president, reports these developments to the board. Cooper himself owns 1.5 percent of the Company's stock and is nearing retirement age, having been employed by the Company for twenty years. Although Pearlstein's Schedule 13D identifies the purpose of his purchases as "investment", Cooper expresses to the board (consisting of five inside directors, including Cooper, and five outside directors) his concern that, although the junk bond market is weak, the Company's stockholders might be tempted to sell to Pearlstein in a hostile tender offer. He rationalizes this based on the Company's recent problems, problems which he is certain can be turned around based on a business plan (prepared last month by the Company's CFO) to further diversify the business, using its large cash resources. Although no specific business areas have been targeted, Cooper explains that he is convinced of his ability to maximize stockholder wealth if given sufficient time. He does not, however, want the threat of Pearlstein breathing down his neck, which he believes will hamper his ability to develop the business.

After some deliberation, the board resolves to refer the matter to you, the Company's outside counsel. Prepare a memorandum to the board explaining its obligations and its options. In so doing, you should assess the legal risks of each option the board might select.

Paramount Communications, Inc. v. Time, Inc.

CCH Fed. Sec. L. Rep. 94,514 (Del. Ch. 1990), *aff'd*, 571 A.2d 1140 (Del. 1990)

ALLEN, Chancellor

Pending are motions in several related lawsuits seeking, principally, a preliminary injunction restraining Time Incorporated from buying stock under a June 16, 1989, offer to purchase 100 million shares of common stock (comprising 51% of the outstanding common stock) of Warner Communications Inc. at $70 per share cash. That offer may close no earlier than July 17, 1989. The only condition to that closing is the submission of tenders of at least 100 million of Warner's outstanding shares. The offer contains no financing condition and in all events the $10.4 billion necessary to finance the purchase and related re-financings has been obtained.[a] The motion does not seek to require Time to dismantle its "poison pill" takeover defense or to take other action sought in the complaints.[1]

Plaintiffs in these lawsuits include Paramount Communications Inc. and its KDS Acquisition Corp. subsidiary, which is itself currently extending an offer to purchase up to all shares of Time at $200 per share; various holders of modest amounts of Time common stock, who purport to represent Time shareholders as a class; and several very substantial Time shareholders who sue on their own behalf. Defendants are Time Incorporated, all 12 of its current and three recently resigned directors, as well as Warner Communications Inc.

On this motion, the court is required to express an opinion on the question whether the directors of Time, who plainly have been granted the legal power to complete a public tender offer transaction that would be the first stage in accomplishing a thoughtfully planned consolidation of the business of Time with that of Warner Communications, have a supervening fiduciary obligation to desist from doing so in order that it be made more likely that the shareholders of Time will be afforded an opportunity to accept the public tender offer for all shares extended by Paramount's KDS subsidiary. The record in this case indicates ... that it is very unlikely that the market price of Time stock immediately following consummation of the now planned two-stage Warner transaction will equal the initial $175 price offered by Paramount.

It is the gist of plaintiffs' position in the various lawsuits now before this court that Time's board of directors does have such a supervening fiduciary duty and has failed to understand or, more accurately, has chosen to ignore that fact, in order to force the Warner transaction upon the corporation and its shareholders—a transaction that,

---

a. References to the record have been deleted.
1. In their complaints, plaintiffs seek, among other relief, to require the board to excuse a follow-up merger between Time and any Paramount affiliate from certain voting requirements of the Time certificate of incorporation and of Section 203 of the Delaware General Corporation Law; to require the board to redeem the company's preferred stock purchase rights that impede the closing of any offer; and to rescind a certain Share Exchange Agreement between Time and Warner, which is touched upon below.

plaintiffs assert, the shareholders would not approve, if given the opportunity to vote on the matter. The board of Time is doing this, it is urged, not for any legitimate reason, but because it prefers that transaction which secures and entrenches the power of those in whose hands management of the corporation has been placed.

It is the gist of the position of the directors of Time that they have no fiduciary duty to desist from accomplishing the transaction in question in these circumstances. They contend, quite broadly speaking, that their duty is to exercise their judgment prudently (*i.e.*, deliberately, in an informed manner) in the good faith pursuit of legitimate corporate goals. This, they say, the record shows they have done. Moreover, they assert that the result of that judgment is a proposed transaction of extraordinary benefit and promise to Time and its shareholders. It is quite reasonable, they contend, for the board to prefer it, on behalf of the corporation and its shareholders, to the sale of the company presently for $200 per share cash.... In short, the directors ... [see] no reason for this court to force them, under the guise of a fiduciary obligation, to take another, more popular course of action.

These same points are made by Warner, which is also a defendant. In addition, Warner asserts its own rights under the contracts in question....

Before attempting to define the legal issues raised by these motions, it is appropriate to turn to a statement of the facts as they appear at this time....

[I.ᵃ]

Time is a Delaware corporation with its principal offices in New York City. Time's traditional business is publication of magazines and books; however, Time also provides pay television programming through its Home Box Office, Inc. and Cinemax subsidiaries. In addition, Time owns and operates cable television franchises through its subsidiary, American Television and Communication Corporation. During the relevant time period, Time's board consisted of sixteen directors. Twelve of the directors were "outside," non-employee directors. Four of the directors were also officers of the company....[3]

As early as 1983 and 1984, Time's executive board began considering expanding Time's operations into the entertainment industry. In 1987, Time established a special committee of executives to consider and propose corporate strategies for the 1990s. The consensus of the committee was that Time should move ahead in the area of ownership and creation of video programming. This expansion, as the Chancellor noted, was predicated upon two considerations: first, Time's desire to have greater control, in terms of quality and price, over the film products delivered by way of its cable network and franchises; and second, Time's concern over the increasing globalization of the world economy. Some of Time's outside directors, especially Luce and Temple, had opposed this move as a threat to the editorial integrity and journalistic focus of Time.[4] De-

---

a. Space limitations have led us to delete Chancellor Allen's thorough elaboration of the facts. The facts set forth in Section I of the opinion are presented by the Delaware Supreme Court in its affirmance, 571 A.2d 1140, 1143-49 (1989).

3. Four directors ... have since resigned from Time's board. The Chancellor found, with the exception of [Arthur] Temple, their resignations to reflect more a willingness to step down than disagreement or dissension over the Time-Warner merger. Temple did not choose to continue to be associated with a corporation that was expanding into the entertainment field....

4. The primary concern of Time's outside directors was the preservation of the "Time Culture." They believed that Time had become recognized in this country as an institution built upon a foundation of journalistic integrity. Time's management made a studious effort to refrain from involvement in Time's editorial policy. Several of Time's outside directors feared that a merger with an en-

spite this concern, the board recognized that a vertically integrated video enterprise to complement Time's existing HBO and cable networks would better enable it to compete on a global basis.

In late spring of 1987, a meeting took place between Steve Ross, CEO of Warner Brothers, and [N.J. Nicholas, Jr., the president and chief operating officer] of Time. Ross and Nicholas discussed the possibility of a joint venture between the two companies through the creation of a jointly-owned cable company. Time would contribute its cable system and HBO. Warner would contribute its cable system and provide access to Warner Brothers Studio. The resulting venture would be a larger, more efficient cable network.... Ultimately the parties abandoned this plan, determining that it was impractical for several reasons....

On August 11, 1987, Gerald M. Levin, Time's vice chairman and chief strategist, wrote [Chairman and CEO] J. Richard Munro a confidential memorandum in which he strongly recommended a strategic consolidation with Warner. In June 1988, Nicholas and Munro sent to each outside director a copy of the "comprehensive long-term planning document" prepared by the committee of Time executives that had been examining strategies for the 1990s. The memo included reference to and a description of Warner as a potential acquisition candidate.

Thereafter, Munro and Nicholas held meetings with Time's outside directors to discuss, generally, long-term strategies for Time and, specifically, a combination with Warner. Nearly a year later, Time's board reached the point of serious discussion of the "nuts and bolts" of a consolidation with an entertainment company. On July 21, 1988, Time's board met, with all outside directors present. The meeting's purpose was to consider Time's expansion into the entertainment industry on a global scale. Management presented the board with a profile of various entertainment companies in addition to Warner, including Disney, 20th Century Fox, Universal, and Paramount.

Without any definitive decision on choice of a company, the board approved in principle a strategic plan for Time's expansion. The board gave management the "go-ahead" to continue discussions with Warner concerning the possibility of a merger. With the exception of Temple and Luce, most of the outside directors agreed that a merger involving expansion into the entertainment field promised great growth opportunity for Time. Temple and Luce remained unenthusiastic about Time's entry into the entertainment field....

The board's consensus was that a merger of Time and Warner was feasible, but only if Time controlled the board of the resulting corporation and thereby preserved a management committed to Time's journalistic integrity.... Some board members expressed concern over whether such a business combination would place Time "*in play.*" The board discussed the wisdom of adopting further defensive measures to lessen such a possibility.[5]

Of a wide range of companies considered by Time's board as possible merger candidates, Warner Brothers, Paramount, Columbia, M.C.A., Fox, MGM, Disney, and Orion, the board, in July 1988, concluded that Warner was the superior candidate for a consolidation.[b] ...

---

tertainment company would divert Time's focus from news journalism and threaten the Time Culture.

5. Time had in place a panoply of defensive devices, including a staggered board, a "poison pill" preferred stock rights plan triggered by an acquisition of 15% of the company, a fifty-day notice period for shareholder motions, and restrictions on shareholders' ability to call a meeting or act by consent.

b. The lengthy reasons why Warner stood out have been excluded due to space limitations.

In August 1988, Levin, Nicholas, and Munro, acting on instructions from Time's board, continued to explore a business combination with Warner. By letter dated August 4, 1988, management informed the outside directors of proposed corporate governance provisions to be discussed with Warner. The provisions incorporated the recommendations of several of Time's outside directors.

From the outset, Time's board favored an all-cash or cash and securities acquisition of Warner as the basis for consolidation. Bruce Wasserstein, Time's financial advisor, also favored an outright purchase of Warner. However, Steve Ross, Warner's CEO, was adamant that a business combination was only practicable on a stock-for-stock basis. Warner insisted on a stock swap in order to preserve its shareholders' equity in the resulting corporation. Time's officers, on the other hand, made it abundantly clear that Time would be the acquiring corporation and that Time would control the resulting board. Time refused to permit itself to be cast as the "acquired" company.

Eventually Time acquiesced in Warner's insistence on a stock-for-stock deal, but talks broke down over corporate governance issues. Time wanted Ross' position as a co-CEO to be temporary and wanted Ross to retire in five years. Ross, however, refused.... Time's request of a guarantee that Time would dominate the CEO succession ... as inconsistent with the concept of a Time-Warner merger "of equals." ... Time, and particularly its outside directors, viewed the corporate governance provisions as critical for preserving the "Time Culture" through a pro-Time management at the top. See *supra* note 4.

Throughout the fall of 1988 Time pursued its plan of expansion into the entertainment field [by speaking with several parties, including Paramount].... Time steadfastly maintained it was not placing itself up for sale.

Warner and Time resumed negotiations in January 1989. The catalyst for the resumption of talks was a private dinner between Steve Ross and Time outside director, Michael Dingman. Dingman was able to convince Ross that the transitional nature of the proposed co-CEO arrangement did not reflect a lack of confidence in Ross. Ross agreed.... Negotiations resumed and many of the details of the original stock-for-stock exchange agreement remained intact. In addition, Time's senior management agreed to long-term contracts.

Time insider directors Levin and Nicholas met with Warner's financial advisors to decide upon a stock exchange ratio. Time's board had recognized the potential need to pay a premium in the stock ratio in exchange for dictating the governing arrangement of the new Time-Warner. Levin and outside director Finkelstein were the primary proponents of paying a premium to protect the "Time Culture." The board discussed premium rates of 10%, 15% and 20%. Wasserstein also suggested paying a premium for Warner due to Warner's rapid growth rate. The market exchange ratio of Time stock for Warner stock was .38 in favor of Warner. Warner's financial advisors informed its board that any exchange rate over .400 was a fair deal and any exchange rate over .450 was "one hell of a deal." The parties ultimately agreed upon an exchange rate favoring Warner of .465. On that basis, Warner stockholders would have owned approximately 62%[7] of the common stock of Time-Warner.

On March 3, 1989, Time's board, with all but one director in attendance, met and unanimously approved the stock-for-stock merger with Warner. Warner's board like-

---

7. As was noted in the briefs and at oral argument, this figure is somewhat misleading because it does not take into consideration the number of individuals who owned stock in both companies.

wise approved the merger. The agreement called for Warner to be merged into a wholly-owned Time subsidiary with Warner becoming the surviving corporation. The common stock of Warner would then be converted into common stock of Time at the agreed upon ratio. Thereafter, the name of Time would be changed to Time-Warner, Inc.

The rules of the New York Stock Exchange required that Time's issuance of shares to effectuate the merger be approved by a vote of Time's stockholders. The Delaware General Corporation Law required approval of the merger by a majority of the Warner stockholders. Delaware law did not require any vote by Time stockholders....

The resulting company would have a 24-member board, with 12 members representing each corporation. The company would have co-CEO's, at first Ross and Munro, then Ross and Nicholas, and finally, after Ross' retirement, ... Nicholas alone. The board would create an editorial committee with a majority of members representing Time. A similar entertainment committee would be controlled by Warner board members. A two-thirds supermajority vote was required to alter CEO successions but an earlier proposal to have supermajority protection for the editorial committee was abandoned....

At its March 3, 1989 meeting, Time's board adopted several defensive tactics. Time entered an automatic share exchange agreement with Warner. Time would receive 17,292,747 shares of Warner's outstanding common stock (9.4%) and Warner would receive 7,080,016 shares of Time's outstanding common stock (11.1%). Either party could trigger the exchange.... Time also agreed to a "no-shop" clause, preventing Time from considering any other consolidation proposal, thus relinquishing its power to consider other proposals, regardless of their merits. Time did so at Warner's insistence. Warner did not want to be left "on the auction block" for an unfriendly suitor, if Time were to withdraw from the deal.

Time's board simultaneously established a special committee of outside directors, Finkelstein, Kearns, and Opel, to oversee the merger. The committee's assignment was to resolve any impediments that might arise in the course of working out the details of the merger and its consummation.

.... [Time's] board scheduled the stockholder vote for June 23; and a May 1 record date was set. On May 24, 1989, Time sent out extensive proxy statements to the stockholders regarding the approval vote on the merger.... [B]y the end of May, the Time-Warner merger appeared to be an accomplished fact.

On June 7, 1989, these wishful assumptions were shattered by Paramount's surprising announcement of its all-cash offer to purchase all outstanding shares of Time for $175 per share. The following day, June 8, the trading price of Time's stock rose from $126 to $170 per share. Paramount's offer was said to be "fully negotiable."[8]

Time found Paramount's "fully negotiable" offer to be in fact subject to at least three conditions. First, Time had to terminate its merger agreement and stock exchange agreement with Warner, and remove certain other of its defensive devices, including the redemption of Time's shareholder rights. Second, Paramount had to obtain the required cable franchise transfers from Time in a fashion acceptable to Paramount in its sole discretion. Finally, the offer depended upon a judicial determination that section

---

8. Subsequently, it was established that Paramount's board had decided as early as March 1989 to move to acquire Time. However, Paramount management intentionally delayed publicizing its proposal until Time had mailed to its stockholders its Time-Warner merger proposal along with the required proxy statements.

203 of the General Corporate Law of Delaware (The Delaware Anti-Takeover Statute) was inapplicable to any Time-Paramount merger. . . .

On June 8, 1989, Time formally responded to Paramount's offer. Time's chairman and CEO, J. Richard Munro, sent an aggressively worded letter to Paramount's CEO, Martin Davis. Munro's letter attacked Davis' personal integrity and called Paramount's offer "smoke and mirrors." . . .

Over the following eight days, Time's board met three times to discuss Paramount's $175 offer. The board viewed Paramount's offer as inadequate and concluded that its proposed merger with Warner was the better course of action. Therefore, the board declined to open any negotiations with Paramount and held steady its course toward a merger with Warner.

In June, Time's board of directors met several times. During the course of their June meetings, Time's outside directors met frequently without management, officers or directors being present. At the request of the outside directors, corporate counsel was present during the board meetings and, from time to time, the management directors were asked to leave the board sessions. During the course of these meetings, Time's financial advisors informed the board that, on an auction basis, Time's per share value was materially higher than [Paramount's] $175 per share offer. After this advice, the board concluded that Paramount's $175 offer was inadequate.

At these June meetings, certain Time directors expressed their concern that Time stockholders would not comprehend the long-term benefits of the Warner merger. Large quantities of Time shares were held by institutional investors. The board feared that even though there appeared to be wide support for the Warner transaction, Paramount's cash premium would be a tempting prospect to these investors. In mid-June, Time sought permission from the New York Stock Exchange to alter its rules and allow the Time-Warner merger to proceed without stockholder approval. Time did so at Warner's insistence. The New York Stock Exchange rejected Time's request on June 15; and on that day, the value of Time stock reached $182 per share.

The following day, June 16, Time's board met to take up Paramount's offer. The board's prevailing belief was that Paramount's bid posed a threat to Time's control of its own destiny and retention of the "Time Culture." Even after Time's financial advisors made another presentation of Paramount and its business attributes, Time's board maintained its position that a combination with Warner offered greater potential for Time. Warner provided Time a much desired production capability and an established international marketing chain. Time's advisors suggested various options, including defensive measures. . . . Finally, Time's board formally rejected Paramount's offer.[11]

At the same meeting, Time's board decided to recast its consolidation with Warner into an outright cash and securities acquisition of Warner by Time; and Time so informed Warner. Time accordingly restructured its proposal to acquire Warner as follows: Time would make an immediate all-cash offer for 51% of Warner's outstanding stock at $70 per share. The remaining 49% would be purchased at some later date for a mixture of cash and securities worth $70 per share. To provide the funds required for its outright acquisition of Warner, Time would assume 7-10 billion dollars worth of debt, thus eliminating one of the principal transaction-related benefits of the original merger agreement. Nine billion dollars of the total purchase price would be allocated to the purchase of Warner's goodwill.

---

11. Meanwhile, Time had already begun erecting impediments to Paramount's offer. Time encouraged local cable franchises to sue Paramount to prevent it from easily obtaining the franchises.

Warner agreed but insisted on certain terms. Warner sought a control premium and guarantees that the governance provisions found in the original merger agreement would remain intact. Warner further sought agreements that Time would not employ its poison pill against Warner and that, unless enjoined, Time would be legally bound to complete the transaction. Time's board agreed to these last measures only at the insistence of Warner....

On June 23, 1989, Paramount raised its all-cash offer to buy Time's outstanding stock to $200 per share. Paramount still professed that all aspects of the offer were negotiable. Time's board met on June 26, 1989 and formally rejected Paramount's $200 per share second offer. The board reiterated its belief that, despite the $25 increase, the offer was still inadequate. The Time board maintained that the Warner transaction offered a greater long-term value for the stockholders and, unlike Paramount's offer, did not pose a threat to Time's survival and its "culture." Paramount then filed this action in the Court of Chancery.]

II.

* * *

Before turning to an analysis of the merits of plaintiffs' complaint, I pause to make one observation that should be apparent. It is not part of the function of the court to evaluate whether the Time-Warner deal is a good deal for Time shareholders or a poor one....

III.

On June 16, the board of directors of Time, upon what would appear competent advice, resolved that it would commit the corporation to the revised Warner transaction. It then implemented its decision in a way intended to assure that no future event would upset achievement of the goal embraced. I am convinced that in doing so, the board understood that it was foreclosing for the present, as a practical matter, the option for Time shareholders to realize $175 cash for their shares—indeed it understood that $175 could be realized from Mr. Davis and perhaps substantially more from him or others— and, more significantly, the board understood that immediately following the effectuation of a Warner merger, the stock market price of Time stock was likely to be materially lower than the $175 then "on the table," perhaps $150, but more likely, within the wide range of $106-$188....

The board explains its choice ... by reference to the view that the long-term value of a Time-Warner combination would be superior not only to the premium $175 presently available to the shareholders, but to any current sale price in the ranges it had been told could be achieved. This is the heart of the matter: the board chose less current value in the hope (assuming that good faith existed, and the record contains no evidence to support a supposition that it does not) that greater value would make that implicit sacrifice beneficial in the future.

That decision raises many subsidiary, but two overarching questions: First, does it make any sense, given what we understand or think we understand about markets, to posit the existence of a distinction between managing for current value maximization and managing for longer-term value creation—a distinction which implies, unless I am wrong, that current stock market values fail to reflect "accurately" achievable future value? The second overarching question ... is this: who, under the evolving law of fiduciary obligations is, or should be, the agency for making such a choice in circumstances of the sort presented here—the board or the shareholders? The legal analysis that follows addresses this second overarching question in terms of two related sets of doctrines.

A.

The legal analysis that follows treats the distinction that the Time board implicitly drew between current share value maximization and long-term share value maximization....

* * *

Directors may operate on the theory that the stock market valuation is "wrong" in some sense, without breaching faith with shareholders. No one, after all, has access to more information concerning the corporation's present and future condition. It is far from irrational and certainly not suspect for directors to believe that a likely immediate market valuation of the Time-Warner merger will undervalue the stock. The record in this case refers to instances in which directors did function on a theory that they understood better than the public market for the firm's shares what the value of their firm was, and were shown by events to be correct....

On the level of legal doctrine, it is clear that under Delaware law, directors are under no obligation to act so as to maximize the immediate value of the corporation or its shares, except in the special case in which the corporation is in a "Revlon mode." *Mills Acquisition Co. v. Macmillan, Inc.*, Del. Supr., Nos. 415 & 416 [599 A.2d 1261] (May 3, 1989).... Thus, Delaware law does recognize that directors, when acting deliberately, in an informed way, and in the good faith pursuit of corporate interests, may follow a course designed to achieve long-term value even at the cost of immediate value maximization.[15]

The legally critical question this case presents then involves *when* must a board shift from its ordinary long-term profit maximizing mode to the radically altered state recognized by the *Revlon* in which its duty, broadly stated, is to exercise its power in the good faith pursuit of immediate maximization of share value. Surely, when as in *Revlon* itself and other cases construing its command, most notably *Macmillan*, the board decides to enter a change in control transaction, it has elected to enter the Revlon zone. But it now appears resolved that a subjective disinclination to sell the company will not prevent that duty from arising where an extraordinary transaction including, at a minimum, a change in corporate control is involved:

> [*Revlon's* requirements pertain] whether the "sale" takes the form of an active auction, a management buyout, or a "restructuring" such as that which the Court of Chancery enjoined in *Macmillan I.*

Mills Acquisition Co. v. Macmillan, Inc....

Thus, more specifically, the first overarching question presented by these facts reduces legally to the inquiry whether the board was, on June 16, involuntarily in that special state—what one can call, as a shorthand, the "Revlon mode"—in which it was required to maximize immediate share value.... If the board was itself under no duty to choose to maximize current value, then the second overarching question must be addressed in terms of the legal questions presented.

---

15. It is this recognition that, in part, permits a corporation to make reasonable charitable contributions, to grant scholarships or take other action that will not have a direct or immediate positive impact upon the financial performance of the firm.

B.

The second overarching question is where legally (an easy question) and equitably (more subtle problem) the locus of decision-making power does or should reside in circumstances of this kind. The argument of plaintiffs is that the directors' duty of loyalty to shareholders requires them at such a time to afford to the shareholders the power and opportunity to designate whether the company should now be sold. This position is supported with two distinct legal arguments. First, certain of the plaintiffs argue that the commitment of the original Warner transaction to a shareholder vote gave rise to a fiduciary obligation to permit the shareholders to decide the matter. The reformatting of the deal in order to avoid the risks of shareholder non-approval is thus seen as a breach of a duty of loyalty. Principally involved in this analysis are cases dealing with the exercise of the franchise....

The second and more difficult doctrinal setting for the question of whose choice is it, is presented by *Unocal Corp. v. Mesa Petroleum Co.*, Del. Supr., 493 A.2d 946 (1985) and a string of Chancery opinions construing its test to require, in certain circumstances, the taking of action—typically the redemption of a so-called poison pill—to permit shareholders to choose between two functionally equivalent alternative transactions....

IV.

Were the Time Directors Under an Obligation to Seek, in Good Faith, Only to Maximize Current Share Value on June 16?: Plaintiffs' Revlon Argument

A.

Plaintiffs' first argument, restated most simply, is that the original merger agreement constituted an implicit decision by the board of Time to transfer control of the company to Warner, or more correctly its shareholders, and when the board decided to consider doing that, its duties changed from long-term management of the corporation for the benefit of the company's shareholders to the narrow and specific goal of present maximization of share value. That is, it entered a "Revlon mode." ... The class action plaintiffs assert that any change in corporate control triggers this special duty. The individual shareholder plaintiffs urge a different theory as triggering the special Revlon duty. They contend that the original merger, if effectuated, would have precluded the Time shareholders from ever (that is, in the foreseeable future) realizing a control premium transaction, and thus, in its impact upon Time shareholders, the merger contemplated by the March 3 agreement would have implicitly represented the same loss of a control premium as would a change in control transaction with no premium. Thus, these plaintiffs assert that even if the stock for stock merger did not represent a change in control, the same duty to maximize current value should attach to it as to a "sale."

Plaintiffs, having purportedly shown that the board really was in a Revlon mode, then go on to argue that the board violated its Revlon duty by not seeking a *current* value maximizing transaction and by entering into a number of agreements that were intended to preclude or impede the emergence of current value maximizing alternatives. These agreements include the "dry up" fee payments, the Share Exchange Agreement and the restrictions on supplying information to or entering into discussions with anyone seeking to acquire control of Time.

Defendants respond first that the board did not consider that it was appropriate in March or thereafter to "sell" the company; the purpose of the original merger was quite the opposite in that it sought to preserve and improve the company's long-term performance. Second, defendants say that if something other than their subjective intention is relevant, it simply is not the case that the stock for stock merger they authorized represented a change in control. It is irrelevant in their view that some 62% of the equity of Time would be owned by former Warner shareholders after the merger, that Mr. Ross would serve as co-CEO or that half of the members of the enlarged board would be former Warner directors. There was no control block of Time shares before the agreement and there would be none after it, they point out. Before the merger agreement was signed, control of the corporation existed in a fluid aggregation of unaffiliated shareholders representing a voting majority—in other words, in the market. After the effectuation of the merger it contemplated, control would have remained in the market, so to speak.

As to the individual plaintiffs' theory, defendants say it is flawed in law and in fact. Legally, they contend that a transaction that is otherwise proper cannot be deemed to trigger the radical "Revlon mode" obligations simply because it has the effect of making an attempted hostile takeover of the corporation less likely. All manner of transactions might have that effect and our cases, it is said, have explicitly rejected the notion that a would-be acquiror can compel a target to maintain itself in status quo while its offer proceeds....

Factually, defendants claim that this record does not establish a reasonable probability that the initial merger, if it had been consummated, would have precluded a future change in control transaction. The merged Time-Warner company would be large, it is true (a "private market" value approaching $30 billion, it is said), but recent history has shown that huge transactions can be done....

In *Mills Acquisition Co. v. Macmillan, Inc.*, ... [559 A.2d 1261 (Del. 1989)], the Supreme Court, while noting that there was no need for it to address in detail the question when *Revlon* duties arose, did note that:

> Clearly not every offer or transaction affecting the corporate structure invokes the *Revlon* duties. A refusal to entertain offers may comport with a valid exercise of business judgment.... Circumstances may dictate that an offer be rebuffed, given the nature and timing of the offer; its legality, feasibility and effect on the corporation and the stockholders; the alternatives available and their effect on the various constituencies, particularly the stockholders; the company's long-term strategic plans; and any special factors bearing on stockholder and public interests. Unocal, 493 A.2d 954-56.... In *Ivanhoe* we recognized that a change in corporate structure under the special facts and circumstances of that case did not invoke *Revlon*. 535 A.2d at 1345.

Mills Acquisition Co. v. Macmillan, Inc., supra....

Elsewhere in *Macmillan* our Supreme Court did indicate that a board may find itself in a Revlon mode without reaching an express resolve to "sell" the company....

Thus, I do not find it dispositive of anything that the Time board did not expressly resolve to sell the company. I take from *Macmillan*, however, and its citation of the earlier *Macmillan I* opinion in this court, that a corporate transaction that does represent a change in corporate control does place the board in a situation in which it is charged with the single duty to maximize current share value. I cannot conclude, however, that the initial merger agreement contemplates a change in control of Time. I am entirely persuaded of the soundness of the view that it is irrelevant for purposes of making such determination that 62% of Time-Warner stock would have been held by former Warner shareholders.

If the appropriate inquiry is whether a change in control is contemplated, the answer must be sought in the specific circumstances surrounding the transaction. Surely under some circumstances a stock for stock merger could reflect a transfer of corporate control. That would, for example, plainly be the case here if Warner were a private company. But where, as here, the shares of both constituent corporations are widely held, corporate control can be expected to remain unaffected by a stock for stock merger. This in my judgment was the situation with respect to the original merger agreement.... [N]either corporation could be said to be acquiring the other. Control of both remained in a large, fluid, changeable and changing market.

The existence of a block of stock in the hands of a single shareholder or a group with loyalty to each other does have real consequences to the financial value of "minority" stock. The law offers some protection to such shares through the imposition of a fiduciary duty upon controlling shareholders. But here, effectuation of the merger would not have subjected Time shareholders to the risks and consequences of holders of minority shares. This is a reflection of the fact that no control passed to anyone in the transaction contemplated. The shareholders of Time would have "suffered" dilution, of course, but they would suffer the same type of dilution upon the public distribution of new stock.

B.

More subtle is ... [the] argument that the preclusion of a future change in control transaction ought to be deemed to trigger Revlon duties, to which I now turn.

The argument, as I understand it, is that the original Time-Warner merger, even if it represented no change in control, precluded a future control premium or private market transaction and that as a consequence of that fact, the directors' fiduciary duties required them to capture a control premium now—to sell the company....

It is plain that the original transaction did not legally preclude or impede a later sale or change in control transaction. It does seem reasonable to assume, however, that effectuation of the merger would, as a practical consequence, reduce the likelihood of such a transaction substantially. Our cases, however, have stated the obvious: a would-be acquiror (or the target company's shareholders) has no right to stay the exercise of director power under Section 141 pending the resolution of an attempt to acquire control. So long as the board acts in good faith and deliberately, its acts during such period will be undisturbed unless they are found to be defensive, in which event they must be shown to be reasonable in relation to a threat posed by the offer under *Unocal*....

The individual plaintiffs' argument is an argument for extension of the *Revlon* case beyond sales or other change in control transactions. I have earlier expressed the view that *Revlon* was not a radical departure from existing Delaware, or other, law (*i.e.*, it has "always" been the case that when a trustee or other fiduciary sells an asset for cash, his duty is to seek the single goal of getting the best available price), as well as the view that to be in a *Revlon* mode is for a director to be in a radically altered state. The suggested rule, however, would constitute an expansion of *Revlon* beyond the traditional principle alluded to above which underlies that case. Plaintiffs can cite no authority compelling or commanding this expansion, which would dramatically restrict the functioning of the board whenever an offer was made. Under our law, the validity of "defensive" measures is addressed under a *Unocal* analysis, not under the narrower *Revlon* case.

V.

Did the Combination of Circumstances Existing on June 16 Impose Upon the Time Board a Fiduciary Obligation to Afford to Shareholders a Choice With Respect to Whether the Corporation Should be "Sold" or Managed for the Long-Term?

This is the second overarching question referred to above. Two legal theories are advanced by plaintiffs in support of their position that the board was under a duty to provide, or at least not practically preclude, a choice to accept the Paramount offer or another, higher offer for sale of the entire company now. The first, simpler, theory relates to the franchise; the second to the analysis of "defensive" corporate acts envisioned by the important *Unocal* case....

A. *The recasting of the transaction in a form that avoided a shareholder vote when the vote seemed destined to go against management*

The principle is well established in Delaware law that manipulation of the corporate machinery for the accomplishment of inequitable purposes will not be countenanced....

Primary reliance is placed upon the recent decision in [*Blasius Indus., Inc. v. Atlas Corp.*, 564 A.2d 651 (Del. Ch. 1988)]. There, a board acted in apparent good faith to prevent an already commenced consent solicitation from having the effect that it was intended to have by the consenting shareholders. Specifically, the board used its legal power to fill vacancies on the board so that the holders of a (presumed) majority of shares could not appoint the number of directors, through the consent "vote," necessary to confer effective control upon the consent-designated directors.

It was there held that such action, even if taken in the good faith belief that it was necessary to protect the corporate enterprise from likely harm from the untenable business plan espoused by the shareholders initiating the consent, involved the basic allocation of power between shareholders and directors; and that action, designed and effectuated to thwart the election of directors by consent, was not the sort of question that was entitled to the presumption of validity of the business judgment rule ... but required the board to demonstrate a compelling justification for such action. *See Blasius.... But see American Rent-A-Car, Inc. v. Cross*, Del. Ch., C.A. No. 7583 (May 9, 1984)....

Plaintiffs' reliance upon *Blasius* is misplaced here. There are critical distinctions between the facts of that case and this one. There, the shareholders were in the process of exercising statutorily conferred rights to elect directors through the consent process. *See* 8 *Del. C.* §228. In contrast, Delaware law created no right in these circumstances to vote upon the original Warner merger.[18] Indeed, a merger transaction requires board determination approving an agreement of merger. *See* 8 *Del. C.* §251(b). I am aware of no principle, statute or rule of corporation law that would hold that once a board approves an agreement of merger, it loses power to reconsider that action prior to a shareholder vote. Equally fundamentally, Delaware law creates no power in shareholders to authorize a merger without the prior affirmative action of the board of directors. Thus, a board resolution rescinding approval of an agreement of merger and removing the matter from the agenda of an annual meeting is altogether different from a resolution designed to interfere with the statutory shareholder power to act through consent.

---

18. Recall that it was only NYSE rules that prompted the proposed submission of that transaction to the Time annual meeting.

This case is closer to (indeed *a fortiori* of) *American Rent-A-Car, Inc., supra*, in which this court declined to enjoin action authorized by a bylaw which was amended by the board at a time when it seemed quite likely to fail of stockholder approval....

I therefore conclude that plaintiffs have not shown that the June 16 decision to recast the transaction entailed any intrusion upon the effective exercise of a right possessed by the shareholders, either under our statutes or under the corporation's charter. The June 16 decision can therefore not be seen as implicating the policy of protection of the corporate franchise, which our law has studiously sought to protect.

B. *The claim that the Warner tender offer is a disproportionate response to a noncoercive Paramount offer that threatens no cognizable injury to Time or its shareholders*

1. *Does Unocal apply?*

Powerful circumstances in this case include the fact that the original Time-Warner merger agreement was, or appears at this stage to have been, chiefly motivated by strategic business concerns; that it was an arm's-length transaction; and, that while its likely effect on reducing vulnerability to unsolicited takeovers may not have been an altogether collateral fact, such effect does not appear to be predominating.[20] Time urges that judicial review of the propriety of the Warner tender offer should involve the same business judgment form of review as would have been utilized in a challenge to the authorization of the original merger agreement....

[However], a rather lengthy list of cases from this court has construed *Unocal* to mean that its form of review applies, at the least, to all actions taken after a hostile takeover attempt has emerged that are found to be defensive in character.[21] *See, e.g., AC Acquisition Corp. v. Anderson, Clayton & Co.*, Del. Ch., 519 A.2d 103, Allen, C. (1986); *Robert M. Bass Group, Inc. v. Edward P. Evans*, Del. Ch., 552 A.2d 1227 (1988).... Thus, while the preexistence of a potential transaction may have pertinence in evaluating whether implementing it or a modified version of it after the board is under attack is a reasonable step in the circumstances, that fact has not been thought in this court to authorize dispensing with the *Unocal* form of analysis. The risks that *Unocal* was shaped to protect against are equally present in such instances.

Factually it is plain, indeed Time's Schedule 14D-9 filing admits, that the reformatting of the stock for stock merger into a leveraged purchase transaction was in reaction to the emergence of the Paramount offer and its likely effect on the proposed Warner transaction....

2. *Does the Paramount all cash, all shares offer represent a threat to an interest the board has an obligation or a right to protect by defensive action?*

Unocal involved a partial offer for cash; consideration in the second-step merger was to be highly subordinated securities. Equally significant, the facts there justified "a reasonable

---

20. This fact distinguishes in a material way the case of *AC Acquisition Corp. v. Anderson, Clayton & Co.*, Del. Ch., 519 A.2d 103 (1986) which originated from a threat to the existing control arrangement. Other material distinctions are that the two transactions there involved were competing versions of a "bust up" plan for the corporation as it had existed and the board could not determine that either was inadequate.

21. When I say at the least, I refer to fact that the *Unocal* form of analysis will also be utilized when a preemptive defensive measure is deployed, where the principal purpose of the action (and not simply a collateral, practical effect) is defensive in a change of control sense. *E.g., Moran v. Household International, Inc.*, Del. Supr., 500 A.2d 1346 (1985).

inference" that the "principal objective [of the offeror was] to be bought off." Thus, the case presented dramatically and plainly a threat to both the shareholders and the corporation.

In two cases decided during the last year, this court has held under similar circumstances that an all cash, all shares offer falling within a range of value that a shareholder might reasonably prefer, to be followed by a prompt second-step merger for cash, could not, so long as it involved no deception, be construed as a sufficient threat to shareholder interests to justify as reasonable board action that would permanently foreclose shareholder choice to accept that offer. See *Grand Metropolitan PLC v. The Pillsbury Company*, Del. Ch., C.A. No. 10319 [588 A.2d 1049], Duffy, J. (December 16, 1988); *City Capital Associates v. Interco Incorporated*, Del. Ch., 551 A.2d 787 (1988). *Cf. Shamrock Holdings, Inc. v. Polaroid Corp.*, Del. Ch., C.A. Nos. 10075, 10079, 10582 and 10585, Berger, V.C. (March 17, 1989), slip op. at 29-32. *Those cases held that in the circumstances presented, "whatever danger there is relates to shareholders and that concerns price only." Pillsbury, supra,*... or that "in the special case of a tender offer for all shares, the threat posed, if any, is not importantly to corporate policies ... but rather ... is most directly to shareholder interests." *Interco*, 551 A.2d at 796.

Plaintiffs argue from these cases that since the Paramount offer is also for all shares and for cash, with a promised second-step merger offering the same consideration, the only interests the board may legitimately seek to protect are the interests of shareholders in having the option to accept the best available price in a sale of their stock. Plaintiffs admit that this interest would justify defensive action at this stage. The board may leave its stock rights plan in place to provide it time to conduct an auction or to arrange any other alternative that might be thought preferable to the shareholders. But, they say, this stockholder interest cannot justify defensive action (the revised merger) that is totally unrelated to a threat to shareholders.

In my opinion, the authorities relied upon do not establish that Time, as a corporate entity, has no distinct legally cognizable interest that the Paramount offer endangers. In each of those cases, the board sought to assure continued control by compelling a transaction that itself would have involved the sale of substantial assets, an enormous increase in debt and a large cash distribution to shareholders. In other words, in those cases, management was presenting and seeking to "cram down" a transaction that was the functional equivalent of the very leveraged "bust up" transaction that management was claiming presented a threat to the corporation.

Here, in sharp contrast, the revised transaction, even though "reactive" in important respects, has its origin and central purpose in *bona fide* strategic business planning, and not in questions of corporate control. *Compare AC Acquisition Corp., supra* (recapitalization had its genesis in a threat to corporate control posed by the imminent termination of trusts that had exercised effective control for years); *Robert M. Bass Group v. Evans, supra* (recapitalization under consideration prior to acquisition proposal would have shifted control to management group of a substantial portion of corporation's assets). To be sure, Time's management and its board had, at all times, one eye on the takeover market, considered that market in all they did, and took steps to afford themselves the conventional defenses. But I do not regard that fact as darkly as do plaintiffs. It is inevitable today for businessmen to be mindful of this factor. At this stage, I do not regard the record as establishing, as was done in *AC Acquisitions, Bass, Interco* or *Pillsbury*, that there is a reasonable likelihood that such concern provided the primary motivation for the corporate transaction. Nor is this transaction an alternative to the sale Paramount proposes (*i.e.*, the functional equivalent) in the way the enjoined transactions in the cited cases can be said to be equivalents of sales.

The more apt parallel than the cited cases is provided by the recent decision in *Shamrock Holdings, Inc. v. Polaroid Corp.*, Del. Ch., C.A. Nos. 10075 and 10079 [559 A.2d 257], Berger, V.C. (January 6, 1989). There, this court found "entirely fair" a transaction (the establishment of an Employee Stock Ownership Plan) that had a significant anti-takeover effect, largely because it was a transaction that had been planned prior to the emergence of the acquisition attempt, plainly could be thought to serve long-term profit maximizing goals, and did not appear motivated primarily as a device to affect or secure control.

Similarly here, I conclude that the achievement of the long-term strategic plan of the Time-Warner consolidation is plainly a most important corporate policy; while the transaction effectuating that policy is reactive in important respects (and thus must withstand a *Unocal* analysis), the policy itself has, in a most concrete way, its origin in non-defensive, *bona fide* business considerations.... Moreover, the Paramount offer and the Warner merger are not, conceptually, alternative transactions; they are alternatives at the moment only because Paramount has conditioned its offer as it has.

In my opinion, where the board has not elected explicitly or implicitly to assume the special burdens recognized by *Revlon*, but continues to manage the corporation for long-term profit pursuant to a preexisting business plan that itself is not primarily a control device or scheme, the corporation has a legally cognizable interest in achieving that plan. Whether steps taken to protect transactions contemplated by such plan are reasonable in all of the circumstances is another matter, to which I now turn.

3. Is the Warner tender offer a reasonable step in the circumstances?

This step requires an evaluation of the importance of the corporate objective threatened; alternative methods for protecting that objective; impacts of the "defensive" action and other relevant factors. In this effort it is prudent to keep in mind that the innovative and constructive rule of *Unocal* must be cautiously applied lest the important benefits of the business judgment rule (including designation of authority to make business and financial decisions to agencies, *i.e.*, boards of directors, with substantive expertise) be eroded or lost by slow degrees....

In this instance, the objective—realization of the company's major strategic plan—is reasonably seen as of unquestionably great importance by the board. Moreover, the reactive step taken was effective but not overly broad. The board did only what was necessary to carry forward a preexisting transaction in an altered form. That "defensive" step does not legally preclude the successful prosecution of a hostile tender offer. And while effectuation of the Warner merger may practically impact the likelihood of a successful takeover of the merged company, it is not established in this record that that is foreclosed as a practical matter. Recent experience suggests it may be otherwise....

I therefore conclude that the revised merger agreement and the Warner tender offer do represent actions that are reasonable in relation to the specific threat posed to the Warner merger by the Paramount offer.

* * *

Reasonable persons can and do disagree as to whether it is the better course from the shareholders' point of view collectively to cash out their stake in the company now at this (or a higher) premium cash price. However, there is no persuasive evidence that the board of Time has a corrupt or venal motivation in electing to continue with its long-term plan even in the face of the cost that that course will no doubt entail for the company's shareholders in the short run. In doing so, it is exercising perfectly conventional powers to cause the corporation to buy assets for use in its business. Because of the timing involved, the board has no need here to rely upon a self-created power designed to assure a veto on all changes in control.

The value of a shareholder's investment, over time, rises or falls chiefly because of the skill, judgment and perhaps luck—for it is present in all human affairs—of the management and directors of the enterprise. When they exercise sound or brilliant judgment, shareholders are likely to profit; when they fail to do so, share values likely will fail to appreciate. In either event, the financial vitality of the corporation and the value of the company's shares is in the hands of the directors and managers of the firm. The corporation law does not operate on the theory that directors, in exercising their powers to manage the firm, are obligated to follow the wishes of a majority of shares. In fact, directors, not shareholders, are charged with the duty to manage the firm. *See Smith v. Van Gorkom*, Del. Supr., 488 A.2d 858 (1985)....

In the decision they have reached here, the Time board may be proven in time to have been brilliantly prescient or dismayingly wrong. In this decision, as in other decisions affecting the financial value of their investment, the shareholders will bear the effects for good or ill. That many, presumably most, shareholders would prefer the board to do otherwise than it has done does not, in the circumstances of a challenge to this type of transaction, in my opinion, afford a basis to interfere with the effectuation of the board's business judgment.

* * *

Having therefore concluded that plaintiffs have not shown a reasonable probability that they possess a right in these circumstances to require the board to abandon or delay the long-planned Warner transaction so that the stockholders might enhance their prospects of a control premium or private market transaction now, I need not discuss the issue raised by Warner concerning its rights as an intensely interested third party. The application [for a preliminary injunction] shall be denied.

IT IS SO ORDERED.

Notes and Questions

1. In Paramount Comm., Inc. v. Time Inc., 571 A.2d 1140 (Del. 1989), the Delaware Supreme Court affirmed the chancellor's denial of a preliminary injunction. In doing so, the court declined to adopt the chancellor's analysis of the Time board's long-term (versus short-term) business horizon, noting (a) that the question of long-term versus short-term values is "largely irrelevant" to the issue of whether the board's action was in the corporation's best interests, and (b) that "absent a limited set of circumstances defined under *Revlon*, a board of directors, while always required to act in an informed manner, is not under any *per se* duty to maximize shareholder value in the short term...." In addition, in determining that no change of control had occurred, the court declined to apply the chancellor's concept of control inhering in the market and instead rested its decision on the lack of substantial evidence to demonstrate that Time's negotiations with Warner made the sale of the corporation inevitable. Finally, in analyzing the "threat" posed by Paramount for purposes of analyzing the recasting of the Warner deal under *Unocal*, the court rejected plaintiffs' approach predicated solely on dollar values:

> Plaintiffs' position represents a fundamental misconception of our standard
> of review under *Unocal* principally because it would involve the court in substi-

tuting its judgment as to what is a "better" deal for that of a corporation's board of directors. To the extent that the Court of Chancery has recently done so in certain of its opinions, we hereby reject such approach as not in keeping with a proper *Unocal* analysis. *See, e.g., Interco*, 551 A.2d 787, and its progeny....

The usefulness of *Unocal* as an analytical tool is precisely its flexibility in the face of a variety of fact scenarios. *Unocal* is not intended as an abstract standard; neither is it a structured and mechanistic procedure of appraisal. Thus, we have said that directors may consider, when evaluating the threat posed by a takeover bid, the "inadequacy of the price offered, nature and timing of the offer, questions of illegality, the impact on 'constituencies' other than shareholders ... the risk of nonconsummation, and the quality of securities being offered in the exchange." 493 A.2d at 955. The open-ended analysis mandated by *Unocal* is not intended to lead to a simple mathematical exercise: that is, of comparing the discounted value of Time-Warner's expected trading price at some future date with Paramount's offer and determining which is the higher. Indeed, in our view, precepts underlying the business judgment rule militate against a court's engaging in the process of attempting to appraise and evaluate the relative merits of a long-term versus a short-term investment goal for shareholders. To engage in such an exercise is a distortion of the *Unocal* process and, in particular, the application of the second part of *Unocal's* test, discussed below.

In this case, the Time board reasonably determined that inadequate value was not the only legally cognizable threat that Paramount's all-cash, all-shares offer could present. Time's board concluded that Paramount's eleventh hour offer posed other threats. One concern was that Time shareholders might elect to tender into Paramount's cash offer in ignorance or a mistaken belief of the strategic benefit which a business combination with Warner might produce. Moreover, Time viewed the conditions attached to Paramount's offer as introducing a degree of uncertainty that skewed a comparative analysis. Further, the timing of Paramount's offer to follow issuance of Time's proxy notice was viewed as arguably designed to upset, if not confuse, the Time stockholders' vote. Given this record evidence, we cannot conclude that the Time board's decision of June 6 that Paramount's offer posed a threat to corporate policy and effectiveness was lacking in good faith or dominated by motives of either entrenchment or self-interest.

Id. at 1153.

2. When the chancellor states that "Time shareholders might elect to tender into Paramount's cash offer in ignorance or a mistaken belief of the strategic benefit which a business combination with Warner might produce," who is to blame for this? Doesn't Time shoulder the disclosure burden relating to the proposed Time-Warner merger?

3. We believe that the chancellor's opinion in *Paramount* contains one of the strongest expressions to date of the Delaware philosophy of the corporation, a philosophy largely reflected (albeit less frankly) in the Supreme Court's opinion. What *is* that philosophy and its component parts? What is the nature of the corporate form, and the underlying function or functions it serves? *Compare* Johnson, The Delaware Judiciary and the Meaning of Corporate Life and Corporate Law, 68 Tex. L. Rev. 865 (1990) (criticizing failure of scholars, courts, and legislatures to develop stated theoretical and normative

models of the corporation and criticizing generally the dominant shareholder-centric approach), *with* Butler and Ribstein, Opting Out of Fiduciary Duties: A Response to the Anti-Contractarians, 65 Wash. L. Rev. 1 (1990) (arguing in favor of a nexus of contracts approach consisting of a series of bilateral bargained-for, and constructively bargained-for, exchanges).

4. In *Time*, Time's board bent over backwards to make sure Time wasn't "put up for sale," thus triggering *Revlon* duties. But when are *Revlon* duties triggered? In Arnold v. Society for Savings Bancorp, Inc., 650 A.2d 1270, 1289-90 (Del. 1994), the Delaware Supreme Court had this to say on the issue:

> .... The directors of a corporation "have the obligation of acting reasonably to seek the transaction offering the best value reasonably available to the stockholders[,]" Paramount Communications, Inc. v. QVC Network, Inc., Del. Supr., 637 A.2d 34, 43 (1994), in at least the following three scenarios: (1) "when a corporation initiates an active bidding process seeking to sell itself or to effect a business reorganization involving a clear break-up of the company," Paramount Communications, Inc. v. Time Inc., Del. Supr., 571 A.2d 1140, 1150 (1990) ... ; (2) "where, in response to a bidder's offer, a target abandons its long-term strategy and seeks an alternative transaction involving the break-up of the company," id.; or (3) when approval of a transaction results in a "sale or change of control," QVC, 637 A.2d at 42-43, 47. In the latter situation, there is no "sale or change in control" when "'[c]ontrol of both [companies] remain[s] in a large, fluid, changeable and changing market.'" Id. at 47 (citation and emphasis omitted).[44]

(ii) Poison Pills
City Capital Assocs. v. Interco Inc.
551 A.2d 787 (Del. Ch. 1988)

ALLEN, Chancellor.

This case, before the court on an application for a preliminary injunction, involves the question whether the directors of Interco Corporation are breaching their fiduciary duties to the stockholders of that company in failing to now redeem certain stock rights originally distributed as part of a defense against unsolicited attempts to take control of the company. In electing to leave Interco's "poison pill" in effect, the board of Interco seeks to defeat a tender offer for all of the shares of Interco for $74 per share cash, extended by plaintiff Cardinal Acquisition Corporation. The $74 offer is for all shares and the offeror expresses an intent to do a back-end merger at the same price promptly if its offer is accepted. Thus, plaintiffs' offer must be regarded as noncoercive.

As an alternative to the current tender offer, the board is endeavoring to implement a major restructuring of Interco that was formulated only recently. The board has grounds to conclude that the alternative restructuring transaction may have a

---

44. See also Marcel Kahan, Paramount or Paradox: The Delaware Supreme Court's Takeover Jurisprudence, 19 J. Corp. L. 583, 595 (1994) ("What is important about the fact that 'control' remains in the hands of unaffiliated shareholders, 'in the market,' is that all these unaffiliated shareholders have virtually identical interests with respect to the company: to maximize the value of their shares.").

value to shareholders of at least $76 per share. The restructuring does not involve a Company self-tender, a merger or other corporate action requiring shareholder action or approval.

It is significant that the question of the board's responsibility to redeem or not to redeem the stock rights in this instance arises at what I will call the end-stage of this takeover contest. That is, the negotiating leverage that a poison pill confers upon this company's board will, it is clear, not be further utilized by the board to increase the options available to shareholders or to improve the terms of those options. Rather, at this stage of this contest, the pill now serves the principal purpose of "protecting the restructuring"—that is, precluding the shareholders from choosing an alternative to the restructuring that the board finds less valuable to shareholders.

Accordingly, this case involves a further judicial effort to pick out the contours of a director's fiduciary duty to the corporation and its shareholders when the board has deployed the recently innovated and powerful antitakeover device of flip-in or flip-over stock rights. That inquiry is, of course, necessarily a highly particularized one.

In *Moran v. Household International, Inc.*, Del. Supr., 500 A.2d 1346 (1985), our Supreme Court acknowledged that a board of directors of a Delaware corporation has legal power to issue corporate securities that serve principally not to raise capital for the firm, but to create a powerful financial disincentive to accumulate shares of the firm's stock. Involved in that case was a board "reaction to what [it] perceived to be the threat in the market place of coercive two-tier tender offers." 500 A.2d at 1356. In upholding the board's power under Sections 157 and 141 of our corporation law to issue such securities or rights, the court, however, noted that:

> When the Household Board of Directors is faced with a tender offer and a request to redeem rights, they will not be able to arbitrarily reject the offer. They will be held to the same fiduciary standards any other board of directors would be held to in deciding to adopt a defensive mechanism, the same standard they were held to in originally approving the Rights Plan. *See Unocal*, 493 A.2d at 954-55, 958.

Moran v. Household International, Inc., Del. Supr., 500 A.2d at 1354. Thus, the Supreme Court in *Moran* has directed us specifically to its decision in *Unocal Corp. v. Mesa Petroleum Co.*, Del. Supr., 493 A.2d 946 (1985) as supplying the appropriate legal framework for evaluation of the principal question posed by this case.[1]

In addition to seeking an order requiring the Interco board to now redeem the Company's outstanding stock rights, plaintiffs seek an order restraining any steps to implement the Company's alternative restructuring transaction.

For the reasons that follow, I hold that the board's determination to leave the stock rights in effect is a defensive step that, in the circumstances of this offer and at this stage of the contest for control of Interco, cannot be justified as reasonable in relationship to a threat to the corporation or its shareholders posed by the offer; that the restructuring

---

1. In saying that *Unocal* supplies the framework for decision of this aspect of the case, I reject plaintiffs' argument that the board bears a burden to demonstrate the entire fairness of its decision to keep the pill in place while its recapitalization is effectuated.... While the recapitalization does represent a transaction in which the 14 person board (and most intensely, its seven inside members) has an interest—in the sense referred to in *Unocal*—it does not represent a self-dealing transaction in the sense necessary to place upon the board the heavy burden of the intrinsic fairness test. *See Weinberger v. UOP, Inc.*, Del. Supr., 457 A.2d 701 (1983)....

itself does represent a reasonable response to the perception that the offering price is "inadequate"; and that the board, in proceeding as it has done, has not breached any duties derivable from the Supreme Court's opinion in *Revlon v. MacAndrews & Forbes Holdings, Inc.*, Del. Supr., 506 A.2d 173 (1986).

* * *

I.

Interco Incorporated.

Interco is a diversified Delaware holding company that comprises 21 subsidiary corporations in four major business areas: furniture and home furnishings, footwear, apparel and general retail merchandising.... The Company's sales for fiscal 1988 were $3.34 billion, with earnings of $3.50 a share. It has approximately 36 million shares of common stock outstanding.[2]

The Company's subsidiaries operate as autonomous units. Rather than seeing the subsidiaries as parts of an integrated whole, the constituent companies are viewed by Interco management as "a portfolio of assets whose investment merits have to be periodically reviewed." ... Owing to the lack of integration between its operating divisions, the Company is, in management's opinion, particularly vulnerable to a highly leveraged "bust-up" takeover of the kind that has become prevalent in recent years. To combat this perceived danger, the Company adopted a common stock rights plan, or poison pill, in late 1985, which included a "flip-in" provision.

The board of directors of Interco is comprised of 14 members, seven of whom are officers of the Company or its subsidiaries.

The Rales Brothers' Accumulation of Interco Stock; The Interco Board's Response.

In May, 1988, Steven and Mitchell Rales began acquiring Interco stock through CCA. The stock had been trading in the low 40's during that period. Alerted to the unusual trading activity taking place in the Company's stock, the Interco board met on July 11, 1988 ... [and] redeemed the rights issued pursuant to the 1985 rights plan and adopted a new rights plan that contemplated both "flip-in" and "flip-over" rights.

In broad outline, the "flip-in" provision contained in the rights plan adopted on July 11 provides that, if a person reaches a threshold shareholding of 30% of Interco's outstanding common stock, rights will be exercisable entitling each holder of a right to purchase from the Company that number of shares per right as, at the triggering time, have a market value of twice the exercise price of each right.[3] The "flip-over" feature of the rights plan provides that, in the event of a merger of the Company or the acquisition of 50% or more of the Company's assets or earning power, the rights may be exer-

---

2. Plaintiff City Capital Associates Limited Partnership ("CCA" or "City Capital") is a Delaware limited partnership. The partnership is owned by two limited partners, Patrick W. Allender and Michael G. Ryan, each of whom owns a 1% interest, and two general partners, City GP I, Inc. and City GP II, Inc., each of which owns a 49% interest in City Capital. Steven M. Rales is the sole shareholder of GP I, and his brother Mitchell P. Rales, is the sole shareholder of GP II. Moving down the business structure, City Capital owns 100% of Cardinal Holdings Corporation which, in turn, owns 100% of Cardinal Acquisition Corporation. Cardinal Acquisition is the entity extending the offer to purchase. Unless otherwise noted, references to CCA are meant to include the offeror.

3. Rights, however, will not be exercisable in the event that an acquiror who holds 20% or less of Interco's common stock acquires not less than 80% of its outstanding stock in a single transaction.

cised to acquire common stock of the acquiring company having a value of twice the exercise price of the right. The exercise price of each right is $160. The redemption price is $.01 per share.

On July 15, 1988, soon after the adoption of the new rights plan, a press release was issued announcing that the Chairman of the Company's board, Mr. Harvey Saligman, intended to recommend a major restructuring of Interco to the board at its next meeting.

On July 27, 1988, the Rales brothers filed a Schedule 13D with the Securities and Exchange Commission disclosing that, as of July 11, they owned, directly or indirectly, 3,140,300 shares, or 8.7% of Interco's common stock. On that day, CCA offered to acquire the Company by merger for a price of $64 per share in cash, conditioned upon the availability of financing. On August 8, before the Interco board had responded to this offer, CCA increased its offering price to $70 per share, still contingent upon receipt of the necessary financing.

At the Interco board's regularly scheduled meeting on August 8, Wasserstein Perella, Interco's investment banker, informed the board that, in its view, the $70 CCA offer was inadequate and not in the best interests of the Company and its shareholders. This opinion was based on a series of analyses, including discounted cash flow, comparable transaction analysis, and an analysis of premiums paid over existing stock prices for selected tender offers during early 1988. Wasserstein Perella also performed an analysis based upon selling certain Interco businesses and retaining and operating others. This analysis generated a "reference range" for the Company of $68-$80 per share. Based on all of these analyses, Wasserstein Perella concluded the offer was inadequate. The board then resolved to reject the proposal. Also at that meeting, the board voted to decrease the threshold percentage needed to trigger the flip-in provision of the rights plan from 30% to 15% and elected to explore a restructuring plan for the Company.

The Initial Tender Offer for Interco Stock.

On August 15, the Rales brothers announced a public tender offer for all of the outstanding stock of Interco at $70 cash per share. The offer was conditioned upon (1) receipt of financing, (2) the tender of sufficient shares to give the offeror a total holding of at least 75% of the Company's common stock on a fully diluted basis at the close of the offer, (3) the redemption of the rights plan, and (4) a determination as to the inapplicability of 8 *Del. C.* §203.[4]

The board met to consider the tender offer at a special meeting a week later on August 22. Wasserstein Perella had engaged in further studies since the meeting two weeks earlier. It was prepared to give a further view about Interco's value.... Now the studies showed a "reference range" for the whole Company of $74-$87. The so-called reference ranges do not purport to be a range of fair value; but just what they purport to be is (deliberately, one imagines) rather unclear....

In all events, after hearing the banker's opinion, the Interco board resolved to recommend against the tender offer. In rejecting the offer, the board also declined to redeem the rights plan or to render 8 *Del. C.* §203 inapplicable to the offer. Finally, the board refused to disclose confidential information requested by CCA in connection with its

---

4. CCA sued Interco in the federal district court for a determination that Section 203 was an invalid enactment under the federal Constitution. It was unsuccessful in that attempt. *See City Capital Associates LP v. Interco Incorporated,* 696 F. Supp. 1551 (D. Del. 1988).

tender offer unless and until CCA indicated a willingness to enter into a confidentiality and standstill agreement with the Company.[5]

The remainder of the meeting was devoted to an exploration of strategic alternatives to the CCA proposal..., ["]including, without limitation, the recapitalization, restructuring or other reorganization of the company, the sale of assets of the company in addition to the Apparel Manufacturing Group, and other extraordinary transactions, to maximize the value of the company to the stockholders...."

On August 23, 1988, a letter was sent to CCA informing it that Interco intended to explore alternatives to the offer and planned to make confidential information available to third parties in connection with that endeavor.... Interco's proposal was met with an August 26, 1988 counterproposal by CCA suggesting an alternative confidentiality agreement—without standstill provisions.

Apart from the exchange of letters, there were no communications between CCA and Interco between the time the $70 offer was made on August 22 and a later, higher offer at $72 per share was made on September 10....

[O]n September 10, the Rales brothers did amend their offer, increasing the price offered to $72 per share. The Interco board did not consider that offer until September 19 when its investment banker was ready to report on a proposed restructuring. At that meeting, the board rejected the $72 offer on grounds of financial inadequacy and adopted the restructuring proposal.

The Proposed Restructuring.

Under the terms of the restructuring designed by Wasserstein Perella, Interco would sell assets that generate approximately one-half of its gross sales and would borrow $2.025 billion. It would make very substantial distributions to shareholders, by means of a dividend, amounting to a stated aggregate value of $66 per share. The $66 amount would consist of (1) a $25 dividend payable November 7 to shareholders of record on October 13, consisting of $14 in cash and $11 in face amount of senior subordinated debentures, and (2) a second dividend, payable no earlier than November 29, which was declared on October 19, of (a) $24.15 in cash, (b) $6.80 principal amount of subordinated discount debentures, (c) $5.44 principal amount of junior subordinated debentures, (d) convertible preferred stock with a liquidation value of $4.76, and (e) a remaining equity interest or stub that Wasserstein Perella estimates (based on projected earnings of the then remaining businesses) will trade at a price of at least $10 per share. Thus, the total value of the restructuring to shareholders would, in the opinion of Wasserstein Perella, be at least $76 per share on a fully distributed basis.

The board had agreed to a compensation arrangement with Wasserstein Perella that gives that firm substantial contingency pay if its restructuring is successfully completed. Thus, Wasserstein Perella has a rather straightforward and conventional conflict of interest when it opines that the inherently disputable value of its restructuring is greater than the all cash alternative offered by plaintiffs. The market has not, for whatever reason, thought the prospects of the Company quite so bright. It has, in recent weeks, consistently valued Interco stock at about $70 a share....

---

5. The standstill agreement would commit CCA not to make any tender offer for three years unless asked to do so by the Company; it apparently does not have an out should CCA seek to make an offer for all shares at a price higher than an offer endorsed by the board.

Steps have now been taken to effectuate the restructuring. On September 15, the Company announced its plans to sell the Ethan Allen furniture division, which is said by the plaintiffs to be the Company's "crown jewel." ...

Since Interco announced the terms of the restructuring on September 20, it has made two changes with respect to it. It announced on September 27 first that the dividend declared on October 13, 1988 would accrue interest at 12% per annum from that date to the payment date; and second, that the second phase dividend would similarly accrue interest (currently expected to be at a rate of 13¾% per annum) from the date of its declaration.

The Present CCA Offer and the Interco Board's Reaction.

In its third supplemental Offer to Purchase dated October 18, 1988, CCA raised its bid to $74. Like the preceding bid, the proposal is an all cash offer for all shares with a contemplated back-end merger for the same consideration.

At its October 19, 1988 board meeting, the board rejected the $74 offer as inadequate and agreed to recommend that shareholders reject the offer. The board based its rejection both on its apparent view that the price was inadequate and on its belief that the proposed restructuring will yield shareholder value of at least $76 per share.

II.

This case was filed on July 27, 1988.... As indicated above, the relief now sought has two principal elements. First, CCA seeks an order requiring the Interco board to redeem the defensive stock rights and effectively give the Interco shareholders the opportunity to choose as a practical matter. Second, it seeks an order restraining further steps to implement the restructuring, including any steps to sell Ethan Allen.

In order to justify that relief, plaintiffs offer several theories. First, it is their position that this case involves an interested board which has acted to entrench itself at the expense of the stockholders of the Company. Second, because they assert that the board comprises interested directors, plaintiffs also assert that the proposed restructuring transaction involves self-dealing, and that the board is therefore obligated, under *Weinberger*..., to establish the entire fairness of the restructuring and its refusal to rescind the stock rights, which plaintiffs assert it cannot do. Third, plaintiffs urge that under the approach first adopted by the Delaware Supreme Court in *Unocal*, the board's action is said *not* to be reasonable in relation to any threat posed by the plaintiffs because, they say, their noncoercive, all cash offer does not pose a threat. Fourth and last, plaintiffs claim that the proposed restructuring does not importantly differ from a sale of the Company, and that under *Revlon*..., the Interco directors have a duty to obtain the highest available price for the Company's stockholders in the market, which the directors have not done.

Interco answers that only the *Unocal* standard applies in this case. Defendants urge that the *Weinberger* entire fairness test is inapposite because there has been no self-dealing. (*See* n.1, *supra*.) Similarly, defendants claim that no *Revlon* duties have arisen because the restructuring does not amount to a sale of the Company and the Company is not, in fact, for sale.... Defendants state that the Interco board is proceeding in good faith to protect the best interests of the Company's stockholders. The board believes that CCA's offer is inadequate, and therefore constitutes a threat to the Company's stockholders; it is their position that the restructuring and the poison pill are, therefore, reasonable reactions to the threat posed. Moreover, defendants assert that leaving the pill in place to protect the restructuring is reasonable because the restructuring will achieve better value for stockholders than will be garnered by shareholders' acceptance of the plaintiffs' inadequate offer.

III.

* * *

It is appropriate ...[,] before subjecting the board's decision not to redeem the pill to the form of analysis mandated by *Unocal*, to identify what relevant facts are not contested or contestable, and what relevant facts may appropriately be assumed against the party prevailing on this point. They are as follows:

First. The value of the Interco restructuring is inherently a debatable proposition, most importantly (but not solely) because the future value of the stub share is unknowable with reasonable certainty.

Second. The board of Interco believes in good faith that the restructuring has a value of "at least" $76 per share.

Third. The City Capital offer is for $74 per share cash.

Fourth. The board of Interco has acted prudently to inform itself of the value of the Company.[7]

Fifth. The board believes in good faith that the City Capital offer is for a price that is "inadequate."

Sixth. City Capital cannot, as a practical matter, close its tender offer while the rights exist; to do so would be to self-inflict an enormous financial injury that no reasonable buyer would do.

Seventh. Shareholders of Interco have differing liquidity preferences and different expectations about likely future economic events.

Eighth. A reasonable shareholder could prefer the restructuring to the sale of his stock for $74 in cash now, but a reasonable shareholder could prefer the reverse.

Ninth. The City Capital tender offer is in no respect coercive. It is for all shares, not for only a portion of shares. It contemplates a prompt follow-up merger, if it succeeds, not an indefinite term as a minority shareholder. It proposes identical consideration in a follow-up merger, not securities or less money.

Tenth. While the existence of the stock rights has conferred time on the board to consider the City Capital proposals and to arrange the restructuring, the utility of those rights as a defensive technique has, given the time lines for the restructuring and the board's actions to date, now been effectively exhausted except in one respect: the effect of those rights continues to "protect the restructuring."

These facts are sufficient to address the question whether the board's action in electing to leave the defensive stock rights plan in place qualifies for the deference embodied in the business judgment rule.

---

7. This fact is assumed for these purposes; surely it is consistent with the record. The board has not, however, endeavored to determine what is the maximum price that CCA might pay. They say it is not part of their duty to enter into the negotiation that would be necessary to "know" that fact. Insofar as this fact relates to plaintiffs' *Revlon* argument, it is further discussed *infra*....

IV.

... *Unocal* ... recognized that in defending against unsolicited takeovers, there is an "omnipresent specter that a board may be acting primarily in its own interest." 493 A.2d at 954. That fact distinguishes takeover defense measures from other acts of a board which, when subject to judicial review, are customarily upheld once the court finds the board acted in good faith and after an appropriate investigation.... *Unocal* recognizes that human nature may incline *even one acting in subjective good faith* to rationalize as right that which is merely personally beneficial. Thus, it created a new intermediate form of judicial review to be employed when a transaction is neither self-dealing nor wholly disinterested. That test has been helpfully referred to as the "proportionality test."[8]

The test is easy to state. Where it is employed, it requires a threshold examination "before the protections of the business judgment rule may be conferred." 493 A.2d 954. That threshold requirement is in two parts. First, directors claiming the protections of the rule "must show that they had reasonable grounds for believing that a danger to corporate policy and effectiveness existed." The second element of the test is the element of balance. "If a defensive measure is to come within the ambit of the business judgment rule, it must be reasonable in relationship to the threat posed." 493 A.2d 955.

Delaware courts have employed the *Unocal* precedent cautiously.[9] The promise of that innovation is the promise of a more realistic, flexible and, ultimately, more responsible corporation law.... The danger that it poses is, of course, that courts—in exercising some element of substantive judgment—will too readily seek to assert the primacy of their own view on a question upon which reasonable, completely disinterested minds might differ....

A.

Turning to the first element of the *Unocal* form of analysis, it is appropriate to note that, in the special case of a tender offer for all shares, the threat posed, if any, is not importantly to corporate policies..., but rather the threat, if any, is most directly to shareholder interests. Broadly speaking, threats to shareholders in that context may be of two types: threats to the voluntariness of the choice offered by the offer, and threats to the substantive, economic interest represented by the stockholding.

1. *Threats to voluntariness.* It is now universally acknowledged that the structure of an offer can render mandatory in substance that which is voluntary in form. The so-called "front-end" loaded partial offer—already a largely vanished breed—is the most extreme example of this phenomenon. An offer may, however, be structured to have a coercive effect on a rational shareholder in any number of different ways. Whenever a tender offer is so structured, a board may, or perhaps should, perceive a threat to a stockholder's interest in exercising choice to remain a stockholder in the firm. The threat posed by structurally coercive offers is typically amplified by an offering price that the target board responsibly concludes is substantially below a fair price.[10]

---

8. *See* Gilson & Kraakman, *Delaware's Intermediate Standard for Defensive Tactics: Is There Substance To The Proportionality Review?*, [44 Bus. Law. 247 (1989)]....

9. Only two cases have found defensive steps disproportionate to a threat posed by a takeover attempt. *See AC Acquisitions Corp. v. Anderson, Clayton & Co.*, Del. Ch. 519 A.2d 103 (1986); *Robert M. Bass Group, Inc. v. Evans*, Del. Ch., [552 A.2d 1227 (1988)].

10. A different form of threat relating to the voluntariness of the shareholder's choice would arise in a structurally noncoercive offer that contained false or misleading material information.

Each of the cases in which our Supreme Court has addressed a defensive corporate measure under the *Unocal* test involved the sharp and palpable threat to shareholders posed by a coercive offer....

2. *Threats from "inadequate" but noncoercive offers.* The second broad classification of threats to shareholder interests that might be posed by a tender offer for all shares relates to the "fairness" or "adequacy" of the price.[11] It would not be surprising or unreasonable to claim that where an offer is not coercive or deceptive (and, therefore, what is in issue is essentially whether the consideration it offers is attractive or not), a board—even though it may expend corporate funds to arrange alternatives or to inform shareholders of its view of fair value—is not authorized to take preclusive action. By preclusive action I mean action that, as a practical matter, withdraws from the shareholders the option to choose between the offer and the status quo or some other board sponsored alternative.

Our law, however, has not adopted that view and experience has demonstrated the wisdom of that choice. We have held that a board is not required simply by reason of the existence of a noncoercive offer to redeem outstanding poison pill rights.... The reason is simple. Even where an offer is noncoercive, it may represent a "threat" to shareholder interests in the special sense that an active negotiator with power, in effect, to refuse the proposal may be able to extract a higher or otherwise more valuable proposal, or may be able to arrange an alternative transaction or a modified business plan that will present a more valuable option to shareholders.... Our cases, however, also indicate that in the setting of a noncoercive offer, absent unusual facts, there may come a time when a board's fiduciary duty will require it to redeem the rights and to permit the shareholders to choose....

B.

In this instance, there is no threat of shareholder coercion. The threat is to shareholders' economic interests posed by an offer the board has concluded is "inadequate." If this determination is made in good faith (as I assumed it is here ...), it alone will justify leaving a poison pill in place, even in the setting of a noncoercive offer, for a period while the board exercises its good faith business judgment to take such steps as it deems appropriate to protect and advance shareholder interests in light of the significant development that such an offer doubtless is. That action may entail negotiation on behalf of shareholders with the offeror, the institution of a *Revlon*-style auction for the Company, a recapitalization or restructuring designed as an alternative to the offer, or other action.[13]

Once that period has closed, and it is apparent that the board does not intend to institute a *Revlon*-style auction,[14] or to negotiate for an increase in the unwanted offer, and that it has taken such time as it required in good faith to arrange an alternative value-maximizing transaction, then, in most instances, the legitimate role of the poison pill in the context of a noncoercive offer will have been fully satisfied.[15] The only function then left for the pill

---

11. Timing questions may be seen as simply a special case of price inadequacy. That is, the price offered is seen as inadequate because the firm's prospects will appear better later; thus, a fair price now would be higher than that offered.

13. I leave aside the rare but occasionally encountered instance in which the board elects to do nothing at all with respect to an any and all tender offer.

14. If a board elects to conduct an auction of a company, the deployment or continuation of a poison pill will serve as a method to permit the board to act as an effective auctioneer.

15. The role of a poison pill in an auction setting may presumably be affected by provisions in the bid documents. For example, should a disinterested board or committee agree in good faith to a provision requiring that a pill remain in place following bidding (which they might do in order to elicit bidders), such a commitment would presumably validly bind the corporation.

at this end-stage is to preclude the shareholders from exercising a judgment about their own interests that differs from the judgment of the directors, who will have some interest in the question. What then is the "threat" in this instance that might justify such a result? Stating that "threat" at this stage of the process most specifically, it is this: *Wasserstein Perella may be correct in their respective valuations of the offer and the restructuring but a majority of the Interco shareholders may not accept that fact and may be injured as a consequence.*

C.

Perhaps there is a case in which it is appropriate for a board of directors to in effect permanently foreclose their shareholders from accepting a noncoercive offer for their stock by utilization of the recent innovation of "poison pill" rights. If such a case might exist by reason of some special circumstance, a review of the facts here show [sic] this not to be it. The "threat" here, when viewed with particularity, is far too mild to justify such a step in this instance.

Even assuming Wasserstein Perella is correct that when received (and following a period in which full distribution can occur), each of the debt securities to be issued in the restructuring will trade at par, that the preferred stock will trade at its liquidation value, and that the stub will trade initially at $10 a share, the difference in the values of these two offers is only 3%, and the lower offer is all cash and sooner. Thus, the threat, at this stage of the contest, cannot be regarded as very great....

More importantly, it is incontestable that the Wasserstein Perella value is itself a highly debatable proposition. Their prediction of the likely trading range of the stub share represents one obviously educated guess. Here, the projections used in that process were especially prepared for use in the restructuring. Plaintiffs claim they are rosy to a fault, citing, for example, a $75 million cost reduction from remaining operations once the restructuring is fully implemented. This cost reduction itself is $2 per share; 20% of the predicted value of the stub. The Drexel Burnham analysis, which offers no greater claim to correctness, estimates the stub will trade at between $4.53 and $5.45. Moreover, Drexel opines that the whole package of restructure consideration has a value between $68.28 and $70.37 a share, which, for whatever reason, is quite consistent with the stock market price of a share of Interco stock during recent weeks.

The point here is not that, in exercising some restrained substantive review of the board's decision to leave the pill in place, the court finds Drexel's opinion more persuasive than Wasserstein Perella's. I make no such judgment. What is apparent—indeed inarguable—is that one could do so. More importantly, without access to Drexel Burnham's particular analysis, a shareholder could prefer a $74 cash payment now to the complex future consideration offered through the restructuring. The defendants understand this; it is evident.

The information statement sent to Interco shareholders to inform them of the terms of the restructuring accurately states and repeats the admonition ... [that] ["t]here can be no assurances as to actual trading values of [the stub shares] ... [and] newly-issued securities and equity securities in highly leveraged companies....["]

Yet, recognizing the relative closeness of the values and the impossibility of knowing what the stub share will trade at, the board, having arranged a value maximizing restructuring, elected to preclude shareholder choice. It did so not to buy time in order to negotiate or arrange possible alternatives, but asserting in effect a right and duty to save shareholders from the consequences of the choice they might make, if permitted to choose.

Without wishing to cast any shadow upon the subjective motivation of the individual defendants…, I conclude that reasonable minds not affected by an inherent, entrenched interest in the matter, could not reasonably differ with respect to the conclusion that the CCA $74 cash offer did not represent a threat to shareholder interests sufficient in the circumstances to justify, in effect, foreclosing shareholders from electing to accept that offer.

…. To acknowledge that directors may employ the recent innovation of "poison pills" to deprive shareholders of the ability effectively to choose to accept a noncoercive offer, after the board has had a reasonable opportunity to explore or create alternatives, or attempt to negotiate on the shareholders' behalf, would, it seems to me, be so inconsistent with widely shared notions of appropriate corporate governance as to threaten to diminish the legitimacy and authority of our corporation law.

I thus conclude that the board's decision not to redeem the rights following the amendment of the offer to $74 per share cannot be justified in the way *Unocal* requires. This determination does not rest upon disputed facts … and I conclude that affirmative relief is therefore permissible at this stage.

* * *

Notes and Questions

1. What is the theory of the corporation on which the *Interco* opinion is based? Is this theory consistent with the theory developed in *Unocal*?

2. In *Paramount Comm., Inc. v. Time Inc.*, 571 A.2d 1140 (Del. 1989) (*"Time-Warner"*), the Delaware Supreme Court explicitly rejected the chancellor's treatment of *Unocal* in *Interco*, at least as that treatment was presented in *Time-Warner*. Relying, in part, on *Interco*, Paramount argued that the only possible threat its any-and-all cash offer posed was "inadequate value." The court's response to this argument is presented in note 1 following the Chancery Court's opinion in Paramount Comm., Inc. v. Time, Inc., *supra* section 2b(i).

3. To illustrate the dilutive effects of a poison pill, assume a plan is triggered if a bidder acquires 15% of the company's common shares. Each common share, other than common shares owned by the bidder, carries with it one right that becomes exercisable upon triggering. The right entitles the holder to purchase, for a price equal to one-half the prevailing market price of the common shares, one share of preferred stock with voting rights equivalent to the common shares. Assume the following about the company: (i) it has 130 million common shares outstanding; (ii) the common shares are trading at $50 per share; and (iii) the bidder purchases 19.5 million common shares (15% of the common shares outstanding), together with 15% of the rights outstanding (leaving a maximum of 110.5 million rights exercisable, since rights owned by the bidder are not exercisable).

Upon hitting the 15% trigger, each of the 110.5 million rights not owned by the bidder entitles its holder to purchase, for $25, $50 worth of preferred stock. If all rights were exercised there would be outstanding 110.5 million shares of preferred stock (assuming the company does not "cash out" any fractional preferred stock interests) with voting power equivalent to 110.5 million common shares and the bidder would be diluted from 15% (19.5 million shares divided by 130 million shares) to effectively 8.1% (19.5 million shares divided by 240.5 million shares).

In addition, given that the market price was $50 per share before exercise of the rights ($6.5 billion market value) and that exercise of the rights would add to the company $2.76 billion in cash (110.5 million times the $25 exercise price), the resulting market value per share most likely would be no more than $38.25 ($9.26 billion divided by 240.5 million shares). Assuming the bidder's average per share purchase price on its 19.5 million common shares was $50 and all 110.5 million rights were exercised, the market value of the bidder's investment in the company would fall from $975 million to $746 million, resulting in a $229 million (or 23.4%) loss.

With respect to the company's other common shareholders, before the plan is triggered and the rights are exercised, they owned 85% of the company with a total market value of $6.5 billion (their aggregate portion being $5.525 billion). Following triggering and exercise, they own 91.9% of the company with a total market value of $9.2 billion (their aggregate portion being $8.45 billion). That increase in their allocable portion of the total market value of $2.925 billion was purchased for a total of $2.76 billion in cash, yielding a handsome $165 million aggregate gain ($1.49 per share).

4. The Delaware Supreme Court first approved the use of poison pills in Moran v. Household Int'l, Inc., 500 A.2d 1346 (Del. 1985). For a case invalidating a poison pill under New Jersey law that would increase the voting power of existing stockholders (other than an acquiror), see Asarco Inc. v. Holmes A Court, 611 F. Supp. 468 (D.N.J. 1985).

5. Thousands of companies, including most major corporations, have adopted some form of rights plan (poison pill) and hundreds of corporations have classified or staggered boards, charter provisions precluding corporate combinations except at some minimum specified price, and/or charter provisions requiring a supermajority vote to approve a business combination. In connection with any proposed business combination, a chief role of counsel is to investigate the various takeover defense mechanisms that the target has in place and to plan strategies according to the limitations that such mechanisms pose. One common example of the consequence of such research and planning is that hostile tender offers are routinely conditioned on a company's existing poison pill being redeemed by the target board or invalidated by a court.

For a powerful argument that the combination of a poison pill and a staggered board of directors makes a target company virtually impervious to attack, see Bebchuk, Coates & Subramanian, The Powerful Antitakeover Force of Staggered Boards: Theory, Evidence, and Policy, 54 Stan. L. Rev. 887 (2002).

Carmody v. Toll Brothers, Inc.
723 A.2d 1180 (Del. Ch. 1998)

JACOBS, Vice Chancellor:

At issue on this Rule 12(b)(6) motion to dismiss is whether a most recent innovation in corporate antitakeover measures—the so-called "dead hand" poison pill rights plan—is subject to legal challenge on the basis that it violates the Delaware General Corporation Law and/or the fiduciary duties of the board of directors who adopted the plan. As explained more fully below, a "dead hand" rights plan is one that cannot be redeemed except by the incumbent directors who adopted the plan or their designated successors....

The firm whose rights plan is being challenged is Toll Brothers (sometimes referred to as "the company"), a Pennsylvania-based Delaware corporation that designs, builds, and markets single family luxury homes in thirteen states and five regions in the United States.... The company's board of directors has nine members, four of whom (including Bruce and Robert Toll [the founders]) are senior executive officers. The remaining five members of the board are "outside" independent directors.

* * *

The home building industry of which the company is a part is highly competitive. For some time that industry has been undergoing consolidation through the acquisition process.... Inherent in any ... expansion-through-acquisition environment is the risk of a hostile takeover. To protect against that risk, the company's board of directors adopted the Rights Plan.

The Rights Plan was adopted on June 12, 1997, at which point Toll Brothers' stock was trading at approximately $18 per share—near the low end of its established price range of $16 3/8 to $25 3/16 per share. After considering the industry economic and financial environment and other factors, the Toll Brothers board concluded that other companies engaged in its lines of business might perceive the company as a potential target for an acquisition. The Rights Plan was adopted with that problem in mind, but not in response to any specific takeover proposal or threat....

The Rights Plan would operate as follows: there would be a dividend distribution of one preferred stock purchase right (a "Right") for each outstanding share of common stock as of July 11, 1997. Initially the Rights would attach to the company's outstanding common shares, and each Right would initially entitle the holder to purchase one thousandth of a share of a newly registered series Junior A Preferred Stock for $100. The Rights would become exercisable, and would trade separately from the common shares, after the "Distribution Date," which is defined as the earlier of (a) ten business days following a public announcement that an acquiror has acquired, or obtained the right to acquire, beneficial ownership of 15% or more of the company's outstanding common shares (the "Stock Acquisition Date"), or (b) ten business days after the commencement of a tender offer or exchange offer that would result in a person or group beneficially owning 15% or more of the company's outstanding common shares. Once exercisable, the Rights remain exercisable until their Final Expiration Date (June 12, 2007, ten years after the adoption of the Plan), unless the Rights are earlier redeemed by the company.

The dilutive mechanism of the Rights is "triggered" by certain defined events. One such event is the acquisition of 15% or more of Toll Brothers' stock by any person or group of affiliated or associated persons. Should that occur, each Rights holder (except the acquiror and its affiliates and associates) becomes entitled to buy two shares of Toll Brothers common stock or other securities at half price. That is, the value of the stock received when the Right is exercised is equal to two times the exercise price of the Right. In that manner, this so-called "flip in" feature of the Rights Plan would massively dilute the value of the holdings of the unwanted acquiror.

The Rights also have a standard "flip over" feature, which is triggered if after the Stock Acquisition Date, the company is made a party to a merger in which Toll Brothers is not the surviving corporation, or in which it is the surviving corporation and its common stock is changed or exchanged. In either event, each Rights holder becomes entitled to purchase common stock of the acquiring company, again at half-price, thereby impairing the acquiror's capital structure and drastically diluting the interest of the acquiror's other stockholders.

The complaint alleges that the purpose and effect of the company's Rights Plan, as with most poison pills, is to make any hostile acquisition of Toll Brothers prohibitively expensive, and thereby to deter such acquisitions unless the target company's board first approves the acquisition proposal. The target board's "leverage" derives from another critical feature found in most rights plans: the directors' power to redeem the Rights at any time before they expire, on such conditions as the directors "in their sole discretion" may establish. To this extent there is little to distinguish the company's Rights Plan from the "standard model." What is distinctive about the Rights Plan is that it authorizes only a specific, defined category of directors—the "Continuing Directors"—to redeem the Rights. The dispute over the legality of this "Continuing Director" or "dead hand" feature of the Rights Plan is what drives this lawsuit.

In substance, the "dead hand" provision operates to prevent any directors of Toll Brothers, except those who were in office as of the date of the Rights Plan's adoption (June 12, 1997) or their designated successors, from redeeming the Rights until they expire on June 12, 2007. That consequence flows directly from the Rights Agreement's definition of a "Continuing Director," which is:

> (i) any member of the Board of Directors of the Company, while such person is a member of the Board, who is not an Acquiring Person, or an Affiliate [as defined] or Associate [as defined] of an Acquiring Person, or a representative or nominee of an Acquiring Person or of any such Affiliate or Associate, and was a member of the Board prior to the date of this Agreement, or (ii) any Person who subsequently becomes a member of the Board, while such Person is a member of the Board, who is not an Acquiring Person, or an Affiliate [as defined] or Associate [as defined] of an Acquiring Person, or a representative or nominee of an Acquiring Person or of any such Affiliate or Associate, if such Person's nomination for election or election to the Board is recommended or approved by a majority of the Continuing Directors.

According to the complaint, this "dead hand" provision has a twofold practical effect. First, it makes an unsolicited offer for the company more unlikely by eliminating a proxy contest as a useful way for a hostile acquiror to gain control, because even if the acquiror wins the contest, its newly-elected director representatives could not redeem the Rights. Second, the "dead hand" provision disenfranchises, in a proxy contest, all shareholders that wish the company to be managed by a board empowered to redeem the Rights, by depriving those shareholders of any practical choice except to vote for the incumbent directors....

The plaintiff's complaint attacks the "dead hand" feature of the Toll Brothers poison pill on both statutory and fiduciary duty grounds. The statutory claim is that the "dead hand" provision unlawfully restricts the powers of future boards by creating different classes of directors—those who have the power to redeem the poison pill, and those who do not. Under 8 Del. C. §§141 (a) and (d), any such restrictions and director classifications must be stated in the certificate of incorporation. The complaint alleges that because those restrictions are not stated in the Toll Brothers charter, the "dead hand" provision of the Rights Plan is *ultra vires* and, consequently, invalid on its face.

The complaint also alleges that even if the Rights Plan is not *ultra vires*, its approval constituted a breach of the Toll Brothers board's fiduciary duty of loyalty in several respects. It is alleged that the board violated its duty of loyalty because (a) the "dead hand" provision was enacted solely or primarily for entrenchment purposes; (b) it was also a disproportionate defensive measure, since it precludes the shareholders from receiving tender offers and engaging in a proxy contest, in contravention of the principles of *Unocal Corp. v. Mesa Petroleum Co.*, as elucidated in *Unitrin, Inc. v. American General Corp.* and (c) the "dead hand" provision purposefully interferes with the shareholder voting franchise without any compelling justification, in derogation of the principles articulated in *Blasius Indus. v. Atlas Corp....*

The validity of antitakeover measures is normally evaluated under the Unocal/Unitrin standard. But where the defensive measures purposefully disenfranchise shareholders, the board will be required to satisfy the more exacting *Blasius* standard, which our Supreme Court has articulated as follows:

> A board's unilateral decision to adopt a defensive measure touching "upon issues of control" that purposefully disenfranchises its shareholders is strongly suspect under Unocal, and cannot be sustained without a "compelling justification."

Stroud v. Grace, Del. Supr., 606 A.2d 75, 92 n.3 (1992).

The complaint alleges that the "dead hand" provision purposefully disenfranchises the company's shareholders without any compelling justification. The disenfranchisement would occur because even in an election contest fought over the issue of the hostile bid, the shareholders will be powerless to elect a board that is both willing and able to accept the bid....

A claim that the directors have unilaterally "created a structure in which shareholder voting is either impotent or self defeating" is necessarily a claim of purposeful disenfranchisement. Given the Supreme Court's rationale for upholding the validity of the poison pill in *Moran*, and the primacy of the shareholder vote in our scheme of corporate jurisprudence, any contrary view is difficult to justify. In *Moran*, the Supreme Court upheld the adoption of a poison pill, in part because its effect upon a proxy contest would be "minimal," but also because if the board refused to redeem the plan, the shareholders could exercise their prerogative to remove and replace the board. In *Unocal* the Supreme Court reiterated that view that the safety valve which justifies a board being allowed to resist a hostile offer a majority of shareholders might prefer, is that the shareholders always have their ultimate recourse to the ballot box. Those observations reflect the fundamental value that the shareholder vote has primacy in our system of corporate governance because it is the "ideological underpinning upon which the legitimacy of directorial power rests." ...

The defendants contend that the complaint fails to allege a valid stockholder disenfranchisement claim, because the Rights Plan does not on its face limit a dissident's ability to propose a slate or the shareholders' ability to cast a vote. The defendants also urge that even if the Plan might arguably have that effect, it could occur only in a very specific and unlikely context, namely, where (i) the hostile bidder makes a fair offer that it is willing to keep open for more than one year, (ii) the current board refuses to redeem the Rights, and (iii) the offeror wages two successful proxy fights and is committed to wage a third.

This argument, in my opinion, begs the issue and is specious. It begs the issue because the complaint does not claim that the Rights Plan facially restricts the shareholders' voting rights. What the complaint alleges is that the "dead hand" provision will either preclude a hostile bidder from waging a proxy contest altogether, or, if there should be a contest, it will coerce those shareholders who desire the hostile offer to succeed to vote for those directors who oppose it—the incumbent (and "Continuing") directors. Besides missing the point, the argument is also specious, because the hypothetical case the defendants argue must exist for any disenfranchisement to occur, rests upon the unlikely assumption that the hostile bidder will keep its offer open for more than one year. Given the market risks inherent in financed hostile bids for public corporations, it is unrealistic to assume that many bidders would be willing to do that.

For these reasons, the plaintiff's *Blasius*-based breach of fiduciary duty claim is cognizable under Delaware law.

The final issue is whether the complaint states a legally cognizable claim that the inclusion of the "dead hand" provision in the Rights Plan was an unreasonable defensive measure within the meaning of *Unocal*. I conclude that it does....

Quickturn Design Systems, Inc. v. Shapiro
721 A.2d 1281, 1289-1291 (Del. 1998)

HOLLAND, Justice:

.... At the time Mentor commenced its bid, Quickturn had in place a Rights Plan that contained a so-called "dead hand" provision. That provision had a limited "continuing director" feature that became operative only if an insurgent that owned more than 15% of Quickturn's common stock successfully waged a proxy contest to replace a majority of the board. In that event, only the "continuing directors" (those directors in office at the time the poison pill was adopted) could redeem the rights.

During the same August 21, 1998 meeting at which it amended the special meeting by-law, the Quickturn board also amended the Rights Plan to eliminate its "continuing director" feature, and to substitute a "no hand" or "delayed redemption provision" [DRP] into its Rights Plan. The Delayed Redemption Provision provides that, if a majority of the directors are replaced by stockholder action, the newly elected board cannot redeem the rights for six months if the purpose or effect of the redemption would be to facilitate a transaction with an "Interested Person."[21]

It is undisputed that the DRP would prevent Mentor's slate, if elected as the new board majority, from redeeming the Rights Plan for six months following their election, because a redemption would be "reasonably likely to have the purpose or effect of facilitating a Transaction" with Mentor, a party that "directly or indirectly proposed, nominated or financially supported" the election of the new board. Consequently, by adopting the DRP, the Quickturn board built into the process a six month delay period in addition to the 90 to 100 day delay mandated by the By-Law Amendment....

In this appeal, Mentor argues that the judgment of the Court of Chancery should be affirmed because the Delayed Redemption Provision is invalid as a matter of Delaware law. According to Mentor, the Delayed Redemption Provision, like the "dead hand" feature in the Rights Plan that was held to be invalid in [*Carmody v. Toll Brothers, Inc.*, 723

---

21. The "no hand" or Delayed Redemption Provision ... states:
    (b) Notwithstanding the provisions of Section 23(a), in the event that a majority of the Board of Directors of the Company is elected by stockholder action at an annual or special meeting of stockholders, then until the 180th day following the effectiveness of such election (including any postponement or adjournment thereof), the Rights shall not be redeemed if such redemption is reasonably likely to have the purpose or effect of facilitating a Transaction with an Interested Person.

A.2d 1180 (Del. Ch. 1998)] will impermissibly deprive any newly elected board of both its statutory authority to manage the corporation under 8 Del. C. §141(a) and its concomitant fiduciary duty pursuant to that statutory mandate. We agree....

One of the most basic tenets of Delaware corporate law is that the board of directors has the ultimate responsibility for managing the business and affairs of a corporation. Section 141(a) requires that any limitation on the board's authority be set out in the certificate of incorporation. The Quickturn certificate of incorporation contains no provision purporting to limit the authority of the board in any way. The Delayed Redemption Provision, however, would prevent a newly elected board of directors from completely discharging its fundamental management duties to the corporation and its stockholders for six months. While the Delayed Redemption Provision limits the board of directors' authority in only one respect, the suspension of the Rights Plan, it nonetheless restricts the board's power in an area of fundamental importance to the shareholders—negotiating a possible sale of the corporation. Therefore, we hold that the Delayed Redemption Provision is invalid under Section 141(a), which confers upon any newly elected board of directors full power to manage and direct the business and affairs of a Delaware corporation.

The Delayed Redemption Provision would prevent a new Quickturn board of directors from managing the corporation by redeeming the Rights Plan to facilitate a transaction that would serve the stockholders' best interests, even under circumstances where the board would be required to do so because of its fiduciary duty to the Quickturn stockholders....

Note

The literature on the use of poison pills includes Velasco, The Enduring Illegitimacy of The Poison Pill, 27 Iowa J. Corp. L. 381 (2002); Lipton & Rowe, Pills, Polls and Professors: A Reply to Professor Gilson, 27 Del. J. Corp. L. 1 (2002); Braendel, Defeating Poison Pills Through Enactment of a State Shareholder Protection Statute, 25 Del. J. Corp. L. 651 (2000); Letsou, Symposium: Contemporary Issues in the Law of Business Organizations: Are Dead Hand (and No Hand) Poison Pills Really Dead?, 68 U. Cin. L. Rev. 1101 (2000).

(iii) Greenmail

Heckmann v. Ahmanson
214 Cal. Rptr. 177 (Cal. Ct. App. 1985)

JOHNSON, Associate Justice.

Plaintiffs, stockholders in Walt Disney Productions, are suing to recover the payoff in the greenmailing[1] of Disney. Defendants are the Disney directors who paid the greenmail and the "Steinberg Group"[2] to whom the money, approximately $325 million, was paid.

---

1. A greenmailer creates the threat of a corporate takeover by purchasing a significant amount of the company's stock. He then sells the shares back to the company at a premium when its executives, in fear of [losing] their jobs, agree to buy him out....

2. The "Steinberg Group" consists of defendants, Saul P. Steinberg, Reliance Financial Services Corp., Reliance Group, Inc., Reliance Group Holdings, Inc., Reliance Insurance Co., Reliance Insurance Co. of New York, United Pacific Insurance Co., United Pacific Life Insurance Co., and United Pacific Insurance Company of New York.

Plaintiffs obtained a preliminary injunction which, in effect, imposes a trust on the profit from the Disney-Steinberg transaction, approximately $60 million, and requires the Steinberg Group to render periodic accountings of the disposition of the entire proceeds. The Steinberg Group appeals from this preliminary injunction. We affirm.

* * *

FACTS AND PROCEEDINGS BELOW

In March 1984 the Steinberg Group purchased more than two million shares of Disney stock. Probably interpreting this as the opening shot in a takeover war, the Disney directors countered with an announcement Disney would acquire Arvida Corporation for $200 million in newly-issued Disney stock and assume Arvida's $190 million debt.[3] The Steinberg Group countered this move with a stockholders' derivative action in federal court to block the Arvida transaction. Nonetheless, on June 6, 1984, the Arvida transaction was consummated.

Undeterred by its failure to halt Disney's purchase of Arvida, the Steinberg Group proceeded to acquire some two million additional shares of Disney stock, increasing its ownership position to approximately 12 percent of the outstanding Disney shares. On June 8, 1984, the Steinberg Group advised Disney's directors of its intention to make a tender offer for 49 percent of the outstanding shares at $67.50 a share and its intention to later tender for the balance at $72.50 a share. The directors' response was swift. On the evening of the same day, the directors proposed Disney repurchase all the stock held by the Steinberg Group. Agreement was reached on June 11.

Under the agreement with the Steinberg Group, Disney purchased all the stock held by the group for $297.4 million and reimbursed the estimated costs incurred in preparing the tender offer, $28 million, for a total of $325.4 million, or about $77 per share. The Steinberg Group garnered a profit of about $60 million. In return, the Steinberg Group agreed not to purchase Disney stock and to dismiss its individual causes of action in the Arvida litigation. It did not dismiss the derivative claims.

Disney borrowed the entire sum necessary to repurchase its shares. This transaction, coupled with the debt assumed in the Arvida purchase, increased Disney's total indebtedness to $866 million, two-thirds of Disney's entire shareholder equity. Upon the announcement of its agreement with the Steinberg Group, the price of Disney stock dropped below $50 per share. Thus, the Steinberg Group received a price 50 percent above the market price following the transaction.

The gravamen of the action against the Steinberg Group is that it used its tender offer and the Arvida litigation to obtain a premium price for its shares in violation of its fiduciary duties to Disney and the other shareholders. The complaint seeks, among other things, rescission of Disney's repurchase agreement with the Steinberg Group, an accounting and a constructive trust upon all funds the Steinberg Group received from Disney.

After due notice and hearing, the trial court issued a preliminary injunction enjoining the Steinberg Group from transferring, investing or disposing of the profit[4] from its

---

3. Like the puff fish, a corporate delicacy will often attempt to avoid being swallowed up by making itself appear less attractive to a potential predator....

4. The profit, for purposes of the preliminary injunction, was defined as the difference paid by defendants for the stock, approximately $63.25 per share, and the total amount received under the repurchase agreement, approximately $77.50 per share, together with income earned on that amount from the date of receipt. This totals approximately $60 million.

sale of Disney stock except in accordance with the standards applicable to a prudent trustee under Civil Code section 2261....

DISCUSSION

* * *

II. PLAINTIFFS DEMONSTRATED A REASONABLE PROBABILITY OF SUCCESS ON THE MERITS ENTITLING THEM TO A CONSTRUCTIVE TRUST UPON THE PROFITS THE STEINBERG GROUP RECEIVED FROM ITS SALE OF DISNEY STOCK.

A. *Liability of the Steinberg Group as an Aider and Abettor of the Disney Directors' Breach of Fiduciary Duty.*

Although we have found no case in which a greenmailer was ordered to return his illgotten gains, precedent for such a judgment exists in California law.

In *Jones v. H. F. Ahmanson & Co.* (1969) 1 Cal. 3d 93, 108-109, 81 Cal. Rptr. 592, 460 P.2d 464, ... the majority stockholders set up a holding company in a manner which made the minority shares unmarketable.... The court held the facts alleged in the complaint stated a cause of action for breach of fiduciary duty. "[D]efendants chose a course of action in which they used their control of the Association to obtain an advantage not made available to all stockholders. They did so without regard to the resulting detriment to the minority stockholders and in the absence of any compelling business purpose." (1 Cal. 3d at p. 114, 81 Cal. Rptr. 592, 460 P.2d 464.)

While there may be many valid reasons why corporate directors would purchase another company or repurchase the corporation's shares, the naked desire to retain their positions of power and control over the corporation is not one of them.[5] ...

If the Disney directors breached their fiduciary duty to the stockholders, the Steinberg Group could be held jointly liable as an aider and abettor. The Steinberg Group knew it was reselling its stock at a price considerably above market value to enable the Disney directors to retain control of the corporation. It knew or should have known Disney was borrowing the $325 million purchase price. From its previous dealings with Disney, including the Arvida transaction, it knew the increased debt load would adversely affect Disney's credit rating and the price of its stock. If it were an active participant in the breach of duty and reaped the benefit, it cannot disclaim the burden.... "Where there is a common plan or design to commit a tort, all who participate are jointly liable whether or not they do the wrongful acts." (*Certified Grocers of California, Ltd. v. San Gabriel Valley Bank* (1983) 150 Cal. App. 3d 281, 289, 197 Cal. Rptr. 710.)

The Steinberg Group contends there was no evidence presented to the trial court that the repurchase agreement was motivated by the Disney directors' desire to perpetuate their own control instead of a good faith belief the corporate interest would be served thereby....

At this point in the litigation, it is not necessary the court be presented with a "smoking gun." We believe the evidence presented to the court was sufficient to demonstrate a probability of success on the merits. The acts of the Disney directors—and particularly their timing—are difficult to understand except as defensive strategies against a hostile takeover....

---

5. We recognize the Disney directors were not parties to the proceedings on the preliminary injunction nor this appeal and have not had the opportunity to tell their side of the story.

Once it is shown a director received a personal benefit from the transaction, which appears to be the case here, the burden shifts to the director to demonstrate not only the transaction was entered in good faith, but also to show its inherent fairness from the viewpoint of the corporation and those interested therein.... The only evidence presented by the Disney directors was the conclusory statement of one of its attorneys that "[t]he Disney objective in purchasing [the] stock was to avoid the damage to Disney and its shareholders which would have been the result of [the] announced tender offer." This vague assertion falls short of evidence of good faith and inherent fairness....

DISPOSITION

The array of law and facts advanced by plaintiffs evaluated against defendants' counter-contentions demonstrates a reasonable probability that plaintiffs will be successful although, we stress, the final decision must await trial and a trial might well produce a different result. As to hardship, we believe the trial court reasonably concluded detriment to the plaintiffs if the proceeds and profits are dissipated or untraceable exceeds any hardship to the Steinberg Group in complying with the investment and accounting provisions of the preliminary injunction.

The order granting a preliminary injunction is affirmed.

THOMPSON, Acting P.J., and HARRIS, J.,* concur.

Macey and McChesney, A Theoretical Analysis of Corporate Greenmail
95 Yale L.J. 13, 29-32, 33, 34-36 (1985)[a]

By increasing the premium a first offeror must pay and/or by reducing the likelihood of her offer succeeding, defensive tactics (including those that encourage creation of auctions) reduce a bidder's incentive to locate attractive targets and invest in first offers. Defensive tactics employed once the initial bid is made afford subsequent bidders an even greater opportunity to free-ride on information generated by the first bidder. It is not just prospective initial bidders who are harmed, however. Fewer bids also harm shareholders of potential targets. Thus, as Easterbrook and Fischel observe, the reduced incentive to scrutinize firms for undervaluation affects the entire market for corporate control....

But greenmail is unlike other defensive tactics, in that greenmail actually *solves* the free-rider problem that lowers the probability of an ultimate takeover. The minority shareholder, by hypothesis, is the first to develop the information that the firm is undervalued. To maximize the premium it will receive, the firm must buy off the minority, paying in greenmail at least the expected value to her of the minority takeover. There is thus no free ride and no disincentive to the production of information, because greenmail compensates the minority for developing the information that the firm is undervalued. Target firm shareholders obtain the ability to run an auction after their firm is identified, but must purchase the right to do so from the one who provided the information in the first place.

* Assigned by the Chairperson of the Judicial Council.

a. Reprinted by permission of The Yale Law Journal Company and Fred B. Rothman & Company from The Yale Law Journal, Vol. 95, pp. 13-61.

The implications of greenmail in avoiding free-rider problems are worth elaborating. The potential for free-riding on information arises because, absent greenmail, the returns for acquiring information normally can be captured only by a successful takeover bid. Gilson notes that the initial offeror's bid must cover two entirely separate costs: the bidder's search costs to discover the target, plus the amount paid to obtain control. If the only way to reap any return for the investment in information is to implement the takeover, unsuccessful takeovers leave the information discovery uncompensated. Potential bidders will reduce the amount of search, and the production of information will be sub-optimal.

Under these circumstances, both demanders and suppliers of information have an incentive to establish a separate compensation system for the information itself, to "unbundle" or "de-couple" the production of information about a firm's value from the takeover itself. More information about firm values will then be produced, which benefit the firms themselves, and producers of that information will be more assured of compensation. Greenmail is one arrangement that de-couples compensation for information from completion of a takeover. The possibility of receiving greenmail gives greater assurance to the information producer that she will be compensated for the value of the information, even if she ultimately does not acquire control. The result is the production of more information and better monitoring of management performance.

Separate compensation also permits sellers of information to specialize. One who develops information about profitable takeover candidates may want simply to sell the information, rather than to manage the undervalued firm herself. There are gains from specialization in separating the discovery of information from acquisition and management of target firms....

In short, there are gains to be made from trading among the parties if specialization is efficient. A bidder could pay a finder's fee directly to one who locates profitable acquisition opportunities. This is essentially the way investment banks are compensated, but one observes non-institutional developers of information performing the same function of selling information to takeover bidders. Third parties are not the only ones who would demand the information developed, however. The target firm's incumbent majority also might be willing to pay for it, either to put it to use themselves or to pass it along to potential bidders or merger partners. Target firms may in some situations be more efficient at locating higher-valued users of the firm's resources. If so, target firms predictably would be the ones to purchase with greenmail the newly developed information from the minority shareholder.

* * *

When greenmail is paid, the target firm's resources go to the firm or individual who has conferred an informational benefit upon the shareholders. In this respect, the payment of greenmail differs from other sorts of defensive tactics. Like greenmail, other defensive tactics benefit target shareholders by permitting them to avoid an initial tender offer they think is too low. But unlike greenmail, these other tactics discourage initial offers by raising the cost of such offers. The potential for obtaining greenmail, by contrast, encourages rather than discourages bidders to invest resources in ferreting out information about target firms, even where that information may be of more value to a third party than to the initial offeror.

* * *

Greenmail, like other defensive tactics, does lower the amount bidders will offer for the target firm.... Unlike other defensive tactics (e.g., litigation), which consume real resources, greenmail is purely a transfer payment. There may be costs of bargaining over the exact terms between the firm and the greenmailer, but these are trivial compared to the costs of litigation or other defensive tactics. And even these are not deadweight social losses, but costs of producing and pricing a valuable resource: information. Thus, as with the free-rider argument, the general case against defensive tactics does not apply to greenmail; greenmail does not consume valuable resources.

* * *

B. *Greenmail in the Absence of a Credible Takeover Threat: The Role of Standstill Agreements*

.... The question remains, why does a potential greenmailer take a position in the firm and threaten a takeover as a prelude to selling information? Assume that an outsider develops valuable information, but has no desire to initiate a takeover. The information is saleable, either to the firm itself or to potential third-party takeover bidders. One might wonder, in this case, why producers of information do not sell the information to one of these parties directly, without acquiring shares or threatening takeovers.

If a corporate outsider has valuable information, she would prefer to sell it directly to the firm if its value is greater than what she could expect from a takeover bid. There arise important bargaining problems, however, that might prevent M from selling the information she has discovered. The seller may be bluffing, as to either the value or even the existence of the information claimed.... Once the information is revealed, the producer of information effectively loses any enforceable property right in the information, and exposes herself to the same free-rider problems discussed above concerning an initial bid. By the same token, if the purchaser is asked to take it "on faith" that the information is really valuable, he exposes himself to being bluffed by someone who actually has no valuable information.

There is an alternative open to both buyers and sellers that would facilitate the efficient exchange of information. The developer of the information could indicate her good faith (the fact that she is not bluffing) by buying a bond that she would forfeit if she had acted in bad faith. Buying into the firm acts as the equivalent of a bond. The minority position works to bond the information seller in two ways. First, the minority holding entails an opportunity cost in the capital that, if her idea is without value, could have been invested more profitably elsewhere. Second, maintaining a substantial minority position has important effects on the investment portfolio of the information seller. Concentrating a significant percentage of the total portfolio in a single asset limits the minority shareholder's ability to diversify away asset-specific risk. By showing that she is willing to incur these costs, the seller makes credible her claim of having valuable information.

In both respects, the minority equity position works like a surety bond to guarantee the quality of her information. The information may still not be revealed, however, until the shareholder receives a management position within the firm, which ensures that the firm will use her idea and compensate her for its value as the value of the stock rises. Additional compensation to the developer of the idea may come from the normal emoluments paid to directors and managers if she joins the firm in either or both of those capacities.

This is, in fact, what is accomplished by standstill agreements, a form of greenmail in which the substantial minority shareholder agrees to maintain a certain level of investment but also to limit her percentage ownership in the firm for a certain period of time....

This hypothesis concerning standstill agreements runs against the common perception that the agreements are simply ways to limit minority interference with the firm by freezing the minority's equity position at its current level. While that may be their function in some cases, standstill agreements can also work as a bonding mechanism permitting the transfer of information. If the bonding hypothesis explains at least some standstill agreements, we would expect to find situations in which standstill contracts were used to *increase* the size of the minority holding. If the size of the minority's current stock holding is insufficient to bond her, the majority would insist on increasing the level of her equity. In fact, such equity-increasing standstill agreements are observed, even with corporate "raiders" whose involvement with the firm, one might have thought, majority shareholders would want to limit.

Standstill agreements as bonds have positive private and social costs, however, in the financial and human capital tied up in the minority's ownership of the firm. Particularly when outsiders specialize in the development of information, not ownership of firms, these bonding arrangements may be unnecessarily costly.... The market provides another solution for these "repeat greenmailers": their reputation for developing reliable information itself acts as a bond to prospective purchasers of information. Certain individuals, such as Victor Posner, Carl Icahn and Saul Steinberg are well-known greenmailers. When these people come to the management of a target firm and claim to have unearthed valuable information, they may demand an outright payment for the information that is not tied to any long-term employment contract. There is no danger to the target firm of a bluff from a greenmailer when the loss to the greenmailer's reputational capital from bluffing exceeds the gain from a one-time greenmail payment. Put another way, if a greenmailer is found to be bluffing, word will spread and her future demands for greenmail will go unheeded. One would predict, therefore, that greenmailers with substantial investments in brand-name capital would more frequently be able to sell their shares outright rather than "post bond" by entering into standstill agreements.

Notes and Questions

1. Warren Buffett, the chair of Berkshire Hathaway Inc. and one of the most successful investors in history, offered his opinion of greenmail in one of his famous letters to Berkshire shareholders. After endorsing repurchases of stock from all shareholders that are sound as a capital allocation decision (*i.e.*, where the stock is trading in the market at below the company's intrinsic value then the shareholders benefit from repurchases), in his 1984 letter, Buffett wrote as follows:

> Our endorsement of repurchases is limited to those dictated by price/value relationships and does not extend to the "greenmail" repurchase—a practice we find odious and repugnant. In these transactions, two parties achieve their personal ends by exploitation of an innocent and unconsulted third party. The players are: (1) the "shareholder" extortionist who, even before the ink on his stock certificate dries, delivers his "your-money-or-your-life" message to managers; (2) the corporate insiders who quickly seek peace at any price—as long as the price is paid by someone else; and (3) the shareholders whose money is used by (2) to make (1) go away. As the dust settles, the mugging, transient shareholder gives his speech on "free enterprise", the muggee management gives its speech on "the best interests of the company", and the innocent shareholder standing by mutely funds the payoff.

Does Buffett overlook the informational benefits of greenmail or are Macey and McChesney wrong to believe that they exist? If it is possible that in some but not all cases a greenmailer does produce information and in some but not all cases a greenmailer is the corporate equivalent of a mugger, are there any mechanisms for identifying who's who in a particular setting? Can legal rules be designed to distinguish who's who and to respond appropriately? Are directorial fiduciary duty and enhanced judicial scrutiny possible legal responses? Are they satisfactory?

2. The court in Samuel M. Feinberg Testamentary Trust v. Carter, 652 F. Supp. 1066 (S.D.N.Y. 1987) (applying New York law) refused to dismiss a cause of action for breach of fiduciary duty based on the repurchase by B. F. Goodrich Company of a large block of its common stock from well-known raider Carl Icahn. But see Heine v. The Signal Companies, 1977 U.S. Dist. LEXIS 17071 (S.D.N.Y.); Cheff v. Mathes, 199 A.2d 548 (Del. 1964); Nathan & Sobel, Corporate Stock Repurchases in the Context of Unsolicited Takeover Bids, 35 Bus. Law. 1545, 1564-66 (1980).

3. Ang & Tucker, The Shareholder Wealth Effects of Corporate Greenmail, 11 J. Fin. Res. 265 (1988), summarize the economic literature on the detriments and benefits of "targeted block share repurchases." The authors test several hypotheses and conclude that (i) "greenmailed firms that are acquired exhibit abnormal returns only similar to those of other merger and tender offer targets. Also, the probability of subsequent acquisition appears to be unrelated to the targeted repurchase." Id. at 266. They further conclude that managers who pay greenmail are significantly more likely to lose their jobs than other managers, whether or not the firm ultimately is acquired.

They point out, however, that their results as to the wealth effects of greenmail do not necessarily lead to the conclusion that greenmail ought to be regulated, since ultimately they find it to have no significant wealth effects. Id. at 278. They do, however, assert that their findings with regard to management turnover supports the Fama thesis we examined supra in chapter 1, section 2.

4. A number of states have adopted statutes regulating greenmail. For example, N.Y. Bus. Corp. Law § 513(e) provides:

> (e) No resident domestic corporation which is subject to the provisions of section nine hundred twelve of this chapter shall purchase or agree to purchase more than ten percent of the stock of the resident domestic corporation from a shareholder for more than the market value[a] thereof unless such purchase or agreement to purchase is approved by the affirmative vote of the board of directors followed by the affirmative vote of the holders of a majority of all outstanding shares entitled to vote thereon at a meeting of shareholders unless the certificate of incorporation requires a greater percentage of the outstanding shares to approve.
>
> The provisions of this paragraph shall not apply when the resident domestic corporation offers to purchase shares from all holders of stock or for stock which the holder has been the beneficial owner of for more than two years....

In a similar vein, Minnesota law provides:

> Subd. 3. Limitation on share purchases. Except for redemptions under section 302A.671, subdivision 6 [control share acquisitions], a publicly held

---

a. "Market value" is defined as the highest closing sale price during the thirty days preceding the purchase (or agreement) date. N.Y. Bus. Corp. Law § 912(a)(11).

corporation shall not, directly or indirectly, purchase or agree to purchase any shares entitled to vote from a person (or two or more persons who act as a partnership, limited partnership, syndicate, or other group pursuant to any written or oral agreement, arrangement, relationship, understanding, or otherwise for the purpose of acquiring, owning, or voting shares of the publicly held corporation) who beneficially owns more than five percent of the voting power of the publicly held corporation for more than the market value thereof if the shares have been beneficially owned by the person or persons for less than six months, unless the purchase or agreement to purchase is approved at a meeting of shareholders by the affirmative vote of the holders of a majority of the voting power of all shares entitled to vote or the publicly held corporation makes an offer, of at least equal value per share, to all holders of shares of the class or series and to all holders of any class or series into which the securities may be converted.

Minn. Stat. Ann. §302A.553 (2005).

Similar statutes have been adopted in Arizona, Ariz. Rev.-Stat. Ann. §10-2704 (2004); Michigan, Mich. Stat. Ann. §450.1799 (2005); Nevada, Nev. Rev. Stat. Ann. ch. 78.3792 (2004); and Wisconsin, Wis. Stat. Ann. §180.1134 (2004).

5. In the case of the Minnesota statute, the limitation on greenmail repurchases is defined in terms of a price "more than the market value" of the shares, presumably at the time of the repurchase. Does this provision achieve the apparent objective of the statute to prohibit greenmail or does it in effect make it legitimate? The answer depends on whether the market value (price) at the time of repurchase would already somehow incorporate the expected premium to be paid to the greenmailer. If it does, then the statute makes greenmail legal, rather than illegal. See Gilson, Drafting an Effective Greenmail Prohibition, 88 Colum. L. Rev. 329, 338 (1988).

6. On the federal level, concern about the adverse impact of greenmail led to the enactment of a penalty tax payable by the greenmailer. See 26 U.S.C. §5881 (2000). In addition, corporations paying greenmail are prohibited from deducting the cost of greenmail payments. See 26 U.S.C. §162(k) (2000 & Supp. II 2002).

Problem — Legislating Against Greenmail

Draft a statute prohibiting greenmail. In so doing, consider (a) whether the statute ought to be mandatory and apply to all corporations (or at least all corporations of a certain type), or enabling, and apply only to those corporations which elect to include it in their charters; (b) ways in which your definition of "premium" can be drafted to deal with the issue of whether the expected premium would already be reflected in the stock's price (reconsider the discussion of beta from chapter 3, section 5b(i)); and (c) assuming that it is sensible to distinguish between selective repurchases that constitute greenmail in its pernicious variety and those that do not, can your draft statute facilitate that distinction?

(iv) Deal Protection Measures

A corollary to protecting the shareholder franchise (see supra chapter 8, section 7) concerns the role boards of directors play in bringing merger proposals to a shareholder vote. Delaware law was amended in 1998 to authorize boards of directors to submit mergers to a shareholder vote even if the board no longer recommends that shareholders approve it. Del. Gen. Corp. Law §251(c). Even so, courts show concern that boards retain sufficient flexibility prior to such a vote to exercise their fiduciary duties in determining whether a proposed merger is in the best interests of the corporation and its shareholders.

The following two cases examine this issue in the context of deal protection measures. These contractual devices included in some merger agreements are designed to give a bidder some assurance that it will clinch the deal, not serve as a mere stalking horse for potential competing bidders. After all, a bidder invests substantial time and resources in lining up a merger. Those efforts set a value for the target firm that other bidders can then use to free ride on the bidder's investment.

Devices include covenants that the board will use "best efforts" to obtain shareholder approval or at least to recommend shareholders approve. They extend to contractual limits on a board's right to talk with third parties about a business combination ("no-talk" provisions) or actively to solicit competing bids ("no-shop" provisions). They can also include a broader range of "lock-up" devices, such as granting the bidder options to buy selected target assets.

The challenge is to design measures providing requisite bidder assurance without target directors abdicating their fiduciary duties. Customarily, deal protection covenants are accompanied by a specific contractual provision that expressly authorizes a board to take actions the deal protection measures otherwise would prohibit if necessary to fulfill the board's fiduciary duties (a "fiduciary out" provision). But even without a "fiduciary out" provision, which would control: contractual provisions or fiduciary principles? Which *should* control?

ACE Limited v. Capital Re Corp.

747 A.2d 95 (Del. Ch. 2000)

STRINE, Vice Chancellor.

Plaintiff ACE Limited ("ACE") has filed a motion requesting a temporary restraining order ("TRO") against defendant Capital Re Corporation ("Capital Re"). ACE requests that I issue an order that restrains Capital Re from taking any action to terminate the June 10, 1999 Agreement and Plan of Merger between and among ACE, Capital Re, and CapRe Acquisition Corporation (the "Merger Agreement"). Capital Re's board of directors wishes to terminate the Merger Agreement and accept an all cash, all shares bid that it believes is financially superior to the Merger Agreement. ACE contends that Capital Re cannot, under the Merger Agreement's no-talk and termination provisions, validly terminate the Merger Agreement.

* * *

Capital Re, a Delaware corporation, is a specialty reinsurance corporation in the business of municipal and non-municipal guaranty reinsurance, mortgage guaranty reinsurance, title reinsurance, and trade credit reinsurance. ACE is a Cayman Islands holding company that, through subsidiaries, engages in the insurance and reinsurance industries internationally.

According to ACE, Capital Re was in a capital crunch earlier this year. Although Capital Re does not admit that this was the reason, it says that for more than a year it has been exploring a possible business combination or capital infusion. During this exploration, Capital Re engaged ACE in discussions about strategic options. As a result of those discussions, ACE provided Capital Re with a cash infusion of $75 million in February 1999 in exchange for newly issued Capital Re shares, which ultimately amounted to 12.3% of the company's outstanding common shares.

This infusion was apparently insufficient to calm the markets because in March of 1999 Moody's Investors Service, Inc. downgraded Capital Re's financial rating from AAA to AA2. ACE contends that a further downgrading would have seriously affected Capital Re's earnings and that Capital Re therefore contacted ACE in May of 1999 to discuss solutions, including a possible business combination with ACE.

Negotiations following this contact bore fruit in the form of the binding Merger Agreement between ACE and Capital Re, which was publicly announced on June 11, 1999. The terms of the Merger Agreement provide for Capital Re stockholders to receive .6 of a share of ACE stock for each share of Capital Re they hold. On June 10, 1999, the value of .6 of a share of ACE was over $17.00.

At the time the Capital Re board executed the Merger Agreement, it knew that ACE, which owns 12.3% of Capital Re's stock, had stockholder voting agreements with stock-holders holding another 33.5% of Capital Re's shares. According to ACE, "representatives of Capital Re significantly participated in the negotiation of, and in obtaining, the shareholder agreements" and Capital Re encouraged the 33.5% holders to sign the agreements. These agreements obligated the 33.5% holders to support the merger if the Capital Re board of directors did not terminate the Merger Agreement in accordance with its provisions. Put simply, ACE would control nearly 46% of the vote going into the merger vote and therefore needed very few of the remaining votes to prevail. Thus the Capital Re board knew when it executed the Merger Agreement that unless it termi-nated the Merger Agreement, ACE would have, as a virtual certainty, the votes to con-summate the merger even if a materially more valuable transaction became available.

Although ACE and Capital Re both agree that the merger, if effectuated, will not result in a "change of control" of Capital Re ...[,] the merger is obviously a transac-tion of great significance for Capital Re's stockholders and for ACE. The parties therefore bargained over the circumstances in which the Capital Re board could con-sider another party's acquisition or merger proposal and/or terminate the Merger Agreement.

For its part, ACE says it wanted the "strongest, legally binding commitment from Capital Re, consistent with the Capital Re board's fiduciary duties." This was natural given the investment ACE had made in Capital Re and the significant resources and or-ganizational energy necessary to consummate the merger....

On the other hand, the Capital Re board knew that the "fiduciary out" in the Merger Agreement was crucial if it was to protect its stockholders' rights.... Because the merger would be consummated even if circumstances had greatly changed and even if a much more valuable offer was available unless the board could validly terminate the agreement, Capital Re claims that the board was careful to negotiate sufficient flexibil-ity for itself to terminate the Merger Agreement if necessary to protect the Capital Re stockholders.

The negotiations on this issue resulted in two important sections of the contract. The first, §6.3 (the "no talk"), generally operates to prohibit Capital Re and "its officers, directors, agents, representatives, advisors or other intermediaries" from "soliciting, ini-tiating, encouraging, ... or taking any action knowingly to facilitate the submission of any inquiries, proposals, or offers ... from any person." Of most importance on this motion, §6.3 also restricts Capital Re from participating in discussions or negotiations with or even providing information to a third party in connection with an "unsolicited bona fide Transaction Proposal," unless the following conditions are met:

• Capital Re's board concludes "in good faith … based on the advice of its outside financial advisors, that such Transaction Proposal is reasonably likely to be or to result in a Superior Proposal";

• Capital Re's board concludes "in good faith … based on the written advice of its outside legal counsel, that participating in such negotiations or discussions or furnishing such information is required in order to prevent the Board of Directors of the Company from breaching its fiduciary duties to its stockholders under the [Delaware General Corporation Law]";

• the competing offeror enters into a confidentiality agreement no less favorable to Capital Re than its confidentiality agreement with ACE, a copy of which must be provided to ACE; and

• the company's directors provide ACE with contemporaneous notice of their intent to negotiate or furnish information with the competing offeror....

ACE argues that Capital Re has violated the plain language of the Merger Agreement. Its major claim is that Capital Re was forbidden to engage in discussions with XL Capital unless it received written legal advice from outside counsel opining that the board's fiduciary duties mandated such discussions. Because the board did not receive such advice, its decision to enter negotiations with XL Capital and to start a bidding war between ACE and XL Capital is, in ACE's view, a clear breach of contract....

Although perhaps not so clear as to preclude another interpretation, §6.3 of the Agreement is on its face better read as leaving the ultimate "good faith" judgment about whether the board's fiduciary duties required it to enter discussions with XL Capital to the board itself. Though the board must "base" its judgment on the "written advice" of outside counsel, the language of the contract does not preclude the board from concluding, even if its outside counsel equivocates (as lawyers sometimes tend to do) as to whether such negotiations are fiduciarily mandated.

Here, the Capital Re board had good economic reason to believe that consummation of the merger in the face of the XL Capital offer was adverse to the interests of the Capital Re stockholders. The board knew that if it did not explore the XL Capital offer, the Capital Re stockholders—including the 33.5% holders—would be forced into the merger even though the merger's value had plummeted since June 10, 1999 and even though the XL Capital offer was more valuable. Given these circumstances, it seems likely that in the end a fact-finder will conclude that the board had a good faith basis for determining that it must talk with XL Capital and not simply let the Capital Re stockholders ride the merger barrel over the financial falls. Furthermore, even if the contract is read as ACE wishes, Silver's [outside counsel, Hogan & Hartson] written legal advice, when taken as a totality, coupled with his oral advice, and viewed in light of the necessarily hurried deliberative process undertaken by the Capital Re board on October 6, 1999, might well be found to be a sufficient basis for a good faith decision by the board....

Restatement (Second) of Contracts §193 explicitly provides that a "promise by a fiduciary to violate his fiduciary duty or a promise that tends to induce such a violation is unenforceable on public policy grounds." ... If §6.3 of the Merger Agreement in fact required the Capital Re board to eschew even discussing another offer unless it received an opinion of counsel stating that such discussions were required, and if ACE demanded such a provision, it is likely that §6.3 will ultimately be found invalid. It is one thing for a board of directors to agree not to play footsie with other potential bidders or to stir up an auction. That type of restriction is perfectly understandable, if not necessary, if good faith business transactions are to be encouraged. It is quite another thing for a board of directors to enter into a merger agreement that precludes the board from considering any other offers unless a lawyer is willing to sign an opinion indicating that his client board is "required" to consider that offer in the less than precise corporate law context of a merger agreement that does not implicate *Revlon* but may preclude other transactions in a manner that raises eyebrows under *Unocal*. Such a contractual commitment is particularly suspect when a failure to consider other offers guarantees the consummation of the original transaction, however more valuable an alternative transaction may be and however less valuable the original transaction may have become since the merger agreement was signed.

In one sense, such a provision seems innocuous. I mean, can't the board find someone willing to give the opinion? What is wrong with a contract that simply limits a board from discussing another offer unless the board's lawyers are prepared to opine that such discussions are required?

But in another sense, the provision is much more pernicious in that it involves an abdication by the board of its duty to determine what its own fiduciary obligations require at precisely that time in the life of the company when the board's own judgment is most important. In the typical case, one must remember, the target board is defending the original deal in the face of an arguably more valuable transaction. In that context, does it make sense for the board to be able to hide behind their lawyers?

More fundamentally, one would think that there would be limited circumstances in which a board could prudently place itself in the position of not being able to entertain and consider a superior proposal to a transaction dependent on a stockholder vote. The circumstances in this case would not seem to be of that nature, because the board's inability to consider another offer in effect precludes the stockholders (including the 33.5% holders) from accepting another offer. For the superior proposal "out" in §§6.3 and 8.3 of the Merger Agreement to mean anything, the board must be free to explore such a proposal in good faith. A ban on considering such a proposal, even one with an exception where legal counsel opines in writing that such consideration is "required," comes close to self-disablement by the board. Our case law takes a rather dim view of restrictions that tend to produce such a result.

Indeed, ACE admits that it pushed Capital Re to the outer limits of propriety, but it claims to have stopped short of pushing Capital Re beyond that limit. But as I read ACE's view of what §6.3 means in the context of this Merger Agreement, ACE comes close to saying that §6.3 provides no "out" at all....

.... When corporate boards assent to provisions in merger agreements that have the primary purpose of acting as a defensive barrier to other transactions not sought out by the board, some of the policy concerns that animate the *Unocal* standard of review might be implicated. In this case, for example, if §6.3 is read as precluding board consideration of alternative offers—no matter how much more favorable—in this non-change of control context, the Capital Re board's approval of the Merger Agreement is as formidable a barrier to another offer as a non-redeemable poison pill. Absent an escape clause, the Merger Agreement guarantees the success of the merger vote and precludes any other alternative, no matter how much more lucrative to the Capital Re stockholders and no matter whether the Capital Re board itself prefers the other alternative. As a practical matter, it might therefore be possible to construct a plausible argument that a no-escape merger agreement that locks up the necessary votes constitutes an unreasonable preclusive and coercive defensive obstacle within the meaning of *Unocal*.

But *Unocal* to one side, one can state with much more doctrinal certainty that the Capital Re board was still required to exercise its bedrock duties of care and loyalty when it entered the Merger Agreement. If the board mistakenly entered into a merger agreement believing erroneously that it had negotiated an effective out giving it the ability to consider more favorable offers, its mistake might well be found to be a breach of its duty of care. In this context where the board is making a critical decision affecting stockholder ownership and voting rights, it is especially important that the board negotiate with care and retain sufficient flexibility to ensure that the stockholders are not unfairly coerced into accepting a less than optimal exchange for their shares....

Examined under either doctrinal rubric, §6.3 as construed by ACE is of quite dubious validity. As a sophisticated party who bargained for, nay demanded, §6.3 of the Merger Agreement, ACE was on notice of its possible invalidity. This factor therefore cuts against its claim that its contract rights should take precedence over the interests of the Capital Re stockholders who could be harmed by enforcement of §6.3.

Omnicare, Inc. v. NCS Healthcare, Inc.
818 A.2d 914 (Del. 2003)

HOLLAND, Justice:

.... The board of directors of NCS, an insolvent publicly traded Delaware corporation, agreed to the terms of a merger with Genesis. Pursuant to that agreement, all of the NCS creditors would be paid in full and the corporation's stockholders would exchange their shares for the shares of Genesis, a publicly traded Pennsylvania corporation. Several months after approving the merger agreement, but before the stockholder vote was scheduled, the NCS board of directors withdrew its prior recommendation in favor of the Genesis merger.

In fact, the NCS board recommended that the stockholders reject the Genesis transaction after deciding that a competing proposal from Omnicare was a superior transaction. The competing Omnicare bid offered the NCS stockholders an amount of cash equal to more than twice the then current market value of the shares to be received in the Genesis merger. The transaction offered by Omnicare also treated the NCS corporation's other stakeholders on equal terms with the Genesis agreement.

The merger agreement between Genesis and NCS contained a provision authorized by Section 251(c) of Delaware's corporation law. It required that the Genesis agreement be placed before the corporation's stockholders for a vote, even if the NCS board of directors no longer recommended it. At the insistence of Genesis, the NCS board also agreed to omit any effective fiduciary clause from the merger agreement. In connection with the Genesis merger agreement, two stockholders of NCS, who held a majority of the voting power, agreed unconditionally to vote all of their shares in favor of the Genesis merger. Thus, the combined terms of the voting agreements and merger agreement guaranteed, ab initio, that the transaction proposed by Genesis would obtain NCS stockholder's approval....

The defendant Jon H. Outcalt is Chairman of the NCS board of directors. Outcalt owns 202,063 shares of NCS Class A common stock and 3,476,086 shares of Class B common stock. The defendant Kevin B. Shaw is President, CEO and a director of NCS. At the time the merger agreement at issue in this dispute was executed with Genesis, Shaw owned 28,905 shares of NCS Class A common stock and 1,141,134 shares of Class B common stock.

Beginning in late 1999, ... NCS began to experience greater difficulty in collecting accounts receivables, which led to a precipitous decline in the market value of its stock. NCS common shares that traded above $20 in January 1999 were worth as little as $5 at the end of that year. By early 2001, NCS was in default on approximately $350 million in debt, including $206 million in senior bank debt and $102 million of its 5 3/4% Convertible Subordinated Debentures (the "Notes"). After these defaults, NCS common stock traded in a range of $0.09 to $0.50 per share until days before the announcement of the transaction at issue in this case.

* * *

In December 2000, NCS ... retained Brown, Gibbons, Lang & Company as its exclusive financial advisor. During this period, NCS's financial condition continued to deteriorate. In April 2001, NCS received a formal notice of default and acceleration from the trustee for holders of the Notes. As NCS's financial condition worsened, the Noteholders formed a committee to represent their financial interests (the "Ad Hoc Committee")....

In the summer of 2001, NCS invited Omnicare, Inc. to begin discussions with Brown Gibbons regarding a possible transaction. On July 20, Joel Gemunder, Omnicare's President and CEO, sent Shaw a written proposal to acquire NCS in a bankruptcy sale under Section 363 of the Bankruptcy Code. This proposal was for $225 million subject to satisfactory completion of due diligence....

In August 2001, Omnicare increased its bid to $270 million, but still proposed to structure the deal as an asset sale in bankruptcy. Even at $270 million, Omnicare's proposal was substantially lower than the face value of NCS's outstanding debt....

There was no further contact between Omnicare and NCS between November 2001 and January 2002. Instead, Omnicare began secret discussions with Judy K. Mencher, a representative of the Ad Hoc Committee. In these discussions..., the Ad Hoc Committee notified the NCS board that Omnicare had proposed an asset sale in bankruptcy for $313,750,000.

In January 2002, Genesis was contacted by members of the Ad Hoc Committee concerning a possible transaction with NCS....

Genesis previously lost a bidding war to Omnicare in a different transaction. This led to bitter feelings between the principals of both companies. More importantly, this bitter experience for Genesis led to its insistence on exclusivity agreements and lock-ups in any potential transaction with NCS.

NCS's operating performance was improving by early 2002. As NCS's performance improved, the NCS directors began to believe that it might be possible for NCS to enter into a transaction that would provide some recovery for NCS stockholders' equity. In March 2002, NCS decided to form an independent committee of board members who were neither NCS employees nor major NCS stockholders (the "Independent Committee"). The NCS board thought this was necessary because, due to NCS's precarious financial condition, it felt that fiduciary duties were owed to the enterprise as a whole rather than solely to NCS stockholders.

Sells and Osborne were selected as the members of the committee, and given authority to consider and negotiate possible transactions for NCS. The entire four member NCS board, however, retained authority to approve any transaction. The Independent Committee retained the same legal and financial counsel as the NCS board.

The Independent Committee met for the first time on May 14, 2002. At that meeting Pollack suggested that NCS seek a "stalking-horse merger partner" to obtain the highest possible value in any transaction. The Independent Committee agreed with the suggestion.

Two days later, on May 16, 2002, ... Genesis made it clear that if it were going to engage in any negotiations with NCS, it would not do so as a "stalking horse." As one of its advisors testified, "We didn't want to be someone who set forth a valuation for NCS which would only result in that valuation ... being publicly disclosed, and thereby creating an environment where Omnicare felt to maintain its competitive monopolistic positions, that they had to match and exceed that level." Thus, Genesis "wanted a degree of certainty that to the extent [it] was willing to pursue a negotiated merger agreement..., [it] would be able to consummate the transaction [it] negotiated and executed."

In June 2002, Genesis proposed a transaction that would take place outside the bankruptcy context....

* * *

At the June 26 meeting, Genesis's representatives demanded that, before any further negotiations take place, NCS agree to enter into an exclusivity agreement with it. As Hager from Genesis explained it: "[I]f they wished us to continue to try to move this process to a definitive agreement, that they would need to do it on an exclusive basis with us. We were going to, and already had incurred significant expense, but we would incur additional expenses..., both internal and external, to bring this transaction to a definitive signing. We wanted them to work with us on an exclusive basis for a short period of time to see if we could reach agreement." On June 27, 2002, Genesis's legal counsel delivered a draft form of exclusivity agreement for review and consideration by NCS's legal counsel.

The Independent Committee met on July 3, 2002, to consider the proposed exclusivity agreement. Pollack presented a summary of the terms of a possible Genesis merger, which had continued to improve....

NCS director Sells testified, Pollack told the Independent Committee at a July 3, 2002 meeting that Genesis wanted the Exclusivity Agreement to be the first step towards a completely locked up transaction that would preclude a higher bid from Omnicare....

After NCS executed the exclusivity agreement, Genesis provided NCS with a draft merger agreement, a draft Noteholders' support agreement, and draft voting agreements for Outcalt and Shaw, who together held a majority of the voting power of the NCS common stock. Genesis and NCS negotiated the terms of the merger agreement over the next three weeks. During those negotiations, the Independent Committee and the Ad Hoc Committee persuaded Genesis to improve the terms of its merger.

The parties were still negotiating by July 19, and the exclusivity period was automatically extended to July 26. At that point, NCS and Genesis were close to executing a merger agreement and related voting agreements. Genesis proposed a short extension of the exclusivity agreement so a deal could be finalized. On the morning of July 26, 2002, the Independent Committee authorized an extension of the exclusivity period through July 31.

By late July 2002, Omnicare came to believe that NCS was negotiating a transaction, possibly with Genesis or another of Omnicare's competitors, that would potentially present a competitive threat to Omnicare. Omnicare also came to believe, in light of a run-up in the price of NCS common stock, that whatever transaction NCS was negotiating probably included a payment for its stock. Thus, the Omnicare board of directors met on the morning of July 26 and, on the recommendation of its management, authorized a proposal to acquire NCS that did not involve a sale of assets in bankruptcy.

On the afternoon of July 26, 2002, Omnicare faxed to NCS a letter outlining a proposed acquisition. The letter suggested a transaction in which Omnicare would retire NCS's senior and subordinated debt at par plus accrued interest, and pay the NCS stockholders $3 cash for their shares. Omnicare's proposal, however, was expressly conditioned on negotiating a merger agreement, obtaining certain third party consents, and completing its due diligence.

Mencher saw the July 26 Omnicare letter and realized that, while its economic terms were attractive, the "due diligence" condition substantially undercut its strength. In an effort to get a better proposal from Omnicare, Mencher telephoned Gemunder and told him that Omnicare was unlikely to succeed in its bid unless it dropped the "due diligence outs." She explained this was the only way a bid at the last minute would be able to succeed. Gemunder considered Mencher's warning "very real," and followed up with his advisors. They, however, insisted that he retain the due diligence condition "to protect [him] from doing something foolish." Taking this advice to heart, Gemunder decided not to drop the due diligence condition.

Late in the afternoon of July 26, 2002, NCS representatives received voicemail messages from Omnicare asking to discuss the letter. The exclusivity agreement prevented NCS from returning those calls. In relevant part, that agreement precluded NCS from "engaging or participating in any discussions or negotiations with respect to a Competing Transaction or a proposal for one." The July 26 letter from Omnicare met the definition of a "Competing Transaction."

Despite the exclusivity agreement, the Independent Committee met to consider a response to Omnicare. It concluded that discussions with Omnicare about its July 26 letter presented an unacceptable risk that Genesis would abandon merger discussions. The Independent Committee believed that, given Omnicare's past bankruptcy proposals and unwillingness to consider a merger, as well as its decision to negotiate exclusively with the Ad Hoc Committee, the risk of losing the Genesis proposal was too substantial. Nevertheless, the Independent Committee instructed Pollack to use Omnicare's letter to negotiate for improved terms with Genesis.

Genesis responded to the NCS request to improve its offer as a result of the Omnicare fax the next day. On July 27, Genesis proposed substantially improved terms. First, it proposed to retire the Notes in accordance with the terms of the indenture, thus eliminating the need for Noteholders to consent to the transaction. This change involved paying all accrued interest plus a small redemption premium. Second, Genesis increased the exchange ratio for NCS common stock to one-tenth of a Genesis common share for each NCS common share, an 80% increase. Third, it agreed to lower the proposed termination fee in the merger agreement from $10 million to $6 million. In return for these concessions, Genesis stipulated that the transaction had to be approved by midnight the next day, July 28, or else Genesis would terminate discussions and withdraw its offer.

The Independent Committee and the NCS board both scheduled meetings for July 28. The committee met first. Although that meeting lasted less than an hour, the Court of Chancery determined the minutes reflect that the directors were fully informed of all material facts relating to the proposed transaction. After concluding that Genesis was sincere in establishing the midnight deadline, the committee voted unanimously to recommend the transaction to the full board.

The full board met thereafter. After receiving similar reports and advice from its legal and financial advisors, the board concluded that "balancing the potential loss of the Genesis deal against the uncertainty of Omnicare's letter, results in the conclusion that the only reasonable alternative for the Board of Directors is to approve the Genesis transaction." The board first voted to authorize the voting agreements with Outcalt and Shaw, for purposes of Section 203 of the Delaware General Corporation Law ("DGCL"). The board was advised by its legal counsel that "under the terms of the merger agreement and because NCS shareholders representing in excess of 50% of the outstanding voting power would be required by Genesis to enter into stockholder voting agreements contemporaneously with the signing of the merger agreement, and would agree to vote their shares in favor of the merger agreement, shareholder approval of the merger would be assured even if the NCS Board were to withdraw or change its recommendation. These facts would prevent NCS from engaging in any alternative or superior transaction in the future." ...

After listening to a summary of the merger terms, the board then resolved that the merger agreement and the transactions contemplated thereby were advisable and fair and in the best interests of all the NCS stakeholders. The NCS board further resolved to recommend the transactions to the stockholders for their approval and adoption. A definitive merger agreement between NCS and Genesis and the stockholder voting agreements were executed later that day. The Court of Chancery held that it was not a per se breach of fiduciary duty that the NCS board never read the NCS/Genesis merger agreement word for word.

Among other things, the NCS/Genesis merger agreement provided ... NCS would submit the merger agreement to NCS stockholders regardless of whether the NCS board continued to recommend the merger [and] NCS would not enter into discussions with third parties concerning an alternative acquisition of NCS, or provide non-public information to such parties, unless (1) the third party provided an unsolicited, bona fide written proposal documenting the terms of the acquisition; (2) the NCS board believed in good faith that the proposal was or was likely to result in an acquisition on terms superior to those contemplated by the NCS/Genesis merger agreement; and (3) before providing non-public information to that third party, the third party would execute a confidentiality agreement at least as restrictive as the one in place between NCS and Genesis....

Outcalt and Shaw, in their capacity as NCS stockholders, entered into voting agreements with Genesis. NCS was also required to be a party to the voting agreements by Genesis. Those agreements provided, among other things, that ... [n]either Outcalt nor Shaw would transfer their shares prior to the stockholder vote on the merger agreement [and] Outcalt and Shaw agreed to vote all of their shares in favor of the merger agreement....

On July 29, 2002, hours after the NCS/Genesis transaction was executed, Omnicare faxed a letter to NCS restating its conditional proposal and attaching a draft merger agreement. Later that morning, Omnicare issued a press release publicly disclosing the proposal.

On August 1, 2002, Omnicare filed a lawsuit attempting to enjoin the NCS/Genesis merger, and announced that it intended to launch a tender offer for NCS's shares at a price of $3.50 per share. On August 8, 2002, Omnicare began its tender offer....

* * *

On October 6, 2002, Omnicare irrevocably committed itself to a transaction with NCS. Pursuant to the terms of its proposal, Omnicare agreed to acquire all the outstanding NCS Class A and Class B shares at a price of $3.50 per share in cash. As a result of this irrevocable offer, on October 21, 2002, the NCS board withdrew its recommendation that the stockholders vote in favor of the NCS/Genesis merger agreement. NCS's financial advisor withdrew its fairness opinion of the NCS/Genesis merger agreement as well.

The Genesis merger agreement permits the NCS directors to furnish non-public information to, or enter into discussions with, "any Person in connection with an unsolicited bona fide written Acquisition Proposal by such person" that the board deems likely to constitute a "Superior Proposal." That provision has absolutely no effect on the Genesis merger agreement. Even if the NCS board "changes, withdraws or modifies" its recommendation, as it did, it must still submit the merger to a stockholder vote....

The Delaware corporation statute provides that the board's management decision to enter into and recommend a merger transaction can become final only when ownership action is taken by a vote of the stockholders. Thus, the Delaware corporation law expressly provides for a balance of power between boards and stockholders which makes merger transactions a shared enterprise and ownership decision. Consequently, a board of directors' decision to adopt defensive devices to protect a merger agreement may implicate the stockholders' right to effectively vote contrary to the initial recommendation of the board in favor of the transaction....

[I]n applying enhanced judicial scrutiny to defensive devices designed to protect a merger agreement, a court must first determine that those measures are not preclusive or coercive before its focus shifts to the "range of reasonableness" in making a proportionality determination. If the trial court determines that the defensive devices protecting a merger are not preclusive or coercive, the proportionality paradigm of *Unocal* is applicable....

Unocal requires that any defensive devices must be proportionate to the perceived threat to the corporation and its stockholders if the merger transaction is not consummated. Defensive devices taken to protect a merger agreement executed by a board of directors are intended to give that agreement an advantage over any subsequent transactions that materialize before the merger is approved by the stockholders and consummated. This is analogous to the favored treatment that a board of directors may properly give to encourage an initial bidder when it discharges its fiduciary duties under *Revlon*....

[T]he NCS directors' decision to adopt defensive devices to completely "lock up" the Genesis merger mandated "special scrutiny" under the two-part test set forth in *Unocal*.... The second stage of the *Unocal* test requires the NCS directors to demonstrate that their defensive response was "reasonable in relation to the threat posed." This inquiry involves a two-step analysis. The NCS directors must first establish that the merger deal protection devices adopted in response to the threat were not "coercive" or "preclusive," and then demonstrate that their response was within a "range of reasonable responses" to the threat perceived.... *Unitrin.* If defensive measures are either preclusive or coercive they are draconian and impermissible. In this case, the deal protection devices of the NCS board were both preclusive and coercive....

Although the minority stockholders were not forced to vote for the Genesis merger, they were required to accept it because it was a fait accompli. The record reflects that the defensive devices employed by the NCS board are preclusive and coercive in the sense that they accomplished a fait accompli. In this case, despite the fact that the NCS board has withdrawn its recommendation for the Genesis transaction and recommended its rejection by the stockholders, the deal protection devices approved by the NCS board operated in concert to have a preclusive and coercive effect. Those tripartite defensive measures—the Section 251(c) provision, the voting agreements, and the absence of an effective fiduciary out clause—made it "mathematically impossible" and "realistically unattainable" for the Omnicare transaction or any other proposal to succeed, no matter how superior the proposal.

The defensive measures that protected the merger transaction are unenforceable not only because they are preclusive and coercive but, alternatively, they are unenforceable because they are invalid as they operate in this case. Given the ... voting agreements, the provision in the merger agreement requiring the board to submit the transaction for a stockholder vote and the omission of a fiduciary out clause in the merger agreement completely prevented the board from discharging its fiduciary responsibilities to the minority stockholders when Omnicare presented its superior transaction....

The NCS board was required to contract for an effective fiduciary out clause to exercise its continuing fiduciary responsibilities to the minority stockholders. The issues in this appeal do not involve the general validity of either stockholder voting agreements or the authority of directors to insert a Section 251(c) provision in a merger agreement. In this case, the NCS board combined those two otherwise valid actions and caused them to operate in concert as an absolute lock up, in the absence of an effective fiduciary out clause in the Genesis merger agreement.

In the context of this preclusive and coercive lock up case, the protection of Genesis' contractual expectations must yield to the supervening responsibility of the directors to discharge their fiduciary duties on a continuing basis. The merger agreement and voting agreements, as they were combined to operate in concert in this case, are inconsistent with the NCS directors' fiduciary duties. To that extent, we hold that they are invalid and unenforceable.

VEASEY, Chief Justice, with whom STEELE, Justice, joins dissenting:

The beauty of the Delaware corporation law, and the reason it has worked so well for stockholders, directors and officers, is that the framework is based on an enabling statute with the Court of Chancery and the Supreme Court applying principles of fiduciary duty in a common law mode on a case-by-case basis. Fiduciary duty cases are inherently fact-intensive and, therefore, unique. This case is unique in two important respects. First, the peculiar facts presented render this case an unlikely candidate for substantial repetition. Second, this is a rare 3-2 split decision of the Supreme Court.

In the present case, we are faced with a merger agreement and controlling stockholders' commitment that assured stockholder approval of the merger before the emergence of a subsequent transaction offering greater value to the stockholders. This does not adequately summarize the unique facts before us, however....

The process by which this merger agreement came about involved a joint decision by the controlling stockholders and the board of directors to secure what appeared to be the only value-enhancing transaction available for a company on the brink of bankruptcy. The Majority adopts a new rule of law that imposes a prohibition on the NCS board's ability to act in concert with controlling stockholders to lock up this merger. The Majority reaches this conclusion by analyzing the challenged deal protection measures as isolated board actions. The Majority concludes that the board owed a duty to the NCS minority stockholders to refrain from acceding to the Genesis demand for an irrevocable lock-up notwithstanding the compelling circumstances confronting the board and the board's disinterested, informed, good faith exercise of its business judgment.

Because we believe this Court must respect the reasoned judgment of the board of directors and give effect to the wishes of the controlling stockholders, we respectfully disagree with the Majority's reasoning that results in a holding that the confluence of board and stockholder action constitutes a breach of fiduciary duty. The essential fact that must always be remembered is that this agreement and the voting commitments of Outcalt and Shaw concluded a lengthy search and intense negotiation process in the context of insolvency and creditor pressure where no other viable bid had emerged. Accordingly, we endorse the Vice Chancellor's well-reasoned analysis that the NCS board's action before the hostile bid emerged was within the bounds of its fiduciary duties under these facts.

.... It is now known, of course, after the case is over, that the stockholders of NCS will receive substantially more by tendering their shares into the topping bid of Omnicare than they would have received in the Genesis merger, as a result of the post-agreement Omnicare bid and the injunctive relief ordered by the Majority of this Court. Our jurisprudence cannot, however, be seen as turning on such ex post felicitous results. Rather, the NCS board's good faith decision must be subject to a real-time review of the board action before the NCS-Genesis merger agreement was entered into.

The Majority has adopted the Vice Chancellor's findings and has assumed arguendo that the NCS board fulfilled its duties of care, loyalty, and good faith by entering into the Genesis merger agreement. Indeed, this conclusion is indisputable on this record. The problem is that the Majority has removed from their proper context the contractual merger protection provisions. The lock-ups here cannot be reviewed in a vacuum. A court should review the entire bidding process to determine whether the independent board's actions permitted the directors to inform themselves of their available options and whether they acted in good faith.

* * *

.... In exchange for offering the NCS stockholders a return on their equity and creditor payment, Genesis demanded certainty that the merger would close. If the NCS board would not have acceded to the Section 251(c) provision, if Outcalt and Shaw had not agreed to the voting agreements and if NCS had insisted on a fiduciary out, there would have been no Genesis deal! Thus, the only value-enhancing transaction available would have disappeared. NCS knew that Omnicare had spoiled a Genesis acquisition in the past, and it is not disputed by the Majority that the NCS directors made a reasoned decision to accept as real the Genesis threat to walk away....

A lock-up permits a target board and a bidder to "exchange certainties." Certainty itself has value. The acquirer may pay a higher price for the target if the acquirer is assured consummation of the transaction. The target company also benefits from the certainty of completing a transaction with a bidder because losing an acquirer creates the perception that a target is damaged goods, thus reducing its value....

The Majority invalidates the NCS board's action by announcing a new rule that represents an extension of our jurisprudence. That new rule can be narrowly stated as follows: A merger agreement entered into after a market search, before any prospect of a topping bid has emerged, which locks up stockholder approval and does not contain a "fiduciary out" provision, is per se invalid when a later significant topping bid emerges.

As we have noted, this bright-line, per se rule would apply regardless of (1) the circumstances leading up to the agreement and (2) the fact that stockholders who control voting power had irrevocably committed themselves, as stockholders, to vote for the merger. Narrowly stated, this new rule is a judicially-created "third rail" that now becomes one of the given "rules of the game," to be taken into account by the negotiators and drafters of merger agreements. In our view, this new rule is an unwise extension of existing precedent....

In our view, the Majority misapplies the *Unitrin* concept of "coercive and preclusive" measures to preempt a proper proportionality balancing. Thus, the Majority asserts that "in applying enhanced judicial scrutiny to defensive devices designed to protect a merger agreement, ... a court must ... determine that those measures are not preclusive or coercive...." Here, the deal protection measures were not adopted unilaterally by the board to fend off an existing hostile offer that threatened the corporate policy and effectiveness of NCS. They were adopted because Genesis—the "only game in town"—would not save NCS, its creditors and its stockholders without these provisions.

The Majority—incorrectly, in our view—relies on *Unitrin* to advance its analysis. The discussion of "draconian" measures in *Unitrin* dealt with unilateral board action, a repurchase program, designed to fend off an existing hostile offer by American General.... Outcalt and Shaw were fully informed stockholders. As the NCS controlling stockholders, they made an informed choice to commit their voting power to the merger. The minority stockholders were deemed to know that when controlling stockholders have 65% of the vote they can approve a merger without the need for the minority votes. Moreover, to the extent a minority stockholder may have felt "coerced" to vote for the merger, which was already a fait accompli, it was a meaningless coercion—or no coercion at all—because the controlling votes, those of Outcalt and Shaw, were already "cast." Although the fact that the controlling votes were committed to the merger "precluded" an overriding vote against the merger by the Class A stockholders, the pejorative "preclusive" label applicable in a *Unitrin* fact situation has no application here. Therefore, there was no meaningful minority stockholder voting decision to coerce....

We respectfully disagree with the Majority's conclusion that the NCS board breached its fiduciary duties to the Class A stockholders by failing to negotiate a "fiduciary out" in the Genesis merger agreement. What is the practical import of a "fiduciary out?" It is a contractual provision, articulated in a manner to be negotiated, that would permit the board of the corporation being acquired to exit without breaching the merger agreement in the event of a superior offer.

In this case, Genesis made it abundantly clear early on that it was willing to negotiate a deal with NCS but only on the condition that it would not be a "stalking horse." Thus, it wanted to be certain that a third party could not use its deal with NCS as a floor against which to begin a bidding war. As a result of this negotiating position, a "fiduciary out" was not acceptable to Genesis. The Majority Opinion holds that such a negotiating position, if implemented in the agreement, is invalid per se where there is an absolute lock-up. We know of no authority in our jurisprudence supporting this new rule, and we believe it is unwise and unwarranted....

It is regrettable that the Court is split in this important case. One hopes that the Majority rule announced here—though clearly erroneous in our view—will be interpreted narrowly and will be seen as *sui generis*. By deterring bidders from engaging in negotiations like those present here and requiring that there must always be a fiduciary out, the universe of potential bidders who could reasonably be expected to benefit stockholders could shrink or disappear. Nevertheless, if the holding is confined to these unique facts, negotiators may be able to navigate around this new hazard....

STEELE, Justice, dissenting:

Here the board of directors acted selflessly pursuant to a careful, fair process and determined in good faith that the benefits to the stockholders and corporation flowing from a merger agreement containing reasonable deal protection provisions outweigh any speculative benefits that might result from entertaining a putative higher offer. A court asked to examine the decisionmaking process of the board should decline to interfere with the consummation and execution of an otherwise valid contract....

The contract terms that NCS' board agreed to included no insidious, camouflaged side deals for the directors or the majority stockholders nor transparent provisions for entrenchment or control premiums. At the time the NCS board and the majority stockholders agreed to a voting lockup, the terms were the best reasonably available for all the stockholders, balanced against a genuine risk of no deal at all. The cost benefit analysis entered into by an independent committee of the board, approved by the full board and independently agreed to by the majority stockholders cannot be second guessed by courts with no business expertise that would qualify them to substitute their judgment for that of a careful, selfless board or for majority stockholders who had the most significant economic stake in the outcome....

Delaware corporate citizens now face the prospect that in every circumstance, boards must obtain the highest price, even if that requires breaching a contract entered into at a time when no one could have reasonably foreseen a truly "Superior Proposal." The majority's proscriptive rule limits the scope of a board's cost benefit analysis by taking the bargaining chip of foregoing a fiduciary out "off the table" in all circumstances....

Lockup provisions attempt to assure parties that have lost business opportunities and incurred substantial costs that their deal will close. I am concerned that the majority decision will remove the certainty that adds value to any rational business plan. Perhaps transactions that include "force-the-vote" and voting agreement provisions that make approval a foregone conclusion will be the only deals invalidated prospectively. Even so, therein lies the problem. Instead of thoughtful, retrospective, restrained flexibility focused on the circumstances existing at the time of the decision, have we now moved to a bright line regulatory alternative?

* * *

---

c. Transactions with Controlling Stockholders

Problem—Freezing-Out the Dissenting Stockholder

Ishmael and Queequeg incorporated Pequod, Inc. (the "Company"), in the State of Panic, for the purpose of developing and marketing a synthetic substitute for spermaceti which Queequeg had developed and patented for industrial use. Queequeg acquired 55% of the shares, and Ishmael acquired the balance. Shortly after incorporation, Ahab, a chemist who the founders considered to be a key employee, bought a total of 6 percent of the stock from Queequeg and Ishmael, resulting in the following ownership: Queequeg, 52%; Ishmael, 42%; Ahab, 6%. The Company purchased land and a building to commence its operations. Queequeg served as the president of the Company, although he spent no more than approximately 25% of his time on the Company's business and drew no salary. Ishmael served full time as vice president and general manager of the Company and was paid a salary of $65,000 a year.

Business went poorly. A nationwide distaste for sea mammal products tainted the Company's synthetic product and demand was very low. Although the founders knew that the answer lay in a revision of their marketing strategy, they didn't know quite how to do it. As the Company continued to fail, Ishmael agreed to reduce his salary to $10,000, following which he devoted little time to the business.

Two years ago, after two years of continued poor operations, Queequeg entered into negotiations with officials of Moby Dick, Inc., looking toward the sale of the Company. Moby Dick is engaged in the production of synthetic animal products generally, and had been able successfully to market its products in the face of increasing animal rights activism.

Under the plan, for twenty months the Company would license Moby Dick to market its patented spermaceti product. In addition, the stockholders of the Company would grant Moby Dick the option to purchase all of the Company's stock for $5,000,000, to facilitate which each of the Company's stockholders would place his stock in escrow. Moby Dick agreed that if it failed to exercise the option, it would return all information relating to the synthetic spermaceti and would refrain from marketing similar products for a period of five years. Finally, Moby Dick agreed to hire Queequeg as its vice president in charge of sea mammal products at a salary of $500,000 a year.

Ishmael objected to the plan. He insisted that the $500,000 salary that Queequeg was to receive was, in reality, consideration for the purchase of the shares and that all stockholders should share in that payment. This presented a problem. If Ishmael didn't participate, Moby Dick would be unable to acquire all of the Company's stock and would back out of the deal. Queequeg and Ahab were concerned that without the transaction the Company would become bankrupt. Consequently, they developed a plan pursuant to which they would incorporate a new corporation, Whitejacket, Inc., the common stock of which would be issued to Queequeg and Ahab. Thereafter, the Company would be merged into Whitejacket, in consideration of which the stockholders of the Company would receive non-voting redeemable preferred stock in Whitejacket. Since the statutory law of the State of Panic required only majority approval of a merger, they knew it would succeed. Following the merger, the option agreement that had been negotiated between the Company and Moby Dick would be entered into by Whitejacket and Moby Dick.

Queequeg and Ahab consult you with respect to their plan. Is the plan lawful? Are there other ways of accomplishing the result desired by Queequeg and Ahab with less legal risk?

Problem — Freeze-Out by Dissolution

Schuyler, Hamilton, and Putnam were the controlling stockholders of Rochambeau Corp., incorporated in the State of Confusion (the "Company"). Together they owned 75% of the Company's common stock, the only class of stock outstanding. The balance of the Company's stock was publicly owned, and traded (although thinly) over-the-counter. Last year, the Company's book value per share was $54.85, and its high and low trading prices were $41 and $36.25, respectively.

On February 1 of this year, Arnold Corporation ("Arnold") offered to buy all of the Company's stock at $57 per share. All three of the controlling stockholders, and a large portion of the public stockholders, tendered, so that by March 15, Arnold had acquired 99.2% of the Company's stock. Wayne, a public stockholder, was one of the stockholders who refused to tender his shares. After Arnold acquired its stock in the Company, the board of directors (consisting of Schuyler, Hamilton, and Putnam) resigned seriatim, replacing themselves with Arnold's nominees.

On June 30 of this year, the Company held its duly noticed annual meeting, at which a resolution was adopted calling for its dissolution. Under the terms of the plan, the Company would make a distribution of $57 in cash to each of the remaining public stockholders, and would distribute all of its remaining assets to Arnold (which would also assume the Company's liabilities). Wayne objected to the plan, and refused to accept the $57 per share offered him by the Company. The Company proceeded with the plan and Arnold, having acquired the Company's assets, transferred them to a newly formed Arnold subsidiary, Cornwallis, Inc.

Wayne has come to you for advice. He would like to sue Arnold for, as he puts it, "stealing" the business. You listen to his story, and promise to write him a memorandum setting forth your opinion as to the desirability of litigating the matter. Do so.

In considering your advice to Wayne, be sure to consider (i) the causes of action that might be asserted; (ii) the defenses available to Arnold; and (iii) the possible alternatives to litigation that might achieve Wayne's goals. You should also be sensitive to the fact that the case is one of first impression in the courts of Confusion, which often look to other American jurisdictions in adjudicating corporate law matters. Finally, assume that Confusion's statutory law is identical to that of (i) Delaware; (ii) the Revised Model Business Corporation Act. How does this affect your advice?

Weinberger v. UOP, Inc.
457 A.2d 701 (Del. Super. Ct. 1983)

MOORE, Justice:

[A] former shareholder of UOP, Inc. . . . challenged the elimination of UOP's minority shareholders by a cash-out merger between UOP and its majority owner, The Signal Companies, Inc. . . . The present Chancellor held that the terms of the merger were fair to the plaintiff and the other minority shareholders of UOP. Accordingly, he entered judgment in favor of the defendants.

* * *

In ruling for the defendants, the Chancellor re-stated his earlier conclusion that the plaintiff in a suit challenging a cash-out merger must allege specific acts of fraud, misrepresentation, or other items of misconduct to demonstrate the unfairness of the merger terms to the minority. We approve this rule and affirm it.

The Chancellor also held that even though the ultimate burden of proof is on the majority shareholder to show by a preponderance of the evidence that the transaction is fair, it is first the burden of the plaintiff attacking the merger to demonstrate some basis for invoking the fairness obligation. We agree with that principle. However, where corporate action has been approved by an informed vote of a majority of the minority shareholders, we conclude that the burden entirely shifts to the plaintiff to show that the transaction was unfair to the minority.... But in all this, the burden clearly remains on those relying on the vote to show that they completely disclosed all material facts relevant to the transaction.

Here, the record does not support a conclusion that the minority stockholder vote was an informed one. Material information, necessary to acquaint those shareholders with the bargaining positions of Signal and UOP, was withheld under circumstances amounting to a breach of fiduciary duty. We therefore conclude that this merger does not meet the test of fairness, at least as we address that concept, and no burden thus shifted to the plaintiff by reason of the minority shareholder vote. Accordingly, we reverse and remand for further proceedings consistent herewith.

* * *

Our treatment of these matters has necessarily led us to a reconsideration of the business purpose rule announced in the trilogy of *Singer v. Magnavox Co.*, [Del. Supr., 380 A.2d 967 (1977)]; *Tanzer v. International General Industries, Inc.*, Del. Supr., 379 A.2d 1121 (1977); and *Roland International Corp. v. Najjar*, Del. Supr., 407 A.2d 1032 (1979). For the reasons hereafter set forth we consider that the business purpose requirement of these cases is no longer the law of Delaware.

I.

* * *

Signal is a diversified, technically based company operating through various subsidiaries. Its stock is publicly traded on the New York, Philadelphia and Pacific Stock Exchanges. UOP, formerly known as Universal Oil Products Company, was a diversified industrial company engaged in various lines of business, including petroleum and petro-chemical services and related products, construction, fabricated metal products, transportation equipment products, chemicals and plastics, and other products and services including land development, lumber products and waste disposal. Its stock was publicly held and listed on the New York Stock Exchange.

In 1974 Signal sold one of its wholly-owned subsidiaries for $420,000,000 in cash.... While looking to invest this cash surplus, Signal became interested in UOP as a possible acquisition. Friendly negotiations ensued, and Signal proposed to acquire a controlling interest in UOP at a price of $19 per share. UOP's representatives sought $25 per share. In the arm's length bargaining that followed, an understanding was reached whereby Signal agreed to purchase from UOP 1,500,000 shares of UOP's authorized but unissued stock at $21 per share.

This purchase was contingent upon Signal making a successful cash tender offer for 4,300,000 publicly held shares of UOP, also at a price of $21 per share. This combined method of acquisition permitted Signal to acquire 5,800,000 shares of stock, representing 50.5% of UOP's outstanding shares. The UOP board of directors advised the company's shareholders that it had no objection to Signal's tender offer at that price. Immediately before the announcement of the tender offer, UOP's common stock had been trading on the New York Stock Exchange at a fraction under $14 per share.

[T]he resulting tender offer was greatly oversubscribed. However, Signal limited its total purchase of the tendered shares so that, when coupled with the stock bought from UOP, it had achieved its goal of becoming a 50.5% shareholder of UOP.

Although UOP's board consisted of thirteen directors, Signal nominated and elected only six. Of these, five were either directors or employees of Signal. The sixth, a partner in the banking firm of Lazard Freres & Co., had been one of Signal's representatives in the negotiations and bargaining with UOP concerning the tender offer and purchase price of the UOP shares.

However, the president and chief executive officer of UOP retired during 1975, and Signal caused him to be replaced by James V. Crawford, a long-time employee and senior executive vice president of one of Signal's wholly-owned subsidiaries. Crawford succeeded his predecessor on UOP's board of directors and also was made a director of Signal.

By the end of 1977 Signal basically was unsuccessful in finding other suitable investment candidates for its excess cash, and by February 1978 considered that it had no other realistic acquisitions available to it on a friendly basis. Once again its attention turned to UOP.

The trial court found that at the instigation of certain Signal management personnel, including William W. Walkup, its board chairman, and Forrest N. Shumway, its president, a feasibility study was made concerning the possible acquisition of the balance of UOP's outstanding shares. This study was performed by two Signal officers, Charles S. Arledge, vice president (director of planning), and Andrew J. Chitiea, senior vice president (chief financial officer). Messrs. Walkup, Shumway, Arledge and Chitiea were all directors of UOP in addition to their membership on the Signal board.

Arledge and Chitiea concluded that it would be a good investment for Signal to acquire the remaining 49.5% of UOP shares at any price up to $24 each. Their report was discussed ... [with] Signal's senior management. In particular, they talked about the proper price to be paid if the acquisition was pursued, purportedly keeping in mind that as UOP's majority shareholder, Signal owed a fiduciary responsibility to both its own stockholders as well as to UOP's minority....

[Signal's] executive committee meeting was set for February 28, 1978. As a courtesy, UOP's president, Crawford, was invited to attend, although he was not a member of Signal's executive committee. On his arrival, and prior to the meeting, Crawford was asked to meet privately with Walkup and Shumway. He was then told of Signal's plan to acquire full ownership of UOP and was asked for his reaction to the proposed price range of $20 to $21 per share. Crawford said he thought such a price would be "generous," and that it was certainly one which should be submitted to UOP's minority shareholders for their ultimate consideration....

Thus, Crawford voiced no objection to the $20 to $21 price range, nor did he suggest that Signal should consider paying more than $21 per share for the minority interests. Later, at the executive committee meeting the same factors were discussed, with Crawford repeating the position he earlier took with Walkup and Shumway....

.... Signal's executive committee authorized its management "to negotiate" with UOP "for a cash acquisition of the minority ownership in UOP, Inc., with the intention of presenting a proposal to [Signal's] board of directors ... on March 6, 1978." ...

[Thereafter, Signal issued two press releases. One noted ongoing negotiations between Signal and UOP for the cash acquisition of the 49.5% of UOP that Signal did not own. The other stated that Signal's management would recommend a price range of $20 to $21 per share for the UOP minority interest.]

* * *

Between Tuesday, February 28, 1978 and Monday, March 6, 1978, a total of four business days, Crawford spoke by telephone with all of UOP's non-Signal, i.e., outside, directors. Also during that period, Crawford retained Lehman Brothers to render a fairness opinion as to the price offered the minority for its stock[, as] ... Lehman Brothers had been acting as UOP's investment banker for many years ... [and] James W. Glanville, a long-time director of UOP and a partner in Lehman Brothers, had acted as a financial advisor to UOP for many years....

Crawford telephoned Glanville, ... [whose] immediate personal reaction was that a price of $20 to $21 would certainly be fair, since it represented almost a 50% premium over UOP's market price....

During this period Crawford also had several telephone contacts with Signal officials. In only one of them, however, was the price of the shares discussed. In a conversation with Walkup, Crawford advised that as a result of his communications with UOP's non-Signal directors, it was his feeling that the price would have to be the top of the proposed range, or $21 per share, if the approval of UOP's outside directors was to be obtained. But again, he did not seek any price higher than $21.

* * *

[Based on Lehman Brothers' due diligence, it] concluded that "the price of either $20 or $21 would be a fair price for the remaining shares of UOP." ...

* * *

On March 6, 1978, both the Signal and UOP boards were convened to consider the proposed merger. Telephone communications were maintained between the two meetings. Walkup, Signal's board chairman, and also a UOP director, attended UOP's meeting with Crawford in order to present Signal's position and answer any questions that UOP's non-Signal directors might have. Arledge and Chitiea, along with Signal's other designees on UOP's board, participated by conference telephone. All of UOP's outside directors attended the meeting either in person or by conference telephone.

First, Signal's board unanimously adopted a resolution authorizing Signal to propose to UOP a cash merger of $21 per share as outlined in a certain merger agreement and other supporting documents. This proposal required that the merger be approved by a majority of UOP's outstanding minority shares voting at the stockholders meeting at which the merger would be considered, and that the minority shares voting in favor of the merger, when coupled with Signal's 50.5% interest would have to comprise at least two-thirds of all UOP shares. Otherwise the proposed merger would be deemed disapproved.

UOP's board then considered the proposal. Copies of the agreement were delivered to the directors in attendance, and other copies had been forwarded earlier to the directors participating by telephone. They also had before them UOP financial data for 1974-1977, UOP's most recent financial statements, market price information, and budget projections for 1978. In addition they had Lehman Brothers' hurriedly prepared fairness opinion letter finding the price of $21 to be fair. Glanville, the Lehman Brothers partner, and UOP director, commented on the information that had gone into preparation of the letter.

Signal also suggests that the Arledge-Chitiea feasibility study, indicating that a price of up to $24 per share would be a "good investment" for Signal, was discussed at the UOP directors' meeting. The Chancellor made no such finding.... Furthermore, it is clear beyond peradventure that nothing in that report was ever disclosed to UOP's minority shareholders prior to their approval of the merger.

After consideration of Signal's proposal, Walkup and Crawford left the meeting to permit a free and uninhibited exchange between UOP's non-Signal directors. Upon their return a resolution to accept Signal's offer was then proposed and adopted. While Signal's men on UOP's board participated in various aspects of the meeting, they abstained from voting. However, the minutes show that each of them "if voting would have voted yes."

* * *

Despite the swift board action of the two companies, the merger was not submitted to UOP's shareholders until their annual meeting on May 26, 1978. In the notice of that meeting and proxy statement sent to shareholders in May, UOP's management and board urged that the merger be approved. The proxy statement also advised:

> The price was determined after *discussions* between James V. Crawford, a director of Signal and Chief Executive Officer of UOP, and officers of Signal which took place during meetings on February 28, 1978, and in the course of several subsequent telephone conversations. (Emphasis added.)

In the original draft of the proxy statement the word "negotiations" had been used rather than "discussions." However, when the Securities and Exchange Commission sought details of the "negotiations" as part of its review of these materials, the term was deleted and the word "discussions" was substituted. The proxy statement indicated that the vote of UOP's board in approving the merger had been unanimous. It also advised the shareholders that Lehman Brothers had given its opinion that the merger price of $21 per share was fair to UOP's minority. However, it did not disclose the hurried method by which this conclusion was reached.

As of the record date of UOP's annual meeting, there were 11,488,302 shares of UOP common stock outstanding, 5,688,302 of which were owned by the minority. At the meeting only 56%, or 3,208,652, of the minority shares were voted. Of these, 2,953,812, or 51.9% of the total minority, voted for the merger, and 254,840 voted against it. When Signal's stock was added to the minority shares voting in favor, a total of 76.2% of UOP's outstanding shares approved the merger while only 2.2% opposed it.

By its terms the merger became effective on May 26, 1978, and each share of UOP's stock held by the minority was automatically converted into a right to receive $21 cash.

II.

A.

A primary issue mandating reversal is the preparation by two UOP directors, Arledge and Chitiea, of their feasibility study for the exclusive use and benefit of Signal. This document was of obvious significance to both Signal and UOP. Using UOP data, it described the advantages to Signal of ousting the minority at a price range of $21-$24 per share....

* * *

Having written [the report], solely for the use of Signal, it is clear from the record that neither Arledge nor Chitiea shared this report with their fellow directors of UOP. We are satisfied that no one else did either. This conduct hardly meets the fiduciary standards applicable to such a transaction....

The Arledge-Chitiea report speaks for itself in supporting the Chancellor's finding that a price of up to $24 was a "good investment" for Signal. It shows that a return on the investment at $21 would be 15.7% versus 15.5% at $24 per share. This was a difference of only two-tenths of one percent, while it meant over $17,000,000 to the minority. Under such circumstances, paying UOP's minority shareholders $24 would have had relatively little long-term effect on Signal, and the Chancellor's findings concerning the benefit to Signal, even at a price of $24, were obviously correct....

Certainly, this was a matter of material significance to UOP and its shareholders. Since the study was prepared by two UOP directors, using UOP information for the exclusive benefit of Signal, and nothing whatever was done to disclose it to the outside UOP directors or the minority shareholders, a question of breach of fiduciary duty arises. This problem occurs because there were common Signal-UOP directors participating, at least to some extent, in the UOP board's decision-making processes without full disclosure of the conflicts they faced.[7]

B.

In assessing this situation, the Court of Chancery was required to:

> examine what information defendants had and to measure it against what they gave to the minority stockholders, in a context in which 'complete candor' is required. In other words, the limited function of the Court was to determine whether defendants had disclosed all information in their possession germane to the transaction in issue. And by 'germane' we mean, for present purposes, information such as a reasonable shareholder would consider important in deciding whether to sell or retain stock.

* * *

> Completeness, not adequacy, is both the norm and the mandate under present circumstances.

Lynch v. Vickers Energy Corp., Del. Supr., 383 A.2d 278, 281 (1977) (*Lynch I*).... [T]hese Signal designated directors on UOP's board still owed UOP and its shareholders an uncompromising duty of loyalty....

Given the absence of any attempt to structure this transaction on an arm's length basis, Signal cannot escape the effects of the conflicts it faced, particularly when its designees on UOP's board did not totally abstain from participation in the matter. There is no "safe harbor" for such divided loyalties in Delaware. When directors of a Delaware corporation are on both sides of a transaction, they are required to demonstrate their utmost good faith and the most scrupulous inherent fairness of the bargain....

There is no dilution of this obligation where one holds dual or multiple directorships, as in a parent-subsidiary context.... Thus, individuals who act in a dual capacity as directors of two corporations, one of whom is parent and the other subsidiary, owe the same duty of good management to both corporations, and in the absence of an independent negotiating structure (see note 7, *supra*), or the directors' total abstention

---

7. Although perfection is not possible, or expected, the result here could have been entirely different if UOP had appointed an independent negotiating committee of its outside directors to deal with Signal at arm's length.... Since fairness in this context can be equated to conduct by a theoretical, wholly independent, board of directors acting upon the matter before them, it is unfortunate that this course apparently was neither considered nor pursued.... Particularly in a parent-subsidiary context, a showing that the action taken was as though each of the contending parties had in fact exerted its bargaining power against the other at arm's length is strong evidence that the transaction meets the test of fairness....

from any participation in the matter, this duty is to be exercised in light of what is best for both companies.... The record demonstrates that Signal has not met this obligation.

C.

The concept of fairness has two basic aspects: fair dealing and fair price. The former embraces questions of when the transaction was timed, how it was initiated, structured, negotiated, disclosed to the directors, and how the approvals of the directors and the stockholders were obtained. The latter aspect of fairness relates to the economic and financial considerations of the proposed merger, including all relevant factors: assets, market value, earnings, future prospects, and any other elements that affect the intrinsic or inherent value of a company's stock.... However, the test for fairness is not a bifurcated one as between fair dealing and price. All aspects of the issue must be examined as a whole since the question is one of entire fairness. However, in a non-fraudulent transaction we recognize that price may be the preponderant consideration outweighing other features of the merger. Here, we address the two basic aspects of fairness separately because we find reversible error as to both.

D.

Part of fair dealing is the obvious duty of candor required by *Lynch I, supra*. Moreover, one possessing superior knowledge may not mislead any stockholder by use of corporate information to which the latter is not privy.... With the well-established Delaware law on the subject, and the Court of Chancery's findings of fact here, it is inevitable that the obvious conflicts posed by Arledge and Chitiea's preparation of their "feasibility study," derived from UOP information, for the sole use and benefit of Signal, cannot pass muster.

The Arledge-Chitiea report is but one aspect of the element of fair dealing. How did this merger evolve? It is clear that it was entirely initiated by Signal. The serious time constraints under which the principals acted were all set by Signal. It had not found a suitable outlet for its excess cash and considered UOP a desirable investment, particularly since it was now in a position to acquire the whole company for itself. For whatever reasons, and they were only Signal's, the entire transaction was presented to and approved by UOP's board within four business days. Standing alone, this is not necessarily indicative of any lack of fairness by a majority shareholder. It was what occurred, or more properly, what did not occur, during this brief period that makes the time constraints imposed by Signal relevant to the issue of fairness.

The structure of the transaction, again, was Signal's doing. So far as negotiations were concerned, it is clear that they were modest at best. Crawford, Signal's man at UOP, never really talked price with Signal, except to accede to its management's statements on the subject, and to convey to Signal the UOP outside directors' view that as between the $20-$21 range under consideration, it would have to be $21....

As we have noted, the matter of disclosure to the UOP directors was wholly flawed by the conflicts of interest raised by the Arledge-Chitiea report. All of those conflicts were resolved by Signal in its own favor without divulging any aspect of them to UOP.

This cannot but undermine a conclusion that this merger meets any reasonable test of fairness. The outside UOP directors lacked one material piece of information generated by two of their colleagues, but shared only with Signal. True, the UOP board had the Lehman Brothers' fairness opinion, but that firm has been blamed by the plaintiff for the hurried task it performed, when more properly the responsibility for this lies with Signal. There was no disclosure of the circumstances surrounding the rather cursory preparation of the Lehman Brothers' fairness opinion. Instead, the impression was given UOP's minority that a careful study had been made, when in fact speed was the hallmark....

Finally, the minority stockholders were denied the critical information that Signal considered a price of $24 to be a good investment. Since this would have meant over $17,000,000 more to the minority, we cannot conclude that the shareholder vote was an informed one. Under the circumstances, an approval by a majority of the minority was meaningless....

Given these particulars and the Delaware law on the subject, the record does not establish that this transaction satisfies any reasonable concept of fair dealing, and the Chancellor's findings in that regard must be reversed.

E.

Turning to the matter of price, plaintiff also challenges its fairness.... [a]

While a plaintiff's monetary remedy ordinarily should be confined to the more liberalized appraisal proceeding herein established, we do not intend any limitation on the historic powers of the Chancellor to grant such other relief as the facts of a particular case may dictate. The appraisal remedy we approve may not be adequate in certain cases, particularly where fraud, misrepresentation, self-dealing, deliberate waste of corporate assets, or gross and palpable overreaching are involved.... Under such circumstances, the Chancellor's powers are complete to fashion any form of equitable and monetary relief as may be appropriate, including rescissory damages. Since it is apparent that this long completed transaction is too involved to undo, and in view of the Chancellor's discretion, the award, if any, should be in the form of monetary damages based upon entire fairness standards, i.e., fair dealing and fair price.

* * *

III.

Finally, we address the matter of business purpose. The defendants contend that the purpose of this merger was not a proper subject of inquiry by the trial court. The plaintiff says that no valid purpose existed—the entire transaction was a mere subterfuge designed to eliminate the minority. The Chancellor ruled otherwise, but in so doing he clearly circumscribed the thrust and effect of *Singer*. *Weinberger v. UOP*, 426 A.2d at 1342-43, 1348-50. This has led to the thoroughly sound observation that the business purpose test "may be ... virtually interpreted out of existence, as it was in *Weinberger*."[9]

The requirement of a business purpose is new to our law of mergers and was a departure from prior case law. *See Stauffer v. Standard Brands, Inc., supra; David J. Greene & Co. v. Schenley Industries, Inc., supra.*

In view of the fairness test which has long been applicable to parent-subsidiary mergers, *Sterling v. Mayflower Hotel Corp.*, Del. Supr., 93 A.2d 107, 109-10 (1952), the expanded appraisal remedy now available to shareholders, and the broad discretion of

---

a. The court's discussions of the proper valuation procedure and the determinants of fair price are set forth *supra* at chapter 3, section 4a(i)(A).

9. Weiss, *The Law of Take Out Mergers: A Historical Perspective*, 56 N.Y.U. L. Rev. 624, 671, n.300 (1981).

the Chancellor to fashion such relief as the facts of a given case may dictate, we do not believe that any additional meaningful protection is afforded minority shareholders by the business purpose requirement of the trilogy of *Singer, Tanzer, Najjar*, and their progeny. Accordingly, such requirement shall no longer be of any force or effect.

The judgment of the Court of Chancery, finding both the circumstances of the merger and the price paid the minority shareholders to be fair, is reversed. The matter is remanded for further proceedings consistent herewith. Upon remand the plaintiff's post-trial motion to enlarge the class should be granted.

REVERSED AND REMANDED.

Notes and Questions

1. In Rabkin v. Philip A. Hunt Chem. Corp., 498 A.2d 1099 (Del. 1985), the court was faced with an action for breach of fiduciary duty as a result of the merger of Hunt into Olin Corporation, the holder of a majority of Hunt's shares acquired by Olin a year earlier from Turner and Newall Industries, Inc., Hunt's former controlling stockholder. As part of the stock purchase, Olin had agreed to pay Hunt's minority stockholders the same per share consideration it paid to Turner and Newall if it acquired the minority stock within one year thereafter. The merger occurred shortly after the expiration of the one-year period under circumstances indicating that "Olin always anticipated owning 100% of Hunt." *Id.* at 1101. The court held that it was error to dismiss plaintiffs' complaint on the authority of *Weinberger*, since defendants' conduct arguably violated both the fair price and fair dealing requirements of *Weinberger*. On remand, however, the Chancery Court decided that Olin had not deliberately timed the merger to evade its one-year time limit and dismissed the case anyway. Rabkin v. Olin Corp., 1990 WL 47648 (Del. Ch. 1990).

2. In *Weinberger*, the court abandoned the "business purpose test," which treated a freeze-out merger lacking a legitimate business purpose as a *per se* breach of fiduciary duty. The court reasoned that the entire fairness test, the appraisal remedy, and the "broad discretion of the chancellor to fashion ... relief" provide adequate protection to minority stockholders. In so ruling, the court overruled Singer v. Magnavox, 380 A.2d 969 (Del. 1977), Tanzer v. Int'l General Indus., Inc., 379 A.2d 1121 (Del. 1977), and Roland Int'l Corp. v. Najjar, 407 A.2d 1032 (Del. 1979). In *Singer*, the court held that a controlling parent breached its fiduciary duty to the subsidiary's minority stockholders by effectuating a merger for the sole purpose of eliminating the minority. Lack of a proper business purpose made the merger *per se* invalid; if proper purpose was proved the court would go on to scrutinize the transaction for entire fairness. (The court applied the entire fairness test instead of the business judgment rule because the controlling parent and the board of the subsidiary (which it elected) stood on both sides of the transaction.)

The question of whose interests the business purpose must serve, an issue left unresolved in *Singer*, was answered by the court in *Tanzer*. The purpose of the *Tanzer* merger was to facilitate the parent's long-term debt financing by eliminating the minority. The court held that a business purpose of the controlling parent was sufficient to satisfy *Singer*, although, of course, it must be *bona fide*, and the parent corporation must otherwise meet the burden of entire fairness as mandated by *Singer*.

Finally, in *Najjar*, the court applied the *Singer* rule to require a legitimate business purpose even for short-form mergers. (The short-form merger technique, illustrated by

Del. Gen. Corp. Law § 253, permits a parent corporation owning at least 90 percent of the shares of each class of its subsidiary's stock to effectuate a merger without the need for a stockholder vote, merely by filing a certificate of merger approved by the board of the parent.)

Other jurisdictions have applied the business purpose test. The New York Court of Appeals (the state's high court) held that a merger that benefits the individual majority stockholders (for example, creating tax advantages for the majority) had a legitimate business purpose. Pruitt v. Rockefeller Center Properties, Inc., 167 A.D.2d 14 (1st Dep't 1991); Alpert v. 28 William St. Corp., 63 N.Y.2d 557, 473 N.E.2d 19, 483 N.Y.S.2d 667 (1984). *See also* Klurfeld v. Equity Enterprises, Inc., 79 A.D.2d 124, 436 N.Y.S.2d 303 (2d Dep't 1981).

In Gabhart v. Gabhart, 267 Ind. 370, 370 N.E.2d 345 (1977), the Indiana Supreme Court held that a proposed freeze-out merger lacking any valid purpose (i.e., a purpose that advanced the corporation's interest) would be enjoined as a de facto dissolution. The court, however, rejected *Singer's* application of the entire fairness test, stating that it would not inquire into "entire fairness" after a valid business purpose had been proven. "Under Delaware law, it appears that every proposed merger would be subject to having its bona fides determined by judicial review. We do not believe the judiciary should intrude into corporate management to that extent." 370 N.E.2d at 356.

See also Albright v. Bagandahl, 391 F. Supp. 754 (D. Utah 1974), in which the court, apparently applying Utah law, set aside a merger on the ground that termination of a minority stockholder's interest was not a legitimate corporate purpose and, therefore, a breach of the majority stockholder's fiduciary duty.

Some jurisdictions make a distinction between long- and short-form mergers. For example, in Yanow v. Teal Industries, Inc., 178 Conn. 263, 422 A.2d 311 (1979), the court rejected the business purpose test for short-form mergers, given the purpose of short-form mergers to provide the parent corporation with a means of eliminating minority shareholders. Similarly, in Deutsch v. Blue Chip Stamps, 116 Cal. App. 3d 97, 172 Cal. Rptr. 21 (1981), the court stated that California's short-form merger statute was enacted to permit majority stockholders to cash out the minority. Indeed, this purpose was noted with respect to the Delaware short-form merger statute (Del. Gen. Corp. Law § 253) in Green v. Sante Fe Indus., Inc., 70 N.Y.2d 244, 514 N.E.2d 105, 519 N.Y.S.2d 793 (1987), a New York case which applied Delaware law to find no breach of fiduciary duty by a majority stockholder which effected a short-form merger with no corporate purpose other than to freeze-out the minority. The court noted, 519 N.Y.S.2d at 798 (citing Stauffer v. Standard Brands, 187 A.2d 78, 80 (Del. Ch. 1962)): "[n]o corporate purpose was statutorily required for a short-form merger, rather the very purpose of such merger was to 'provide the parent corporation with a means of eliminating the minority shareholders' interest in the enterprise.'"

3. Compare *Weinberger's* rejection of the business purpose test with the opinion of the Massachusetts Supreme Judicial Court in Coggins v. New England Patriots Football Club, Inc., 397 Mass. 525, 492 N.E.2d 1112, 1116-19 (1986). Coggins sued on behalf of a class seeking to rescind the cash-out merger of the New England Patriots Football Club, Inc. into a newly created corporation for the purpose of enabling the Patriots' controlling stockholder to assign to the corporation his personal debts incurred in obtaining control of the Patriots. In reviewing the trial court's determination that plaintiffs were to be awarded rescissory damages, the court had to determine the appropriate scope of review of the merger, which it did as follows:

Scope of Judicial Review. In deciding this case, we address an important corporate law question: What approach will a Massachusetts court reviewing a cash freeze-out merger employ? This question has been considered by courts in a number of other states....

The parties have urged us to consider the views of a court with great experience in such matters, the Supreme Court of Delaware. We note that the Delaware court announced one test in 1977, but recently has changed to another.... We note that the "fairness" test to which the Delaware court now has adhered is, as we later show, closely related to the views expressed in our decisions. Unlike the Delaware court, however, we believe that the "business-purpose" test is an additional useful means under our statutes and case law for examining a transaction in which a controlling stockholder eliminates the minority interest in a corporation.... This concept of fair dealing is not limited to close corporations but applies to judicial review of cash freeze-out mergers....

* * *

Factors in judicial review. The defendants concentrate their arguments on the finding of the Superior Court judge that the offered price for nonvoting shares was inadequate. They claim that his conclusion that rescissory damages are due these plaintiffs is based wholly on a finding of price inadequacy. The trial judge, however, considered the totality of circumstances, including the purpose of the merger, the accuracy and adequacy of disclosure in connection with the merger, and the fairness of the price. The trial judge correctly considered the totality of circumstances, even though he failed to attach adequate significance to each of these factors and to structure them correctly in his analysis.

Judicial scrutiny should begin with recognition of the basic principle that the duty of a corporate director must be to further the legitimate goals of the corporation. The result of a freeze-out merger is the elimination of public ownership in the corporation. The controlling faction increases its equity from a majority to 100%, using corporate processes and corporate assets. The corporate directors who benefit from this transfer of ownership must demonstrate how the legitimate goals of the corporation are furthered. A director of a corporation violates his fiduciary duty when he uses the corporation for his or his family's personal benefit in a manner detrimental to the corporation.... Because the danger of abuse of fiduciary duty is especially great in a freeze-out merger, the court must be satisfied that the freeze-out was for the advancement of a legitimate corporate purpose. If satisfied that elimination of public ownership is in furtherance of a business purpose, the court should then proceed to determine if the transaction was fair by examining the totality of the circumstances.

The plaintiffs here adequately alleged that the merger of the Old Patriots and New Patriots was a freeze-out merger undertaken for no legitimate business purpose, but merely for the personal benefit of Sullivan. While we have recognized the right to "selfish ownership" in a corporation, such a right must be balanced against the concept of the majority stockholder's fiduciary obligation to the minority stockholders.... Consequently, the defendants bear the burden of proving, first, that the merger was for a legitimate business purpose, and, second, that, considering totality of circumstances, it was fair to the minority.

4. In evaluating the propriety of a freeze-out merger, should the way in which a controlling stockholder obtained control be significant? For example, is there a relevant

distinction between the case where a controlling stockholder acquired control through a series of open-market purchases of a widely held corporation and where she was the corporation's founder (and controlling stockholder) and later sold to others a minority portion of the corporation's shares?

5. What is the relevance of business purpose once the legislature has decided that some proportion of the shares of a corporation can eliminate the others over the latters' objection? *Compare* Brudney & Chirelstein, A Restatement of Corporate Freezeouts, 87 Yale L.J. 1354, 1356-57 n.9 (1978), *with* Easterbrook & Fischel, Close Corporations and Agency Costs, 38 Stan. L. Rev. 271, 296 (1986).

6. Are the business purpose test and the entire fairness test predicated on the same theory of the nature and purpose of the corporation? If not, what are the differences?

7. If the two tests are different, is one or the other more appropriate in a jurisdiction that has enacted a constituency statute? (*See supra* chapter 5, section 7, for a discussion of constituency statutes.)

8. Is any legal evaluation of a freeze-out merger necessary or appropriate where the minority shares were publicly traded before the merger? *See* Armstrong v. Marathon Oil Co., 66 Ohio App.3d 127, 583 N.E.2d 462 (1990) (under Ohio statute, benchmark for appraising the fair cash value of publicly traded minority stock was price at which stock traded on the day before the merger, adjusted to eliminate the effects of the pending merger). *Cf.* Del. Gen. Corp. Law §262(b)(1) (stock market exception to the appraisal remedy).

In re Siliconix Inc. Shareholders Litigation
2001 WL 716787 (Del. Ch. 2001) (unpublished opinion)

NOBLE, Vice Chancellor.

I. INTRODUCTION

Lead Plaintiff Raymond L. Fitzgerald ("Fitzgerald"), a shareholder in Defendant Siliconix incorporated ("Siliconix") brings this consolidated action, *inter alia*, to challenge the stock-for-stock tender offer by Defendant Vishay Intertechnology, Inc. ("Vishay") through its wholly-owned subsidiary, Vishay TEMIC Semiconductor Acquisition Holdings Corp. ("Acquisition") for the 19.6% equity interest in Siliconix that Acquisition does not already own.[2]

Fitzgerald has moved to enjoin preliminarily the tender ... because of alleged breaches by Vishay and the directors of Siliconix of their fiduciary duties to Siliconix shareholders.

In support of his motion, Fitzgerald makes these arguments. First, Fitzgerald alleges that the Defendants' disclosures to the minority shareholders contained material misrepresentations and omitted material facts. Second, he contends that the offered price is unfair; and, because of disclosure violations and the coercive nature of the tender proposal, Defendants cannot satisfy the burden therefore imposed upon them to demonstrate the fairness of the price. Finally, as a result of alleged repeated breaches of fiduciary duties and the oppressive structure of the proposed tender, Fitzgerald argues that the tender must be judged by the entire fairness test, a standard, Fitzgerald asserts, that Defendants cannot satisfy.

----

2. For simplicity, I will refer to Vishay and Acquisition collectively as Vishay.

.... I now conclude that, based on the current record, Fitzgerald has not demonstrated a reasonable probability of success on the merits of his claims. Accordingly, his motion for a preliminary injunction must be denied.

II. FACTUAL HISTORY
A. The Parties.

* * *

Vishay, which is listed on the New York Stock Exchange, is a manufacturer of passive electronic components and semiconductor components. It owns 80.4% of the equity in Siliconix.

Siliconix is listed on the NASDAQ. It designs, markets, and manufactures power and analog semiconductor products....

Defendant Felix Zandman ("Zandman") is the chairman, chief executive officer, and controlling stockholder of Vishay.

Defendant King Owyang is a director, president, and chief executive officer of Siliconix. He was appointed to these positions by Vishay in 1998 following Vishay's acquisition of its equity interest in Siliconix.

Defendants Mark Segall ("Segall") and Timothy Talbert ("Talbert") are directors of Siliconix and served on the Special Committee formed to evaluate a Vishay proposal to acquire the minority interests in Siliconix.

The other individual Defendants are directors of Siliconix and are either employees of Vishay or have an on-going close business relationship with Vishay.

B. Background to the Tenders.

Since acquiring its interest in Siliconix, Vishay has assisted in marketing Siliconix' products, and the company itself is frequently referred to as "Vishay Siliconix." Siliconix has been successful since Vishay's acquisition [but its stock price has been depressed due to negative investor sentiment towards technology stocks generally]....

Early this year, Vishay began to consider acquiring the remaining Siliconix stock that it did own. According to Vishay, it determined that it should evaluate opportunities to reduce costs and seek synergies that could be achieved through an acquisition of the minority Siliconix shares. Fitzgerald's view is that Vishay started to look seriously at acquiring Siliconix because its price was starting to rise from its December low and its prospects were improving. If Vishay did not act quickly, it would be forced to pay significantly more for the Siliconix minority interests.

C. The Cash Tender Offer.

On February 22, 2001, Vishay publicly announced a proposed, all-cash tender offer for the publicly-held Siliconix common stock at a price of $28.82 per share. It also announced that if it obtained over 90% of the Siliconix stock, it would consider a short-form merger of Siliconix into a Vishay subsidiary for the same price. Vishay determined the price by applying a 10% premium to the then market price of Siliconix stock. Vishay made no effort to value Siliconix. Fitzgerald maintains that the tender offer price of $28.82 per share was grossly inadequate and asserts that the public announcement was an effort to keep the price artificially depressed. Among other factors, he points out that the price represented a 20.1% discount from Siliconix' average closing price for the six-month period prior to the announcement of the cash tender offer.

D. *Appointment of the Special Committee.*

In its February 22, 2001 press release, Vishay requested the opportunity to "discuss its tender offer with a special committee of independent, non-management Siliconix directors who are unaffiliated with Vishay." In response, the Siliconix board designated a Special Committee consisting of directors Segall and Talbert. Both members of the Special Committee had done extensive work with Vishay. Segall had been its attorney until shortly before the tender. Talbert had been active in providing banking services to Vishay in the 1980s. Both were friends of Vishay management, including particularly Avi Eden ("Eden"), who was Vishay's principal representative for the Siliconix tender effort.... Members of the Special Committee were to be paid a separate $50,000 fee and there were discussions about a "special fee" to be determined later....

Fitzgerald maintains that the actions of the Special Committee, throughout its existence, have constituted nothing more than a sham—essentially two Vishay loyalists, supinely pursuing their engagement without vigor or effectiveness.

The Defendants' version of the conduct of the Special Committee, as one would expect, is quite different. Its mandate was to take reasonable and necessary steps to evaluate the transaction and to negotiate with Vishay.

Following its appointment, the Special Committee sought outside professional assistance. After discussions with representatives of at least five investment banking firms, the Special Committee engaged Lehman Brothers ("Lehman") as its financial advisor. After consulting with three prominent law firms, the Special Committee chose Heller, Ehrman, White & McAuliffe ("Heller Ehrman") to provide legal counsel. Neither Lehman nor Heller Ehrman had any relationship with Siliconix or Vishay.

Fitzgerald points out that Segall discussed the retention of both the financial expert and the legal advisor with Eden. Fitzgerald would have the Court believe that this was an opportunity for Eden to veto any of the advisors. The Special Committee, on the other hand, would have the Court believe that this was simply a double check on potential conflicts of interest. Although I cannot resolve this dispute, I do accept that both Lehman and Heller Ehrman were independent.

The Special Committee met regularly with its advisors. Although recognizing that Vishay could not be compelled to sell its stake in Siliconix and that Vishay could commence a unilateral offer at any time, nonetheless, according to the Defendants, the Special Committee attempted to evaluate Vishay's February cash tender proposal and to negotiate the best terms, including price, that it could obtain for the minority shareholders.

On April 5, 2001, the Special Committee and its advisors met with Vishay. The Special Committee expressed the view that [$28.82] per share was not a fair price for Siliconix. The parties agreed to resume their discussions after Lehman had completed its due diligence and valuation work on Siliconix and the special committee had had an opportunity to review that work.

E. *The Stock-for-Stock Exchange.*

In the meantime, Siliconix' stock had risen above the $28.82 per share cash offer price. Vishay management was unwilling to increase the cash offer and therefore started to consider a stock-for-stock transaction. On May 2, 2001, the Special Committee again met with Vishay. Vishay was again told that the Special Committee did not consider $28.82 per share adequate, and Vishay floated the possibility of a stock-for-stock deal.

Because of the stock-for-stock possibility, Lehman was directed by the Special Committee to analyze Vishay to form a view as to what the value of the Vishay stock would be in terms of such an offer. Fitzgerald alleges that Lehman at this meeting took the position that it would have endorsed an offer in the range of $34 to $36. The Special Committee advised Vishay that the $28.82 price was inadequate. Vishay drafted a merger agreement for consideration by the Special Committee, and the parties conducted on-going negotiations for several weeks about a potential merger.

* * *

On May 23, 2001, Vishay informed the Special Committee that it was considering proceeding with a stock-for-stock exchange offer without first obtaining the Special Committee's approval. Two days later, Vishay announced the exchange offer under which it would exchange 1.5 shares of Vishay common stock for every share of Siliconix common stock. The exchange ratio was simply the ratio of the Siliconix and Vishay stock prices as of the February 22 proposal. Unlike the February 22 cash tender announcement, the share exchange carried no market premium for the Siliconix shareholders.

* * *

Vishay's offer contained a non-waivable "majority of the minority" provision providing that Vishay would not proceed with its tender offer unless a majority of those shareholders not affiliated with Vishay tendered their shares. Vishay also stated that it intended to effect a short-form merger following a successful tender offer, but it noted that it is not required to do so and that there might be circumstances under which it would not do so. [Vishay's] Registration Statement also advised the minority shareholders that if Vishay pursued the short-form merger, it would be at the same per share consideration as the exchange offer and that objecting shareholders could invoke their appraisal rights under Delaware law.

* * *

The Special Committee advised Vishay that is was unlikely to approve the 1.5 exchange ratio as fair, but the record is unclear what steps were taken to seek enhancement of the terms of the tender offer....

On June 8, 2001, Siliconix filed with the Securities and Exchange Commission its Schedule 14D-9 setting forth its disclosures concerning Vishay's offer. It reported that the Special Committee has determined to remain neutral and make no recommendation with respect to the tender offer. The Special Committee never requested Lehman to prepare a fairness opinion as to the exchange offer. According to Segall, the Special Committee did not seek a fairness opinion because until May 23, 2001, it was still negotiating terms with Vishay. Until the terms were finalized, it would have been premature to seek a fairness opinion. Segall notes that after the process changed from a negotiated agreement to a unilateral tender offer, the Special Committee did not seek a fairness opinion because it did not consider it customary or appropriate to obtain a fairness opinion in the context of the unilateral tender offer.

Fitzgerald argues that the Special Committee knew that if it asked for Lehman's opinion, Lehman would render an opinion that the exchange ratio was inadequate, especially given Lehman's reservations about giving a fairness opinion at below $34 per share. Fitzgerald's reference to Lehman's reluctance to give a fairness opinion below $34 per share is based upon some notes made by a meeting attendee. On the other hand, Lehman's principal representative on the Siliconix project does not recall expressing such an opinion, even tentatively....

III. ANALYSIS

* * *

B. *Probability of Success.*

I first set forth the established legal principles dealing with when a tender offeror may be under a duty to offer a fair price. I next address Fitzgerald's argument that the proposed transaction must be judged under the entire fairness standard, not only because of its potential impact on the merits of the dispute, but also because of its potential to expand the scope of Defendants' disclosure obligations. I then turn to the critical issues associated with the adequacy of the disclosures made by Defendants to the minority shareholders. I conclude with an assessment of whether the pending tender offer is coercive.

1. *Fair Price Issues.*

In responding to a voluntary tender offer, shareholders of Delaware corporations are free to accept or reject the tender based on their own evaluation of their best interests. "That choice will normally depend upon each stockholder's individual investment objectives and his evaluation of the merits of the offer."[20] However, this Court will intervene to protect the rights of the shareholders to make a voluntary choice. The issue of voluntariness of the tender depends on the absence of improper coercion and the absence of disclosure violations. Thus, "as a general principle, our law holds that a controlling shareholder extending an offer for minority-held shares in the controlled corporation is under no obligation, absent evidence that material information about the offer has been withheld or misrepresented or that the offer is coercive in some significant way, to offer any particular price for the minority-held stock."[21]

Accordingly, Vishay was under no duty to offer any particular price, or a "fair" price, to the minority shareholders of Siliconix unless actual coercion or disclosure violations are shown by Fitzgerald. In short, as long as the tender offer is pursued properly, the free choice of the minority shareholders to reject the tender offer provides sufficient protection. Because I conclude that there were no disclosure violations and the tender is not coercive, Vishay was not obligated to offer a fair price in its tender.

2. *Entire Fairness Standard.*

Fitzgerald argues that a preliminary injunction should issue because the Defendants cannot demonstrate that the transaction is entirely fair. He contends that both the fair dealing and the fair price prongs of the entire fairness standard are implicated because the Siliconix directors (including the Special Committee members) breached their duty of care and their duty of loyalty to the Siliconix shareholders.... However, unless coercion or disclosure violations can be shown, no defendant has the duty to demonstrate the entire fairness of this proposed tender transaction.

It may seem strange that the scrutiny given to tender offer transactions is less than the scrutiny that may be given to, for example, a merger transaction which is accompanied by more general breaches of fiduciary duty by the directors of the acquired corporation. From the standpoint of a Siliconix shareholder, there may be little substantive

---

20. *Eisenberg v. Chicago Milwaukee Corp.*, Del. Ch., 537 A.2d 1051, 1056 (1987).
21. *In re Ocean Drilling & Exploration Co. Shareholders Litig.* ("*Ocean Drilling*"), 1991 Del. Ch. LEXIS 82, *9-10, Del. Ch., Consol. C.A. No. 11898, Chandler, V.C. (Apr. 30, 1991)....

difference if the tender is successful and Vishay proceeds, as it has indicated that it most likely will, with the short-form merger. The Siliconix shareholders may reject the tender, but, if the tender is successful and the short-form merger accomplished, the shareholder, except for the passage of time, will end up in the same position as if he or she had tendered or if the transaction had been structured as a merger, *i.e.*, as the holder of 1.5 Vishay shares for every Siliconix share held before the process began (or as someone pursuing appraisal rights) and with no continuing direct economic interest in the Siliconix business enterprise.

The difference in judicial approach can be traced to two simple concepts. The first is that accepting or rejecting a tender is a decision to be made by the individual shareholder, and at least as to the tender itself, he will, if he rejects the tender, still own the stock of the target company following the tender.[23] The second concept is that the acquired company in the merger context enters into a merger agreement, but the target company in the tender context does not confront a comparable corporate decision because the actual target of a tender is not the corporation (or its directors), but, instead, is its shareholders. Indeed, the board of the tender target is not asking its shareholders to approve any corporate action by the tender target. That, however, does not mean that the board of the company to be acquired in a tender has no duties to shareholders.

But addressing that question in the circumstances of this case involves one in considering an anomaly. Public tender offers are, or rather can be, change in control transactions that are functionally similar to merger transactions with respect to the critical question of control over the corporate enterprise. Yet, under the corporation law, a board of directors which is given the critical role of initiating and recommending a merger to the shareholders (see *8 Del. C. § 251*) traditionally has been accorded no statutory role whatsoever with respect to a public tender offer for even a controlling number of shares. This distinctive treatment of board power with respect to merger and tender offers is not satisfactorily explained by the observation that the corporation law statutes were basically designed in a period when large scale public tender offers were rarities; our statutes are too constantly and carefully massaged for such an explanation to account for much of the story. More likely, one would suppose, is that conceptual notion that tender offers essentially represent the sale of shareholders' separate property and such sales—even when aggregated into a single change in control transaction—require no "corporate" action and do not involve distinctively "corporate" interests.

... Fitzgerald maintains that the Siliconix board (or perhaps its Special Committee) was required by *McMullin v. Beran*[][27] to take a position on whether the Siliconix shareholders should accept the tender and to inform them of that decision and the reasons for it. The board's failure, which Fitzgerald maintains reflects breaches of both the duty of care and the duty of loyalty, to provide this assistance to the shareholders likewise mandates an entire fairness evaluation.

McMullin teaches, *inter alia*, that in the context of a merger of a subsidiary with a third party (thereby effecting a complete sale of the subsidiary) where the controlling

---

23. Of course, if a short-form merger is effected, the time for continued holding of the stock may be short.

27. *McMullin v. Beran*, Del. Supr., 765 A.2d 910 (2000). In *McMullin*, ARCO owned 80.1% of the common stock of ARCO Chemical. It sought the sale of the entire Chemical company through a merger of Chemical into a subsidiary of Lyondell. The directors of Chemical approved the merger agreement before submitting it to all of Chemical's stockholders.

shareholder wants the merger to occur and the minority shareholders are powerless to prevent it: (i) the directors of the subsidiary have "an affirmative duty to protect those minority shareholders' interests";[29] (ii) the board cannot "abdicate [its] duty by leaving it to the shareholders alone" to determine how to respond;[30] and (iii) the board has a duty to assist the minority shareholders by ascertaining the subsidiary's value as a going concern so that the shareholders may be better able to assess the acquiring party's offer and, thus, to assist in determining whether to pursue appraisal rights.[31]

Many of the pertinent factors in *McMullin* are similar to the Siliconix circumstances. In *McMullin*, the controlling shareholder owned a little more than 80% of the subsidiary, and half of the subsidiary's directors were employed by the parent. In both cases, the ultimate question for the minority shareholders was whether to acquiesce in the proposed transaction or to rely upon the appraisal remedy. Although there are many similarities, there is one large difference: *McMullin* involved a merger of the subsidiary into a third-party, a transaction for which the subsidiary board sought the approval of the minority shareholders.

The question thus becomes: does *McMullin* apply with full force, as Fitzgerald seems to contend, to a tender offer by a controlling shareholder for the remaining 20% of the stock held by the minority (where a short-form merger may follow) or does it primarily define or confirm standards governing mergers under the facts of that case?

When one looks at both the *McMullin* and Siliconix transactions from the perspective of the minority shareholders, their need for (and their ability to benefit from) the guidance and information to be provided by their boards in accordance with the principles of *McMullin* is virtually indistinguishable. The most likely ultimate puzzle for the minority shareholder, as noted above, is (a) take the consideration offered or (b) seek appraisal. However, this analysis must focus on the source of the duties motivating the result in *McMullin*. The Supreme Court was careful to note throughout its opinion that the duties involved were statutory duties imposed by 8 *Del. C.* §251 (relating to mergers) and the "attendant" fiduciary duties. The Court emphasized that fiduciary duties are "context specific" and the context of *McMullin* was, of course, a merger. In the face of a carefully crafted opinion, I cannot read into it a new approach to assessing the conduct of directors of a tender target.... In addition, the minority shareholders in *McMullin* were powerless; the parent was voting for the merger and it did not matter how they voted. Here, the Siliconix minority shareholders have the power to thwart the tender offer because it will go forward only if a majority of the minority shares are tendered. Accordingly, I conclude that *McMullin* cannot be read to require application of the entire fairness test to evaluate the proposed transaction.[36]

To the extent that *McMullin* may be read to require the subsidiary board to guide the minority shareholders in their decision to accept or reject a tender, I note that there

---

29. *McMullin v. Beran, supra*, 765 A.2d at 920.

30. *Id.*, 765 A.2d at 919.

31. *Id.*, 765 A.2d at 922.

36. Defendants also assert that, to the extent that Delaware law may be construed to require actions or disclosures by the board of the tender target beyond the truthful and complete disclosures required for Schedule 14D-9, it would be preempted by federal securities law. In particular, it is my understanding that Defendants argue that Delaware law cannot impinge upon the rights of the board to recommend acceptance or rejection of the tender or to express no opinion or state that it is unable to take a position. Because of my disposition of the substantive issues in this preliminary proceeding, I need not now reach Defendants' preemption contentions. (*See* 17 C.F.R. §240-14e-2(a)).

may exist circumstances where there is no answer to the question of whether to accept or reject. Sometimes the facts in favor of and against acceptance of the tender will balance out. On this preliminary record, I am not persuaded that the Special Committee's decision not to take a position was not reasonably supported by the information available to it. There are a number of competing factors. For example, the tender consideration, whether in reference to the frequently mentioned $34 per share or the Lehman analysis reciting a wide range of potential values, is at the low end. On the other hand, factors such as liquidity and the possibility that the Siliconix price might decline if the Vishay offer is withdrawn may be interpreted as supporting a tender. Regardless of how one assesses the Special Committee's obligation to make a recommendation, once the Siliconix board set forth the reasons for that decision in its Schedule 14D-9, its full and complete disclosure obligation was in effect. The sufficiency of those disclosures is considered subsequently.

I will now turn to the issues of disclosure and coercion, as to at least one of which Fitzgerald must demonstrate a reasonable probability of success, if he is to prevail on his motion for a preliminary injunction.

3. *Disclosure.*

A majority stockholder, in this instance, Vishay, who makes a tender to acquire the stock of the minority shareholders owes the minority shareholders a fiduciary duty to disclose accurately all material facts surrounding the tender. The significance of that is enhanced where, as here, the acquiring Company effectively controls the acquired company. When the directors of the tender target company communicate with the shareholders, for example, through a Schedule 14D-9, they must, while complying with their ever-present duties of due care, good faith and loyalty, communicate honestly. A fact is material if there is a "substantial likelihood" that its disclosure "would have been viewed by the reasonable investor as having significantly altered the 'total mix' of information made available."[41] Delaware law does not require disclosure of "all available information" simply because available information "might be helpful."[42] The plaintiff has the burden of demonstrating materiality. In the context of a preliminary injunction proceeding regarding a tender offer, the issue becomes whether there is a reasonable probability that a material omission or misstatement has been made "that would make a reasonable shareholder more likely to tender his shares."[44]

With these principles in mind, I will turn to the alleged disclosure violations. Fitzgerald alleges relatively few instances of misleading disclosures; most of his challenges allege a failure to disclose material facts.

[The court then considered at great length Fitzgerald's arguments that Vishay's Registration Statement and Siliconix's Schedule 14D-9 were misleading. Fitzgerald's primary argument was that those documents painted an unduly pessimistic picture of Siliconix's future.]

In conclusion, I have not found that, on this preliminary record, Fitzgerald had made the necessary showing to establish any disclosure violation. Accordingly, I will now turn to a consideration of whether or not the tender is coercive.

* * *

---

41. *Skeen v. Jo-Ann Stores, Inc., Del. Supr., 750 A.2d 1170, 1174 (2000).*
42. *Id.*
44. *Ocean Drilling, supra,* mem. Op. at 3.

4. *Coercion.*

A tender offer is coercive if the tendering shareholders are "wrongfully induced by some act of the defendant to sell their shares for reasons unrelated to the economic merits of the sale."[78] The wrongful acts must "[influence] in some material way" the shareholder's decision to tender.[79] I now turn to the instances alleged by Fitzgerald to constitute actionable coercion.

[The court then considered Fitzgerald's coercion claim at great length. Fitzgerald primarily claimed that Vishy's tender offer was coercive because it was launched when Siliconix's stock price was depressed and that Vishay refused to commit to effecting a short-form merger upon completion of its tender offer.]

* * *

In some sense, Fitzgerald laments the position of a minority shareholder in a corporation where one shareholder controls more than 80% of the stock. If the tender is successful and he does not tender, Fitzgerald will either be a member of an even smaller minority or his stock will be the object of a short-form merger that will divest him of his pure stake in Siliconix. Perhaps these circumstances are not happy ones, but they are allowed by law and inherent in the nature of his holdings and, thus, while perhaps encouraging him to tender, do not constitute actionable coercion.

Accordingly, Fitzgerald has not succeeded in demonstrating, at this time, that he has a reasonable probability of success on the merits of his claims.

* * *

For the foregoing reasons, an Order denying Fitzgerald's Motion for a Preliminary Injunction will be entered.

* * *

Notes and Questions

1. In re Pure Resources, Inc., Shareholders Litigation, 808 A.2d 421 (Del. Ch. 2002), presented a plaintiff stockholder challenge to the fairness of a controlling stockholder's tender offer similar to that presented in *Siliconix*. Although following the reasoning of *Siliconix*, the Delaware Chancery Court expanded on the conditions under which a controlling stockholder's tender offer for minority shares would be deemed non-coercive:

> The potential for coercion and unfairness posed by controlling stock-holders who seek to acquire the balance of the company's shares by acquisition requires some equitable reinforcement.... [O]ur law should consider an acquisition tender offer by a controlling stockholder non-coercive only when: 1) it is subject to a non-waivable majority of the minority tender condition; 2) the controlling stockholder promises to consummate a prompt § 253 [short form] merger at the same price if it obtains more than 90 percent of the shares; and 3) the controlling stockholder has made no retributive threats. Those protections ... minimize the distorting influence of the tendering process on voluntary choices. They also recognize the

---

78. *Ivanhoe Partners v. Newmont Mining Corp.*, Del. Ch., 533 A.2d 585, 605, *aff'd.*, Del. Supr., 535 A.2d 1334 (1987)....

79. *Ivanhoe Partners v. Newmont Mining Corp., supra*, 533 A.2d at 605-06.

adverse conditions that confront stockholders who find themselves owning what have become very thinly traded shares. These conditions also provide a partial cure to the disaggregation problem, by providing a realistic non-tendering goal the minority can achieve to prevent the offer from proceeding altogether.

The informational and timing advantages possessed by controlling stockholders also require some countervailing protection if the minority is to truly be afforded the opportunity to make an informed, voluntary tender decision. In this regard, the majority stockholder owes a duty to permit the independent directors on the target board both free rein and adequate time to react to the tender offer, by (at the very least) hiring their own advisors, providing the minority with a recommendation as to the advisability of the offer, and disclosing adequate information for the minority to make an informed judgment. For their part, the independent directors have a duty to undertake these tasks in good faith and diligently, and to pursue the best interests of the minority.

When a tender offer is non-coercive in the sense I have identified and the independent directors of the target are permitted to make an informed recommendation and provide fair disclosure, the law should be chary about superimposing the full fiduciary requirement of entire fairness upon the statutory tender offer process.

Id. at 445-46.

How does the court's non-coercive prescription measure up to the Federal tender offer provisions contained in the Williams Act and in SEC rules and regulations? While presumably a Federal court would allow the three non-coercive conditions listed above to stand (as additive as opposed to contradictory to the Federal tender offer scheme), what about the measures designed to address the informational and timing advantages possessed by controlling stockholders? Under Securities Exchange Act Rule 14e-2, a target's board must notify its stockholders of its position on a pending tender offer not later than 10 business days from the commencement of that offer. A target's board naturally sets forth its position on its Schedule 14D-9 filed with the SEC and distributed to its stockholders. But what if, in the words of the Delaware Chancery Court in *Pure Resources*, a target's board needs more "time to react to the tender offer, by (at the very least) hiring their own advisors, providing the minority with a recommendation as to the advisability of the offer, and disclosing adequate information for the minority to make an informed judgment"?

2. Does the entire fairness standard apply to short-form mergers? In Glassman v. Unocal Exploration Corp., 777 A.2d 242 (Del. 2001), the Delaware Supreme Court stated:

[T]he short-form merger statute, as enacted in 1937, authorized a parent corporation to merge with its wholly-owned subsidiary by filing and recording a certificate evidencing the parent's ownership and its merger resolution. In 1957, the statute was expanded to include parent/subsidiary mergers where the parent company owns at least 90% of the stock of the subsidiary. The 1957 amendment also made it possible, for the first time and only in a short-form merger, to pay the minority cash for their shares, thereby eliminating their ownership interest in the company. In its current form, which has not changed significantly since 1957, 8 *Del. C.* § 253 provides in relevant part:

(a) In any case in which at least 90 percent of the outstanding shares of each class of the stock of a corporation ... is owned by another corporation..., the corporation having such stock ownership may ... merge the other corporation ... into itself ... by executing, acknowledging and filing, in accordance with § 103 of this title, a certificate of such ownership and merger setting forth a copy of the resolution of its board of directors to so merge and the date of the adoption; provided, however, that in case the parent corporation shall not own all the outstanding stock of ... the subsidiary corporation[], ... the resolution ... shall state the terms and conditions of the merger, including the securities, cash, property or rights to be issued, paid delivered or granted by the surviving corporation upon surrender of each share of the subsidiary corporation ...

* * *

(d) In the event that all of the stock of a subsidiary Delaware corporation ... is not owned by the parent corporation immediately prior to the merger, the stockholders of the subsidiary Delaware corporation party to the merger shall have appraisal rights as set forth in Section 262 of this Title.

* * *

Mindful of this history, we must decide whether a minority stockholder may challenge a short-form merger by seeking equitable relief through an entire fairness claim. Under settled principles, a parent corporation and its directors undertaking a short-form merger are self-dealing fiduciaries who should be required to establish entire fairness, including fair dealing and fair price. The problem is that § 253 authorizes a summary procedure that is inconsistent with any reasonable notion of fair dealing. In a short-form merger, there is no agreement of merger negotiated by two companies; there is only a unilateral act—a decision by the parent company that its 90% owned subsidiary shall no longer exist as a separate entity. The minority stockholders receive no advance notice of the merger; their directors do not consider or approve it; and there is no vote. Those who object are given the right to obtain fair value for their shares through appraisal.

The equitable claim plainly conflicts with the statute. If a corporate fiduciary follows the truncated process authorized by § 253, it will not be able to establish the fair dealing prong of entire fairness. If, instead, the corporate fiduciary sets up negotiating committees, hires independent financial and legal experts, etc., then it will have lost the very benefit provided by the statute—a simple, fast and inexpensive process for accomplishing a merger. We resolve this conflict by giving effect the intent of the General Assembly. In order to serve its purpose, § 253 must be construed to obviate the requirement to establish entire fairness.

* * *

Although fiduciaries are not required to establish entire fairness in a short-form merger, the duty of full disclosure remains, in the context of this request for stockholder action. Where the only choice for the minority stockholders is whether to accept the merger consideration or seek appraisal, they must be given all the factual information that is material to that decision. The Court of Chancery carefully considered plaintiffs' disclosure claims and applied settled law in rejecting them. We affirm this aspect of the appeal on the basis of the trial court's decision.

Id. at 244 & 247-48.

Section 3
Antitakeover Legislation

A large number of states have enacted antitakeover protections as part of their corporations statutes, arguably in response to the dislocating effect of takeovers on a variety of local constituents. *See* Johnson & Millon, Missing the Point About State Takeover Statutes, 87 Mich. L. Rev. 846 (1989). Whether or not one agrees that this is the purpose of such statutes, *see, e.g.*, Booth, The Promise of State Takeover Statutes, 86 Mich. L. Rev. 1635 (1988); Romano, The Political Economy of Takeover Statutes, 73 Va. L. Rev. 111 (1987), it is clearly the purpose of the most dramatic of these enactments, the Pennsylvania Control Share Acquisition Act of 1990 (the "Act"), which substantially revised Pennsylvania's antitakeover legislation. This note describes the Pennsylvania statute and the other principal types of antitakeover legislation.

(i) *Pennsylvania Act*

On April 27, 1990, Pennsylvania adopted what may be the most far-reaching, and is certainly the most controversial, antitakeover legislation in the United States. 15 Pa. Cons. Stat. §§1721, 2561, 2571, 2581 (1990). (Portions of this statute were amended and recodified in December 1990. This Note describes the statute as amended.) This new legislation (a) permits Pennsylvania corporations to force bidders to disgorge their profits on shares purchased and sold within a specified period, (b) revises provisions relating to the scope of directors' fiduciary duties, and (c) includes a control share acquisition statute.[1]

a. *Disgorgement*

The predominant approach in state tender offer legislation is to deprive the bidder of voting rights in the acquired shares absent target stockholder approval (control share acquisition statutes) or to provide minimum substantive and procedural requirements for takeover transactions (business combination statutes). Although the Act includes a statute of the former type, at its heart lies its most controversial provision, the disgorgement statute. §§2571-2575. This statute provides that profits (§2573) realized by "controlling persons or groups" (§2573) on the sale of equity securities (§2573) of a corporation covered by the statute (a "registered corporation")[2] within eighteen months of becoming a controlling person or group "shall belong to and be recoverable by the corporation" (§2574) if the securities were acquired within twenty-four months before or eighteen months after such person or group became a control person. This statute goes beyond mere changes in control, and is aimed at preventing greenmail and attempts by bidders to put the corporation "in play" for the purpose of realizing short-term profits on its stock (§2572). The statute expressly dis-

---

1. The statute also includes provisions concerning the corporation's obligations with respect to labor agreements and severance pay for employees who are terminated following a takeover which are not discussed herein.

2. A "registered corporation" is one that has voting securities and either is registered under the Securities Exchange Act of 1934 or is otherwise subject to the Act's reporting requirements.

claims a purpose to limit "legitimate shareholder activity that does not involve putting a corporation "in play" or involv[ing] seeking to acquire control of the corporation," (§2572(b)), particularly proxy contests. Actions to compel disgorgement may be brought by the corporation, or derivatively by a stockholder if the corporation fails to bring suit within sixty days after written demand (§2575(a)). Successful litigants are entitled to attorneys' fees.

b. *Constituency Statute*

As a further part of its antitakeover package, the Pennsylvania legislature amended Pennsylvania's constituency statute (§1721, now codified at §1715) which, in a predecessor provision (now surviving as §1716), formed an important part of the court's approval (in refusing to issue a preliminary injunction) of constituency consideration by the board in Baron v. Strawbridge & Clothier, 646 F. Supp. 690 (E.D. Pa. 1986). Although §1716 continues to apply to corporations opting out of the new section, §1715(a) permits directors, in the discharge of their duties, to consider the interests of "any or all groups affected" by its action, "including shareholders, employees, suppliers, customers and creditors of the corporation, and ... communities in which offices or other establishments of the corporation are located," with no single group's interest to be required to be considered "as a dominant or controlling interest or factor." In cementing this approach, the statute provides that consideration of such interests does not violate the standard of care or right to rely of the board of directors, which duties are "solely to the business of the corporation" (§1717).

Enforcement of these last duties is restricted to derivative actions brought by the corporation or by stockholders (§1717), and may not be sought in direct actions. Finally, the statute seeks to emphasize this constituency protection in control contests by explicitly rejecting the heightened standard of scrutiny applied to defensive measures by the Delaware courts (§1715(d)).

The potential scope of the statute is diminished, however, by §1711(b), which permits registered Pennsylvania corporations to opt out of the new constituency provisions (by bylaw amendment adopted by the board of directors) by July 26, 1990, and permits other corporations to opt out (by bylaw amendment adopted by the board of directors) by April 27, 1991, or in their original articles of incorporation or by amendment to the articles within ninety days after first becoming a registered corporation. Corporations which are not "registered" may opt out in the same manner, subject to a one-year grace period rather than one of ninety days.

c. *Control Share Acquisition Statute*

The control share acquisition statute, the third major component of the Act, permits registered corporations to opt out of its provisions in much the same manner as §1715. Like control share provisions adopted in other states, the Pennsylvania statute denies voting rights to control shares (which are shares otherwise entitling the owner to cast a certain threshold percentage of the votes in an election of the corporation's directors (§2562)) unless approved by "the holders of a majority of the voting power entitled to vote in two separate votes ..." consisting of (i) all of the disinterested shares of the corporation and (ii) all of the voting shares of the corporation (§2563). The definition of "disinterested shares" (§2562) includes shares beneficially owned by executive officers and inside directors of the target, as well as those owned by the acquiror, thereby neutralizing any advantage that might be held by the target's management. The statute goes further than other control share statutes, however, and also excludes arbitrageurs who would be biased in favor of the takeover by including within the definition of disinterested shares only those shares "beneficially owned by the same holder ... continuously" for a period ending before the proposed takeover would have resulted in significant arbitrage activity. *See also* Rosenbaum & Parker, The Pennsylvania Takeover Act of 1990: Summary and Analysis 36 (1990). Rosenbaum and Parker further note several other unusual features of the Act, including the exclusion from the definition of disinterested shares of those shares owed by an ESOP in which the employees lack the right confidentially to direct the voting, *id.* at 37, and the right of the corporation to redeem control shares at their then-market price (under certain conditions) within twenty-four months after specified triggering events, which obviously subjects the acquiror to the disgorgement provisions within the first eighteen months after controlling person status was obtained. *Id.* at 39-40.

(ii) *Other Forms of Antitakeover Legislation*

In addition to (or in lieu of) control share acquisition statutes (described generally in connection with the Pennsylvania Act), a number of states have adopted business combination statutes. New York Business Corporation Law §912 illustrates this type of statute. The statute defines "business combination" as consisting of a variety of recapitalization transactions, including mergers, consolidations, significant asset transfers, significant stock issuances, liquidations, recapitalizations, and loans or other forms of financial assistance with or to an "interested shareholder" and its affiliates (§912(a)(5)). "Interested shareholder" is defined in §912(a)(10) to include 20 percent beneficial owners and corporate affiliates who beneficially owned 20 percent of the corporation's stock within a five-year period ending on the relevant date. The statute prohibits business combinations with an interested stockholder for five years following the date on which that status was attained except (i) upon the approval of a majority of the target's board prior to the acquisition by the interested shareholder of its shares; (ii) upon approval of a majority of the target's disinterested shareholders (apparently including, for these purposes, shares owned by the target's directors); or (iii) for business combinations effected at "fair prices," determined in accordance with the statutory formula (§912(b),(c)). The effect of the statute clearly is to preclude a bidder's obtaining complete ownership of a target through a transaction following a tender offer without meeting the requisite conditions. Other types of business combination statutes simply require prior target board approval to permit the bidder to effect a business combination. Lieberman & Bartell, The Rise in State Antitakeover Laws, 23 Sec. & Comm. Reg. 149, 153 (September 5, 1990).

The different types of takeover provisions are often combined, and may further be combined with disclosure requirements imposed on the bidder. For example, some states have adopted fair price provisions in combination with control share acquisition statutes rather than business combination statutes (*e.g.*, Florida) or have combined control share acquisition statutes and business combination statutes (*e.g.*, Idaho, Kansas, Massachusetts). Two states (Maine and Utah) require a bidder who acquires more than a specified percentage of the target's stock to purchase all of its remaining shares at the same premium paid for the initial acquisition.

A third type of antitakeover legislation permits boards of directors to adopt poison pills. For example, §6.05 of the Illinois Business Corporation Act permits the corporation to issue rights or options with terms that may void their exercise by bidders. Absent such a statute (or definitive case law) "the typical state corporate law provision prohibiting discrimination among shareholders by the same class could be held to forbid a poison pill capital structure." Lieberman and Bartell, *supra* at 154.

(iii) *Court Review of Antitakeover Legislation*

The states were not able to adopt their various versions of takeover legislation without surmounting a series of challenges to their constitutionality on Commerce Clause grounds and on Supremacy Clause grounds. *See* Warren, Developments in State Takeover Regulation, MITE and its Aftermath, 40 Bus. Law. 671 (1985).

The Supreme Court first addressed the issues in Edgar v. MITE Corp., 457 U.S. 624 (1982), in which a deeply divided court invalidated an Illinois takeover statute, principally on Commerce Clause grounds. The states responded with a "second generation" of statutes that sought to cure the constitutional infirmities of the Illinois statute at issue in *MITE* and other "first generation" statutes by narrowing their scope. The Supreme Court upheld the constitutionality of Indiana's second generation statute in CTS Corp. v. Dynamics Corp. of Amer., 481 U.S. 69 (1987).

A "third generation" of state statutes followed, patterned on the Indiana statute but also being broader in scope. The Supreme Court has yet to pass on the constitutionality of the third generation of statutes. Lower courts have by and large upheld their validity, *e.g.*, BNS, Inc. v. Koppers Corp., 683 F. Supp. 458 (D. Del. 1988) (Delaware law); Amanda Acquisition Corp. v. Universal Foods Corp., 877 F.2d 496 (7th Cir. 1989) (Wisconsin law), although a couple of decisions have found some versions or aspects to be unconstitutional, *e.g.*, Hyde Park Partners, L.P. v. Connolly, [CCH] Fed. Sec. L. Rep. ¶ 93,619 at 97,792 (1st Cir. 1988) (Massachusetts law); RTE Corp. v. Mark IV Indus., [CCH] Fed. Sec. L. Rep. ¶ 93,789 at 98,722 (E.D. Wis. 1988) (Wisconsin law).

(iv) *A Selected Bibliography on Antitakeover Legislation*

As in many areas of corporate law where the stakes are high and the legal issues thorny, the scholarly literature addressing antitakeover legislation is voluminous. Most scholarly attention seems to have been centered on constituency statutes. The following is a somewhat arbitrary selection of pieces of interest.

Of general interest: Bebchuk, The Case For Increasing Shareholder Power, 118 Harv. L. Rev. 833 (2005); Walsh, The Fiduciary Foundation of Corporate Law, 27 Iowa J. Corp. L. 333 (2002); Subramanian, The Influence of Antitakeover Statutes on Incorporation Choice: Evidence on The "Race" Debate and Antitakeover Overreaching, 150 U. Pa. L. Rev. 1795 (2002).

With respect to the Pennsylvania Act: Day, Corporate Governance, Conrail, and the Market: Getting on the Right Track!, 26 Iowa J. Corp. L. 1 (2000); Murray, Comment: Money Talks, Constituents Walk: Pennsylvania's Corporate Constituency Statute Can Maximize Shareholders' Wealth, 48 Buffalo L. Rev. 629 (2000); Silberman, How Do Pennsylvania Directors Spell Relief? Act 36, 17 Del. J. Corp. L. 115 (1991).

With respect to constituency statutes: Paredes, The Firm and the Nature of Control: Toward a Theory of Takeover Law, 29 Iowa J. Corp. L. 103 (2003); Adams & Matheson, A Statutory Model for Corporate Constituency Concerns, 49 Emory L.J. 1085 (2000); Symposium: Corporate Malaise—Stakeholder Statutes: Cause or Cure, 21 Stetson L. Rev. 1 (1991).

Problem — Enforcing Constituency Legislation

Red Letter Corporation, a corporation organized in the State of Confusion ("Red Letter"), is a publicly held company with 30,000,000 shares of common stock outstanding, trading in the market at $25. Dimmesdale Co. ("Dimmesdale") announces a hostile tender offer for Red Letter at $35. The Red Letter board, after determining the Dimmesdale offer to be grossly inadequate, announces an exchange offer for up to 10,000,000 shares pursuant to which it offers to exchange for each share of stock a note with a principal amount of $40 at an interest rate two basis points above prime. The notes have protective covenants limiting Red Letter's ability to incur additional debt, sell assets or pay dividends without the approval of a majority of Red Letter's independent directors.

The exchange offer is fully subscribed. Dimmesdale increases its offer to $40. In response, Red Letter's board negotiates an agreement with Prynne, Inc. ("Prynne") for a leveraged buyout pursuant to which Prynne will sell off significant assets of Red Letter. Red Letter agrees to waive the note covenants to permit Prynne's acquisition to occur. Immediately, the trading price of the notes, which had traded at par, drops to $33, and noteholders begin to threaten the board with litigation. After intensive negotiations and a bidding war, the Red Letter board agrees to permit Prynne to acquire Red Letter for $1 per share more than Dimmesdale's final price. Upon this announcement, the notes stabilize at $34 in the market.

As part of the deal, Prynne announces its intention to close Red Letter's factory in the city of Chillingworth and lay off workers in all of its factories in order to be able to service the debt it will incur in the transaction. Red Letter is the largest employer in Chillingworth. Red Letter contributes heavily to Chillingworth's tax base and a variety of local charities, and each August sponsors the Chillingworth Music Festival, which is a major source of tourism in Chillingworth. Separate actions seeking an injunction against acceptance of the Prynne offer are brought in chancery court of the State of Confusion (located in the House of the Seven Gables) against the Red Letter board by the noteholders as a class, Red Letter's principal trade union (on behalf of its employee-members), and the Town of Chillingworth. The actions are brought under Confusion's constituency statute, which reads in relevant part as follows:

> A director, officer or incorporator of a corporation shall perform his duties as such, including, in the case of a director, his duties as a member of a committee of the board upon which he may serve, in good faith and in a manner he reasonably believes to be in the best interests of the corporation, and with such care as an ordinarily prudent person in a like position would use under similar circumstances. In determining what he reasonably believes to be in the best interests of the corporation, a director may consider the interest of the corporation's employees, suppliers, creditors and customers, the economy of the state, region and nation, community and societal considerations, and the long-term and short-term interests of the corporation and its stockholders, including the possibility that these interests may be best served by the continued independence of the corporation.

i) How would each plaintiff draft its complaint?

ii) You represent the Red Letter board. How would you respond to the plaintiff's causes of action?

iii) You are the chancellor. Write your opinion disposing of these matters.

iv) Assume that the actions were brought seeking damages following the closing of the Prynne deal. How would your opinion change?

Section 4
De Facto Merger Doctrine (Redux)

We first encountered the de facto merger doctrine and the doctrine of independent legal significance in chapter 6, section 3, dealing with the rights of preferred stockholders. There, we saw companies with preferred stock outstanding using mergers to convert preferred stockholders into common stockholders. This eliminated the companies' obligations relating to the preferred stockholders, which often included a sizeable dividend arrearage.

Companies, however, also resort to transactional mechanics, including mergers, in an attempt to deny common stockholders appraisal rights or, in some instances, the ability to vote on a given transaction. With that in mind, consider the following cases.

Hariton v. Arco Electronics, Inc.
188 A. 2d 123 (Del. 1963)

SOUTHERLAND, Chief Justice.

This case involves a sale of assets under § 271 of the corporation law, 8 Del.C.... It may be stated as follows:

A sale of assets is effected under § 271 in consideration of shares of stock of the purchasing corporation. The agreement of sale embodies also a plan to dissolve the selling corporation and distribute the shares so received to the stockholders of the seller, so as to accomplish the same result as would be accomplished by a merger of the seller into the purchaser. Is the sale legal?

The facts are these:

The defendant Arco and Loral Electronics Corporation, a New York corporation, are both engaged, in somewhat different forms, in the electronic equipment business. In the summer of 1961 they negotiated for an amalgamation of the companies. As of October 27, 1961, they entered into a 'Reorganization Agreement and Plan.' The provisions of this Plan pertinent here are in substance as follows:

1. Arco agrees to sell all its assets to Loral in consideration (inter alia) of the issuance to it of 283,000 shares of Loral.

2. Arco agrees to call a stockholders meeting for the purpose of approving the Plan and the voluntary dissolution.

3. Arco agrees to distribute to its stockholders all the Loral shares received by it as a part of the complete liquidation of Arco.

At the Arco meeting all the stockholders voting (about 80%) approved the Plan. It was thereafter consummated.

Plaintiff, a stockholder who did not vote at the meeting, sued to enjoin the consummation of the Plan on the grounds (1) that it was illegal, and (2) that it was unfair. The second ground was abandoned. Affidavits and documentary evidence were filed, and defendant moved for summary judgment and dismissal of the complaint. The Vice Chancellor granted the motion and plaintiff appeals.

.... Plaintiff's argument that the sale is illegal runs as follows:

The several steps taken here accomplish the same result as a merger of Arco into Loral. In a 'true' sale of assets, the stockholder of the seller retains the right to elect whether the selling company shall continue as a holding company. Moreover, the stockholder of the selling company is forced to accept an investment in a new enterprise without the right of appraisal granted under the merger statute. § 271 cannot therefore be legally combined with a dissolution proceeding under § 275 and a consequent distribution of the purchaser's stock. Such a proceeding is a misuse of the power granted under § 271, and a de facto merger results.

The foregoing is a brief summary of plaintiff's contention.

Plaintiff's contention that this sale has achieved the same result as a merger is plainly correct. The same contention was made to us in Heilbrunn v. Sun Chemical Corporation, Del., 150 A.2d 755. Accepting it as correct, we noted that this result is made possible by the overlapping scope of the merger statute and section 271.... We also adverted to the increased use, in connection with corporate reorganization plans, of § 271 instead of the merger statute. Further, we observed that no Delaware case has held such procedure to be improper, and that two cases appear to assume its legality.... But we were not required in the Heilbrunn case to decide the point.

We now hold that the reorganization here accomplished through § 271 and a mandatory plan of dissolution and distribution is legal. This is so because the sale-of-assets statute and the merger statute are independent of each other. They are, so to speak, of equal dignity, and the framers of a reorganization plan may resort to either type of corporate mechanics to achieve the desired end. This is not an anomalous result in our corporation law. As the Vice Chancellor pointed out, the elimination of accrued dividends, though forbidden under a charter amendment ...[,] may be accomplished by a merger. Federal United Corporation v. Havender, 24 Del.Ch. 318, 11 A.2d 331.

In Langfelder v. Universal Laboratories, D.C., 68 F. Supp. 209, Judge Leahy commented upon 'the general theory of the Delaware Corporation Law that action taken pursuant to the authority of the various sections of that law constitute acts of independent legal significance and their validity is not dependent on other sections of the Act.' 68 F. Supp. 211, footnote.

* * *

Plaintiff concedes, as we read his brief, that if the several steps taken in this case had been taken separately they would have been legal. That is, he concedes that a sale of assets, followed by a separate proceeding to dissolve and distribute, would be legal, even though the same result would follow. This concession exposes the weakness of his contention. To attempt to make any such distinction between sales under § 271 would be to create uncertainty in the law and invite litigation.

We are in accord with the Vice Chancellor's ruling, and the judgment below is affirmed.

Rath v. Rath Packing Company
136 N.W. 2d 410 (Iowa 1965)

GARFIELD, Chief Justice.

The question presented is whether an Iowa corporation may carry out an agreement with another corporation, designated 'Plan and Agreement of Reorganization,' which amounts to a merger in fact of the two without approval of holders of two thirds of its outstanding shares, as provided by section 496A.70, Code 1962, [Iowa Bus. Corp. Act ("I.C.A.")], and its articles of incorporation. The question is one of first impression of Iowa. We must disagree with the trial court's holding that this may be done.

Plaintiffs, minority shareholders of Rath, brought this action in equity to enjoin carrying out the agreement on the ground, so far as necessary to consider, it provides for a merger in fact with Needham Packing Co., which requires approval of two thirds of the holders of outstanding Rath shares and that was not obtained. The trial court ... entered judgment of dismissal on the pleadings. It held approval of the plan by holders of a majority of Rath shares was sufficient. Plaintiffs appeal.

Plaintiffs own more than 6000 shares of Rath Packing Co., an Iowa corporation.... Rath has 993,185 shares outstanding held by about 4000 owners. It is engaged in meat packing and processing, mostly pork and allied products....

Needham Packing Co. is a corporation organized in 1960 under Delaware law with its principal plant in Sioux City, Iowa. Its total shares outstanding, including debentures and warrants convertible into stock, are 787,907, held by about 1000 owners. Both Rath and Needham stock is traded on the American Stock Exchange. Needham is also engaged in meat packing, mostly beef....

Pursuant to authority of Rath's board prior to April 2, 1965, it entered into the questioned agreement with Needham, designated 'Plan and Agreement of Reorganization,' under which Rath agreed to: (1) amend its articles to double the number of shares of its common stock, create a new class of preferred shares and change its name to Rath-Needham Corporation; (2) issue to Needham 5.5 shares of Rath common and two shares of its 80-cent preferred stock for each five shares of Needham stock in exchange for all Needham's assets, properties, business, name and good will, except a fund not exceeding $175,000 to pay expenses in carrying out the agreement and effecting Needham's dissolution and distribution of the new Rath-Needham stock to its shareholders, any balance remaining after 120 days to be paid over to Rath; (3) assume all Needham's debts and liabilities; and (4) elect two Needham officers and directors to its board.

Under the plan Needham agreed to: (1) transfer all its assets to Rath; (2) cease using its name; (3) distribute the new Rath Needham shares to its stockholders, liquidate and dissolve; and (4) turn over to Rath its corporate and business records.

If the plan were carried out, assuming the new preferred shares were converted into common, the thousand Needham shareholders would have about 54 per cent of the outstanding common shares of Rath-Needham and the four thousand Rath shareholders would have about 46 per cent.

Under the plan the book value of each share of Rath common stock, as of January 2, 1965, would be reduced from $27.99 to $15.93, a reduction of about 44 per cent. Each share of Needham common would be increased in book value, as of December 26, 1964, from $6.61 to $23.90, assuming conversion of the new Rath-Needham preferred.

In the event of liquidation of Rath-Needham, Needham shareholders would be preferred to Rath's under the plan, by having a prior claim to the assets of Rath-Needham to an amount slightly in excess of the book value of all Needham shares. Needham shareholders are also preferred over Rath's under the plan in distribution of income by the right of the former to receive preferred dividends of 80 cents a share—about five per cent of Needham's book value. Shortly prior to the time terms of the plan were made public Rath and Needham shares sold on the American Exchange for about the same price. Almost immediately thereafter the price of Needham shares increased and Rath's decreased so the former sold for 50 per cent more than the latter.

At a meeting of Rath shareholders on April 26, 1965, 60.1 per cent of its outstanding shares, 77 per cent of those voted, were voted in favor of these two proposals: (1) to amend the articles to authorize a class of 80¢ preferred stock and increase the authorized common from $1,500,000 shares ($10 par) to 3,000,000 shares (no par); and (2) upon acquisition by Rath of the assets, properties, business and good will of Needham to change Rath's name to Rath-Needham Corporation and elect as its directors Lloyd and James Needham. Holders of 177,000 shares voted against these proposals and 218,000 shares were not voted. The plan was not approved by the shareholders except as above stated.

Rath officers vigorously solicited proxies for the meeting by personal travel, telephone and through a professional proxy soliciting agency. This action was commenced five days prior to the meeting and four days thereafter a supplement and amendment to the petition were filed.

I. We will summarize the provisions of Code Chapter 496A, I.C.A., so far as material to the appeal.

Section 496A.74 provides that a foreign corporation and a domestic one may merge if permitted by laws of the state where the former is organized and '1. Each domestic corporation shall comply with the provisions of this chapter with respect to the merger * * * of domestic corporations * * *.'

Section 496A.68 states that two or more domestic corporations may merge pursuant to a plan approved in the manner provided in this chapter. The board of each corporation shall approve a plan setting forth: (1) the names of the merging corporations and the survivor; (2) terms of the merger; (3) manner of converting shares of each merging corporation into shares of the survivor; (4) any changes in the articles of incorporation of the survivor; (5) other provisions of the merger deemed necessary or desirable.

Section 496A.70 provides for approval of the plan of merger by the shareholders of each merging corporation and '[a]t each such meeting, a vote of the shareholders shall be taken on the proposed plan * * *. * * * The plan * * * shall be approved upon receiving the affirmative vote of the holders of at least two-thirds of the outstanding shares of each such corporation, * * *.'

* * *

Section 496A.77 states that any shareholder shall have the right to dissent from any merger to which the corporation is a party.

Section 496A.78 gives a dissenting shareholder, by following the procedure there outlined, the right to be paid the fair value of his shares as of the day prior to that on which the corporate action was approved.

The above sections are those on which plaintiffs rely. They contend these statutes specifically provide for effecting a merger and the same result cannot legally be attained at least without approval of the holders of two thirds of the shares and according to dissenters 'appraisal rights' i.e., the right to receive the fair value of their stock by compliance with the specified procedure.

Defendants contend and the trial court held compliance with the above sections was not required and defendants could legally proceed under other sections of chapter 496A which merely authorize amendments to articles of incorporation and issuance of stock. The sections just referred to provide (section 496A.55) that a corporation may amend its articles in any respects desired and in particular: change its name, change the number of shares of any class, change shares having a par value to those without par and create new classes of shares with preferences over shares then authorized.

Section 496A.56 states articles may be amended by giving shareholders notice of a meeting at which the amendments are to be considered, with a summary of the proposed changes, and upon receiving the affirmative vote of holders of a majority of the stock entitled to vote. The articles of amendment shall be filed with the secretary of state and county recorder (496A.59) and be effective upon issuance by the former of the certificate of amendment (496A.60).

Section 496A.17 provides that shares, with or without par, may be issued for such consideration as the board fixes.

Section 496A.18 states that shares may be paid for in money or property, tangible or intangible, and in the absence of fraud the judgment of the board as to value of the consideration received shall be conclusive.

II. The principal point of law defendants asked to have adjudicated under rule 105, R.C.P., is that the provisions of chapter 496A last referred to are legally independent of, and of equal dignity with, those relating to mergers and the validity of the action taken by defendants is not dependent upon compliance with the merger sections under which the same result might be attained. The trial court accepted this view.

It is clear the view just expressed emanates from the opinion in Hariton v. Arco Electronics, Inc., Del., 188 A.2d 123, the only precedent called to our attention which sustains the decision appealed from. Virtually the only basis for the conclusion Hariton reaches is the statement of the law point these defendants raised. The opinion contains little discussion and cites no authority that supports the decision.

We can agree all provisions of our chapter 496A are of equal dignity. But we cannot agree any provisions of the act are legally independent of others if this means that in arriving at the correct interpretation thereof and the legislative intent expressed therein we are not to consider the entire act and, so far as possible, construe its various provisions in the light of their relation to the whole act.... Nor should other fundamental rules of statutory construction be ignored in determining the scope and effect of any provision of chapter 496A.

We may also observe that the trial court 'concluded the 'safeguards' written into the codes of most states, including Iowa and Delaware, with respect to rights of dissenting shareholders in connection with mergers are based on outmoded concepts of economic realities, particularly in the case of an enterprise such as Rath which is regularly traded on the American Exchange and has a diversified stock ownership with over 4000 shareholders....

If the soundness of this view were admitted, the statutory safeguards should of course be removed by legislative, not judicial action....

III. The 'Plan and Agreement of Reorganization' clearly provides for what amounts to a merger of Rath and Needham under any definition of merger we know.

* * *

If, as we hold, this agreement provides for what amounts to a merger of Rath and Needham, calling it a Plan and Agreement of Reorganization does not change its essential character. A fundamental maxim of equity, frequently applied, is that equity regards substance rather than form. Kurtz v. Humboldt Trust & Savings Bank, 231 Iowa 1347, 1349, 4 N.W.2d 363, 364, and citations....

It is our duty to look behind the form to the substance of the challenged transaction....

IV. The power of a corporation to merge must be derived from the law of the state which created it. There must be some plain enactment authorizing the merger, for legislative authority is just as essential to a merger as to creation of the corporation in the first instance.... Legislative authority for a merger will not be implied but must be clearly, distinctly and expressly conferred....

At common law no merger could take place without unanimous consent of the stockholders. However, statutes in all jurisdictions now authorize mergers upon a vote of less than all stockholders. A shareholder who dissents to a merger may obtain the value of his stock if the right thereto is provided by statute, if procedure is established therefor and is followed by him....

The merger sections of chapter 496A clearly and expressly confer the necessary power to merge. Section 496A.74, supra, expressly requires compliance 'with the provisions of this chapter with respect to the merger * * * of domestic corporations.' Nothing in the sections dealing with amending articles and issuing stock purports to authorize a merger. They make no reference to merger. The most that may fairly be claimed is that they impliedly confer the required power to merge. But this is insufficient.

V. In seeking the scope and effect of the two sets of sections relied upon at least one fundamental rule of statutory construction is applicable. As stated, the merger sections specifically provide for a particular thing—mergers. The sections authorizing amendment of articles and issuance of stock apply to all amendments and stock issues, whether or not amending the articles or issuing stock is part of a merger, as they may or may not be. As applied to mergers, the sections on which plaintiffs rely are specific provisions, those on which defendants rely are not....

'It is an old and familiar principle * * * that where there is in the same statute a specific provision, and also a general one which in its most comprehensive sense would include matters embraced in the former, the particular provision must control, and the general provision must be taken to effect only such cases within its general language as are not within the provisions of the particular provision. Additional words of qualification needed to harmonize a general and a prior special provision in the same statute should be added to the general provision, rather than to the special one.' 20 Am.Jur., Statutes, section 367.

* * *

A closely related rule, many times applied by us, is that where a general statute, if standing alone, would include the same matter as a special statute and thus conflict with it, the latter will prevail and the former must give way. The special provision will be considered an exception to or qualification of the general one....

'Another rule which has been applied, is that where one section of a statute treats specially and solely of a matter, that section prevails in reference to that matter over other sections in which only incidental reference is made thereto, * * *.' 50 Am.Jur., Statutes, section 366.

It is apparent that if the sections pertaining to amending articles and issuing stock are construed to authorize a merger by a majority vote of shareholders they conflict with the sections specifically dealing with the one matter of mergers which require a two-thirds vote of shareholders. The two sets of sections may be harmonized by holding, as we do, that the merger sections govern the matter of merger and must be regarded as an exception to the sections dealing with amending articles and issuing stock, which may or may not be involved in a merger.

The construction we give these sections is in accord with the cardinal rule that, if reasonably possible, effect will be given to every part of a statute....

The merger sections make it clear the legislature intended to require a two-thirds vote of shareholders and accord so called appraisal rights to dissenters in case of a merger. It is unreasonable to ascribe to the same legislature an intent to provide in the same act a method of evading the required two-thirds vote and the grant of such appraisal rights. The practical effect of the decision appealed from is to render the requirements of a two-thirds vote and appraisal rights meaningless in virtually all mergers. It is scarcely an exaggeration to say the decision amounts to judicial repeal of the merger sections in most instances of merger.

It is obvious, as defendants' counsel frankly stated in oral argument, that corporate management would naturally choose a method which requires only majority approval of shareholders and does not grant dissenters the right to be paid the fair value of their stock. The legislature could hardly have intended to vest in corporate management the option to comply with the requirements just referred to or to proceed without such compliance, a choice that would invariably be exercised in favor of the easier method.

Seen in support of the views just stated Applestein v. United Board & Carton Corp., 60 N.J. Super. 333, 159 A.2d 146, 153, Affd. 33 N.J. 72, 161 A.2d 474; Chicago, S.F. & C.R. Co. v. Ashling, supra, 160 Ill. 373, 43 N.E. 373, 375. If defendants' view were to prevail 'we obtain the anomalous result of one part of the corporation law rendering nugatory another part of the same law in accomplishing the same result.' Applestein case. The Ashling opinion expresses a similar view.

VI. 15 Fletcher, Cyc. Corporations, 1961 Revised Volume section 7165.5, page 307, contains this: 'However, where a particular corporate combination is in legal effect a merger or a consolidation, even though the transaction may be otherwise labeled by the parties, the courts treat the transaction as a de facto merger or consolidation so as to confer upon dissenting stockholders the right to receive cash payment for their shares.' Decisions from several jurisdictions are cited in support. Only Heilbrunn v. Sun Chemical Corp., 37 Del.Ch. 552, 146 A.2d 757, Affd. 38 Del.Ch. 321, 150 A.2d 755, 758, is cited as contra.

Basis of the Heilbrunn decision is the court's declared failure to see how any injury was inflicted on shareholders of a corporation that purchased the assets of another. No opinion was expressed as to whether shareholders of the selling corporation could obtain equitable relief. The Delaware court first decided that question in Hariton v. Arco Electronics, supra, Del., 188 A.2d 123.

We think the precedents which support the statement quoted from Fletcher are sound....

VII. The trial court thought that while no Iowa case is directly in point, the policy of Iowa law is in accord with its decision, citing Traer v. Lucas Prospecting Co., 124 Iowa 107, 115-119, 99 N.W. 290, and Graeser v. Phoenix Finance Co., 218 Iowa 1112, 254 N.W. 859. Defendants also cite Price v. Holcomb, 89 Iowa 123, 137, 56 N.W. 407, and Beidenkopf v. Des Moines Life Insurance Co., 160 Iowa 629, 142 N.W. 434, 46 L.R.A.,N.S., 290. We find no conflict between the conclusion we reach and these precedents. Each of them may be distinguished on the ground the transaction there involved did not amount to a merger nor obligate any corporation to dissolve....

* * *

VIII. As indicated at the outset, Article XI of Rath's articles of incorporation provides: 'The corporation shall not merge with or consolidate into any other corporation * * * except upon obtaining the vote in favor thereof of the holders of record of two-thirds (2/3) of the shares of common stock * * *.' Article XII requires the affirmative vote of the holders of two thirds of the shares of common stock to amend Article XI.

In view of our holding in the previous divisions hereof it is unnecessary to consider the effect of these charter provisions. However, we will say that ... it would seem they afford plaintiffs added ground for relief....

IX. We hold entry of judgment of dismissal on the pleadings was error, that defendants should be enjoined from carrying out the 'Plan and Agreement of Reorganization' until such time, if ever, as it is approved by the holders of at least two thirds of the outstanding shares of Rath and in the event of such approval plaintiffs, if they dissent to such plan and follow the procedure provided by Code section 496A.78, I.C.A., shall be entitled to be paid the fair value of their shares in Rath. For decree in harmony with this opinion the cause is—Reversed and remanded.

Notes and Questions

1. Which court, *Hariton* or *Rath*, has the better legal argument? The better argument as a matter of policy?

2. In Giammalvo v. Sunshine Mining Co., 1994 Del. Ch. LEXIS 6, Vice Chancellor Berger granted summary judgment to defendants on a preferred stockholder's charge that defendants had violated redemption provisions of Sunshine's charter by repurchasing stock from a single stockholder, and that such repurchases were de facto redemptions that had to be accomplished pursuant to the charter provisions. In so doing, she noted that the contract permitted such repurchases, and suggested that the repurchases made in lieu of redemption were supported by analogy to the equal dignity rule; in other words, that each contractual provision was of independent legal significance. Does the logic of the *Hariton* court support this analogy?

3. Shidler v. All Amer. Life & Fin. Corp., 298 N.W.2d 318 (Iowa 1980), involved an issue over class voting requirements with respect to a merger between General United Group, Incorporated (GUG), an Iowa corporation, and All American Delaware Corporation (All American), a Delaware corporation which was a wholly owned subsidiary of All American Life & Casualty Company (Casualty), an Illinois corporation. At the time of the merger, GUG had outstanding three classes of stock: preferred stock and class B common stock, both of which were convertible into common stock, and common stock. Casualty, the parent of All American, also owned all of GUG's preferred and class B common, and a relatively small amount of common stock.

Pursuant to the merger agreement, all of the outstanding shares of GUG's common stock not owned by Casualty would be converted into the right to receive $3.25 cash. The proxy statement sent to the stockholders indicated that approval of the merger required the vote of 2/3 of the common and class B common, voting as one class. Since 10,623,150 shares of class B (owned by Casualty) were outstanding and only 2,959,650 shares of common, approval of the merger under this requirement was assumed. Section 496A.70 of the Iowa Corporation Law provided as follows:

> Each outstanding share of each such corporation shall be entitled to vote on the proposed plan of merger or consolidation, whether or not such share has voting rights under the provisions of the articles of incorporation of such corporation. The plan of merger or consolidation shall be approved upon receiving the affirmative vote of the holders of at least two-thirds of the outstanding shares of each such corporation, unless any class of shares of any such corporation is entitled to vote as a class thereon, in which event, as to such corporation, the plan of merger or consolidation shall be approved upon receiving the affirmative vote of the holders of at least two-thirds of the outstanding shares of each class of shares entitled to vote as a class thereon and of the total outstanding shares. Any class of shares of any such corporation shall be entitled to vote as a class if the plan of merger or consolidation, as the case may be, contains any provision which, if contained in a proposed amendment to articles of incorporation, would entitle such class of shares to vote as a class.

The reference in this section to a merger containing a provision which, as an amendment to articles, would require class voting also necessitates consideration of portions of section 496A.57 on amendments:

> The holders of the outstanding shares of a class shall be entitled to vote as a class upon a proposed amendment, whether or not entitled to vote thereon by the provisions of the articles of incorporation, if the amendment would:
>
> 1. Increase or decrease the aggregate number of authorized shares of such class.
>
> * * *
>
> 3. Effect an exchange, reclassification, or cancellation of all or part of the shares of such class.

Plaintiff challenged the merger, arguing that the statute required the common stock to vote separately as a class. The court proceeded to address this claim:

> Plaintiffs argue that several clauses in section 496A.57 entitled the common to be voted separately. We go no farther than paragraph 3 of that section and specifically to the word "cancellation." Suppose that no merger had been proposed, but an amendment to the articles had been submitted which required that all certificates of GUG common shares be surrendered to a depository for cash, that thereafter the shares of common stock would cease to be stock of the corporation, and that the stock transfer books would be closed. Would not this stock be canceled in a realistic sense? One day the owner of common stock owns a part of an ongoing enterprise; the next day he does not, he instead has money. His shares are recalled and no further trading is permitted in them; the books are closed. To "cancel" means to "revoke, annul, invalidate." *Webster's Third New International Dictionary* 325 (1969). Other definitions are, "To revoke or recall; to annul or destroy, make void or invalid, or set aside. To rescind; abandon; repeal; surrender; waive; terminate." *Black's Law Dictionary* 186 (5th ed. 1979)....
>
> Rath v. Rath Packing Co., 257 Iowa 1277, 136 N.W.2d 410 (1965) enjoins us to look at the merger statutes realistically. We think in the first place that if these common shares had been called in for cash by amendment to the articles without a merger, they would have been entitled to be voted as a class under

section 496A.57(3). That this stock would be entitled to be voted if its characteristics are altered, but not if it is completely extinguished for cash, does not appear reasonable. Section 496A.57 does not say the cancellation must be "without consideration."

Section 496A.70 provides in the second place that a class of stock is entitled to vote separately if the plan of merger "contains any provision which, if contained in a proposed amendment to articles of incorporation, would entitle such class of shares to vote as a class." We thus conclude that together these section [sic] entitled this common stock to be voted separately as a class.

III. Defendants voice several arguments contrary to this construction of the statutes. One is that this was a "cash out" merger. They say the common stock was not changed or reduced; it was eliminated and money was substituted. But we find nothing in sections 496A.70 and 496A.57 which differentiates cash out mergers from other varieties. Indeed, the cash out merger is drastic: the stockholder is compelled to give up his stock altogether and separate himself from the ongoing organization; he is ejected. Did not the General Assembly intend that such a class of stock should be entitled to vote separately on its fate?

Defendants further contend that if the General Assembly had intended each class of stock to have separate voting rights on mergers, it could have easily so provided as some states have done. But the Assembly did not desire to give each class separate voting rights automatically. It desired to give a class separate voting rights if that stock was affected in ways designated in section 496A.57, one of which is cancellation.

Then defendants urge that the merger plan does not use the word "cancel" or "cancellation" regarding this stock, and they say section 496A.57 does not apply unless the merger plan contains a provision "identical" to one of those in the section. We think this argument flies in the face of the *Rath* rationale of realism. The substance, not the precise words, controls. A merger draftsman cannot avoid section 496A.57 by calling an actual cancellation something else.

Defendants also insist that under section 496A.76 the assets of GUG could have been sold, the proceeds could have been distributed, and GUG could have been dissolved without a separate class vote; the holders of common stock would then have no stock, but money instead. Why then, defendants ask, may not substantially the same thing be done by merger?

We may assume arguendo that a separate class vote would not be required in such a proceeding, and we lay aside the point that a sale, distribution, and dissolution normally have substantially different consequences than a merger. But the controlling point is that for reasons it found sufficient, the General Assembly made the requirements of section 496A.70 on merger and of section 496A.76 on sale of assets materially different. We may not make the sections identical by judicial legislation....

We do not find defendants' arguments against the applicability of section 496A.57(3) to be convincing.

IV. As a separate argument, defendants contend that a section of chapter 496A and a clause of GUG's articles, read together, prohibit class voting of the common stock. Section 496A.138 provided at the time of the attempted merger:

Whenever, with respect to any action to be taken by the shareholders of a corporation, the articles of incorporation require the vote or concurrence of the holders of a greater or lesser proportion of the shares, or of any class or series thereof, than required by this chapter with respect to such action, the provisions of the articles of incorporation shall control.

(The words "or lesser" were deleted by 1978 Sess., 67 G.A., ch. 1186, § 3.)

GUG's articles stated at the time:

The holders of the Common Stock and Class B Common Stock shall be entitled at all times to one vote per share and the holders of all classes of common stock of the corporation shall vote together as one class on all matters.

We may assume for the purpose of answering the certified question that during the period section 496A.138 contained the words "or lesser," a clause in corporate articles could lawfully have reduced the two-thirds vote requirement of section 496A.70 to a lesser proportion. The difficulty with defendants' argument, however, is that the quoted portion of the articles on which defendants rely does not deal with the proportion; it does not purport to lessen the two-thirds requirement.

The quoted portion of the articles does however purport to prohibit class voting as between common and class B common. This clause was undoubtedly inserted to give control to Casualty. But the articles cannot override the statutes.... Section 496A.138 deals with proportions, not class voting. Its words, "or of any class or series thereof," do not authorize a prohibition of class voting. Rather, they constitute an adjective phrase modifying "shares," and "shares" is in an adjective clause modifying "proportion." On the other hand, section 496A.70 provides that any class of shares "shall" be entitled to vote as a class if the merger contains a provision which, as an amendment to articles, would entitle the class to vote separately; and section 496A.57(3) entitles a class to vote separately upon an amendment to cancel shares, "whether or not entitled to vote thereon by the provisions of the articles of incorporation...."

We are not persuaded by defendants' argument.

V. Finally, defendants urge plaintiffs' claim that the common was entitled to vote as a class is really academic for two reasons. One is that Casualty could have converted its other GUG stock to common and thus obtained a two-thirds affirmative vote by the common on the merger. The other is that under section 496A.138, Casualty could have changed the articles to reduce the two-thirds requirement in section 496A.70 to a lesser proportion and thus carried the merger election.

We lay aside the fact that a conversion of Casualty's other shares to common shares would have involved several other considerations, and that a change in the articles to reduce the two-thirds requirement would today run into the 1978 repeal of the words "or lesser" in section 496A.138. The significant point is that when the vote on the merger actually occurred in May 1973, Casualty had not in fact converted its other stock or reduced the two-thirds requirement. We deal with the election as it occurred, not as it might have occurred. Many corporations have various classes or series of shares which have rights of conversion into other shares. Corporate elections under chapter 496A cannot stand or fall on what would have happened if certain hypothetical conversions had previously taken place or if changes in the articles had previously been made; they must stand or fall on what in fact took place. We do not find merit in defendants' final argument.

We thus answer the question propounded as follows:

> The Iowa law required that the General United Group, Incorporated (GUG) merger into All American Delaware Corporation in May of 1973 be approved by an affirmative vote of at least two-thirds (2/3) of the outstanding GUG Common Stock shares voting separately as a class and by at least two-thirds (2/3) of the total outstanding GUG shares.

298 N.W.2d at 324. In evaluating *Shidler* in light of a perceived trend toward judicial disenfranchisement of shareholders Professor Buxbaum notes:

> Fortunately, the recent case of *Shidler v. All American Life & Financial Corp.* is a refreshing reminder that, through its reserved power, the judiciary can adapt to particular circumstances by interpreting a general statutory enjoinder to consider shareholder participation rights as the norm, with some exceptions. The Iowa Supreme Court interpreted a state statute's requirement that a class of shareholders approve a cancellation of shares on a class basis to apply to cash merger transactions. Indeed, in *Shidler* the statute, which provided voting rights to any class whose shares would be canceled in a reorganization, superseded the bargained-for article provisions purporting to merge the class into one class for voting purposes.
>
> This resolution of a recurrent tension between statutory and contractual treatment of shareholder participation rights recalls and confirms the earlier suggestion that underlying judicial attitudes towards the "proper" place of the preferred shareholder in the owner-manager hierarchy determine the judicial approach to these so-called "interpretation" questions. The particular results are always defensible, but the overall disenfranchising trend is clearly discernible.

Buxbaum, The Internal Division of Powers in Corporate Governance, 73 Calif. L. Rev. 1671, 1692-93 (1985). Do you agree with Professor Buxbaum? Why or why not?

Epilogue and Concluding Problem — Reconceptualizing the Corporation

In 1989 economist Michael Jensen published an influential and controversial article in the Harvard Business Review proclaiming the obsolescence of the public corporation, at least for corporations "where long-term growth is slow, where internally generated funds outstrip the opportunities to invest them profitably, or where downsizing is the most productive long-term strategy." Jensen, Eclipse of the Public Corporation, Harvard Business Review, 61 (September/October 1989). In the article Jensen argued that the substantial restructuring of American industry in the late 1980s was less a result of private greed and manipulative and speculative conduct than a recognition of, and substantial correction for, the inadequacies of the public corporation form for conducting the business of mature industries. In particular, he viewed the privatization of American business as a means of eliminating agency costs without eliminating the "vital functions" of risk diversification and liquidity. The mechanism for accomplishing this change is the "LBO Association," consisting of (i) a sponsoring partnership which "counsels and monitors management," (ii) corporate managers with large equity holdings in their operating units, and (iii) institutional investors that fund the buyout through equity and debt purchases.

Central to the success of this restructuring is the use of debt. In responding to those who view as troublesome the dramatic increase in debt financing described in this book, Jensen makes three important points:

> First, the trebling of the market value of public-company equity over the last decade means that corporate borrowing had to increase to avoid a major deleveraging.

> Second, debt creation without retention of the proceeds of the issue helps limit the ways to free cash flow by compelling managers to pay out funds they would otherwise retain. Debt is in effect a substitute for dividends.... Third, debt is a powerful agent for change.

He sees debt as disciplining management to reduce overhead and retain only those operations that contribute to the company's actual wealth.

In this view, the increased risk of failure occasioned by heavy leveraging is not a bad thing. On the contrary, Jensen suggests that the early debt defaults and, sometimes, bankruptcies of certain LBOs present an early opportunity to permit creditors to restructure a corporation that is performing inadequately, with such inadequate performance signaled by its inability to meet its financial obligations.

Finally, LBOs permit significant gains to stockholders and, according to Jensen, do not necessarily result in expropriation of bondholder wealth. To the extent they do, he suggests that the problem of expropriation is unlikely to continue over the long term as contractual devices developed by bondholders prevent such transfers.

The fact that LBO companies are private permits management's incentives to be much more closely aligned with those of the owners (including management, LBO sponsors, and debtholders). As a result, he concludes that substantial savings result from LBO transactions, and the resulting companies are able to take a much longer-term view of their businesses than is the case with traditional public corporations whose stockholders are focused on short-term value maximization.

What are the implications of Jensen's thesis for the nature of the corporation and the purpose of corporate law in general? For the rights of various constituent groups? In light of Jensen's analysis, as well as all of the materials you have considered in this book, we ask you as a final matter to consider this issue in connection with the following problem:

The Bondolian legislature has expressed some curiosity over the dramatic capital restructuring of corporate America during the 1980s. They are especially anxious to learn whether the structure of American corporate law (which, upon your advice, they largely have imitated) is adequate to the task of regulating this new reality. In particular, the legislature's committee on corporate law has asked you to evaluate the desirability of adopting a constituency statute much like Section 717(b) of the New York Business Corporation Law (set forth *supra* at chapter 5, section 7). Draft a memorandum to the committee responding to the legislature's concern. In so doing, you should also be sure to describe any other ideas you may have for ensuring the fair and efficient functioning of Bondolian corporations.

Index